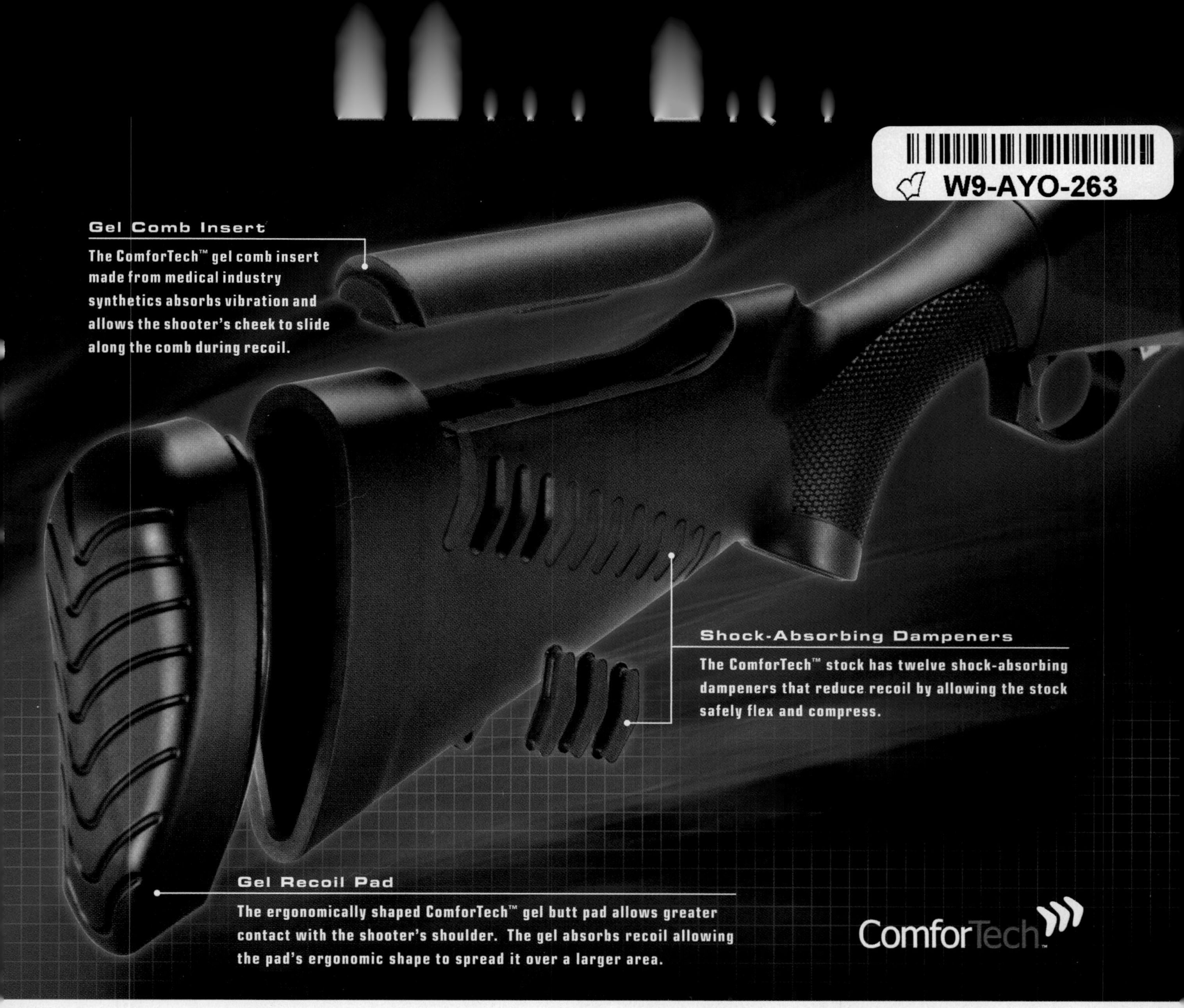

Gel Comb Insert

The ComforTech™ gel comb insert made from medical industry synthetics absorbs vibration and allows the shooter's cheek to slide along the comb during recoil.

Shock-Absorbing Dampeners

The ComforTech™ stock has twelve shock-absorbing dampeners that reduce recoil by allowing the stock safely flex and compress.

Gel Recoil Pad

The ergonomically shaped ComforTech™ gel butt pad allows greater contact with the shooter's shoulder. The gel absorbs recoil allowing the pad's ergonomic shape to spread it over a larger area.

ComforTech™

COMFORTECH™ TECHNOLOGY REDUCES FELT RECOIL BY 40%

BENELLI SEMI-AUTOMATIC SHOTGUNS weigh a pound less than most other semi-automatic shotguns. Consequently, the challenge was to reduce felt recoil without adding weight. The Benelli engineer solved the problem, reducing felt recoil by as much as 40%, without moving parts, without effecting the gun's superb balance *and* without adding weight. Benelli calls it ComforTech,™ but the engineers simply say: Problem Identified – Problem Solved — BENELLI TECHNOLOGY.

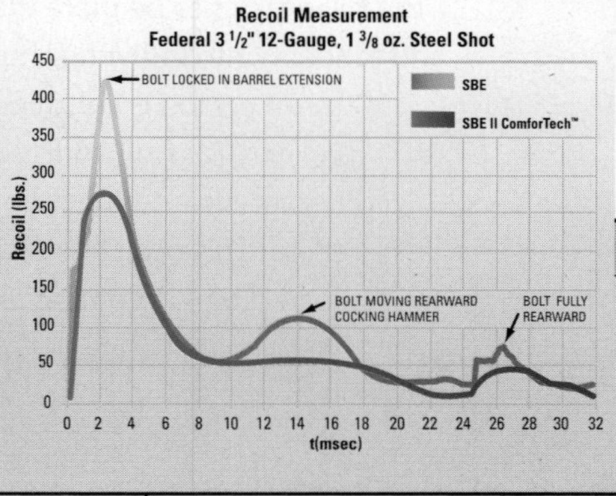

Recoil Measurement
Federal 3 1/2" 12-Gauge, 1 3/8 oz. Steel Shot

BOLT LOCKED IN BARREL EXTENSION
SBE
SBE II ComforTech™
Recoil (lbs.)
BOLT MOVING REARWARD COCKING HAMMER
BOLT FULLY REARWARD
t(msec)

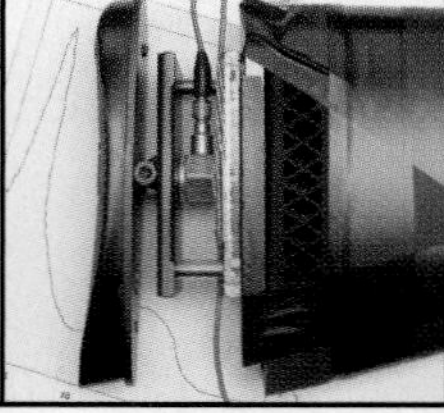

BENELLI ENGINEERING

Before Benelli engineers could solve the problem of recoil they first had to develop specialized instruments that could measure the force levels of a gun's kick during the few milliseconds of recoil.

benelliusa.com

PERFORMANCE WORTH THE PRICE

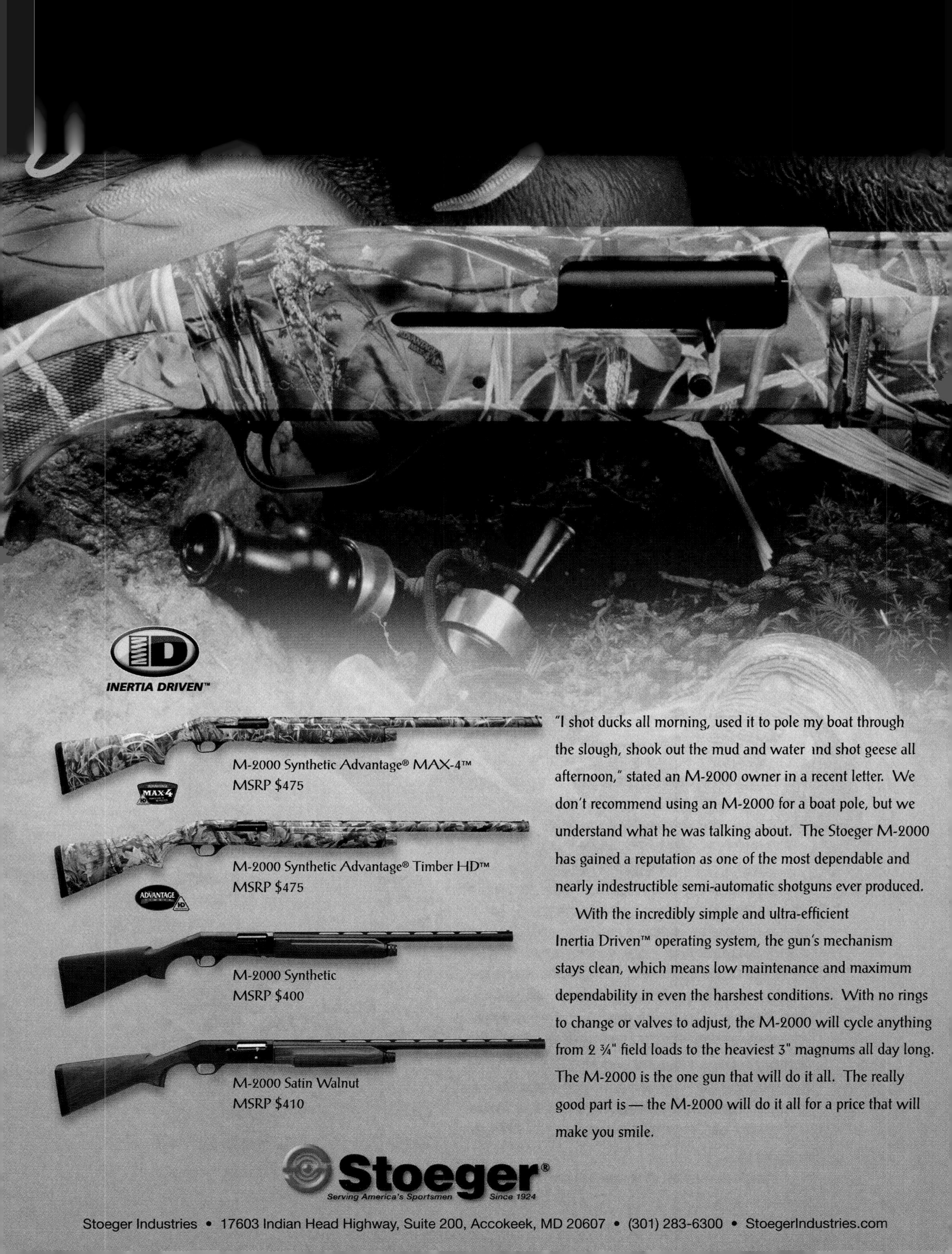

INERTIA DRIVEN™
M-2000 Synthetic Advantage® MAX-4™
MSRP $475
MAX-4
M-2000 Synthetic Advantage® Timber HD™
MSRP $475
ADVANTAGE
M-2000 Synthetic
MSRP $400
M-2000 Satin Walnut
MSRP $410
"I shot ducks all morning, used it to pole my boat through the slough, shook out the mud and water ınd shot geese all afternoon," stated an M-2000 owner in a recent letter. We don't recommend using an M-2000 for a boat pole, but we understand what he was talking about. The Stoeger M-2000 has gained a reputation as one of the most dependable and nearly indestructible semi-automatic shotguns ever produced.
With the incredibly simple and ultra-efficient Inertia Driven™ operating system, the gun's mechanism stays clean, which means low maintenance and maximum dependability in even the harshest conditions. With no rings to change or valves to adjust, the M-2000 will cycle anything from 2 ¾" field loads to the heaviest 3" magnums all day long. The M-2000 is the one gun that will do it all. The really good part is — the M-2000 will do it all for a price that will make you smile.
Stoeger®
Serving America's Sportsmen
Since 1924
Stoeger Industries • 17603 Indian Head Highway, Suite 200, Accokeek, MD 20607 • (301) 283-6300 • StoegerIndustries.com

For more than 80 years Stoeger Publishing has been dedicated to the production of the best outdoor titles available. In addition to our classic annuals, Shooter's Bible and Gun Trader's Guide, our catalog of books includes more than 80 titles on hunting, firearms, shooting, reloading, collecting, fishing, game and fish cookery and birding. Books from Stoeger will make a fine addition to any sportsman's library.

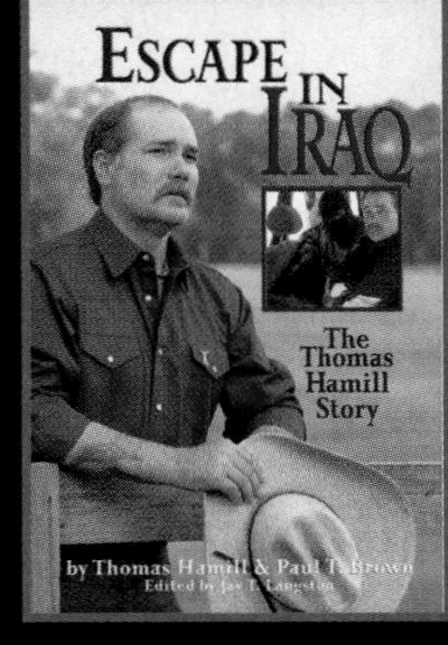

ESCAPE IN IRAQ
The Thomas Hamill Story

Thomas Hamill and Paul T. Brown

Chronicles the extraordinary experience of American civilian, Thomas Hamill, a truck convoy commander delivering fuel to the U.S. armed forces in Iraq. His convoy was attacked and he was wounded and taken prisoner by masked gunmen who held him hostage in Iraq for 24 days before he made a miraculous escape. His is an inspirational story of danger, courage, faith and family.

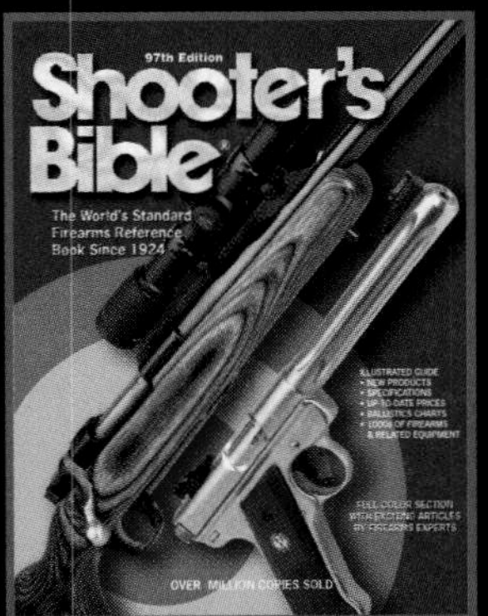

SHOOTER'S BIBLE

97th Edition

As the most widely-recognized publication on firearms and accessories, Shooter's Bible provides an invaluable reference for both hunters and collectors. The 97th Edition includes expanded selections and articles and the latest information on what's new from the world's foremost makers of guns and shooting accessories.

THE HANDLOADER'S MANUAL OF CARTRIDGE CONVERSIONS

John J. Donnelley and Bryce M. Towsley

Stoeger's classic guide has been revised and updated with a new format and additional cartridge data. The Handloader's Manual provides the data and drawings needed to convert modern materials into more than 900 rifle and pistol cartridge cases.

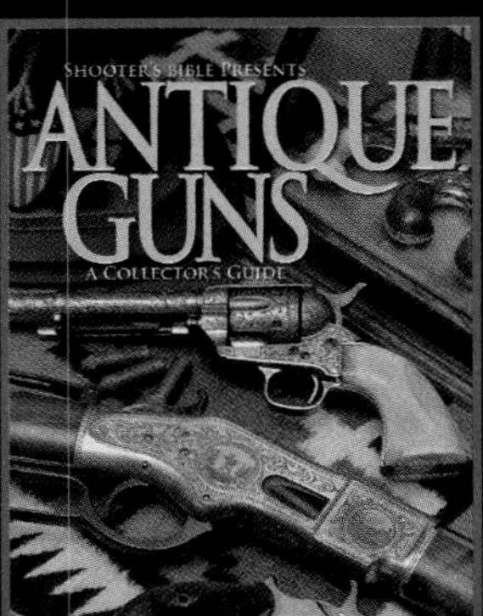

Shooter's Bible Presents

ANTIQUE GUNS
A Collector's Guide

Edited by Stephen D. Carpenteri

Antique Guns is a concise and meticulously researched guide for identifying and pricing antique firearms. Antique Guns covers many of the pre-1900 American and European firearms that interest most present-day collectors and dealers.

MODEL 1911
AUTOMATIC PISTOL

Robert Campbell

This firearms expert presents an in-depth exploration into the development, and continued career of America's most popular modern handgun—the Colt Model 1911. The author has tested and analyzed both the original models and popular modern varieties and provides a concise look at performance, design and engineering.

For a complete list of Stoeger books call: 1-877-GUN-BOOK or visit us on the web at www.stoegerpublishing.com

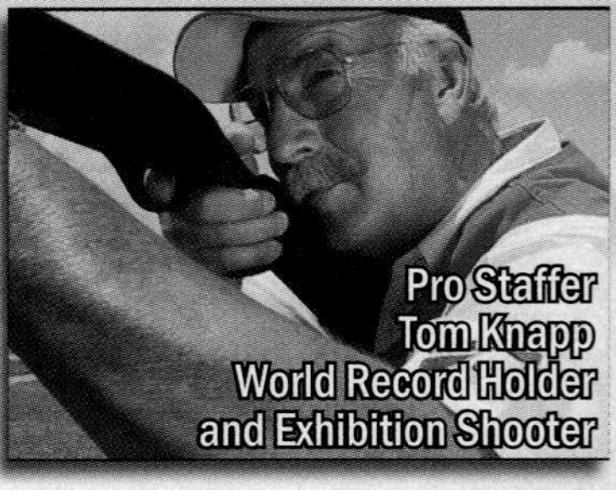

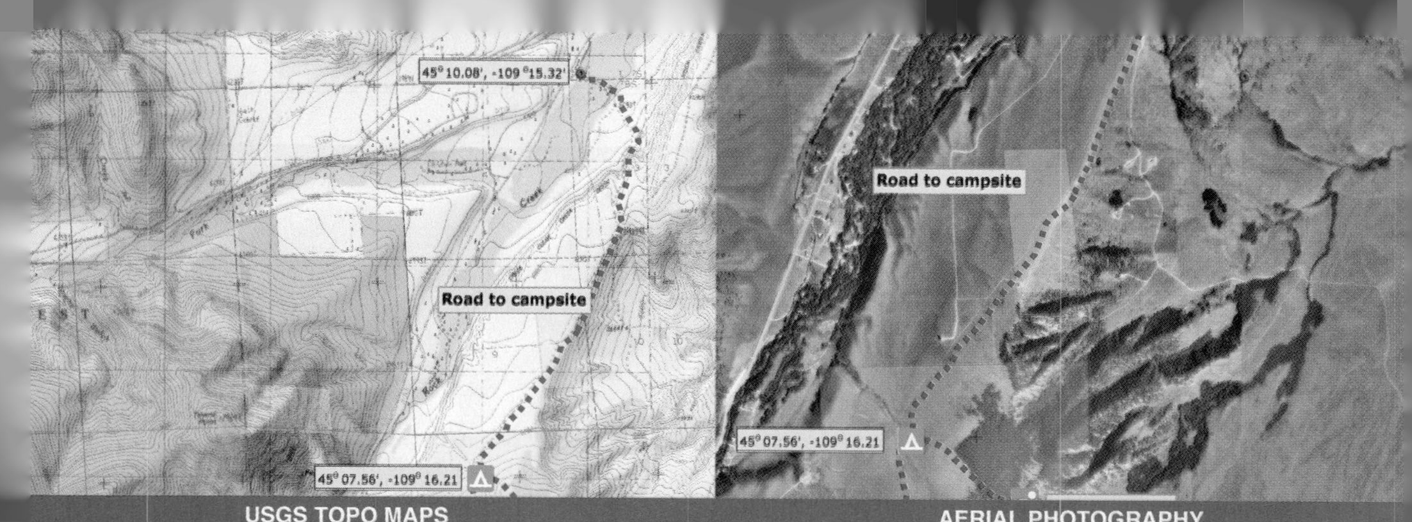
45° 10.08', -109° 15.32'
Road to campsite
45° 07.56', -109° 16.21
Road to campsite
45° 07.56', -109° 16.21
USGS TOPO MAPS
AERIAL PHOTOGRAPHY

Colt Model 1911 Semi-Automatic Pistol

Adopted by the U.S. Ordnance Department in 1911, the Colt semi-automatic pistol was originally manufactured by Colt and the government's Springfield Armory. In 1917, with the US entry into World War I, the government contracted with Colt for one million pistols and contracts were signed for the production of a total of two million more pistols with Remington-UMC, North American Arms, Savage, Winchester, National Cash Register Co., Burroughs Adding Machine, Lamston Monotype, and Caron Bros. A total of 629,000 pistols were completed by the war's end in1918. Production was resumed in 1924 with a series of design modifications introduced during the inter-war period resulting in the Model 1911 A1. From the onset of World War II until its end in 1945 Colt, Remington UMC, Remington-Rand, Ithaca, Singer, and Union Switch and Signal Company manufactured nearly 2 million M1911A1s.

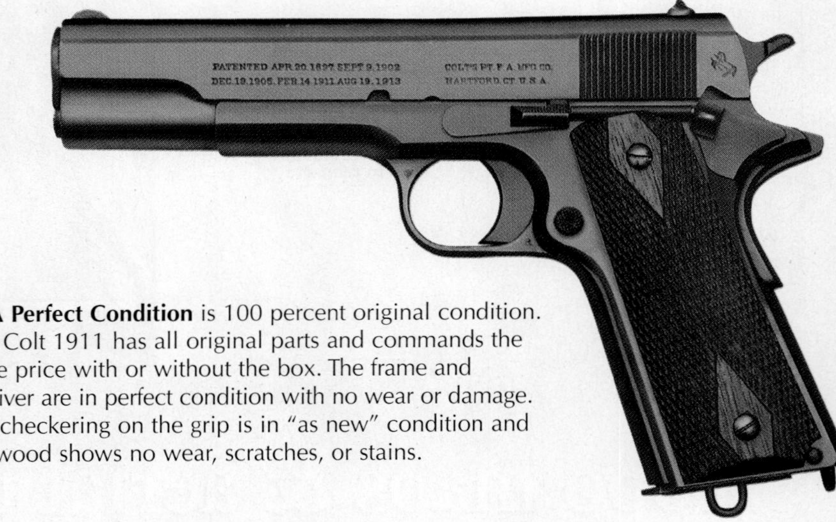

NRA Perfect Condition is 100 percent original condition. This Colt 1911 has all original parts and commands the same price with or without the box. The frame and receiver are in perfect condition with no wear or damage. The checkering on the grip is in "as new" condition and the wood shows no wear, scratches, or stains.

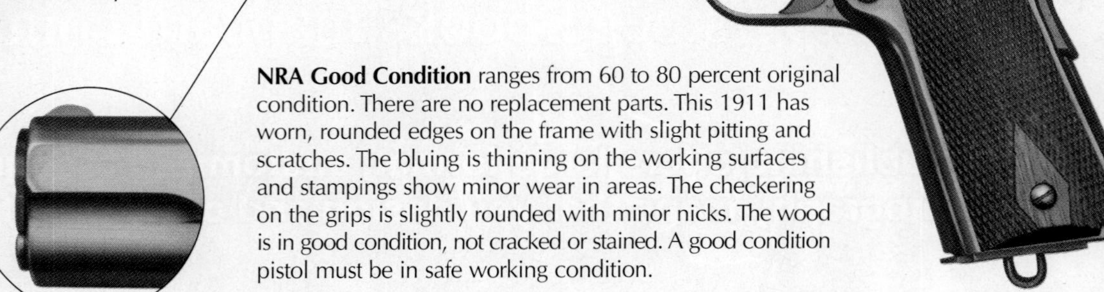

NRA Good Condition ranges from 60 to 80 percent original condition. There are no replacement parts. This 1911 has worn, rounded edges on the frame with slight pitting and scratches. The bluing is thinning on the working surfaces and stampings show minor wear in areas. The checkering on the grips is slightly rounded with minor nicks. The wood is in good condition, not cracked or stained. A good condition pistol must be in safe working condition.

NRA Fair Condition ranges from 20 to 60 percent original condition. This Model 1911 is in well-worn condition with the frame retaining only 40 percent of its original finish. Some major and minor parts have been replaced and scratches and pitting from rust and corrosion are evident on the frame and slide. Serial numbers and other markings are shallow and difficult to identify. While the grips on this pistol are not badly scratched or soiled, they show worn checkering and several large and small dents. The gun must function and shoot properly.

Winchester Model 94

Winchester produced approximately 2,550,000 Model 94 lever action rifles between 1894 and 1962. The Model 94 was manufactured in both rifle and carbine versions with several configurations that included pistol- and straight-grip stocks, various grades of wood, and several different barrel lengths and magazine capacities. Crescent and shotgun style buttstocks and takedown barrels were also offered. The Model 94 was produced in 25-35, 30, 30-30, 32-40 and 38-55 calibers.

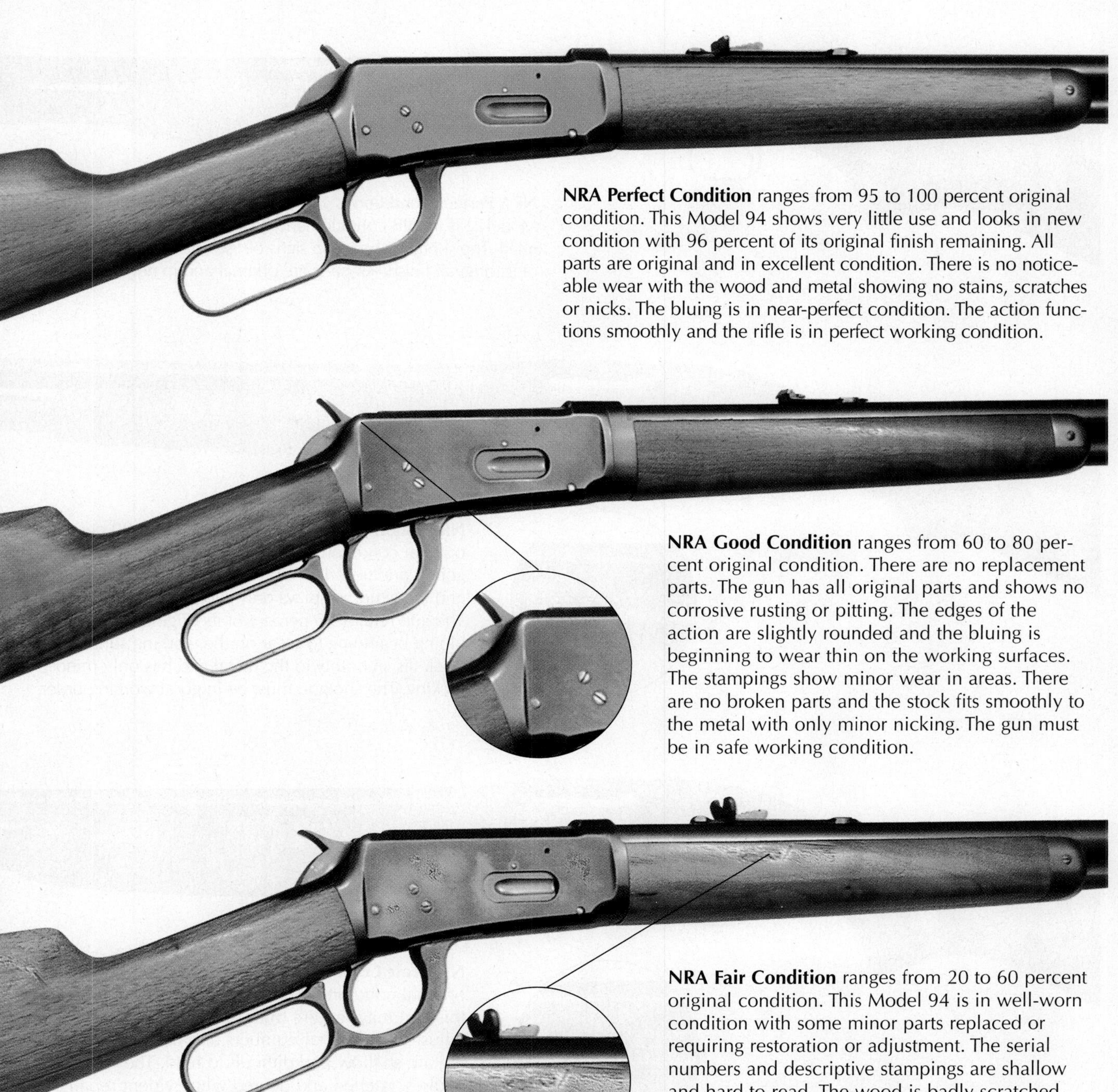

NRA Perfect Condition ranges from 95 to 100 percent original condition. This Model 94 shows very little use and looks in new condition with 96 percent of its original finish remaining. All parts are original and in excellent condition. There is no noticeable wear with the wood and metal showing no stains, scratches or nicks. The bluing is in near-perfect condition. The action functions smoothly and the rifle is in perfect working condition.

NRA Good Condition ranges from 60 to 80 percent original condition. There are no replacement parts. The gun has all original parts and shows no corrosive rusting or pitting. The edges of the action are slightly rounded and the bluing is beginning to wear thin on the working surfaces. The stampings show minor wear in areas. There are no broken parts and the stock fits smoothly to the metal with only minor nicking. The gun must be in safe working condition.

NRA Fair Condition ranges from 20 to 60 percent original condition. This Model 94 is in well-worn condition with some minor parts replaced or requiring restoration or adjustment. The serial numbers and descriptive stampings are shallow and hard to read. The wood is badly scratched and dented with evident repairs. There is corrosive pitting and scratches but the gun remains in safe firing condition.

Winchester Model 12

When introduced in 1912, the hammerless Model 12 slide-action shotgun was offered only in 20-guage with a 2½-inch chamber. In 1914 12- and 16-guage versions were introduced followed by a 28-guage in 1937. The Model 12 was available with various chokes and with walnut, straight or pistol grip stock and forearm. Winchester sold more than 1,900,000 Model 1912s during the shotgun's 51-year history.

NRA Perfect Condition is 100 percent original condition. This Model12 is in NIB condition and has not been previously sold at retail. The shotgun shows no signs of use and retains 100 percent of its original finish. All parts are original and in new condition.

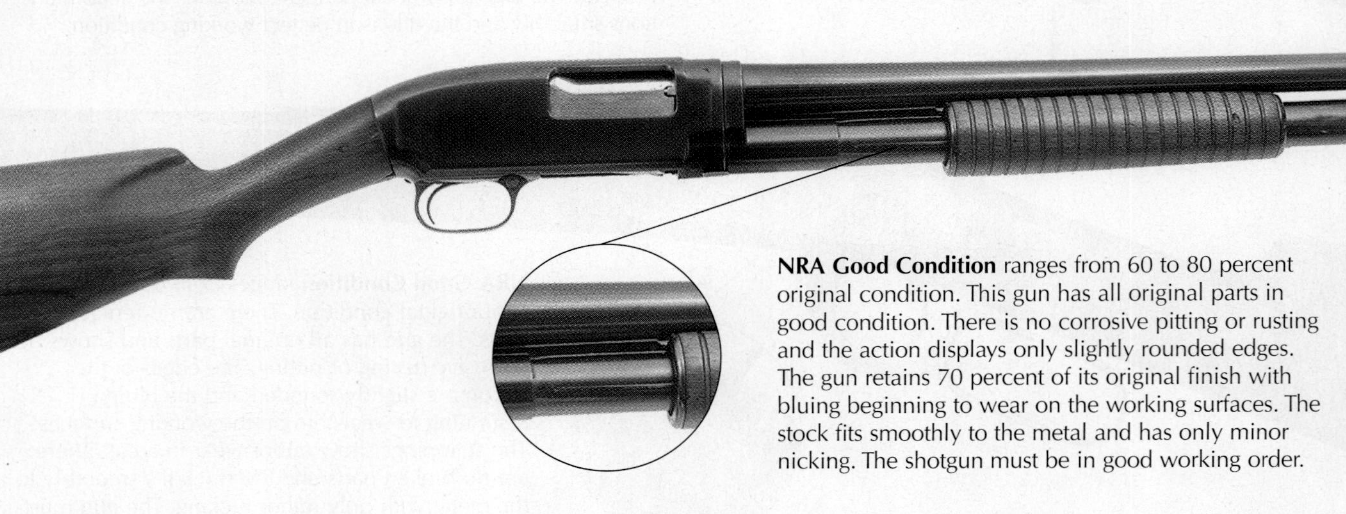

NRA Good Condition ranges from 60 to 80 percent original condition. This gun has all original parts in good condition. There is no corrosive pitting or rusting and the action displays only slightly rounded edges. The gun retains 70 percent of its original finish with bluing beginning to wear on the working surfaces. The stock fits smoothly to the metal and has only minor nicking. The shotgun must be in good working order.

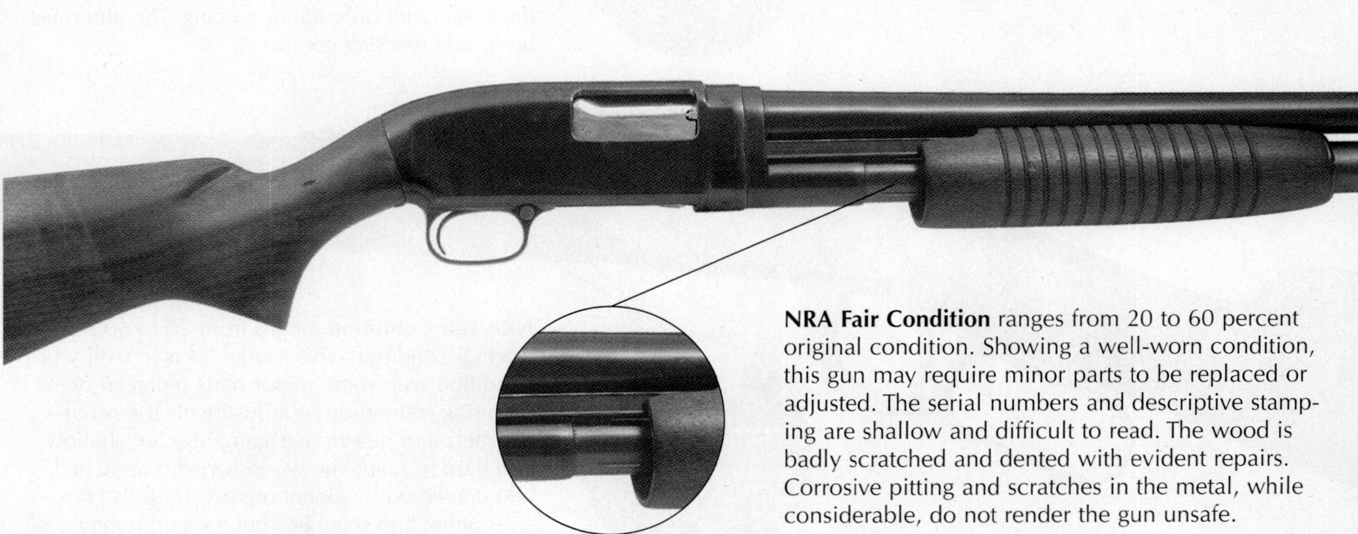

NRA Fair Condition ranges from 20 to 60 percent original condition. Showing a well-worn condition, this gun may require minor parts to be replaced or adjusted. The serial numbers and descriptive stamping are shallow and difficult to read. The wood is badly scratched and dented with evident repairs. Corrosive pitting and scratches in the metal, while considerable, do not render the gun unsafe.

Twenty-Eighth Edition
Completely Revised And Updated

Gun Trader's Guide

STOEGER PUBLISHING COMPANY
Accokeek, Maryland

STOEGER PUBLISHING COMPANY
is a division of Benelli U.S.A.

Benelli U.S.A.
Vice President and General Manager: Stephen Otway
Vice President of Marketing and Communications: Stephen McKelvain

Stoeger Publishing Company
President: Jeffrey K. Reh
Managing Editor: Harris J. Andrews
Creative Director: Cynthia T. Richardson
Marketing & Communications Manager: Alex Bowers
Imaging Specialist: William Graves
National Sales Manager: Jennifer Thomas
Special Accounts Manager: Julie Brownlee
Publishing Assistant: Amy Jones

Edited by: Stephen D. Carpenteri

ISBN:0-88317-317-4 BK0502
Library of Congress Control number: 2005902513

Manufactured in the United States of America

Distributed to the book trade and to the sporting goods trade by:
Stoeger Industries, Stoeger Publishing Company
17603 Indian Head Highway, Suite 200
Accokeek, Maryland 20607-2501

OTHER PUBLICATIONS:
Shooter's Bible
The World's Standard Firearms Reference Book
Gun Trader's Guide
Complete Fully Illustrated Guide to Modern Firearms with Current Market Values

Hunting & Shooting:
Advanced Black Powder Hunting
The Bowhunter's Guide
Complete Book of Whitetail Hunting
Cowboy Action Shooting
Hunting Whitetails East and West
Hunting the Whitetail Rut
Hounds of the World
Hunting and Shooting with the Modern Bow
Hunt Club Management Guide
Hunting America's Wild Turkey
Great Shooters of the World
Labrador Retrievers
Shotgunning for Deer
Taxidermy Guide
Tennessee Whitetails
Trailing the Hunter's Moon
The Turkey Hunter's Tool Kit: Shooting Savvy
The Ultimate in Rifle Accuracy
Whitetail Strategies

Collecting Books:
The Truth About Spring Turkey Hunting According to "Cuz"
The Whole Truth About Spring Turkey Hunting According to "Cuz"
Sporting Collectibles
The Working Folding Knife
The Lore of Spices

Firearms:
Antique Guns
The Book of the Twenty-Two
Complete Guide to Compact Handguns
Complete Guide to Service Handguns
Firearms Disassembly with Exploded Views
FN Browning Armorer to the World
Gunsmithing at Home
How to Buy & Sell Used Guns
Heckler & Koch: Armorers of the Free World
Legendary Sporting Rifles
Model 1911 Automatic Pistol
Modern Beretta Firearms
Muzzleloading Big game Rifles
Spanish Handguns
The Walther Handgun Story

Reloading:
Complete Reloading Guide
The Handloader's Manual of Cartridge Conversions
Modern Sporting Rifle Cartridges

Fishing:
Bassing Bible
Big Bass Zone
Catfishing: Beyond the Basics
The Complete Book of Flyfishing
Deceiving Trout
Fiberglass Rod Making
Fishing Made Easy
Fishing Online: 1,000 Best Web Sites
Flyfishning for Trout A to Z
The Fly Fisherman's Entomological Pattern Book
The Flytier's Companion
The Flytier's Manual
Flytier's Master Class
Handbook of Fly Tying
To Rise a Trout
Ultimate Bass Boats

Cooking game:
The Complete Book of Dutch Oven Cooking
Dress 'Em Out
Fish & Shellfish Care & Cookery
Game Cookbook
Wild About Venison
Wild About Game Birds
Wild About Waterfowl
Wild About Freshwater Fish
Wild About Seafood
World's Best Catfish Bookbook

Nature:
Birder's Bible
Conserving Wild America
Freedom Matters
The Pocket Survival guide
U.S. Guide to Venomous Snakes
Wild About Babies

Fiction:
Wounded Moon

Non Fiction:
Escape In Iraq: The Thomas Hamill Story

Front Cover:
The firearms shown on the cover were produced by the Colt Patent Firearms Company in Hartford, Connecticut. The revolvers shown are Model 1877 Double Action pistols manufactured between 1877 and 1909. They were available in various finishes, calibers and barrel lengths. Engraving was available as well as ivory, pearl, rosewood and hard rubber grips.

The Model 1878 Damascus Double Barrel Hammer Shotgun was produced from 1878 through 1889 in 10 and 12 gauge. They were offered in standard and deluxe grades with engraving and checkered burl walnut stocks.

Lightning Magazine Slide Action rifles and carbines were produced from 1884 through 1902. They were offered in small, medium and large frame models. The large frame model was intended for large game in calibers up to 50-95 Express.

Special thanks to the National Rifle Association, for access to their image archives.

Introduction

This 28th edition of Stoeger's *Gun Trader's Guide* is designed to provide the professional and amateur gun enthusiast with more specifications and photographs of collectible firearms than ever before. In the past 50 years, the *Gun Trader's Guide* has grown to over 550 pages and now lists more than 6,000 firearms and variations.

The first edition of the *Gun Trader's Guide* contained some 1,360 listings accompanied by 100 illustrations. Now, after 27 revisions, the book has evolved into one of the most complete catalogs of the rifles, shotguns and handguns of the late 19th and 20th centuries.

The current edition of the *Gun Trader's Guide* has been expanded to include more listings than ever before, with nearly 2,750 illustrations. Hundreds of thousands of gun buffs have made the *Gun Trader's Guide* their primary reference for identification and comparison of sporting, military and law enforcement firearms, including rare and unusual collectibles and commemoratives.

The format of the *Gun Trader's Guide* is simple and straightforward, listing thousands of firearms manufactured since the late 1800s in the United States and abroad. Most entries include complete specifications including model number and name, caliber/gauge, barrel length, overall length, weight, distinguishing features, variations and the dates of manufacture (when they can be accurately determined) and date of discontinuation. Many illustrative photos accompany the text to help the reader with identifications and comparisons.

SIMPLIFIED STRUCTURE

Production data includes:

- Specifications
- Variations of different models
- Dates of manufacture
- Current values
- Tabbed sections for user friendly reference
- Complete index of all firearms

The *Gun Trader's Guide* is revised annually to ensure that its wealth of information is both current and detailed. The principal features that contribute to the unique nature of this firearms reference guide include the extensive pictorial format and accompanying comprehensive specifications. It provides a convenient procedure for identifying vintage firearms while simultaneously determining and verifying their current value.

Values shown are based on national averages obtained by conferring with hundreds of different gun dealers, traders, collectors and auctioneers, not by applying an arbitrary mathematical formula that could produce unrealistic figures. The values listed accurately reflect the prices being charged nationwide at the time of publication.

In some rare cases, however, like the Winchester Model 1873 "One of One Thousand" rifle or the Parker AA1 Special shotgun in 28 gauge, where very little (if any) trading took place, active gun collectors were consulted to obtain current market values.

ORGANIZATION OF LISTINGS

In the early editions of the *Gun Trader's Guide,* firearms were frequently organized chronologically by date of production within manufacturers' listings because firearms aficionados know that many gunmaking companies used the date that a particular model was introduced as the model number. For example, the Colt U.S. Model 1911 semiautomatic pistol was introduced in 1911; the French Model 1936 military rifle was introduced in 1936; and the Remington Model 32 shotgun debuted in 1932. However, during the first quarter of the 20th century, gunmakers began assigning names and numbers that did not relate to the year that gun was introduced. As these recent models and their variations multiplied through the years, it became increasingly difficult to track them by date, especially for the less-experienced collector.

Also, some Winchester and Remington firearms are grouped differently in this edition. For example, The Winchester Model 1894, in its many variations, has been produced since 1894 and is still being manufactured under "Model 94" by U.S. Repeating Arms Co. In general, Winchester used the year of introduction to name its firearms; that is, Model 1890, 1892, 1894, 1895, etc. Shortly after World War I, Winchester dropped the first two digits and listed the models as 90, 92, 94, 95 etc. Later, guns were given model numbers that had no relation to the date of manufacture. Marlin and several other manufacturers used a similar approach in handling model designations.

Consequently, Winchester rifles are grouped alphanumerically in two different groups: Early Winchesters, manufactured before 1920 under the 4-digit model/date designations; and those manufactured after 1920 with their revised model format designations. If any difficulty is encountered in locating a particular model, the different models and their variations are cross-referenced in the index.

Past readers have reported difficulty in finding certain Remington rifles. In this edition, Remington rifles have been grouped according to action type: That is, single-shot rifles, slide actions, autoloaders, etc. Our surveys revealed this to be the easiest way to locate a specific firearm. Again, use the index if difficulty in finding a particular model is encountered.

In researching data for this edition, we found that not all manufacturers' records were available and some information was unobtainable. For example, many early firearms production records were destroyed in a fire that ravaged the Winchester plant. Some manufacturers' records have simply been lost, or were simply not maintained accurately. These circumstances resulted in some minor deviations in the presentation format of certain model listings. For example, production dates may not be listed when manufacturing records are unavailable. As an alternative, approximate dates of manufacture may be listed to reflect the availability of guns from a manufacturer or distributor. These figures may represent disposition dates indicating when that particular model was shipped to a distributor or importer. Frequently, especially with foreign manufacturers, production records are unavailable. Therefore, availability information is often based on importation records, that reflect domestic distribution only.

This is simply to advise the reader of the procedure and policy used regarding these published dates and further establish the distinction between "production dates," which are based on manufacturers' records and "availability dates," which are based on distribution records in the absence of recorded production data.

To further ensure that we have the most accurate information available, we encourage and solicit the users of the *Gun Trader's Guide* to communicate with our research staff at the Stoeger offices and forward any verifiable information they may have, especially in relation to older, out-of-production models.

CAUTION TO READERS

To comply with new Federal regulations, all manufacturers who produce firearms intended for disposition to the general public and designed to accept large capacity ammunition feeding devices are required to redesign those models to limit their capacities to 10 rounds or less, or discontinue production or importation. This amendment to the Gun Control Act of 1968 prohibits the manufacture, transfer or possession of all such devices manufactured after October 13, 1994. The grandfather clause of this amendment exempts all such devices lawfully possessed at the time the legislation became law. These pre-ban arms (manufactured before October 13, 1994) may therefore be bought, sold or traded without any additional restrictions imposed by this law.

All post-ban feeding devices must meet the new requirements. For the purposes of this book models previously designed to accept high capacity feeding devices will be listed at their original specifications and capacities if only the feeding device was modified to reduce that capacity.

Regarding shotguns, the reader should be aware that shotgun barrels must be 18 inches or longer except when used by military or law enforcement personnel. A special permit from the Bureau of Alcohol, Tobacco and Firearms is required for all others.

ACKNOWLEDGEMENTS

The publisher wishes to express special thanks to the many collectors, dealers, manufacturers, shooting editors and other industry professionals who provided product information and willingly shared their knowledge in making this the best *Gun Trader's Guide* ever.

Also, our appreciation is extended to the firearm firms and distributors' public relations and production personnel, and all the research personnel who we work with throughout the year. We are especially grateful to everyone for their assistance and cooperation in compiling information for the *Gun Trader's Guide* and for allowing us to reproduce photographs and illustrations of their collectible firearms.

Finally, our thanks to all the dedicated readers who take the time to write us with comments, suggestions and queries about various firearms. We appreciate your input and encourage you to continue.

Readers may send comments or suggestions to:

Editor,
Gun Trader's Guide,
Stoeger Publishing Company,
17603 Indian Head Highway,
Suite 200, Accokeek, MD
20607-2501.

How To Use This Guide

Are you planning on buying or selling a used rifle, shotgun or handgun? Perhaps you just want to establish the value of a favorite gun in your collection. No matter what your interest in collectible modern firearms, today's enthusiast inevitably turns to the Gun Trader's Guide to determine specifications, date of manufacture and the updated value of a specific firearm.

Opening the book, the collector asks himself two questions: "How much is my used gun worth?" and "How was that price determined?"

Prices contained in this book are "retail;" that is, the price the consumer may expect to pay for a similar item. However, many variables must be considered when buying or selling any used gun. Scarcity, demand, geographical location, the buyer's position and the gun's condition govern the selling price of a particular gun. Sentiment often shades the value of a particular gun in the seller's mind, but the market value of Grandpa's old .30/30 can not be logically catalogued nor effectively marketed (except possibly to someone else in the family!).

TEST SALE

To illustrate how the price of a particular gun may fluctuate, let us consider the popular Winchester Model 94 and see what its value might be.

The model 1894 (or Model 94) is a lever-action, solid-frame repeater. Round or octagon barrels of 26 inches were standard when the rifle was first introduced in 1894. However, half-octagon barrels were available for a slight increase in price. Various magazine lengths were also available.

Fancy-grade versions in all Model 94 calibers were available with 26-inch round nickel steel barrels. This grade featured a checkered fancy walnut pistol grip stock and forearm, and was available with either shotgun or rifle-type butt plates.

In addition, Winchester produced this model in carbine-style with a saddle ring on the left side of the receiver. The carbine had a 20-inch round barrel and full or half magazine. Some carbines were supplied with standard-grade barrels while others were made of nickel steel. Trapper models were also available with shortened 14-, 16- or 18-inch barrels.

In later years, the Rifle and Trapper models were discontinued and only the carbine remained. Eventually, the saddle ring was eliminated from this model and the carbine buttstock was replaced with a shotgun-type butt stock and shortened forend.

After World War II, the finish on Winchester Model 94 carbines changed to strictly hot caustic bluing; thus, pre-war models usually demand a premium over post-war models.

Then, in 1964, beginning with serial number 2,700,000, the action on the Winchester Model 94 was redesigned for easier manufacture. Many collectors and firearms enthusiasts considered this (and other) design changes to be inferior to former models. Therefore, the term "pre-64" has become the watchword for collectors when it comes to setting values on Winchester-made firearms.

Whether this evaluation is correct or not is not the issue. The justification for a price increase of pre-1964 models was that they were no longer available. This diminished availability placed them immediately in the "scarce" class and made them increasingly more desirable to collectors.

Shortly after the 1964 transition, Winchester began producing Model 94 commemorative models in great numbers, adding to the confusion of the concept of "limited production." Increased availability adversely affected the annual appreciation and price stability of these commemorative models. The negative response generated by this marketing practice was increased when the Winchester company was sold in the 1980s. The name of this long-established American firearms manufacturer was changed to U. S. Repeating Arms Company and still manufactures the Model 94 in both standard, carbine and big bore models. Later, the Angle-Eject model was introduced, a design change that allowed for the mounting of scope sights directly above the action.

With the above facts in mind, let's explore the *Gun Trader's Guide* to establish the approximate value of your particular Model 94. We will assume that you recently inherited the rifle, which has Winchester Model 94 inscribed on the barrel. Turn to the Rifle Section of the book and look under the W listings until you find Winchester. (The Contents section will also indicate where the Winchester Rifle section begins.) The index (at the back of the book) is another possible means of locating your rifle.

The listings in the *Gun Trader's Guide* are arranged within each manufacturer's entry, first by model numbers in consecutive numerical order followed by model names in alphabetical order. At first glance, you see that there are two model designations that may apply: the original designation (Model 1894) or the revised, shorter designation (Model 94). Which of these designations applies to your recently acquired Winchester?

The first step in the process is to try to match the appearance of your model with an illustration in the book. The photos may all look alike at first glance, but close evaluation and careful attention to detail will enable you to eliminate models that are not applicable. Further examination of your gun might reveal a curved or crescent-shaped butt plate. By careful observation of your gun's characteristics and close visual comparison of the photographic examples, you may logically conclude that your gun is the Winchester Model 94 Lever Action Rifle. (Please note that the guns shown in the *Gun Trader's Guide* are not always shown in proportion to one another; that is, a carbine barrel might not appear to be shorter than a rifle barrel.)

When the dealer offers you about half of what you expected, you are shocked!

You have now tentatively determined your model, but, to be sure, you should read through the specifications for that model and establish that the barrel on the pictured rifle is 26 inches long; round, octagonal or half-octagonal.

Upon measuring, you find that the barrel on your rifle is approximately 26 inches, perhaps a trifle under; and it is round. Additionally, your rifle is marked .38-55 (the caliber designation). The caliber offerings listed in the specifications include .38-55, so you are further convinced that this is your gun. You may read on to determine that this rifle was manufactured from 1894 to 1937. After that date, only the shorter-barreled carbine was offered by Winchester, and then only in .25-35, .30-30 and .32 Special.

At this point you know you have a Winchester Model 94 rifle manufactured before World War II. You read the value and take the rifle to your dealer to initiate a sale. Here is a look at some of the scenarios you may encounter:

SCENARIO I

If the rifle is truly in excellent condition, that is, if it retains at least 95 percent of its original finish on both the metal and wood and has a perfect bore, then the gun does in fact have a collectible value as noted. However, keep in mind that the dealer is in business to make a profit. If he pays you the full value of the gun, he will have to charge more than this when he sells it in order to realize a reasonable profit. If more than the fair market value is charged, the gun will not sell or someone will pay more for the gun than it is actually worth.

Therefore, expect a reputable dealer to offer you less than the published value for the gun. The exact amount will vary for a variety of reasons. For example, if the dealer already has a dozen or so of the same model on his shelf and they do not sell well, his offer will be considerably lower. On the other hand, if the dealer does not have any of this model in stock and knows several collectors who want it, chances are his offer will be considerably higher.

SCENARIO II

Perhaps you overlooked the true state of the rifle's condition. Suppose the gun apparently is flawless but not much of the original bluing remains. There are several shiny, bare-metal spots mixed with a brown patina over the remaining metal. Also, much

While any gun's exterior condition is a big factor in determining its value, internal parts also play an important role in pricing. Photograph courtesy of Browning Firearms, 2000

of the original varnish on the wood has been worn off from extended use. Consequently, the rifle is not in "excellent" condition, and is worth less than the value shown in this book.

SCENARIO III

Your Winchester Model 94 rifle looks nearly new, as if it were just out of the box, and the rifle works perfectly. Therefore, you are convinced that the dealer should pay you the full value of the gun (less a reasonable profit of 25 to 35 percent). When the dealer offers you about half what you expect, you are shocked!

Although the rifle looks new to you, the experienced dealer has detected that the gun has been refinished. Perhaps you did not notice the rounding of the formerly sharp edges on the receiver, of the slight funneling of some screw holes — all dead giveaways that the rifle has been refinished. If so, your rifle is not in "excellent" condition as you originally assumed, and is therefore worth less than "book" value.

A knowledgeable gun dealer will check each firearm to determine that it functions properly, and the condition of interior parts may also be a factor in determining the value of any firearm.

Now, if you are somewhat of an expert and know for certain that your rifle has never been refinished or otherwise repaired or damaged, there is still at least 95 percent of its original finish left, and you believe you have a firearm worth full book value, understand that a dealer will still offer you from 25 percent to 50 percent less for it due to profit margins, over-stocked goods, etc.

OTHER OPTIONS

One alternative is to advertise your gun in a local newspaper and sell the firearm directly to a private collector. However, this approach may prove both frustrating and expensive. In addition, there may be federal and local restrictions on the sale of firearms in your area, so check with the local police chief or sheriff before you proceed.

If you experience such complications, chances are the next time you have a firearm to sell you will be more than happy to take it to a dealer and let him make his fair share of profit.

STANDARDS OF CONDITION

The condition of a firearm is an important factor in determining its value. In some rare and unusual models, a variation in condition from "Excellent" to "Very Good" can mean a value difference of several thousand dollars. Therefore, you must be able to determine the gun's condition before you can accurately evaluate the value of the firearm.

Several sets of standards are available, but the National Rifle Association Standards of Condition of Modern Firearms are probably the most popular. In recent years, condition has been established by the percentage of original finish remaining on the wood and metal of the firearm. Let's see how these standards are applied.

EXCELLENT

When a collectible firearm has been expertly refinished to Excellent condition, a rule of thumb is to deduct 50 percent from the value listed in this book. If the job is poorly done, deduct 80 percent or more.

For the purpose of assigning comparative values as a basis for trading, firearms listed in this book are assumed to be in Excellent condition if they have 95 percent or more remaining original finish, no noticeable marring of wood or metal, and the bore has no pits or rust.

To the novice, this translates to a practically new gun, almost as though you had just removed the firearm from its shipping box. The trained eye, however, will see the difference between "new" or "mint" condition and merely "excellent."

VERY GOOD

Any other defects, no matter how minor, diminish the value of a firearm below those listed in this book. For example, if more than 5 percent of the original finish is gone and there are minor surface dents or scratches, regardless of how small, the gun is no longer in Excellent condition. Instead, it is considered to be in Very Good condition provided the gun is in perfect working order. Despite the minor defects, the gun will still look relatively new to the untrained buyer.

GOOD

If the gun is in perfect working condition and functions properly but has minor wear on working surfaces (perhaps some bad scratches on the wood or metal), the gun is considered to be in Good condition, one grade below Very Good, according to NRA standards. Again, the price shown in this book for that particular firearm must be reduced to reflect its true value.

The two remaining NRA conditions fall under the headings of Fair and Poor. These guns normally have little value unless they are of historical importance or a dealer simply must have them to complete his collection. The value of such guns is then determined by the price the buyer is willing to pay.

Previous editions of the *Gun Trader's Guide* offered multiplication factors to use for firearms in other than Excellent condition. These factors are listed below, but be aware that the figures given are not etched in stone. Instead, they provide another rough means of establishing the value of a particular firearm.

For guns in other than Excellent condition, multiply the price shown in this book for the model in question by the following factors:

MULTIPLICATION FACTORS FOR GUNS NOT IN EXCELLENT CONDITION

Condition	**X Factor**
(NiB) Mint or New	1.25
(Ex) Excellent	1.00
Very Good	.85
(Gd) Good	.68
Fair	.35
Poor	.15

PARTING THOUGHTS

Remember, the word "guide" in *Gun Trader's Guide* should be taken literally. This book is meant to be a reference only and is not the gospel of the collectible gun trade. We sincerely hope, however, that you find this publication helpful when you decide to buy or sell a used or collectible firearm.

Also, keep in mind that gun values vary from region to region. For this reason, we recommend that you attend gun shows and auctions near you to develop a better understanding of gun values and pricing in your part of the country. And, whenever you travel, check the prices of guns you're familiar with to determine their value in other parts of the country. The difference can be surprising!

NATIONAL RIFLE ASSOCIATION STANDARDS OF CONDITION

- **New:**
  Not previously sold at retail. In same condition as current factory production.
- **New, discontinued:**
  Same as New, but a discontinued model.
- **Perfect:**
  In new condition in every respect, sometimes referred to as mint.
- **Excellent:**
  New condition. Used very little, no noticeable marring of wood or metal, bluing perfect (except at muzzle or sharp edges).
- **Very Good:**
  In perfect working condition, no appreciable wear on working surfaces. No broken parts, no corrosion or pitting, only minor surface dents or scratches.
- **Good:**
  In safe working condition, minor wear on working surfaces. No broken parts, no corrosion or pitting that will interfere with proper functioning.
- **Fair:**
  In safe working condition but well worn, perhaps requiring replacement of minor parts or other adjustments that should be reported by the seller. No rust, but may have corrosion pits that do not render the gun unsafe or inoperable.
- **Poor:**
  Badly worn, rusty and battered, perhaps requiring major adjustment or repairs to return to operating condition.

Contents

Colt Model 1911

Winchester Model 94 Traditional

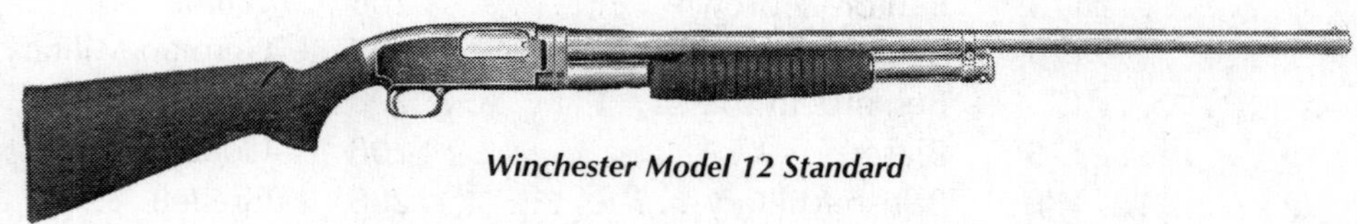

Winchester Model 12 Standard

Twenty-Eighth Edition
GUN TRADER'S GUIDE

Handguns

NOTE: *The following abbreviations are used throughout the Handgun section: DA = Double Action; SA = Single Action; LR = LR; WMR = Winchester Magnum Rimfire; adj. = Adjustable; avail. = Available; bbl., = Barrel; disc. = Discontinued; TT = Target Trigger; TH = Target Hammer*

Accu-Tek Model AT-.380

AA ARMS — Monroe, North Carolina

AP-9 SERIES

Semiautomatic recoil-operated pistol w/polymer integral grip/frame design. Fires from a closed bolt. Caliber: 9mm Parabellum. 10- or 20*-round magazine, 3- , 5- or 11-inch bbl., 11.8 inches overall w/5-inch bbl., Weight: 3.5 lbs. Fixed blade, protected post front sight adjustable for elevation, winged square notched rear. Matte phosphate/blue or nickel finish. Checkered polymer grip/frame. Made 1988 to date.

AP9 model
(pre-94 w/ventilated bbl., shroud . . NiB $443 Ex $340 Gd $221
AP9 Mini model
(post-94 w/o bbl., shroud). . . . . NiB $232 Ex $211 Gd $134
AP9 Target model
(pre-94 w/11-inch bbl.). . . . . NiB $438 Ex $365 Gd $252
Nickel finish, add. $25

ACCU-TEK — Chino, California

MODEL AT-9 AUTO PISTOL

Caliber: 9mm Para. 8-round magazine, Double action only. 3.2-inch bbl., 6.25 inches overall. Weight: 28 oz. Fixed blade front sight, adj. rear w/3-dot system. Firing pin block with no external safety. Stainless or black over stainless finish. Checkered black nylon grips. Announced 1992, but made1995 to date.

Satin stainless model . . . . NiB $273 Ex $211 Gd $134
Matte black stainless . . . . NiB $243 Ex $195 Gd $135

Accu-Tek Model BL-9

MODEL AT-25 AUTO PISTOL

Similar to Model AT380 except chambered .25 ACP w/7-round magazine, Made 1992-96.

Lightweight w/aluminum frame. . . . . NiB $159 Ex $134 Gd $82
Bright stainless (disc. 1991). . . . . NiB $163 Ex $140 Gd $97
Satin stainless model . . . . NiB $167 Ex $135 Gd $94
Matte black stainless . . . . NiB $160 Ex $129 Gd $88

MODEL AT-32 AUTO PISTOL

Similar to Model AT-.380 except chambered .32 ACP. Made 1990 to date.

Lightweight w/aluminum
Frame (disc. 1991). . . . . NiB $134 Ex $108 Gd $75
Satin stainless model . . . . NiB $185 Ex $159 Gd $108
Matte black stainless . . . . NiB $185 Ex $159 Gd $108

Accu-Tek HC-380SS

MODEL AT-40 DA AUTO PISTOL

Caliber: .40 S&W. Seven-round magazine, 3.2-inch bbl., 6.25 inches overall. Weight: 28 oz. Fixed blade front sight, adj. rear w/3-dot system. Firing pin block with no external safety. Stainless or black over stainless finish. Checkered black nylon grips. Announced 1992, but made 1995-96.

Satin stainless model . . . . NiB $273 Ex $206 Gd $144
Matte black stainless . . . . NiB $273 Ex $206 Gd $144

MODEL AT-380 AUTO PISTOL

Caliber: .380 ACP. Five-round magazine, 2.75-inch bbl., 5.6 inches overall. Weight: 20 oz. External hammer w/slide safety. Grooved black composition grips. Alloy or stainless frame w/steel slide. Black, satin aluminum or stainless finish. Made 1992 to date.

Standard alloy frame (disc. 1992) . . . NiB $166 Ex $134 Gd $83
Satin stainless model . . . . NiB $261 Ex $211 Gd $149
Matte black stainless . . . . NiB $261 Ex $211 Gd $149

MODELS BL-9, BL 380 .... NiB $185 Ex $149 Gd $103
Ultra compact DAO semiautomatic pistols. Calibers: .380 ACP, 9mm Para. 5-round magazine, 3-inch bbl., 5.6 inches overall. Weight: 24 oz. Fixed sights. Carbon steel frame and slide w/black finish. Polymer grips. Made 1997 to date.

MODELS CP-9, CP-40, CP-45
Compact, double action only, semiautomatic pistols. Calibers: 9mm Parabellum, .40 S&W, .45 ACP, 8-, 7- or 6-round magazine, 3.2-inch bbl., 6.25 inches overall. Weight: 28 oz. Fixed blade front sight, adj. rear w/3-dot system. Firing-pin block with no external safety. Stainless or black over stainless finish. Checkered black nylon grips. Made1997 to date.
Black stainless model........... NiB $232 Ex $175 Gd $123
Satin stainless model............ NiB $232 Ex $175 Gd $123

MODEL HC-380SS AUTO PISTOL.... NiB $262 Ex $211 Gd $159
Caliber: .380 ACP. 13-round magazine, 2.75-inch bbl., 6 inches overall. Weight: 28 oz. External hammer w/slide safety. Checkered black composition grips. Stainless finish. Made 1993 to date.

ACTION ARMS — Philadelphia, Pennsylvania

See also listings under CZ pistols. Action Arms stopped importing firearms in 1994.

AT-84 DA AUTOMATIC PISTOL ... NiB $573 Ex $501 Gd $450
Caliber: 9mm Para. 15-round magazine, 4.75-inch bbl., 8 inches overall. Weight: 35 oz. Fixed front sight, drift-adj. rear. Checkered walnut grips. Blued finish. Made in Switzerland 1987-89.

AT-84P DA AUTO PISTOL .... NiB $692 Ex $553 Gd $362
Compact version of the Model AT-84. Only a few prototypes were manufactured in 1985. No resale value established.

AT-88P DA AUTO PISTOL .... NiB $654 Ex $525 Gd $361
Compact version of the AT-88S w/3.7-inch bbl. Only a few prototypes of this model were manufactured in 1985. Note: The AT-88 pistol series was later manufactured by Sphinx-Muller as the AT-2000 series.

AT-88S DA AUTOMATIC PISTOL... NiB $578 Ex $475 Gd $316
Calibers: 9mm Para. or .41 Action Express, 10-round magazine, 4.6-inch bbl., 8.1 inches overall. Weight: 35.3 oz. Fixed blade front sight, adj. rear. Checkered walnut grips. Imported 1989-91.

ADVANTAGE ARMS — St. Paul, Minnesota

MODEL 422 .... NiB $180 Ex $139 Gd $87
Hammerless, top-break, 4-bbl., derringer w/rotating firing pin. Calibers: .22 LR and .22 Mag., 4-round capacity, 2.5 inch bbl., 4.5 inches overall. Weight: 15 oz. Fixed sights. Walnut grips. Blued, nickel or PDQ matte black finish. Made 1985-87.

S. A. ALKARTASUNA FABRICA DE ARMAS — Guernica, Spain

"RUBY" AUTOMATIC PISTOL..... NiB $283 Ex $263 Gd $159
Caliber: .32 Automatic (7.65mm). Nine-round magazine, 3.63-inch bbl., 6.38 inches overall. Weight: About 34 oz. Fixed sights. Blued finish. Checkered wood or hard rubber grips. Made 1917-22. Note: Mfd. by a number of Spanish firms, the Ruby was a secondary standard service pistol of the French Army in World Wars I and II. Specimens made by Alkartasuna bear the "Alkar" trademark.

Action Arms AT-84 with Prototype of Model AT-84P in background

AMERICAN ARMS — Kansas City, Missouri

BISLEY SA REVOLVER .... NiB $453 Ex $365 Gd $273
Umberti reproduction of Colt's Bisley. Caliber: .45 LC. Six-round cylinder, 4.75-, 5.5- or 7.7-inch bbl., Case-hardened steel frame. Fixed blade front sight, grooved top strap rear. Hammer block safety. Imported 1997 to date.

CX-22 DA AUTOMATIC PISTOL
Similar to Model PX-.22 except w/8-round magazine, 3.33-inch bbl., 6.5 inches overall. Weight: 22 oz. Made 1990 to 1995.
Standard w/chrome
Slide (disc. 1990)............... NiB $211 Ex $165 Gd $108
Classic model .... NiB $191 Ex $154 Gd $107

EP-380 DA AUTOMATIC PISTOL .... NiB $478 Ex $449 Gd $417
Caliber: .380 Automatic. Seven-round magazine, 3.5-inch bbl., 6.5 inches overall. Weight: 25 oz. Fixed front sight, square notch adj. rear. Stainless finish. Checkered wood grips. Made 1989-91.

ESCORT DA AUTO PISTOL....... NiB $283 Ex $211 Gd $118
Caliber: .380 ACP. 7-round magazine, 3.38-inch bbl., 6.13 inches overall. Weight: 19 ounces. Fixed, low-profile sights. Stainless steel frame, slide, and trigger. Nickel-steel bbl., Soft polymer grips. Loaded chamber indicator. Made 1995-97 .

MATEBA AUTO REVOLVER
Unique combination action design allows both slide and cylinder to recoil together causing cylinder to rotate. Single or double action. Caliber: .357 Mag. Six-round cylinder, 4- or 6-inch bbl., 8.77 inches overall w/4-inch bbl., Weight: 2.75 lbs. Steel/alloy frame. Ramped blade front sight, adjustable rear. Blue finish. Smooth walnut grips. Imported 1997 to date.
Mateba model (w/4-inch bbl.).... NiB $1087 Ex $874 Gd $603
Mateba model (w/6-inch bbl.).... NiB $1152 Ex $926 Gd $638

P-98 DA AUTOMATIC PISTOL .... NiB $200 Ex $169 Gd $128
Caliber: .22 LR. Eight-round magazine, 5-inch bbl., 8.25 inches overall. Weight: 25 oz. Fixed front sight, square notch adj. rear. Blued finish. Serrated black polymer grips. Made 1989-96.

American Arms Regulator Deluxe Model

American Derringer Model 1

American Derringer Model 3

PK-22 DA AUTOMATIC PISTOL. . . . . NiB $175 Ex $149 Gd $123
Caliber: .22 LR. Eight-round magazine, 3.33-inch bbl., 6.33 inches overall. Weight: 22 oz. Fixed front sight, V-notch rear. Blued finish. Checkered black polymer grips. Made 1989-96.

PX-22 DA AUTOMATIC PISTOL . . . NiB $175 Ex $149 Gd $123
Caliber: .22 LR. Seven-round magazine, 2.75-inch bbl., 5.33 inches overall. Weight: 15 oz. Fixed front sight, V-notch rear. Blued finish. Checkered black polymer grips. Made 1989-96.

PX-25 DA AUTOMATIC PISTOL . . . NiB $185 Ex $149 Gd $134
Same general specifications as the Model PX-22 except chambered for .25 ACP. Made 1991-92.

REGULATOR SA REVOLVER
Similar in appearance to the Colt Single-Action Army. Calibers: .357 Mag., .44-.40, .45 Long Colt. Six-round cylinder, 4.75- or 7.5-inch bbl., blade front sight, fixed rear. Brass trigger guard/backstrap on Standard model. Casehardened steel on Deluxe model. Made 1992 to date.
Standard model . . . . NiB $340 Ex $267 Gd $170

(cont'd.) **REGULATOR SA REVOLVER**
Standard combo set (45 LC/.45 ACP & .44-.40/.44 Spec.). . . . NiB $365 Ex $288 Gd $206
Deluxe model . . . . .NiB $332 Ex $267 Gd $185
Deluxe combo set (.45 LC/.45 ACP & .44-40/.44 Spec.) . . . . NiB $386 Ex $334 Gd $190
Stainless steel . . . . NiB $364 Ex $293 Gd $203

BUCKHORN SA REVOLVER
Similar to Regulator model except chambered .44 Mag. w/4.75-, 6- or 7.7-inch bbl., Fixed or adjustable sights. Hammer block safety. Imported 1993-96.
Buckhorn model (standard sights) . . NiB $345 Ex $273 Gd $190
W/adjustable sights, add $15

SABRE DA AUTOMATIC PISTOL
Calibers: 9mm Para., .40 S&W. Eight-round magazine (9mm), 9-round (.40 S&W), 3.75-inch bbl., 6.9 inches overall. Weight: 26 oz. Fixed blade front sight, square, notch adj. rear. Black polymer grips. Blued or stainless finish. Advertised 1991 but not imported.
Blued finish . . . . NiB $408 Ex $328 Gd $226
Stainless steel . . . . NiB $447 Ex $349 Gd $248

SPECTRE DA AUTO PISTOL
Blowback action, fires closed bolt. Calibers: 9mm Para., .40 S&W, .45 ACP. 30-round magazine, 6-inch bbl., 13.75 inches overall. Weight: 4 lbs. 8 oz. Adj. post front sight, fixed U-notch rear. Black nylon grips. Matte black finish. Imported 1990-94.
9mm Para. . . . . NiB $525 Ex $448 Gd $401
.40 S&W (disc. 1991) . . . . NiB $422 Ex $340 Gd $235
.45 ACP . . . . NiB $480 Ex $391 Gd $278

WOODMASTER SA AUTO PISTOL. . . . . . . NiB $230 Ex $185 Gd $128
Caliber: .22 LR. 10-round magazine, 5.88-inch bbl., 10.5 inches overall. Weight: 31 oz. Fixed front sight, square-notch adj. rear. Blued finish. Checkered wood grips. Disc. 1989.

454 SSA REVOLVER. . . . . NiB $919 Ex $729 Gd $533
Umberti SSA chambered 454. Six-round cylinder, 6-inch solid raised rib or 7.7-inch top-ported bbl., satin nickel finish. Hammer block safety. Imported 1996-97.

AMERICAN DERRINGER CORPORATION — Waco, Texas

MODEL 1, STAINLESS
Single-action pocket pistol similar to the Remington O/U derringer. Two-shot capacity. More than 60 calibers from .22 LR to .45-70. Three-inch bbl., 4.82 inches overall, weight: 15 oz. Automatic bbl., selection. Satin or high-polished stainless steel. Rosewood grips. Made 1980 to date.
.45 Colt, .44-40 Win., .44 Special, .410 . . . . NiB $407 Ex $362 Gd $294
.45-70, .44 Mag., 41 Mag., .30-30 Win., .223 Rem. . . . . NiB $493 Ex $477 Gd $371
.357 Max., .357 Mag., .45 Win. Mag., 9mm Para. . . . . NiB $356 Ex $332 Gd $244
.38 Special, .38 Super, .32 Mag., .22 LR, .22 WRM. . . . . NiB $340 Ex $313 Gd $192

MODEL 2 STEEL "PEN" PISTOL
Calibers: .22 LR, .25 Auto, .32 Auto (7.65mm). single-shot. Two-inch bbl., 5.6 inches overall (4.2 inches in pistol format). Weight: 5 oz. Stainless finish. Made 1993-94.
.22 LR . . . . NiB $178 Ex $143 Gd $102
.25 Auto. . . . . NiB $183 Ex $148 Gd $107
.32 Auto. . . . . NiB $209 Ex $158 Gd $117

MODEL 3 STAINLESS STEEL . . . . NiB $102 Ex $83 Gd $56
Single-shot. Calibers: .32 Mag. or .38 Special. 2.5-inch bbl., 4.9 inches overall. Weight: 8.5 oz. Rosewood grips. Made 1984-95.

MODEL 4 DOUBLE DERRINGER
Calibers: .357 Mag., .357 Max., .44 Mag., .45 LC, .45 ACP (upper bbl., and 3-inch .410 shotshell (lower bbl.). 4.1-inch bbl, 6 inches overall. Weight: 16.5 oz. Stainless steel. Staghorn grips. Made 1984 to date.
.357 Mag., .357 Max . . . . NiB $443 Ex $387 Gd $265
.44 Mag., .45 LC, .45 ACP . . . . NiB $535 Ex $476 Gd $316
Engraved, add $1125

MODEL 6
Caliber: .22 Mag., .357 Mag., .45 LC, .45 ACP or .45 LC/.410 or .45 Colt. Bbl.: 6 inches, 8.2 inches overall. Weight: .22 oz. Satin or high-polished stainless steel w/rosewood grips. Made 1986 to date.
.22 Magnum . . . . NiB $459 Ex $352 Gd $285
.357, .45 ACP, .45 LC. . . . . NiB $459 Ex $352 Gd $296
.45/LC/.410 O/U. . . . . NiB $469 Ex $357 Gd $316
Engraved, add $1295

MODEL 7
Same general specifications as the Model 1 except high-strength aircraft aluminum is used to replace some of the stainless steel parts, which reduces its weight to 7.5 oz. Made 1986 to date.
.22 LR, .22 WMR. . . . . NiB $396 Ex $163 Gd $112
Calibers .32, .38 and .44 . . . . NiB $520 Ex $469 Gd $408

MODEL 10
Same general specifications as the Model 7 except chambered for .38 Special, .45 ACP or .45 Long Colt.
.38 Special or .45 ACP. . . . . NiB $342 Ex $285 Gd $234
.45 Long Colt. . . . . NiB $393 Ex $285 Gd $234
Model 11 . . . . NiB $203 Ex $163 Gd $112
Same general specifications as Model 7 except with a matte gray finish only, weight: 11 oz. Made 1980 to date.

25 AUTOMATIC PISTOL
Calibers: .25 ACP or .250 Mag. Bbl.: 2.1 inches, 4.4 inches overall. Weight: 15.5 oz. Smooth rosewood grips. Limited production.
.25 ACP blued
(est. production 50). . . . . NiB $569 Ex $416 Gd $314
.25 ACP stainless
(est. production 400). . . . . NiB $416 Ex $324 Gd $263
.250 Mag. stainless
(est. production 100). . . . . NiB $579 Ex $518 Gd $401

MODEL 38 DA DERRINGER
Hammerless, double action, double bbl (o/u). Calibers: .22 LR, .38 Special, 9mm Para., .357 Mag., .40 S&W. Three-inch bbl., weight: 14.5 oz. Made 1990 to date.
.22 LR or .38 Special . . . . NiB $455 Ex $418 Gd $368
9mm Para. NiB $252 Ex $205 Gd $142
.357 Mag. NiB $495 Ex $455 Gd $399
.40 S&W . . . . NiB $298 Ex $241 Gd $167

ALASKAN SURVIVAL MODEL. . . . . NiB $495 Ex $454 Gd $317
Same general specifications as the Model 4 except upper bbl., chambered for .45-70 or 3-inch .410 and .45 Colt lower bbl. Also available in .45 Auto, .45 Colt, .44 Special, .357 Mag. and .357 Max. Made 1985 to date.

COP DA DERRINGER . . . . NiB $260 Ex $229 Gd $199
Hammerless, double-action, four-bbl., derringer. Caliber: .357 Mag. 3.15-inch bbl., 5.5 inches overall. Weight: 16 oz. Blade front sight,

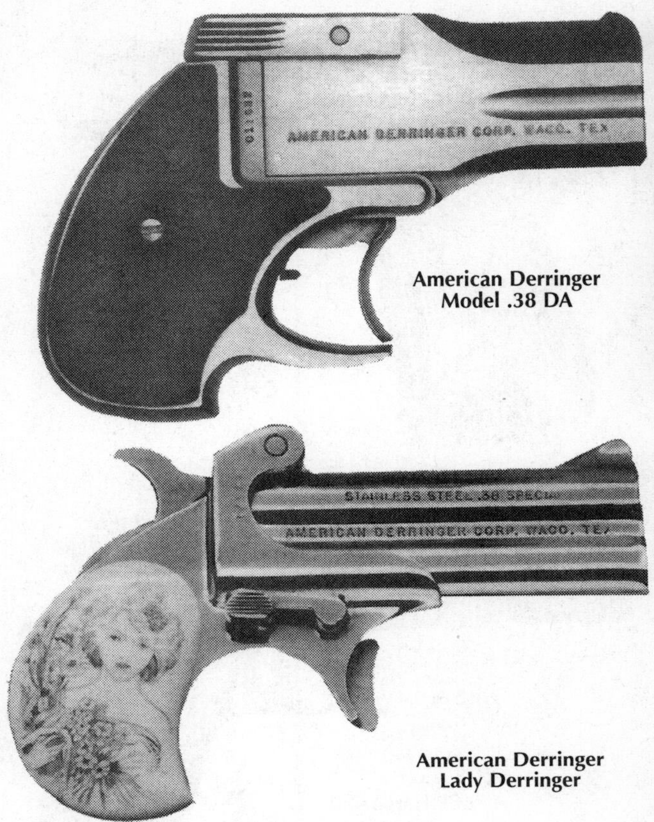

American Derringer Model .38 DA

American Derringer Lady Derringer

***(cont'd.)* COP DA DERRINGER**
open notched rear. Rosewood grips. Intro. 1990 but only limited production occurred.

LADY DERRINGER
Same general specifications as Model 1 except w/custom-tuned action fitted w/scrimshawed synthetic ivory grips. Calibers: .32 H&R Mag., .32 Special, .38 Special (additional calibers on request). Deluxe Grade engraved and highly polished w/French fitted jewelry box. Made 1991 to date.
Lady Derringer . . . . NiB $376 Ex $346 Gd $305
Deluxe. . . . . NiB $391 Ex $362 Gd $320
Engraved . . . . NiB $947 Ex $876 Gd $825

MINI-COP DA DERRINGER . . . . . . NiB $274 Ex $213 Gd $152
Same general specifications as the American Derringer Cop except chambered for .22 Magnum. Made 1990-95.

SEMMERLING LM-4
Manually operated repeater. Calibers: .45 ACP or 9mm. Five-round (.45 ACP) or 7-round magazine (9mm)., 3.6-inch bbl., 5.2 inches overall. Weight: 24 oz. Made 1997 to date. Limited availability.
Blued finish . . . . NiB $2606 Ex $2097 Gd $1446
Stainless steel . . . . NiB $3441 Ex $2765 Gd $1900

TEXAS COMMEMORATIVE
Same general specifications as Model 1 except w/solid brass frame, stainless bbls. and rosewood grips. Calibers: .22 LR, .32 Mag., .38 Special, .44-40 Win. or .45 Colt. Made 1991 to date.
.38 Special . . . . NiB $384 Ex $343 Gd $267
.44-40 or .45 Colt . . . . NiB $471 Ex $420 Gd $394

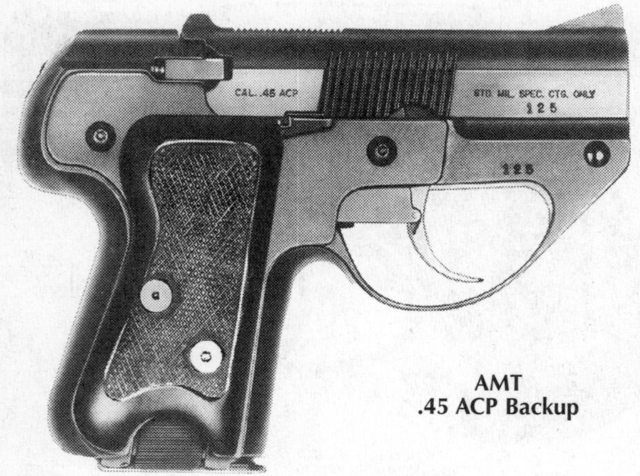

AMT
.45 ACP Backup

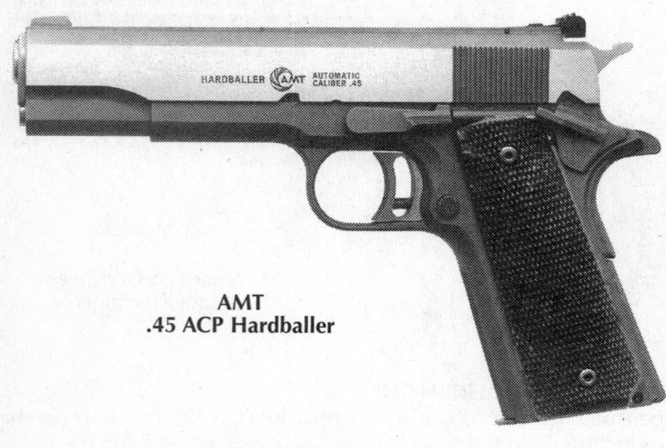

AMT
.45 ACP Hardballer

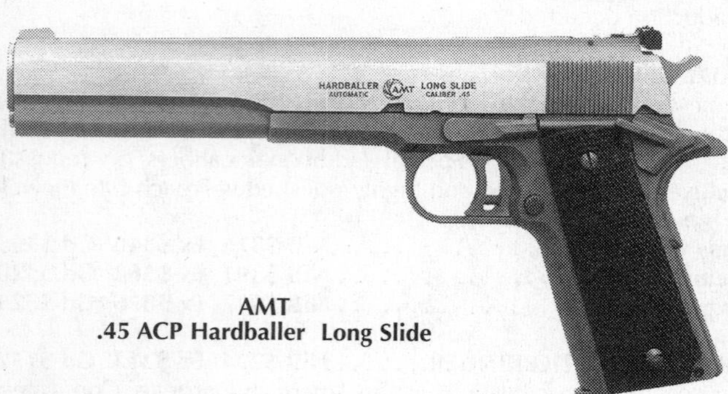

AMT
.45 ACP Hardballer Long Slide

AMERICAN FIREARMS MFG. CO., INC. — San Antonio, Texas

25 AUTO PISTOL
Caliber: .25 Auto. 8-round magazine, 2.1-inch bbl., 4.4 inches overall. Weight: 14.5 oz. Fixed sights. Stainless or blued ordnance steel. Smooth walnut grips. Made 1966-74.
Stainless steel model . . . . NiB $231 Ex $189 Gd $134
Blued steel model . . . . NiB $175 Ex $149 Gd $113

380 AUTO PISTOL. . . . . NiB $733 Ex $681 Gd $604
Caliber: .380 Auto. 8-round magazine, 3.5-inch bbl., 5.5 inches overall. Weight: 20 oz. Stainless steel. Smooth walnut grips. Made 1972-74.

AMT (ARCADIA MACHINE & TOOL) — Irwindale, California (Previously Irwindale Arms, Inc.)

NOTE: *The AMT Backup II automatic pistol was introduced in 1993 as a continuation of the original .380 backup with the traditional double action function and a redesigned double safety.*

45 ACP HARDBALLER
Caliber: .45 ACP. Seven-round magazine, 5-inch bbl., 8.5 inches overall. Weight: 39 oz. Adj. or fixed sights. Serrated matte slide rib w/loaded chamber indicator. Extended combat safety, adj. trigger and long grip safety. Wraparound Neoprene grips. Stainless steel. Made 1978 to date.
.45 ACP Hardballer . . . . NiB $473 Ex $319 Gd $195
Long slide conversion kit
(disc. 1997), add $300

45 ACP HARDBALLER LONG SLIDE
Similar to the standard AMT Hardballer except w/2-inch-longer bbl. and slide. Also chambered for .400 Cor-Bon. Made 1980 to date.
.45 ACP long slide . . . . NiB $447 Ex $369 Gd $241
.400 Cor-Bon long slide
(Intro.1998). . . . . NiB $427 Ex $344 Gd $237
5-inch conversion kit
(disc. 1997), add $300

1911 GOVERNMENT MODEL
AUTO PISTOL . . . . NiB $340 Ex $288 Gd $211
Caliber: .45 ACP. Seven-round magazine, 5-inch bbl., 8.5 inches overall. Weight: 38 ounces. Fixed sights. Wraparound Neoprene grip. Made 1979 to date.

AUTOMAG II
AUTOMATIC PISTOL . . . . NiB $417 Ex $293 Gd $180
Caliber: .22 Mag. Seven- or 9-round magazine, bbl., lengths: 3.38-4.5-, 6-inch. Weight: 32 oz. Fully adj. Millett sights. Stainless finish. Smooth black composition grips. Made 1986 to date.

AUTOMAG III
AUTOMATIC PISTOL . . . . NiB $549 Ex $471 Gd $368
Calibers: .30 M1 and 9mm Win. Mag. Eight-round magazine., 6.38-inch bbl., 10.5 inches overall. Weight: 43 ounces. Millet adj. sights. Stainless finish. Carbon fiber grips. Made 1989 to date.

AUTOMAG IV
AUTOMATIC PISTOL . . . . NiB $553 Ex $466 Gd $368
Calibers: 10mm Mag., .45 Win. Mag. 8- or 7-round magazine, 6.5- or 8.63-inch bbl., 10.5 inches overall. Weight: 46 oz. Millet adj. sights. Stainless finish. Carbon fiber grips. Made 1990 to date.

AUTOMAG V
AUTOMATIC PISTOL . . . . NiB $893 Ex $763 Gd $685
Caliber: .50 A.E. Five-round magazine, 7-inch bbl., 10.5 inches overall. Weight: 46 oz. Custom adj. sights. Stainless finish. Carbon fiber grips. Made 1994-95.

BACKUP AUTOMATIC PISTOL
Caliber: .22LR, .380 ACP. Eight-round (.22LR) or 5-round (.380 ACP) magazine, 2.5-inch bbl., 5 inches overall. Weight: 18 oz. Open sights. Carbon fiber or walnut grips. Stainless steel finish. Made 1990 to date.
.22 LR (disc. 1987) . . . . NiB $317 Ex $199 Gd $142
.380 ACP (disc. 1993) . . . . NiB $265 Ex $188 Gd $132

BACKUP II
AUTOMATIC PISTOL . . . . NiB $273 Ex $201 Gd $159
Caliber: .380 ACP, 5-round magazine, 2.5-inch bbl., 5 inches overall. Weight: 18 oz. Open sights. Stainless steel finish. Carbon-fiber grips. Made 1993 to date.

BACKUP DAO AUTO PISTOL
Calibers: .380 ACP, .38 Super, 9mm Para., .40 Cor-Bon, .40 S&W, .45 ACP. Six-round (.380, .38 Super 9mm) or 5-round (.40 Cor-Bon, .40 S&W, .45 ACP) magazine, 2.5-inch bbl., 5.75-inches overall. Weight: 18 oz. (.380 ACP) or 23 oz. Open fixed sights. Stainless steel finish. Carbon fiber grips. Made 1992 to date.
.380 ACP . . . . NiB $237 Ex $185 Gd $144
.38 Super, 9mm . . . . NiB $262 Ex $201 Gd $129
.40 Cor-Bon, .40 S&W,
.45 ACP . . . . NiB $256 Ex $206 Gd $142

BULL'S EYE
TARGET MODEL . . . . NiB $421 Ex $361 Gd $315
Caliber: .40 S&W. Eight-round magazine, 5-inch bbl., 8.5 inches overall. Weight: 38 oz. Millet adjustable sights. Wide adj. trigger. Wraparound Neoprene grips. Made 1990-92.

JAVELINA . . . . NiB $587 Ex $484 Gd $370
Caliber: 10mm. Eight-round magazine, 7-inch bbl., 10.5 inches overall. Weight: 48 oz. Long grip safety, beveled magazine well, wide adj. trigger. Millet adj. sights. Wraparound Neoprene grips. Stainless finish. Made 1991-93.

LIGHTNING AUTO PISTOL
Caliber: .22 LR. 10-round magazine, 5-, 6.5-, 8.5-, 10-inch bbl., 10.75 inches overall (6.5-inch bbl.). Weight: 45 oz. (6.5-inch bbl.). Millett adj. sights. Checkered rubber grips. Stainless finish. Made 1984-87.
Standard model . . . . NiB $365 Ex $261 Gd $159
Bull's-Eye model . . . . NiB $435 Ex $365 Gd $299

ON DUTY DA PISTOL
Calibers: .40 S&W, 9mm Para., .45 ACP. 15-round (9mm), 13-shot (.40 S&W) or 9-round (.45 ACP) magazine, 4.5-inch bbl., 7.75 inches overall. Weight: 32 oz. Hard anodized aluminum frame. Stainless steel slide and bbl., Carbon fiber grips. Made 1991-94.
9mm or .40 S&W . . . . NiB $402 Ex $309 Gd $262
.45 ACP . . . . NiB $443 Ex $365 Gd $211

SKIPPER AUTO PISTOL . . . . NiB $391 Ex $293 Gd $262
Calibers: .40 S&W and .45 ACP. Seven-round magazine, 4.25-inch bbl., 7.5 inches overall. Weight: 33 oz. Millet adj. sights. Walnut grips. Matte finish stainless steel. Made 1990-92.

ANSCHUTZ PISTOLS — Ulm, Germany Mfd. by J.G. Anschutz GmbH Jagd und Sportwaffenfabrik

Currently imported by Accuracy International, Boseman, MT and AcuSport Corporation, Bellefontaine, OH

MODEL 64P
Calibers: .22 LR or .22 Magnum. Five- or 4-round magazine, 10-inch bbl., 64MS action w/two-stage trigger. Target sights optional. Rynite black synthetic stock. Imported 1998 to date.
.22 LR . . . . NiB $492 Ex $380 Gd $322
.22 Mag. . . . . NiB $524 Ex $509 Gd $452
W/tangent

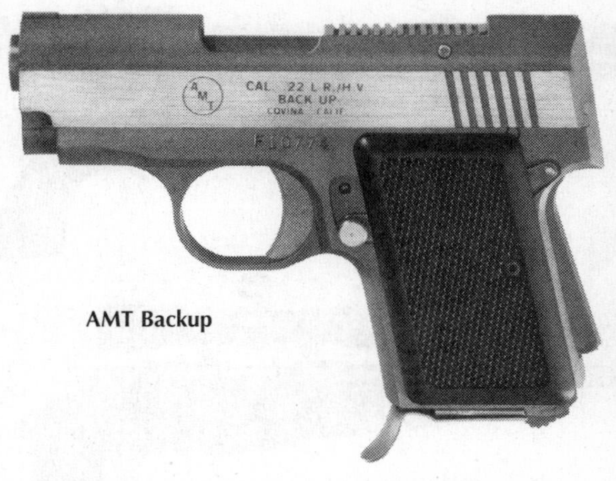

AMT Backup

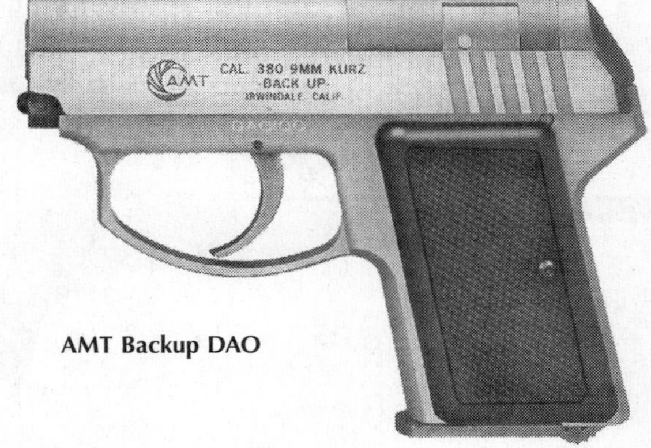

AMT Backup DAO

AMT Bull's Eye Target

AMT Skipper

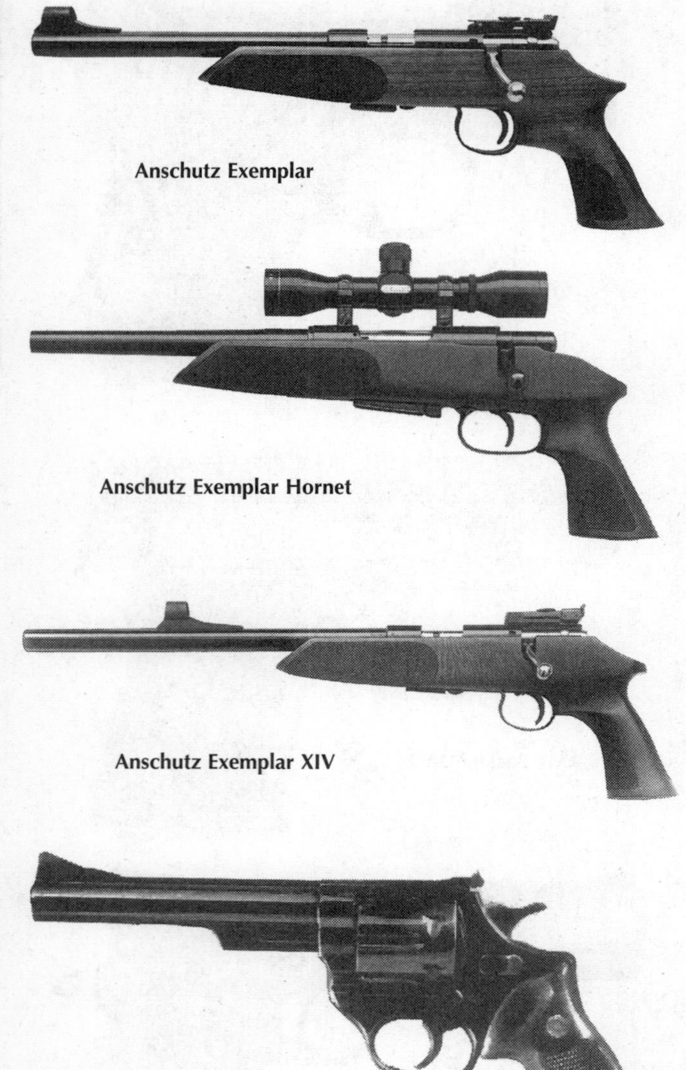
Anschutz Exemplar

Anschutz Exemplar Hornet

Anschutz Exemplar XIV

Astra Model .44 DA

EXEMPLAR (1416P/1451P) BOLT-ACTION PISTOL
Caliber: .22 LR, single-shot or 5-round clip. Seven- or 10-inch bbl., 19 inches overall (10-inch bbl.). Weight: 3.33 lbs. Match 64 action. Slide safety. Hooded ramp post front sight, adjustable open notched rear. European walnut contoured grip. Exemplar made 1987-95 and 1400 series made 1997 to date. Note: The .22 WMR chambering was also advertised but never manufactured.
Exemplar w/7- or 10-inch bbl. . . . . NiB $422 Ex $370 Gd $313
Left-hand model (disc. 1997). . . . . . NiB $531 Ex $479 Gd $396
Model 1451P (single-shot). . . . . NiB $433 Ex $349 Gd $241
Model 1416P (5-round repeater). . . NiB $421 Ex $339 Gd $234

EXEMPLAR HORNET . . . . NiB $879 Ex $682 Gd $583
Based on the Anschutz Match 54 action, tapped and grooved for scope mounting with no open sights. Caliber: .22 Hornet, 5-round magazine, 10-inch bbl., 20 inches overall. Weight: 4.35 lbs. Checkered European walnut grip. Winged safety. Made 1990 to 1995.

EXEMPLAR XIV . . . . NiB $531 Ex $479 Gd $396
Same general specifications as the standard Exemplar bolt-action pistol except w/14-inch bbl., weight: 4.15 lbs. Made 1989-95.

ARMSCOR (Arms Corp.) — Manila, Philippines *Currently imported by K.B.I., Harrisburg, PA. (Imported 1991-95 by Ruko Products, Inc., Buffalo NY. Previously by Armscor Precision, San Mateo, CA.)*

MODEL M1911-A1
AUTOMATIC PISTOL . . . . NiB $407 Ex $366 Gd $223
Caliber: .45 ACP. Eight-round magazine, 5-inch bbl., 8.75 inches overall. Weight: 38 oz. Blade front sight, drift adjustable rear w/3-dot system. Skeletonized tactical hammer and trigger. Extended slide release and beavertail grip safety. Parker-ized finish. Checkered composition or wood stocks. Imported 1996-97.

MODEL 200DC/TC
DA REVOLVER. . . . . NiB $173 Ex $153 Gd $127
Caliber: .38 Special. Six-round cylinder, 2.5-, 4-, or 6-inch bbl.; 7.3, 8.8, or 11.3 inches overall. Weight: 22, 28, or 34 oz. Ramp front and fixed rear sights. Checkered mahogany or rubber grips. Imported 1996 to date.

ASAI AG — Advanced Small Arms Industries Solothurn, Switzerland

Currently imported by Magnum Research Inc., Minneapolis, MN.
See listings under Magnum Research Pistols

ASTRA PISTOLS — Guernica, Spain Manufactured by Unceta y Compania

Currently imported by E.A.A. Corporation, Sharpes, FL.

MODEL 357 DA REVOLVER . . . . . NiB $260 Ex $224 Gd $189
Caliber: .357 Magnum. Six-round cylinder. 3-, 4-, 6-, 8.5-inch bbl., 11.25 inches overall (with 6-inch bbl.). Weight: 42 oz. (with 6-inch bbl.). Ramp front sight, adj. rear sight. Blued finish. Checkered wood grips. Imported 1972-88.

MODEL 44 DA REVOLVER
Similar to Astra ..357 except chambered for .44 Magnum. Six- or 8.5-inch bbl., 11.5 inches overall (6-inch bbl.). Weight: 44 oz. (6-inch bbl.). Imported 1980-93.
Blued finish (disc. 1987) . . . . NiB $291 Ex $245 Gd $219
Stainless finish (disc. 1993) . . . . NiB $296 Ex $245 Gd $219

MODEL 41 DA REVOLVER . . . . . . .NiB $291 Ex $250 Gd $168
Same general specifications as Model 44 except in .41 Mag. Imported 1980-85.

MODEL 45
DA REVOLVER. . . . . NiB $296 Ex $245 Gd $219
Similar to Astra .357 except chambered for .45 Colt or .45 ACP. Six- or 8.5-inch bbl., 11.5 inches overall (with 6-inch bbl.). Weight: 44 oz. (6-inch bbl.). Imported 1980-87.

MODEL 200 FIRECAT
VEST POCKET AUTO PISTOL . . . . . NiB $260 Ex $209 Gd $194
Caliber: .25 Automatic (6.35mm). Six-round magazine, 2.25-inch bbl., 4.38 inches overall. Weight: 11.75 oz. Fixed sights. Blued finish. Plastic grips. Made 1920 to date. U.S. importation disc. in 1968.

MODEL 202 FIRECAT
VEST POCKET AUTO PISTOL . . . . . NiB $496 Ex $420 Gd $369
Same general specifications as the Model 200 except chromed and engraved w/pearl grips. U.S. importation disc. 1968.

MODEL 400 AUTO PISTOL. . . . . . NiB $420 Ex $379 Gd $165
Caliber: 9mm Bayard Long (.38 ACP, 9mm Browning Long, 9mm Glisenti, 9mm Para. and 9mm Steyr cartridges may be used interchangeably in this pistol because of its chamber design). Nine-round magazine., 6-inch bbl., 10 inches overall. Weight: 35 oz. Fixed sights. Blued finish. Plastic grips. Made 1922-45. Note: This pistol, as well as Astra Models 600 and 3000, is a modification of the Browning Model 1912.

MODEL 600 MIL./POLICE-TYPE
AUTO PISTOL . . . . NiB $415 Ex $338 Gd $206
Calibers: .32 Automatic (7.65mm), 9mm Para. Magazine: 10-round (.32 cal.) or 8-round (9mm)., 5.25-inch bbl., 8 inches overall. Weight: About 33 oz. Fixed sights. Blued finish. Checkered wood or plastic grips. Made 1944-.45.

MODEL 800 CONDOR
MILITARY AUTO PISTOL. . . . . . . NiB $1529 Ex $1147 Gd $764
Similar to Models 400 and 600 except has an external hammer. Caliber: 9mm Para. Eight-round magazine, 5.25-inch bbl., 8.25 inches overall. Weight: 32.5 oz. Fixed sights. Blued finish. Plastic grips. Imported 1958-65.

MODEL 2000 CAMPER
AUTOMATIC PISTOL . . . . NiB $384 Ex $272 Gd $180
Same as Model 2000 Cub except chambered for .22 Short only, has 4-inch bbl., overall length, 6.25 inches, weight: 11.5 oz. Imported 1955-60.

MODEL 2000 CUB
POCKET AUTO PISTOL. . . . . NiB $260 Ex $199 Gd $127
Calibers: .22 Short, .25 Auto. Six-round magazine, 2.25-inch bbl., 4.5 inches overall. Weight: About 11 oz. Fixed sights. Blued or chromed finish. Plastic grips. Made 1954 to date. U.S. importation disc. 1968.

MODEL 3000
POCKET AUTO PISTOL. . . . . NiB $520 Ex $500 Gd $239
Calibers: .22 LR, .32 Automatic (7.65mm), .380 Auto (9mm Short). Ten-round magazine (.22 cal.), 7-round (.32 cal.), 6-round (.380 cal.). Four-inch bbl., 6.38 inches overall. Weight: About 22 oz. Fixed sights. Blued finish. Plastic grips. Made 1947-56.

MODEL 3003
POCKET AUTO PISTOL. . . . . NiB $1050 Ex $693 Gd $520
Same general specifications as the Model 3000 except chromed and engraved w/pearl grips. Disc. 1956.

MODEL 4000
ALCON AUTO PISTOL . . . . NiB $525 Ex $423 Gd $260
Similar to Model 3000 except has an external hammer. Calibers: .22 LR, .32 Automatic (7.65mm), .380 Auto (9mm Short). Ten-round magazine (.22 LR), 8-round (.32 Auto), 7-round (.380 Auto), 3.66-inch bbl., 6.5-inches overall. Weight: 20 oz. (.22 cal.) or 24.75 oz. (.32 and .380). Fixed sights. Blued finish. Plastic grips. Made 1956-71.

MODEL A-60 DA
AUTOMATIC PISTOL . . . . NiB $419 Ex $368 Gd $235
Similar to the Constable except in .380 only, w/13-round magazine and slide-mounted ambidextrous safety. Blued finish only. Imported 1980-91.

Astra Model 3003 Pocket

Astra Model 4000 Falcon

Astra Model A-80

MODEL A-70 COMPACT AUTO PISTOL
Calibers: 9mm Para., .40 S&W. Eight-round (9mm) or 7-round (.40 S&W) magazine., 3.5-inch bbl., 6.5 inches overall. Blued, nickel or stainless finish. Weight: 29.3 oz. Imported 1992-96.
Blued finish . . . . NiB $285 Ex $260 Gd $178
Nickel finish . . . . NiB $316 Ex $291 Gd $209
Stainless finish. . . . . NiB $377 Ex $337 Gd $285

MODEL A-75 DECOCKER AUTO PISTOL
Similar to the Model 70 except in 9mm, .40 S&W and .45 ACP w/decocking system and contoured pebble-textured grips. Imported 1993-97.
Blued finish, 9mm or .40 S&W . . . . NiB $291 Ex $260 Gd $194
Nickel finish, 9mm or .40 S&W. . . . NiB $306 Ex $260 Gd $178
Stainless, 9mm or .40 S&W. . . . . . NiB $296 Ex $260 Gd $189
Blued finish, .45 ACP. . . . . NiB $321 Ex $260 Gd $168
Nickel finish, .45 ACP . . . . NiB $345 Ex $280 Gd $168
Stainless, .45 ACP . . . . NiB $387 Ex $336 Gd $234

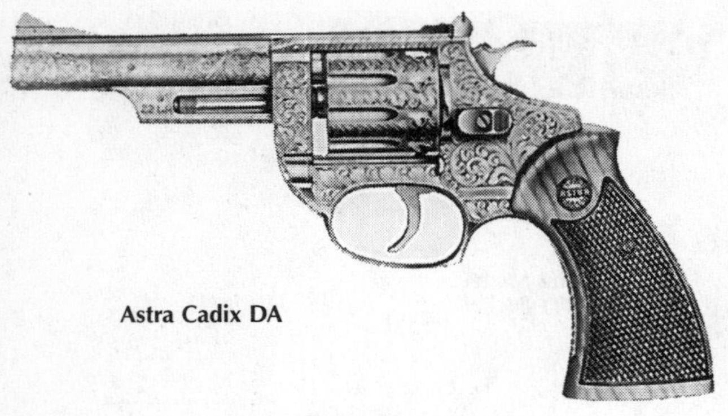
Astra Cadix DA

Astra Constable DA

Auto-Ordnance 1927 A-5 w/drum magazine

MODEL A-75 ULTRALIGHT . . . . . . NiB $316 Ex $270 Gd $183
Similar to the standard Model 75 except 9mm only w/24-oz. alloy frame. Imported 1994-97.

MODEL A-80 AUTO PISTOL . . . . . . NiB $387 Ex $336 Gd $224
Calibers: 9mm Para., .38 Super, .45 ACP. 15-round magazine or 9-round (.45 ACP). Bbl.: 3.75 inches., 7 inches overall. Weight: 36 oz. Imported 1982-89. See illustration previous page.

MODEL A-90 DA
AUTOMATIC PISTOL . . . . NiB $418 Ex $341 Gd $234
Calibers: 9mm Para., .45 ACP. 15-round (9mm) or 9-round (.45 ACP) magazine, 3.75-inch bbl., 7 inches overall. Weight: about 40 oz. Fixed sights. Blued finish. Checkered plastic grips. Imported 1985-90.

MODEL A-100 DA AUTO PISTOL
Same general specifications as the Model A-90 except selective double action chambered for 9mm Para., .40 S&W or .45 ACP. Imported 1991-97.

***(cont'd)* MODEL A-100 DA AUTO PISTOL**
Blued finish . . . . NiB $392 Ex $341 Gd $239
Nickel finish . . . . NiB $418 Ex $354 Gd $224
For night sights, add $85

CADIX DA REVOLVER
Calibers: .22 LR, .38 Special. Nine-round (.22 LR) or 5-round (.38 cal.) cylinder. Four- or 6-inch bbl., Weight: About 27 oz. (6-inch bbl.). Ramp front sight, adj. rear sight. Blued finish. Plastic grips. Imported 1960-68.
Standard model . . . . NiB $204 Ex $173 Gd $107
Lightly engraved model . . . . NiB $324 Ex $260 Gd $178
Heavily engraved model (shown) . . . . . NiB $636 Ex $510 Gd $349

CONSTABLE DA AUTO PISTOL
Calibers: .22 LR, .32 Automatic (7.65mm), .380 Auto (9mm Short). Magazine capacity: 10-round (.22 LR), 8-round (.32), 7-round (.380). 3.5-inch bbl., 6.5 inches overall. Weight: about 24 oz. Blade front sight, windage adj. rear. Blued or chromed finish. Imported 1965-92.
Stainless finish . . . . NiB $359 Ex $288 Gd $199
Blued finish . . . . NiB $308 Ex $248 Gd $171
Chrome finish (disc. 1990) . . . . NiB $327 Ex $263 Gd $181

AUTAUGA ARMS — Prattville, Alabama

MODEL 32 (MK II)
DAO AUTOMATIC PISTOL . . . . NiB $343 Ex $241 Gd $185
Caliber: .32 ACP. Six-round magazine, 2-inch bbl., weight: 11.36 oz.. Double action only. Stainless steel. Black polymer grips. Made 1997 to date.

AUTO-ORDNANCE CORPORATION — West Hurley, New York

1911 A1 GOVERNMENT AUTO PISTOL
Copy of Colt 1911 A1 semiautomatic pistol. Calibers: 9mm Para., .38 Super, 10mm, .45 ACP. 9-round (9mm, .38 Super) or 7-round 10mm, .45 ACP) magazine. Five-inch bbl., 8.5 inches overall. Weight: 39 oz. Fixed blade front sight, rear adj. Blued, satin nickel or Duo-Tone finish. Checkered plastic grips. Made 1983-99.
.45 ACP caliber . . . . NiB $376 Ex $310 Gd $228
9mm, 10mm, .38 Super. . . . . NiB $385 Ex $320 Gd $214

1911A1 .40 S&W PISTOL . . . . NiB $376 Ex $310 Gd $228
Similar to the Model 1911 A1 except has 4.5-inch bbl., w/7.75-inch overall length. Eight-round magazine, weight: 37 oz. Blade front and adj. rear sights w/3-dot system. Checkered black rubber wraparound grips. Made 1991-99.

1911 "THE GENERAL". . . . . NiB $397 Ex $335 Gd $213
Caliber: .45 ACP. Seven-round magazine, 4.5-inch bbl., 7.75 inches overall. Weight: 37 oz. Blued nonglare finish. Made 1992-99.

1927 A-5 SEMIAUTOMATIC PISTOL
Similar to Thompson Model 1928A submachine gun except has no provision for automatic firing and does not have detachable buttstock. Caliber: .45 ACP, 5-, 15-, 20- and 30-round detachable box magazines. 30-round drum also available. 13-inch finned bbl., 26 inches overall. Weight: About 6.75 lbs. Adj. rear sight, blade front. Blued finish. Walnut grips. Made 1977-94.
W/box magazine . . . . NiB $895 Ex $718 Gd $491
W/drum magazine (illustrated) . . . . NiB $1221 Ex $978 Gd $668

ZG-51 PIT BULL
AUTOMATIC PISTOL . . . . NiB $402 Ex $325 Gd $228
Caliber: .45 ACP. Seven-round magazine, 3.5-inch bbl., 7 inches overall. Weight: 32 oz. Fixed front sight, square-notch rear. Blued finish. Checkered plastic grips. Made 1991-99.

LES BAER — Hillsdale, Illinois

1911 CONCEPT SERIES AUTOMATIC PISTOL
Similar to Government 1911 built on steel or alloy full-size or compact frame. Caliber: .45 ACP. Seven-round magazine, 4.25- or 5-inch bbl. Weight: 34 to 37 oz. Adjustable low mount combat or BoMar target sights. Blued, matte black, Two-Tone or stainless finish. Checkered wood grips. Made 1996 to date.
Concept models I & II. . . . . NiB $1161 Ex $933 Gd $641
Concept models III, IV & VII. . . . NiB $1276 Ex $1025 Gd $703
Concept models V, VI & VIII . . . . NiB $1327 Ex $1065 Gd $731
Concept models IX & X. . . . . NiB $1340 Ex $1076 Gd $738

1911 PREMIER SERIES AUTOMATIC PISTOL
Similar to the Concept series except also chambered for .38 Super, 9x23 Win., .400 Cor-Bon and .45 ACP. 5- or 6-inch bbl. Weight: 37 to .40 oz. Made 1996 to date.
Premier II
(9x23 w/5-inch bbl.) . . . . NiB $1436 Ex $1157 Gd $800
Premier II (.400
Cor-Bon w/5-inch bbl.) . . . . NiB $1309 Ex $1055 Gd $731
Premier II (.45 ACP
w/5-inch bbl.) . . . . NiB $1219 Ex $983 Gd $682
Premier II (.45 ACP
S/S w/5-inch bbl.) . . . . NiB $1347 Ex $1085 Gd $751
Premier II (.45/.400
combo w/5-inch bbl.) . . . . NiB $1507 Ex $1213 Gd $838
Premier II (.38
Super w/6-inch bbl.) . . . . NiB $1691 Ex $1361 Gd $939
Premier II (.400
Cor-Bon w/6-inch bbl.) . . . . NiB $1525 Ex $1228 Gd $848
Premier II (.45 ACP
w/6-inch bbl.) . . . . NiB $1436 Ex $1157 Gd $800

S.R.P. AUTOMATIC PISTOL
Similar to F.B.I. Contract "Swift Response Pistol" built on a (customer-supplied) Para-Ordance over-sized frame or a 1911 full-size or compact frame. Caliber: .45 ACP. Seven-round magazine, 5-inch bbl., weight: 37 oz. Ramp front and fixed rear sights, w/Tritium Sight insert.
SRP 1911Government
or Commanche model. . . . . NiB $2069 Ex $1662 Gd $1142
SRP P-12 model. . . . . NiB $2362 Ex $1896 Gd $1301
SRP P-13 model. . . . . NiB $2139 Ex $1718 Gd $1179
SRP P-14 model. . . . . NiB $2012 Ex $1616 Gd $1110

1911 ULTIMATE MASTER COMBAT SERIES AUTOMATIC PISTOL
Model 1911 in Combat Competition configuration. Calibers: .38 Super, 9x23 Win., .400 Cor-Bon and .45 ACP. Five- or 6-inch NM bbl., weight: 37 to 40 oz. Made 1996 to date.
Ultimate MC (.38 or 9x23
w/5-inch bbl.) . . . . NiB $2149 Ex $1728 Gd $1189
Ultimate MC (.400 Cor-Bon
w/5-inch bbl.) . . . . NiB $1989 Ex $1600 Gd $1103
Ultimate MC (.45 ACP
w/5-inch bbl.) . . . . NiB $1894 Ex $1524 Gd $1051
Ultimate MC (.38 or 9x23
w/6-inch bbl.) . . . . NiB $2206 Ex $1774 Gd $1221
Ultimate MC (.400 Cor-Bon
w/6-inch bbl.) . . . . NiB $2053 Ex $1651 Gd $1137
Ultimate MC (.45 ACP
w/6-inch bbl.) . . . . NiB $1951 Ex $1570 Gd $1082
Ultimate "Steel Special"
(.38 Super Bianchi SPS). . . . . . . NiB $2461 Ex $1978 Gd $1360
Ultimate "PARA" (.38, 9x23
or .45 IPSC comp) . . . . NiB $2499 Ex $2008 Gd $1380
W/Triple-Port Compensator, add. $95

Auto-Ordnance ZG-51 Pit Bull

1911 CUSTOM CARRY SERIES AUTOMATIC PISTOL
Model 1911 in Combat Carry configuration built on steel or alloy full-size or compact frame. 4.5- or 5-inch NM bbl., chambered for .45 ACP. Weight: 34 to 37 oz.
Custom carry (steel frame
w/4.24- or 5-inch bbl.) . . . . NiB $1384 Ex $1116 Gd $773
Custom carry (alloy frame
w/4.24-inch bbl.). . . . . NiB $1607 Ex $1295 Gd $895

BAUER FIREARMS CORPORATION — Fraser, MI

.25 AUTOMATIC PISTOL. . . . . NiB $158 Ex $138 Gd $97
Stainless steel. Caliber: .25 Automatic. Six-round magazine, 2.13-inch bbl., 4 inches overall. Weight: 10 oz. Fixed sights. Checkered walnut or simulated pearl grips. Made 1972-84.

BAYARD PISTOLS — Herstal, Belgium Mfd. by Anciens Etablissements Pieper

MODEL 1908
POCKET AUTOMATIC PISTOL . . . . NiB $366 Ex $264 Gd $136
Calibers: .25 Automatic (6.35mm). .32 Automatic (7.65mm), .380 Automatic (9mm Short). Six-round magazine, 2.25-inch bbl., 4.88 inches overall. Weight: About 16 oz. Fixed sights. Blued finish. Hard rubber grips. Intro. 1908. Disc. 1923.

MODEL 1923 POCKET
.25 AUTOMATIC PISTOL. . . . . NiB $366 Ex $305 Gd $162
Caliber: .25 Automatic (6.35mm). 2.13-inch bbl., 4.31 inches overall. Weight: 12 oz. Fixed sights. Blued finish. Checkered hard-rubber grips. Intro. 1923. Disc. 1930.

MODEL 1923 POCKET
AUTOMATIC PISTOL . . . . NiB $374 Ex $305 Gd $162
Calibers: .32 Automatic (7.65mm), .380 Automatic (9mm Short). Six-round magazine, 3.31-inch bbl., 5.5 inches overall. Weight: About 19 oz. Fixed sights. Blued finish. Checkered hard-rubber grips. Intro. 1923. Disc. 1940.

MODEL 1930 POCKET
.25 AUTOMATIC PISTOL. . . . . NiB $366 Ex $264 Gd $131
This is a modification of the Model 1923, which it closely resembles.

BEEMAN PRECISION ARMS, INC. — Santa Rosa, CA

P08 AUTOMATIC PISTOL . . . . NiB $415 Ex $349 Gd $185
Caliber: .22 LR. 10-round magazine, 3.8-inch bbl., 7.8 inches overall. Weight: 25 oz. Fixed sights. Blued finish. Checkered hardwood grips. Imported 1969-91.

Benelli MP90S

Benelli MP95E

Beretta Model 21

MINI P08 AUTOMATIC PISTOL . . . NiB $389 Ex $313 Gd $217
Caliber: Same general specifications as P08 except shorter 3.5-inch bbl., 7.4 inches overall. Weight: 20 oz. Imported 1986-91.

SP METALLIC SILHOUETTE PISTOLS
Caliber: .22 LR. Single-shot. Bbl. lengths: 6-, 8-, 10- or 15-inches. Adj. rear sight. Receiver contoured for scope mount. Walnut target grips w/adj. palm rest. Models SP made 1985-86 and SPX 1993-94.
SP Standard W/8-or 10-inch bbl. . . . NiB $257 Ex $207 Gd $144
SP Standard W/12-inch bbl. . . . . . . NiB $302 Ex $241 Gd $167
SP Standard W/15-inch bbl. . . . . . . NiB $320 Ex $258 Gd $178
SP Deluxe W/8-or 10-inch bbl. . . . . NiB $308 Ex $248 Gd $171
SP Deluxe W/12-inch bbl. . . . . NiB $327 Ex $263 Gd $181
SP Deluxe W/15-inch bbl. . . . . NiB $346 Ex $278 Gd $192
SPX Standard W/10-inch bbl. . . . . . NiB $639 Ex $513 Gd $352
SPX Deluxe W/10-inch bbl. . . . . NiB $869 Ex $696 Gd $476

BEHOLLA PISTOL — Suhl, Germany Mfd. by both Becker and Holländer and Stenda-Werke GmbH

POCKET AUTOMATIC PISTOL . . . . NiB $234 Ex $189 Gd $117
Caliber: .32 Automatic (7.65mm). Seven-round magazine, 2.9-inch bbl., 5.5 inches overall. Weight: 22 oz. Fixed sights. Blued finish. Serrated wood or hard rubber grips. Made by Becker and Hollander 1915-1920, by Stenda-Werke circa 1920-25. Note: Essentially the same pistol was manufactured concurrently w/the Stenda version as the "Leonhardt" by H. M. Gering and as the "Menta" by August Menz.

BENELLI PISTOLS — Urbino, Italy *Imported by Benelli USA*

MP90S WORLD CUP TARGET PISTOL
Semiautomatic blowback action. Calibers: .22 Short, .22LR, .32 W.C. Five-round magazine, 4.33-inch fixed bbl. 6.75 inches overall. Weight: 36 oz. Post front sight, adjustable rear. Blue finish. Anatomic shelf-style grip. Imported 1992 to 2001.
MP90S (.22 LR) . . . . NiB $1295 Ex $1106 Gd $591
MP90S (.22 Short, disc. 1995). . . . NiB $1087 Ex $875 Gd $603
MP90S (.32 WC) . . . . NiB $1344 Ex $1081 Gd $743
W/conversion kit, add $550

MP95E SPORT TARGET PISTOL
Similar to the MP90S except with 5- or 9-round magazine, 4.25- inch bbl., Blue or chrome finish. Checkered target grip. Imported 1994 to date.
Blue MP95 (.22 LR) . . . . NiB $731 Ex $602 Gd $370
Blue MP95 (.32 WC) . . . . NiB $719 Ex $576 Gd $395
Chrome, add $85

BERETTA USA CORP. — Accokeek, Maryland

Beretta firearms are manufactured by Fabbrica D'Armi Pietro Beretta S. p. A. in the Gardone Val Trompia (Brescia), Italy. This prestigious firm has been in business since 1526. In 1977, Beretta U.S.A. Corp., a manufacturing and importing facility, opened in Accokeek, MD. (Previously imported by Garcia Corp., J.L. Galef & Son, Inc. and Berben Corporation.) Note: Beretta also owns additional firearms manufacturing companies including: Benelli, Franchi, Sako, Stoeger, Tikka and Uberti.

MODEL 20 DOUBLE-ACTION AUTO PISTOL. . . . . NiB $170 Ex $149 Gd $98
Caliber: .25 ACP. Eight-round magazine, 2.5-inch bbl., 4.9 inches overall. Weight: 10.9 oz. Plastic or walnut grips. Fixed sights. Made 1984-85.

MODEL 21 DOUBLE-ACTION AUTO PISTOL
Calibers: .22 LR and .25 ACP. Seven-round (.22 LR) or 8-round (..25 ACP) magazine, 2.5-inch bbl., 4.9 inches overall. Weight: About 12 oz. Blade front sight, V-notch rear. Walnut grips. Made 1985 to date.
Blued finish . . . . NiB $205 Ex $165 Gd $113
Nickel finish (.22 LR only) . . . . NiB $243 Ex $196 Gd $135
Model 21EL engraved model . . . . . NiB $320 Ex $257 Gd $177

MODEL 70 AUTOMATIC PISTOL . . NiB $237 Ex $190 Gd $131
Improved version of Model 1935. Steel or lightweight alloy. Calibers: .32 Auto (7.65mm), .380 Auto (9mm Short). Eight-round (.32) or 7-round (.380) magazine, 3.5-inch bbl., 6.5 inches overall. Weight: Steel, 22.25 oz.; alloy, 16 oz. Fixed sights. Blued finish. Checkered plastic grips. Made 1959-85. Note: Formerly marketed in U.S. as "Puma" (alloy model in .32) and "Cougar" (steel model in .380). Disc.

MODEL 70S. NiB $252 Ex $221 Gd $139
Similar to Model 70T except chambered for .22 Auto and .380 Auto. Longer bbl. guide and safety lever blocking hammer. Front blade and rear sight fixed on breechblock. Weight: 1 lb., 7 oz. Made 1977-85.

MODEL 70T
AUTOMATIC PISTOL . . . . NiB $288 Ex $262 Gd $159
Similar to Model 70. Caliber: .32 Automatic (7.65mm). Nine-round magazine, 6-inch bbl., 9.5 inches overall. Weight: 19 oz. adj. rear sight, blade front sight. Blued finish. Checkered plastic grips. Intro. in 1959. disc.

MODEL 71
AUTOMATIC PISTOL . . . . NiB $232 Ex $206 Gd $134
Same general specifications as alloy Model 70. Caliber: .22 LR. Six-inch bbl., 8-round magazine, Adj. rear sight frame. Single action. Made 1959-89. Note: Formerly marketed in U.S. as the "Jaguar Plinker."

MODEL 72 . . . . NiB $232 Ex $206 Gd $129
Same as Model 71 except has 6-inch bbl., weight: 18 oz. Intro. in 1959. Disc. Note: Formerly marketed in U.S as "Jaguar Plinker."

MODEL 76 AUTO TARGET PISTOL
Caliber: .22 LR. 10-round magazine, 6-inch bbl., 8.8 inches overall. Weight: 33 oz. adj. rear sight, front sight w/interchangeable blades. Blued finish. Checkered plastic or wood grips. Made 1966-85. Note: Formerly marketed in the U.S. as the "Sable."
Model 76 w/plastic grips. . . . . NiB $385 Ex $309 Gd $212
Model 76W w/wood grips. . . . . NiB $449 Ex $360 Gd $247

MODEL 81 DOUBLE-
ACTION AUTO PISTOL. . . . . NiB $324 Ex $262 Gd $170
Caliber: .32 Automatic (7.65mm). 12-round magazine, 3.8-inch bbl., 6.8 inches overall. Weight: 23.5 oz. Fixed sights. Blued finish. Plastic grips. Made principally for the European market 1975-84, w/similar variations as implemented on the Model 84.

MODEL 82 DOUBLE-
ACTION AUTO PISTOL. . . . . NiB $308 Ex $247 Gd $170
Caliber: .32 ACP. Similar to the Model 81 except with a slimmer-profile frame designed to accept a single column 9-round magazine. Matte black finish. Importation disc. 1984.

MODEL 84 DOUBLE-
ACTION AUTO PISTOL. . . . . NiB $314 Ex $268 Gd $164
Same as Model 81 except made in caliber .380 Automatic w/13-round magazine, 3.82-inch bbl., 6.8 inches overall. Weight: 23 oz. Fixed front and rear sights. Made 1975-82.

MODEL 84B DA AUTO PISTOL . . . NiB $309 Ex $262 Gd $180
Improved version of Model 84 w/strengthened frame and slide, and firing-pin block safety added. Ambidextrous reversible magazine release. Blued or nickel finish. Checkered black plastic or wood grips. Other specifications same. Made c. 1982-84.

MODEL 84(BB) DOUBLE-ACTION AUTO PISTOL
Improved version of Model 84B w/further-strengthened slide, frame and recoil spring. Caliber: .380 ACP. 13-round magazine, 3.82-inch bbl., 6.8 inches overall. Weight: 23 oz. Checkered black plastic or wood grips. Blued or nickel finish. Notched rear and blade front sight. Made c. 1984-94.
Blued w/plastic grips. . . . . NiB $448 Ex $360 Gd $238
Blued w/wood grips . . . . NiB $467 Ex $376 Gd $258
Nickel finish w/wood grips . . . . NiB $513 Ex $412 Gd $283

Beretta Model 71

Beretta Model 72

Beretta Model 84

MODEL 84 CHEETAH SEMI-AUTO PISTOL
Similar to the Model 84 BB except with required design changes as mandated by regulation, including reduced magazine capacity (10-round magazine) and marked as 9mm short (.380) as a marketing strategy to counter increased availability of 9mm chamberings from other manufacturers. Made 1994 to date. See illustration next page.
Blued w/plastic grips. . . . . NiB $428 Ex $345 Gd $238
Blued w/wood grips . . . . NiB $467 Ex $376 Gd $258
Nickel finish w/wood grips . . . . NiB $505 Ex $407 Gd $280

MODEL 85 DOUBLE-
ACTION AUTO PISTOL. . . . . NiB $458 Ex $360 Gd $206
Similar to the Model 84 except designed with a slimmer-profile frame to accept a single column 8-round magazine, no ambidextrous magazine release. Matte black finish. Weight: 21.8 oz. Introduced in 1977 following the Model 84. See illustration next page.

MODEL 85B DA AUTO PISTOL . . . NiB $463 Ex $370 Gd $237
Improved version of the Model 85. Imported 1982-85.

Beretta Model 84 Cheetah (Nickel finish)

Beretta Model 85

Beretta Model 85BB

Beretta Model 86 Cheetah

MODEL 85BB DOUBLE-ACTION PISTOL
Improved version of the Model 85B w/strengthened frame and slide. Caliber: .380 ACP. Eight-round magazine, 3.82 inch bbl., 6.8 inches overall. Weight: 21.8 oz. Blued or nickel finish. Checkered black plastic or wood grips. Imported 1985-94.
Blued finish
w/plastic grips . . . . **NiB $394 Ex $317 Gd $218**
Blued finish
w/wood grips . . . . **NiB $440 Ex $353 Gd $243**
Nickel finish
w/wood grips . . . . **NiB $491 Ex $394 Gd $271**

MODEL 85 CHEETAH SEMI-AUTO PISTOL
Similar to the Model 85 BB except with required design changes as mandated by regulation and marked as 9mm short (.380) as a marketing strategy to counter increased availability of 9mm chamberings from other manufacturers. Made 1994 to date.
Blued w/plastic grips . . . . **NiB $394 Ex $317 Gd $206**
Blued w/wood grips . . . . **NiB $447 Ex $363 Gd $256**
Nickel w/wood grips . . . . **NiB $491 Ex $405 Gd $287**

MODEL 85F DOUBLE-ACTION PISTOL
Similar to the Model 85BB except has re-contoured trigger guard and manual ambidextrous safety w/decocking device. Bruniton finish. Imported in 1990.
Matte black Bruniton
finish w/plastic grips . . . . **NiB $398 Ex $321 Gd $208**
Matte black Bruniton
finish w/wood grips . . . . **NiB $464 Ex $378 Gd $267**

MODEL 86 CHEETAH
DA AUTO PISTOL . . . . **NiB $512 Ex $403 Gd $208**
Caliber: .380 auto. Eight-round magazine, 4.4- inch bbl., 7.3 inches overall. Weight: 23.3 oz. Bruniton finish w/wood grips. Made 1986-89. (Reintroduced 1990 in the Cheetah series.)

MODEL 87 CHEETAH AUTO PISTOL
Similar to the Model 85 except in .22 LR w/8- or 10- shot magazine (Target) and optional extended 6-inch bbl. (Target in single action). Overall length: 6.8 to 8.8 inches. Weight: 20.1 oz. to 29.4 oz (Target). Checkered wood grips. Made 1987 to date.
Blued finish
(double-action) . . . . **NiB $512 Ex $403 Gd $208**
Target model
(single action) . . . . **NiB $466 Ex $378 Gd $264**

MODEL 89
GOLD STANDARD TARGET
AUTOMATIC PISTOL . . . . **NiB $661 Ex $537 Gd $347**
Caliber: .22 LR. Eight-round magazine, 6-inch bbl., 9.5 inches overall. Weight: 41 oz. Adj. target sights. Blued finish. Target-style walnut grips. Made 1988 to date.

MODEL 90
DA AUTO PISTOL . . . . **NiB $288 Ex $209 Gd $139**
Caliber: .32 Auto (7.65mm). Eight-round magazine, 3.63-inch bbl., 6.63 inches overall. Weight: 19.5 oz. Fixed sights. Blued finish. Checkered plastic grips. Made 1969-83.

MODEL 92 DA AUTO
PISTOL (1ST SERIES) . . . . **NiB $676 Ex $571 Gd $288**
Caliber: 9mm Para. 15-round magazine, 4.9-inch bbl., 8.5 inches overall. Weight: 33.5 oz. Fixed sights. Blued finish. Plastic grips. Initial production of 5,000 made in 1976.

MODEL 92D DA AUTO PISTOL
Same general specifications as Model 92F except DA only w/bobbed hammer and 3-dot sight. Made 1992 to date.
Model 92D . . . . **NiB $481 Ex $378 Gd $290**
With Tritium sight system add **$80**

MODEL 92F COMPACT DA AUTOMATIC PISTOL . . . . **NiB $605 Ex $492 Gd $214**
Caliber: 9mm Para. 12-round magazine, 4.3-inch bbl., 7.8 inches overall. Weight: 31.5 oz. Wood grips. Square-notched rear sight, blade front integral w/slide. Made 1986-93.

MODEL 92F COMPACT L TYPE M DA AUTOMATIC PISTOL
Same general specifications as the original 92F Compact except 8-round magazine, Weight: 30.9 oz. Bruniton matte finish. Made 1998 to date.
Model 92F Compact L Type M. . . . . **NiB $607 Ex $494 Gd $216**
Model 92F Compact L Type M Inox. . . . . **NiB $607 Ex $494 Gd $216**
W/Tritium sight system, add. **$80**

MODEL 92F DA AUTOMATIC PISTOL
Same general specifications as Model 92 except w/slide-mounted safety and repositioned magazine release. Replaced Model 92SB. Blued or stainless finish. Made 1985 to date.
Blued finish . . . . **NiB $607 Ex $494 Gd $226**
Stainless finish. . . . . **NiB $607 Ex $494 Gd $226**
Model 92F-EL gold. . . . . **NiB $740 Ex $612 Gd $450**

MODEL 92FS DA AUTOMATIC PISTOL
Calibers: 9mm, 9mmx19 and .40 S&W. 15- round magazine, 4.9-inch bbl., 8.5 inches overall. Weight: 34.4 to 35.3 oz. Ambidextrous safety/decock lever. Chrome-lined bore w/combat trigger guard. Bruniton finish w/plastic grips or Inox finish w/rubber grips. Made 1991 to date.
Model 92FS . . . . **NiB $659 Ex $525 Gd $303**
Model 92FS, Inox . . . . **NiB $684 Ex $581 Gd $303**
Model 92FS — Brigadier (Made 1999 to date) . . . . **NiB $567 Ex $458 Gd $318**
Model 92FS — Brigadier Inox . . . . **NiB $684 Ex $581 Gd $308**
Model 92FS — Centurion (Made 1992 to date) . . . . **NiB $684 Ex $581 Gd $308**
Model 92FS — 470th Anniver. (Made 1999) . . . . **NiB $2203 Ex $1955 Gd $1157**

MODEL 92S DA AUTO PISTOL (2ND SERIES) . . . . **NiB $689 Ex $586 Gd $277**
Revised version of Model 92 w/ambidextrous slide-mounted safety modification intended for both commercial and military production. Evolved to Model 92S-1 for U.S. Military trials. Made 1980-85.

MODEL 92SB DA AUTO PISTOL (3RD SERIES). . . . . . **NiB $710 Ex $617 Gd $319**
Same general specifications as standard Model 92 except has slide-mounted safety and repositioned magazine release. Made 1981-85.

MODEL 92 SB-F DA AUTO PISTOL . . . . **NiB $689 Ex $586 Gd $277**
Caliber: 9mm Para. 15-round magazine, bbl.: 4.9 inches, 8.5 inches overall. Weight: 34 oz. Plastic or Beretta Model 92 SB-F DA Auto Pistol wood grips. Square-notched rear sight, blade front sight integral w/slide. This model, also called Model 92S-1, is the standard-issue sidearm for the U.S. Armed Forces. Made 1985 to date.

Beretta Model 90

Beretta Model 92F

Beretta Model 92 Compact L Type M

Beretta Model 92FS Brigadier Inox

Beretta Model 96

Beretta Model 949 Olimpionico

Beretta Model 950BS Jetfire

MODEL 96 DOUBLE-ACTION AUTO PISTOL
Same general specifications as Model 92F except in .40 S&W. 10-round magazine (9-round in Compact model). Made 1992 to date.
Model 96 D (DA only) .... **NiB $430 Ex $345 Gd $236**
Model 96 Centurion (compact) .... **NiB $478 Ex $376 Gd $237**
W/Tritium sights, add **$80**
W/Tritium sights system, add **$95**

MODEL 101 .... **NiB $262 Ex $232 Gd $134**
Same as Model 70T except caliber .22 LR, has 10-round magazine, Intro. in 1959. Disc.

MODEL 318
(1934) AUTO PISTOL .... **NiB $288 Ex $252 Gd $139**
Caliber: .25 Automatic (6.35mm). Eight-round magazine, 2.5-inch bbl., 4.5 inches overall. Weight: 14 oz. Fixed sights. Blued finish. Plastic grips. Made 1934 to c. 1939.

MODEL 949
OLIMPIONICO AUTO PISTOL .... **NiB $695 Ex $581 Gd $221**
Calibers: .22 Short, .22 LR. Five-round magazine, 8.75-inch bbl., 12.5 inches overall. Weight: 38 oz. Target sights. Adj. bbl., weight. Muzzle brake. Checkered walnut grips w/thumbrest. Made 1959-64.

MODEL 950B AUTO PISTOL ...... **NiB $168 Ex $129 Gd $77**
Same general specifications as Model 950CC except caliber .25 Auto, has 7-round magazine, Made 1959 to date. Note: Formerly marketed in the U.S. as "Jetfire."

MODEL 950BS JETFIRE SA PISTOL
Calibers: .25 ACP or .22 Short (disc.1992). Seven- or 8-round magazine, 2.4- or 4- inch bbl., 4.5 to 4.7 inches overall. Weight: 9.9 oz. Fixed blade front and V-notch rear sights. Matte Blue or Inox (Stainless) finish. Checkered black plastic grips. Made 1987 to date.
Blued finish .... **NiB $166 Ex $132 Gd $93**
Nickel finish .... **NiB $217 Ex $175 Gd $120**
Inox finish .... **NiB $191 Ex $154 Gd $107**
W/4-inch bbl.,
(.22 Short) .... **NiB $199 Ex $159 Gd $110**

MODEL 950CC
AUTO PISTOL .... **NiB $144 Ex $123 Gd $77**
Caliber: .22 Short. Six-round magazine, hinged 2.38-inch bbl., 4.75 inches overall. Weight: 11 oz. Fixed sights. Blued finish. Plastic grips. Made 1959 to date. Note: Formerly marketed in the U.S. as "Minx M2."

MODEL 950CC
SPECIAL AUTO PISTOL .... **NiB $144 Ex $123 Gd $77**
Same general specifications as Model 950CC Auto except has 4-inch bbl. Made 1959 to date. Note: Formerly marketed in the U.S. as "Minx M4."

MODEL 951 (1951)
MILITARY AUTO PISTOL .... **NiB $299 Ex $247 Gd $170**
Caliber: 9mm Para. Eight-round magazine, 4.5-inch bbl., 8 inches overall. Weight: 31 oz. Fixed sights. Blued finish. Plastic grips. Made 1952 to date. Note: This is the standard pistol of the Italian Armed Forces, also used by Egyptian and Israeli armies and by the police in Nigeria. Egyptian and Israeli models usually command a premium. Formerly marketed in the U.S. as the "Brigadier."

MODEL 1915
AUTO PISTOL .... **NiB $998 Ex $741 Gd $329**
Calibers: 9mm Glisenti and .32 ACP (7.65mm). Eight-round magazine, 4-inch bbl., 6.7 inches overall (9mm), 5.7 inches (.32 ACP). Weight: 30 oz. (9mm), 20 oz. (.32 ACP). Fixed sights. Blued finish. Wood grips. Made 1915-1922. An improved postwar 1915/1919 version in caliber .32 ACP was later offered for sale in 1922 as the Model 1922.

MODEL 1923
AUTO PISTOL .... **NiB $1050 Ex $895 Gd $277**
Caliber: 9mm Glisenti (Luger). Eight-round magazine, 4-inch bbl., 6.5 inches overall. Weight: 30 oz. Fixed sights. Blued finish. Plastic grips. Made c. 1923-36.

MODEL 1934 AUTO PISTOL
Caliber: .380 Automatic (9mm Short). Seven-round magazine, 3.38-inch bbl., 5.88 inches overall. Weight: 24 oz. Fixed sights. Blued finish. Plastic grips. Official pistol of the Italian Armed Forces. Wartime pieces not as well made and finished as commercial models. Made 1934-59.
Commercial model .... **NiB $396 Ex $345 Gd $206**
War model .... **NiB $370 Ex $340 Gd $195**

MODEL 1935 AUTO PISTOL
Caliber: .32 ACP (7.65mm). Eight-round magazine, 3.5-inch bbl., 5.75 inches overall. Weight: 24 oz. Fixed sights. Blued finish. Plastic grips. A roughly-finished version of this pistol was produced during WW II. Made 1935-1959.
Commercial model . . . . **NiB $370 Ex $334 Gd $190**
War model. . . . . **NiB $319 Ex $267 Gd $164**

MODEL 3032 DA SEMIAUTOMATIC TOMCAT
Caliber: .32 ACP. Seven-round magazine, 2.45-inch bbl., 5 inches overall. Weight: 14.5 oz. Fixed sights. Blued or stainless finish. Made 1996 to date.
Matte blue. . . . . **NiB $278 Ex $211 Gd $129**
Polished blue . . . . **NiB $323 Ex $268 Gd $197**
Stainless. **NiB $348 Ex $283 Gd $201**

Beretta
Model 3032 Tomcat

MODEL 8000/8040/8045 COUGAR DA PISTOL
Calibers: 9mm, .40 S&W and .45 Auto. Eight- or 10- shot magazine, 3.6 to 3.7- inch bbl., 7- to 7.2 inches overall. Weight: 32 to 32.6 oz. Short recoil action w/rotating barrel. Fixed sights w/3-dot Tritium system. Textured black composition grips. Matte black Bruniton finish w/alloy frame. Made 1994 to date.
8000 Cougar D (9mm DAO). . . . . **NiB $631 Ex $574 Gd $322**
8000 Cougar F (9mm DA) . . . . **NiB $631 Ex $574 Gd $322**
8040 Cougar D (.40 S&W DAO). . . . . **NiB $631 Ex $574 Gd $322**
8040 Cougar F (.40 S&W DA) . . . . **NiB $631 Ex $574 Gd $322**
8045 Cougar D (.45 Auto DAO) . . . . **NiB $652 Ex $579 Gd $332**
8045 Cougar F (.45 Auto DA) . . . . **NiB $652 Ex $579 Gd $332**

Beretta
Model 8000 Cougar D

MODEL 8000/8040/8045 MINI COUGAR DA PISTOL
Calibers: 9mm, .40 S&W and .45 Auto. Six- 8- or 10-round magazine, 3.6- to 3.7- inch bbl., 7 inches overall. Weight: 27.4 to 30.4 oz. Fixed sights w/3-dot Tritium system. Ambidextrous safety/decocker lever. Matte black Bruniton finish w/anodized aluminum alloy frame. Made 1998 to date.
8000 Mini Cougar D (9mm DAO) . . . . **NiB $659 Ex $525 Gd $267**
8000 Mini Cougar F (9mm DA) . . . . **NiB $679 Ex $545 Gd $277**
8040 Mini Cougar D (.40 S&W DAO) . . . . **NiB $679 Ex $545 Gd $277**
8040 Mini Cougar F (.40 S&W DA) . . . . **NiB $679 Ex $545 Gd $277**
8045 Mini Cougar D (.45 Auto DAO). . . . . **NiB $669 Ex $535 Gd $252**
8045 Mini Cougar F (.45 Auto DA). . . . . **NiB $679 Ex $545 Gd $277**

Beretta
Model 8000 Cougar F

MODEL 9000S SUBCOMPACT PISTOL SERIES
Calibers: 9mm, .40 S&W. 10-round magazine, 3.5- inch bbl., 6.6 inches overall. Weight: 25.7 to 27.5 oz. Single/double and double-action only. Front and rear dovetail sights w/3- dot system. Chrome-plated barrel w/Techno-polymer frame. Geometric locking system w/tilt barrel. Made 1999 to date. See illustration next page.
Type D (9mm) . . . . **NiB $516 Ex $437 Gd $276**
Type D (.40 S&W) . . . . **NiB $530 Ex $427 Gd $277**
Type F (9mm). . . . . **NiB $556 Ex $457 Gd $283**
Type F (.40 S&W). . . . . **NiB $566 Ex $472 Gd $292**

Beretta
Model 8040 Mini Cougar D

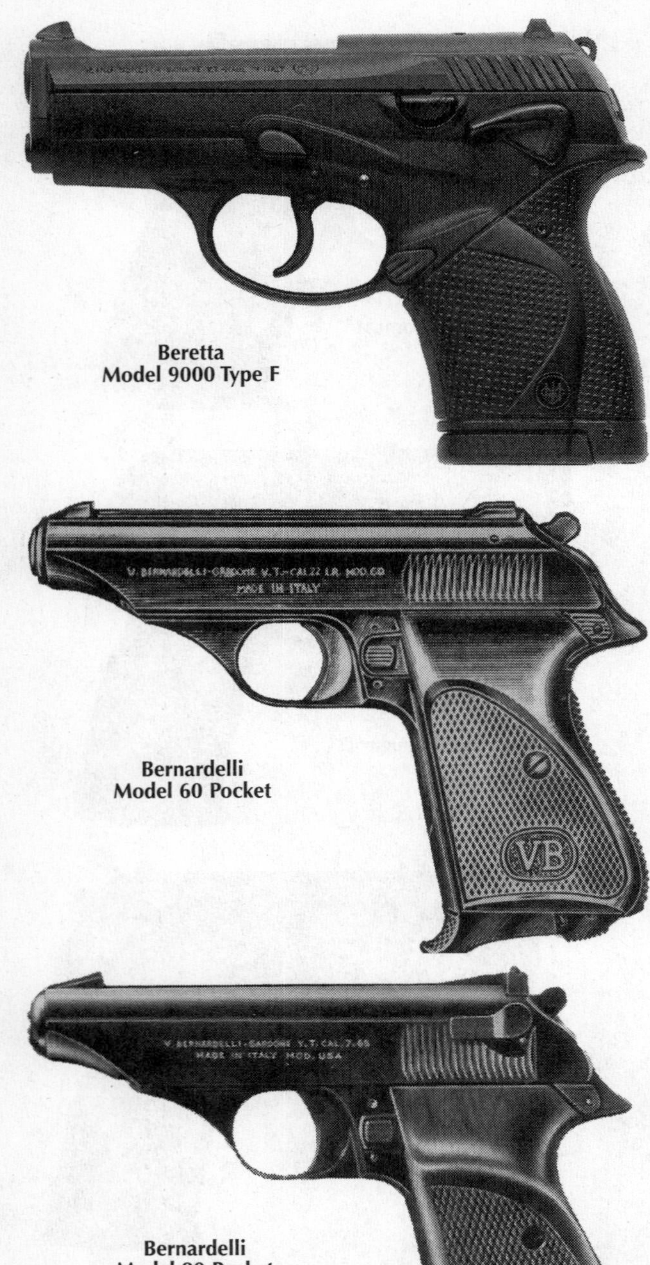

Beretta
Model 9000 Type F

Bernardelli
Model 60 Pocket

Bernardelli
Model 80 Pocket

VINCENZO BERNARDELLI, S.P.A. Gardone V. T. (Brescia), Italy

Currently imported by Armsport, Inc., Miami, FL

MODEL 60 POCKET AUTOMATIC PISTOL . . . . NiB $232 Ex $206 Gd $139
Calibers: .22 LR, .32 Auto (7.65mm), .380 Auto (9mm Short). Eight-round magazine (.22 and .32), 7-round (.380). 3.5-inch bbl., 6.5 inches ovr-all. Weight: About 25 oz. Fixed sights. Blued finish. Bakelite grips. Made 1959-90.

MODEL 68 AUTOMATIC PISTOL . . . NiB $149 Ex $129 Gd $87
Caliber: 6.35. Five- and 8-round magazine, 2.13-inch bbl., 4.13 inches overall. Weight: 10 oz. Fixed sights. Blued or chrome finish. Bakelite or pearl grips. This model, like its .22-caliber counterpart, was known as the "Baby" Bernardelli. Disc. 1970.

MODEL 69 AUTOMATIC TARGET PISTOL . . . . NiB $602 Ex $499 Gd $319
Caliber: .22 LR. 10-round magazine, 5.9-inch bbl., 9 inches overall. Weight: 2.2 lbs. Fully adj. target sights. Blued finish. Stippled right- or left-hand wraparound walnut grips. Made 1987 to date. Note: This was previously Model 100.

MODEL 80 AUTOMATIC PISTOL . . . . NiB $196 Ex $170 Gd $108
Calibers: .22 LR, .32 ACP (7.65mm), .380 Auto (9mm Short). Magazine capacity: 10-round (.22), 8-round (.32), 7-round (.380). 3.5-inch bbl., 6.5 inches overall. Weight: 25.6 oz. adj. rear sight, white dot front sight. Blued finish. Plastic thumbrest grips. Note: Model 80 is a modification of Model 60 designed to conform w/U.S. import regulations. Made 1968-88.

MODEL 90 SPORT TARGET . . . . NiB $221 Ex $196 Gd $118
Same as Model 80 except has 6-inch bbl., 9 inches overall, weight: 26.8 oz. Made 1968-90.

MODEL 100 TARGET AUTOMATIC PISTOL . . . . NiB $417 Ex $345 Gd $226
Caliber: .22 LR. 10-round magazine, 5.9-inch bbl., 9 inches overall. Weight: 37.75 oz. Adj. rear sight, interchangeable front sights. Blued finish. Checkered walnut thumbrest grips. Made 1969-86. Note: Formerly Model 69.

MODEL AMR AUTO PISTOL . . . . . . NiB $417 Ex $345 Gd $216
Simlar to Model USA except with 6-inch bbl. and target sights. Imported 1992-94.

"BABY" AUTOMATIC PISTOL . . . . . NiB $262 Ex $185 Gd $108
Calibers: .22 Short, .22 Long. Five-round magazine, 2.13-inch bbl., 4.13 inches overall. Weight: 9 oz. Fixed sights. Blued finish. Bakelite grips. Made 1949-68.

MODEL P010 AUTOMATIC PISTOL . . . . NiB $710 Ex $607 Gd $375
Caliber: .22 LR. Five- and 10-round magazine, 5.9-inch bbl. w/7.5-inch sight radius. Weight: 40 oz. Interchangeable front sight, adj. rear. Blued finish. Textured walnut grips. Made 1988-92 and 1995-97.

P018 COMPACT MODEL . . . . NiB $515 Ex $489 Gd $247
Slightly smaller version of the Model P018 standard DA automatic except has 14-round magazine and 4-inch bbl., 7.68 inches overall. Weight: 33 oz. Walnut grips only. Imported 1987-96.

P018 DOUBLE-ACTION AUTOMATIC PISTOL
Caliber: 9mm Para. 16-round magazine, 4.75-inch bbl., 8.5 inches overall. Weight: 36 oz. Fixed combat sights. Blued finish. Checkered plastic or walnut grips. Imported 1987-96.
W/plastic grips . . . . NiB $515 Ex $427 Gd $252
W/walnut grips . . . . NiB $544 Ex $442 Gd $303

P. ONE DA AUTO PISTOL

Caliber: 9mm Parabellum or .40 S&W. 10- or 16-round magazine, 4.8-inch bbl., 8.35 inches overall. Weight: 34 oz. Blade front sight, adjustable rear w/3-dot system. Matte black or chrome finish. Checkered walnut or black plastic grips. Imported 1993-97.

Model P One blue finish . . . . NiB $612 Ex $515 Gd $303
Model P One chrome finish. . . . . . . NiB $644 Ex $525 Gd $371
W/walnut grips, add $35

P. ONE PRACTICAL VB AUTO PISTOL

Similar to Model P One except chambered for 9x21mm w/2-, 4- or 6-port compensating system for IPSC competition. Imported 1993-97.

Model P One
Practical (2 port) . . . . NiB $1055 Ex $978 Gd $705
Model P One
Practical (4 port) . . . . NiB $1162 Ex $962 Gd $682
Model P One
Practical (6 port) . . . . NiB $1578 Ex $1282 Gd $903
W/chrome finish, add $60

SPORTER AUTOMATIC PISTOL . . . . . NiB $319 Ex $288 Gd $185

Caliber .22 LR. Eight-round magazine, bbl., lengths: 6-, 8- and 10-inch, 13 inches overall (10-inch bbl.). weight: About 30 oz. (10-inch bbl.) Target sights. Blued finish. Walnut grips. Made 1949-68.

MODEL USA AUTO PISTOL

Single-action, blowback. Calibers: .22 LR, .32 ACP, .380 ACP. Seven-round magazine or 10-round magazine (.22 LR). 3.5-inch bbl., 6.5 inches overall. Weight: 26.5 oz. Ramped front sight, adjustable rear. Blue or chrome finish. Checkered black bakelite grips w/thumbrest. Imported 1991-97.

Model USA blue finish . . . . NiB $396 Ex $309 Gd $220
Model USA chrome finish . . . . NiB $485 Ex $402 Gd $294

VEST POCKET AUTOMATIC PISTOL . . . . NiB $262 Ex $206 Gd $134

Caliber: .25 Auto (6.35mm). Five- or 8-round magazine, 2.13-inch bbl., 4.13 inches overall. Weight: 9 oz. Fixed sights. Blued finish. Bakelite grips. Made 1945-68.

BERSA PISTOLS — Argentina

Currently imported by Eagle Imports, Wanamassa, NJ (Previously by Interarms & Outdoor Sports)

MODEL 83 DOUBLE-ACTION AUTO PISTOL

Similar to the Model 23 except for the following specifications: Caliber: .380 ACP. Seven-round magazine, 3.5-inch bbl., Front blade sight integral on slide, square-notch rear adj. for windage. Blued or satin nickel finish. Custom wood grips. Imported 1988-94.

Blued finish . . . . NiB $245 Ex $189 Gd $158
Satin nickel . . . . NiB $305 Ex $255 Gd $192

MODEL 85 DOUBLE-ACTION AUTO PISTOL

Same general specifications as Model 83 except 13-round magazine, Imported 1988-94. See illustration next page.

Blued finish . . . . NiB $296 Ex $255 Gd $148
Satin nickel . . . . NiB $394 Ex $326 Gd $240

MODEL 86 DOUBLE-ACTION AUTO PISTOL

Same general specifications as Model 85 except available in matte blued finish and w/Neoprene grips. Imported 1992-94.

Matte blued finish . . . . NiB $326 Ex $275 Gd $168
Nickel finish . . . . NiB $386 Ex $316 Gd $226

Bernardelli P010

Bernardelli "Baby"

Bernardelli P018

MODEL 95 DA AUTOMATIC PISTOL

Caliber: .380 ACP. Seven-round magazine, 3.5-inch bbl., weight: 23 oz. Wraparound rubber grips. Blade front and rear notch sights. Imported 1995 to date.

Blued finish . . . . NiB $239 Ex $173 Gd $117
Nickel finish . . . . NiB $262 Ex $196 Gd $140

Bersa Model 85

Bersa Model 383

Bersa Thunder .380

Bersa Thunder .380 Deluxe

MODEL 97
AUTO PISTOL . . . . NiB $336 Ex $291 Gd $178
Caliber: .380 ACP. Seven-round magazine, 3.3-inch bbl., 6.5 inches overall. Weight: 28 oz. Intro. 1982. Disc.

MODEL 223
Same general specifications as Model 383 except in .22 LR w/10-round magazine capacity. Disc. 1987.
Double action . . . . NiB $209 Ex $178 Gd $117
Single action . . . . NiB $199 Ex $168 Gd $114

MODEL 224
Caliber: .22 LR. 10-round magazine, 4-inch bbl., weight: 26 oz. Front blade sight, square-notched rear adj. for windage. Blued finish. Checkered nylon or custom wood grips. Made 1984. SA. disc. 1986.
Double-action . . . . NiB $209 Ex $178 Gd $117
Single action . . . . NiB $114 Ex $177 Gd $111

MODEL 226
Same general specifications as Model 224 but w/6-inch bbl. Disc. 1987.
Double action . . . . NiB $209 Ex $178 Gd $117
Single action . . . . NiB $199 Ex $168 Gd $114

MODEL 383 AUTO PISTOL
Caliber: .380 Auto. Seven-round magazine, 3.5-inch bbl. Front blade sight integral on slide, square-notched rear sight adj. for windage. Custom wood grips on double-action, nylon grips on single action. Blued or satin nickel finish. Made 1984. SA. disc. 1989.
Double action . . . . NiB $127 Ex $102 Gd $56
Single action . . . . NiB $168 Ex $128 Gd $81
Satin nickel . . . . NiB $210 Ex $168 Gd $94

MODEL 622
AUTO PISTOL . . . . NiB $164 Ex $132 Gd $92
Caliber: .22 LR. Seven-round magazine, 4- or 6-inch bbl., 7 or 9 inches overall. Weight: 2.25 lbs. Blade front sight, square-notch rear adj. for windage. Blued finish. Nylon grips. Made 1982-87.

MODEL 644
AUTO PISTOL. . . . . NiB $239 Ex$204 Gd $127
Caliber: .22 LR. 10-round magazine, 3.5-inch bbl., weight: 26.5 oz. 6.5 inches overall. Adj. rear sight, blade front. Contoured black nylon grips. Made 1980-88.

THUNDER 9
AUTO PISTOL . . . . NiB $245 Ex $204 Gd $127
Caliber: 9mm Para. 15-round magazine, 4-inch bbl., 7.38 inches overall. Weight: 30 oz. Blade front sight, adj. rear w/3-dot system. Ambidextrous safety and decocking device. Matte blued finish. Checkered black polymer grips. Made 1993-96.

THUNDER .22
AUTO PISTOL (MODEL 23)
Caliber: .22 LR, 10-round magazine, 3.5-inch bbl., 6.63 inches overall. Weight: 24.5 oz. Notched-bar dovetailed rear, blade integral w/slide front. Black polymer grips. Made 1989 to date.
Blued finish . . . . NiB $239 Ex $204 Gd $117
Nickel finish . . . . NiB $252 Ex $204 Gd $139

THUNDER .380 AUTO PISTOL
Caliber: .380 ACP. Seven-round magazine, 3.5-inch bbl., 6.63 inches overall. Weight: 25.75 oz. Notched-bar dovetailed rear, blade integral w/slide front. Blued, satin nickel, or Duo-Tone finish. Made 1995 to date.
Blued finish . . . . NiB $234 Ex $250 Gd $122
Satin nickel finish . . . . NiB $274 Ex $224 Gd $161
Duo-Tone finish . . . . NiB $261 Ex $214 Gd $154

THUNDER .380 PLUS AUTO PISTOL
Same general specifications as standard Thunder .380 except has 10-round magazine and weight: 26 oz. Made 1995-97.
Matte finish . . . . NiB $241 Ex $194 Gd $134
Satin nickel finish . . . . NiB $292 Ex $234 Gd $161
Duo-Tone finish . . . . NiB $273 Ex $219 Gd $151

BROLIN ARMS — La Verne, California

"LEGEND SERIES" SA AUTOMATIC PISTOL
Caliber: .45 ACP. Seven-round magazine, 4- or 5-inch bbl., weight: 32-36 oz. Walnut grips. Single action, full size, compact, or full size frame compact slide. Matte blued finish. Lowered and flared ejection port. Made 1995 to date.
Model L45 . . . . NiB $448 Ex $387 Gd $244
Model L45C . . . . NiB $464 Ex $403 Gd $270
Model L45T . . . . NiB $474 Ex $414 Gd $280

"PATRIOT SERIES" SA AUTOMATIC PISTOL
Caliber: .45 ACP. Seven-round magazine, 3.25- and 4-inch bbl., weight: 33-37 oz. Wood grips. Fixed rear sights. Made 1996 to date.
Model P45 . . . . NiB $612 Ex $499 Gd $321
Model P45C (disc. 1997) . . . . NiB $637 Ex $647 Gd $576
Model P45T (disc. 1997) . . . . NiB $647 Ex $525 Gd $301

"PRO-STOCK AND PRO-COMP" SA PISTOL
Caliber: .45 ACP. Eight-round magazine, 4- or 5-inch bbl., weight: 37 oz. Single action, blued or two-tone finish. Wood grips. Bomar adjustable sights. Made 1996-97.
Model Pro comp . . . . NiB $720 Ex $582 Gd $402
Model Pro stock . . . . NiB $643 Ex $531 Gd $358

TAC SERIES
Caliber: .45 ACP. Eight-round magazine, 5-inch bbl., 8.5 inches overall. Weight: 37 oz. Low profile combat or Tritium sights. Beavertail grip safety. Matte blue, chrome or two-tone finish. Checkered wood or contoured black rubber grips. Made 1997 to date.
Model TAC 11 service . . . . NiB $633 Ex $526 Gd $327
Model TAC 11 compact . . . . NiB $643 Ex $531 Gd $327
W/Tritium sights, add $95

BRONCO PISTOL — Eibar, Spain
Manufactured by Echave y Arizmendi

MODEL 1918 POCKET
AUTOMATIC PISTOL . . . . NiB $199 Ex $174 Gd $87
Caliber: .32 ACP (7.65mm). Six-round magazine 2.5-inch bbl., 5 inches overall. Weight: 20 oz. Fixed sights. Blued finish. Hard rubber grips. Made c.1918-.25.

SEMIAUTOMATIC PISTOL . . . . NiB $184 Ex $138 Gd $111
Caliber: .25 ACP, 6-round magazine, 2.13-inch bbl., 4.13 inches overall. Weight: 11 oz. Fixed sights. Blued finish. Hard rubber grips. Made 1919-35.

Browning
Model 25 Automatic

BROWNING PISTOLS — Morgan, Utah

The following Browning pistols have been manufactured by Fabrique Nationale d'Armes de Guerre (now Fabrique Nationale Herstal) of Herstal, Belgium, by Arms Technology Inc. of Salt Lake City and by J. P. Sauer & Sohn of Eckernforde, W. Germany. (See also FN Browning and J.P. Sauer & Sohn listings.)

.25 AUTOMATIC PISTOL
Same general specifications as FN Browning Baby (see separate listing). Standard Model, blued finish, hard rubber grips. Light Model, nickel-plated, Nacrolac pearl grips. Renaissance Engraved Model, nickel-plated, Nacrolac pearl grips. Made by FN 1955-69.
Standard model . . . . NiB $527 Ex $475 Gd $228
Lightweight model . . . . NiB $537 Ex $475 Gd $228
Renaissance model . . . . NiB $1026 Ex $794 Gd $434

.32 AND .380 AUTOMATIC PISTOL, 1955 TYPE
Same general specifications as FN Browning .32 (7.65mm) and .380 Pocket Auto. Standard Model, Renaissance Engraved Model as furnished in .25 Automatic. Made by FN 1955-69.
Standard model (.32 ACP) . . . . NiB $466 Ex $380 Gd $257
Standard model (.380 ACP) . . . . . . NiB $396 Ex $329 Gd $226
Renaissance model . . . . NiB $998 Ex $844 Gd $612

.380 AUTOMATIC PISTOL, 1971 TYPE
Same as .380 Automatic, 1955 Type except has longer slide, 4.44-inch bbl., is 7.06 inches overall, weight: 23 oz. Rear sight adj. for windage and elevation, plastic thumbrest grips. Made 1971-75.
Standard model . . . . NiB $427 Ex $329 Gd $226
Renaissance model . . . . NiB $1024 Ex $818 Gd $535

BDA DA AUTOMATIC PISTOL
Similar to SIG-Sauer P220. Calibers: 9mm Para., .38 Super Auto, .45 Auto. Nine-round magazine (9mm and .38), 7-round (.45 cal), 4.4-inch bbl., 7.8 inches overall. Weight: 29.3 oz. Fixed sights. Blued finish. Plastic grips. Made 1977-79 by J. P. Sauer.
BDA model, 9mm, .45 ACP . . . . . . NiB $499 Ex $427 Gd $277
BDA model, .38 Super . . . . NiB $509 Ex $411 Gd $319

BDA-.380 DA AUTOMATIC PISTOL
Caliber: .380 Auto. 10- or 13-round magazine, bbl. length: 3.81 inches., 6.75 inches overall. Weight: 23 oz. Fixed blade front sight, square-notch drift-adj. rear sight. Blued or nickel finish. Smooth walnut grips. Made 1982-97 by Beretta. See illustration next page.
Blued finish . . . . NiB $483 Ex $375 Gd $226
Nickel finish . . . . NiB $469 Ex $386 Gd $278

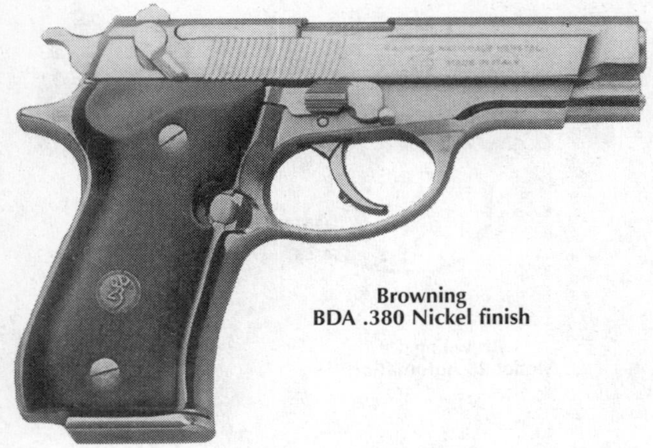

Browning
BDA .380 Nickel finish

Browning
BDM 9mm DA

Browning
Buck Mark 22 Field (5.5)

Browning
Buck Mark 22 Bullseye

Browning
Buck Mark 22 Plus

BDM SERIES AUTOMATIC PISTOLS
Calibers: 9mm Para., 10-round magazine, 4.73-inch bbl., 7.85 inches overall. Weight: 31 oz., windage adjustable sights w/3-dot system. Low profile removable blade front sights. Matte blued, Bi-Tone or silver chrome finish. Selectable shooting mode and decocking safety lever. Made 1991 to date.

BDM Standard. . . . . NiB $520 Ex $322 Gd $295
BDM Practical. . . . . NiB $528 Ex $427 Gd $298
BDM-D Silver Chrome . . . . NiB $534 Ex $432 Gd $302

BUCK MARK .22 AUTOMATIC PISTOL
Caliber: .22 LR. 10-round magazine, 5.5- inch bbl., 9.5 inches overall. Weight: 32 oz. Black molded grips. Adj. rear sight. Blued or nickel finish. Made 1985 to date.

Blued finish . . . . NiB $231 Ex $190 Gd $113
Nickel finish . . . . NiB $292 Ex $242 Gd $178

BUCK MARK .22 BULLSEYE PISTOL
Same general specifications as the standard Buck Mark 22 except w/7.25-inch fluted barrel, 11.83 inches overall. Weight: 36 oz. Adjustable target trigger. Undercut post front sight, click-adjustable Pro-Target rear. Laminated, Rosewood, black rubber or composite grips. Made 1996 to date.

Standard model
(composite grips). . . . . NiB $345 Ex $283 Gd $195
Target model . . . . NiB $422 Ex $319 Gd $195

BUCK MARK .22
BULLSEYE TARGET . . . . NiB $432 Ex $329 Gd $205
Caliber: .22 LR. 10-round magazine, 7.25- inch fluted bbl., 11.83 inches overall. Weight: 31 oz. Rosewood wrap-around finger groove grips w/matte blued finish. Made 1996 to date.

BUCK MARK .22 FIELD
(5.5) AUTO PISTOL. . . . . NiB $355 Ex $267 Gd $174
Calibers: .22 LR. 10-round magazine, 5.5- inch bbl., 9.58 inches overall. Weight: 35.5 oz. Standard sights. Matte Blue finish. Made 1991 to date.

BUCK MARK .22 MICRO AUTOMATIC PISTOL
Same general specifications as standard Buck Mark .22 except w/4-inch bbl., 8 inches overall. Weight: 32 oz. Molded composite grips. Ramp front sight, Pro Target rear sight. Made 1992 to date.

Blued finish . . . . NiB $278 Ex $221 Gd $116
Nickel finish . . . . NiB $298 Ex $265 Gd $189

Browning
Buck Mark .22 Silhouette

Browning
Buck Mark .22 Target (5.5)

BUCK MARK .22 MICRO PLUS AUTO PISTOL
Same specifications as the Buck Mark .22 Micro except ambidextrous, laminated wood grips. Made 1996 to date.
Blued finish . . . . **NiB $278 Ex $221 Gd $118**
Nickel finish . . . . **NiB $311 Ex $260 Gd $197**

BUCK MARK .22 PLUS AUTOMATIC PISTOL
Same general specifications as standard Buck Mark .22 except for black molded, impregnated hardwood grips. Made 1987 to date.
Blued finish . . . . **NiB $278 Ex $221 Gd $108**
Nickel finish . . . . **NiB $317 Ex $266 Gd $203**

BUCK MARK .22 TARGET (5.5) AUTO PISTOL
Caliber: .22 LR. 10-round magazine, 5.5- inch bbl., 9.6 inches overall. Weight: 35.5 oz. Pro target sights. Wrap-around walnut or contoured finger groove grips. Made 1990 to date.
Matte blue finish . . . . **NiB $375 Ex $303 Gd $169**
Nickel finish (1994 to date). . . . . . . **NiB $450 Ex $373 Gd $277**
Gold finish (1991-99) . . . . **NiB $492 Ex $412 Gd $310**

BUCK MARK .22 SILHOUETTE . . . . **NiB $376 Ex $299 Gd $159**
Same general specifications as standard Buck Mark .22 except for 9.88-inch bbl. Weight: 53 oz. Target sights mounted on full-length scope base, and laminated hardwood grips and forend. Made 1987 to date.

Browning
Buck Mark .22 Micro Plus

BUCK MARK .22
UNLIMITED SILHOUETTE . . . . **NiB $453 Ex $355 Gd $221**
Same general specifications as standard Buck Mark .22 Silhouette except w/14-inch bbl., 18.69 inches overall. Weight: 64 oz. Interchangeable post front sight and Pro Target rear. Nickel finish. Made 1992 to date.

BUCK MARK .22
VARMINT AUTO PISTOL. . . . . **NiB $339 Ex $278 Gd $180**
Same general specifications as standard Buck Mark .22 except for 9.88-inch bbl. Weight: 48 oz. No sights, full-length scope base, and laminated hardwood grips. Made 1987 to date.

Browning Challenger
Standard Model

CHALLENGER AUTOMATIC PISTOL
Caliber: .22 LR. 10-round magazine, bbl. lengths: 4.5 and 6.75-inches. 11.44 inches overall (with 6.75-inch bbl.). Weight: 38 oz. (6.75-inch bbl.). Removable blade front sight, screw adj. rear. Standard finish, blued, also furnished gold inlaid (Gold model) and engraved and chrome-plated (Renaissance model). Checkered walnut grips. Finely figured and carved grips on Gold and Renaissance models. Standard made by FN 1962-75, higher grades. Intro. 1971. Disc.
Standard model . . . . **NiB $411 Ex $349 Gd $231**
Gold model . . . . **NiB $1518 Ex $1312 Gd $600**
Renaissance model . . . . **NiB $1518 Ex $1312 Gd $600**

CHALLENGER II
AUTOMATIC PISTOL . . . . **NiB $232 Ex $201 Gd $118**
Same general specifications as Challenger Standard model w/6.75-inch bbl. except changed grip angle and impregnated hardwood grips. Original Challenger design modified for lower production costs. Made by ATI 1976-83.

Browning Challenger
Renaissance Model

Browning
Challenger III Sporter .22

Browning
Hi-Power Mark III

Browning
9mm Hi-Power w/Molded Grips

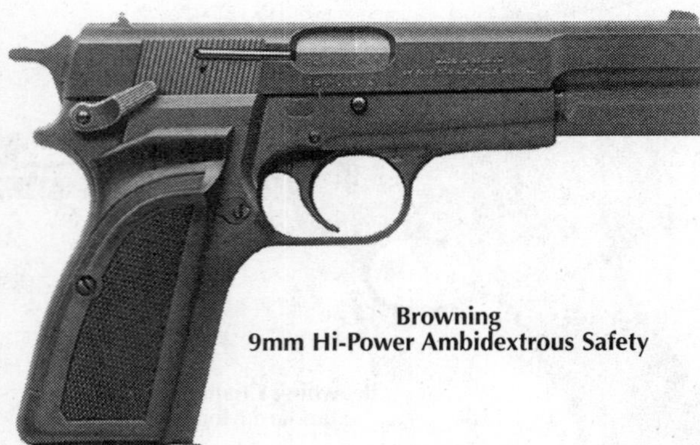

Browning
9mm Hi-Power Ambidextrous Safety

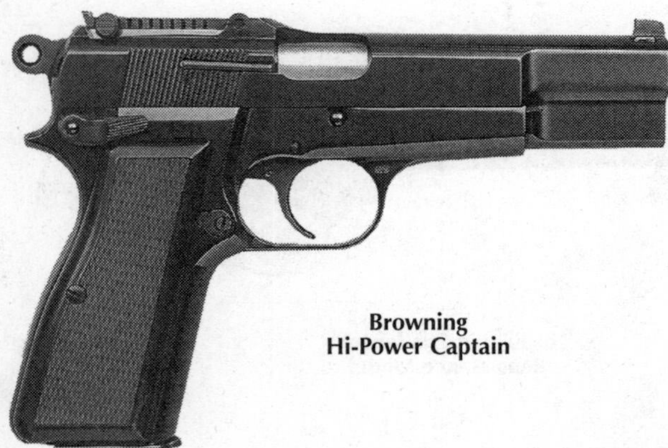

Browning
Hi-Power Captain

CHALLENGER III AUTOMATIC PISTOL . . . . NiB $232 Ex $201 Gd $118
Same general description as Challenger II except has 5.5 inch bull bbl., alloy frame and new sight system. Weight: 35 oz. Made 1982-84. Sporter Model w/6.75-inch bbl.. Made 1984-86.

HI-POWER AUTOMATIC PISTOL
Same general specifications as FN Browning Model 1935 except chambered for 9mm Para., .30 Luger and .40 S&W. 10- or 13-round magazine, 4.63-inch bbl., 7.75 inches overall. Weight: 32 oz. (9mm) or 35 oz. (.40 S&W). Fixed sights, also available w/rear sight adj. for windage and elevation, and ramp front sight. Ambidextrous safety added after 1989. Standard model blued, chrome-plated or Bi-Tone finish. Checkered walnut, contour-molded Polyamide or wraparound rubber grips. Renaissance Engraved model chrome-plated, w/Nacrolac pearl grips. Made by FN from1955 to date.

Standard model, fixed sights, 9mm . . . . NiB $751 Ex $617 Gd $452
Standard model, fixed sights, .40 S&W (intro. 1986). . . . . NiB $761 Ex $735 Gd $555
Standard model, .30 Luger (1986-89). . . . . NiB $735 Ex $632 Gd $426
Renaissance model, fixed sights. . . . . NiB $1430 Ex $1369 Gd $555
W/adjustable rear sight, add $50
W/ambidextrous safety, add $95
W/moulded grips, deduct $40
W/tangent rear sight (1965-78), add* $295
W/T-Slot grip & tangent sight (1965-78), add* $595
***Check FN agent to certify value**

HI-POWER CAPITAN AUTOMATIC. . . . . NiB $653 Ex $540 Gd $360
Similar to the standard Hi-Power except fitted w/adj. 500-meter tangent rear sight and rounded serrated hammer. Made 1993 to date.

HI-POWER MARK III AUTOMATIC PISTOL . . . . NiB $581 Ex $432 Gd $334
Calibers: 9mm and .40 S&W. 10-round magazine, 4.75-inch bbl., 7.75 inches overall. Weight: 32 oz. Fixed sights with molded grips. Durable non-glare matte blue finish. Made 1985 to date.

Browning
Hi-Power Practical

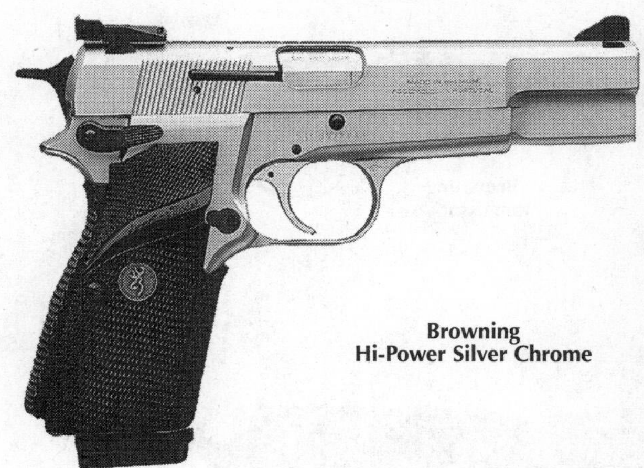
Browning
Hi-Power Silver Chrome

HI-POWER PRACTICAL AUTOMATIC PISTOL
Similar to the standard Hi-Power except has silver-chromed frame and blued slide w/Commander-style hammer. Made 1991 to date.
W/fixed sights . . . . **NiB $612 Ex $473 Gd $334**
W/adj. sights . . . . **NiB $645 Ex $533 Gd $390**

HI-POWER SILVER CHROME AUTOMATIC PISTOL . . . . **NiB $741 Ex $591 Gd $349**
Calibers: 9mm and .40 S&W. 10-round magazine, 4.75-inch bbl., 7.75 inches overall. Weight: 36 oz. Adjustable sights with Pachmayer grips. Silver-chromed finish. Made 1991 to date.

HI-POWER 9MM CLASSIC
Limited Edition 9mm Hi-Power, w/silver-gray finish, high-grade engraving and finely-checkered walnut grips w/double border. Proposed production of the Classic was 5000 w/less than half that number produced. Gold Classic limited to 500 w/two-thirds proposed production in circulation. Made 1985-86.
Gold classic . . . . **NiB $2609 Ex $2095 Gd $1438**
Standard classic . . . . **NiB $1321 Ex $1065 Gd $737**

Browning
Hi-Power 9mm Classic

INTERNATIONAL MEDALIST AUTOMATIC TARGET PISTOL . . . . **NiB $896 Ex $751 Gd $432**
Modification of Medalist to conform w/International Shooting Union rules. 5.9-inch bbl., Smaller grip with no forearm. Weight: 42 oz. Made 1970-73.

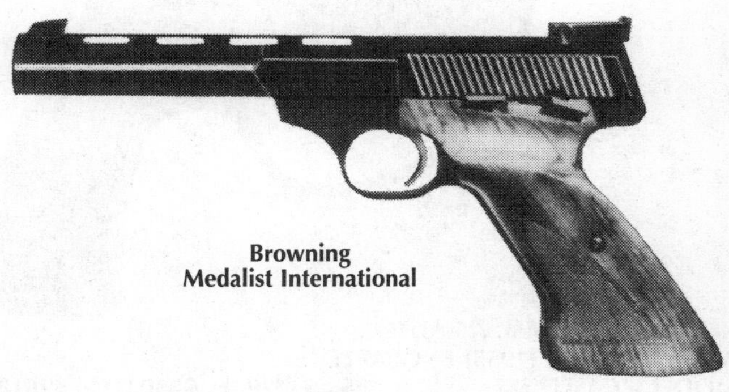
Browning
Medalist International

MEDALIST AUTOMATIC TARGET PISTOL
Caliber: .22 LR. 10-round magazine, 6.75-inch bbl. w/vent rib, 11.94 inches overall. Weight: 46 oz. Removable blade front sight, click-adj. micrometer rear. Standard finish, blued also furnished gold-inlaid (Gold Model) and engraved and chrome-plated (Renaissance Model). Checkered walnut grips w/thumbrest (for right- or left-handed shooter). Finely figured and carved grips on Gold and Renaissance Models. Made by FN 1962-75. Higher grades. Intro. 1971.
Standard model . . . . **NiB $906 Ex $751 Gd $493**
Gold model . . . . **NiB $2038 Ex $1729 Gd 937**
Renaissance model . . . . **NiB $2480 Ex $2038 Gd $1288**

Browning
Medalist Automatic Target Pistol

NOMAD AUTOMATIC PISTOL . . . . **NiB $339 Ex $287 Gd $184**
Caliber: .22 LR. 10-round magazine, bbl. lengths: 4.5 and 6.75-inches, 8.94 inches overall (4.5-inch bbl.). Weight: 34 oz. (with 4.5-inch bbl.). Removable blade front sight, screw adj. rear. Blued finish. Plastic grips. Made by FN 1962-74.

Browning Renaissance

Charter Arms Bonnie

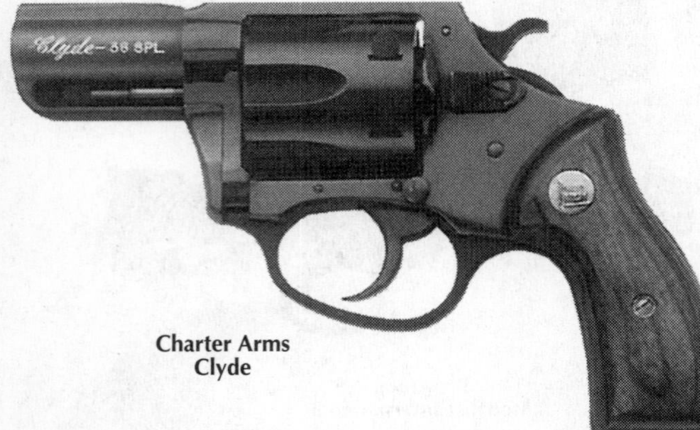

Charter Arms Clyde

RENAISSANCE 9MM, .25 AUTO AND .380 AUTO (1955) ENGRAVED MODELS, CASED SET . . . . NiB $4729 Ex $3803 Gd $2618
One pistol of each of the three models in a special walnut carrying case, all chrome-plated w/Nacrolac pearl grips. Made by FN 1955-69.

BRYCO ARMS INC. — Irvine, California Distributed by Jennings Firearms. Inc. Carson City, NV

MODELS J22, J25 AUTO PISTOL
Calibers: .22 LR, .25 ACP. Six-round magazine, 2.5-inch bbl., about 5 inches overall. Weight: 13 oz. Fixed sights. Chrome, satin nickel or black Teflon finish. Walnut, grooved black Cycolac or resin-impregnated wood grips. Made from 1981 to date.
Model J-22. . . . . NiB $88 Ex $71 Gd $50
Model J-25 (disc. 1995). . . . . NiB $73 Ex $61 Gd $46

MODELS M25, M32, M38 AUTO PISTOL
Calibers: .25 ACP, .32 ACP, .380 ACP. Six-round magazine, 2.81-inch bbl., 5.31 inches overall. Weight: 11oz. to 15 oz. Fixed sights. Chrome, satin nickel or black Teflon finish. Walnut, grooved, black Cycolac or resin-impregnated wood grips. Made from 1988 to date.
Model M25 (disc.) . . . . NiB $71 Ex $56 Gd $46
Model M32 . . . . NiB $101 Ex $81 Gd $57
Model M38 . . . . NiB $113 Ex $92 Gd $61

MODEL M48 AUTO PISTOL . . . . NiB $92 Ex $81 Gd $56
Calibers: .22 LR, .32 ACP, .380 ACP. Seven-round magazine, 4-inch bbl., 6.69 inches overall. Weight: 20 oz. Fixed sights. Chrome, satin nickel or black Teflon finish. Smooth wood or black Teflon grips. Made from 1989-95.

MODEL M58 AUTO PISTOL . . . . NiB $92 Ex $81 Gd $56
Caliber: .380 ACP. 10-round magazine, 3.75-inch bbl., 5.5 inches overall. Weight: 30 oz. Fixed sights. Chrome, satin nickel, blued or black Teflon finish. Smooth wood or black Teflon grips. Made 1993-95.

MODEL M59 AUTO PISTOL . . . . NiB $102 Ex $92 Gd $56
Caliber: 9mm Para. 10-round magazine, 4-inch bbl., 6.5 inches overall. Weight: 33 oz. Fixed sights. Chrome, satin nickel, blued or black Teflon finish. Smooth wood or black Teflon grips. Made 1994-96.

MODEL NINE SA AUTO PISTOL . . . . NiB $127 Ex $107 Gd $66
Similar to Bryco/Jennings Model M59 except w/redesigned slide w/loaded chamber indicator and frame mounted ejector. Weight: 30 oz. Made 1997 to date.

MODEL T-.22 TARGET PISTOL . . . . NiB $120 Ex $97 Gd $67
Similar to Bryco/Jennings Model M48 except chambered for .22 LR only, w/target configuration sights and redesigned slide w/loaded chamber indicator and hold open. Made 1997 to date.

BUDISCHOWSKY PISTOL — Mt. Clemens, Michigan, Mfd. by Norton Armament Corporation

TP-70 DA AUTOMATIC PISTOL
Calibers: .22 LR, .25 Auto. Six-round magazine, 2.6-inch bbl., 4.65 inches overall. Weight: 12.3 oz. Fixed sights. Stainless steel. Plastic grips. Made 1973-77.
.22 LR . . . . NiB $352 Ex $295 Gd $219
.25 Auto. . . . . NiB $341 Ex $270 Gd $188

CALICO LIGHT WEAPONS SYSTEMS — Bakersfield, California

MODEL 110 AUTO PISTOL. . . . . . . NiB $667 Ex $599 Gd $438
Caliber: .22 LR. 100-round magazine, 6-inch bbl., 17.9 inches overall. Weight: 3.75 lbs. Adj. post front sight, fixed U-notch rear. Black finish aluminum frame. Molded composition grip. Made 1986-94.

MODEL M-950 AUTO PISTOL . . . . NiB $489 Ex $412 Gd $293
Caliber 9mm Para. 50- or 100-round magazine, 7.5-inch bbl., 14 inches overall. Weight: 2.25 lbs. Adj. post front sight, fixed U-notch rear. Glass-filled polymer grip. Made 1989-94.

CHARTER ARMS CORPORATION — Stratford, Connecticut

MODEL 40 AUTOMATIC PISTOL..... NiB $285 Ex $260 Gd $142
Caliber: .22 RF. Eight-round magazine, 3.3-inch bbl., 6.3 inches overall. Weight: 21.5 oz. Fixed sights. Checkered walnut grips. Stainless steel finish. Made 1985-86.

MODEL 79K
DA AUTOMATIC PISTOL .... NiB $346 Ex $321 Gd $209
Calibers: .380 or .32 Auto. Seven-round magazine, 3.6-inch bbl., 6.5 inches overall. Weight: 24.5 oz. Fixed sights. Checkered walnut grips. Stainless steel finish. Made 1985-86.

BONNIE AND CLYDE SET........ NiB $453 Ex $392 Gd $260
Matching pair of shrouded 2.5-inch bbl., revolvers chambered for .32 Magnum and .38 Special. Blued finish w/scrolled name on bbls.. Made 1989-90.

BULLDOG .44 DA REVOLVER
Caliber: .44 Special. Five-round cylinder, 2.5- or 3-inch bbl., 7 or 7.5 inches overall. Weight: 19 or 19.5 oz. Fixed sights. Blued, nickel-plated or stainless finish. Checkered walnut Bulldog or square buttgrips. Made from 1973-96.
Blued finish/
Pocket Hammer (2.5-inch) .... NiB $234 Ex $204 Gd $97
Blued finish/
Bulldog grips (3-inch disc. 1988).... NiB $214 Ex $169 Gd $117
Electroless nickel............... NiB $241 Ex $194 Gd $134
Stainless steel/
Bulldog grips (disc. 1992) .... NiB $204 Ex $163 Gd $107
Neoprene grips/
Pocket Hammer................ NiB $209 Ex $168 Gd $116

BULLDOG .357 DA REVOLVER .... NiB $194 Ex $158 Gd $97
Caliber: .357 Magnum. Five-round cylinder, 6-inch bbl., 11 inches overall. Weight: 25 oz. Fixed sights. Blued finish. Square, checkered walnut grips. Intro. 1977-96.

BULLDOG NEW POLICE DA REVOLVER
Same general specifications as Bulldog Police except chambered for .44 Special. Five-round cylinder, 2.5- or 3.5-inch bbl. Made 1990-92.
Blued finish.................... NiB $241 Ex $180 Gd $128
Stainless finish (2.5-inch bbl. only)........ NiB $183 Ex $148 Gd $97

BULLDOG POLICE DA REVOLVER
Caliber: .38 Special or .32 H&R Magnum. Six-round cylinder, 4-inch bbl., 8.5 inches overall. Weight: 20.5 oz. Adj. rear sight, ramp front. Blued or stainless finish. Square checkered walnut grips. Made 1976-93. Shroud dropped on new model.
Blued finish.................. NiB $214 Ex $170 Gd $117
Stainless finish................ NiB $204 Ex $165 Gd $106
.32 H&R Magnum (disc.1992)..... NiB $219 Ex $173 Gd $117

BULLDOG PUG DA REVOLVER
Caliber: .44 Special. Five-round cylinder, 2.5 inch bbl., 7.25 inches overall. Weight: 20 oz. Blued or stainless finish. Fixed ramp front sight, fixed square-notch rear. Checkered Neoprene or walnut grips. Made 1988-93.
Blued finish.................. NiB $234 Ex $204 Gd $133
Stainless finish................ NiB $234 Ex $204 Gd $133

BULLDOG TARGET DA REVOLVER
Calibers: .357 Magnum, .44 Special (latter intro. in 1977). Four-inch bbl., 8.5 inches overall. Weight: 20.5 oz. in .357. Adj. rear sight, ramp front. Blued finish. Square checkered walnut grips. Made 1976-92.
Blued finish (disc.1989).......... NiB $199 Ex $157 Gd $108
Stainless steel .... NiB $234 Ex $158 Gd $92

Charter Arms Bulldog Police

Charter Arms Bulldog Police

Charter Arms Bulldog Target

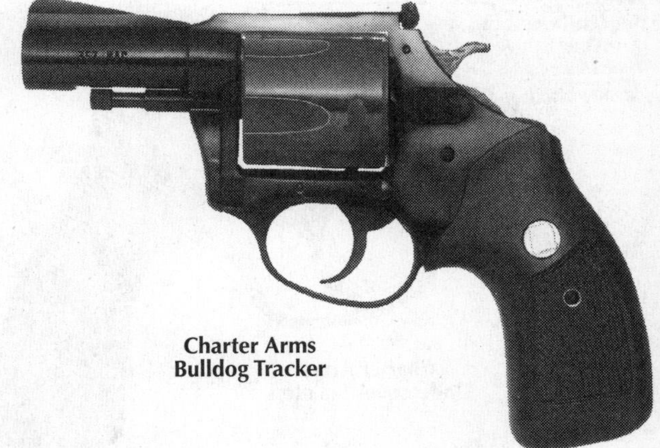
Charter Arms Bulldog Tracker

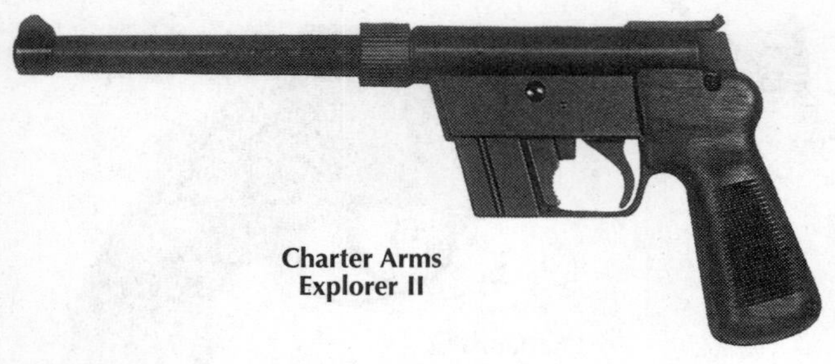
Charter Arms
Explorer II

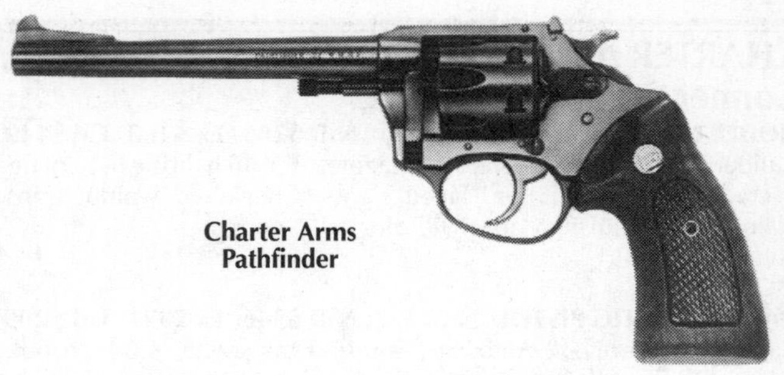
Charter Arms
Pathfinder

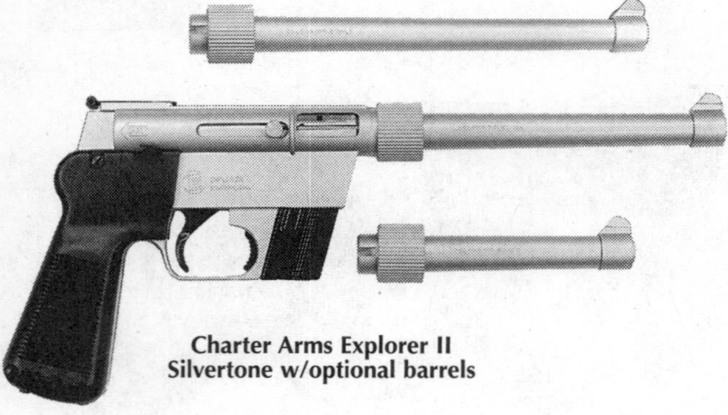
Charter Arms Explorer II
Silvertone w/optional barrels

Charter Arms Police Undercover
.32 H&R Magnum

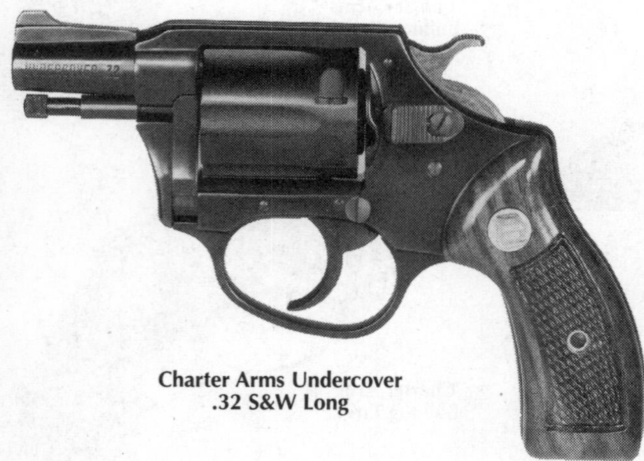
Charter Arms Undercover
.32 S&W Long

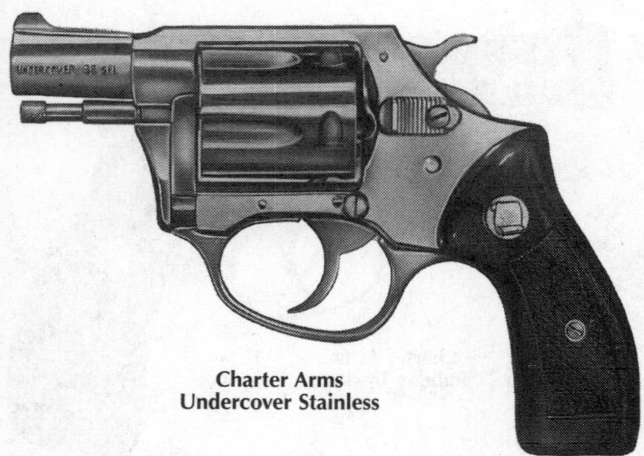
Charter Arms
Undercover Stainless

BULLDOG TRACKER
DA REVOLVER. . . . . NiB $193 Ex $158 Gd $97
Caliber: .357 Mag. Five-round cylinder, 2.5-, 4- or 6-inch bbl., 11 inches overall (6-inch bbl.). Weight: 21 oz. (2.5-inch bbl.). Adj. rear sight, ramp front. Checkered walnut grips. Blued finish. 4- or 6-inch bbl., Disc.1986. Reintroduced 1989-92. See illustration previous page.

EXPLORER II SEMIAUTO SURVIVAL PISTOL
Caliber: .22 RF. Eight-round magazine, 6-, 8- or 10-inch bbl., 13.5 inches overall (6-inch bbl.). Weight: 28 oz. finishes: Black, heat cured, semigloss textured enamel or silvertone anticorrosion. Disc.1987.
Standard model . . . . NiB $97 Ex $87 Gd $56
Silvertone (w/optional
6- or 10-inch bbl.) . . . . NiB $119 Ex $106 Gd $66

OFF-DUTY DA REVOLVER
Calibers: .22 LR or .38 Special. Six-round (.22 LR) or 5-round (.38 Spec.) cylinder. Two-inch bbl., 6.25 inches overall. Weight: 16 oz. Fixed rear sight, Partridge-type front sight. Plain walnut grips. Matte black, nickel or stainless steel finish. Made 1992-96.
Matte black finish . . . . NiB $178 Ex $153 Gd $92
Nickel finish . . . . NiB $209 Ex $159 Gd $107
Stainless steel . . . . NiB $198 Ex $161 Gd $107

PATHFINDER DA REVOLVER
Calibers: .22 LR, .22 WMR. Six-round cylinder, bbl. lengths: 2-, 3-, 6-inches, 7.13 inches overall (in 3-inch bbl.), and regular grips. Weight: 18.5 oz. (3-inch bbl.). Adj. rear sight, ramp front. Blued or stainless finish. Plain walnut regular, checkered Bulldog or square buttgrips. Made 1970 to date. Note: Originally designated "Pocket Target," name was changed in 1971 to "Pathfinder." Grips changed in 1984. Disc.1993.
Blued finish . . . . NiB $193 Ex $158 Gd $97
Stainless finish . . . . NiB $193 Ex $158 Gd $97

CHARTER ARMS PIT BULL DA REVOLVER
Calibers: 9mm, .357 Magnum, .38 Special. Five-round cylinder, 2.5-, 3.5- or 4-inch bbl., 7 inches overall (2.5-inch bbl.). Weight: 21.5 to 25 oz. All stainless steel frame. Fixed ramp front sight, fixed square-notch rear. Checkered Neoprene grips. Blued or stainless finish. Made 1989-93.
Blued finish . . . . NiB $240 Ex $189 Gd $107
Stainless finish . . . . NiB $250 Ex $199 Gd $107

CHARTER ARMS UNDERCOVER DA REVOLVER
Caliber: .38 Special. Five-round cylinder,. bbl., lengths: 2-, 3-, 4-inches, 6.25 inches overall (2-inch bbl.), and regular grips. Weight: 16 oz. (2-inch bbl.). Fixed sights. Plain walnut, checkered Bulldog or square buttgrips. Made 1965-96.
Blued or nickel-plated finish . . . . NiB $183 Ex $153 Gd $92
Stainless finish . . . . NiB $269 Ex $204 Gd $117

CHARTER ARMS UNDERCOVER
Same general specifications as standard Undercover except chambered for .32 H&R Magnum or .32 S&W Long, has 6-round cylinder and 2.5-inch bbl.
.32 H&R Magnum (blued) . . . . NiB $183 Ex $153 Gd $92
.32 H&R Magnum
nickel. . . . . NiB $183 Ex $153 Gd $92
.32 H&R Magnum (stainless) . . . . . . NiB $270 Ex $204 Gd $158
.32 S&W Long (blued) disc. 1989. . . . . NiB $270 Ex $204 Gd $158

CHARTER ARMS UNDERCOVER POCKET POLICE DA REVOLVER
Same general specifications as standard Undercover except has 6-round cylinder and pocket-type hammer. Blued or stainless steel finish. Made 1969-81.
Blued finish . . . . NiB $163 Ex $148 Gd $97
Stainless steel . . . . NiB $219 Ex $180 Gd $131

CHARTER ARMS UNDERCOVER POLICE DA REVOLVER
Same general specifications as standard Undercover except has 6-round cylinder. Made 1984-89. Reintroduced 1993.
Blued, .38 Special . . . . NiB $217 Ex $186 Gd $110
Stainless, .38 Special . . . . NiB $216 Ex $176 Gd $125
.32 H&R Magnum . . . . NiB $197 Ex $163 Gd $115

CHARTER ARMS UNDER-
COVERETTE DA REVOLVER . . . . . . NiB $166 Ex $151 Gd $100
Same as Undercover model w/2-inch bbl. except caliber .32 S&W Long, 6-round cylinder, blued finish only. Weight: 16.5 oz. Made 1972-83.

CIMARRON F.A. CO. — Fredricksburg, Texas

CIMARRON EL PISTOLERO
SINGLE-ACTION REVOLVER. . . . . . NiB $423 Ex $326 Gd $198
Calibers: .357 Mag., .45 Colt. Six-round cylinder, 4.75- 5.5- or 7.5-inch bbl., polished brass backstrap and triggerguard. Otherwise, same as Colt Single-Action Army revolver w/parts being interchangeable. Made 1997-98.

COLT MANUFACTURING CO., INC. — Hartford, Connecticut

Previously Colt Industries, Firearms Division. Production of some Colt handguns spans the period before World War II to the postwar years. Values shown for these models are for earlier production. Those manufactured c. 1946 and later generally are less desirable to collectors and values are approximately 30 percent lower.

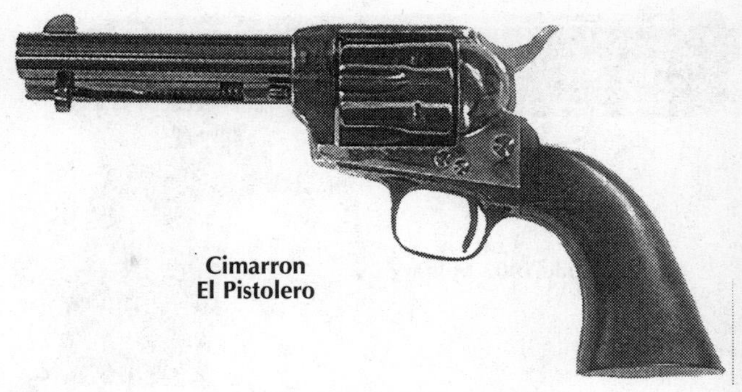

Cimarron
El Pistolero

NOTE: *For ease in finding a particular firearm, Colt handguns are grouped into three sections: Automatic Pistols, Single-Shot Pistols, Derringers and Revolvers. For a complete listing, please refer to the Index.*

AUTOMATIC PISTOLS

COLT MODEL 1900 .38 AUTOMATIC PISTOL
Caliber: .38 ACP (modern high-velocity cartridges should not be used in this pistol). Seven-round magazine, 6-inch bbl., 9 inches overall. Weight: 35 oz. Fixed sights. Blued finish. Hard rubber and plain or checkered walnut grips. Sharp-spur hammer. Combination rear sight and safety unique to the Model 1900 (early production). In mid-1901 a solid rear sight was dovetailed into the slide. (SN range 1-4274) Made 1900-03. Note: 250 models were sold to the military (50 Navy and 200 Army).
Early commercial model
(w/sight/safety) . . . . NiB $6963 Ex $5078 Gd $1856
Late commercial model
(W/dovetailed sight) . . . . NiB $6000 Ex $4023 Gd $2735
Army Model w/U.S. inspector
marks (1st Series - SN 90-150
w/inspector mark J.T.T). . . . . NiB $16,380 Ex $10,920 Gd $8719
(2nd Series - SN 1600-1750
w/inspector mark R.A.C.) . . . . NiB $10,237 Ex $8190 Gd $5569
Navy model (Also marked
w/USN-I.D. number) . . . . NiB $18,018 Ex $11,953 Gd $8982

COLT MODEL 1902 MILITARY .38 AUTOMATIC PISTOL
Caliber: .38 ACP (modern high-velocity cartridges should not be used in this pistol). Eight-round magazine, 6-inch bbl., 9 inches overall. Weight: 37 oz. Fixed sights w/blade front and V-notch rear. Blued finish. Checkered hard rubber grips. Round back hammer, changed to spur type in 1908. No safety but fitted w/standard military swivel. About 18,000 produced with split SN ranges. The government contract series (15,001-15,200) and the commercial sales series (15,000 receding to 11,000) and (30,200-47,266). Made 1902-29.
Early military model (w/front
slide serrations) . . . . NiB $3663 Ex $3403 Gd $3195
Late military model (w/rear
slide serrations) . . . . NiB $2902 Ex $2363 Gd $2155
Marked "U.S. Army" (SN 15,001-
15,200) . . . . NiB $8915 Ex $6835 Gd $4495

COLT MODEL 1902 SPORTING
.38 AUTOMATIC PISTOL. . . . . . NiB $3715 Ex $2415 Gd $1011
Caliber: .38 ACP (modern high-velocity cartridges should not be used in this pistol). Seven-round magazine, 6-inch bbl., 9 inches overall. Weight: 35 oz. Fixed sights w/blade front and V-notch rear. Blued finish. Checkered hard rubber grips. Round back hammer was standard but some spur hammers were installed during late production. No safety and w/o swivel as found on military model. Total production about 7,500 w/split SN ranges (4275-10,999) and (30,000-30,190) Made 1902-08.

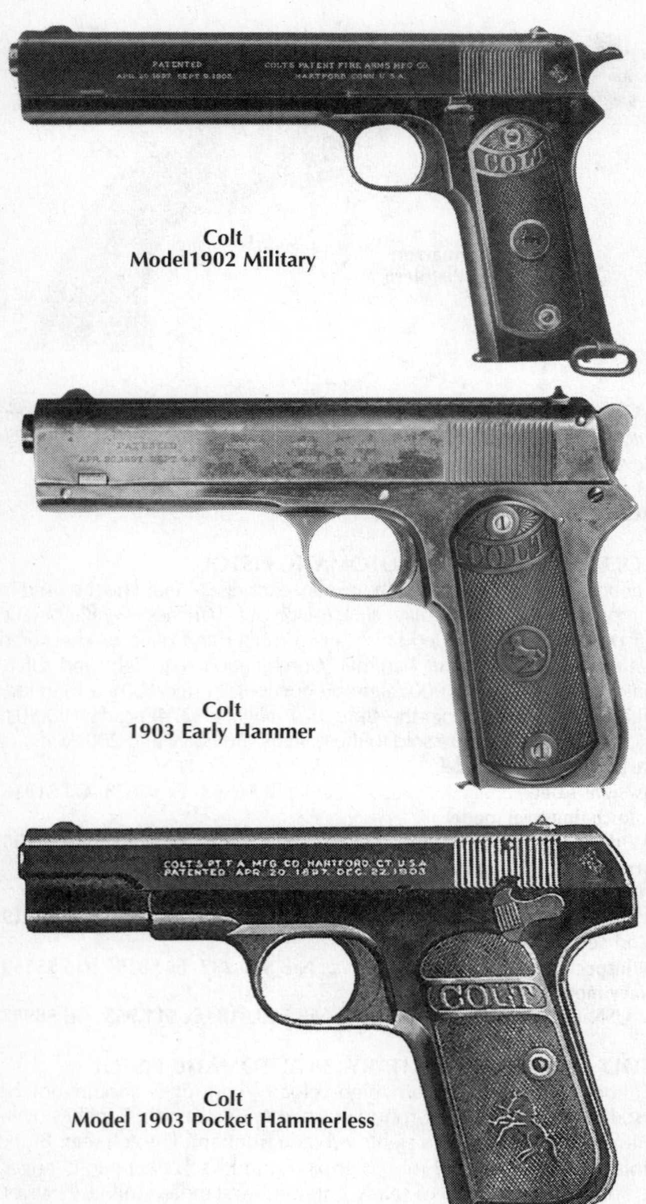

Colt
Model1902 Military

Colt
1903 Early Hammer

Colt
Model 1903 Pocket Hammerless

MODEL 1903 POCKET .32 AUTOMATIC PISTOL FIRST ISSUE - COMMERCIAL SERIES

Caliber: .32 Auto. Eight-round magazine, 4-inch bbl., 7 inches overall. Weight: 23 oz. Fixed sights. Blued or nickel finish. Checkered hard rubber grips. Hammerless (concealed hammer). Slide lock and grip safeties. Fitted w/barrel bushing but early models have no magazine safety. Total production of the Model 1903 reached 572,215. The First Issue production occurred 1903-08 (SN range 1-72,000).

Blued finish . . . . NiB $919 Ex $612 Gd $446
Nickel finish . . . . NiB $1012 Ex $633 Gd $461

MODEL 1903 POCKET .32 AUTOMATIC PISTOL SECOND ISSUE - COMMERCIAL SERIES

Same as First Issue but with 3.75-inch bbl. and small extractor. Production occurred 1908-10 (SN range 72,001 -105,050).

Blued finish . . . . NiB $670 Ex $498 Gd $358
Nickel finish . . . . NiB $693 Ex $556 Gd $389

MODEL 1903 POCKET .32 AUTOMATIC PISTOL, THIRD ISSUE - COMMERCIAL SERIES

Caliber: .32 Auto. Similar to Second Issue w/3.75-inch bbl. except with integral barrel bushing and locking lug at muzzle end of bbl. Production occurred 1910-26 (SN range 105,051-468,096).

Blued finish . . . . NiB $580 Ex $445 Gd $295
Nickel finish . . . . NiB $620 Ex $470 Gd $270

MODEL 1903 POCKET .32 AUTOMATIC PISTOL FOURTH ISSUE - COMMERCIAL SERIES

Caliber: .32 Auto. Similar to Third Issue except a slide lock safety change was made when a Tansley-style disconnector was added on all pistols above SN 468,097, which prevents firing of cartridge in chamber when the magazine is removed. Blued or nickel finish. Checkered walnut grips. These design changes were initiated 1926-.45 (SN range 105,051-554,446)

Blued finish . . . . NiB $576 Ex $465 Gd $323
Nickel finish . . . . NiB $639 Ex $515 Gd $357

MODEL 1903 POCKET (HAMMER) .38 AUTOMATIC PISTOL

Caliber: .38 ACP (modern high-velocity cartridges should not be used in this pistol). Similar to Model 1902 Sporting .38 but w/shorter frame, slide and 4.5-inch bbl. Overall dimension reduced to 7.5 inches. Weight: 31 oz. Fixed sights w/blade front and V-notch rear. Blued finish. Checkered hard rubber grips. Round back hammer, changed to spur type in 1908. No safety. (SN range 16,001-47,226 with some numbers above 30,200 assigned to 1902 Military). Made 1903-1929.

Early model
(round hammer) . . . . NiB $2220 Ex $1930 Gd $945
Late model
(spur hammer). . . . . NiB $1785 Ex $1195 Gd $695

MODEL 1903 POCKET HAMMERLESS (CONCEALED HAMMER) .32 AUTOMATIC PISTOL - MILITARY

Caliber: .32 ACP. Eight-round magazine, Similar to Model 1903 Pocket .32 except concealed hammer and equipped w/magazine safety. Parkerized or blued finish. (SN range with "M" prefix M1-M200,000) Made 1941-.45.

Blued service model (marked
"U.S. Property") . . . . NiB $1525 Ex $1040 Gd $740
Parkerized service model (marked
"U.S. Property") . . . . NiB $1515 Ex $540 Gd $690
Blued documented
Officer's model . . . . NiB $3465 Ex $3690 Gd $1590
Parkerized documented
Officer's model . . . . NiB $2415 Ex $2090 Gd $1490

MODEL 1905 .45 AUTOMATIC PISTOL

Caliber: .45 (Rimless) Automatic. Seven-round magazine, 5-inch bbl., 8 inches overall. Weight: 32.5 oz. Fixed sights w/blade front and V-notch rear. Blued finish. Checkered walnut, hard rubber or pearl grips. Predecessor to Model 1911 Auto Pistol and contributory to the development of the .45 ACP cartridge. (SN range 1-6100) Made 1905-11.

Commercial model . . . . NiB $5500 Ex $3250 Gd $1500
W/slotted backstrap
(500 produced) . . . . NiB $8250 Ex $7500 Gd $6000
W/shoulder stock/holster . . . . $7500 to $10,000

MODEL 1905 .45 (1907)
CONTRACT PISTOL. . . . . NiB $12,000 Ex $9500 Gd $6250

Variation of the Model 1905 produced to U.S. Military specifications, including loaded chamber indicator, grip safety and lanyard loop. Only 201 were produced, but 200 were delivered and may be identified by the chief inspector's initials "K.M." (SN range 1-201) Made 1907-08.

MODEL 1908 POCKET .25 HAMMERLESS AUTO PISTOL

Caliber: .25 Auto. Six-round magazine, 2-inch bbl., 4.5 inches overall. Weight: 13 oz. Flat-top front, square-notch rear sight in groove. Blued, nickel or Parkerized finish. Checkered hard rubber grips on early models, checkered walnut on later type, special pearl grips illustrated. Both a grip safety and slide lock safety are included on all models. The Tansley-style safety disconnector was added in 1916 at pistol No. 141000. (SN range 1-409,061) Made 1908-41.

Blued finish . . . . NiB $966 Ex $758 Gd $602
Nickel finish . . . . NiB $1018 Ex $862 Gd $706
Marked "U.S. Property" (w/blued finish). . . . . NiB $3301 Ex $1715 Gd $1329
Marked "U.S. Property" (w/parkerized finish). . . . . NiB $2672 Ex $2162 Gd $1486

MODEL 1908 POCKET .380 AUTOMATIC PISTOL

Similar to Pocket .32 Auto w/3.75-inch bbl. except chambered for .380 Auto w/seven-round magazine. Weight: 23 oz. Blue, nickel or Parkerized finish. (SN range 1-138,009) Made 1908-45.

First Issue (made 1908-11, w/bbl., lock and bushing, w/SN 1-6,250). . . . . NiB $914 Ex $706 Gd $342
Second Issue (made 1911-28, w/o bbl., lock and bushing, w/SN 6,251-92,893) . . . . NiB $862 Ex $550 Gd $290
Third Issue (made 1928-45, w/safety disconnector, w/SN 92,894-138,009). . . . . NiB $582 Ex $472 Gd $331
Parkerized service model (Marked "U.S. Property" made 1942-45, w/SN "M" prefix.) . . . . . NiB $2405 Ex $1781 Gd $1521
Documented officer's model (service model w/military assignment papers) . . . . NiB $2896 Ex $2336 Gd $1620

NOTE: *During both World Wars, Colt licensed other firms to make these pistols under government contract, including Ithaca Gun Co., North American Arms Co., Ltd. (Canada), Remington-Rand Co., Remington-UMC, Singer Sewing Machine Co., and Union Switch & Signal Co. M1911 also produced at Springfield Armory.*

MODEL 1911 AUTOMATIC PISTOL

Caliber: .45 Auto. Seven-round magazine, 5-inch bbl., 8.5 inches overall. Weight: 39 oz. Fixed sights. Blued finish on Commercial model. Parkerized or similar finish on most military pistols. Checkered walnut grips (early production), plastic grips (later production). Checkered, arched mainspring housing and longer grip safety spur adopted in 1923 (on M1911A1).

Model 1911 commercial (C-series) . . . . NiB $1843 Ex $1491 Gd $1042
Model 1911A1 commercial (Pre-WWII) . . . . NiB $3714 Ex $2987 Gd $2057

U.S. GOVERNMENT MODEL 1911

Colt manufacture. . . . . NiB $1380 Ex $1172 Gd $844
North American manufacture . . . . NiB $25,868 Ex $20,693 Gd $14,071
Remington-UMC manufacture. . . . . NiB $2307 Ex $1859 Gd $1285
Springfield manufacture . . . . . . NiB $2269 Ex $1828 Gd $1265
Navy Model M1911 type. . . . . . NiB $2991 Ex $2405 Gd $1656

U.S. GOVERNMENT MODEL 1911A1

Singer manufacture . . . . . . NiB $25,936 Ex $20,748 Gd $14,109
Colt, Ithaca, Remington-Rand manufacture. . . . . NiB $987 Ex $799 Gd $558
Union Switch & Signal manufacture . . . . NiB $1484 Ex $1199 Gd $835

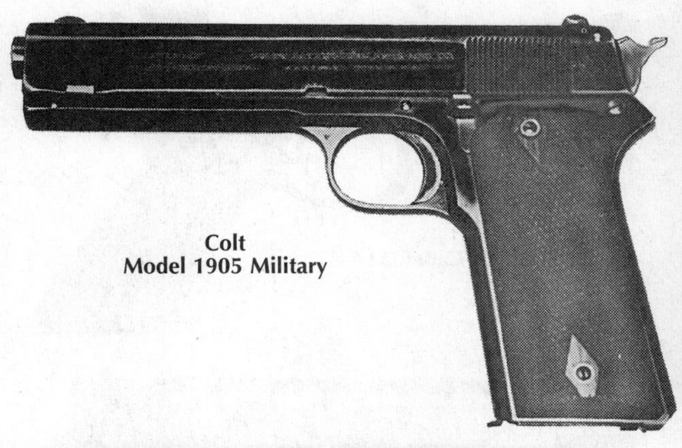

Colt
Model 1905 Military

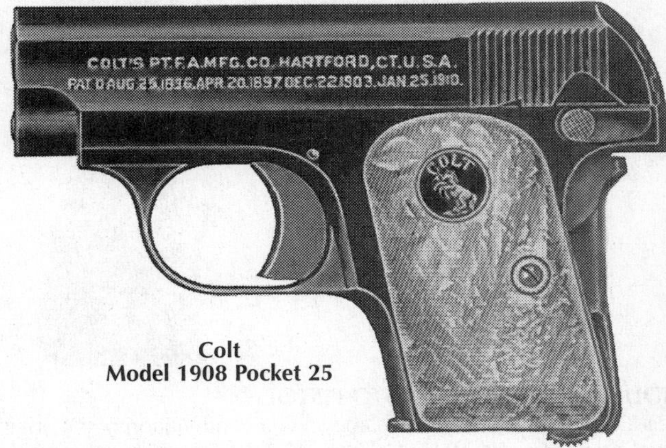

Colt
Model 1908 Pocket 25

Colt
Model 1911

Colt
1991 A1

Colt Cadet .22

Colt All American Model 2000

MODEL M1991 A1 SEMIAUTO PISTOL
Reissue of Model 1911A1 (see above) w/a continuation of the original serial number range 1945. Caliber: .45 ACP. Seven-round magazine, 5-inch bbl., 8.5 inches overall. Weight: 39 oz. Fixed blade front sight, square notch rear. Parkerized finish. Black composition grips. Made 1991 to date. (Commander and Compact variations intro. 1993).
Standard model. . . . . NiB $914 Ex $857 Gd $654
Commander w/4.5-inch bbl., ... NiB $654 Ex $592 Gd $3542
Compact w/3.5-inch bbl., (six-round). . . . . NiB $758 Ex $654 Gd $498

.22 CADET AUTOMATIC PISTOL . . . . . NiB $245 Ex $197 Gd $136
Caliber: 22 LR. 10-round magazine, 4.5-inch vent rib bbl., 8.63 inches overall. Weight: 33.5 oz. Blade front sight, dovetailed rear. Stainless finish. Textured black polymer grips w/Colt medallion. Made 1993-95. Note: The Cadet Model name was disc. under litigation but the manufacturer continued to produce this pistol configuration as the Model "Colt 22". For this reason the "Cadet" model will command slight premiums.

.22 SPORT AUTOMATIC PISTOL . . . . . NiB $416 Ex $312 Gd $161
Same specifications as Cadet Model except renamed Colt .22 w/composition monogrip or wraparound black rubber grip. Made 1995-98.

.22 TARGET PISTOL. . . . . NiB $312 Ex $265 Gd $135
Similar to Colt 22 Sport Model except w/6-inch vent rib bbl., 10.12 inches overall. Weight: 40.5 oz. Partridge style front sight, adjustable white outline rear on full length grooved rib. Made 1995 to date.

ACE AUTOMATIC PISTOL
Caliber: .22 LR (regular or high speed). 10-round magazine. Built on the same frame as the Government Model .45 Auto w/same safety features, etc. Hand-honed action, target bbl., adj. rear sight. 4.75-inch bbl., 8.25. inches overall. Weight: 38 oz. Made 1930-.40.
Commercial model . . . . NiB $2016 Ex $1612 Gd $1096
Service model (1938-42) . . . . . . NiB $2854 Ex $2283 Gd $1553

ALL AMERICAN
MODEL 2000 DA PISTOL . . . . NiB $800 Ex $696 Gd $436
Hammerless semiautomatic w/blued slide and polymer or alloy receiver fitted w/roller-bearing trigger. Caliber: 9mm Para. 15-round magazine, 4.5-inch bbl., 7.5 inches overall. Weight: 29 oz. (Polymer) or 33 oz (Alloy). Fixed blade front sight, square-notch rear w/3-dot system. Matte blued slide w/black polymer or anodized aluminum receiver. Made 1992-94.

AUTOMATIC .25 PISTOL
As a result of the 1968 Firearms Act restricting the importation of the Colt Pocket Junior that was produced in Spain, Firearms International was contracted by Colt to manufacture a similar blowback action with the same exposed hammer configuration. Both the U.S. and Spanish-made. .25 automatics were recalled to correct an action malfunction. Returned firearms were fitted with a rebounding firing pin to prevent accidental discharges. Caliber: .25 ACP. Six-round magazine, 2.25-inch bbl., 4.5 inches overall. Weight: 12.5 oz. Integral blade front, square-notch rear sight groove. Blued finish. Checkered wood grips w/Colt medallion. Made 1970-75.
Model as issued. . . . . NiB $322 Ex $270 Gd $114
Model recalled
& refitted. . . . . NiB $332 Ex $270 Gd $114

CHALLENGER
AUTOMATIC PISTOL . . . . NiB $525 Ex $421 Gd $218
Same basic design as Woodsman Target, Third Issue but lacks some of the refinements. Fixed sights. Magazine catch on butt as in old Woodsman. Does not stay open on last shot. Lacks magazine safety. 4.5- or 6-inch bbl., 9 to 10.5 inches overall. Weight: 30 oz. (4.5-inch bbl.) or 31.5 oz. (6-inch bbl.) Blued finish. Checkered plastic grips. Made 1950-55.

COMBAT COMMANDER AUTOMATIC PISTOL
Same as Lightweight Commander except has steel frame w/blued or nickel-plated finish. Weight: 36 oz. Made 1950-76.
9mm Para. . . . . NiB $664 Ex $535 Gd $370
.38 Super, .45 ACP. . . . . NiB $768 Ex $618 Gd $427

COMMANDER LIGHTWEIGHT AUTOMATIC PISTOL
Same basic design as Government Model except w/shorter 4.25-inch bbl., and a special lightweight "Coltalloy" receiver and mainspring housing. Calibers: .45 Auto, .38 Super Auto, 9mm Para. Seven-round magazine (.45 cal.), nine-round (.38 Auto and 9mm), 8 inches overall. Weight: 26.5 oz. Fixed sights. Round spur hammer. Improved safety lock. Blued finish. Checkered plastic or walnut grips. Made 1950-76.
9mm Para. . . . . NiB $655 Ex $529 Gd $368
.38 Super, .45 ACP. . . . . NiB $707 Ex $571 Gd $401

CONVERSION
UNIT—.22-.45. . . . . NiB $2863 Ex $2303 Gd $1587
Converts Service Ace .22 to National Match .45 Auto. Unit consists of match-grade slide assembly and bbl., bushing, recoil spring, recoil spring guide and plug, magazine and slide stop. Made 1938-42.

CONVERSION
UNIT — .45-.22 . . . . NiB $528 Ex $430 Gd $305
Converts Government Model .45 Auto to a .22 LR target pistol. Unit consists of slide assembly, bbl., floating chamber (as in Service Ace), bushing, ejector, recoil spring, recoil spring guide and plug, magazine and slide stop. The component parts differ and are not interchangable between post war, series 70, series 80, ACE I and ACE II units. Made 1938 to date.

DELTA ELITE SEMIAUTO PISTOL
Caliber: 10 mm. Five-inch bbl., 8.5 inches overall. Eight-round magazine, Weight: 38 oz. Checkered Neoprene combat grips w/Delta medallion. Three-dot, high-profile front and rear combat sights. Blued or stainless finish. Made 1987-96.
First Edition
(500 Ltd. edition). . . . . NiB $1204 Ex $1011 Gd $673
Blued finish . . . . NiB $658 Ex $534 Gd $376
Matte stainless finish . . . . NiB $684 Ex $555 Gd $390
Ultra stainless finish . . . . NiB $788 Ex $638 Gd $447

DELTA GOLD CUP SEMIAUTO PISTOL
Same general specifications as Delta Elite except in match configuration w/Accro adjustable rear sight. Made 1989-93 and 1995-96.
Blued finish (disc. 1991) . . . . NiB $756 Ex $612 Gd $429
Stainless steel finish. . . . . NiB $971 Ex $820 Gd $664

GOLD CUP MARK III
NATIONAL MATCH . . . . NiB $1132 Ex $919 Gd $633
Similar to Gold Cup National Match .45 Auto except chambered for .38 Special Mid Range. Five-round magazine, Made 1961-74.

GOLD CUP NATIONAL
MATCH .45 AUTO. . . . . NiB $1028 Ex $872 Gd $516
Match version of Government Model .45 Auto w/same general specifications except: match grade bbl., w/new design bushing, flat mainspring housing, long wide trigger w/adj. stop, hand-fitted slide w/improved ejection port, adj. rear sight, target front sight, checkered walnut grips w/gold medallions. Weight: 37 oz. Made 1957-70.

GOVERNMENT MODEL 1911/1911A1
See Colt Model 1911.

HUNTSMAN . . . . NiB $490 Ex $386 Gd $282
Same specifications as the Challenger. Made 1955-76.

MK I & IL/SERIES '90 DOUBLE
EAGLE COMBAT COMMANDER . . . . . NiB $612 Ex $493 Gd $341
Calibers: .40 S&W, .45 ACP. Seven-round magazine, 4.25-inch bbl., 7.75 inches overall. Weight: 36 oz. Fixed blade front sight, square-notch rear. Checkered Xenoy grips. Stainless finish. Made 1992-96.

MK IL/SERIES '90 DOUBLE EAGLE DA SEMIAUTO PISTOL
Calibers: .38 Super, 9mm, .40 S&W, 10mm, .45 ACP. Seven-round magazine. Five-inch bbl., 8.5 inches overall. Weight: 39 oz. Fixed or Accro adj. sights. Matte stainless finish. Checkered Xenoy grips. Made 1991-96.
.38 Super, 9mm, .40
S&W (fixed sights). . . . . NiB $652 Ex $526 Gd $364
.45 ACP (adjustable sights) . . . . NiB $648 Ex $524 Gd $366
.45 ACP (fixed sights) . . . . NiB $622 Ex $487 Gd $351
10mm (adjustable sights). . . . . NiB $642 Ex $519 Gd $363
10mm (fixed sights). . . . . NiB $616 Ex $498 Gd $348

MK IL/SERIES '90 DOUBLE
EAGLE OFFICER'S ACP . . . . NiB $648 Ex $526 Gd $366
Same general specifications as Double Eagle Combat Commander except chambered for .45 ACP only, 3.5-inch bbl., 7.25 inches overall. Weight: 35 oz. Also available in lightweight (25 oz.) w/blued finish (same price). Made 1990-93.

MK IV/SERIES '70 COMBAT COMMANDER
Same general specifications as the Lightweight Commander except made 1970-83.
Blued finish . . . . NiB $625 Ex $503 Gd $342
Nickel finish . . . . NiB $692 Ex $468 Gd $372

Colt Delta Gold Cup

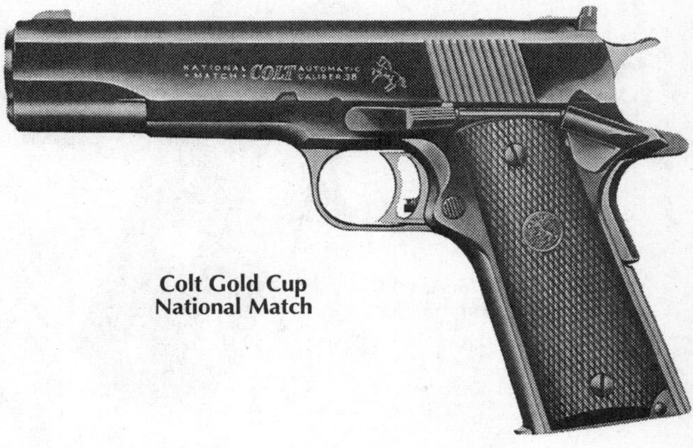
Colt Gold Cup National Match

Colt MK II/Series '90 Double Eagle Officer's ACP

MK IV/SERIES '70 GOLD CUP
NATIONAL MATCH .45 AUTO . . . NiB $1018 Ex $841 Gd $654
Match version of MK IV/Series '70 Government Model. Caliber: .45 Auto only. Flat mainspring housing. Accurizor bbl., and bushing. Solid rib, Colt-Elliason adj. rear sight undercut front sight. Adj. trigger, target hammer. 8.75 inches overall. Weight: 38.5 oz. Blued finish. Checkered walnut grips. Made 1970-84.

MK IV/SERIES '70 GOV'T.
AUTO PISTOL . . . . NiB $862 Ex $654 Gd $394
Calibers: .45 Auto, .38 Super Auto, 9mm Para. Seven-round magazine in .45, 9-round in .38 and 9mm. Five-inch bbl., 8.38 inches overall. Weight: 38 oz., (.45); 39 oz. in .38 and 9mm. Fixed rear sight and ramp front sight. Blued or nickel-plated finish. Checkered walnut grips. Made 1970-84.

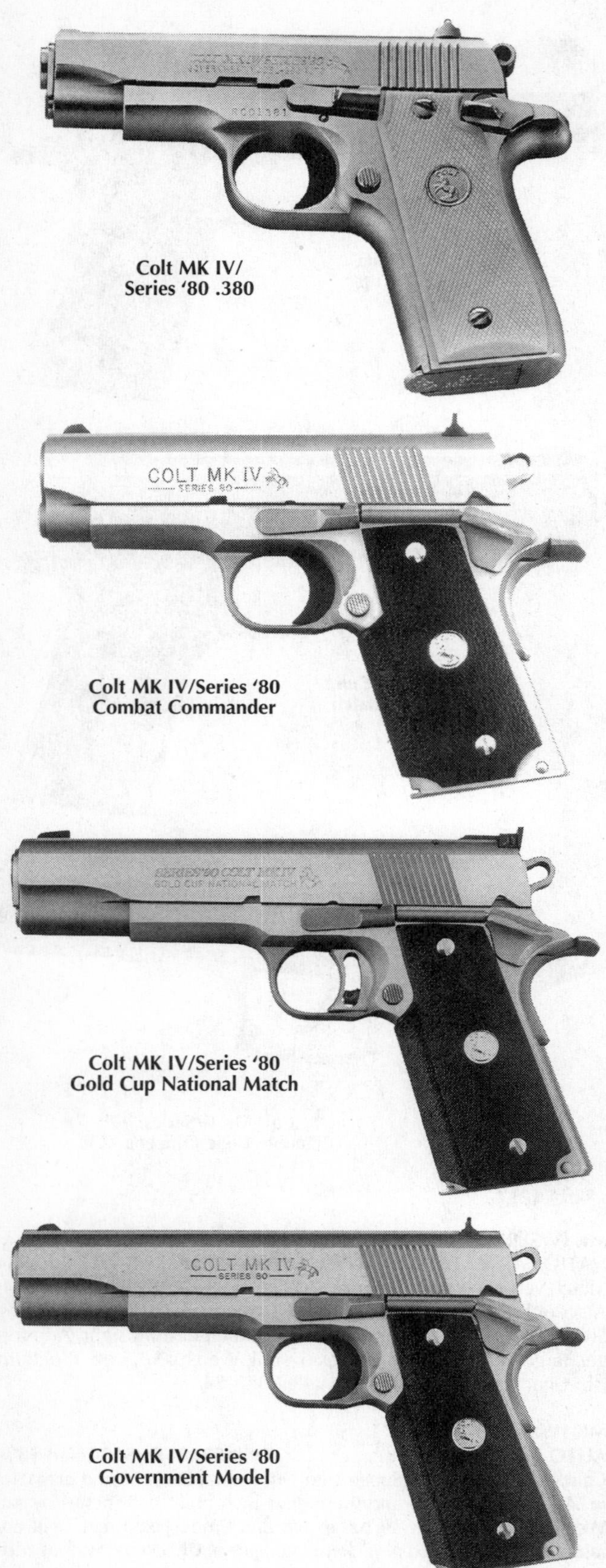

Colt MK IV/ Series '80 .380

Colt MK IV/Series '80 Combat Commander

Colt MK IV/Series '80 Gold Cup National Match

Colt MK IV/Series '80 Government Model

MK IV/SERIES '80 .380 AUTOMATIC PISTOL
Caliber: .380 ACP, 3.29-inch bbl., 6.15 inches overall. Weight: 21.8 oz. Composition grips. Fixed sights. Made since 1984 to date.
Blued finish
(disc.1997). NiB $459 Ex $324 Gd $220
Bright nickel
(disc.1995). NiB $532 Ex $391 Gd $241
Satin nickel
Coltguard (disc.1989) . . . . NiB $511 Ex $355 Gd $235
Stainless finish . . . . NiB $516 Ex $365 Gd $251

MK IV/SERIES '80 COMBAT COMMANDER
Updated version of the MK IV/Series '70 w/same general specifications. Blued, two-tone or stainless steel w/"pebbled" black Neoprene wraparound grips. Made since 1979.
Blued finish
(disc.1996). NiB $608 Ex $509 Gd $332
Satin nickel
(disc.1987). NiB $649 Ex $534 Gd $357
Stainless finish . . . . NiB $670 Ex $524 Gd $380
Two-tone finish . . . . NiB $695 Ex $545 Gd $384

MK IV/SERIES '80 COMBAT ELITE
Same general specifications as MK IV/Series '80 Combat Commander except w/Elite enhancements. Calibers: .38 Super, .40 S&W, .45 ACP. Stainless frame w/blued steel slide. Accro adj. sights and beavertail grip safety. Made 1992-96.
.38 Super,
.45 ACP . . . . NiB $789 Ex $675 Gd $373
.40 S&W . . . . NiB $758 Ex $654 Gd $342

MK IV/SERIES '80 GOLD CUP NATIONAL MATCH
Same general specifications as Match '70 version except w/additional finishes and "pebbled" wraparound Neoprene grips. Made 1983-96.
Blued finish . . . . NiB $930 Ex $748 Gd $384
Bright blued
finish . . . . NiB $971 Ex $682 Gd $457
Stainless finish . . . . NiB $769 Ex $623 Gd $394

MK IV/SERIES '80 GOVERNMENT MODEL
Same general specifications as Government Model Series '70 except also chambered in .40 S&W, w/"pebbled" wraparound Neoprene grips, blued or stainless finish. Made since 1983.
Blued finish . . . . NiB $755 Ex $545 Gd $337
Bright blued
finish . . . . NiB $826 Ex $571 Gd $466
Bright stainless
finish . . . . NiB $748 Ex $644 Gd $342
Matte stainless finish . . . . NiB $745 Ex $539 Gd $352

MK IV/SERIES '80 LIGHT-
WEIGHT COMMANDER . . . . NiB $639 Ex $504 Gd $332
Updated version of the MK IV/Series '70 w/same general specifications.

MK IV/SERIES '80 MUSTANG .380 AUTOMATIC
Caliber: .380 ACP. Five- or 6-round magazine, 2.75-inch bbl., 5.5 inches overall. Weight: 18.5 oz. Blued, nickel or stainless finish. Black composition grips. Made 1986-97.
Blued finish . . . . NiB $442 Ex $343 Gd $244
Nickel finish
(disc.1994). NiB $498 Ex $342 Gd $251
Satin nickel
Coltguard (disc.1988) . . . . NiB $488 Ex $322 Gd $242
Stainless finish . . . . NiB $508 Ex $342 Gd $251

MK IV/SERIES '80 MUSTANG PLUS II
Caliber: .380 ACP, 7-round magazine, 2.75-inch bbl., 5.5 inches overall. Weight: 20 oz. Blued or stainless finish w/checkered black composition grips. Made 1988-96.
Blued finish . . . . NiB $452 Ex $353 Gd $257
Stainless finish . . . . NiB $508 Ex $352 Gd $242

MK IV/SERIES '80 MUSTANG POCKETLITE
Same general specifications as the Mustang 30 except weight: 12.5 oz. w/aluminum alloy receiver. Blued, chrome or stainless finish. Optional wood grain grips. Made since 1988.
Blued finish . . . . NiB $454 Ex $355 Gd $256
Lady Elite
(two-tone) finish . . . . NiB $479 Ex $433 Gd $292
Stainless finish . . . . NiB $510 Ex $354 Gd $264
Teflon/stainless finish . . . . NiB $537 Ex $350 Gd $251

MK IV/SERIES '80 OFFICER'S ACP AUTOMATIC PISTOL
Calibers: .40 S&W and .45 ACP, 3.63-inch bbl., 7.25 inches overall. Weight: 34 oz. Made 1984-97. .40 S&W, disc.1992.
Blued finish
(disc.1996). . . . . NiB $561 Ex $458 Gd $318
Matte finish . . . . NiB $538 Ex $433 Gd $310
Satin nickel finish . . . . NiB $624 Ex $501 Gd $339
Stainless steel . . . . NiB $586 Ex $472 Gd $328

MK IV/SERIES '80
SA LIGHTWEIGHT CONCEALED
CARRY OFFICER . . . . NiB $633 Ex $511 Gd $347
Caliber: .45 ACP. Seven-round magazine, 4.25-inch bbl., 7.75 inches overall. Weight: 35 oz. Aluminum alloy receiver w/stainless slide. Dovetailed low-profile sights w/3-dot system. Matte stainless finish w/blued receiver. Wraparound black rubber grip w/finger grooves. Made since 1998.

MK IV/SERIES '90 DEFENDER
SA LIGHTWEIGHT . . . . NiB $623 Ex $499 Gd $331
Caliber: .45 ACP. Seven-round magazine, 3-inch bbl., 6.75 inches over-all. Weight: 22.5 oz. Aluminum alloy receiver w/stainless slide. Dovetailed low-profile sights w/3-dot system. Matte stainless finish w/Nickel-Teflon receiver. Wraparound black rubber grip w/finger grooves. Made since 1998.

MK IV/SERIES 90
PONY DAO PISTOL . . . . NiB $514 Ex $422 Gd $283
Caliber: .380 ACP. Six-round magazine, 2.75-inch bbl., 5.5 inches overall. Weight: 19 oz. Ramp front sight, dovetailed rear. Stainless finish. Checkered black composition grips. Made since 1997.

MK IV/SERIES 90
PONY POCKETLITE. . . . . NiB $494 Ex $406 Gd $269
Similar to standard weight Pony Model except w/aluminum frame. Brushed stainless and Teflon finish. Made 1997 to date.

NATIONAL MATCH AUTOMATIC PISTOL
Identical to the Government Model .45 Auto but w/hand-honed action, match-grade bbl., adj. rear and ramp front sights or fixed sights. Made 1932-40.
W/adjustable
sights . . . . NiB $2886 Ex $2316 Gd $1610
W/fixed sights . . . . NiB $2084 Ex $1645 Gd $1148

NRA CENTENNIAL
.45 GOLD CUP
NATIONAL MATCH . . . . NiB $1500 Ex $1234 Gd $860
Only 2500 produced in 1971.

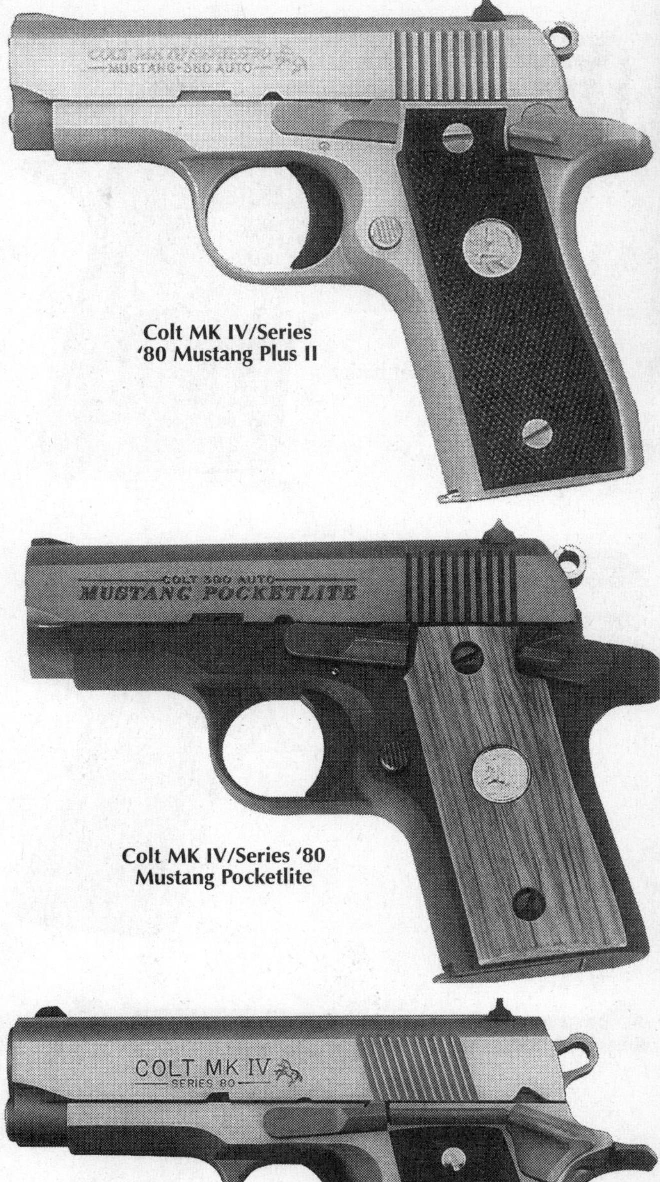

Colt MK IV/Series '80 Mustang Plus II

Colt MK IV/Series '80 Mustang Pocketlite

Colt MK IV/Series '80 Officer's ACP

POCKET JUNIOR MODEL
AUTOMATIC PISTOL . . . . NiB $384 Ex $290 Gd $176
Made in Spain by Unceta y Cia (Astra). Calibers: .22 Short, .25 Auto. Six-round magazine, 2.25 inch bbl., 4.75 inches overall. Weight: 12 oz. Fixed sights. Checkered walnut grips. Note: In 1980, this model was subject to recall to correct an action malfunction. Returned firearms were fitted with a rebounding firing pin to prevent accidental discharges. Made 1958-68. See illustration next page.

Colt Pocket Junior

Colt Woodsman
Match Target Second Issue

SUPER .38 AUTOMATIC PISTOL
Identical to Government Model .45 Auto except for caliber and magazine capacity. Caliber: .38 Automatic. Nine-round magazine, Made 1928-70.
Pre-war . . . . NiB $2857 Ex $2299 Gd $1697
Post-war. . . . . NiB $1120 Ex $607 Gd $639

SUPER MATCH .38 AUTOMATIC PISTOL
Identical to Super .38 Auto but w/hand-honed action, match grade bbl., adjustable rear sight and ramp front sight or fixed sights. Made 1933-46.
W/adjustable sights . . . . NiB $6979 Ex $5507 Gd $3840
W/fixed sights . . . . NiB $4701 Ex $3787 Gd $2606

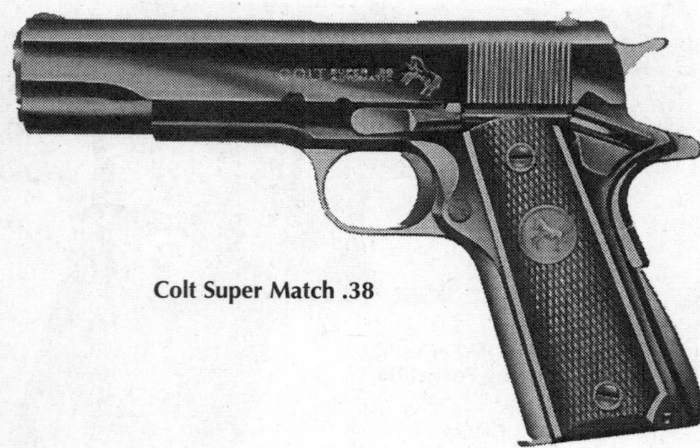
Colt Super Match .38

TARGETSMAN. . . . . NiB $719 Ex $657 Gd $303
Similar to Woodsman Target but has "economy" adj. rear sight, lacks automatic slide stop. Made 1959-76.

WOODSMAN MATCH TARGET AUTOMATIC PISTOL FIRST ISSUE. . . . . NiB $1501 Ex $1449 Gd $825
Same basic design as other Woodsman models. Caliber: .22 LR. 10-round magazine, 6.5-inch bbl., slightly tapered w/flat sides, 11 inches overall. Weight: 36 oz. Adjustable rear sight. Blued finish. Checkered walnut one-piece grip w/extended sides. Made 1938-42.

Colt Targetsman

WOODSMAN MATCH TARGET AUTO PISTOL, SECOND ISSUE . . . . NiB $929 Ex $752 Gd $482
Same basic design as Woodsman Target Third Issue. Caliber: .22 LR (reg. or high speed). 10-round magazine, Six-inch flat-sided heavy bbl., 10.5 inches overall. Weight: 40 oz. Click adj. rear sight, ramp front. Blued finish. Checkered plastic or walnut grips. Made 1948-76.

WOODSMAN MATCH TARGET "4 1/2" AUTOMATIC PISTOL . . . . NiB $877 Ex $555 Gd $409
Same as Match Target second issue except w/4.5-inch bbl., 9 inches overall. Weight: 36 oz. Made 1950-76.

Colt Woodsman
Match Target First Issue

WOODSMAN SPORT MODEL AUTOMATIC PISTOL, FIRST ISSUE. . . . . NiB $970 Ex $788 Gd $528
Caliber: .22 LR (reg. or high speed). Same as Woodsman Target second issue except has 4.5-inch bbl., adjustable rear sight w/fixed or adjustable front sight. Weight: 27 oz., 8.5 inches overall. Made 1933-48.

WOODSMAN SPORT MODEL AUTOMATIC PISTOL, SECOND ISSUE . . . . NiB $970 Ex $788 Gd $528
Same as Woodsman Target third Issue but w/4.5-inch bbl., 9 inches overall. Weight: 30 oz. Made 1948-76.

WOODSMAN TARGET MODEL AUTOMATIC, FIRST ISSUE . . . . NiB $788 Ex $736 Gd $372
Caliber: .22 LR (reg. velocity). 10-round magazine, 6.5-inch bbl., 10.5 inches overall. Weight: 28 oz. Adjustable sights. Blued finish. Checkered walnut grips. Made 1915-.32. Note: The mainspring housing of this model is not strong enough to permit safe use of high-speed cartridges. Change to a new heat-treated mainspring housing was made at pistol No. 83,790. Many of the old models were converted by installation of new housings. The new housing may be distinguished from the earlier type by the checkering in the curve under the breech. The new housing is grooved straight across, while the old type bears a diagonally-checkered oval.

WOODSMAN TARGET MODEL AUTOMATIC, SECOND ISSUE . . . . NiB $711 Ex $555 Gd $347
Caliber: .22 LR (reg. or high speed). Same as original model except has heavier bbl., and high-speed mainspring housing. (See note under Woodsman, First Issue). Weight: 29 oz. Made 1932-48.

WOODSMAN TARGET MODEL AUTOMATIC, THIRD ISSUE . . . . . . NiB $561 Ex $436 Gd $254
Same basic design as previous Woodsman pistols but w/longer grip, magazine catch on left side, larger thumb safety, slide stop, slide stays open on last shot, magazine disconnector thumbrest grips. Caliber: .22 LR (reg. or high speed). 10-round magazine, 6-inch bbl., 10.5 inches overall. Weight: 32 oz. Click adjustable rear sight, ramp front sight. Blued finish. Checkered plastic or walnut grips. Made 1948-76.

WORLD WAR I 50TH ANNIVERSARY COMMEMORATIVE SERIES
Limited production replica of Model 1911 .45 Auto engraved w/battle scenes, commemorating Battles at Chateau Thierry, Belleau Wood Second Battle of the Marne, Meuse Argonne. In special presentation display cases. Production: 7,400 Standard model, 75 Deluxe, 25 Special Deluxe grade. Match numbered sets offered. Made in 1967, 68, 69. Values indicated are for commemoratives in new condition.
Standard grade . . . . NiB $982 Ex $794 Gd $553
Deluxe grade . . . . NiB $2004 Ex $1615 Gd $1118
Special Deluxe grade . . . . NiB $3911 Ex $3143 Gd $2161

WORLD WAR II COMMEMORATIVE .45 AUTO . . . . NiB $1022 Ex $866 Gd $674
Limited production replica of Model 1911A1 .45 Auto engraved w/respective names of locations where historic engagements occurred during WW II, as well as specific issue and theater identification. European model has oak leaf motif on slide, palm leaf design frames the Pacific issue. Cased. 11,500 of each model were produced. Made in 1970. Value listed is for gun in new condition.

WORLD WAR II 50TH ANNIVERSARY COMMEMORATIVE. . . . . NiB $2306 Ex $1942 Gd $1449
Same general specifications as the Colt World War II Commemorative .45 Auto except slightly different scroll engraving, 24-karat gold-plate trigger, hammer, slide stop, magazine catch, magazine catch lock, safety lock and four grip screws. Made in 1995 only.

WORLD WAR II D-DAY INVASION COMMEMORATIVE . . . . NiB $1391 Ex $1318 Gd $932
High-luster and highly decorated version of the Colt Model 1911A1. Caliber: .45 ACP. Same general specifications as the Colt Model 1911 except for 24-karat gold-plated hammer, trigger, slide stop, magazine catch, magazine catch screw, safety lock and four grip screws. Also has scrolls and inscription on slide. Made in 1991 only.

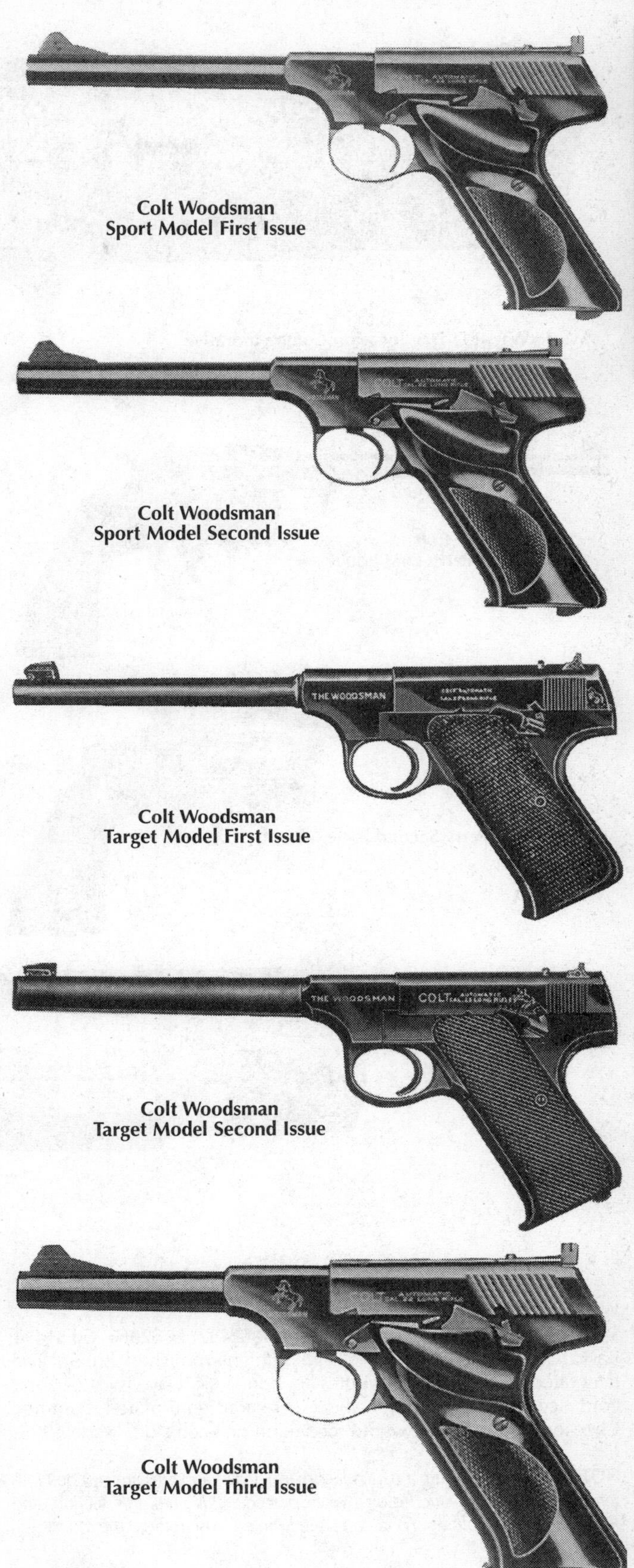
Colt Woodsman Sport Model First Issue

Colt Woodsman Sport Model Second Issue

Colt Woodsman Target Model First Issue

Colt Woodsman Target Model Second Issue

Colt Woodsman Target Model Third Issue

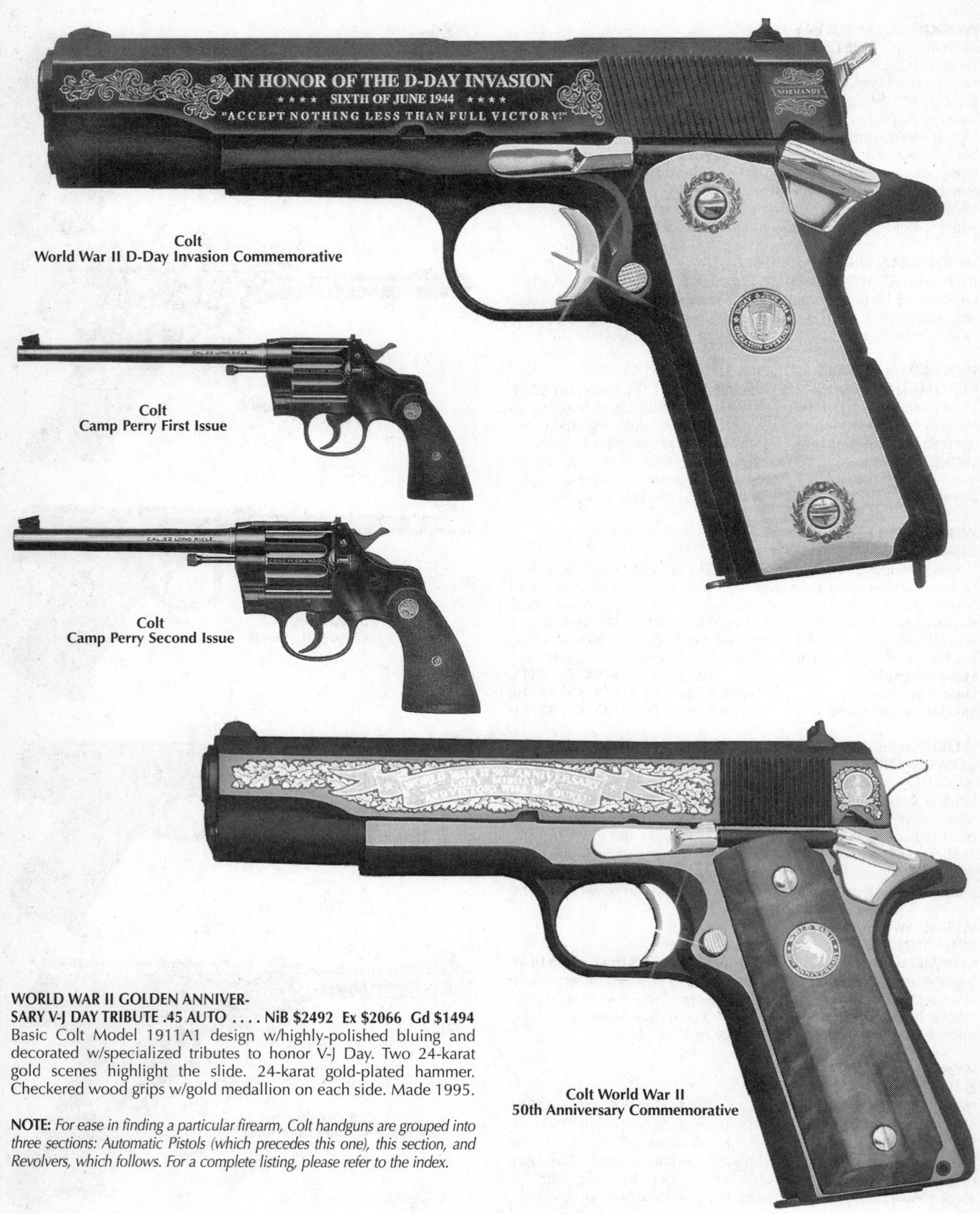

Colt
World War II D-Day Invasion Commemorative

Colt
Camp Perry First Issue

Colt
Camp Perry Second Issue

Colt World War II
50th Anniversary Commemorative

WORLD WAR II GOLDEN ANNIVERSARY V-J DAY TRIBUTE .45 AUTO . . . . NiB $2492 Ex $2066 Gd $1494
Basic Colt Model 1911A1 design w/highly-polished bluing and decorated w/specialized tributes to honor V-J Day. Two 24-karat gold scenes highlight the slide. 24-karat gold-plated hammer. Checkered wood grips w/gold medallion on each side. Made 1995.

NOTE: *For ease in finding a particular firearm, Colt handguns are grouped into three sections: Automatic Pistols (which precedes this one), this section, and Revolvers, which follows. For a complete listing, please refer to the index.*

SINGLE-SHOT PISTOLS & DERRINGERS

CAMP PERRY MODEL SINGLE-SHOT PISTOL, FIRST ISSUE . . . . NiB $1729 Ex $1402 Gd $961
Built on Officers' Model frame. Caliber: .22 LR (embedded head chamber for high-speed cartridges after 1930). 10 inch bbl., 13.75 inches overall. Weight: 34.5 oz. Adj. target sights. Hand-finished action. Blued finish. Checkered walnut grips. Made 1926-34.

CAMP PERRY MODEL SECOND ISSUE . . . . NiB $1501 Ex $1241 Gd $877
Same general specifications as First Issue except has shorter hammer fall and 8-inch bbl., 12 inches overall. Weight: 34 oz. Made 1934-41 (about 440 produced).

CIVIL WAR CENTENNIAL MODEL PISTOL
Single-shot replica of Colt Model 1860 Army Revolver. Caliber: .22 Short. Six-inch bbl., weight: 22 oz. Blued finish w/gold-plated frame, grip frame, and trigger guard, walnut grips. Cased. 24,114 were produced. Made in 1961.
Single pistol . . . . NiB $271 Ex $220 Gd $155
Pair w/consecutive serial numbers . . . . NiB $613 Ex $485 Gd $335

DERRINGER NO. 4
Replica of derringer No. 3 (1872 Thuer Model). Single-shot w/side-swing bbl., Caliber: .22 Short, 2.5-inch bbl., 4.9 inches overall. Weight: 7.75 oz. Fixed sights. Gold-plated frame w/blued bbl., and walnut grips or completely nickel- or gold-plated w/simulated ivory or pearl grips. Made 1959-63. 112,000 total production. (SN w/D or N suffix)
Single pistol (gun only) . . . . NiB $136 Ex $110 Gd $77
Single pistol (cased w/accessories) . . . . NiB $396 Ex $292 Gd $162

DERRINGER NO. 4 COMMEMORATIVE MODELS
Limited production version of .22 derringers issued, w/appropriate inscription, to commemorate historical events. Additionally, non-firing models (w/unnotched bbls.) were furnished in books, picture frames and encased in plexiglass as singles or in cased pairs..
No. 4 Presentation Derringers
(Non-firing w/accessories) . . . . NiB $4000
Ltd. Ed. Book Series
(W/nickel-plated derringers) . . . . NiB $374
1st Presentation Series
(Leatherette covered metal case) . . . . NiB $348
2nd Presentation Series
(Single wooden case) . . . . NiB $244
2nd Presentation Series
(Paired wooden case) . . . . NiB $374
1961 Issue Geneseo, Illinois,
125th Anniversary (104 produced) . . . . NiB $733
1962 Issue Fort McPherson,
Nebraska, Centennial (300 produced) . . . . NiB $452

LORD AND LADY DERRINGERS (NO. 5)
Same as Derringer No. 4. Lord model with blued bbl., w/gold-plated frame and walnut grips. Lady model is gold-plated w/simulated pearl grips. Furnished in cased pairs. Made 1970-72. (SN w/Der sufix)
Lord derringer, pair in case . . . . . . NiB $473 Ex $381 Gd $265
Lady derringer, pair in case . . . . . . NiB $485 Ex $382 Gd $272
Lord and Lady derringers,
one each, in case . . . . NiB $504 Ex $407 Gd $282

ROCK ISLAND ARSENAL CENTENNIAL PISTOL . . . . NiB $426 Ex $421 Gd $234
Limited production (550 pieces) version of Civil War Centennial Model single-shot .22 pistol, made exclusively for Cherry's Sporting Goods, Geneseo, Illinois, to commemorate the centennial of the Rock Island Arsenal in Illinois. Cased. Made in 1962.

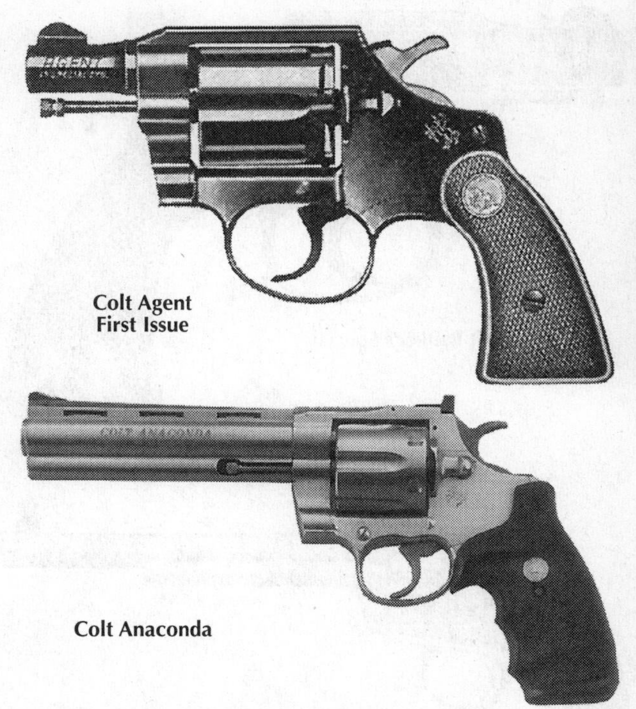

Colt Agent
First Issue

Colt Anaconda

NOTE: *This section of Colt handguns contains only revolvers. For automatic pistols or single-shot pistols and derringers, please see the two sections that precede this. For a complete listing, please refer to the Index.*

REVOLVERS

.38 DS II REVOLVER . . . . NiB $451 Ex $356 Gd $243
Caliber: .38 Special. Six-round cylinder, 2-inch bbl., 7 inches overall. Weight: 21 oz. Ramp front sight, fixed notch rear. Satin stainless finish. Black rubber combat grip w/finger grooves. Made 1997 to date.

AGENT DA REVOLVER, FIRST ISSUE . . . . NiB $457 Ex $405 Gd $254
Same as Cobra, first issue except has short-grip frame .38 Special only, weight: 14 oz. Made 1955-72.

AGENT (LW) DA REVOLVER, SECOND ISSUE . . . . NiB $426 Ex $395 Gd $223
Same as Colt Agent, first issue except has shrouded ejector rod and alloy frame. Made 1973-86.

ANACONDA DA REVOLVER
Calibers: .44 Mag., .45 Colt., bbl. lengths: 4, 6 or 8 inches; 11.63 inches overall (with 6-inch bbl.). Weight: 53 oz. (6-inch bbl.). Adj. white outline rear sight, red insert ramp-style front. Matte stainless or Realtree gray camo finish. Black Neoprene combat grips w/finger grooves. Made since 1990.
Matte stainless . . . . NiB $686 Ex $525 Gd $322
Realtree gray camo
finish (disc. 1996) . . . . NiB $738 Ex $556 Gd $348
Custom model
(.44 Mag. w/ported bbl.) . . . . NiB $925 Ex $639 Gd $327
First Edition model
(Ltd. Edition 1000) . . . . NiB $998 Ex $790 Gd $426
Hunter model
(.44 Mag. w/2x scope) . . . . NiB $1159 Ex $951 Gd $566

Colt Banker's Special

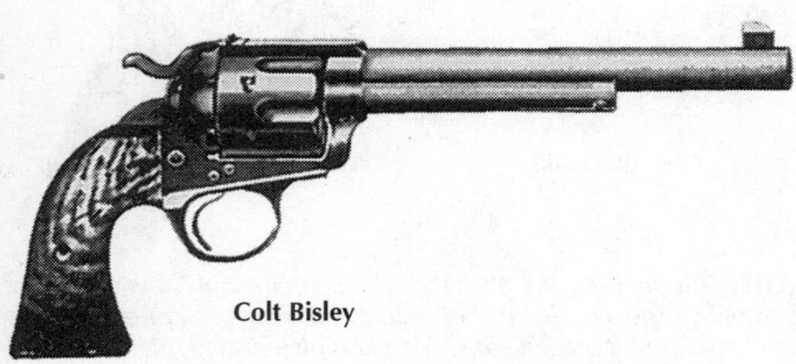
Colt Bisley

Colt Buntline Special .45

Colt Commando Special

ANACONDA TITANIUM DA REVOLVER
Same general specifications as the standard Anaconda except chambered .44 Mag. only w/titanium-plated finish, gold-plated trigger, hammer and cylinder release. Limited edition of 1,000 distributed by American Historical Foundation w/personalized inscription. Made 1996.
One of 1000 . . . . NiB $2489 Ex $1996 Gd $1366
Presentation case, add. $200

ARMY SPECIAL DA REVOLVER . . . . . . NiB $779 Ex $701 Gd $441
.41-caliber frame. Calibers: .32-20, .38 Special (.41 Colt). Six-round cylinder, right revolution. Bbl., lengths: 4-, 4.5, 5-, and 6-inches, 9.25 inches overall (4-inch bbl.). Weight: 32 oz. (4-inch bbl.). Fixed sights. Blued or nickel-plated finish. Hard rubber grips. Made 1908-27. Note: This model has a somewhat heavier frame than the New Navy, which it replaced. Serial numbers begin w/300,000. The heavy .38 Special High Velocity loads should not be used in .38 Special arms of this model.

BANKER'S SPECIAL DA REVOLVER
This is the Police Positive w/a 2-inch bbl., otherwise specifications same as that model, rounded butt intro. in 1933. Calibers: .22 LR (embedded head-cylinder for high speed cartridges intro. 1933), .38 New Police. 6.5 inches overall. Weight: 23 oz. (.22 LR), 19 oz. (.38). Made 1926-.40.
.38 caliber . . . . NiB $1126 Ex $915 Gd $130
.22 caliber . . . . NiB $2153 Ex $1746 Gd $1230

BISLEY MODEL SA REVOLVER
Variation of the Single-Action Army, developed for target shooting w/modified grips, trigger and hammer. Calibers: General specifications same as SA Army. Target Model made w/flat-topped frame and target sights. Made 1894-1915.
Standard model . . . . NiB $8224 Ex $6587 Gd $4492
Target model (flat-top) . . . . . NiB $12,176 Ex $9770 Gd $6692

BUNTLINE SPECIAL .45 . . . . NiB $1262 Ex $1022 Gd $714
Same as standard SA Army except has 12-inch bbl., caliber .45 Long Colt. Made 1957-75.

COBRA DA REVOLVER,
ROUND BUTT, FIRST ISSUE . . . . . . NiB $488 Ex $394 Gd $275
Lightweight Detective Special w/same general specifications as that model except w/Colt-alloy frame. Two-inch bbl., calibers: .38 Special, .38 New Police, .32 New Police. Weight: 15 oz., (.38 cal.). Blued finish. Checkered plastic or walnut grips. Made 1951-73.

COBRA DA REVOLVER,
SECOND ISSUE . . . . NiB $488 Ex $384 Gd $228
Lightweight version of Detective Special, Second Issue has aluminum alloy frame. 16.5 oz. Made 1973-81.

COBRA DA REVOLVER
SQUARE BUTT . . . . NiB $462 Ex $358 Gd $228
Lightweight Police Positive Special w/same general specifications except has Colt-alloy frame, 4-inch bbl., Calibers: .38 Special, .38 New Police, .32 New Police. Weight: 17 oz. in .38 caliber. Blued finish. Checkered plastic or walnut grips. Made 1951-73.

COMMANDO SPECIAL
DA REVOLVER. . . . . NiB $462 Ex $358 Gd $254
Caliber: .38 Special. Six-round cylinder, 2-inch bbl., 6.88 inches overall. Weight: 21.5 oz. Fixed sights. Low-luster blued finish. Made 1982-86.

DETECTIVE SPECIAL DA REVOLVER, FIRST ISSUE
Similar to Police Positive Special w/2-inch bbl., otherwise specifications same as that model, rounded butt intro. 1933. .38 Special only in pre-war issue. Blued or nickel-plated finish. Weight: 17 oz. 6.75 inches overall. Made 1926-46.
Blued finish . . . . NiB $493 Ex $389 Gd $285
Nickel finish . . . . NiB $878 Ex $717 Gd $535

Colt Cobra
Round Butt First Issue

Colt
Detective Special First Issue

DETECTIVE SPECIAL DA REVOLVER, 2ND ISSUE
Similar to Detective special first issue except w/2- or 3-inch bbl., and also chambered .32 New Police, .38 New Police. Wood, plastic or over-sized grips. Made 1947-72.
Blued finish . . . . NiB $487 Ex $395 Gd $279
Nickel finish . . . . NiB $545 Ex $442 Gd $299
W/three-inch bbl., add $95

DETECTIVE SPECIAL DA REVOLVER, 3RD ISSUE
"D" frame, shrouded ejector rod. Caliber: .38 Special. Six-round cylinder, 2-inch bbl., 6.88 inches overall. Weight: 21.5 oz. Fixed rear sight, ramp front. Blued or nickel-plated finish. Checkered walnut wraparound grips. Made 1973-84.
Blued finish . . . . NiB $488 Ex $384 Gd $280
Nickel finish . . . . NiB $498 Ex $405 Gd $285
W/three-inch bbl., add $75

DETECTIVE SPECIAL DA REVOLVER, 4TH ISSUE
Similar to Detective Special, Third Issue except w/alloy frame. Blued or chrome finish. Wraparound black neoprene grips w/Colt medallion. Made 1993-95.
Blued finish . . . . NiB $462 Ex $431 Gd $280
Chrome finish . . . . NiB $467 Ex $384 Gd $257
DAO model (bobbed hammer) . . . . NiB $498 Ex $405 Gd $285

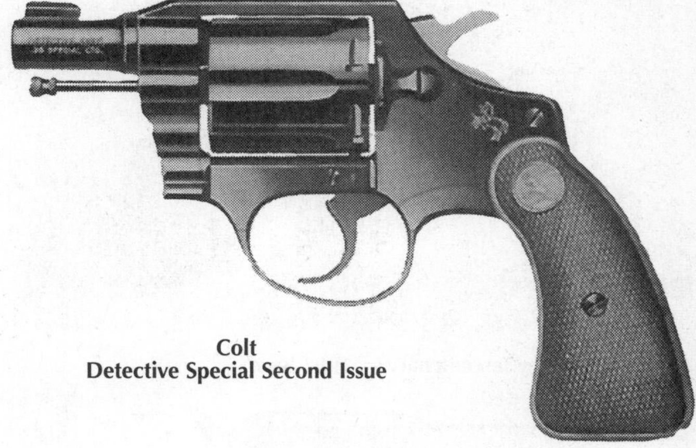

Colt
Detective Special Second Issue

DIAMONDBACK DA REVOLVER
"D" frame, shrouded ejector rod. Calibers: .22 LR, .22 WRF, .38 Special. Six-round cylinder, 2.5-, 4- or 6-inch bbl., w/vent rib, 9 inches overall (with 4-inch bbl). Weight: 31.75 oz. (.22 cal., 4-inch bbl.), 28.5 oz. (.38 cal.). Ramp front sight, adj. rear. Blued or nickel finish. Checkered walnut grips. Made 1966-84.
Blued finish . . . . NiB $701 Ex $597 Gd $285
Nickel finish . . . . NiB $632 Ex $488 Gd $332
.22 Mag. model . . . . NiB $665 Ex $514 Gd $346
W/2.5-inch bbl., add $75

DA ARMY (1878) REVOLVER. . . . NiB $5550 Ex $5030 Gd $2690
Also called DA Frontier. Similar in appearance to the smaller Lightning Model but has heavier frame of different shape, round disc on left side of frame, lanyard loop in butt. Calibers: .38-40, .44-40, .45 Colt. Six-round cylinder, bbl. lengths: 3.5- and 4-inches (w/o ejector), 4.75-, 5.5- and 7.5-inches w/ejector. 12.5 inches overall (7.5-inch bbl.). Weight: 39 oz. (.45 cal., 7.5-inch bbl.). Fixed sights. Hard rubber bird's-head grips. Blued or nickel finish. Made 1878-1905.

Colt
Diamondback

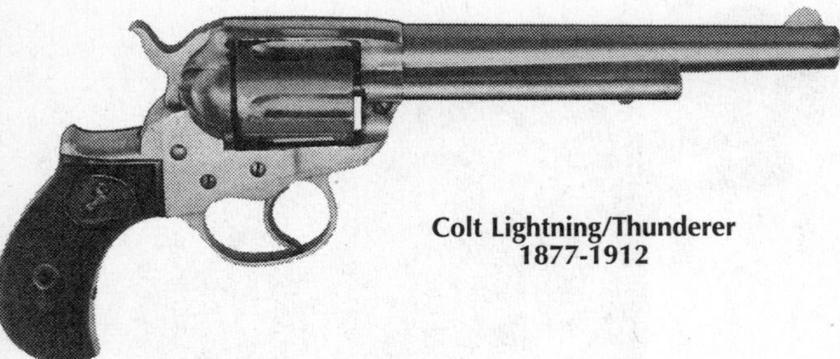

Colt Lightning/Thunderer
1877-1912

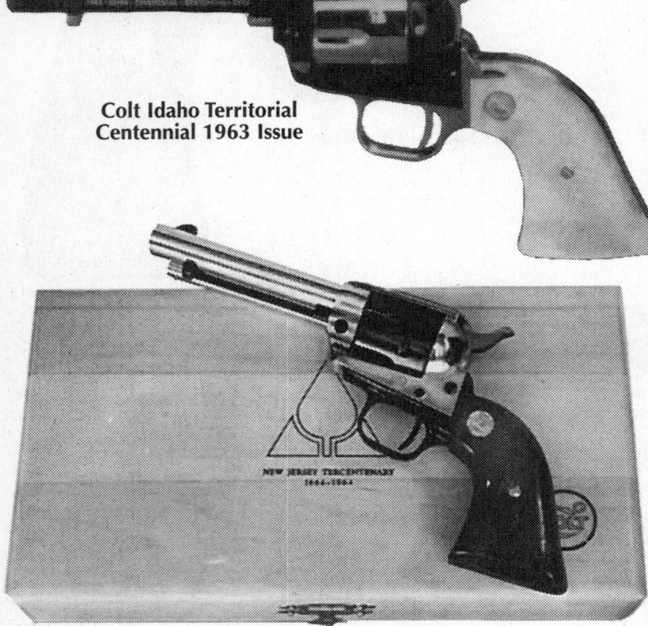

Colt Idaho Territorial Centennial 1963 Issue

Colt New Jersey Tercentenary — 1964 issue

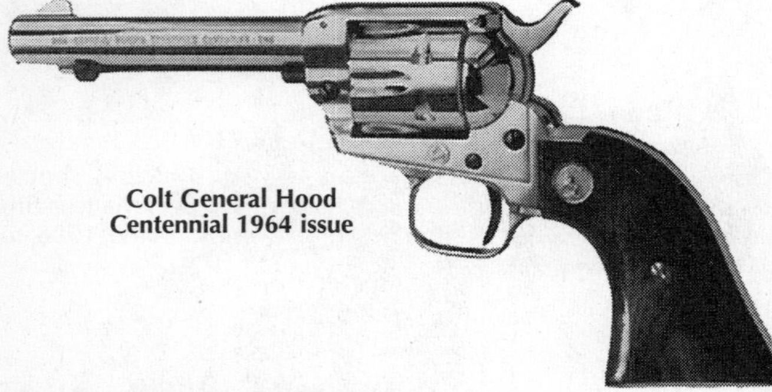

Colt General Hood Centennial 1964 issue

FRONTIER SCOUT REVOLVER

SA Army replica, scale. Calibers: .22 Short, Long, LR or .22 WMR (interchangeable cylinder available). Six-round cylinder, 4.75-inch bbl., 9.9 inches overall. Weight: 24 oz. Fixed sights. Plastic grips. Originally made w/bright alloy frame. Since 1959 w/steel frame and blued finish or all-nickel finish w/composition, wood or Staglite grips. Made 1958-71.

Blued finish, plastic grips. . . . . NiB $399 Ex $322 Gd $218
Nickel finish, wood grips. . . . . NiB $447 Ex $369 Gd $249
Buntline model, add $60
Extra interchangeable cylinder, add $75

FRONTIER SCOUT REVOLVER COMMEMORATIVE MODELS

Limited production versions of Frontier Scout issued, w/appropriate inscription, to commemorate historical events. Cased. Note: Values indicated are for commemoratives in new condition.

1961 ISSUES
Kansas Statehood Centennial (6201 produced). . . . . NiB $477
Pony Express Centennial (1007 produced). . . . . NiB $519

1962 ISSUES
Columbus, Ohio, Sesquicentennial (200 produced) . . . . NiB $659
Fort Findlay, Ohio, Sesquicentennial (130 produced) . . . . NiB $799
Fort Findlay Cased Pair, .22 Long Rifle and .22 Magnum (20 produced) . . . . NiB $3168
New Mexico Golden Anniversary . . . . NiB $563
West Virginia Statehood Centennial (3452 produced) . . . . NiB $477

1963 ISSUES
Arizona Territorial Centennial (5355 produced). . . . . NiB $467
Battle of Gettysburg Centennial (1019 produced). . . . . NiB $477
Carolina Charter Tercentenary (300 produced). . . . . NiB $467
Fort Stephenson, Ohio, Sesquicentennial (200 produced). . . . . NiB $659
General John Hunt Morgan Indiana Raid . . . . NiB $742
Idaho Territorial Centennial (902 produced) . . . . NiB $467

1964 ISSUES
California Gold Rush (500 produced) . . . . NiB $488
Chamizal Treaty (450 produced) . . . . NiB $493
General Hood Centennial (1503 produced) . . . . NiB $477
Montana Territorial Centennial (2300 produced) . . . . NiB $467
Nevada "Battle Born" (981 produced) . . . . NiB $477
Nevada Statehood Centennial (3984 produced) . . . . NiB $462
New Jersey Tercentenary (1001 produced) . . . . NiB $457
St. Louis Bicentennial (802 produced) . . . . NiB $477
Wyoming Diamond Jubilee (2357 produced) . . . . NiB $467

1965 ISSUES
Appomattox Centennial (1001 produced) . . . . NiB $467
Forty-Niner Miner (500 produced) . . . . NiB $477
General Meade Campaign (1197 produced) . . . . NiB $477
Kansas Cowtown Series—Wichita 500 produced) . . . . NiB $467
Old Fort Des Moines Reconstruction (700 produced) . . . . NiB $488
Oregon Trail (1995 produced). . . . . NiB $477
St. Augustine Quadricentennial (500 produced) . . . . NiB $488

1966 ISSUES
Colorado Gold Rush (1350 produced) . . . . NiB $488
Dakota Territory (1000 produced) . . . . NiB $467
Indiana Sesquicentennial (1500 produced) . . . . NiB $462
Kansas Cowtown Series—Abilene (500 produced) . . . . NiB $467
Kansas Cowtown Series—Dodge City (500 produced) . . . . NiB $477
Oklahoma Territory (1343 produced) . . . . NiB $467

1967 ISSUES
Alamo (4500 produced) . . . . NiB $477
Kansas Cowtown Series—Coffeyville (500 produced). . . . NiB $467
Kansas Trail Series—Chisholm Trail (500 produced). . . . NiB $477
Lawman Series—Bat Masterson (3000 produced) . . . . NiB $488

1968 ISSUES
Kansas Trail Series—Santa Fe Trail (501 produced). . . . NiB $467
Kansas Trail Series—Pawnee Trail (501 produced). . . . NiB $457
Lawman Series—Pat Garrett (3000 produced). . . . NiB $498
Nebraska Centennial (7001 produced). . . . NiB $462

1969 ISSUES
Alabama Sesquicentennial (3001 produced) . . . . NiB $462
Arkansas Territory Sesquicentennial (3500 produced) . . . . NiB $457
California Bicentennial (5000 produced). . . . NiB $441
General Nathan Bedford Forrest (3000 produced) . . . . NiB $467
Golden Spike (11,000 produced). . . . NiB $488
Kansas Trail Series—Shawnee Trail (501 produced) . . . . NiB $462
Lawman Series—Wild Bill Hickock (3000 produced) . . . . NiB $498

1970 ISSUES
Kansas Fort Series—Fort Larned (500 produced) . . . . NiB $467
Kansas Fort Series—Fort Hays (500 produced) . . . . NiB $467
Kansas Fort Series—Fort Riley (500 produced). . . . NiB $467
Lawman Series—Wyatt Earp (3000 produced) . . . . NiB $571
Maine Sesquicentennial (3000 produced). . . . NiB $457
Missouri Sesquicentennial (3000 produced) . . . . NiB $462

1971 ISSUES
Kansas Fort Series—Fort Scott (500 produced) . . . . NiB $467

1972 ISSUES
Florida Territory Sesquicentennial (2001 produced) . . . NiB $462

1973 ISSUES Azizona ranger
(3001 produced) . . . . NiB $653 Ex $566 Gd $348

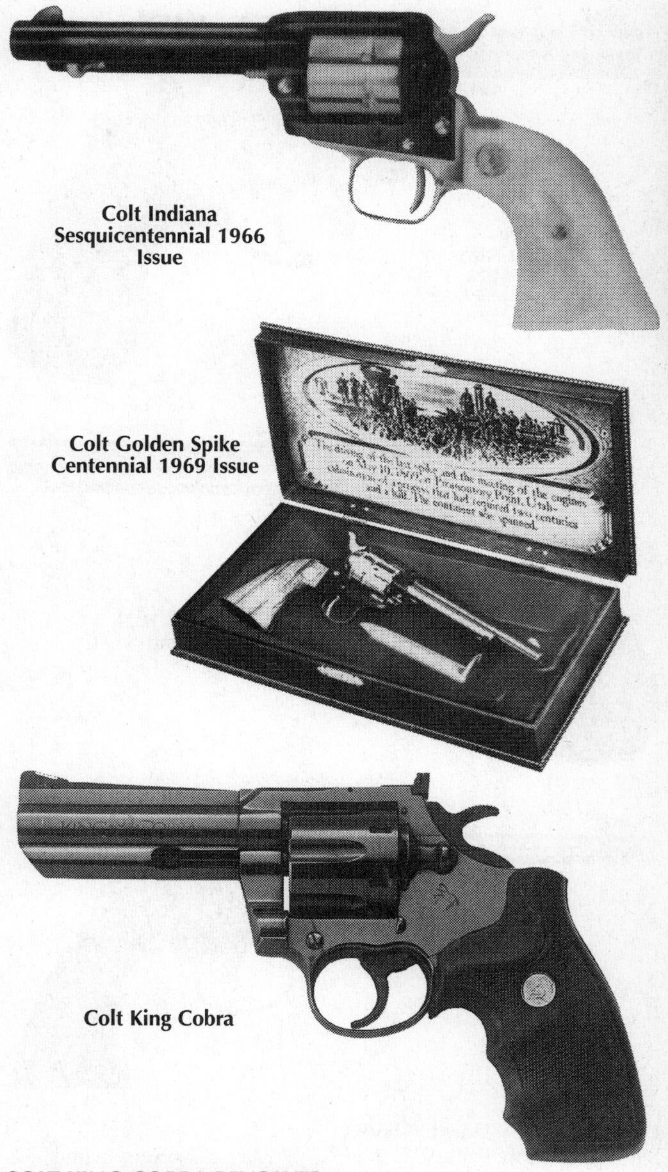
Colt Indiana Sesquicentennial 1966 Issue

Colt Golden Spike Centennial 1969 Issue

Colt King Cobra

COLT KING COBRA REVOLVER

Caliber: .357 Mag., bbl. lengths: 2.5-, 4-, 6- or 8-inches, 9 inches overall (with 4-inch bbl.). Weight: 42 oz., average. Matte stainless steel finish. Black Neoprene combat grips. Made 1986 to date. 2.5-inch bbl. and "Ultimate" bright or blued finish. Made 1988-92.

Matte stainless. . . . NiB $466 Ex $372 Gd $259
Ultimate bright stainless . . . . NiB $508 Ex $399 Gd $282
Blued. . . . NiB $446 Ex $394 Gd $238

LAWMAN MK III DA REVOLVER

"J" frame, shrouded ejector rod on 2-inch bbl., only. Caliber: .357 Magnum. Six-round cylinder, bbl. lengths: 2-, 4-inch. 9.38 inches overall (w/4-inch bbl.), Weight: (with 4-inch bbl.), 35 oz. Fixed rear sight, ramp front. Service trigger and hammer or target trigger and wide-spur hammer. Blued or nickel-plated finish. Checkered walnut service or target grips. Made 1969-1982.

Blued finish . . . . NiB $425 Ex $321 Gd $191
Nickel finish . . . . NiB $446 Ex $347 Gd $207

Colt Lawman MK V

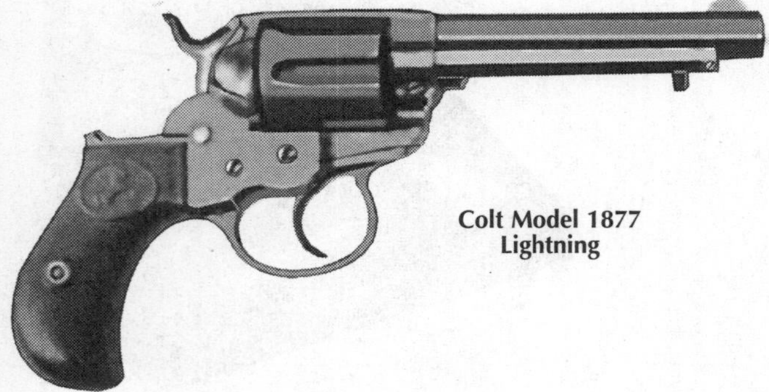
Colt Model 1877 Lightning

Colt New Navy

LAWMAN MK V DA REVOLVER
Similar to Trooper MK V. Caliber: .357 Mag. Six-round cylinder, 2- or 4-inch bbl., 9.38 inches overall (4-inch bbl.). Weight: 35 oz. (4-inch bbl.). Fixed sights. Checkered walnut grips. Made 1983-85.
Blued finish . . . . NiB $294 Ex $246 Gd $164
Nickel finish . . . . NiB $325 Ex $259 Gd $176

MAGNUM CARRY DA REVOLVER . . . . NiB $426 Ex $343 Gd $244
Similar to Model DS II except chambered for .357 Magnum. Made 1998 to date.

MARINE CORPS MODEL (1905) DA REVOLVER
General specifications same as New Navy Second Issue except has round butt, was supplied only in .38 caliber (.38 Short & Long Colt, .38 Special) w/6-inch bbl. (SN range 10,001-10,926) Made 1905-09.
Marine Corps model . . . . NiB $2957 Ex $2385 Gd $1631
Marked "USMC" . . . . NiB $3893 Ex $3269 Gd $2255

METROPOLITAN MK III DA REVOLVER . . . . NiB $452 Ex $353 Gd $248
Same as Official Police MK III except has 4-inch bbl. w/service or target grips. Weight: 36 oz. Made 1969-72.

MODEL 1877 LIGHTNING REVOLVER . . . . . . NiB $1847 Ex $1484 Gd $1020
Also called Thunderer Model. Calibers: .38 and .41 centerfire. Six-round cylinder, bbl. lengths: 2.5-, 3.5-, 4.5- and 6-inch without ejector, 4.5- and 6-inch w/ejector, 8.5 inches overall (3.5-inch bbl.). Weight: 23 oz. (.38 cal., with 3.5-inch bbl.) Fixed sights. Blued or nickel finish. Hard rubber bird's-head grips. Made 1877-09.

NEW FRONTIER BUNTLINE SPECIAL
Same as New Frontier SA Army except has 12-inch bbl.,
Second generation (1962-75) . . . NiB $1324 Ex $1065 Gd $734
Third generation (1976-92) . . . . . . NiB $1102 Ex $888 Gd $613

NEW FRONTIER SA ARMY REVOLVER
Same as SA Army except has flat-top frame, adj. target rear sight, ramp front sight, smooth walnut grips. 5.5- or 7.5-inch bbl., Calibers: .357 Magnum, .44 Special, .45 Colt. Made 1961-92.
Second generation (1961-75) . . . NiB $1309 Ex $1049 Gd $685
Third generation (1976-92) . . . . . . NiB $1101 Ex $893 Gd $633

NEW FRONTIER SA .22 REVOLVER . . . . . . NiB $384 Ex $280 Gd $166
Same as Peacemaker .22 except has flat-top frame, adj. rear sight, ramp front sight. Made 1971-76; reintro. 1982-86.

NEW NAVY (1889) DA, FIRST ISSUE
Also called New Army. Calibers: .38 Short & Long Colt, .41 Short & Long Colt. Six-round cylinder, left revolution. Bbl. lengths: 3-, 4.5- and 6-inches, 11.25 inches overall (with 6-inch bbl.). Weight: 32 oz. with 6-inch bbl. Fixed sights, knife-blade and V-notch. Blued or nickel-plated finish. Walnut or hard rubber grips. Made 1889-94. Note: This model, which was adopted by both the Army and Navy, was Colt's first revolver of the solid frame, swing-out cylinder type. It lacks the cylinder-locking notches found on later models made on this .41 frame; ratchet on the back of the cylinder is held in place by a double projection on the hand.
First issue. . . . . NiB $1884 Ex $1521 Gd $1057
First issue w/3-inch bbl. . . . . . . NiB $2606 Ex $2098 Gd $1449
Navy contract, marked "U.S.N.(SN 1-1500). . . . . NiB $3444 Ex $2769 Gd $1906

NEW NAVY (1892) DA, SECOND ISSUE
Also called New Army. General specifications same as First Issue except has double cylinder notches and double locking bolt. Calibers: .38 Special added in 1904 and .32-20 in 1905. Made 1892-07. Note: The heavy .38 Special High Velocity loads should not be used in .38 Special arms of this model.
Second issue . . . . NiB $1634 Ex $1323 Gd $926
Second issue w/3-inch bbl. . . . . NiB $2356 Ex $1900 Gd $1318
Navy contract, marked "U.S.N". . . . . . NiB $2674 Ex $2155 Gd $1491

NEW POCKET DA REVOLVER . . . . NiB $684 Ex $555 Gd $390
Caliber: .32 Short & Long Colt. Six-round cylinder. bbl. lengths: 2.5, 3.5- and 6-inches. 7.5 inches overall w/3.5-inch bbl., Weight: 16 oz., with 3.5-inch bbl. Fixed sights, knife-blade and V-notch. Blued or nickel finish. Rubber grips. Made 1893-05.

NEW POLICE DA REVOLVER . . . . . NiB $586 Ex $524 Gd $352
Built on New Pocket frame but w/larger grip. Calibers: .32 Colt New Police, .32 Short & Long Colt. Bbl. lengths: 2.5-, 4- and 6-inches, 8.5 inches overall (with 4-inch bbl.). Weight: 17 oz., with 4-inch bbl. Fixed knife-blade front sight, V-notch rear. Blued or nickel finish. Rubber grips. Made 1896-05.

NEW POLICE TARGET DA REVOLVER. . . . . NiB $1469 Ex $1313 Gd $793
Target version of the New Police w/same general specifications. Target sights. Six-inch bbl., blued finish only. Made 1896-05.

NEW SERVICE DA REVOLVER

Calibers: .38 Special, .357 Magnum (intro. 1936), .38-40, .44-40, .44 Russian, .44 Special, .45 Auto, .45 Colt, .450 Eley, .455 Eley, .476 Eley. Six-round cylinder, bbl. lengths: 4-, 5- and 6-inch in .38 Special and .357 Magnum, 4.5-, 5.5- and 7.5 inches in other calibers; 9.75 inches overall (with 4.5-inch bbl.). Weight: 39 oz. (.45 cal. with 4.5-inch bbl.). Fixed sights. Blued or nickel finish. Checkered walnut grips. Made 1898-42. Note: More than 500,000 of this model in caliber .45 Auto (designated "Model 1917 Revolver") were purchased by the U.S. Gov't. during WW I. These arms were later sold as surplus to National Rifle Association members through the Director of Civilian Marksmanship. Price was $16.15 plus packing charge. Supply exhausted during the early 1930s.

Commercial model . . . . NiB $1744 Ex $1407 Gd $976
Magnum . . . . NiB $1132 Ex $918 Gd $643
1917 Army. . . . . NiB $1094 Ex $887 Gd $623

NEW SERVICE TARGET . . . . NiB $1235 Ex $1095 Gd $684

Target version of the New Service. Calibers: Originally chambered for .44 Russian, .450 Eley, .455 Eley and .476 Eley, later models in .44 Special, .45 Colt and .45 Auto. Six- or 7.5-inch bbl., 12.75 inches overall (7.5-inch bbl.). Adj. target sights. Hand-finished action. With blued finish. Checkered walnut grips. Made 1900-40.

OFFICERS' MODEL MATCH . . . . . . NiB $776 Ex $646 Gd $360

Same general design as Officers' Model revolvers. Has tapered heavy bbl., wide hammer spur, Adjustable rear sight ramp front sight, large target grips of checkered walnut. Calibers: .22 LR, .38 Special. Six-inch bbl., 11.25 inches overall. Weight: 43 oz. (in .22 cal.), 39 oz. (.38 cal.). Blued finish. Made 1953-70.

OFFICERS' MODEL SPECIAL. . . . . . NiB $820 Ex $560 Gd $352

Target version of Officers' Model Second Issue w/similar characters except w/heavier, nontapered bbl. redesigned hammer. Ramp front sight, Colt Officers' Model Special "Coltmaster" rear sight adj. for windage and elevation. Calibers: .22 LR, .38 Special. Six-inch bbl. 11.25 inches overall. Weight: 39 oz. (in .38 cal.), 43 oz., (.22 cal.). Blued finish. Checkered plastic grips. Made 1949-53.

OFFICERS' MODEL TARGET DA REVOLVER, FIRST ISSUE . . . . . . NiB $1249 Ex $1009 Gd $703

Caliber: .38 Special. Six-inch bbl., hand-finished action, adj. target sights. Checkered with walnut grips. General specifications same as New Navy, Second Issue. Made 1904-08.

OFFICERS' MODEL TARGET, SECOND ISSUE

Calibers: .22 LR (intro. 1930, embedded head-cylinder for high-speed cartridges after 1932), .32 Police Positive (made 1932-1942), .38 Special. Six-round cylinder, bbl. lengths: 4-, 4.5-, 5-, 6- and 7.5-inch (in .38 Special) or 6-inch only (.22 LR and .32 PP), 11.25 inches overall (6-inch bbl. in .38 Special). Adj. target sights. Blued finish. Checkered walnut grips. Hand-finished action. General features same as Army Special and Official Police of same date. Made 1908-49 (w/exceptions noted).

Second issue (.38 caliber) . . . . NiB $1029 Ex $831 Gd $576
Second issue (.32 caliber) . . . . . . NiB $1627 Ex $1309 Gd $901
Second issue (.22 caliber) . . . . NiB $1141 Ex $919 Gd $636
W/shorter bbls. (4-, 4.5- or 5-inches), add 40%

OFFICIAL POLICE DA REVOLVER

Calibers: .22 LR (intro. 1930, embedded head-cylinder for high-speed cartridges after 1932), .32-20 (disc. 1942), .38 Special, .41 Long Colt (disc. 1930). Six-round cylinder, bbl. lengths: 4-, 5-, and 6-inch or 2-inch and 6-inch heavy bbl. in .38 Special only; .22 LR w/4- and 6-inch bbls. only; 11.25 inches overall. Weight: 36

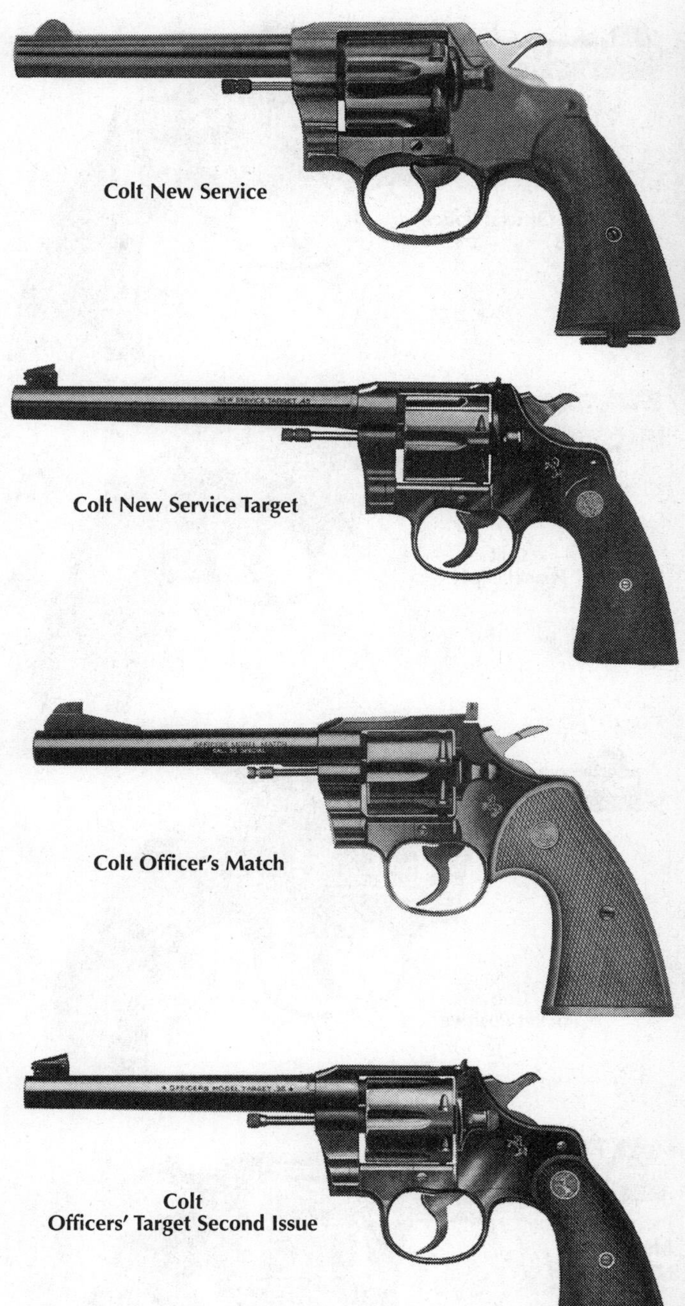

Colt New Service

Colt New Service Target

Colt Officer's Match

Colt
Officers' Target Second Issue

***(cont'd)* OFFICIAL POLICE DA REVOLVER**

oz. (standard 6-inch bbl.) in .38 Special. Fixed sights. Blued or nickel-plated finish. Checkered walnut grips on all revolvers of this model except some of postwar production had checkered plastic grips. Made 1927-69. Note: This model is a refined version of the Army Special, which it replaced in 1928 at about serial number 520,000. The Commando .38 Special was a wartime adaptation of the Official Police made to government specifications. Commando can be identified by its sandblasted blued finish. Serial numbers start w/number 1-50,000 (1942-45). See illustration next page.

Commercial model (pre-war) . . . . . NiB $560 Ex $456 Gd $323
Commercial model (post-war). . . . . NiB $496 Ex $404 Gd $288
Commando model. . . . . NiB $592 Ex $482 Gd $341

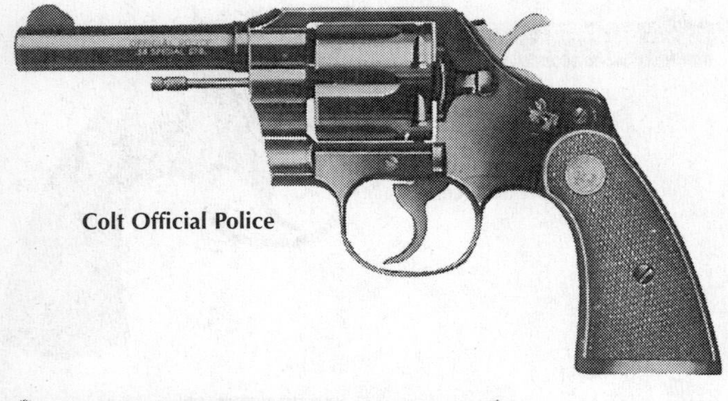
Colt Official Police

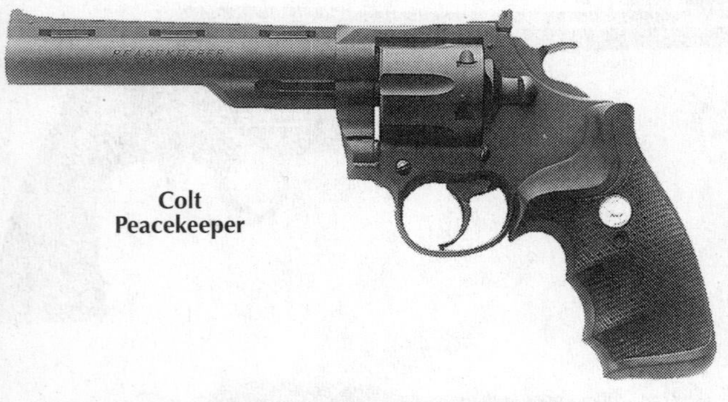
Colt Peacekeeper

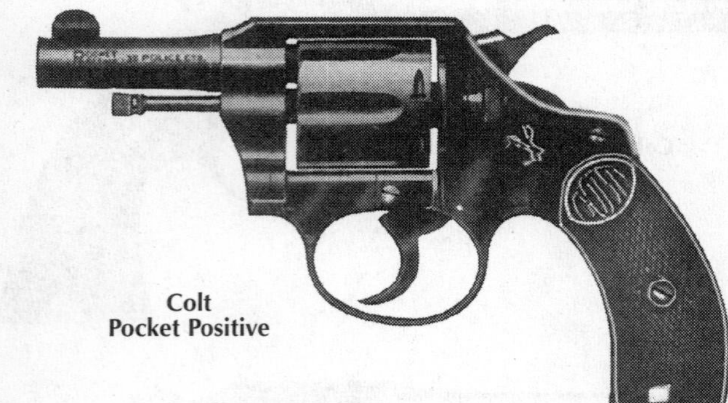
Colt Pocket Positive

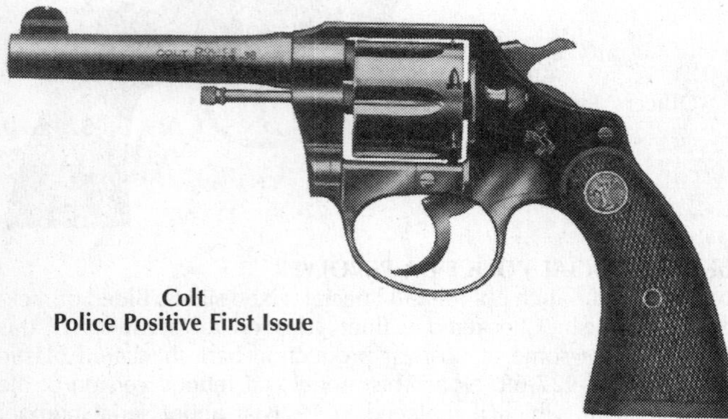
Colt Police Positive First Issue

OFFICIAL POLICE MK III DA REVOLVER . . . . NiB $270 Ex $218 Gd $150
"J" frame, without shrouded ejector rod. Caliber: .38 Special. Six-round cylinder. bbl., lengths: 4-, 5-, 6-inches, 9.25 inches overall w/4-inch bbl., weight: 34 oz. (4-inch bbl.). Fixed rear sight, ramp front. Service trigger and hammer or target trigger and wide-spur hammer. Blued or nickel-plated finish. Checkered walnut service grips. Made 1969-75.

PEACEKEEPER DA REVOLVER . . . . . NiB $436 Ex $363 Gd $171
Caliber: .357 Mag. Six-round cylinder, 4- or 6-inch bbl., 11.25 inches overall (6-inch bbl.). Weight: 46 oz. (with 6-inch bbl.). Adj. white outline rear sight, red insert ramp-style front. Non-reflective matte blued finish. Made 1985-89.

PEACEMAKER .22 SECOND AMENDMENT COMMEMORATIVE. . . . . NiB $597 Ex $493 Gd $233
Caliber: .22, revolver w/7.5-inch bbl., nickel-plated frame, bbl. ejector rod assembly, hammer and trigger, blued cylinder, backstrap and trigger guard. Black pearlite grips. bbl., inscribed "The Right to Keep and Bear Arms." Presentation case. Limited edition of 3000 issued in 1977. Top value is for revolver in new condition.

PEACEMAKER .22 SA REVOLVER . . NiB $389 Ex $285 Gd $233
Calibers: .22 LR and .22 WMR. Furnished w/cylinder for each caliber, 6-round. Bbl.: 4.38-, 6- or 7.5-inches, 11.25 inches overall (with 6-inch bbl.). Weight: 30.5 oz. (with 6-inch bbl.). Fixed sights. Black composite grips. Made 1971-76.

POCKET POSITIVE DA REVOLVER. . . . . NiB $571 Ex $509 Gd $337
General specifications same as New Pocket except this model has positive lock feature (see Police Positive). Calibers: .32 Short & Long Colt (disc. 1914), .32 Colt New Police (.32 S&W Short & Long). Fixed sights, flat top and square notch. Blue or nickel finish. Made 1905-40.
Blue finish . . . . NiB $539 Ex $436 Gd $305
Nickel finish . . . . NiB $643 Ex $519 Gd $371

POLICE POSITIVE DA, FIRST ISSUE
Improved version of the New Police w/the "Positive Lock," which prevents the firing pin coming in contact w/the cartridge except when the trigger is pulled. Calibers: .32 Short & Long Colt (disc. 1915), .32 Colt New Police (.32 S&W Short & Long), .38 New Police (.38 S&W). Six-round cylinder, bbl. lengths: 2.5- (.32 cal. only), 4- 5- and 6-inches; 8.5 inches overall (with 4-inch bbl.). Weight 20 oz. (with 4-inch bbl.). Fixed sights. Blued or nickel finish. Rubber or checkered walnut grips. Made 1905-47.
Blue finish . . . . NiB $476 Ex $384 Gd $268
Nickel finish . . . . NiB $540 Ex $436 Gd $303

POLICE POSITIVE DA, SECOND ISSUE
Same as Detective Special second issue except has 4-inch bbl., 9 inches overall, weight: 26.5 oz. Intro. in 1977. Note: Original Police Positive (First Issue) has a shorter frame, is not chambered for .38 Special.
Blue finish . . . . NiB $462 Ex $374 Gd $260
Nickel finish . . . . NiB $534 Ex $431 Gd $300

POLICE POSITIVE SPECIAL DA REVOLVER . . . . NiB $534 Ex $431 Gd $300
Based on the Police Positive w/frame lengthened to permit longer cylinder. Calibers: .32-20 (disc. 1942), .38 Special, .32 New Police and .38 New Police (intro. 1946). Six-round cylinder; bbl. lengths: 4-(only length in current production), 5- and 6-inch; 8.75 inches overall (with 4-inch bbl.). Weight: 23 oz. (with 4-inch bbl. in .38 Special). Fixed sights. Checkered grips of hard rubber, plastic or walnut. Made 1907-73.

COLT POLICE POSITIVE TARGET DA REVOLVER. . . . . NiB $809 Ex $654 Gd $456
Target version of the Police Positive. Calibers: .22 LR (intro. 1910, embedded-head cylinder for high-speed cartridges after 1932), .22 WRF (1910-35), .32 Short & Long Colt, (1915), .32 New Police (.32 S&W Short & Long). Six-inch bbl., blued finish only, 10.5 inches overall. Weight: 26 oz. in .22 cal. Adj. target sights. Checkered walnut grips. Made 1905-40.

PYTHON DA REVOLVER

"I" frame, shrouded ejector rod. Calibers: .357 Magnum, .38 Special. Six-round cylinder, 2.5-, 4-, 6- or 8-inch vent rib bbl., 11.25 inches overall (with 6-inch bbl.). Weight: 44 oz. (6-inch bbl.). Adj. rear sight, ramp front. Blued, nickel or stainless finish. Checkered walnut target grips. Made 1955 to date. Ultimate stainless finish made 1985 to date.

Blued finish . . . . NiB $966 Ex $841 Gd $347
Royal blued finish . . . . NiB $670 Ex $555 Gd $407
Nickel finish. . . . . NiB $658 Ex $545 Gd $400
Stainless finish . . . . NiB $736 Ex $642 Gd $443
Ultimate stainless finish . . . . NiB $997 Ex $841 Gd $399
Hunter model (w/2x scope) . . . . NiB $1531 Ex $1354 Gd $808
Silhouette model (w/2x scope) . . . . NiB $1589 Ex $1405 Gd $756

SHOOTING MASTER DA REVOLVER

Deluxe target arm based on the New Service model. Calibers: Originally made only in .38 Special, .44 Special, .45 Auto and .45 Colt added in 1933, .357 Magnum in 1936. Six-inch bbl., 11.25 inches overall. Weight: 44 oz., in (.38 cal.), adj. target sights. Hand-finished action. Blued finish. Checkered walnut grips. Rounded butt. Made 1932-41.

Shooting Master .38 Special. . . . . NiB $1380 Ex $1224 Gd $808
Shooting Master .357 Mag. . . . . NiB $1427 Ex $1151 Gd $797
Shooting Master .44 Special, .45 ACP, .45LC. . . . . NiB $3839 Ex $3527 Gd $2071

SA ARMY REVOLVER

Also called Frontier Six-Shooter and Peacemaker. Available in more than 30 calibers including: .22 Rimfire (Short, Long, LR), .22 WRF, .32 Rimfire, .32 Colt, .32 S&W, .32-20, .38 Colt, .38 S&W, .38 Special, .357 Magnum, .38-40, .41 Colt, .44 Rimfire, .44 Russian, .44 Special, .44-40, .45 Colt, .45 Auto, .450 Boxer, 450 Eley, .455 Eley, .476 Eley. Six-round cylinder. Bbl. lengths: 4.75, 5 .5 and 7.5 inches w/ejector or 3 and 4 inches w/o ejector. 10.25 inches overall (with 4.75-inch bbl.). Weight: 36 oz. (.45 cal. w/4.75-inch bbl.). Fixed sights. Also made in Target Model w/flat top-strap and target sights. Blued finish w/casehardened frame or nickel-plated. One-piece smooth walnut or checkered black rubber grips. Note: S.A. Army Revolvers w/serial numbers above 165,000 (circa 1896) are adapted to smokeless powder and cylinder pin screw was changed to spring catch at about the same time. The "First Generation" of SA Colts included both blackpowder and smokeless configurations and were manufactured from 1873 to 1940. Production resumed in 1955 w/serial number 1001SA and continued through 1975 to complete the second series, which is referred to as the "Second Generation." In 1976, the "Third Generation" of production began and continues to to date. However, several serial number rollovers occurred at 99,999. For example, in 1978 the "SA" suffix became an "SA" prefix and again in 1993, when the serial number SA99,999 was reached, the serialization format was changed again to include both an "S" prefix and an "A" suffix. Although the term "Fourth Generation" is frequently associated with this rollover, no series change actually occurred, therefore, the current production is still a "Third Generation" series. Current calibers: .357 Magnum, .44 Special, .45 Long Colt.

Pinched frame (1873 only). . . . . NiB $82,616 Ex $66,092 Gd $44,943

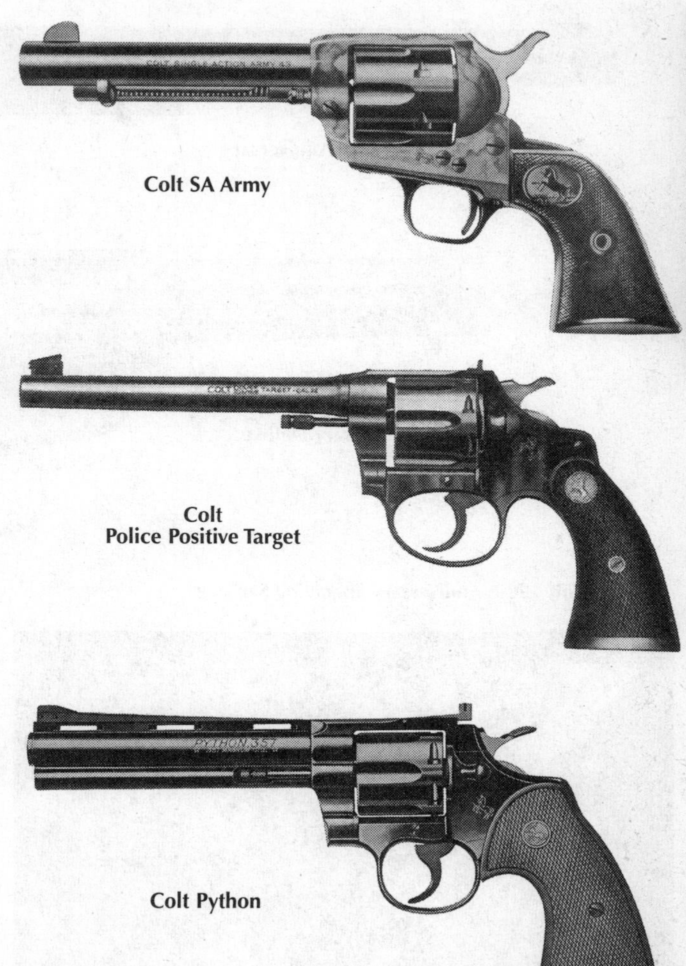

Colt SA Army

Colt Police Positive Target

Colt Python

(cont'd.) **SA ARMY REVOLVER**

Early commercial (1873-77) . . . . NiB $42,576 Ex $34,060 Gd $23,161
Early military (1873-77) . . . . NiB $48,750 Ex $39,000 Gd $26,520
Large bore rimfire (1875-80) . . . . NiB $39,650 Ex $31,720 Gd $21,570
Small bore rimfire (1875-80) . . . . NiB $30,550 Ex $24,440 Gd $16,619
Frontier six-shooter, .44-40 (1878-82) . . . . NiB $46,216 Ex $36,972 Gd $25,141
Storekeeper's model, no ejector (1883-98) . . . . NiB $48,750 Ex $39,000 Gd $26,520
Sheriff's model (1883-98) . . . . NiB $46,150 Ex $36,920 Gd $25,106
Target model, flat top strap, target sights . . . . NiB $25,350 Ex $20,280 Gd $13,790
U.S. Cavalry model, .45 (1873-92) . . . . NiB $44,850 Ex $35,880 Gd $24,398

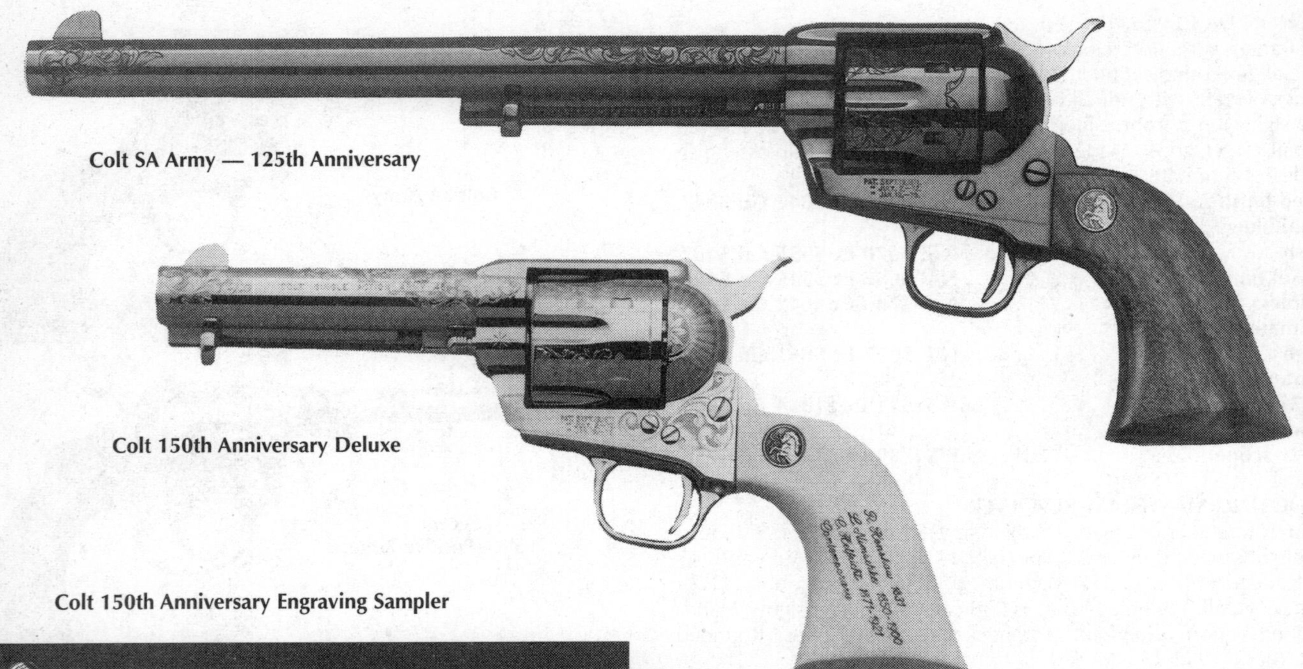

Colt SA Army — 125th Anniversary

Colt 150th Anniversary Deluxe

Colt 150th Anniversary Engraving Sampler

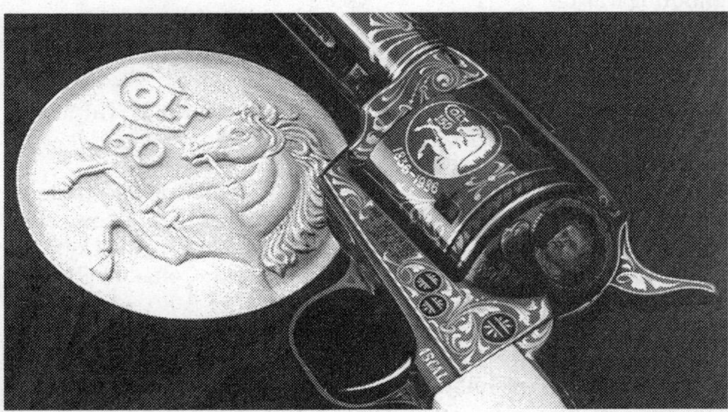

In the previous section the GTG deviates from the observed practice of listing only the value of firearms produced after 1900. This deliberate departure from the standard format is intended to provide a general reference and establish proper orientation for the reader, because the Colt SSA had its origins in the last quarter of the 19th century. Consequently, antique firearms produced prior to 1898 have been listed as a preface and introduction to the first series of production (what is now recognized as "1st Generation") in order to systematically demonstrate the progressive and sequential development of the multi-generation Colt SAA. Therefore, the previous general values have been provided to establish a point of reference to allow a more comprehensive examination of the evolution of the Colt SAA. However, please note that the following values apply only to original models, not to similar S.A.A. revolvers of more recent manufacture.

Standard model, pre-war
(1st generation) . . . . $12,950 to $65,000
Standard model
(1955-75)
(2nd generation) . . . . NiB $2344 Ex $1895 Gd $1321
Standard model
(1976 to date) . . . . NiB $1128 Ex $915 Gd $643

SA ARMY — 125TH ANNIVERSARY.... NiB $1844 Ex $1495 Gd $1049
Limited production deluxe version of SA Army issued in commemoration of Colt's 125th Anniversary. Caliber: .45 Long Colt., 7.5-inch bbl., cold-plated frame trigger, hammer, cylinder pin, ejector rod tip, and grip medallion. Presentation case w/anniversary medallion. Serial numbers "50AM." 7368 were made in 1961. See illustration previous page.

SA ARMY COMMEMORATIVE MODELS
Limited production versions of SA Army .45 issued, w/appropriate inscription to commemorate historical events. Cased. Note: Values indicated are for commemorative revolvers in new condition.

1963 ISSUES
Arizona Territorial Centennial (1280 produced).... NiB $1548
West Virginia Statehood Centennial (600 produced).... NiB $1470

1964 ISSUES
Chamizal Treaty (50 produced).... NiB $1573
Colonel Sam Colt Sesquicentennial Presentation (4750 produced).... NiB $1548
Deluxe Presentation (200 produced).... NiB $2809
Special Deluxe Presentation (50 produced).... NiB $4417
Montana Territorial Centennial (851 produced).... NiB $1548
Nevada "Battle Born" (100 produced).... NiB $1620
Nevada Statehood Centennial (1877 produced).... NiB $1517
New Jersey Tercentenary (250 produced).... NiB $1505
Pony Express Presentation (1004 produced).... NiB $1620
St. Louis Bicentennial (450 produced).... NiB $1548
Wyatt Earp Buntline (150 produced).... NiB $2783

1965 ISSUES
Appomattox Centennial (500 produced).... NiB $1578
Old Fort Des Moines Reconstruction (200 produced).... NiB $1500

1966 ISSUES
Abercrombie & Fitch Trailblazer —Chicago (100 produced).... NiB $1387
Abercrombie & Fitch Trailblazer —New York (200 produced).... NiB $1362
Abercrombie & Fitch Trailblazer —San Francisco (100 produced).... NiB $1387
California Gold Rush (130 produced).... NiB $1578
General Meade (200 produced).... NiB $1578
Pony Express Four Square (4 guns).... NiB $6587

1967 ISSUES
Alamo (1000 produced).... NiB $1568
Lawman Series—Bat Masterson (500 produced).... NiB $1743

1968 ISSUES
Lawman Series—Pat Garrett (500 produced).... NiB $1568

Colt SA Army Flat Top

1969 ISSUES
Lawman Series—Wild Bill Hickok (500 produced).... NiB $1568

1970 ISSUES
Lawman Series—Wyatt Earp (501 produced).... NiB $2773
Missouri Sesquicentennial (501 produced).... NiB $1568
Texas Ranger (1000 produced).... NiB $2467

1971 ISSUES
NRA Centennial, .357 or .45 (5001 produced).... NiB $1568

1975 ISSUES
Peacemaker Centennial .45 (1501 produced).... NiB $1593
Peacemaker Centennial .44-40 (1501 produced).... NiB $1696
Peacemaker Centennial Cased Pair (501 produced).... NiB $3235

1979 ISSUES
Ned Buntline .45 (3000 produced).... NiB $1156

1986 ISSUES
Colt 150th Anniversary (standard).... NiB $1846
Colt 150th Anniversay (engraved).... NiB $2876

COLT SA COWBOY REVOLVER.... NiB $488
SSA variant designed for "Cowboy Action Shooting." Caliber: .45 Colt. Six-round cylinder, 5.5-inch bbl., 11 inches overall. Weight: 42 oz. Blade front sight, fixed V-notch rear. Blued finish w/color casehardened frame. Smooth walnut grips. Made 1999 to date.

SA SHERIFF'S MODEL .45
Limited edition replica of Storekeeper's Model in caliber .45 Colt, made exclusively for Centennial Arms Corp. Chicago, Illinois. Numbered "1SM." Blued finish w/casehardened frame or nickel-plated. Walnut grips. Made in 1961.
Blued finish (478 produced).... NiB $2797 Ex $2258 Gd $1568
Nickel finish (25 produced).... NiB $6660 Ex $5348 Gd $3669

THREE-FIFTY-SEVEN DA REVOLVER
Heavy frame. Caliber: .357 Magnum. Six-shot cylinder, 4 or 6-inch bbl. Quickdraw ramp front sight, Accro rear sight. Blued finish. Checkered walnut grips. 9.25 or 11.25 inches overall. Weight: 36 oz. (4-inch bbl.), 39 oz. (6 inch bbl.). Made 1953-61.
W/standard hammer and service grips.... NiB $604 Ex $492 Gd $349
W/wide-spur hammer and target grips.... NiB $642 Ex $523 Gd $369

TROOPER DA REVOLVER
Same specifications as Officers' Model Match except has 4-inch bbl. w/quick-draw ramp front sight, weight: 34 oz. in .38 caliber. Made 1953-69.
W/standard hammer and service grips.... NiB $460 Ex $373 Gd $263
W/wide-spur hammer and target grips.... NiB $523 Ex $425 Gd $298

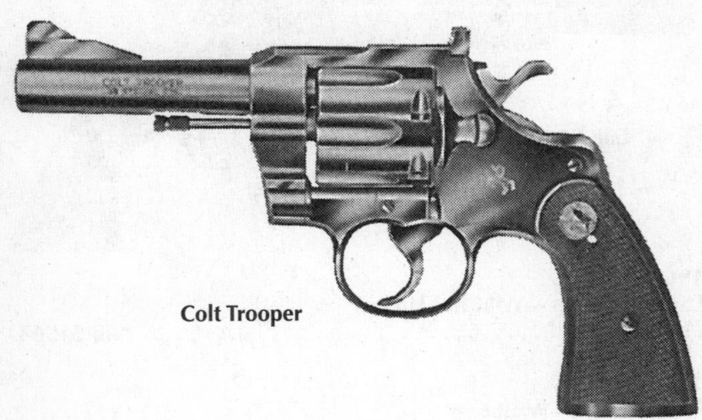
Colt Trooper

Colt Trooper MK V

Colt U.S. Bicentennial Commemorative Set

TROOPER MK III DA REVOLVER
"J"frame, shrouded ejector rod. Calibers: .22 LR, .22 Magnum, .38 Special, .357 Magnum. Six-round cylinder. bbl. lengths: 4-, 6-inches. 9.5 inches overall (with 4-inch bbl.). Weight: 39 oz. (4-inch bbl.). Adj. rear sight, ramp front. Target trigger and hammer. Blued or nickel-plated finish. Checkered walnut target grips. Made 1969-78.
Blued finish . . . . NiB $435 Ex $363 Gd $157
Nickel finish. . . . . NiB $481 Ex $388 Gd $157

TROOPER MK V REVOLVER
Re-engineered Mark III for smoother, faster action. Caliber: .357 Magnum. Six-round cylinder, bbl. lengths: 4-, 6-, 8-inch w/vent rib. Adj. rear sight, ramp front, red insert. Checkered walnut grips. Made 1982-86.
Blued finish . . . . NiB $466 Ex $388 Gd $285
Nickel finish. . . . . NiB $517 Ex $440 Gd $260

VIPER DA REVOLVER . . . . NiB $466 Ex $414 Gd $282
Same as Cobra, Second Issue except has 4-inch bbl., 9 inches overall, weight: 20 oz. Made 1977-84.

U.S. BICENTENNIAL COMMEMORATIVE SET. . . . . NiB $2597
Replica Colt 3rd Model Dragoon revolver w/accessories, Colt SA Army revolver, and Colt Python revolver. Matching roll-engraved unfluted cylinders, blued finish and rosewood grips w/Great Seal of the United States silver medallion. Dragoon revolver has silver grip frame. Serial numbers 0001 to 1776. All revolvers in set have same number. Deluxe drawer-style presentation case of walnut w/book compartment containing a reproduction of "Armsmear." Issued in 1976. Value is for revolvers in new condition.

COONAN ARMS, INC. — Maplewood, Minnesota *(formerly St. Paul, Minnesota)*

MODEL .357 MAGNUM AUTO PISTOL
Caliber: .357 Mag. Seven-round magazine, 5- or 6-inch bbl., 8.3 inches overall (with 5-inch bbl.). Weight: 42 oz. Front ramp interchangeable sight, fixed rear sight, adj. for windage. Black walnut grips. Made 1983-99.
Model A Std. grade w/o grip safety (disc. 1991). NiB $832 Ex $672 Gd $466
Model B Std. grade w/5-inch bbl., ... NiB $608 Ex $491 Gd $343
Model B Std. grade w/6-inch bbl., ... NiB $640 Ex $517 Gd $361
Model B w/5-inch compensated bbl., (Classic). . . . . NiB $1123 Ex $903 Gd $623
Model B w/6-inch compensated bbl. . . . . NiB $897 Ex $723 Gd $500

.357 MAGNUM CADET COMPACT
Similar to the standard .357 Magnum model except w/3.9-inch bbl., on compact frame. Six-round (Cadet), 7- or 8-round magazine (Cadet II). Weight: 39 oz., 7.8 inches overall. Made 1993-99.
Cadet model . . . . NiB $717 Ex $579 Gd $403
Cadet II model. . . . . NiB $837 Ex $677 Gd $388

CZ PISTOLS — Uhersky Brod (formerly Strakonice), Czechoslovakia Mfd. by Ceska Zbrojovka-Nardoni Podnik (formerly Bohmische Waffenfabrik A. G.)

Currently imported by CZ USA, Kansas City, KS. Previously by Magnum Research and Action Arms. Vintage importation is by Century International Arms.

MODEL 27 AUTO PISTOL. . . . . NiB $586 Ex $483 Gd $288
Caliber: .32 Automatic (7.65mm). Eight-round magazine, 4-inch bbl., 6 inches overall. Weight: 23.5 oz. Fixed sights. Blued finish. Plastic grips. Made 1927-51. Note: After the German occupation. (March 1939), Models 27 and .38 were marked w/manufacturer code "fnh." Designation of Model .38 was changed to "Pistole 39(t)."

MODEL .38 AUTO PISTOL (VZ SERIES)
Caliber: .380 Automatic (9mm). Nine-round magazine, 3.75-inch bbl., 7 inches overall. Weight: 26 oz. Fixed sights. Blued finish. Plastic grips. After 1939 designated as T39. Made 1938-.45.
CZ DAO model . . . . NiB $459 Ex $381 Gd $281
CZ SA/DA model. . . . . NiB $1334 Ex $1044 Gd $719

MODEL 50 DA AUTO PISTOL. . . . . . NiB $186 Ex $151 Gd $107
Similar to Walther Model PP except w/frame-mounted safety and trigger guard not hinged. Caliber: .32 ACP (7.65mm), 8-round magazine, 3.13-inch bbl., 6.5 inches overall. Weight: 24.5 oz. Fixed sights. Blued finished. Intro. in 1950. disc. Note: "VZ50" is the official designation of this pistol used by the Czech National Police ("New Model .006" was the export designation but very few were released).

MODEL 52 SA AUTO PISTOL
Roller-locking breech system. Calibers: 7.62mm or 9mm Para. Eight-round magazine, 4.7-inch bbl., 8.1 inches overall. Weight: 31 oz. Fixed sights. Blued finish. Grooved composition grips. Made 1952-56.
7.62mm model . . . . NiB $195 Ex $164 Gd $98
9mm model. NiB $195 Ex $164 Gd $98

MODEL 70 DA AUTO PISTOL. . . . . . NiB $438 Ex $355 Gd $248
Similar to Model 50 but redesigned to improve function and dependability. Made 1962-83.

MODEL 75 DA/DAO AUTOMATIC PISTOL
Calibers: 9mm Para. or .40 S&W w/selective action mode. 10-, 13- or 15-round magazine, 3.9-inch bbl., (Compact) or 4.75-inch bbl., (Standard), 8 inches overall (Standard). Weight: 35 oz. Fixed sights. Blued, nickel, Two-Tone or black polymer finish. Checkered wood or high-impact plastic grips. Made 1994 to date.
Black polymer finish . . . . NiB $400 Ex $324 Gd $227
High-polish blued finish. . . . . NiB $464 Ex $375 Gd $262
Matte blued finish . . . . NiB $426 Ex $344 Gd $240
Nickel finish. . . . . NiB $452 Ex $365 Gd $255
Two-tone finish . . . . NiB $438 Ex $355 Gd $248
W/.22 Kadet conversion, add $250
Compact model, add $35

82 DA AUTO PISTOL. . . . . NiB $329 Ex $303 Gd $180
Similar to the standard CZ 83 model except chambered in 9x18 Makarov. This model currently is the Czech military sidearm.

83 DA AUTOMATIC PISTOL
Calibers: .32 ACP, .380 ACP. 15-round (.32 ACP) or 13-round (.380 ACP) magazine, 3.75-inch bbl., 6.75 inches overall. Weight: 26.5 oz. Fixed sights. Blued (standard); chrome and nickel (optional special edition) w/brushed, matte or polished finish. Checkered black plastic grips. Made 1985 to date.
Standard finish. . . . . NiB $360 Ex $288 Gd $174
Special edition. . . . . NiB $500 Ex $403 Gd $277
Engraved . . . . NiB $1110 Ex $895 Gd $622

85 AUTOMATIC DA PISTOL
Same as CZ 75 except w/ambidextrous slide release and safety. Calibers: 9mm Para., 7.65mm. Made 1986 to date.
Black polymer finish . . . . NiB $459 Ex $370 Gd $259
High-polish blued finish. . . . . NiB $566 Ex $458 Gd $303
Matte blued finish . . . . NiB $509 Ex $355 Gd $252

CZ Model 75 Compact

CZ Model 75 Kadet

CZ Model 83

CZ Model 85 Combat

CZ Model 97B

CZ Model 100

Daewoo DH40

85 COMBAT DA AUTOMATIC PISTOL
Similar to the standard CZ 85 model except w/13-round magazine, combat-style hammer, fully adj. rear sight and walnut grips. Made 1986 to date.

Black polymer finish . . . . **NiB $489 Ex $427 Gd $252**
High-polished blued finish . . . . **NiB $529 Ex $427 Gd $297**
Matte blued finish . . . . **NiB $529 Ex $427 Gd $297**

MODEL 97B DA AUTOLOADING PISTOL. . . . . NiB $561 Ex $494 Gd $303
Similar to the CZ Model 75 except chambered for the .45 ACP cartridge. 10-round magazine, Frame-mounted thumb safety that allows single-action, cocked-and-locked carry. Made 1997 to date.

MODEL 100 DA AUTOMATIC PISTOL . . . . NiB $396 Ex $339 Gd $205
Caliber: 9mm, .40 S&W. 10-round magazine, 3.8-inch bbl., Weight: 25 oz. Polymer grips w/fixed low-profile sights. Made 1996 to date.

MODEL 1945 DA POCKET AUTO PISTOL. . . . . NiB $248 Ex $201 Gd $140
Caliber: .25 Auto (6.35mm). Eight-round magazine, 2.5-inch bbl., 5 inches overall. Weight: 15 oz. Fixed sights. Blued finish. Plastic grips. Intro. 1945. disc.

DUO POCKET AUTO PISTOL . . . . NiB $242 Ex $211 Gd $134
Caliber: .25 Automatic (6.35mm). Six-round magazine, 2.13 inch bbl., 4.5 inches overall. Weight: 14-.5 oz. Fixed sights. Blued or nickel finish. Plastic grips. Made c.1926-60.

DAEWOO PISTOLS — Seoul, Korea
Mfd. by Daewoo Precision Industries Ltd.

Imported by Daewoo Precision Industries, Southhampton, PA, Previously by Nationwide Sports Distributors and KBI, Inc.

DH40 AUTO PISTOL. . . . . NiB $413 Ex $355 Gd $224
Caliber: .40 S&W. 12-round magazine, 4.25-inch bbl., 7 inches overall. Weight: 28 oz. Blade front sight, dovetailed rear w/3-dot system. Blued finish. Checkered composition grips. DH/DP series feature a patented "fastfire" action w/5-6 lb. trigger pull. Made 1994-96.

DH45 AUTO PISTOL. . . . . NiB $652 Ex $530 Gd $364
Caliber: .45 ACP. 13-round magazine, 5-inch bbl., 8.1 inches overall. Weight: 35 oz. Blade front sight, dovetailed rear w/3-dot system. Blued finish. Checkered composition grips. Announced 1994, but not imported.

DP51 AUTO PISTOL . . . . NiB $387 Ex 311 Gd $214
Caliber: 9mm Para. 13-round magazine, 4.1-inch bbl., 7.5 inches overall. Weight: 28 oz. Blade front and square-notch rear sights. Matte black finish. Checkered composition grips. Made 1991-96.

DP52 AUTO PISTOL . . . . NiB $346 Ex $300 Gd $183
Caliber: .22 LR. 10-round magazine, 3.8-inch bbl., 6.7 inches overall. Weight: 23 oz. Blade front sight, dovetailed rear w/3-dot system. Blued finish. Checkered wood grips. Made 1994-96.

DAKOTA/E.M.F. CO. — Santa Ana, California

MODEL 1873 SA REVOLVER
Calibers: .22 LR, .22 Mag., .357 Mag., .45 Long Colt, .30 M1 carbine, .38-40, .32-20, .44-40. Bbl. lengths: 3.5, 4.75, 5.5, 7.5 inches. Blued or nickel finish. Engraved models avail.
Standard model . . . . NiB $351 Ex $275 Gd $224
W/extra cylinder . . . . NiB $699 Ex $586 Gd $441

MODEL 1875 OUTLAW SA REVOLVER . . . . NiB $447 Ex $362 Gd $253
Calibers: .45 Long Colt, .357 Mag., .44-40. 7.5-inch bbl. Casehardened frame, blued finish. Walnut grips. This is an exact replica of the Remington Number 3 revolver produced 1875-89.

MODEL 1890 REMINGTON POLICE
Calibers: .357 Mag., .44-40, .45 Long Colt, 5.75-inch bbl., blued or nickel finish. Similar to Outlaw w/lanyard ring and no bbl. web .
Standard model . . . . NiB $473 Ex $382 Gd $266
Nickel model . . . . NiB $562 Ex $453 Gd $315
Engraved model . . . . NiB $651 Ex $525 Gd $364

BISLEY SA REVOLVER
Calibers: .44-40, .45 Long Colt, .357 Mag, 5.5- or 7.5-inch bbl., disc. 1992. Reintroduced 1994.
Standard model . . . . NiB $377 Ex $311 Gd $219
Target model . . . . NiB $423 Ex $341 Gd $224

HARTFORD SA REVOLVER
Calibers: .22 LR, .32-20, .357 Mag., .38-40, .44-40, .44 Special, .45 Long Colt. These are exact replicas of the original Colts w/steel backstraps, trigger guards and forged frames. Blued or nickel finish. Imported 1990 to date.
Standard model . . . . NiB $377 Ex $300 Gd $204
Engraved model . . . . NiB $656 Ex $530 Gd $369
Hartford Artillery, U.S. Cavalry models . . . . NiB $423 Ex $351 Gd $224

SHERIFF'S MODEL SA REVOLVER . . . . NiB $413 Ex $326 Gd $224
Calibers: .32-20, .357 Mag., .38-40, .44 Special, .44-40, .45 LC. 3.5-inch bbl. Reintroduced 1994.

TARGET SA REVOLVER . . . . NiB $413 Ex $290 Gd $209
Calibers: .45 Long Colt, .357 Mag., .22 LR; 5.5- or 7.5-inch bbl. Polished, blued finish, casehardened frame. Walnut grips. Ramp front, blade target sight, adj. rear sight.

CHARLES DALY HANGUNS — Manila, Philippines. Currently imported by K.B.I., Harrisburg, PA.

MODEL M1911-A1 FIELD FS AUTOMATIC PISTOL
Caliber: .45 ACP. Eight- or 10-round magazine (Hi-Cap), 5-inch bbl., 8.75 inches overall. Weight: 38 oz. Blade front sight, drift adjustable rear w/3-dot system. Skeletonized tactical hammer and trigger. Extended slide release and beavertail grip safety. Matte blue, stainless or Duo finish. Checkered composition or wood stocks. Imported 1996 to date.
Matte blue (Field FS) . . . . NiB $464 Ex $402 Gd $249
Stainless (Empire FS) . . . . NiB $627 Ex $504 Gd $326
Duo (Superior FS) . . . . NiB $498 Ex $402 Gd $280
W/.22 conversion kit, add $200

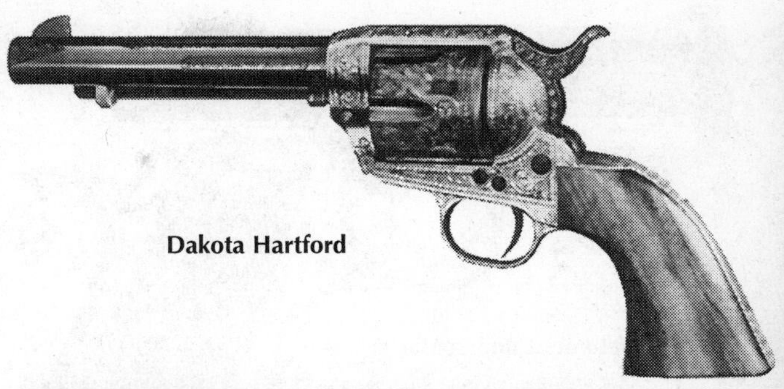
Dakota Hartford

DAVIS INDUSTRIES, INC. — Chino, California

MODEL D DERRINGER
Single-action double derringer. Calibers: .22 LR, .22 Mag., .25 ACP, .32 Auto, .32 H&R Mag., 9mm, .38 Special. Two-round capacity, 2.4-inch or 2.75-inch bbl., 4 inches overall (2.4-inch bbl.). Weight: 9 to 11.5 oz. Laminated wood grips. Black Teflon or chrome finish. Made 1987 to date.
.22 LR or .25 ACP . . . . NiB $86 Ex $71 Gd $52
.22 Mag., .32 H&R Mag., .38 Spec. . . . . . NiB 106 Ex $86 Gd $62
.32 Auto. . . . . NiB $100 Ex $81 Gd $59
9mm Para. . . . . NiB $118 Ex $97 Gd $69

LONG BORE DERRINGER. . . . . NiB $106 Ex $86 Gd $62
Similar to Model D except in calibers .22 Mag., .32 H&R Mag., .38 Special, 9mm Para. 3.75-inch bbl., weight: 16 oz. Made 1995 to date.

MODEL P-.32 . . . . NiB $93 Ex $76 Gd $55
Caliber: .32 Auto. Six-round magazine, 2.8-inch bbl., 5.4 inches overall. Weight: 22 oz. Black Teflon or chrome finish. Laminated wood grips. Made 1987 to date.

MODEL P-.380 . . . . NiB $97 Ex $86 Gd $61
Caliber: .380 Auto. Five-round magazine, 2.8-inch bbl., 5.4 inches overall. Weight: 22 oz. Black Teflon or chrome finish. Made 1990 to date.

DESERT INDUSTRIES, INC. — Las Vegas, Nevada (Previously Steel City Arms, Inc.)

DOUBLE DEUCE DA PISTOL . . . . . NiB $377 Ex $321 Gd $224
Caliber: .22 LR. Six-round magazine, 2.5-inch bbl., 5.5 inches overall. Weight: 15 oz. Matte-finish stainless steel. Rosewood grips.

TWO-BIT SPECIAL PISTOL . . . . NiB $377 Ex $321 Gd $214
Similar to the Double Deuce model except chambered in .25 ACP w/5-shot magazine,

(NEW) DETONICS MFG. CORP — Phoenix, Arizona (Previously Detonics Firearms Industries, Bellevue, WA)

COMBAT MASTER
Calibers: .45 ACP, .451 Detonics Mag. Six-round magazine, 3.5-inch bbl., 6.75 inches overall. Combat-type w/fixed or adjustable sights. Checkered walnut grip. Stainless steel construction. Disc. 1992.
MK I matte stainless, fixed sights, (disc. 1981) . . . . NiB $559 Ex $477 Gd $324
MK II stainless steel finish, (disc. 1979). . . . . NiB $559 Ex $477 Gd $324

Detonics Combat Master

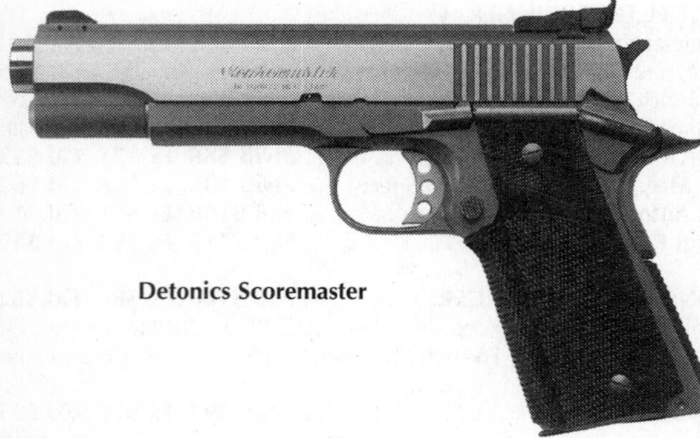
Detonics Scoremaster

Dreyse Model 1907

(cont'd) **COMBAT MASTER**

MK III chrome, (disc. 1980) . . . . NiB $498 Ex $402 Gd $280

MK IV polished blued, adj. sights, (disc. 1981) . . . . NiB $549 Ex $443 Gd $308

MK V matte stainless, fixed sights, (disc. 1985) . . . . NiB $708 Ex $573 Gd $399

MK VI polished ptainless, adj. sights, (disc. 1989). . . . . NiB $765 Ex $618 Gd $431

MK VI in .451 Magnum, (disc. 1986) . . . . NiB $1113 Ex $906 Gd $629

MK VII matte stainless steel, no sights, (disc. 1985) . . . . NiB $977 Ex $785 Gd $540

MK VII in .451 Magnum, (disc. 1980) . . . . NiB $1309 Ex $1055 Gd $731

POCKET 9 . . . . NiB $606 Ex $479 Gd $377
Calibers: 9mm Para., .380. Six-round magazine, three-inch bbl., 5.88 inches overall. Fixed sights. Double- and single-action trigger mechanism. Disc. 1986.

SCOREMASTER . . . . NiB $1053 Ex $895 Gd $742
Calibers: .45 ACP, .451 Detonics Mag. Seven-round magazine. Five- or 6-inch heavyweight match bbl., 8.75 inches overall. Weight: 47 oz. Stainless steel construction, self-centering bbl., system. Disc. 1992.

SERVICE MASTER . . . . NiB $875 Ex $722 Gd $467
Caliber: .45 ACP. Seven-round magazine, 4.25-inch bbl., weight: 39 oz. Interchangeable front sight, Millett rear sight. Disc. 1986.

SERVICE MASTER II. . . . . NiB $983 Ex $805 Gd $524
Same general specifications as standard Service Master except comes in polished stainless steel w/self-centering bbl., system. Disc. 1992.

DOWNSIZER CORPORATION — Santee, California

MODEL WSP
DAO PISTOL . . . . NiB $441 Ex $324 Gd $222
Single-round, tip-up pistol. Calibers: .22 Mag., .32 Mag., .380 ACP. 9mm Parabellum, .357 Mag., .40 S&W, .45 ACP. Six-round cylinder, 2.10-inch bbl. w/o extractor, 3.25 inches overall. Weight: 11 oz. No sights. Stainless finish. Synthetic grips. Made 1994 to date.

DREYSE PISTOLS — Sommerda, Germany Mfd. by Rheinische Metallwaren und Maschinenfabrik ("Rheinmetall")

MODEL 1907
AUTOMATIC PISTOL . . . . NiB $269 Ex $203 Gd $141
Caliber: .32 Auto (7.65mm). Eight-round magazine, 3.5-inch bbl., 6.25 inches overall. Weight: About 24 oz. Fixed sights. Blued finish. Hard rubber grips. Made c. 1907-14.

VEST POCKET
AUTOMATIC PISTOL . . . . NiB $351 Ex $260 Gd $173
Conventional Browning type. Caliber: .25 Auto (6.35mm). Six-round magazine, 2-inch bbl., 4.5 inches overall. Weight: About 14 oz. Fixed sights. Blued finish. Hard rubber grips. Made c. 1909-14.

DWM PISTOL — Berlin, Germany Mfd. by Deutsche Waffen-und-Munitionsfabriken

POCKET AUTOMATIC PISTOL . . . . NiB $800 Ex $647 Gd $451
Similar to the FN Browning Model 1910. Caliber: .32 Automatic (7.65mm). 3.5-inch bbl., 6 inches overall. Weight: About 21 oz. Blued finish. Hard rubber grips. Made c. 1921-31.

ED BROWN — Perry, Montana

"CLASS A LTD" SA
AUTOMATIC PISTOL . . . . NiB $2401 Ex $2013 Gd $919
Caliber: .38 Super, 9mm, 9x23, .45 ACP. Seven-round magazine, 4.25- or 5-inch bbl., weight: 34-39 oz. Rubber checkered or optional Hogue exotic wood grip. M1911 style single action pistol. Fixed front and rear Novak Lo-mount or fully adjustable sights.

"CLASSIC CUSTOM" SA AUTOMATIC PISTOL . . . . NiB $2917 Ex $2402 Gd $1218
Caliber: .45 ACP. Seven-round magazine, 4.25- or 5-inch bbl., weight: 39 oz. Exotic Hogue wood grip w/modified ramp or post front and rear adjustable sights.

"SPECIAL FORCES" SA AUTOMATIC PISTOL . . . . NiB $1290 Ex $1099 Gd $749
Caliber: .45 ACP. Seven-round magazine, 4.25- or 5-inch bbl., weight: 34-39 oz. Rubber checkered, optional exotic wood grips. Single action M1911 style pistol.

ENFIELD REVOLVER — Enfield Lock, Middlesex, England Manufactured by Royal Small Arms Factory

(BRITISH SERVICE) NO. 2 MK 1 REVOLVER . . . . NiB $262 Ex $221 Gd $159
Webley pattern. Hinged frame. Double action. Caliber: .380 British Service (.38 S&W w/200-grain bullet). Six-round cylinder, 5-inch bbl., 10.5 inches overall. Weight: About 27.5 oz. Fixed sights. Blued finish. Vulcanite grips. First issued in 1932, this was the standard revolver of the British Army in WW II. Now obsolete. Note: This model also produced w/spurless hammer as No. 2 Mk 1* and Mk 1**.

ENTREPRISE ARMS — Irwindale, California

"ELITE" SA AUTOMATIC PISTOL . . . . NiB $684 Ex $622 Gd $555
Single action M1911 style pistol. Caliber: .45 ACP. 10-round magazine, 3.25-, 4.25-, 5-inch bbl., (models P325, P425, P500). Weight: 36-40 oz. Ultraslim checkered grips, Tactical 2 high profile sights w/3-dot system. Lightweight adjustable trigger. Blued or matte black oxide finish. Made 1997 to date.

"MEDALIST" SA AUTOMATIC PISTOL
Similar to Elite model except machined to match tolerances and target configuration. Caliber: .45 ACP, .40 S&W. 10-round magazine, 5-inch compensated bbl. w/dovetail front and fully adjustable rear Bo-Mar sights. Weight: 40 oz. Made 1997 to date.
.40 S&W model. . . . . NiB $1064 Ex $859 Gd $597
.45 ACP model. . . . . NiB $930 Ex $751 Gd $522

"TACTICAL" SA AUTOMATIC PISTOL
Similar to Elite model except in combat carry configuration. Dehorned frame and slide w/ambidextrous safety. Caliber: .45 ACP. 10-round magazine, 3.25-, 4.25-, 5-inch bbl., weight: 36-40 oz. Tactical 2 Ghost Ring or Novak Lo-mount sights.
Tactical 2 ghost ring sights . . . . NiB $1023 Ex $920 Gd $585
Novak Lo-Mount . . . . NiB $888 Ex $724 Gd $515
Tactical plus model . . . . NiB $956 Ex $781 Gd $554

BOXER SA AUTOMATIC PISTOL . . . . NiB $1314 Ex $1103 Gd $747
Similar to Medalist model except w/profiled slide configuration and fully adjustable target sights. weight: 42 oz. Made 1997 to date.

"TSM" SA AUTOMATIC PISTOL
Similar to Elite model except in IPSC configuration. Caliber: .45 ACP, .40 S&W. 10-round magazine, 5-inch compensated bbl., w/dovetail front and fully adjustable rear Bo-Mar sights. Weight: 40 oz. Made 1997 to date.

Enfield (British Service)No. 2 MK 1 Revolver

Erma Model ER-772 Match Revolver

***(cont'd)* "TSM" SA AUTOMATIC PISTOL**
TSM I model . . . . NiB $2154 Ex $1948 Gd $818
TSM II model. . . . . NiB $2251 Ex $1819 Gd $1267
TSM III model . . . . NiB $2476 Ex $1999 Gd $1390

ERMA-WERKE — Dachau, Germany

MODEL ER-772 MATCH REVOLVER. . . . . NiB $1211 Ex $979 Gd $588
Caliber: .22 LR. Six-round cylinder, 6-inch bbl., 12 inches overall. Weight: 47.25 oz. Adjustable micrometer rear sight and front sight blade. Adjustable trigger. Interchangeable walnut sporter or match grips. Polished blued finish. Made 1991-94.

MODEL ER-773 MATCH REVOLVER. . . . . NiB $1009 Ex $906 Gd $519
Same general specifications as Model 772 except chambered for .32 S&W. Made 1991-95.

MODEL ER-777 MATCH REVOLVER . . . . NiB $951 Ex $849 Gd514
Caliber: .357 Magnum. Six-round cylinder. 4- or 5.5-inch bbl., 9.7 to 11.3 inches overall. Weight: 43.7 oz. (with 5.5-inch bbl.). Micrometer adj. rear sight. Checkered walnut sporter or match-style grip (interchangeable). Made 1991-95.

MODEL ESP-85A COMPETITION PISTOL
Calibers: .22 LR and .32 S&W Wadcutter. Eight- or 5-round magazine, 6-inch bbl., 10 inches overall. Weight: 40 oz. Adj. rear sight, blade front sight. Checkered walnut grip w/thumbrest. Made 1991-97.
Match model . . . . NiB $1346 Ex $1017 Gd $650
Chrome match. . . . . NiB $1458 Ex $1227 Gd $933
Sporting model . . . . NiB $1168 Ex $950 Gd $672
Conversion unit .22 LR . . . . NiB $1075 Ex $875 Gd $620
Conversion unit .32 S&W . . . . NiB $1175 Ex 1035 Gd $675

European American Armory
Big Bore Bounty Hunter

MODEL KGP68
AUTOMATIC PISTOL . . . . NiB $485 Ex $434 Gd $279
Luger type. Calibers: .32 Auto (7.65mm), .380 Auto (9mm Short). Six-round magazine (.32 Auto), 5-round (.380 Auto), 4-inch bbl., 7.38 inches overall. Weight: 22.5 oz. Fixed sights. Blued finish. Checkered walnut grips. Made 1968-93.

MODEL KGP69
AUTOMATIC PISTOL . . . . NiB $485 Ex $434 Gd $213
Luger type. Caliber: .22 LR. Eight-round magazine, 4-inch bbl., 7.75 inches overall. Weight: 29 oz. fixed sights. Blued finish. Checkered walnut grips. Imported 1969-93.

Erma-Werke
Model KGP69

EUROPEAN AMERICAN ARMORY — Hialeah, Florida

See also listings under Astra Pistols.

EUROPEAN MODEL AUTO PISTOL
Calibers: .32 ACP (SA only), .380 ACP (SA or DA), 3.85-inch bbl., 7.38 overall, 7-round magazine, Weight: 26 oz. Blade front sight, drift-adj. rear. Blued, chrome, blue/chrome, blue/gold, Duo-Tone or Wonder finish. Imported 1991 to date.
Blued .32 caliber (disc. 1995) . . . . . NiB $171 Ex $139 Gd $99
Blue/chrome .32 caliber
(disc. 1995) . . . . NiB $197 Ex $160 Gd $113
Chrome .32 caliber
(Disc. 1995). . . . . NiB $214 Ex $175 Gd $116
Blued .380 caliber . . . . NiB $188 Ex $145 Gd $102
Blue/chrome .380 caliber
(disc. 1993) . . . . NiB $197 Ex $170 Gd $113
DA .380 caliber (disc. 1994) . . . . . . NiB $216 Ex $185 Gd $133
Lady .380 caliber (disc. 1995). . . . . NiB $261 Ex $211 Gd $158
Wonder finish .380 caliber . . . . NiB $188 Ex $155 Gd $102

BIG BORE BOUNTY HUNTER SA REVOLVER
Calibers: .357 Mag., .41 Mag., .44-40, .44 Mag., .45 Colt. Bbl., lengths: 4.63, 5.5, 7.5 inches. Blade front and grooved topstrap rear sights. Blued or chrome finish w/color casehardened or gold-plated frame. Smooth walnut grips. Imported 1992 to date.
Blued finish . . . . NiB $269 Ex $219 Gd $156
Blued w/color-
casehardened frame . . . . NiB $341 Ex $280 Gd $173
Blued w/gold-plated frame . . . . NiB $320 Ex $260 Gd $183
Chrome finish . . . . NiB $357 Ex $295 Gd $217
Gold-plated frame, add $100

Erma Model ESP-85A
Competition Pistol

BOUNTY HUNTER SA REVOLVER
Calibers: .22 LR, .22 Mag. Bbl. lengths: 4.75, 6 or 9 inches. Blade front and dovetailed rear sights. Blued finish or blued w/gold-plated frame. European hardwood grips. Imported 1991 to date.
Blued finish (4.75-inch bbl.) . . . . NiB $93 Ex $76 Gd $55
Blued .22 LR/.22 WRF combo (4.75-inch bbl.) . . . . NiB $112 Ex $92 Gd $65
Blued .22 LR/.22 WRF combo (6-inch bbl.). NiB $118 Ex $97 Gd $69
Blued .22 LR/.22 WRF combo (9-inch bbl.). NiB $125 Ex $102 Gd $72

EA22 TARGET . . . . NiB $373 Ex $301 Gd $208
Caliber: .22 LR. 12-round magazine, 6-inch bbl., 9.10 inches overall. Weight: 40 oz. Ramp front sight, fully adj. rear. Blued finish. Checkered walnut grips w/thumbrest. Made 1991-94.

FAB 92 AUTO PISTOL
Similar to the Witness model except chambered in 9mm only w/slide-mounted safety and no cock-and-lock provision. Imported 1992-95.
FAB 92 standard . . . . NiB $352 Ex $296 Gd $188
FAB 92 compact . . . . NiB $352 Ex $296 Gd $188

STANDARD GRADE REVOLVER
Calibers: .22 LR, .22 WRF, .32 H&R Mag., .38 Special. Two-, 4- or 6-inch bbl., blade front sight, fixed or adj. rear. Blued finish. European hardwood grips w/finger grooves. Imported 1991 to date.
.22 LR (4-inch bbl.) . . . . NiB $182 Ex $148 Gd $104
.22 LR (6-inch bbl.) . . . . NiB $195 Ex $158 Gd $111
.22 LR combo (4-inch bbl.) . . . . . . NiB $259 Ex $209 Gd $146
.22 LR combo (6-inch bbl.) . . . . . . NiB $297 Ex $239 Gd $166
.32 H&R, .38 Special (2-inch bbl.) . NiB $188 Ex $153 Gd $107
.38 Special (4-inch bbl.) . . . . NiB $202 Ex $163 Gd $114
.357 Mag. NiB $219 Ex $183 Gd $112

TACTICAL GRADE REVOLVER
Similar to the Standard model except chambered in .38 Special only. Two- or 4-inch bbl., fixed sights. Available w/compensator. Imported 1991-93.
Tactical revolver . . . . NiB $234 Ex $204 Gd $132
Tactical revolver w/compensator . . . . . NiB $325 Ex $270 Gd $186

WINDICATOR TARGET REVOLVER . . . . . . NiB $443 Ex $341 Gd $214
Calibers: .22 LR, .38 Special, .357 Magnum. Eight-round cylinder in .22 LR, 6-round in .38 Special and .357 Magnum. Six-inch bbl. w/bbl. weights. 11.8 inches overall. Weight: 50.2 oz. Interchangeable blade front sight, fully adj. rear. Walnut competition-style grips. Imported 1991-93.

WITNESS DA AUTO PISTOL
Similar to the Brno CZ-75 w/a cocked-and-locked system. Double or single action. Calibers: 9mm Para. .38 Super, .40 S&W, 10mm; .41 AE and .45 ACP. 16-round magazine (9mm), 12 shot (.38 Super/.40 S&W), or 10-round (10mm/.45 ACP), 4.75-inch bbl., 8.10 inches overall. Weight: 35.33 oz. Blade front sight, rear sight adj. for windage w/3-dot sighting system. Steel or polymer frame. Blued, satin chrome, blue/chrome, stainless or Wonder finish. Checkered rubber grips. EA Series imported 1991 to date.
9mm blue . . . . NiB $367 Ex $296 Gd $204
9mm chrome or blue/chrome. . . . . NiB $380 Ex $306 Gd $211
9mm stainless . . . . NiB $437 Ex $352 Gd $243
9mm Wonder finish. . . . . NiB $392 Ex $316 Gd $218
.38 Super and .40 S&W blued. . . . . NiB $386 Ex $311 Gd $215
.38 Super and .40 S&W chrome or blue/chrome . . . . NiB $429 Ex $346 Gd $240
.38 Super and .40 S&W stainless . . . . NiB $455 Ex $367 Gd $254
.38 Super and .40 S&W Wonder finish . . . . NiB $417 Ex $336 Gd $233
10mm, .41 AE and .45 ACP blued. . . . . . . NiB $480 Ex $387 Gd $268

European American Armory Windicator Target

European American Armory Witness

(cont'd) **WITNESS DA AUTO PISTOL**
10mm, .41 AE and .45 ACP chrome or blue/chrome . . . . NiB $499 Ex $403 Gd $278
10mm, .41 AE and .45 ACP stainless. . . . . . NiB $557 Ex $448 Gd $310
10mm, .41 AE and .45 ACP Wonder finish . . . . NiB $506 Ex $408 Gd $282

COMPACT WITNESS DA AUTO PISTOL (L SERIES)
Similar to the standard Witness series except more compact w/ 3.625-inch bbl., and polymer or steel frame. Weight: 30 oz. Matte blued or Wonder finish. EA Compact series imported 1999 to date.
9mm blue . . . . NiB $382 Ex $321 Gd $219
9mm Wonder finish. . . . . NiB $403 Ex $346 Gd $229
.38 Super and .40 S&W blued. . . . . NiB $392 Ex $316 Gd $220
.38 Super and .40 S&W Wonder finish . . . . NiB $417 Ex $336 Gd $233
10mm, .41 AE and .45 ACP blued. . . . . NiB $482 Ex $387 Gd $268
10mm, .41 AE and .45 ACP Wonder fin. . . . NiB $506 Ex $408 Gd $282
W/ported bbl., add $30

WITNESS CARRY COMP
Double/Single action. Calibers: .38 Super, 9mm Parabellum, .40 S&W, 10mm, .45 ACP. 10-, 12- or 16-round magazine, 4.25-inch bbl., w/1-inch compensator. Weight: 33 oz., 8.10 inches overall. Black rubber grips. Post front sight, drift adjustable rear w/3-dot system. Matte blue, Duo-Tone or Wonder finish. Imported 1992 to date.
9mm, .40 S&W . . . . NiB $448 Ex $382 Gd $219
.38 Super, 10mm, .45 ACP. . . . . NiB $392 Ex $316 Gd $220
W/Duo-Tone finish (disc.), add $25
W/Wonder finish, add $10

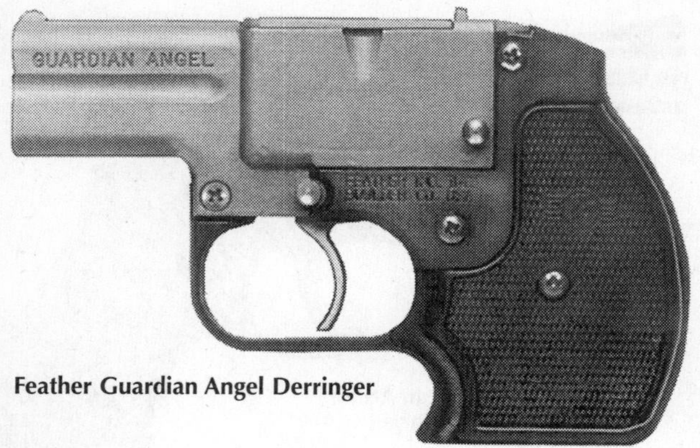
Feather Guardian Angel Derringer

FEG Mark II AP-.22

WITNESS LIMITED CLASS AUTO PISTOL . . . . **NiB $897 Ex $754 Gd $433**
Single action. Calibers: .38 Super, 9mm Parabellum, .40 S&W, .45 ACP. 10-round magazine, 4.75-inch bbl., Weight: 37 oz. Checkered competition-style walnut grips. Long slide w/post front sight, fully adj. rear. Matte blue finish. Imported 1994 to date.

WITNESS SUBCOMPACT DA AUTO PISTOL
Calibers: 9mm Para., .40 S&W, 41 AK, .45 ACP. 13-round magazine in 9mm, 9-round in .40 S&W, 3.66-inch bbl., 7.25 inches overall. Weight: 30 oz. Blade front sight, rear sight adj. for windage. Blued, satin chrome or blue/chrome finish. Imported 1995-97.
9mm blue . . . . **NiB $351 Ex $326 Gd $300**
9mm chrome or blue/chrome . . . . . **NiB $396 Ex $321 Gd $225**
.40 S&W blue . . . . **NiB $396 Ex $321 Gd $225**
.40 S&W chrome or blue/chrome . . **NiB $434 Ex $351 Gd $245**
.41 AE blue . . . . **NiB $467 Ex $377 Gd $263**
.41 AE chrome or blue/chrome . . . . **NiB $498 Ex $402 Gd $280**
.45 ACP blued . . . . **NiB $479 Ex $387 Gd $270**
.45 ACP chrome or blue/chrome . . . **NiB $453 Ex $387 Gd $275**

WITNESS TARGET PISTOLS
Similar to standard Witness model except fitted w/2- or 3-port compensator, competition frame and S/A target trigger. Calibers: 9mm Para., 9x21, .40 S&W, 10mm and .45 ACP, 5.25-inch match bbl., 10.5 inches overall. Weight: 38 oz. Square post front sight, fully adj. rear or drilled and tapped for scope. Blued or hard chrome finish. Low-profile competition grips. Imported 1992 to date.
Silver Team (blued w/2-port compensator) . . . . **NiB $901 Ex $724 Gd $494**
Gold Team (chrome w/3-port compensator) . . . . **NiB $1842 Ex $1448 Gd $1026**

FAS PISTOLS — Malino, Italy Currently imported by Nygord Precision Products *(Previously by Beeman Precision Arms and Osborne's, Cheboygan, MI)*

601 SEMIAUTOMATIC MATCH TARGET PISTOL
Caliber: .22 Short. Five-round top-loading magazine, 5.6-inch ported and ventilated bbl., 11 inches overall. Weight: 41.5 oz. Removable, adj. trigger group. Blade front sight, open-notch fully adj. rear. Stippled walnut wrapaound or adj.target grips.
Right-hand model . . . . **NiB $949 Ex $764 Gd $528**
Left-hand model . . . . **NiB $1070 Ex $917 Gd $535**

602 SEMIAUTOMATIC MATCH TARGET PISTOL
Similar to Model FAS 601 except chambered for .22 LR. Weight: 37 oz.
Right-hand model . . . . **NiB $917 Ex $637 Gd $484**
Left-hand model . . . . **NiB $938 Ex $637 Gd $509**

603 SEMIAUTOMATIC MATCH TARGET PISTOL . . . . **NiB $1019 Ex $917 Gd $535**
Similar to Model FAS 601 except chambered for .32 S&W (wadcutter).

607 SEMIAUTOMATIC MATCH TARGET PISTOL . . . . **NiB $1019 Ex $917 Gd $484**
Similar to Model FAS 601 except chambered for .22 LR, w/removable bbl. weights. Imported 1995 to date.

FEATHER INDUSTRIES, INC. — Boulder, Colorado

GUARDIAN ANGEL DERRINGER
Double-action over/under derringer w/interchangeable drop-in loading blocks. Calibers: .22 LR, .22 WMR, 9mm, .38 Spec. Two-round capacity, 2-inch bbl., 5 inches overall. weight: 12 oz. Stainless steel. Checkered black grip. Made 1988-95.
.22 LR, .22 WMR . . . . **NiB $194 Ex $92 Gd $61**
9mm, .38 Special (disc. 1989) . . . . **NiB $132 Ex $97 Gd $66**

FEG (FEGYVERGYAN) PISTOLS — Budapest, Soroksariut, Hungary *(Currently imported by KBI, Inc. and Century International Arms (Previously by Interarms)*

MARK II AP-.22 DA AUTOMATIC PISTOL . . . . **NiB $271 Ex $235 Gd $153**
Caliber: .22 LR. Eight-round magazine, 3.4-inch bbl., Weight: 23 oz. Drift-adj. sights. Double action, all-steel pistol. Imported 1997 to date.

MARK II AP-.380 DA AUTOMATIC PISTOL . . . **NiB $271 Ex $235 Gd $164**
Caliber: .380. Seven-round magazine, 3.9-inch bbl., weight 27 oz. Drift-adj. sights. Double action, all-steel pistol. Imported 1997 to date.

MARK II APK-.380 DA AUTOMATIC PISTOL . . . . **NiB $271 Ex $235 Gd $164**
Caliber: .380. Seven-round magazine, 3.4-inch bbl., weight: 25 oz. Drift-adj. sights. Double action, all-steel pistol. Imported 1997 to date.

MODEL GKK-9 (92C) AUTO PISTOL . . . . **NiB $352 Ex $317 Gd $194**
Improved version of the double-action FEG Model MBK. Caliber: 9mm Para. 14-round magazine, 4-inch bbl., 7.4 inches overall. Weight: 34 oz. Blade front sight, rear sight adj. for windage. Checkered wood grips. Blued finish. Imported 1992-93.

MODEL GKK-.45 AUTO PISTOL
Improved version of the double-action FEG Model MBK. Caliber: .45 ACP. Eight-round magazine, 4.1-inch bbl., 7.75 inches overall. Weight: 36 oz. Blade front sight, rear sight adj. for windage w/3-dot system. Checkered walnut grips. Blued or chrome finish. Imported 1993-96.
Blued model (disc. 1994) . . . . NiB $328 Ex $266 Gd $186
Chrome model. . . . . NiB $322 Ex $286 Gd $179

MODEL MBK-9HP
AUTO PISTOL . . . . NiB $265 Ex $239 Gd $112
Similar to the double-action Browning Hi-Power. Caliber: 9mm Para. 14-round magazine, 4.6-inch bbl., 8 inches overall. Weight: 36 oz. Blade front sight, rear sight adj. for windage. Checkered wood grips. Blued finish. Imported 1992-93.

MODEL PJK-9HP AUTO PISTOL
Similar to the single-action Browning Hi-Power. Caliber: 9mm Para. 13-round magazine, 4.75-inch bbl., 8 inches overall. Weight: 21 oz. Blade front sight, rear sight adj. for windage w/3-dot system. Checkered walnut or rubber grips. Blued or chrome finish. Imported 1992 to date.
Blued model . . . . NiB $266 Ex $216 Gd $153
Chrome model. . . . . NiB $272 Ex $246 Gd $170

MODEL PSP-.25 AUTO PISTOL
Similar to the Browning .25. Caliber: .25 ACP. Six-round magazine, 2.1-inch bbl., 4.1 inches overall. Weight: 9.5 oz. Fixed sights. Checkered composition grips. Blued or chrome finish.
Blued model . . . . NiB $265 Ex $188 Gd $143
Chrome model. . . . . NiB $265 Ex $188 Gd $143

MODEL SMC-.22 AUTO PISTOL . . . NiB $253 Ex $204 Gd $142
Same general specifications as FEG Model SMC-.380 except in .22 LR. Eight-round magazine, 3.5-inch bbl., 6.1 inches overall. Weight: 18.5 oz. Blade front sight, rear sight adj. for windage. Checkered composition grips w/thumbrest. Blued finish.

MODEL SMC-.380 AUTO PISTOL . . . NiB $219 Ex $194 Gd $127
Similar to the Walther DA PPK w/alloy frame. Caliber: .380 ACP. Six-round magazine, 3.5-inch bbl., 6.1 inches overall. Weight: 18.5 oz. Blade front sight, rear sight adj. for windage. Checkered composition grips w/ thumbrest. Blued finish. Imported 1993 to date.

MODEL SMC-918 AUTO PISTOL. . . . NiB $224 Ex $194 Gd $137
Same general specifications as FEG Model SMC-.380 except chambered in 9x18mm Makarov. Imported 1994-97.

FIALA OUTFITTERS, INC. — New York

REPEATING PISTOL. . . . . NiB $509 Ex $433 Gd $229
Despite its appearance, which closely resembles that of the early Colt Woodsman and High-Standard, this arm is not an automatic pistol. It is hand-operated by moving the slide to eject, cock and load. Caliber: .22 LR. 10-round magazine, bbl. lengths: 3-, 7.5- and 20-inch. 11.25 inches overall (with 7.5-inch bbl.). Weight: 31 oz. (with 7.5-inch bbl.). Target sights. Blued finish. Plain wood grips. Shoulder stock was originally supplied for use w/20-inch bbl. Made 1920-23. Value shown is for pistol w/one bbl. and no shoulder stock.

F.I.E. CORPORATION — Hialeah, Florida

The F.I.E Corporation became QFI (Quality Firearms Corp.) of Opa Locka, Fl., about 1990, when most of F.I.E's models were discontinued.

FEG Model PJK-9HP

F.I.E. Model A27BW

MODEL A27BW "THE BEST" SEMIAUTO . . . . NiB $137 Ex $117 Gd $81
Caliber: .25 ACP. Six-round magazine, 2.5-inch bbl., 6.75 inches overall. Weight: 13 oz. Fixed sights. Checkered walnut grip. Disc. 1990.

ARMINIUS DA STANDARD REVOLVER
Calibers: .22 LR, .22 combo w/interchangeable cylinder, .32 S&W, .38 Special, .357 Magnum. Six, 7 or 8 rounds depending on caliber. Swing-out cylinder. bbl., lengths: 2-, 3-, 4, 6-inch. Vent rib on calibers other than .22, 11 inches overall (with 6-inch bbl.). Weight: 26 to 30 oz. Fixed or micro-adj. sights. Checkered plastic or walnut grips. Blued finish. Made in Germany. disc. See illustration next page.
.22 LR . . . . NiB $87 Ex $76 Gd $56
.22 Combo. . . . . NiB $158 Ex $132 Gd $81
.32 S&W . . . . NiB $168 Ex $126 Gd $85
.38 Special. NiB $119 Ex $141 Gd $96
.357 Magnum . . . . NiB $198 Ex $163 Gd $117

BUFFALO SCOUT SA REVOLVER
Calibers: .22 LR, .22 WRF, .22 combo w/interchangeable cylinder. 4.75-inch bbl., 10 inches overall. Weight: 32 oz. Adjustable sights. Blued or chrome finish. Smooth walnut or black checkered nylon grips. Made in Italy. disc.
Blued standard. NiB $81 Ex $61 Gd $41
Blued convertible . . . . NiB $101 Ex $81 Gd $57
Chrome standard. . . . . NiB $88 Ex $71 Gd $40
Chrome convertible. . . . . NiB $122 Ex 101 Gd $73

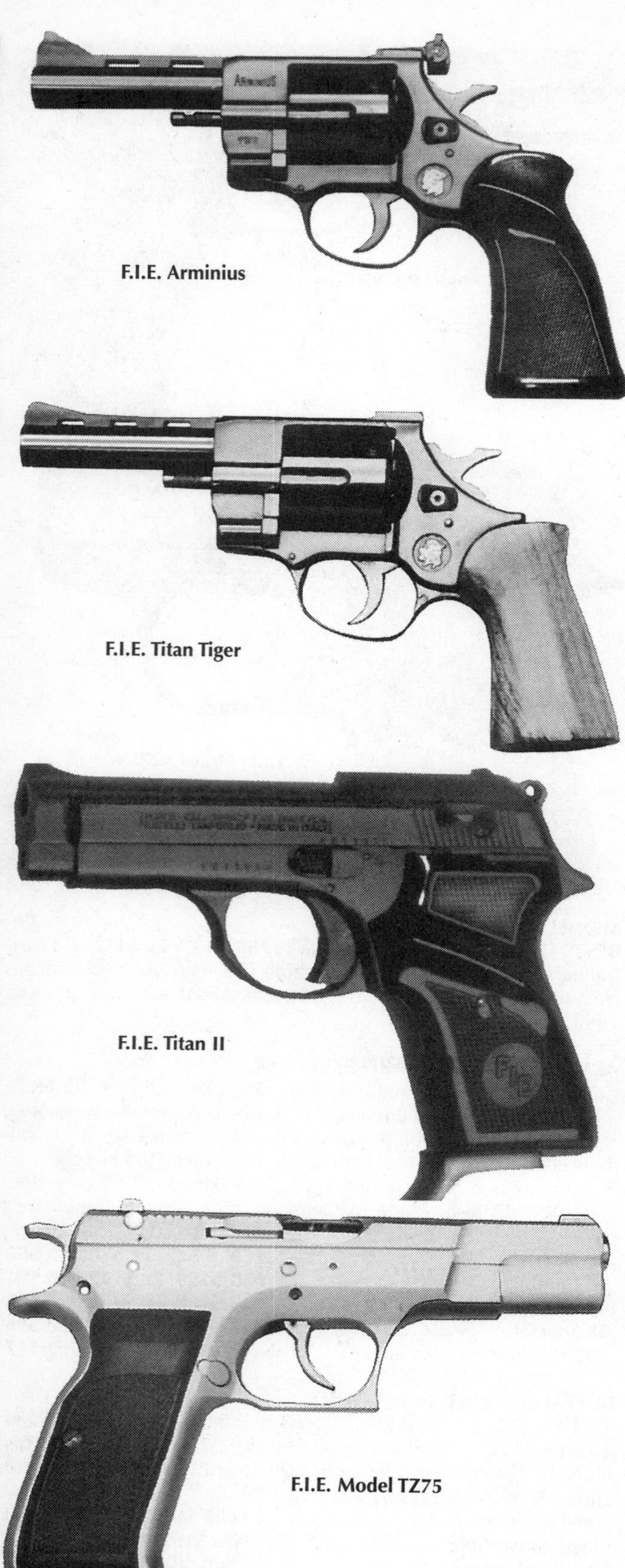

F.I.E. Arminius

F.I.E. Titan Tiger

F.I.E. Titan II

F.I.E. Model TZ75

HOMBRE SA REVOLVER . . . . NiB $229 Ex $189 Gd $117
Calibers: .357 Magnum, .44 Magnum, .45 Colt. Six-round cylinder. bbl. lengths: 6 or 7.5 inches, 11 inches overall (with - inch bbl.). Weight: 45 oz. (6-inch bbl.). Fixed sights. Blued bbl., w/color-casehardened receiver. Smooth walnut grips. Made 1979-90.

SUPER TITAN II
Caliber: .32 ACP or .380 ACP, 3.25-inch bbl., weight: 28 oz. Blued or chrome finish. Disc. 1990.
.32 ACP in blue . . . . NiB $227 Ex $197 Gd $110
.32 ACP in chrome . . . . NiB $206 Ex $166 Gd $115
.380 ACP in blue . . . . NiB $212 Ex $171 Gd $119
.380 ACP in chrome . . . . NiB $231 Ex $191 Gd $129

TEXAS RANGER SINGLE-ACTION REVOLVER
Calibers: .22 LR, .22 WRF, .22 combo w/interchangeable cylinder. bbl., lengths: 4.75-, 6.5-, 9-inch. 10 inches overall (with 4.75-inch bbl.). Weight: 32 oz. (with 4.75-inch bbl.). Fixed sights. Blued finish. Smooth walnut grips. Made 1983-90.
Standard . . . . NiB $90 Ex $79 Gd $49
Convertible . . . . NiB $147 Ex $123 Gd $94

LITTLE RANGER SA REVOLVER
Same as the Texas Ranger except w/3.25-inch bbl. and bird's-head grips. Made 1986-90.
Standard . . . . NiB $87 Ex $76 Gd $56
Convertible . . . . NiB $150 Ex $125 Gd $95

TITAN TIGER DOUBLE-ACTION REVOLVER . . . . NiB $138 Ex $117 Gd $76
Caliber: .38 Special. Six-round cylinder, 2- or 4-inch bbl., 8.25 inches overall (with 4-inch bbl.). Weight: 30 oz. (4-inch bbl.). Fixed sights. Blued finish. Checkered plastic or walnut grips. Made in the U.S. Disc. 1990.

TITAN II SEMIAUTOMATIC
Caiibers: .22 LR, .32 ACP, .380 ACP. 10-round magazine, integral tapered post front sight, windage-adjustable rear sight. European walnut grips. Blued or chrome finish. Disc. 1990.
.22 LR in blue . . . . NiB $138 Ex $112 Gd $61
.32 ACP in blued . . . . NiB $177 Ex $143 Gd $99
.32 ACP in chrome . . . . NiB $227 Ex $187 Gd $136
.380 ACP in blue . . . . NiB $208 Ex $168 Gd $117
.380 ACP in chrome . . . . NiB $233 Ex $188 Gd $131

MODEL TZ75 DA SEMIAUTOMATIC
Double action. Caliber: 9mm. 15-round magazine, 4.5-inch bbl., 8.25 inches overall. Weight: 35 oz. Ramp front sight, windage-adjustable rear sight. European walnut or black rubber grips. Imported 1988-90.
Blued finish . . . . NiB $398 Ex $347 Gd $240
Satin chrome . . . . NiB $471 Ex $378 Gd $262

YELLOW ROSE SA REVOLVER
Same general specifications as the Buffalo Scout except in .22 combo w/interchangeable cylinder and plated in 24-karat gold. Limited Edition w/scrimshawed ivory polymer grips and American walnut presentation case. Made 1987-90.
Yellow Rose .22 combo . . . . NiB $141 Ex $120 Gd $105
Yellow Rose Limited Edition . . . . NiB $263 Ex $222 Gd $161

FIREARMS INTERNATIONAL CORP. — Washington, D.C.

**MODEL D
AUTOMATIC PISTOL . . . . NiB $248 Ex $201 Gd $141**
Caliber: .380 Automatic. Six-round magazine, 3.3-inch bbl., 6.13 inches overall. Weight: 19.5 oz. Blade front sight, windage-adjustable rear sight. Blued, chromed, or military finish. Checkered walnut grips. Made 1974-77.

**REGENT DA
REVOLVER. NiB $127 Ex $104 Gd $84**
Calibers: .22 LR, .32 S&W Long. Eight-round cylinder (.22 LR), or 7-round (.32 S&W). Bbl. lengths: 3-, 4-, 6-inches (.22 LR) or 2.5-, 4-inches (.32 S&W). Weight: 28 oz.(with 4-inch bbl.). Fixed sights. Blued finish. Plastic grips. Made 1966-72.

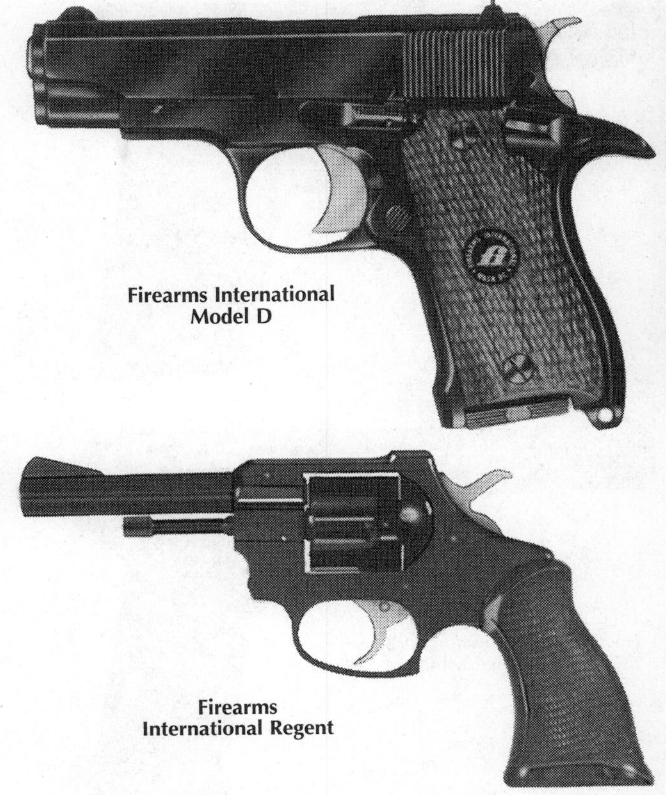
Firearms International Model D

Firearms International Regent

FN BROWNING PISTOLS — Liege, Belgium Mfd. by Fabrique Nationale Herstal

See also Browning Pistols.

6.35MM POCKET AUTO PISTOL
(See FN Browning Baby Auto Pistol)

**MODEL 1900 POCKET
AUTO PISTOL . . . . NiB $537 Ex $439 Gd $228**
Caliber: .32 Automatic (7.65mm). Seven-round magazine, 4-inch bbl., 6.75 inches overall. Weight: 22 oz. Fixed sights. Blued finish. Hard rubber grips. Made 1899-10.

MODEL 1903 MILITARY AUTO PISTOL
Caliber: 9mm Browning Long. Seven-round magazine, 5-inch bbl., 8 inches overall. Weight: 32 oz. Fixed sights. Blued finish. Hard rubber grips. Note: Aside from size, this pistol is of the same basic design as the Colt Pocket .32 and .380 Automatic pistols. Made 1903-39.
**Model 190
Standard . . . . NiB $529 Ex $427 Gd $297**
**Model 1903
(w/slotted backstrap). . . . . NiB $786 Ex $633 Gd $437**
**Model 1903 (w/slotted
backstrap, shoulder stock
and extended magazine) . . . . . . NiB $3162 Ex $2561 Gd $1754**

FN Browning 6.35mm Pocket

**MODEL 1910
POCKET AUTO PISTOL . . . . NiB $375 Ex $350 Gd $231**
Calibers: .32 Auto (7.65mm), .380 Auto (9mm). Seven-round magazine (.32 cal.), or 6-round (.380 cal.), 3.5-inch bbl., 6 inches overall. Weight: 20.5 oz. Fixed sights. Blued finish. Hard rubber grips. Made 1910-54.

**MODEL 1922 (10/.22)
POLICE/MILITARY AUTO**
Calibers: .32 Auto (7.65mm), .380 Auto (9mm). Nine-round magazine (.32 cal.), or 8-round (.380 cal.), 4.5-inch bbl., 7 inches overall. Weight: 25 oz. Fixed sights. Blued finish. Hard rubber grips. Made 1922-59.
**Model 1910
commercial . . . . NiB $431 Ex $354 Gd $225**
**Model 191
Military contract . . . . NiB $528 Ex $426 Gd $296**
**Model 1910 (w/Nazi
proofs 1940-44), add 25%**

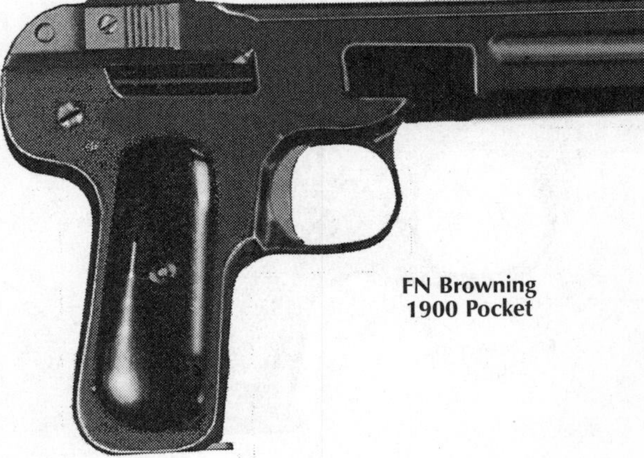
FN Browning 1900 Pocket

FN Browning 1910 Pocket

FN Browning 1922 Police/Military

FN Browning 1935 Military Hi-Power

FN Browning Baby

MODEL 1935 MILITARY HI-POWER PISTOL
Variation of the Browning-Colt .45 Auto design. Caliber: 9mm Para.13-round magazine, 4.63-inch bbl., 7.75 inches overall. Weight: About 35 oz. Adjustable rear sight and fixed front, or both fixed. Blued finish (Canadian manufacture Parkerized). Checkered walnut or plastic grips. Note: Above specifications in general apply to both the original FN production and the pistols made by John Inglis Company of Canada for the Chinese government. A smaller version, w/shorter bbl. and slide and 10-round magazine, was made by FN for the Belgian and Rumanian Governments about 1937-1940. Both types were made at the FN plant during the German occupation of Belgium.
Pre-war commercial (w/fixed sights). . . . . NiB $1055 Ex $849 Gd $643
Pre-war commercial
(w/tangent sight only). . . . . NiB $1931 Ex $1261 Gd $643
Pre-war commercial
(w/tangent sight, slotted backstrap) . . . NiB $2872 Ex $2512 Gd $1327
Pre-war Belgian military contract. . . . . . . NiB $1135 Ex $945 Gd $635
Pre-war Foreign military contract. . . . . NiB $2094 Ex $1683 Gd $1158
War production (w/fixed sights) . . . . NiB $786 Ex $633 Gd $447
War production (w/tangent sight only). . NiB $1321 Ex $1065 Gd $737
War production
(w/tangent sight and slotted backstrap) . . . NiB $3324 Ex $2666 Gd $1826
Post-war/pre-BAC (w/fixed sights) . . . . NiB $658 Ex $530 Gd $367
Post-war/pre-BAC (w/tangent sight only) . . NiB $729 Ex $586 Gd $405
Post-war/pre-BAC
(w/tangent sight, slotted backstrap) . . . . NiB $1301 Ex $1045 Gd $717
Inglis manufacture
Canadian military (w/fixed sights) . . . . NiB $947 Ex $715 Gd $432
Canadian military
(w/fixed sight, slotted) . . . . NiB $1773 Ex $1424 Gd $980
Canadian military
(w/tangent sight, slotted) . . . . NiB $1446 Ex $1164 Gd $803
Canadian military
(marked w/Inglis logo) . . . . NiB $2518 Ex $2033 Gd $1388
Chinese military contract
(w/tangent sight, slotted) . . . . NiB $3259 Ex $2615 Gd $1791
Canadian military
(w/fixed sight, slotted backstrap) . . . . . . NiB $1774 Ex $1426 Gd $981
Canadian military
(marked w/Inglis logo) . . . . NiB $2518 Ex $2033 Gd $1388
W/issue wooden holster, add $400

BABY AUTO PISTOL . . . . NiB $539 Ex $477 Gd $333
Caliber: .25 Automatic (6.35mm). Six-round magazine, 2.13-inch bbl., 4 inches overall. Weight: 10 oz. Fixed sights. Blued finish. Hard rubber grips. Made 1931-83.

FOREHAND & WADSWORTH — Worcester, Massachusetts

REVOLVERS
See listings of comparable Harrington & Richardson and Iver Johnson revolvers for values.

FORT WORTH FIREARMS — Fort Worth, TX

MATCH MASTER STANDARD. . . . . NiB $350 Ex $225 Gd $200
Semi-automatic. Caliber: .22LR. Equipped with 3 7/8-, 4 1/2-, 5 1/2-, 7 1/2- or 10-inch bull bbl., double extractors, includes upper push button and standard magazine release, angled grip, low profile frame. Mfg. 1995-2000.

MATCH MASTER DOVETAIL . . . . . NiB $450 Ex $375 Gd $285
Similar to Match Master except has 3 7/8-, 4 1/2-, or 5 1/2-inch bbl. with dovetail rib.

MATCH MASTER DELUXE . . . . NiB $510 Ex $405 Gd $310
Similar to Match master Standard except has Weaver rib on bbl.
W/10-inch bbl. . . . . Add $100

SPORT KING . . . . NiB $510 Ex $260 Gd $235
Semi-automatic. Caliber: .22 LR. Equipped with 4 1/2- or 5 1/2-inch bbl., blued finish, military grips, drift sights, 10 round magazine. Mfg 1995-2000.

CITATION . . . . NiB $375 Ex $280 Gd $235
Semi-automatic. Caliber: .22 LR. Equipped with 5 1/2-inch bull bbl. or 7 1/2-inch fluted bbl., military grips, 10-round magazine.

TROPHY . . . . NiB $380 Ex $295 Gd $230
Semi-automatic. Caliber: .22 LR. Equipped with 5 1/2- or 7 1/2-inch bull bbl. blued finish, military grips, 10-round magazine.
W/LH action (5 1/2-inch bbl. only) . . . . Add $50

VICTOR . . . . NiB $440 Ex $350 Gd $260
Semi-automatic. Caliber: .22LR. Equipped with 3 7/8-, 4 1/2- (VR or Weaver rib), 8- (Weaver rib) or 10-inch (Weaver rib) bbls.; blued finish, military grips, 10-round magazine.
W/4 1/2- or 4 1/2-inch Weaver rib bbls. . . . . Add $80
W/8- or 10-inch Weaver rib bbls. . . . . Add $175

OLYMPIC . . . . NiB $585 Ex $470 Gd $360
Semi-automatic. Caliber: .22 LR or Short. Equipped with 6 1/2-inch fluted bbl., blued finish, military grips, 10-round magazine.

SHARPSHOOTER . . . . NiB $357 Ex $297 Gd $222
Semi-automatic. Caliber: .22 LR. Equipped with 5 1/2-inch bull bbl.,blued finish, military grips, 10-round magazine.

LE FRANCAIS PISTOLS — St. Etienne, France Produced bv Manufacture Francaise d'Armes et Cycles

ARMY MODEL AUTOMATIC PISTOL . . . NiB $1606 Ex $1189 Gd $773
Similar in operation to the Le Francais .25 Automatics. Caliber: 9mm Browning Long. Eight-round magazine, 5-inch bbl., 7.75 inches overall. Weight: About 34 oz. Fixed sights. Blued finish. Checkered walnut grips. Made from 1928-.38.

POLICEMAN MODEL
AUTOMATIC PISTOL . . . . NiB $897 Ex $846 Gd $336
DA. Hinged bbl., Caliber: .25 Automatic (6.35mm). Seven-round magazine, 3.5-inch bbl., 6 inches overall. Weight: About 12 oz. Fixed sights. Blued finish. Hard rubber grips. Intro. 1914. disc.

STAFF OFFICER MODEL
AUTOMATIC PISTOL . . . . NiB $300 Ex $255 Gd $173
Caliber: .25 Automatic. Similar to the "Policeman" model except does not have cocking-piece head, barrel, is about an inch shorter and weight is an ounce. less. Introduced in 1914. disc.

FREEDOM ARMS — Freedom, Wyoming

MODEL 1997
PREMIER GRADE SA REVOLVER
Calibers: .357 Mag., .41 Mag. or .45 LC. Five- or 6-round cylinder, 4.25-, 5-, 5.5-, 6- or 7.5- inch bbl., removable front blade with adjustable or fixed rear sight. Hardwood or black Micarta grips. Satin stainless finish. Made 1997 to date.
Premier grade 97 . . . . NiB $1739 Ex $1302 Gd $761
For extra cylinder, add $200
For fixed sights, deduct $75

MODEL FA-.44 (83-44) SA REVOLVER
Similar to Model 454 Casull except chambered in .44 Mag. Made from 1988 to date.
Field grade . . . . NiB $1405 Ex $1065 Gd $812
Premier grade . . . . NiB $1739 Ex $1276 Gd $761
Silhouette class (w/10-inch bbl.) . NiB $1410 Ex $1070 Gd $823
Silhouette pac
(10-inch bbl., access.) . . . . NiB $1405 Ex $1065 Gd $812
For fixed sights, deduct $95

MODEL FA-.45 (83-45) SA REVOLVER
Similar to Model 454 Casull except chambered in .45 Long Colt. Made 1988-90.
Field grade . . . . NiB $1261 Ex $952 Gd $591
Premier grade . . . . NiB $1126 Ex $906 Gd $623
For fixed sights, deduct $95

MODEL FA-252 (83-22) SA REVOLVER
Calibers: .22 LR w/optional .22 Mag. cylinder. Bbl. lengths: 5.13 and 7.5 (Varmint Class), 10 inches (Silhouette Class). Adjustable express or competition silhouette sights. Brushed or matte stainless finish. Black Micarta (Silhouette) or black and green laminated hardwood grips (Varmint). Made 1991 to date.
Silhouette class . . . . NiB $1923 Ex $1611 Gd $658
Silhouette class
w/extra .22 Mag. cyl . . . . NiB $1488 Ex $1199 Gd $828
Varmint class . . . . NiB $1135 Ex $915 Gd $635
Varmint class
w/extra .22 Mag. cyl . . . . NiB $1424 Ex $1147 Gd $793

MODEL FA-353 (83-357) SA REVOLVER
Caliber: .357 Mag., bbl. lengths: 4.75, 6, 7.5 or 9 inches. Removable blade front sight, adjustable rear. Brushed or matte stainless finish. Pachmayr Presentation or impregnated hardwood grips.
Field grade . . . . NiB $999 Ex $805 Gd $558
Premier grade . . . . NiB $1614 Ex $1508 Gd $658
Silhouette class
(w/9-inch bbl.) . . . . NiB $1020 Ex $823 Gd $571

MODEL FA-454AS (83-454) REVOLVER
Caliber: .454 Casull (w/optional .45 ACP, .45 LC, .45 Win. Mag. cylinders). Five-round cylinder, bbl. lengths: 4.75, 6, 7.5 or 10 inches. Adjustable express or competition silhouette sights. Pachmayr presentation or impregnated hardwood grips. Brushed or matte stainless steel finish.
Field grade . . . . NiB $1613 Ex $1199 Gd $555
Premier grade . . . . NiB $2075 Ex $1739 Gd $658
Silhouette class (w/10-inch bbl.) . NiB $1028 Ex $828 Gd $573
For extra cylinder, add $250

MODEL FA-454FS REVOLVER
Same general specifications as Model FA-454AS except w/fixed sight.
Field grade . . . . NiB $1643 Ex $1430 Gd $864
Premier grade . . . . NiB $1679 Ex $1456 Gd $864

Freedom Arms FA-252

Freedom Arms FA-454AS

MODEL FA-454 GAS REVOLVER . . . . . . NiB $1643 Ex $1430 Gd $864
Field Grade version of Model FA-454AS except not made w/12-inch bbl., Matte stainless finish, Pachmayr presentation grips. Adj. Sights or fixed sight on 4.75-inch bbl.,

MODEL FA-555 REVOLVER
Similar to Model .454 Casull except chambered in .50 AK. Made 1994 to date.
Field grade . . . . NiB $1456 Ex $1065 Gd $812
Premier grade . . . . NiB $1817 Ex $1327 Gd $967

MODEL FA-BG-22LR MINI-REVOLVER . . . . NiB $185 Ex $143 Gd $108
Caliber: .22 LR. Three-inch tapered bbl., partial high-gloss stainless steel finish. Disc. 1987.

MODEL FA-BG-22M MINI-REVOLVER . . . . NiB $211 Ex $159 Gd $118
Same general specifications as model FA-BG-22LR except in caliber .22 WMR. Disc. 1987.

MODEL FA-BG-22P MINI-REVOLVER . . . . NiB $211 Ex $170 Gd $108
Same general specifications as Model FA-BG-22LR except in .22 percussion. Disc. 1987.

MODEL FA-L-22LR MINI-REVOLVER . . . NiB $170 Ex $159 Gd $82
Caliber: .22 LR, 1.75-inch contoured bbl., partial high-gloss stainless steel finish. Bird's-head-type grips. Disc. 1987.

MODEL FA-L-22M MINI-REVOLVER . . . . NiB $180 Ex $149 Gd $108
Same general specifications as Model FA-L-22LR except in caliber .22 WMR. Disc. 1987.

MODEL FA-L-22P MINI-REVOLVER . . . . NiB $195 Ex $134 Gd $98
Same general specifications as Model FA-L-22LR except in .22 percussion. Disc. 1987.

MODEL FA-S-22LR MINI-REVOLVER . . . NiB $170 Ex $159 Gd $82
Caliber: .22 LR. One-inch contoured bbl., partial high-gloss stainless steel finish. Disc. 1988.

MODEL FA-S-22M MINI-REVOLVER. . . NiB $170 Ex $149 Gd $108
Same general specifications as Model FA-S-22LR except in caliber .22 WMR. Disc. 1988.

MODEL FA-S-22P MINI-REVOLVER . . . . NiB $170 Ex $149 Gd $82
Same general specifications as Model FA-S-22LR except in .22 percussion. Disc. 1988.

FRENCH MILITARY PISTOLS — Cholet, France

Mfd. originally by Société Alsacienne de Constructions Mécaniques (S.A.C.M.). Currently made by Manufacture d'Armes Automatiques, Lotissement Industriel des Pontots, Bayonne

MODEL 1935A AUTOMATIC PISTOL. . . . . . . NiB $292 Ex $241 Gd $114
Caliber: 7.65mm Long. Eight-round magazine, 4.3-inch bbl., 7.6 inches overall. Weight: 26 oz. Two-lug locking system similar to the Colt U.S. M1911A1. Fixed sights. Blued finish. Checkered grips. Made 1935-45. Note: This pistol was used by French troops during WW II and in Indo-China 1945-54.

MODEL 1935S AUTOMATIC PISTOL . . . . NiB $351 Ex $321 Gd $173
Similar to Model 1935A except shorter (4.1-inch bbl., and 7.4 inches overall) and heavier (28 oz.). Single-step lug locking system.

MODEL 1950 AUTOMATIC PISTOL . . . . NiB $434 Ex $351 Gd $245
Caliber: 9mm Para. Nine-round magazine, 4.4-inch bbl., 7.6 inches overall. Weight: 30 oz. Fixed sights, tapered post front and U-notched rear. Similar in design and function to the U.S. .45 service automatic except no bbl., bushing.

MODEL MAB F1 AUTOMATIC PISTOL. . . . . . NiB $591 Ex $540 Gd $234
Similar to Model MAB P-15 except w/6-inch bbl. and 9.6 inches overall. Adjustable target-style sights. Parkerized finish.

MODEL MAB P-8 AUTOMATIC PISTOL. . . . . NiB $521 Ex $423 Gd $297
Similar to Model MAB P-15 except w/8-round magazine,

MODEL MAB P-15 AUTOMATIC PISTOL. . . . NiB $591 Ex $540 Gd $336
Caliber: 9mm Para. 15-round magazine, 4.5-inch bbl., 7.9 inches overall. Weight: 38 oz. Fixed sights, tapered post front and U-notched rear.

FROMMER PISTOLS — Budapest, Hungary
Mfd. by Fémáru-Fegyver-és Gépgyár R.T.

LILLIPUT POCKET AUTOMATIC PISTOL . . . . NiB $428 Ex $326 Gd $173
Caliber: .25 Automatic (6.35mm). Six-round magazine, 2.14-inch bbl., 4.33 inches overall. Weight: 10.13 oz. Fixed sights. Blued finish. Hard rubber grips. Made during early 1920s. Note: Although similar in appearance to the Stop and Baby, this pistol is blowback operated.

STOP POCKET AUTOMATIC PISTOL . . NiB $326 Ex $275 Gd $122
Locked-breech action, outside hammer. Calibers: .32 Automatic (7.65mm), .380 Auto (9mm short). Seven-round (.32 cal.) or 6-round (.380 cal.) magazine, 3.88-inch bbl., 6.5 inches overall. Weight: About 21 oz. Fixed sights. Blued finish. Hard rubber grips. Made 1912-20.

BABY POCKET AUTOMATIC PISTOL . . NiB $270 Ex $234 Gd $117
Similar to Stop model except has 2-inch bbl., 4.75 inches overall. Weight 17.5 oz. Magazine capacity is one round less than Stop Model. Intro. shortly after WW I.

Galena Industries Inc., — Sturgis, South Dakota

Galena Industries purchased the rights to use the AMT trademark in 1998. Many, but not all, original AMT designs were included in the transaction.

AMT BACKUP . . . . NiB $340 Ex $245 Gd $200
Caliber: .380 (small frame, 2.5-inch bbl. only), .38 Super, .357 Sig, .40 S&W, .400 CorBon, .45 ACP, 9mm; magazine capacity: 5 or 6 rounds. Double action, 3-inch bbl., weight: 18 oz. (in .380), or 23 oz.
.38 Super, .357 Sig, .400 CorBon. . . . . Add $50

AUTOMAG II SEMI AUTO . . . . NiB $468 Ex $339 Gd $262
Caliber: .22 WMR, 9-round magazine (except 7-round in 3.38-inch bbl.); 3.38- 4.5- or 6-inch bbls.; weight: About 32 oz.

AUTOMAG III . . . . NiB $571 Ex $442 Gd $339
Similar to Automag II except chambered for the .30 Carbine cartridge, 6.38-inch bbl., stainless steel finish, weight: About 43 oz.

AUTOMAG IV . . . . NiB $654 Ex $499 Gd $396
Caliber: .45 Winchester Magnum; 7-round magazine, 6.5-inch bbl., weight: 46 oz.

AUTOMAG .440 CORBON . . . . NiB $969 Ex $816 Gd $557
Semiautomatic, 7.5-inch bbl., 5-round magazine, checkered walnut grips, matte black finish, weight: 46 oz. Intro. 2000.

GALENA HARDBALLER. . . . . NiB $488 Ex $365 Gd $287
Based on the Colt Model 1911 frame. Caliber: .45 ACP, .40 S&W, .400 CorBon, 7-round magazine capacity, 5-inch bbl., weight: About 38 oz.

GALENA LONGSLIDE . . . . NiB $571 Ex $442 Gd $339
Similar to Hardballer model except caliber: .45 ACP, 7-inch bbl., 7-round magazine capacity, stainless steel finish, weight: About 46 ounces.

GALENA ACCELERATOR . . . . NiB $596 Ex $468 Gd $339
Similar to Hardballer model except caliber: .400 CorBon, 7-inch bbl., 7-round magazine capacity, stainless steel finish, weight: About 46 ounces.

GALENA COMMANDO . . . . NiB $468 Ex $339 Gd $262
Similar to Hardballer model except caliber: .40 S&W, 4-inch bbl., 8-round magazine capacity, stainless steel finish, weight: About 38 ounces.

GALESI PISTOLS — Collebeato (Brescia), Italy Mfd. by Industria Armi Galesi

MODEL 6
POCKET AUTOMATIC PISTOL . . . . . NiB $175 Ex $134 Gd $94
Calibers: .22 Long, .25 Automatic (6.35mm). Six-round magazine, 2.25-inch bbl., 4.38 inches overall. Weight: About 11 oz. Fixed sights. Blued finish. Plastic grips. Made from 1930 to date.

MODEL 9 POCKET
AUTOMATIC PISTOL
Calibers: .22 LR, .32 Auto (7.65mm), .380 Auto (9mm Short). Eight-round magazine, 3.25-inch bbl., 5.88 inches overall. Weight: About 21 oz. Fixed sights. Blued finish. Plastic grips. Made from 1930 to date.

Galesi
Model 6 Pocket

***(cont'd)* MODEL 9 POCKET**
AUTOMATIC PISTOL
Note: Specifications vary, but those shown for .32 Automatic are commom.
.22 LR or
.380 Auto. . . . . NiB $204 Ex $163 Gd $112
.32 Auto. . . . . NiB $173 Ex $153 Gd $102

GLISENTI PISTOL — Carcina (Brescia), Italy Mfd. by Societa Siderurgica Glisenti

MODEL 1910 ITALIAN
SERVICE AUTOMATIC. . . . . NiB $844 Ex $716 Gd $385
Caliber: 9mm Glisenti. Seven-round magazine, 4-inch bbl., 8.5 inches overall. Weight: About 32 oz. Fixed sights. Blued finish. Hard rubber or plastic grips. Adopted 1910 and used through WWII.

GLOCK, INC. — Smyrna, Georgia

NOTE: *Models: 17, 19, 20, 21, 22, 23, 24, 31, 32, 33, 34 and 35 were fitted with a redesigned grip-frame in 1998. Models: 26, 27, 29, 30 and all "C" guns (compensated models) retained the original frame design.*

MODEL 17 DA AUTOMATIC PISTOL
Caliber: 9mm Parabellum. 10-, 17- or 19-round magazine, 4.5-inch bbl., 7.2 inches overall. Weight: 22 oz. w/o magazine, Polymer frame, steel bbl., slide and springs. Fixed or adj. rear sights. Matte, nonglare finish. Made of only 35 components, including three internal safety devices. Imported 1983 to date.
Model 17 (w/fixed sights) . . . . NiB $535 Ex $463 Gd $285
Model 17C (compensated bbl.) . . . . NiB $693 Ex $586 Gd $310
W/adjustable sights, add $30
W/Meprolight sights, add $80
W/Trijicon sights, add $105

MODEL 17L COMPETITION
Same general specifications as Model 17 except weight: 23.35 oz. with 6-inch bbl. 8.85 inches overall. Imported 1988 to date. Imported1983 to date.
Model 1 L7 (w/fixed sights). . . . . . NiB $703 Ex $596 Gd $346
W/ported bbl., (early production), add $35
W/adjustable sights, add $30

Glock Model 19
Compact

Glock
Model 30

MODEL 19 COMPACT

Same general specifications as Model 17 except smaller version with 4-inch bbl., 6.85 inches overall and weight: 21 oz. Imported 1988 to date.

Model 19 (w/fixed sights) . . . . NiB $540 Ex $468 Gd $290
Model 19C (compensated bbl.). . . . . NiB $551 Ex $448 Gd $315
W/adjustable sights, add $30
W/Meprolight sights, add $80
W/Trijicon sights, add $105

MODEL 20 DA AUTO PISTOL

Caliber: 10mm. 15-round, hammerless, 4.6-inch bbl., 7.59 inches overall. Weight: 26.3 oz. Fixed or adj. sights. Matte, nonglare finish. Made from 1991 to date.

Model 20 (w/fixed sights) . . . . NiB $759 Ex $657 Gd $300
Model 19C (compensated bbl.) . . . . NiB $724 Ex $599 Gd $415
W/adjustable sights, add $30
W/Meprolight sights, add $80
W/Trijicon sights, add $105

MODEL 21 AUTOMATIC PISTOL

Same general specifications as Model 17 except chambered in .45 ACP. 13-round magazine, 7.59 inches overall. Weight: 25.2 oz. Imported 1991 to date.

Model 21 (w/fixed sights) . . . . NiB $660 Ex $535 Gd $346
Model 21C (compensated bbl.) . . . . NiB $713 Ex $579 Gd $405
W/adjustable sights, add $30
W/Meprolight sights, add $80
W/Trijicon sights, add $105

MODEL .22 AUTOMATIC PISTOL

Same general specifications as Model 17 except chambered for .40 S&W. 15-round magazine, 7.4 inches overall. Imported 1992 to date.

Model .22 (w/fixed sights). . . . . NiB $684 Ex $535 Gd $331
Model 22C
(compensated bbl.) . . . . NiB $633 Ex $512 Gd $357
W/adjustable sights, add $30
W/Meprolight sights, add $80
W/Trijicon sights, add $105

MODEL 23 AUTOMATIC PISTOL

Same general specifications as Model 19 except chambered for .40 S&W. 13-round magazine, 6.97 inches overall. Imported 1992 to date.

Model 23 (w/fixed sights) . . . . NiB $549 Ex $477 Gd $324
Model 23C (compensated bbl.) . . . . NiB $586 Ex $477 Gd $339
W/adjustable sights, add $30
W/Meprolight sights, add $80
W/Trijicon sights, add $105

MODEL 24 AUTOMATIC PISTOL

Caliber: .40 S&W, 10- and 15-round magazines (the latter for law enforcement and military use only), 8.85 inches overall. Weight: 26.5 oz. Manual trigger safety; passive firing block and drop safety. Made 1995 to date.

Model 24 (w/fixed sights) . . . . NiB $718 Ex $575 Gd $346
Model 24C (compensated bbl.) . . . . NiB $706 Ex $572 Gd $402
W/adjustable sights, add $30

MODEL 26 DA AUTOMATIC PISTOL

Caliber: 9mm, 10-round magazine, 3.47-inch bbl., 6.3 inches overall. Weight: 19.77 oz. Imported 1995 to date.

Model 26 (w/fixed sights) . . . . NiB $505 Ex $473 Gd $346
Model 26C (compensated bbl.) . . . . NiB $589 Ex $479 Gd $338
W/adjustable sights, add $30

MODEL 27 DA AUTO PISTOL

Similar to the Glock Model .22 except subcompact. Caliber: .40 S&W, 10-round magazine, 3.5-inch bbl., Weight: 21.7 oz. Polymer stocks, fixed or fully adjustable sights. Imported 1995 to date.

Model 27 (w/fixed sights) . . . . NiB $533 Ex $461 Gd $334
W/adjustable sights, add $30
W/Meprolight sights, add $80
W/Trijicon sights, add $105

MODEL 28 COMPACT (LAW ENFORCEMENT ONLY)

Same general specifications as Model .25 except smaller version. .380 ACP with 3.5-inch bbl., weight: 20 oz. Imported 1999 to date.

MODEL 29 DA AUTO PISTOL

Similar to the Glock Model 20 except subcompact. Caliber: 10mm. 10-round magazine, 3.8-inch bbl., weight: 27.1 oz. Polymer stocks, fixed or fully adjustable sights. Imported 1997 to date.

Model 29 (w/fixed sights) . . . . NiB $637 Ex $540 Gd $346
W/adjustable sights, add $30
W/Meprolight sights, add $80
W/Trijicon sights, add $100

MODEL 30 DA AUTO PISTOL

Similar to the Glock Model 21 except subcompact. Caliber: .45 ACP. 10-round magazine, 3.8-inch bbl., weight: 26.5 oz. Polymer stocks, fixed or fully adjustable sights. Imported 1997 to date.

Model 27 (w/fixed sights) . . . . NiB $637 Ex $540 Gd $346
W/adjustable sights, add $30
W/Meprolight sights, add $80
W/Trijicon sights, add $105

MODEL 31 DA AUTOMATIC PISTOL
Caliber: .357 Sig., safe action system. 10- 15- or 17-round magazine, 4.49-inch bbl., weight: 23.28 oz. Safe Action trigger system w/3 safeties. Imported 1998 to date.

Model 31
(w/fixed sights) . . . . NiB $526 Ex $454 Gd $327
Model 31C
(compensated bbl.) . . . . NiB $585 Ex $479 Gd $343
W/adjustable sights, add $30
W/Meprolight sights, add $80
W/Trijicon sights, add $105

MODEL .32 DA AUTOMATIC PISTOL
Caliber: .357 Sig., safe action system. 10- 13- or 15-round magazine, 4.02-inch bbl., weight: 21.52 oz. Imported 1998 to date.

Model .32
(w/fixed sights) . . . . NiB $523 Ex $451 Gd $324
Model 32C. . . . . NiB $541 Ex $436 Gd $303
W/adjustable sights, add $30
W/Meprolight sights, add $80
W/Trijicon Sights, add $105

MODEL 33 DA AUTOMATIC PISTOL
Caliber: .357 Sig., safe action system. Nine- or 11-round magazine, 3.46-inch bbl. Weight: 19.75 oz. Imported 1998 to date.

Model 33
(w/fixed sights) . . . . NiB $525 Ex $453 Gd $326
W/adjustable sights, add $30
W/Meprolight sights, add $80
W/Trijicon sights, add $105

MODEL 34 AUTO PISTOL. . . . . . . NiB $704 Ex $602 Gd $367
Similar to Model 17 except w/redesigned grip-frame and extended slide-stop lever and magazine release. 10-, 17- or 19-round magazine, 5.32- inch bbl. Weight: 22.9 oz. Fixed or adjustable sights. Imported 1998 to date.

MODEL 35 AUTO PISTOL. . . . . . . NiB $704 Ex $633 Gd $367
Similar to Model 34 except .40 S&W. Imported 1998 to date.

MODEL 36 DA AUTOMATIC PISTOL
Caliber: .45 ACP., safe action system. Six-round magazine, 3.78-inch bbl., weight: 20.11 oz. Safe Action trigger system w/3 safeties. Imported 1999 to date.

Model 36
(w/fixed sights) . . . . NiB $633 Ex $536 Gd $342
W/adjustable sights, add $30
W/Meprolight sights, add $80
W/Trijicon sights, add $105

DESERT STORM
COMMEMORATIVE. . . . . NiB $1062 Ex $888 Gd $557
Same specifications as Model 17 except "Operation Desert Storm, January 16-February 27, 1991" engraved on side of slide w/list of coalition forces. Limited issue of 1,000 guns. Made in 1991.

GREAT WESTERN ARMS CO. — North Hollywood, California

NOTE: *Values shown are for improved late model revolvers early Great Westerns are variable in quality and should be evaluated accordingly. It should also be noted that, beginning about July 1956, these revolvers were offered in kit form. Values of guns assembled from these kits will, in general, be of less value than factory-completed weapons.*

Grendel Model P-12

DOUBLE BARREL DERRINGER . . . . NiB $322 Ex $296 Gd $169
Replica of Remington Double Derringer. Caliber: .38 S&W. Double bbls. (superposed), 3-inch bbl. Overall length: 5 inches. Fixed sights. Blued finish. Checkered black plastic grips. Made 1953-62.

SA FRONTIER REVOLVER . . . . NiB $526 Ex $475 Gd $271
Replica of the Colt Single Action Army Revolver. Calibers: .22 LR, .357 Magnum, .38 Special, .44 Special, .44 Magnum .45 Colt. Six-round cylinder, bbl. lengths: 4.75-, 5.5 and 7.5-inches. Weight: 40 oz. in .22 cal. w/5.5-inch bbl. Overall length: 11.13 inches w/5.5-inch bbl. Fixed sights. Blued finish. Imitation stag grips. Made 1951-1962.

GRENDEL, INC. — Rockledge, Florida

MODEL P-10 AUTOMATIC PISTOL
Hammerless, blow-back action. DAO with no external safety. Caliber: .380 ACP. 10-round box magazine integrated in grip. Three-inch bbl., 5.3 inches overall. Weight: 15 oz. Matte blue, nickel or green Teflon finish. Made 1988-91.

Blued finish . . . . NiB $151 Ex $135 Gd $895
Nickel finish . . . . NiB $192 Ex $161 Gd $117
Teflon finish. . . . . NiB $202 Ex $166 Gd $120
W/compensated bbl., add $45

MODEL P-12 DA AUTOMATIC PISTOL
Caliber: .380 ACP. 11-round Zytel magazine, 3-inch bbl., 5.3 inches overall. Weight: 13 oz. Fixed sights. Polymer DuPont ST-800 grip. Made 1991-95.

Standard model . . . . NiB $166 Ex $141 Gd $95
Electroless nickel . . . . NiB $213 Ex $176 Gd $129

MODEL P-30 AUTOMATIC PISTOL
Caliber: .22 WMR. 30-round magazine, 5-or 8-inch bbl., 8.5 inches overall w/5-inch bbl., weight: 21 oz. Blade front sight, fixed rear sight. Made 1991-95.

W/5-inch bbl., ... NiB $256 Ex $215 Gd $189
W/8-inch bbl., ... NiB $256 Ex $215 Gd $189

MODEL P-31
AUTOMATIC PISTOL . . . . NiB $368 Ex $332 Gd $205
Caliber: .22 WMR. 30-round Zytel magazine, 11-inch bbl., 17.3 inches overall. Weight: 48 oz. Adj. blade front sight, fixed rear. Checkered black polymer DuPont ST-800 grip and forend. Made 1991-95.

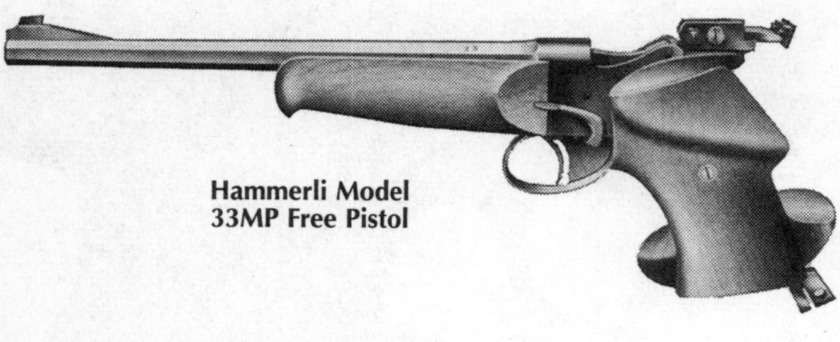

Hammerli Model 33MP Free Pistol

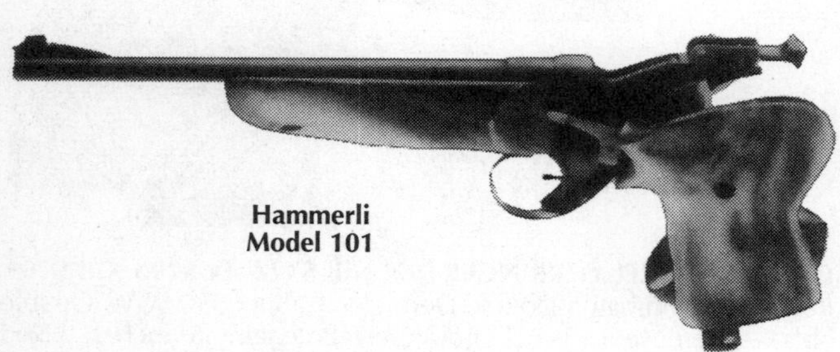

Hammerli Model 101

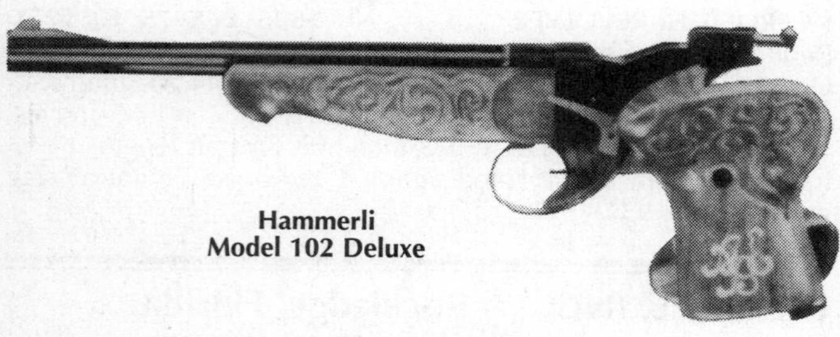

Hammerli Model 102 Deluxe

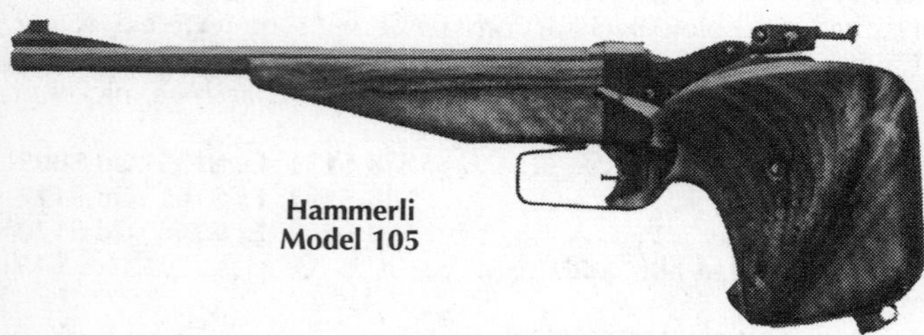

Hammerli Model 105

GUNSITE — Paulden, Arizona

"ADVANCED TACTICAL" SA AUTO PISTOL
Manufactured w/Colt 1991 or Springfield 1991 parts. Caliber: .45 ACP. Eight-round magazine, 3.5-, 4.25-, 5-inch bbl. Weight: 32-38 oz. Checkered or laser-engraved walnut grips. Fixed or Novak Lo-mount sights.
Stainless finish . . . . NiB $1054 Ex $851 Gd $592
Blued finish . . . . NiB $926 Ex $749 Gd $522

"CUSTOM CARRY" SA AUTO PISTOL
Caliber: .45 ACP. Eight-round magazine, 3.5-, 4.25-, 5-inch bbl., Weight: 32-38 oz. Checkered or laser-engraved walnut grips. Fixed Novak Lo-mount sights. Single action, manufactured based on enhanced colt models.
Stainless finish . . . . NiB $1092 Ex $891 Gd $612
Blued finish . . . . NiB $1054 Ex $851 Gd $592

H&R 1871, INC. — Gardner, Massachusetts

NOTE: *In 1991, H&R 1871, Inc. was formed from the residual of the parent company, Harrington & Richardson, and then took over the New England Firearms facility. H&R 1871 produced firearms under both their logo and the NEF brand name until 1999, when the Marlin Firearms Company acquired the assets of H&R 1871. See listings under Harrington & Richardson, Inc.*

HÄMMERLI AG JAGD-UND SPORTWAFFE FABRIK — Lenzburg, Switzerland

Currently imported by Sigarms, Inc., Exeter, NH. Previously by Hammerli, USA; Beeman Precision Arms & Mandall Shooting Supplies.

MODEL 33MP FREE PISTOL . . . . . . NiB $986 Ex $780 Gd $496
System Martini single-shot action, set trigger. Caliber: .22 LR. 11.5-inch octagon bbl., 16.5 inches overall. Weight: 46 oz. Micrometer rear sight, interchangeable front sights. Blued finish. Walnut grips, forearm. Imported 1933-49.

MODEL 100 FREE PISTOL
Same general specifications as Model 33MP. Improved action and sights, redesigned stock. Standard model has plain grips and forearm, deluxe model has carved grips and forearm. Imported 1950-56.
Standard model . . . . NiB $844 Ex $700 Gd $483
Deluxe model . . . . NiB $1040 Ex $813 Gd $535

MODEL 101 . . . . NiB $926 Ex $710 Gd $535
Similar to Model 100 except has heavy round bbl. w/matte finish, improved action and sights, adj. grips. Weight: About 49 oz. Imported 1956-60.

MODEL 102
Same as Model 101 except bbl., has highly polished blued finish. Deluxe model (illustrated) has carved grips and forearm. Made 1956-60.
Standard model . . . . NiB $926 Ex $700 Gd $535
Deluxe model . . . . NiB $1040 Ex $813 Gd $535

MODEL 103 . . . . NiB $975 Ex $815 Gd $470
Same as Model 101 except has lighter octagon bbl. (as in Model 100) w/highly polished blued finish, grips and forearm of select French walnut. Weight: About 46 oz. Imported 1956-60.

MODEL 104 . . . . NiB $803 Ex $700 Gd $380
Similar to Model 102 except has lighter round bbl., improved action redesigned grips and forearm. Weight: 46 oz. Imported 1961-65.

MODEL 105 . . . . NiB $983 Ex $756 Gd $432
Similar to Model 103 except has improved action, redesigned grips and forearm. Imported 1961-65.

MODEL 106 . . . . NiB $957 Ex $731 Gd $411
Similar to Model 104 except has improved trigger and grips. Made 1966-71.

MODEL 107
Similar to Model 105 except has improved trigger and stock. Deluxe model (illustrated) has engraved receiver and bbl., carved grips and forearm. Imported 1966-71.
Standard model . . . . NiB $1040 Ex $813 Gd $411
Deluxe model . . . . NiB $1380 Ex $1040 Gd $483

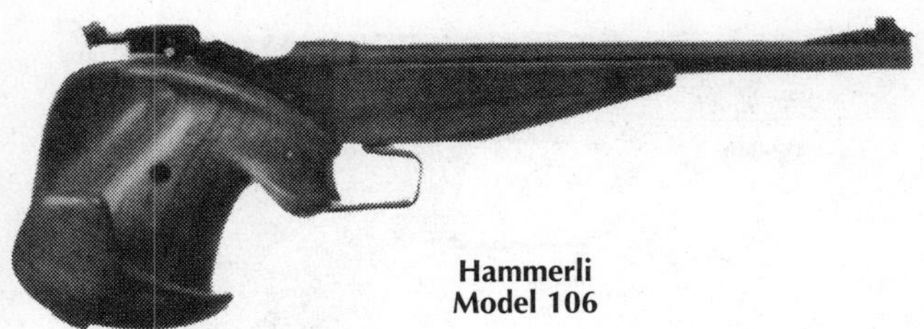
Hammerli
Model 106

Hammerli
Model 107 Deluxe

MODEL 120 HEAVY BARREL
Same as Models 120-1 and 120-2 except has 5.7-inch heavy bbl., weight: 41 oz. Available w/standard or adj. grips. Imported 1972 to date.
W/standard grips. . . . . NiB $638 Ex $576 Gd $329
W/adj. grips. . . . . NiB $689 Ex $535 Gd $329

MODEL 120-1 SINGLE-SHOT FREE PISTOL. . . . . NiB $638 Ex $576 Gd $329
Side lever-operated bolt action. Adj. single-stage or two-stage trigger. Caliber: .22 LR, 9.9-inch bbl., 14.75 inches overall. Weight: 44 oz. Micrometer rear sight, front sight on high ramp. Blued finish bbl., and receiver, lever and grip frame anodized aluminum. Checkered walnut thumbrest grips. Imported 1972 to date.

MODEL 120-2. . . . . NiB $638 Ex $576 Gd $329
Same as Model 120-1 except has hand-contoured grips w/adj. palm rest (available for right or left hand). Imported 1972 to date.

MODELS 150/151 FREE PISTOLS
Improved Martini-type action w/lateral-action cocking lever. Set trigger adj. for weight, length and angle of pull. Caliber: .22 LR, 11.3-inch round free-floating bbl., 15.4 inches overall. Weight: 43 oz. (w/extra weights, 49.5 oz.). Micrometer rear sight, front sight on high ramp. Blued finish. Select walnut forearm and grips w/adj. palm shelf. Imported 1972-93.
Model 150 (disc. 1989) . . . . NiB $1945 Ex $1580 Gd $915
Model 151 (disc. 1993) . . . . NiB $1945 Ex $1580 Gd $915

MODEL 152 ELECTRONIC PISTOL
Same general specifications as Model 150 except w/electronic trigger. Made 1990-92
Right hand . . . . NiB $2095 Ex $1688 Gd $1060
Left hand. . . . . NiB $1966 Ex $1592 Gd $1114

MODELS 160/162 FREE PISTOLS
Caliber: .22 LR. Single-shot. 11.31-inch bbl., 17.5 inches overall. Weight: 46.9 oz. Interchangeable front sight blades, fully adj. match rear. Match-style stippled walnut grips w/adj. palm shelf and polycarbon fiber forend. Imported 1993 to date.
Model 160 w/mechanical Set trigger . . . . NiB $1745 Ex $1559 Gd $864
Model 162 w/ electronic trigger . . . . NiB $1874 Ex $1508 Gd $1038

MODEL 208 STANDARD AUTO PISTOL. . . . . NiB $1688 Ex $1379 Gd $864
Caliber: .22 LR. Eight-round magazine, 5.9-inch bbl., 10 inches overall. Weight: 35 oz. (bbl. weight adds 3 oz.). Micrometer rear sight, ramp front. Blued finish. Checkered walnut grips w/adj. heel plate. Imported 1966-88.

MODEL 208S TARGET PISTOL . . . . . NiB $1842 Ex $1379 Gd $735
Caliber: .22 LR. Eight-round magazine, 6-inch bbl., 10.2 inches overall. Weight: 37.3 oz. Micrometer rear sight, ramp front sight. Blued finish. Stippled walnut grips w/adj. heel plate. Imported 1990 to date.

MODEL 211 . . . . NiB $1636 Ex $1353 Gd $751
Same as Model 208 except has standard thumbrest grips. Imported 1966-91.

Hammerli
Model 120 Heavy Barrel

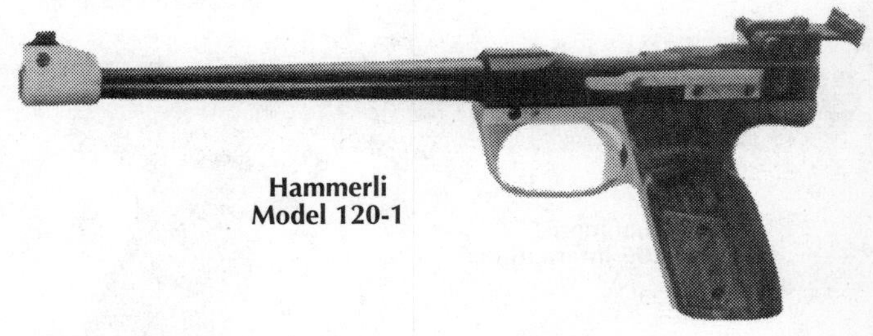
Hammerli
Model 120-1

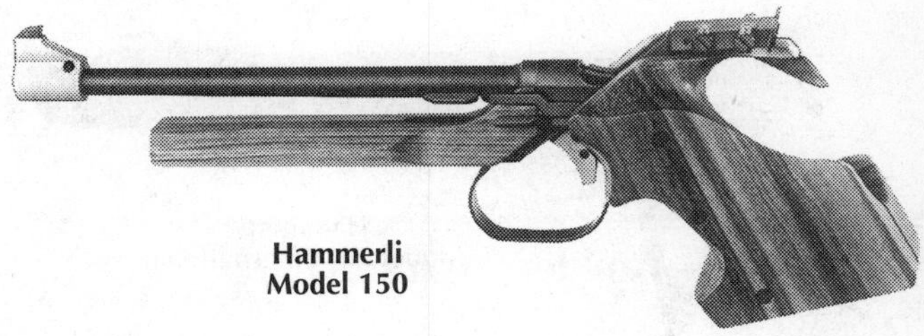
Hammerli
Model 150

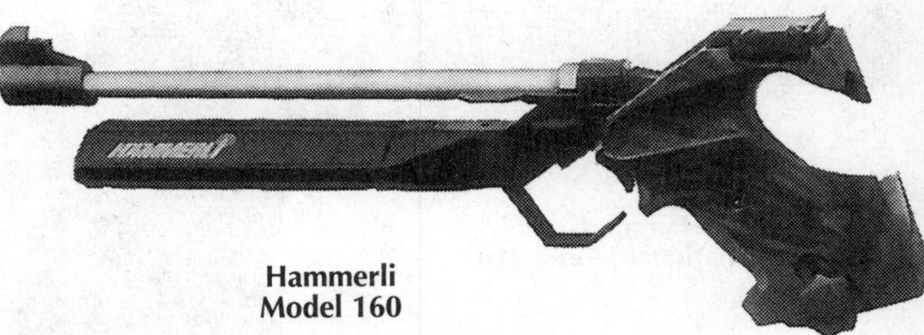

Hammerli
Model 160

Hammerli
Model 208

Hammerli
Model 232 Rapid Fire

Hammerli
Model 215

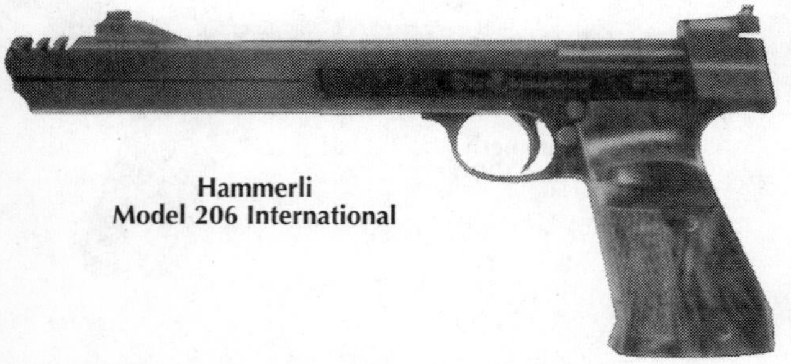

Hammerli
Model 206 International

Hammerli
Model 207 International

Hammerli
International Model 210

MODEL 212
HUNTER'S PISTOL .... NiB $1327 Ex $1152 Gd $709
Caliber: .22 LR, 4.88-inch bbl., 8.5 inches overall. Weight: 31 oz. Blade front sight, square-notched fully adj. rear. Blued finish. Checkered walnut grips. Imported 1984-93.

MODEL 215 .... NiB $1477 Ex $1121 Gd $622
Similar to the Model 208 except w/heavier bbl. and fewer deluxe features. Imported 1990-93.

MODEL 230-1 RAPID
FIRE AUTO PISTOL........... NiB $1477 Ex $1199 Gd $709
Caliber: .22 Short. Five-round magazine, 6.3-inch bbl., 11.6 inches overall. Weight: 44 oz. Micrometer rear sight, post front. Blued finish. Smooth walnut thumbrest grips. Imported 1970-83.

MODEL 230-2................. NiB $781 Ex $699 Gd $689
Same as Model 230-1 except has checkered walnut grips w/adj. heel plate. Imported 1970-83.

MODEL 232 RAPID FIRE
AUTO PISTOL............... NiB $1461 Ex $1183 Gd $693
Caliber: .22 Short. Six-round magazine, 5.1-inch ported bbl., 10.5 inches overall. Weight: 44 oz. Fully adj. target sights. Blued finish. Stippled walnut wraparound target grips. Imported 1984-93.

INTERNATIONAL MODEL
206 AUTO PISTOL.............. NiB $715 Ex $664 Gd $360
Calibers: .22 Short, .22 LR. Six-round (.22 Short) or 8-round (.22 LR) magazine, 7.1-inch bbl. w/muzzle brake, 12.5 inches overall. Weight: 33 oz. (.22 Short), 39 oz. (.22 LR) (supplementary weights add 5 and 8 oz.). Micrometer rear sight, ramp front. Blued finish. Standard thumbrest grips. Imported 1962-69.

INTERNATIONAL
MODEL 207 .... NiB $767 Ex $689 Gd $406
Same as Model 206 except has grips w/adj. heel plate, weight: 2 oz. more. Made 1962-69.

INTERNATIONAL
MODEL 209
AUTO PISTOL................. NiB $844 Ex $751 Gd $520
Caliber: .22 Short. Five-round mag., 4.75-inch bbl., w/muzzle brake and gas-escape holes, 11 inches overall. Weight: 39 oz. (interchangeable front weight adds 4 oz.). Micrometer rear sight, post front. Blued finish. Standard thumbrest grips of checkered walnut. Imported 1966-70.

INTERNATIONAL
MODEL 210 .... NiB $844 Ex $756 Gd $561
Same as Model 209 except has grips w/adj. heel plate, is 0.8-inch longer and weight: 1 ounce more. Made 1966-70.

MODEL 280 TARGET PISTOL
Carbon-reinforced synthetic frame and bbl., housing. Calibers: .22 LR, .32 S&W Long WC. Six-round (.22 LR) or 5-round (.32 S&W) magazine, 4.5-inch bbl. w/interchangeable metal or carbon fiber counterweights. 11.88 inches overall. Weight: 39 oz. Micro-adj. match sights w/interchangeable elements. Imported 1988 to date.
.22 LR . . . . NiB $1537 Ex $1203 Gd $536
.32 S&W Long WC . . . . NiB $1696 Ex $1388 Gd $995
.22/.32 Conversion kit, add $800

VIRGINIAN SA REVOLVER . . . . NiB $571 Ex $535 Gd $287
Similar to Colt Single-Action Army except has base pin safety system (SWISSAFE). Calibers: .357 Magnum, .45 Colt. Six-round cylinder. 4.63-, 5.5- or 7.5-inch bbl., 11 inches overall (with 5.5-inch bbl.). Weight: 40 oz. (with 5.5-inch bbl.). Fixed sights. Blued bbl. and cylinder, casehardened frame, chrome-plated grip frame and trigger guard. One-piece smooth walnut stock. Imported 1973-76 by Interarms, Alexandria, Va.

WALTHER OLYMPIA MODEL 200 AUTOMATIC PISTOL, 1952-TYPE. . . . NiB $710 Ex $653 Gd $427
Similar to 1936 Walther Olympia Funfkampf model. Calibers: .22 Short, .22 LR. Six-round (.22 Short) or 10-round (.22 LR) magazine, 7.5-inch bbl., 10.7 inches overall. Weight: 27.7 oz. (.22 Short, light alloy breechblock), 30.3 oz. (.22 LR). Supplementary weights provided. Adj. target sights. Blued finish. Checkered walnut thumbrest grips. Imported 1952-58.

WALTHER OLYMPIA MODEL 200,1958-TYPE . . . NiB $766 Ex $653 Gd $457
Same as Model 200 1952 type except has muzzle brake, 8-round magazine (.22 LR). 11.6 inches overall. Weight: 30 oz. (.22 Short), 33 oz. (.22 LR). Imported 1958-63.

WALTHER OLYMPIA MODEL 201 . . . . NiB $710 Ex $653 Gd $427
Same as Model 200,1952 Type except has 9.5-inch bbl. Imported 1955-57.

WALTHER OLYMPIA MODEL 202 . . . . NiB $766 Ex $653 Gd $493
Same as Model 201 except has grips w/adj. heel plate. Imported 1955-57.

WALTHER OLYMPIA MODEL 203
Same as corresponding Model 200 (1955 type lacks muzzle brake) except has grips w/adj. heel plate. Imported1955-63.
1955 type . . . . NiB $766 Ex $653 Gd $493
1958 type . . . . NiB $823 Ex $710 Gd $514

WALTHER OLYMPIA MODEL 204
American model. Same as corresponding Model 200 (1956-Type lacks muzzle brake) except in .22 LR only, has slide stop and micrometer rear sight. Imported 1956-63.
1956-type . . . . NiB $797 Ex $684 Gd $535
1958-type . . . . NiB $854 Ex $741 Gd $540

WALTHER OLYMPIA MODEL 205
American model. Same as Model 204 except has grips w/adj. heel plate. Imported 1956-63.
1956-type . . . . NiB $854 Ex $741 Gd $540
1958-type . . . . NiB $911 Ex $797 Gd $571

Hammerli-Walther Olympia Model 203 1958-Type

Hammerli-Walther Olympia Model 205

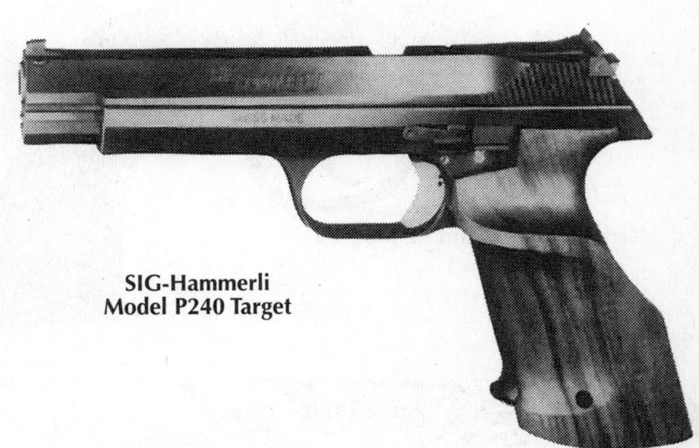
SIG-Hammerli Model P240 Target

MODEL P240 TARGET AUTO PISTOL
Calibers: .32 S&W Long (wadcutter), .38 Special (wadcutter). Five-round magazine, 5.9-inch bbl., 10 inches overall. Weight: 41 oz. Micrometer rear sight, post front. Blued finish/smooth walnut thumbrest grips. Accessory .22 LR conversion unit available. Imported 1975-86.
.32 S&W Long . . . . NiB $1559 Ex $1302 Gd $7061
.38 Special. . . . . NiB $2223 Ex $1786 Gd $1228
.22 LR conversion unit, add . . . . NiB $606 Ex $550 Gd $380

Harrington & Richardson SL .32

Harrington & Richardson USRA Model Single-Shot Target Pistol

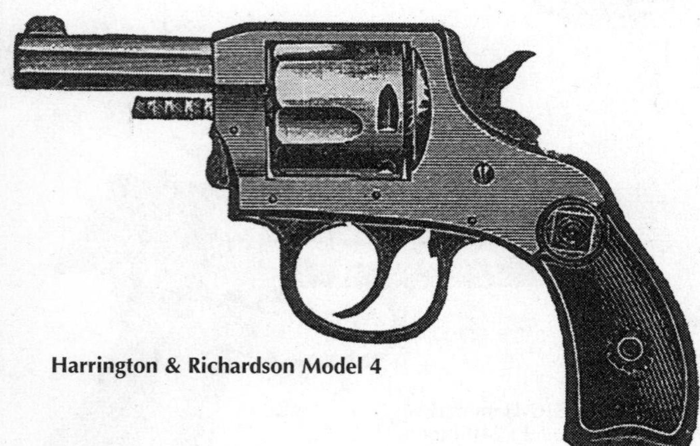
Harrington & Richardson Model 4

Harrington & Richardson Model 5

HARRINGTON & RICHARDSON, INC. — Gardner, Massachusetts Now H&R 1871, Inc., Gardner, Mass.

Formerly Harrington & Richardson Arms Co. of Worcester, Mass. One of the oldest and most distinguished manufacturers of handguns, rifles and shotguns, H&R suspended operations on January 24,1986. In 1987, New England Firearms was established as an independent company producing selected H&R models under the NEF logo. In 1991, H&R 1871, Inc., was formed from the residual of the parent company and then took over the New England Firearms facility. H&R 1871 produced firearms under both its logo and the NEF brand name until 1999, when the Marlin Firearms Company acquired the assets of H&R 1871.

NOTE: *For ease in finding a particular firearm, H&R handguns are grouped into Automatic/Single-Shot Pistols, followed by Revolvers. For a complete listing, please refer to the index.*

AUTOMATIC/SINGLE-SHOT PISTOLS

SL .25 PISTOL . . . . NiB $402 Ex $357 Gd $188
Modified Webley & Scott design. Caliber: .25 Auto. Six-round magazine, 2-inch bbl., 4.5 inches overall. Weight: 12 oz. Fixed sights. Blued finish. Black hard rubber grips. Made 1912-16.

SL .32 PISTOL . . . . NiB $357 Ex $341 Gd $173
Modified Webley & Scott design. Caliber: .32 Auto. Eight-round magazine, 3.5-inch bbl., 6.5 inches overall. Weight: About 20 oz. Fixed sights. Blued finish. Black hard rubber grips. Made 1916-24.

USRA MODEL SINGLE-
SHOT TARGET PISTOL . . . . NiB $479 Ex $453 Gd $249
Hinged frame. Caliber: .22 LR, bbl. lengths: 7-, 8- and 10-inch. Weight: 31 oz. w/10-inch bbl., Adj. target sights. Blued finish. Checkered walnut grips. Made 1928-41.

REVOLVERS

MODEL 4
(1904) DA . . . . NiB $107 Ex $97 Gd $46
Solid frame. Calibers: .32 S&W Long, .38 S&W. Six-round cylinder (.32 cal.), or 5-round (.38 cal.), bbl. Lengths: 2.5-, 4.5- and 6-inch. Weight: About 16 oz. (in .32 cal.) Fixed sights. Blued or nickel finish. Hard rubber grips. Disc. prior to 1942.

MODEL 5 (1905) DA. . . . . NiB $107 Ex $97 Gd $51
Solid frame. Caliber: .32 S&W. Five-round cylinder, bbl., lengths: 2.5-,4.5- and 6-inch. Weight: About 11 oz. Fixed sights. Blued or nickel finish. Hard rubber grips. Disc. prior to 1942.

MODEL 6 (1906) DA. . . . . NiB $107 Ex $97 Gd $51
Solid frame. Caliber: .22 LR. Seven-round cylinder, bbl. lengths: 2.5, 4.5- and 6-inches. Weight: About 10 oz. Fixed sights. Blued or nickel finish. Hard rubber grips. Disc. prior to 1942.

.22 SPECIAL DA. . . . . NiB $178 Ex $153 Gd $81
Heavy hinged frame. Calibers: .22 LR, .22 Mag. Nine-round cylinder, 6-inch bbl., weight: 23 oz. Fixed sights, front gold-plated. Blued finish. Checkered walnut grips. Recessed safety cylinder on later models for high-speed ammunition. Disc. prior to 1942.

MODEL 199 SPORTSMAN SA REVOLVER . . . . NiB $296 Ex $256 Gd $128
Hinged frame. Caliber: .22 LR. Nine-round cylinder, 6-inch bbl., 11 inches overall. Weight: 30 oz. Adj. target sights. Blued finish. Checkered walnut grips. Disc. 1951.

MODEL 504 DA . . . . NiB $177 Ex $157 Gd $111
Caliber: .32 H&R Magnum. Five-round cylinder, 4- or 6-inch bbl., (square butt), 3- or 4-inch bbl., round butt. Made 1984-86.

MODEL 532 DA . . . . NiB $109 Ex $99 Gd $58
Caliber: .32 H&R Magnum. Five-round cylinder, 2.5- or 4-inch bbl., weight: Approx. 20 and 25 oz. respectively. Fixed sights. American walnut grips. Lustre blued finish. Made 1984-86.

MODEL 586 DA . . . . NiB $187 Ex $167 Gd $111
Caliber: .32 H&R Magnum. Five-round cylinder. bbl. lengths: 4.5, 5.5, 7.5, 10 inches. Weight: 30 oz. average. Adj. rear sight, blade front. Walnut finished hardwood grips. Made 1984-86.

MODEL 603 TARGET. . . . . NiB $177 Ex $131 Gd $91
Similar to Model 903 except in .22 WMR. Six-round capacity w/unfluted cylinder. Made 1980-83.

MODEL 604 TARGET. . . . . NiB $182 Ex $142 Gd $91
Similar to Model 603 except w/6-inch bull bbl., weight: 38 oz. Made 1980-83.

MODEL 622/623 DA. . . . . NiB $126 Ex $106 Gd $60
Solid frame. Caliber: .22 Short, Long, LR, 6-round cylinder. bbl., lengths: 2.5-, 4-, 6-inches. Weight: 26 oz. (with 4-inch bbl.). Fixed sights. Blued finish. Plastic grips. Made 1957-86. Note: Model 623 is same except chrome or nickel finish.

MODEL 632/633 GUARDSMAN DA REVOLVER . . . . . NiB $115 Ex $91 Gd $55
Solid Frame. Caliber: .32 S&W Long. Six-round cylinder, bbl., lengths: 2.5- or 4-inch. Weight: 19 oz. (with 2.5-inch bbl.). Fixed sights. Blued or chrome finish. Checkered Tenite grips (round butt on 2.5-inch, square butt on 4-inch). Made 1953-86. Note: Model 633 is the same except for chrome or nickel finish.

MODEL 649/650 DA. . . . . NiB $152 Ex $131 Gd $71
Solid frame. Side loading and ejection. Convertible model w/two 6-round cylinders. Calibers: .22 LR, .22 WMR. 5.5-inch bbl., Weight: 32 oz. Adj. rear sight, blade front. Blued finish. One-piece, Western-style walnut grip. Made 1976-86. Note: Model 650 is same except nickel finish.

MODEL 666 DA . . . . NiB $111 Ex $81 Gd $45
Solid frame. Convertible model w/two 6-round cylinders. Calibers: .22 LR, .22 WMR. Six-inch bbl., weight: 28 oz. Fixed sights. Blued finish. Plastic grips. Made 1976-78.

MODEL 676 DA . . . . NiB $152 Ex $131 Gd $55
Solid frame. Side loading and ejection. Convertible model w/two 6-round cylinders. Calibers: .22 LR, .22 WMR, bbl. lengths: 4.5-, 5.5-, 7.5-, 12-inches. Weight: 32 oz. (with 5.5-inch bbl.). Adj. rear sight, blade front. Blued finish, color-casehardened frame. One-piece, Western-style walnut grip. Made 1976-1980.

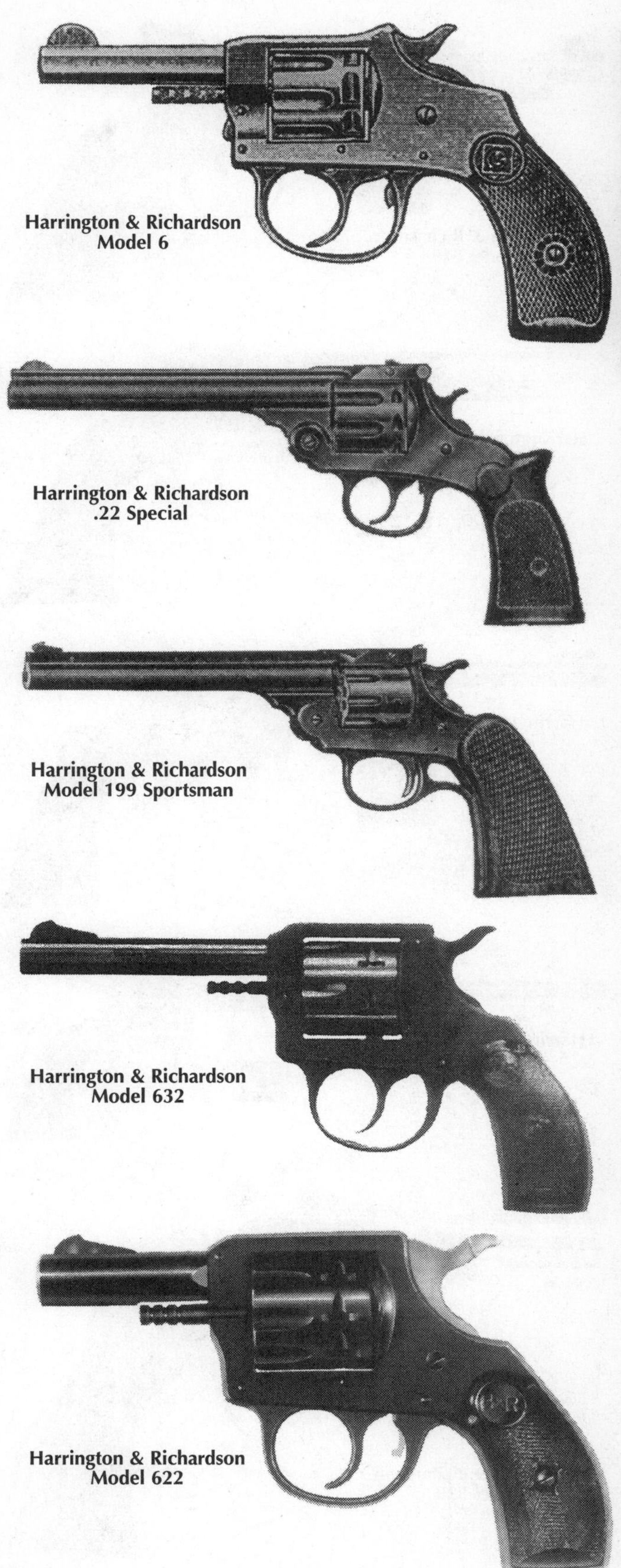

Harrington & Richardson Model 6

Harrington & Richardson .22 Special

Harrington & Richardson Model 199 Sportsman

Harrington & Richardson Model 632

Harrington & Richardson Model 622

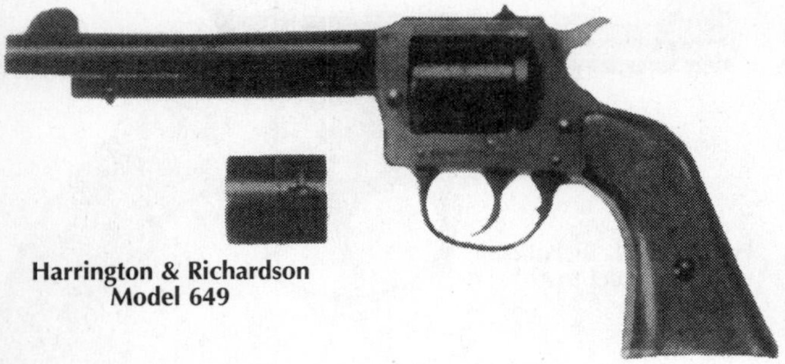

Harrington & Richardson Model 649

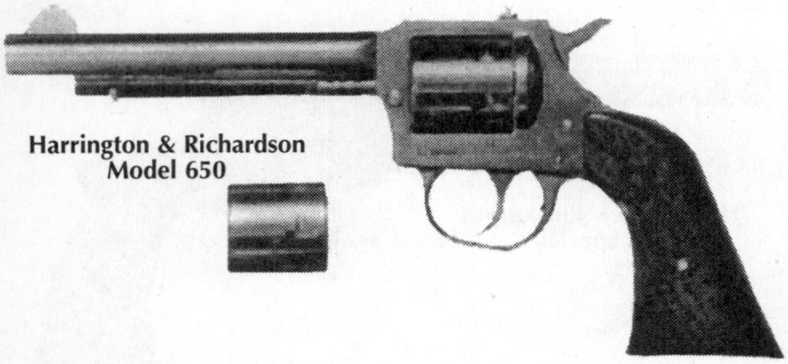

Harrington & Richardson Model 686

Harrington & Richardson Model 830

Harrington & Richardson Model 650

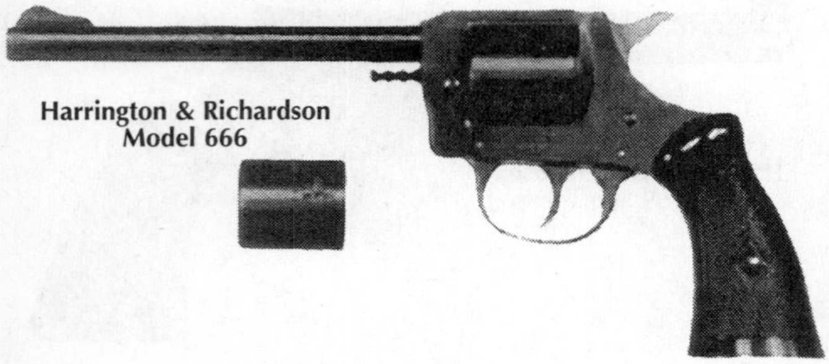

Harrington & Richardson Model 666

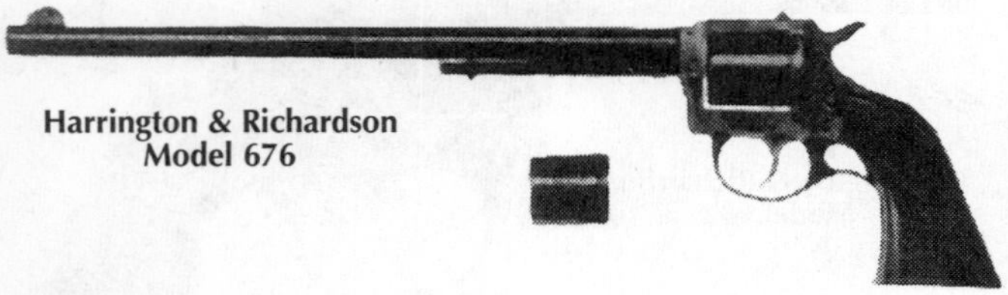

Harrington & Richardson Model 676

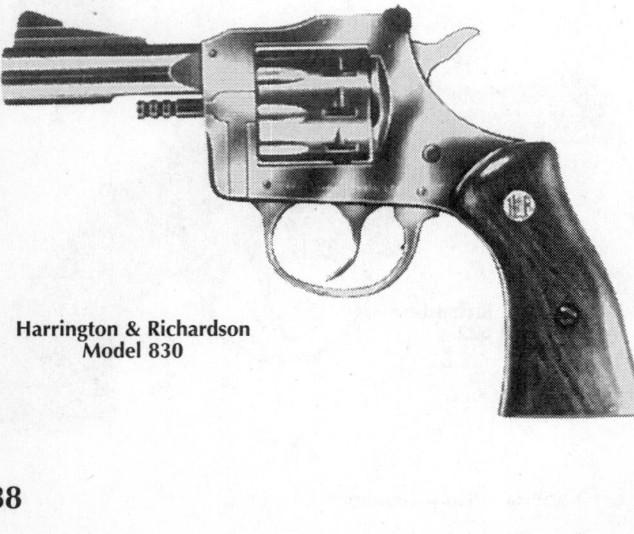

Harrington & Richardson Model 830

MODEL 686 DA . . . . NiB $196 Ex $173 Gd $99
Caliber: .22 LR and .22 WMR. Six-round magazine, 4.5-, 5.5-, 7.5-, 10- or 12-inch bbl. Adj. rear sight, ramp and blade front. Blued, color-casehardened frame. Weight: 31 oz. (with 4.5-inch bbl.). Made 1980-86.

MODEL 732/733 DA. . . . . NiB $137 Ex $109 Gd $63
Solid frame, swing-out 6-round cylinder. Calibers: .32 S&W, .32 S&W Long. bbl., lengths: 2.5-, 4-inch. Weight: 26 oz. (with 4-inch bbl.). Fixed sights (windage adj. rear on 4-inch bbl. model). Blued finish. Plastic grips. Made 1958-86. Note: Model 733 is the same except with nickel finish.

MODEL 826 DA . . . . NiB $140 Ex $114 Gd $68
Caliber: .22 WMR. Six-round magazine, 3-inch bull bbl., ramp and blade front sight, adj. rear. American walnut grips. Weight: 28 oz. Made 1981-83.

MODEL 829/830 DA
Same as Model 826 except in .22 LR caliber. Nine round capacity. Made 1981-83.
Model 829, blued . . . . NiB $140 Ex $119 Gd $73
Model 830, nickel . . . . NiB $145 Ex $124 Gd $78

MODEL 832,1833 DA
Same as Model 826 except in .32 SW Long. Blued or nickel finish. Made 1981-83.
Model 832, blued . . . . NiB $158 Ex $133 Gd $78
Model 833, nickel . . . . NiB $155 Ex $139 Gd $83

MODEL 900/901 DA. . . . . NiB $99 Ex $94 Gd $53
Solid frame, snap-out cylinder. Calibers: .22 Short, Long, LR. Nine-round cylinder, bbl. lengths: 2.5-, 4-, 6-inches. Weight: 26 oz. (with 6-inch bbl.). Fixed sights. Blued finish. Cycolac grips. Made 1962-73. Note: Model 901 (disc. in 1963) is the same except has chrome finish and white Tenite grips.

MODEL 903 TARGET. . . . . NiB $160 Ex $145 Gd $89
Caliber: .22 LR. Nine round capacity. SA/DA, 6-inch target-weight flat-side bbl., swing-out cylinder. Weight: 35 oz. Blade front sight, adj. rear. American walnut grips. Made 1980-83.

MODEL 904 TARGET. . . . . NiB $160 Ex $242 Gd $89
Similar to Model 903 except 4- or 6-inch bull bbl. Weight: 32 oz.

Harrington & Richardson
Model 900

Harrington & Richardson
Model 925

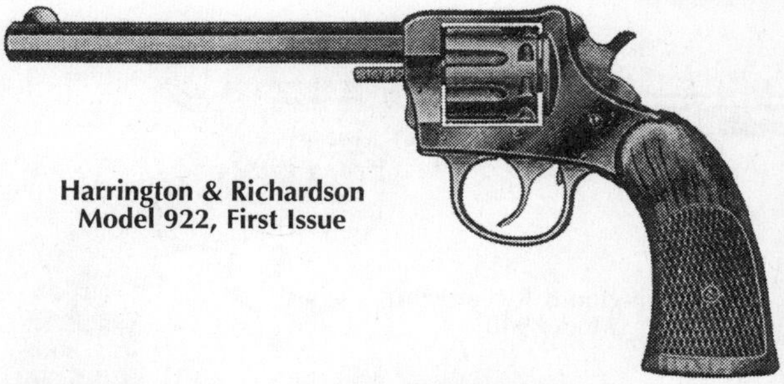

MODEL 905
TARGET. . . . . NiB $193 Ex $153 Gd $110
Same as Model 904 except w/4-inch bbl. only. Nickel finish. Made 1981-83.

MODEL 922
DA REVOLVER
FIRST ISSUE. . . . . NiB $221 Ex $173 Gd $122
Solid frame. Caliber: .22 LR. Nine-round cylinder, 10-inch octagon bbl., (early model) or 6-inches, round bbl. (later production). Weight: 26 oz. (with 6-inch bbl.). Fixed sights. Blued finish. Checkered walnut grips. Safety cylinder on later models. Disc. prior to 1942.

MODEL 922/923
DA REVOLVER,
SECOND ISSUE. . . . . NiB $104 Ex $84 Gd $60
Solid frame. Caliber: .22 LR. Nine-round cylinder, bbl. lengths: 2.5-, 4-, 6-inches. Weight: 24 oz. (with 4-inch bbl.). Fixed sights. Blued finish. Plastic grips. Made 1950-86. Note: Second Issue Model 922 has a different frame from that of the First Issue. Model 923 is same as Model 922, Second Issue except for nickel finish.

MODEL 925
DEFENDER . . . . NiB $148 Ex $120 Gd $85
DA. Hinged frame. Caliber: .38 S&W. Five-round cylinder, 2.5-inch bbl., weight: 22 oz. Adj. rear sight, fixed front. Blued finish. One-piece wraparound grip. Made 1964-78.

MODEL 926 DA . . . . NiB $148 Ex $120 Gd $85
Hinged frame. Calibers: .22 LR, .38 S&W. Nine-round (.22 LR) or 5-round (.38) cylinder, 4-inch bbl., weight: 31 oz. Adj. rear sight, fixed front. Blued finish. Checkered walnut grips. Made 1968-78.

Harrington & Richardson
Model 903

Harrington & Richardson
Model 905

Harrington & Richardson
Model 922, First Issue

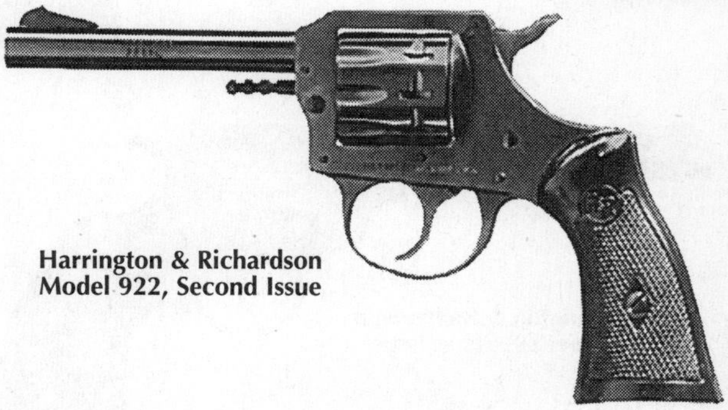

Harrington & Richardson
Model 922, Second Issue

Harrington & Richardson
Model 926

Harrington & Richardson
Model 939

Harrington & Richardson
Model 929

Harrington & Richardson
Model 949

Harrington & Richardson
Model 950

Harrington & Richardson
Model 999, First Issue

Harrington & Richardson
Model 999, Second Issue

MODEL 929/930
SIDEKICK DA REVOLVER. . . . . NiB $122 Ex $100 Gd $71
Caliber: .22 LR. Solid frame, swing-out 9-round cylinder, bbl. lengths: 2.5-, 4-, 6-inches. Weight: 24 oz. (with 4-inch bbl.). Fixed sights. Blued finish. Checkered plastic grips. Made 1956-86. Note: Model 930 is same except with nickel finish.

MODEL 939/940
ULTRA SIDEKICK
DA REVOLVER. . . . . NiB $159 Ex $125 Gd $90
Solid frame, swing-out 9-round cylinder. Safety lock. Calibers: .22 Short, Long, LR. Flat-side 6-inch bbl. w/vent rib. Weight: 33 oz. Adj. rear sight, ramp front. Blued finish. Checkered walnut grips. Made 1958-86, reintroduced by H&R 1871 in 1992. Note: Model 940 is same except has round bbl.

MODEL 949/950
FORTY-NINER
DA REVOLVER. . . . . NiB $146 Ex $115 Gd $79
Solid frame. Side loading and ejection. Calibers: .22 Short, Long, LR. Nine-round cylinder, 5.5- or 7.5 inch bbl., weight: 31 to 38 oz. Adj. rear sight, blade front. Blued or nickel finish. One-piece, Western-style walnut grip. Made 1960-86, reintroduced by H&R 1871 in 1992-99. Note: Model 950 is same except has nickel finish.

MODEL 976 DA . . . . NiB $120 Ex $95 Gd $69
Same as Model 949 except has color-casehardened frame, 7.5-inch bbl. Weight: 36 oz. Intro. 1977. disc.

HARRINGTON & RICHARDSON
MODEL 999 SPORTSMAN
DA REVOLVER, FIRST ISSUE . . . . . . NiB $214 Ex $173 Gd $107
Hinged frame. Calibers: .22 LR, .22 Mag. Same specifications as Model 199 Sportsman Single Action. Disc. before 1942.

MODEL 999 SPORTSMAN
DA REVOLVER
SECOND ISSUE. . . . . NiB $2229 Ex $183 Gd $112
Hinged frame. Caliber: .22 LR. Nine-round cylinder, 6-inch bbl. w/vent rib. Weight: 30 oz. Adj. sights. Blued finish. Checkered walnut grips. Made 1950-86.

(NEW) MODEL 999
SPORTSMAN
DA REVOLVER. . . . . NiB $227 Ex $183 Gd $128
Hinged frame. Caliber: .22 Short, Long, LR. Nine-round cylinder. Six-inch bbl. w/vent rib. Weight: 30 oz. Blade front sight adj. for elevation, square-notched rear adj. for windage. Blued finish. Checkered hardwood grips. Reintroduced by H&R 1871 in 1992.

AMERICAN DA .... NiB $104 Ex $84 Gd $60
Solid frame. Calibers: .32 S&W Long, .38 S&W. Six-round (.32 cal.) or 5-round (.38 cal.) cylinder, bbl. lengths: 2.5-,4.5- and 6-inches. Weight: About 16 oz. Fixed sights. Blued or nickel finish. Hard rubber grips. Disc. prior to 1942.

AUTOMATIC EJECTING DA REVOLVER..... NiB $181 Ex $146 Gd $100
Hinged frame. Calibers: .32 S&W Long, .38 S&W. Six-round (.32 cal.) or 5-round (.38 cal.) cylinder, bbl. lengths: 3.25-, 4-, 5- and 6-inches. Weight: 16 oz. (.32 cal.), 15 oz. (.38 cal.). Fixed sights. Blued or nickel finish. Black hard rubber grips. Disc. prior to 1942.

BOBBY DA .... NiB $316 Ex $260 Gd $168
Hinged frame. Calibers: .32 S&W, .38 S&W. Six-round cylinder (.32 cal.) or 5-round (.38 cal.). Four-inch bbl., 9 inches overall. Weight: 23 oz. Fixed sights. Blued finish. Checkered walnut grips. Disc. 1946. Note: Originally designed and produced for use by London's bobbies.

DEFENDER .38 DA .... NiB $158 Ex $127 Gd $86
Hinged frame. Based on the Sportsman design. Caliber: .38 S&W. Bbl. lengths: 4- and 6-inches, 9 inches overall (with 4-inch bbl.). Weight: 25 oz. with 4-inch bbl. Fixed sights. Blued finish. Black plastic grips. Disc. 1946. Note: This model was manufactured during WW II as an arm for plant guards, auxiliary police, etc.

EXPERT MODEL DA .... NiB $202 Ex $163 Gd $114
Same specifications as .22 Special except has 10-inch bbl., weight: 28 oz. Disc. prior to 1942.

HAMMERLESS DA, LARGE FRAME........ NiB $135 Ex $110 Gd $94
Hinged frame. Calibers: .32 S&W Long 38 S&W. Six-round (.32 cal.), or 5-round (.38 cal.) cylinder, bbl. lengths: 3.25-, 4-, and 6-inches. Weight: About 17 oz. Fixed sights. Blued or nickel finish. Hard rubber grips. Disc. prior to 1942.

HAMMERLESS DA, SMALL FRAME........ NiB $135 Ex $110 Gd $77
Hinged frame. Calibers: .22 LR, .32 S&W. Seven-round (.22 cal.) or 5-round (.32 cal.) cylinder, bbl. lengths: 2-, 3-, 4-, 5- and 6-inches. Weight: About 13 oz. Fixed sights. Blued or nickel finish. Hard rubber grips. Disc. prior to 1942.

HUNTER MODEL DA .... NiB $151 Ex $121 Gd $79
Solid frame. Caliber: .22 LR. Nine-round cylinder, 10-inch octagon bbl., weight: 26 oz. Fixed sights. Blued finish. Checkered walnut grips. Safety cylinder on later models. Note: An earlier Hunter Model was built on the smaller 7-round frame. Disc. prior to 1942.

NEW DEFENDER DA............. NiB $270 Ex $214 Gd $153
Hinged frame. Caliber: .22 LR. Nine-round cylinder, 2-inch bbl., 6.25 inches overall. Weight: 23 oz. Adj. sights. Blued finish. Checkered walnut grips, round butt. Note: Basically, this is the Sportsman DA w/a short bbl., Disc. prior to 1942.

PREMIER DA .... NiB $114 Ex $99 Gd $68
Small hinged frame. Calibers: .22 LR, .32 S&W. Seven-round (.22 LR) or 5-round (.32) cylinder. Bbl. Lengths: 2-, 3-, 4-, 5 and 6-inches. Weight: 13 oz. (in .22 LR), 12 oz. (in .32 S&W). Fixed sights. Blued or nickel finish. Black hard rubber grips. Disc. prior to 1942. (See illustration next page.)

MODEL STR 022 BLANK REVOLVER .... NiB $89 Ex $73 Gd $52
Caliber: .22 RF blanks. Nine-round cylinder, 2.5-inch bbl. Weight: 19 oz. Satin blued finish.

MODEL STR 032 BLANK REVOLVER .... NiB $103 Ex $83 Gd $59
Same general specifications as STR 022 except chambered for .32

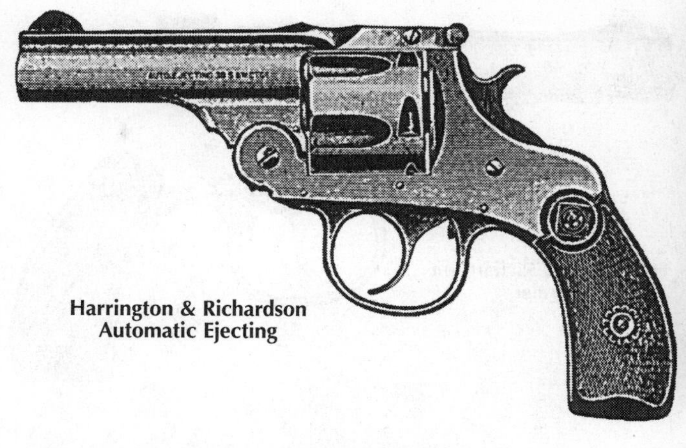

Harrington & Richardson
Automatic Ejecting

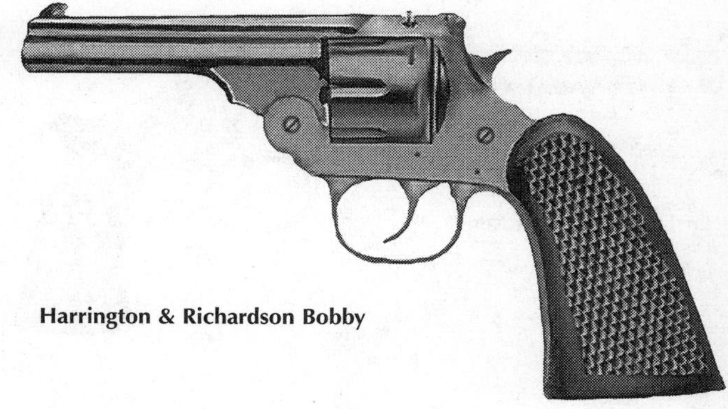

Harrington & Richardson Bobby

Harrington & Richardson
Defender .38

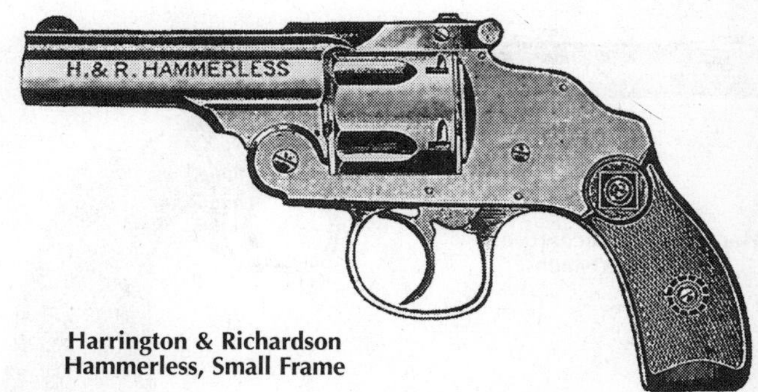

Harrington & Richardson
Hammerless, Small Frame

Harrington & Richardson
Premier

Harrington & Richardson
Vest Pocket

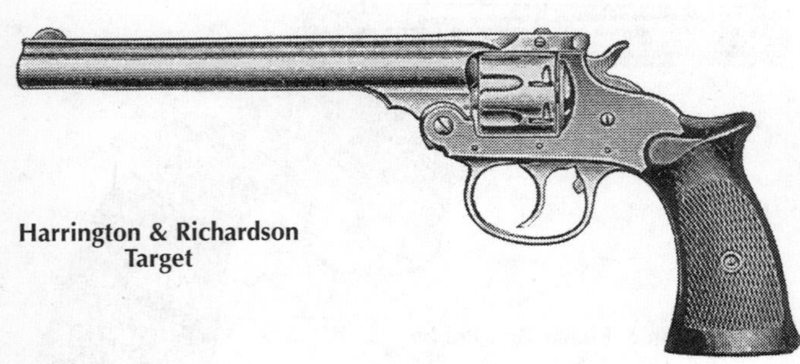

Harrington & Richardson
Target

Harrington & Richardson
Young American

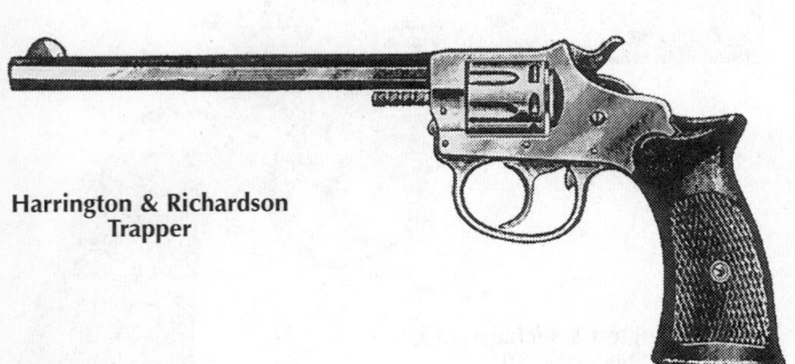

Harrington & Richardson
Trapper

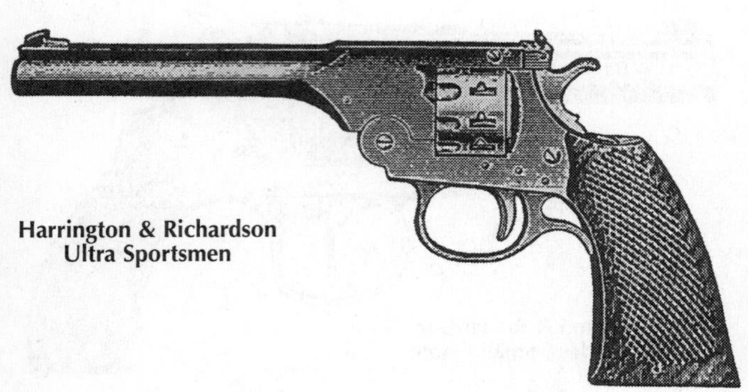

Harrington & Richardson
Ultra Sportsmen

TARGET MODEL DA . . . . NiB $174 Ex $141 Gd $98
Small hinged frame. Calibers: .22 LR, .22 W.R.F. Seven-round cylinder, 6-inch bbl., weight: 16 oz. Fixed sights. Blued finish. Checkered walnut grips. Disc. prior to 1942.

TRAPPER MODEL DA . . . . NiB $161 Ex $130 Gd $90
Solid frame. Caliber: .22 LR. Seven-round cylinder, 6-inch octagon bbl., weight: 12.5 oz. Fixed sights. Blued finish. Checkered walnut grips. Safety cylinder on later models. Disc. prior to 1942.

ULTRA SPORTSMAN. . . . . NiB $239 Ex $190 Gd $139
SA. Hinged frame. Caliber: .22 LR. Nine-round cylinder, 6-inch bbl., weight: 30 oz. Adj. target sights. Blued finish. Checkered walnut grips. This model has short action, wide hammer spur, cylinder is length of a .22 LR cartridge. Disc. prior to 1942.

VEST POCKET DA . . . . NiB $104 Ex $84 Gd $60
Solid frame. Spurless hammer. Calibers: .22 Rimfire, .32 S&W. Seven-round (.22 cal.) or 5-round (.32 cal.) cylinder, 1.13-inch bbl., weight: About 9 oz. Blued or nickel finish. Hard rubber grips. Disc. prior to 1942.

YOUNG AMERICA DA . . . . NiB $104 Ex $84 Gd $60
Solid frame. Calibers: .22 Long, .32 S&W. Seven-round (.22 cal.) or 5-round (.32 cal.) cylinder. Bbl. lengths: 2-, 4.5- and 6-inches. Weight: About 9 oz. Fixed sights. Blued or nickel finish. Hard rubber grips. Disc. prior to 1942.

HARTFORD ARMS & EQUIPMENT CO. — Hartford, Connecticut

Hartford pistols were the forebearer of the original High Standard line. High Standard Mfg. Corp. acquired Hartford Arms & Equipment Co. in 1932. The High Standard Model B is essentially the same as the Hartford Automatic.

AUTOMATIC TARGET PISTOL. . . . . NiB $683 Ex $557 Gd $379
Caliber. .22 LR. 10-round magazine, 6.75-inch bbl., 10.75 inches overall. Weight: 31 oz. Target sights. Blued finish. Black rubber grips. This gun closely resembles the early Colt Woodsman and High Standard pistols. Made 1929-30.

REPEATING PISTOL. . . . . NiB $526 Ex $425 Gd $296
Same general design as the automatic pistol of this manufacture, but this model is a hand-operated repeating pistol on the order of the Fiala. Made 1929-30.

SINGLE-SHOT TARGET PISTOL. . . . NiB $518 Ex $415 Gd $277
Similar in appearance to the Hartford Automatic. Caliber: .22 LR, 6.75-inch bbl., 10.75 inches overall. Weight: 38 oz. Target sights. Mottled frame and slide, blued bbl., Black rubber or walnut grips. Made 1929-30.

HASKELL MANUFACTURING — Lima, Ohio

See listings under Hi-Point.

HAWES FIREARMS — Van Nuys, California

DEPUTY MARSHAL SA REVOLVER
Calibers: .22 LR, also .22 WMR in two-cylinder combination. Six-round cylinder, 5.5-inch bbl., 11 inches overall. Weight: 34 oz. Adj. rear sight, blade front. Blued finish. Plastic or walnut grips. Imported from 1973-81.
.22 LR (plastic grips) . . . . NiB $95 Ex $76 Gd $54
Combination, .22 LR/.22 WMR (plastic). . . . . NiB $101 Ex $81 Gd $57
Walnut grips, add. $10

DEPUTY DENVER MARSHAL
Same as Deputy Marshal SA except has brass frame. Imported from 1973-81.
.22 LR (plastic grips). . . . . NiB $101 Ex $81 Gd $57
Combination, .22 LR/.22 WMR (plastic) . . . . . NiB $101 Ex $81 Gd $57
Walnut grips add $10

DEPUTY MONTANA MARSHAL
Same as Deputy Marshal except has brass grip frame. Walnut grips only. Imported from 1973-81.
.22 LR . . . . NiB $132 Ex $107 Gd $76
Combination, .22 LR/.22 WMR . . . . . NiB $158 Ex $127 Gd $89

DEPUTY SILVER CITY MARSHAL
Same as Deputy Marshal except has chrome-plated frame, brass grip frame, blued cylinder and bbl., Imported from 1973-81.
.22 LR (plastic grips). . . . . NiB $107 Ex $87 Gd $56
Combination, .22 LR/.22 WMR (plastic). . . . NiB $127 Ex $107 Gd $76
Walnut grips add $10

DEPUTY TEXAS MARSHAL
Same as Deputy Marshal except has chrome finish. Imported from 1973-81.
.22 LR (plastic grips). . . . . NiB $112 Ex $97 Gd $71
Combination, .22 LR/.22 WMR (plastic). . . . NiB $143 Ex $122 Gd $81
Walnut grips add. $10

FAVORITE SINGLE-SHOT TARGET PISTOL. . NiB $155 Ex $100 Gd $60
Replica of Stevens No. 35. Tip-up action. Caliber: .22 LR. Eight-inch bbl., 12 inches overall. Weight: 24 oz. Target sights. Chrome-plated frame. Blued bbl., Plastic or rosewood grips (add $5). Imported 1972-76.

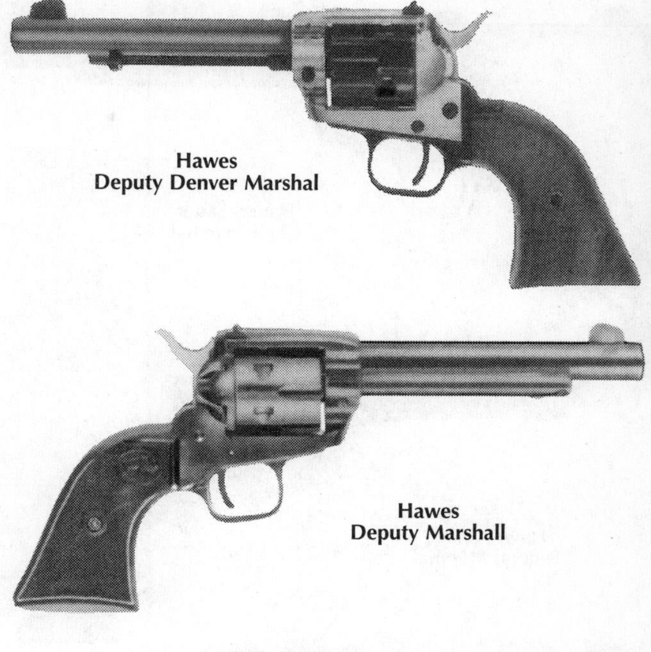

Hawes
Deputy Denver Marshal

Hawes
Deputy Marshall

Hawes
Deputy Montana Marshal

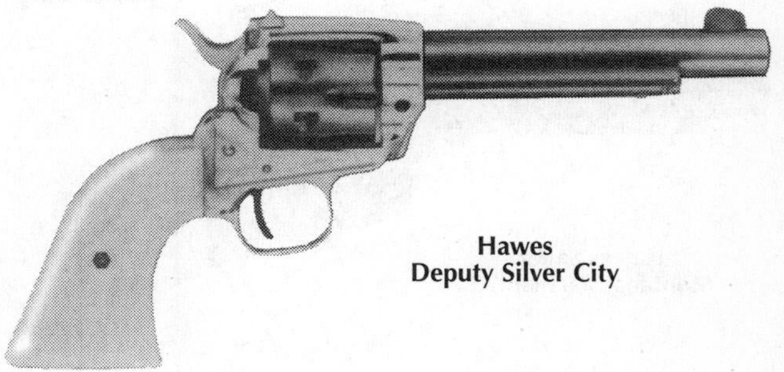

Hawes
Deputy Silver City

Hawes
Deputy Texas Marshal

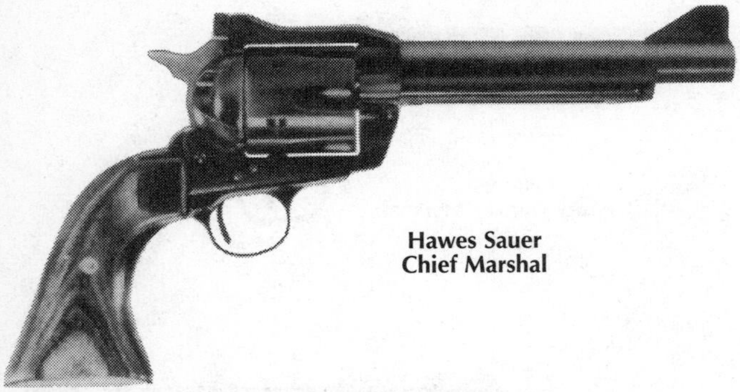

Hawes Sauer Chief Marshal

Hawes Sauer Texas Marshal

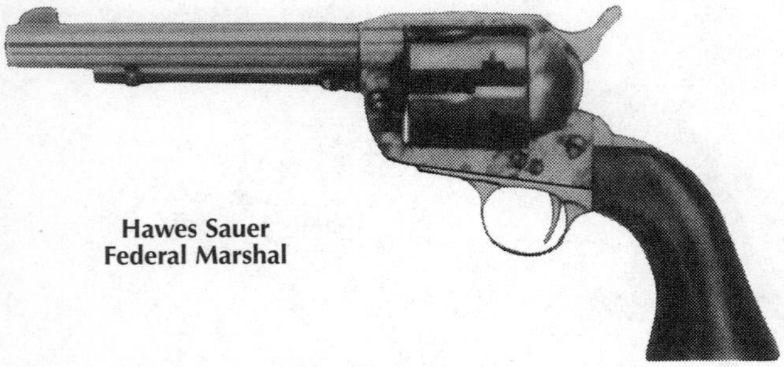

Hawes Sauer Federal Marshal

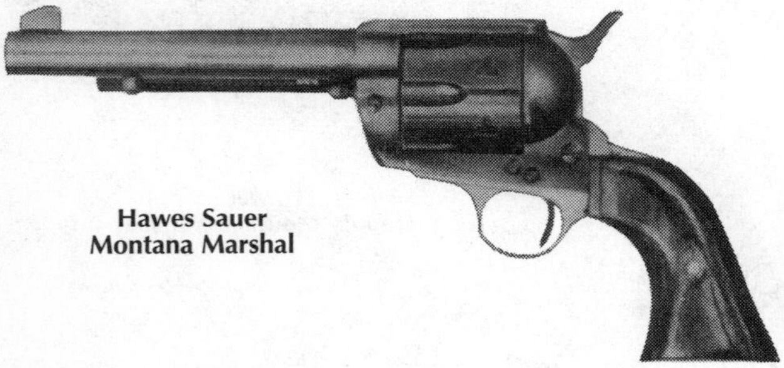

Hawes Sauer Montana Marshal

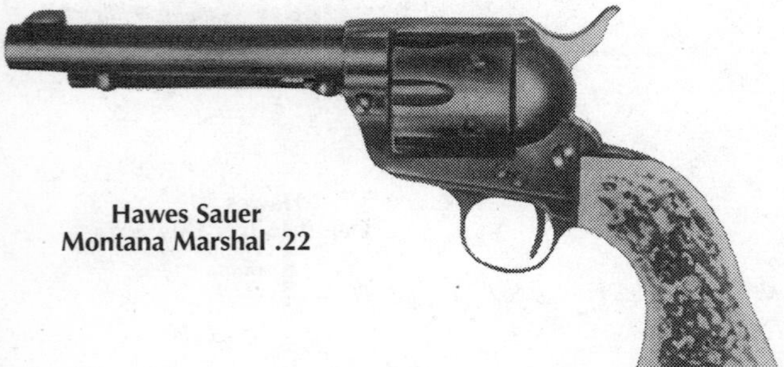

Hawes Sauer Montana Marshal .22

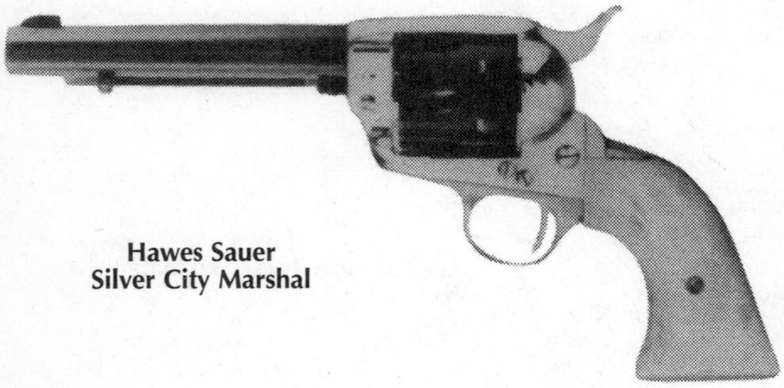

Hawes Sauer Silver City Marshal

SAUER CHIEF MARSHAL SA TARGET REVOLVER

Same as Western Marshal except has adj. rear sight and front sight, oversized rosewood grips. Not made in .22 caliber. Imported from 1973-81.

.357 Magnum or .45 Colt . . . . NiB $273 Ex $222 Gd $157
.44 Magnum . . . . NiB $305 Ex $247 Gd $174
Combination .357 Magnum
and 9mm Para.
.45 Colt and .45 Auto . . . . NiB $304 Ex $258 Gd $145
Combination
.44 Magnum and .44-40 . . . . NiB $298 Ex $247 Gd $171

SAUER FEDERAL MARSHAL

Same as Western Marshal except has color-casehardened frame, brass grip frame, one-piece walnut grip. Not made in .22 caliber. Imported from 1973-81.

.357 Magnum or .45 Colt . . . . NiB $258 Ex $207 Gd $145
.44 Magnum . . . . NiB $293 Ex $227 Gd $153
Combination
.357 Magnum and 9mm Para.,
.45 Colt and .45 Auto . . . . NiB $303 Ex $258 Gd $145
Combination .44 Magnum and .44-40 . . . . NiB $298 Ex $247 Gd $171

SAUER MONTANA MARSHAL

Same as Western Marshal except has brass grip frame. Imported from 1973-81.

.357 Magnum or .45 Colt . . . . NiB $273 Ex $222 Gd $157
.44 Magnum . . . . NiB $305 Ex $247 Gd $174
Combination .357 Magnum and 9mm Para.,
.45 Colt and .45 Auto . . . . NiB $326 Ex $265 Gd $186
Combination .44 Magnum and .44-40 . . . . NiB $339 Ex $275 Gd $193
.22 LR . . . . NiB $267 Ex $217 Gd $154
Combination .22 LR and .22 WMR . . . . NiB $286 Ex $232 Gd $164

SAUER SILVER CITY MARSHAL

Same as Western Marshal except has nickel plated frame, brass grip frame, blued cylinder and bbl., pearlite grips. Imported from 1973-81.

.44 Magnum . . . . NiB $326 Ex $265 Gd $186
Combination .357 Magnum and 9mm Para.
.45 Colt and .45 Auto . . . . NiB $300 Ex $229 Gd $147
Combination .44 Magnum and .44-40 . . . . NiB $326 Ex $239 Gd $173

SAUER TEXAS MARSHAL

Same as Western Marshal except nickel plated, has pearlite grips. Imported from 1973-81.

.357 Magnum or .45 Colt . . . . NiB $302 Ex $244 Gd $171
.44 Magnum . . . . NiB $321 Ex $260 Gd $181
Combination .357 Magnum and 9mm Para.,
.45 Colt and .45 Auto . . . . NiB $346 Ex $280 Gd $196
Combination .44 Magnum and .44-40 . . . . NiB $366 Ex $295 Gd $206
.22 LR . . . . NiB $264 Ex $214 Gd $151
Combination .22 LR and .22 WMR . . . . NiB $294 Ex $224 Gd $153

SAUER WESTERN MARSHAL SA REVOLVER
Calibers: .22 LR (disc.), .357 Magnum, .44 Magnum, .45 Auto. Also in two-cylinder combinations: .22 WMR (disc.), 9mm Para., .44-40, .45 Auto. Six-round cylinder, bbl. lengths: 5.5-inch (disc.), 6-inch, 11.75 inches overall (with 6-inch bbl.). Weight: 46 oz. Fixed sights. Blued finish. Originally furnished w/simulated stag plastic grips. Recent production has smooth rosewood grips. Made from 1968 by J. P. Sauer & Sohn, Eckernforde, Germany. Imported from 1973-81.
.357 Magnum or .45 Colt . . . . NiB $274 Ex $219 Gd $154
.44 Magnum . . . . NiB $309 Ex $254 Gd $174
Combination .357 Magnum and 9mm Para.,
.45 Colt and .45 Auto . . . . NiB $290 Ex $234 Gd $168
Combination .44 Magnum
and .44-40. . . . . NiB $321 Ex $260 Gd $181
.22 LR . . . . NiB $219 Ex $168 Gd $128
Combination .22 LR
and .22 WMR . . . . NiB $239 Ex $204 Gd $148

HECKLER & KOCH — Oberndorf/Neckar, West Germany, and Chantilly, Virginia

MODEL HK4 DA AUTO PISTOL
Calibers: .380 Automatic (9mm Short), .22 LR, .25 Automatic (6.35mm), .32 Automatic (7.65mm) w/conversion kits. Seven-round magazine (.380 Auto), 8-round in other calibers, 3.4-inch bbl., 6.19 inches overall. Weight: 18 oz. Fixed sights. Blued finish. Plastic grip. Disc. 1984.
.22 LR or .380 Automatic . . . . NiB $417 Ex $324 Gd $216
.25 ACP or .32 ACP Automatic . . . . NiB $417 Ex $324 Gd $216
.380 Automatic w/.22
conversion unit . . . . NiB $529 Ex $427 Gd $297
.380 Automatic w/.22, .25, .32
conversion units . . . . NiB $731 Ex $591 Gd $412

MODEL MARK 23
DA AUTO PISTOL . . . . NiB $2219 Ex $1693 Gd $1162
Short-recoil semiautomatic pistol w/polymer frame and steel slide. Caliber: .45 ACP. 10-round magazine, 5.87-inch bbl., 9.65 inches overall. Weight: 43 oz. Seven interchangeable rear sight adjustment units w/3-dot system. Developed primarily in response to specifications by the Special Operations Command (SOCOM) for a Special Operations Forces Offensive Handgun Weapon System. Imported 1996 to date.

MODEL P7K3 DA
AUTO PISTOL
Caliber: .380 ACP. Eight-round magazine, 3.8 inch-bbl., 6.3 inches overall. Weight: About 26 oz. Adj. rear sight. Imported 1988-94.
P7K3 in .380 Cal. . . . . NiB $878 Ex $718 Gd $491
.22 LR conversion kit. . . . . NiB $646 Ex $553 Gd $378
.32 ACP conversion kit . . . . NiB $337 Ex $285 Gd $193

MODEL P7M8. . . . . NiB $910 Ex $734 Gd $508
Squeeze-cock SA semiautomatic pistol. Caliber: 9mm Para. Eight-round magazine, 4.13-inch bbl., 6.73 inches overall. Weight: 29.9 oz. Matte black or nickel finish. Adj. rear sight. Imported 1985 to date. See illustration next page.

MODEL P7M10
Caliber: .40 S&W. Nine-round magazine, 4.2-inch bbl., 6.9 inches overall. Weight: 43 oz. Fixed front sight blade, adj. rear w/3-dot system. Imported 1992-94.
Blued finish . . . . NiB $1065 Ex $813 Gd $571
Nickel finish . . . . NiB $1075 Ex $823 Gd $581

Hawes Sauer Western Marshal

Heckler & Koch Model HK4

Heckler &Koch Model P7K3

Heckler & Koch Mark 23

Heckler & Koch Model P7M8

Heckler & Koch USP45

Heckler & Koch Model P7M13

Heckler & Koch Model P7 (PSP)

Heckler & Koch Model P9S DA

MODEL P7M13 . . . . NiB $948 Ex $747 Gd $526
Caliber: 9mm. 13-round magazine, 4.13-inch bbl., 6.65 inches overall. Weight: 34.42 oz. Matte black finish. Adj. rear sight. Imported 1985-94.

MODEL P7(PSP)
AUTO PISTOL . . . . NiB $787 Ex $634 Gd $438
Caliber: 9mm Para. Eight-round magazine, 4.13-inch bbl., 6.54 inches overall. DA. Weight: About 33.5 oz. Blued finish. Imported 1983-85 and again in 1990 with limited availability.

MODEL P9S
DA AUTOMATIC PISTOL
Calibers: 9mm Para., .45 Automatic. Nine-round (9mm) or 7-round (.45 Auto) magazine. Four-inch bbl., 7.63 inches overall. Weight: 32 ounces. Fixed sights. Blued finish. Contoured plastic grips. Disc. 1986.
9mm . . . . NiB $768 Ex $582 Gd $413
.45 Automatic . . . . NiB $783 Ex $639 Gd $428

MODEL P9S TARGET
COMPETITION KIT
Same as Model P9S Target except comes w/extra 5.5-inch bbl. and bbl. weights. Also available w/walnut competition grip.
W/standard grip . . . . NiB $1185 Ex $922 Gd $659
W/competition grip. . . . . NiB $1256 Ex 1010 Gd $697

MODEL SP89. . . . . NiB $3851 Ex $3078 Gd $2100
Semiautomatic, recoil-operated, delayed roller-locked bolt system. Caliber: 9mm Para. 15-round magazine, 4.5-inch bbl., 13 inches overall. Weight: 68 oz. Hooded front sight, adj. rotary-aperture rear. Imported 1989-93.

MODEL USP
AUTO PISTOL
Polymer integral grip/frame design w/recoil reduction system. Calibers: 9mm Para., .40 S&W or .45 ACP. 15-round (9mm) or 13-round (.40 S&W and .45ACP) magazine, 4.13- or 4.25-inch bbl., 6.88 to 7.87 inches overall. Weight: 26.5-30.4 oz. Blade front sight, adj. rear w/3-dot system. Matte black or stainless finish. Stippled black polymer grip. Available in SA/DA or DAO. Imported 1993 to date.
Matte
Black finish . . . . NiB $689 Ex $525 Gd $370
Stainless. NiB $632 Ex $509 Gd $353
W/Tritium sights, add $95
W/ambidextrous decocking lever, add $20

Heckler & Koch Model USP45 Compact 50th Anniversary

Heckler & Koch Model USP9 Compact (Stainless)

Heckler & Koch Model USP357 Compact

Heckler & Koch Model USP Expert

Heckler & Koch Model USP Tactical

MODEL USP9 COMPACT
Caliber: 9mm. 10- round magazine, 4.25- inch bbl., 7.64 inches overall. Weight: 25.5 oz. Short recoil w/modified Browning action. 3-dot sighting system. Polymer frame w/integral grips. Imported 1997 to date.
Blued finish . . . . NiB $638 Ex $525 Gd $360
Stainless finish . . . . NiB $674 Ex $550 Gd $380
W/ambidextrous decocking lever, add $15

MODEL USP40 COMPACT
Caliber: .40 S&W. 10-round magazine, 3.58- inch bbl., 6.81 inches overall. Weight: 27 oz. Short recoil w/modified Browning action. 3-dot sighting system. Polymer frame w/integral grips. Imported 1997 to date.
Blued finish . . . . NiB $689 Ex $561 Gd $365
Stainless finish . . . . NiB $736 Ex $586 Gd $380
W/ambidextrous decocking lever, add $15

MODEL USP45 COMPACT
Caliber: .45 ACP. Eight-round magazine, 3.8- inch bbl., 7.09 inches overall. Weight: 28 oz. Short recoil w/modified Browning action. 3-dot sighting system. Polymer frame w/integral grips. Imported 1998 to date.
Blued finish . . . . NiB $689 Ex $561 Gd $365
Stainless finish . . . . NiB $736 Ex $586 Gd $380
W/ambidextrous decocking lever, add $15
50th Anniversary (1 of 1,000) . . . . NiB $1316 Ex $1060 Gd $632

MODEL USP EXPERT . . . . NiB $1400 Ex $1060 Gd $782
Caliber: .45 ACP. 10-round magazine, 6.2- inch bbl., 9.65 inches overall. Weight: 30 oz. Adjustable 3-dot target sights. Short recoil modified Browning action w/recoil reduction system. Reinforced polymer frame w/integral grips and match-grade slide. Imported 1999 to date.

MODEL USP TACTICAL . . . . NiB $1101 Ex $859 Gd $576
SOCOM Enhanced version of the USP Standard Model, w/4.92-inch threaded bbl. Chambered for .45 ACP only. Imported 1998 to date.

Heckler & Koch Model VP'7OZ

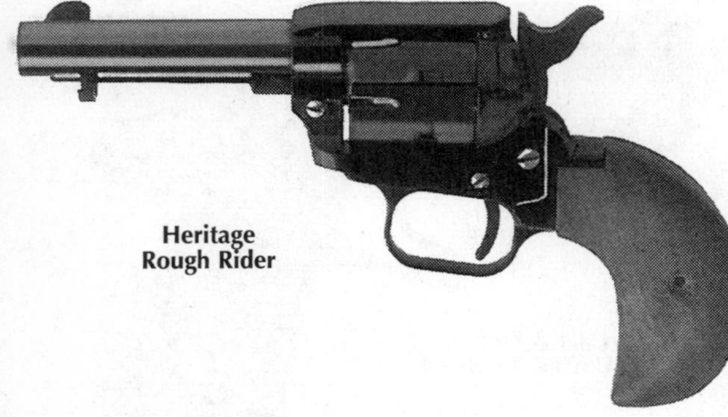
Heritage Rough Rider

Heritage Sentry

MODEL VP 70Z AUTO PISTOL . . . . NiB $588 Ex $460 Gd $331
Caliber: 9mm Para. 18-round magazine, 4.5-inch bbl., 8 inches overall. Weight: 32.5 oz. DA Fixed sights. Blued slide, plastic receiver and grip. Disc. 1986.

HELWAN PISTOLS

See listings under Interarms.

HERITAGE MANUFACTURING — Opa Locka, Florida

MODEL HA25 AUTO PISTOL
Caliber: .25 ACP. Six-round magazine, 2.5-inch bbl., 4.63 inches overall. Weight: 12 oz. Fixed sights. Blued or chrome finish. Made 1993 to date.
Blued . . . . NiB $129 Ex $103 Gd $72
Chrome . . . . NiB $134 Ex $108 Gd $77

ROUGH RIDER SA REVOLVER
Calibers: .22 LR, .22 Mag. Six-round cylinder. bbl. lengths: 2.75, 3.75, 4.75, 6.5 or 9 inches. Weight: 31-38 oz. Blade front sight, fixed rear. High-polished blued finish w/gold accents. Smooth walnut grips. Made 1993 to date.
.22 LR . . . . NiB $118 Ex $93 Gd $72
.22 LR/.22 WRF combo . . . . NiB $149 Ex $118 Gd $87

SENTRY DA REVOLVER
Calibers: .22 LR, .22 Mag., .32 Mag., 9mm or .38 Special. Six- or 8-round (rimfire) cylinder, 2- or 4-inch bbl., 6.25 inches overall (2-inch bbl.). Ramp front sight, fixed rear. Blued or nickel finish. Checkered polymer grips. Made from 1993-97.
Blued . . . . NiB $120 Ex $98 Gd $69
Nickel . . . . NiB $133 Ex $108 Gd $77

STEALTH DA AUTO PISTOL . . . . . . NiB $283 Ex $231 Gd $165
Calibers: 9mm, .40 S&W. 10-round magazine, 3.9-inch bbl., weight: 20.2 oz. Gas-delayed blowback, double action only. Ambidextrous trigger safety. Blade front sight, drift-adj. rear. Black chrome or stainless slide. Black polymer grip frame. Made from 1996 to date.

HI-POINT FIREARMS — Mansfield, Ohio

MODEL JS-9MM
AUTO PISTOL . . . . NiB $127 Ex $102 Gd $66
Caliber: 9mm Para. Eight-round magazine, 4.5-inch bbl., 7.75 inches overall. Weight: 39 oz. Fixed low-profile sights w/3-dot system. Matte blue, matte black or chrome finish. Checkered synthetic grips. Made from 1990-98.

MODEL JS-
9MM COMPETITION PISTOL
(STALLARD). NiB $117 Ex $97 Gd $66
Similar to standard JS-9 except w/4-inch compensated bbl. w/ shortened slide and adj. sights. 10-round magazine, 7.25 inches overall. Weight: 30 oz. Made from 1998 to date.

MODEL JS-9MM/
C-9MM COMPACT PISTOL
(BEEMILLER) . . . . NiB $118 Ex $97 Gd $65
Similar to standard JS-9 except w/3.5-inch bbl. and shortened slide w/alloy or polymer frame. 6.72 inches overall. Weight: 29 oz. or 32 oz. Three-dot-style sights. Made from 1993 to date.

MODEL CF-.380
POLYMER . . . . NiB $81 Ex $61 Gd $41
Caliber: .380 ACP. Eight-round magazine, 3.5-inch bbl., 6.72 inches overall. Weight: 32 oz. Three-dot sights. Made from 1994 to date.

MODEL JS-.40/J
C-.40 AUTO PISTOL
(IBERIA) . . . . NiB $146 Ex $117 Gd $81
Similar to Model JS-9mm except in caliber .40 S&W.

MODEL JS-.45/JH-.45
AUTO PISTOL
(HASKELL). . . . . NiB $163 Ex $127 Gd $87
Similar to Model JS-9mm except in caliber .45 ACP w/7-round magazine and two-tone Polymer finish.

J. C. HIGGINS

See Sears, Roebuck & Company

HIGH STANDARD SPORTING FIREARMS — East Hartford, Connecticut Formerly High Standard Mfg. Co., Hamden, Connecticut

A long-standing producer of sporting arms, High Standard disc. its operations in 1984. See new High Standard models under separate entry, HIGH STANDARD MFG. CO., INC.

NOTE: *For ease in finding a particular firearm, High Standard handguns are grouped into three sections: Automatic pistols (below), deringers and revolvers. For a complete listing, please refer to the Index.*

AUTOMATIC PISTOLS

MODEL A
HAMMERLESS . . . . NiB $785 Ex $627 Gd $433
Caliber: .22 LR. 10-round magazine, bbl. lengths: 4.5-, 6.75-inch. 11.5 inches overall (6.75-inch bbl.). Weight: 36 oz. (in 6.75-inch bbl.). Adj. target sights. Blued finish. Checkered walnut grips. Made 1938-42.

High Standard Model A

MODEL B
AUTOMATIC PISTOL . . . . NiB $469 Ex $382 Gd $306
Original Standard pistol. Hammerless. Caliber: .22 LR. 10-round magazine, bbl. lengths: 4.5-, 6.75-inch, 10.75 inches overall (with 6.75-inch bbl.). Weight: 33 oz. (6.75-inch bbl.). Fixed sights. Blued finish. Hard rubber grips. Made 1932-42.

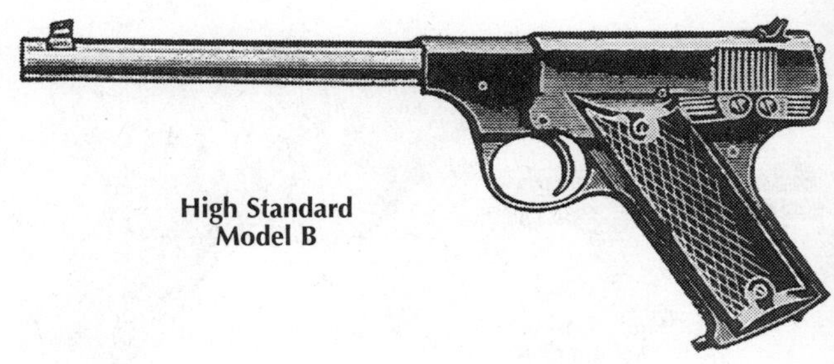

High Standard Model B

MODEL C
AUTOMATIC PISTOL . . . . NiB $938 Ex $739 Gd $484
Same as Model B except in .22 Short. Made 1935-42.

MODEL D
AUTOMATIC PISTOL . . . . NiB $849 Ex $683 Gd $471
Same general specifications as Model A but heavier bbl., weight: 40 oz. (6.75-inch bbl.). Made 1937-42.

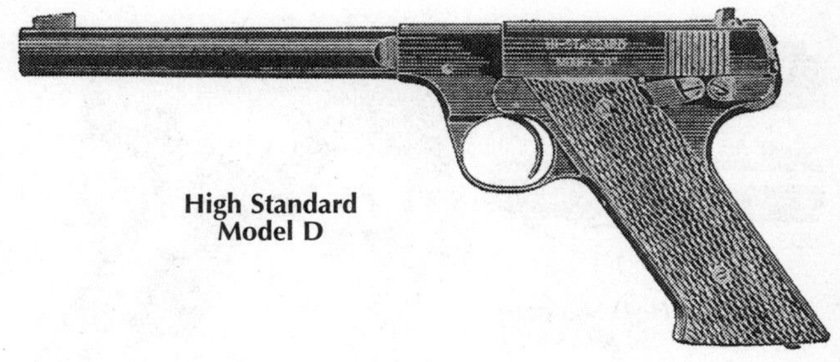

High Standard Model D

DURA-MATIC
AUTOMATIC PISTOL . . . . NiB $322 Ex $260 Gd $180
Takedown. Caliber: .22 LR. 10-round magazine, 4.5 or 6.5 inch interchangeable bbl., 10.88 inches overall (6.5-inch bbl.). Weight: 35 oz. (in 6.5-inch bbl.). Fixed sights. Blued finish. Checkered grips. Made 1952-70.

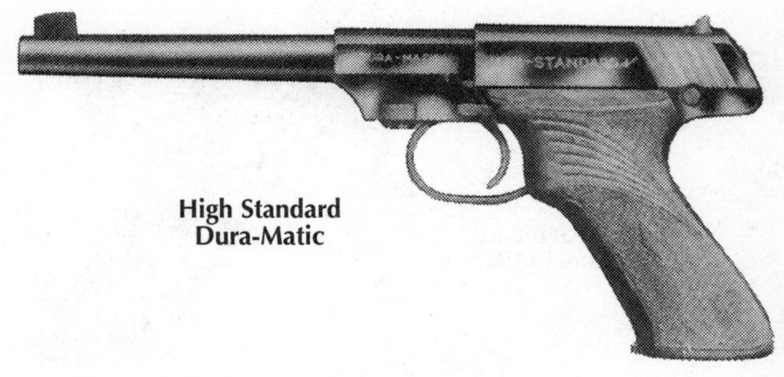

High Standard Dura-Matic

MODEL E
AUTOMATIC PISTOL . . . . NiB $1741 Ex $1344 Gd $1043
Same general specifications as Model A but w/extra heavy bbl. and thumbrest grips. Weight: 42 oz. (6.75-inch bbl.). Made 1937-42.

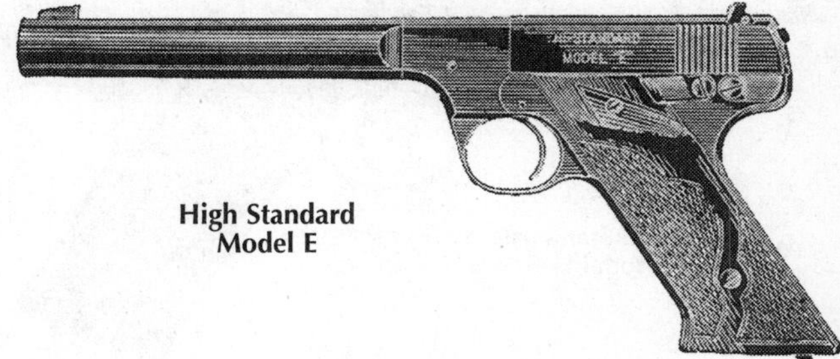

High Standard Model E

FIELD-KING
AUTOMATIC PISTOL
FIRST MODEL
Same general specifications as Sport-King but w/heavier bbl. and target sights. Late model 6.75-inch bbls. have recoil stabilizer and lever take-down feature. Weight: 43 oz. (6.75-inch bbl.). Made 1951-58.
W/one bbl. NiB $668 Ex $566 Gd $352
W/both bbls. . . . . NiB $736 Ex $639 Gd $462

FIELD-KING AUTOMATIC PISTOL
SECOND MODEL
Same general specifications as First Model Field-King but w/button take-down and marked FK 100 or FK 101.
W/one bbl. NiB $649 Ex $522 Gd $241
W/both bbls. . . . . NiB $783 Ex $649 Gd $425

High Standard G-.380

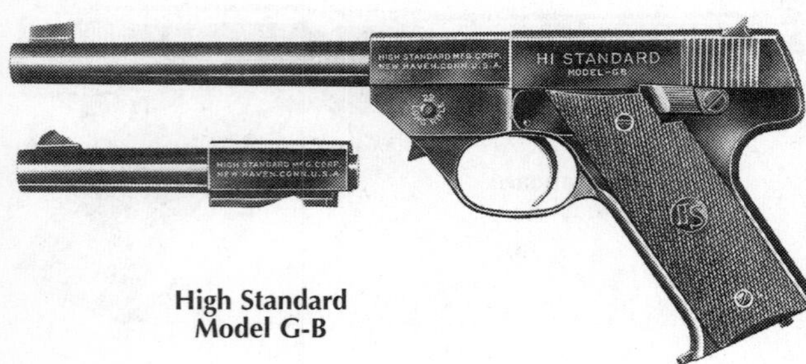

High Standard Model G-B

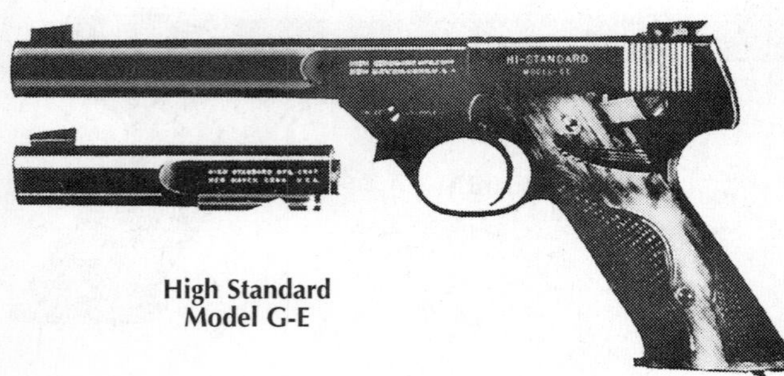
High Standard Model G-E

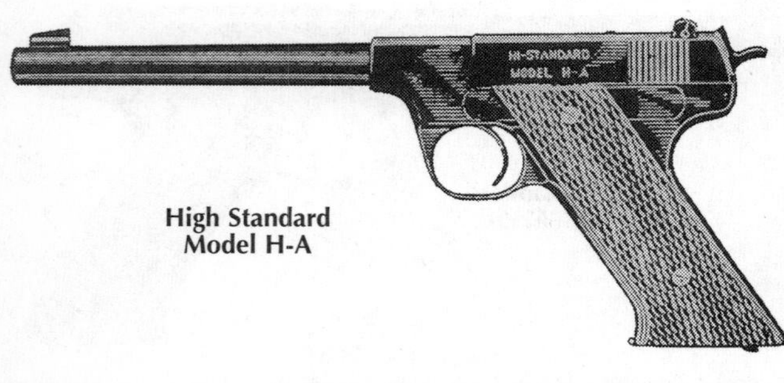

High Standard Model H-A

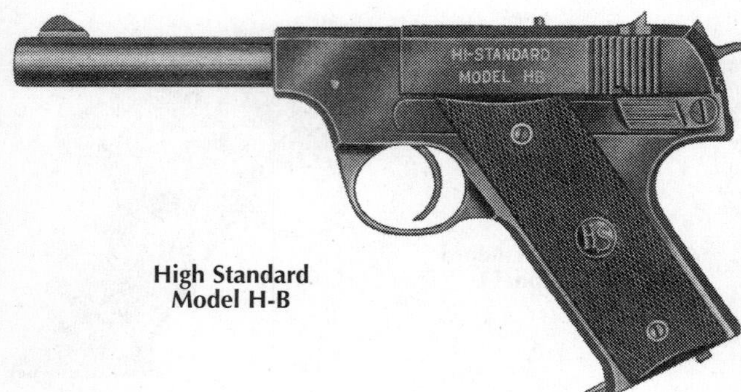

High Standard Model H-B

FLITE-KING AUTOMATIC PISTOL — FIRST MODEL
Same general specifications as Sport-King except in .22. Short w/aluminum alloy frame and slide and marked FK 100 or FK 101. Weight: 26 oz. (6.5-inch bbl.). Made 1953-58.
W/one bbl. . . . . NiB $518 Ex $417 Gd $288
W/both bbls. . . . . NiB $620 Ex $499 Gd $353

FLITE-KING AUTOMATIC PISTOL — SECOND MODEL
Same as Flite-King—First Model except w/steel frame and marked in the 102 or 103 series. Made 1958-66.
Model 102 . . . . NiB $603 Ex $437 Gd $315
Model 103 . . . . NiB $558 Ex $417 Gd $294

MODEL G-.380
AUTOMATIC PISTOL . . . . NiB $594 Ex $514 Gd $350
Lever takedown. Visible hammer. Thumb safety. Caliber: .380 Automatic. Six-round magazine, 5-inch bbl., weight: 40 oz. Fixed sights. Blued finish. Checkered plastic grips. Made 1943-50.

MODEL G-B AUTOMATIC PISTOL
Lever takedown. Hammerless. Interchangeable bbls. Caliber: .22 LR. 10-round magazine, bbl. lengths: 4.5, 6.75 inches, 10.75 inches overall (with 6.75-inch bbl.). Weight: 36 oz. (with 6.75-inch bbl.). Fixed sights. Blued finish. Checkered plastic grips. Made 1948-51.
W/one bbl. . . . . NiB $575 Ex $437 Gd $315
W/both bbls. . . . . NiB $594 Ex $514 Gd $351

MODEL G-D AUTOMATIC PISTOL
Lever takedown. Hammerless. Interchangeable bbls. Caliber: .22 LR. 10-round magazine, bbl. lengths: 4.5, 6.75 inches. 11.5 inches overall (with 6.75-inch bbl.). Weight: 41 oz. (6.75-inch bbl.). Target sights. Blued finish. Checkered walnut grips. Made 1948-51.
W/one bbl. . . . . NiB $952 Ex $731 Gd $530
W/both bbls. . . . . NiB $1089 Ex $859 Gd $612

MODEL G-E AUTOMATIC PISTOL
Same general specifications as Model G-D but w/extra heavy bbl. and thumbrest grips. Weight: 44 oz. (with 6.75-inch bbl.). Made 1949-51.
W/one bbl. . . . . NiB $1389 Ex $1179 Gd $906
W/both bbls. . . . . NiB $1663 Ex $1323 Gd $1045

MODEL H-A
AUTOMATIC PISTOL . . . . NiB $1299 Ex $1153 Gd $787
Same as Model A but w/visible hammer, no thumb safety. Made 1939-42.

MODEL H-B
AUTOMATIC PISTOL . . . . NiB $681 Ex $535 Gd $379
Same as Model B but w/visible hammer, no thumb safety. Made 1940-42.

MODEL H-D
AUTOMATIC PISTOL . . . . NiB $1217 Ex $1027 Gd $708
Same as Model D but w/visible hammer, no thumb safety. Made 1939-42.

MODEL H-DM
AUTOMATIC PISTOL . . . . NiB $698 Ex $581 Gd $433
Also called H-D Military. Same as Model H-D but w/thumb safety. Made 1941-51.

MODEL H-E
AUTOMATIC PISTOL . . . . NiB $2532 Ex $1982 Gd $1060
Same as Model E but w/visible hammer, no thumb safety. Made 1939-42.

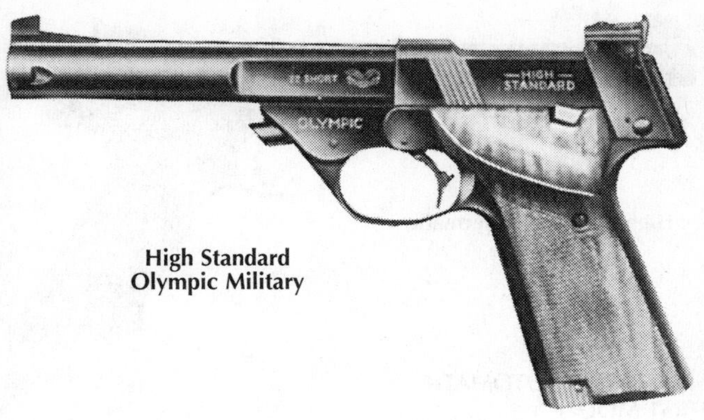

High Standard
Olympic Military

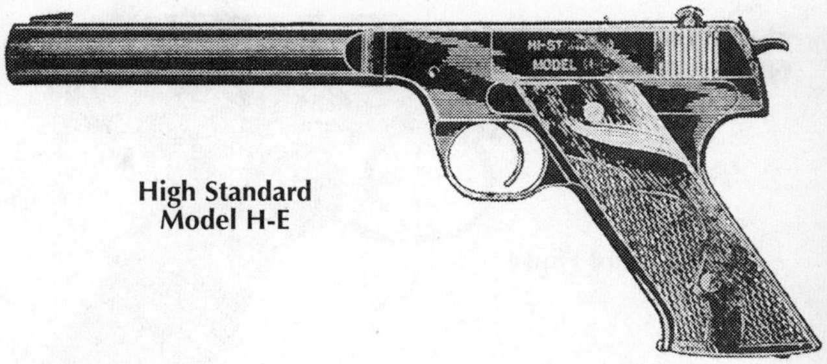

OLYMPIC AUTOMATIC PISTOL FIRST MODEL (G-O)
Same general specifications as Model G-E but in .22 Short w/light alloy slide. Made 1950-51.
W/one bbl. . . . . NiB $1185 Ex $1050 Gd $545
W/both bbls. . . . . NiB $1769 Ex $1420 Gd $976

OLYMPIC AUTOMATIC SECOND MODEL
Same general specifications as Supermatic but in .22 Short w/light alloy slide. Weight: 39 oz. (6.75-inch bbl.). Made 1951-58.
W/one bbl. . . . . NiB $1105 Ex $978 Gd $653
W/both bbls. . . . . NiB $1399 Ex $1137 Gd $828

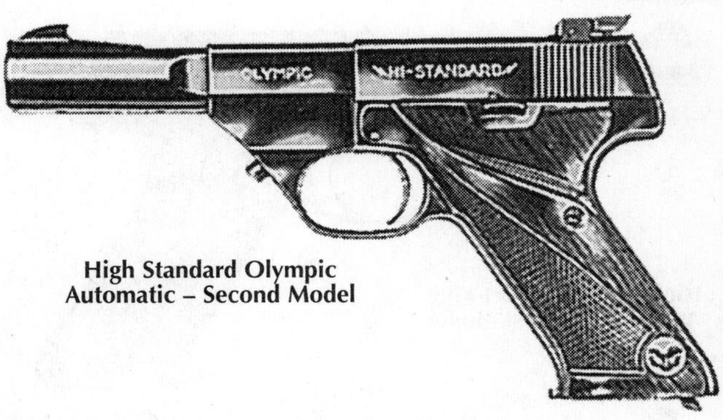

OLYMPIC AUTOMATIC PISTOL THIRD MODEL . . . . NiB $1103 Ex $890 Gd $643
Same as Supermatic Trophy w/bull bbl. except in .22 Short. Made 1963-66.

OLYMPIC COMMEMORATIVE
Limited edition of Supermatic Trophy Military issued to commemorate the only American-made rimfire target pistol ever to win an Olympic gold medal. Highly engraved w/Olympic rings inlaid in gold. Deluxe presentation case. Two versions issued: In 1972 (.22 LR) and 1980 (.22 Short).
1972 issue . . . . NiB $6240 Ex $5210 Gd $3413
1980 issue . . . . NiB $2093 Ex $1744 Gd $1119

OLYMPIC I.S.U . . . . NiB $925 Ex $746 Gd $517
Same as Supermatic Citation except caliber .22 Short, 6.75- or 8-inch tapered bbl. w/stabilizer, detachable weights. Made from 1958-77. Eight-inch bbl. disc. in 1966.

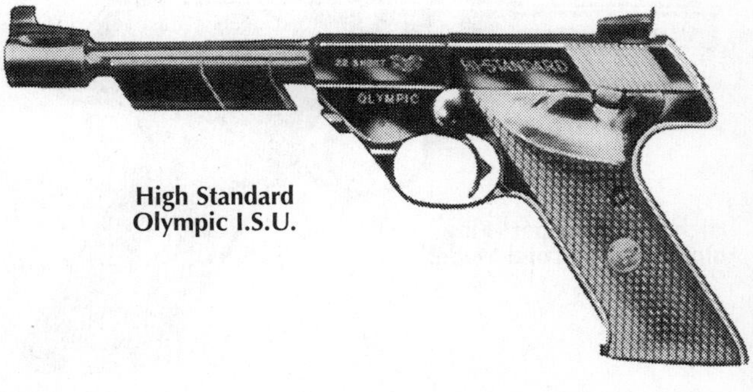

OLYMPIC I.S.U. MILITARY . . . . . NiB $2121 Ex $1071 Gd $622
Same as Olympic I.S.U. except has military grip and bracket rear sight. Intro. in 1965. disc.

OLYMPIC MILITARY . . . . NiB $1072 Ex $877 Gd $681
Same as Olympic — Third Model except has military grip and bracket rear sight. Made in 1965.

PLINKER . . . . NiB $331 Ex $266 Gd $184
Similar to Dura-Matic w/same general specifications. Made 1971-73. See illustration next page.

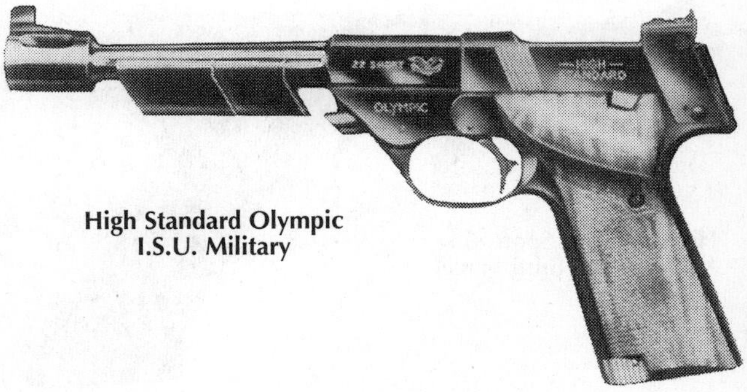

SHARPSHOOTER AUTOMATIC PISTOL . . . . NiB $744 Ex $612 Gd $427
Takedown. Hammerless. Caliber: .22 LR. 10-round magazine, 5.5-inch bull bbl., 9 inches overall. Weight: 42 oz. Micrometer rear sight, blade front sight. Blued finish. Plastic grips. Made 1971-83. See illustration next page.

High Standard
Model H-E

High Standard Olympic
Automatic – First Model

High Standard Olympic
Automatic – Second Model

High Standard
Olympic I.S.U.

High Standard Olympic
I.S.U. Military

High Standard Plinker

High Standard Supermatic

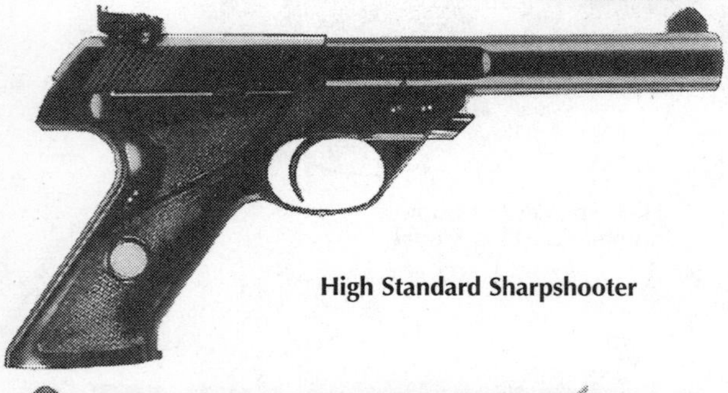

High Standard Sharpshooter

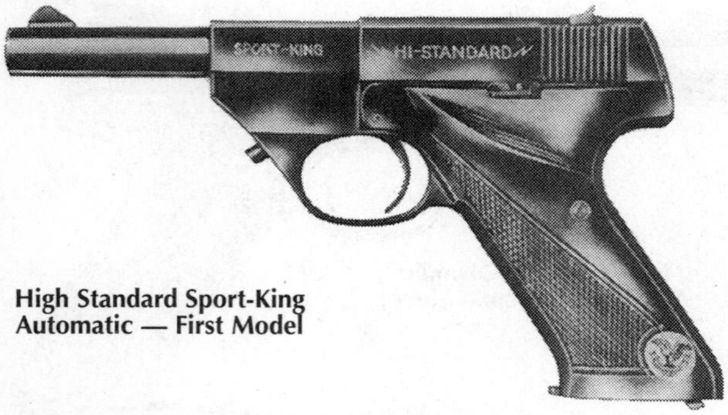

High Standard Sport-King Automatic — First Model

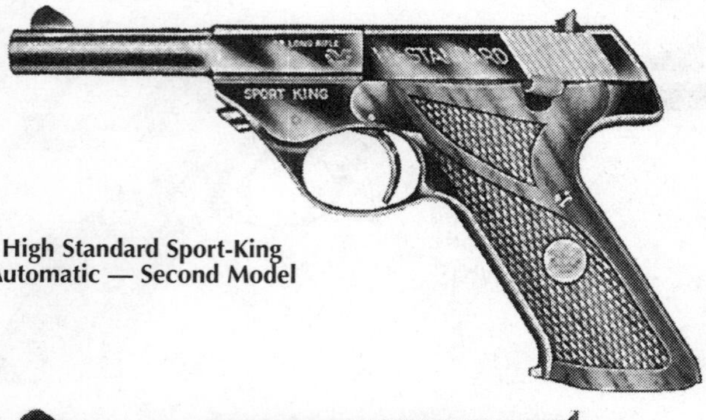

High Standard Sport-King Automatic — Second Model

High Standard Sport-King Automatic — Third Model

SPORT-KING AUTOMATIC FIRST MODEL

Takedown. Hammerless. Interchangeable bbls. Caliber: .22 LR. 10-round magazine, bbl. lengths: 4.5-, 6.75-inches. 11.5 inches overall (with 6.75-inch bbl.). Weight: 39 oz. (with 6.75-inch bbl.). Fixed sights. Blued finish. Checkered plastic thumbrest grips. Made 1951-58. Note: 1951-54 production has lever takedown as in "G" series. Later version (illustrated) has push-button takedown.

W/one bbl. NiB $379 Ex $309 Gd $219
W/both bbls. . . . . NiB $462 Ex $375 Gd $263

SPORT-KING AUTOMATIC PISTOL SECOND MODEL . . . . NiB $405 Ex $329 Gd $232

Caliber: .22 LR. 10-round magazine, 4.5- or 6.75 inch interchangeable bbl. 11.25 inches overall (with 6.75-inch bbl.). Weight: 42 oz. (with 6.75-inch bbl.). Fixed sights. Blued finish. Checkered grips. Made 1958-70.

SPORT-KING AUTOMATIC PISTOL THIRD MODEL . . . . NiB $366 Ex $298 Gd 210

Similar to Sport-King — Second Model w/same general specifications. Blued or nickel finish. Intro. in 1974. disc.

SPORT-KING LIGHTWEIGHT

Same as standard Sport-King except has forged aluminum alloy frame. Weight: 30 oz. w/6.75-inch bbl. Made 1954-65.

W/one bbl. NiB $387 Ex $281 Gd $190
W/both bbls. . . . . NiB $463 Ex $385 Gd $218

SUPERMATIC AUTOMATIC PISTOL

Takedown. Hammerless. Interchangeable bbls. Caliber: .22 LR. 10-round magazine, bbl. lengths: 4.5-, 6.75-inches. Late model 6.75-inch bbls. have recoil stabilizer feature. Weight: 43 oz. (with 6.75-inch bbl.) 11.5 inches overall (with 6.75-inch bbl.). Target sights. Elevated serrated rib between sights. Adj. bbl. weights add 2 or 3 oz. Blued finish. Checkered plastic thumbrest grips. Made 1951-58.

W/one bbl. NiB $740 Ex $597 Gd $416
W/both bbls. . . . . NiB $900 Ex $726 Gd $504

SUPERMATIC CITATION

Same as Supermatic Tournament except 6.75-, 8- or 10-inch tapered bbl. w/stabilizer and two removable weights. Also furnished w/Tournament's 5.5-inch bull bbl., adj. trigger pull, recoil-proof click-adj. rear sight (bbl.-mounted on 8- and 10-inch bbls.), checkered walnut thumbrest grips on bull bbl. model. Currently mfd. w/only bull bbl. Made 1958-66.

W/5.5-inch bull bbl. . . . . NiB $700 Ex $546 Gd $288
W/6.75-inch tapered bbl. . . . . NiB $700 Ex $546 Gd $288
W/8-inch tapered bbl. . . . . NiB $937 Ex $747 Gd $536
W/10-inch tapered bbl. . . . . NiB $1141 Ex $962 Gd $730

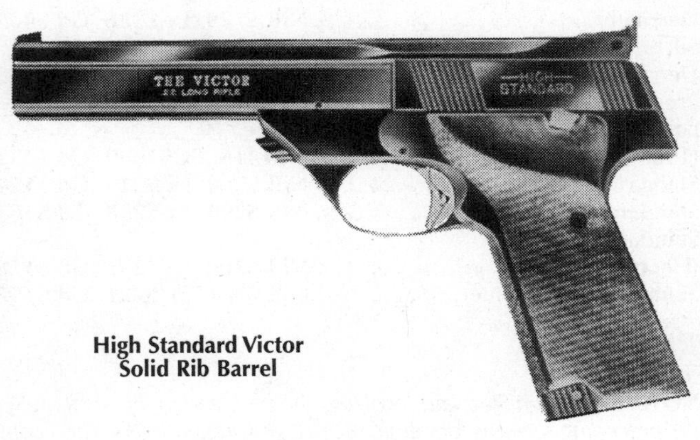

High Standard Victor Solid Rib Barrel

SUPERMATIC CITATION MILITARY
Same as Supermatic Citation except has military grip and bracket rear sight as in Supermatic Trophy. Made from 1965-73.
W/bull bbl. NiB $636 Ex $514 Gd $362
W/fluted bbl. . . . . NiB $871 Ex $722 Gd $532

SUPERMATIC TOURNAMENT . . . . NiB $645 Ex $568 Gd $279
Takedown. Caliber: .22 LR. 10-round magazine, interchangeable 5.5-inch bull or 6.75-inch heavy tapered bbl., notched and drilled for stabilizer and weights. 10 inches overall (with 5.5-inch bbl.). Weight: 44 oz. (5.5-inch bbl.). Click adj. rear sight, undercut ramp front. Blued finish. Checkered grips. Made 1958-66.

SUPERMATIC TOURNAMENT MILITARY . . . . NiB $635 Ex $511 Gd $351
Same as Supermatic Tournament except has military grip. Made 1965-71.

SUPERMATIC TROPHY
Same as Supermatic Citation except with 5.5-inch bull bbl., or 7.25-inch fluted bbl., w/detachable stabilizer and weights, extra magazine, High-luster blued finish, checkered walnut thumbrest grips. Made 1963-66.
W/bull bbl. . . . . NiB $1158 Ex $952 Gd $493
W/fluted bbl. . . . . NiB $1189 Ex $967 Gd $519

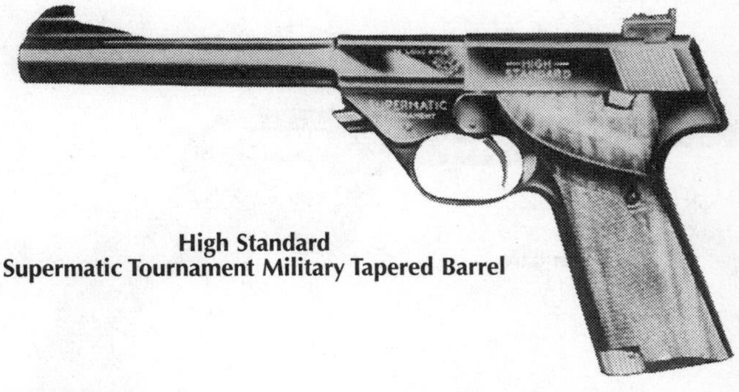

SUPERMATIC TROPHY MILITARY
Same as Supermatic Trophy except has military grip and bracket rear sight. Made 1965-84.
W/bull bbl. NiB $970 Ex $868 Gd $461
W/fluted bbl. . . . . NiB $466 Ex $873 Gd $487

VICTOR AUTOMATIC . . . . NiB $837 Ex $662 Gd $430
Takedown. Caliber: .22 LR. 10-round magazine, 4.5-inch solid or vent rib and 5.5-inch vent rib, interchangeable bbl., 9.75 inches overall (with 5.5-inch bbl.). Weight: 52 oz. (with 5.5-inch bbl.). Rib mounted target sights. Blued finish. Checkered walnut thumbrest grips. Standard or military grip configuration. Made from 1972-84 (standard-grip model, 1974-75).

High Standard Supermatic Citation Bull Barrel

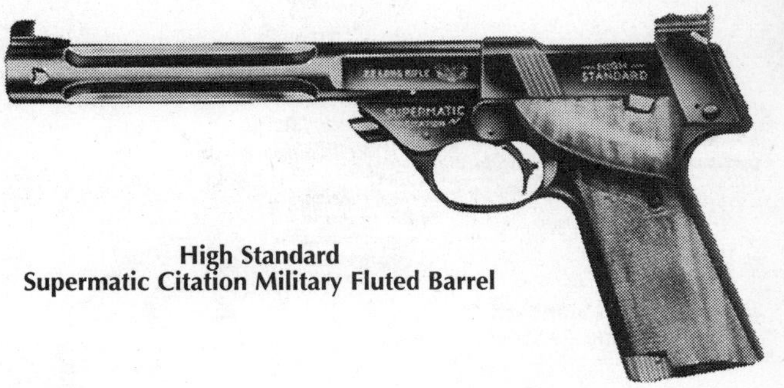

High Standard Supermatic Citation Military Fluted Barrel

High Standard Supermatic Tournament Bull Barrel

High Standard Supermatic Tournament Military Tapered Barrel

High Standard Supermatic Trophy Bull Barrel

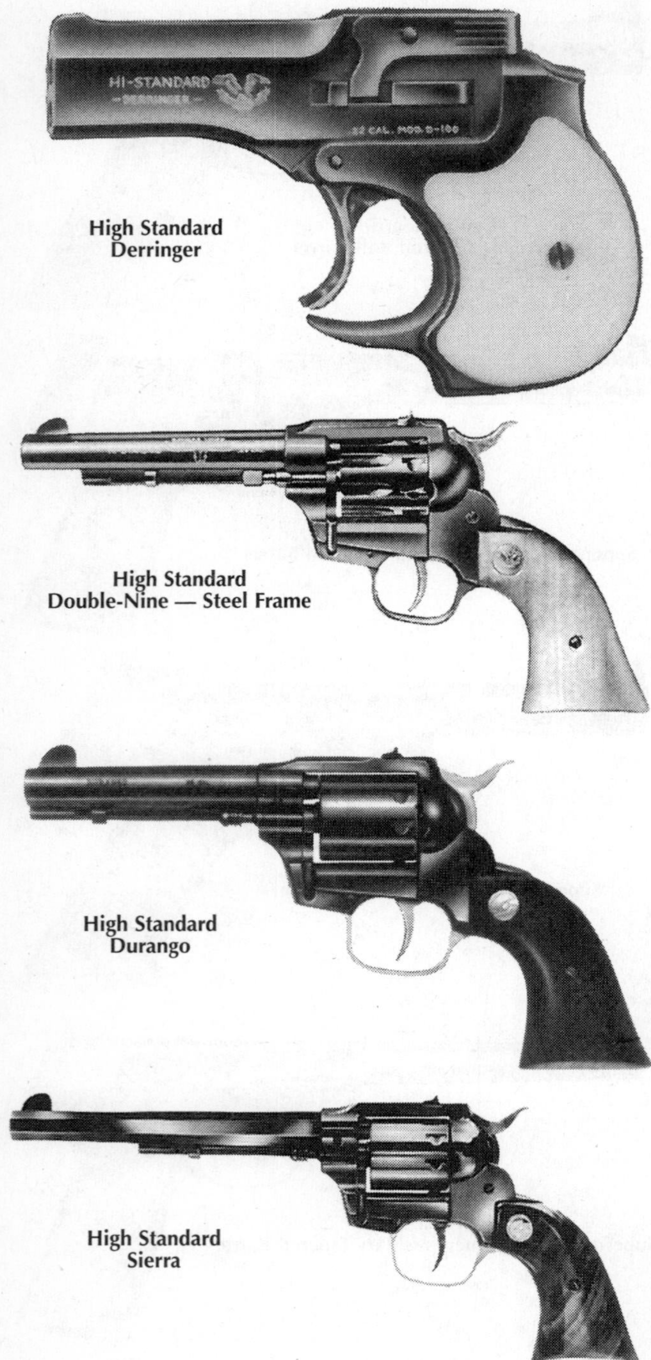

High Standard Derringer

High Standard Double-Nine — Steel Frame

High Standard Durango

High Standard Sierra

NOTE: *High Standard automatic pistols can be found in the preceding section, while revolvers immediately follow this derringer listing.*

DERRINGERS

DERRINGER
Hammerless, double action, two-round, double bbl. (over/under). Calibers: .22 Short, Long, LR or .22 Magnum Rimfire, 3.5-inch bbls., 5 inches overall. Weight: 11 oz. Standard model has blued or nickel finish w/plastic grips. Presentation model is goldplated in walnut case. Standard model made from 1963 (.22 S-L-LR) and 1964 (.22 MRF) to 1984. Gold model, 1965-83.

(cont'd) **DERRINGER**
Gold Presentation One Derringer. NiB $729 Ex $586 Gd $405
Silver Presentation One Derringer. NiB $696 Ex $561 Gd $388
Presentation Set, matched pair, consecutive numbers (1965 only) . . . . NiB $1316 Ex $1060 Gd $732
Standard model (blue). . . . . NiB $268 Ex $219 Gd $154
Standard model (nickel) . . . . NiB $294 Ex $238 Gd $167
Standard model (Electroless nickel). . . . . NiB $309 Ex $252 Gd $178
Standard model (blue). . . . . NiB $271 Ex $221 Gd $157

REVOLVERS

NOTE: *Only High Standard revolvers can be found in this section. See the preceding sections for automatic pistols and derringers. For a complete listing of High Standard handguns, please refer to the Index.*

CAMP GUN. . . . . NiB $277 Ex $226 Gd $160
Same as Sentinel Mark I/Mark IV except has 6-inch bbl., adj. rear sight, target-style checkered walnut grips. Caliber: .22 LR or .22 WMR. Made 1976-83.

DOUBLE-NINE DA REVOLVER —ALUMINUM FRAME
Western-style version of Sentinel. Blued or nickel finish w/simulated ivory, ebony or stag grips, 5.5-inch bbl., 11 inches overall. Weight: 27.25 oz. Made 1959-71.
Blue model . . . . NiB $236 Ex $190 Gd $118
Nickel model. . . . . NiB $247 Ex $200 Gd $126

DOUBLE-NINE—STEEL FRAME
Similar to Double-Nine—Aluminum Frame, w/same general specifications except w/steel frame and has extra cylinder for .22 WMR, walnut grips. Intro. in 1971. disc.
Blue model . . . . NiB $295 Ex $239 Gd $169
Nickel model. . . . . NiB $308 Ex $248 Gd $175

DOUBLE-NINE DELUXE . . . . NiB $304 Ex $248 Gd $174
Same as Double-Nine — Steel Frame except has adj. target rear sight. Intro. in 1971. disc.

DURANGO
Similar to Double-Nine—Steel Frame except .22 LR only, available w/4.5- or 5.5-inch bbl. Made 1971-73.
Blue model . . . . NiB $197 Ex $160 Gd $113
Nickel model. . . . . NiB $210 Ex $169 Gd $118

HIGH SIERRA DA REVOLVER
Similar to Double-Nine—Steel Frame except has 7-inch octagon bbl., w/gold-plated grip frame, fixed or adj. sights. Made 1973-1983.
W/fixed sights . . . . NiB $365 Ex $296 Gd $207
W/adj. sights . . . . NiB $385 Ex $314 Gd $223

HOMBRE
Similar to Double-Nine—Steel Frame except .22 LR only, lacks single-action type ejector rod and tube, has 4.5-inch bbl. Made 1971-73.
Blue model . . . . NiB $191 Ex $157 Gd $111
Nickel model. . . . . NiB $210 Ex $169 Gd $121

KIT GUN DA REVOLVER. . . . . NiB $223 Ex $181 Gd $122
Solid frame, swing-out cylinder. Caliber: .22 LR. Nine-round cylinder, 4-inch bbl., 9 inches overall. Weight: 19 oz. Adj. rear sight, ramp front. Blued finish. Checkered walnut grips. Made 1970-73.

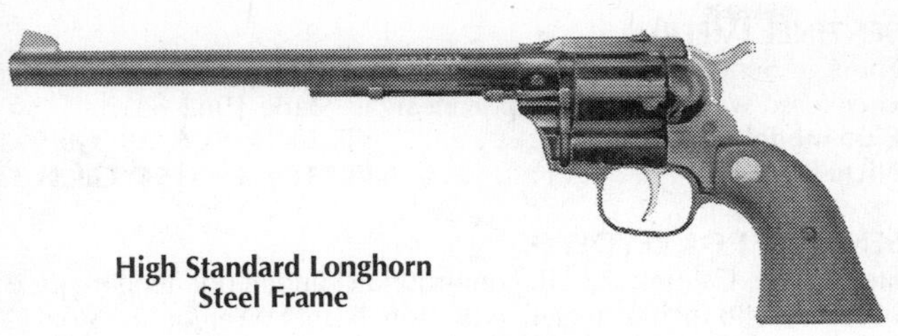

High Standard Longhorn Steel Frame

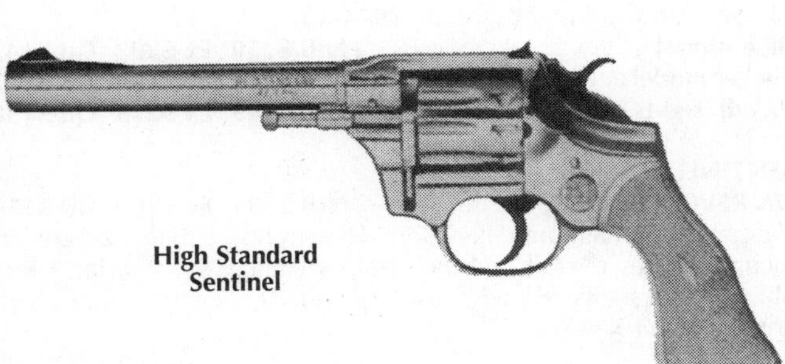

High Standard Sentinel

LONGHORN ALUMINUM FRAME

Similar to Double-Nine—Aluminum Frame except has Longhorn hammer spur, 4.5-, 5.5- or 9.5-inch bbl., Walnut, simulated pearl or simulated stag grips. Blued finish. Made 1960-1971.

W/4.5- or 5.5-inch bbl. . . . . NiB $257 Ex $210 Gd $149
W/9.5-inch bbl . . . . NiB $281 Ex $226 Gd $157

LONGHORN STEEL FRAME

Similar to Double-Nine — Steel Frame except has 9.5-inch bbl. w/fixed or adj. sights. Made 1971-1983

W/fixed sights . . . . NiB $276 Ex $226 Gd $162
W/adj. sights . . . . NiB $412 Ex $344 Gd $247

NATCHEZ . . . . NiB $267 Ex $221 Gd $162

Similar to Double-Nine — Aluminum Frame except 4.5-inch bbl., 10 inches overall, weight: 25.25 oz., blued finish, simulated ivory bird's-head grips. Made 1961-66.

POSSE . . . . NiB $184 Ex $149 Gd $105

Similar to Double-Nine — Aluminum Frame except 3.5-inch bbl., 9 inches overall, weight: 23.25 oz. Blued finish, brass-grip frame and trigger guard, walnut grips. Made 1961-66.

SENTINEL DA REVOLVER

Solid frame, swing-out cylinder. Caliber: .22 LR. Nine-round cylinder, 3- 4- or 6-inch bbl. Nine inches overall (with 4-inch-bbl.). Weight: 19 oz. (with 4-inch bbl.). Fixed sights. Aluminum frame. Blued or nickel finish. Checkered grips. Made 1955-56.

Blue model . . . . NiB $160 Ex $131 Gd $94
Blue/green model . . . . NiB $154 Ex $144 Gd $116
Gold model . . . . NiB $334 Ex $303 Gd $180
Nickel model . . . . NiB $169 Ex $154 Gd $103
Pink model . . . . NiB $350 Ex $314 Gd $180

SENTINEL DELUXE

Same as Sentinel except w/4- or 6-inch bbl., wide trigger, drift-adj. rear sight, two-piece square-butt grips. Made 1957-74. Note: Designated Sentinel after 1971.

Blue model . . . . NiB $154 Ex $139 Gd $103
Nickel model . . . . NiB $180 Ex $164 Gd $113

High Standard Kit Gun

High Standard Longhorn Aluminum Frame

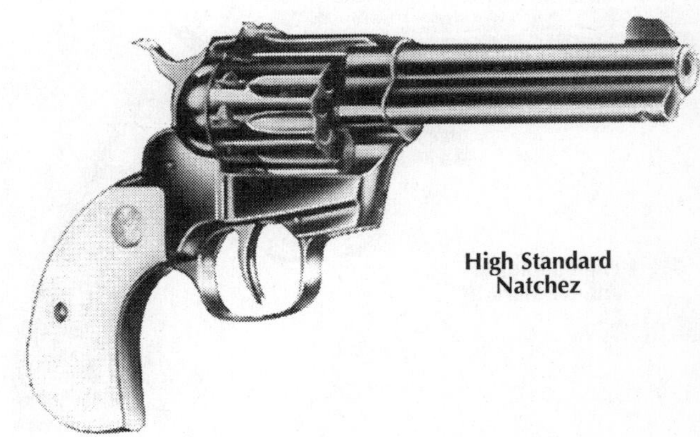

High Standard Natchez

High Standard Posse

High Standard
Sentinel I

High Standard
Sentinel Mark II

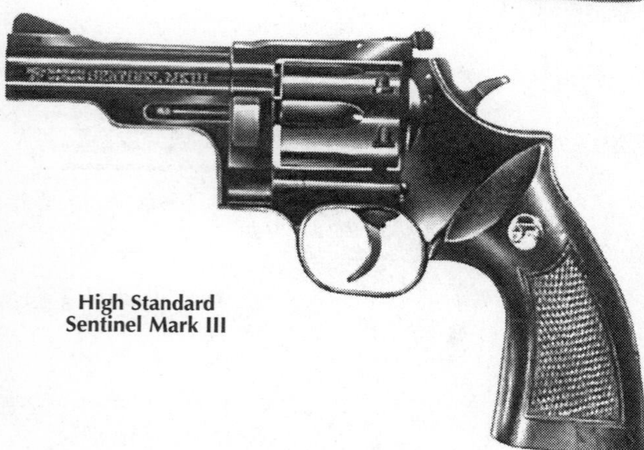

High Standard
Sentinel Mark III

High Standard
Sentinel Snub

SENTINEL IMPERIAL
Same as Sentinel except has onyx-black or nickel finish, two-piece checkered walnut grips, ramp front sight. Made 1962-65.
Blue model . . . . NiB $154 Ex $139 Gd $93
Nickel model . . . . NiB $164 Ex $154 Gd $103

SENTINEL 1 DA REVOLVER
Steel frame. Caliber: .22 LR. Nine-round cylinder, bbl. lengths: 2-, 3-, 4-inch, 6.88 inches overall (with 2-inch bbl.). Weight: 21.5 oz. (2-inch bbl.). Ramp front sight, fixed or adj. rear. Blued or nickel finish. Smooth walnut grips. Made 1974-83.
Blue model . . . . NiB $250 Ex $203 Gd $142
Nickel model . . . . NiB $315 Ex $254 Gd $177
W/adj. sights . . . . NiB $341 Ex $275 Gd $190

SENTINEL MARK II
DA REVOLVER . . . . NiB $295 Ex $269 Gd $156
Caliber: .357 Magnum. Six-round cylinder, bbl. lengths: 2.5-, 4-, 6-inch, 9 inches overall w/4-inch bbl., weight: 38 oz. (with 4-inch bbl.). Fixed sights. Blued finish. Walnut service or combat-style grips. Made 1974-76.

SENTINEL MARK III . . . . NiB $330 Ex $267 Gd $187
Same as Sentinel Mark II except has ramp front and adj. rear sights. Weight: 40 oz. (with 4-inch bbl.). Blued finish. Made 1974-76.

SENTINEL MARK IV
Same as Sentinel Mark I except in .22 WMR. Made 1974-83.
Blue model . . . . NiB $304 Ex $247 Gd $173
Nickel model . . . . NiB $330 Ex $267 Gd $187
W/adj. sights . . . . NiB $363 Ex $293 Gd $205

SENTINEL SNUB
Same as Sentinel Deluxe except w/2.75-inch bbl., (7.25 inches overall, weight: 15 oz.), checkered bird's head-type grips. Made 1957-74.
Blued finish . . . . NiB $159 Ex $154 Gd $103
Nickel finish . . . . NiB $170 Ex $164 Gd $113

HIGH STANDARD MFG. CO., INC. — Houston, Texas Distributed from Hartford, Connecticut

10X AUTOMATIC PISTOL . . . . NiB $973 Ex $767 Gd $458
Caliber: .22 LR. 10-round magazine, 5.5-inch bbl., 9.5 inches overall. Weight: 45 oz. Checkered walnut grips. Blued finish. Made from 1994 to date.

OLYMPIC I.S.U. AUTOMATIC PISTOL
Same specifications as the 1958 I.S.U. issue. See listing under previous High Standard Section.
Olympic I.S.U. model . . . . NiB $586 Ex $483 Gd $226
Olympic I.S.U. military model. . . . . NiB $530 Ex $432 Gd $226
Military model . . . . NiB $452 Ex $365 Gd $255

SPORT KING AUTO PISTOL . . . . NiB $355 Ex $288 Gd $202
Caliber: .22 LR. 10-round magazine, 4.5- or 6.75-inch bbl., 8.5 or 10.75 inches overall. Weight: 44 oz. (with 4.5-inch bbl.), 46 oz. (with 6.75-inch bbl.). Fixed sights, slide mounted. Checkered walnut grips. Parkerized finish. Advertised in 1996 to date. No resale value established.

SUPERMATIC CITATION AUTO PISTOL
Caliber: .22 LR. 10-round magazine, 5.5- or 7.75-inch bbl., 9.5 or 11.75 inches overall. Weight: 44 oz. (with 5.5-inch bbl.), 46 oz. (with 7.75-inch bbl.). Frame-mounted, micro-adj. rear sight, undercut ramp

(cont'd) **SUPERMATIC CITATION AUTO PISTOL**
front sight. Blued or Parkerized finish. Made 1994 to date.
Supermatic Citation model . . . . NiB $447 Ex $355 Gd $211
.22 Short conversion . . . . NiB $350 Ex $288 Gd $200

CITATION MS AUTO PISTOL . . . . . NiB $667 Ex $586 Gd $329
Similar to the Supermatic Citation except has 10-inch bbl., 14 inches overall. Weight: 49 oz. Made 1994 to date.

SUPERMATIC TOURNAMENT. . . . . NiB $400 Ex $324 Gd $227
Caliber: .22 LR. 10-round magazine, bbl. lengths: 4.5, 5.5, or 6.75 inches, overall length: 8.5, 9.5 or 10.75 inches. Weight: 43, 44 or 45 oz. depending on bbl. length. Micro-adj. rear sight, undercut ramp front sight. Checkered walnut grips. Parkerized finish. Made 1994 to date.

SUPERMATIC TROPHY
Caliber: .22 LR. 10-round magazine, 5.5 or 7.25-inch bbl., 9.5 or 11.25 inches overall. Weight: 44 oz. (with 5.5-inch bbl.). Micro-adj. rear sight, undercut ramp front sight. Checkered walnut grips w/thumbrest. Blued or Parkerized finish. Made 1994 to date.
Supermatic Trophy. . . . . NiB $464 Ex $375 Gd $262
.22 Short Conversion. . . . . NiB $350 Ex $288 Gd $200

VICTOR AUTOMATIC
Caliber: .22 LR.10-round magazine, 4.5- or 5.5-inch ribbed bbl., 8.5 or 9.5 inches overall. Weight: 45 oz. (with 4.5-inch bbl.), 46 oz. (with 5.5-inch bbl.). Micro-adj. rear sight, post front. Checkered walnut grips. Blued or Parkerized finish. Made 1994 to date.
Victor Model . . . . NiB $530 Ex $432 Gd $226
.22 Short conversion . . . . NiB $350 Ex $288 Gd $200

HOPKINS & ALLEN ARMS CO. — Norwich, Connecticut

HOPKINS & ALLEN REVOLVERS
See listings of comparable Harrington & Richardson and Iver Johnson models for values.

INGRAM — Mfd. by Military Armament Corp.

See listings under M.A.C. (Military Armament Corp.)

Note: *Military Armament Corp. ceased production of the select-fire automatic, M10 (9mm & .45 ACP) and M11 (.380 ACP) in 1977. Commercial production resumed on semiautomatic versions under the M.A.C. banner until 1982.*

INTERARMS — Alexandria, Virginia

See also Bersa Pistol.

HELWAN BRIGADIER
AUTO PISTOL . . . . NiB $210 Ex $163 Gd $102
Caliber: 9mm Para. Eight-round magazine, 4.25-inch bbl., 8 inches overall. Weight: 32 oz. Blade front sight, dovetailed rear. Blued finish. Grooved plastic grips. Imported 1987-95.

VIRGINIAN DRAGOON SA REVOLVER
Calibers: .357 Magnum, .44 Magnum, .45 Colt. Six-round cylinder. Bbls.: 5- (not available in .44 Magnum), 6-, 7.5-, 8.38-inch (latter only in .44 Magnum w/adj. sights), 11.88 inches overall with (6-inch bbl.). Weight: 48 oz. (with 6-inch bbl.). Fixed sights or micrometer rear and ramp front sights. Blued finish w/color-casetreated frame. Smooth walnut grips. SWISSAFE base pin safety system.

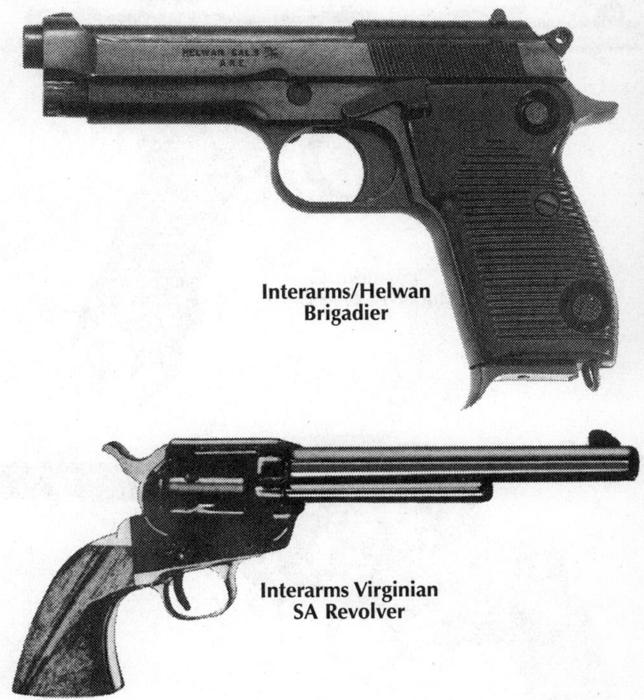

Interarms/Helwan Brigadier

Interarms Virginian SA Revolver

(cont'd) VIRGINIAN DRAGOON SA REVOLVER
Manufactured by Interarms Industries Inc., Midland, VA. 1977-84.
Standard Dragoon . . . . NiB $273 Ex $242 Gd $175
Engraved Dragoon. . . . . NiB $571 Ex $494 Gd $340
Deputy model . . . . NiB $267 Ex $231 Gd $170
Stainless. . . . . NiB $273 Ex $242 Gd $216

VIRGINIAN REVOLVER
SILHOUETTE MODEL . . . . NiB $386 Ex $237 Gd $231
Same general specifications as regular model except designed in stainless steel w/untapered bull bbl., lengths of 7.5, 8.38 and 10.5 inches. Made 1985-86.

VIRGINIAN SA REVOLVER . . . . NiB $519 Ex $417 Gd $287
Similar to Colt Single-Action Army except has base pin safety system. Imported 1973-76. (See also listing under Hämmerli.)

INTRATEC U.S.A., INC. — Miami, Florida

CATEGORY 9 DAO
SEMIAUTOMATIC. . . . . NiB $228 Ex $192 Gd $110
Blowback action w/polymer frame. Caliber: 9mm Par Eight-round magazine, 3-inch bbl., 7.7 inches overall. Weight: 18 oz. Textured black polymer grips. Matte black finish. Made 1993 to date.

CATEGORY 40
DAO SEMIAUTOMATIC . . . . NiB $226 Ex $182 Gd $126
Locking-breech action w/polymer frame. Caliber: .40 S&W. Seven-round magazine, 3.25-inch bbl., 8 inches overall. Weight: 21 oz. Textured black polymer grips. Matte black finish. Made 1994 to date.

CATEGORY 45
DAO SEMIAUTOMATIC . . . . NiB $244 Ex $203 Gd $140
Locking-breech action w/polymer frame. Caliber: .45 ACP. Six-round magazine, 3.25-inch bbl., 8 inches overall. Weight: 21 oz. Textured black polymer grips. Matte black finish. Made 1994 to date.

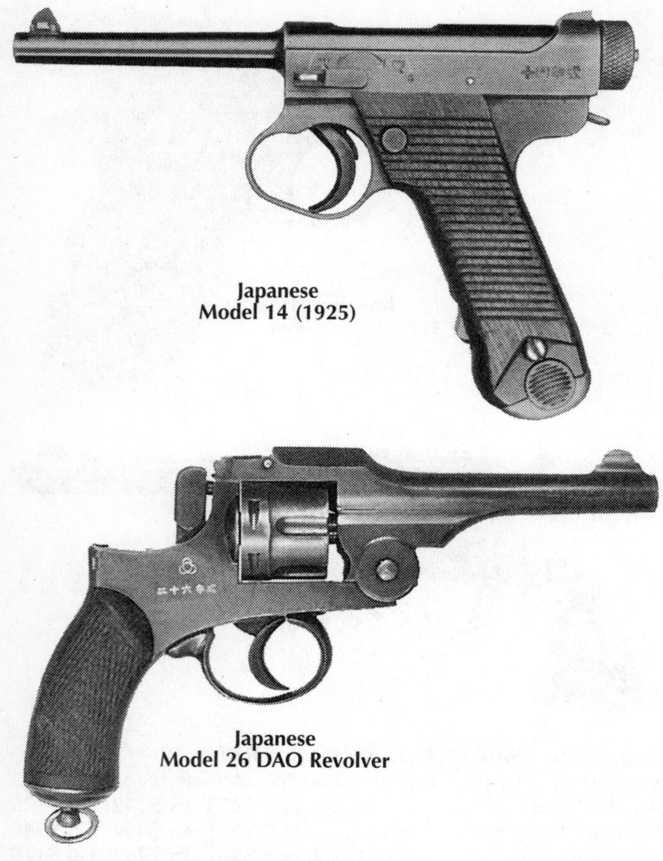
Japanese Model 14 (1925)

Japanese Model 26 DAO Revolver

MODEL PROTEC .22 DA SEMIAUTOMATIC
Caliber: .25 ACP. 10-round magazine, 2.5-inch bbl., 5 inches overall. Weight: 14 oz. Wraparound composition grips. Black Teflon, satin grey or Tec-Kote finish. Advertised in 1992.
ProTec .22 standard . . . . NiB $119 Ex $88 Gd $37
ProTec .22 w/satin or Tec-Kote . . . . NiB $124 Ex $93 Gd $42

MODEL PROTEC .25 DA SEMIAUTOMATIC
Caliber: .25 ACP. Eight-round magazine, 2.5-inch bbl., 5 inches overall. Weight: 14 oz. Fixed sights. Wraparound composition grips. Black Teflon, satin grey or Tec-Kote finish. Made 1991 to date. Note: Formerly Model Tec-.25.
ProTec .25 standard. . . . . NiB $97 Ex $77 Gd $55
ProTec .25 w/satin or Tec-Kote . . . . . . NiB $103 Ex $83 Gd $58

MODEL TEC-9 SEMIAUTOMATIC
Caliber: 9mm Para. 20- or 36-round magazine, 5-inch bbl., weight: 50-51 oz. Open fixed front sight, adj. rear. Military nonglare blued or stainless finish.
Tec-9 w/blued finish . . . . NiB $262 Ex $211 Gd $146
Tec-9 w/nickel finish. . . . . NiB $261 Ex 211 Gd $147
Tec 9S w/stainless finish . . . . NiB $345 Ex $278 Gd $190

MODEL TEC-9M SEMIAUTOMATIC
Same specifications as Model Tec-9 except has 3-inch bbl. without shroud and 20-round magazine, blued or stainless finish.
Tec-9M w/blued finish. . . . . NiB $236 Ex $190 Gd $133
Tec-9MS w/stainless finish. . . . . NiB $313 Ex $252 Gd $175

MODEL TEC-22T SEMIAUTOMATIC
Caliber: .22 LR. 10/.22-type 30-round magazine, 4-inch bbl., 11.19 inches overall. Weight: 30 oz. Protected post front sight, adj. rear sight. Matte black or Tec-Kote finish. Made 1989 to date.

(cont'd) **MODEL TEC-22T SEMIAUTOMATIC**
Tec-22T standard. . . . . NiB $175 Ex $144 Gd $103
Tec-22TK Tec-Kote . . . . NiB $210 Ex $170 Gd $118

MODEL TEC DOUBLE DERRINGER. . . . . NiB $126 Ex $103 Gd $72
Calibers: .22 WRF, .32 H&R Mag., .38 Special. Two-round capacity, 3-inch bbl., 4.63 inches overall. Weight: 13 oz. Fixed sights. Matte black finish. Made 1986-88.

ISRAEL ARMS — Kfar Sabs, Israel
Imported by Israel Arms International, Houston TX

MODEL BUL-M5 LOCKED BREECH (2000) AUTO PISTOL . . . . NiB $427 Ex $293 Gd $257
Similar to the M1911 U.S. Government model. Caliber: .45 ACP. Seven-round magazine, 5-inch bbl., 8.5 inches overall. Weight: 38 oz. Blade front and fixed, low-profile rear sights.

KAREEN MK II (1500) AUTO PISTOL
Single-action only. Caliber: 9mm Para. 10-round magazine, 4.75-inch bbl., 8 inches overall. Weight: 33.6 oz. Blade front sight, rear adjustable for windage. Textured black composition or rubberized grips. Blued, two-tone, matte black finish. Imported 1996 to date.
Blued or matte black finish . . . . NiB $427 Ex $334 Gd $241
Two-tone finish . . . . NiB $633 Ex $494 Gd $361
Meprolite sights, add $40

KAREEN MK II COMPACT (1501) AUTO PISTOL . . . . NiB $417 Ex $350 Gd $252
Similar to standard Kareen MKII except w/3.85-inch bbl., 7.1 inches overall. Weight: 32 oz. Imported 1997 to date.

GOLAN MODEL (2500) AUTO PISTOL
Single or double action. Caliber: 9mm Para., .40 S&W. 10-round magazine, 3.85-inch bbl., 7.1 inches overall. Weight: 34 oz. Steel slide and alloy frame w/ambidextrous safety and decocking lever. Matte black finish. Imported 1997 to date.
9mm Para. . . . . NiB $857 Ex $689 Gd $475
.40 S&W . . . . NiB $696 Ex $561 Gd $388

GAL MODEL (5000) AUTO PISTOL . . . . NiB $364 Ex $293 Gd $203
Caliber: .45 ACP. Eight-round magazine, 4.25-inch bbl., 7.25 inches overall. Weight: 42 oz. Low profile 3-dot sights. Combat-style black rubber grips. Imported 1997 to date.

JAPANESE MILITARY PISTOLS — Tokyo, Japan Manufactured by Government Plant

MODEL 14 (1925) AUTOMATIC PISTOL . . . . NiB $655 Ex $527 Gd $364
Modification of the Nambu Model 1914, changes chiefly intended to simplify mass production. Standard round trigger guard or oversized guard for use w/gloves. Caliber: 8mm Nambu. Eight-round magazine, 4.75-inch bbl., 9 inches overall. Weight: About 29 oz. Fixed sights. Blued finish. Grooved wood grips. Intro. 1925 and mfd. through WW II.

MODEL 26 DAO REVOLVER . . . . . NiB $583 Ex $398 Gd $265
Top-break frame. Caliber: 9mm. Six-round cylinder w/automatic extractor/ejector, 4.7-inch bbl., adopted by the Japanese Army from 1893 to 1914, replaced by the Model 14 Automatic Pistol but remained in service through World War II.

MODEL 94 (1934)
AUTOMATIC PISTOL . . . . NiB $288 Ex $216 Gd $139
Poorly designed and constructed, this pistol is unsafe and can be fired merely by applying pressure on the sear, which is exposed on the left side. Caliber: 8mm Nambu. Six-round magazine, 3.13-inch bbl., 7.13 inches overall. Weight: About 27 oz. Fixed sights. Blued finish. Hard rubber or wood grips. Intro. in 1934, principally for export to Latin American countries, production continued thru WW II.

NAMBU MODEL
1914 AUTOMATIC PISTOL . . . . . NiB $1678 Ex $1472 Gd $730
Original Japanese service pistol, resembles Luger in appearance and Glisenti in operation. Caliber: 8mm Nambu. Seven-round magazine, 4.5-inch bbl., 9 inches overall. Weight: About 30 oz. Fixed front sight, adj. rear sight. Blued finish. Checkered wood grips. Made 1914-1925.

Japanese Model 94 (1934)

JENNINGS FIREARMS INC. — Currently Mfd. by Bryco Arms, Irvine, California Previously by Calwestco, Inc. & B.L. Jennings

See additional listings under Bryco Arms.

MODEL J AUTO PISTOL
Calibers: .22 LR, .25 ACP. Six-round magazine, 2.5-inch bbl., about 5 inches overall. Weight: 13 oz. Fixed sights. Chrome, satin nickel or black Teflon finish. Walnut, grooved black Cycolac or resin-impregnated wood grips. Made from 1981-85 under Jennings and Calwestco logos; from 1985 to date by Bryco Arms.
Model J-22. . . . . NiB $79 Ex $65 Gd $43
Model J-25. . . . . NiB $74 Ex $58 Gd $38

Jennings Model J Auto Pistol

IVER JOHNSON ARMS, INC. — Jacksonville, Arkansas

Operation of this company dates back to 1871, when Iver Johnson and Martin Bye partnered to manufacture metallic cartridge revolvers. Johnson became the sole owner and changed the name to Iver Johnson's Arms & Cycle Works, which it was known as for almost 100 years. Modern management shortened the name, and after several owner changes the firm was moved from Massachusetts, its original base, to Jacksonville, Arkansas. In 1987, the American Military Arms Corporation (AMAC) acquired the operation, which subsequently ceased in 1993.

NOTE: *For ease in finding a particular firearm, Iver Johnson handguns are divided into two sections: Automatic Pistols (below) and Revolvers, which follow. For the complete handgun listing, please refer to the Index.*

AUTOMATIC PISTOLS

9MM DA AUTOMATIC . . . . NiB $390 Ex $314 Gd $217
Caliber: 9mm. Six-round magazine, 3-inch bbl., 6.5 inches overall. Weight: 26 oz. Blade front sight, adj. rear. Smooth hardwood grip. Blued or matte blued finish. Intro. 1986.

COMPACT .25 ACP . . . . NiB $178 Ex $147 Gd $95
Bernardelli V/P design. Caliber: .25 ACP. Five-round magazine, 2.13-inch bbl., 4.13 inches overall. Weight: 9.3 oz. Fixed sights. Checkered composition grips. Blued slide, matte blued frame and color-casehardened trigger. Made 1991 to 93.

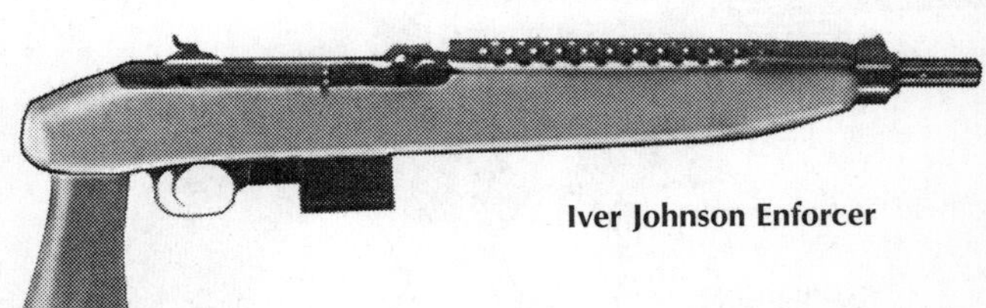
Iver Johnson Enforcer

ENFORCER . . . . NiB $483 Ex $375 Gd $266
Semiautomatic. Caliber: .30 U.S. Carbine. Five-, 15-, or 30-round magazine, 9.5- inch bbl., weight: 5.5 lbs. Adj. sights. Walnut stock. Made mid-1980s to 1993.

PP30 SUPER
ENFORCER AUTOMATIC . . . . NiB $453 Ex $360 Gd $226
Caliber: .30 U.S. Carbine. Fifteen- or 30-round magazine, 9.5-inch bbl., 17 inches overall. Weight: 4 pounds. Adj. peep rear sight, blade front. American walnut stock. Made 1984-86.

PONY AUTOMATIC PISTOL
Caliber: .380 Auto. Six-round magazine, 3.1-inch bbl., 6.1 inches overall. Blue, matte blue, nickel finish or stainless. Weight: 20 oz. Wooden grips. Smallest of the locked breech automatics. Made 1982-88. Reintroduced 1990-93.
Blue or matte
blue model . . . . NiB $329 Ex $277 Gd $194
Nickel model. . . . . NiB $380 Ex $288 Gd $195
Deluxe model . . . . NiB $406 Ex $329 Gd $236

Iver Johnson
Model TP

Iver Johnson
Model 57A Target

Iver Johnson
Model 55 Target

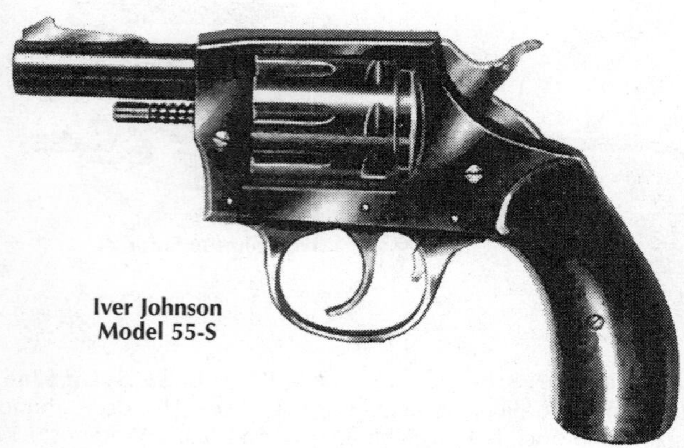

Iver Johnson
Model 55-S

Iver Johnson
Model 56 Blank Revolver

MODEL TP-22 DA AUTOMATIC. . . . . NiB $154 Ex $113 Gd $72
Calibers: .22 LR, Seven-round magazine, 2.85-inch bbl., 5.39 inches overall. Blued finish. Weight: 14.46 oz. Made 1982-93.

MODEL TP25 DA POCKET PISTOL . . . . NiB $190 Ex $154 Gd $108
Double-action automatic. Caliber: .25 ACP. Seven-round magazine, 3-inch bbl., 5.5 inches overall. Weight: 12 oz. Black plastic grips and blued finish. Made 1982-93.

TRAILSMAN AUTOMATIC PISTOL
Caliber: .22 LR. 10-round magazine, 4.5 or 6-inch bbl., 8.75 inches overall (with 4.5-inch bbl.). Weight: 46 oz. Fixed target-type sights. Checkered composition grips. Made 1984-90.
Standard model . . . . NiB $224 Ex $183 Gd $127
Deluxe model . . . . NiB $263 Ex $213 Gd $149

REVOLVERS

MODEL 55 TARGET DA REVOLVER . . . . NiB $144 Ex $113 Gd $72
Solid frame. Caliber: .22 LR. Eight-round cylinder, bbl. lengths: 4.5-, 6-inches. 10.75 inches overall (with 6-inch bbl.). Weight: 30.5 oz. (with 6-inch bbl.). Fixed sights. Blued finish. Walnut grips. Note: Original model designation was 55; changed to 55A when loading gate was added in 1961. Made 1955-77.

MODEL 55-S REVOLVER. . . . . NiB $154 Ex $113 Gd $72
Same general specifications as the Model 55 except for 2.5-inch bbl. and small, molded pocket-size grip.

MODEL 56 BLANK REVOLVER . . . . NiB $93 Ex $77 Gd $55
Solid frame. Caliber: .22 blanks only. Eight-round cylinder, 2.5-inch solid bbl., 6.75 inches overall. Weight: 10 oz.

MODEL 57A TARGET DA REVOLVER. . . . . NiB $123 Ex $108 Gd $72
Solid frame. Caliber: .22 LR. Eight-round cylinder, bbl. lengths: 4.5-, and 6-inches. 10.75 inches overall. Weight: 30.5 oz. with 6-inch bbl. Adj. sights. Blued finish. Walnut grips. Note: Original model designation was 57, changed to 57A when loading gate was added in 1961. Made 1956-75.

MODEL 66 TRAILSMAN DA REVOLVER. . . . . NiB $113 Ex $82 Gd $61
Hinged frame. Rebounding hammer. Caliber: .22 LR. Eight-round cylinder, 6-inch bbl., 11 inches overall. Weight: 34 oz. Adj. sights. Blued finish. Walnut grips. Made 1958-75.

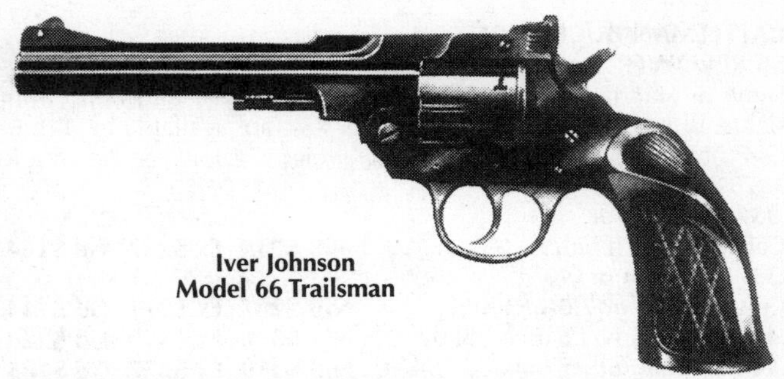
Iver Johnson
Model 66 Trailsman

Iver Johnson
Model 67 Viking

MODEL 67 VIKING DA REVOLVER .... NiB $152 Ex $123 Gd $87
Hinged frame. Caliber: .22 LR. Eight-round cylinder, bbl. lengths: 4.5- and 6-inches, 11 inches overall (with 6-inch bbl.). Weight: 34 oz. (with 6-inch bbl.). Adj. sights. Walnut grips w/thumbrest. Made 1964-75.

MODEL 67S VIKING SNUB REVOLVER .... NiB $154 Ex $113 Gd $72
DA. Hinged frame. Calibers: .22 LR, .32 S&W Short and Long, .38 S&W. Eight-round cylinder in .22, 5-round in .32 and .38 calibers; 2.75-inch bbl. Weight: 25 oz. Adj. sights. Tenite grips. Made 1964-75.

Iver Johnson
Model 67S Viking Snub

MODEL 1900 DA REVOLVER ...... NiB $124 Ex $103 Gd $57
Solid frame. Calibers: .22 LR, .32 S&W, .32 S&W Long, .38 S&W. Seven-round cylinder in .22 cal.,or 6-round (.32 S&W), 5-round (.32 S&W Long, .38 S&W); bbl. lengths: 2.5-, 4.5- and 6-inches. Weight: 12 oz. (in .32 S&W w/2.5-inch bbl.). Fixed sights. Blued or nickel finish. Hard rubber grips. Made 1900-47.

MODEL 1900 TARGET DA REVOLVER.......... NiB $185 Ex $149 Gd $103
Solid frame. Caliber: .22 LR. Seven-round cylinder, bbl. lengths: 6- and 9.5-inches. Fixed sights. Blued finish. Checkered walnut grips. (This earlier model does not have counterbored chambers as in the Target Sealed 8. Made 1925-42.)

Iver Johnson
Model 1900 Target

AMERICAN BULLDOG DA REVOLVER
Solid frame. Calibers: .22 LR, .22 WMR, .38 Special. Six-round cylinder in .22, 5-round in .38. Bbl. lengths: 2.5-, 4-inch. 9 inches overall (with 4-inch bbl.). Weight: 30 oz. (with 4-inch bbl.). Adj. sights. Blued or nickel finish. Plastic grips. Made 1974-76.
.38 Special.................... NiB $175 Ex $144 Gd $92
Other calibers................. NiB $154 Ex $113 Gd $72

ARMSWORTH MODEL 855 SA.... NiB $242 Ex $175 Gd $128
Hinged frame. Caliber: .22 LR. Eight-round cylinder, 6-inch bbl., 10.75 inches overall. Weight: 30 oz. Adj. sights. Blued finish. Checkered walnut one-piece grip. Adj. finger rest. Made 1955-57.

CADET DA REVOLVER .... NiB $152 Ex $128 Gd $77
Solid frame. Calibers: .22 LR, .22 WMR, .32 S&W Long, .38 S&W, .38 Special. Six- or 8-round cylinder in .22, 5-round in other calibers, 2.5-inch bbl., 7 inches overall. Weight: 22 oz. Fixed sights. Blued finish or nickel finish. Plastic grips. Note: Loading gate added in 1961, .22 cylinder capacity changed from 8 to 6 rounds in 1975. Made 1955-77.

Iver Johnson
Cadet

CATTLEMAN SA REVOLVER
Patterned after the Colt Army SA revolver. Calibers: .357 Magnum, .44 Magnum, .45 Colt. Six-round cylinder. Bbl. lengths: 4.75-, 5.5- (not available in .44), 6- (.44 only), 7.25-inch. Weight: About 41 oz. Fixed sights. Blued bbl., and cylinder color-casehardened frame, brass grip frame. One-piece walnut grip. Made by Aldo Uberti, Brescia, Italy, 1973-78.
.44 Magnum .... NiB $267 Ex $216 Gd $139
Other calibers................. NiB $237 Ex $194 Gd $123

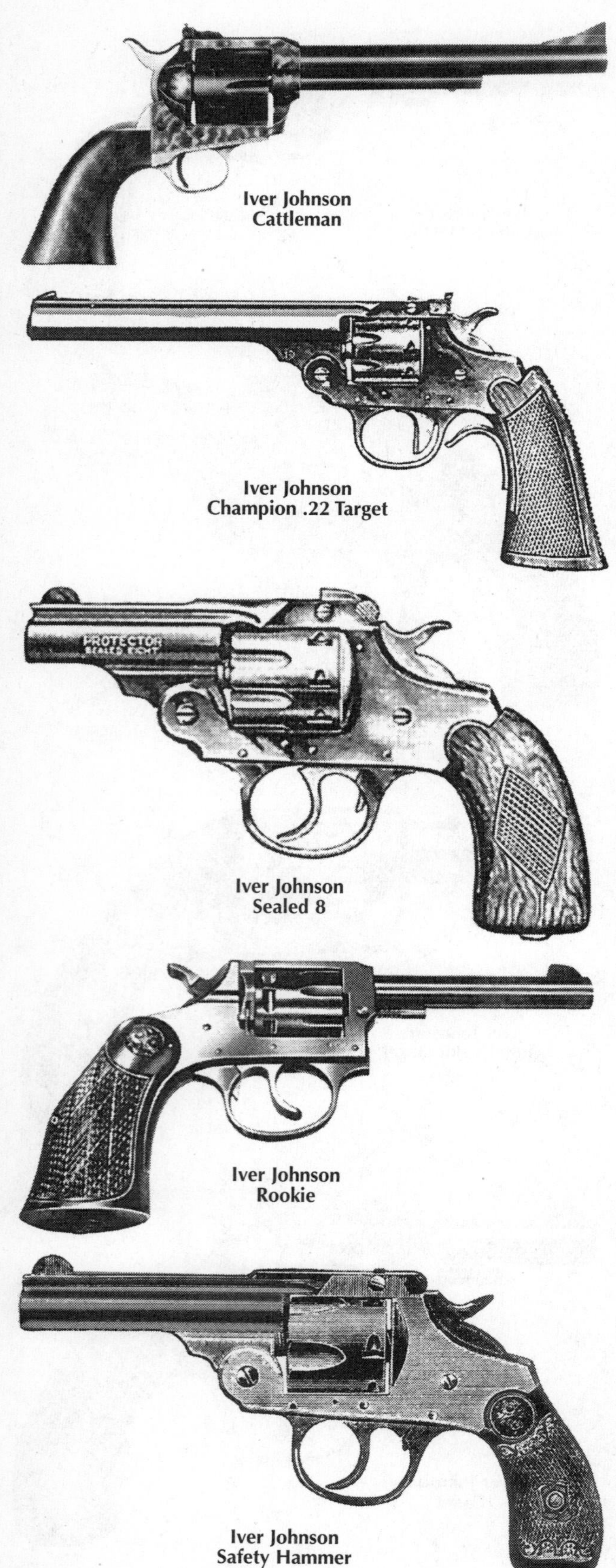

Iver Johnson Cattleman

Iver Johnson Champion .22 Target

Iver Johnson Sealed 8

Iver Johnson Rookie

Iver Johnson Safety Hammer

CATTLEMAN BUCKHORN SA REVOLVER
Same as standard Cattleman except has adj. rear and ramp front sights. Bbl. lengths: 4.75- (.44 only), 5.75- (not available in .44), 6- (.44 only), 7.5- or 12-inches bbl., weight: About 44 oz. Made 1973-78.

.357 Magnum or .45 Colt w/12-inch bbl. . . . . NiB $319 Ex $237 Gd $164
.357 Magnum or .45 Colt w/5.75- or 7.5-inch bbl. . . . . . NiB $267 Ex $211 Gd $144
.44 Magnum, w/12-inch bbl. . . . . . . NiB $396 Ex $319 Gd $220
.44 Magnum, other bbls. . . . . NiB $319 Ex $267 Gd $185

CATTLEMAN BUNTLINE SA REVOLVER
Same as Cattleman Buckhorn except has 18-inch bbl., walnut shoulder stock w/brass fittings. Weight: About 56 oz. Made 1973-78.

.44 Magnum . . . . NiB $512 Ex $414 Gd $287
Other calibers . . . . NiB $461 Ex $372 Gd $259

CATTLEMAN TRAIL BLAZER . . . . . . NiB $202 Ex $160 Gd $109
Similar to Cattleman Buckhorn except .22 caliber has interchangeable .22 LR and .22 WMR cylinders, 5.5- or 6.5-inch bbl., weight: About 40 oz. Made 1973-78.

CHAMPION .22 TARGET SA . . . . NiB $248 Ex $201 Gd $140
Hinged frame. Caliber: .22 LR. Eight-round cylinder. Single action. Counterbored chambers as in Sealed 8 model, 6-inch bbl., 10.75 inches overall. Weight: 28 oz. Adj. target sights. Blued finish. Checkered walnut grips, adj. finger rest. Made 1938-48.

DELUXE TARGET . . . . NiB $247 Ex $201 Gd $149
Same as Sportsman except has adj. sights. Made 1975-76.

PROTECTOR SEALED 8 DA REVOLVER . . . . NiB $190 Ex $139 Gd $102
Hinged frame. Caliber: .22 LR. Eight-round cylinder, 2.5-inch bbl., 7.25 inches overall. Weight: 20 oz. Fixed sights. Blued finish. Checkered walnut grips. Made 1933-49.

ROOKIE DA REVOLVER. . . . . NiB $113 Ex $92 Gd $72
Solid frame. Caliber: .38 Special. Five-round cylinder, 4-inch bbl., 9-inches overall. Weight: 30 oz. Fixed sights. Blued or nickel finish. Plastic grips. Made 1975-77.

SAFETY HAMMER DA REVOLVER. . . . . NiB $154 Ex $123 Gd $82
Hinged frame. Calibers: .22 LR, .32 S&W, .32 S&W Long, .38 S&W. Seven-round cylinder in .22 cal.,or 6-round (.32 S&W Long), 5-round (.32 S&W, .38 S&W). bbl. lengths: 2, 3, 3.25, 4, 5 or 6 inches. Weight w/4-inch bbl.: 15 oz. (.22, .32 S&W), 19.5 oz. (.32 S&W Long) or 19 oz. (.38 S&W). Fixed sights. Blued or nickel finish. Hard rubber, round butt grips or square butt, rubber or walnut grips available. Note: .32 S&W Long and .38 S&W models built on heavy frame. Made 1892-1950.

SAFETY HAMMERLESS DA REVOLVER. . . . . NiB $164 Ex $134 Gd $87
Similar to the Safety Hammer Model except w/shrouded hammerless frame. Made 1895-1950.

SIDEWINDER
DA REVOLVER. . . . . NiB $154 Ex $139 Gd $82
Solid frame. Caliber: .22 LR. Six- or 8-round cylinder, bbl. lengths: 4.75, 6 inches; 11.25 inches overall (with 6-inch bbl.). Weight: 31 oz. (with 6-inch bbl.). Fixed sights. Blued or nickel finish w/plastic staghorn grips or color-casehardened frame w/walnut grips. Note: Cylinder capacity changed from 8 to 6 rounds in 1975. Intro. 1961. disc.

SIDEWINDER "S" . . . . NiB $164 Ex $139 Gd $97
Same as Sidewinder except has interchangeable cylinders in .22 LR and .22 WMR, adj. sights. Intro. 1974. disc.

SPORTSMAN
DA REVOLVER. . . . . NiB $143 Ex $113 Gd $82
Solid frame. Caliber: .22 LR. Six-round cylinder. Bbl. lengths: 4.75-, 6-inches, 10.75 inches overall (with 6-inch bbl.). Weight: 30.5 oz. (with 6-inch bbl.). Fixed sights. Blued finish. Plastic grips. Made 1974-76.

SUPERSHOT 9
DA REVOLVER. . . . . NiB $159 Ex $134 Gd $77
Same as Supershot Sealed 8 except has nine non-counterbored chambers. Made 1929-49.

SUPERSHOT .22 DA REVOLVER . . . . . NiB $112 Ex $92 Gd $61
Hinged frame. Caliber: .22 LR. Seven-round cylinder, 6-inch bbl. Fixed sights. Blued finish. Checkered walnut grips. This earlier model does not have counterbored chambers as in the Supershot Sealed 8. Made 1929-49.

SUPERSHOT MODEL 844 DA. . . . . NiB $190 Ex $149 Gd $102
Hinged frame. Caliber: .22 LR. Eight-round cylinder, bbl. lengths: 4.5- or 6-inch, 9.25 inches overall (with 4.5-inch bbl.). Weight: 27 oz. (4.5-inch bbl.). Adj. sights. Blued finish. Checkered walnut one-piece grip. Made 1955-56.

SUPERSHOT SEALED
8 DA REVOLVER . . . . NiB $190 Ex $149 Gd $103
Hinged frame. Caliber: .22 LR. Eight-round cylinder, 6-inch bbl., 10.75 inches overall. Weight: 24 oz. Adj. target sights. Blued finish. Checkered walnut grips. Postwar model does not have adj. finger rest as earlier version. Made 1931-57.

SWING-OUT DA REVOLVER
Calibers: .22 LR, .22 WMR, .32 S&W Long, .38 Special. Six-round cylinder in .22, 5-round in .32 and .38. Two, 3-, 4-inch plain bbl., or 4- 6-inch vent rib bbl., 8.75 inches overall (with 4-inch bbl.). Fixed or adj. sights. Blued or nickel finish. Walnut grips. Made in 1977.
W/plain barrel, fixed sights . . . . NiB $164 Ex $134 Gd $92
W/vent rib, adj. sights. . . . . NiB $154 Ex $185 Gd $113

TARGET 9 DA REVOLVER. . . . . NiB $196 Ex $159 Gd $112
Same as Target Sealed 8 except has nine non-counterbored chambers. Made 1929-46.

TARGET SEALED 8 DA REVOLVER . . . . NiB $185 Ex $144 Gd $108
Solid frame. Caliber: .22 LR. Eight-round cylinder, bbl. lengths: 6- and 10-inches. 10.75 inches overall (with 6-inch bbl.). Weight: 24 oz. (with 6-inch bbl.). Fixed sights. Blued finish. Checkered walnut grips. Made 1931-57.

TRIGGER-COCKING SA TARGET . . . . NiB $254 Ex $203 Gd $146
Hinged frame. First pull on trigger cocks hammer, second pull releases hammer. Caliber: .22 LR. Eight-round cylinder, counterbored chambers, 6-inch bbl., 10.75 inches overall. Weight: 24 oz. Adj. target sights. Blued finish. Checkered walnut grips. Made 1940-47.

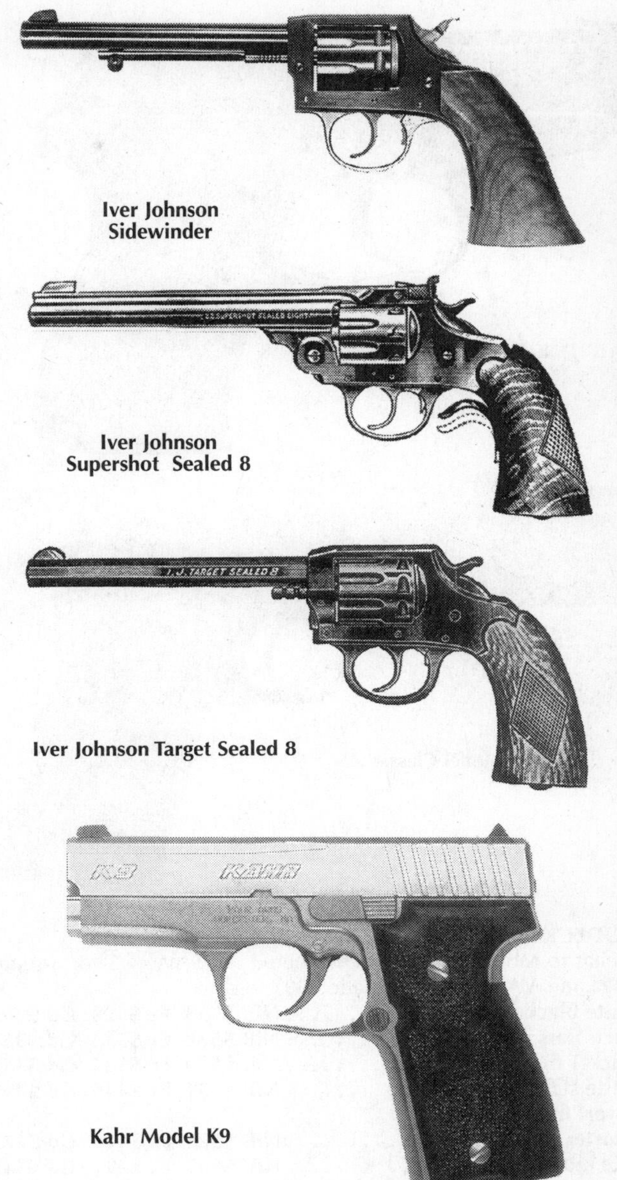

Iver Johnson Sidewinder

Iver Johnson Supershot Sealed 8

Iver Johnson Target Sealed 8

Kahr Model K9

KAHR ARMS — Blauvelt, New York

MODEL K9
DAO AUTO PISTOL
Caliber: 9mm Para. Seven-round magazine, 3.5-inch bbl., 6 inches overall. Weight: 24 oz. Fixed sights. Matte black, electroless nickel, Birdsong Black-T or matte stainless finish. Wraparound textured polymer or hardwood grips. Made 1994 to date.
Duo-Tone finish . . . . NiB $703 Ex $565 Gd $389
Matte black finish . . . . NiB $580 Ex $452 Gd $313
Electroless nickel finish . . . . NiB $606 Ex $488 Gd $336
Black-T finish. . . . . NiB $823 Ex $606 Gd $447
Matte stainless finish . . . . NiB $561 Ex $452 Gd $312
Lady K9 model. . . . . NiB $542 Ex $436 Gd $301
Elite model . . . . NiB $574 Ex $462 Gd $319
Tritium Night Sights, add. $90

Kel-Tec Model P-11

Kimber Model Classic .45

MODEL K40 DAO AUTO PISTOL
Similar to Model K9 except chambered .40 S&W w/5- or 6-round magazine, Weight: 26 oz. Made 1997 to date.
Matte black finish . . . . NiB $533 Ex $429 Gd $295
Electroless nickel finish . . . . NiB $634 Ex $512 Gd $355
Black-T finish. . . . . NiB $670 Ex $532 Gd $356
Matte stainless finish . . . . NiB $559 Ex $445 Gd $298
Covert model
(shorter grip-frame). . . . . NiB $528 Ex $419 Gd $279
Elite model . . . . NiB $603 Ex $491 Gd $348
Tritium Night Sights, add. $90

MODEL MK9 DAO AUTO PISTOL
Similar to Model K9 except w/Micro-Compact frame. Six- or 7-round magazine, 3- inch bbl., 5.5 inches overall. Weight: 22 oz. Stainless or Duo-Tone finish. Made 1998 to date.
Duo-Tone finish. . . . . NiB $722 Ex $584 Gd $408
Matte stainless
finish . . . . NiB $603 Ex $491 Gd $337
Elite model . . . . NiB $605 Ex $491 Gd $337
Tritium Night
Sights, add. $90

KBI, INC — Harrisburg, Pennsylvania

MODEL PSP-.25 AUTO PISTOL. . . . NiB $245 Ex $188 Gd $121
Caliber: .25 ACP. Six-round magazine, 2.13-inch bbl., 4.13 inches overall. Weight: 9.5 oz. All-steel construction w/dual safety system. Made 1994 to date.

KEL-TEC CNC INDUSTRIES, INC. — Cocoa, Florida

MODEL P-11 DAO PISTOL
Caliber: 9mm Parabellum or .40 S&W. 10-round magazine, 3.1-inch bbl., 5.6 inches overall. Weight: 14 oz. Blade front sight, drift adjustable rear. Aluminum frame w/steel slide. Checkered black, gray, or green polymer grips. Matte blue, nickel, stainless steel or Parkerized finish. Made 1995 to date.
9mm . . . . NiB $282 Ex $231 Gd $168
.40 S&W . . . . NiB $284 Ex $226 Gd $152
Parkerized finish, add $40
Nickel finish, add (disc. 1995). $30
Stainless finish, add
(1996 to date) $55
Tritium Night Sights, add. $80
.40 cal. conversion kit, add $175

KIMBER MANUFACTURING, INC. — Yonkers, New York (Formerly Kimber of America, Inc.)

MODEL CLASSIC .45
Similar to Government 1911 built on steel, polymer or alloy full-size or compact frame. Caliber: .45 ACP. Seven-, 8-, 10- or 14-round magazine, 4- or 5-inch bbl., 7.7 or 8.75 inches overall. Weight: 28 oz. (Compact LW), 34 oz. (Compact or Polymer) or .38 oz. (Custom FS). McCormick low-profile combat or Kimber adj. target sights. Blued, matte black oxide or stainless finish. Checkered custom wood or black synthetic grips. Made from 1994 to date.
Custom (matte black) . . . . NiB $633 Ex $530 Gd $339
Custom Royal (polished blue) . . . . . NiB $691 Ex $556 Gd $383
Custom stainless (satin stainless). . . NiB $653 Ex $525 Gd $362
Custom Target (matte black) . . . . . . NiB $665 Ex $535 Gd $368
Target Gold Match
(polished blue). . . . . NiB $913 Ex $694 Gd $505
Target stainless Match
(polished stainless) . . . . NiB $732 Ex $834 Gd $571
Polymer (matte black) . . . . NiB $742 Ex $597 Gd $411
Polymer Stainless
(satin stainless slide) . . . . NiB $891 Ex $710 Gd $491
Polymer Target
(matte black slide). . . . . NiB $833 Ex $669 Gd $460
Compact (matte black) . . . . NiB $588 Ex $473 Gd $327
Compact stainless (satin stainless) . . . . . . NiB $653 Ex $525 Gd $362
Compact LW (matte
black w/alloy frame) . . . . NiB $673 Ex $509 Gd $355

KORTH PISTOLS — Ratzeburg, Germany

Currently imported by Keng's Firearms Specialty, Inc. Previously by Beeman Precision Arms; Osborne's and Mandall Shooting Supply

REVOLVERS COMBAT, SPORT, TARGET
Calibers: .357 Mag. and .22 LR w/interchangeable combination cylinders of .357 Mag./9mm Para. or .22 LR/.22 WMR also .22 Jet, .32 S&W and .32 H&R Mag. Bbls: 2.5-, 3-, 4-inch (combat) and 5.25- or 6-inch (target). Weight: 33 to 42 oz. Blued, stainless, matte silver or polished silver finish. Checkered walnut grips. Imported 1967 to date.
Standard rimfire model . . . . NiB $3284 Ex $2605 Gd $1740
Standard centerfire model. . . . . NiB $3331 Ex $2610 Gd $1781
ISU Match Target model . . . . . . NiB $4057 Ex $3295 Gd $2193
Custom stainless finish, add. $450
Matte silver finish, add $650
Polished silver finish, add $950

SEMIAUTOMATIC PISTOL

Calibers: 30 Luger, 9mm Para., .357 SIG, .40 S&W, 9x21mm. 10- or 14-round magazine, 4- or 5-inch bbl., all-steel construction, recoil-operated. Ramp front sight, adj. rear. Blued, stainless, matte silver or polished silver finish. Checkered walnut grips. Imported 1988 to date.

Standard model . . . . NiB $4934 Ex $3937 Gd $2706
Matte silver finish, add $650
Polished silver finish, add $950

Lahti Automatic Pistol

LAHTI PISTOLS — Mfd. by Husqvarna Vapenfabriks A. B. Huskvarna, Sweden, and Valtion Kivaar Tedhas ("VKT") Jyväskyla, Finland

AUTOMATIC PISTOL

Caliber: 9mm Para. Eight-round magazine, 4.75-inch bbl., weight: About 46 oz. Fixed sights. Blued finish. Plastic grips. Specifications given are those of the Swedish Model 40 but also apply in general to the Finnish Model L-35, which differs only slightly. A considerable number of Swedish Lahti pistols were imported and sold in the U.S. The Finnish model, somewhat better made, is rare. Finnish Model L-35 adopted 1935. Swedish Model 40 adopted 1940 and mfd. through 1944.

Finnish L-35 model . . . . NiB $2396 Ex $1871 Gd $1248
Swedish 40 model . . . . NiB $501 Ex $377 Gd $233

L.A.R. Mark I Grizzly

L.A.R. MANUFACTURING, INC. — West Jordan, Utah

MARK I GRIZZLY WIN. MAG. AUTOMATIC PISTOL

Calibers: .357 Mag., .45 ACP, .45 Win. Mag. Seven-round magazine, 6.5-inch bbl., 10.5 inches overall. Weight: 48 oz. Fully adj. sights. Checkered rubber combat-style grips. Blued finish. Made from 1983 to date. 8- or 10-inch bbl., Made 1987-99.

.357 Mag. (6.5 inch barrel) . . . . . . NiB $1124 Ex $848 Gd $647
.45 Win. Mag.(6.5 inch barrel) . . . . NiB $972 Ex $792 Gd $534
8-inch barrel . . . . NiB $1255 Ex $1049 Gd $766
10-inch barrel . . . . NiB $1332 Ex $1075 Gd $755

MARK IV GRIZZLY
AUTOMATIC PISTOL . . . . NiB $1054 Ex $869 Gd $585

Same general specifications as the L.A.R. Mark I except chambered for .44 Magnum, has 5.5- or 6.5-inch bbl., beavertail grip safety, matte blued finish. Made 1991-99.

MARK V AUTO PISTOL . . . . NiB $946 Ex $740 Gd $534

Similar to the Mark I except chambered in 50 Action Express. Six-round magazine, 5.4- or 6.5-inch bbl., 10.6 inches overall (with 5.4-inch bbl.). Weight: 56 oz. Checkered walnut grips. Made 1993-99.

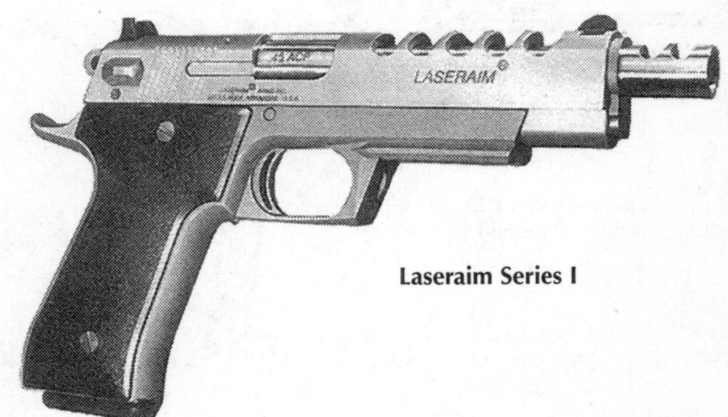

Laseraim Series I

LASERAIM TECHNOLOGIES INC. Little Rock, Arkansas

SERIES I SA AUTO PISTOL

Calibers: .40 S&W, .45 ACP, 10mm. Seven or 8- round magazine, 3.875- or 5.5-inch dual-port compensated bbl., 8.75 or 10.5 inches overall. Weight: 46 or 52 oz. Fixed sights w/Laseraim or adjustable Millet sights. Textured black composition grips. Extended slide release, ambidextrous safety and beveled magazine well. Stainless or matte black Teflon finish. Made 1993 to date.

Series I w/adjustable sights . . . . NiB $432 Ex $330 Gd $228
Series I w/fixed sights . . . . NiB $391 Ex $299 Gd $218
Series I w/fixed sights (HotDot) . . . NiB $534 Ex $432 Gd $299
Series I Dream Team (RedDot) . . . . NiB $779 Ex $626 Gd $422
Series I Illusion (Laseraim) . . . . NiB $840 Ex $646 Gd $432

Laseraim
Velocity 400 Series w/Laser Sight

Laseraim Series III
w/LA93 Illusion III Scope

Llama Model IIIA
Deluxe Chrome Engraved First Issue

Llama Model IIIA
Deluxe Blue Engraved Second Issue

SERIES II SA AUTO PISTOL
Similar to Series I except w/stainless finish and no bbl., compensator. Made 1993-96.
Series II w/adjustable sights . . . . . . NiB $361 Ex $299 Gd $207
Series II w/fixed sights. . . . . NiB $338 Ex $271 Gd $189
Series II Dream Team. . . . . NiB $654 Ex $521 Gd $360
Series II Illusion. . . . . NiB $692 Ex $551 Gd $380

SERIES III SA AUTO PISTOL
Similar to Series II except w/serrated slide and 5-inch compensated bbl., only. Made 1994 to date.
Series III w/
adjustable sights . . . . NiB $571 Ex $460 Gd $318
Series III w/fixed sights . . . . NiB $520 Ex $419 Gd $290

VELOCITY SERIES SA AUTO PISTOL
Similar to Series I except chambered for .357 Sig. or .400 Cor-Bon, 3.875-inch unported bbl., (compact) or 5.5-inch dual-port compensated bbl. Made 1997 to date. See illustration previous page.
Compact model (unported) . . . . NiB $362 Ex $294 Gd $202
Government model (ported) . . . . . . NiB $425 Ex $342 Gd $236
W/wireless laser
(HotDot), add $150

LIGNOSE PISTOLS — Suhl, Germany Aktien-Gesellschaft "Lignose" Abteilung

The following Lignose pistols were manufactured from 1920 to the mid-1930s. They were also marketed under the Bergmann name.

EINHAND MODEL 2A
POCKET AUTO PISTOL. . . . . NiB $316 Ex $285 Gd $112
As the name implies, this pistol is designed for one-hand operation, pressure on a "trigger" at the front of the guard retracts the slide. Caliber: .25 Auto. (6.35 mm). Six-round magazine, 2-inch bbl., 4.75 inches overall. Weight: About 14 oz. Blued finish. Hard rubber grips.

MODEL 2 POCKET
AUTO PISTOL . . . . NiB $347 Ex $265 Gd $194
Conventional Browning type. Same general specifications as Einhand Model 2A but lacks the one-hand operation.

EINHAND MODEL
3A POCKET AUTO PISTOL . . . . NiB $408 Ex $316 Gd $219
Same as the Model 2A except has longer grip, 9-round magazine, weight: About 16 oz.

LLAMA HANDGUNS — Mfd. by Gabilondo y Cia, Vitoria, Spain (Imported by S.G.S., Wanamassa, New Jersey)

NOTE: *For ease in finding a particular Llama handgun, the listings are divided into two groupings: Automatic Pistols (below) and Revolvers, which follow. For a complete listing of Llama handguns, please refer to the index.*

AUTOMATIC PISTOLS

MODEL IIIA
AUTOMATIC PISTOL . . . . NiB $226 Ex $201 Gd $145
Caliber: .380 Auto. Seven-round magazine, 3.69-inch bbl., 6.5 inches overall. Weight: 23 oz. Adj. target sights. Blued finish. Plastic grips. Intro. 1951. disc.

MODELS IIIA, XA, XV DELUXE
Same as standard Model IIIA, XA and XV except engraved w/blued or chrome finish and simulated pearl grips. Disc. 1984.
Chrome-engraved finish.......... NiB $339 Ex $275 Gd $193
Blue-engraved finish .... NiB $307 Ex $249 Gd $176

MODEL VIII
AUTOMATIC PISTOL .... NiB $382 Ex $265 Gd $203
Caliber: .38 Super. Nine-round magazine, 5-inch bbl., 8.5 inches overall. Weight: 40 oz. Fixed sights. Blued finish. Wood grips. Intro. in 1952. Disc.

MODELS VIII, IXA, XI DELUXE
Same as standard Models VIII, IXA and XI except finish (chrome engraved or blued engraved) and simulated pearl grips. Disc. 1984.
Chrome-engraved finish.......... NiB $434 Ex $351 Gd $245
Blue-engraved finish .... NiB $467 Ex $377 Gd $263

MODEL IXA AUTOMATIC PISTOL.... NiB $326 Ex $249 Gd $163
Same as model VIII except .45 Auto, 7-round magazine,

MODEL XA AUTOMATIC PISTOL..... NiB $222 Ex $192 Gd $111
Same as model IIIA except .32 Auto, 8-round magazine,

MODEL XI AUTOMATIC PISTOL ..... NiB $320 Ex $258 Gd $178
Same as model VIII except 9mm Para.

MODEL XV AUTOMATIC PISTOL..... NiB $263 Ex $212 Gd $135
Same as model XA except .22 LR.

MODELS BE-IIIA, BE-XA, BE-XV...... NiB $357 Ex $285 Gd $194
Same as models IIIA, XA and XV except w/blued-engraved finish. Made 1977-84.

MODELS BE-VIII,
BE-IXA, BE-XI DELUXE .... NiB $418 Ex $336 Gd $232
Same as models VIII, IXA and XI except w/blued-engraved finish. Made 1977-84.

MODELS C-IIIA, C-XA, C-XV ..... NiB $403 Ex $316 Gd $209
Same as models IIIA, XA and XV except in satin chrome.

MODELS C-VIII, C-IXA, C-XI ..... NiB $403 Ex $316 Gd $209
Same as models VIII, IXA and XI except in satin chrome.

MODELS CE-IIIA,
CE-XA, CE-XV .... NiB $443 Ex $377 Gd $255
Same as models IIIA, XA and XV except w/chrome engraved finish. Made 1977-84.

MODELS CE-VIII,
CE-IXA, CE-XI .... NiB $413 Ex $316 Gd $250
Same as models VIII, IXA and XI, w/except chrome engraved finish. Made 1977-84.

COMPACT FRAME
AUTO PISTOL .... NiB $418 Ex $321 Gd $214
Calibers: 9mm Para., .38 Super, .45 Auto. Seven-, 8- or 9-round magazine, 5-inch bbl., 7.88 inches overall. Weight: 34 oz. Blued, satin-chrome or Duo-Tone finishes. Made 1990 to date. Duo-Tone disc. 1993.

DUO-TONE LARGE
FRAME AUTO PISTOL........... NiB $392 Ex $326 Gd $219
Caliber: .45 ACP. Seven-round magazine, 5-inch bbl., 8.5 inches overall. Weight: 36 oz. Adj. rear sight. Blued finished w/satin chrome. Polymer black grips. Made 1990-93.

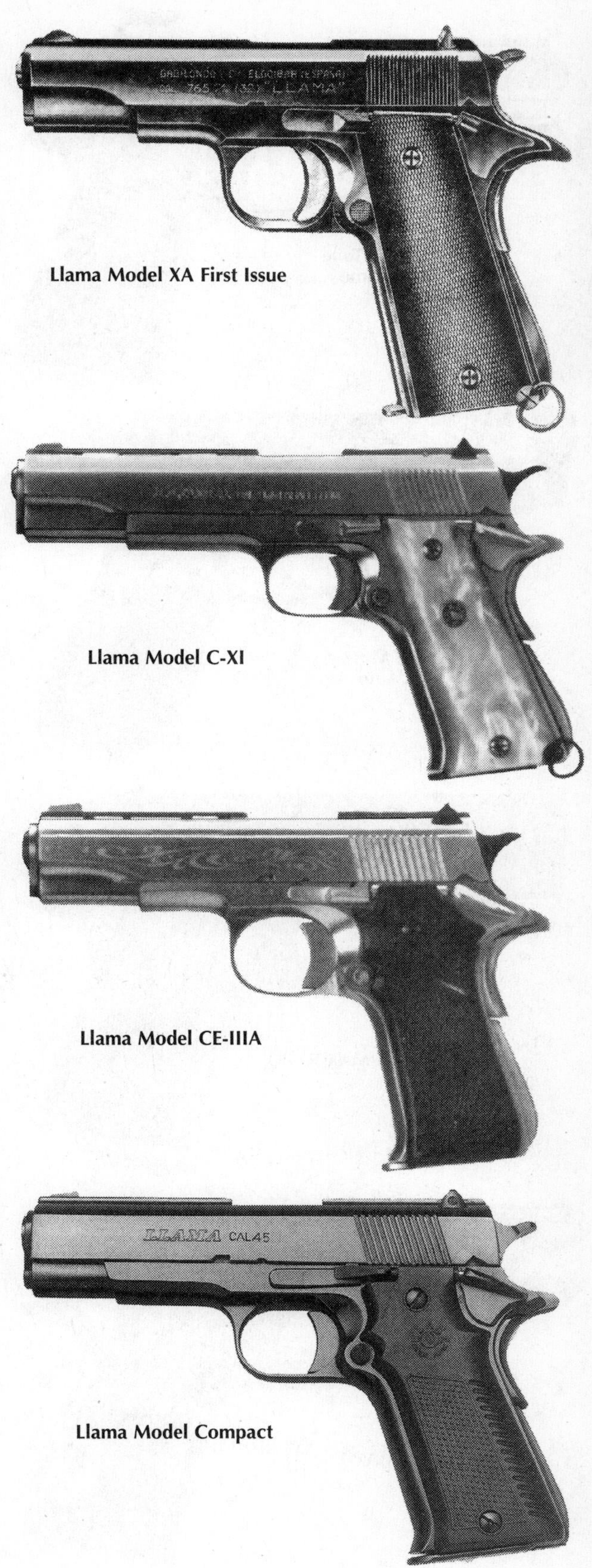

Llama Model XA First Issue

Llama Model C-XI

Llama Model CE-IIIA

Llama Model Compact

Llama Duo-Tone Large Frame

Llama M-82 DA Auto

Llama MINI-MAX II

Llama MAX-I

DUO-TONE SMALL FRAME AUTO PISTOL. . . . . NiB $357 Ex $265 Gd $173
Calibers: .22 LR, .32 and .380 Auto. Seven- or 8-round magazine, 3.69 inch bbl., 6.5 inches overall. Weight: 23 oz. Square-notch rear sight, Partridge-type front. Blued finish w/chrome. Made 1990-93.

MODEL G-IIIA DELUXE . . . . NiB $1104 Ex $887 Gd $610
Same as Model IIIA except gold damascened w/simulated pearl grips. Disc. 1982.

LARGE-FRAME AUTOMATIC PISTOL (IXA)
Caliber: .45 Auto. Seven-round magazine, 5-inch bbl., weight: 2 lbs., 8 oz. Adj. rear sight, Partridge-type front. Walnut grips or teakwood on satin chrome model. Later models w/polymer grips. Made from 1984 to date.
Blued finish . . . . NiB $352 Ex $245 Gd $163
Satin chrome finish . . . . NiB $398 Ex $316 Gd $214

M-82 DA AUTOMATIC PISTOL. . . . . NiB $724 Ex $571 Gd $362
Caliber: 9mm Para. 15-round magazine, 4.25-inch bbl., 8 inches overall. Weight: 39 oz. Drift-adj. rear sight. Matte blued finish. Matte black polymer grips. Made from 1988-93.

M-87 COMPETITION PISTOL . . . . NiB $1071 Ex $858 Gd $586
Caliber: 9mm Para. 15-round magazine, 5.5-inch bbl., 9.5 inches overall. Weight: 40 oz. Low-profile combat sights. Satin nickel finish. Matte black grip panels. Built-in ported compensator to minimize recoil and muzzle rise. Made 1989-93.

MICRO-MAX SA AUTOMATIC PISTOL
Caliber: .380 ACP. Seven-round magazine, 3.125-inch bbl., weight: 23 oz. Blade front sight, drift adjustable rear w/3-dot system. Matte blue or satin chrome finish. Checkered polymer grips. Imported 1997 to date.
Matte blue finish . . . . NiB $275 Ex $224 Gd $159
Satin chrome finish . . . . NiB $311 Ex $250 Gd $179

MINI-MAX SA AUTOMATIC PISTOL
Calibers: 9mm, .40 S&W or .45 ACP. Six- or 8-round magazine, 3.5-inch bbl., 8.3 inches overall. Weight: 35 oz. Blade front sight, drift adjustable rear w/3-dot system. Matte blue, Duo-Tone or satin chrome finish. Checkered polymer grips. Imported 1996 to date.
Duo-Tone finish. . . . . NiB $316 Ex $265 Gd $173
Matte blue finish . . . . NiB $279 Ex $239 Gd $153
Satin chrome finish . . . . NiB $341 Ex $265 Gd $183
Stainless (disc.) . . . . NiB $361 Ex $290 Gd $204

MINI-MAX II SA AUTOMATIC PISTOL
Cal: .45 ACP only. 10-round mag., 3.625 inch bbl., 7.375 inch overall. Wt: 37 oz. Blade front sight, drift adj. rear w/3-dot system. Shortened barrel and grip. Matte and Satin Chrome finish. Imp. 1998.
Matte blue finish . . . . NiB $430 Ex $347 Gd $239
Satin chrome finish . . . . NiB $465 Ex $372 Gd $260

MAX-I SA AUTOMATIC PISTOL
Calibers: 9mm or .45 ACP. 7- or 9-round magazine, 4.25- to 5.125 inch bbl., weight: 34 or 36 oz. Blade front sight, drift adj. rear w/3-dot system. Matte blue, Duo-Tone or satin chrome finish. Checkered black rubber grips. Imported 1995 to date.
Duo-Tone finish. . . . . NiB $275 Ex $224 Gd $148
Matte blue finish . . . . NiB $275 Ex $224 Gd $143
Satin chrome finish . . . . NiB $311 Ex $245 Gd $153

MAX-II SA AUTOMATIC PISTOL
Same as the MAX-I with 4.25 bbl. except w/10-round mag. Weight: 39 oz. Matte blue or satin chrome finish. Imp. 1996 to date.
Matte blue finish . . . . NiB $265 Ex $214 Gd $150
Satin Chrome finish. . . . . NiB $301 Ex $245 Gd $158

OMNI 45 DOUBLE-ACTION AUTOMATIC PISTOL .... NiB $418 Ex $336 Gd $224
Caliber: .45 Auto. Seven-round magazine, 4.25-inch bbl., 7.75 inches overall. Weight: 40 oz. Adj. rear sight, ramp front. Highly polished deep blued finish. Made 1984-86.

OMNI 9MM DOUBLE-ACTION AUTOMATIC................. NiB $457 Ex $367 Gd $253
Same general specifications as .45 Omni except chambered for 9mm w/13-round magazine. Made 1983-86.

SINGLE-ACTION AUTOMATIC PISTOL .... NiB $428 Ex $336 Gd $222
Calibers: .38 Super, 9mm, .45 Auto. Nine-round magazine (7-round for .45 Auto), 5-inch bbl., 8.5 inches overall. Weight: 2 lbs., 8 oz. Intro. in 1981.

SMALL-FRAME AUTOMATIC PISTOL
Calibers: .380 Auto (7-round magazine), .22 RF (8-round magazine), 3.69-inch bbl., weight: 23 oz. Partridge-blade front sight, adj. rear. Blued or satin-chrome finish.
Blued finish .... NiB $341 Ex $265 Gd $173
Satin-chrome finish .... NiB $403 Ex $316 Gd $214

REVOLVERS

MARTIAL DOUBLE-ACTION REVOLVER .... NiB $260 Ex $214 Gd $143
Calibers: .22 LR, .38 Special. Six-round cylinder, bbl. lengths: 4-inch (.38 Special only) or 6-inch; 11.25 inches overall (w/6-inch bbl.). Weight: About 36 oz. w/6-inch bbl. Target sights. Blued finish. Checkered walnut grips. Made 1969-76.

MARTIAL DOUBLE-ACTION DELUXE
Same as standard Martial except w/satin chrome, chrome-engraved, blued engraved or gold damascened finish. Simulated pearl grips. Made 1969-78.
Satin-chrome finish .... NiB $321 Ex $265 Gd $163
Chrome-engraved finish......... NiB $377 Ex $306 Gd $204
Blue-engraved finish .... NiB $367 Ex $296 Gd $204
Gold-damascened finish .... NiB $1545 Ex $1256 Gd $938

COMANCHE I DOUBLE-ACTION REVOLVER................... NiB $275 Ex $224 Gd $163
Same general specifications as Martial .22. Made 1977-83.

COMANCHE II .... NiB $260 Ex $214 Gd $143
Same general specifications as Martial .38. Made 1977-83.

COMANCHE III DOUBLE-ACTION REVOLVER.................. NiB $275 Ex $224 Gd $148
Caliber: .357 Magnum. Six-round cylinder, 4-inch bbl., 9.25 inches overall. Weight: 36 oz. Adj. rear sight, ramp front. Blued finish. Checkered walnut grips. Made from 1975-95. Note: Prior to 1977, this model was designated "Comanche."

COMANCHE III CHROME................... NiB $355 Ex $270 Gd $190
Same gen. specifications as Comanche III except has satin chrome finish, 4- or 6-inch bbl. Made 1979-92.

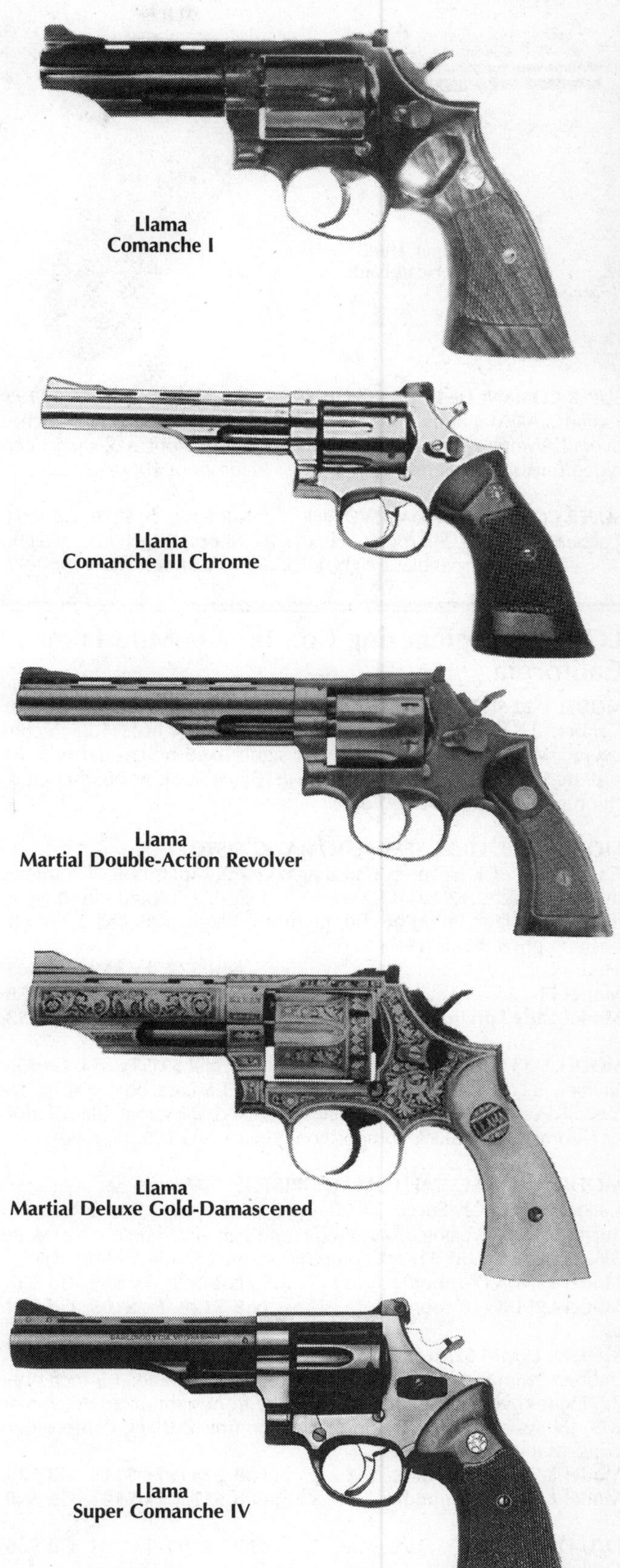

Llama
Comanche I

Llama
Comanche III Chrome

Llama
Martial Double-Action Revolver

Llama
Martial Deluxe Gold-Damascened

Llama
Super Comanche IV

Luger 1900
American Eagle

SUPER COMANCHE IV DA REVOLVER . . . NiB $357 Ex $290 Gd $199
Caliber: .44 Magnum. Six-round cylinder, 6-inch bbl., 11.75 inches overall. Weight: 50 oz. Adj. rear sight, ramp front. Polished deep blued finish. Checkered walnut grips. Made from 1980-93.

SUPER COMANCHE V DA REVOLVER . . . . NiB $341 Ex $270 Gd $191
Caliber: .357 Mag. Six-round cylinder, 4-, 6- or 8.5-inch bbl., weight: 48 ozs. Ramped front blade sight, click-adj. Rear. Made from 1980-89.

LORCIN Engineering Co., Inc. — Mira Loma, California

MODEL L-22 SEMIAUTOMATIC PISTOL . . . . . NiB $84 Ex $69 Gd $50
Caliber: 22 LR. Nine-round magazine, 2.5-inch bbl., 5.25 inches overall. Weight: 16 oz. Blade front sight, fixed notch rear w/3-dot system. Black Teflon or chrome finish. Black, pink or pearl composition grips. Made 1990 to date.

MODEL L-25, LT-.25 SEMIAUTOMATIC PISTOL
Caliber: 25 ACP. Seven-round magazine, 2.4-inch bbl., 4.8 inches overall. Weight: 12 oz. (LT-25) or 14.5 oz. (L-25). Blade front sight, fixed rear. Black Teflon or chrome finish. Black, pink or pearl composition grips. Made 1989 to date.
Model L-25 . . . . NiB $72 Ex $59 Gd $43
Model LT-25. . . . . NiB $84 Ex $69 Gd $50
Model Lady Lorcin. . . . . NiB $91 Ex $74 Gd $53

MODEL L-32 SEMIAUTOMATIC PISTOL . . . . . NiB $91 Ex $74 Gd $53
Caliber: 32 ACP. Seven-round magazine, 3.5-inch bbl., 6.6 inches overall. Weight: 27 oz. Blade front sight, fixed notch rear. Black Teflon or chrome finish. Black composition grips. Made 1992 to date.

MODEL L-380 SEMIAUTOMATIC PISTOL
Caliber: .380 ACP. Seven- or 10-round magazine, 3.5-inch bbl., 6.6 inches overall. Weight: 23 oz. Blade front sight, fixed notch rear. Matte Black finish. Grooved black composition grips. Made 1994 to date.
Model L9MM (7-round). . . . . NiB $98 Ex $79 Gd $57
Model L9MM (10-round). . . . . NiB $129 Ex $105 Gd $74

MODEL L9MM SEMIAUTOMATIC PISTOL
Caliber: 9mm Parabellum. 10- or 13-round magazine, 4.5-inch bbl., 7.5 inches overall. Weight: 31 oz. Blade front sight, fixed notch rear w/3-dot system. Black Teflon or chrome finish. Black composition grips. Made 1992 to date.
Model L-380 (10-round) . . . . NiB $141 Ex $115 Gd $79
Model L-380 (13-round) . . . . NiB $171 Ex $141 Gd $90

O/U DERRINGER . . . . NiB $104 Ex $84 Gd $60
Caliber: .38 Special/.357 Mag., .45LC. Two-round derringer. 3.5-inch bbls.

(cont'd) **O/U DERRINGER**
6.5 inches overall. Weight: 12 oz. Blade front sight, fixed notch rear. Stainless finish. Black composition grips. Made 1996 to date.

LUGER PISTOLS

Mfd. by Deutsche Waffen und Munitionsfabriken (DWM), Berlin, Germany. Previously by Koniglich Gewehrfabrik Erfurt, Heinrich Krieghoff Waffenfabrik, Mauser-Werke, Simson & Co., Vickers Ltd., Waffenfabrik, Bern.

1900 AMERICAN EAGLE . . . . NiB $3108 Ex $1756 Gd $924
Caliber: 7.65 mm. Eight-round magazine; thin, 4.75-inch; tapered bbl.; 9.5 inches overall. Weight: 32 oz. Fixed rear sight, dovetailed front sight. Grip safety. Checkered walnut grips. Early-style toggle, narrow trigger, wide guard, no stock lug. American Eagle over chamber. Estimated 8000 production.

1900 COMMERCIAL . . . . NiB $3160 Ex $2640 Gd $1418
Same specifications as Luger 1900 American Eagle except DWM on early-style toggle, no chamber markings. Estimated 8000 production.

1900 SWISS. . . . . NiB $3940 Ex $3160 Gd $1444
Same specifications as Luger 1900 American Eagle except Swiss cross in sunburst over chamber. Estimated 9000 production.

1902 AMERICAN EAGLE . . . . . . NiB $8890 Ex $6810 Gd $3690
Caliber: 9mm Para. Eight-round magazine, 4-inch heavy tapered bbl., 8.75 inches overall. Weight: 30 oz. Fixed rear sight, dovetailed front sight. Grip safety. Checkered walnut grips. American Eagle over chamber, DWM on early-style toggle, narrow trigger, wide guard, no stock lug. Estimated 700 production.

1902 CARBINE . . . . NiB $13,338 Ex $10,670 Gd $7255
Caliber: 7.65mm. Eight-round magazine, 11.75-inch tapered bbl., 16.5 inches overall. Weight: 46 oz. Adj. 4-position rear sight, long ramp front sight. Grip safety. Checkered walnut grips and forearm. DWM on early-style toggle, narrow trigger, wide guard, no chamber markings, stock lug. Estimated 3200 production.
Model 1902 carbine (gun only). . . . . NiB $8993 Ex $6795 Gd $4621
Model 1902 carbine
(gun only, American Eagle). . . . . NiB $11,926 Ex $9542 Gd $6488
W/issued stock and matching numbers, add $4550
W/original stock and non-matching numbers, add $2550

1902 CARTRIDGE COUNTER . . . . NiB $27,040 Ex $17,160 Gd $8996
Caliber: 9mm Para. Eight-round magazine, Heavy, tapered 4-inch bbl., 8.75 inches overall. Weight: 30 oz. Fixed rear sight, dovetailed front sight. Grip safety. Checkered walnut grips. DWM on dished toggle w/lock, American Eagle over chamber when marked. No stock lug. Estimated production unknown.

1902 COMMERCIAL . . . . NiB $8986 Ex $7301 Gd $3763
Same basic specifications as Luger 1902 Cartridge Counter except DWM on early-style toggle, narrow trigger, wide guard, no chamber markings, no stock lug. Estimated 400 production.

1902 AMERICAN EAGLE . . . . . . NiB $9547 Ex $7301 Gd $3931
Same basic specifications as Luger 1902 Commercial except American Eagle over chamber, DWM on early-style toggle, narrow trigger, wide guard, no stock lug. Estimated 700 production.

1902 AMERICAN EAGLE
CARTRIDGE COUNTER . . . . NiB $26,936 Ex $17,160 Gd $9048
Same basic specifications as Luger 1902 Cartridge Counter except American Eagle over chamber, DWM on early-style toggle, narrow trigger, wide guard, no stock lug. Estimated 700 production.

1904 GL "BABY" .... Nib $195,000 Ex $156,000 Gd $106,080
Caliber: 9mm Para. Seven-round magazine, 3.25-inch bbl., 7.75 inches overall. Weight: Approx. 20 oz. Serial number 10077B. "GL" marked on rear of toggle. Georg Luger's personal sidearm. Only one made in 1904.

1904 NAVAL (REWORKED) ...... Nib $13,056 Ex $10,444 Gd $7102
Caliber: 9mm Para. Eight-round magazine, bbl., length altered to 4 inches., 8.75 inches overall. Weight: 30 oz. Adj. two-position rear sight, dovetailed front sight. Thumb lever safety. Checkered walnut grips. Heavy tapered bbl., DWM on new-style toggle w/lock, 1902 over chamber. W/or without grip safety and stock lug. Estimated 800 production.

1906 (11.35).......... Nib $117,000 Ex $93,600 Gd $63,648
Caliber: .45 ACP. Six-round magazine, 5-inch bbl., 9.75 inches overall. Weight: 36 oz. Fixed rear sight, dovetailed front sight. Grip safety. Checkered walnut grips. GL monogram on rear toggle link, larger frame w/altered trigger guard and trigger, no proofs, no markings over chamber. No stock lug. Estimated production is 2. Note: This version of the Luger pistol is the most valuable next to the "GL" Baby Luger.

1906 AMERICAN EAGLE (7.65)...................... Nib $2977 Ex $2145 Gd $1053
Caliber: 7.65mm. Eight-round magazine, thin 4.75-inch tapered bbl., 9.5 inches overall. Weight: 32 oz. Fixed rear sight, dovetailed front sight. Grip safety. Checkered walnut grips. DWM on new-style toggle, American Eagle over chamber. No stock lug. Estimated 8000 production.

1906 AMERICAN EAGLE (9MM)...... Nib $2847 Ex $2296 Gd $1308
Same basic specifications as the 7.65mm 1906 except in 9mm Para. w/4-inch barrel, 8.75 inches overall, weight: 30 ounces. Estimated 3500 production.

1906 BERN (7.65MM)........ Nib $2571 Ex $2259 Gd $1437
Same basic specifications as the 7.65mm 1906 American Eagle except checkered walnut grips w/.38-inch borders, Swiss Cross on new-style toggle, Swiss proofs, no markings over chamber, no stock lug. Estimated 17,874 production.

1906 BRAZILIAN (7.65MM).......... Nib $2650 Ex $1922 Gd $778
Same general specifications as the 7.65mm 1906 American Eagle except w/Brazilian proofs, no markings over chamber, no stock lug. Estimated 4500 produced.

1906 BRAZILIAN (9MM)...... Nib $2586 Ex $2078 Gd $1429
Same basic specifications as the 9mm 1906 American Eagle except w/Brazilian proofs, no markings over chamber, no stock lug. Production unknown, but less than 4000 is estimated by collectors.

1906 COMMERCIAL
Calibers: 7.65mm, 9mm. Same specifications as the 1906 American Eagle versions (above) except no chamber markings and no stock lug. Estimated production: 6000 (7.65mm) and 3500 (9mm).
7.65mm................... Nib $2962 Ex $1974 Gd $1298
9mm .... Nib $2962 Ex $1974 Gd $1298

1906 DUTCH .... Nib $1936 Ex $1558 Gd $1075
Caliber: 9mm Para. Same specifications as the 9mm 1906 American Eagle except tapered bbl., w/proofs, no markings over chamber, no stock lug. Estimated 3000 production.

1906 LOEWE AND COMPANY....... Nib $4681 Ex $3757 Gd $2576
Caliber: 7.65mm. Eight-round magazine, 6-inch tapered bbl., 10.75 inches overall. Weight: 35 oz. Adj. two-position rear sight, dovetailed front sight. Grip safety. Checkered walnut grips. Loewe & Company over chamber, Naval proofs, DWM on new-style toggle, no stock lug. Estimated production unknown.

1906 NAVAL
Caliber: 9mm Para. Eight-round magazine, 6-inch tapered bbl., 10.75 inches overall. Weight: 35 oz. Adj. two-position rear sight, dovetailed front sight. Grip safety and thumb safety w/lower marking (1st issue), higher marking (2nd issue). Checkered walnut grips. No chamber markings, DWM on new-style toggle w/o lock, but w/stock lug. Est. production: 9000 (lst issue); 2,000 (2nd issue).
First issue .... Nib $3900 Ex $3100 Gd $1300
Second issue .... Nib $4100 Ex $3500 Gd $1300

1906 NAVAL COMMERCIAL......... Nib $3900 Ex $3100 Gd $1300
Same as the 1906 Naval except lower marking on thumb safety, no chamber markings. DWM on new-style toggle, w/stock lug and commercial proofs. Estimated 3000 production.

1906 PORTUGUESE ARMY .... Nib $1860 Ex $1460 Gd $560
Same specifications as the 7.65mm 1906 American Eagle except w/Portuguese proofs, crown and crest over chamber. No stock lug. Estimated 3500 production.

1906 PORTUGUESE NAVAL......... Nib $9560 Ex $6060 Gd $2060
Same as the 9mm 1906 American Eagle except w/Portuguese proofs, crown and anchor over chamber, no stock lug.

1906 RUSSIAN............ Nib $15,000 Ex $9950 Gd $5500
Same general specifications as the 9mm 1906 American Eagle except thumb safety has markings concealed in up position, DWM on new-style toggle, DWM bbl., proofs, crossed rifles over chamber. Estimated production unknown.

1906 SWISS................ Nib $2443 Ex $1793 Gd $1243
Same general specifications as the 7.65mm 1906 American Eagle Luger except Swiss Cross in sunburst over chamber, no stock lug. Estimated 10,300 production.

1906 SWISS (REWORK)....... Nib $2430 Ex $1780 Gd $1230
Same basic specifications as the 7.65mm 1906 Swiss except in bbl. lengths of 3.63, 4 and 4.75 inches, overall length 8.38 inches (with 4-inch bbl.). Weight 32 oz. (with 4-inch bbl.). DWM on new-style toggle, bbl., w/serial number and proof marks, Swiss Cross in sunburst or shield over chamber, no stock lug. Estimated production unknown.

1906 SWISS POLICE......... Nib $2430 Ex $1780 Gd $1230
Same general specifications as the 7.65mm 1906 Swiss except DWM on new-style toggle, Swiss Cross in matted field over chamber, no stock lug. Estimated 10,300 production.

1908 BULGARIAN............ Nib $2530 Ex $1830 Gd $780
Caliber: 9mm Para. Eight-round magazine, 4-inch tapered bbl., 8.75 inches overall. Weight: 30 oz. Fixed rear sight dovetailed front sight. Thumb safety w/lower marking concealed. Checkered walnut grips. DWM chamber marking, no proofs, crown over shield on new-style toggle lanyard loop, no stock lug. Estimated production unknown.

1908 COMMERCIAL .... Nib $1227 Ex $827 Gd $527
Same basic specifications as the 1908 Bulgarian except higher marking on thumb safety. No chamber markings, commercial proofs, DWM on new-style toggle, no stock lug. Estimated 4000 production.

1908 ERFURT MILITARY....... Nib $1246 Ex $1022 Gd $736
Caliber: 9mm Para. Eight-round magazine, 4-inch tapered bbl., 8.75 inches overall. Weight: 30 oz. Fixed rear sight dovetailed front sight. Thumb safety w/higher marking concealed. Checkered walnut grips. Serial number and proof marks on barrel, crown and Erfurt on new-style toggle, dated chamber, but no stock lug. Estimated production unknown.

Luger 1923 Stoeger

1908 MILITARY
Same general specifications as the 9mm 1908 Erfurt Military Luger except first and second issue have thumb safety w/higher marking concealed, serial number on bbl., no chamber markings, proofs on frame, DWM on new-style toggle but no stock lug. Estimated production: 10,000 (first issue) and 5000 (second issue). Third issue has serial number and proof marks on barrel, dates over chamber, DWM on new-style toggle but no stock lug. Estimated 3000 production.
First issue . . . . Nib $1278 Ex $842 Gd $550
Second issue . . . . Nib $1278 Ex $810 Gd $446
Third issue . . . . Nib $1590 Ex $1018 Gd $654

1908 NAVAL . . . . Nib $4173 Ex $3363 Gd $2305
Same basic specifications as the 9mm 1908 military Lugers except w/6-inch bbl, adj. two-position rear sight, no chamber markings, DWM on new-style toggle, w/stock lug. Estimated 26,000 production.

1908 NAVAL (COMMERCIAL) . . . . Nib $4757 Ex $3197 Gd $1637
Same specifications as the 1908 Naval Luger except no chamber markings or date. Commercial proofs, DWM on new-style toggle, w/stock lug. Estimated 1900 produced.

1914 ERFURT ARTILLERY . . . . . . Nib $2650 Ex $1870 Gd $908
Caliber: 9mm Para. Eight-shot magazine, 8-inch tapered bbl., 12.75 inches overall. Weight: 40 oz. Artillery rear sight, Dovetailed front sight. Thumb safety w/higher marking concealed. Checkered walnut grips. Serial number and proof marks on barrel, crown and Erfurt on new-style toggle, dated chamber, w/stock lug. Estimated production unknown.

1914 ERFURT MILITARY . . . . Nib $1278 Ex $862 Gd $550
Same specifications as the 1914 Erfurt Artillery except w/4-inch bbl., and corresponding length, weight, etc.; fixed rear sight. Estimated 3000 production.

1914 NAVAL . . . . Nib $3424 Ex $2384 Gd $1084
Same specifications as 9mm 1914 Lugers except has 6-inch bbl. w/corresponding length and weight, adj. two-position rear sight. Dated chamber, DWM on new-style toggle, w/stock lug. Estimated 40,000 produced.

1914-1918 DWM ARTILLERY . . . . . . Nib $2328 Ex $1912 Gd $950
Caliber: 9mm Para. Eight-shot magazine, 8-inch tapered bbl., 12.75 inches overall. Weight: 40 oz. Artillery rear sight, dovetailed front sight. Thumb safety w/higher marking concealed. Checkered walnut grips. Serial number and proof marks on barrel, DWM on new-style toggle, dated chamber, w/stock lug. Estimated 3000 production.

1914-1918 DWM MILITARY . . . . . Nib $1744 Ex $862 Gd $550
Same specifications as the 9mm 1914-1918 DWM Artillery except w/4-inch tapered bbl., and corresponding length, weight, etc., and fixed rear sight. Production unknown.

1920 CARBINE
Caliber: 7.65mm. Eight-round magazine, 11.75-inch tapered bbl., 15.75 inches overall. Weight: 44 oz. Four-position rear sight, long ramp front sight. Grip (or thumb) safety. Checkered walnut grips and forearm. Serial numbers and proof marks on barrel, no chamber markings, various proofs, DWM on new-style toggle, w/stock lug. Estimated production unknown.
Model 1920 Carbine (gun only) . . . . Nib $5706 Ex $4978 Gd $2690
Model 1920 Carbine (W/shoulder stock), add $2500

1920 NAVY CARBINE . . . . Nib $3771 Ex $3029 Gd $2081
Caliber: 7.65mm. Eight-round magazine, 11.75-inch tapered bbl., 15.75 inches overall. Two-position sliding rear sight. Naval military proofs and no forearm. Production unknown.

1920 COMMERCIAL . . . . Nib $886 Ex $678 Gd $392
Calibers: 7.65mm, 9mm Para. Eight-round magazine, 3.63-, 3.75-, 4-, 4.75-, 6-, 8-, 10-, 12-, 16-, 18- or 20-inch tapered bbl., overall length: 8.375 to 24.75 inches. Weight: 30 oz. (with 3.63-inch bbl.). Varying rear sight configurations, dovetailed front sight. Thumb safety. Checkered walnut grips. Serial numbers and proof marks on barrel, no chamber markings, various proofs, DWM or crown over Erfurt on new-style toggle, w/stock lug. Production not documented.

1920 DWM OR ERFURT MILITARY . . . . . . Nib $968 Ex $760 Gd $526
Caliber: 9mm Para. Eight-round magazine, 4-inch tapered barrel, 8.75 inches overall. Weight: 30 oz. Fixed rear sight dovetailed front sight. Thumb safety. Checkered walnut grips. Serial numbers and proof marks on barrel, dated chamber, various proofs, DWM or crown over Erfurt on new-style toggle, w/stock lug. Esimated 3000 production.

1920 POLICE . . . . Nib $1265 Ex $990 Gd $683
Same specifications as 9mm 1920 DWM w/some dated chambers, various proofs, DWM or crown over Erfurt on new-style toggle, identifying marks on grip frame, w/stock lug. Estimated 3000 production.

1923 COMMERICAL . . . . Nib $878 Ex $566 Gd $316
Calibers: 7.65mm and 9mm Para. Eight-round magazine, 3.63-, 3.75-, 4-, 6-, 8-, 12- or 16-inch tapered bbl., overall length: 8.38 inches (with 3.63-inch bbl.). Weight: 30 oz. (with 3.63-inch bbl.). Various rear sight configurations, dovetailed front sight. Thumb lever safety. Checkered walnut grips. DWM on new-style toggle, serial number and proofs on barrel, no chamber markings, w/stock lug. Estimated 15,000 production.

1923 DUTCH COMMERICAL . . . . Nib $1704 Ex $1496 Gd $664
Same basic specifications as 1923 Commercial Luger w/same caliber offerings, but only 3.63- or 4-inch bbl. Fixed rear sight, thumb lever safety w/arrow markings. Production unknown.

1923 KRIEGHOFF COMMERCIAL . . . . . Nib $1756 Ex $1392 Gd $841
Same specifications as 1923 Commercial Luger, w/same caliber offerings but bbl., lengths of 3.63, 4, 6, and 8 inches. "K" marked on new-style toggle. Serial number, proofs and Germany on barrel. No chamber markings, but w/ stock lug. Production unknown.

1923 SAFE AND LOADED . . . . . . Nib $1548 Ex $1080 Gd $560
Same caliber offerings, bbl., lengths and specifications as the 1923 Commercial except thumb lever safety, safe markings, w/stock lug. Estimated 10,000 production.

1923 STOEGER
Same general specifications as the 1923 Commercial Luger with the same caliber offerings and bbl., lengths of 3.75, 4, 6, 8 and up to 24 inches. Thumb lever safety. DWM on new-style toggle, serial number and/or proof marks on barrel. American Eagle over chamber but no stock lug. Estimated production less than 1000 (also see Stoeger listings). Note: Qualified appraisals should be obtained on all Stoeger Lugers with bbl. lengths over 8 inches to ensure accurate values.
3.75-, 4-, or 6-inch bbl........ Nib $2894 Ex $2323 Gd $1543
8-inch bbl.................. Nib $3876 Ex $3108 Gd $2126

1926 "BABY" PROTOTYPE . . Nib $110,500 Ex $88,400 Gd $60,112
Calibers: 7.65mm Browning and 9mm Browning (short). Five-round magazine, 2.31-inch bbl., about 6.25 inches overall. Small-sized-frame and toggle assembly. Prototype for a Luger "pocket pistol," but never manufactured commercially. Checkered walnut grips, slotted for safety. Only four known to exist, but as many as a dozen could have been made.

1929 SWISS................. Nib $1853 Ex $1177 Gd $683
Caliber: 7.65mm. Eight-round magazine, 4.75-inch tapered bbl., 9.5 inches overall. Weight: 32 oz. Fixed rear sight, dovetailed front sight. Long grip safety and thumb lever w/S markings. Stepped receiver and straight grip frame. Checkered plastic grips. Swiss Cross in shield on new-style toggle. Serial numbers and proofs on barrel, no markings over chamber and no stock lug. Estimated 1900 produuction.

1934 KRIEGHOFF COMMERCIAL (SIDE FRAME) .... Nib $2890 Ex $2214 Gd $862
Caliber: 7.65mm or 9mm Para. Eight-round magazine, bbl. lengths: 4, 6, and 8 inches, overall length: 8.75 (with 4-inch bbl.). Weight: 30 oz. (with 4-inch bbl.). Various rear sight configurations w/dovetailed front sight. Thumb lever safety. Checkered brown plastic grips. Anchor w/H K Krieghoff Suhl on new-style toggle, but no chamber markings. Tapered bbl., w/serial number and proofs; w/stock lug. Estimated 1700 production.

1934 KRIEGHOFF S
Caliber: 9mm Para. Eight-round magazine, 4-inch tapered bbl., 8.75 inches overall. Weight: 30 oz. Fixed rear sight, dovetailed front sight. Thumb lever safety. Anchor w/H K Krieghoff Suhl on new-style toggle, S dated chamber, bbl., proofs and stock lug. Early model: Checkered walnut or plastic grips. Estimated 2500 production. Late model: Checkered brown plastic grips. Est. 1200 production.
Early model................ Nib $3544 Ex $2843 Gd $1946
Late model................. Nib $2576 Ex $2068 Gd $1419

1934 BYF.................... Nib $1274 Ex $962 Gd $546
Caliber: 9mm Para. Eight-round magazine, 4-inch tapered bbl., 8.75 inches overall. Weight: 30 oz. Fixed rear sight, dovetailed front sight. Thumb lever safety. Checkered walnut or plastic grips. byf on new-style toggle, serial number and proofs on bbl., 41-42 dated chamber and w/stock lug. Estimated 3000 productlon.

1934 MAUSER S/42 K........ Nib $4721 Ex $3993 Gd $1601
Caliber: 9mm Para. Eight-round magazine, 4-inch tapered bbl., 8.75 inches overall. Weight: 30 oz. Fixed rear sight dovetailed front sight. Thumb lever safety. Checkered walnut or plastic grips. 42 on new-style toggle, serial number and proofs on barrel, 1939-.40 dated chamber markings and w/stock lug. Estimated 10,000 production.

1934 MAUSER S/42 (DATED)..... Nib $1060 Ex $826 Gd $436
Same specifications as Luger 1934 Mauser 42 except 41 dated chamber markings and w/stock lug. Production unknown.

Luger S42

1934 MAUSER BANNER (MILITARY)..... Nib $2727 Ex $1895 Gd $1011
Same specifications as Luger 1934 Mauser 42 except Mauser in banner on new-style toggle, tapered bbl., w/serial number and proofs usually, dated chamber markings and w/stock lug. Production unknown.

1934 MAUSER COMMERCIAL........... Nib $1577 Ex $1107 Gd $641
Same specifications as Luger 1934 Mauser 42 except checkered walnut grips. Mauser in banner on new-style toggle, tapered bbl., usually w/serial number and proofs, no chamber markings, but w/stock lug. Production unknown.

1934 MAUSER DUTCH........ Nib $2933 Ex $1789 Gd $541
Same specifications as Luger 1934 Mauser 42 except checkered walnut grips. Mauser in banner on new-style toggle, tapered bbl., w/caliber, 1940 dated chamber markings and w/stock lug. Production unknown.

1934 MAUSER LATVIAN...... Nib $2989 Ex $2042 Gd $1792
Caliber: 7.65mm. Eight-round magazine, 4-inch tapered bbl., 8.75 inches overall. Weight: 30 oz. Fixed square-notched rear sight, dovetailed Partridge front sight. Thumb lever safety. Checkered walnut stocks. Mauser in banner on new-style toggle,1937 dated chamber markings and w/stock lug. Production unknown.

1934 MAUSER (OBERNDORF)....... Nib $2950 Ex $2364 Gd $1615
Same as 1934 Mauser 42 except checkered walnut grips. Oberndorf 1934 on new-style toggle, tapered bbl., w/proofs and caliber, Mauser banner over chamber and w/stock lug (also see Mauser).

1934 SIMSON-S TOGGLE...... Nib $1945 Ex $1373 Gd $593
Same as 1934 Mauser 42 except checkered walnut grips, S on new-style toggle, tapered bbl., w/serial number and proofs, no chamber markings; w/stock lug. Estimated 10,000 production.

42 MAUSER BANNER (BYF) ..... Nib $1273 Ex $961 Gd $545
Same specifications as Luger 1934 Mauser 42 except weight: 32 oz. Mauser in banner on new-style toggle, tapered bbl., w/serial number and proofs usually, dated chamber markings and w/stock lug. Estimated 3,500 production.

ABERCROMBIE AND FITCH......... Nib $6040 Ex $4584 Gd $1048
Calibers: 7.65mm and 9mm Para. Eight-round magazine, 4.75-inch tapered bbl., 9.5 inches overall. Weight: 32 oz. Fixed rear sight, dovetailed front sight. Grip safety. Checkered walnut grips. DWM on new-style toggle Abercrombie & Fitch markings on barrel, Swiss Cross in sunburst over chamber, no stock lug. Est. 100 production.

Luna Model 200 Free Pistol

DUTCH ROYAL AIR FORCE .... Nib $2929 Ex $1785 Gd $537
Caliber: 9mm Para. Eight-round magazine, 4-inch tapered bbl., 8.75 inches overall. Weight: 30 oz. Fixed rear sight dovetailed front sight. Grip safety and thumb safety w/markings and arrow. Checkered walnut grips. DWM on new-style toggle, bbl., dated w/serial number and proofs, no markings over chamber, no stock lug. Estimated 4000 production.

DWM (G DATE)............... Nib $1395 Ex $953 Gd $485
Caliber: 9mm Para. Eight-round magazine, 4-inch tapered bbl., 8.75 inches overall. Weight: 30 oz. Fixed rear sight, dovetailed front sight. Thumb lever safety. Checkered walnut grips. DWM on new-style toggle, serial number and proofs on barrel, G (1935 date) over chamber and w/stock lug. Production unknown.

DWM AND ERFURT .... Nib $1181 Ex $948 Gd $650
Caliber: 9mm Para. Eight-round magazine, 4- or 6-inch tapered bbl., overall length: 8.75 or 10.75 inches. Weight: 30 or 38 oz. Fixed rear sight, dovetailed front sight. Thumb safety. Checkered walnut grips. Serial numbers and proof marks on barrel, double dated chamber, various proofs, DWM or crown over Erfurt on new-style toggle and w/stock lug. Production unknown.

KRIEGHOFF 36 .... Nib $3136 Ex $2513 Gd $1716
Caliber: 9mm Para. Eight-round magazine, 4-inch tapered bbl., 8.75 inches overall. Weight: 30 oz. Fixed rear sight, dovetailed front sight. Thumb lever safety. Checkered brown plastic grips. Anchor w/H K Krieghoff Suhl on new-style toggle, 36 dated chamber, serial number and proofs on barrel and w/stock lug. Estimated 700 production.

KRIEGHOFF-DATED
1936-1945................ Nib $3204 Ex $2622 Gd $1062
Same specifications as Luger Krieghoff 36 except 1936-45 dated chamber, bbl. proofs. Est. 8600 production.

KRIEGHOFF (GRIP SAFETY) ... Nib $4768 Ex $3811 Gd $2608
Same specifications as Luger Krieghoff 36 except grip safety and thumb lever safety. No chamber markings, tapered bbl., w/serial number, proofs and caliber, no stock lug. Production unknown.

MAUSER BANNER
(GRIP SAFETY)............. Nib $2725 Ex $1893 Gd $1009
Caliber: 7.65mm. Eight-round magazine, 4.75-inch tapered bbl., 9.5 inches overall. Weight: 30 oz. Fixed rear sight, dovetailed front sight. Grip safety and thumb lever safety. Checkered walnut grips. Mauser in banner on new-style toggle, serial number and proofs on barrel, 1939 dated chamber markings, but no stock lug. Production unknown.

MAUSER BANNER 42 (DATED).... Nib $1577 Ex $1109 Gd $641
Caliber: 9mm Para. Eight-round magazine, 4-inch tapered bbl., 8.75 inches overall. Weight: 30 oz. Fixed rear sight, dovetailed front sight. Thumb lever safety. Checkered walnut or plastic grips. Mauser in banner on new-style toggle serial number and proofs on bbl., (usually) 1942 dated chamber markings and stock lug. Production unknown.

MAUSER BANNER
(SWISS PROOF)............. Nib $3316 Ex $2588 Gd $1340
Same specifications as Luger Mauser Banner 42 above except checkered walnut grips and 1939 dated chamber.

MAUSER FREISE............. Nib $4662 Ex $3738 Gd $2528
Same specifications as Mauser Banner 42 except checkered walnut grips, tapered bbl. w/proofs on sight block and Freise above chamber. Production unknown.

S/42
Caliber: 9mm Para. Eight-round magazine, 4-inch tapered barrel. 8.75 inches overall. Weight: 30 oz. Fixed rear sight, dovetailed front sight. Thumb lever safety. Checkered walnut grips. S/42 on new-style toggle, serial number and proofs on barrel and w/stock lug. Dated Model: Has dated chamber; estimated 3000 production. G Date: Has G (1935 date) over chamber; estimated 3000 production. K Date: Has K (1934 date) over chamber; prod. figures unknown.
Dated model .... Nib $1049 Ex $815 Gd $425
G date model................ Nib $1147 Ex $919 Gd $628
K date model.............. Nib $2453 Ex $1980 Gd $1360

RUSSIAN
COMMERCIAL............. Nib $2810 Ex $2250 Gd $1534
Caliber: 7.65mm. Eight-round magazine, 3.63-inch tapered bbl., 8.38 inches overall. Weight: 30 oz. Fixed rear sight, dovetailed front sight. Thumb lever safety. Checkered walnut grips. DWM on new-style toggle, Russian proofs on barrel, no chamber markings but w/stock lug. Production unknown.

SIMSON AND COMPANY
Calibers: 7.65mm and 9mm Para. Eight-round magazine, Weight: 32 oz. Fixed rear sight, dovetailed front sight. Thumb lever safety. Checkered walnut grips. Simson & Company Suhl on new-style toggle, serial number and proofs on barrel, date over chamber and w/stock lug. Estimated 10,000 production.
Simson and Company (9mm w/1925 date).......... Nib $2630 Ex $2110 Gd $732
Simson and Company (undated).................. Nib $1524 Ex $848 Gd $484
Simson and Company (S code).................... Nib $1940 Ex $1368 Gd $588

VICKERS-DUTCH .... Nib $2934 Ex $2102 Gd $854
Caliber: 9mm Para. Eight-round magazine, 4-inch tapered bbl., 8.75 inches overall. Weight: 30 oz. Fixed rear sight, dovetailed front sight. Grip safety and thumb lever w/arrow markings. Checkered walnut grips (coarse). Vickers LTD on new-style toggle, no chamber markings, dated barrel but no stock lug. Estimated 10,000 production.

LUNA FREE PISTOL — Zella-Mehlis, Germany Originally mfd. by Ernst Friedr. Buchel and later by Udo Anschutz

MODEL 200 FREE PISTOL...... Nib $1163 Ex 1049 Gd $643
Single-shot. System Aydt action. Set trigger. Caliber: .22 LR. Eleven-inch bbl., weight: 40 oz. Target sights. Blued finish. Checkered and carved walnut grip and forearm; improved design w/adj. hand base on later models of Udo Anschutz manufacture. Made prior to WWII.

M.A.C. (Military Armament Corp.) — Stephensville, Texas, Dist. by Defense Systems International, Marietta, Georgia. Previously by Cobray, SWD and RPB Industries

INGRAM MODEL 10 AUTO PISTOL
Select fire (NFA-Title II-Class III) SMG based on Ingram M10 blowback system using an open bolt design with or without telescoping stock. Calibers: 9mm or .45 ACP. Cyclic rate: 750 RPM (9mm) or 900 RPM (.45 ACP). 32- or 30-round magazine, 5.75-inch threaded bbl. (to accept muzzle brake) bbl. extension or suppressor, 10.5 inches overall w/o stock or 10.6 (w/telescoped stock) and 21.5 (w/extended stock). Weight: 6.25 pounds. Front protected post sight, fixed aperture rear sight. Garand-style safety in trigger guard.

9mm model . . . . Nib $894 Ex $816 Gd $582
.45 ACP model . . . . Nib $894 Ex $816 Gd $582
W/bbl. extension, add $195
W/suppressor, add $495

INGRAM MODEL 10A1S SEMIAUTOMATIC
Similar to the Model 10 except (Class I) semiautomatic w/closed bolt design to implement an interchangable component system to easily convert to fire 9mm and .45 ACP.

9mm model . . . . Nib $313 Ex $293 Gd $214
.45 ACP model . . . . Nib $323 Ex $297 Gd $214
W/bbl. extension, add $150
W/fake suppressor, add $195

INGRAM MODEL 11 SEMIAUTOMATIC
Similar to the Model 10A1 except (Class I) semiautomatic chambered .380 ACP.

.380 ACP model . . . . Nib $684 Ex $627 Gd $507
W/bbl. extension, add $150
W/fake suppressor, add $195

MAGNUM RESEARCH INC. — Minneapolis, Minnesota

BABY EAGLE SEMIAUTOMATIC . . . . Nib $439 Ex $371 Gd $225
DA. Calibers: 9mm, .40 S&W, .41 AE. 15-shot magazine (9mm), 9-round magazine (.40 S&W), 10-round magazine (.41 AE), 4.75-inch bbl., 8.15 inches overall. Weight: 35.4 oz. Combat sights. Matte blued finish. Imported 1991-96 and 1999 to date.

DESERT EAGLE MK VII SEMIAUTOMATIC
Gas-operated. Calibers: .357 Mag., .41 Mag., .44 Mag., .50 Action Express (AE). Eight- or 9-round magazine, 6-inch w/standard bbl., or 10- and 14-inch w/polygonal bbl., 10.6 inches overall (with 6-inch bbl.). Weight: 52 oz. (w/alum. alloy frame) to 67 oz. (w/steel frame). Fixed or adj. combat sights. Combat-type trigger guard. finish: Military black oxide, nickel, chrome, stainless or blued. Wraparound rubber grips. Made by Israel Military Industries 1984-95.

.357 standard (steel) or alloy (6-inch bbl.) . . . Nib $898 Ex $690 Gd $425
.357 stainless steel (6-inch bbl.) . . . . . Nib $956 Ex $768 Gd $527
.41 Mag. standard (steel) or alloy 6-inch bbl.) . . . . Nib $892 Ex $716 Gd $491
.41 Mag. stainless steel (6-inch bbl.) . . . Nib $860 Ex $690 Gd $474
.44 Mag. standard (steel) or alloy (6-inch bbl.) . . . . Nib $840 Ex $674 Gd $463
.44 Mag. stainless steel (6-inch bbl.) . . . Nib $918 Ex $737 Gd $506
.50 AE Magnum standard . . . . Nib $990 Ex $794 Gd $544
Add for 10-inch bbl. . . . . Nib $125 Ex $100 Gd $68
Add for 14-inch bbl. . . . . Nib $156 Ex $125 Gd $85

Magnum Research Model Desert Eagle Mark XIX (Shown w/Optional Leupold Scope

Magnum Research Model One Pro .45

MODEL DESERT EAGLE MARK XIX SEMI-AUTOMATIC PISTOL
Interchangeable component system based on .50-caliber frame. Calibers: .357 Mag., .44 Mag., .50 AE. Nine-, 8-, 7-round magazine, 6- or 10-inch bbl. w/dovetail design and cross slots to accept scope rings. Weight: 70.5 oz. (6-inch bbl.) or 79 oz. 10.75 or 14.75 inches overall. Sights: Post front and adjustable rear. Blue, chrome or nickel finish; available brushed, matte or polished. Hogue soft rubber grips. Made 1995 to date.

.357 Mag. (W/6-inch bbl.) . . . . Nib $1078 Ex $922 Gd $428
.44 Mag. (W/6-inch bbl.) . . . . Nib $1006 Ex $808 Gd $553
.50 AE (W/6-inch bbl.) . . . . Nib $1046 Ex $839 Gd $574
W/10-inch bbl., add $50
Two caliber conversion (bbl., bolt & mag.), add $395
XIX Platform System 3 caliber-conversion w/6 bbls.) . . . . Nib $2872 Ex $2301 Gd $1571
XIX6 System (two caliber-conversion w/2 6-inch bbls.) . . . . Nib $1914 Ex $1526 Gd $1043
XIX10 System (two cal.-conv. w/ two 10 inch bbls.) . . . . . . Nib $2068 Ex $1658 Gd $1134
Custom shop finish, add 15%
24K gold finish, add 35%

(ASAI) MODEL ONE PRO .45 PISTOL
Calibers: .45 ACP or .400 COR-BON, 3.75- inch bbl., 7.04 or 7.83 (IPSC Model) inches overall. Weight: 23.5 (alloy frame) or 31.1 oz. 10-round magazine. Short recoil action. SA or DA mode w/de-cocking lever. Steel or alloy grip-frame. Textured black polymer grips. Imported 1998 to date.

Model 1P45 . . . . Nib $587 Ex $472 Gd $324
Model 1C45/400 (compensator kit), add $175
Model 1C400NC (400 conversion kit), add $125

Magnum Research SSP-91 Lone Eagle Pistol
(w/Optional Leupold Scope)

SSP-91 LONE EAGLE PISTOL

Single-shot action w/interchangeable rotating breech bbl., assembly. Calibers: .22 LR, .22 Mag., .22 Hornet, .22-250, .223 Rem., .243 Win., 6mm BR, 7mm-08, 7mm BR, .30-06, .30-30, .308 Win., .35 Rem., .357 Mag., .44 Mag., .444 Marlin. 14-inch interchangeable bbl. assembly, 15 inches overall. Weight: 4.5 lbs. Black or chrome finish. Made 1991 to date.

SSP-91 S/S pistol (complete gun w/black finish)..... NiB $3405 Ex $338 Gd $202
SSP-91 S/S pistol (complete gun w/chrome finish) .. NiB $591 Ex $504 Gd $393
Extra 14-inch bbl., action w/black finish...... NiB $660 Ex $597 Gd $515
Extra 14-inch bbl., action w/chrome finish.... NiB $754 Ex $680 Gd $585
Ambidextrous stock assembly............. NiB $98 Ex $78 Gd $53
W/muzzle brake, add $65
W/open sights, add...................................... $30

MAUSER PISTOLS — Oberndorf, Germany Waffenfabrik Mauser of Mauser-Werke A.G.

MODEL 80-SA AUTOMATIC...... NiB $478 Ex $348 Gd $208

Caliber: 9mm Para. 13-round magazine, 4.66-inch bbl., 8 inches overall. Weight: 31.5 oz. Blued finish. Hardwood grips. Made 1991-94.

MODEL 90 DA AUTOMATIC ..... NiB $473 Ex $348 Gd $208

Caliber: 9mm Para. 14-round magazine, 4.66-inch bbl., 8 inches overall. Weight: 35 oz. Blued finish. Hardwood grips. Made 1991-94.

MODEL 90 DAC COMPACT ...... NiB $478 Ex $348 Gd $208

Caliber: 9mm Para. 14-round magazine, 4.13-inch bbl., 7.4 inches overall. Weight: 33.25 oz. Blued finish. Hardwood grips. Made 1991-94.

MODEL 1898 (1896) MILITARY AUTO PISTOL

Caliber: 7.63mm Mauser, but also chambered for 9mm Mauser and 9mm Para. w/the latter being identified by a large red "9" in the grips. 10-round box magazine, 5.25-inch bbl., 12 inches overall. Weight: 45 oz. Adj. rear sight. Blued finish. Walnut grips. Made 1897-1939. Note: Specialist collectors recognize a number of variations at significantly higher values. Price here is for more common commercial and military types with original finish.

Commercial model (pre-war) .... NiB $3411 Ex $2631 Gd $993
Commercial model (wartime) .... NiB $1903 Ex $1435 Gd $551
Red 9 Commercial model (fixed sight) ..... NiB $1175 Ex $905 Gd $447
Red 9 WWI Contract (tangent sight)....... NiB $2059 Ex $1487 Gd $697
W/stock sssembly (matching SN), add $550

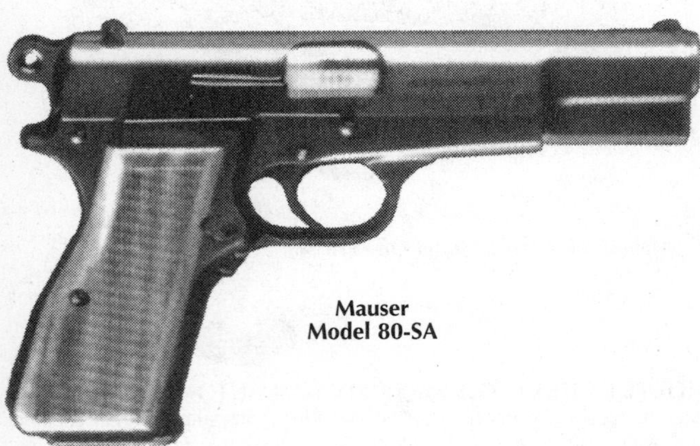
Mauser
Model 80-SA

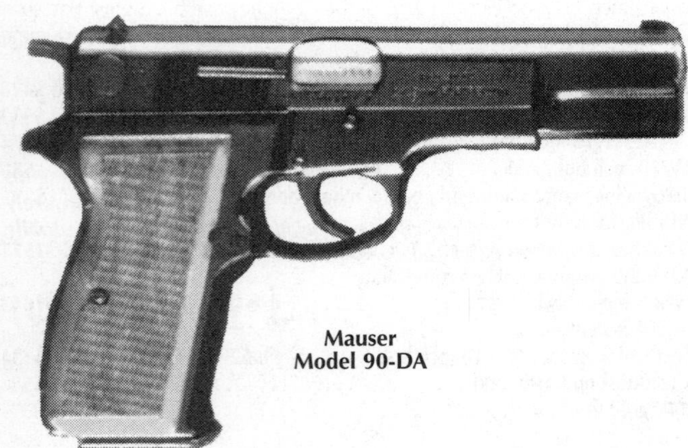
Mauser
Model 90-DA

MODEL HSC DA AUTO PISTOL

Calibers: .32 Auto (7.65mm), .380 Auto (9mm Short). Eight-round (.32) or 7-round (.380) magazine, 3.4-inch bbl., 6.4 inches overall. Weight: 23.6 oz. Fixed sights. Blued or nickel finish. Checkered walnut grips. Made 1938-.45 and from 1968-96.

Commercial model (low grip screw)...... NiB $4196 Ex $3156 Gd $1960
Commercial model (wartime) .... NiB $426 Ex $348 Gd $197
Nazi military model (pre-war)............. NiB $790 Ex $582 Gd $218
Nazi military model (wartime) .... NiB $478 Ex $374 Gd $197
French production (postwar)............... NiB $400 Ex $322 Gd $162
Mauser production (postwar) .... NiB $374 Ex $317 Gd $166
Recent importation (Armes De Chasse) ...... NiB $504 Ex $452 Gd $260
Recent importation (Interarms)............ NiB $348 Ex $296 Gd $166
Recent importation (European Amer. Arms) ... NiB $286 Ex $244 Gd $140
Recent importation (Gamga, USA) .... NiB $421 Ex $353 Gd $239
American Eagle model (1 of 5000) .... NiB $466 Ex $374 Gd $258

LUGER LANGE PISTOL 08

Caliber: 9mm Para. Eight-inch bbl., Checkered grips. Blued finish. Accessorized w/walnut shoulder stock, front sight tool, spare magazine, leather case. Currently in production. Commemorative version made in limited quantities w/ivory grips and 14-carat gold monogram plate.

MOUNTAIN EAGLE SEMIAUTOMATIC

Caliber: .22 LR. 15-round polycarbonate resin magazine, 6.5-inch injection-molded polymer and steel bbl., 10.6 inches overall. Weight: 21 oz. Ramp blade front sight, adj. rear. Injection-molded, checkered and textured grip. Matte black finish. Made 1992-96.

Mountain Eagle (standard, 6.5-inch bbl.) .. NiB $196 Ex $159 Gd $111
Mountain Eagle (compact 4.5-inch bbl.)... NiB $184 Ex $148 Gd $104

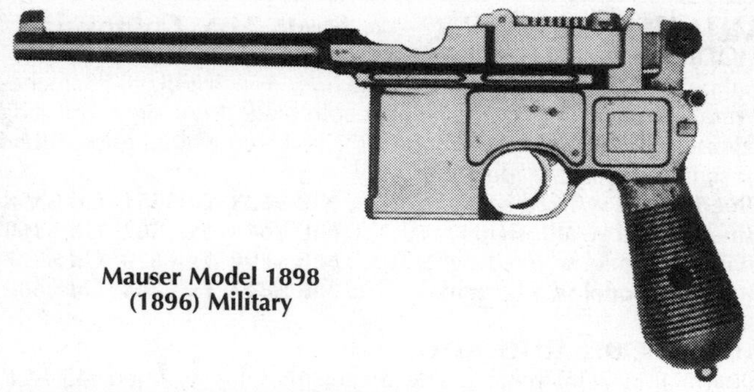
Mauser Model 1898 (1896) Military

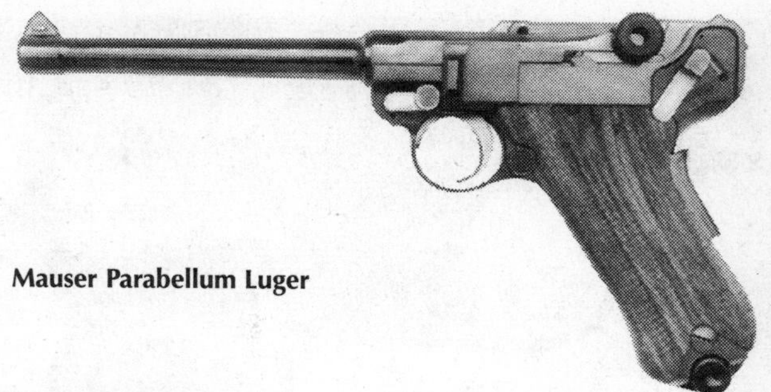
Mauser Parabellum Luger

(cont'd) **LUGER LANGE PISTOL 08**
Commemorative model (100 produced) . . . NiB $2632 Ex $2113 Gd $1449
Commemorative matched pair . . . . NiB $5232 Ex $4193 Gd $2864
Cartridge counter model. . . . . NiB $3412 Ex $2707 Gd $1874
Carbine model (w/matching buttstock) . NiB $6344 Ex $5082 Gd $3468

PARABELLUM LUGER AUTO PISTOL
Current commercial model. Swiss pattern with grip safety. Calibers: 7.65mm Luger, 9mm Para. Eight-round magazine, bbl. lengths: 4-, 6-inch, 8.75 inches overall (with 4-inch bbl.). Weight: 30 oz. (with 4-inch bbl.). Fixed sights. Blued finish. Checkered walnut grips. Made from 1970 to date. Note: Pistols of this model sold in the U.S. have the American Eagle stamped on the receiver.
Standard model (blue) . . . . NiB $1088 Ex $833 Gd $618

POCKET MODEL 1910 AUTO PISTOL
Caliber: .25 Auto (6.35mm). Nine-round magazine, 3.1-inch bbl., 5.4 inches overall. Weight: 15 oz. Fixed sights. Blued finish. Checkered walnut or hard rubber grips. Made 1910-34.
Model 1910 (standard) . . . . NiB $451 Ex $321 Gd $155
Model 1910 (w/side latch) . . . . NiB $471 Ex $378 Gd $260

POCKET MODEL 1914 AUTOMATIC. . . . . NiB $451 Ex $321 Gd $160
Similar to Pocket Model 1910. Caliber: .32 Auto (7.65mm). Eight-round magazine, 3.4-inch bbl., 6 inches overall. Weight: 21 oz. Fixed sights. Blued finish. Checkered walnut or hard rubber grips. Made 1914-34

POCKET MODEL 1934 . . . . NiB $477 Ex $347 Gd $165
Similar to Pocket Models 1910 and 1914 in the respective calibers. Chief difference is in the more streamlined, one-piece grips. Made 1934-39.

WTP MODEL I AUTO PISTOL. . . . . NiB $526 Ex $349 Gd $157
"Westentaschen-Pistole" (Vest Pocket Pistol). Caliber: .25 Automatic (6.35mm). Six-round magazine, 2.5-inch bbl., 4 inches overall. Weight: 11.5 oz. Blued finish. Hard rubber grips. Made 1922-37.

WTP MODEL II AUTO PISTOL . . . . NiB $687 Ex $557 Gd $219
Similar to Model I but smaller and lighter. Caliber: .25 Automatic (6.35mm). Six-round magazine, 2-inch bbl., 4 inches overall. Weight: 9.5 oz. Blued finish. Hard rubber grips. Made 1938-40.

MERWIN HULBERT & CO., — New York, NY

FIRST MODEL
FRONTIER ARMY . . . . NiB $3671 Ex $1903 Gd $811
Single action, .44 caliber, 7.5-inch bbl. Square butt, open top, scoop flutes on cylinder, two screws above trigger guard

SECOND MODEL
FRONTIER ARMY . . . . NiB $5244 Ex $1812 Gd $980
Similar to First Model except has only one screw above trigger guard.

SECOND MODEL
POCKET ARMY . . . . NiB $5255 Ex $1355 Gd $887
Similar to Second Model except has bird's-head butt instead of square butt, 3.5- or 7-inch (scarce) bbl. May be marked "Pocket Army."

THIRD MODEL
FRONTIER ARMY . . . . NiB $5255 Ex $1355 Gd $887
Caliber: .44, 7-inch round bbl. with no rib, single action. Square butt, top strap, usually has conventional fluting on cylinder but some have scoop flutes.

THIRD MODEL
FRONTIER ARMY . . . . NiB $4995 Ex $1199 Gd $835
Similar to Third Model Frontier Army SA except is double action.

THIRD MODEL
POCKET ARMY . . . . .NiB $4995 Ex $1199 Gd $835
Caliber: .44, 3.5- or 7.5-inch bbl. with no rib. Single action, bird's-head butt, top strap.

THIRD MODEL
POCKET ARMY . . . . NiB $4735 Ex $1095 Gd $783
Similar to Third Model Pocket Army SA except is double action.

FOURTH MODEL
FRONTIER ARMY . . . . NiB $6815 Ex $3695 Gd $1875
Caliber: .44, 3.5- 5- or 7-inch unique ribbed bbl. Single action, square butt, top strap, conventional flutes on cylinder.

FOURTH MODEL
FRONTIER ARMY
Similar to Fourth Model Frontier Army SA except is double action.
. . . . . .NiB $6315 Ex $3175 Gd $1771

(The following handguns are foreign copies of Merwin Hulbert Co. guns and may be marked as such, or as "Sistema Merwin Hulbert," but rarely with the original Hopkins & Allen markings. These guns will usually bring half or less of a comparable genuine Merwin Hulbert product.)

FIRST POCKET MODEL. . . . . NiB $1582 Ex $490 Gd $256
Caliber: .38 Special, 5-round cylinder (w/cylinder pin exposed at front of frame), single action. Spur trigger; round loading hole in recoil shield, no loading gate.

SECOND POCKET MODEL . . . . . NiB $1426 Ex. $412 Gd $230
Similar to First Pocket Model except has sliding loading gate.

THIRD POCKET MODEL . . . . .NiB $1318 Ex $382 Gd $210
Similar to First Pocket Model except has enclosed cylinder pin.

THIRD POCKET
MODEL W/TRIGGER GUARD. . . . NiB $1318 Ex $408 Gd $236
Similar to First Pocket Model except w/conventional trigger guard.

Mauser WTP Model I

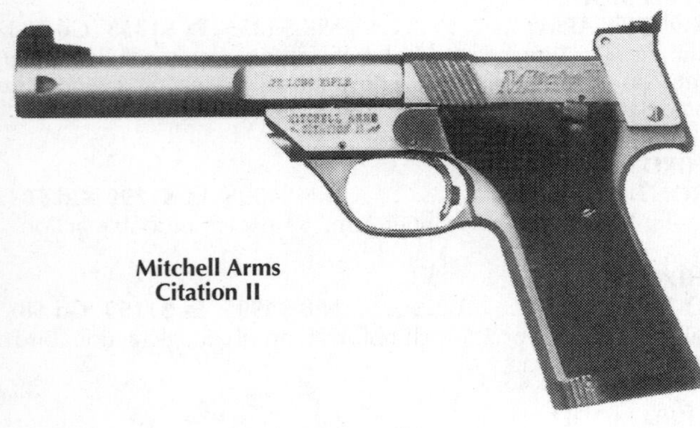
Mitchell Arms
Citation II

Mitchell Arms
Sharpshooter II

MEDIUM FRAME
POCKET MODEL.............. NiB $1006 Ex $340 Gd $200
Caliber: .38 Spec., 5-round cylinder, DA, may have hammer spur.

MEDIUM FRAME
POCKET MODEL 32 .... Nib $1162 Ex $382 Gd $226
Similar to Medium Frame Pocket Model except .32 caliber, 7-round cylinder, double action. ....

TIP-UP MODEL 22 .... NiB $1162 Ex $538 Gd $278
Similar to S&W Model One except .22 caliber, 7-round cylinder, spur trigger. Scarce. ....

MITCHELL ARMS, INC. — Santa Ana, California

MODEL 1911 GOLD SIGNATURE
Caliber: .45 ACP. Eight-round magazine, 5-inch bbl., 8.75 inches overall. Weight: 39 oz. Interchangeable blade front sight, drift-adj. combat or fully adj. rear. Smooth or checkered walnut grips. Blued or stainless finish. Made 1994-96.
Blued model w/fixed sights....... NiB $623 Ex $551 Gd $358
Blued model w/adj. sights........ NiB $643 Ex $562 Gd $368
Stainless model w/fixed sights..... NiB $796 Ex $679 Gd $577
Stainless model w/adj. sights...... NiB $827 Ex $704 Gd $602

ALPHA MODEL AUTO PISTOL
Dual action w/interchangeable trigger modules. Caliber: .45 ACP. Eight-round magazine, 5-inch bbl., 8.75 inches overall. Weight: 39 oz. Interchangeable blade front sight, drift-adj. rear. Smooth or checkered walnut grips. Blued or stainless finish. Made from 1994 to date.Advertised 1995, but not manufactured.
Blued model w/fixed sights................ NiB $910 Ex $732 Gd $504
Blued model w/adj. sights.................. NiB $944 Ex $759 Gd $523
Stainless model w/fixed sights............. NiB $944 Ex $759 Gd $523
Stainless model w/adj. sights............... NiB $975 Ex $784 Gd $539

AMERICAN EAGLE PISTOL .... NiB $607 Ex $488 Gd $336
Stainless-steel re-creation of the American Eagle Parabellum auto pistol. Caliber: 9mm Para. Seven-round magazine, 4-inch bbl., 9.6 inches overall. Weight: 26.6 oz. Blade front sight, fixed rear. Stainless finish. Checkered walnut grips. Made 1993-94.

CITATION II AUTO PISTOL ...... NiB $412 Ex $310 Gd $182
Re-creation of the High Standard Supermatic Citation Military. Caliber: .22 LR. 10-round magazine, 5.5-inch bull bbl. or 7.25 fluted bbl., 9.75 inches overall (5.5-inch bbl.). Weight: 44.5 oz. Ramp front sight, slide-mounted micro-adj. rear. Satin blued or stainless finish. Checkered walnut grips w/thumbrest. Made 1992-96.

OLYMPIC L.S.U. AUTO PISTOL.... NiB $854 Ex $574 Gd $294
Similar to the Citation II model except chambered in .22 Short, 6.75-inch round tapered bbl. w/stabilizer and removable counterweights. Made 1992-96.

SHARPSHOOTER II AUTO PISTOL....... NiB $336 Ex $296 Gd $183
Re-creation of the High Standard Sharpshooter. Caliber: .22 LR. 10-round magazine, 5-inch bull bbl., 10.25 inches overall. Weight: 42 oz. Ramp front sight, slide-mounted micro-adj. rear. Satin blued or stainless finish. Checkered walnut grips w/thumbrest. Made 1992-96.

MODEL SA SPORT KING II....... NiB $280 Ex $225 Gd $155
Caliber: .22 LR. 10-round magazine, 4.5- or 6.75-inch bbl., 9 or 11.25 inches overall. Weight: 39 or 42 oz. Checkered walnut or black plastic grips. Blade front sight and drift adjustable rear. Made 1993-94.

SA ARMY REVOLVER
Calibers: .357 Mag., .44 Mag., .45 Colt/.45 ACP. Six-round cylinder. bbl., lengths: 4.75, 5.5, 7.5 inches, weight: 40-43 oz. Blade front sight, grooved top strap or adj. rear. Blued or nickel finish w/color-casehardened frame. Brass or steel backstrap/trigger guard. Smooth one-piece walnut grips. Imported 1987-94 and 1997 to date.
Standard model w/blued finish.......... NiB $386 Ex $311 Gd $215
Standard model w/nickel finish.......... NiB $424 Ex $342 Gd $235
Standard model w/stainless backstrap..... NiB $457 Ex $367 Gd $253
.45 Combo w/blued finish .... NiB $514 Ex $413 Gd $284
.45 Combo w/nickel finish .... NiB $552 Ex $443 Gd $305

TROPHY II AUTO PISTOL........ NiB $443 Ex $367 Gd $183
Similar to the Citation II model except w/gold-plated trigger and gold-filled markings. Made 1992-96.

VICTOR II AUTO PISTOL . . . . NiB $514 Ex $413 Gd $284
Re-creation of the High Standard Victor w/full-length vent rib. Caliber: .22 LR. 10-round magazine, 4.5- or 5.5-inch bbl., 9.75 inches overall (with 5.5-inch bbl.). Weight: 52 oz. (with 5.5-inch bbl.). Rib-mounted target sights. Satin blued or stainless finish. Checkered walnut grips w/thumbrest. Made 1992-96.

GUARDIAN ANGEL
DERRINGER . . . . NiB $134 Ex $109 Gd $76
Hammerless, double-action O/U derringer w/interchangeable drop-in breech block. Calibers: .22 LR, .22 WRM. Two-round capacity. Two-inch bbl., 5 inches overall. Weight: 12 oz. Blue, nickel or gold finish. Blade front and fixed rear sights. Checkered black grips. Made 1996-97.

GUARDIAN II . . . . NiB $250 Ex $201 Gd $139
Caliber: .38 Special, Six-round cylinder, 2-, 4- or 6-inch bbl., 8.5 inches overall (with 4-inch bbl.). Weight: 32 oz (with 4-inch bbl.). Blade ramp front and fixed rear sights. Checkered combat or target grips. Blued finish. Made 1995.

GUARDIAN III . . . . NiB $287 Ex $236 Gd $150
Same specifications as Guardian II model except w/adjustable rear sights. Made 1995.

TITAN II DA . . . . NiB $318 Ex $252 Gd $175
Caliber: .357 Mag. Six-round cylinder. 2-, 4- or 6-inch bbl., 7.75 inches overall (with 4-inch bbl.). Weight: 38 oz (with 4-inch bbl.). Blade front and fixed rear sights. Crane mounted cylinder release. Blued or stainless finish. Made 1995.

TITAN III DA . . . . NiB $359 Ex $282 Gd $191
Same specification as the Titan II except w/adjustable rear sight. Made 1995.

MKE PISTOL — Ankara, Turkey
Mfd. by Makina ve Kimya Endüstrisi Kurumu

KIRIKKALE DA
AUTOMATIC PISTOL . . . . NiB $379 Ex $308 Gd $180
Similar to Walther PP. Calibers: .32 Auto (7.65mm), .380 Auto (9mm Short). Seven-round magazine, 3.9-inch bbl., 6.7 inches overall. Weight: 24 oz. Fixed sights. Blued finish. Checkered plastic grips. Made 1948-88. Note: This is a Turkish Army standard service pistol.

MOA CORPORATION — Dayton, Ohio

MAXIMUM SINGLE-SHOT PISTOL
Calibers: .22 Hornet to .454 Casull Mag. Armoloy, Chromoloy or stainless falling block action fitted w/blued or stainless 8.75-, 10- or 14-inch Douglas bbl., weight: 60-68 oz. Smooth walnut grips. Made 1986 to date.
Chromoloy receiver
(blued bbl.) . . . . NiB $843 Ex $727 Gd $382
Armoloy receiver (blued bbl.) . . . . . NiB $854 Ex $757 Gd $405
Stainless receiver (blued bbl.) . . . . . NiB $951 Ex $854 Gd $609
W/stainless bbl., add $95
W/extra bbl., add $250

MAXIMUM CARBINE PISTOL
Similar to Maximum Pistol except w/18-inch bbl. Made 1986-88 and 1994 to date.
MOA Maximum (blued bbl.) . . . . . . NiB $869 Ex $691 Gd $467
MOA Maximum (stainless bbl.) . . . . NiB $941 Ex $765 Gd $523

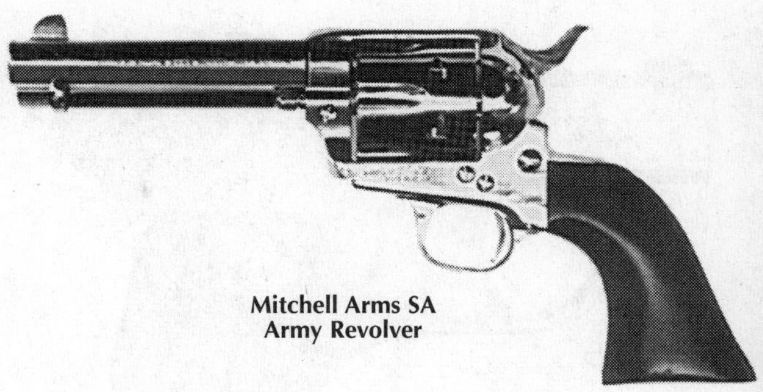
Mitchell Arms SA Army Revolver

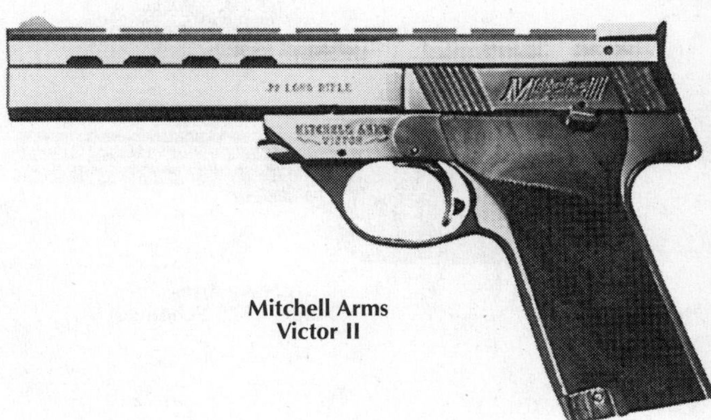
Mitchell Arms Victor II

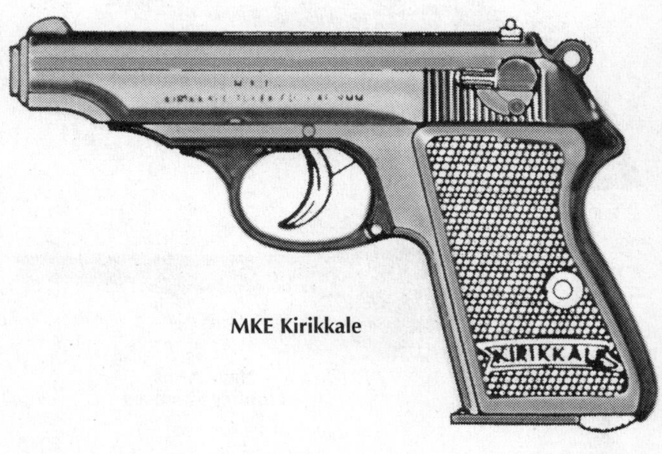

MKE Kirikkale

MOA Maximum Carbine Pistol

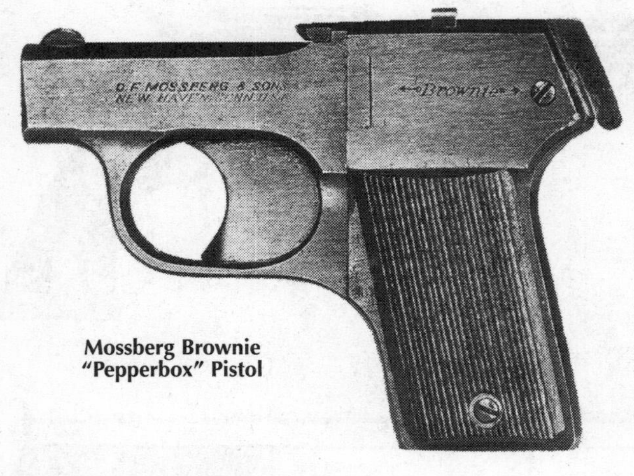

Mossberg Brownie "Pepperbox" Pistol

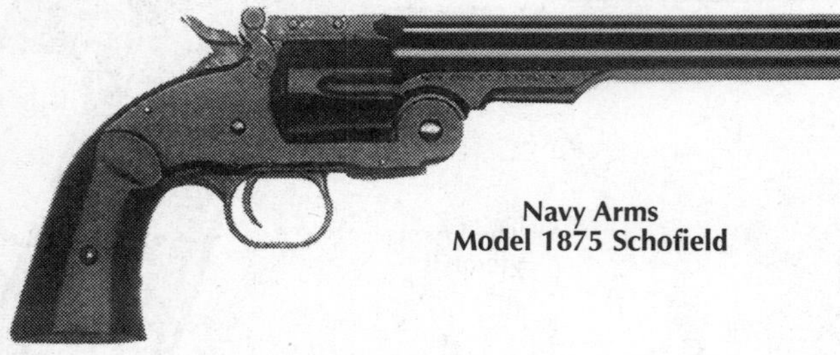
Navy Arms Model 1875 Schofield

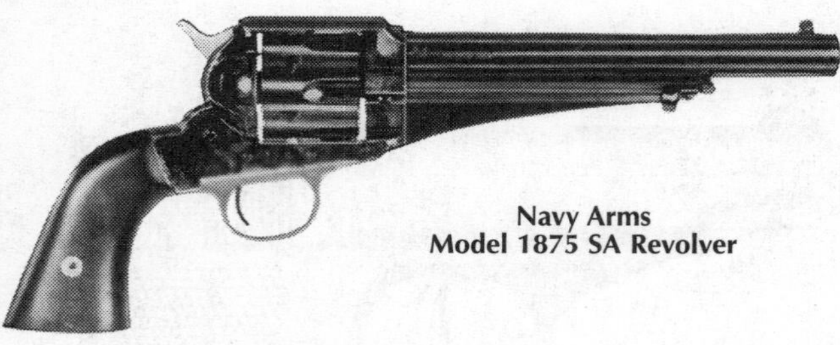
Navy Arms Model 1875 SA Revolver

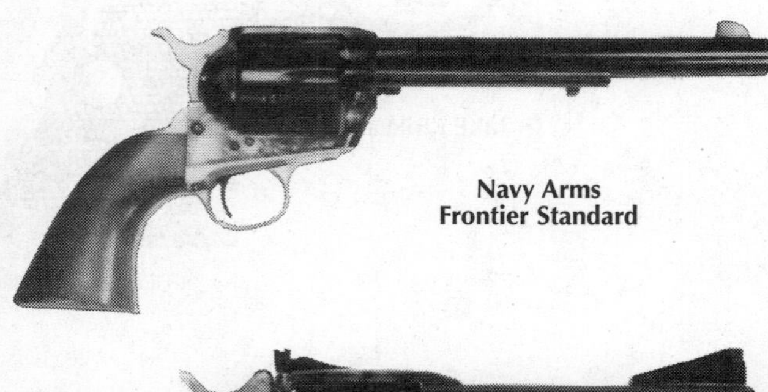
Navy Arms Frontier Standard

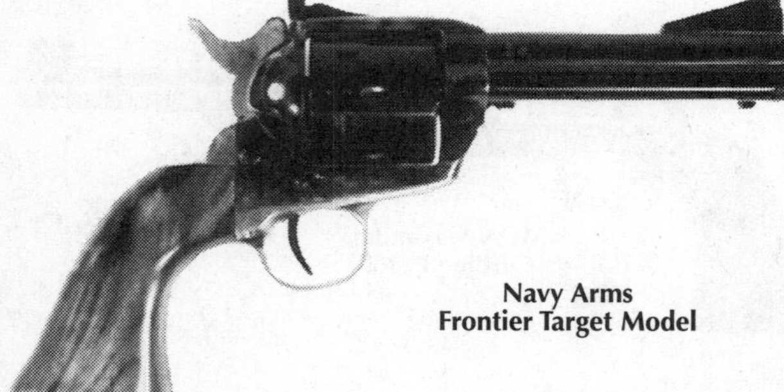
Navy Arms Frontier Target Model

O.F. MOSSBERG & SONS, INC. — North Haven, Connecticut

BROWNIE "PEPPERBOX" PISTOL. . . . . . . NiB $367 Ex $316 Gd $183
Hammerless, top-break, double-action, four bbls. w/revolving firing pin. Caliber: .22 LR, 2.5-inch bbls., weight: 14 oz. Blued finish. Serated grips. Approximately 37,000 made 1919-.32.

NAMBU PISTOLS

See Listings under Japanese Military Pistols.

NAVY ARMS COMPANY — Martinsburg, West Virginia

MODEL 1873 SA REVOLVER
Calibers: .44-40, .45 Colt. Six-round cylinder, bbl. lengths: 3, 4.75, 5.5, 7.5 inches, 10.75 inches overall (with 5.5-inch bbl.). Weight: 36 oz. Blade front sight, grooved topstrap rear. Blued w/color-case-hardened frame or nickel finish. Smooth walnut grips. Made 1991 to date.
Blued finish w/brass backstrap . . . . NiB $365 Ex $298 Gd $164
U.S. Artillery model w/5-inch bbl. . . . NiB $396 Ex $319 Gd $220
U.S. Cavalry model w/7-inch bbl. . . NiB $428 Ex $345 Gd $238
Bisley model . . . . NiB $365 Ex $314 Gd $164
Sheriff's model (disc. 1998). . . . . . . NiB $360 Ex $288 Gd $164

MODEL 1875 SCHOFIELD REVOLVER
Replica of S&W Model 3, top-break single-action w/auto ejector. Calibers: .44-40 or .45 LC. Six-round cylinder, 5- or 7-inch bbl., 10.75 or 12.75 inches overall. Weight: 39 oz. Blade front sight, square-notched rear. Polished blued finish. Smooth walnut grips. Made 1994 to date.
Cavalry model (7-inch bbl.) . . . . NiB $628 Ex $551 Gd $267
Deluxe Cavalry model
(engraved) . . . . NiB $1499 Ex $1202 Gd $806
Wells Fargo model (5-inch bbl.) . . . NiB $648 Ex $520 Gd $357
Deluxe Wells Fargo
model (engraved). . . . . NiB $1466 Ex $1177 Gd $806
Hideout model (3.5-inch bbl.). . . . . NiB $622 Ex $499 Gd $343

MODEL 1875 SA REVOLVER. . . . . . NiB $390 Ex $314 Gd $217
Replica of Remington Model 1875. Calibers: .357 Magnum, .44-40, .45 Colt. Six-round cylinder, 7.5-inch bbl., 13.5 inches overall. Weight: About 48 oz. Fixed sights. Blued or nickel finish. Smooth walnut grips. Made in Italy c.1955-1980. Note: Originally marketed in the U.S. as Replica Arms Model 1875 (that firm was acquired by Navy Arms Co).

FRONTIER SA REVOLVER . . . . NiB $307 Ex $247 Gd $171
Calibers: .22 LR, .22 WMR, .357 Mag., .45 Colt. Six-round cylinder, bbl. lengths: 4.5-, 5.5-, 7.5-inches, 10.25 inches overall (with 4.5-inch bbl.). Weight: About 36 oz. (with 4.5-inch bbl.). Fixed sights. Blued bbl., and cylinder, color-casehardened frame, brass grip frame. One-piece smooth walnut grip. Imported 1975-79.

FRONTIER TARGET MODEL . . . . . . NiB $332 Ex $267 Gd $185
Same as standard Frontier except has adj. rear sight and ramp front sight. Imported 1975-79.

BUNTLINE FRONTIER. . . . . NiB $493 Ex $396 Gd $273
Same as Target Frontier except has detachable shoulder stock and 16.5-inch bbl. Calibers: .357 Magnum and .45 Colt only. Made 1975-79.

LUGER (STANDARD) AUTOMATIC . . . . NiB $168 Ex $136 Gd $95
Caliber: .22 LR, standard or high velocity. 10-round magazine, bbl. length: 4.5 inches, 8.9 inches overall. Weight: 1 lb., 13.5 oz. Square blade front sight w/square notch, stationary rear sight. Walnut checkered grips. Non-reflecting black finish. Made 1986-88.

ROLLING BLOCK
SINGLE-SHOT PISTOL . . . . NiB $360 Ex $304 Gd $185
Calibers: .22 LR, .22 Hornet, .357 Magnum. Eight-inch bbl., 12 inches overall. Weight: About 40 oz. Adjustable sights. Blued bbl., color-casehardened frame, brass trigger guard. Smooth walnut grip and forearm. Imported 1965-80.

TT-OLYMPIA PISTOL . . . . NiB $265 Ex $240 Gd $162
Reproduction of the Walther Olympia Target Pistol. Caliber: .22 LR. Eight inches overall 4.6-inch bbl., weight: 28 oz. Blade front sight, adj. rear. Blued finish. Checkered hardwood grips. Imported 1992-94.

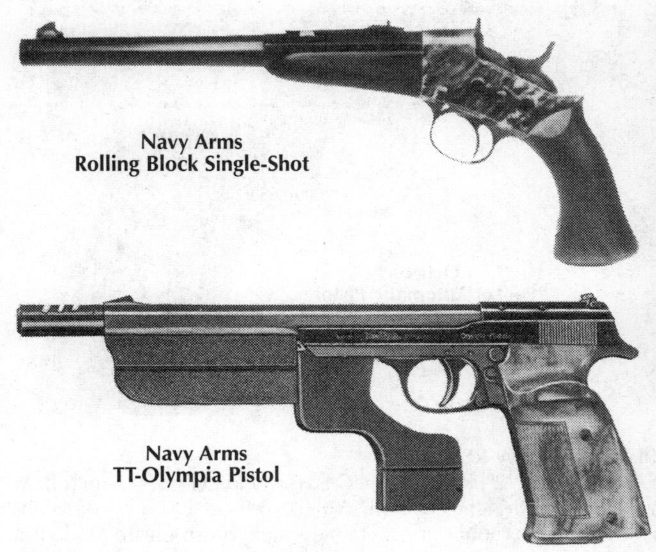

Navy Arms
Rolling Block Single-Shot

Navy Arms
TT-Olympia Pistol

NEW ENGLAND FIREARMS — Gardner, Massachusetts

In 1987, New England Firearms was established as an independent company producing select H&R models under the NEF logo. In 1991, H&R 1871, Inc. was formed from the residual of the parent company and took over the New England Firearms facility. H&R 1871 produced firearms under both their logo and the NEF brand name until 1999, when the Marlin Firearms Company acquired the assets of H&R 1871.

MODEL R73 REVOLVER . . . . NiB $135 Ex $104 Gd $68
Caliber: .32 H&R Mag. Five-round cylinder, 2.5- or 4-inch bbl., 8.5 inches overall (with 4-inch bbl.). Weight: 26 oz. (with 4 inch bbl.). Fixed or adjustable sights. Blued or nickel finish. Walnut-finish hardwood grips. Made from 1988-99.

New England Firearms
Model R73 Revolver

MODEL R92 REVOLVER . . . . NiB $135 Ex $104 Gd $68
Same general specifications as Model R73 except chambered for .22 LR. Nine-round cylinder. Weight: 28 oz. w/4 inch bbl., Made 1988-99.

MODEL 832 STARTER PISTOL . . . . . . NiB $98 Ex $79 Gd $55
Calibers: .22 Blank, .32 Blank. Nine- and 5-round cylinders, respectively. Push-pin swing-out cylinder. Solid wood grips w/NEF medallion insert.

New England Firearms
Model 832 Starter Pistol

ULTRA REVOLVER. . . . . NiB $167 Ex $135 Gd $94
Calibers: .22 LR, .22 Mag. Nine-round cylinder in .22 LR, 6-round cylinder in .22 Mag., 4- or 6-inch ribbed bull bbl., 10.75 inches overall (with 6-inch bbl.). Weight: 36 oz. (with 6-inch bbl.). Blade front sight, adj. square-notched rear. Blued or nickel finish. Walnut-finish hardwood grips. Made from 1989-99.

LADY ULTRA REVOLVER. . . . . NiB $160 Ex $124 Gd $78
Same basic specifications as the Ultra except in .32 H&R Mag. w/5-round cylinder and 3-inch ribbed bull bbl., 7.5 inches overall. Weight: 31 oz. Made 1992 -99.

NORTH AMERICAN ARMS — Provo, Utah

MODEL 22LR . . . . NiB $165 Ex $133 Gd $93
Same as Model 22S except chambered for .22 LR., is 3.88-inches overall, weight: 4.5 oz. Made 1976 to date.

MODEL 22S MINI REVOLVER. . . . . NiB $178 Ex $144 Gd $100
Single-Action. Caliber: .22 Short. Five-round cylinder, 1.13-inch bbl., 3.5-inches overall. Weight: 4 oz. Fixed sights. Stainless steel. Plastic grips. Made from 1975 to date.

MODEL 450 MAGNUM EXPRESS
Single-Action. Calibers: .450 Magnum Express, .45 Win. Mag. Five-round cylinder, 7.5- or 10.5-inch bbl., matte or polished stainless steel finish. Walnut grips. Presentation case. Disc. 1986.
Matte stainless model . . . . NiB $1245 Ex $990 Gd $735
Polished stainless model . . . . . . NiB $1449 Ex $1143 Gd $888
W/10-inch bbl., add $250
W/combo cylinder, add. $225

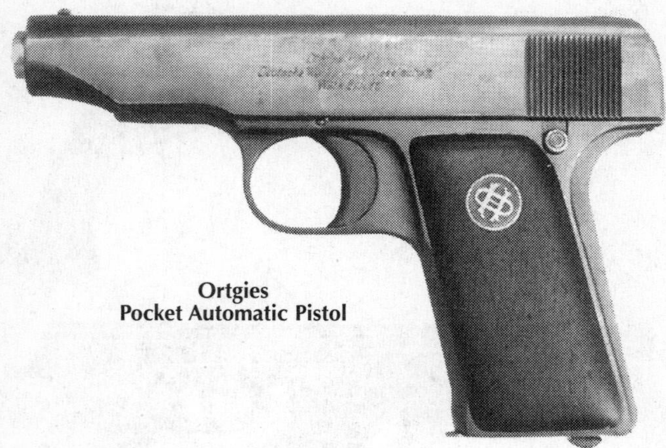
Ortgies
Pocket Automatic Pistol

BLACK WIDOW REVOLVER
SA. Calibers: .22 LR., .22 WMR. Five-round cylinder, 2-inch heavy vent bbl., 5.88-inches overall. Weight: 8.8 oz. Fixed or adj. sights. Full-size black rubber grips. Stainless steel brush finish. Made from 1990 to date.
Adj. sight model . . . . NiB $269 Ex $227 Gd $135
Adj. sight combo model . . . . NiB $309 Ex $253 Gd $181
Fixed sight model . . . . NiB $218 Ex $176 Gd $121
Fixed sight combo model. . . . . NiB $298 Ex $248 Gd $184

GUARDIAN DAO PISTOL. . . . . NiB $370 Ex $299 Gd $304
Caliber: .32 ACP. Six-round magazine, 2-inch bbl., 4.4 inches overall. Weight: 13.5 oz. Fixed sights. Black synthetic grips. Stainless steel. Made 1997 to date.

MINI-MASTER TARGET REVOLVER
SA. Calibers: .22 LR., .22 WMR. Five-round cylinder, 4-inch heavy vent rib bbl., 7.75-inches overall. Weight: 10.75 oz. Fixed or adj. sights. Black rubber grips. Stainless steel brush finish. Made from 1990 to date.
Adj. sight model . . . . NiB $258 Ex $212 Gd $181
Adj. sight combo model . . . . NiB $366 Ex $302 Gd $220
Fixed sight model . . . . NiB $257 Ex $207 Gd $144
Fixed sight combo model. . . . . NiB $333 Ex $276 Gd $203

NORWEGIAN MILITARY PISTOLS
Mfd. by Kongsberg Vaapenfabrikk, Government Arsenal at Kongsberg, Norway

MODEL 1914
AUTOMATIC PISTOL . . . . NiB $422 Ex $339 Gd $233
Similar to Colt Model 1911 .45 Automatic w/same general specifications except has lengthened slide stop. Made 1919-46.

NORWEGIAN
MODEL 1912 . . . . NiB $2698 Ex $2163 Gd $1478
Same as the model 1914 except has conventional slide stop. Only 500 were made.

OLYMPIC ARMS, INC.
Olympia Washington

OA-93 AR SEMIAUTOMATIC PISTOL
AR-15 style receiver with no buffer tube or charging handle. Caliber: .223 Rem. or 7.62x39mm. Five-, 20- or 30-round detachable

***(cont'd)* OA-93 AR SEMIAUTOMATIC PISTOL**
magazine, 6-, 9- or 14-inch stainless steel bbl., 15.75 inches overall w/6-inch bbl., weight: 4 lbs., 3 oz. Flattop upper with no open sights. Vortex flash suppressor. A2 stowaway pistol grip and forward pistol grip. Made 1993-94. Note: All post-ban versions of OA-93 style weapons are classified by BATF as "Any Other Weapon" and must be transferred by a Class III dealer. Values listed here are for limited-production, pre-ban guns.
Model OA-93
(.223 Rem.) . . . . NiB $3598 Ex $2884 Gd $2629
Model OA-93
(7.62x39mm). . . . . NiB $4414 Ex $4210 Gd $3904

OA-96 AR SEMI-
AUTOMATIC PISTOL . . . . NiB $892 Ex $800 Gd $714
Similar to Model OA-93 AR except w/6.5-inch bbl. only chambered for .223 Rem. Additional compliance modifications include a fixed (nonremovable) well-style magazine and no forward pistol grip. Made 1996 to date.

ORTGIES PISTOLS — Erfurt, Germany
Manufactured by Deutsche Werke A.G.

POCKET AUTO-
MATIC PISTOL . . . . NiB $316 Ex $265 Gd $194
Calibers: .32 Auto (7.65mm), .380 Auto (9mm). Seven-round magazine (.380 cal.), 8-round (.32 cal.), 3.25-inch bbl., 6.5-inches overall. Weight: 22 oz. Fixed sights. Blued finish. Plain walnut grips. Made in 1920's.

VEST POCKET
AUTOMATIC PISTOL . . . . NiB $290 Ex $234 Gd $163
Caliber: .25 Auto (6.35mm). Six-round magazine, 2.75-inch bbl., 5.19 inches overall. Weight: 13.5 oz. Fixed sights. Blued finish. Plain walnut grips. Made in 1920's.

PHOENIX ARMS — Ontario, California

MODEL HP22/HP25
SA AUTO PISTOLS. . . . . NiB $129 Ex $77 Gd $49
Caliber: .22 LR, .25 ACP. 10-round magazine, 3-inch bbl., 5.5 inches overall. Weight: 20 oz. Checkered synthetic grips. Blade front sight, adjustable rear. Blue, chrome or nickel finish. Made 1994 to date.

MODEL HP
RANGE-MASTER TARGET SA
AUTO PISTOL . . . . NiB $139 Ex $110 Gd $79
Similar to Model HP .22 except w/5.5-inch target bbl. and extended magazine, Ramp front sight, adjustable notch rear on vent rib. Checkered synthetic grips. Blue or satin nickel finish. Made 1998 to date.

MODEL HP
RANGE-MASTER DELUXE TARGET
SA AUTO PISTOL . . . . NiB $237 Ex $141 Gd $100
Similar to Model HP Rangemaster Target model except w/dual-2000 laser sight and custom wood grips. Made 1998 to date.

"RAVEN" SA
AUTO PISTOL. . . . . NiB $78 Ex $59 Gd $44
Caliber: .25 ACP. Six-round magazine, 2.5 inch bbl., 4.75 inches overall. Weight: 15 oz. Ivory, pink pearl, or black slotted stocks. Fixed sights. Blue, chrome or nickel finish. Made 1993 to date.

PARA-ORDNANCE MFG. INC. — Scarborough, Ontario, Canada

LIMITED EDITION SERIES

Custom-tuned and fully accessorized "Limited Edition" versions of standard "P" Models. Enhanced-grip frame and serrated slide fitted w/match-grade bbl., and full-length recoil spring guide system. Beavertail grip safety and skeletonized hammer. Ambidextrous safety and trigger-stop adjustment. Fully adjustable or contoured low-mount sights. For pricing see individual models.

MODEL P-10 SA AUTO PISTOL

Super compact. Calibers: .40 S&W, .45 ACP. 10-round magazine, 3-inch bbl., weight: 24 oz. (alloy frame) or 31 oz. (steel frame). Ramp front sight and drift adjustable rear w/3-dot system. Steel or alloy frame. Matte black, Duo-Tone or stainless finish. Made 1997 to date.

Alloy model . . . . NiB $666 Ex $537 Gd $357
Duo-Tone model . . . . NiB $660 Ex $532 Gd $383
Stainless steel model . . . . NiB $749 Ex $614 Gd $441
Steel model . . . . NiB $644 Ex $522 Gd $365
Limited model (tuned & accessorized), add $125

P-12 COMPACT AUTO PISTOL

Calibers: .45 ACP. 11-round magazine, 3.5-inch bbl., 7-inches overall. Weight: 24 oz. (alloy frame). Blade front sight, adj. rear w/3-dot system. Textured composition grips. Matte black alloy or steel finish. Made 1990 to date.

Model P1245 (alloy) . . . . NiB $680 Ex $548 Gd $399
Model P1245C (steel) . . . . NiB $808 Ex $650 Gd $448
Limited model (tuned & accessorized), add $125

P-13 AUTO PISTOL

Same general specifications as Model P-12 except w/12-round magazine, 4.5-inch bbl., 8-inches overall. Weight: 25 oz. (alloy frame). Blade front sight, adj. rear w/3-dot system. Textured composition grips. Matte black alloy or steel finish. Made 1990 to date.

Model P1345 (alloy) . . . . NiB $810 Ex $588 Gd $382
Model P1345C (steel) . . . . NiB $821 Ex $662 Gd $457
Limited model
(tuned & accessorized), add $125

P-14 AUTO PISTOL

Caliber: .45 ACP. 13-round magazine, 5-inch bbl., 8.5 inches overall. Weight: 28 oz. Alloy frame. Blade front sight, adj. rear w/3-dot system. Textured composition grips. Matte black alloy or steel finish. Made from 1990 to date.

Model P1445 (alloy) . . . . NiB $666 Ex $537 Gd $357
Model P1445C (steel) . . . . NiB $735 Ex $594 Gd $414
Limited model (tuned
& accessorized), add $125

MODEL P-15 AUTO PISTOL

Caliber: .40 S&W. 10-round magazine, 4.25-inch bbl., 7.75 inches overall. Weight: 28 to 36 oz. Steel, alloy or stainless receiver. Matte black, Duotone or stainless finish. Made 1996-99.

Model P1540 (alloy) . . . . NiB $666 Ex $537 Gd $470
Model P1540C (steel) . . . . NiB $631 Ex $511 Gd $358
Duotone stainless model . . . . NiB $706 Ex $578 Gd $415
Stainless model . . . . NiB $747 Ex $614 Gd $444

MODEL P-16 SA AUTO PISTOL

Caliber: .40 S&W. 10- or 16-round magazine, 5-inch bbl., 8.5 inches overall. Weight: 40 oz. Ramp front sight and drift adjustable rear w/3-dot system. Carbon steel or stainless frame. Matte black, Duotone or stainless finish. Made 1997 to date.

Blue steel model . . . . NiB $681 Ex $552 Gd $382
Duotone model . . . . NiB $702 Ex $573 Gd $408

Para-Ordnance
P-12 Compact

Para-Ordnance
P-14 Auto Pistol

Plainfield
Model 71

***(cont'd)* MODEL P-16 SA AUTO PISTOL**

Stainless model . . . . NiB $820 Ex $702 Gd $388
Limited model (tuned
& accessorized), add $125

MODEL P-18 SA AUTO PISTOL

Caliber: 9mm Parabellum. 10- or 18-round magazine, 5-inch bbl., 8.5 inches overall. Weight: 40 oz. Dovetailed front sight and fully adjustable rear. Bright stainless finish. Made 1998 to date.

Stainless model . . . . NiB $769 Ex $614 Gd $485
Limited model (tuned
& accessorized), add $125

Plainfield Model 72

Radom P-35

Record-Match
Model 200 Free Pistol

PLAINFIELD MACHINE COMPANY — Dunellen, New Jersey

This firm disc. operation about 1982.

MODEL 71 AUTOMATIC PISTOL

Calibers: .22 LR, .25 Automatic w/conversion kit available. 10-round magazine (.22 LR) or 8-round (.25 Auto), 2.5-inch bbl., 5.13 inches overall. Weight: 25 oz. Fixed sights. Stainless steel frame/slide. Checkered walnut grips. Made 1970-82. See illustration previous page.

.22 LR or .25 Auto only . . . . NiB $164 Ex $143 Gd $98
W/conversion kit . . . . NiB $195 Ex $164 Gd $103

MODEL 72 AUTOMATIC PISTOL

Same as Model 71 except has aluminum slide, 3.5-inch bbl., 6 inches overall. Made 1970-82

.22 LR or .25 Auto only . . . . NiB $174 Ex $149 Gd $82
W/conversion kit . . . . NiB $189 Ex $154 Gd $108

PROFESSIONAL ORDNANCE, INC. — Lake Havasu City, Arizona

MODEL CARBON-15 TYPE 20
SEMIAUTOMATIC PISTOL . . . . . . NiB $840 Ex $763 Gd $505

Similar to Carbon-15 Type 97 except w/unfluted barrel. Weight: 40 oz. Matte black finish. Made 1999 to date.

MODEL CARBON-15 TYPE 97
SEMIAUTOMATIC PISTOL . . . . . . NiB $917 Ex $866 Gd $531

AR-15 operating system w/recoil reduction system. Caliber: .223 Rem. 10-round magazine, 7.25-inch fluted bbl., 20 inches overall. Weight: 46 oz. Ghost ring sights. Carbon-fiber upper and lower receivers w/Chromoly bolt carrier. Matte black finish. Checkered composition grip. Made 1996 to date.

RADOM PISTOL — Radom, Poland Manufactured by the Polish Arsenal

P-35 AUTOMATIC PISTOL

Variation of the Colt Government Model .45 Auto. Caliber: 9mm Para. Eight-round magazine, 4.75-inch bbl., 7.75 inches overall. Weight: 29 oz. Fixed sights. Blued finish. Plastic grips. Made 1935 thru WWII.

Commercial model
(Polish Eagle) . . . . NiB $2370 Ex $1620 Gd $483
Nazi military model
(W/slotted backstrap) . . . . NiB $916 Ex $716 Gd $212
Nazi military model
(W/takedown lever) . . . . NiB $560 Ex $385 Gd $201
Nazi military model
(No takedown lever or slot) . . . . NiB $397 Ex $315 Gd $194
Nazi military model (Parkerized) . . . . NiB $1045 Ex $839 Gd $221

RANDALL FIREARMS COMPANY — Sun Valley, California

The short-lived Randall firearms Company (1982 to 1984) was a leader in the production of stainless steel semi-autimatic handguns, particularly in left-handed configurations. Prices shown are for production models. Add 50% for prototype models (t-prefix on serial numbers) and $125 for guns with serial numbers below 2000. Scare models (C311, C332, etc., made in lots of four pieces or less) valued substantially higher to avid collectors.

MODEL A111 . . . . NiB $1000 Ex $825 Gd $550

Caliber: .45 Auto. Barrel: 5 inches. Round-slide top; right-hand model. Sights: Fixed. Total production: 3,431 pieces.

MODEL A112 . . . . NiB $1275 Ex $875 Gd $675

Calibers: 9mm. Barrel: 5 inches. Round-slide top; right-hand model. Sights: Fixed.

MODEL A121 . . . . NiB $1050 Ex $850 Gd $725

Caliber: .45 Auto. Barrel: 5 inches. Flat-slide top; right-hand model. Sights: Fixed.

MODEL A122 . . . . NiB $1825 Ex $1500 Gd $1200

Calibers: 9mm. Barrel: 5 inches. Flat-slide top; right-hand model. Sights: Fixed. Total production: 18 pieces.

MODEL A131 . . . . NiB $1075 Ex $850 Gd $625

Caliber: .45 Auto. Barrel: 5 inches. Flat-slide top; right-hand model. Sights: Millet. Total production: 2.083 pieces.

MODEL A211 **. . . . . NiB $1125 Ex $900 Gd $725**
Caliber: .45 Auto. Barrel: 4.25 inches. Round-slide top; right-hand model. Sights: Fixed.

MODEL A232 **. . . . . NiB $2125 Ex $1875 Gd $1400**
Caliber: 9mm. Barrel: 4.25 inches. Flat-slide top; right-hand model. Sights: Fixed.

MODEL A331 **. . . . . NiB $1725 Ex $1475 Gd $1150**
Caliber: .45 Auto. Barrel: 4.25 inches. Flat-slide top; right-hand model. Sights: Fixed.

MODEL B111 **. . . . . NiB $1855 Ex $1500 Gd $1225**
Caliber: .45 Auto. Barrel: 5 inches. Round-slide top; left-hand model. Sights: Fixed. Toatal production: 297 pieces

MODEL B131 **. . . . . NiB $2100 Ex $1725 Gd $1350**
Caliber: .45 Auto. Barrel: 5 inches. Flat-slide top; left-hand model. Sights: Millet. Total production: 225 pieces.

MODEL B311 **. . . . . NiB $2150 Ex $1800 Gd $1425**
Caliber: .45 Auto. Barrel: 4.25 inches. Round-slide top; left-hand model. Sights: Fixed. Total production: 52 pieces.

MODEL B312 LEMAY **. . . . . NiB $4000 Ex $3200 Gd $2600**
Caliber: 9mm. Barrel: 4.25 inches. Round-slide top; left-hand model. Sights: Fixed. Total production: 9 pieces.

MODEL B331 **. . . . . NiB $2450 Ex $2100 Gd $1625**
Caliber: .45 Auto. Barrel: 4.25 inches. Flat-slide top; left-hand model. Sights: Millet. Total production: 45 pieces.

RECORD-MATCH PISTOLS — Zella-Mehlis, Germany, Manufactured by Udo Anschütz

MODEL 200 FREE PISTOL **. . . . . NiB $1040 Ex $983 Gd $741**
Basically the same as Model 210 except w/different stock design and conventional set trigger, spur trigger guard. Made prior to WW II.

MODEL 210 FREE PISTOL **. . . . . NiB $1380 Ex $1318 Gd $742**
System Martini action, set trigger w/button release. Caliber: .22 LR. Single-shot, 11-inch bbl., weight: 46 oz. Target sights micrometer rear. Blued finish. Carved and checkered walnut forearm and stock w/adj. hand base. Also made w/dual action (Model 210A); weight 35 oz. Made prior to WWII.

REISING ARMS CO. — Hartford, Connecticut

TARGET AUTOMATIC PISTOL **. . . . . NiB $501 Ex $372 Gd $192**
Hinged frame. Outside hammer. Caliber: .22 LR. 12-round magazine, 6.5-inch bbl., fixed sights. Blued finish. Hard rubber grips. Made 1921-24.

REMINGTON ARMS COMPANY — Ilion, New York

MODEL 51 AUTOMATIC PISTOL
Calibers: .32 Auto, .380 Auto. Seven-round magazine, 3.5-inch bbl., 6.63 inches overall. Weight: 21 oz. Fixed sights. Blued finish. Hard rubber grips. Made 1918-34.
.32 ACP . . . . NiB $802 Ex $674 Gd $365
.380 ACP . . . . NiB $699 Ex $571 Gd $313

MODEL 95 DOUBLE DERRINGER
SA. Caliber: 41 Short Rimfire. Three-inch double bbls. (superposed), 4.88 inches overall. Early models have long hammer spur and two-

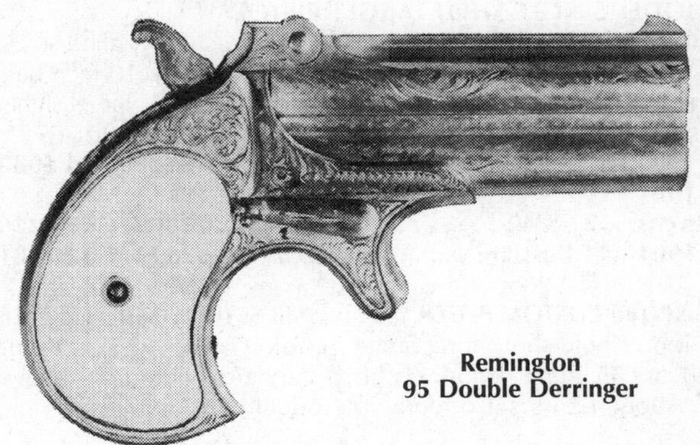
Remington
95 Double Derringer

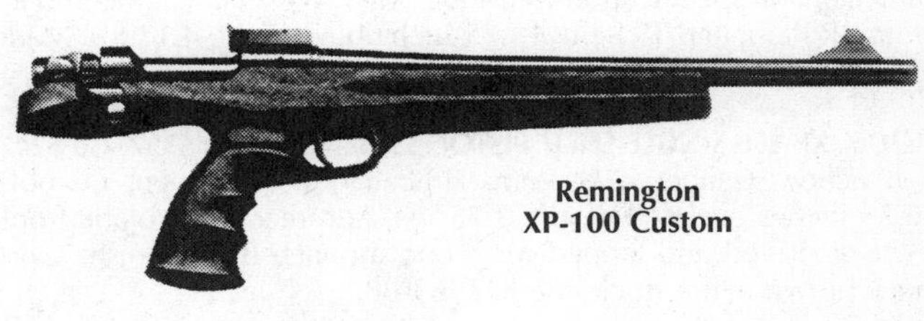
Remington
XP-100 Custom

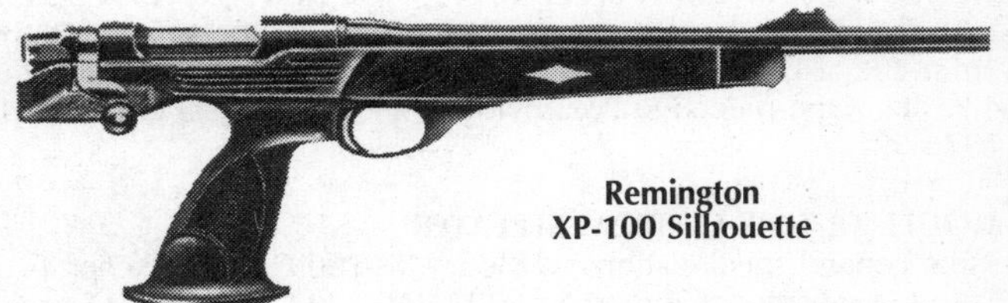
Remington
XP-100 Silhouette

***(cont'd)* MODEL 95 DOUBLE DERRINGER**
armed extractor, but later guns have short hammer spur and sliding extractor (a few have no extractor). Fixed blade front sight and grooved rear. finish: Blued, blued w/nickel-plated frame or fully nickel-plated; also w/factory engraving. Grips: Walnut, checkered hard rubber, pearl, ivory. Weight: 11 oz. Made 1866-1935. Approximately 150,000 were manufactured. Note: During the 70 years of its production, serial numbering of this model was repeated two or three times. Therefore, aside from hammer and extractor differences between the earlier and later models, the best clue to the age of a Double Derringer is the stamping of the company's name on the top of the bbl., or side rib. Prior to 1888, derringers were stamped "E. Remington & Sons, Ilion, N.Y." on one side rib and "Elliot's Patent Dec. 12, 1865" on the other (Type I-early & mid-production) and on the top rib (Type I-late production). In 1888-1911, "Remington Arms Co., Ilion, N.Y." and patent date were stamped on the top rib (Type II) and from 1912-35 "Remington Arms - U.M.C. Co., Ilion, N.Y." and patent date were stamped on the top rib.
Model 95 (Early Type I,
w/o extractor) . . . . NiB $2090 Ex $2038 Gd $751
Model 95 (Mid Type I,
w/extractor) . . . . NiB $2244 Ex $2090 Gd $849
Model 95 (Late Type I,
w/extractor) . . . . NiB $2296 Ex $2090 Gd $854
Model 95 (Type II
produced 1988-11) . . . . NiB $1884 Ex $1472 Gd $648
Model 95 (Type III,
produced 1912-35) . . . . NiB $915 Ex $746 Gd $517
Factory-engraved model w/ivory
or pearl grips, add 35%

NEW MODEL SINGLE-SHOT TARGET PISTOL
Also called Model 1901 Target. Rolling-block action. Calibers: .22 Short & Long, .25 Stevens, .32 S&W, .44 S&W Russian. 10-inch half-octagon bbl., 14 inches overall. Weight: 45 oz. (.22 cal.). Target sights. Blued finish. Checkered walnut grips and forearm. Made 1901-09.
Model 1901 (.22 caliber). . . . . . . NiB $2575 Ex $2280 Gd $980
Model 1901
(.25 Stevens, .32 S&W) . . . . NiB $2254 Ex $1802 Gd $1226
Model 1901 (.44 Russian) . . . . . NiB $2781 Ex $2523 Gd $1081

MODEL XP-100 CUSTOM PISTOL . . . . NiB $510 Ex $407 Gd $216
Bolt-action, single-shot, long-range pistol. Calibers: .223 Rem., 7mm-08 or .35 Rem. 14.5-inch bbl., standard contour or heavy. Weight: About 4.25 lbs. Currently in production.

MODEL XP-100 SILHOUETTE. . . . . NiB $560 Ex $448 Gd $305
Same general specifications as Model XP-100 except chambered for 7mm BR Rem. and 35 Rem. 14.75-inch bbl., weight: 4.13 lbs. Made 1987-92.

MODEL XP-100 SINGLE-SHOT PISTOL . . .NiB $444 Ex $357 Gd $247
Bolt action. Caliber: 221 Rem. Fireball. 10.5-inch vent rib bbl., 16.75 inches overall. Weight: 3.75 lbs. Adj. rear sight, blade front, receiver drilled and tapped for scope mounts. Blued finish. One-piece brown nylon stock. Made 1963-88.

MODEL XP-100 VARMINT SPECIAL . . . . . . NiB $522 Ex $419 Gd $228
Bolt-action, single-shot, long-range pistol. Calibers: .223 Rem., 7mm BR. 14.5-inch bbl., 21.25 inches overall. Weight: About 4.25 lbs. One-piece Du Pont nylon stock w/universal grips. Made 1986-92.

MODEL XP-100R CUSTOM REPEATER
Same general specifications as Model XP-100 Custom except 4- or 5- round repeater chambered for .22-250, .223 Rem., .250 Savage, 7mm-08 Rem., .308 Win., .35 Rem. and .350 Rem. Mag. Kevlar-reinforced synthetic or fiberglass stock w/blind magazine and sling swivel studs. Made 1992-94 and 1998 to date.
Model XP-100R (fiberglass stock) . . . . NiB $696 Ex $561 Gd $388
Model XP-100R KS (kevlar stock) . . . . NiB $633 Ex $586 Gd $380

XP-22R
RIMFIRE REPEATER . . . . NiB $564 Ex $455 Gd $316
Bolt-action clip repeater built on Model 541-style action. Calibers: .22 Short, Long, LR. Five-round magazine, 14.5-inch bbl., weight: 4.25 lbs. Rem. synthetic stock. Announced 1991 but not produced.

RG REVOLVERS — Mfg. By Rohm Gmbh, Germany *(Imported by R.G. Industries, Miami, Florida)*

MODEL 23
SA/DA. 6-round magazine, swing-out cylinder. Caliber: .22 LR. 1.75- or 3.38-inch bbl., Overall length: 5.13 and 7.5 inches. Weight: 16-17 oz. Fixed sights. Blued or nickel finish. Disc. 1986.
Blued finish . . . . NiB $102 Ex $87 Gd $57
Nickel finish . . . . NiB $102 Ex $87 Gd $57

MODEL 38S
SA/DA. Caliber: .38 Special. Six-round magazine, swing-out cylinder. Three- or 4-inch bbl., overall length: 8.25 and 9.25 inches. Weight: 32-34 oz. Windage-adj. rear sight. Blued finish. Disc. 1986.
W/plastic grips . . . . NiB $138 Ex $112 Gd $78
W/wood grips . . . . NiB $157 Ex $127 Gd $89

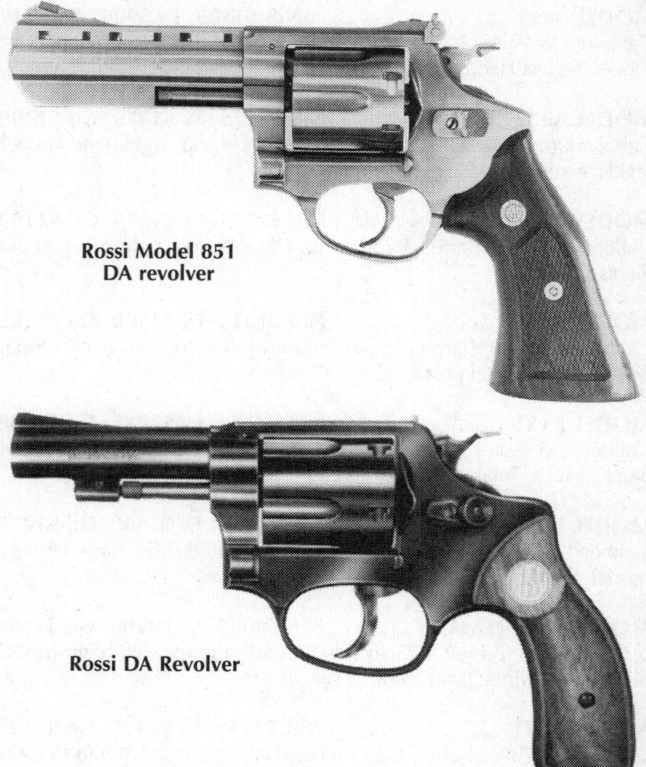
Rossi Model 851 DA revolver

Rossi DA Revolver

ROSSI REVOLVERS — Sáo Leopoldo, Brazil Manufactured by Amadeo Rossi S.A. *(Imported by Interarms, Alexanderia, Virginia)*

MODEL 31 DA REVOLVER . . . . NiB $127 Ex $112 Gd $77
Caliber: .38 Special. Five-round cylinder, 4-inch bbl., weight: 20 oz. Blued or nickel finish. Disc. 1985.

MODEL 51 DA REVOLVER . . . . NiB $132 Ex $117 Gd $87
Caliber: .22 LR. Six-round cylinder, 6-inch bbl., weight: 28 oz. Blued finish. Disc. 1985.

MODEL 68 . . . . NiB $172 Ex $142 Gd $77
Caliber: .38 Special. Five-round magazine, 2- or 3-inch bbl., overall length: 6.5 and 7.5 inches. Weight: 21-23 oz. Blued finish. Nickel finish available w/3-inch bbl. Disc. 1998.

MODEL 84 DA REVOLVER . . . . NiB $197 Ex $162 Gd $132
Caliber: .38 Special. Six-round cylinder, 3-inch bbl., 8 inches overall. Weight: 27.5 oz. Stainless steel finish. Imported 1984-86.

MODEL 85 DA REVOLVER . . . . NiB $213 Ex $172 Gd $119
Same as Model 84 except has vent rib. Imported 1985-86.

MODEL 88 DA REVOLVER
Caliber: .38 Special. Five-round cylinder, 2- or 3-inch bbl., weight: 21 oz. Stainless steel finish. Imported 1988-98.
Model 88 (disc.) . . . . NiB $202 Ex $152 Gd $117
Model 88 Lady Rossi
(round butt) . . . . NiB $226 Ex $182 Gd $126

MODEL 88/2 DA REVOLVER. . . . . . NiB $188 Ex $152 Gd $106
Caliber: .38 Special. Five-round cylinder, 2- or 3-inch bbl., 6.5 inches overall. Weight: 21 oz. Stainless steel finish. Imported 1985-87.

MODEL 89 DA REVOLVER . . . . **NiB $182 Ex $142 Gd $122**
Caliber: .32 S&W. Six-round cylinder, 3-inch bbl., 7.5 inches overall. Weight: 17 oz. Stainless steel finish. Imported 1989-90.

MODEL 94 DA REVOLVER . . . .**NiB $175 Ex $155 Gd $109**
Caliber: .38 Special. Six-round cylinder, 3-inch bbl., 8 inches overall. Weight: 29 oz. Imported 1985-88.

MODEL 95 (951) REVOLVER . . . . . **NiB $204 Ex $165 Gd $116**
Caliber: .38 Special. Six-round magazine, 3-inch bbl., 8 inches overall. Weight: 27.5 oz. Vent rib. Blued finish. Imported 1985-90.

MODEL 351/352 REVOLVERS
Caliber: .38 Special. Five-round cylinder, 2-inch bbl., 6.87 inches overall. Weight: 22 oz. Ramp front and rear adjustable sights. Stainless or matte blued finish. Imported 1999 to date.
Model 351 (matte blue finish) . . . . . **NiB $267 Ex $216 Gd $145**
Model 352 (stainless finish) . . . . **NiB $216 Ex $175 Gd $123**

MODEL 461/462 REVOLVERS
Caliber: .357 Magnum. Six-round cylinder, 2-inch heavy bbl., 6.87 inches overall. Weight: 26 oz. Rubber grips w/ serrated ramp front sight. Stainless or matte blued finish. Imported 1999 to date.
Model 461 (matte blue finish) . . . . . **NiB $267 Ex $216 Gd $145**
Model 462 (stainless finish) . . . . **NiB $297 Ex $247 Gd $180**

MODEL 511 DA REVOLVER . . . . . . **NiB $206 Ex $175 Gd $139**
Similar to the Model 51 except in stainless steel. Imported 1986-1990.

MODEL 515 DA REVOLVER . . . . . . **NiB $222 Ex $180 Gd $126**
Calibers: .22 LR, .22 Mag. Six-round cylinder, 4-inch bbl., 9 inches overall. Weight: 30 oz. Red ramp front sight, adj. square-notched rear. Stainless finish. Checkered hardwood grips. Imported from 1992 to date.

MODEL 518 DA REVOLVER . . . . . . **NiB $210 Ex $170 Gd $120**
Similar to the Model 515 except in caliber .22 LR. Imported 1993 to date.

MODEL 677 DA REVOLVER . . . . . . **NiB $232 Ex $190 Gd $136**
Caliber: .357 Mag. Six-round cylinder, 2-inch bbl., 6.87 inches overall. Weight: 26 oz. Serrated front ramp sight, channel rear. Matte blue finish. Contoured rubber grips. Imported 1997 to date.

MODEL 720 DA REVOLVER . . . . . . **NiB $235 Ex $190 Gd $133**
Caliber: .44 Special. Five-round cylinder, 3-inch bbl., 8 inches overall. Weight: 27.5 oz. Red ramp front sight, adj. square-notched rear. Stainless finish. Checkered Neoprene combat-style grips. Imported from 1992 to date.

MODEL 841 DA REVOLVER . . . . . . **NiB $222 Ex $180 Gd $126**
Same general specifications as Model 84 except has 4-inch bbl., (9 inches overall), weight: 30 oz. Imported 1985-86.

MODEL 851 DA REVOLVER . . . . . . **NiB $220 Ex $180 Gd $129**
Same general specifications as Model 85 except w/3-or 4-inch bbl., 8 inches overall (with 3-inch bbl.). Weight: 27.5 oz. (with 3-inch bbl.). Red ramp front sight, adj. square-notched rear. Stainless finish. Checkered hardwood grips. Imported 1991 to date.

MODEL 877 DA REVOLVER . . . . . . **NiB $243 Ex $201 Gd $147**
Same general specifications as Model 677 except stainless steel. Made 1996 to date.

MODEL 941 DA REVOLVER . . . . . . **NiB $203 Ex $165 Gd $116**
Caliber: .38 Special. Six-round cylinder, 4-inch bbl., 9 inches overall. Weight: 30 oz. Blued finish. Imported 1985-86.

Rossi Model 971
DA Revolver

MODEL 951 DA REVOLVER . . . . . . **NiB $226 Ex $185 Gd $133**
Previous designation M95 w/same general specifications.

MODEL 971 DA REVOLVER
Caliber: .357 Magnum. Six-round cylinder, 2.5-, 4- or 6-inch bbl., 9 inches overall (with 4-inch bbl.). Weight: 36 oz. (with 4-inch bbl.). Blade front sight, adj. square-notched rear. Blued or stainless finish. Checkered hardwood grips. Imported 1990 to date.
Blued finish . . . . **NiB $212 Ex $170 Gd $119**
Stainless finish . . . . **NiB $222 Ex $180 Gd $126**
W/compensated bbl., add **$15**

MODEL 971 VRC DA REVOLVER . . . . **NiB $284 Ex $231 Gd $145**
Same general specifications as Model 971 stainless except w/ventilated rib and compensated bbl. Made 1996 to date.

CYCLOPS DA REVOLVER . . . . **NiB $405 Ex $321 Gd $237**
Caliber: .357 Mag. Six-round cylinder, 6- or 8-inch compensated slab-sided bbl., 11.75 or 13.75 inches overall. Weight: 44 oz. or 51 oz. Undercut blade front sight, fully adjustable rear. B-Square scope mount and rings. Stainless steel finish. Checkered rubber grips. Made 1997 to date.

DA REVOLVER . . . . **NiB $171 Ex $139 Gd $99**
Calibers: .22 LR, .32 S&W Long, .38 Special. Five-round (.38) or 6-round cylinder (other calibers), bbl. lengths: 3-, 6-inches. Weight: 22 oz. (3-inch bbl.). Adj. Rear sight, ramp front. Blued or nickel finish. Wood or plastic grips. Imported 1965-91.

SPORTSMAN'S .22 . . . . **NiB $235 Ex $190 Gd $133**
Caliber: .22 LR. Six-round magazine, 4-inch bbl., 9 inches overall. Weight: 30 oz. Stainless steel finish. Disc. 1991.

RUBY PISTOL
Manufactured by Gabilondo y Urresti, Eibar, Spain, and others

7.65MM AUTOMATIC PISTOL . . . . **NiB $288 Ex $222 Gd $89**
Secondary standard service pistol of the French Army in world wars I and II. Essentially the same as the Alkartasuna (see separate listing). Other manufacturers: Armenia Elgoibarresa y Cia., Eceolaza y Vicinai y Cia., Hijos de Angel Echeverria y Cia., Bruno Salaverria y Cia., Zulaika y Cia., all of Eibar, Spain-Gabilondo y Cia., Elgoibar Spain; Ruby Arms Company, Guernica, Spain. Made 1914-.22.

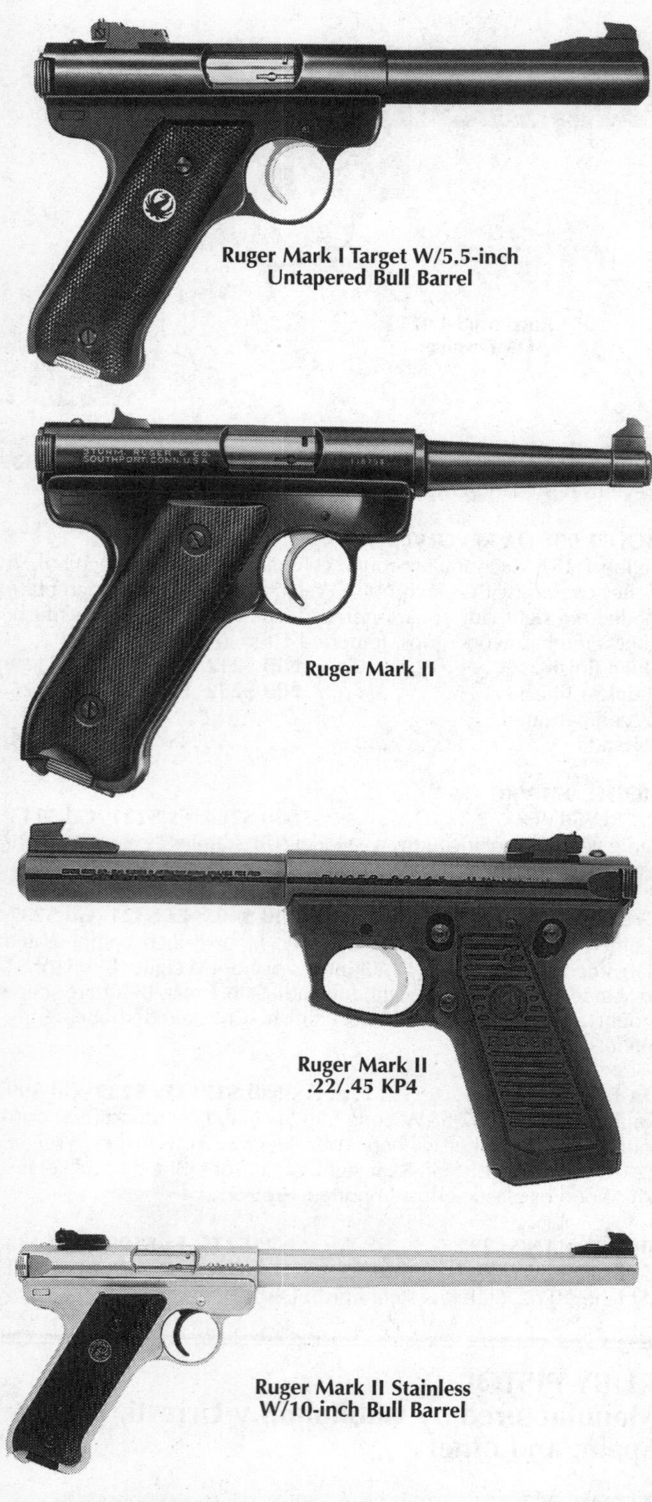

Ruger Mark I Target W/5.5-inch Untapered Bull Barrel

Ruger Mark II

Ruger Mark II .22/.45 KP4

Ruger Mark II Stainless W/10-inch Bull Barrel

RUGER HANDGUNS — Southport, Connecticut Manufactured by Sturm, Ruger & Co.

Rugers made in 1976 are designated "Liberty" in honor of the U.S. Bicentennial and bring a premium of approximately 25 percent in value over regular models.

NOTE: *For ease in finding a particular Ruger handgun, the listings are divided into two groups: Automatic/Single-Shot Pistols (below) and Revolvers, which follow. For a complete listing, please refer to the index.*

AUTOMATIC/SINGLE-SHOT PISTOLS

HAWKEYE SINGLE-SHOT PISTOL ..... NiB $1357 Ex $1151 Gd $636
Built on a SA revolver frame w/cylinder replaced by a swing-out breechblock and fitted w/a bbl., w/integral chamber. Caliber: .256 Magnum. 8.5-inch bbl., 14.5 inches overall. Weight: 45 oz. Blued finish. Ramp front sight, click adj. rear. Smooth walnut grips. Made 1963-65 (3300 produced).

MARK I TARGET MODEL AUTOMATIC PISTOL
Caliber: .22 LR. 10-round magazine, 5.25- and 6.88-inch heavy tapered or 5.5-inch untapered bull bbl., 10.88 inches overall (with 6.88-inch bbl.). Weight: 42 oz. (in 5.5- or 6.88-inch bbl.). Undercut target front sight, adj. rear. Blued finish. Hard rubber grips or checkered walnut thumbrest grips. Made 1951-81.
Standard .... NiB $275 Ex $224 Gd $152
W/red medallion .... NiB $533 Ex $456 Gd $301
Walnut grips, add $15

MARK II AUTOMATIC PISTOL
Caliber: .22 LR, standard or high velocity 10-round magazine, 4.75- or 6-inch tapered bbl., 8.31 inches overall (with 4.75-inch bbl.). Weight: 36 oz. Fixed front sight, square notch rear. Blued or stainless finish. Made 1982 to date.
Blued........................... NiB $301 Ex $265 Gd $142
Stainless .... NiB $348 Ex $296 Gd $126
Bright stainless (ltd.
prod. 5,000 in 1982)................. NiB $527 Ex $425 Gd $295

MARK II .22/.45 AUTOMATIC PISTOL
Same general specifications as Ruger Mark II .22 LR except w/blued or stainless receiver and bbl., in four lengths: 4-inch tapered w/adj. sights (P4), 4.75-inch tapered w/fixed sights (KP4), 5.25-inch tapered w/adj. sights (KP 514) and 5.5-inch bull (KP 512). Fitted w/Zytel grip frame of the same design as the Model 1911 45 ACP. Made 1993 to date.
Model KP4 (4.75-inch bbl.)............ NiB $239 Ex $214 Gd $136
Model KP512, KP514
(w/5.5- or 5.25-inch bbl.)............. NiB $292 Ex $261 Gd $203
Model P4, P512
(Blued w/4- or 5.5-inch bbl.) .... NiB $230 Ex $188 Gd $133

MARK II BULL BARREL MODEL
Same as standard Mark II except for bull bbl. (5.5- or 10-inch). Weight: About 2.75 lbs.
Blued finish .... NiB $256 Ex $209 Gd $148
Stainless finish (intro. 1985) ...... NiB $340 Ex $275 Gd $193

MARK II GOVERNMENT MODEL AUTO PISTOL
Civilian version of the Mark II used by U.S. Armed Forces. Caliber: .22 LR. 10-round magazine, 6.88-inch bull bbl., 11.13 inches overall. Weight: 44 oz. Blued or stainless finish. Made from 1986 to date.
Blued model (MK687G commercial) ..... NiB $363 Ex $296 Gd $162
Stainless steel model
(KMK678G commercial)............... NiB $353 Ex $286 Gd $200
W/U.S. markings (military model) .... NiB $584 Ex $533 Gd $358

MARK II TARGET MODEL
Caliber: .22 LR. 10-round magazine, 4-, 5.5- and 10-inch bull bbl. or 5.25- and 6.88-inch heavy tappered bbl., weight: 38 oz. to 52 oz. 11.13 inches overall (with 6.88-inch bbl.). Made from 1982 to date.
Blued.......................... NiB $301 Ex $262 Gd $147
Stainless steel .... NiB $368 Ex $296 Gd $126

Ruger Mark II
Target Model

Ruger P-89
DAC/DAO

MODEL P-85 AUTOMATIC PISTOL

Caliber: 9mm. DA, recoil-operated. 15-round capacity, 4.5 inch bbl., 7.84 inches overall. Weight: 32 oz. Fixed rear sight, square-post front. Available w/decocking levers, ambidextrous safety or in DA only. Blued or stainless finish. Made 1987-92.

Blued finish .... NiB $362 Ex $321 Gd $223
Stainless steel finish............. NiB $377 Ex $331 Gd $305

MODEL P-89 AUTOMATIC PISTOL

Caliber: 9mm. DA w/slide-mounted safety levers. 15-round magazine, 4.5-inch bbl., 7.84 inches overall. Weight: 32 oz. Square-post front sight, adj. rear w/3-dot system. Blued or stainless steel finish. Grooved black Xenoy grips. Made from 1992 to date.

P-89 blued.................... NiB $408 Ex $357 Gd $223
P-89 stainless .... NiB $455 Ex $388 Gd $326

MODEL P-89 DAC/DAO AUTO PISTOLS

Similar to the standard Model P-89 except the P-89 DAC has ambidextrous decocking levers. The P-89 DAO operates in double-action-only mode. Made 1991 to date.

P-89 DAC blued................ NiB $408 Ex $352 Gd $223
P-89 DAC stainless .... NiB $455 Ex $374 Gd $274
P-89 DAO stainless .... NiB $455 Ex $374 Gd $274

Ruger P-90

MODEL P-90, KP90 DA AUTOMATIC PISTOL

Caliber: .45 ACP. Seven-round magazine, 4.5-inch bbl., 7.88 inches overall. Weight: 33.5 oz. Square-post front sight adj. square-notched rear w/3-dot system. Grooved black Xenoy composition grips. Blued or stainless finish. DAC model has ambidextrous decocking levers. Made 1991 to date.

Model P-90 blued .... NiB $455 Ex $377 Gd $223
Model P-90 DAC (decockers) ..... NiB $465 Ex $388 Gd $233
Model KP-90 DAC stainless....... NiB $465 Ex $395 Gd $336
Model KP-90 DAC (decockers) .... NiB $470 Ex $398 Gd $341

MODEL P-91 DA AUTOMATIC PISTOL

Same general specifications as the Model P-90 except chambered for .40 S&W w/12-round double-column magazine, Made 1992-94.

Model P-91 Standard........... NiB $414 Ex $362 Gd $305
Model P-91 DAC (decockers) ..... NiB $429 Ex $347 Gd $282
Model P-91 DAO (DA only) ...... NiB $435 Ex $352 Gd $282

MODEL P-93 COMPACT AUTO PISTOL

Similar to the standard Model P-89 except w/3.9-inch bbl., (7.3 inches overall) and weight: 31 oz. Stainless steel finish. Made 1993 to date.

Model P-93 DAC (decocker) (disc. 1994)..... NiB $480 Ex $398 Gd $269
Model P-93 DAO (DA only) .... NiB $460 Ex $367 Gd $259

Ruger P-93
Compact

MODEL P-94 AUTOMATIC PISTOL

Similar to the Model P-91 except w/4.25-inch bbl., Calibers: 9mm or .40 S&W. Blued or stainless steel finish. Made 1994 to date.

Model KP-94 DAC (S/S decocker).......... NiB $480 Ex $384 Gd $347
Model KP-94 DAO (S/S dble. action only) .... NiB $455 Ex $388 Gd $342
Model P-94 DAC (Blued decocker).......... NiB $429 Ex $341 Gd $305
Model P-94 DAO (blued dble. action only) ... NiB $419 Ex $325 Gd $285

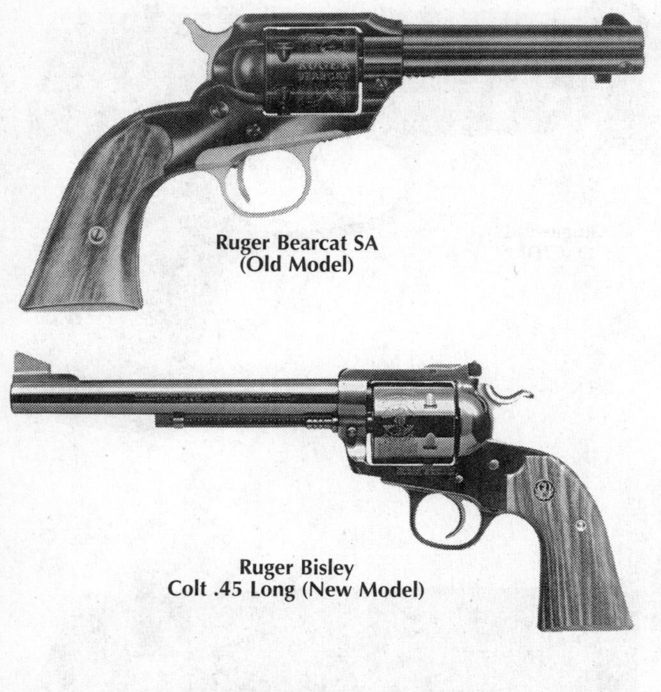
Ruger Bearcat SA (Old Model)

Ruger P-97

Ruger Bisley Colt .45 Long (New Model)

Ruger Bisley Single-Six Small Frame

Ruger Blackhawk

Ruger Blackhawk SA .44

MODEL P-95 AUTOMATIC PISTOL

Caliber: 9mm Parabellum. 10-round magazine, 3.9-inch bbl., 7.3 inches overall. Weight: 27 oz. Square-post front sight, drift adjustable rear w/3-dot system. Molded polymer grip-frame fitted w/stainless or chrome-moly slide. Ambidextrous decocking levers (P-95D) or double action only (DAO). Matte black or stainless finish. Made 1997 to date.

P-95 blued . . . . NiB $373 Ex $306 Gd $183
P-95 stainless. . . . . NiB $409 Ex $332 Gd $188

MODEL P-97 AUTOMATIC PISTOL

Caliber: .45 ACP. Eight-round magazine, 4.5- inch bbl., 7.25 inches overall. Weight: 30.5 oz. Square-post front sight adj. square-notched rear w/3-dot system. Grooved black Xenoy composition grips. Blued or stainless finish. DAC model has ambidextrous decocking levers. Made 1999 to date.

Model KP-97
DAO stainless . . . . NiB $425 Ex $342 Gd $224
Model KP-97
DAC (decockers) . . . . NiB $425 Ex $342 Gd $224

STANDARD MODEL AUTOMATIC PISTOL

Caliber: .22 LR. Nine-round magazine, 4.75- or 6-inch bbl., 8.75 inches overall (with 4.75-inch bbl.). Weight: 36 oz. (with 4.75 inch bbl.). Fixed sights. Blued finish. Hard rubber or checkered walnut grips. Made from 1949 to date. Note: After the death of Alexander Sturm in 1951, the color of the eagle on the grip medallion was changed from red to black as a memorial. Known as the "Red Eagle Automatic," this early type is now a collector's item. Made 1951-81.

W/red eagle medallion . . . . NiB $561 Ex $458 Gd $257
W/black eagle medallion. . . . . NiB $221 Ex $200 Gd $123
Walnut grips, add $15

NOTE: *This section contains only Ruger Revolvers. Automatic and Single-Shot Pistols may be found on the preceding pages. For a complete listing of Ruger handguns, please refer to the index.*

REVOLVERS

BEARCAT SA (OLD MODEL)

Aluminum frame. Caliber: .22 LR. Six-round cylinder, 4-inch bbl., 8.88 inches overall. Weight: 17 oz. Fixed sights. Blued finish. Smooth walnut grips. Made 1958-73.

W/brass trigger guard . . . . NiB $378 Ex $327 Gd $224
W/aniodized
aluminum trigger . . . . NiB $636 Ex $615 Gd $327

BEARCAT, SUPER (OLD MODEL)........ NiB $376 Ex $315 Gd $212
Same general specifications as Bearcat except has steel frame. Weight: 25 oz. Made 1971-73.

NEW MODEL BEARCAT REVOLVER
Same general specifications as Super Bearcat except all steel frame and trigger guard. Interlocked mechanism and transfer bar. Calibers: .22 LR and .22WMR. Interchangeable 6-round cylinders (disc. 1996). Smooth walnut stocks w/Ruger medallion. Made 1994 to date.
Convertible model (disc.
1996 after factory recall) .... NiB $376 Ex $299 Gd $222
Standard model (.22 LR only) .... NiB $335 Ex $273 Gd $170

BISLEY SA REVOLVER, LARGE FRAME
Calibers: .357 Mag., .41 Mag. .44 Mag., .45 Long Colt. 7.5-inch bbl., 13 inches overall. Weight: 48 oz. Non-fluted or fluted cylinder, no engraving. Ramp front sight, adj. rear. Satin blued or stainless. Made 1986 to date.
Blued finish .... NiB $451 Ex $363 Gd $203
Vaquero/Bisley (blued w/case colored fr.) .... NiB $451 Ex $363 Gd $203
Vaquero/Bisley (stainless steel) ... NiB $443 Ex $348 Gd $214
W/ivory grips, add.............................. $35

BISLEY SINGLE-SIX REVOLVER, SMALL FRAME
Calibers: .22 LR and .32 Mag. Six-round cylinder, 6.5-inch bbl., 11.5 inches overall. Weight: 41 oz. Fixed rear sight, blade front. Blue finish. Goncalo Alves grips. Made 1986 to date.
.22 caliber .... NiB $363 Ex $275 Gd $172
.32 H&R Mag. .... NiB $415 Ex $327 Gd $286

BLACKHAWK SA CONVERTIBLE (OLD MODEL)
Same as Blackhawk except has extra cylinder. Caliber combinations: .357 Magnum and 9mm Para., .45 Colt and .45 Automatic. Made 1967-72.
.357/9mm combo (early w/o prefix SN)... NiB $430 Ex $378 Gd $219
.357/9mm combo (late w/prefix SN) ..... NiB $424 Ex $342 Gd $238
.45 LC/.45 ACP combo
(1967-85 & 1999 to date)............. NiB $533 Ex $481 Gd $317

BLACKHAWK SA REVOLVER (OLD MODEL)
Calibers: .30 Carbine, .357 Magnum, .41 Magnum, .45 Colt. Six-round cylinder, bbl. lengths: 4.63-inch (.357, .41, .45 caliber), 6.5-inch (.357, .41 caliber), 7.5-inch (.30, .45 caliber). 10.13 inches overall (.357 Mag. w/4.63-inch bbl.). Weight: 38 oz. (.357 w/4.63-inch bbl.). Ramp front sight, adj. rear. Blued finish. Checkered hard rubber or smooth walnut grips. Made 1956-73.
.30 Carbine, .357 Mag........... NiB $430 Ex $378 Gd $219
.41 Mag. .... NiB $430 Ex $327 Gd $219
.45 Colt .... NiB $451 Ex $389 Gd $224

BLACKHAWK SA "FLAT-TOP" REVOLVER (OLD MODEL)
Similar to standard Blackhawk except w/"Flat Top" cylinder strap. Calibers: .357 or .44 Magnum. Six-round fluted cylinder, 4.625-, 6.5-, 7.5- or 10-inch bbl., adj. rear sight, ramp front. Blued finish. Black rubber or smooth walnut grips. Made 1956-63.
.357 Mag. (w/4.625-inch bbl.) .... NiB $533 Ex $471 Gd $250
.357 Mag. (w/6.5-inch bbl.) .... NiB $739 Ex $585 Gd $327
.357 Mag. (w/10-inch bbl.)........... NiB $1254 Ex $1100 Gd $636
.44 Mag. (w/fluted cylinder/ 4.625-inch bbl.) .. NiB $739 Ex $585 Gd $327
.44 Mag. (w/fluted cylinder/ 6.5-inch bbl.).... NiB $791 Ex $636 Gd $378
.44 Mag. (w/fluted cylinder/ 10-inch bbl.) .. NiB $1254 Ex $1100 Gd $636

GP-100 DA REVOLVER
Caliber: .357 Magnum. Three- to 4-inch heavy bbl., or 6-inch standard or heavy bbl., Overall length: 9.38 or 11.38 inches. Cushioned grip panels. Made from 1986 to date.
Blued finish .... NiB $430 Ex $342 Gd $209
Stainless steel finish............. NiB $456 Ex $353 Gd $250

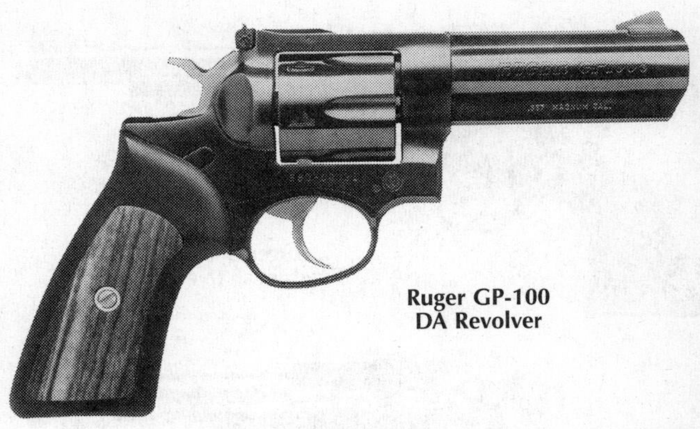

Ruger GP-100
DA Revolver

Ruger New Model Blackhawk Convertible

Ruger Blackhawk High-Gloss Stainless
(New Model) .357 Magnum

NEW MODEL BLACKHAWK CONVERTIBLE
Same as New Model Blackhawk except has extra cylinder. Blued finish only. Caliber combinations: .357 Magnum/9mm Para., .44 Magnum/.44-40, .45 Colt/.45 ACP. (Limited Edition Buckeye Special .32-20/.32 H&R Mag. or .38-40/10mm). Made 1973 to date.
.32-20/.32 H&R Mag. (1989-90) .... NiB $399 Ex $322 Gd $183
.38-40/10mm (1990-91) .... NiB $372 Ex $301 Gd $211
.357/9mm combo .... NiB $399 Ex $322 Gd $182
.44/.44-40 combo (disc.1982) .... NiB $436 Ex $353 Gd $246
.45 LC/.45 ACP combo (disc. 1985) ...... NiB $404 Ex $327 Gd $228

NEW MODEL BLACKHAWK SA REVOLVER
Interlocked mechanism. Calibers: .30 Carbine, .357 Magnum, .357 Maximum, .41 Magnum, .44 Magnum, .44 Special, .45 Colt. Six-round cylinder, bbl. lengths: 4.63-inch (.357, .41, .45 Colt); 5.5 inch (.44 Mag., .44 Spec.); 6.5-inch (.357, .41, .45 Long Colt); 7.5-inch (.30, .45, .44 Special, .44 Mag.); 10.5-inch in .44 Mag; 10.38 inches overall (.357 Mag. w/4.63-inch bbl.). Weight: 40 oz. (.357 w/4.63-inch bbl.). Adj. rear sight, ramp front. Blued finish or stainless steel; latter only in .357 or .45 LC. Smooth walnut grips. Made 1973 to date.
Blued finish........................ NiB $378 Ex $270 Gd $157
High-gloss stainless (.357 Mag., .45 LC) . . . NiB $372 Ex $301 Gd $211
Satin stainless (.357 Mag., .45 LC) .... NiB $359 Ex $291 Gd $203
.357 Maximum SRM (1984-85).......... NiB $399 Ex $322 Gd $198

Ruger Blackhawk
Blued finish (New Model)

Ruger Redhawk

Ruger Single-Six SSM
(New Model)

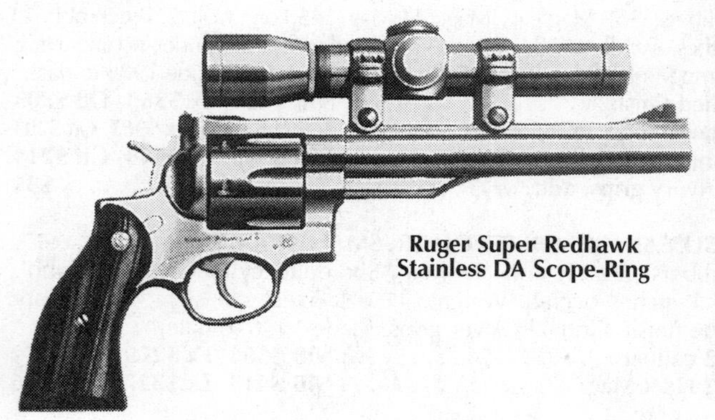
Ruger Super Redhawk
Stainless DA Scope-Ring

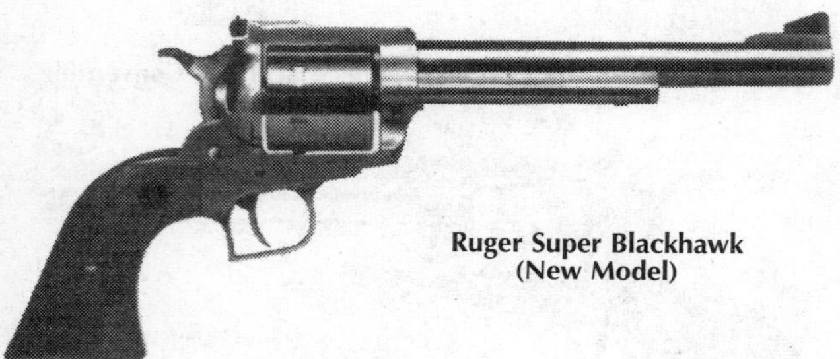
Ruger Super Blackhawk
(New Model)

Ruger Super Single-Six
Convertible (New Model)

Ruger Police Service-Six
Stainless Steel

NEW MODEL SINGLE-SIX SSM REVOLVER. . . . . NiB $325 Ex $299 Gd $170
Same general specifications as standard Single-Six except chambered for .32 H&R Magnum cartridge. Bbl. lengths: 4.63, 5.5, 6.5 or 9.5 inches.

NEW MODEL SUPER BLACKHAWK SA REVOLVER
Interlocked mechanism. Caliber: .44 Magnum. Six-round cylinder, 5.5-inch, 7.5-inch and 10.5-inch bull bbl. 13.38 inches overall. Weight: 48 oz. Adj. rear sight, ramp front. Blued and stainless steel finish. Smooth walnut grips. Made 1973 to date, 5.5-inch bbl. made 1987 to date.
Blued finish . . . . NiB $402 Ex $325 Gd $212
High-gloss stainless (1994-96). . . . . NiB $396 Ex $320 Gd $223
Satin stainless steel . . . . NiB $383 Ex $309 Gd $216

NEW MODEL SUPER SINGLE-SIX CONVERTIBLE REVOLVER
SA w/interlocked mechanism. Calibers: .22 LR and .22 WMR. Interchangeable 6-round cylinders. Bbl. lengths: 4.63, 5.5, 6.5, 9.5 inches. 10.81 inches overall (with 4.63 inch bbl.). Weight: 33 oz. (with 4.63-inch bbl.). Adj. rear sight, ramp front. Blued finish or stainless steel; latter only w/5.5- or 6.5-inch bbl., smooth walnut grips. Made 1972 to date.
Blued finish . . . . NiB $315 Ex $243 Gd $129
High-gloss stainless (1994-96). . . . . NiB $254 Ex $207 Gd $146
Stainless steel . . . . NiB $353 Ex $279 Gd $222

POLICE SERVICE-SIX
Same general specifications as Speed-Six except has square butt. Stainless steel models and 9mm Para. caliber available w/only 4-inch bbl., Made 1971-88.
.38 Special, blued finish . . . . NiB $271 Ex $241 Gd $189
.38 Special, stainless steel . . . . NiB $292 Ex $256 Gd $230
.357 Magnum or 9mm Para., blued finish . . . . NiB $271 Ex $241 Gd $189
.357 Magnum, stainless steel. . . . . . NiB $297 Ex $261 Gd $230

REDHAWK DA REVOLVER
Calibers: .357 Mag., .41 Mag., .45 LC, .44 Mag. Six-round cylinder, 5.5- and 7.5-inch bbl., 11 and 13 inches overall, respectively. Weight: About 52 oz. Adj. rear sight, interchangeable front sights. Stainless finish. Made 1979 to date; .357 Mag. disc. 1986. Alloy steel model w/blued finish intro. in 1986 in .41 Mag. and .44 Mag. calibers.
Blued finish . . . . NiB $522 Ex $358 Gd $213
Stainless steel . . . . NiB $558 Ex $445 Gd $363

SUPER REDHAWK STAINLESS DA SCOPE-RING REVOLVER
Calibers: .44 Mag., .454 Casull and .45 LC. Six-round cylinder, 7.5- to 9.5- inch bbl., 13 to 15 inches overall. Weight: 53 to 58 oz. Integral scope mounting system w/stainless rings. Adjustable rear sight. Cushioned grip panels. Made 1987 to date.
Model .44 Mag. 7.5- inch bbl., stainless. . . . . NiB $594 Ex $491 Gd $363
Model .44 Mag. 9.5- inch bbl., stainless. . . . . NiB $594 Ex $491 Gd $363
Model .454 Casull & 45 LC Stainless/target gray stainless . . . . . NiB $687 Ex $564 Gd $435

SECURITY-SIX DA REVOLVER
Caliber: .357 Magnum, handles .38 Special. Six-round cylinder, bbl. lengths: 2.25-, 4-, 6-inch, 9.25 inches overall (with 4-inch bbl.). Weight: 33.5 oz. (with 4-inch bbl.). Adj. rear sight, ramp front. Blued finish or stainless steel. Square butt. Checkered walnut grips. Made 1971-85.
Blued finish . . . . NiB $285 Ex $234 Gd $168
Stainless steel . . . . NiB $331 Ex $270 Gd $193

SINGLE-SIX SA REVOLVER (OLD MODEL)
Calibers: .22 LR, .22 WMR. Six-round cylinder. bbl., lengths: 4.63, 5.5, 6.5, 9.5 inches, 10.88 inches overall (with 5.5-inch bbl.). Weight: About 35 oz. Fixed sights. Blued finish. Checkered hard rubber or smooth walnut grips. Made 1953-73. Note: Pre-1956 model w/flat loading gate is worth about twice as much as later version.
Standard . . . . NiB $326 Ex $249 Gd $135
Convertible (w/two cylinders, .22 LR/.22 WMR). . . . . NiB $480 Ex $429 Gd $223

SINGLE-SIX — LIGHTWEIGHT . . . . NiB $532 Ex $429 Gd $197
Same general specifications as Single-Six except has 4.75-inch bbl., lightweight alloy cylinder and frame, 10 inches overall length, weight: 23 oz. Made in 1956.

SP101 DA REVOLVER
Calibers: .22 LR, .32 Mag., 9mm, .38 Special+P, .357 Mag. Five- or 6-round cylinder, 2.25-, 3.06- or 4-inch bbl., weight: 25-34 oz. Stainless steel finish. Cushioned grips. Made 1988 to date. See illustration next page.
Standard model . . . . NiB $414 Ex $269 Gd $264
DAO model (DA only, spurless hammer) . . . . NiB $393 Ex $305 Gd $264

SPEED-SIX DA REVOLVER
Calibers: .38 Special, .357 Magnum, 9mm Para. Six-round cylinder, 2.75-, 4-inch bbl., (9mm available only w/2.75-inch bbl.). 7.75 inches overall (2.75-inch bbl.). Weight: 31 oz. (with 2.75-inch bbl.). Fixed sights. Blued or stainless steel finish; latter available in .38 Special (with 2.75 inch bbl.), .357 Magnum and 9mm w/either bbl., Round butt. Checkered walnut grips. Made 1973-87.
.38 Special, blued finish . . . . NiB $254 Ex $225 Gd $175
.38 Special, stainless steel . . . . NiB $305 Ex $266 Gd $139
.357 Magnum or 9mm Para., blued finish . . . . NiB $323 Ex $271 Gd $202
.357 Magnum or 9mm Para., stainless steel. . . . . NiB $323 Ex $271 Gd $202

Ruger
Super Redhawk Stainless

Ruger
Single-Six

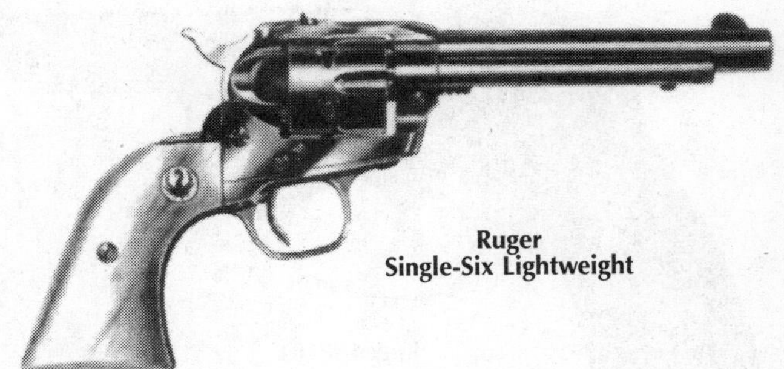
Ruger
Single-Six Lightweight

Ruger
Super Single-Six Convertible

Ruger Single-Six Fixed Sight

Ruger Vaquero Stainless Steel

Ruger Vaquero Blued

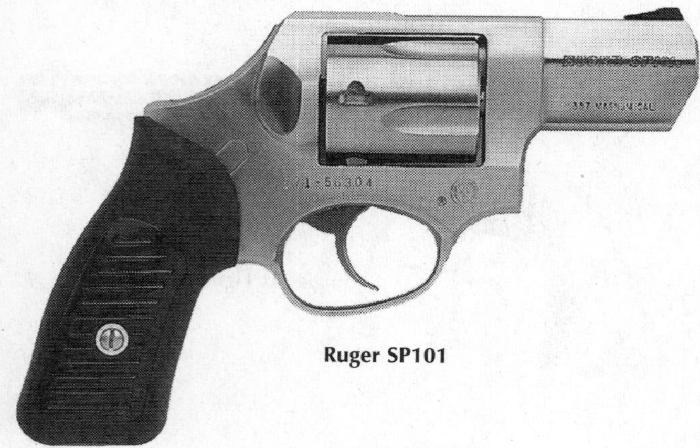

Ruger SP101

SUPER BLACKHAWK
SA .44 MAGNUM REVOLVER (OLD MODEL)

SA w/heavy frame and unfluted cylinder. Caliber: .44 Magnum. Six-round cylinder. 6.5- or 7.5-inch bbl., Adj. rear sight, ramp front. Steel or brass grip frame w/square-back trigger guard. Smooth walnut grips. Blued finish. Made 1956-73.

W/6.5-inch bbl., ... NiB $415 Ex $322 Gd $193
W/7.5-inch bbl., ... NiB $415 Ex $322 Gd $193
W/brass gripframe .... NiB $913 Ex $734 Gd $505

VAQUERO SA REVOLVER

Calibers: .357 Mag., .44-40, .44 Magnum, .45 Colt. Six-round cylinder. Bbl. lengths: 4.625, 5.5, 7.5 inches, 13.63 inches overall (with 7.5-inch bbl.). Weight: 41 oz. (with 7.5-inch bbl.). Blade front sight, grooved topstrap rear. Blued w/color casehardened frame or polished stainless finish. Smooth rosewood grips w/Ruger medallion. Made 1993 to date.

Blued w/color-case
hardened frame .... NiB $451 Ex $348 Gd $296
Stainless finish .... NiB $451 Ex $348 Gd $296
W/ivory grips, add $41

RUSSIAN SERVICE PISTOLS Mfd. by Government plants at Tula and elsewhere

Tokarev-type pistols have also been made in Hungary, Poland, Yugoslavia, People's Republic of China, N. Korea.

MODEL 30 TOKAREV SERVICE AUTOMATIC

Modified Colt-Browning type. Caliber: 7.62mm Russian Auto (also uses 7.63mm Mauser Auto cartridge). Eight-round magazine, 4.5-inch bbl., 7.75 inches overall. Weight: About 29 oz. Fixed sights. Made 1930 mid-1950s. Note: A slightly modified version w/improved locking system and different disconnector was adopted in 1933.

Standard Service Model TT30 ..... NiB $348 Ex $313 Gd $185
Standard Service Model TT33 ..... NiB $348 Ex $313 Gd $185
Recent imports (distinguished
by importer marks) .... NiB $160 Ex $129 Gd $78

MODEL PM
MAKAROV AUTO PISTOL........ NiB $476 Ex $425 Gd $211

Double-action, blowback design. Caliber: 9mm Makarov. Eight-round magazine, 3.8-inch bbl., 6.4 inches overall. Weight: 26 oz. Blade front sight, square-notched rear. Checkered composition grips.

Standard Service Model PM
(Pistole Makarov).............. NiB $495 Ex $399 Gd $277
Recent imports (distinguished
by importer marks) .... NiB $202 Ex $163 Gd $114

SAKO HANDGUNS — Riihimaki, Finland Manufactured by Oy Sako Ab

.22-.32 OLYMPIC PISTOL (TRIACE)

Calibers: .22 LR, .22 Short, .32 S&W Long. Five-round magazine, 6- or 8.85- (.22 Short) inch bbl., weight: About 46 oz. (.22 LR); 44 oz. (.22 Short); 48 oz. (.32). Steel frame. ABS plastic, anatomically designed grip. Non-reflecting matte black upper surface and chromium-plated slide. Equipped w/carrying case and tool set. Limited importation 1983-89.

Sako .22 or .32
Single pistol................ NiB $1353 Ex $1200 Gd $690
Sako Triace, triple-barrel set
w/wooden grip .... NiB $2577 Ex $2271 Gd $1251

SAUER HANDGUNS
Mfd. through WW II by J. P. Sauer & Sohn, Suhl, Germany. Now mfd. by J. P. Sauer & Sohn, GmbH, Eckernförde, West Germany

See also listings under Sig Sauer.

MODEL 1913 POCKET AUTOMATIC PISTOL .... NiB $311 Ex $240 Gd $158
Caliber: .32 Automatic (7.65mm). Seven-round magazine, 3-inch bbl., 5.88 inches overall. Weight: 22 oz. Fixed sights. Blued finish. Black hard rubber grips. Made 1913-30.

MODEL 1930 POCKET AUTOMATIC PISTOL
Authority Model (Behorden Model). Successor to Model 1913, has improved grip and safety. Caliber: .32 Auto (7.65mm). Seven-round magazine, 3-inch bbl., 5.75 inches overall. Weight: 22 oz. Fixed sights. Blued finish. Black hard rubber grips. Made 1930-38. Note: Some pistols made w/indicator pin showing when cocked. Also mfd. w/dual slide and receiver; this type weight: about 7 oz. less than the standard model.
Steel model .... NiB $342 Ex $245 Gd $158
Dural (alloy) model .... NiB $1573 Ex $1260 Gd $877

MODEL 38H DA AUTOMATIC PISTOL
Calibers: .25 Auto (6.35mm), .32 Auto (7.65mm), .380 Auto (9mm). Specifications shown are for .32 Auto model. Seven-round magazine, 3.25-inch bbl., 6.25 inches overall. Weight: 20 oz. Fixed sights. Blued finish. Black plastic grips. Also made in dual model weighing about 6 oz. less. Made 1938-1945. Note: This pistol, designated Model .38, was mfd. during WW II for military use. Wartime models are inferior in design to earlier production, as some lack safety lever.
.22 caliber .... NiB $411 Ex $309 Gd $131
.32 ACP .... NiB $413 Ex $341 Gd $199
.32 ACP (w/Nazi proofs) .... NiB $514 Ex $413 Gd $284
.380 ACP .... NiB $3540 Ex $2787 Gd $1308

POCKET .25 (1913) AUTOMATIC PISTOL .... NiB $316 Ex $255 Gd $158
Smaller version of Model 1913, issued about same time as .32 caliber model. Caliber: .25 Auto (6.35mm). Seven-round magazine, 2.5-inch bbl., 4.25 inches overall. Weight: 14.5 oz. Fixed sights. Blued finish. Black hard rubber grips. Made 1913-30.

SINGLE-ACTION REVOLVERS
See listings under Hawes.

Sako Model .22-.32 Olympic

Sauer 1930 Pocket

Savage Model 101

SAVAGE ARMS CO. — Utica, New York

MODEL 101 SA SINGLE-SHOT PISTOL .... NiB $163 Ex $132 Gd $71
Barrel integral w/swing-out cylinder. Calibers: .22 Short, Long, LR. 5.5-inch bbl. Weight: 20 oz. Blade front sight, slotted rear, adj. for windage. Blued finish. Grips of compressed, impregnated wood. Made 1960-68.

MODEL 501/502F "STRIKER" SERIES PISTOLS
Calibers: .22 LR., and .22 WMR. 5- or 10- round magazine, 10-inch bbl., 19 inches overall. Weight: 4 lbs. Drilled and tapped sights for scope mount (installed). Ambidextrous rear grip. Made 2000 to date.
Model 501F, .22 LR .... NiB $199 Ex $178 Gd $138
Model 502F, .22 WMR.......... NiB $219 Ex $194 Gd $143

MODEL 510/516 "STRIKER" SERIES PISTOLS
Calibers: 223 Rem., .22-250 Rem., .243 Win., 7mm-08 Rem., .260 Rem., and .308 Win. Three-round magazine, 14-inch bbl., .22.5 inches overall. Drilled and tapped for scope mounts. Left hand bolt with right hand ejection. Stainless steel finish. Made 1998 to date.

(cont'd.) **MODEL 510/516 "STRIKER" SERIES PISTOLS**
Model 510F .... NiB $403 Ex $352 Gd $194
Model 516FSAK................ NiB $494 Ex $408 Gd $352
Model 516FSS .... NiB $398 Ex $352 Gd $336
Model 516BSAK .... NiB $494 Ex $408 Gd $352
Model 516BSS.................. NiB $556 Ex $449 Gd $367

MODEL 1907 AUTOMATIC PISTOL
Caliber: .32 ACP, 10-round magazine, 3.25-inch bbl., 6.5 inches overall. Weight: 19 oz. Checkered hard rubber or steel grips marked "Savage Quality," circling an Indian-head logo. Optional pearl grips. Blue, nickel, silver or gold finish. Made 1908-20.
Blued model (.32 ACP)......... NiB $443 Ex $316 Gd $127
Blued model (.380 ACP) .... NiB $571 Ex $469 Gd $214
W/ optional nickel,
silver or gold finish, add....................... $750-$1200
W/optional pearl grips, add .... $225-$950

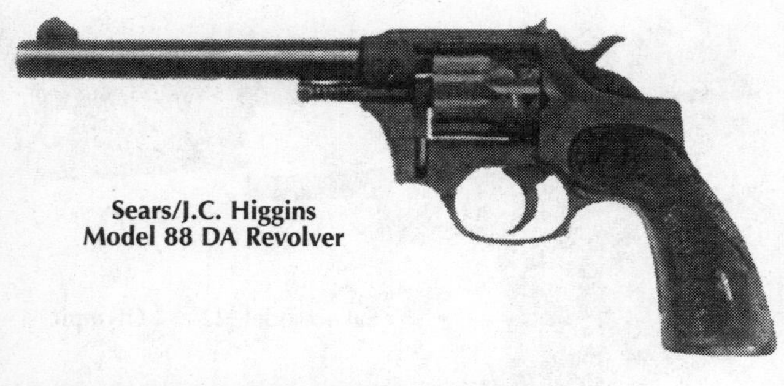
Sears/J.C. Higgins Model 88 DA Revolver

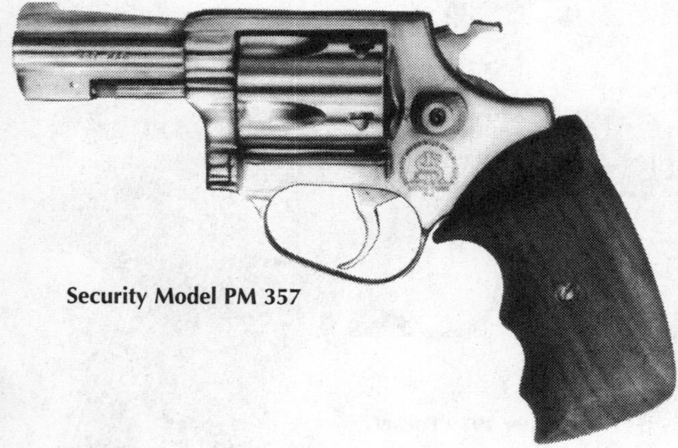
Security Model PM 357

Security Model PPM 357

Security Model PSS38

MODEL 1910 AUTOMATIC PISTOL
Calibers: .32 Auto, .380 Auto. 10-round magazine (.32 cal.), 9-round (.380 cal.). 3.75-inch bbl., (.32 cal.), 4.25-inch (.380 cal.). 6.5 inches overall (.32 cal.), 7 inches (.380 cal.). Weight: About 23 oz. Fixed sights. Blued finish. Hard rubber grips. Made in hammerless type w/grip safety or w/exposed hammer spur. Made 1910-17.
.32 ACP . . . . NiB $322 Ex $271 Gd $179
.380 ACP . . . . NiB $495 Ex $404 Gd $271

MODEL 1915 AUTOMATIC PISTOL
Same general specifications as the Savage Model 1907 except the Model 1915 is hammerless and has a grip safety. It is also chambered for both the .32 and .380 ACP. Made 1915-17.
.32 ACP . . . . NiB $551 Ex $471 Gd $245
.380 ACP . . . . NiB $685 Ex $551 Gd $380

U.S. ARMY TEST MODEL 1910 . NiB $7698 Ex $5658 Gd $2598
Caliber: .45 ACP, Seven-round magazine w/exposed hammer. An enlarged version of the Model 1910 manufactured for military trials between 1907 and 1911. Note: Most "Trial Pistols" were refurbished and resold as commercial models. Values are for original Government Test Issues Models.

MODEL 1917 AUTOMATIC PISTOL
Same specifications as 1910 Model except has spur-type hammer and redesigned, heavier grip. Made 1917-28.
.32 ACP . . . . NiB $316 Ex $265 Gd $122
.380 ACP . . . . NiB $673 Ex $596 Gd $265

SEARS, ROEBUCK & COMPANY — Chicago, Illinois

J.C. HIGGINS MODEL 80
AUTO PISTOL . . . . NiB $187 Ex $136 Gd $106
Caliber: .22 LR. 10-round magazine, 4.5- or 6.5-inch interchangeable bbl., 10.88 inches overall (with 6.5-inch bbl.). Weight: 41 oz. (with 6.5-inch bbl.). Fixed Partridge sights. Blued finish. Checkered grips w/thumbrest.

J.C. HIGGINS MODEL 88
DA REVOLVER. . . . . NiB $126 Ex $101 Gd $70
Caliber: .22 LR. Nine-round cylinder, 4- or 6-inch bbl., 9.5 inches (with 4-inch bbl.). Weight: 23 oz. (with 4-inch bbl.). Fixed sights. Blued or nickel finish. Checkered plastic grips.

J.C. HIGGINS RANGER
DA REVOLVER. . . . . NiB $152 Ex $121 Gd $80
Caliber: .22 LR. Nine-round cylinder, 5.5-inch bbl., 10.75 inches overall. Weight: 28 oz. Fixed sights. Blued or chrome finish. Checkered plastic grips.

SECURITY INDUSTRIES OF AMERICA — Little Ferry, New Jersey

MODEL PM 357 DA REVOLVER . . . . . NiB $240 Ex $189 Gd $138
Caliber: .357 Magnum. Five-round cylinder, 2.5-inch bbl., 7.5 inches overall. Weight: 21 oz. Fixed sights. Stainless steel. Walnut grips. Made 1975-78.

MODEL PPM357 DA REVOLVER . . . . . NiB $240 Ex $189 Gd $138
Caliber: .357 Magnum. Five-round cylinder, 2-inch bbl., 6.13 inches overall. Weight: 18 oz. Fixed sights. Stainless steel. Walnut grips. Made from 1976-78. Note: Spurless hammer (illustrated) was disc. in 1977; this model has the same conventional hammer as other Security revolvers.

MODEL PSS 38
DA REVOLVER. . . . . NiB $189 Ex $164 Gd $123
Caliber: .38 Special. Five-round cylinder, 2-inch bbl., 6.5 inches overall. Weight: 18 oz. Fixed sights. Stainless steel. Walnut grips. Intro. 1973. disc.

R. F. SEDGLEY. INC. — Philadelphia, Pennsylvania

BABY HAMMERLESS
EJECTOR REVOLVER . . . . NiB $592 Ex $480 Gd $225
DA. Solid frame. Folding trigger. Caliber: .22 Long. Six-round cylinder, 4 inches overall. Weight: 6 oz. Fixed sights. Blued or nickel finish. Rubber grips. Made c. 1930-39.

L. W. SEECAMP, INC. — Milford, Connecticut

MODEL LWS .25
DAO PISTOL . . . . NiB $428 Ex $351 Gd $244
Caliber: .25 ACP. Seven-round magazine, 2-inch bbl., 4.125 inches overall. Weight: 12 oz. Checkered black polycarbonate grips. Matte stainless finish. No sights. Made 1981-85.

MODEL LWS .32 DAO PISTOL
Caliber: .32 ACP. Six-round magazine, 2-inch bbl., 4.25 inches overall. Weight: 12.9 oz. Ribbed sighting plane with no sights. Checkered black Lexon grips. Stainless steel. Made 1985 to date. Limited production results in inflated resale values.
Matte stainless finish . . . . NiB $608 Ex $557 Gd $425
Polished stainless finish . . . . NiB $624 Ex $568 Gd $430

SHERIDAN PRODUCTS, INC. — Racine, Wisconsin

KNOCKABOUT
SINGLE-SHOT PISTOL . . . . NiB $112 Ex $102 Gd $50
Tip-up type. Caliber: .22 LR, Long, Short; 5-inch bbl., 6.75 inches overall. Weight: 24 oz. Fixed sights. Checkered plastic grips. Blued finish. Made 1953-60.

SIG PISTOLS — Neuhausen am Rheinfall, Switzerland, Mfd. by SIG Schweizerische Industrie-Gesellschaft

See also listings under SIG-Sauer.

MODEL P210-1
AUTOMATIC PISTOL . . . . NiB $2093 Ex $1758 Gd $1042
Calibers: .22 LR, 7.65mm Luger, 9mm Para. Eight-round magazine, 4.75-inch bbl., 8.5 inches overall. Weight: 33 oz. (.22 cal.) or 35 oz. (7.65mm, 9mm). Fixed sights. Polished blued finish. Checkered wood grips. Made 1949-86.

MODEL P210-2 . . . . NiB $1578 Ex $1346 Gd $805
Same as Model P210-1 except has sandblasted finish, plastic grips. Not avail. in .22 LR. Disc. 1987.

MODEL P210-5
TARGET PISTOL . . . . NiB $2088 Ex $1835 Gd $1039
Same as Model P210-2 except has 6-inch bbl., micrometer adj. rear sight, target front sight, adj. trigger stop, 9.7 inches overall. Weight: About 38.3 oz. Disc. 1997.

SIG
Model P210-1

SIG
Model P210-6 Target Pistol

MODEL P210-6 TARGET PISTOL . . . . . . NiB $1964 Ex $1578 Gd $934
Same as Model P210-2 except has micrometer adj. rear sight, target front sight, adj. trigger stop. Weight: About 37 oz. Disc. 1987.

P210 .22 CONVERSION UNIT . . . . NiB $794 Ex $631 Gd $435
Converts P210 pistol to .22 LR. Consists of bbl., w/recoil spring, slide and magazine,

SIG SAUER HANDGUNS Mfd. by J. P. Sauer & Sohn of West Germany, SIG of Switzerland, and other manufacturers

MODEL P220 DA/DAO AUTOMATIC PISTOL
Calibers: 22LR, 7.65mm, 9mm Para., .38 Super, .45 Automatic. Seven-round in .45, 9-round in other calibers, 4.4-inch bbl., 8 inches overall. Weight: 26.5 oz.(9mm). Fixed sights. Blue, electroless nickel, K-Kote, Duo/nickel or Ilaflon finish. Alloy frame. Checkered plastic grips. Imported 1976 to date. Note: Also sold in U.S. as Browning BDA. See illustration next page.
Blue finish . . . . NiB $721 Ex $608 Gd $391
Duo/nickel finish. . . . . NiB $762 Ex $603 Gd $437
Nickel finish . . . . NiB $793 Ex $700 Gd $464
K-Kote finish . . . . NiB $762 Ex $603 Gd $385
Ilaflon finish . . . . NiB $762 Ex $603 Gd $437
.22 conversion kit, add $680
W/Siglite sights, add $92

MODEL P220 SPORT AUTOMATIC . . . . NiB $1252 Ex $1020 Gd $814
Similar to Model P220 except .45 ACP only w/4.5-inch compensated bbl., 10-round magazine, adj. target sights. Weight: 46.1 oz. Stainless finish. Made 1999 to date.

SIG Sauer P220

SIG Sauer P225

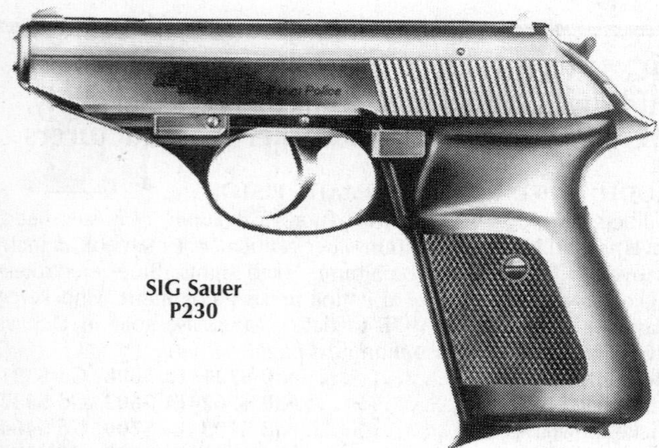
SIG Sauer P230

MODEL P225 DA AUTOMATIC
Caliber: 9mm Para. Eight-round magazine, 3.85-inch bbl., 7 inches overall. Weight: 26.1 oz. Blue, nickel, K-Kote, Duo/nickel or Ilaflon finish.
Blued finish . . . . NiB $562 Ex $484 Gd $381
Duo/nickel finish. . . . . NiB $608 Ex $531 Gd $428
Nickel finish . . . . NiB $634 Ex $557 Gd $454
K-Kote finish . . . . NiB $634 Ex $557 Gd $454
W/Siglite sights, add $105

MODEL P226 DA/DAO AUTOMATIC
Caliber: .357 SIG, 9mm Para., .40 S&W, 10- or 15-round magazine, 4.4-inch bbl., 7.75 inches overall. Weight: 29.5 oz. Alloy frame. Blue, electroless nickel, K-Kote, Duo/nickel or Nitron finish. Imported 1983 to date.
Blued finish . . . . NiB $790 Ex $656 Gd $388
Duo/nickel finish. . . . . NiB $831 Ex $739 Gd $414
Nickel finish . . . . NiB $737 Ex $594 Gd $413
K-Kote finish . . . . NiB $704 Ex $629 Gd $396
Nitron finish
(Blacken stainless) . . . . NiB $711 Ex $574 Gd $399
W/Siglite sights, add $85

MODEL P228 DA AUTOMATIC
Same general specifications as Model P226 except w/3.86-inch bbl., 7.13 inches overall. 10- or 13-round magazine, Imported 1990-97.
Blued finish . . . . NiB $723 Ex $620 Gd $388
Duo/nickel finish. . . . . NiB $765 Ex $662 Gd $431
Electroless nickel finish . . . . NiB $795 Ex $692 Gd $461
K-Kote finish . . . . NiB $770 Ex $667 Gd $435
For Siglite nite sights, add $102

MODEL P229 DA/DAO AUTOMATIC
Same general specifications as Model P228 except w/3.86-inch bbl., 10- or 12-round magazine, weight: 32.5 oz. Nitron or Satin Nickel finish. Imported 1991 to date.
Nitron finish
(Blackened stainless) . . . . NiB $775 Ex $672 Gd $388
Satin nickel finish . . . . NiB $816 Ex $713 Gd $430
For Siglite nite sights, add $100

MODEL P229
SPORT AUTOMATIC . . . . NiB $1243 Ex $986 Gd $805
Similar to Model P229 except .357 SIG only w/4.5-inch compensated bbl., adj. target sights. Weight: 43.6 oz. Stainless finish. Made 1998 to date.

MODEL P230 DA AUTOMATIC PISTOL
Calibers: .22 LR, .32 Auto (7.65mm), .380 Auto (9mm Short), 9mm Ultra. 10-round magazine in .22, 8-round in .32, 7-round in 9mm; 3.6-inch bbl., 6.6 inches overall. Weight: 18.2 oz. or 22.4 oz. (steel frame). Fixed sights. Blued or stainless finish. Plastic grips. Imported 1976-96.
Blued finish . . . . NiB $457 Ex $354 Gd $240
Stainless finish (P230SL) . . . . NiB $513 Ex $431 Gd $410

MODEL P232 DA/DAO AUTOMATIC PISTOL
Caliber: .380 ACP. Seven-round magazine, 3.6-inch bbl., 6.6 inches overall. Weight: 16.2 oz. or 22.4 oz. (steel frame). Double/single action or double action only. Blade front and notch rear drift adjustable sights. Alloy or steel frame. Automatic firing pin lock and heelmounted magazine release. Blue, Duo or stainless finish. Stippled black composite stocks. Imported 1997 to date.
Blued finish . . . . NiB $482 Ex $421 Gd $243
Duo finish . . . . NiB $503 Ex $441 Gd $263
Stainless finish . . . . NiB $519 Ex $462 Gd $390
For Siglite nite sights, add $40

MODEL P239 DA/DAO AUTOMATIC PISTOL
Caliber: .357 SIG, 9mm Parabellum or .40 S&W. Seven- or 8-round magazine, 3.6-inch bbl., 6.6 inches overall. Weight: 28.2 oz. Double/single action or double action only. Blade front and notch rear adjustable sights. Alloy frame w/stainless slide. Ambidextrous frame- mounted magazine release. Matte black or Duo finish. Stippled black composite stocks. Made 1996 to date.
Matte black finish . . . . NiB $534 Ex $472 Gd $246
DAO finish. . . . . NiB $573 Ex $462 Gd $320
For Siglite nite sights, add $100

SMITH & WESSON, INC. — Springfield, Massachusetts

NOTE: *For ease in locating a particular S&W handgun, the listings are divided into two groupings: Automatic/Single-Shot Pistols (below) and Revolvers (page 153). For a complete handgun listing, please refer to the index.*

AUTOMATIC/SINGLE-SHOT PISTOLS

.32 AUTOMATIC PISTOL. . . . . . NiB $2909 Ex $2188 Gd $1570
Caliber: .32 Automatic. Same general specifications as .35 caliber model, but barrel is fastened to the receiver instead of hinged. Made 1924-37.

MODEL .22 SPORT SERIES
Caliber: .22 LR. 10-round magazine, 4-, 5.5- or 7-inch standard (A-series) or bull bbl., (S-series). Single action. Eight, 9.5 or 11 inches overall. Weight: 28 oz. to 33 oz. Partridge front sight, fully adjustable rear. Alloy frame w/stainless slide. Blued finish. Black polymer or Dymondwood grips. Made 1997 to date.
Model 22A (w/4-inch bbl.) . . . . NiB $228 Ex $203 Gd $125
Model 22A (w/5.5-inch bbl.). . . . . . NiB $258 Ex $232 Gd $154
Model 22A (w/7-inch bbl.) . . . . NiB $297 Ex $272 Gd $194
Model 22S (w/5.5-inch bbl.) . . . . . . NiB $331 Ex $306 Gd $228
Model 22S (w/7-inch bbl.) . . . . NiB $273 Ex $213 Gd $149
W/bull bbl., add $40
W/Dymondwood grips, add $75

35 (1913) AUTOMATIC PISTOL . . . NiB $219 Ex $690 Gd $407
Caliber: 35 S&W Auto. Seven-round magazine, 3.5-inch bbl., (hinged to frame). 6.5 inches overall. Weight: 25 oz. Fixed sights. Blued or nickel finish. Plain walnut grips. Made 1913-21.

MODEL 39 9MM DA AUTO PISTOL
Calibers: 9mm Para. Eight-round magazine, 4-inch barrel. Overall length: 7.44-inches. Steel or alloy frames. Weight: 26.5 oz. (w/alloy frame). Click adjustable rear sight, ramp front. Blued or nickel finish. Checkered walnut grips. Made 1954-82. Note: Between 1954 and 1966, 927 pistols were produced w/steel instead of alloy. In 1970, Model 39-1 w/alloy frame and steel slide. In 1971, Model 39-2 was introduced as an improved version of the original Model 39 w/modified extractor.
Model 39 (early production) 1954-70
First series (SN range 1000-2600) . . . . . NiB $1514 Ex $1319 Gd $676
9mm blue(w/steel frame & slide, produced 1966) . . . . NiB $1268 Ex $1036 Gd $629
9mm blue (w/alloy frame) . . . . NiB $434 Ex $351 Gd $244
Nickel finish, add $35
Models 39-1, 39-2 (late production)
1970-82 9mm blue (w/alloy frame) . . . . . . NiB $387 Ex $273 Gd $222
Nickel finish, add $35

MODEL 41 .22 AUTOMATIC PISTOL
Caliber: .22 LR, .22 Short (not interchangeably). 10-round magazine, bbl. lengths: 5-, 5.5-, 7.75-inches; latter has detachable muzzle brake, 12 inches overall (with 7.75-inch bbl.). Weight: 43.5 oz. (with 7.75-inch bbl.). Click adj. rear sight, undercut Partridge front. Blued finish. Checkered walnut grips w/thumbrest. 1957 to date.
.22 LR model . . . . NiB $715 Ex $561 Gd $267
.22 Short model (w/counter-weights & muzzle brake) . . . . NiB $1155 Ex $929 Gd $641
W/extended sight, add $95
W/muzzle brake, add $45

Smith & Wesson Model 22A Sport Series

Smith & Wesson Model 22S Sport Series w/Dymondwood Grips

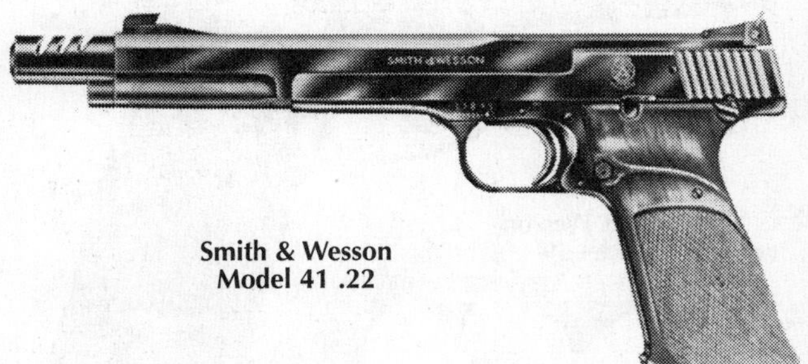

Smith & Wesson Model 41 .22

MODEL 46 .22 AUTO PISTOL. . . . . NiB $484 Ex $366 Gd $227
Caliber: .22 LR. 10-round magazine, bbl. lengths: 5-, 5.5-, 7-inches. 10.56 inches overall (with 7-inch bbl.). Weight: 42 oz. (with 7-inch bbl.). Click adj. rear sight, undercut Partridge front. Blued finish. Molded nylon grips w/thumbrest. Only 4,000 produced. Made 1959-68. See illustration next page.

MODEL 52 .38 MASTER AUTO
Caliber: .38 Special (midrange wadcutter only). Five-round magazine, 5-inch bbl., overall length: 8.63 inches. Weight: 41 oz. Micrometer click rear sight, Partridge front on ramp base. Blued finish. Checkered walnut grips. Made 1961-94. See illustration next page.
Model 52 (1961-63) . . . . NiB $928 Ex $823 Gd $434
Model 52-1 (1963-71) . . . . NiB $722 Ex $593 Gd $331
Model 52-2 (1971-93) . . . . NiB $722 Ex $593 Gd $331
Model 52-A USA Marksman (fewer than 100 mfg.) . . . . NiB $3130 Ex $2666 Gd $1791

Smith & Wesson
Model 46

Smith & Wesson
Model 439

Smith & Wesson
Model 52

Smith & Wesson
Model 59

Smith & Wesson
Model 422

MODEL 59
9MM DA AUTO

Similar specifications as Model 39 except has 14-round staggered column magazine, checkered nylon grips. Made 1971-82.

Model 59, blue . . . . NiB $417 Ex $370 Gd $241
Model 59, nickel . . . . NiB $454 Ex $401 Gd $252
Model 59
(early production
w/smooth grip frame) . . . . NiB $600 Ex $483 Gd $335

MODEL 61
ESCORT POCKET AUTOMATIC PISTOL

Caliber: .22 LR. Five-round magazine, 2.13-inch bbl., 4.69 inches overall. Weight: 14 oz. Fixed sights. Blued or nickel finish. Checkered plastic grips. Made 1970-73.

Model 61, blue . . . . NiB $267 Ex $226 Gd $123
Model 61, nickel . . . . NiB $293 Ex $247 Gd $123

MODEL 410
AUTO PISTOL . . . . NiB $488 Ex $357 Gd $197

Caliber: .40 S&W. Double action. 10-round magazine, 4-inch bbl., 7.5 inches overall. Weight: 28.5 oz. Alloy frame w/steel slide. Post front sight, fixed rear w/3-dot system. Matte blue finish. Checkered synthetic grips w/straight backstrap. Made 1996 to date.

MODEL 411
AUTO PISTOL . . . . NiB $470 Ex $403 Gd $300

Similar to S&W Model 915 except in caliber .40 S&W. 11-round magazine, made 1994-96.

MODEL 422 SA
AUTO PISTOL

Caliber: .22 LR. 10-round magazine, 4.5- or 6-inch bbl., 7.5 inches overall (with 4.5-inch bbl.). Weight: 22-23.5 oz. Fixed or adjustable sights. Checkered plastic or walnut grips. Blued finish. Made from 1987-96.

Standard model . . . . NiB $203 Ex $166 Gd $115
Target model . . . . NiB $245 Ex $192 Gd $120

MODEL 439
9MM AUTOMATIC

DA. Caliber: 9mm Para. Two 8-round magazines, 4-inch bbl., 7.44 inches overall. Alloy frame. Weight: 30 oz. Serrated ramp square front sight, square notch rear. Checkered walnut grips. Blued or nickel finish. Made 1979-88.

Model 439, blue . . . . NiB $409 Ex $336 Gd $228
Model 439, nickel . . . . NiB $444 Ex $371 Gd $311
W/adjustable sights, add $24

Smith & Wesson
Model 645

Smith & Wesson
Model 459

MODEL 457
COMPACT AUTO PISTOL . . . . NiB $501 Ex $366 Gd $206
Caliber: .45 ACP. Double action. Seven-round magazine, 3.75-inch bbl., 7.25 inches overall. Weight: 29 oz. Alloy frame w/steel slide. Post front sight, fixed rear w/3-dot system. Bobbed hammer. Matte blue finish. Wraparround synthetic grip w/straight backstrap. Made 1996 to date.

MODEL 459 DA AUTOMATIC
Caliber: 9mm Para. Two 14-round magazines, 4-inch bbl., 7.44 inches overall. Alloy frame. Weight: 28 oz. Blued or nickel finish. Made 1979-87.
Model 459, blue . . . . NiB $443 Ex $376 Gd $268
Model 459, nickel . . . . NiB $489 Ex $423 Gd $299
FBI Model (brushed finish) . . . . NiB $690 Ex $639 Gd $361

Smith & Wesson
Model 469

MODEL 469
(MINI) AUTOMATIC . . . . NiB $403 Ex $351 Gd $248
DA. Caliber: 9mm Para. Two 12-round magazines, 3.5-inch bbl., 6.88 inches overall. Weight: 26 oz. Yellow ramp front sight, dovetail mounted square-notch rear. Sandblasted blued finish. Optional ambidextrous safety. Made 1982-88.

MODEL 539 DA AUTOMATIC
Similar to Model 439 except w/steel frame. Caliber: 9mm Para. Two 8-round magazines, 4-inch bbl., 7.44 inches overall. Weight: 36 oz. Blued or nickel finish. Made 1980-83.
Model 539, blue . . . . NiB $484 Ex $428 Gd $330
Model 539, nickel . . . . NiB $521 Ex $464 Gd $356
W/adjustable sights, add $30

MODEL 559 DA AUTOMATIC
Similar to Model 459 except w/steel frame. Caliber: 9mm Para. Two 14-round magazines, 4-inch bbl., 7.44 inches overall. Weight: 39.5 oz. Blued or nickel finish. (3750 produced) Made 1980-83.
Model 559, blue . . . . NiB $521 Ex $469 Gd $278
Model 559, nickel . . . . NiB $551 Ex $505 Gd $309
W/adjustable sights, add $30

MODEL 622 SA AUTO PISTOL
Same general specifications as Model 422 except w/stainless finish. Made from 1989-96.
Standard model . . . . NiB $244 Ex $197 Gd $182
Target model . . . . NiB $300 Ex $249 Gd $197

Smith & Wesson
Model 639

MODEL 639 AUTOMATIC . . . . NiB $455 Ex $331 Gd $305
Caliber: 9mm Para. Two 12-round magazines, 3.5-inch bbl., 6.9 inches overall. Weight: 36 oz. Stainless. Made 1982-88.

Smith & Wesson Model 659

Smith & Wesson Model 745

Smith & Wesson Model 1026

MODEL 645 DA AUTOMATIC

Caliber: .45 ACP. Eight-round. 5-inch bbl., overall length: 8.5 inches. Weight: Approx. 38 oz. Red ramp front, fixed rear sights. Stainless. Made 1986-88. See illustration previous page.

Model 645 (w/fixed sights) . . . . NiB $509 Ex $396 Gd $329
Model 645 (w/adjustable sights) . . . NiB $535 Ex $422 Gd $355

MODEL 659 9MM AUTOMATIC

DA. Similar to S&W Model 459 except weight: 39.5 oz. and finish is satin stainless steel finish. Made 1983-88.

Model 659 (w/fixed sights) . . . . NiB $478 Ex $365 Gd $329
Model 659 (w/adjustable sights). . . . . NiB $504 Ex $391 Gd $355

MODEL 669 AUTOMATIC. . . . . NiB $458 Ex $334 Gd $233

Caliber: 9mm. 12-round magazine, 3.5 inch bbl., 6.9 inches overall. Weight: 26 oz. Serrated ramp front sight w/red bar, fixed rear. Nonglare stainless steel finish. Made 1986-88.

MODEL 745 AUTOMATIC PISTOL

Caliber: .45 ACP. Eight-round magazine, 5-inch bbl., 8.63 inches overall. Weight: 38.75 oz. Fixed sights. Blued slide, stainless frame. Checkered walnut grips. Similar to the model 645, but w/o DA capability. Made 1987-90.

W/standard competition features . . . . NiB $612 Ex $473 Gd $365
IPSC Commemorative (first 5,000) . . . . NiB $721 Ex $581 Gd $402

MODEL 908/909/910 AUTO PISTOLS

Caliber: 9mm Parabellum. Double action. Eight-round (Model 908), 9-round (Model 909) or 10-round (Model 910) magazine; 3.5- or 4-inch bbl.; 6.83 or 7.38 inches overall. Weight: 26 oz. to 28.5 oz. Post front sight, fixed rear w/3-dot system. Matte blue steel slide w/alloy frame. Delrin synthetic wrap-around grip w/straight backstrap. Made 1994 to date.

Model 908. NiB $454 Ex $336 Gd $197
Model 909 (disc 1996) . . . . NiB $388 Ex $300 Gd $197
Model 910 . . . . NiB $454 Ex $336 Gd $197

MODEL 915 AUTO PISTOL . . . . . . NiB $377 Ex $280 Gd $197

DA. Caliber: 9mm Para. 15-round magazine, 4-inch bbl., 7.5 inches overall. Weight: 28.5 oz. Post front sight, fixed square-notched rear w/3-dot system. Xenoy wraparound grip. Blued steel slide and alloy frame. Made 1992-94.

MODEL 1000 SERIES DA AUTO

Caliber: 10mm. Nine-round magazine, 4.25- or 5-inch bbl., 7.88 or 8.63 inches overall. Weight: About 38 oz. Post front sight, adj. or fixed square-notched rear w/3-dot system. One-piece Xenoy wraparound grips. Stainless slide and frame. Made 1990-94.

Model 1006 (fixed sights, 5 inch bbl.) . . . . NiB $675 Ex $562 Gd $433
Model 1006 (Adj. sights, 5 inch bbl.) . . . . . NiB $703 Ex $590 Gd $461
Model 1026 (fixed sights, 5 inch bbl., decocking lever) . . . . NiB $670 Ex $562 Gd $433
Model 1066 (fixed sights, 4.25 inch bbl.) . . . . NiB $649 Ex $551 Gd $428
Model 1076 (fixed sights, 4.25 inch bbl., frame-mounted decocking lever, straight backstrap). . . . . NiB $685 Ex $567 Gd $433
Model 1076 (same as above w/Tritium night sight) . . . . NiB $727 Ex $608 Gd $474
Model 1086 (same as model 1076 in DA only) . . . . NiB $753 Ex $551 Gd $428

MODEL 2206 SA AUTOMATIC PISTOL

Similar to Model 422 except w/stainless-steel slide and frame, weight: 35-39 oz. Partridge front sight on adj. sight model; post w/white dot on fixed sight model. Plastic grips. Made 1990-96.

Standard model . . . . NiB $311 Ex $244 Gd $192
Target model . . . . NiB $383 Ex $295 Gd $249

MODEL 2213 SPORTSMAN AUTO . . . . NiB $275 Ex $218 Gd $177

Caliber: .22 LR. Eight-round magazine, 3-inch bbl., 6.13 inches overall. Weight: 18 oz. Partridge front sight, fixed square-notched rear w/3-dot system. Black synthetic molded grips. Stainless steel slide w/alloy frame. Made 1992-99.

MODEL 2214 SPORTSMAN AUTO . . . . NiB $249 Ex $203 Gd $146

Same general specifications as Model 2214 except w/blued slide and matte black alloy frame. Made from 1990-99.

MODEL 3904/3906 DA AUTO PISTOL
Caliber: 9mm. Eight-round magazine, 4-inch bbl., 7.5 inches overall. Weight: 25.5 oz. (Model 3904) or 34 oz. (Model 3906). Fixed or adj. sights. Delrin one-piece wraparound, checkered grips. Alloy frame w/blued carbon steel slide (Model 3904) or satin stainless (Model 3906). Made 1989-91.

Model 3904 w/adjustable sights........ NiB $504 Ex $437 Gd $355
Model 3904 w/fixed sights............ NiB $483 Ex $417 Gd $308
Model 3904 w/Novak LC sight .... NiB $509 Ex $401 Gd $277
Model 3906 w/adjustable sights .... NiB $574 Ex $497 Gd $425
Model 3906 w/Novak LC sight .... NiB $545 Ex $468 Gd $396

Smith & Wesson Model 3906

MODEL 3913/3914 DA AUTOMATIC
Caliber: 9mm Parabellum (Luger). Eight-round magazine, 3.5-inch bbl., 6.88 inches overall. Weight: 25 oz. Post front sight, fixed or adj. square-notched rear. One-piece Xenoy wraparound grips w/straight backstrap. Alloy frame w/stainless or blued slide. Made 1990 to date.

Model 3913 stainless .... NiB $655 Ex $501 Gd $413
Model 3913LS Lady Smith stainless
w/contoured trigger guard .... NiB $671 Ex $516 Gd $413
Model 3913TSW (intro. 1998) .... NiB $655 Ex $511 Gd $413
Model 3914 blued compact
(disc 1995) .... NiB $501 Ex $407 Gd $302

Smith & Wesson Model 3953

MODEL 3953/3954 DA AUTO PISTOL
Same general specifications as Model 3913/3914 except double action only. Made from 1991 to date.

Model 3953 stainless,
double action only .... NiB $655 Ex $511 Gd $413
Model 3954 blued, double
action only (disc. 1992).................. NiB $480 Ex $413 Gd $310

MODEL 4000 SERIES DA AUTO
Caliber: .40 S&W. 11-round magazine, 4-inch bbl., 7.88 inches overall. Weight: 28-30 oz. w/alloy frame or 36 oz. w/stainless frame. Post front sight, adj. or fixed square-notched rear w/2 white dots. Straight backstrap. One-piece Xenoy wraparound grips. Blued or stainless finish. Made between 1990-93.

Model 4003 stainless w/alloy frame ..... NiB $625 Ex $532 Gd $429
Model 4003 TSW w/
S&W Tactical options .... NiB $784 Ex $687 Gd $393
Model 4004 blued w/alloy frame .... NiB $569 Ex $460 Gd $320
Model 4006 stainless
frame, fixed sights.................. NiB $578 Ex $496 Gd $310
Model 4006 stainless
frame, Adj. sights .... NiB $697 Ex $583 Gd $434
Model 4006 TSW w/
S&W Tactical options .... NiB $789 Ex $686 Gd $393
Model 4013 stainless frame,
fixed sights .... NiB $635 Ex $522 Gd $316
Model 4013 TSW w/
S&W Tactical options .... NiB $774 Ex $619 Gd $455
Model 4014 blued, fixed sights
(disc. 1993)........................ NiB $547 Ex $460 Gd $305
Model 4026 w/decocking
Lever (disc. 1994).................. NiB $661 Ex $561 Gd $434
Model 4043 DA only, stainless
w/alloy frame .... NiB $784 Ex $681 Gd $393
Model 4044 DA only,
blued w/alloy frame .... NiB $578 Ex $496 Gd $326
Model 4046 DA only, stainless
frame, fixed sights.................. NiB $702 Ex $582 Gd $438
Model 4046 TSW w/
S&W Tactical options .... NiB $804 Ex $695 Gd $386
Model 4046 DA only, stainless
frame, Tritium night sight .... NiB $941 Ex $834 Gd $559

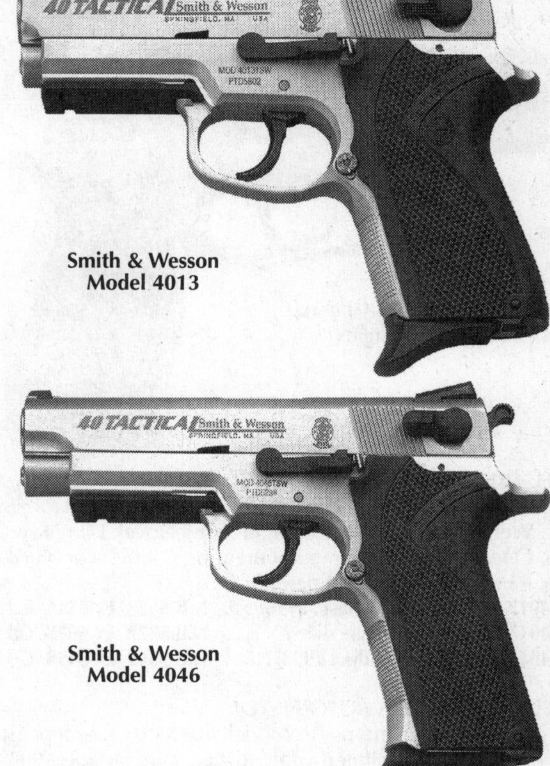

Smith & Wesson Model 4013

Smith & Wesson Model 4046

Smith & Wesson Model 4053

Smith & Wesson Model 4586

Smith & Wesson Model 5904 w/Adjustable Sights

MODEL 4013/4014 DA AUTOMATIC

Caliber: .40 S&W. Eight-round capacity, 3.5-inch bbl., 7 inches overall. Weight: 26 oz. Post front sight, fixed Novak LC rear w/3-dot system. One-piece Xenoy wraparound grips. Stainless or blued slide w/alloy frame. Made 1991 to date.

Model	NiB	Ex	Gd
Model 4013 w/stainless slide (disc. 1996)	$633	$514	$308
Model 4013 Tactical w/stainless slide	$772	$617	$453
Model 4014 w/blued slide (disc. 1993)	$545	$458	$262

MODEL 4053/4054 DA AUTO PISTOL

Same general specifications as Model 4013/4014 except double action only. Alloy frame fitted w/blued steel slide. Made 1991-97.

(cont'd) MODEL 4053/4054 DA AUTO PISTOL

Model	NiB	Ex	Gd
Model 4053 DA only w/stainless slide	$545	$458	$406
Model 4053 TSW w/ S&W Tactical options	$772	$617	$447
Model 4054 DA only w/blued slide (disc. 1992)	$545	$458	$406

MODEL 4500 SERIES DA AUTOMATIC

Caliber: .45 ACP. Six-, 7- or 8-round magazine, bbl. lengths: 3.75, 4.25 or 5 inches; 7.13 to 8.63 inches overall. Weight: 34.5 to 38.5 oz. Post front sight, fixed Novak LC rear w/3-dot system or adj. One-piece Xenoy wraparound grips. Satin stainless finish. Made 1990 to date.

Model	NiB	Ex	Gd
Model 4505 w/fixed sights, 5-inch bbl.	$612	$535	$329
Model 4505 w/Novak LC sight, 5-inch bbl.	$640	$563	$357
Model 4506 w/fixed sights, 5-inch bbl.	$720	$586	$442
Model 4506 w/Novak LC sight, 5-inch bbl.	$754	$620	$473
Model 4513T (TSW) w/3.75-inch bbl. Tactical Combat	$695	$571	$432
Model 4516 w/3.75-inch bbl.	$695	$566	$380
Model 4526 w/5-inch bbl., alloy frame, decocking lever, fixed sights	$674	$566	$432
Model 4536, decocking lever	$679	$576	$442
Model 4546, w/3.75-inch bbl., DA only	$679	$576	$442
Model 4553T (TSW) w/3.75-inch bbl. Tactical Combat	$640	$563	$352
Model 4556, w/3.75-inch bbl., DA only	$612	$535	$329
Model 4563 TSW w/4.25-inch bbl. Tactical Combat	$695	$571	$432
Model 4566 w/4.25-inch bbl., ambidextrous safety, fixed sights	$664	$561	$380
Model 4566 TSW w/4.25-inch bbl. Tactical Combat	$695	$571	$432
Model 4576 w/4.25-inch bbl., decocking lever	$674	$566	$380
Model 4583T TSW w/4.25-inch bbl. Tactical Combat	$640	$563	$442
Model 4586 w/4.25-inch bbl., DA only	$720	$586	$432
Model 4586 TSW w/4.25-inch bbl. Tactical Combat	$695	$571	$370

MODEL 5900 SERIES DA AUTOMATIC

Caliber: 9mm. 15-round magazine, 4-inch bbl., 7.5 inches overall. Weight: 26-38 oz. Fixed or adj. sights. One-piece Xenoy wraparound grips. Alloy frame w/stainless-steel slide (Model 5903) or blued slide (Model 5904) stainless-steel frame and slide (Model 5906). Made 1989/90 to date.

Model	NiB	Ex	Gd
Model 5903 w/adjustable sights	$736	$597	$303
Model 5903 w/Novak LC rear sight	$736	$597	$303
Model 5903 TSW w/4-inch bbl., Tactical Combat	$736	$597	$303
Model 5904 w/adjustable sights	$574	$463	$321
Model 5904 w/Novak LC rear sight	$566	$447	$308
Model 5905 w/Adjustable Sights	$586	$468	$355
Model 5905 w/Novak LC rear sight	$674	$566	$380
Model 5906 w/adjustable sights	$669	$561	$355
Model 5906 w/Novak LC rear sight	$648	$458	$329
Model 5906 w/Tritium night sight	$772	$653	$509
Model 5906 TSW w/4-inch bbl., Tactical Combat	$767	$669	$489
Model 5924 anodized frame, blued slide	$607	$458	$262
Model 5926 Stain. frame, decocking lever	$695	$566	$432
Model 5943 alloy frame/ stainless slide, DA only	$669	$561	$350
Model 5943 TSW w/4-inch bbl., DA only	$638	$514	$356
Model 5944 alloy frame/ blued slide, DA only	$576	$473	$339
Model 5946 stainless frame/slide, DA only	$633	$432	$308
Model 5946 TSW w/4-inch bbl., DA only	$640	$563	$164

MODEL 6900 COMPACT SERIES

Double action. Caliber: 9mm. 12-round magazine, 3.5-inch bbl., 6.88 inches overall. Weight: 26.5 oz. Ambidextrous safety. Post front sight, fixed Novak LC rear w/3-dot system. Alloy frame w/blued carbon steel slide (Model 6904) or stainless steel slide (Model 6906). Made 1989 to date.

Model 6904 . . . . NiB $611 Ex $446 Gd $315
Model 6906 w/fixed sights . . . . NiB $627 Ex $512 Gd $415
Model 6906 w/Tritium night sight . . . . NiB $750 Ex $550 Gd $477
Model 6926 same as model 6906 w/decocking lever . . . . NiB $637 Ex $518 Gd $315
Model 6944 same as model 6904 in DA only . . . . NiB $549 Ex $462 Gd $266
Model 6946 same as model 6906 in DA only ,fixed sights . . . . NiB $637 Ex $518 Gd $315
Model 6946 w/Tritium night sight . . . . NiB $699 Ex $575 Gd $374

SIGMA SW380 AUTOMATIC PISTOL . . . . . NiB $318 Ex $276 Gd $199

Caliber: .380 ACP. Double-action only. Six-round magazine, 3-inch bbl., weight: 14 oz. Black integral polymer gripframe w/checkered back and front straps. Fixed channel sights. Polymer frame w/hammerless steel slide. Made 1996 to date.

SIGMA SW9 SERIES AUTOMATIC PISTOL

Caliber: 9mm Parabellum. Double action only. 10-round magazine, 3.25-, 4- or 4.5-inch bbl., weight: 17.9 oz. to 24.7 oz. Polymer frame w/hammerless steel slide. Post front sight and drift adjustable rear w/3-dot system. Gray or black integral polymer gripframe w/checkered back and front straps. Made 1994 to date.

Model SW9C (compact w/3.25-inch bbl.) . . . . NiB $487 Ex $390 Gd $297
Model SW9F (blue slide w/4.5-inch bbl.) . . . . . NiB $524 Ex $426 Gd $315
Model SW9M (compact w/3.25-inch bbl.) . . . . NiB $328 Ex $317 Gd $199
Model SW9V (stainless slide w/4-inch bbl.) . . . NiB $390 Ex $328 Gd $276
Tritium night sight, add $210

SW40 SERIES AUTOMATIC PISTOL

Same general specifications as SW9 series except chambered for .40 S&W w/4- or 4.5-inch bbl., weight: 24.4 to 26 oz. Made 1994 to date.

Model SW40C (compact w/4inch bbl.) . . . . . . NiB $485 Ex $388 Gd $295
Model SW40F (blue slide w/4.5inch bbl.). . . . . NiB $485 Ex $388 Gd $295
Model SW40V (stainless slide w/4inch bbl.) . . . . NiB $393 Ex $331 Gd $279
Tritium night sight, add $210

MODEL 1891 SINGLE-SHOT TARGET PISTOL, FIRST MODEL

Hinged frame. Calibers: .22 LR, .32 S&W, .38 S&W. Bbl. lengths: 6-, 8- and 10-inches, approx. 13.5 inches overall (with 10-inch bbl.). Weight: About 25 oz. Target sights, barrel catch rear adj. for windage and elevation. Blued finish. Square butt, hard rubber grips. Made 1893-1905. Note: This model was available also as a combination arm w/accessory .38 revolver bbl. and cylinder enabling conversion to a pocket revolver. It has the frame of the .38 SA revolver Model 1891 w/side flanges, hand and cylinder stop slots.

Single-shot pistol, .22 LR . . . . NiB $846 Ex $691 Gd $357
Single-shot pistol, .32 S&W or .38 S&W. . . . . NiB $1178 Ex $947 Gd $652
Combination set, revolver and single-shot barrel. . . . . NiB $1306 Ex $1050 Gd $722

MODEL 1891 SINGLE-SHOT TARGET PISTOL, SECOND MODEL . . . . NiB $1158 Ex $797 Gd $411

Similar to the First Model except side flanges, hand and stop slots eliminated, cannot be converted to revolver, redesigned rear sight. Caliber: .22 LR only, 10-inch bbl. only. Made 1905-09.

PERFECTED SINGLE-SHOT TARGET PISTOL

Similar to Second Model except has double-action lockwork. Caliber: .22 LR only, 10-inch bbl. Checkered walnut grips, extended

Smith & Wesson Model 1

(cont'd) **PERFECTED SINGLE-SHOT TARGET PISTOL**

square-butt target type. Made 1909-23. Note: In 1920 and thereafter, this model was made w/barrels having bore diameter of .223 instead of .226 and tight, short chambering. The first group of these pistols was produced for the U.S. Olympic Team of 1920, thus the designation Olympic Model.

Pre-1920 type . . . . NiB $1776 Ex $797 Gd $334
Olympic model . . . . NiB $1467 Ex $1050 Gd $638

STRAIGHT LINE SINGLE-SHOT TARGET PISTOL . . . . NiB $1827 Ex $1261 Gd $591

Frame shaped like that of an automatic pistol, barrel swings to the left on pivot for extracting and loading, straight-line trigger and hammer movement. Caliber: .22 LR. 10-inch bbl., 11.25 inches overall. Weight: 34 oz. Target sights. Blued finish. Smooth walnut grips. Supplied in metal case w/screwdriver and cleaning rod. Made 1925-36.

NOTE: *The following section contains only S&W Revolvers. For a complete listing of S&W handguns, please refer to the index.*

REVOLVERS

MODEL 1 HAND EJECTOR DA REVOLVER. . . . . NiB $749 Ex $646 Gd $425

First Model. Forerunner of the .32 Hand Ejector and Regulation Police models, this was the first S&W revolver of the solid-frame, swing-out cylinder type. Top strap of this model is longer than those of later models, and it lacks the usual S&W cylinder latch. Caliber: .32 S&W Long. Bbl., lengths: 3.25-, 4.25-, and 6-inches. Fixed sights. Blued or nickel finish. Round butt, hard rubber stocks. Made 1896-1903.

NO. 3 SA FRONTIER. . . . . NiB $9376 Ex $6224 Gd $2001

Caliber: .44-40 WCF. Bbl., lengths: 4-, 5- and 6.5-inch. Fixed or target sights. Blued or nickel finish. Round, hard rubber or checkered walnut grips. Made 1885-1908.

NO. 3 SA (NEW MODEL) . . . . . NiB $3894 Ex $3123 Gd $2136

Hinged frame. Six-round cylinder. Caliber: .44 S&W Russian. Bbl., lengths: 4-, 5-, 6-, 6.5-, 7.5- and 8-inches. Fixed or target sights. Blued or nickel finish. Round, hard rubber or checkered walnut grips. Made 1878-1908. Note: Value shown is for standard model. Specialist collectors recognize numerous variations w/a range of higher values.

NO. 3 SA TARGET. . . . . NiB $6735 Ex $3387 Gd $1266

Hinged frame. Six-round cylinder. Calibers: .32/.44 S&W, .38/.44 S&W Gallery & Target. 6.5-inch bbl. only. Fixed or target sights. Blued or nickel finish. Round, hard rubber or checkered walnut grips. Made 1887-1910.

Smith & Wesson
Model 10 (Two-inch Barrel)

Smith & Wesson
Model 12 (Two-inch Barrel)

Smith & Wesson Model 13
(Heavy Barrel)

Smith & Wesson
Model 14

MODEL 10 .38 MILITARY & POLICE DA
Also called Hand Ejector Model of 1902, Hand Ejector Model of 1905, Model K. Manufactured substantially in its present form since 1902, this model has undergone numerous changes, most of them minor. Round- or square-butt models, the latter intro. in 1904. Caliber: .38 Special. Six-round cylinder, bbl. lengths: 2-(intro. 1933), 4-, 5-, 6- and 6.5-inch (latter disc. 1915) also 4-inch heavy bbl., (intro. 1957); 11.13 inches overall (square-butt model w/6-inch bbl.). Round-butt model is 1/4-inch shorter, weight: About 1/2 oz. less. Fixed sights. Blued or nickel finish. Checkered walnut grips, hard rubber available in round-butt style. Current Model 10 has short action. Made 1902 to date. Note: S&W Victory Model, wartime version of the M & P .38, was produced for the U.S. Government from 1940 to the end of the war. A similar revolver, designated .38/200 British Service Revolver, was produced for the British Government during the same period. These arms have either brush-polish or sandblast blued finish, and most of them have plain, smooth walnut grips, lanyard swivels.
Model of 1902 (1902-05) . . . . NiB $646 Ex $512 Gd $234
Model of 1905 (1905-40) . . . . NiB $543 Ex $425 Gd $234
.38/200 British Service (1940-45) . . . NiB $388 Ex $291 Gd $141
Victory Model (1942-45). . . . . NiB $395 Ex $322 Gd $228
Model of 1944 (1945-48) . . . . NiB $254 Ex $208 Gd $151
Model 10 (1948 - date) . . . . NiB $388 Ex $291 Gd $141

MODEL 10 .38 MILITARY
& POLICE HEAVY BARREL . . . . NiB $388 Ex $291 Gd $141
Same as standard Model 10 except has heavy 4-inch bbl., weight: 34 oz. Made 1957 to date.

MODEL 12 .38 M
& PAIRWEIGHT. . . . . NiB $404 Ex $296 Gd $172
Same as standard Military & Police except has light alloy frame, furnished w/2- or 4-inch bbl. only, weight: 18 oz. (w/2-inch bbl.). Made 1952-86.

MODEL 12/13 (AIR FORCE MODEL)
DA REVOLVER. . . . . NiB $854 Ex $777 Gd $519
Special "Air Force" Model designed with alloy cylinder and frame to be used as a "Survival Weapon" for air crews. Athough this weapon was actually a first-series Model 12, the Air Force stamped "M13" on the top strap. Issued 1953 but recalled for function problems in 1954.

MODEL 13 .357
MILITARY/POLICE. . . . . NiB $339 Ex $257 Gd $149
Same as Model 10 .38 Military & Police Heavy Barrel except chambered for .357 Magnum and .38 Special w/3- or 4-inch bbl. Round or square butt configuration. Made 1974-98.

MODELS 14 (K38) AND 16 (K32) MASTERPIECE REVOLVERS
Calibers: .22 LR, .22 Magnum Rimfire, .32 S&W Long, .38 Special. Six-round cylinder. DA/SA. Bbl. lengths: 4- (.22 WMR only), 6-, 8.38-inch (latter not available in K32), 11.13 inches overall (with 6-inch bbl.). Weight: 38.5 oz. (with 6-inch bbl.). Click adj. rear sight, Partridge front. Blued finish. Checkered walnut grips. Made 1947 to date. (Model 16 disc. 1974, w/only 3,630 produced; reissued 1990-93.)
Model 14 (K-38 double-
action) . . . . NiB $329 Ex $277 Gd $174
Model 14 (K-38 single action,
6-inch bbl.) . . . . NiB $355 Ex $288 Gd $185
Model 14 (K-38 single action,
8.38-inch bbl.) . . . . NiB $387 Ex $314 Gd $220
Model 16 (K-32 double-
action) 1st Issue. . . . . NiB $1430 Ex $1225 Gd $812
Model 16 (K-32 double-
action) . . . . NiB $460 Ex $305 Gd $218

MODELS 15 (.38) AND 18 (.22) COMBAT MASTERPIECE DA REVOLVERS
Same as K-.22 and K-.38 Masterpiece but w/2- (.38) or 4-inch bbl., and Baughman quick-draw front sight. 9.13 inches overall w/4-inch bbl., Weight: 34 oz. (.38 cal.). Made 1950 to date.
Model 15 . . . . NiB $370 Ex $226 Gd $205
Model 18 (disc. 1985) . . . . NiB $380 Ex $303 Gd $216
W/target options TH & TT, add $35

MODEL 17 K-.22 MASTERPIECE DA REVOLVER
Caliber: 22LR. Six-round cylinder, Bbl lengths: 4, 6 or 8.38 inches. 11.13 inches overall (with 6-inch bbl.). Weight: 38 oz. (with 6-inch bbl.). Partridge-type front sight, S&W micrometer click rear. Checkered walnut Service grips with S&W momogram. S&W blued finish. Made 1947-93 and 1996-98.
Model 17 (4-inch bbl.) . . . . .NiB $615 Ex $538 Gd $332
Model 17 (6-inch bbl.) . . . . NiB $615 Ex $538 Gd $332
Model 17 (8.38-inch bbl.) . . . . NiB $641 Ex $589 Gd $414
W/target options TH & TT, add $35

MODEL 19 .357 COMBAT MAGNUM DA REVOLVER
Caliber: .357 Magnum. Six-round cylinder, bbl. lengths: 2.5 (round butt), 4, or 6 inches, 9.5 inches overall (with 4-inch bbl.). Weight: 35 oz. (with 4-inch bbl.). Click adj. rear sight, ramp front. Blued or nickel finish. Target grips of checkered Goncalo Alves. Made 1956 to date (2.5- and 6-inch bbls. were disc. in 1991).
Model 19 (2.5-inch bbl.) . . . . NiB $375 Ex $293 Gd $195
Model 19 (4-inch bbl.) . . . . NiB $385 Ex $303 Gd $204
Model 19 (6-inch bbl.) . . . . NiB $391 Ex $308 Gd $210
Model 19 (8.38-inch bbl.) . . . . NiB $374 Ex $303 Gd $213
W/target options TH & TT, add $60

MODEL 20 .38/.44 HEAVY DUTY DA
Caliber: .38 Special. Six-round cylinder, bbl. lengths: 4, 5 and 6.5 inches;10.38 inches overall (with 5-inch bbl.). Weight: 40 oz. (with 5-inch bbl.). Fixed sights. Blued or nickel finish. Checkered walnut grips. Short action after 1948. Made 1930-56 and 1957-67.
Pre-World War II . . . . NiB $629 Ex $521 Gd $366
Postwar . . . . NiB $376 Ex $310 Gd $170

MODEL 21 1950 .44 MILITARY DA REVOLVER
Postwar version of the 1926 Model 44 Military. Caliber: .44 Special, 6-round cylinder. Bbl. lengths: 4-, 5- and 6.5-inches. 11.75 inches overall (w/6.5-inch bbl.) Weight: 39.5 oz. (w/6.5-inch bbl.). Fixed front sight w/square-notch rear sight; target model has micrometer click rear sight adj. for windage and elevation. Checkered walnut grips w/S&W monogram. Blued or nickel finish. Made 1950-67.
Model 21 (4- or 5-inch bbl.) . . . . NiB $1843 Ex $1663 Gd $710
Model 21 (6.5-inch bbl.) . . . . NiB $2745 Ex $2474 Gd $1045

MODEL .22 1950 ARMY DA . . . . . . NiB $1843 Ex $1663 Gd $710
Postwar version of the 1917 Army w/same general specifications except redesigned hammer. Made 1950-67.

.22/.32 TARGET DA REVOLVER
Also known as the "Bekeart Model." Design based upon ".32 Hand Ejector." Caliber: .22 LR (recessed head cylinder for high-speed cartridges intro. 1935). Six-round cylinder, 6-inch bbl., 10.5 inches overall. Weight: 23 oz. Adj. target sights. Blued finish. Checkered walnut grips. Made 1911-53. Note: In 1911, San Francisco gun dealer Phil Bekeart, who suggested this model, received 292 pieces. These are the true "Bekeart Model" revolvers and are marked with separate identification numbers on the base of the wooden grip.
.22/.32 Target model . . . . NiB $329 Ex $277 Gd $154
.22/.32 Target model (early prod. 1-3000) . . . . NiB $466 Ex $337 Gd $213
.22/.32 Target model (Bekeart model). . . . . . . NiB $1135 Ex $929 Gd $234

.22/.32 KIT GUN. . . . . NiB $320 Ex $253 Gd $191
Same as .22/.32 Target except has 2- or 4-inch bbl., round grips, 6 or 8 inches overall, weight: 19-21oz. Made 1935-53.

Smith & Wesson
Model 15

Smith & Wesson
Model 17 K-22

Smith & Wesson
Model 18 (See Model 15 for description)

Smith & Wesson
Model 19 (Round Butt)

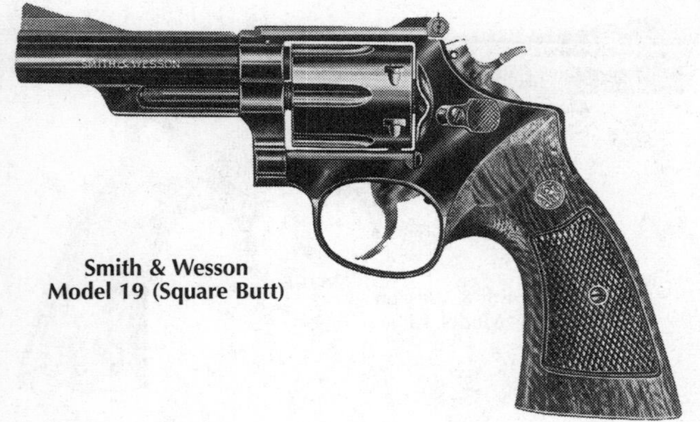
Smith & Wesson
Model 19 (Square Butt)

Smith & Wesson
Model 22/32 Kit Gun

Smith & Wesson
Model 20

Smith & Wesson
Model 22/32 Target Revolver

Smith & Wesson
Model 21

Smith & Wesson
Model 23

Smith & Wesson
Model 22

MODEL 23 .38/.44 OUTDOORSMAN DA REVOLVER
Target version of the .38/44 Heavy Duty. 6.5- or 8.75-inch bbl., weight: 41.75 oz. Target sights, micrometer-click rear on postwar models. Blued or nickel finish. 1950 transition model has ribbed barrel, redesigned hammer. Made 1930-67.
Prewar model (plain bbl.) . . . . NiB $699 Ex $596 Gd $318
Postwar (ribbed bbl.). . . . . NiB $833 Ex $710 Gd $376

MODEL 24 1950 .44 TARGET DA REVOLVER
Postwar version of the 1921 Model .44 with 4-, 5- or 6.5-inch ribbed bbl., redesigned hammer, micrometer click rear sight. Matte or polished blue finish. Made 1950-67. Model 24 reintroduced 1983 only.
Model 24 (1950)
w/4-inch bbl. . . . . NiB $1028 Ex $853 Gd $564
Model 24 (1950)
w/5-inch bbl. . . . . NiB $1041 Ex $868 Gd $580
Model 24 (1950)
w/6.5-inch bbl. . . . . NiB $755 Ex $631 Gd $425
Model 24 (1950) w/polished
blue finish, add 20%
Model 24 (1950)
w/nickel finish, add. 50%
Model 24
.44 Target reintroduced
(7,500 produced in 1983-84)
Model 24 (w/4-inch bbl.) . . . . NiB $491 Ex $466 Gd $363
Model 24 (w/6.5-inch bbl.). . . . . NiB $440 Ex $414 Gd $321
Model 24-3 .44
Lew Horton Special (produced in 1983)
Model 24-3 (w/3-inch bbl.). . . . . NiB $419 Ex $363 Gd $285

MODEL .25 1955 .45 TARGET DA REVOLVER
Same as 1950 Model .44 Target, but chambered for .45 ACP, .45 Auto Rim or .45 LC w/4-, 6- or 6.5-inch bbl. Made 1955 to 1991 in several variations. Note: In 1961, the .45 ACP was designated Model .25-2, and in 1978 the .45 LC was designated Model .25-5.

Model 25 1955 .45 Target
Model 25 (.45 ACP w/4- or 6-inch bbl.) . . . . . . NiB $490 Ex $439 Gd $233
Model 25 (.45 ACP w/6.5-inch pinned bbl.) . . . NiB $693 Ex $593 Gd $387
Model 25 (.45 LC early production) . . . . NiB $1420 Ex $1266 Gd $648
Model 25-2 .45 ACP
Model 25 (w/3-inch bbl., Lew Horton Special) NiB $537 Ex $485 Gd $408
Model 25 (w/4-inch bbl.). . . . . NiB $492 Ex $398 Gd $277
Model 24-3 (w/6.5-inch bbl.) . . . . NiB $505 Ex $408 Gd $285
Model 25-5 .45 LC
Model 25 (w/4-inch bbl.). . . . . NiB $492 Ex $398 Gd $277
Model 24-3 (w/6.5-inch bbl.) . . . . NiB $531 Ex $429 Gd $299

MODEL 26 1950 .45 LIGHT TARGET DA REVOLVER
Similar to 1950 Model Target except w/lighter bbl. Note: Lighter profile was not well received. (Only 2768 produced)

Model 26 (.45 ACP or .45 Auto Rim
w/6.5-inch bbl.). . . . . NiB $814 Ex $701 Gd $304
Model 26 (.45 LC, < 200 produced) . . . . NiB $2412 Ex $2072 Gd $883
W/4- or 5-inch bbl., add. 25%

MODEL 27 .357 MAGNUM DA
Caliber: .357 Magnum. Six-round cylinder, bbl. lengths: 3.5-, 4-, 5-, 6-, 6.5-and 8.38-inches, 11.38 inches overall (with 6-inch bbl.). Weight: 44 oz. (with 6-inch bbl.). Adj. target sights, Baughman quick-draw ramp front sight on 3.5-inch bbl., Blued or nickel finish. Checkered walnut grips. Made 1935-94. Note: Until 1938, the .357 Magnum was custom made in any barrel length from 3.5-inch to 8.75-inch. Each of these revolvers was accompanied by a registration certificate and has its registration number stamped on the inside of the yoke. Postwar magnums have a redesigned hammer w/shortened fall and the new S&W micrometer click rear sight.

Prewar registered model
(Reg number on yoke) . . . . NiB $1311 Ex $1055 Gd $727
Prewar model without registration number . . . NiB $414 Ex $332 Gd $234
Early model w/pinned bbl., recessed cyl.. . . . . NiB $454 Ex $363 Gd $255
Late model w/8.38-inch bbl. . . . . NiB $423 Ex $340 Gd $242
Late model, w/3.5-5-inch bbl. . . . . NiB $461 Ex $399 Gd $270
Late model, other bbl. lengths. . . . . NiB $461 Ex $399 Gd $270

MODEL 28 HIGHWAY PATROLMAN
Caliber: .357 Magnum. Six-round cylinder, bbl. lengths: 4- or 6-inches, 11.25 inches overall (with 6-inch bbl.). Weight: 44 oz. (with 6-inch bbl.). Adj.rear sight, ramp front. Blued finish. Checkered walnut grips, Magna or target type. Made 1954-86.

Prewar registered model
(reg number on yoke) . . . . NiB $1311 Ex $1055 Gd $727
Prewar model without registration number . . . NiB $925 Ex $746 Gd $517
Early model w/pinned bbl.,
recessed cylinder, 5-screws . . . . NiB $383 Ex $335 Gd $275
Late model, all bbl. lengths . . . . NiB $299 Ex $263 Gd $217

MODEL 29 .44 MAGNUM DA REVOLVER
Caliber: .44 Magnum. Six-round cylinder. bbl., lengths: 4-, 5-, 6.5-, 8.38-inches. 11.88 inches overall (with 6.5-inch bbl.). Weight: 47 oz. (with 6.5-inch bbl.). Click adj. rear sight, ramp front. Blued or nickel finish. Checkered Goncalo Alves target grips. Made 1956-98.

Early Production Standard Series (disc. 1983)
3-Screw model (1962-83) . . . . NiB $697 Ex $594 Gd $337
4-Screw model (1957-61) . . . . NiB $744 Ex $697 Gd $466
5-Screw model (1956-57) . . . . NiB $961 Ex $775 Gd $536
W/5-inch bbl., 3- or 4-screw models, add 95%

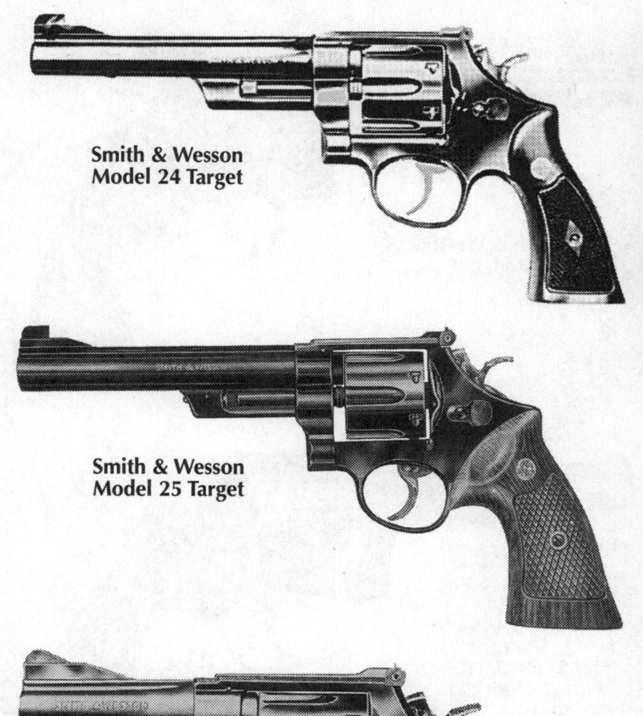
Smith & Wesson Model 24 Target

Smith & Wesson Model 25 Target

Smith & Wesson Model 27

Smith & Wesson Model 28

(cont'd) **MODEL 29 .44 MAGNUM DA REVOLVER**
Late Production standard series (disc. 1998)
Model 29 (w/4- or 6.5-inch bbl.) . . . . NiB $469 Ex $380 Gd $267
Model 29 (w/3-inch bbl., Lew Horton Special) . . NiB $463 Ex $385 Gd $329
Model 29 (w/8.38-inch bbl.) . . . . NiB $522 Ex $419 Gd $332
Model 29 Classic (w/5- or 6.5-inch bbl.) . . . . . NiB $514 Ex $411 Gd $303
Model 29 Classic (w/8.38-inch bbl.). . . . . NiB $522 Ex $425 Gd $332
Model 29 Classic DX (w/6.5-inch bbl.). . . . . . . NiB $669 Ex $566 Gd $334
Model 29 Classic DX (w/8.38-inch bbl.) . . . . . NiB $677 Ex $574 Gd $342
Model 29 Magna Classic (w/7.5-inch ported bbl.)
. . . . . NiB $904 Ex $776 Gd $436
Model 29 Silhouette (w/10.63-inch bbl.) . . . . . NiB $595 Ex $518 Gd $336

Smith & Wesson
Model 29

Smith & Wesson
Model 31

Smith & Wesson
Model 32

Smith & Wesson
Model 34

MODEL 30 .32 HAND EJECTOR DA REVOLVER . . . . NiB $319 Ex $278 Gd $190
Caliber: .32 S&W Long. Six-round cylinder, bbl. lengths: 2- (intro. 1949), 3-, 4- and 6-inches, 8 inches overall (with 4-inch bbl.). Weight: 18 oz. (with 4-inch bbl.). Fixed sights. Blued or nickel finish. Round, checkered walnut or hard rubber grips. Made 1903-76.

MODELS 31 & 33 REGULATION POLICE DA REVOLVER
Same basic type as .32 Hand Ejector except has square buttgrips. Calibers: .32 S&W Long (Model 31) .38 S&W (Model 33). Six-round cylinder in .32 cal., 5-round in .38 caliber. Bbl., lengths: 2- (intro. 1949), 3-, 4- and 6-inches in .32 cal., 4-inch only in .38 cal., 8.5 inches overall (with 4-inch bbl.). Weight: 18 oz. (.38 cal. w/4-inch bbl.), 18.75 oz. (.32 cal. w/4-inch bbl.). Fixed sights. Blued or nickel finish. Checkered walnut grips. Made from 1917. Model 33 disc. in 1974; Model 31 disc. in 1992.
Model 31 . . . . NiB $309 Ex $252 Gd $190
Model 33 . . . . NiB $345 Ex $293 Gd $190

.32 DOUBLE-ACTION REVOLVER . . . . NiB $454 Ex $407 Gd $165
Hinged frame. Caliber: .32 S&W. Five-round cylinder, bbl. lengths: 3-, 3.5- and 6-inches. Fixed sights. Blued or nickel finish. Hard rubber grips. Made from 1880-1919. Note: Value shown applies generally to the several varieties. Exception is the rare first issue of 1880 (identified by squared sideplate and serial no. 1 to 30) valued up to $2,500.

MODEL .32 TERRIER DA . . . . NiB $356 Ex $243 Gd $145
Caliber: .38 S&W. Five-round cylinder, 2-inch bbl., 6.25 inches overall. Weight: 17 oz. Fixed sights. Blued or nickel finish. Checkered walnut or hard rubber grips. Built on .32 Hand Ejector frame. Made 1936-74.

.32-20 MILITARY & POLICE DA . . .NiB $418 Ex $289 Gd $222
Same as M & P 38 except chambered for .32-20 Winchester cartridge. First intro. in the 1899 model, M & P revolvers were produced in this caliber until about 1940. Values same as M & P .38 models.

MODEL 34 1953 .22/.32 KIT GUN. . . . . NiB $321 Ex $254 Gd $192
Same general specifications as previous .22/.32 Kit Gun except w/2-inch or 4-inch bbl. and round or square grips, blued or nickel finish. Made 1936-91.

MODEL 35 1953 .22/.32 TARGET. . . . . NiB $456 Ex $327 Gd $224
Same general specifications as previous model .22/.32 Target except has micrometer-click rear sight. Magna type target grips. Weight: 25 oz. Made 1953-74.

MODEL 36 CHIEFS SPECIAL DA
Based on .32 Hand Ejector w/frame lengthened to permit longer cylinder for .38 Special cartridge. Caliber: .38 Special. Five-round cylinder, bbl. lengths: 2- or 3-inches, 6.5 inches overall (with 2-inch bbl.). Weight: 19 oz. Fixed sights. Blued or nickel finish. Checkered walnut grips, round or square butt. Made 1952 to date.
Blued model . . . . NiB $319 Ex $252 Gd $175
Nickel model. . . . . NiB $327 Ex $264 Gd $187
Early model (5-screw, small trigger guard, SN 1-2500) . . . . NiB $397 Ex $321 Gd $217

MODEL 37 AIRWEIGHT CHIEFS SPECIAL .... **NiB $440 Ex $312 Gd $209**
Same general specifications as standard Chiefs Special except has light alloy frame, weight: 12.5 oz. w/2-inch bbl., blued finish only. Made 1954 to date.

MODEL 38 BODYGUARD AIRWEIGHT DA REVOLVER
Shrouded hammer. Light alloy frame. Caliber: .38 Special. Five-round cylinder, 2- or 3-inch bbl., 6.38 inches overall (w/2-inch bbl). Weight: 14.5 oz. Fixed sights. Blued or nickel finish. Checkered walnut grips. Made 1955-98.
Blued model .... **NiB $375 Ex $283 Gd $190**
Nickel model .... **NiB $391 Ex $298 Gd $206**
Early model (pinned & recessed, pre-1981) .... **NiB $337 Ex $272 Gd $190**

.38 DA REVOLVER .... **NiB $535 Ex $380 Gd $221**
Hinged frame. Caliber: .38 S&W. Five-round cylinder, bbl. lengths: 4-, 4.25-, 5-, 6-, 8- and 10-inch. Fixed sights. Blued or nickel finish. Hard rubber grips. Made 1880-1911. Note: Value shown applies generally to the several varieties. Exceptions are the first issue of 1880 (identified by squared sideplate and serial no. 1 to 4,000) and the 8- and 10-inch bbl. models of the third issue (1884-95).

MODEL .38 HAND EJECTOR DA
Military & Police — First Model. Resembles Colt New Navy in general appearance, lacks bbl., lug and locking bolt common to all later S&W hand ejector models. Caliber: .38 Long Colt. Six-round cylinder, bbl. lengths: 4-, 5-, 6- and 6.5-inch, 11.5 inches overall (with 6.5-inch bbl.). Fixed sights. Blued or nickel finish. Round, checkered walnut or hard rubber grips. Made 1899-1902.
Standard model (civilian issue) .... **NiB $696 Ex $593 Gd $238**
Army Model (marked U.S. Army Model, 1000 issued) ..... **NiB $1990 Ex $1681 Gd $677**
Navy Model (marked USN, 1000 issued) .... **NiB $1472 Ex $1678 Gd $674**

.38 MILITARY & POLICE TARGET DA .... **NiB $639 Ex $484 Gd $237**
Target version of the Military & Police w/standard features of that model. Caliber: .38 Special, six-inch bbl. Weight: 32.25 oz. Adj. target sights. Blued finish. Checkered walnut grips. Made 1899-1940. For values, add $175 for corresponding M&P 38 models.

MODEL .38 PERFECTED DA ...... **NiB $845 Ex $536 Gd $227**
Hinged frame. Similar to earlier .38 DA Model but heavier frame, side latch as in solid-frame models, improved lockwork. Caliber: .38 S&W. Five-round cylinder, bbl. lengths: 3.25, 4, 5 and 6 inches. Fixed sights. Blued or nickel finish. Hard rubber grips. Made 1909-20.

MODEL .40 CENTENNIAL DA HAMMERLESS REVOLVER ..... **NiB $503 Ex $452 Gd $282**
Similar to Chiefs Special but has Safety Hammerless-type mechanism w/grip safety. Two-inch bbl. Weight: 19 oz. Made 1953-74.

MODEL 42 CENTENNIAL AIRWEIGHT
Same as standard Centennial model except has light alloy frame, weight: 13 oz. Made 1954-74.
Blued model .... **NiB $507 Ex $456 Gd $286**
Nickel model .... **NiB $1054 Ex $1002 Gd $590**

MODEL 43 1955 .22/.32 KIT GUN AIRWEIGHT .... **NiB $456 Ex $378 Gd $209**
Same as Model 34 Kit Gun except has light alloy frame, square grip. Furnished w/3.5-inch bbl., weight: 14.25 oz. Made 1954-74.

Smith & Wesson Model 36

Smith & Wesson Model 37

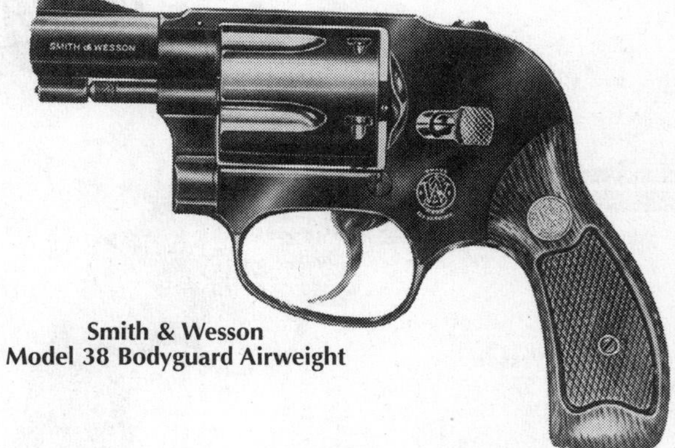
Smith & Wesson Model 38 Bodyguard Airweight

MODEL 44 1926 MILITARY DA REVOLVER
Same as the early New Century model with extractor rod casing but lacking the "Triple Lock" feature. Caliber: .44 S&W Special. Six-round cylinder, bbl. lengths: 4, 5 and 6.5 inches, 11.75 inches overall (with 6.5-inch bbl.). Weight: 39.5 oz. (with 6.5-inch bbl.). Fixed sights. Blued or nickel finish. Checkered walnut grips. Made 1926-41.
Standard model .... **NiB $922 Ex $743 Gd $514**
Target model w/6.5-inch bbl., target sights, blued .... **NiB $3836 Ex $3076 Gd $2104**

.44 AND .38 DA REVOLVERS
Also called Wesson Favorite (lightweight model), Frontier (caliber .44-40). Hinged frame. Six-round cylinder. Calibers: .44 S&W Russian, .38-40, .44-40. Bbl. lengths: 4-, 5-, 6- and 6.5-inch. Weight: 37.5 oz. (with 6.5-inch bbl.). Fixed sights. Blued or nickel finish. Hard rubber grips. Made 1881-1913, Frontier disc. 1910.
Standard model, .44 Russian ... **NiB $4702 Ex $2024 Gd $767**
Standard model, .38-40 .... **NiB $4702 Ex $2024 Gd $767**
Frontier model .... **NiB $4702 Ex $2024 Gd $767**
Favorite model .... **NiB $10,300 Ex $8240 Gd $2884**

Smith & Wesson
Model 48

Smith & Wesson
Model 49 Bodyguard

Smith & Wesson
Model 57

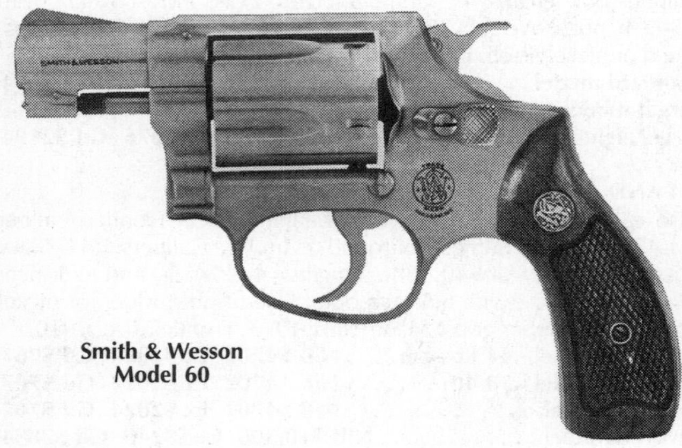
Smith & Wesson
Model 60

Smith & Wesson
Model 63

Smith & Wesson
Model 64

.44 HAND EJECTOR MODEL DA REVOLVER
First Model, New Century, also called "Triple Lock" because of its third cylinder lock at the crane. Six-round cylinder. Calibers: .44 S&W Special, .450 Eley, .455 Mark II. Bbl. lengths: 4-, 5-, 6.5- and 7.5-inch. Weight: 39 oz. (with 6.5-inch bbl.). Fixed sights. Blued or nickel finish. Checkered walnut grips. Made 1907-66.
Second Model is basically the same as New Century except crane lock ("Triple Lock" feature) and extractor rod casing eliminated. Calibers: .44 S&W Special .44-40 Win. .45 Colt. Bbl. lengths: 4-, 5-, 6.5- and 7.5-inch; 11.75 inches overall (with 6.5-inch bbl.). Weight: 38 oz. (with 6.5-inch bbl.). Fixed sights. Blued or nickel finish. Checkered walnut grips. Made 1915-37.
First Model series w/triple lock (1907-15)
Standard model,
.44 S&W Special . . . . NiB $2390 Ex $1978 Gd $912
Standard model w/
special calibers . . . . NiB $2390 Ex $1978 Gd $922
British 455
Target model . . . . NiB $3346 Ex $3088 Gd $709
Second Model series w/o triple lock (1915-37)
Standard model,
.44 S&W Special . . . . NiB $1778 Ex $1598 Gd $763
Standard model
w/special calibers . . . . NiB $2370 Ex $1958 Gd $892
Third Model series (see S&W Model .44/1926)
Fourth Model series (see S&W Model .44/1950)

.44 HAND EJECTOR,
SECOND MODEL
DA REVOLVER. . . . . NiB $716 Ex $634 Gd $320
Basically the same as New Century except crane lock ("Triple Lock" feature) and extractor rod casing eliminated. Calibers: .44 S&W Special .44-40 Win. .45 Colt. Bbl. lengths: 4-, 5-, 6.5- and 7.5-inches, 11.75 inches overall (with 6.5-inch bbl.). Weight: .38 oz. (with 6.5-inch bbl.). Fixed sights. Blued or nickel finish. Checkered walnut grips. Made 1915-37.

MODEL 48 (K-.22) MASTERPIECE M.R.F. DA REVOLVER
Caliber: .22 Mag. and .22 RF. Six-round cylinder, bbl. lengths: 4, 6 and 8.38 inches, 11.13 inches overall (w/ 6-inch bbl.). Weight: 39 oz. Adj. rear sight, ramp front. Made 1959-86.
Model 48 (4- or 6-inch bbl.) . . . . . . NiB $295 Ex $267 Gd $192
Model 48 (8.38-inch bbl.) . . . . NiB $331 Ex $311 Gd $208
W/target options TH & TT, add $50

MODEL 49 BODYGUARD
Same as Model 38 Bodyguard Airweight except has steel frame, weight: 20.5 oz. Made 1959-96.
Blued model . . . . NiB $321 Ex $280 Gd $177
Nickel model. . . . . NiB $347 Ex $306 Gd $203

MODEL 51 1960 .22/.32 KIT GUN . . . . . . NiB $432 Ex $380 Gd $252
Same as Model 34 Kit Gun except chambered for .22 WMR 3.5-inch bbl., weight: 24 oz. Made 1960-74.

MODEL 53 .22 MAGNUM DA
Caliber: .22 Rem. Jet C.F. Magnum. Six-round cylinder (inserts permit use of .22 Short, Long, or LR cartridges). Bbl. lengths: 4, 6, 8.38 inches, 11.25 inches overall (with 6-inch bbl.). Weight: 40 oz. (with 6-inch bbl.). Micrometer-click rear sight ramp front. Checkered walnut grips. Made 1960-74.
Model 53 (4- or 6-inch bbl.) . . . . . . NiB $781 Ex $693 Gd $431
Model 53 (8.38-inch bbl.) . . . . NiB $802 Ex $724 Gd $441
W/target options TH & TT, add $35

MODEL 57 41 MAGNUM DA REVOLVER
Caliber: 41 Magnum. Six-round cylinder, bbl. lengths: 4-, 6-, 8.38-inch. Weight: 40 oz. (with 6-inch bbl.). Micrometer click rear sight, ramp front. Target grips of checkered Goncalo Alves. Made 1964-93.
Model 57 (w/4- or 6-inch bbl.) . . . . NiB $376 Ex $279 Gd $196
Model 57 (w/8.63-inch bbl.). . . . . NiB $397 Ex $299 Gd $217
Model 57 (w/pinned bbl., recessed cylinder), add 10%

MODEL 58 41 MILITARY
& POLICE DA REVOLVER . . . . NiB $526 Ex $476 Gd $320
Caliber: 41 Magnum. Six-round cylinder, 4-inch bbl. 9.25 inches overall. Weight: 41 oz. Fixed sights. Checkered walnut grips. Made 1964-82.

MODEL 60 STAINLESS DA
Caliber: .38 Special or .357 Magnum. Five-round cylinder, bbl. lengths: 2, 2.1 or 3 inches, 6.5 or 7.5 inches overall. Weight: 19 to 23 oz. Square-notch rear sight, ramp front. Satin finish stainless steel. Made 1965-96 (.38 Special) and 1996 to date .357/.38).
.38 Special (disc. 1996). . . . . NiB $382 Ex $279 Gd $218
.357 Mag. . . . . NiB $434 Ex $326 Gd $238
Lady Smith (W/smaller grip) . . . . . . NiB $465 Ex $316 Gd $243

MODEL 63 (1977) KIT GUN DA . . . . NiB $398 Ex $274 Gd $223
Caliber: .22 LR. Six-round cylinder, 2- or 4-inch bbl., 6.5 or 8.5 inches overall. Weight: 19 to 24.5 oz. Adj. rear sight, ramp front. Stainless steel. Checkered walnut or synthetic grips.

MODEL 64 .38 M&P STAINLESS. . . . . NiB $424 Ex $295 Gd $228
Same as standard Model 10 except satin-finished stainless steel, square butt w/4-inch heavy bbl., or round butt w/2-inch bbl. Made 1970 to date.

MODEL 65 .357 MILITARY/POLICE STAINLESS
Same as Model 13 except satin-finished stainless steel. Made 1974 to date.
Model 65 M&P. . . . . NiB $429 Ex $279 Gd $233
Model 65 Lady Smith (W/smaller grip) . . . . . . NiB $465 Ex $331 Gd $254

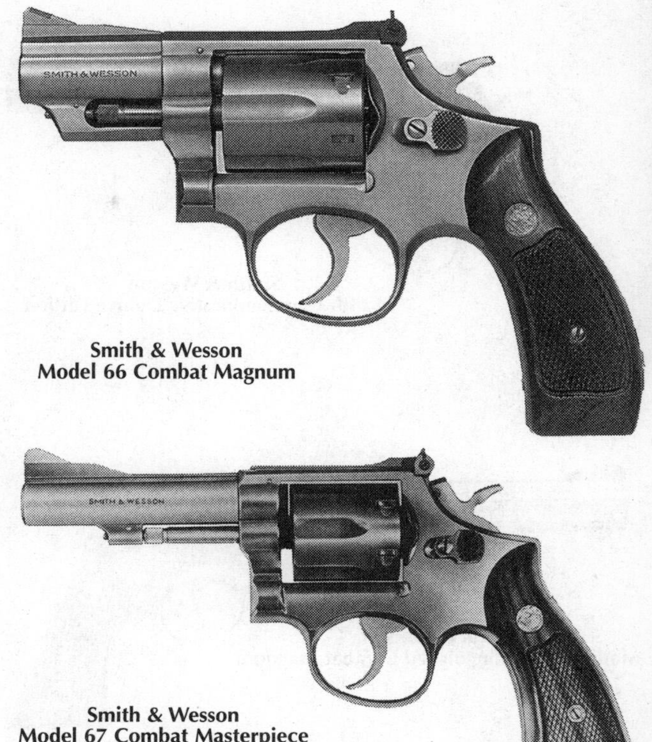

Smith & Wesson
Model 66 Combat Magnum

Smith & Wesson
Model 67 Combat Masterpiece

MODEL 66 .357 COMBAT MAGNUM STAINLESS
Same as Model 19 except satin-finished stainless steel. Made 1971 to date.
Model 66 (2.5-inch bbl.) . . . . NiB $497 Ex $353 Gd $245
Model 66 (3-inch bbl.) . . . . NiB $485 Ex $341 Gd $254
Model 66 (4-inch bbl.) . . . . NiB $485 Ex $341 Gd $254
Model 66 (6-inch bbl.) . . . . NiB $506 Ex $433 Gd $284
W/target options TH & TT, add $48

MODEL 67 .38 COMBAT
MASTERPIECE STAINLESS . . . . NiB $491 Ex $341 Gd $254
Same as Model 15 except satin-finished stainless steel available only w/4-inch bbl. Made 1972-88 and 1991 to date.

MODEL 68 .38 COMBAT
MASTERPIECE STAINLESS . . . . NiB $802 Ex $674 Gd $540
Same as Model 66 except w/4- or 6-inch bbl., chambered for .38 Special. Made to accommodate CA Highway Patrol because they were not authorized to carry .357 magnums. Made 1976-83. (7500 produced)

125th Anniversary Commemorative
Issued to celebrate the 125th anniversary of the 1852 partnership of Horace Smith and Daniel Baird Wesson. Standard Edition is Model 25 revolver in .45 Colt w/6.5-inch bbl., bright blued finish, gold-filled bbl., roll mark "Smith & Wesson 125th Anniversary," sideplate marked w/gold-filled Anniversary seal, smooth Goncalo Alves grips, in presentation case w/nickel silver Anniversary medallion and book, "125 Years w/Smith & Wesson," by Roy Jinks. Deluxe Edition is same except revolver is Class A engraved w/gold-filled seal on sideplate, ivory grips, Anniversary medallion is sterling silver and book is leather bound. Limited to 50 units. Total issue is 10,000 units, of which 50 are Deluxe Edition and two are a Custom Deluxe Edition and not for sale. Made in 1977.
Standard edition . . . . NiB $796 Ex $643 Gd $447
Deluxe edition. . . . . NiB $2228 Ex $1791 Gd $1213

Smith & Wesson
125th Commemorative Deluxe Edition

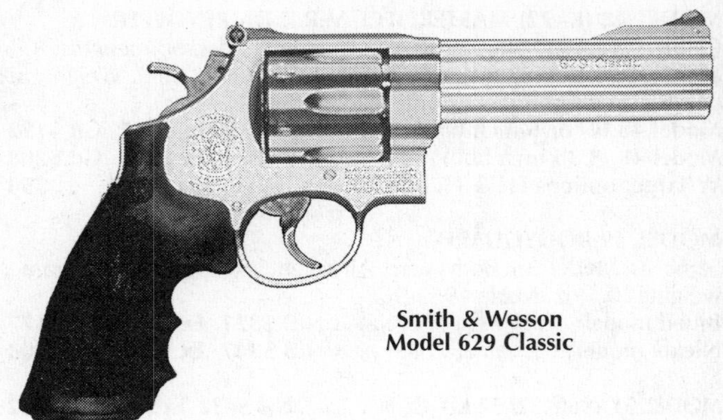
Smith & Wesson
Model 629 Classic

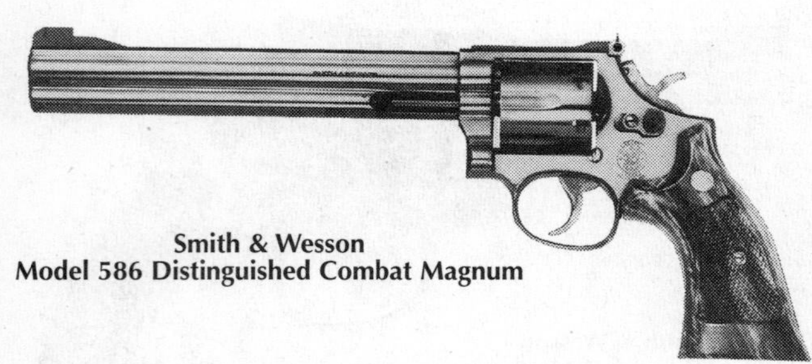
Smith & Wesson
Model 586 Distinguished Combat Magnum

Smith & Wesson
Model 625

Smith & Wesson
Model 629

317 AIRLITE DA REVOLVER
Caliber: .22 LR. Eight-round cylinder, 1.88- or 3-inch bbl., 6.3 or 7.2 inches overall. Weight: 9.9 oz. or 11 oz. Ramp front sight, notched frame rear. Aluminum, carbon fiber, stainless and titanium construction. Brushed aluminum finish. Synthetic or Dymondwood grips. Made 1997 to date.
Model 317
(w/1.88-inch bbl.) . . . . NiB $462 Ex $333 Gd $251
Model 317
(w/3-inch bbl.) . . . . NiB $462 Ex $333 Gd $251
Model 317
(w/Dymondwood grips), add. $68

MODEL 520
DA REVOLVER. . . . . NiB $353 Ex $301 Gd $147
Caliber: .357 Mag. Six-round cylinder. N-Frame w/4-inch bbl. Weight: 40 oz. Fixed sights. In 1980, 3000 were made for the N.Y. State Police, but that agency did not purchase those firearms. (Sold commercially).

MODEL 547
DA REVOLVER. . . . . NiB $322 Ex $291 Gd $209
Caliber: 9mm. Six-round cylinder, bbl. length: 3 or 4 inches, 7.31 inches overall. Weight: 32 oz. Square-notch rear sight, ramp front. Disc. 1986.

MODEL 581 REVOLVER
Caliber: .357 Magnum. Bbl. lengths: 4 inches, weight: 34 oz. Serrated ramp front sight, square notch rear. Checkered walnut grips. Made 1985-92.
Blued finish . . . . NiB $295 Ex $244 Gd $177
Nickel finish . . . . NiB $316 Ex $267 Gd $197

MODEL 586 DISTINGUISHED COMBAT MAGNUM
Caliber: .357 Magnum. Six-round cylinder, bbl. lengths: 4, 6 and 8.38 inches, overall length: 9.75 inches (with 4-inch bbl.). Weight: 42, 46, 53 oz., respectively. Red ramp front sight, micrometer-click adj. rear. Checkered grip. Blued or nickel finish. Made 1980-99.
Model 586
(w/4- or 6-inch bbl.) . . . . NiB $398 Ex $311 Gd $208
Model 586
(w/8.63-inch bbl.) . . . . NiB $421 Ex $333 Gd $230
Model 586 (w/adjustable
front sight), add. $35
Model 586
(w/nickel finish), add. $45

MODEL 610 DA REVOLVER . . . . . . NiB $681 Ex $537 Gd $429
Similar to Model 625 except in caliber 10mm. Magna classic grips. Made 1990-91 and 1998 to date.

MODEL 617 DA REVOLVER
Similar to Model 17 except in stainless. Made 1990 to date.
Semi-target model w/4- or 6-inch bbl. . . . . NiB $504 Ex $350 Gd $252
Target model w/6-inch bbl. . . . . NiB $504 Ex $350 Gd $252
Target model w/8.38-inch bbl. . . . . NiB $504 Ex $350 Gd $252
W/10-round cylinder, add $94

MODEL 624 DOUBLE-ACTION REVOLVER
Same general specifications as Model 24 except satin finished stainless steel. Limited production of 10,000. Made 1985-86.
Model 624 w/4-inch bbl. . . . . NiB $368 Ex $275 Gd $250
Model 624 w/6.5-inch bbl. . . . . NiB $393 Ex $290 Gd $264
Model 624 w/3-inch bbl., round butt (Lew Horton spec.) . . . . NiB $425 Ex $378 Gd $425

MODEL 625 DA REVOLVER . . . . . . NiB $514 Ex $370 Gd $262
Same general specifications as Model 25 except 3-, 4- or 5-inch bbl., round-butt Pachmayr grips and satin stainless steel finish. Made 1989 to date.

MODEL 627 DA REVOLVER . . . . . . NiB $514 Ex $370 Gd $262
Same general specifications as Model 27 except satin stainless steel finish. Made 1989-91.

MODEL 629 DA REVOLVER
Same as Model 29 in .44 Magnum except in stainless steel. Classic made 1990 to date.
Model 629 (3-inch bbl., Backpacker) . . . . NiB $613 Ex $480 Gd $357
Model 629 (4- and 6-inch bbl.) . . . . NiB $637 Ex $503 Gd $377
Model 629 (8.38-inch bbl.) . . . . NiB $653 Ex $499 Gd $396
Model 629 Classic (5- and 6.5-inch bbl.) . . . . . NiB $640 Ex $491 Gd $377
Model 629 Classic (8.38-inch bbl.) . . . . NiB $666 Ex $516 Gd $403
Model 629 Classic DX (6.5-inch bbl.) . . . . NiB $841 Ex $676 Gd $547
Model 629 Classic DX (8.38-inch bbl.) . . . . . . NiB $874 Ex $709 Gd $580
Model 629 Magna Classic (w/7.5-inch ported bbl.) . . . . NiB $1020 Ex $820 Gd $565

MODEL 631 DA REVOLVER
Similar to Model 31 except chambered for .32 H&R Mag. Goncalo Alves combat grips. Made 1991-92.
Fixed sights, 2-inch bbl. . . . . NiB $370 Ex $303 Gd $226
Adjustable sights, 4-inch bbl. . . . . NiB $374 Ex $303 Gd $213
Lady Smith, 2-inch bbl. NiB $396 Ex $324 Gd $252
Lady Smith, 2-inch bbl. (black stainless). . . . . . NiB $400 Ex $324 Gd $227

MODEL 632 CENTENNIAL DA
Same general specifications as Model 640 except chambered for .32 H&R Mag. 2- or 3-inch bbl., weight: 15.5 oz. Stainless slide w/alloy frame. Fixed sights. Santoprene combat grips. Made in 1991-92.
Model 632 w/2-inch bbl. . . . . NiB $344 Ex $267 Gd $221
Model 632 w/3-inch bbl. . . . . NiB $344 Ex $267 Gd $221

MODEL 637 CHIEFS SPECIAL AIRWEIGHT DA . . . . NiB $437 Ex $303 Gd $236
Same general specifications as Model 37 except w/clear anodized fuse alloy frame and stainless cylinder. 560 made in 1991 and reintroduced in 1996.

MODEL 638 BODYGUARD AIRWEIGHT DA . . . . NiB $453 Ex $329 Gd $257
Same general specifications as Model .38 except w/clear anodized fuse alloy frame and stainless cylinder. 1200 made in 1989 and reintroduced in 1998.

MODEL 640 CENTENNIAL DA . . . . NiB $453 Ex $209 Gd $257
Caliber: .38 Special. Five-round cylinder, 2, 2.1 or 3-inch bbl., 6.31 inches overall. Weight: 20-22 oz. Fixed sights. Stainless finish. Smooth hardwood service grips. Made 1990 to date.

Smith & Wesson
Model 640

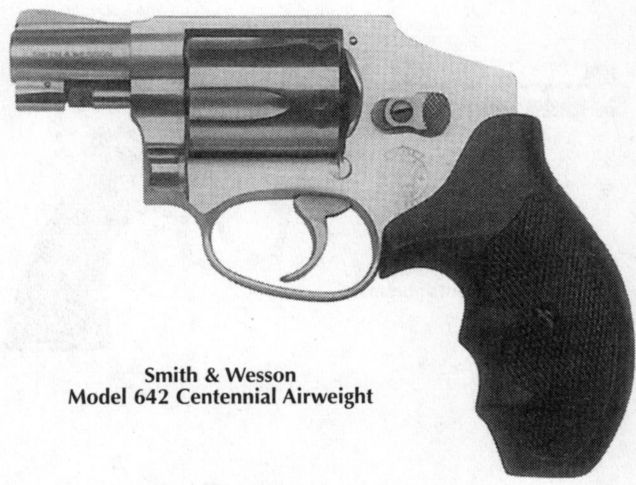
Smith & Wesson
Model 642 Centennial Airweight

MODEL 642 CENTENNIAL AIRWEIGHT DA REVOLVER
Same general specifications as Model 640 except w/stainless steel/aluminum alloy frame and finish. Weight 15.8 oz. Santoprene combat grips. Made 1990-93 and reintroduced 1996.
Model 642 Centennial . . . . NiB $453 Ex $329 Gd $247
Model 642 Lady Smith (W/smaller grip). . . . . NiB $453 Ex $329 Gd $247

MODEL 648 DA REVOLVER. . . . . NiB $380 Ex $277 Gd $221
Same general specifications as Models 17/617 except in stainless and chambered for .22 Mag. Made 1990-93.

MODEL 649 BODYGUARD DA. . . . . NiB $478 Ex $329 Gd $247
Caliber: .38 Special. Five-round cylinder, bbl. length: 2 inches, 6.25 inches overall. Weight: 20 oz. Square-notch rear sight ramp front. Stainless frame and finish. Made 1986 to date.

MODEL 650 REVOLVER. . . . . NiB $271 Ex $220 Gd $210
Caliber: .22 Mag. Six-round cylinder, 3-inch bbl., 7 inches overall. Weight: 23.5 oz. Serrated ramp front sight, fixed square-notch rear. Round butt, checkered walnut monogrammed grips. Stainless steel finish. Made 1983-86.

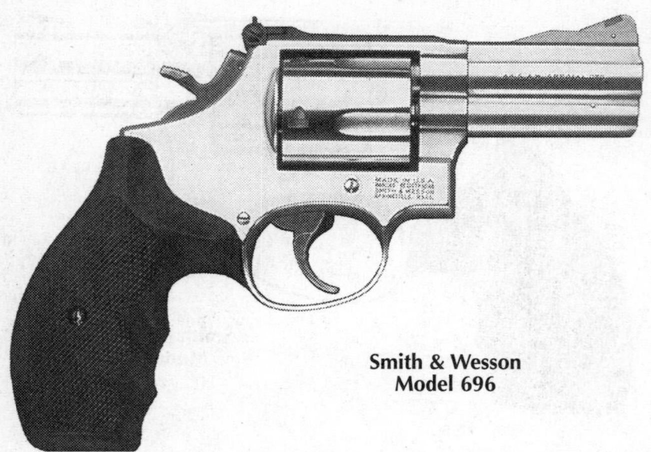

Smith & Wesson
Model 696

MODEL 651 STAINLESS DA

Caliber: .22 Mag. Rimfire. Six-round cylinder, bbl. length: 3 and 4 inches, 7 and 8.63 inches, respectively, overall. Weight: 24.5 oz. Adj. rear sight, ramp front. Made 1983-87 and 1990-98. Note: Optional .22 LR cylinder available during early production.

Model 651 w/3- or 4-inch bbl. . . . . NiB $382 Ex $273 Gd $212
Model 651 w/extra cylinder . . . . . . NiB $588 Ex $505 Gd $402

MODEL 657 REVOLVER

Caliber: 41 Mag. Six-round cylinder. Bbl. lengths: 4, 6 or 8.4 inches; 9.6, 11.4, and 13.9 inches overall. Weight: 44.2, 48 and 52.5 oz. Serrated black ramp front sight on ramp base click rear, adj. for windage and elevation. Satin finished stainless steel. Made 1986 to date.

W/4- or 6-inch bbl. . . . . NiB $571 Ex $406 Gd $319
W/8.4-inch bbl. . . . . NiB $588 Ex $424 Gd $336

MODEL 681 . . . . NiB $346 Ex $254 Gd $217

Same as S&W Model 581 except in stainless finish only. Made 1991-93.

MODEL 686

Same as S&W Model 586 Distinguished Combat Magnum except in stainless finish w/additional 2.5-inch bbl. Made 1991 to date.

Model 686 (w/2.5-inch bbl.) . . . . NiB $509 Ex $380 Gd $350
Model 686 (w/4- or 6-inch bbl.) . . . . NiB $535 Ex $406 Gd $375
Model 686 (w/8.63-inch bbl.) . . . . NiB $566 Ex $437 Gd $427
Model 686 (w/adjustable front sight), add. $35

Smith & Wesson
Model K-22 Outdoorsman

MODEL 686 PLUS

Same as standard Model 686 Magnum except w/7-round cylinder and 2.5-, 4- or 6-inch bbl. Made 1996 to date.

Model 686 Plus (w/2.5-inch bbl.) . . . . NiB $525 Ex $360 Gd $277
Model 686 Plus (w/4-inch bbl.) . . . . NiB $547 Ex $383 Gd $298
Model 686 Plus (w/6-inch bbl.) . . . . NiB $438 Ex $355 Gd $248

MODEL 696 . . . . NiB $520 Ex $344 Gd $277

Caliber: .44 S&W Special. L-Frame w/five-round cylinder, 3-inch shrouded bbl., 8.38 inches overall. Weight: 48 oz. Red ramp front sight, micrometer-click adj. rear. Checkered synthetic grip. Satin stainless steel. Made 1997 to date.

MODEL 940 CENTENNIAL DA . . . . NiB $420 Ex $291 Gd $245

Same general specifications as Model 640 except chambered for 9mm. Two- or 3-inch bbl., Weight: 23-25 oz. Santoprene combat grips. Made 1991 to date.

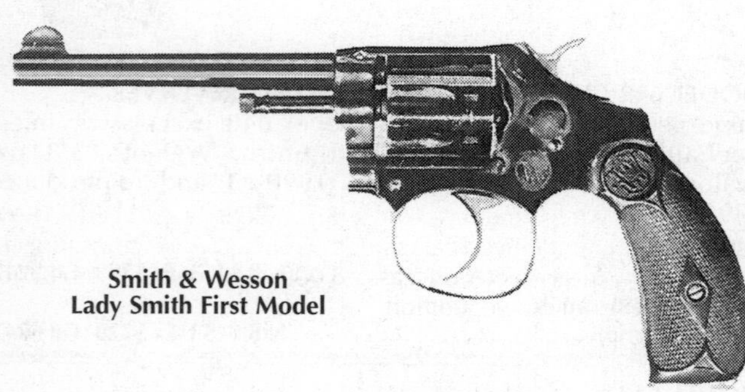

Smith & Wesson
Lady Smith First Model

MODEL 1891 SA REVOLVER

Hinged frame. Caliber: .38 S&W. Five-round cylinder, bbl. lengths: 3.25, 4, 5 and 6-inches. Fixed sights. Blued or nickel finish. Hard rubber grips. Made 1891-1911. Note: Until 1906, an accessory single-shot target bbl. (see Model 1891 Single-Shot Target Pistol) was available for this revolver.

Revolver only. . . . . NiB $2409 Ex $1740 Gd $843
Set w/.22 single-shot bbl. . . . . . NiB $3130 Ex $2100 Gd $1585

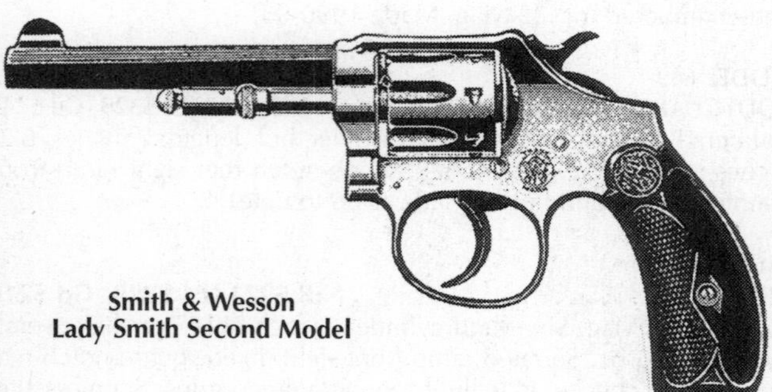

Smith & Wesson
Lady Smith Second Model

1917 ARMY DA REVOLVER

Caliber: .45 Automatic, using 3-cartridge half-moon clip or .45 Auto Rim, without clip. Six-round cylinder, 5.5-inch bbl., 10.75 inches overall. Weight: 36.25 oz. Fixed sights. Blued finish (blue-black finish on commercial model, brush polish on military). Checkered walnut grips (commercial model, smooth on military). Made under U.S. Government contract 1917-19 and produced commercially 1919-1941. Note: About 175,000 of these revolvers were produced during WW I. The DCM sold these to NRA members during the 1930s at $16.15 each.

Commercial model . . . . NiB $693 Ex $539 Gd $318
Military model. . . . . NiB $848 Ex $642 Gd $251

K-22 MASTERPIECE DA........ NiB $1267 Ex $1112 Gd $649
Improved version of K-22 Outdoorsman w/same specifications but w/micrometer-click rear sight, short action and antibacklash trigger. Fewer than 1100 manufactured in 1940.

K-22 OUTDOORSMAN DA....... NiB $612 Ex $535 Gd $314
Design based on the .38 Military & Police Target. Caliber: .22 LR. Six-round cylinder, 11.13 inches overall. Weight: 35 oz. Adj. target sights. Blued finish. Checkered walnut grip. Made 1931-40.

K32 AND K38 HEAVY MASTERPIECES
Same as K32 and K38 Masterpiece but w/heavy bbl. Weight: 38.5 oz. Made 1950-53. Note: All K32 and K38 revolvers made after September 1953 have heavy bbls. and the "Heavy Masterpiece" designation was disc. Values for Heavy Masterpiece models are the same as shown for Models 14 and 16. (See separate listing).

K-32 TARGET DA REVOLVER......... NiB $1420 Ex $1153 Gd $802
Same as .38 Military & Police Target except chambered for .32 S&W Long cartridge, slightly heavier bbl., weight: 34 oz. Only 98 produced. Made 1938-.40.

LADY SMITH (MODEL M HAND EJECTOR) DA REVOLVER
Caliber: .22 LR. Seven-round cylinder, bbl. length: 2.25-, 3-, 3.5- and 6-inch (Third Model only), approximately 7 inches overall w/3.5-inch bbl., weight: About 9.5 oz. Fixed sights, adj. target sights available on Third Model. Blued or nickel finish. Round butt, hard rubber grips on First and Second models; checkered walnut or hard rubber square buttgrips on Third Model. First Model —1902-06: Cylinder locking bolt operated by button on left side of frame, no bbl., lug and front locking bolt. Second Model —1906-11: Rear cylinder latch eliminated, has bbl. lug, forward cylinder lock w/draw-bolt fastening. Third Model —1911-21: Same as Second Model except has square grips, target sights and 6-inch bbl. available. Note: Legend has it that a straight-laced D.B. Wesson ordered discontinuance of the Lady Smith when he learned of the little revolver's reputed popularity w/ladies of the evening. The story, which undoubtedly has enhanced the appeal of this model to collectors, is not true: The Lady Smith was disc. because of difficulty of manufacture and high frequency of repairs.
First model .... NiB $2944 Ex $1914 Gd $508
Second model .... NiB $2120 Ex $1605 Gd $498
Third model, w/fixed sights,
2.25- or 3.5-inch bbl. .... NiB $2120 Ex $1605 Gd $508
Third model, w/fixed sights,
6-inch bbl. .... NiB $2120 Ex $1579 Gd $498
Third model, w/adj. sights,
6-inch bbl. .... NiB $4077 Ex $1698 Gd $776

REGULATION POLICE
DA (I FRAME) .... NiB $645 Ex $522 Gd $366
Calibers: .32 S&W (6-round) or .38 S&W (5-round) built on .32 Hand Ejector frames. Two-, 3-, 3.25-, 4-, 4.25- or 6-inch bbl., weight: 20-24 oz. Fixed sights. Blue or nickel finish. Checkered walnut grips. Made 1917-57. Note: After 1957 "J" Frames replaced the older "I" Frames and designations changed to Model 31 and 33 respectively.
Regulation Police, .32 S&W....... NiB $368 Ex $316 Gd $152
Regulation Police, .38 S&W....... NiB $368 Ex $316 Gd $152

REGULATION POLICE TARGET DA
Target version of the Regulation Police w/standard features of that model. Calibers: .32 S&W Long or .38 S&W. 6-inch bbl., 10.25 inches overall. Weight: 20 oz. Adjustable target sights. Blue or nickel finish. Checkered walnut grips. Made about 1917-57.
Regulation Police Target, .32 S&W .... NiB $705 Ex $603 Gd $294
Regulation Police Target, .38 S&W .... NiB $705 Ex $603 Gd $294

Smith & Wesson
Regulation Police Target

Smith & Wesson
Safety Hammerless

SAFETY HAMMERLESS
REVOLVER .... NiB $1273 Ex $861 Gd $372
Also called New Departure Double Action. Hinged frame. Calibers: .32 S&W, .38 S&W. Five-round cylinder, bbl. lengths: 2, 3- and 3.5-inch (.32 cal.) or 2-, 3.25-, 4-, 5- and 6-inch (.38 cal.); 6.75 inches overall (.32 cal. w/3-inch bbl.) or 7.5 inches (.38 cal. w/3.25-inch bbl.). Weight: 14.25 oz. (.32 cal. w/3-inch bbl.) or 18.25 oz. (.38 cal. 2.5-inch bbl.). Fixed sights. Blued or nickel finish. Hard rubber grips. Made 1888-1937 (.32 cal.); 1887-1941 (.38 cal. w/various minor changes.)

TEXAS RANGER
COMMEMORATIVE............ NiB $1273 Ex $979 Gd $703
Issued to honor the 150th anniversary of the Texas Rangers. Model 19 .357 Combat Magnum w/4-inch bbl., sideplate stamped w/Texas Ranger Commemorative Seal, smooth Goncalo Alves grips. Special Bowie knife in presentation case. 8,000 sets made in 1973. Top value is for set in new condition.

SPHINX ENGINEERING SA. — Porrentruy, Switzerland

MODEL AT-380 DA PISTOL
Caliber: .380 ACP. 10-round magazine, 3.27- inch bbl., 6.03 inches overall. Weight: 25 oz. Stainless steel frame w/blued slide or Palladium finish. Slide latch w/ambidextrous magazine release. Imported 1993-96.
Model AT-380 two-tone
(w/blued slide) .... NiB $471 Ex $409 Gd $307
Model AT-380 N/pall
(w/Palladium finish) .... NiB $543 Ex $482 Gd $380

NOTE: *The AT-88 pistol series was previously manufactured by ITM in Switzerland and imported by Action Arms before Sphinx-Muller resumed production of these firearms, now designated as the AT-2000 series.*

Springfield Armory
1911-A1 Post '90 Series Trophy Model

Springfield Armory
1911-A1 PDP Series Defender

Springfield Armory
1911-A1 Champion

Springfield Armory
1911-A1 Compact

Sphinx
Model AT2000S Scope Optional

MODEL AT2000S DA AUTOMATIC PISTOL

Calibers: 9mm Parabellum, .40 S&W. 15- or 11-round magazine respectively, 4.53-inch bbl., (S-standard), 3.66-inch bbl., (P-compact), 3.34-inch bbl., (H-subcompact), 8.25 inches overall. Weight: 36.5 oz. Fixed sights w/3-dot system. Stainless frame w/blued slide or Palladium finish. Ambidextrous safety. Checkered walnut or neoprene grips. Imported 1993-96.

Model AT2000S (standard) . . . . NiB $1013 Ex $794 Gd $488
Model AT2000P (compact) . . . . NiB $896 Ex $666 Gd $447
Model AT2000H (subcompact) . . . . NiB $896 Ex $666 Gd $447
.40 S&W, add $90
For Palladium finish (disc. 1994). . . . . . NiB $233 Ex $210 Gd $180

MODEL AT2000C/2000CS COMPETITOR

Similar to the Model AT2000S except also chambered for 9x21mm. 10-round magazine, 5.31-inch compensated bbl., 9.84 inches overall. Weight: 40.56 oz. Fully adjustable BoMar or ProPoint sights. Made 1993-96.

Model 2000C (w/BoMar sight) . . . . NiB $1790 Ex $1331 Gd $898
Model 2000CS (w/ProPoint sight). . . . . . NiB $1790 Ex $1331 Gd $898

MODEL AT2000GM/GMS GRAND MASTER

Similar to the AT2000C except single action only w/square trigger guard and extended beavertail grip. Imported 1993-96.

Model 2000GM (w/BoMar sight) . . . . NiB $2323 Ex $1865 Gd $1279
Model 2000GMS (w/ProPoint sight). . . . . . NiB $2450 Ex $1967 Gd $1349

SPRINGFIELD, INC. — Geneseo, Illinois (Formerly Springfield Armory)

MODEL M1911 SERIES AUTO PISTOL

Springfield builds the "PDP" (Personal Defense Pistol) Series based on the self-loading M 1911-A1 pistol (military specifications model) as adopted for a standard service weapon by the U.S. Army. With enhancements and modifications they produce a full line of firearms including Ultra-Compacts, Lightweights, Match Grade and Competition Models. For values see specific models.

MODEL 1911-A1 GOVERNMENT

Calibers: 9mm Para., .38 Super, .40 S&W, 10mm or .45 ACP., 7-, 8-, 9- or 10-round magazine, 4- or 5-inch bbl., 8.5 inches overall. Weight: 36 oz. Fixed combat sights. Blued, Parkerized or Duo-Tone finish. Checkered walnut grips. Note: This is an exact duplicate of the Colt M1911-A1 that was used by the U.S. Armed Forces as a service weapon.

Blued finish . . . . NiB $432 Ex $391 Gd $310
Parkerized finish . . . . NiB $432 Ex $391 Gd $310

MODEL 1911-A1 (PRE '90 SERIES)
Calibers: 9mm Parabellum, .38 Super, 10mm, .45 ACP. Seven-, 8-, 9- or 10-round magazine, bbl. length: 3.63, 4, 4.25 or 5 inches, 8.5 inches overall. Weight: 36 oz. Fixed combat sights. Blued, Duo-Tone or Parkerized finish. Checkered walnut stocks. Made 1985-90.
Government model (blued) . . . . NiB $430 Ex $389 Gd $308
Government model (Parkerized) . . . NiB $430 Ex $389 Gd $308
Bullseye model (wadcutter) . . . . . NiB $1479 Ex $1260 Gd $801
Combat Commander model (blued) . . . NiB $466 Ex $415 Gd $302
Combat Commander model
(Parkerized) . . . . NiB $466 Ex $415 Gd $302
Commander model (blued) . . . . NiB $481 Ex $445 Gd $313
Commander model (Duo-Tone) . . . . NiB $481 Ex $476 Gd $343
Commander model (Parkerized) . . . NiB $481 Ex $445 Gd $313
Compact model (blued) . . . . NiB $512 Ex $476 Gd $308
Compact model (Duo-Tone) . . . . . . NiB $563 Ex $527 Gd $359
Compact model (Parkerized) . . . . . . NiB $481 Ex $445 Gd $277
Defender model (blued) . . . . NiB $547 Ex $501 Gd $343
Defender model (Parkerized) . . . . . NiB $517 Ex $467 Gd $308
Defender model (Custom Carry) . . . NiB $846 Ex $769 Gd $499
National Match model (Hardball) . . NiB $826 Ex $693 Gd $499
Trophy Master (Competition) . . . NiB $1356 Ex $1152 Gd $795
Trophy Master (Distinguished) . . NiB $2070 Ex $1738 Gd $1075
Trophy Master (Competition) . . . NiB $1727 Ex $1509 Gd $938

MODEL 1911-A1 (POST '90 SERIES)
SA linkless operating system w/steel or alloy frame. Calibers: 9mm Parabellum, .38 Super, .40 S&W, 10mm, .45 ACP. Seven-, 8-, 9- or 10-round magazine, bbl. length: 3.63, 4, 4.25 or 5 inches; 8.5 inches overall. Weight: 28 oz. to 36 oz. Fixed combat sights. Blued, Duo-Tone, Parkerized or stainless finish. Checkered composition or walnut stocks. Made 1990 to date.
Mil-Spec model (blued) . . . . NiB $496 Ex $404 Gd $308
Mil-Spec model (Parkerized) . . . . . . NiB $496 Ex $404 Gd $308
Standard model (blued) . . . . NiB $487 Ex $394 Gd $275
Standard model (Parkerized) . . . . . . NiB $685 Ex $532 Gd $379
Standard model (stainless) . . . . NiB $710 Ex $557 Gd $430
Trophy model (blued) . . . . NiB $1019 Ex $820 Gd $463
Trophy model (Duo-Tone) . . . . NiB $999 Ex $831 Gd $474
Trophy model (stainless) . . . . NiB $1061 Ex $893 Gd $536

MODEL 1911-A1 PDP SERIES
PDP Series (Personal Defense Pistol). Calibers: .38 Super, .40 S&W, .45 ACP. Seven-, 8-, 9-, 10-, 13- or 17-round magazine, bbl. length: 4, 5, 5.5 or 5.63 inches, 9 to 11 inches overall w/compensated bbl. Weight: 34.5 oz. to 42.8 oz. Post front sight, adjustable rear w/3-dot system. Blued, Duo-Tone, Parkerized or stainless finish. Checkered composition or walnut stocks. Made 1991 to date.
Defender model (blued) . . . . NiB $897 Ex $780 Gd $489
Defender model (Duo-Tone) . . . . . . NiB $897 Ex $780 Gd $489
Defender model (Parkerized) . . . . . NiB $897 Ex $780 Gd $489
.45 ACP Champion Comp model
(blued) . . . . NiB $769 Ex $570 Gd $361
.45 ACP Compact Comp HC model
(blued) . . . . NiB $855 Ex $764 Gd $520
.38 Sup Factory Comp model
(blued) . . . . NiB $825 Ex $734 Gd $489
.45 ACP Factory Comp model
(blued) . . . . NiB $825 Ex $734 Gd $489
.38 Sup Factory Comp HC model
(blued) . . . . NiB $825 Ex $734 Gd $489
.45 ACP Factory Comp HC model
(blued) . . . . NiB $825 Ex $734 Gd $489

MODEL M1911-A1 CHAMPION
Calibers: .38 ACP, .45 ACP. Six- or 7-round magazine, 4-inch bbl.

Springfield Armory
M1911-A1 Ultra Compact Parkerized

(cont'd) **MODEL M1911-A1 CHAMPION**
Weight: 26.5 to 33.4 oz. Low profile post front sight and drift adjustable rear w/3-dot sighting system. Commander-style hammer and slide. Checkered walnut grips. Blue, Bi-Tone, Parkerized or stainless finish. Made 1992 to date.
.380 ACP standard
(disc. 1995) . . . . NiB $404 Ex $328 Gd $226
.45 ACP Parkerized . . . . NiB $481 Ex $379 Gd $226
.45 ACP blued . . . . NiB $481 Ex $389 Gd $251
.45 ACP Bi-Tone
(B/H Model) . . . . NiB $739 Ex $540 Gd $331
.45 ACP stainless . . . . NiB $744 Ex $535 Gd $433
.45 super tuned . . . . NiB $922 Ex $591 Gd $489

MODEL M1911-A1 COMPACT
Similar to the standard M1911 w/champion length slide on a steel or alloy frame w/a shortened grip. Caliber: .45 ACP. Six- or 7-round magazine (10+ law enforcement only), 4-inch bbl. weight: 26.5 to 32 oz. Low profile sights w/3-dot system. Checkered walnut grips. Matte blue, Duo-Tone or Parkerized finish. Made 1991-96.
Compact Parkerized . . . . NiB $453 Ex $392 Gd $259
Compact blued . . . . NiB $521 Ex $459 Gd $327
Compact Duo-Tone . . . . NiB $453 Ex $392 Gd $259
Compact stainless . . . . NiB $772 Ex $594 Gd $517
Compact comp (ported) . . . . NiB $880 Ex $772 Gd $492
High capacity blue . . . . NiB $584 Ex $446 Gd $370
High capacity stainless . . . . NiB $624 Ex $547 Gd $409

MODEL M1911-A1 ULTRA COMPACT
Similar to M1911 Compact except chambered for .380 ACP or .45 ACP. 6- or 7-round magazine, 3.5-inch bbl., weight: 22 oz. to 30 oz. Matte Blue, Bi-Tone, Parkerized (military specifiactions) or stainless finish. Made 1995 to date. See illustration next page.
.380 ACP Ultra (disc. 1996) . . . . . . NiB $715 Ex $521 Gd $307
.45 ACP Ultra Parkerized . . . . NiB $715 Ex $521 Gd $307
.45 ACP Ultra blued . . . . NiB $715 Ex $521 Gd $307
.45 ACP Ultra Bi-Tone . . . . NiB $827 Ex $634 Gd $419
.45 ACP Ultra stainless . . . . NiB $797 Ex $572 Gd $470
.45 ACP ultra high
capacity Parkerized . . . . NiB $787 Ex $572 Gd $343
.45 ACP ultra high
capacity blue . . . . NiB $787 Ex $572 Gd $343
.45 ACP ultra high
capacity stainless . . . . NiB $797 Ex $572 Gd $470
.45 ACP V10 ultra
comp Parkerized . . . . NiB $741 Ex $532 Gd $317
.45 ACP V10 ultra comp blue . . . . . NiB $741 Ex $532 Gd $317
.45 ACP V10 ultra comp stainless . . NiB $797 Ex $572 Gd $470
.45 ACP V10 ultra super tuned . . . . NiB $980 Ex $827 Gd $470

Springfield Armory
M1911-A1 Ultra Compact Bi-Tone

Springfield Armory
P9 Combat

Springfield Armory
M1911-A1 Ultra Compact Stainless

Springfield Armory Panther

Springfield Armory
M1911-A1 Ultra Compact Super Tuned

FIRECAT
AUTOMATIC PISTOL
Calibers: 9mm, .40 S&W. Eight-round magazine (9mm) or 7-round magazine (.40 S&W), 3.5-inch bbl., 6.5 inches overall. Weight: 25.75 oz. Fixed sights w/3-dot system. Checkered walnut grip. Matte blued finish. Made 1991-93.

9mm . . . . NiB $529 Ex $457 Gd $304
.40 S&W . . . . NiB $529 Ex $457 Gd $304

PANTHER
AUTO PISTOL . . . . NiB $570 Ex $483 Gd $304
Calibers: 9mm, .40 S&W. 15-round magazine (9mm) or 11-round magazine (.40 S&W), 3.8-inch bbl., 7.5 inches overall. Weight: 28.95 oz. Blade front sight, rear adj. for windage w/3-dot system. Checkered walnut grip. Matte blued finish. Made 1991-93.

MODEL P9 DA COMBAT SERIES
Calibers: 9mm, .40 S&W, .45 ACP. Magazine capacity: 15-round (9mm), 11-round (.40 S&W) or 10-round (.45 ACP), 3.66-inch bbl., (Compact and Sub-Compact), or 4.75-inch bbl., (Standard), 7.25 or 8.1 inches overall. Weight: 32 to 35 oz. Fixed sights w/3-dot system. Checkered walnut grip. Matte blued, Parkerized, stainless or Duo-Tone finish. Made 1990-94.

Compact model (9mm,
Parkerized) . . . . NiB $463 Ex $406 Gd $269
Sub-Compact model (9mm,
Parkerized) . . . . NiB $503 Ex $447 Gd $310
Standard model (9mm,
Parkerized) . . . . NiB $483 Ex $406 Gd $269
W/blued finish, add. $25
W/Duo-Tone finish, add $235
W/stainless finish, add. $20
.40 S&W, add. $35
.45 ACP add. $95

MODEL P9 COMPETITION SERIES
Same general specifications as Model P9 except in target configuration w/5-inch bbl., (LSP Ultra) or 5.25-inch bbl. Factory Comp model w/dual port compensator system, extended safety and magazine release.
Factory Comp model (9mm Bi-Tone)................ NiB $633 Ex $511 Gd $356
Factory Comp model (9mm stainless)................ NiB $747 Ex $603 Gd $419
LSP Ultra model (9mm Bi-Tone)................ NiB $582 Ex $471 Gd $329
LSP Ultra model (9mm stainless)................ NiB $620 Ex $501 Gd $349
.40 S&W, .45 ACP: add............................ $90

STALLARD ARMS — Mansfield, Ohio

See listings under Hi-Point.

STAR PISTOLS — Eibar, Spain
Star, Bonifacio Echeverria, S.A.

MODEL 30M DA AUTO PISTOL... NiB $381 Ex $325 Gd $243
Caliber: 9mm Para. 15-round magazine, 4.38-inch bbl., 8 inches overall. Weight: 40 oz. Steel frame w/combat features. Adj. sights. Checkered composition grips. Blued finish. Made 1984-91.

MODEL 30PK DA AUTO PISTOL........ NiB $381 Ex $325 Gd $243
Same gen. specifications as Star Model 30M except 3.8-inch bbl., weight: 30 oz. Alloy frame. Made 1984-89.

MODEL 31P DA AUTO PISTOL
Same general specifications as Model 30M except removable backstrap houses complete firing mechanism. Weight: 39.4 oz. Made 1990-94.
Blued finish.................. NiB $381 Ex $325 Gd $238
Starvel finish................. NiB $412 Ex $355 Gd $269

MODEL 31 PK DA AUTO PISTOL........ NiB $381 Ex $325 Gd $238
Same general specifications as Model 31P except w/alloy frame. Weight: 30 oz. Made 1990-97.

MODEL A AUTOMATIC PISTOL... NiB $355 Ex $304 Gd $178
Modification of the Colt Government Model .45 Auto, which it closely resembles, but lacks grip safety. Caliber: .38 Super. Eight-round magazine, 5-inch bbl., 8 inches overall. Weight: 35 oz. Fixed sights. Blued finish. Checkered grips. Made 1934-97. (No longer imported.)

MODELS AS, BS, PS............. NiB $361 Ex $330 Gd $238
Same as Models A, B and P except have magazine safety. Made in 1975.

MODEL B..................... NiB $355 Ex $279 Gd $167
Same as Model A except in 9mm Para. Made 1934-75.

MODEL BKM.................. NiB $340 Ex $299 Gd $197
Similar to Model BM except has aluminum frame weight: 25.6 oz. Made 1976-92.

MODEL BKS STARLIGHT AUTOMATIC PISTOL........... NiB $291 Ex $154 Gd $169
Light alloy frame. Caliber: 9mm Para. Eight-round magazine, 4.25-inch bbl., 7 inches overall. Weight: 25 oz. Fixed sights. Blued or chrome finish. Plastic grips. Made 1970-81.

Star Model 30M

Star Model 30PK

Star Model AS

Star Model BKS

MODEL BM AUTOMATIC PISTOL
Caliber: 9mm. Eight-round magazine, 3.9-inch bbl., 6.95 inches overall. Weight: 34.5 oz. Fixed sights. Checkered walnut grips. Blued or Starvel finish. Made 1976-92.
Blued finish . . . . **NiB $307 Ex $266 Gd $174**
Starvel finish . . . . **NiB $341 Ex $300 Gd $209**

MODEL CO POCKET AUTOMATIC PISTOL . . . . **NiB $271 Ex $220 Gd $128**
Caliber: .25 Automatic (6.35mm), 2.75-inch bbl., 4.5 inches overall. Weight: 13 oz. Fixed sights. Blued finish. Plastic grips. Made 1941-57.

MODEL CU STARLET POCKET PISTOL . . . . **NiB $256 Ex $220 Gd $128**
Light alloy frame. Caliber: .25 Auto (6.35mm). Eight-round magazine, 2.38-inch bbl., 4.75 inches overall. Weight: 10.5 oz. Fixed sights. Blued or chrome-plated slide w/frame anodized in black, blue, green, gray or gold. Plastic grips. Made 1957-97. (U.S. importation disc. 1968.)

MODEL F AUTOMATIC PISTOL . . . . **NiB $351 Ex $249 Gd $122**
Caliber: .22 LR. 10-round magazine, 4.5-inch bbl., 7.5 inches overall. Weight: 25 oz. Fixed sights. Blued finish. Plastic grips. Made 1942-67.

MODEL F OLYMPIC RAPID-FIRE. . . . . **NiB $487 Ex $359 Gd $150**
Caliber: .22 Short. Nine-round magazine, 7-inch bbl., 11.06 inches overall. Weight: 52 oz. w/weights. Adj. target sight. Adj. 3-piece bbl. weight. Aluminum alloy slide. Muzzle brake. Plastic grips. Made 1942-67.

MODEL FM . . . . **NiB $334 Ex $257 Gd $120**
Similar to Model FR except has heavier frame w/web in front of trigger guard, 4.25-inch heavy bbl., Weight: 32 oz. Made 1972-91.

MODEL FR . . . . **NiB $359 Ex $257 Gd $120**
Similar to Model F w/same general specifications but restyled, has slide stop and adj. rear sight. Made 1967-72.

MODEL FRS. . . . . **NiB $385 Ex $283 Gd $120**
Same as Model FR except has 6-inch bbl., weight: 28 oz. Also avail. in chrome finish. Made 1967-91.

MODEL FS. **NiB $359 Ex $257 Gd $120**
Same as regular Model F but w/6-inch bbl. and adj. sights. Weight: 27 oz. Made 1942-67.

MODEL H . . . . **NiB $395 Ex $283 Gd $120**
Same as Model HN except .32 Auto (7.65mm), 7-round magazine, weight: 20 oz. Made 1934-41.

MODEL HK LANCER AUTOMATIC PISTOL . . . . **NiB $270 Ex $239 Gd $142**
Similar to Starfire w/same general specifications except .22 LR. Made 1955-68.

MODEL HN AUTOMATIC PISTOL . . . . **NiB $408 Ex $296 Gd $128**
Caliber: .380 Auto (9mm Short). Six-round magazine, 2.75-inch bbl., 5.56 inches overall. Weight: 20 oz. Fixed sights. Blued finish. Plastic grips. Made 1934-41.

Star Model F

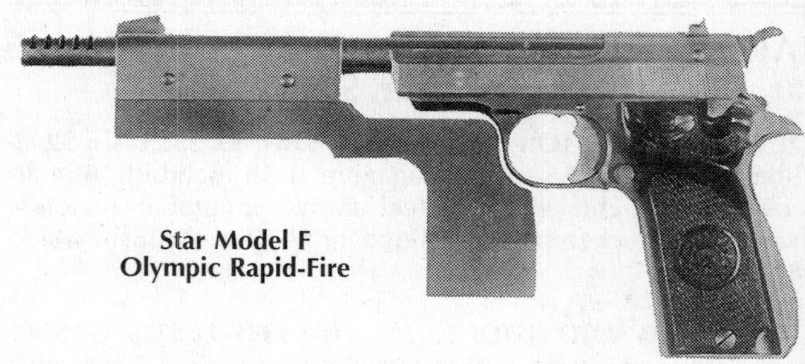
Star Model F Olympic Rapid-Fire

Star Model FS

MODEL I AUTOMATIC PISTOL . . . . **NiB $385 Ex $283 Gd 1q25**
Caliber: .32 Auto (7.65mm). Nine-round magazine, 4.81-inch bbl., 7.5 inches overall. Weight: 24 oz. Fixed sights. Blued finish. Plastic grips. Made 1934-36.

MODEL IN . . . .**NiB $433 Ex $300 Gd $127**
Same as Model I except caliber .380 Auto (9mm Short), 8-round magazine, weight: 24.5 oz. Made 1934-36.

MODEL M MILITARY AUTOMATIC PISTOL . . . . **NiB $357 Ex $306 Gd $189**
Modification of the Colt Government Model .45 Auto, which it closely resembles, but without grip safety. Calibers: 9mm Bergmann (Largo), .45 ACP, 9mm Para. Eight-round magazine except 7-shot in .45 caliber, 5-inch bbl., 8.5 inches overall. Weight: 36 oz. Fixed sights. Blued finish. Checkered grips. Made 1934-39.

MODELS M40, M43, M45 FIRESTAR AUTO PISTOLS
Calibers: 9mm, .40 S&W, .45 ACP. Seven-round magazine (9mm) or 6-round (other calibers). 3.4-inch bbl., 6.5 inches overall. Weight: 30.35 oz. Blade front sight, adj. rear w/3-dot system. Checkered rubber grips. Blued or Starvel finish. Made 1990-97.
M40 blued (.40 S&W) . . . . NiB $323 Ex $277 Gd $175
M40 Starvel (.40 S&W) . . . . NiB $343 Ex $297 Gd $195
M43 blued (9mm) . . . . NiB $323 Ex $282 Gd $195
M43 Starvel (9mm) . . . . NiB $343 Ex $297 Gd $195
M45 blued (.45 ACP). . . . . NiB $353 Ex $323 Gd $195
M45 Starvel (.45 ACP). . . . . NiB $374 Ex $343 Gd $216

MEGASTAR AUTOMATIC PISTOL
Calibers: 10mm, .45 ACP. 12-round magazine, 4.6-inch bbl., 8.44 inches overall. Weight: 47.6 oz. Blade front sight, adj. rear. Checkered composition grip. finishes: Blued or Starvel. Made from 1992-97.
Blued finish, 10mm or .45 ACP. . . . . NiB $486 Ex $409 Gd $407
Starvel finish, 10mm or .45 ACP. . . . . NiB $516 Ex $439 Gd $337

MODEL P . . . . NiB $377 Ex $311 Gd $183
Same as Model A except caliber .45 Auto, has 7-round magazine. Made 1934-75.

MODEL PD AUTOMATIC PISTOL
Caliber: .45 Auto. Six-round magazine, 3.75-inch bbl., 7 inches overall. Weight: 25 oz. Adj. rear sight, ramp front. Blued or Starvel finish. Checkered walnut grips. Made 1975-92.
Blued finish . . . . NiB $374 Ex $318 Gd $195
Starvel finish . . . . NiB $394 Ex $338 Gd $216

MODEL S. NiB $259 Ex $224 Gd $122
Same as Model SI except caliber .380 Auto (9mm), 7-round magazine, weight: 19 oz. Made 1941-65.

MODEL SL AUTOMATIC PISTOL . . . . NiB $300 Ex $259 Gd $173
Reduced-size modification of the Colt Government Model .45 Auto, lacks grip safety. Caliber: .32 Auto (7.65mm). Eight-round magazine, 4-inch bbl., 6.5 inches overall. Weight: 20 oz. Fixed sights. Blued finish. Plastic grips. Made 1941-65.

STARFIRE DK AUTOMATIC PISTOL . . . . . NiB $496 Ex $384 Gd $211
Light alloy frame. Caliber: .380 Automatic (9mm Short). Seven-round magazine, 3.13-inch bbl.. 5.5 inches overall. Weight: 14.5 oz. Fixed sights. Blued or chrome-plated slide w/frame anodized in black, blue, green, gray or gold. Plastic grips. Made 1957-97. U.S. importation disc. 1968.

MODEL SUPER A AUTOMATIC PISTOL . . . NiB $430 Ex $358 Gd $180
Caliber: .38 Super. Improved version of Model A but has disarming bolt permitting easier takedown, cartridge indicator, magazine safety, take-down magazine, improved sights w/luminous spots for aiming in darkness. This is the standard service pistol of the Spanish Armed Forces, adopted 1946.

MODEL SUPER B AUTOMATIC PISTOL
Caliber: 9mm Para. Similar to Model B except w/improvements described under Model Super A. Made c. 1946-89/90.
Super blued finish . . . . NiB $353 Ex $277 Gd $165
Starvel finish . . . . NiB $384 Ex $308 Gd $195

MODELS SUPER M, SUPER P . . . . . NiB $836 Ex $693 Gd $326
Calibers: .45 ACP, 9mm Parabellum or 9mm Largo, (Super M) and 9mm Parabellum (Super P). Improved versions of the Models M & P w/same general specifications, but has disarming bolt permitting easier takedown, cartridge indicator, magazine safety, take-down magazine, improved sights w/luminous spots for aiming in darkness.

MODELS SUPER SL, SUPER S . . . . . NiB $294 Ex $540 Gd $167
Same general specifications as the regular Model SI and S except w/improvements described under Super Star. Made c. 1946-72.

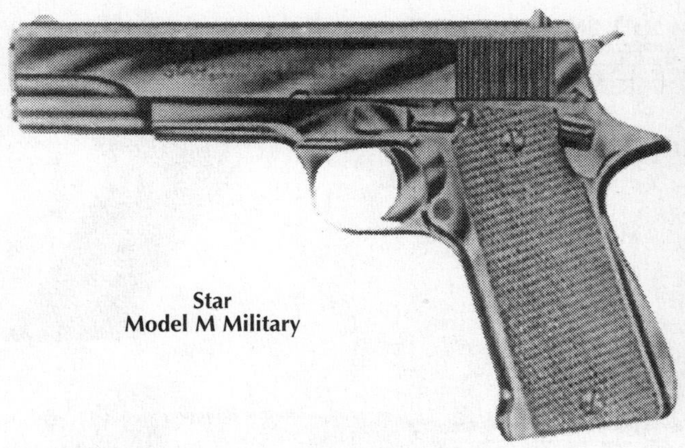
Star
Model M Military

Star
Model PD

MODEL SUPER SM . . . . NiB $294 Ex $254 Gd $192
Similar to Model Super S except has adj. rear sight, wood grips. Made 1973-81.

SUPER TARGET MODEL . . . . NiB $1306 Ex $1000 Gd $541
Same as Super Star model except w/adj. target rear sight. (Disc.)

ULTRASTAR DA AUTOMATIC PISTOL . . . . NiB $321 Ex $275 Gd $188
Calibers: 9mm Parabellum or .40 S&W. Nine-round magazine, 3.57-inch bbl., 7 inches overall. Weight: 26 oz. Blade front, adjustable rear w/3-dot system. Polymer frame. Blue metal finish. Checkered black polymer grips. Imported 1994-97.

STENDA-WERKE PISTOL — Suhl, Germany

POCKET AUTOMATIC PISTOL . . . . NiB $249 Ex $193 Gd $122
Essentially the same as the Beholla (see listing of that pistol for specifications). Made c. 1920-.25. Note: This pistol may be marked "Beholla" along w/the Stenda name and address.

STERLING ARMS CORPORATION — Gasport, New York

MODEL 283 TARGET 300
AUTO PISTOL . . . . NiB $169 Ex $113 Gd $98
Caliber: .22 LR. 10-round magazine, bbl. lengths: 4.5-, 6- 8-inch. 9 inches overall w/4.5-inch bbl., Weight: 36 oz. w/4.52-inch bbl. Adj. sights. Blued finish. Plastic grips. Made 1970-71.

Sterling
Model 283Target 300

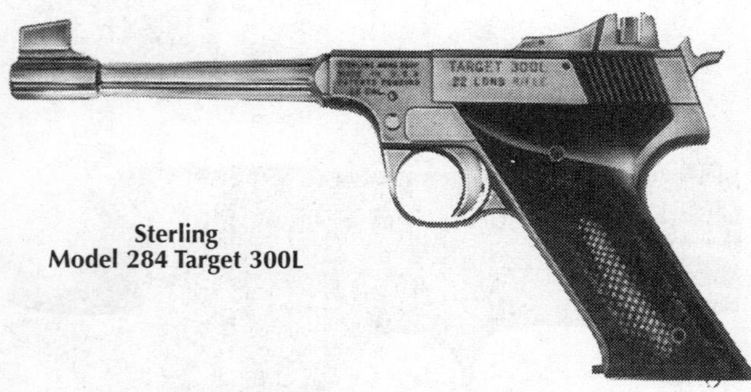

Sterling
Model 284 Target 300L

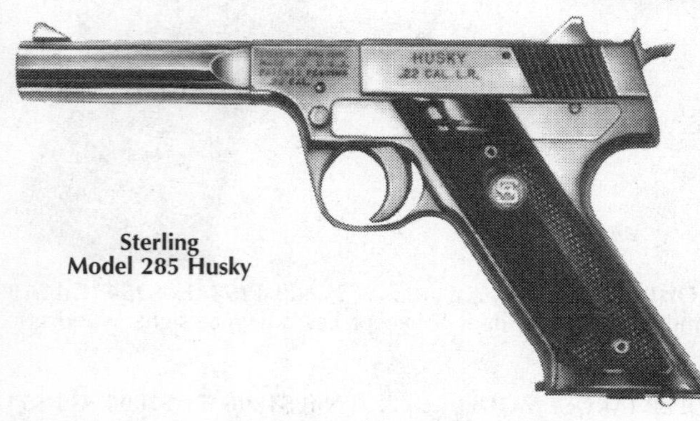

Sterling
Model 285 Husky

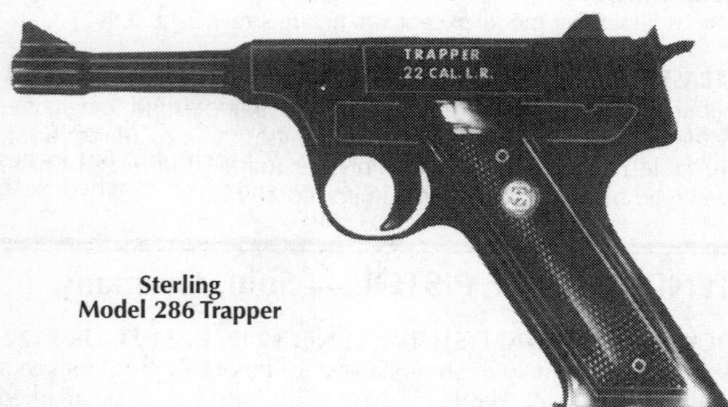

Sterling
Model 286 Trapper

MODEL 284 TARGET 300L . . . . NiB $186 Ex $135 Gd $100
Same as Model 283 except has 4.5- or 6-inch Luger-type bbl. Made 1970-71.

MODEL 285 HUSKY . . . . NiB $186 Ex $135 Gd $100
Same as Model 283 except has fixed sights, 4.5-inch bbl only. Made 1970-71.

MODEL 286 TRAPPER . . . . NiB $186 Ex $135 Gd $100
Same as Model 284 except w/fixed sights. Made 1970-71.

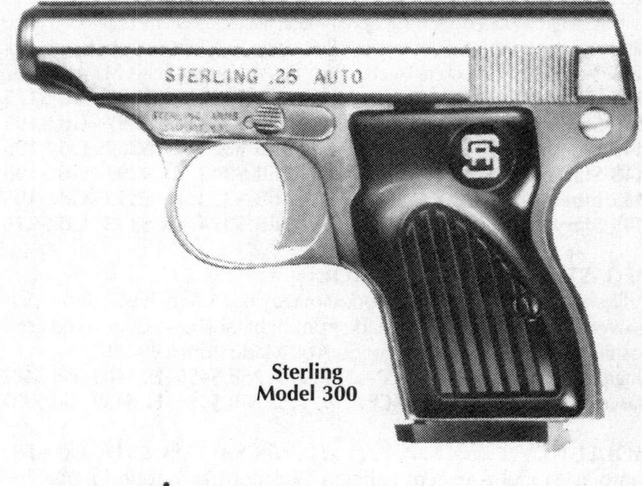

Sterling
Model 300

Sterling
Model 400

MODEL 287 PPL-.380
AUTOMATIC PISTOL . . . . NiB $135 Ex $110 Gd $77
Caliber: .380 Auto. Six-round magazine, 1-inch bbl., 5.38 inches overall. Weight: 22.5 oz. Fixed sights. Blued finish. Plastic grips. Made 1971-72.

MODEL 300
AUTOMATIC PISTOL . . . . NiB $135 Ex $105 Gd $59
Caliber: .25 Auto. Six-round magazine, 2.33-inch bbl., 4.5 inches overall. Weight: 13 oz. Fixed sights. Blued or nickel finish. Plastic grips. Made 1972-83.

MODEL 300S. . . . . NiB $143 Ex $110 Gd $69
Same as Model 300 except in stainless steel. Made 1976-83.

MODEL 302 . . . . NiB $135 Ex $105 Gd $59
Same as Model 300 except in .22 LR. Made 1973-83.

MODEL 302S. . . . . NiB $135 Ex $105 Gd $59
Same as Model 302 except in stainless steel. Made 1976-83.

MODEL 400 DA
AUTOMATIC PISTOL . . . . NiB $181 Ex $151 Gd $120
Caliber: .380 Auto. Seven-round magazine, 3.5-inch bbl., 6.5 inches overall. Weight: 24 oz. Adj. rear sight. Blued or nickel finish. Checkered walnut grips. Made 1975-83.

MODEL 400S. . . . . NiB $207 Ex $161 Gd $120
Same as Model 400 except stainless steel. Made 1977-83.

MODEL 450 DA
AUTO PISTOL . . . . NiB $237 Ex $207 Gd $161
Caliber: .45 Auto. Eight-round magazine, 4-inch bbl., 7.5 inches overall. Weight: 36 oz. Adj. rear sight. Blued finish. Smooth walnut grips. Made 1977-83.

MODEL PPL-22
AUTOMATIC PISTOL . . . . NiB $186 Ex $135 Gd $100
Caliber: .22 LR. 10-round magazine, 1-inch bbl., 5.5 inches overall. Weight: About 24 oz. Fixed sights. Blued finish. Wood grips. Only 382 made 1970-71.

J. STEVENS ARMS & TOOL CO. — Chicopee Falls, Mass.

This firm was established in Civil War era by Joshua Stevens, for whom the company was named. In 1936 it became a subsidiary of Savage Arms.

NO. 10
SINGLE-SHOT
TARGET PISTOL . . . . NiB $240 Ex $220 Gd $138
Caliber: .22 LR. 8-inch bbl., 11.5 inches overall. Weight: 37 oz. Target sights. Blued finish. Hard rubber grips. In external appearance this arm resembles an automatic pistol but it has a tip-up action. Made 1919-39.

NO. 35
OFFHAND MODEL SINGLE-SHOT
TARGET PISTOL . . . . NiB $378 Ex $327 Gd $210
Tip-up action. Caliber: .22 LR. Bbl. lengths: 6, 8, 10, 12.25 inches. Weight: 24 oz. w/6-inch bbl. Target sights. Blued finish. Walnut grips. Note: This pistol is similar to the earlier "Gould" model. Made 1907-39.

OFFHAND NO. 35 SINGLE-SHOT
PISTOL/SHOTGUN. . . . . NiB $378 Ex $327 Gd $174
Same general specifications as the standard No. 35 pistol except chambered for the .410 shotshell. Six-, 8-, 10-, or 12-inch half-ocatagonal bbl., iron frame either blued, nickel plated, or casehardened. BATF Class 3 license required to purchase. Made 1923-42.

NO. 36
SINGLE-SHOT PISTOL . . . . NiB $762 Ex $589 Gd $385
Tip-up action. Calibers: .22 Short and LR, .22 WRF, .25 Stevens, .32 Short Colt, .38 Long Colt, .44 Russian. 10- or 12-inch half-octagonal bbl., iron or brass frame w/nickel plated finish. Blued bbl. Checkered walnut grips. Made 1880-1911.

NO. 37
SINGLE-SHOT PISTOL . . . . NiB $936 Ex $767 Gd $487
Similar specifications to the No. 38 except the finger spur on the trigger guard has been omitted. Made 1889-1903.

NO. 38
SINGLE-SHOT PISTOL . . . . NiB $453 Ex $418 Gd $300
Tip-up action. Calibers: .22 Short and LR, .22 WRF, .25 Stevens, .32 Stevens, .32 Short Colt. Iron or brass frame. Checkered grips. Made 1884-1903.

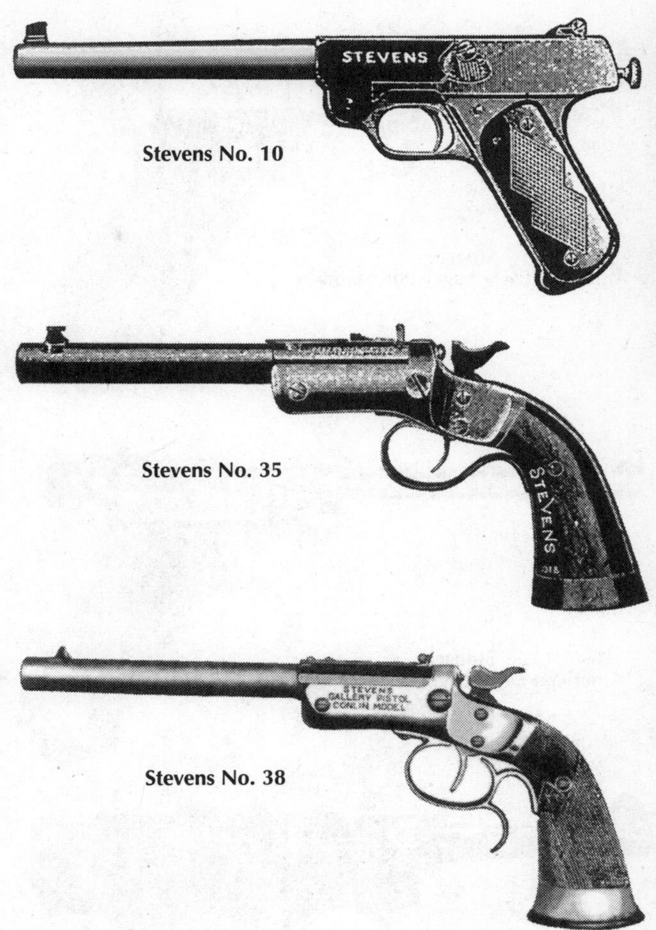

Stevens No. 10

Stevens No. 35

Stevens No. 38

NO. 41
TIP-UP SINGLE-SHOT PISTOL . . . . NiB $300 Ex $249 Gd $168
Tip-up action. Caliber: .22 Short, 3.5-inch half-octagonal bbl. Blued metal parts w/optional nickel frame. Made 1896-1915.

STEYR PISTOLS — Steyr, Austria

GB SEMIAUTOMATIC PISTOL
Caliber: 9mm Para. 18-round magazine, 5.4-inch bbl., 8.9 inches overall. Weight: 2.9 lbs. Post front sight, fixed, notched rear. Double, gas-delayed, blow-back action. Made 1981-88.
Commercial model . . . . NiB $642 Ex $565 Gd $369
Military model
(Less than 1000 imported). . . . . . . NiB $590 Ex $487 Gd $415

M12 AUTOMATIC PISTOL
Caliber: 9mm Steyr. Eight-round fixed magazine, charger loaded; 5.1-inch bbl., 8.5 inches overall. Weight: 35 oz. Fixed sights. Blued finish. Checkered wood grips. Made 1911-19. Adopted by the Austro-Hungarian Army in 1912. Note: Confiscated by the Germans in 1938, an estimated 250,000 of these pistols were converted to 9mm Para. and stamped w/an identifying "08" on the left side of the slide. Mfd. by Osterreichische Waffenfabrik-Gesellschaft.
Commercial model (9mm Steyr) . . . NiB $487 Ex $410 Gd $328
Military model (9mm Steyr-
Austro-Hungarian Army) . . . . NiB $493 Ex $415 Gd $173
Military model (9mm Parabellum
Conversion marked "08") . . . . NiB $957 Ex $802 Gd $432

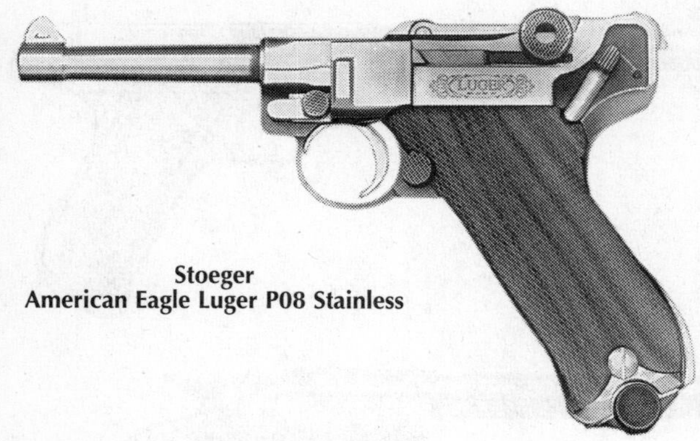

Stoeger
American Eagle Luger P08 Stainless

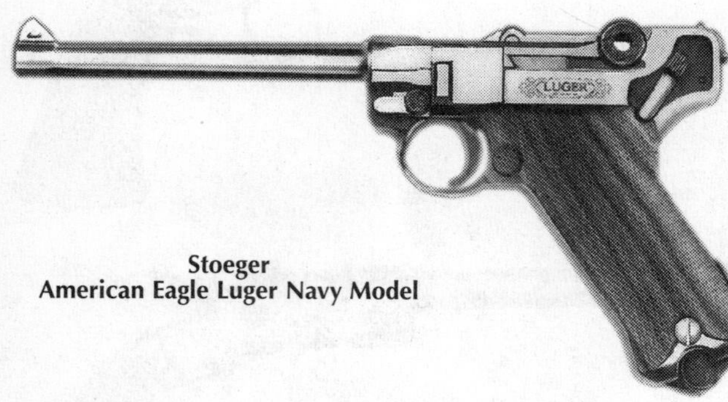

Stoeger
American Eagle Luger Navy Model

Stoeger
Standard Luger

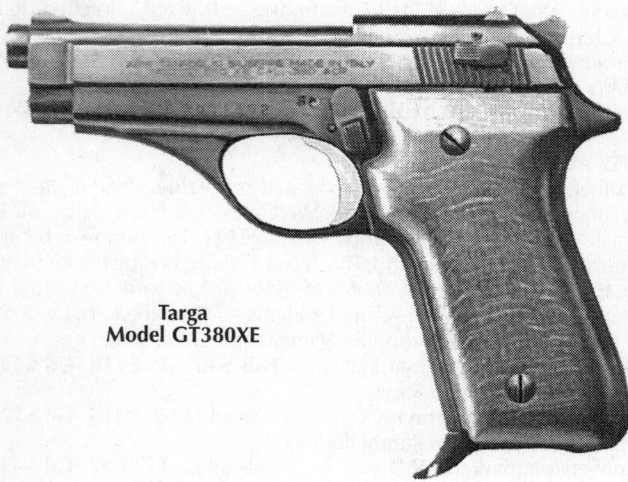

Targa
Model GT380XE

STOEGER LUGERS
Formerly mfd. by Stoeger Industries, So. Hackensack, N.J.; later by Classic Arms, Union City, N.J.

AMERICAN EAGLE LUGER
Caliber: 9mm Para. Seven-round magazine, 4- or 6-inch bbl., 8.25 inches overall (with 4-inch bbl.). or 10.25 inches (with 6-inch bbl.). Weight: 30 or 32 oz. Checkered walnut grips. Stainless steel w/brushed or matte black finish. Made from 1994 to date.
Model P-08 stainless (4-inch bbl.). . . . . NiB $681 Ex $385 Gd $314
Navy model (6-inch bbl.). . . . . NiB $681 Ex $385 Gd $314
W/matte black finish, add $50

STANDARD LUGER .22 AUTOMATIC PISTOL . . . . NiB $157 Ex $131 Gd $80
Caliber: .22 LR. 10-round magazine, 4.5- or 5.5-inch bbl., 8.88 inches overall (with 4.5-inch bbl.). Weight: 29.5 oz. (with 4.5-inch bbl.). Fixed sights. Black finish. Smooth wood grips. Made 1969-86.

STEEL FRAME LUGER .22 AUTO PISTOL . . . . NiB $162 Ex $136 Gd $96
Caliber: .22 LR. 10-round magazine, 4.5-inch bbl., 8.88 inches overall. Blued finish. Checkered wood grips. Features one piece forged and machined steel frame. Made 1980-86.

TARGET LUGER .22 AUTO PISTOL . . . . NiB $193 Ex $187 Gd $145
Same as Standard Luger .22 except has target sights 9.38 inches overall w/4.5-inch bbl., Checkered wood grips. Made 1975-86.

TARGA PISTOLS — Italy
Manufactured by Armi Tanfoglio Guiseppe

MODEL GT26S AUTO PISTOL . . . . NiB $105 Ex $85 Gd $61
Caliber: .25 ACP. Six-round magazine, 2.5-inch bbl., 4.63 inches overall. Weight: 15 oz. fixed sights. Checkered composition grips. Blued or chrome finish. Disc. 1990.

MODEL GT32 AUTO PISTOL
Caliber: .32 ACP. Six-round magazine, 4.88-inch bbl., 7.38 inches overall. Weight: 26 oz. fixed sights. Checkered composition or walnut grips. Blued or chrome finish.
Blued finished . . . . NiB $136 Ex $111 Gd $80
Chrome finish . . . . NiB $152 Ex $116 Gd $91

MODEL GT380 AUTOMATIC PISTOL
Same as the Targa GT32 except chambered for .380 ACP.
Blued finish . . . . NiB $156 Ex $126 Gd $89
Chrome finish . . . . NiB $168 Ex $136 Gd $96

MODEL GT380XE AUTOMATIC PISTOL . . . . NiB $187 Ex $147 Gd $106
Caliber: .380 ACP. 11-round magazine, 3.75-inch bbl., 7.38 inches overall. Weight: 28 oz. Fixed sights. Blued or satin nickel finish. Smooth wooden grips. Made 1980-90.

Taurus Model .44

Taurus Model 66

FORJAS TAURUS S.A. — Porto Alegre, Brazil

MODEL 44 DA REVOLVER
Caliber: .44 Mag. Six-round cylinder, 4-, 6.5-, or 8.38-inch bbl. Weight: 44.75 oz., 52.5 or 57.25 oz. Brazilian hardwood grips. Blued or stainless steel finish. Made 1994 to date.
Blued finish .... NiB $427 Ex $350 Gd $182
Stainless..................... NiB $483 Ex $391 Gd $320

MODEL 65 DA REVOLVER
Caliber: .357 Magnum. 6-round cylinder, 3- or 4-inch bbl., weight: 32 oz. Front ramp sight, square notch rear. Checkered walnut target grip. Royal blued or satin nickel finish. Imported 1992-97 and 1999 to date.
Blue......................... NiB $371 Ex $284 Gd $121
Stainless..................... NiB $376 Ex $289 Gd $131

MODEL 66 DA REVOLVER
Calibers: .357 Magnum, .38 Special. Six-round cylinder, 3-, 4- and 6-inch bbl., weight: 35 oz. Serrated ramp front sight, rear click adj. Checkered walnut grips. Royal blued or nickel finish. Imported 1992-97 and 1999 to date.
Blue......................... NiB $330 Ex $259 Gd $162
Stainless..................... NiB $391 Ex $269 Gd $218

MODEL 73 DA REVOLVER .... NiB $186 Ex $161 Gd $110
Caliber: .32 Long. Six-round cylinder, 3-inch heavy bbl., weight: 20 oz. Checkered grips. Blued or satin nickel finish. Disc. 1993.

MODEL 74 TARGET GRADE DA REVOLVER .... NiB $197 Ex $186 Gd $120
Caliber: .32 S&W Long. Six-round cylinder, 3-inch bbl., 8.25 inches overall. Weight: 20 oz. Adj. rear sight, ramp front. Blued or nickel finish. Checkered walnut grips. Made 1971-90.

MODEL 80 DA REVOLVER
Caliber: .38 Special. Six-round cylinder, bbl. lengths: 3, 4 inches, 9.25 inches overall (with 4-inch bbl.). Weight: 30 oz. (with 4-inch bbl.) Fixed sights. Blued or nickel finish. Checkered walnut grips. Made 1996-97.
Blued........................ NiB $204 Ex $156 Gd $ 95
Stainless..................... NiB $258 Ex $192 Gd $141

MODEL 82 HEAVY BARREL
Same as Model 80 except has heavy bbl., weight: 33 oz. w/4-inch bbl., Made 1971 to date.
Blued........................ NiB $207 Ex $161 Gd $100
Stainless..................... NiB $212 Ex $171 Gd $110

MODEL 83 HEAVY BARREL TARGET GRADE
Same as Model 84 except has heavy bbl., weight: 34.5 oz. Made 1977 to date. See illustration next page.
Blued........................ NiB $229 Ex $168 Gd $107
Stainless..................... NiB $265 Ex $199 Gd $148

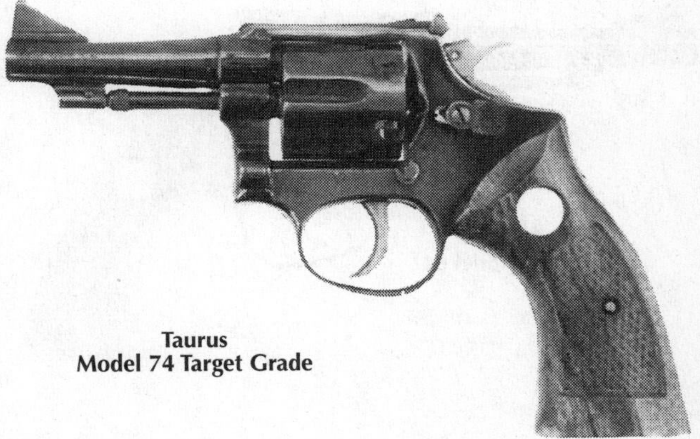
Taurus
Model 74 Target Grade

Taurus Model 80

Taurus Model 82

Taurus Model 83

Taurus
Model 85 w/Spur Hammer

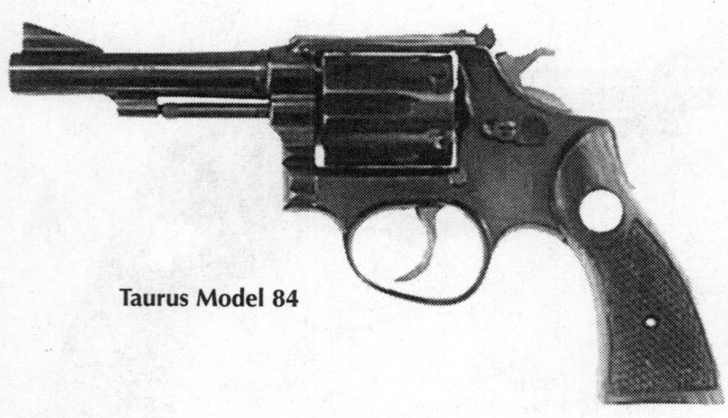
Taurus Model 84

Taurus
Model 85 Concealed Hammer

Taurus Model 86

MODEL 84 TARGET GRADE REVOLVER . . . . NiB $267 Ex $211 Gd $145
Caliber: .38 Special. Six-round cylinder, 4-inch bbl., 9.25 inches overall. Weight: 31 oz. Adj. rear sight, ramp front. Blued or nickel finish. Checkered walnut grips. Made 1971-89.

MODEL 85 DA REVOLVER
Caliber: .38 Special. Five-round cylinder, 2- or 3-inch. bbl., weight: 21 oz. Fixed sights. Checkered walnut grips. Blued, satin nickel or stainless-steel finish. Currently in production. Model 85CH is the same as the standard version except for concealed hammer.
Blued or satin nickel . . . . NiB $282 Ex $216 Gd $97
Stainless steel . . . . NiB $343 Ex $252 Gd $178

MODEL 86 TARGET MASTER DA REVOLVER . . . . NiB $287 Ex $216 Gd $145
Caliber: .38 Special. Six-round cylinder, 6-inch bbl., 11.25 inches overall. Weight: 34 oz. Adj. rear sight, Partridge-type front. Blued finish. Checkered walnut grips. Made 1971-94.

MODEL 94 TARGET GRADE
Same as Model 74 except .22 LR. w/9-round cylinder, 3- or 4-inch bbl., weight: 25 oz. Blued or stainless finish. Made 1971 to date.
Blued finish . . . . NiB $262 Ex $196 Gd $109
Stainless finish . . . . NiB $308 Ex $226 Gd $165

MODEL 96 TARGET MASTER . . . . . NiB $292 Ex $216 Gd $145
Same as Model 86 except in .22 LR. Made 1971 to date.

MODEL 431 DA REVOLVER
Caliber: .44 Spec. Five-round cylinder, 3- or 4-inch solid-rib bbl. w/ejector shroud. Weight: 35 oz. w/4-inch bbl., Serrated ramp front sight, notched topstrap rear. Blued or stainless finish. Made 1992-97.
Blued finish . . . . NiB $236 Ex $185 Gd $114
Stainless finish . . . . NiB $303 Ex $231 Gd $185

MODEL 441 DA REVOLVER
Similar to the Model 431 except w/6-inch bbl. and fully adj. target sights. Weight: 40 oz. Made 1991-97.
Blued finish . . . . NiB $257 Ex $196 Gd $114
Stainless finish . . . . NiB $374 Ex $267 Gd $206

MODEL 445 DA REVOLVER
Caliber: .44 Special. Five-round cylinder, 2-inch bbl., 6.75 inches overall. Weight: 28.25 oz. Serrated ramp front sight, notched frame rear. Standard or concealed hammer. Santoprene I grips. Blue or stainless finish. Imported 1997 to date.
Blue model . . . . NiB $287 Ex $221 Gd $114
Stainless model . . . . NiB $379 Ex $241 Gd $170

MODEL .454 DA RAGING BULL REVOLVER
Caliber: .454 Casull. Five-round cylinder, ported 6.5- or 8.4-inch vent rib bbl., 12 inches overall (w/6.5-inch bbl.). Weight: 53 or 63 oz. Partridge front sight, micrometer adj. rear. Santoprene I or walnut grips. Blue or stainless finish. Imported 1997 to date.
Blue model . . . . NiB $839 Ex $686 Gd $512
Stainless model . . . . NiB $824 Ex $752 Gd $676

MODEL 669/669VR DA REVOLVER
Caliber: .357 Mag. Six-round cylinder, 4- or 6-inch solid-rib bbl. w/ejector shroud Model 669VR has vent rib bbl., weight: 37 oz. w/4-inch bbl., Serrated ramp front sight, micro-adj. rear. Royal blued or stainless finish. Checkered Brazilian hardwood grips. Made 1989 to date.
Model 669 blued. . . . . NiB $279 Ex $208 Gd $131
Model 669 stainless. . . . . NiB $345 Ex $264 Gd $208
Model 669VR blued. . . . . NiB $289 Ex $218 Gd $141
Model 669VR stainless . . . . NiB $356 Ex $274 Gd $218

MODEL 741/761 DA REVOLVER
Caliber: .32 H&R Mag. Six-round cylinder, 3- or 4-inch solid-rib bbl. w/ejector shroud. Weight: 20 oz. w/3-inch bbl., Serrated ramp front sight, micro-adj. rear. Blued or stainless finish. Checkered Brazilian hardwood grips. Made 1991-97.
Model 741 blued. . . . . NiB $223 Ex $172 Gd $121
Model 741 stainless . . . . NiB $294 Ex $233 Gd $167
Model 761 (6-inch bbl., blued, 34 oz.) . . . . NiB $269 Ex $203 Gd $116

MODEL 941 TARGET REVOLVER
Caliber: .22 Magnum. Eight-round cylinder. Solid-rib bbl. w/ejector shroud. Micro-adj. rear sight. Brazilian hardwood grips. Blued or stainless finish.
Blued finish . . . . NiB $282 Ex $211 Gd $114
Stainless finish. . . . . NiB $318 Ex $252 Gd $170

MODEL PT .22 DA AUTOMATIC PISTOL . . . . NiB $186 Ex $146 Gd $79
Caliber: .22 LR. Nine-round magazine, 2.75-inch bbl., weight: 12.3 oz. Fixed open sights. Brazilian hardwood grips. Blued finish. Made 1991 to date.

MODEL PT .25 DA AUTOMATIC PISTOL . . . . NiB $186 Ex $146 Gd $79
Same general specifications as Model PT 22 except in .25 ACP w/eight-round magazine, Made from 1992 to date.

MODEL PT58 SEMI-AUTOMATIC PISTOL . . . . NiB $350 Ex $299 Gd $213
Caliber: .380 ACP. Twelve-round magazine, 4-inch bbl., 7.2 inches overall. Weight: 30 oz. Blade front sight, rear adj. for windage w/3-dot sighting system. Blued, satin nickel or stainless finish. Made 1988-96.

MODEL PT 92AF SEMIAUTOMATIC PISTOL
Double action. Caliber: 9mm Para. Fifteen-round magazine, 5-inch bbl., 8.5 inches overall. Weight: 24 oz. Blade front sight, notched bar rear. Smooth Brazilian walnut grips. Blued, satin nickel or stainless finish. Made 1991 to date.
Blued finish . . . . NiB $461 Ex $369 Gd $221
Satin nickel finish . . . . NiB $501 Ex $410 Gd $262
Stainless finish. . . . . NiB $471 Ex $379 Gd $308

Taurus Model 669

Taurus Model PT .22

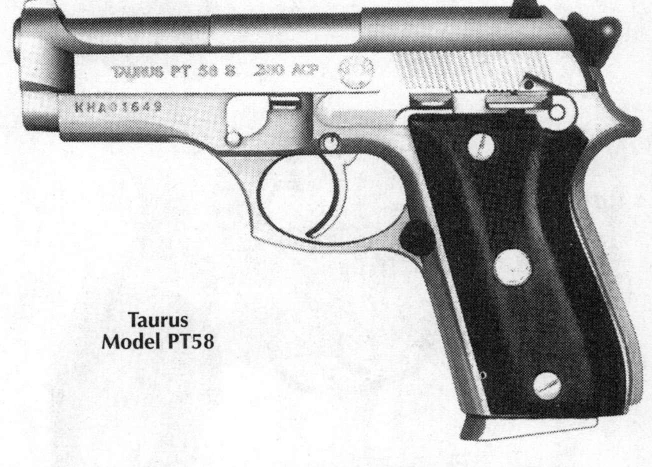

Taurus Model PT58

Taurus Model PT92

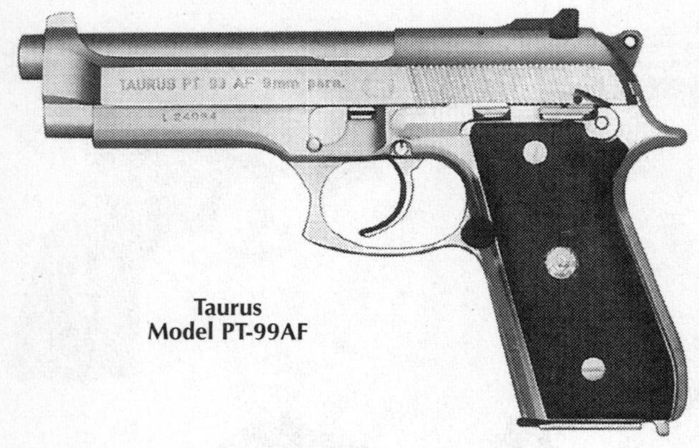

Taurus
Model PT-99AF

Taurus
Model PT-908

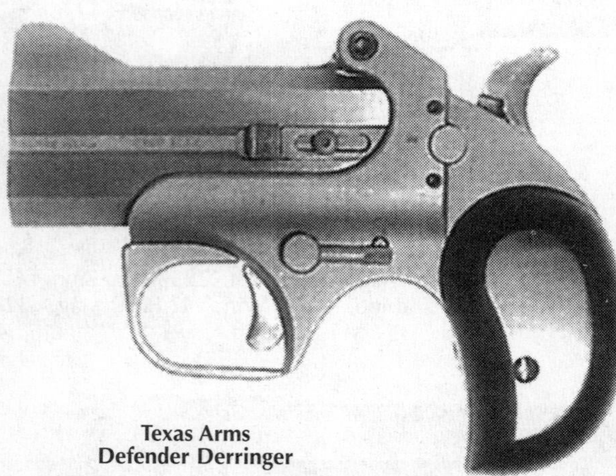
Texas Arms
Defender Derringer

MODEL PT-92AFC COMPACT PISTOL
Same general specifications as Model PT-92AF except w/13-round magazine, 4.25-inch bbl., 7.5 inches overall. Weight: 31 oz. Made 1991-96
Blued finish . . . . NiB $363 Ex $212 Gd $215
Satin nickel finish . . . . NiB $400 Ex $350 Gd $254
Stainless finish . . . . NiB $430 Ex $337 Gd $276

MODEL PT 99AF SEMI-AUTOMATIC PISTOL . . . . NiB $495 Ex $383 Gd $225
Same general specifications as Model PT-92AF except rear sight is adj. for elevation and windage, and finish is blued or satin nickel.

MODEL PT 100 DA AUTOMATIC PISTOL
Caliber: .40 S&W. Eleven-round magazine, 5-inch bbl., weight: 34 oz. Fixed front sight, adj. rear w/3-dot system. Smooth hardwood grip. Blued, satin nickel or stainless finish. Made 1991-97.
Blued finish . . . . NiB $482 Ex $375 Gd $227
Satin finish. NiB $472 Ex $416 Gd $268
Stainless finish . . . . NiB $436 Ex $385 Gd $252

MODEL PT 101 DA AUTOMATIC PISTOL
Same general specifications as Model 100 except w/micrometer click adj. sights. Made 1992-96.
Blued finish . . . . NiB $497 Ex $385 Gd $227
Satin nickel finish . . . . NiB $543 Ex $431 Gd $273
Stainless finish . . . . NiB $502 Ex $426 Gd $303

MODEL PT 111 MILLENNIUM DAO PISTOL
Caliber: 9mm Parabellum. 10-round magazine, 3.12-inch bbl., 6 inches overall. Weight: 19.1 oz. Fixed low-profile sights w/3-dot system. Black polymer grip/frame. Blue or stainless slide. Imported 1998 to date.
Blue model . . . . NiB $380 Ex $212 Gd $156
Stainless model . . . . NiB $380 Ex $314 Gd $156

MODEL PT 908 SEMIAUTOMATIC PISTOL
Caliber: 9mm Para. Eight-round magazine, 3.8-inch bbl., 7 inches overall. Weight: 30 oz. Post front sight, drift-adj. combat rear w/3-dot system. Blued, satin nickel or stainless finish. Made 1993-97.
Blued finish . . . . NiB $355 Ex $309 Gd $212
Satin nickel finish . . . . NiB $355 Ex $319 Gd $212
Stainless finish . . . . NiB $564 Ex $446 Gd $298

MODEL PT 911 COMPACT SEMIAUTOMATIC PISTOL
Caliber: 9mm Parabellum. 10-round magazine, 3.75-inch bbl., 7.05 inches overall. Weight: 28.2 oz. Fixed low-profile sights w/3-dot system. Santoprene II grips. Blue or stainless finish. Imported 1997 to date.
Blue model . . . . NiB $443 Ex $362 Gd $209
Stainless model . . . . NiB $566 Ex $448 Gd $300

MODEL PT 938 COMPACT SEMIAUTOMATIC PISTOL
Caliber: 380 ACP. 10-round magazine, 3.72-inch bbl., 6.75 inches overall. Weight: 27 oz. Fixed low-profile sights w/3-dot system. Santoprene II grips. Blue or stainless finish. Imported 1997 to date.
Blue model . . . . NiB $428 Ex $362 Gd $204
Stainless model . . . . NiB $383 Ex $311 Gd $218

MODEL PT 940 COMPACT SEMIAUTOMATIC PISTOL
Caliber: .40 S&W. 10-round magazine, 3.75-inch bbl., 7.05 inches overall. Weight: 28.2 oz. Fixed low-profile sights w/3-dot system. Santoprene II grips. Blue or stainless finish. Imported 1997 to date.
Blue model . . . . NiB $453 Ex $382 Gd $214
Stainless model . . . . NiB $464 Ex $387 Gd $316

MODEL PT 945 COMPACT SEMIAUTOMATIC PISTOL
Caliber: .45 ACP. Eight-round magazine, 4.25-inch bbl., 7.48 inches overall. Weight: 29.5 oz. Fixed low-profile sights w/3-dot system. Santoprene II grips. Blue or stainless finish. Imported 1995 to date.
Blue model . . . . NiB $479 Ex $392 Gd $234
Stainless model . . . . NiB $504 Ex $413 Gd $336

TEXAS ARMS — Waco, Texas

DEFENDER DERRINGER . . . . NiB $300 Ex $260 Gd $163
Calibers: 9mm, .357 Mag., .44 Mag., .45 ACP, .45 Colt/.410. Three-inch bbl., 5 inches overall. Weight: 21 oz. Blade front sight, fixed rear. Matte gun-metal gray finish. Smooth grips. Made 1993 to date.

TEXAS LONGHORN ARMS — Richmond, Texas

"THE JEZEBEL" PISTOL .... NiB $280 Ex $226 Gd $158
Top-break, single-shot. Caliber: .22 Short, Long or LR. Six-inch half-round bbl., 8 inches overall. Weight: 15 oz. Bead front sight, adj. rear. One-piece walnut grip. Stainless finish. Intro. in 1987.

SA REVOLVER CASED SET
Set contains one each of the Texas Longhorn Single Actions. Each chambered in the same caliber and w/the same serial number. Intro. in 1984.
Standard set................ NiB $5672 Ex $4550 Gd $3114
Engraved set .... NiB $7394 Ex $5927 Gd $4050

SOUTH TEXAS ARMY LIMITED EDITION SA REVOLVER ...... NiB $1758 Ex $1304 Gd $1023
Calibers: All popular centerfire pistol calibers. Six-round cylinder, 4.75-inch bbl.,10.25 inches overall. Weight: 40 oz. Fixed sights. Color casehardened frame. One-piece deluxe walnut grips. Blued bbl., Intro. in 1984.

SESQUICENTENNIAL SA REVOLVER..... NiB $2445 Ex $1962 Gd $1344
Same as South Texas Army Limited Edition except engraved and nickel-plated w/one-piece ivory grip. Intro. in 1986.

TEXAS BORDER SPECIAL SA REVOLVER .... NiB $1550 Ex $1245 Gd $855
Same as South Texas Army Limited Edition except w/3.5-inch bbl. and bird's-head grips. Intro. in 1984.

WEST TEXAS FLAT TOP TARGET SA REVOLVER .... NiB $1551 Ex $1301 Gd $1008
Same as South Texas Army Limited Edition except w/choice of bbl. lengths from 7 .5 to 15 inches. Same special features w/flat-top style frame and adj. rear sight. Intro. in 1984.

THOMPSON PISTOL — West Hurley, New York Mfd. by Auto-Ordnance Corporation

MODEL 27A-5 SEMIAUTOMATIC PISTOL
Similar to Thompson Model 1928A submachine gun except has no provision for automatic firing, does not have detachable buttstock. Caliber: .45 Auto, 20-round detachable box magazine (5-, 15- and 30-round box magazines, 39-round drum also available), 13-inch finned bbl., overall length: 26 inches. Weight: About 6.75 lbs. Adj. rear sight, blade front. Blued finish. Walnut grips. Intro. 1977. See Auto-Ordnance in Handgun Section.

THOMPSON/CENTER ARMS — Rochester, New Hampshire

CONTENDER SINGLE-SHOT PISTOL
Break frame, underlever action. Calibers: (rimfire) .22 LR. .22 WMR, 5mm RRM; (standard centerfire), .218 Bee, .22 Hornet, .22 Rem. Jet, .221 Fireball, .222 Rem., .25-35, .256 Win. Mag., .30 M1 Carbine, .30-30, .38 Auto, .38 Special .357 Mag./Hot Shot, 9mm Para., .45 Auto, .45 Colt, .44 Magnum/Hot Shot; (wildcat centerfire) .17 Ackley Bee, .17 Bumblebee, .17 Hornet, .17 K Hornet, .17 Mach IV, .17-.222, .17-.223, .22 K Hornet, .30 Herrett, .357 Herrett, .357-4 B&D. Interchangeable bbls.: 8.75- or 10-inch standard octagon (.357 Mag., .44 Mag. and .45 Colt available w/detachable choke for use w/Hot Shot cartridges); 10-inch w/vent rib and detachable internal choke tube for Hot Shots, .357 and .44 Magnum only; 10-inch

Thompson
Contender Single-Shot Pistol

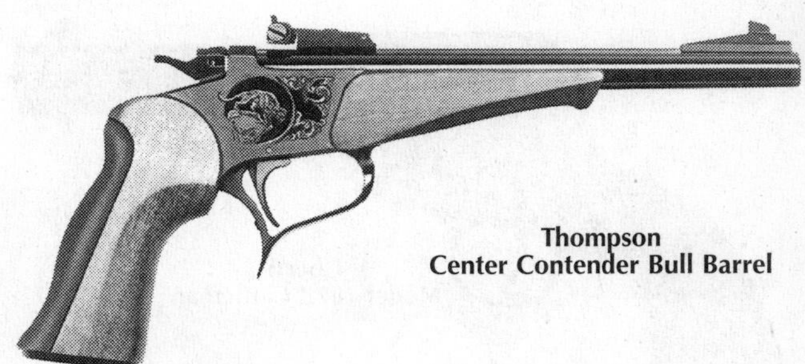
Thompson
Center Contender Bull Barrel

***(cont'd)* CONTENDER SINGLE-SHOT PISTOL**
bull bbl., .30 or .357 Herrett only. 13.5 inches overall w/10-inch bbl., Weight: 43 oz. (w/standard 10-inch bbl.). Adj. rear sight, ramp front; vent rib model has folding rear sight, adj. front; bull bbl., available w/or w/o sights. Lobo 1.5/ scope and mount (add $40 to value). Blued finish. Receiver photoengraved. Checkered walnut thumbrest grip and forearm (pre-1972 model has different grip w/silver grip cap). Made 1967 to date, w/the following revisions and variations.
Standard model.................. NiB $326 Ex $275 Gd $163
Vent rib model .... NiB $428 Ex $326 Gd $188
Bull bbl. model, w/sights .... NiB $408 Ex $321 Gd $183
Bull bbl. model, without sights ...... NiB $397 Ex $306 Gd $168
Extra standard bbl................ NiB $249 Ex $198 Gd $96
Extra vent rib or bull bbl........... NiB $295 Ex $209 Gd $112

CONTENDER BULL BARREL ...... NiB $408 Ex $321 Gd $183
Caliber offerings of the bull bbl. version expanded in 1973 and 1978, making it the Contender model w/the widest range of caliber options: .22 LR, .22 Win. Mag., .22 Hornet, .223 Rem., 7mm T.C.U., 7x30 Waters, .30 M1 Carbine, .30-30 Win., .32 H&R Mag., .32-20 Win., .357 Rem. Max., .357 Mag., 10mm Auto, .44 Magnum, .445 Super Magnum. 10-inch heavy bbl., Partridge-style iron sights. Contoured Competitor grip. Blued finish.

CONTENDER INTERNAL CHOKE MODEL
Originally made in 1968-69 w/octagonal bbl., this Internal Choke version in .45 Colt/.410 caliber only was reintroduced in 1986 w/10-inch bull bbl. Vent rib also available. Fixed iron rear sight, bead front. Detachable choke screws into muzzle. Blued finish. Contoured American black walnut Competitor grip, also since 1986, has nonslip rubber insert permanently bonded to back of grip.
W/bull bbl..................... NiB $428 Ex $341 Gd $204
W/vent rib .... NiB $453 Ex $367 Gd $256

CONTENDER OCTAGON BARREL ...... NiB $375 Ex $280 Gd $193
The original Contender design, this octagonal bbl., version began to see the discontinuance of caliber offerings in 1980. Now it is available in .22 LR only, 10-inch octagonal bbl., Partridge-style iron sights. Contoured Competitor grip. Blued finish.

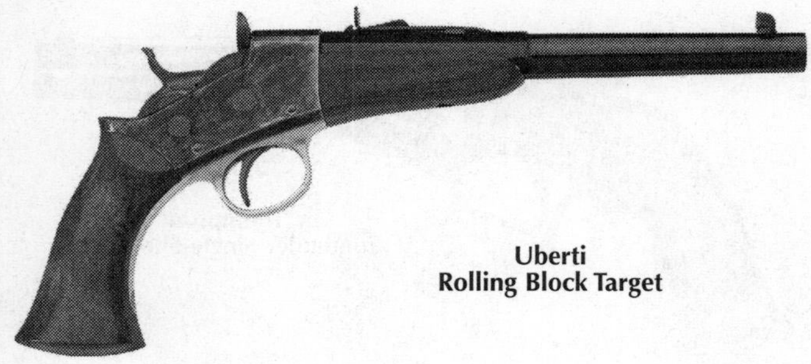

Uberti
Rolling Block Target

Uberti
Model 1873 Cattleman

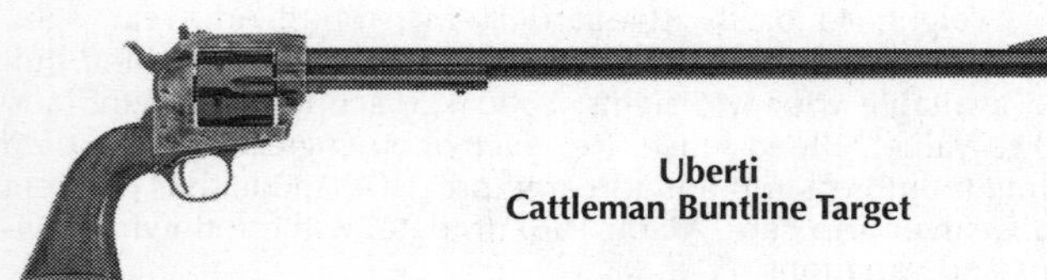

Uberti
Cattleman Buntline Target

CONTENDER STAINLESS

Similar to the standard Contender models except stainless steel w/blued sights. Black Rynite forearm and ambidextrous finger-groove grip. Made from 1993 to date.

Standard SS model (10-inch bbl.) .... **NiB $467 Ex $344 Gd $247**
SS Super 14.......................... **NiB $457 Ex $354 Gd $258**
SS Super 16.......................... **NiB $482 Ex $360 Gd $263**

CONTENDER SUPER 14/16

Calibers: .22 LR, .222 Rem., .223 Rem., 6mm T.C.U., 6.5mm T.C.U., 7mm T.C.U., 7x30 Waters, .30 Herrett, .30-30 Win., .357 Herrett, .357 Rem. Max., .35 Rem., 10mm Auto, .44 Mag., .445 Super Mag. 14- or 16.25-inch bull bbl., 18 or 20.25 inches overall. Weight: 43-65 oz. Partridge-style ramp front sight, adj. target rear. Blued finish. Made 1978 to date.

Super 14 .... **NiB $380 Ex $283 Gd $196**
Super 16 .... **NiB $395 Ex $288 Gd $201**

CONTENDER TC ALLOY II

Calibers: .22 LR, .223 Rem., .357 Magnum, .357 Rem. Max., .44 Magnum, 7mm T.C.U., .30-30 Win., .45 Colt/.410 (w/internal choke), .35 Rem. and 7-30 Waters (14-inch bbl.). 10- or 14-inch bull bbl. or 10-inch vent rib bbl. (w/internal choke). All metal parts permanently electroplated w/T/C Alloy II, which is harder than stainless steel, ensuring smoother action, 30 percent longer bbl. life. Other design specifications the same as late model Contenders. Made 1986-89.

T/C Alloy II 10-inch bull bbl. .... **NiB $385 Ex $324 Gd $268**
T/C Alloy II vent rib bbl. w/choke .... **NiB $437 Ex $354 Gd $248**
T/C Alloy II Super 14 .... **NiB $470 Ex $380 Gd $266**

ENCORE SINGLE-SHOT PISTOL

Similar to the standard Contender models except w/10-, 12- or 15-inch bbl., Calibers: .22-250 Rem., .223 Rem., .243 Win., .260 Rem., .270 Win., 7mm BR Rem., 7mm-08 Rem., 7.62x39mm, .308 Win., .30-06 Spfd., .44 Rem. Mag., .444 Marlin, .45-70 Govt., .45 LC/410. Blue or stainless finish. Walnut or composition, ambidextrous finger-groove grip. Hunter Model w/2.5-7x pistol scope. Note: Encore bbls. are not interchangeable with Contenter models. Made from 1998 to date.

Encore model w/10-inch
bbl. (blue, disc.) .... **NiB $462 Ex $395 Gd $222**
Encore model w/12-inch bbl. (blue) ...... **NiB $462 Ex $395 Gd $222**
Encore model w/15-inch bbl. (blue) ...... **NiB $470 Ex $405 Gd $230**
Hunter model w/2.5-7x scope .... **NiB $737 Ex $633 Gd $390**
Encore model (stainless), add **$55**

UBERTI HANDGUNS — Mfd. by Aldo Uberti, Ponte Zanano, Italy *(Imported by Uberti USA, Inc.)*

MODEL 1871 ROLLING BLOCK
TARGET PISTOL .... **NiB $362 Ex $300 Gd $188**

Single shot. Calibers: .22 LR, .22 Magnum, .22 Hornet and .357 Magnum; 9.5-inch bbl., 14 inches overall. Weight: 44 oz. Ramp front sight, fully adjustable rear. Smooth walnut grip and forearm. Color casehardened frame w/brass trigger guard. Blued half-octagon or full round barrel.

MODEL 1873 CATTLEMAN SA REVOLVER

Calibers: .357 Magnum, .38-40, .44-40, .44 Special, .45 Long Colt, .45 ACP. Six-round cylinder, Bbl length: 3.5, 4.5, 4.75, 5.5, 7.5 or 18 inches; 10.75 inches overall (5.5-inch bbl.). Weight: 38 oz. (5.5-inch bbl.). Color casehardened steel frame w/steel or brass back strap and trigger guard. Nickel-plated or blued barrel and cylinder. Imported 1997 to date.

First issue .... **NiB $392 Ex $336 Gd $198**
Bisley .... **NiB $392 Ex $336 Gd $198**
Bisley (flattop) .... **NiB $392 Ex $336 Gd $198**
Buntline (reintroduced 1992) .... **NiB $392 Ex $336 Gd $198**
Quick Draw .... **NiB $392 Ex $336 Gd $198**
Sabre (bird head) .... **NiB $392 Ex $336 Gd $198**
Sheriff's model .... **NiB $392 Ex $336 Gd $198**
Convertible cylinder, add **$51**
Stainless steel, add **$125**
Steel backstrap and trigger guard, add **$55**
Target sights, add **$60**

MODEL 1875 REMINGTON OUTLAW

Replica of Model 1875 Remington. Calibers: .357 Mag., .44-40, .45 ACP, .45 Long Colt. Six-round cylinder, 5.5- to 7.5-inch bbl., 11.75 to 13.75 inches overall. Weight: 44 oz. (with 7.5 inch bbl). Color casehardened steel frame w/steel or brass back strap and trigger guard. Blue or nickel finish.

Blue model .... **NiB $423 Ex $321 Gd $173**
Nickel model (disc. 1995).............. **NiB $535 Ex $448 Gd $290**
Convertible cylinder
(.45 LC/.45 ACP), add................................ **$92**

MODEL 1890 REMINGTON POLICE

Similar to Model 1875 Remington except without the web under the ejector housing.

Blue Model .... **NiB $423 Ex $321 Gd $173**
Nickel Model (disc. 1995) .... **NiB $530 Ex $443 Gd $285**
Convertible Cylinder (.45 LC/.45 ACP), add........................ **$92**

ULTRA LIGHT ARMS, INC — Granville, WV.

MODEL 20 SERIES PISTOLS
Calibers: .22-250 thru .308 Win. Five-round magazine, 14-inch bbl., weight: 4 lbs. Composite Kevlar, graphite reinforced stock. Benchrest grade action available in right- or left-hand models. Timney adjustable trigger w/three function safety. Bright or matte finish. Made 1987-99.
Model 20 Hunter's Pistol (disc. 1989). . . NiB $1351 Ex $1203 Gd $693
Model 20 Reb Pistol (disc. 1999) . . . . . . NiB $1534 Ex $1254 Gd $718

UNIQUE PISTOLS — Hendaye, France
Mfd. by Manufacture d'Armes des Pyrénées
Currently imported by Nygord Precision Products(Previously by Beeman Precision Arms)

MODEL B/CF AUTOMATIC PISTOL . . . . . . NiB $223 Ex $212 Gd $145
Calibers: .32 ACP, .380 ACP. Nine-round (.32) or 8-round (.38) magazine, 4-inch bbl., 6.6 inches overall. Weight: 24.3 oz. Blued finish. Plain or thumbrest plastic grips. Intro. 1954. Disc.

MODEL D2 . . . . NiB $329 Ex $277 Gd $221
Same as Model D6 except has 4.5-inch bbl., 7.5 inches overall, weight: 24.5 oz. Made 1954 to date.

MODEL D6 AUTOMATIC PISTOL. . . . . NiB $329 Ex $277 Gd $164
Caliber: .22 LR. 10-round magazine, 6-inch bbl., 9.25 inches overall. Weight: About 26 oz. Adj. sights. Blued finish. Plain or thumbrest plastic grips. Intro. in 1954. Disc.

MODEL DES/32U RAPID FIRE PISTOL
Caliber: .32 S&W Long (wadcutter). Five- or 6-round magazine, 5.9-inch bbl., weight: .40.2 oz. Blade front sight, micro-adj. rear. Trigger adj. for weight and position. Blued finish. Stippled handrest grips. Imported 1990 to date.
Right-hand model . . . . NiB $1424 Ex $1289 Gd $671
Left-hand model . . . . NiB $1471 Ex $1353 Gd $735

MODEL DES/69-U TARGET PISTOL
Caliber: .22 LR. Five-round magazine, 5.9-inch bbl., w/250 gm counterweight. 10.6 inches overall. Trigger adjusts for position and pull. Weight: 35.3 oz. Blade front sight, micro-adj. rear. Checkered walnut thumbrest grips w/adj. handrest. Blued finish. Imported 1969 to date.
Right-hand model . . . . NiB $1212 Ex $1052 Gd $537
Left-hand model . . . . NiB $1237 Ex $1083 Gd $573

MODEL DES/VO RAPID FIRE
MATCH AUTOMATIC PISTOL . . . . NiB $1057 Ex $820 Gd $568
Caliber: .22 Short. Five-round magazine, 5.9-inch bbl., 10.4 inches overall. Weight: 43 oz. Click adj. rear sight blade front. Checkered walnut thumbrest grips w/adj. handrest. Trigger adj. for length of pull. Made 1974 to date.

KRIEGS MODELL L AUTOMATIC PISTOL . . . . NiB $351 Ex $273 Gd $181
Caliber: .32 Auto (7.65mm). Nine-round magazine, 3.2-inch bbl., 5.8 inches overall. Weight: 26.5 oz. Fixed sights. Blued finish. Plastic grips. Mfd. during German occupation of France 1940-45. Note: Bears the German military acceptance marks and may have grips marked "7.65m/m 9 SCHUSS."

MODEL L AUTOMATIC PISTOL . . . . NiB $273 Ex $222 Gd $119
Calibers: .22 LR, .32 Auto (7.65mm), .380 Auto (9mm Short). 10-round magazine in .22, 7 in .32, 6 in .380; 3.3-inch bbl.; 5.8 inches overall. Weight: 16.5 oz. (.380 Auto w/light alloy frame), 23 oz. (w/steel frame). Fixed sights. Blued finish. Plastic grips. Intro. 1955. Disc.

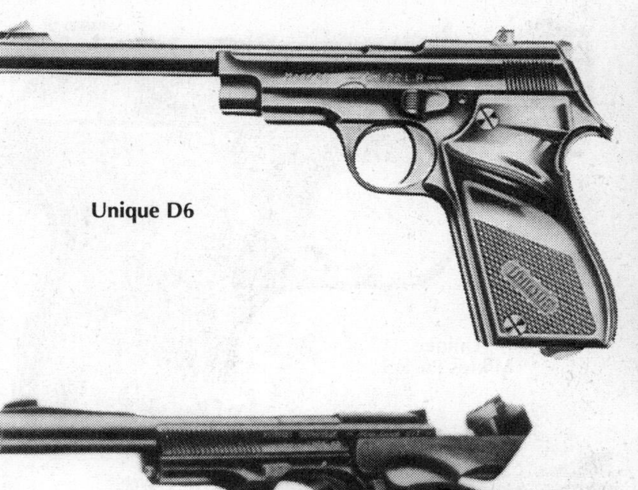
Unique D6

Unique
DES/69 Standard Match

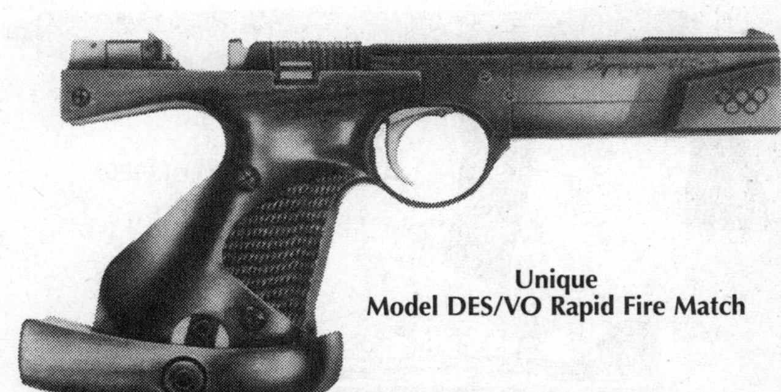
Unique
Model DES/VO Rapid Fire Match

MODEL MIKROS POCKET
AUTOMATIC PISTOL . . . . NiB $215 Ex $169 Gd $112
Calibers: .22 Short, .25 Auto (6.35mm). Six-round magazine, 2.25-inch bbl., 4.44 inches overall. Weight: 9.5 oz. (light alloy frame), 12.5 oz. (steel frame.). Fixed sights. Blued finish. Plastic grips. Intro. 1957. Disc. See illustration next page.

MODEL RR
AUTOMATIC PISTOL . . . . NiB $194 Ex $184 Gd $122
Postwar commercial version of WWII Kriegsmodell w/same general specifications. Intro. 1951. Disc.

MODEL 2000-U MATCH PISTOL
Caliber: .22 Short. Designed for U.I.T. rapid fire competitution. Five-round top-inserted magazine, 5.5-inch bbl., w/five vents for recoil reduction. 11.4 inches overall. Weight: 43.4 oz. Special light alloy frame, solid steel slide and shock absorber. Stippled French walnut w/adj. handrest. Imported 1990-96.
Right-hand model . . . . NiB $1372 Ex $1114 Gd $608
Left-hand model . . . . NiB $1403 Ex $1145 Gd $579

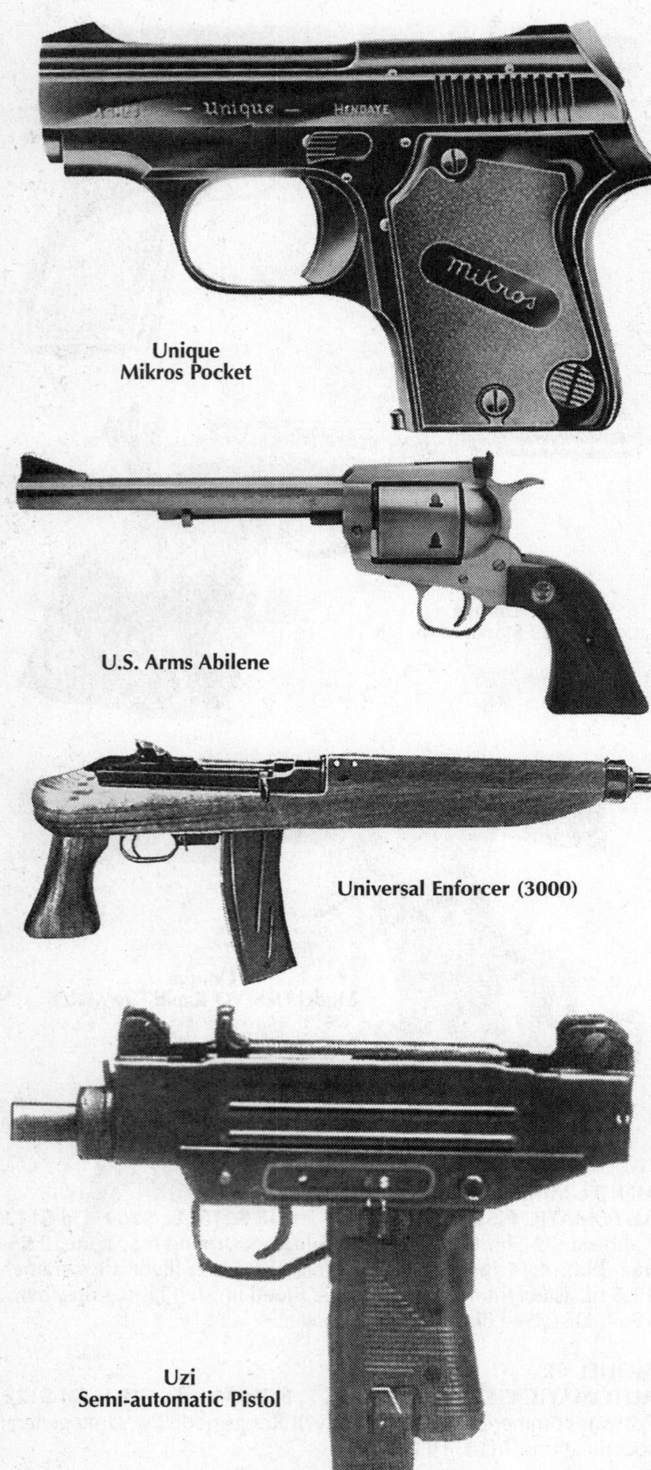

Unique
Mikros Pocket

U.S. Arms Abilene

Universal Enforcer (3000)

Uzi
Semi-automatic Pistol

UNITED STATES ARMS CORPORATION — Riverhead, New York

ABILENE SA REVOLVER

Safety Bar action. Calibers: .357 Mag., .41 Mag., .44 Mag., .45 Colt and .357/9mm convertible model w/two cylinders. Six-round cylinder, bbl. lengths: 4.63-, 5.5-, 6.5-inch, 7.5- and 8.5-inches in .44 Mag. only. Weight: About 48 oz. Adj. rear sight, ramp front. Blued finish or stainless steel. Smooth walnut grips. Made 1976-83.

.44 Magnum, blued finish . . . . NiB $330 Ex $279 Gd $192
.44 Magnum, stainless steel. . . . . . . NiB $381 Ex $320 Gd $228
Other calibers, blued finish. . . . . . . NiB $311 Ex $253 Gd $180
.357 Magnum, stainless steel. . . . . . NiB $375 Ex $304 Gd $215
Convertible, .357 Mag./9mm
Para., blued finish . . . . NiB $330 Ex $279 Gd $192

UNIVERSAL FIREARMS CORPORATION — Hialeah, Florida

This company was purchased by Iver Johnson Arms in the mid-1980s, when the Enforcer listed below was disc.. An improved version was issued under the Iver Johnson name (see separate listing).

ENFORCER (3000)
SEMIAUTOMATIC PISTOL . . . . NiB $291 Ex $240 Gd $174

M-1 Carbine-type action. Caliber: 30 Carbine. Five-, 15- or 30-round clip magazine, 10.25-inch bbl., 17.75 inches overall. Weight: 4.5 lbs. (with 30-round magazine). Adj. rear sight, blade front. Blued finish. Walnut stock w/pistol grip and handguard. Made 1964-83.

UZI PISTOLS — Mfd. by Israel Military Industries, Israel

(Currently imported by UZI America)

SEMIAUTOMATIC PISTOL . . . . . . NiB $1003 Ex $886 Gd $682

Caliber: 9mm Para. 20-round magazine, 4.5-inch bbl., about 9.5 inches overall. Weight: 3.8 lbs. Front post-type sight, rear open-type, both adj. Disc. 1993.

"EAGLE" SERIES
SEMIAUTOMATIC DA PISTOL

Caliber: 9mm Parabellum, .40 S&W, .45 ACP (Short Slide). 10-round magazine, 3.5-, 3.7- and 4.4-inch bbl., weight: 32 oz. to 35 oz. Blade front sight, drift adjustable tritium rear. Matte blue finish. Black synthetic grips. Imported 1997 to date.

Compact model
(DA or DAO) . . . . NiB $509 Ex $463 Gd $351
Polymer compact model . . . . NiB $509 Ex $463 Gd $351
Full-size model . . . . NiB $509 Ex $463 Gd $351
Short slide model. . . . . NiB $509 Ex $463 Gd $351

WALTHER PISTOLS — Manufactured by German, French and Swiss firms

The following Walther pistols were made before and during World War II by Waffenfabrik Walther, Zella-Mehlis (Thür.), Germany.

MODEL 1
AUTOMATIC PISTOL . . . . NiB $692 Ex $564 Gd $255

Caliber: .25 Auto (6.35mm). Six-round. 2.1-inch bbl., 4.4 inches overall. Weight: 12.8 oz. Fixed sights. Blued finish. Checkered hard rubber grips. Intro. 1908.

MODEL 2
AUTOMATIC PISTOL

Caliber: .25 Auto (6.35mm). Six-round magazine, 2.1-inch bbl., 4.2 inches overall. Weight: 9.8 oz. Fixed sights. Blued finish. Checkered hard rubber grips. Intro. 1909.

Standard model. . . . . NiB $486 Ex $461 Gd $162
Pop-up sight model . . . . NiB $1467 Ex $1055 Gd $596

MODEL 3 AUTOMATIC PISTOL....... NiB $1575 Ex $1317 Gd $596
Caliber: .32 Auto (7.65mm). Six-round magazine, 2.6-inch bbl., 5 inches overall. Weight: 16.6 oz. Fixed sights. Blued finish. Checkered hard rubber grips. Intro. 1910.

MODEL 4 AUTOMATIC PISTOL......... NiB $429 Ex $352 Gd $170
Caliber: .32 Auto (7.65mm). Eight-round magazine, 3.5-inch bbl., 5.9 inches overall. Weight: 18.6 oz. Fixed sights. Blued finish. Checkered hard rubber grips. Made 1910-18.

MODEL 5 AUTOMATIC PISTOL......... NiB $517 Ex $455 Gd $156
Improved version of Model 2 w/same general specifications, distinguished chiefly by better workmanship and appearance. Intro. in 1913.

MODEL 6 AUTOMATIC PISTOL...... NiB $6242 Ex $4697 Gd $1143
Caliber: 9mm Para. Eight-round magazine, 4.75-inch bbl., 8.25 inches overall. Weight: 34 oz. Fixed sights. Blued finish. Checkered hard rubber grips. Made 1915-17. Note: The powerful 9mm Para. cartridge is too much for the simple blow-back system of this pistol, so firing is not recommended.

MODEL 7 AUTOMATIC PISTOL......... NiB $700 Ex $546 Gd $237
Caliber: .25 Auto. (6.35mm). Eight-round magazine, 3-inch bbl., 5.3 inches overall. Weight: 11.8 oz. Fixed sights. Blued finish. Checkered hard rubber grips. Made 1917-18.

MODEL 8 AUTOMATIC PISTOL......... NiB $572 Ex $490 Gd $180
Caliber: .25 Auto. (6.35mm). Eight-round magazine, 2.88-inch bbl., 5.13 inches overall. Weight: 12.38 oz. Fixed sights. Blued finish. Checkered plastic grips. Made 1920-45.

MODEL 8 LIGHTWEIGHT AUTOMATIC PISTOL........... NiB $535 Ex $433 Gd $303
Same as standard Model Eight except about 25 percent lighter due to use of aluminum alloys.

MODEL 9 VEST POCKET AUTOMATIC PISTOL........... NiB $648 Ex $571 Gd $195
Caliber: .25 Auto (6.35mm). Six-round magazine, 2-inch bbl., 3.94 inches overall. Weight: 9 oz. Fixed sights. Blued finish. Checkered plastic grips. Made 1921-45.

MODEL HP DOUBLE-ACTION AUTOMATIC
Prewar commercial version of the P38 marked with an "N" proof over an "Eagle" or "Crown." The "HP" is an abbreviation of "Heeres Pistole" (Army Pistol). Caliber: 9mm Para. 8-round magazine, 5-inch bbl., 8.38 inches overall. Weight: About 34.5 oz. Fixed sights. Blued finish. Checkered wood or plastic grips. The Model HP is distinguished by its notably fine material and workmanship. Made 1937-44. (SN range 1000-25900)

First production (Swedish Trials model H1000-H2000).............. NiB $3086 Ex $2480 Gd $1706
Standard commercial production (2000-24,000)..................... NiB $1569 Ex $1363 Gd $843
War production - marked "P38" (24,000-26,000)................... NiB $1260 Ex $1049 Gd $693
W/Nazi proof "Eagle/359," add $240

OLYMPIA FUNFKAMPF MODEL AUTOMATIC......... NiB $1805 Ex $1470 Gd $594
Caliber: .22 LR. 10-round magazine, 9.6-inch bbl., 13 inches overall. Weight: 33 oz., less weight. Set of 4 detachable weights. Adj. target sights. Blued finish. Checkered grips. Intro. 1936.

OLYMPIA HUNTING MODEL AUTOMATIC......... NiB $1676 Ex $1264 Gd $481
Same general specifications as Olympia Sport Model but w/4-inch bbl., Weight: 28.5 oz.

Walther Model 5

Walther Model 8

Walther Model 9

OLYMPIA RAPID FIRE MODEL AUTOMATIC......... NiB $1676 Ex $1264 Gd $584
Caliber: .22 Short. Six-round magazine, 7.4-inch bbl., 10.7 inches overall. Weight: (without 12.38 oz. detachable muzzle weight,) 27.5 oz. Adj. target sights. Blued finish. Checkered grips. Made about 1936-40.

OLYMPIA SPORT MODEL AUTOMATIC.......... NiB $1032 Ex $878 Gd $461
Caliber: .22 LR. 10-round magazine, 7.4-inch bbl., 10.7 inches overall. Weight: 30.5 oz., less weight. Adj. target sights. Blued finish. Checkered grips. Set of four detachable weights was supplied at extra cost. Made about 1936-40.

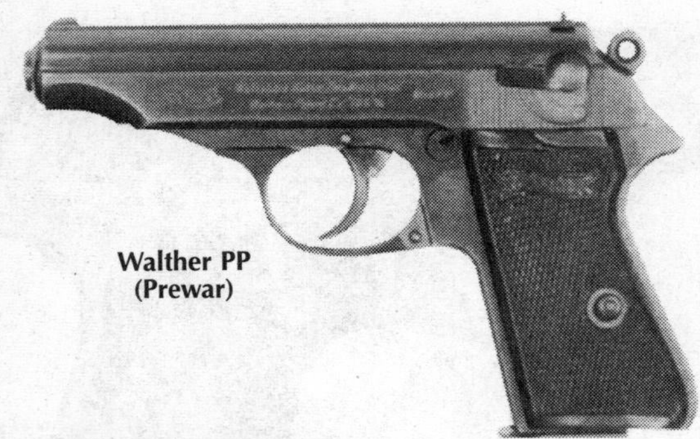
Walther PP (Prewar)

P38 MILITARY DA AUTOMATIC

Modification of the Model HP adopted as an official German Service arm in 1938 and produced throughout WW II by Walther (code "ac"), Mauser (code "byf") and a few other manufacturers. General specifications and appearance same as Model HP, but w/a vast difference in quality, the P38 being a mass-produced military pistol. Some of the late wartime models were very roughly finished and tolerances were quite loose.

War Production w/Walther banner (1940)

Zero Ser. 1st Iss. (SN 01-01,000) .... NiB $7825 Ex $5971 Gd $2160
Zero Ser. 2nd Iss. (SN 01,000-03,500) .... NiB $6280 Ex $4889 Gd $2057
Zero Ser. 3rd Iss. (SN 03,500-013,000) ...... NiB $2892 Ex $2120 Gd $884

WALTHER CONTRACT PISTOLS (LATE 1940-44)

"480" code Series (SN 1-7,600) .... NiB $5507 Ex $3705 Gd $1336
"ac" code Ser. w/no date (SN 7,350-9,700)... NiB $5765 Ex $4426 Gd $1954
"ac" code Ser. w/.40 below code (SN 9,700-9,900A) .... NiB $4220 Ex $3705 Gd $1645
"ac40" code inline Ser. (SN 1-9,900B)....... NiB $2160 Ex $1748 Gd $718
"ac" code Ser. w/41 below code (SN 1-4,5001) .. NiB $1620 Ex $1465 Gd $796
"ac" code Ser. w/42 below code (SN 4,5001-9,300K) .... NiB $1362 Ex $1208 Gd $590
"ac" code Ser. w/43 date (inline or below)..... NiB $678 Ex $523 Gd $369
"ac" code Ser. w/45 (inline or below)......... NiB $626 Ex $523 Gd $343

MAUSER CONTRACT PISTOLS (LATE 1942-44)

"byf" code Ser. w/42 date (19,000 prod.) ..... NiB $1203 Ex $1100 Gd $688
"bcf" code Ser. w/43, 44 or 45 date (inline or below) .... NiB $749 Ex $646 Gd $491
"svw" code Ser. (French prod. w/Nazi proofs)... NiB $1171 Ex $991 Gd $501
"svw" code Ser. (French prod. w/star proof) .... NiB $488 Ex $401 Gd $282

SPREEWERKE CONTRACT PISTOLS (LATE 1942-45)

"cyq" code 1st Ser. w/Eagle over 359 (500 prod.) .... NiB $1714 Ex $1390 Gd $963
"cyq" code Standard Ser. (300,000 prod.) ..... NiB $854 Ex $468 Gd $365
"cyq" code "0" Ser. (5,000 prod.)............ NiB $1086 Ex $1081 Gd $494

MODEL PP DA AUTOMATIC PISTOL

Polizeipistole (Police Pistol). Calibers: .22 LR (5.6mm), .25 Auto (6.35mm), .32 Auto (7.65mm), .380 Auto (9mm). Eight-round magazine, (7-round in .380), 3.88-inch bbl., 6.94 inches overall. Weight: 23 oz. Fixed sights. Blued finish. Checkered plastic grips. 1929-45. Post-War production and importation 1952 to present.

NOTE: Wartime models are inferior in quality to prewar commercial pistols.

COMMERCIAL MODEL W/CROWN "N" PROOF

.22 cal. (w/comm. Crown "N" proof)....... NiB $1085 Ex $935 Gd $617
.25 cal. (w/comm. Crown "N" proof)....... NiB $3617 Ex $3253 Gd $1605
.32 cal. (w/comm. Crown "N" proof)......... NiB $554 Ex $492 Gd $301
.32 cal. (w/Dural (alloy) frame)............. NiB $530 Ex $548 Gd $340

(cont'd) **Commercial Model w/Crown "N" Proof**

.32 cal. (w/Verchromt Fin., pre-war)......... NiB $1130 Ex $1542 Gd $600
.32 cal. (A.F.Stoeger Contract, pre-war) ...... NiB $1799 Ex $1336 Gd $538
.32 cal. (Allemagne French contract, pre-war) .... NiB $1336 Ex $1130 Gd $538
.380 cal. (w/Comm. Crown "N" proof) ...... NiB $1387 Ex $1125 Gd $641
.380 cal. (w/Verchromt Fin., pre-war)........ NiB $2572 Ex $2263 Gd $849

WARTIME MODEL WITH EAGLE "N" PROOF

.32 cal. (w/Waffenampt proofs)............... NiB $611 Ex $524 Gd $593
.32 cal. (w/Eagle "C" Nazi Police markings)..... NiB $895 Ex $761 Gd $436
.32 cal. (w/Eagle "F" Nazi Police markings) ..... NiB $898 Ex $761 Gd $436
.32 cal. (w/NSKK markings) .... NiB $3061 Ex $2211 Gd $821
.32 cal. (w/NSDAP Gruppe markings)....... NiB $2443 Ex $2083 Gd $769
.380 cal. (w/Waffenampt proofs)........ NiB $1347 Ex $1085 Gd $725

COMMERCIAL MODEL (POST-WAR)

.22 cal. (German manufacture)............. NiB $1008 Ex $879 Gd $467
.32 cal. (German manufacture)............. NiB $905 Ex $544 Gd $412
.380 cal. (German manufacture)............ NiB $1033 Ex $879 Gd $338
.22 cal. (French manufacture) .... NiB $503 Ex $447 Gd $210
.32 cal. (French manufacture) .... NiB $503 Ex $447 Gd $210
.380 cal. (French manufacture)............... NiB $550 Ex $487 Gd $226
.22, .32 or .380 Cal. (other foreign manuf.) ..... NiB $349 Ex $282 Gd $194

MODEL PP SPORT DA AUTOMATIC PISTOL

Target version of the Model PP. Caliber: .22 LR. Eight-round magazine, 5.75- to 7.75 inch bbl. w/adjustable sights. Blue or nickel finish. Checkered plastic grips w/thumbrest. Made 1953-70.

PP Sport (Walther manufacture)........... NiB $956 Ex $853 Gd $596
PP Sport (Manurhin manufacture).......... NiB $776 Ex $724 Gd $498
PP Sport C model (comp./single act.)........ NiB $977 Ex $894 Gd $596
W/nickel finish, add $170
W/matched bbl., weights, add $75

MODEL PP DELUXE ENGRAVED

These elaborately engraved models are available in blued finish, silver- or gold-plated.

Blued finish .... NiB $1496 Ex $1311 Gd $1105
Silver-plated............... NiB $1826 Ex $1404 Gd $1208
Gold-plated .... NiB $2037 Ex $1713 Gd $1311
W/ivory grips, add........................... $250
W/presentation case, add $700
.22 caliber, add $50
.380 caliber, add 95%

MODEL PP LIGHTWEIGHT

Same as standard Model PP except about 25 percent lighter due to use of aluminum alloys (Dural). Values 40 percent higher. (See individual listings).

WALTHER MODEL PP SUPER DA PISTOL............ NiB $897 Ex $729 Gd $515

Caliber: 9x18mm. Seven-round magazine, 3.6-inch bbl., 6.9 inches overall. Weight: 30 oz. Fixed sights. Blued finish. Checkered plastic grips. Made 1974-81.

MODEL PP 7.65MM PRESENTATION............ NiB $1942 Ex $1568 Gd $1091

Made of soft aluminum alloy in green-gold color, these pistols were not intended to be fired.

MODEL PPK DOUBLE-ACTION AUTOMATIC PISTOL

Polizeipistole Kriminal (Detective Pistol). Calibers: .22 LR (5.6mm), .25 Auto (6.35mm), .32 Auto (7.65mm), .380 Auto (9mm). Seven-round magazine, (6-round in .380), 3.25-inch bbl., 5.88 inches overall. Weight: 19 oz. Fixed sights. Blued finish. Checkered plastic grips. ***Note: Wartime models are inferior in workmanship to prewar commercial pistols. Made 1931-45.***

NOTE: *After both World Wars, the Walther manufacturing facility was required to cease the production of "restricted" firearms as part of the armistice agreements. Following WW II, Walther moved its manufacturing facility from the original location in Zella/Mehilis, Germany to Ulm/Donau. In 1950, the firm Manufacture de Machines du Haut Rhine at Mulhouse, France was licensed by Walther and started production of PP and PPK models at the Manurhin facility in 1952. The MK II Walthers as produced at Manurhin were imported into the U.S. until 1968 when CGA importation requirements restricted the PPK firearm configuration from further importation. As a result, Walther developed the PPK/S to conform to the new regulations and licensed Interarms to produce the firearm in the U.S. from 1986-99. From 1984-86, Manurhin imported PP and PPK/S type firearms under the Manurhin logo. Additional manufacturing facilities (both licensed & unlicensed) that produced PP and PPK type firearms were established after WW II in various locations and other countries including: China, France, Hungary, Korea, Romania and Turkey. In 1996, Walther was sold to Umarex Sportwaffen GmbH and manufacturing facilities were relocated in Arnsberg, Germany. In 1999, Walther formed a partnership with Smith and Wesson and selected Walther firearms are licensed for production in the U.S.*

COMMERCIAL MODEL W/EAGLE "N" PROOF (PREWAR)

.22 cal. (w/Comm. Eagle "N" proof)	NiB $1387	Ex $1233	Gd $584
.25 cal. (w/Comm. Eagle "N" proof)	NiB $5250	Ex $3190	Gd $2778
.32 cal. (w/Comm. Eagle "N" proof)	NiB $714	Ex $508	Gd $405
.380 cal. (w/Comm. Eagle "N" proof)	NiB $2675	Ex $2160	Gd $924

WARTIME MODEL W/EAGLE "N" PROOF

.22 cal. (w/Comm. Eagle "N" proof)	NiB $1381	Ex $1125	Gd $797
.22 cal. (w/Dural frame)	NiB $1645	Ex $1336	Gd $1233
.32 cal. (w/Comm. Eagle "N" proof)	NiB $606	Ex $503	Gd $297
.32 cal. (w/Dural frame)	NiB $844	Ex $684	Gd $478
.32 cal. (w/Verchromt Fin., Pre-War)	NiB $2263	Ex $1748	Gd $769
.380 cal. (w/Comm. Eagle "N" proof)	NiB $2778	Ex $2160	Gd $821
.380 cal. (w/Dural frame)	NiB $2984	Ex $2263	Gd $872
.380 cal. (w/Verchromt Fin., Pre-War)	NiB $3344	Ex $2572	Gd $1877
.22 cal. (w/Comm. Eagle "N" proof)	NiB $771	Ex $761	Gd $539
.32 cal. (w/Waffenampt proofs)	NiB $1003	Ex $719	Gd $359
.32 cal. (w/Eagle "C" Nazi Police markings)	NiB $1003	Ex $719	Gd $318
.32 cal. (w/Eagle "F" Nazi Police markings)	NiB $1357	Ex $997	Gd $456
.32 cal. (w/NSKK markings)	NiB $2154	Ex $1743	Gd $1218
.32 cal. (w/NSDAP Gruppe markings)	NiB $2057	Ex $1542	Gd $1104
.380 cal. (w/Waffenampt proofs)	NiB $1336	Ex $1027	Gd $769

COMMERCIAL MODEL (POST-WAR)

.22 cal. (German manufacture)	NiB $1013	Ex $884	Gd $369
.32 cal. (German manufacture)	NiB $910	Ex $549	Gd $343
.380 cal. (German manufacture)	NiB $1028	Ex $549	Gd $446
.22 cal. (French manufacture)	NiB $2160	Ex $872	Gd $486
.32 cal. (French manufacture)	NiB $822	Ex $616	Gd $385
.380 cal. (French manufacture)	NiB $1131	Ex $797	Gd $410
.22, .32 or .380 cal. (other foreign manuf.)	NiB $314	Ex $257	Gd $183

COMMERCIAL MODEL (U.S. PRODUCTION)

.380 cal. (w/blue finish)	NiB $519	Ex $406	Gd $360
.380 cal. (w/nickel finish)	NiB $519	Ex $406	Gd $360
.32 or .380 Cal. (stainless steel)	NiB $519	Ex $406	Gd $360

MODEL PPK DELUXE ENGRAVED

These elaborately engraved models are available in blued finish, chrome-, silver- or gold-plated.

Blued finish	NiB $1799	Ex $1439	Gd $1104
Chrome-plated	NiB $2881	Ex $1490	Gd $1125
Silver-plated	NiB $2083	Ex $1542	Gd $2478

Walther PPK (WW II)

Walther PPK Silver-Plated

(cont'd) **MODEL PPK DELUXE ENGRAVED**

Gold-plated	NiB $2417	Ex $1825	Gd $1336
W/ivory grips, add			$250
W/Presentation case, add			$700
.22 cal, add			$50
.25 cal, add			$100
.380 cal, add			$95

MODEL PPK LIGHTWEIGHT

Same as standard Model PPK except about 25 percent lighter due to aluminum alloys. Values 50 percent higher.

MODEL PPK 7.65MM PRESENTATION .... NiB $1722 Ex $1264 Gd $769

Made of soft aluminum alloy in green-gold color, these pistols were not intended to be fired.

MODEL PPK/S DA AUTOMATIC PISTOL

Designed to meet the requirements of the U.S. Gun Control Act of 1968, this model has the frame of the PP and the shorter slide and bbl., of the PPK. Overall length: 6.1 inches. Weight: 23 oz. Other specifications are the same as those of standard PPK except steel frame only. German, French and U.S. production 1971 to date. U.S. version made by Interarms 1978-99.

.22 cal. (German manufacture)	NiB $1181	Ex $872	Gd $486
.32 cal. (German manufacture)	NiB $872	Ex $666	Gd $404
.380 cal. (German manufacture)	NiB $1181	Ex $847	Gd $409
.22 cal. (French manufacture)	NiB $807	Ex $575	Gd $420
.32 cal. (French manufacture)	NiB $812	Ex $498	Gd $358
.380 cal. (French manufacture)	NiB $858	Ex $549	Gd $405
.22, .32 or .380 cal., blue (U.S. manufacture)	NiB $549	Ex $436	Gd $317
.22, .32 or .380 cal., stainless (U.S. manuf.)	NiB $549	Ex $436	Gd $395

NOTE: *Interarms (Interarmco) acquired a license from Walther in 1978 to manufacturer PP and PPK models at the Ranger Manufacturing Co., Inc. in Gadsden, Alabama. In 1988 the Ranger facility was licensed as EMCO and continued to produce Walther firearms for Interarms until 1996. From 1996-99, Black Creek in Gadsden, Alabama produced Walther pistols for Interarms. In 1999, Smith & Wesson acquired manufacturing rights for Walther firearms at the Black Creek facility.*

MODELS PPK/S DELUXE ENGRAVED
These elaborately engraved models are available in blued finish, chrome-, silver- or gold-plated.
Blued finish . . . . NiB $1507 Ex $1095 Gd $1043
Chrome-plated . . . . NiB $1394 Ex $1095 Gd $786
Silver-plated. . . . . NiB $1558 Ex $1146 Gd $1840
Gold-plated . . . . NiB $1733 Ex $1399 Gd $973

NOTE: *The following Walther pistols are now manufactured by Carl Walther, Waffenfabrik, Ulm/Donau, Germany.*

SELF-LOADING
SPORT PISTOL . . . . NiB $761 Ex $709 Gd $478
Caliber: .22 LR. 10-round magazine, bbl. lengths: 6- and 9-inch, 9.88 inches overall w/6-inch bbl. Target sights. Blued finish. One-piece, wood or plastic grips, checkered. Intro. in 1932.

MODEL FREE PISTOL . . . . NiB $1862 Ex $1425 Gd $771
Single-Shot. Caliber: .22 LR. 11.7-inch heavy bbl., Weight: 48 oz. Adj. grips and target sights w/electronic trigger. Importation disc. 1991.

MODEL GSP TARGET AUTOMATIC PISTOL
Calibers: .22 LR, .32 S&W Long Wadcutter. Five-round magazine, 4.5-inch bbl., 11.8 inches overall. Weights: 44.8 oz. (.22 cal.) or 49.4 oz. (.32 cal.). Adj. target sights. Black finish. Walnut thumbrest grips w/adj. handrest. Made 1969-94.
.22 LR . . . . NiB $1497 Ex $1296 Gd $549
.32 S&W Long
Wadcutter . . . . NiB $1703 Ex $1193 Gd $570
Conversion unit.
.22 Short
or .22 LR add. . . . . NiB $967 Ex $848 Gd $869

MODEL OSP RAPID
FIRE TARGET PISTOL. . . . . NiB $1579 Ex $1116 Gd $549
Caliber: .22 Short. Five-round magazine, 4.5-inch bbl., 11.8 inches overall. Weight: 42.3 oz. Adj. target sights. Black finish. Walnut thumbrest grips w/adj. handrest. .22 LR conversion unit available (add $275). Made 1968-94.

MODEL P4 (P38-LV)
DA PISTOL . . . . NiB $726 Ex $623 Gd $309
Similar to P38 except has an uncocking device instead of a manual safety. Caliber: 9mm Para. 4.3-inch bbl., 7.9 inches overall. Other general specifications same as for current model P38. Made 1974-82.

MODEL P5 DA PISTOL . . . . NiB $808 Ex $679 Gd $448
Alloy frame w/frame-mounted decocking levers. Caliber: 9mm Para. Eight-round magazine, 3.5-inch bbl., 7 inches overall. Weight: 28 oz. blued finish. Checkered walnut or synthetic grips. Made 1988 to date.

MODEL P5
COMPACT PISTOL . . . . NiB $988 Ex $860 Gd $422
Similar to model P5 except w/3.1-inch bbl. and weight: 26 oz. Made 1988-96.

Walther Free Pistol

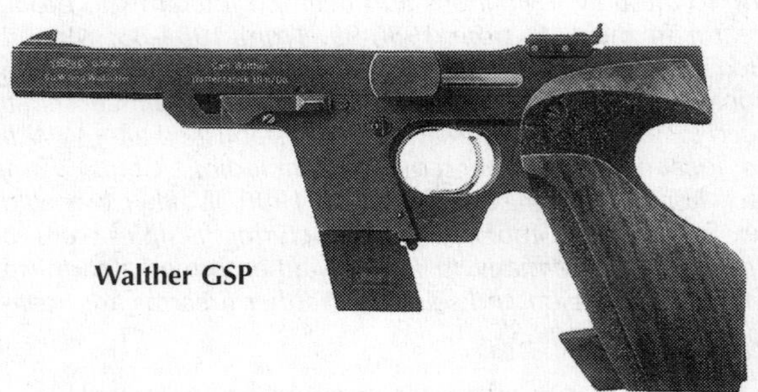
Walther GSP

Walther P5

MODEL P38 (P1) DA AUTOMATIC
Postwar commercial version of the P38, has light alloy frame. Calibers: .22 LR, 7.65mm Luger, 9mm Para. Eight-round magazine, bbl., lengths: 5.1-inch in .22 caliber, 4.9- inch in 7.65mm and 9mm, 8.5 inches overall. Weight: 28.2 oz. Fixed sights. Nonreflective black finish. Checkered plastic grips. Made 1957-89. Note: The "P1" is W. German Armed Forces official pistol.
.22 LR . . . . NiB $731 Ex $618 Gd $370
Other calibers . . . . NiB $679 Ex $576 Gd $314

MODEL P38 DELUXE ENGRAVED PISTOL
Elaborately engraved, available in blued or chrome-, silver- or gold-plated finish.
Blued finish . . . . NiB $1929 Ex $1440 Gd $847
Chrome-plated . . . . NiB $1594 Ex $1259 Gd $822
Silver-plated . . . . NiB $1568 Ex $1259 Gd $867
Gold-plated . . . . NiB $1929 Ex $1545 Gd $1105

MODEL P38K . . . . NiB $756 Ex $658 Gd $323
Short-barreled version of current P38, the "K" standing for "kurz" (meaning short). Same general specifications as standard model except 2.8-inch bbl., 6.3 inches overall, weight: 27.2 oz. Front sight is slide mounted. Caliber: 9mm Para. Made 1974-80.

MODEL P 88 DA AUTOMATIC PISTOL . . . . NiB $1425 Ex $1270 Gd $534
Caliber: 9mm Para. 15-round magazine, 4-inch bbl., 7.38 inches overall. Weight: 31.5 oz. Blade front sight, adj. rear. Checkered black synthetic grips. External hammer w/ambidextrous decocking levers. Alloy frame w/matte blued steel slide. Made 1987-93.

MODEL P 88 DA COMPACT
Similar to the standard P 88 Model except w/10- or 13-round magazine, 3.8-inch bbl., 7.1 inches overall. Weight: 29 oz. Imported 1993 to date.
Model P88 (early importation) . . . . NiB $920 Ex $792 Gd $534
Model P88 (post 94 importation) . . . . NiB $817 Ex $689 Gd $457

MODEL P99 DA AUTOMATIC PISTOL . . . . NiB $616 Ex $539 Gd $385
Calibers: 9mm Para., .40 S&W or 9x21mm. 10-round magazine, 4-inch bbl., 7.2 inches overall. Weight: 22-25 oz. Ambidextrous magazine release, decocking lever and 3-function safety. Interchangeable front post sight, micro-adj. rear. Polymer gripframe w/blued slide. Imported 1997 to date.

MODEL TPH DA POCKET PISTOL
Light alloy frame. Calibers: .22 LR, .25 ACP (6.35mm). Six-round magazine, 2.25-inch bbl., 5.38 inches overall. Weight: 14 oz. Fixed sights. Blued finish. Checkered plastic grips. Made 1968 to date. Note: Few Walther-made models reached the U.S. because of import restrictions. A U.S.-made version was mfd. by Interarms from 1986-99.
German model . . . . NiB $858 Ex $704 Gd $338
U.S. model . . . . NiB $411 Ex $375 Gd $241

NOTE: The Walther Olympia Model pistols were manufactured 1952-1963 by Hämmerli AG Jagd-und Sportwaffenfabrik, Lenzburg, Switzerland, and marketed as "Hämmerli-Walther." See Hämmerli listings for specific data.

OLYMPIA MODEL 200 AUTO PISTOL, 1952 TYPE . . . . NiB $725 Ex $663 Gd $442
Similar to 1936 Walther Olympia Funfkampf Model.

For the following Hammerli-Walther Models (200, 201, 202, 203, 204, and 205) See listings under Hammerli Section.

WARNER PISTOL — Norwich, Connecticut Warner Arms Corp. (or Davis-Warner Arms Co.)

INFALLIBLE POCKET AUTOMATIC PISTOL . . . . NiB $503 Ex $400 Gd $143
Caliber: .32 Auto. Seven-round magazine, 3-inch bbl., 6.5 inches overall. Weight: About 24 oz. Fixed sights. Blued finish. Hard rubber grips. Made 1917-19.

Walther P38

Walther P38K

Walther P88

Walther TPH (Current)

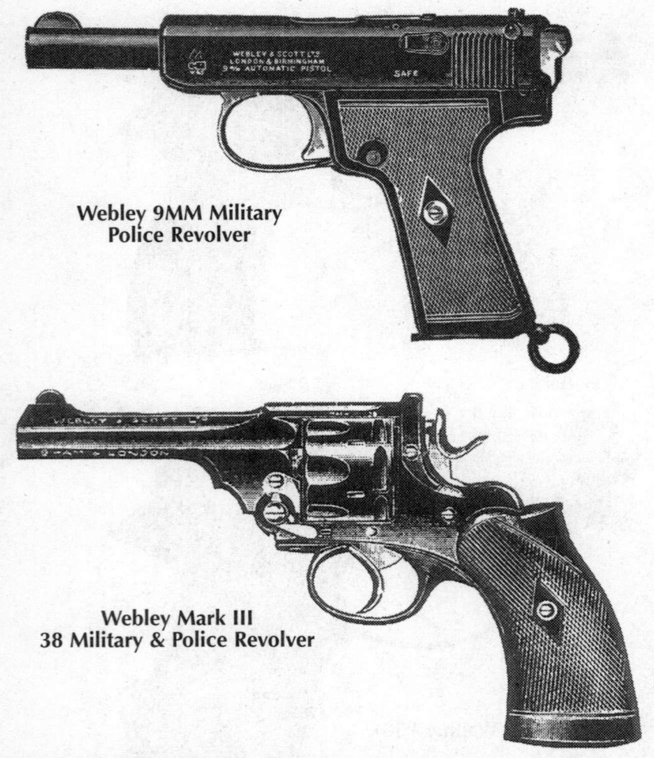

Webley 9MM Military Police Revolver

Webley Mark III 38 Military & Police Revolver

WEBLEY & SCOTT LTD. — London and Birmingham, England

MODEL 9MM MILITARY & POLICE AUTOMATIC........ NiB $1025 Ex $922 Gd $536
Caliber: 9mm Browning Long. Eight-round magazine, 8 inches overall. Weight: 32 oz. Fixed sights. Blued finish. Checkered Vulcanite grips. Made 1909-30.

MODEL 25 HAMMER AUTOMATIC .... NiB $359 Ex $281 Gd $153
Caliber: .25 Automatic. Six-round magazine, overall length: 4.75 inches. Weight: 11.75 oz. No sights. Blued finish. Checkered Vulcanite grips. Made 1906-40.

MODEL 25 HAMMERLESS AUTOMATIC................ NiB $410 Ex $256 Gd $153
Caliber: .25 Automatic. Six-round magazine, overall length: 4.25 inches, weight: 9.75 oz. Fixed sights. Blued finish. Checkered Vulcanite grips. Made 1909-.40.

MARK I 455 AUTOMATIC PISTOL .... NiB $1861 Ex $1398 Gd $625
Caliber: .455 Webley Auto. Seven-round magazine, 5-inch bbl., 8.5 inches overall. Weight: About 39 oz. Fixed sights. Blued finish. Checkered Vulcanite grips. Made 1913-31. Reissued during WWII. Total production about 9,300. Note: Mark I No. 2 is same pistol w/adj. rear sight and modified manual safety.

MARK III 38 MILITARY & POLICE REVOLVER .... NiB $385 Ex $329 Gd $169
Hinged frame. DA. Caliber: .38 S&W. Six-round cylinder, bbl. lengths: 3- and 4-inches. 9.5 inches overall (with 4-inch bbl.). Weight: 21 oz. (with 4-inch bbl.). Fixed sights. Blued finish. Checkered walnut or Vulcanite grips. Made 1897-45.

MARK IV 22 CALIBER TARGET REVOLVER............ NiB $733 Ex $604 Gd $244
Same frame and general appearance as Mark IV .38. Caliber: .22 LR. Six-round cylinder, 6-inch bbl., 10.13 inches overall. Weight: 34 oz. Target sights. Blued finish. Checkered grips. Disc. 1945.

MARK IV 38 MILITARY & POLICE REVOLVER .... NiB $490 Ex $413 Gd $220
Identical in appearance to the double-action Mark IV .22 w/hinged frame except chambered for .38 S&W. Six-round cylinder, bbl. length: 3-, 4- and 5-inches; 9.13 inches overall (with 5-inch bbl.). Weight: 27 oz. (with 5-inch bbl.). Fixed sights. Blued finish. Checkered grips. Made 1929-c. 1957.

MARK VI NO. 1 BRITISH SERVICE REVOLVER .... NiB $336 Ex $284 Gd $192
DA. Hinged frame. Caliber: 455 Webley. Six-round cylinder, bbl. lengths: 4-, 6- and 7.5-inches; 11.25 inches overall (with 6-inch bbl.). Weight: 38 oz. (with 6-inch bbl.). Fixed sights. Blued finish. Checkered walnut or Vulcanite grips. Made 1915-1947.

MARK VI 22 TARGET REVOLVER............ NiB $490 Ex $413 Gd $212
Same frame and general appearance as the Mark VI 455. Caliber: .22 LR. Six-round cylinder, 6-inch bbl., 11.25 inches overall. Weight: 40 oz. Target sights. Blued finish. Checkered walnut or Vulcanite grips. Disc. 1945.

METROPOLITAN POLICE AUTOMATIC PISTOL .... NiB $490 Ex $336 Gd $197
Calibers: .32 Auto, .380 Auto. Eight-round (.32) or 7-round (.380) magazine, 3.5-inch bbl., 6.25 inches overall. weight: 20 oz. Fixed sights. Blued finish. Checkered Vulcanite grips. Made 1906-40 (.32) and 1908-20 (.380).

RIC MODEL DA REVOLVER .... NiB $327 Ex $280 Gd $136
Royal Irish Constabulary or Bulldog Model. Solid frame. Caliber: .455 Webley. Five-round cylinder, 2.25-inch bbl., weight: 21 oz. Fixed sights. Blued finish. Checkered walnut or vulcanite grips. Disc.

SEMIAUTOMATIC SINGLE-SHOT PISTOL .... NiB $1015 Ex $809 Gd $526
Similar in appearance to the Webley Metropolitan Police Automatic, this pistol is "semiautomatic" in the sense that the fired case is extracted and ejected and the hammer cocked as in a blow-back automatic pistol; it is loaded singly and the slide manually operated in loading. Caliber: .22 Long, 4.5- or 9-inch bbl., 10.75 inches overall (with 9-inch bbl.). Weight: 24 oz. (with 9-inch bbl.). Adj. sights. Blued finish. Checkered Vulcanite grips. Made 1911-27.

SINGLE-SHOT TARGET PISTOL ...... NiB $410 Ex $281 Gd $127
Hinge frame. Caliber: .22 LR. 10-inch bbl., 15 inches overall. Weight: 37 oz. Fixed sights on earlier models, current production has adj. rear sight. Blued finish. Checkered walnut or Vulcanite grips. Made 1909 to date.

FOSBERY AUTOMATIC REVOLVER
Hinged frame. Recoil action revolves cylinder and cocks hammer. Caliber: 455 Webley. Six-round cylinder, 6-inch bbl., 12 inches overall. Weight: 42 oz. Fixed or adjustable sights. Blued finish. Checkered walnut grips. Made 1901-1939. Note: A few were produced in caliber .38 Colt Auto w/an 8-shot cylinder (very rare).
1901 model............... NiB $6280 Ex $5765 Gd $3190
1902 model............... NiB $5765 Ex $4220 Gd $1645
1904 model............... NiB $5665 Ex $4220 Gd $1645
.38 Colt (8-round), add 100%
Target model w/adjustable sights, add .... .20%

WESSON FIREARMS CO., INC. — Palmer, Massachusetts Formerly Dan Wesson Arms, Inc.

MODEL 8 SERVICE
Same general specifications as Model 14 except caliber .38 Special. Made 1971-75. Values same as for Model 14.

MODEL 8-2 SERVICE
Same general specifications as Model 14-2 except caliber .38 Special. Made 1975 to date. Values same as for Model 14-2.

MODEL 9 TARGET
Same as Model 15 except caliber .38 Special. Made 1971-75. Values same as for Model 15.

MODEL 9-2 TARGET
Same as Model 15-2 except caliber .38 Special. Made 1975 to date. Values same as for Model 15-2.

MODEL 9-2H HEAVY BARREL
Same general specifications as Model 15-2H except caliber .38 Special. Made 1975 to date. Values same as for Model 15-2H. Disc. 1983.

MODEL 9-2HV VENT RIB HEAVY BARREL
Same as Model 15-2HV except caliber .38 Special. Made 1975 to date. Values same as for Model 15-2HV.

MODEL 9-2V VENT RIB
Same as Model 15-2V except caliber .38 Special. Made 1975 to date. Values same as for Model 15-2H.

MODEL 11 SERVICE DA REVOLVER
Caliber: .357 Magnum. Six-round cylinder. bbl. lengths: 2.5-, 4-, 6-inches interchangeable bbl. assemblies, 9 inches overall (with 4-inch bbl.). Weight: 38 oz. (with 4-inch bbl.). Fixed sights. Blued finish. Interchangeable grips. Made 1970-71. Note: The Model 11 has an external bbl., nut.
W/one bbl. assembly and grip. . . . . NiB $214 Ex $186 Gd $141
Extra bbl. assembly, add $60
Extra grip, add $45

MODEL 12 TARGET
Same general specifications as Model 11 except has adj. sights. Made 1970-71.
W/one-bbl. assembly and grip. . . . . NiB $261 Ex $217 Gd $154
Extra bbl. assembly, add $60
Extra grip, add $25

MODEL 14 SERVICE DA REVOLVER
Caliber: .357 Magnum. Six-round cylinder, bbl. length: 2.25-, 3.75, 5.75-inches; interchangeable bbl. assemblies, 9 inches overall (with 3.75-inch bbl.). Weight: 36 oz. (with 3.75-inch bbl.). Fixed sights. Blued or nickel finish. Interchangeable grips. Made 1971-75. Note: Model 14 has recessed bbl., nut.
W/one-bbl. assembly and grip. . . . . NiB $240 Ex $202 Gd $154
Extra bbl. assembly, add $60
Extra grip, add $25

MODEL 14-2 SERVICE DA REVOLVER
Caliber: .357 Magnum. Six-round cylinder, bbl. lengths: 2.5-, 4-, 6-, 8-inch; interchangeable bbl. assemblies, 9.25 inches overall (with 4-inch bbl.) Weight: 34 oz. (with 4-inch bbl.). Fixed sights. Blued finish. Interchangeable grips. Made 1975 to date. Note: Model 14-2 has recessed bbl. nut.

Dan Wesson
Model 14-2 Service

***(cont'd)* MODEL 14-2 SERVICE DA REVOLVER**
W/one bbl. assembly (8 inch) and grip . . . . . NiB $230 Ex $184 Gd $133
W/one bbl. assembly (other lengths) and grip. . . . . NiB $230 Ex $184 Gd $133
Extra bbl. assembly, 8 inch, add $65
Extra bbl. assembly, other lengths, add $50
Extra grip, add $25

MODEL 15 TARGET
Same general specifications as Model 14 except has adj. sights. Made 1971-75.
W/one bbl. assembly and grip. . . . . NiB $286 Ex $235 Gd $138
Extra bbl. assembly, add $60
Extra grip, add $25

MODEL 15-2 TARGET
Same general specifications as Model 14-2 except has adj. rear sight and interchangeable blade front; also avail. w/10-, 12- or 15-inch bbl., Made 1975 to date.
W/one bbl. assembly (8 inch) and grip . NiB $300 Ex $249 Gd $141
W/one bbl. assembly (10 inch) and grip . . NiB $300 Ex $249 Gd $141
W/one bbl. assembly (12 inch)/grip. Disc. . . . . NiB $300 Ex $249 Gd $141
W/one bbl. assembly (15 inch)/grip. Disc. . . . . NiB $300 Ex $249 Gd $141
W/one-bbl. assembly (other lengths)/grip. . . . . NiB $189 Ex $154 Gd $108
Extra bbl. assembly (8 inch), add $65
Extra bbl. assembly (10 inch), add $65
Extra bbl. assembly (12 inch). Disc., add $65
Extra bbl. assembly (15 inch). Disc., add $65
Extra bbl. assembly (other lengths), add $65
Extra grip, add. $25

MODEL 15-2H HEAVY BARREL
Same as Model 15-2 except has heavy bbl., assembly weight: with 4-inch bbl., 38 oz. Made 1975-83.
W/one bbl. assembly (8 inch) and grip . . . . . NiB $215 Ex $179 Gd $123
W/one bbl. assembly (10 inch) and grip . . . . . NiB $215 Ex $179 Gd $123
W/one bbl. assembly (12 inch) and grip . . . . . NiB $215 Ex $179 Gd $123
W/one bbl. assembly (15 inch) and grip . . . . . NiB $215 Ex $179 Gd $123
W/one bbl. assembly (other lengths)/grip . . . . . NiB $215 Ex $179 Gd $123
Extra bbl. assembly (8 inch), add $65
Extra bbl. assembly (10 inch), add $65
Extra bbl. assembly (12 inch), add $65
Extra bbl. assembly (15 inch), add $65
Extra bbl. assembly (other lengths), add $65
Extra grip, add $25

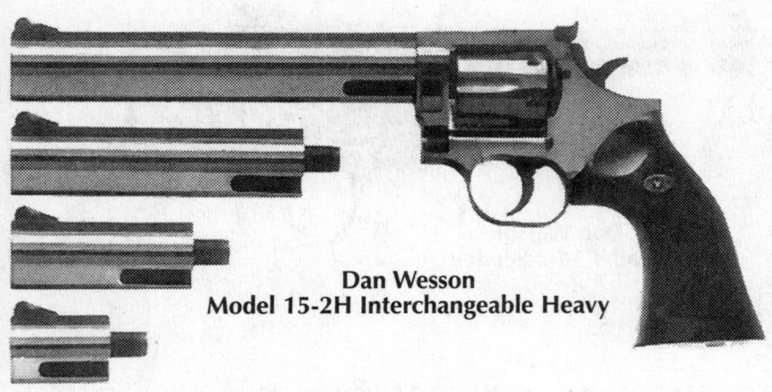
Dan Wesson
Model 15-2H Interchangeable Heavy

MODEL 15-2HV VENT RIB HEAVY BARREL
Same as Model 15-2 except has vent rib heavy bbl. assembly; weight: (w/4-inch bbl.) 37 oz. Made 1975 to date.
W/one bbl. assembly (8 inch) and grip ...... NiB $251 Ex $215 Gd $138
W/one bbl. assembly (10 inch) and grip ..... NiB $251 Ex $215 Gd $138
W/one bbl. assembly (12 inch) and grip ..... NiB $251 Ex $215 Gd $138
W/one bbl. assembly (15 inch) and grip .... NiB $266 Ex $251 Gd $174
W/one bbl. assembly (other lengths) and grip .... NiB $230 Ex $184 Gd $129
Extra bbl. assembly (8 inch), add $65
Extra bbl. assembly (10 inch), add $65
Extra bbl. assembly (12 inch), add $65
Extra bbl. assembly (15 inch), add $65
Extra bbl. assembly (other lengths), add $65
Extra grip, add $25

MODEL 15-2V VENT RIB
Same as Model 15-2 except has vent rib bbl. assembly, weight: 35 oz. (with 4-inch bbl.). Made 1975 to date. Values same as for 15-2H.

HUNTER PACS
Dan Wesson Hunter Pacs are offered in all Magnum calibers and include heavy vent rib 8-inch shrouded bbl., Burris scope mounts, bbl. changing tool in a case.
HP22M-V.................... NiB $800 Ex $621 Gd $402
HP22M-2.................... NiB $653 Ex $530 Gd $372
HP722M-V.................... NiB $755 Ex $611 Gd $427
HP722M-2.................... NiB $730 Ex $590 Gd $413
HP32-V.................... NiB $704 Ex $572 Gd $399
HP32-2.................... NiB $615 Ex $499 Gd $350
HP732-V.................... NiB $737 Ex $596 Gd $416
HP732-2.................... NiB $692 Ex $560 Gd $392
HP15-V.................... NiB $692 Ex $560 Gd $392
HP15-2.................... NiB $641 Ex $519 Gd $364
HP715-V.................... NiB $743 Ex $601 Gd $420
HP715-2.................... NiB $692 Ex $560 Gd $392
HP41-V.................... NiB $609 Ex $494 Gd $347
HP741-V.................... NiB $794 Ex $642 Gd $448
HP741-2.................... NiB $692 Ex $560 Gd $392
HP44-V.................... NiB $781 Ex $632 Gd $441
HP44-2.................... NiB $692 Ex $560 Gd $392
HP744-V.................... NiB $857 Ex $693 Gd $483
HP744-2.................... NiB $832 Ex $672 Gd $468
HP40-V.................... NiB $539 Ex $438 Gd $309
HP40-2.................... NiB $755 Ex $611 Gd $427
HP740-V.................... NiB $896 Ex $723 Gd $503
HP740-2.................... NiB $832 Ex $672 Gd $468
HP375-V.................... NiB $526 Ex $428 Gd $302
HP375-2.................... NiB $871 Ex $704 Gd $490
HP45-V.................... NiB $666 Ex $540 Gd $379

WHITNEY FIREARMS COMPANY — Hartford, Connecticut

WOLVERINE AUTOMATIC PISTOL
Dural frame/shell contains all operating components. Caliber: .22 LR. 10-round magazine, 4.63-inch bbl., 9 inches overall. Weight: 23 oz. Partridge-type sights. Blued or nickel finish. Plastic grips. Made 1955-62.
Wolverine model, blue .... NiB $463 Ex $385 Gd $231
Wolverine model, nickel .... NiB $643 Ex $514 Gd $262

WICHITA ARMS — Wichita, Kansas

CLASSIC PISTOL
Caliber: Chambered to order. Bolt-action, single-round. 11.25-inch octagonal bbl., 18 inches overall. Weight: 78 oz. Open micro sights. Custom-grade checkered walnut stock. Blued finish. Made 1980-97.
Standard .... NiB $3478 Ex $2417 Gd $2160
Presentation grade (engraved) .... NiB $5507 Ex $3756 Gd $2932

HUNTER PISTOL.............. NiB $1347 Ex $961 Gd $781
Bolt-action, single-shot. Calibers: .22 LR, .22 WRF, 7mm Super Mag., 7-30 Waters, .30-30 Win., .32 H&R Mag., .357 Mag., .357 Super Mag. 10.5-inch bbl., 16.5 inches overall, weight: 60 oz. No sights (scope mount only). Stainless steel finish. Walnut stock. Made 1983-94.

INTERNATIONAL PISTOL......... NiB $728 Ex $506 Gd $388
Top-break, single-shot. SA. Calibers: 7-30 Waters, 7mm Super Mag., 7R (.30-30 Win. necked to 7mm), .30-30 Win. .357 Mag., .357 Super Mag., .32 H&R Mag., .22 Mag., .22 LR. 10- and 14-inch bbl. (10.5 inch for centerfire calibers). Weight: 50-71 oz. Partridge front sight, adj. rear. Walnut forend and grips.

MK-40 SILHOUETTE PISTOL .... NiB $1596 Ex $1111 Gd $905
Calibers: .22-250, 7mm IHMSA, .308 Win. Bolt-action, single-shot. 13-inch bbl., 19.5 inches overall. Weight: 72 oz. Wichita Multi-Range sight system. Aluminum receiver w/blued bbl., gray Fiberthane glass stock. Made 1981 to date.

SILHOUETTE PISTOL (WSP) .... NiB $1961 Ex $1580 Gd $1286
Calibers: .22-250, 7mm IHMSA 308 Win. Bolt-action, single-shot. 14.94-inch bbl., 21.38 inches overall. Weight: 72 oz. Wichita Multi-Range sight system. Blued finish. Walnut or gray Fiberthane glass stock. Walnut center or rear grip. Made 1979 to date.

WILKINSON ARMS — Parma, Idaho

"LINDA" SEMI-AUTOMATIC PISTOL .... NiB $724 Ex $673 Gd $389
Caliber: 9mm Para. Luger. 31-round magazine, 8.25-inch bbl., 12.25 inches overall. Weight: 77 oz. Rear peep sight w/blade front. Blued finish. Checkered composition grips.

"SHERRY" SEMI-AUTOMATIC PISTOL .... NiB $275 Ex $226 Gd $133
Caliber: .22 LR. Eight-round magazine, 2.13-inch bbl., 4.38 inches overall. Weight: 9.25 oz. Crossbolt safety. Fixed sights. Blued or blue-gold finish. Checkered composition grips.

Twenty-Eighth Edition
GUN TRADER'S GUIDE

Rifles

Action Arms Timber Wolfe

Alpha Arms Custom

Alpha Arms Alaskan

Alpha Arms Jaguar

AA ARMS — Monroe, North Carolina

AR-9 SEMIAUTOMATIC CARBINE . . . . NiB $775 Ex $647 Gd $367
Semiautomatic recoil-operated rifle w/side-folding metal stock design. Fires from a closed bolt. Caliber: 9mm Parabellum. 20-round magazine. 16.25-inch bbl., 33 inches overall. Weight: 6.5 lbs. Fixed blade, protected postfront sight adjustable for elevation, winged square notched rear. Matte phosphate/blue or nickel finish. Checkered polymer grip/frame. Made 1991-94.

ACTION ARMS — Philadelphia, Pennsylvania

MODEL B SPORTER
SEMI-AUTOMATIC CARBINE . . . . . NiB $566 Ex $494 Gd $316
Similar to Uzi Carbine (see separate listing) except w/thumbhole stock. Caliber: 9mm Parabellum, 10-round magazine. 16-inch bbl. Weight: 8.75 lbs. Post front sight; adj. rear. Imported 1993-94.

TIMBER WOLFE REPEATING RIFLE
Calibers: .357 Mag./.38 Special and .44 Mag. slide-action. Tubular magazine holds 10 and 8 rounds, respectively. 18.5-inch bbl. 36.5 inches overall. Weight: 5.5 lbs. Fixed blade front sight; adj. rear. Receiver w/integral scope mounts. Checkered walnut stock. Imported 1989-94.

(cont'd.) **TIMBER WOLFE REPEATING RIFLE**
Blued model . . . . NiB $296 Ex $239 Gd $163
Chrome model, add. $50
.44 Mag., add $100

ALPHA ARMS, INC. — Dallas, Texas

CUSTOM BOLT-ACTION RIFLE . . . . NiB $1565 Ex $1234 Gd $775
Calibers: .17 Rem. thru .338 Win. Mag. Right or left-hand action in three action lengths w/three-lug locking system and 60-degree bolt rotation. 20- to 24-inch round or octagonal bbl. Weight: 6 to 7 lbs. No sights. Presentation-grade California Claro walnut stock w/hand-rubbed oil finish, custom inletted sling swivels and ebony forend tip. Made 1984-89.

ALASKAN BOLT-ACTION RIFLE . . . . NiB $1565 Ex $1234 Gd $775
Similar to Custom model except w/stainless-steel bbl. and receiver w/all other parts coated w/Nitex. Weight: 6.75 to 7.25 lbs. Open sights w/bbl-band sling swivel. Classic-style Alpha wood stock w/Niedner-style steel grip cap and solid recoil pad. Made 1984-89.

GRAND SLAM
BOLT-ACTION RIFLE. . . . . NiB $1234 Ex $979 Gd $673
Same as Custom model except w/Alphawood (fiberglass and wood) classic-style stock featuring Niedner-style grip cap. Weight: 6.5 lbs. Left-hand models. Made 1984-89.

JAGUAR BOLT-ACTION RIFLE
Same as Custom Rifle except designed on Mauser-style action w/claw extractor drilled and tapped for scope. Originally designated Alpha Model 1. Calibers: .243, 7mm-08, .308 original chambering (1984-85) up to .338 Win. Mag. in standard model; .338 thru .458 Win. Mag. in Big Five model (1984-85). Teflon-coated trigger guard/floorplate assembly. Made 1984-88.
Jaguar Grade I . . . . NiB $979 Ex $775 Gd $561
Jaguar Grade II . . . . NiB $1183 Ex $571 Gd $520
Jaguar Grade III. . . . . NiB $1234 Ex $979 Gd $673
Jaguar Grade IV. . . . . NiB $1336 Ex $979 Gd $673
Big Five model. . . . . NiB $1591 Ex $1132 Gd $877

AMERICAN ARMS — N. Kansas City, Missouri

1860 HENRY . . . . NiB $862 Ex $647 Gd $367
Replica of 1860 Henry rifle. Calibers: .44-40 or .45 LC. 24.25-inch half-octagonal bbl. 43.75 inches overall. Weight: 9.25 lbs. Brass frame and appointments. Straight-grip walnut buttstock.

1866 WINCHESTER
Replica of 1866 Winchester. Calibers: .44-40 or .45 LC. 19-inch round tapered bbl. (carbine) or 24.25-inch tapered octagonal bbl. (rifle). 38 to 43.25 inches overall. Weight: 7.75 or 8.15 lbs. Brass frame, elevator and buttplate. Walnut buttstock and forend.
Carbine . . . . NiB $673 Ex $571 Gd $352
Rifle. . . . . NiB $673 Ex $571 Gd $352

1873 WINCHESTER
Replica of 1873 Winchester rifle. Calibers: .44-40 or .45 LC. 24.25-inch tapered octagonal bbl. w/tubular magazine. Color casehardened steel frame w/brass elevator and ejection port cover. Walnut buttstock w/steel buttplate.
Standard model . . . . NiB $800 Ex $647 Gd $367
Deluxe model . . . . NiB $1042 Ex $836 Gd $571

AMERICAN SPIRIT ARMS CORP.— Scottsdale, Arizona

ASA BULL BARREL FLATTOP RIFLE . . . NiB $965 Ex $640 Gd $465
Semi-automatic. Caliber: ..223 Rem. Patterned after AR-15. Forged steel lower receiver, aluminum flattop upper receiver, 24-inch stainless bull barrel, free-floating aluminum hand guard, includes Harris bipod.

ASA BULL BARREL A2 RIFLE . . . . NiB $890 Ex $665 Gd $465
Similar to Flattop Rifle except has A2 upper receiver with carrying handle and sights. Introduced 1999.

OPEN MATCH RIFLE . . . . NiB $1365 Ex $965 Gd $665
Caliber: .223 Rem. Bbl.: 16-inch fluted and ported stainless steel match with round shroud. Flattop without sights, forged upper and lower receiver, match trigger. Introduced 2001.

LIMITED MATCH RIFLE . . . . NiB $1315 Ex $840 Gd $540
Caliber: .223 Rem. Bbl.: 16-inch fluted stainless steel match with round shroud. National Match front and rear sights; match trigger.

DCM SERVICE RIFLE. . . . . NiB $1315 Ex $990 Gd $540
Caliber: .223 Rem. Bbl.: 20-inch stainless steel match type with free-floating shroud. National Match front and rear sights; match trigger; pistol grip.

ASA M4 RIFLE. . . . . NiB $865 Ex $610 Gd $415
Caliber: .223 Rem. Non-collapsible stock, M4 hand guard, 16-inch bbl. w/muzzle brake; aluminum flattop upper receiver.

ASA A2 RIFLE . . . . NiB $835 Ex $565 Gd $440
Caliber: .223 Rem. A2 receiver; 20-inch National Match barrel. Introduced 1999.

ASA CARBINE. . . . . NiB $985 Ex $640 Gd $540
Caliber: .223 Rem. or Short. Side-charging, flattop receiver; M4 hand guard; 16-inch National Match bbl. w/slotted muzzle brake.

POST-BAN CARBINE. . . . . NiB $845 Ex $595 Gd $440
Caliber: .223 Rem. Wilson 16-inch National Match bbl.; non-collapsible stock. Introduced 1999.

BULL BARREL A2 INVADER . . . . NiB $970 Ex $660 Gd $480
Caliber: .223 Rem. Similar to ASA 24-inch bull bbl. rifle except has 16-inch stainless steel bbl.. Introduced 1999.

A2 CAR CARBINE. . . . . NiB $965 Ex $660 Gd $490
Caliber: 9mm Parabellum. Forged receiver, non-collapsible stock. Bbl.: 16-inch Wilson w/o muzzle brake, bird cage flash hider (pre-ban) or muzzle brake (post-ban).

FLATTOP CAR RIFLE. . . . . NiB $965 Ex $740 Gd $540
Caliber: 9mm Parabellum. Similar to A2 CAR Rifle except flattop design w/o sights. Introduced 2002.

ASA TACTICAL RIFLE . . . . NiB $1690 Ex $1010 Gd $690
Caliber: .308 Win. Bbl.: 16-inch stainless steel regular or match; side-charging handle; pistol grip.
Match model (w/fluted bbl. match trigger, chrome finish) . Add $525

ASA 24-INCH MATCH RIFLE . . . . . . NiB $1690 Ex $1010 Gd $690
Caliber: .308 Win. Bbl.: 24-inch stainless steel match with or w/o fluting/porting. Side-charging handle; pistol grip. Introduced 2002.

AMT (ARCADIA MACHINE & TOOL) — Irwindale, California

BOLT-ACTION REPEATING RIFLE
Winchester-type push-feed or Mauser-type controlled-feed short-, medium- or long-action. Calibers: .223 Remington, .22-250 Remington, .243 A, .243 Winchester, 6mm PPC, .25-06 Remington, 6.5x08, .270 Winchester, 7x57 Mauser, 7mm-08 Remington, 7mm Remington Mag., 7.62x39mm, .308 Winchester, .30-06, .300 Winchester Mag., .338 Winchester Mag., .375 H&H, .416 Remington, .416 Rigby, .458 Winchester Mag. 22- to 28-inch number 3 contour bbl. Weight: 7.75 to 8.5 lbs. Sights: None furnished; drilled and tapped for scope mounts. Classic composite or Kevlar stock. Made 1996-97.
Standard model . . . . NiB $828 Ex $649 Gd $471
Deluxe model . . . . NiB $1032 Ex $8128 Gd $522

BOLT-ACTION SINGLE-SHOT RIFLE
Winchester-type cone breech push-feed or Mauser-type controlled-feed action. Calibers: .22 Hornet, .22 PPC, .222 Remington, .223 Remington, .22-250 Remington, .243 A, .243 Winchester, 6mm PPC, 6.5x08, .270 Win., 7mm-08 Remington, .308 Winchester 22- to 28-inch #3 contour bbl. Weight: 7.75 to 8.5 lbs. Sights: None furnished; drilled and tapped for scope mounts. Classic composite or Kevlar stock. Made 1996-97.
Standard model. . . . . NiB $853 Ex $675 Gd $522
Deluxe model . . . . NiB $1027 Ex $828 Gd $624

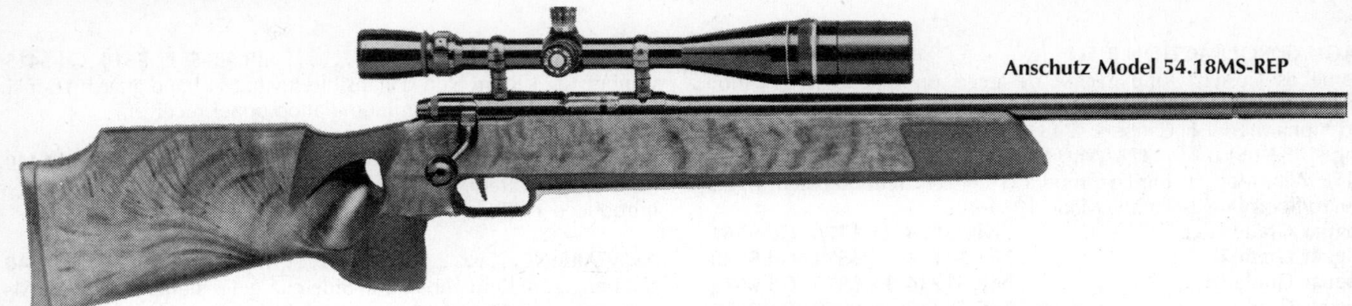
Anschutz Model 54.18MS-REP

CHALLENGER AUTOLOADING TARGET RIFLE SERIES I, II & III
Similar to Small Game Hunter except w/McMillan target fiberglass stock. Caliber: .22 LR. 10-round magazine. 16.5-, 18-, 20- or 22-inch bull bbl. Drilled and tapped for scope mount; no sights. Stainless steel finish. Made 1994-98.
Challenger I Standard .... NiB $726 Ex $522 Gd $343
Challenger II w/muzzle brake..... NiB $860 Ex $700 Gd $496
Challenger III w/bbl extension .... NiB $765 Ex $624 Gd $444
W/jewelled trigger, add.......................... $200

LIGHTNING 25/22
AUTOLOADING RIFLE .... NiB $236 Ex $190 Gd $124
Caliber: .22 LR. 25-round magazine. 18-inch tapered or bull bbl. Weight: 6 lbs. 37 inches overall. Sights: Adj. rear; ramp front. Folding stainless-steel stock w/matte finish. Made 1984-94.

LIGHTNING SMALL GAME HUNTER SERIES
Similar to AMT 25/22 except w/conventional matte black fiberglass/nylon stock. 10-round rotary magazine. 22-inch bbl. 40.5 inches overall. Weight: 6 lbs. Grooved for scope; no sights. Made 1987-94 (Series I), 1992-93 (Series II).
Hunter I.................... NiB $218 Ex $179 Gd $118
Hunter II (w/22-inch
heavy target bbl.) .... NiB $235 Ex $190 Gd $128

MAGNUM HUNTER AUTO RIFLE .... NiB $382 Ex $307 Gd $211
Similar to Lightning Small Game Hunter II model except chambered in .22 WRF w/22-inch match-grade bbl. Made 1993 to date.

ANSCHUTZ RIFLES — Ulm, Germany Mfd. by J.G. Anschutz GmbH Jagd und Sportwaffenfabrik

Currently imported by AcuSport Corp.; Accuracy International; Champion's Choice; Champion Shooter's Supply, Go Sportsmen's Supply, Inc.; Gunsmithing Inc. (Previously by Precision Sales Int'l., Inc.)

Anschutz models 1407 ISU, 1408-ED, 1411, 1413, 1418, 1432, 1433, 1518 and 1533 were marketed in the U.S by Savage Arms. Further, Anschutz models 1403, 1416, 1422D, 1441, 1516 and 1522D were sold as Savage/Anschutz with Savage model designations (see also listings under Savage Arms

MODEL 54 18MS .... NiB $1251 Ex $993 Gd $684
Bolt-action, single-shot, Caliber: .22 LR. 22-inch bbl. European hardwood stock w/cheekpiece. Stipple-checkered forend and Wundhammer swell pistol-grip. Receiver grooved, drilled and tapped for scope blocks. Weight: 8.4 lbs. Imported 1982-97.

MODEL 54.18MS-REP REPEATING RIFLE
Same as model 54.18MS except w/repeating action and 5-round magazine. 22- to 30-inch bbl. 41-49 inches overall. Avg. weight: 7 lbs., 12 oz. Hardwood or synthetic gray thumbhole stock. Imported 1989-97.

***(cont'd.)* MODEL 54.18MS-REP REPEATING RIFLE**
Standard MS-REP model .... NiB $1405 Ex $1148 Gd $736
Left-hand model .... NiB $1277 Ex $1045 Gd $684

MODEL 64S BOLT-ACTION SINGLE-SHOT RIFLE
Bolt-action, single-shot. Caliber: .22 LR. 26-inch bbl. Checkered European hardwood stock w/Wundhammer swell pistol-grip and adj. buttplate. Single-stage trigger. Aperture sights. Weight: 8.25 lbs. Imported 1963-82.
Standard .... NiB $525 Ex $371 Gd $267
Left-hand model .... NiB $525 Ex $371 Gd $293

MODEL 64MS BOLT-ACTION SINGLE-SHOT RIFLE
Bolt-action, single-shot. Caliber: .22 LR. 21.25-inch bbl. European hardwood silhouette-style stock w/cheekpiece. Forend base and Wundhammer swell pistol-grip, stipple-checkered. Adj. two-stage trigger. Receiver grooved, drilled and tapped for scope blocks. Weight: 8 lbs. Imported 1982-96.
Standard or Featherweight
(disc. 1988) .... NiB $808 Ex $705 Gd $344
Left-hand model .... NiB $834 Ex $710 Gd $463

MODEL 64MSR BOLT-ACTION REPEATER
Similar to Anschutz Model 64MS except repeater w/5-round magazine. Imported 1996 to date.
Standard model................ NiB $808 Ex $705 Gd $422
Left-hand model .... NiB $834 Ex $705 Gd $422

MODEL 520/61 SEMIAUTOMATIC...... NiB $416 Ex $267 Gd $113
Caliber: .22 LR. 10-round magazine. 24-inch bbl. Sights: Folding leaf rear, hooded ramp front. Receiver grooved for scope mounting. Rotary-style safety. Monte Carlo stock and beavertail forend, checkered. Weight: 6.5 lbs. Imported 1982-83.

MODEL 525 AUTOLOADER
Caliber: .22 LR. 10-round magazine. 20- or 24-inch bbl. 39 to 43 inches overall. Weight: 6.1 to 6.5 lbs. Adj. folding rear sight; hooded ramp front. Checkered European hardwood Monte Carlo style buttstock and beavertail forend. Sling swivel studs. Imported since 1982.
Carbine model
(disc. 1986) .... NiB $401 Ex $267 Gd $164
Rifle model (24-inch bbl.) .... NiB $493 Ex $396 Gd $273

MODEL 1403B .... NiB $885 Ex $679 Gd $370
A lighter-weight model designed for Biathlon competition. Caliber: .22 LR. 21.5-inch bbl. Adj. two-stage trigger. Adj. grooved wood buttplate, stipple-checkered deep thumb-rest flute and straight pistol-grip. Weight: 9 lbs. w/sights. Imported 1982-1992.

MODEL 1403D MATCH SINGLE-SHOT TARGET RIFLE
Caliber: .22 LR. 25-inch bbl. 43 inches overall. Weight: 8.6 lbs. No sights, receiver grooved for Anschutz target sights. Walnut-finished hardwood target stock w/adj. buttplate. Importation disc. 1992.
Standard model................ NiB $648 Ex $520 Gd $357
W/match sights .... NiB $905 Ex $726 Gd $497

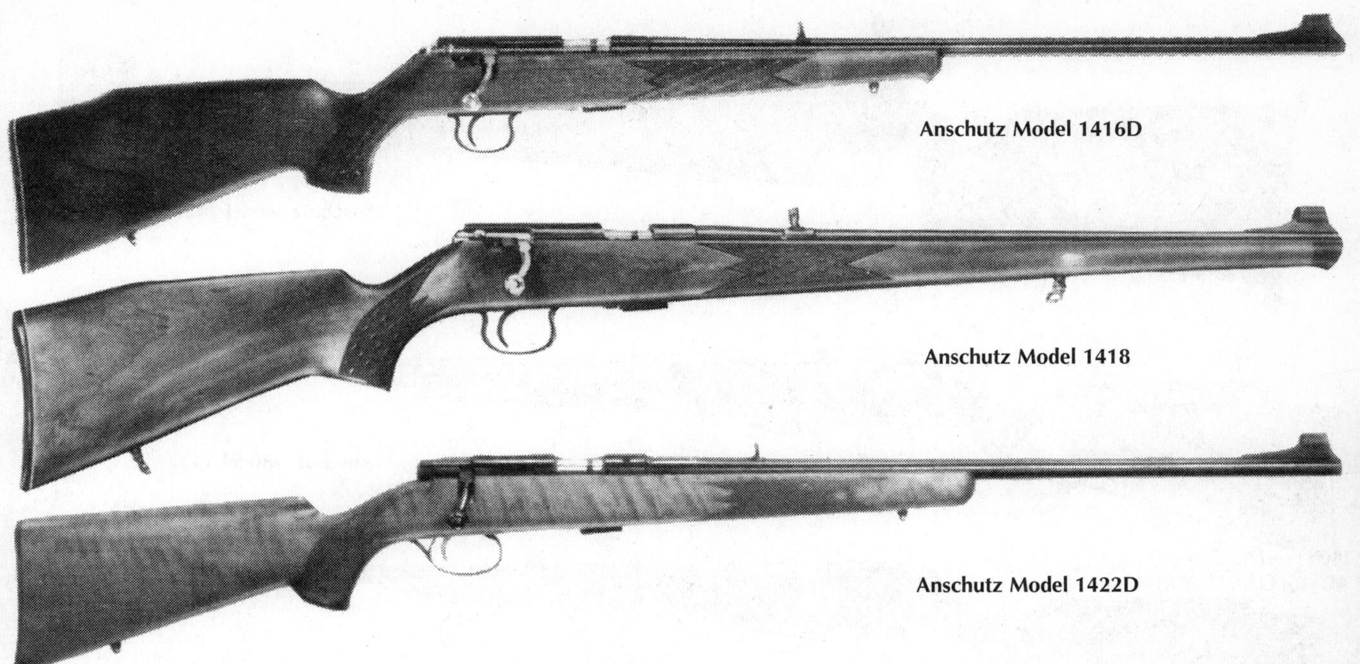

Anschutz Model 1416D

Anschutz Model 1418

Anschutz Model 1422D

MODEL 1407 ISU MATCH 54 RIFLE
Bolt-action, single-shot, caliber: .22 LR. 26.88-inch bbl. Scope bases. Receiver grooved for Anschutz sights. Single-stage adj. trigger. Select walnut target stock w/deep forearm for position shooting, adj. buttplate, hand stop and swivel. Weight: 10 lbs. Imported 1970-81.
Standard model . . . . NiB $576 Ex $499 Gd $242
Left-hand model . . . . NiB $576 Ex $499 Gd $242
W/international sights, add $65

MODEL 1408-ED
SUPER RUNNING BOAR . . . . NiB $422 Ex $370 Gd $319
Bolt-action, single-shot, caliber: .22 LR. 23.5-inch bbl. w/sliding weights. No metallic sights. Receiver drilled and tapped for scope-sight bases. Single-stage adj. trigger. Oversize bolt knob. Select walnut stock w/thumbhole, adj. comb and buttplate. Weight: 9.5 lbs. Intro. 1976. Disc.

MODEL 1411 MATCH 54 RIFLE
Bolt-action, single-shot. Caliber: .22 LR. 27.5-inch extra heavy bbl. w/mounted scope bases. Receiver grooved for Anschutz sights. Single-stage adj. trigger. Select walnut target stock w/cheekpiece (adj. in 1973 and later production), full pistol-grip, beavertail forearm, adj. buttplate, hand stop and swivel. Model 1411-L has left-hand stock. Weight: 11 lbs. Disc.
W/Non-adj. cheekpiece. . . . . NiB $422 Ex $370 Gd $216
W/adj. cheekpiece. . . . . NiB $590 Ex $473 Gd $325
with Anschutz
International Sight set . . . . NiB $325 Ex $139 Gd $98

MODEL 1413 SUPER MATCH 54 RIFLE
Freestyle international target rifle w/specifications similar to those of Model 1411, except w/special stock w/thumbhole, adj. pistol grip, adj. cheekpiece in 1973 and later production, adj. hook buttplate, adj. palmrest. Model 1413-L has left-hand stock. Weight: 15.5 lbs. Disc.
W/Non-adj. cheekpiece. . . . . NiB $757 Ex $679 Gd $350
W/Adj. cheekpiece . . . . NiB $634 Ex $510 Gd $319
With Anschutz
International Sight set $275

MODEL 1416D . . . . NiB $544 Ex $525 Gd $319
Bolt-action sporter. Caliber: .22 LR. 22.5-inch bbl. Sights: Folding leaf rear; hooded ramp front. Receiver grooved for scope mounting. Select European stock w/cheekpiece, skip-checkered pistol grip and forearm. Weight: 6 lbs. Imported 1982 to date.

MODEL 1416D CLASSIC/CUSTOM SPORTERS
Same as Model 1416D except w/American classic-style stock (Classic) or modified European-style stock w/Monte Carlo roll-over cheekpiece and Schnabel forend (Custom). Weight: 5.5 lbs. (Classic); 6 lbs. (Custom). Imported 1986 to date.
Model 1416D Classic . . . . NiB $602 Ex $484 Gd $332
Model 1416D Classic,
"True" left-hand . . . . NiB $648 Ex $520 Gd $357
Model 1416D Custom. . . . . NiB $583 Ex $468 Gd $313
Model 1416D fiberglass (1991-92). . . . NiB $711 Ex $571 Gd $392

MODEL 1418 BOLT-ACTION
SPORTER. NiB $368 Ex $291 Gd $162
Caliber: .22 LR. 5- or 10-round magazine. 19.75-inch bbl. Sights: Folding leaf rear; hooded ramp front. Receiver grooved for scope mounting. Select walnut stock, Mannlicher type w/cheekpiece, pistol-grip and forearm skip checkered. Weight: 5.5 lbs. Intro. 1976. Disc.

MODEL 1418D BOLT-ACTION
SPORTER. NiB $932 Ex $819 Gd $473
Caliber: .22 LR. 5- or 10-round magazine. 19.75-inch bbl. European walnut Monte Carlo stock, Mannlicher type w/cheekpiece, pistol-grip and forend skip-line checkered, buffalo horn Schnabel tip. Weight: 5.5 lbs. Imported from 1982-95 and 1998 to date.

MODEL 1422D CLASSIC/CUSTOM RIFLE
Bolt-action sporter. Caliber: .22 LR. Five-round removable straight-feed clip magazine. 24-inch bbl. Sights: Folding leaf rear; hooded ramp front. Select European walnut stock, classic type (Classic); Monte Carlo w/hand-carved rollover cheekpiece (Custom). Weight: 7.25 lbs. (Classic) 6.5 lbs. (Custom). Imported 1982-89.
Model 1422D Classic . . . . NiB $757 Ex $602 Gd $370
Model 1422D Custom. . . . . NiB $834 Ex $757 Gd $422

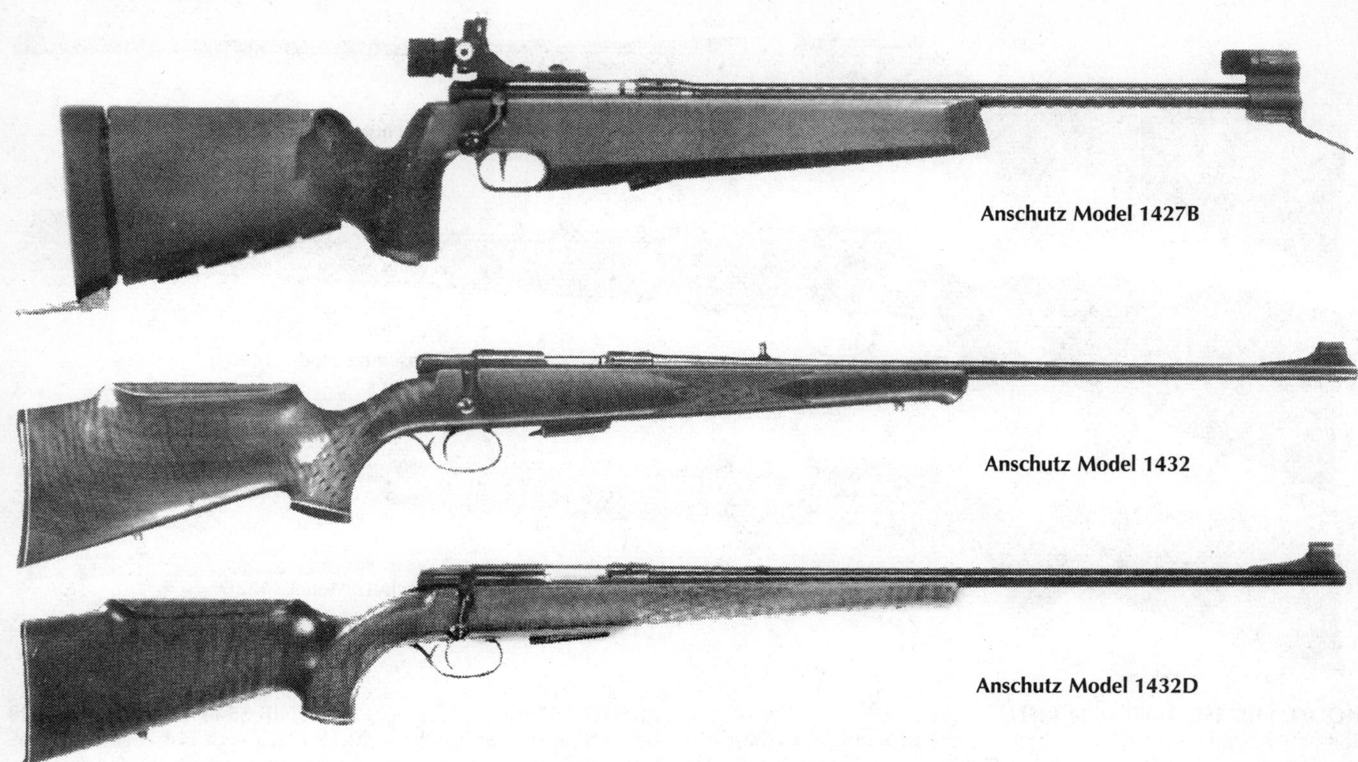

Anschutz Model 1427B

Anschutz Model 1432

Anschutz Model 1432D

MODEL 1427B BIATHLON RIFLE
Bolt-action clip repeater. Caliber: .22 LR. 21.5-inch bbl. Two-stage trigger w/wing-type safety. Hardwood stock w/deep fluting, pistol grip and deep forestock with adj. hand stop rail. Target sights w/adjustable weights. Advertised in 1981 but imported from 1982 to date as Model 1827B. (See that model designation for current values)

MODEL 1430D MATCH . . . . NiB $705 Ex $576 Gd $350
Improved version of Model 64S. Bolt-action, single-shot. Caliber: .22 LR. 26-inch medium-heavy bbl. Walnut Monte Carlo stock w/cheekpiece, adj. buttplate, deep midstock tapered to forend. Pistol-grip and contoured thumb groove w/stipple checkering. Single-stage adj. trigger. Target sights. Weight: 8.38 lbs. Imported 1982-83.

MODEL 1432 BOLT-ACTION SPORTER
Caliber: .22 Hornet. 5-round box magazine. 24-inch bbl. Sights: Folding leaf rear, hooded ramp front. Receiver grooved for scope mounting. Select walnut stock w/Monte Carlo comb and cheekpiece, pistol-grip and forearm skip-checkered. Weight: 6.75 lbs. Imported 1974-87. (Reintroduced as 1700/1730 series)
Early model
(1974-85). NiB $1243 Ex $892 Gd $635
Late model
(1985-87). NiB $1073 Ex $841 Gd $558

MODEL 1432D CLASSIC/CUSTOM RIFLE
Bolt-action sporter similar to Model 1422D except chambered for Caliber: .22 Hornet. 4-round magazine. 23.5-inch bbl. Weight: 7.75 lbs. (Classic); 6.5 lbs. (Custom). Classic stock on Classic model; fancy-grade Monte Carlo w/hand-carved rollover cheekpiece (Custom). Imported 1982-87. (Reintroduced as 1700/1730 series)
Model 1432D Classic . . . . NiB $1246 Ex $895 Gd $638
Model 1432D Custom. . . . . NiB $1075 Ex $844 Gd $561

MODEL 1433 BOLT-ACTION SPORTER . . . . . NiB $1055 Ex $844 Gd $586
Caliber: .22 Hornet. 5-round box magazine. 19.75-inch bbl. Sights: Folding leaf rear, hooded ramp front. Receiver grooved for scope mounting. Single-stage or double-set trigger. Select walnut Mannlicher stock; cheekpiece, pistol-grip and forearm skip-checkered. Weight: 6.5 lbs. Imported 1976-86.

MODEL 1448D CLAY BIRD. . . . . . . NiB $310 Ex $279 Gd $191
Similar to Model 1449 except chambered for Caliber: .22 LR. w/22.5-inch smooth bore bbl. and no sights. Walnut-finished hardwood stock. Imported 1999 to date.

MODEL 1449 YOUTH SPORTER . . . . NiB $243 Ex $197 Gd $135
Bolt-action sporter version of Model 2000. Caliber: .22 LR. 5-round box magazine. 16.25-inch bbl. Weight: 3.5 lbs. Hooded ramp front sight, addition. Walnut-finished hardwood stock. Imported 1989-92.

MODEL 1450B TARGET RIFLE . . . . NiB $654 Ex $473 Gd $319
Biathlon rifle developed on 2000 Series action. 19.5-inch bbl. Weight: 5.5 lbs. Adj. buttplate. Target sights. Imported 1993-94.

MODEL 1451 E/R SPORTER/TARGET
Bolt-action, single-shot (1451E) or repeater (1451R). Caliber: .22 LR. 22- or 22.75-inch bbl. w/o sights. Select hardwood stock w/stippled pistolgrip and vented forearm. beavertail forend, adj. cheekpiece, and deep thumb flute. Weight: 6.5 lbs. Imported 1996 to date.
Model 1451E (disc. 1997) . . . . NiB $422 Ex $319 Gd $216
Model 1451R . . . . NiB $438 Ex $405 Gd $250

MODEL 1451D CLASSIC/CUSTOM RIFLE
Same as Model 1451R except w/walnut-finished hardwood stock (Classic) or modified European-style walnut stock w/Monte Carlo rollover cheekpiece and Schnabel forend (Custom). Weight: 5 lbs. Imported 1996 to date.
Model 1451D Classic (Super) . . . . . NiB $315 Ex $238 Gd $160
Model 1451D Custom. . . . . NiB $454 Ex $413 Gd $274

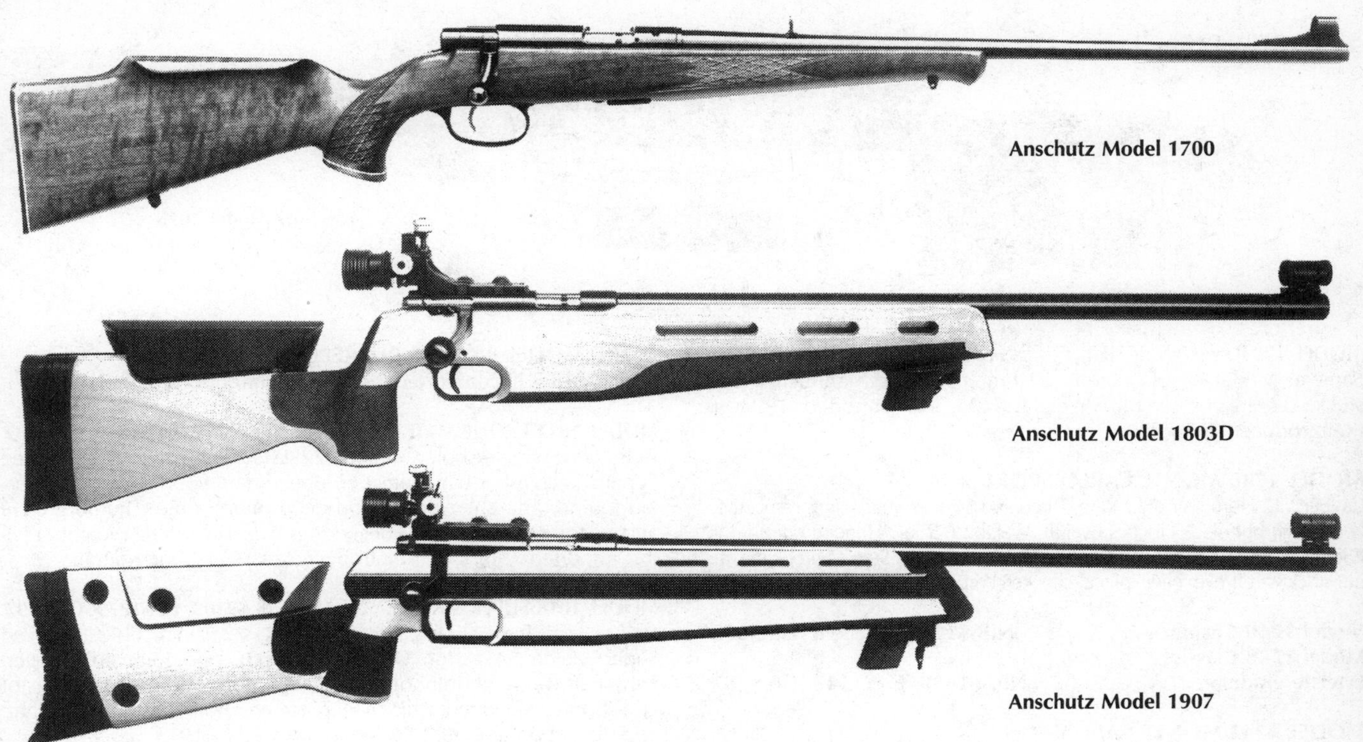

Anschutz Model 1700

Anschutz Model 1803D

Anschutz Model 1907

MODEL 1451 ST- R RIFLE . . . . NiB $443 Ex $403 Gd $288
Same as Model 1451R except w/two-stage trigger and walnut-finished hardwood uncheckered stock. Imported 1999 to date.

MODEL 1516D CLASSIC/CUSTOM RIFLE
Same as Model 1416D except chambered for Caliber: .22 Magnum RF, with American classic-style stock (Classic) or modified European-style stock w/Monte Carlo rollover cheekpiece and Schnabel forend (Custom). Weight: 5.5 lbs. (Classic), 6 lbs. (Custom). Imported 1986 to date.
Model 1516D Classic . . . . NiB $660 Ex $510 Gd $335
Model 1516D Custom . . . . NiB $685 Ex $560 Gd $360

MODELS 1516D/1518D LUXUS RIFLES
The alpha designation for these models was changed from Custom to Luxus in 1996-98. (See current Custom listings for Luxus values.)

MODELS 1518/1518D SPORTING RIFLES
Same as Model 1418 except chambered for .22 Magnum RF, 4-round box magazine. Model 1518 intro. 1976. Disc. Model 1518D has full Mannlicher-type stock. Imported 1982 to date.
Model 1518 . . . . NiB $710 Ex $590 Gd $360
Model 1518D . . . . NiB $905 Ex $710 Gd $485
W/set trigger, add $125

MODEL 1522D CLASSIC/CUSTOM RIFLE
Same as Model 1422D except chambered for .22 Magnum RF, 4-round magazine. Weight: 6.5 lbs. (Custom). Fancy-grade Classic or Monte Carlo stock w/hand-carved rollover cheekpiece. Imported 1982-89. (Reintroduced as 1700D/1730D series)
Model 1522D Classic . . . . NiB $1015 Ex $815 Gd $565
Model 1522D Custom . . . . NiB $1015 Ex $815 Gd $565

MODEL 1532D CLASSIC/CUSTOM RIFLE
Same as Model 1432D except chambered for .222 Rem. Three-round mag. Weight: 6.5 lbs. (Custom). Classic stock on Classic Model; fancy-grade Monte Carlo stock w/handcarved rollover cheekpiece (Custom). Imported 1982-89. (Reintroduced as 1700D/174 D0 series)
Model 1532D Classic . . . . NiB $905 Ex $710 Gd $360
Model 1532D Custom . . . . NiB $1200 Ex $910 Gd $610

MODEL 1533 . . . . NiB $1014 Ex $764 Gd $514
Same as Model 1433 except chambered for .222 Rem. Three-shot box magazine. Imported 1976-94.

MODEL 1700 SERIES BOLT-ACTION REPEATER
Match 54 Sporter. Calibers: .22 LR., .22 Magnum, .22 Hornet, .222 Rem. Five-shot removable magazine 24-inch bbl. 43 inches overall. Weight: 7.5 lbs. Folding leaf rear sight, hooded ramp front. Select European walnut stock w/cheekpiece and Schnabel forend tip. Imported 1989 to date.
Standard Model 1700
Bavarian — rimfire cal. . . . . NiB $925 Ex $865 Gd $505
Standard Model 1700
Bavarian — centerfire cal. . . . . NiB $1245 Ex $970 Gd $620
Model 1700D Classic (Classic
stock, 6.75 lbs.) rimfire cal. . . . . NiB $1095 Ex $915 Gd $620
Model 1700D Classic — centerfire cal. . . . . . NiB $1208 Ex $970 Gd $666
Model 1700D Custom — rimfire cal. . . . . NiB $1014 Ex $815 Gd $561
Model 1700D Custom — centerfire cal.. . . . . NiB $1239 Ex $995 Gd $683
Model 1700D Graphite Cust. (McMillan graphite
reinforced stock, 22 inch bbl., intro. 1991) . . NiB $1070 Ex $895 Gd $570
Select walnut and gold trigger . . . . add $181
Model 1700 FWT Feather-
weight (6.5 lbs.) rimfire calibers . . . . NiB $1051 Ex $845 Gd $581
Model 1700 FWT — centerfire cal. . . . . NiB $1220 Ex $1070 Gd $670

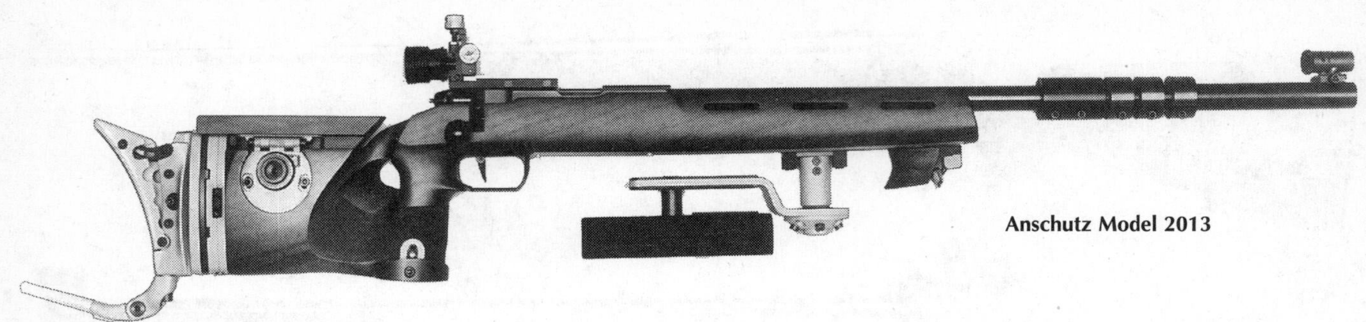
Anschutz Model 2013

MODEL 1733D MANNLICHER. . . . . . . NiB $1313 Ex $1101 Gd $792
Same as Model 1700D except w/19-inch bbl. and Mannlicher-style stock. 39 inches overall. Weight: 6.25 lbs. Imported 1993-96 (Reintroduced in 1998).

MODEL 1740 MONTE CARLO SPORTER
Caliber: .22 Hornet or .222 Rem. Three and 5-round magazines respectively. 24-inch bbl. 43.25 inches overall. Weight: 6.5 lbs. Hooded ramp front, folding leaf rear. Drilled and tapped for scope mounts. Select European walnut stock w/roll-over cheekpiece, checkered grip and forend. Imported 1997 to date.
Model 1740 Custom . . . . NiB $1264 Ex $998 Gd $638
Model 1740 Classic
(Meistergrade) . . . . NiB $1430 Ex $1148 Gd $787

MODEL 1743 MONTE CARLO
SPORTER . . . . NiB $1282 Ex $1050 Gd $689
Similar to Model 1740 except w/Mannlicher full stock. Imported 1997 to date.

MODEL 1803D MATCH SINGLE-SHOT TARGET RIFLE
Caliber: .22 LR. 25.5-inch bbl. 43.75 inches overall. Weight: 8.5 lbs. No sights; receiver grooved, drilled and tapped for scope mounts. Blonde or walnut-finished hardwood stock w/adj. cheekpiece, stippled grip and forend. Left-hand version. Imported 1987-92.
Right-hand model
(Reintroduced as 1903D) . . . . NiB $937 Ex $782 Gd $473
Left-hand model . . . . NiB $1008 Ex $808 Gd $553

MODEL 1807 ISU
STANDARD MATCH . . . . NiB $1282 Ex $998 Gd $638
Bolt-action single-shot. Caliber: 22 LR. 26-inch bbl. Improved Super Match 54 action. Two-stage match trigger. Removable cheekpiece, adj. buttplate, thumbpiece and forestock w/stipple-checkered. Weight: 10 lbs. Imported 1982-88. (Reintroduced as 1907 ISU)

MODEL 1808ED SUPER RUNNING TARGET
Bolt-action single-shot. Caliber: .22 LR. 23.5-inch bbl. w/sliding weights. Improved Super Match 54 action. Heavy beavertail forend w/adj.cheekpiece and buttplate. Adj. single-stage trigger. Weight: 9.5 lbs. Imported from 1982-96.
Right-hand model . . . . NiB $1555 Ex $1256 Gd $792
Left-hand model . . . . NiB $1597 Ex $1282 Gd $878

MODEL 1808MS-R
METALLIC SILHOUETTE . . . . NiB $1925 Ex $1462 Gd $844
Bolt-action repeater. Caliber: .22 LR. 19.2-inch bbl. w/o sights. Thumbhole Monte Carlo stock w/grooved forearm enhanced w/ "Anschutz" logo. Weight: 8.2 lbs. Imported from 1998 to date.

MODEL 1810 SUPER MATCH II . . . . . . NiB $1900 Ex $1359 Gd $844
A less detailed version of the Super Match 1813 model. Tapered forend w/deep receiver area. Select European hardwood stock.

***(cont'd.)* MODEL 54.18MS-REP REPEATING RIFLE**
Weight: 13.5 lbs. Imported 1982-88 (reintroduced as 1910 series).

MODEL 1811 PRONE MATCH . . . . NiB $1750 Ex $1539 Gd $782
Bolt-action single-shot. Caliber: .22 LR. 27.5-inch bbl. Improved Super Match 54 action. Select European hardwood stock w/beavertail forend, adj. cheekpiece, and deep thumb flute. Thumb groove and pistol grip w/stipple checkering. Adj. buttplate. Weight: 11.5 lbs. Imported 1982-88. (Reintroduced as 1911Prone Match)

MODEL 1813 SUPER MATCH. . . . . NiB $2209 Ex $1879 Gd $797
Bolt-action single-shot. Caliber: .22 LR. 27.5-inch bbl. Improved Super Match 54 action w/light firing pin, one-point adj. trigger. European walnut thumbhole stock, adj. palm rest, forend and pistol grip stipple checkered. Adj. cheekpiece and hook buttplate. Weight: 15.5 lbs. Imported 1982-88. (Reintroduced as 1913 Super Match)

MODEL 1827 BIATHLON RIFLE
Bolt-action clip repeater. Caliber: .22 LR. 21.5-inch bbl. 42.5 inches overall. Weight: 8.5 to 9 lbs. Slide safety. Adj. target sight set w/snow caps. European walnut stock w/cheekpiece, stippled pistol grip and forearm w/adj. weights. Fortner straight pull bolt option offered in 1986. Imported 1982 to date.
Mdl. 1827B w/Sup. Mat. 54 action . . . . NiB $2291 Ex $2085 Gd $952
Model 1827B, left-hand . . . . NiB $2037 Ex $1652 Gd $1160
Model 1827BT w/Fortner
Option, right-hand . . . . NiB $2394 Ex $2188 Gd $949
Model 1827BT, left-hand . . . . NiB $2553 Ex $2054 Gd $1440
Model 1827BT w/laminated stock, add $175
W/stainless steel bbl., add $205

MODEL 1907 ISU INTERNATIONAL MATCH RIFLE
Updated version of Model 1807 w/same general specifications as Model 1913 except w/26-inch bbl. 44.5 inches overall. Weight: 11 lbs. Designed for ISU 3-position competition. Fitted w/vented beechwood or walnut, blonde or color-laminated stock. Imported 1989 to date.
Right-hand model . . . . NiB $1498 Ex $1307 Gd $792
Left-hand model . . . . NiB $1684 Ex $1369 Gd $966
W/laminated stock, add $135
W/walnut stock, add $100
W/stainless steel bbl., add $130

MODEL 1910 INTERNATIONAL SUPER MATCH RIFLE
Updated version of Model 1810 w/same general specifications Model 1913 except w/less-detailed hardwood stock w/tapered forend. Weight: 13.5 lbs. Imported 1989 to date.
Right-hand model . . . . NiB $2492 Ex $2003 Gd $1029
Left-hand model . . . . NiB $2486 Ex $2023 Gd $1432

MODEL 1911 PRONE MATCH RIFLE
Updated version of Model 1811 w/same general specifications Model 1913 except w/specialized prone match hardwood stock w/beavertail forend. Weight: 11.5 lbs. Imported 1989 to date.
Right-hand model . . . . NiB $1800 Ex $1710 Gd $795

Anschutz Achiever

MODEL 1912
LADIES' SPORT RIFLE . . . . NiB $1760 Ex $1544 Gd $792
Similar to the Model 1907 designed for ISU 3-position competition w/same general U.I.T. specifications except w/shorter dimensions to accomodate smaller competitors. Weight: 11.4 lbs. Imported 1999 to date.

MODEL 1913 STANDARD RIFLE . . . . . . NiB $1522 Ex $1153 Gd $792
Similar to 1913 Super Match w/economized appointments. Imported 1997 to date.

MODEL 1913 SUPER MATCH RIFLE
Bolt-action single-shot Super Match (updated version of Model 1813). Caliber: .22 LR. 27.5-inch bbl. Weight: 14.2 lbs. Adj. two-stage trigger. Vented International thumbhole stock w/adj. cheekpiece, hand and palm rest, fitted w/10-way butthook. Imported 1989 to date.
Right-hand model . . . . NiB $2203 Ex $1874 Gd $792
Left-hand model . . . . NiB $2274 Ex $1822 Gd $1246
W/laminated stock, add $130
W/stainless steel bbl., add $140

MODEL 2007 ISU STANDARD RIFLE
Bolt-action single-shot. Caliber: .22 LR. 19.75-inch bbl. 43.5 to 44.5 inches overall. Weight: 10.8 lbs. Two-stage trigger. Standard ISU stock w/adj. cheekpiece. Imported 1992 to date.
Right-hand model . . . . NiB $1900 Ex $1436 Gd $823
Left-hand model . . . . NiB $2007 Ex $1627 Gd $1141
W/stainless steel bbl., add $140

MODEL 2013
LADIES' SPORT RIFLE . . . . NiB $2106 Ex $1925 Gd $834
Similar to the Model 2007 designed for ISU 3-position competition w/same general U.I.T. specifications except w/shorter dimensions to accomodate smaller competitors. Weight: 11.4 lbs. Imported 1999 to date.

MODEL 2013
BENCHREST RIFLE (BR-50) . . . . . NiB $1704 Ex $1539 Gd $792
Bolt-action single-shot. Caliber: .22 LR. 19.6-inch bbl. 43 inches overall. Weight: 10.3 lbs. Adjustable trigger for single or two-stage function. Benchrest-configuration stock. Imported 1999 to date.
MODEL 2013 SILHOUETTE RIFLE . . . . NiB $2090 Ex $1565 Gd $844
Bolt-action single-shot. Caliber: .22 LR. 20-inch bbl. 45.5 inches overall. Weight: 11.5 lbs. Two-stage trigger. Thumbhole black synthetic or laminated stock w/adj. cheekpiece, hand and palm rest. Imported 1994 to date.

MODEL 2013 SUPER MATCH RIFLE
Bolt-action single-shot. Caliber: .22 LR. 19.75- or 27.1-inch bbl. 43 to 50.1 inches overall. Weight: 15.5 lbs. Two-stage trigger. International thumbhole, black synthetic or laminated stock w/adj. cheekpiece, hand and palm rest; fitted w/10-way butthook. Imported 1992 to date.
Right-hand model . . . . NiB $2440 Ex $2204 Gd $1050
Left-hand model . . . . NiB $2419 Ex $1956 Gd $1365
W/laminated stock, add $180

ACHIEVER BOLT-ACTION RIFLE . . . . NiB $366 Ex $289 Gd $160
Caliber: .22 LR. 5-round magazine. Mark 2000-type repeating action. 19.5-inch bbl. 36.5 inches overall. Weight: 5 lbs. Adj. open rear sight; hooded ramp front. Plain European hardwood target-style stock w/vented forend and adj. buttplate. Imported since 1987.

ACHIEVER ST-SUPER TARGET . . . . . NiB $495 Ex $366 Gd $212
Same as Achiever except single-shot w/22-inch bbl. and adj. stock. 38.75 inches overall. Weight: 6.5 lbs. Target sights. Imported since 1994.

BR-50 BENCH REST RIFLE . . . . . . NiB $2018 Ex $1581 Gd $937
Single-shot. Caliber: .22 LR. 19.75-inch bbl. (23 inches w/muzzle weight). 37.75-42.5 inches overall. Weight: 11 lbs. Grooved receiver, no sights. Walnut-finished hardwood or synthetic benchrest stock w/adj. cheekpiece. Imported 1994-97. (Reintroduced as Model 2013 BR-50)

KADETT BOLT-ACTION
REPEATING RIFLE . . . . NiB $315 Ex $212 Gd $135
Caliber: .22 LR. 5-round detachable box magazine. 22-inch bbl. 40 inches overall. Weight: 5.5 lbs. Adj. folding leaf rear sight; hooded ramp front. Checkered European hardwood stock w/walnut-finish. Imported 1987-88.

MARK 2000 MATCH . . . . NiB $413 Ex $305 Gd $186
Takedown, bolt-action single-shot. Caliber: .22 LR. 26-inch heavy bbl. Walnut stock w/deep-fluted thumb-groove, Wundhammer swell pistol grip, beavertail forend. Adj. buttplate, single-stage adj. trigger. Weight: 8 lbs. Imported 1982-89.

ARMALITE, INC. — Geneseo, Illinois (Formerly Costa Mesa, California)

Armalite was in Costa Mesa, California from 1959-73. Following the acquisition by Eagle Arms in 1995, production resumed under the Armalite, Inc. Logo in Geneseo, Illinois.
Production by ARMALITE

AR-7 EXPLORER SURVIVAL RIFLE . . . NiB $144 Ex $118 Gd $67
Takedown. Semiautomatic. Caliber: .22 LR. Eight-round box magazine. 16-inch cast aluminum bbl. w/steel liner. Sights: Peep rear; blade front. Brown plastic stock, recessed to stow barrel, action, and magazine. Weight: 2.75 lbs. Will float stowed or assembled. Made 1959-1973 by Armalite; 1974-90 by Charter Arms; 1990-97 by Survival Arms, Cocoa, FL.; 1997 to date by Henry Repeating Arms Co., Brooklyn, NY.

AR-7 EXPLORER CUSTOM RIFLE . . . NiB $196 Ex $160 Gd $82
Same as AR-7 Survival Rifle except w/deluxe walnut stock w/cheekpiece and pistol grip. Weight: 3.5 lbs. Made 1964-70.

Armalite AR-10

Armalite AR-10 (T) Target Carbine

Armalite M-15A2 National Match

Armalite M-15A2 HBAR

AR-180 SEMIAUTOMATIC RIFLE

Commercial version of full automatic AR-18 Combat Rifle. Gas-operated semiautomatic. Caliber: .223 Rem. (5.56mm). Five, 20-, 30-round magazines. 18.25-inch bbl. w/flash hider/muzzle brake. Sights: Flip-up "L" type rear, adj. for windage; post front, adj. for elevation. Accessory: 3x scope and mount (add $60 to value). Folding buttstock of black nylon, rubber buttplate and pistol grip, heat dissipating fiberglass forend (hand guard), swivels, sling. 38 inches overall, 28.75 inches folded. Weight: 6.5 lbs. Note: Made by Armalite Inc. 1969-72, manufactured for Armalite by Howa Machinery Ltd., Nagoya, Japan, 1972-73; by Sterling Armament Co. Ltd., Dagenham, Essex, England, 1976 to 94. Importation disc.

Armalite AR-180 (Mfg. by Armalite-Costa Mesa) . . . . NiB $1256 Ex $1050 Gd $741
Armalite AR-180 (Mfg. by Howa) . . . . . . NiB $1430 Ex $1147 Gd $787

***(cont'd.)* AR-180 SEMIAUTOMATIC RIFLE**

Armalite AR-180 (Mfg. by Sterling) . . . . . NiB $1044 Ex $839 Gd $577
W/3x scope and mount, add. $225

Production by ARMALITE, Inc.

AR-10 (A) SEMIAUTOMATIC SERIES

Gas-operated semiautomatic action. Calibers: .243 Win. or .308 Win. (7.62 x 51mm). 10-round magazine. 16- or 20-inch bbl. 35.5 or 39.5 inches overall. Weight: 9 to 9.75 lbs. Post front sight, adj. aperature rear. Black or green composition stock. Made 1995 to date.

AR-10 A2 (Std. carbine). . . . . NiB $1900 Ex $1591 Gd $638
AR-10 A2 (Std. rifle) . . . . NiB $1230 Ex $1045 Gd $612
AR-10 A4 (S.P. carbine) . . . . NiB $1282 Ex $1045 Gd $612
AR-10 A4 (S.P. rifle). . . . . NiB $1282 Ex $1045 Gd $612

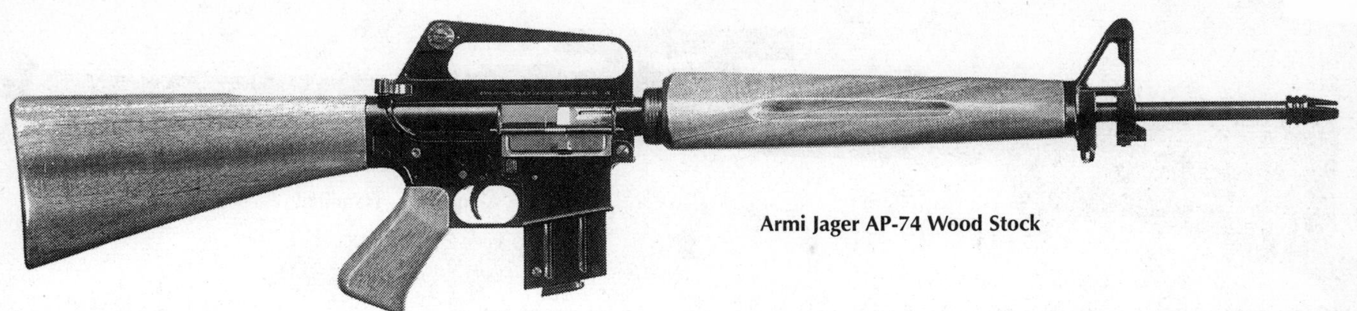
Armi Jager AP-74 Wood Stock

AR-10 (T) TARGET
Similar to Armalite Model AR-10A except in National Match configuration w/three-slot short Picatinny rail system and case deflector. 16- or 24-inch bbl. Weight: 8.25 to 10.4 lbs. Composite stock and handguard. No sights. Optional National Match carry handle and detachable front sight. Made 1995 to date.
AR-10 T (Rifle)............... NiB $1900 Ex $1591 Gd $947
AR-10 T (Carbine)............ NiB $1900 Ex $1591 Gd $947

MODEL AR-50 SS BOLT-ACTION RIFLE...................... NiB $2389 Ex $2028 Gd $1256
Caliber: .50 BMG. 31-inch bbl. w/muzzle brake. 59 inches overall. Weight: 41 lbs. Modified octagonal-form receiver, drilled and slotted for scope rail. Single-stage trigger. Triple front-locking bolt lug w/spring-loaded plunger for automatic ejection. Magnesium phosphate steel, hard-anodized aluminum finish. Made 1999 to date.

M15 SERIES
Gas-operated semiautomatic w/A2-style forward-assist mechanism and push-type pivot pin for easy takedown. Caliber: .223. 7-round magazine. 16-, 20- or 24-inch bbl. Weight: 7-9.2 lbs. Composite or retractable stock. Fully adj. sights. Black anodized finish. Made 1995 to date.
M-15A2 (Carbine) .... NiB $865 Ex $737 Gd $581
M-15A2 (Service Rifle)............... NiB $916 Ex $787 Gd $592
M-15A2 (National Match)........... NiB $1277 Ex $1040 Gd $684
M-15A2 (Golden Eagle heavy bbl.)........... NiB $1251 Ex $1004 Gd $644
M-15A2 M4C (retractable stock, disc. 1997)......... NiB $1199 Ex $932 Gd $607
M-15A4 (Action Master, disc. 1997)..... NiB $1077 Ex $865 Gd $593
M-15A4 (Predator) .... NiB $916 Ex $787 Gd $592
M-15A4 (S.P. Rifle) .... NiB $890 Ex $736 Gd $478
M-15A4 (S.P. Carbine)................. NiB $839 Ex $684 Gd $427
M-15A4T (Eagle Eye Carbine).......... NiB $1251 Ex $993 Gd $684
M-15A4T (Eagle Eye Rifle)............ NiB $1302 Ex $968 Gd $684

ARMI JAGER — Turin, Italy

AP-74 COMMANDO............ NiB $265 Ex $204 Gd $132
Similar to standard AP-74 but styled to resemble original version of Uzi 9mm submachine gun w/wood buttstock. Lacks carrying handle and flash suppressor. Has different type front sight mount and guards, wood stock, pistol grip and forearm. Intro. 1976. Disc.

AP-74 SEMIAUTOMATIC RIFLE
Styled after U.S. M16 military rifle. Caliber: .22 LR, .32 Auto (pistol cartridge). Detachable clip magazine; capacity: 14 rounds caliber .22 LR, 9 rounds .32 ACP. 20-inch bbl. w/flash suppressor. Weight: 6.5 lbs. M16 type sights. Stock, pistol-grip and forearm of black plastic, swivels and sling. Intro. 1974. Disc.
.22 LR....................... NiB $317 Ex $265 Gd $162
.32 Auto...................... NiB $343 Ex $291 Gd $173

AP-74 WOOD STOCK MODEL
Same as standard AP-74 except w/wood stock, pistol-grip and forearm weight: 7 lbs. Disc.
.22 LR .... NiB $394 Ex $317 Gd $204
.32 Auto...................... NiB $420 Ex $317 Gd $204

ARMSCOR (Arms Corp.) — Manila, Philippines *(Imported until 1991 by Armscor Precision, San Mateo, CA; 1991-95 by Ruko Products, Inc., Buffalo NY: Currently imported by K.B.I., Harrisburg, PA)*

MODEL 20 AUTO RIFLE
Caliber: .22 LR. 15-round magazine. 21-inch bbl. 39.75 inches overall. Weight: 6.5 lbs. Sights: Hooded front; adj. rear. Checkered or plain walnut finished mahogany stock. Blued finish. Imported 1990-91. (Reinstated by Ruko in the M series.)
Model 20 (checkered stock) .... NiB $127 Ex $103 Gd $72
Model 20C (carbine-style stock) ..... NiB $114 Ex $93 Gd $65
Model 20P (plain stock) .... NiB $102 Ex $82 Gd $58

MODEL 1600 AUTO RIFLE
Caliber: .22 LR. 15-round magazine. 19.5-inch bbl. 38 inches overall. Weight: 6 lbs. Sights: Post front; aperture rear. Plain mahogany stock. Matte black finish. Imported 1987-91. (Reinstated by Ruko in the M series.)
Standard model................. NiB $149 Ex $108 Gd $77
Retractable stock model .... NiB $159 Ex $123 Gd $82

MODEL AK22 AUTO RIFLE
Caliber: .22 LR. 15- or 30-round magazine. 18.5-inch bbl. 36 inches overall. Weight: 7 lbs. Sights: Post front; adj. rear. Plain mahogany stock. Matte black finish. Imported 1987-91.
Standard model................ NiB $195 Ex $174 Gd $108
Folding stock model .... NiB $210 Ex $179 Gd $133

MODEL M14 SERIES BOLT-ACTION RIFLE
Caliber: .22 LR. 10-round magazine. 23-inch bbl. Weight: 6.25 lbs. Open sights. Walnut or walnut finished mahogany stock. Imported 1991-97.
M14P Standard model............. NiB $103 Ex $77 Gd $53
M14D Deluxe model (checkered stock, disc. 1995) .... NiB $89 Ex $72 Gd $61

MODEL M20 SERIES SEMIAUTOMATIC RIFLE
Caliber: .22 LR. 10- or 15-round magazine. 18.25- or 20.75-inch bbl. Weight:5.5 to 6.5 lbs. 38 to 40.5 inches overall. Hooded front sight w/windage adj. rear. Walnut finished mahogany stock. Imported 1990-97.
M20C carbine model .... NiB $108 Ex $88 Gd $57
M20P standard model.................. NiB $100 Ex $77 Gd $57
M20S Sporter Deluxe (checkered mahogany stock)...................... NiB $133 Ex $118 Gd $67
M20SC Super Classic (checkered walnut stock) .... NiB $261 Ex $205 Gd $88

A-Square — Hannibal

MODEL M1400 BOLT-ACTION RIFLE
Similar to Model 14P except w/checkered stock w/Schnabel forend. Weight: 6 lbs. Imported 1990-97.
M1400LW (Lightweight, disc. 1992) . . . . . . NiB $200 Ex $169 Gd $108
M1400S (Sporter) . . . . NiB $133 Ex $108 Gd $77
M1400SC (Super Classic) . . . . NiB $255 Ex $205 Gd $143

MODEL M1500 BOLT-ACTION RIFLE
Caliber: .22 Mag. 5-round magazine. 21.5-inch bbl. Weight: 6.5 lbs. Open sights. Checkered mahogany stock. Imported 1991-97.
M1500 (standard) . . . . NiB $133 Ex $108 Gd $77
M1500LW (Euro-style walnut stock, disc. 1992) . . . . NiB $184 Ex $159 Gd $108
M1500SC (Monte Carlo stock) . . . . NiB $190 Ex $159 Gd $118

MODEL M1600 AUTO RIFLE
Rimfire replica of Armalite Model AR 180 (M16) except chambered for Caliber .22 LR. 15-round magazine. 18-inch bbl. Weight: 5.25 lbs. Composite or retractable buttstock w/composite handguard and pistol grip. Carrying handle w/adj. aperture rear sight and protected post front. Black anodized finish. Imported 1991-97.
M-1600 (standard w/fixed stock) . . . . . . NiB $153 Ex $123 Gd $86
M-1600R (retractable stock) . . . . NiB $165 Ex $133 Gd $93

MODEL M1800 BOLT-ACTION RIFLE
Caliber: .22 Hornet. 5-round magazine. 22-inch bbl. Weight: 6.6 lbs. Checkered hardwood or walnut stock. Sights: Post front; adj. rear. Imported 1995 to date.
M-1800 (standard) . . . . NiB $261 Ex $190 Gd $133
M-1800SC (checkered walnut stock) . . . . . NiB $363 Ex $292 Gd $210

MODEL M2000 AUTO RIFLE
Similar to Model 20P except w/checkered mahogany stock and adj. sights. Imported 1991 to date.
M2000S (standard) . . . . NiB $133 Ex $108 Gd $75
M2000SC (checkered walnut stock) . . . . . . NiB $242 Ex $195 Gd $135

ARNOLD ARMS — Arlington, Washington

AFRICAN SAFARI
Calibers: .243 to .458 Win. Magnum. 22- to 26-inch bbl. Weight: 7-9 lbs. Scope mount standard or w/optional M70 Express sights. Chrome-moly in four finishes. "A" and "AA" Fancy Grade English walnut stock with number 5 standard wraparound checkering pattern. Ebony forend tip. Made 1996 to date.
With "A" Grade English walnut: matte blue . . . . NiB $4486 Ex $3595 Gd $2455
Std. polish . . . . NiB $4741 Ex $3769 Gd $2593
Hi-Luster . . . . NiB $4939 Ex $3957 Gd $2700
Stainless steel matte . . . . NiB $4486 Ex $3595 Gd $2454
With "AA" Grade English Walnut: C-M matte blue . . . . NiB $4461 Ex $3574 Gd $2440
Std. polish . . . . NiB $4741 Ex $3799 Gd $2593
Hi-Luster . . . . NiB $4939 Ex $3957 Gd $2700
Stainless steel matte . . . . NiB $4486 Ex $3594 Gd $2455

ALASKAN TROPHY
Calibers: .300 Magnum to .458 Win. Magnum. 24- to 26-inch bbl. Weight: 7-9 lbs. Scope mount w/Express sights standard. Stainless steel or chrome-moly Apollo action w/fibergrain or black synthetic stock. Barrel band on 357 H&H and larger magnums. Made 1996 to date.
Matte finish . . . . NiB $3083 Ex $2473 Gd $1692
Std. polish . . . . NiB $3339 Ex $2676 Gd $1830
Stainless steel . . . . NiB $3154 Ex $2529 Gd $1729

A-SQUARE COMPANY INC. — Louisville, Kentucky (Formerly Bedford, KY)

CAESAR BOLT-ACTION RIFLE
Custom rifle built on Remington's 700 receiver. Calibers: Same as Hannibal, Groups I, II and III. 20- to 26-inch bbl. Weight: 8.5 to 11 lbs. Express 3-leaf rear sight, ramp front. Synthetic or classic Claro oil-finished walnut stock w/flush detachable swivels and Coil-Chek recoil system. Three-way adj. target trigger; 3-position safety. Right- or left-hand. Made 1984 to date.
Synthetic stock model . . . . NiB $3223 Ex $2605 Gd $1781
Walnut stock model. . . . . NiB $2862 Ex $2193 Gd $1575

GENGHIS KHAN BOLT-ACTION RIFLE
Custom varmint rifle developed on Winchester's M70 receiver; fitted w/heavy tapered bbl. and Coil-Chek stock. Calibers: .22-250 Rem., .243 Win., .25-06 Rem., 6mm Rem. Weight: 8-8.5 lbs. Made 1994 to date.
Synthetic stock model . . . . NiB $3944 Ex $3110 Gd $2141
Walnut stock model. . . . . NiB $3274 Ex $2656 Gd $1832

HAMILCAR BOLT-ACTION RIFLE
Similar to Hannibal Model except lighter. Calibers: .25-06, .257 Wby., 6.5x55 Swedish, .270 Wby., 7x57, 7mm Rem., 7mm STW, 7mm Wby., .280 Rem., .30-06, .300 Win., .300 Wby., .338-06, 9.3x62. Weight: 8-8.5 lbs. Made 1994 to date.
Synthetic stock model . . . . NiB $3758 Ex $3012 Gd $2058
Walnut stock model. . . . . NiB $3314 Ex $2656 Gd $1816

HANNIBAL BOLT-ACTION RIFLE
Custom rifle built on reinforced P-17 Enfield receiver. Calibers: Group I: 30-06; Group II: 7mm Rem. Mag., .300 Win. Mag., .416 Taylor, .425 Express, .458 Win. Mag.; Group III: .300 H&H, .300 Wby. Mag., 8mm Rem. Mag., .340 Wby. Mag., .375 H&H, .375 Wby. Mag., .404 Jeffery, .416 Hoffman, .416 Rem Mag., .450 Ackley, .458 Lott; Group IV: .338 A-Square Mag., .375 A-Square Mag., .378 Wby. Mag., .416 Rigby, .416 Wby. Mag., .460 Short Square Mag., .500 A-Square Mag. 20- to 26-inch bbl. Weight: 9 to 11.75 lbs. Express 3-leaf rear sight, ramp front. Classic Claro oil-finished walnut stock or synthetic stock w/flush detachable swivels and Coil-Chek recoil system. Adj. trigger w/2-position safety. Made 1983 to date.
Synthetic stock model . . . . NiB $3699 Ex $2965 Gd $2126
Walnut stock model. . . . . NiB $3500 Ex $2806 Gd $1928

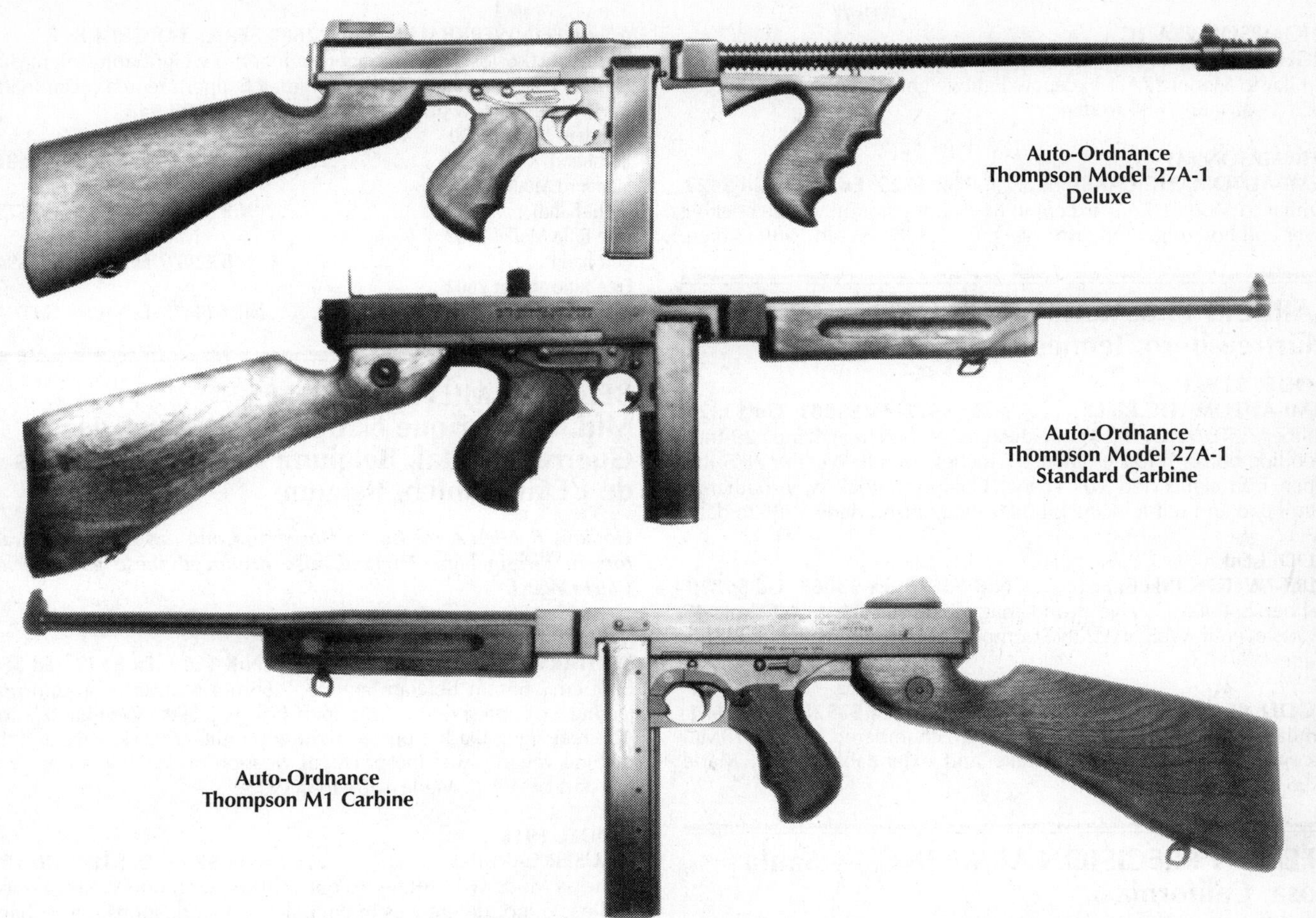

Auto-Ordnance
Thompson Model 27A-1
Deluxe

Auto-Ordnance
Thompson Model 27A-1
Standard Carbine

Auto-Ordnance
Thompson M1 Carbine

AUSTRIAN MILITARY RIFLES — Steyr, Austria Manufactured at Steyr Armory

MODEL 90
STEYR-MANNLICHER RIFLE . . . . . . NiB $286 Ex $161 Gd $108
Straight-pull bolt action. Caliber: 8mm. 5-round magazine. Open sights. 10-inch bayonet. Cartridge clip forms part of the magazine mechanism. Some of these rifles were provided with a laced canvas hand guard, others were of wood.

MODEL 90
STEYR-MANNLICHER CARBINE . . . NiB $286 Ex $190 Gd $108
Same general specifications as Model 90 rifle except w/19.5-inch bbl., weight 7 lbs. No bayonet stud or supplemental forend grip.

MODEL 95
STEYR-MANNLICHER CARBINE . . . NiB $286 Ex $190 Gd $108
Same general specifications as Model 95 rifle except w/19.5-inch bbl., weight 7 lbs. Post front sight; adj. rear carbine sight.

MODEL 95
STEYR-MANNLICHER
SERVICE RIFLE. . . . . NiB $261 Ex $139 Gd $103
Straight-pull bolt action. Caliber: 8x50R Mannlicher (many of these rifles were altered during World War II to use the 7.9mm German service ammunition). 5-round Mannlicher-type box magazine. 30-inch bbl. Weight: 8.5 lbs. Sights: Blade front; rear adj. for elevation. Military-type full stock.

AUTO-ORDNANCE CORPORATION — West Hurley, New York (Manufacturing rights acquired by Kahr Arms 1999)

THOMPSON MODEL 22-27A-3 . . . NiB $726 Ex $602 Gd $422
Same-bore version of Deluxe Model 27A-1. Same general specifications except 22 LR w/lightweight alloy receiver, weight 6.5 lbs. Magazines include 5-, 20-, 30- and 50-round box types, 80-round drum. Made 1977-94.

THOMPSON MODEL 27A-1 DELUXE
Same as Standard Model 27A-1 except w/finned bbl. w/compensator, adj. rear sight, pistol-grip forestock. Caliber: .22 LR, l0mm (1991-93) or 45 ACP. Weight: 11.5 lbs. Made 1976-99.
.22 LR (Limited production) . . . . NiB $1293 Ex $1037 Gd $709
10mm or 45 ACP . . . . NiB $727 Ex $604 Gd $475
50-round drum magazine, add $250
100-round drum magazine, add $450
Violin carrying case, add. $100

THOMPSON MODEL 27A-1
STANDARD SEMIAUTO CARBINE. . . . . . NiB $628 Ex $576 Gd $370
Similar to Thompson submachine gun ("Tommy Gun") except has no provision for automatic firing. Caliber: .45 Auto. 20-round detachable box magazine (5-,15- and 30-round box magazines, 39-round drum also available). 16-inch plain bbl. Weight: 14 lbs. Sights: Aperture rear; blade front. Walnut buttstock, pistol grip and grooved forearm, sling swivels. Made 1976-86.

THOMPSON 27A-1C
LIGHTWEIGHT CARBINE . . . . NiB $751 Ex $602 Gd $413
Similar to Model 27A-1 except w/lightweight alloy receiver. Weight: 9.25 lbs. Made 1984 to date.

THOMPSON M1
SEMI-AUTOMATIC CARBINE . . . . . NiB $725 Ex $602 Gd $422
Similar to Model 27A-1 except in M-1 configuration w/side cocking lever and horizontal forearm. Weight: 11.5 lbs. Made 1986 to date.

BARRETT FIREARMS MFG., INC. — Murfreesboro, Tennessee

MODEL 82 A-1
SEMI-AUTOMATIC RIFLE . . . . . NiB $6977 Ex $5381 Gd $3321
Caliber: .50 BMG. 10-round detachable box magazine. 29-inch recoiling bbl. w/muzzle brake. 57 inches overall. Weight: 28.5 lbs. Open iron sights and 10x scope. Composit stock w/Sorbothance recoil pad and self-leveling bipod. Blued finish. Made 1985 to date.

MODEL 90
BOLT-ACTION RIFLE . . . . NiB $3578 Ex $3063 Gd $1879
Caliber: .50 BMG. Five round magazine. 29-inch match bbl. 45 inches overall. Weight: 22 lbs. Composite stock w/retractable bipod. Made 1990-95.

MODEL 95 BOLT-ACTION . . . . NiB $4634 Ex $3578 Gd $2651
Similar to Model 90 bullpup design chambered for .50 BMG except w/improved muzzle brake and extendable bipod. Made 1995 to date.

BEEMAN PRECISION ARMS INC. — Santa Rosa, California

Since 1993 all European firearms imported by Beeman have been distributed by Beeman Outdoor Sports, Div., Roberts Precision Arms, Inc., Santa Rosa, CA.

WEIHRAUCH HW MODELS 60J AND 60J-ST
BOLT-ACTION RIFLES
Calibers: .22 LR (60J-ST), .222 Rem. (60J). 22.8-inch bbl. 41.7 inches overall. Weight: 6.5 lbs. Sights: Hooded blade front; open adj. rear. Blued finish. Checkered walnut stock w/cheekpiece. Made 1988-94.
Model 60J . . . . NiB $473 Ex $710 Gd $576
Model 60J-ST . . . . NiB $590 Ex $473 Gd $325

WEIHRAUCH HW MODEL 60M
SMALL BORE RIFLE . . . . NiB $628 Ex $525 Gd $340
Caliber: .22 LR. Single-shot. 26.8-inch bbl. 45.7 inches overall. Weight: 10.8 lbs. Adj. trigger w/push-button safety. Sights: Hooded blade front on ramp, precision aperture rear. Target-style stock w/stippled forearm and pistol grip. Blued finish. Made 1988-94.

WEIHRAUCH HW
MODEL 660 MATCH RIFLE . . . . NiB $885 Ex $757 Gd $370
Caliber: .22 LR. 26-inch bbl. 45.3 inches overall. Weight: 10.7 lbs. Adj. match trigger. Sights: globe front, precision aperture rear. Match-style walnut stock w/adj. cheekpiece and buttplate. Made 1988-94.

FEINWERKBAU MODEL 2600 SERIES TARGET RIFLE
Caliber: .22 LR. Single-shot. 26.3-inch bbl. 43.7 inches overall.

***(cont'd)* FEINWERKBAU MODEL 2600 SERIES TARGET RIFLE**
Weight: 10.6 lbs. Match trigger w/fingertip weight adjustment dial. Sights: Globe front; micrometer match aperture rear. Laminated hardwood stock w/adj. cheekpiece. Made 1988-94.
Standard Model 2600
(left-hand) . . . . NiB $1633 Ex $1252 Gd $840
Standard Model 2600
(right-hand) . . . . NiB $1458 Ex $1149 Gd $737
Free Rifle Model 2602
(left-hand) . . . . NiB $2076 Ex $1664 Gd $943
Free Rifle Model 2602
(right-hand) . . . . NiB $20676 Ex $1664 Gd $943

BELGIAN MILITARY RIFLES Mfd. by Fabrique Nationale D'Armes de Guerre, Herstal, Belgium; Fabrique D'Armes de L'Etat, Lunich, Belgium

Hopkins & Allen Arms Co. of Norwich, Conn., as well as contractors in Birmingham, England, also produced these guns during World War I.

MODEL 1889 MAUSER
MILITARY RIFLE . . . . NiB $210 Ex $139 Gd $88
Caliber: 7.65mm Belgian Service (7.65mm Mauser). 5-round projecting box magazine. 30.75-inch bbl. w/jacket. Weight: 8.5 lbs. Adj. rear sight, blade front. Straight-grip military stock. This, and the carbine version, was the principal weapon of the Belgian Army at the start of WWII. Made 1889 to c.1935.

MODEL 1916
MAUSER CARBINE . . . . NiB $235 Ex $184 Gd $98
Same as Model 1889 Rifle except w/20.75-inch bbl. Weighs 8 lbs. and has minor differences in the rear sight graduations, lower band closer to the muzzle and swivel plate on side of buttstock.

MODEL 1935 MAUSER
MILITARY RIFLE . . . . NiB $312 Ex $235 Gd $133
Same general specifications as F.N. Model 1924; minor differences. Caliber: 7.65mm Belgian Service. Mfd. by Fabrique Nationale D'Armes de Guerre.

MODEL 1936 MAUSER
MILITARY RIFLE . . . . NiB $235 Ex $190 Gd $130
An adaptation of Model 1889 w/German M/98-type bolt, Belgian M/89 protruding box magazine. Caliber: 7.65mm Belgian Service. Mfd. by Fabrique Nationale D'Armes de Guerre.

BENTON & BROWN FIREARMS, INC. — Fort Worth, Texas

MODEL 93 BOLT-ACTION RIFLE
Similar to Blaser Model R84 (the B&B rifle is built on the Blaser action, see separate listing) with an interchangeable bbl. system. Calibers: .243 Win., 6mm Rem., .25-06, .257 Wby., .264 Win., .270 Win., .280 Rem., 7mm Rem Mag., .30-06, .308, .300 Wby., .300 Win. Mag., .338 Win., .375 H&H. 22- or 24-inch bbl. 41 or 43 inches overall. Bbl.-mounted scope rings and one-piece base; no sights. Two-piece walnut or fiberglass stock. Made 1993 to date.
Walnut stock model. . . . . NiB $1812 Ex $1658 Gd $927
Fiberglass stock model. . . . . NiB $1606 Ex $1246 Gd $885
Extra bbl. assembly, add $475
Extra bolt assembly, add $425

Beretta 501
Bolt-Action Sporter

Beretta AR-70

BERETTA U.S.A. CORP. — Accokeek, Maryland, Manufactured by Fabbrica D'Armi Pietro Beretta, S.p.A., Gardone Val Trompia (Brescia), Italy

455 SxS EXPRESS DOUBLE RIFLE
Sidelock action w/removable sideplates. Calibers: .375 H&H, .458 Win. Mag., .470 NE, .500 NE (3 inches), .416 Rigby. Bbls.: 23.5 or 25.5-inch. Weight: 11 lbs. Double triggers. Sights: Blade front; V-notch folding leaf rear. Checkered European walnut forearm and buttstock w/recoil pad. Color casehardened receiver w/blued bbls. Made 1990 to date.
Model 455 . . . . NiB $40,938 Ex $32,750 Gd $22,270
Model 455EELL. . . . . NiB $51,875 Ex $41,500 Gd $28,220

500 BOLT-ACTION SPORTER
Centerfire bolt-action rifle w/Sako A I short action. Calibers: .222 Rem., .223 Rem. Five round magazine. 23.63-inch bbl. Weight: 6.5 lbs. Available w/ or w/o iron sights. Tapered dovetailed receiver. European walnut stock. Disc. 1986.
Standard . . . . NiB $623 Ex $525 Gd $370
DL Model . . . . NiB $1491 Ex $1194 Gd $815
500 EELL
Engraved . . . . NiB $1555 Ex $1349 Gd $886
W/iron sights, add 10%

501 BOLT-ACTION SPORTER
Same as Model 500 except w/Sako A II medium action. Calibers: .243 Win., .308 Win. Weight: 7.5 lbs. Disc. 1986.
Standard . . . . NiB $648 Ex $520 Gd $357
Standard
w/iron sights . . . . NiB $623 Ex $576 Gd $370
DL model. . . . . NiB $1483 Ex $1204 Gd $844
501 EELL (engraved) . . . . NiB $1616 Ex $1359 Gd $895
W/iron sights, add 10%

502 BOLT-ACTION SPORTER
Same as Model 500 except w/Sako A III long action. Calibers: .270 Win., 7mm Rem. Mag., .30/06, 375 H&H. Weight: 8.5 lbs. Disc. 1986.
Standard model . . . . NiB $721 Ex $581 Gd $402
DL model. . . . . NiB $1668 Ex $1307 Gd $895
502 EELL (engraved) . . . . NiB $1816 Ex $1457 Gd $997
W/iron sights, add 10%

AR-70 SEMIAUTOMATIC RIFLE . . . . NiB $1925 Ex $1694 Gd $998
Caliber: .223 Rem. (5.56mm). 30-round magazine. 17.75-inch bbl. Weight: 8.25 lbs. Sights: Rear peep adj. for windage and elevation; blade front. High-impact synthetic buttstock. Imported 1984-89.

EXPRESS S686/S689 SABLE O/U RIFLE
Calibers: .30-06 Spfld., 9.3x74R, and .444 Marlin. 24-inch bbl. Weight: 7.7 lbs. Drilled and tapped for scope mount. European-style cheek rest and ventilated rubber recoil pad. Imported 1995 to date.
Model S686/S689 Silver Sable II. . . . . NiB $4563 Ex $3605 Gd $2060
Model S689 Gold Sable . . . . NiB $6180 Ex $5150 Gd $2987
Model S686/S689 EELL
Diamond Sable. . . . . NiB $12,875 Ex $9270 Gd $6180
W/extra bbl. set, add $325
W/detachable claw mounts, add $595

EXPRESS SSO O/U EXPRESS DOUBLE RIFLE
Sidelock. Calibers: .375 H&H Mag., .458 Win. Mag., 9.3 x 74R. 23-24- or 25.5-inch blued bbls. Weight: 11 lbs. Double triggers. Express sights w/blade front and V-notch folding leaf rear. Optional Zeiss scope w/claw mounts. Color casehardened receiver w/scroll engraving, game scenes and gold inlays on higher grades. Checkered European walnut forearm and buttstock w/cheekpiece and recoil pad. Imported 1985 to date.
Model SS0 (disc. 1989) . . . . NiB $9270 Ex $8137 Gd $5150
Model SS05 (disc. 1990) . . . . NiB $10,300 Ex $8755 Gd $6180
Model SS06 Custom . . . . NiB $26,265 Ex $20,085 Gd $12,360
Model SS06 EELL Gold Custom . . . . NiB $29,767 Ex $26,265 Gd $14,935
Extra bbl. assembly, add $6250
Claw mounts, add $550

Blaser Model R84

MATO
Calibers: .270 Win., .280 Rem., 7mm Rem. Mag, .300 Win. Mag., .338 Win. Mag., .375 H&H. 23.6-inch bbl. Weight: 8 lbs. Adjustable trigger. Drop-out box magazine. Drilled and tapped for scope w/ or w/o adj. sights. Walnut or synthetic stock. Manufactured based on Mauser 98 action. Made in 1997 to date.
Standard model . . . . NiB $1256 Ex $947 Gd $638
Deluxe model . . . . NiB $1925 Ex $1565 Gd $844
.375 H&H w/iron sights, add. $300

SMALL BORE SPORTING CARBINE/TARGET RIFLE
Semiautomatic w/bolt handle in raised or conventional single-shot bolt-action w/handle in lowered position. Caliber: .22 LR. Four, 5-, 8-, 10- or 20-round magazines. 20.5-inch standard or heavy bbl. Sights: 3-leaf folding rear, partridge front. Target or sporting stock w/checkered pistol grip and forend and sling swivels. Weight: 5.5 to 6 lbs.
Sporter model (Super Sport X) . . . . NiB $396 Ex $319 Gd $211
Target model (Olympia X) . . . . NiB $270 Ex $448 Gd $293

BERNARDELLI, VINCENZO — Brescia, Italy

Currently headquartered in Brescia, Italy, Bernardelli arms were manufactured from 1721 to 1997 in Gardone, Italy. Imported and distributed by Armsport, Inc., Miami, Florida. Also handled by Magnum Research, Inc., Quality Arms, Inc., Armes De Chasse, Stoeger and Action Arms.

EXPRESS VB . . . . NiB $5550 Ex $4550 Gd $3500
Double barrel. Calibers: Various. Side-by-side sidelock action. Ejectors, double triggers. Imported 1990 to1997.
Deluxe model (w/double triggers), add $1000

EXPRESS 2000 . . . . NiB $3000 Ex $1950 Gd $1390
Calibers: .30-06, 7x65R, 8x57JRS, 9.3x74R. Over/under boxlock design. Single or double triggers, extractors. Checkered walnut stock and forearm. Imported 1994 to 1997.
Single trigger, add. $150

MINERVA EXPRESS . . . . NiB $5275 Ex $4200 Gd $3795
Caliber: Various. Exposed hammers. Extractors, double triggers. Moderate engraving. Imported 1995 to 1997.

CARBINA .22. . . . . NiB $610 Ex $450 Gd $275
Semi-auto. Caliber: .22 rimfire. Blow-back action. Imported 1990 to 1997.

MODEL 120 . . . . NiB $2115 Ex $1650 Gd $1100
Combination gun; over-under boxlock; 12 gauge over .22 Hornet, .222 Rem., 5.6x50R Mag., .243 Win., 6.5x57R, .270 Win., 7x57R, .308 Win., .30-06, 6.5x55, 7x65R, 8x57JRS, 9.3x74R. Iron sights. Checkered walnut stock and forearm. Double triggers, automatic ejectors or extractors. Ventilated recoil pad. Engraved action. Made in Italy. Discontinued.

MODEL 190 . . . . NiB $1375 Ex $1050 Gd $995
Combination gun; over-under boxlock. Calibers: 12, 16 or 20 ga. Over .222 Rem., .243 Win., .30-06, .308 Win., 5.6x50R Mag., .5.6x57R, 6.5x55, 6.5x57R, 7x57R, 7x65R, 8x57JRS, 9.3x74R. Iron sights. Checkered walnut stock. Double triggers; extractors. Made in Italy. Introduced 1969, discontinued 1989.

***(cont'd)* MODEL 190**

MODEL 2000 . . . . NiB $2200 Ex $1750 Gd $1275
Combination gun; over-under boxlock action. Calibers: 12, 16 or 20 ga. Over .222 Rem., .22 Hornet, 5.6x50R Mag., .243 Win., 6.5x55, 6.5x57R, .270 Win., 7x57R, .308 Win., .30-06, 8x57JRS, 9.3x74R. Bbl: 23 inches. Sights: Blade front, open rear. Hand checkered, oil-finished select European walnut stock, double-set triggers, auto ejectors. Silvered, engraved action. Made in Italy. Introduced 1990, discontinued 1991.
Extra bbl. assembly, add $500

BLASER USA, INC. — Fort Worth, Texas Mfd. by Blaser Jagdwaffen GmbH, Germany *(Imported by Sigarms, Exeter, NH; Autumn Sales, Inc., Fort Worth, TX)*

MODEL R84 BOLT-ACTION RIFLE
Calibers: .22-250, .243, 6mm Rem., .25-06, .270, .280 Rem., .30-06- .257 Wby. Mag., .264 Win. Mag., 7mm Rem Mag., .300 Win. Mag., .300 Wby. Mag., .338 Win. Mag., .375 H&H. Interchangeable bbls. w/standard or Magnum bolt assemblies. Bbl. length: 23 inches (standard); 24 inches (Magnum). 41 to 42 inches overall. Weight: 7 to 7.25 lbs. No sights. Bbl.-mounted scope system. Two-piece Turkish walnut stock w/solid black recoil pad. Imported 1989-94.
Model R84 Standard . . . . NiB $2183 Ex $1668 Gd $1045
Model R84 Deluxe
(game scene). . . . . NiB $3007 Ex $1977 Gd $1246
Model R84 Super Deluxe
(Gold and silver inlays). . . . . NiB $3625 Ex $1997 Gd $1379
Left-hand model, add $125
Extra bbl. assembly, add $650

MODEL R93 SAFARI SERIES BOLT-ACTION REPEATER
Similar to Model R84 except restyled action w/straight-pull bolt, unique safety and searless trigger mechanism. Additional chamberings: 6.5x55, 7x57, .308, .416 Rem. Optional open sights. Imported 1994-98.
Model R93 Safari . . . . NiB $3702 Ex $3110 Gd $1977
Model R93 Safari Deluxe . . . . NiB $4140 Ex $3934 Gd $3110
Model R84 Safari
Super Deluxe . . . . NiB $4655 Ex $4140 Gd $3264
Extra bbl. assembly, add $525

MODEL R93 CLASSIC SERIES BOLT-ACTION REPEATER
Similar to Model R93 Safari except w/expanded model variations. Imported 1998 to date.
Model R93 Attache
(Premium wood, fluted bbl.). . . . . NiB $4346 Ex $3676 Gd $2904
Model R93 Classic
(.22-250 to .375 H&H) . . . . NiB $3361 Ex $2693 Gd $1838
Model R93 Classic Safari (.416 Rem.). . . . . NiB $3748 Ex $3002 Gd $2048
Model R93 LX (.22-250 to .416 Rem.) . . . . . NiB $1688 Ex $1354 Gd $927
Model R93 Synthetic (.22-250
to .375 H&H) . . . . NiB $1301 Ex $1045 Gd $717
Extra bbl. assembly, add $550

Brno Model II

Brno Model 21H
Bolt-Action Sporting Rifle

Brno Model 22F

Brno Hornet
Bolt-Action Sporting Rifle

BRITISH MILITARY RIFLES
Mfd. at Royal Small Arms Factory, Enfield Lock, Middlesex, England, as well as private contractors

RIFLE NO. 1 MARK III. . . . . NiB $265 Ex $163 Gd $112
Short magazine Lee-Enfield (S.M.L.E.). Bolt action. Caliber: .303 British. 10-round box magazine. 25.25-inch bbl. Weight: 8.75 lbs. Sights: Adj. rear; blade front w/guards. Two-piece, full-length military stock. Note: The earlier Mark III (approved 1907) is virtually the same as Mark III (adopted 1918) except for sights and different magazine cut-off that was eliminated on the latter.

RIFLE NO. 3 MARK I (PATTERN 14) . . . . . . NiB $290 Ex $214 Gd $112
Modified Mauser-type bolt action. Except for caliber .303 British and long-range sight, this rifle is the same as U.S. Model 1917 Enfield. See listing of the latter for general specifications.

RIFLE NO. 4 MARK I. . . . . NiB $239 Ex $188 Gd $112
Post-World War I modification of the S.M.L.E. intended to simplify mass production. General specifications same as Rifle No. 1 Mark III except w/aperture rear sight and minor differences in construction and weighs 9.25 lbs.

LIGHT RIFLE NO. 4 MARK I . . . . . . NiB $188 Ex $137 Gd $102
Modification of the S.M.L.E. Caliber: .303 British. 10-round box magazine. 23-inch bbl. Weight: 6.75 lbs. Sights: Micrometer click rear peep; blade front. One-piece military-type stock w/recoil pad. Made during WWII.

RIFLE NO. 5 MARK I. . . . . NiB $316 Ex $214 Gd $137
Jungle Carbine. Modification of the S.M.L.E. similar to Light Rifle No. 4 Mark I except w/20.5-inch bbl. w/flash hider, carbine-type stock. Made during WWII, originally designed for use in the Pacific Theater.

BRNO SPORTING RIFLES — Brno, Czech Republic, Manufactured by Ceska Zbrojovka
Imported by Euro-Imports, El Cajon, CA (Previously by Bohemia Arms & Magnum Research)

See also CZ rifles.

MODEL I BOLT-ACTION SPORTING RIFLE. . . . . NiB $630 Ex $553 Gd $372
Caliber: .22 LR. Five round detachable magazine. 22.75-inch bbl. Weight: 6 lbs. Sights: three-leaf open rear; hooded ramp front. Sporting stock w/checkered pistol grip, swivels. Made 1946-73.

MODEL II BOLT-ACTION SPORTING RIFLE. . . . . NiB $681 Ex $578 Gd $372
Same as Model I except w/deluxe grade stock. Made 1949-57.

MODEL III BOLT-ACTION TARGET RIFLE . . . . NiB $733 Ex $681 Gd $424
Same as Model I except w/heavy bbl. and target stock. Made 1948-56.

MODEL IV BOLT-ACTION TARGET RIFLE . . . . NiB $784 Ex $619 Gd $424
Same as Model III except w/improved target trigger mechanism. Made 1956-62.

MODEL V BOLT-ACTION SPORTING RIFLE. . . . . NiB $733 Ex $558 Gd $372
Same as Model I except w/improved trigger mechanism. Made 1956-73.

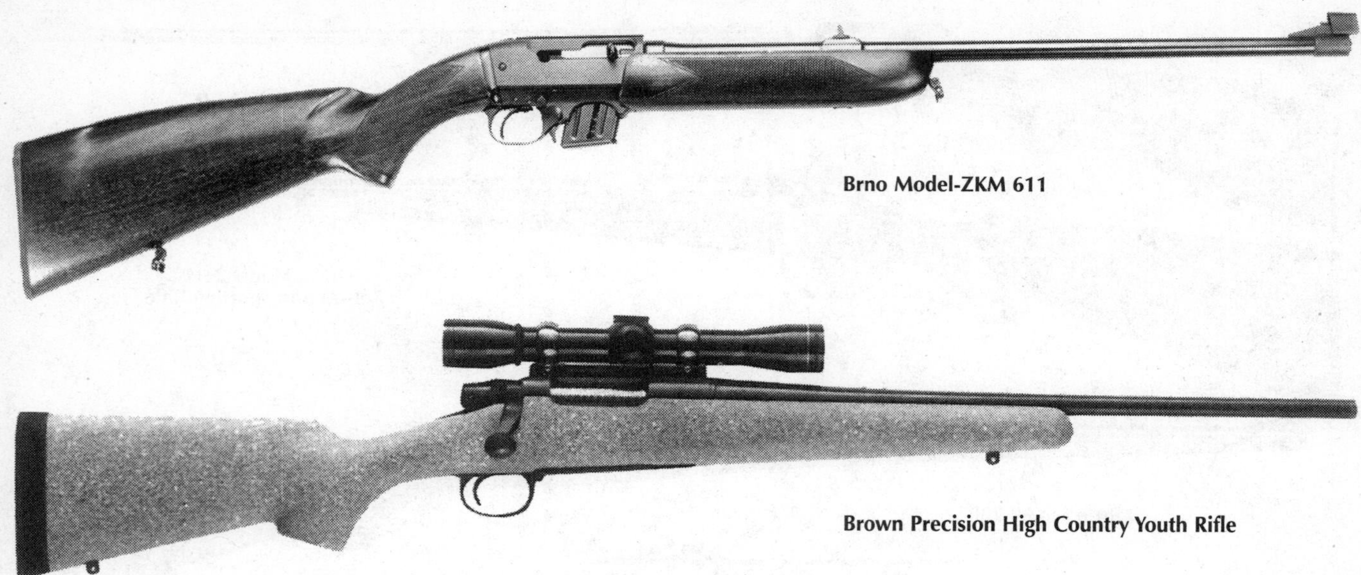

Brno Model-ZKM 611

Brown Precision High Country Youth Rifle

MODEL 21H BOLT-ACTION SPORTING RIFLE. . . . . NiB $784 Ex $630 Gd $424
Mauser-type action. Calibers: 6.5x57mm, 7x57mm 8x57mm. Five round box magazine. 20.5-inch bbl. Double set trigger. Weight: 6.75 lbs. Sights: Two-leaf open rear-hooded ramp front. Half-length sporting stock w/cheekpiece, checkered pistol-grip and forearm, swivels. Made 1946-55.

MODEL 22F. . . . . NiB 1036 Ex $831 Gd $569
Same as Model 21H except w/full-length Mannlicher-type stock, weight: 6 lbs., 14 oz. Disc.

MODEL 98 STANDARD
Calibers: .243 Win., .270 Win., .30-06, .308 Win., .300 Win. Mag., 7x57mm, 7x64mm, or 9.3x62mm. 23.8-inch bbl. Overall 34.5 inches. Weight: 7.25 lbs. Checkered walnut stock w/Bavarian cheekpiece. Imported 1998 to date.
Standard calibers . . . . NiB $456 Ex $367 Gd $254
Calibers .300 Win., Mag., 9.3x62mm . . . . . NiB $507 Ex $409 Gd $282
W/single set trigger, add $100

MODEL 98 MANNLICHER
Similar to Model 98 Standard except full length stock and set triggers. Imported 1998 to date.
Standard calibers . . . . NiB $624 Ex $489 Gd $333
Calibers .300 Win. Mag., 9.3x62mm. . . . . . NiB $688 Ex $553 Gd $380

ZBK-110 SINGLE-SHOT
Calibers: .22 Hornet, .222 Rem., 5.6x52R, 5.6x50 Mag., 6.5x57R, 7x57R, and 8x57JRS. 23.8-inch bbl. Weight: 6.1 lbs. Walnut checkered buttstock and forearm w/Bavarian cheekpiece. Imported 1998 to date.
Standard model. . . . . NiB $238 Ex $181 Gd $130
Lux model . . . . NiB $392 Ex $263 Gd $186
Calibers 7x57R and 8x57 JRS, add $25
W/interchangeable 12 ga. shotgun bbl., add $132

HORNET BOLT-ACTION SPORTING RIFLE. . . . . NiB $988 Ex $860 Gd $473
Miniature Mauser action. Caliber: .22 Hornet. Five-round detachable box magazine. 23-inch bbl. Double set trigger. Weight: 6.25 lbs.

***(cont'd.)* HORNET BOLT-ACTION SPORTING RIFLE**
Sights: Three-leaf open rear hooded ramp front. Sporting stock w/checkered pistol grip and forearm, swivels. Made 1949-74. Note: This rifle was also marketed in U.S. as "Z-B Mauser Varmint Rifle." (Reintroduced as Model ZKB 680)

MODEL ZKB 680 BOLT-ACTION RIFLE. . . . . NiB $489 Ex $392 Gd $269
Calibers: .22 Hornet, .222 Rem. Five-round detachable box magazine. 23.5-inch bbl. Weight: 5.75 lbs. Double-set triggers. Adj. open rear sight, hooded ramp front. Walnut stock. Imported 1985-92.

MODEL ZKM 611 SEMIAUTOMATIC RIFLE
Caliber: .22 WMR. Six-round magazine. 20-inch bbl. 37 inches overall. Weight: 6.2 lbs. Hooded front sight; mid-mounted rear sight. Checkered walnut or beechwood stock. Single thumbscrew takedown. Grooved receiver for scope mounting. Imported 1992 to date.
Standard beechwood model . . . . . . NiB $424 Ex $341 Gd $234
Deluxe walnut model . . . . NiB $526 Ex $418 Gd $263

BROWN PRECISION COMPANY — Los Molinos, California

MODEL 7 SUPER LIGHT SPORTER . . . . . NiB $1031 Ex $933 Gd $675
Lightweight sporter built on a Remington Model 7 barreled action w/18-inch factory bbl. Weight: 5.25 lbs. Kevlar stock. Made 1984-92.

HIGH COUNTRY BOLT-ACTION SPORTER
Custom sporting rifles built on Blaser, Remington 700, Ruger 77 and Winchester 70 actions. Calibers: .243 Win., .25-06, .270 Win., 7mm Rem. Mag., .308 Win., .30-06. Five-round magazine (4-round in 7mm Mag.). 22- or 24-inch bbl. Weight: 6.5 lbs. Fiberglass stock w/recoil pad, sling swivels. No sights. Made 1975 to date.
Standard High Country . . . . NiB $1153 Ex $998 Gd $741
Custom High Country . . . . NiB $2080 Ex $1658 Gd $947
Left-hand action, add. $200
Stainless bbl., add $200
70, 77 or Blaser actions, add. $125
70 SG action, add $350

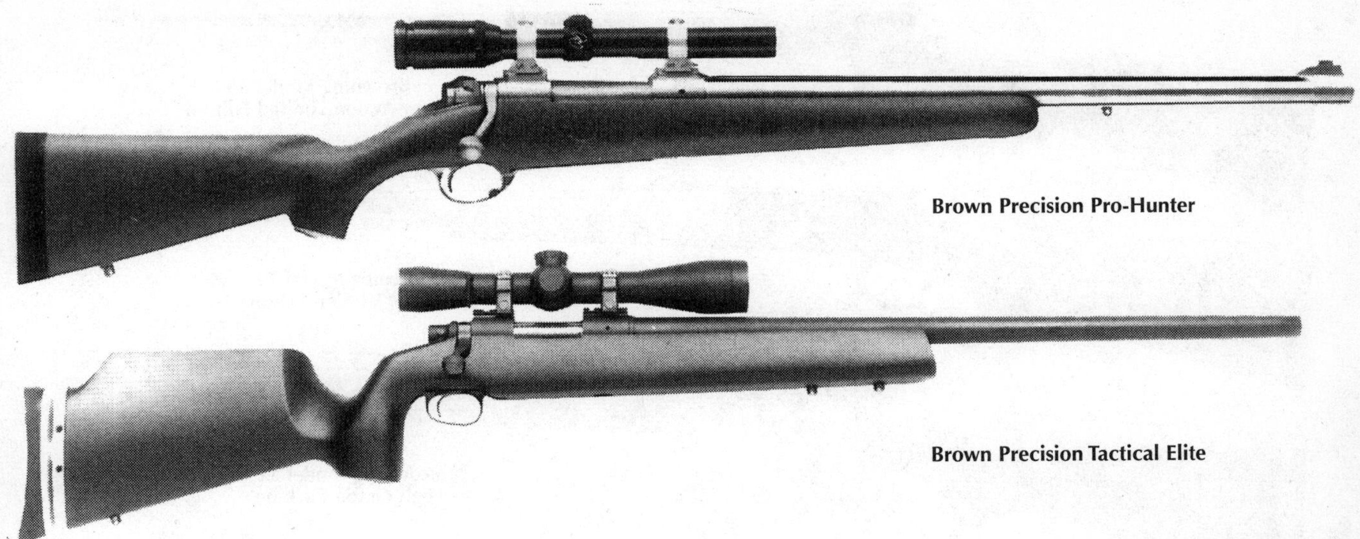

Brown Precision Pro-Hunter

Brown Precision Tactical Elite

HIGH COUNTRY YOUTH RIFLE .... **NiB $1248 Ex $939 Gd $630**
Similar to standard Model 7 Super Light except w/Kevlar or graphite stock, scaled-down to youth dimensions. Calibers: .223, .243, 6mm, 7mm-08, .308. Made 1992 to date.

PRO-HUNTER BOLT-ACTION RIFLE
Custom sporting rifle built on Remington 700 or Winchester 70 SG action fitted w/match-grade Shilen bbl. chambered in customer's choice of caliber. Matte blued, nickel or Teflon finish. Express-style rear sight hooded ramp front. Synthetic stock. Made 1989 to date
Standard Pro-Hunter.............. **NiB $2442 Ex $2030 Gd $1155**
Pro-Hunter Elite (1993 to date) ...... **NiB $3472 Ex $2700 Gd $1824**

PRO-VARMINTER BOLT-ACTION RIFLE
Custom varminter built on a Remington 700 or 40X action fitted w/Shilen stainless steel benchrest bbl. Varmint or benchrest-style stock. Made 1993 to date.
Standard Pro-Varminter .... **NiB $1864 Ex $1410 Gd $947**
Pro-Hunter w/Rem 40X action ...... **NiB $2440 Ex $1864 Gd $1246**

SELECTIVE TARGET MODEL ..... **NiB $1238 Ex $939 Gd $604**
Tactical law-enforcement rifle built on a Remington 700V action. Caliber: .308 Win. 20-, 22- or 24-inch bbl. Synthetic stock. Made 1989-92.

TACTICAL ELITE RIFLE .... **NiB $2600 Ex $2291 Gd $1261**
Similar to Selective Target Model except fitted w/select match-grade Shilen benchrest heavy stainless bbl. Calibers: .223, .308, .300 Win. Mag. Black or camo Kevlar/graphite composite fiberglass stock w/adj. buttplate. Non-reflective black Teflon metal finish. Made 1993 to date.

BROWNING RIFLES — Morgan, Utah Mfd. for Browning by Fabrique Nationale d'Armes de Guerre (now Fabrique Nationale Herstal), Herstal, Belgium; Miroku Firearms Mfg. Co., Tokyo, Japan; A.T.I., Salt Lake City, Ut; Oy Sako Ab, Riihimaki, Finland.

.22 AUTOMATIC RIFLE, GRADE I
Similar to discontinued Remington Model 241A. Autoloading. Take-down. Calibers: .22 LR. .22 Short (not interchangeably). Tubular magazine in buttstock holds 11 LR. 16 Short. Bbl. lengths: 19.25 inches (.22 LR), 22.25 inches (.22 Short). Weight: 4.75 lbs. (.22 LR); 5 lbs. (.22 Short). Receiver scroll engraved. Open rear sight, bead front. Checkered pistol-grip buttstock, semibeavertail forearm. Made 1965-72 by FN; 1972 to date by Miroku. Note: Illustrations are of rifles manufactured by FN.
FN manufacture................ **NiB $602 Ex $422 Gd $216**
Miroku manufacture .... **NiB $319 Ex $216 Gd $164**

.22 AUTOMATIC RIFLE, GRADE II
Same as Grade I except satin chrome-plated receiver engraved w/small game animal scenes, gold-plated trigger select walnut stock and forearm. .22 LR only. Made 1972-84.
FN manufacture.............. **NiB $1015 Ex $675 Gd $474**
Miroku manufacture .... **NiB $423 Ex $347 Gd $217**

.22 AUTOMATIC RIFLE, GRADE III
Same as Grade I except satin chrome-plated receiver elaborately hand-carved and engraved w/dog and game-bird scenes, scrolls and leaf clusters: gold-plated trigger, extra-fancy walnut stock and forearm, skip-checkered. .22 LR only. Made 1972-84.
FN manufacture............ **NiB $2076 Ex $1664 Gd $1040**
Miroku manufacture .... **NiB $840 Ex $521 Gd $423**

.22 AUTOMATIC, GRADE VI...... **NiB $733 Ex $527 Gd $347**
Same general specifications as standard .22 Automatic except for engraving, high-grade stock w/checkering and glossy finish. Made by Miroku 1986 to date.

MODEL 52 BOLT-ACTION RIFLE .... **NiB $733 Ex $578 Gd $372**
Limited edition of Winchester Model 52C Sporter. Caliber: .22 LR. Five-round magazine. 24-inch bbl. Weight: 7 lbs. Micro-Motion trigger. No sights. Checkered select walnut stock w/rosewood forend and metal grip cap. Blued finish. Only 5000 made in 1991-92.

MODEL 53 LEVER-ACTION RIFLE .... **NiB $758 Ex $630 Gd $414**
Limited edition of Winchester Model 53. Caliber: .32-20. Seven-round tubular half-magazine. 22-inch bbl. Weight: 6.5 lbs. Adj. rear sight, bead front. Select walnut checkered pistol-grip stock w/high-gloss finish. Classic-style forearm. Blued finish. Only 5000 made in 1990. See illustration next page.

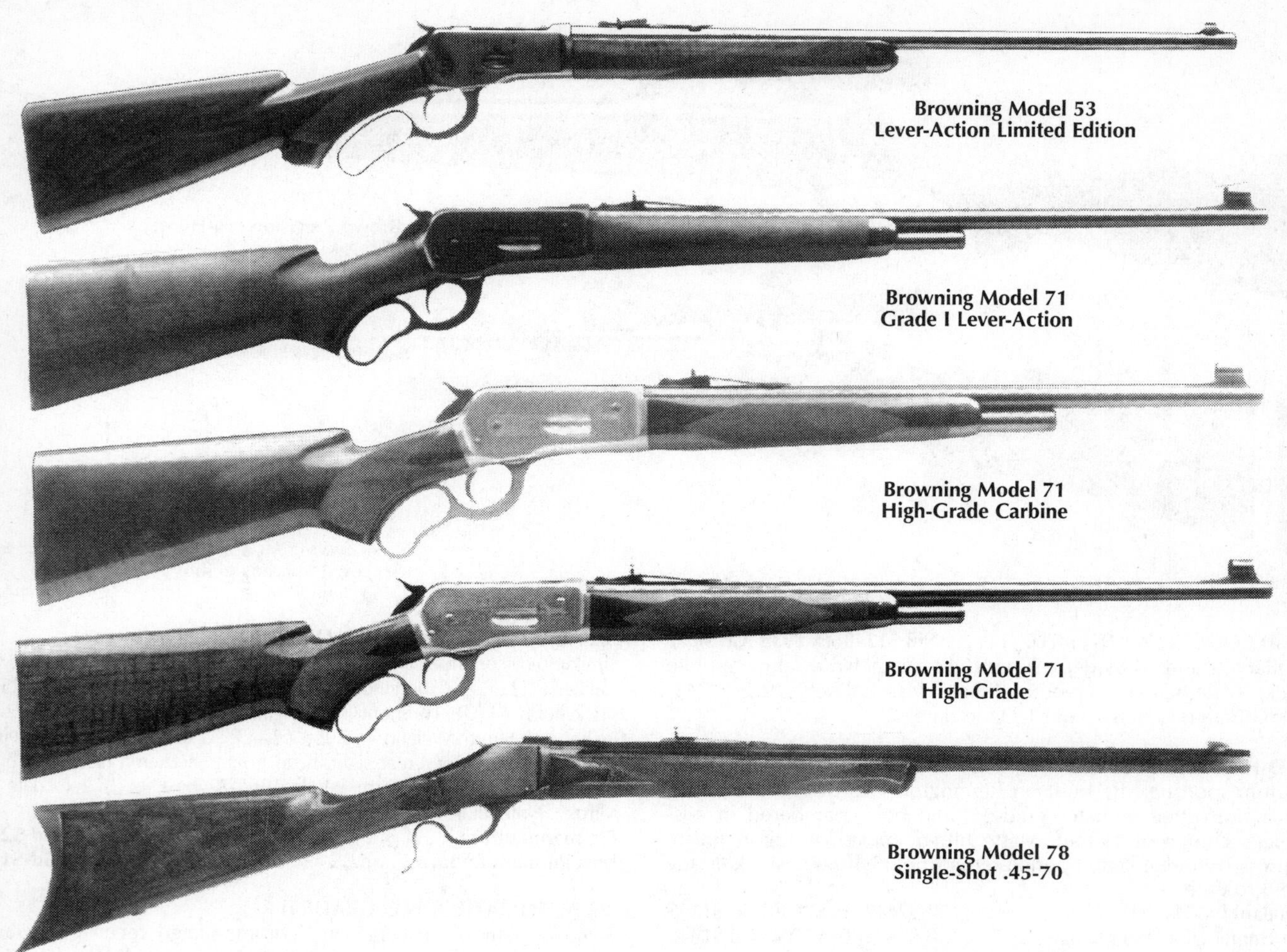

MODEL 65 GRADE I LEVER-ACTION RIFLE .... NiB $733 Ex $475 Gd $372
Caliber: .218 Bee. 7-round tubular half-magazine. 24-inch bbl. Weight: 6.75 lbs. Sights: Adj. buckhorn-style rear, hooded bead front. Select walnut pistol-grip stock w/high-gloss finish. Semibeavertail forearm. Limited edition of 3500 made in 1989.

MODEL 65 HIGH GRADE RIFLE .... NiB $1814 Ex $939 Gd $630
Same general specifications as Model 65 Grade I except w/engraving and gold-plated animals on grayed receiver. Cut checkering on pistol grip and forearm. Limited edition of 1500 made in 1989.

MODEL 71 GRADE I CARBINE .... NiB $733 Ex $553 Gd $372
Same general specifications as Model 71 Grade I Rifle except carbine w/20-inch round bbl. and weighs 8 lbs. Limited edition of 4000 made in 1986-87.

MODEL 71 GRADE I LEVER-ACTION RIFLE........... NiB $826 Ex $630 Gd $424
Caliber: .348 Win. 4-round magazine. 24-inch round bbl. Weight: 8 lbs., 2 oz. Open buckhorn sights. Select walnut straight grip stock w/satin finish. Classic-style forearm, flat metal buttplate. Limited edition of 3000 made in 1986-87.

MODEL 71 HIGH-GRADE CARBINE ..... NiB $1196 Ex $1020 Gd $578
Same general specifications as Model 71 High Grade Rifle, except carbine w/20-inch round bbl. Limited edition of 3000 made in 1986-88.

MODEL 71 HIGH-GRADE RIFLE .... NiB $1274 Ex $990 Gd $707
Caliber: .348 Win. Four round magazine. 24-inch round bbl. Weight: 8 lbs., 2 oz. Engraved receiver. Open buckhorn sights. Select walnut checkered pistol-grip stock w/high-gloss finish. Classic-style forearm, flat metal buttplate. Limited edition of 3000 made in 1987.

78 BICENTENNIAL SET....... NiB $3617 Ex $2973 Gd $1969
Special Model 78 .45-70 w/same specifications as standard type, except sides of receiver engraved w/bison and eagle, scroll engraving on top of receiver, lever, both ends of bbl. and buttplate; high-grade walnut stock and forearm. Accompanied by an engraved hunting knife and stainless steel commemorative medallion, all in an alder wood presentation case. Each item in set has matching serial number beginning with "1776" and ending with numbers 1 to 1,000. Edition limited to 1,000 sets. Made in 1976.

78 SINGLE-SHOT RIFLE
Falling-block lever-action similar to Winchester 1885 High Wall single-shot rifle. Calibers: .22-250, 6mm Rem., .243 Win., .25-06, 7mm Rem. Mag., .30-06, .45-70 Govt. 26-inch octagon or heavy round bbl.; 24-inch octagon bull bbl. on .45-70 model. Weight: 7.75 lbs. w/octagon bbl.; w/round bbl., 8.5 lbs.; .45-70, 8.75 lbs. Furnished w/o sights except .45-70 model w/open rear sight, blade front. Checkered fancy walnut stock and forearm. .45-70 model w/straight-grip stock and curved buttplate; others have Monte Carlo comb and cheekpiece, pistol-grip w/cap, recoil pad. Made 1973-83 by Miroku. Reintroduced in 1985 as Model 1885.
All calibers except .45-70 .... NiB $784 Ex $656 Gd $414
.45-70 .... NiB $862 Ex $681 Gd $424

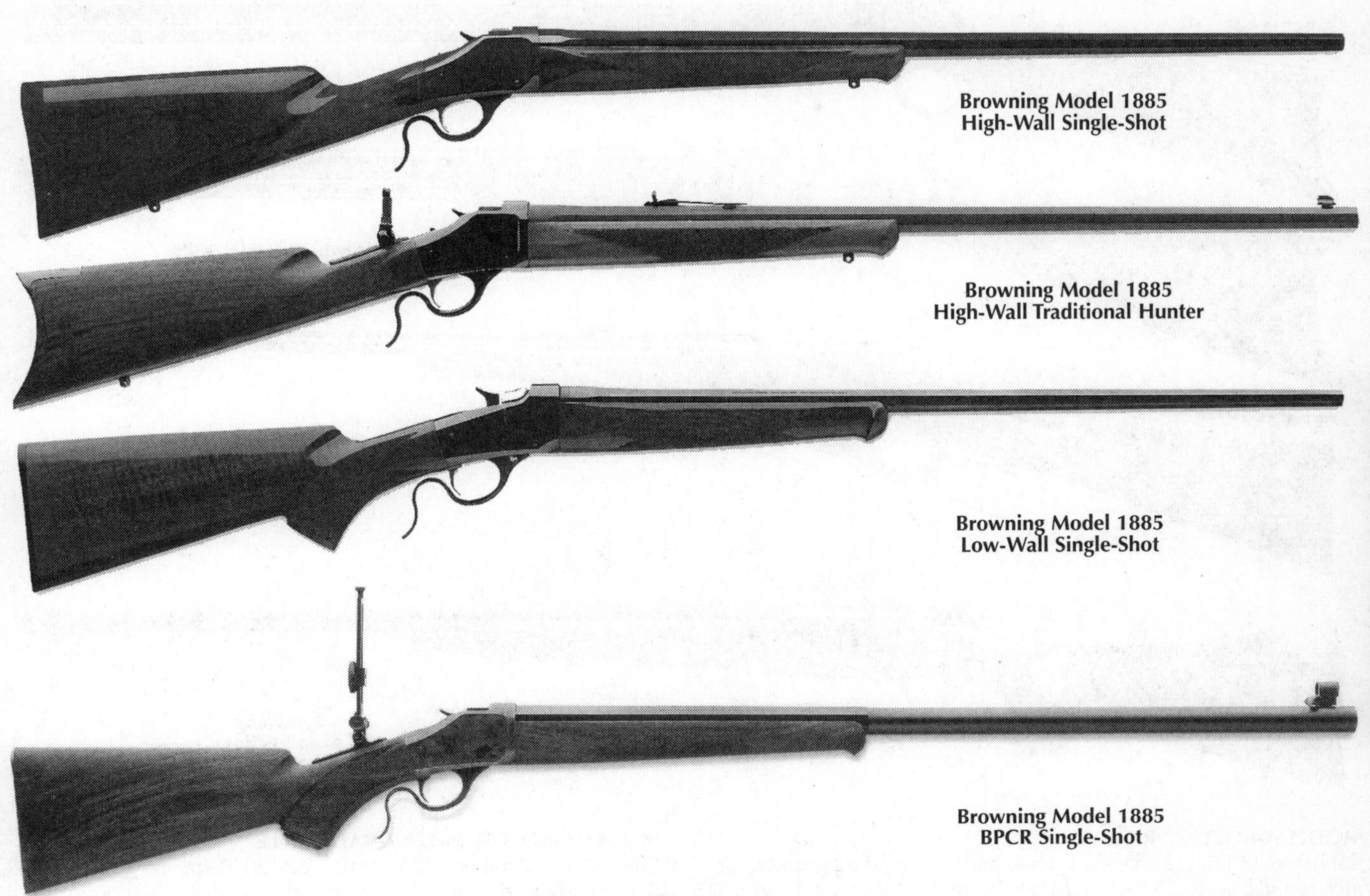
Browning Model 1885 High-Wall Single-Shot

Browning Model 1885 High-Wall Traditional Hunter

Browning Model 1885 Low-Wall Single-Shot

Browning Model 1885 BPCR Single-Shot

MODEL 1885 SINGLE-SHOT RIFLE
Calibers: .22 Hornet, .223, .243, (Low Wall); .357 Mag., .44 Mag., .45 LC (L/W Traditional Hunter); .22-250, .223 Rem., .270 Win., 7mm Rem. Mag., .30-06, .454 Casull Mag., .45.70 (High Wall); .30.30 Win., .38-55 WCF, .45 Govt. (H/W Traditional Hunter); .40-65, .45 Govt. and .45.90 (BPCR). 24-, 28-, 30 or 34-inch round, octagonal or octagonal and round bbl. 39.5, 43.5, 44.25 or 46.125 inches overall. Weight: 6.25, 8.75, 9, 11, or 11.75 lbs. respectively. Blued or color casehardened receiver. Gold-colored adj. trigger. Drilled and tapped for scope mounts w/no sights or vernier tang rear sight w/globe front and open sights on .45-70 Govt. Walnut straight-grip stock and Schnabel forearm w/cut checkering and high-gloss or oil finish. Made 1985 to date.

Low Wall model w/o sights (Intro. 1995) . . NiB $782 Ex $679 Gd $448
Traditional Hunter model (Intro. 1998) . . . NiB $937 Ex $885 Gd $499
High Wall model w/o sights (Intro. 1985) . . . . NiB $731 Ex $576 Gd $422
Traditional Hunter model (Intro. 1997) . . NiB $1024 Ex $818 Gd $483
BPCR model w/no ejector (Intro. 1996) . . . . NiB $1616 Ex $1307 Gd $942
BPCR Creedmoor Model .45-90 (Intro. 1998) . . . . NiB $1616 Ex $1256 Gd $895

MODEL 1886 MONTANA CENTENNIAL RIFLE . . . . NiB $1925 Ex $1555 Gd $973
Same general specifications as Model 1886 High Grade lever-action except w/specially engraved receiver designating Montana Centennial; also different stock design. Made in 1986 in limited issue by Miroku.

MODEL 1886 GRADE I LEVER-ACTION RIFLE . . . . NiB $1246 Ex $921 Gd $689
Caliber: .45-70 Govt., 8-round magazine. 26-inch octagonal bbl. 45 inches overall. Weight: 9 lbs., 5 oz. Deep blued finish on receiver. Open buckhorn sights. Straight-grip walnut stock. Classic-style forearm. Metal buttplate. Satin finish. Made in 1986 in limited issue 7,000 by Miroku.

MODEL 1886 HIGH-GRADE LA RIFLE . . . . NiB $1513 Ex $1153 Gd $839
Same general specifications as the Model 1886 Grade I except receiver is grayed, steel embellished w/scroll; elk and American bison engraving. High-gloss stock. Made in 1986 in limited issue of 3,000 by Miroku.

MODEL 1895 GRADE I LA RIFLE . . . . NiB $782 Ex $731 Gd $679
Caliber: .30-06, .30-40 Krag. Four round magazine. 24-inch round bbl. 42 inches overall. Weight: 8 lbs. French walnut stock and Schnabel forend. Sights: Rear buckhorn; gold bead on elevated ramp front. Made in 1984 in limited issue of 8,000 (2,000 chambered for .30-40 Krag and 6,000 chambered for .30-06). Mfd. by Miroku.

MODEL 1895 HIGH-GRADE LA RIFLE. . . . . NiB $1406 Ex $1252 Gd $891
Same general specifications as Model 1895 Grade I except engraved receiver and Grade III French walnut stock and forend w/fine checkering. Made in 1985 in limited issue of 1000 in each caliber by Miroku.

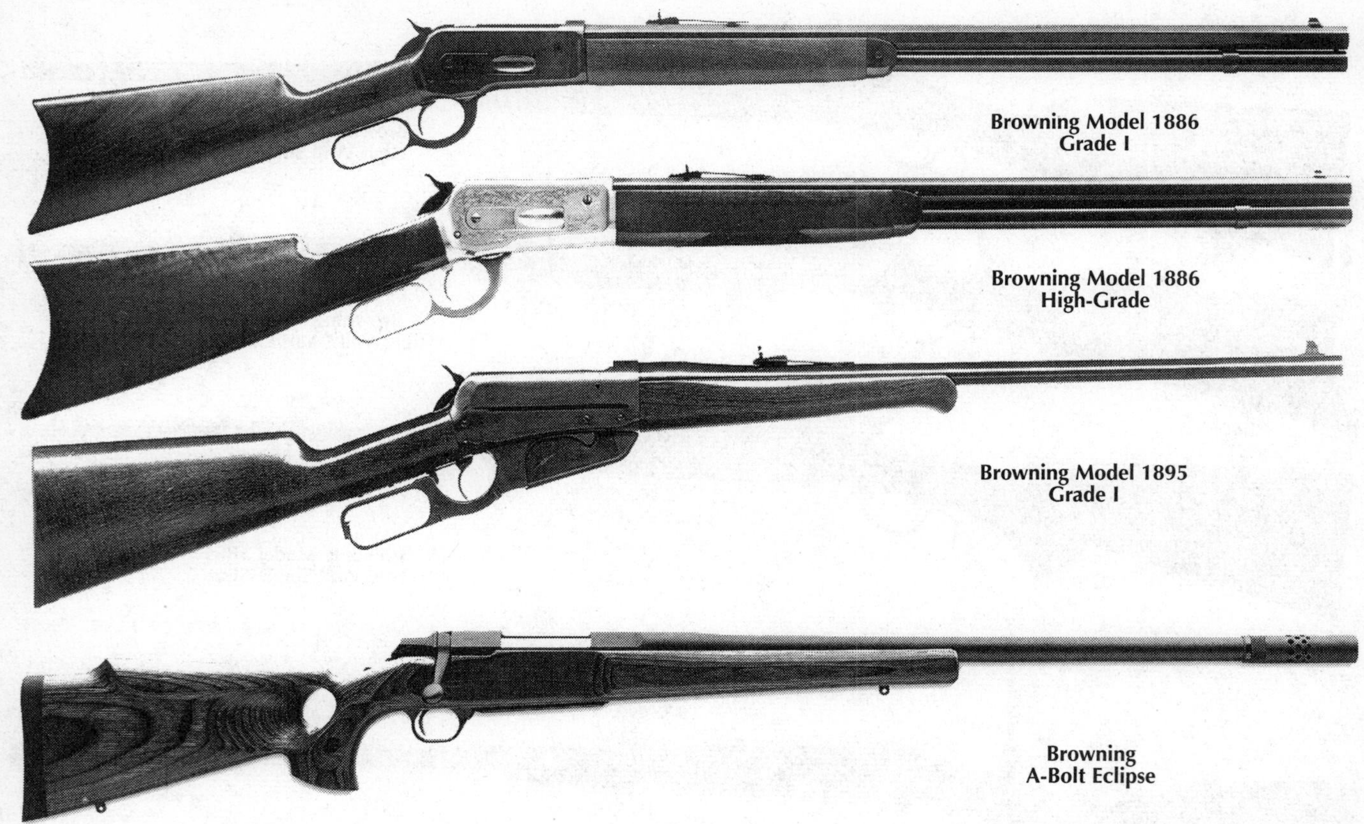

Browning Model 1886
Grade I

Browning Model 1886
High-Grade

Browning Model 1895
Grade I

Browning
A-Bolt Eclipse

MODEL A-BOLT .22 RIFLE

Calibers: .22 LR. .22 Magnum. Five- and 15-round magazines. 22-inch round bbl. 40.25 inches overall. Weight: 5 lbs., 9 oz. Gold-colored adj. trigger. Laminated walnut stock w/checkering. Rosewood forend grip cap; pistol grip. With or w/o sights. Ramp front and adj. folding leaf rear on open sight model. 22 LR made 1985-96; 22 Magnum, 1990-96.

Grade I .22 LR . . . . **NiB $370 Ex $285 Gd $201**
Grade I .22 Magnum . . . . **NiB $448 Ex $365 Gd $216**
Deluxe Grade
Gold Medallion . . . . **NiB $551 Ex $422 Gd $309**

MODEL A-BOLT ECLIPSE BOLT RIFLE

Same general specifications as Hunter Grade except fitted w/gray and black laminated thumbhole stock. Available in both short and long action w/two bbl. configurations w/BOSS. Mfd. by Miroku 1996 to date.

Eclipse w/standard bbl. . . . . **NiB $885 Ex $757 Gd $618**
Eclipse Varmint w/heavy bbl. . . . . **NiB $1037 Ex $887 Gd $759**
Eclipse M-1000
(Target .300 Win. Mag.) . . . . **NiB $1194 Ex $929 Gd $681**

MODEL A-BOLT EURO-BOLT RIFLE

Same general specifications as Hunter Grade except w/checkered satin-finished walnut stock. W/continental-style cheekpiece, palm-swell grip and Schnabel forend. Mannlicher-style spoon bolt handle and contoured bolt shroud. 22- or 26-inch bbl. w/satin blued finish. Weight: 6.8 to 7.4 lbs. Calibers: .22-250 Rem., .243 Win., .270 Win., .30.06, .308 Win., 7mm Rem. Mag. Mfd. by Miroku 1993-94; 1994-96 (Euro-Bolt II).

Euro-Bolt . . . . **NiB $618 Ex $473 Gd $314**
Euro-Bolt II . . . . **NiB $654 Ex $576 Gd $417**
BOSS option, add **$90**

MODEL A-BOLT HUNTER GRADE RIFLE

Calibers: .22 Hornet, .223 Rem., .22-250 Rem., .243 Win., .257 Roberts, 7mm-08 Rem., .308 Win., (short action) .25-06 Rem., .270 Win., .280 Rem., .284 Win., .30-06, 7mm Rem. Mag., .300 Win. Mag., .338 Win. Mag. Four-round magazine (standard), 3-round (magnum). 22-inch bbl. (standard), 24-inch (magnum). Weight: 7.5 lbs. (standard), 8.5 lbs. (magnum). With or w/o sights. Classic-style walnut stock. Produced in two action lengths w/nine locking lugs, fluted bolt w/60 degree rotation. Mfd. by Miroku 1985-93; 1994 to date (Hunter II).

Hunter . . . . **NiB $628 Ex $576 Gd $412**
Hunter II . . . . **NiB $726 Ex $525 Gd $448**
Hunter Micro. . . . . **NiB $731 Ex $576 Gd $473**
BOSS option, add **$90**
Open sights, add **$50**

MODEL A-BOLT MEDALLION GRADE RIFLE

Same as Hunter Grade except w/high-gloss deluxe stock rosewood grip cap and forend; high-luster blued finish. Also in .375 H&H w/open sights. Left-hand models available in long action only. Mfd. by Miroku 1988-93; 1994 to date (Medallion II). Bighorn Sheep Ltd. Ed.

(600 made 1986, .270 Win.) . . . . **NiB $1307 Ex $998 Gd $689**
Gold Medallion Deluxe Grade . . . . **NiB $686 Ex $551 Gd $378**
Gold Medallion II Deluxe Grade . . . . **NiB $711 Ex $571 Gd $392**
Medallion, Standard Grade . . . . **NiB $551 Ex $473 Gd $293**
Medallion II, Standard Grade . . . . **NiB $557 Ex $448 Gd $308**
Medallion, .375 H&H . . . . **NiB $927 Ex $705 Gd $422**
Medallion II, .375 H&H . . . . **NiB $937 Ex $679 Gd $473**
Micro Medallion . . . . **NiB $602 Ex $473 Gd $319**
Micro Medallion II . . . . **NiB $628 Ex $499 Gd $345**
Pronghorn Antelope Ltd. Ed.
(500 made 1987, .243 Win.) . . . . **NiB $1156 Ex $1008 Gd $828**
BOSS option, add **$90**

Browning A-Bolt .22

Browning A-Bolt Euro-Bolt

Browning A-Bolt Hunter

Browning A-Bolt Hunter with BOSS

Browning A-Bolt Medallion Custom Trophy

Browning A-Bolt Medallion White Gold

Browning A-Bolt Medallion

Browning A-Bolt Medallion (Left-Handed)

Browning A-Bolt Composite Stalker

Browning A-Bolt Stainless Stalker

Browning BAR, Grade IV

Browning BAR, Grade V

MODEL A-BOLT STALKER RIFLE
Same general specifications as Model A-Bolt Hunter Rifle except w/checkered graphite-fiberglass composite stock and matte blued or stainless metal. Non-glare matte finish of all exposed metal surfaces. 3 models: Camo Stalker orig. w/multi-colored laminated wood stock, matte blued metal; Composite Stalker w/graphite-fiberglass stock, matte blued metal; w/composite stock, stainless metal. Mfd. by Miroku 1987-93; 1994 to date. (Stalker II).

Camo Stalker (orig. laminated stock) . . . . . NiB $580 Ex $421 Gd $246
Composite Stalker. NiB $622 Ex $477 Gd $349
Composite Stalker II . . . . NiB $622 Ex $477 Gd $349
Stainless Stalker . . . . NiB $658 Ex $555 Gd $452
Stainless Stalker II. NiB $683 Ex $580 Gd $477
Stainless Stalker, .375 H&H . . . . NiB $832 Ex $709 Gd $580
BOSS option, add $90
Left-hand model, add $90

MODEL A-BOLT
VARMINT II RIFLE . . . . NiB $735 Ex $683 Gd $524
Same general specifications as Stalker model except w/22-inch heavy bbl. w/BOSS system and varmint-style black laminated wood stock. Calibers: .22-250, .223 or .308. No sights. Bright blue or satin finish. Mfd. by Miroku 1994 to date.

MODEL B-92 LEVER-ACTION RIFLE . . . . . NiB $477 Ex $416 Gd $220
Calibers: .357 Mag. and .44 Rem. Mag. 11-round magazine. 20-inch round bbl. 37.5 inches overall. Weight: 5.5 to 6.4 lbs. Seasoned French walnut stock w/high gloss finish. Cloverleaf rear sight; steel post front. Made 1979-89 by Miroku.

BAR AUTOMATIC RIFLE,
GRADE I, STANDARD CALIBERS. . . . . NiB $725 Ex $555 Gd $400
Gas-operated semiautomatic. Calibers: .243 Win., .270 Win., .280 Rem., .308 Win., .30-06. Four-round box magazine. 22-inch bbl. Weight: 7.5 lbs. Folding leaf rear sight, hooded ramp front. French walnut stock and forearm checkered, QD swivels. Made 1967-92 by FN.

BAR, GRADE I, MAGNUM CALIBERS . . . . NiB $735 Ex $683 Gd $519
Same as BAR in standard calibers, except w/24-inch bbl.chambered 7mm Rem. Mag. or .300 Win. Mag. .338 Win. Mag. w/3-round box magazine and recoil pad. Weight: 8.5 lbs. Made 1969-92 by FN.

BAR, GRADE II
Same as Grade I except receiver engraved w/big-game heads (deer and antelope on standard-caliber rifles, ram and grizzly on Magnum-caliber) and scrollwork, higher grade wood. Made 1967-74 by FN.
Standard calibers. . . . . NiB $935 Ex $790 Gd $584
Magnum calibers. . . . . NiB $1043 Ex $765 Gd $528

BAR, GRADE III
Same as Grade I except receiver of grayed steel engraved w/big-game heads (deer and antelope on standard-caliber rifles, moose and elk on Magnum-caliber) framed in fine-line scrollwork, gold-plated trigger, stock and forearm of highly figured French walnut, hand-checkered and carved. Made 1971-74 by FN.
Standard calibers. . . . . NiB $996 Ex $935 Gd $533
Magnum calibers. . . . . NiB $1256 Ex $1179 Gd $664

BAR, GRADE IV
Same as Grade I except receiver of grayed steel engraved w/full detailed rendition of running deer and antelope on standard-caliber rifles, moose and elk on Magnum-caliber gold-plated trigger, stock and forearm of highly figured French walnut, hand checkered and carved. Made 1971-86 by FN.
Standard calibers. . . . . NiB $1630 Ex $1307 Gd $895
Magnum calibers. . . . . NiB $1887 Ex $1513 Gd $1036

BAR, GRADE V
Same as Grade I except receiver w/complete big-game scenes executed by a master engraver and inlaid w/18K gold (deer and antelope on standard-caliber rifles, moose and elk on Magnum caliber), gold-plated trigger, stock and forearm of finest French walnut, intricately hand-checkered and carved. Made 1971-74 by FN.
Standard calibers. . . . . NiB $3175 Ex $2543 Gd $1736
Magnum calibers. . . . . NiB $3625 Ex $2955 Gd $2028

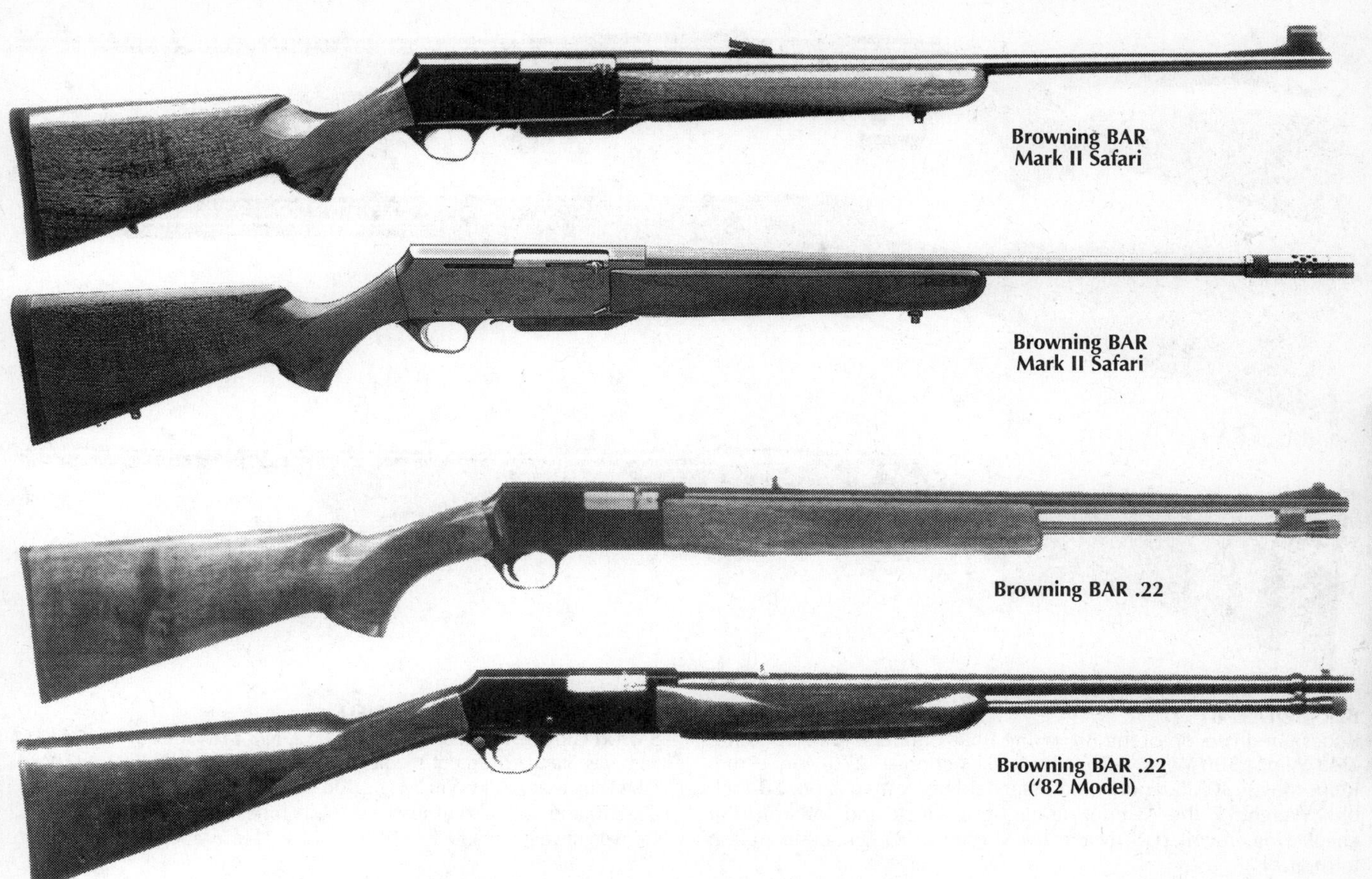
Browning BAR Mark II Safari

Browning BAR Mark II Safari

Browning BAR .22

Browning BAR .22 ('82 Model)

MODEL BAR MARK II SAFARI AUTOMATIC RIFLE
Same general specifications as standard BAR semiautomatic rifle, except w/redesigned gas and buffer systems, new bolt release lever, and engraved receiver. Made 1993 to date.
Standard calibers .... **NiB $679 Ex $618 Gd $422**
Magnum calibers..................... **NiB $757 Ex $654 Gd $448**
Lightweight (Alloy receiver w/20-inch bbl.)....................... **NiB $602 Ex $515 Gd $319**
BAR Mk II Grade III (intro. 1996)..... **NiB $2183 Ex $2003 Gd $1153**
BAR Mk II Grade IV (intro. 1996)..... **NiB $2384 Ex $1745 Gd $1307**
W/BOSS option, add **$60**
W/open sights, add **$15**

BAR .22 AUTOMATIC RIFLE
Semiautomatic. Caliber: .22 LR. Tubular magazine holds 15 rounds. 20.25-inch bbl. Weight: 6.25 lbs. Sights: Folding-leaf rear, gold bead front on ramp. Receiver grooved for scope mounting. French walnut pistol-grip stock and forearm checkered. Made 1977-85.
Grade I .... **NiB $370 Ex $309 Gd $175**
Grade II....................... **NiB $448 Ex $412 Gd $216**

BBR LIGHTNING BOLT-ACTION RIFLE ... **NiB $551 Ex $448 Gd $334**
Bolt-action rifle w/short bolt throw of 60 degrees. Calibers: .25-06 Rem., .270 Win., .30-06, 7mm Rem. Mag., .300 Win. Mag. 24-inch bbl. Weight: 8 lbs. Made 1979-84.

BL-.22 LEVER-ACTION REPEATING RIFLE
Short-throw lever-action. Caliber: .22 LR, Long, Short. Tubular magazine holds 15 LR, 17 Long 22 Short rounds. 20-inch bbl. Weight: 5 lbs. Sights: Folding leaf rear; bead front. Receiver grooved for scope

***(cont'd.)* BL .22 LEVER-ACTION REPEATING RIFLE**
mounting. Walnut straight-grip stock and forearm, bbl. band. Made 1970 to date by Miroku.
Grade I .... **NiB $345 Ex $211 Gd $144**
Grade I7 w/scroll engraving.............. **NiB $360 Ex $242 Gd $175**

BLR LEVER-ACTION REPEATING RIFLE
Calibers: (short action only) .243 Win., .308 Win., .358 Win. Four round detachable box magazine. 20-inch bbl. Weight: 7 lbs. Sights: Windage and elevation adj. open rear; hooded ramp front. Walnut straight-grip stock and forearm, checkered, bbl. band, recoil pad. Made 1966 by BAC/USA; 1969-73 by FN; 1974-80 by Miroku. Note: USA manufacture of this model was limited to prototypes and pre-production guns only and may be identified the "MADE IN USA" roll stamp on the bbl.
FN model...................... **NiB $726 Ex $499 Gd $345**
Miroku model .... **NiB $448 Ex $319 Gd $216**
USA model .... **NiB $1153 Ex $998 Gd $586**

BLR LIGHTNING MODEL
Lightweight version of the Browning BLR '81 w/forged alloy receiver and redesigned trigger group. Calibers: Short Action— .22-250 Rem., .223 Rem., .243 Win., 7mm-08 Rem., .308 Win.; Long Action— .270 Win., 7mm Rem. Mag., .30-06, .300 Win. Mag. Three or 4-round detachable box magazine. 20-, 22- or 24-inch bbl. Weight: 6.5 to 7.75 lbs. Pistol-grip style walnut stock and forearm, cut checkering and recoil pad. Made by Miroku 1995 to date.
BLR Lightning model short action........ **NiB $473 Ex $412 Gd $216**
BLR Lightning model long action .... **NiB $499 Ex $448 Gd $293**

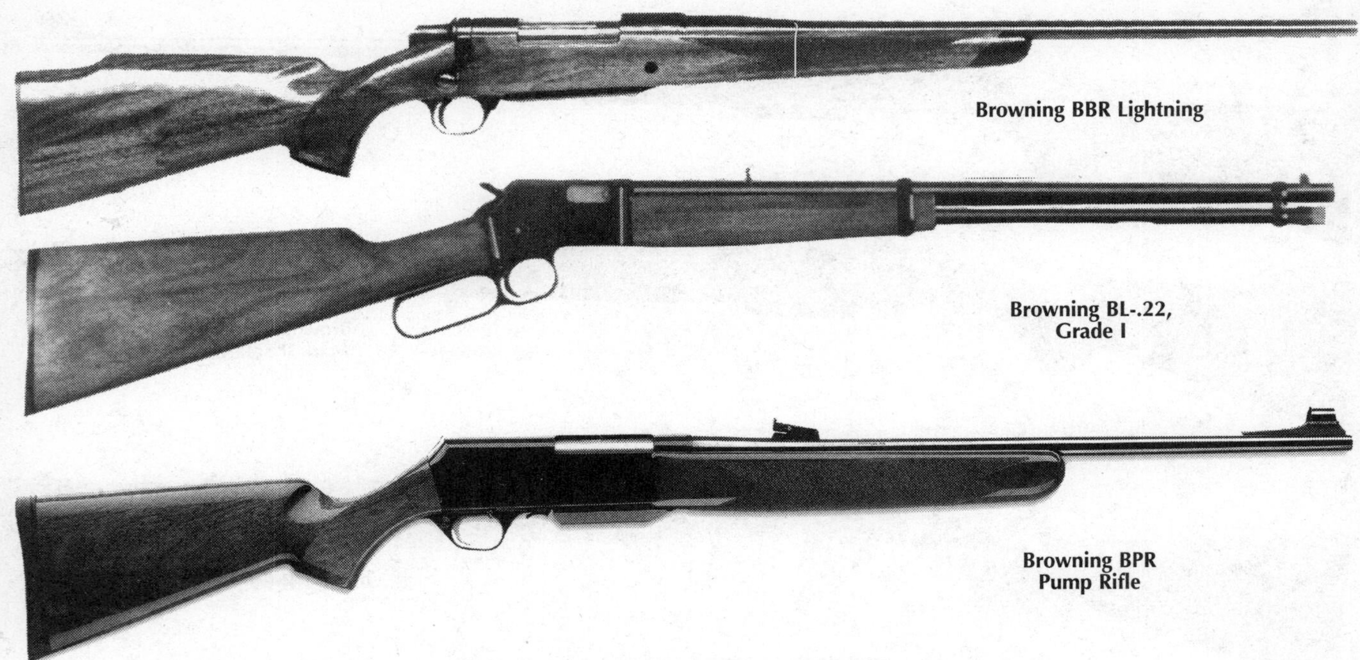

Browning BBR Lightning

Browning BL-.22, Grade I

Browning BPR Pump Rifle

BLR MODEL '81

Redesigned version of the Browning BLR. Calibers: .222-50 Rem., .243 Win., .308 Win., .358 Win; Long Action— .270 Win., 7mm Rem. Mag., .30-06. Fourround detachable box magazine. 20-inch bbl. Weight: 7 lbs. Walnut straight-grip stock and forearm, cut checkering, recoil pad. Made by Miroku 1981-95; Long Action intro. 1991.

BLR Model '81 short action....... NiB $576 Ex $417 Gd $267
BLR Model '81 long action .... NiB $618 Ex $422 Gd $309

BPR-22 PUMP RIFLE

Hammerless slide-action repeater. Specifications same as for BAR-.22, except also available chambered for .22 Magnum RF; magazine capacity, 11 rounds. Made 1977-82 by Miroku.

Model I .... NiB $267 Ex $216 Gd $154
Model II....................... NiB $473 Ex $417 Gd $242

BPR PUMP RIFLE

Slide-action repeater based on proven BAR designs w/forged alloy receiver and slide that cams down to clear bbl. and receiver. Calibers: .243 Win., .308 Win., .270 Win., .30-06, 7mm Rem. Mag. .300 Win. Mag. Three or 4-round detachable box magazine. 22- or 24-inch bbl. w/ramped front sight and open adj. rear. Weight: 7.2 to 7.4 lbs. Made 1997 to date by Miroku.

BPR Model standard calibers...... NiB $836 Ex $662 Gd $425
BPR Model magnum calibers...... NiB $919 Ex $687 Gd $456

HIGH-POWER BOLT-ACTION RIFLE, MEDALLION GRADE .... NiB $1717 Ex $1558 Gd $940

Same as Safari Grade except receiver and bbl. scroll engraved, ram's head engraved on floorplate; select walnut stock w/rosewood forearm tip, grip cap. Made 1961-74.

HIGH-POWER BOLT-ACTION RIFLE, OLYMPIAN GRADE .... NiB $3738 Ex $3352 Gd $1832

Same as Safari Grade except bbl. engraved; receiver, trigger guard and floorplate satin chrome-plated and engraved w/game scenes appropriate to caliber; finest figured walnut stock w/rosewood forearm tip and grip cap, latter w/18K-gold medallion. Made 1961-74.

HIGH-POWER BOLT-ACTION RIFLE, SAFARI GRADE, MEDIUM ACTION..... NiB $1045 Ex $792 Gd $561

Same as Standard except medium action. Calibers: .22-250, .243 Win., .264 Win. Mag., .284 Win. Mag., .308 Win. Bbl.: 22-inch lightweight bbl.; .22-250 and .243 also available w/24-inch heavy bbl. Weight: 6 lbs., 12 oz. w/lightweight bbl.; 7 lbs. 13 oz. w/heavy bbl. Made 1963-74 by Sako.

HIGH-POWER BOLT-ACTION RIFLE, SAFARI GRADE, SHORT ACTION....... NiB $1045 Ex $792 Gd $561

Same as Standard except short action. Calibers: .222 Rem., .222 Rem. Mag. 22-inch lightweight or 24-inch heavy bbl. No sights. Weight: 6 lbs., 2 oz. w/lightweight bbl.; 7.5 lbs. w/heavy bbl. Made 1963-74 by Sako.

HIGH-POWER BOLT-ACTION RIFLE, SAFARI GRADE, STANDARD ACTION . . NiB $1333 Ex $1045 Gd $839

Mauser-type action. Calibers: .270 Win., .30-06, 7mm Rem. Mag., .300 H&H Mag., .300 Win. Mag., .308 Norma Mag. .338 Win. Mag., .375 H&H Mag., .458 Win. Mag. Cartridge capacity: 6 rounds in .270, .30-06; 4 in Magnum calibers. Bbl. length: 22 in., in .270, .30-06; 24 in., in Magnum calibers. Weight: 7 lbs., 2 oz., in .270, .30-06; 8.25 lbs. in Mag. calibers. Folding leaf rear sight, hooded ramp front. Checkered stock w/pistol grip, Monte Carlo cheekpiece, QD swivels; recoil pad on Magnum models. Made 1959-74 by FN.

"T-BOLT" T-1 .22 REPEATING RIFLE

Straight-pull bolt action. Caliber: .22 LR. Five round clip magazine. 24-inch bbl. Peep rear sight w/ramped blade front. Plain walnut stock w/pistol grip and laquered finish. Weight: 6 lbs. Also left-hand model. Made 1965-74 by FN.

Right-hand model .... NiB $473 Ex $412 Gd $242
Left-hand model .... NiB $499 Ex $417 Gd $242

"T-BOLT" T-2

Same as T-1 Model except w/checkered fancy figured walnut stock. Made 1966-74 by FN. (Reintroduced briefly during the late 1980's with oil-finished stock)

Original model .... NiB $499 Ex $417 Gd $242
Reintroduced model .... NiB $448 Ex $370 Gd $216

Browning
BL-22 II

Browning
BLR Model '81

Browning High-Power
Bolt-Action Rifle, Medallion Grade

Browning High-Power
Safari Grade Medium Action, Heavy Barrel

Browning High-Power
Safari Grade Short Action, Heavy Barrel

Browning High-Power
Safari Grade Standard Action

F.N. BROWNING FAL SEMIAUTOMATIC RIFLE
Same as F.N. FAL Semiautomatic Rifle. See F.N. listing for specifications. Sold by Browning for a brief period c. 1960.

F.N. FAL standard model (G-series)...................... **NiB $3912 Ex $2779 Gd $1981**
F.N. FAL lightweight model (G-series)...................... **NiB $4711 Ex $4165 Gd $2625**
F.N. FAL heavy bbl.. model (G-series)...................... **NiB $7286 Ex $5998 Gd $4636**
BAC FAL model...................... **NiB $3011 Ex $2676 Gd $1688**

BSA GUNS LTD. — Birmingham, England (Previously Imported by Samco Global Arms, BSA Guns Ltd and Precision Sports)

NO. 12 MARTINI SINGLE-SHOT TARGET RIFLE................ **NiB $602 Ex $473 Gd $345**
Caliber .22 LR. 29-inch bbl. Weight: 8.75 lbs. Parker-Hale Model 7 rear sight and Model 2 front sight. Straight-grip stock, checkered forearm. Note: This model was also available w/open sights or w/BSA No. 20 and 30 sights. Made before WWII.

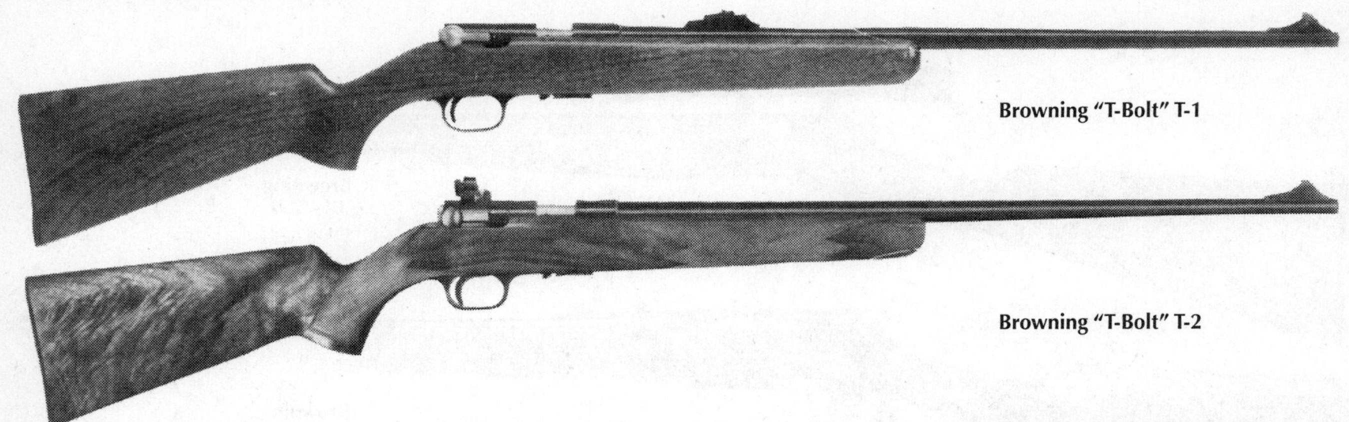

Browning "T-Bolt" T-1

Browning "T-Bolt" T-2

MODEL 12/15 MARTINI HEAVY .... NiB $623 Ex $473 Gd $309
Same as Standard Model 12/15 except w/extra heavy bbl., weighs 11 lbs.

MODEL 12/15 MARTINI SINGLE-SHOT TARGET RIFLE ..... NiB $551 Ex $417 Gd $293
Caliber: .22 LR. 29-inch bbl. Weight: 9 lbs. Parker-Hale No. PH-7A rear sight and No. FS-22 front sight. Target stock w/high comb and cheekpiece, beavertail forearm. Note: This is a post-WWII model; however, a similar rifle, the BSA-Parker Model 12/15, was produced c. 1938.

NO. 13 MARTINI SINGLE-SHOT TARGET RIFLE................. NiB $525 Ex $417 Gd $267
Caliber: .22 LR. Lighter version of the No.12 w/same general specifications except w/25-inch bbl., weighs 6.5lbs. Made before WWII.

NO. 13 SPORTING RIFLE
Same as No. 13 Target except fitted w/Parker-Hale "Sportarget" rear sight and bead front sight. Also available in .22 Hornet. Made before WWII.
.22 Long Rifle .... NiB $576 Ex $417 Gd $278
.22 Hornet................... NiB $782 Ex $623 Gd $417

MODEL 15 MARTINI SINGLE-SHOT TARGET RIFLE.......... NiB $551 Ex $417 Gd $267
Caliber: .22 LR. 29-inch bbl. Weight: 9.5 lbs. BSA No. 30 rear sight and No. 20 front sight. Target stock w/cheekpiece and pistol-grip, long, semi-beavertail forearm. Made before WWII.

CENTURION MODEL MATCH RIFLE .... NiB $520 Ex $370 Gd $267
Same general specifications as Model 15 except w/"Centurion" match bbl. Made before WWII.

CF-2 BOLT-ACTION HUNTING RIFLE .... NiB $422 Ex $345 Gd $211
Mauser-type action. Calibers: 7mm Rem. Mag., .300 Win. Mag. Three-round magazine. 23.6-inch bbl. Weight: 8 lbs. Sights: Adj. rear; hooded ramp front. Checkered walnut stock w/Monte Carlo comb, rollover cheekpiece, rosewood forend tip, recoil pad, sling swivels. Made 1975-87. See Ithaca-BSA CF-2.

CF-2 STUTZEN RIFLE .... NiB $520 Ex $370 Gd $267
Calibers: .222 Rem., .22-250, .243 Win., .270 Win., .308 Win. .30-06. Four round capacity (5 in 222 Rem.). 20.6-inch bbl. 41.5 inches (approx.) overall length. Weight: 7.5 to 8 lbs. Williams front and rear sights. Hand-finished European walnut stock. Monte Carlo cheekpiece and Wundhammer palm swell. Double-set triggers. Importation disc. 1987.

CFT TARGET RIFLE .... NiB $834 Ex $629 Gd $454
Single-shot bolt action. Caliber: 7.62mm. 26.5-inch bbl. About 47.5 inches overall. Weight: 11 lbs., incl. accessories. Bbl. and action weight: 6 lbs., 12 oz. Importation disc. 1987.

MAJESTIC DELUXE FEATHERWEIGHT BOLT-ACTION HUNTING RIFLE
Mauser-type action. Calibers: .243 Win., .270 Win., .308 Win., .30-06, .458 Win. Mag. Four round magazine. 22-inch bbl. w/BESA recoil re-ducer. Weight: 6.25 lbs.; 8.75 lbs. in 458. Folding leaf rear sight, hooded ramp front. Checkered European-style walnut stock w/cheekpiece, pistol-grip, Schnabel forend, swivels, recoil pad. Made 1959-65.
.458 Win. Mag. caliber .... NiB $576 Ex $448 Gd $293
Other calibers .... NiB $473 Ex $417 Gd $242

BSA MAJESTIC DELUXE STANDARD WEIGHT .... NiB $448 Ex $267 Gd $195
Same as Featherweight model except heavier bbl. w/o recoil reducer. Calibers: .22 Hornet, .222 Rem., .243 Win., 7x57mm, .308 Win., .30-06. Weight: 7.25 to 7.75 lbs. Disc.

MARTINI-INTERNATIONAL ISU MATCH RIFLE.............. NiB $968 Ex $736 Gd $494
Similar to MK III, but modified to meet International Shooting Union "Standard Rifle" specifications. 28-inch standard weight bbl. Weight: 10.75 lbs. Redesigned stock and forearm, latter attached to bbl. w/"V" section alloy strut. Intro. 1968. Disc.

MARTINI-INTERNATIONAL MARK V MATCH RIFLE .... NiB $993 Ex $762 Gd $525
Same as ISU model except w/heavier bbl. Weight: 12.25 lbs. Intro. 1976. Disc.

MARTINI-INTERNATIONAL MATCH RIFLE SINGLE-SHOT HEAVY PATTERN .... NiB $709 Ex $559 Gd $453
Caliber: .22 LR. 29-inch heavy bbl. Weight: 14 lbs. Parker-Hale "International" front and rear sights. Target stock w/full cheekpiece and pistol-grip, broad beavertail forearm, handstop, swivels. Right- or left-hand models. Mfd. 1950-53.

MARTINI-INTERNATIONAL MATCH RIFLE — LIGHT PATTERN......... NiB $684 Ex $556 Gd $427
Same general specifications as Heavy Pattern except w/26-inch lighter weight bbl. Weight: 11 lbs. Disc.

MARTINI-INTERNATIONAL MK II MATCH RIFLE .... NiB $890 Ex $571 Gd $453
Same general specifications as original model. Heavy and Light Pattern. Improved trigger mechanism and ejection system. Redesigned stock and forearm. Made 1953-59.

MARTINI-INTERNATIONAL MK III MATCH RIFLE .... NiB $993 Ex $762 Gd $524
Same general specifications as MK II Heavy Pattern. Longer action frame w/I-section alloy strut to which forearm is attached; bbl. is fully floating. Redesigned stock and forearm. Made 1959-67.

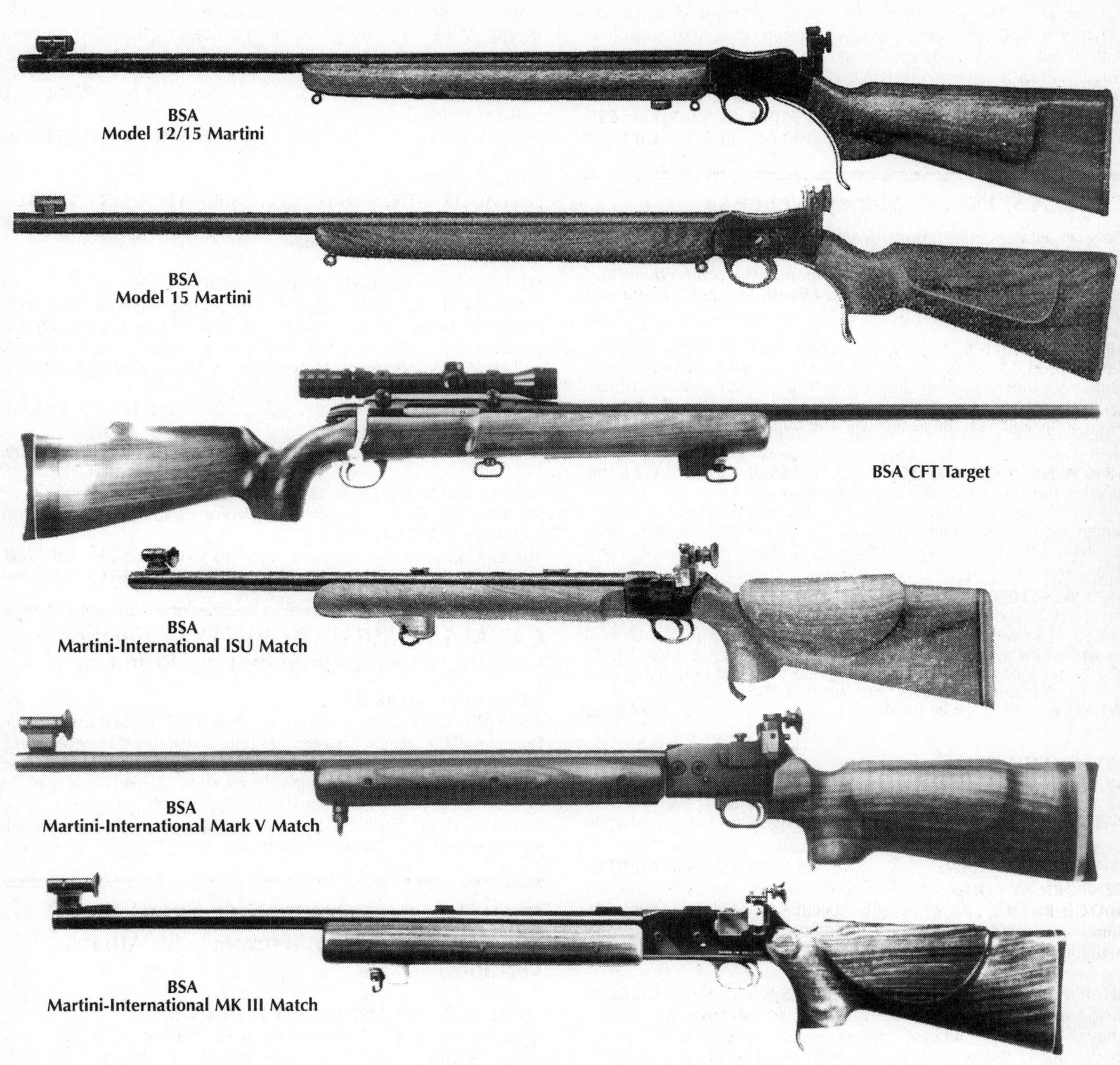

BSA
Model 12/15 Martini

BSA
Model 15 Martini

BSA CFT Target

BSA
Martini-International ISU Match

BSA
Martini-International Mark V Match

BSA
Martini-International MK III Match

MONARCH DELUXE BOLT-ACTION HUNTING RIFLE . . . . **NiB $345 Ex $309 Gd $211**
Same as Majestic Deluxe Standard Weight model except w/redesigned stock of U.S. style w/contrasting hardwood forend tip and grip cap. Calibers: .222 Rem., .243 Win., .270 Win., 7mm Rem. Mag., .308 Win., .30-06. 22-inch bbl. Weight: 7 to 7.25 lbs. Made 1965-74.

MONARCH DELUXE VARMINT RIFLE . . . . **NiB $448 Ex $370 Gd $242**
Same as Monarch Deluxe except w/24-inch heavy bbl. and weighs 9 lbs. Calibers: .222 Rem., .243 Win. See illustration next page.

BUSHMASTER FIREARMS — (Quality Parts Company), Windham, Maine

M17S BULLPUP . . . . **NiB $862 Ex $728 Gd $501**
Caliber: .223. 21.5-inch bbl. Weight: 8.2 lbs. Polymer stocks. Handle w/fixed open sights w/Weaver-type rail for any optics. Semi-auto, self-compensating short stroke gas piston. Forward trigger/grip w/rear chamber. Bullpup style. Alloy receiver. Synthetic lower receiver is hinged to upper w/hinged takedown system. Accepts M-16 type magazines. Made 1992 to date.

MODEL XM15 E2S SERIES
Caliber: .223. 16-, 20-, 24- or 26-inch bbl. Weight: 7 to 8.6 lbs. Polymer stocks. Adjustable sights w/dual flip-up aperture; optional flattop rail accepts scope. Direct gas-operated w/rotating bolt. Forged alloy receiver. All steel-coated w/manganese phosphate. Accepts M-16 type magazines. Made 1989 to date.
XM15 E2S Carbine. . . . . NiB $1095 Ex $915 Gd $658
XM15 E2S Target Rifle . . . . NiB $1147 Ex $864 Gd $606

CABELA'S, INC. — Sidney, Nebraska

Cabela's is a sporting goods dealer and catalog company headquartered in Sidney, Nebraska. Cabela's imports black powder cartridge Sharps replicas, revolvers and other reproductions and replicas manufactured in Italy by A. Uberti, Pedersoli, Pietta and others.

1858 HENRY REPLICA . . . . NiB $625 Ex $550 Gd $475
Lever-action. Modeled after the original Henry rifle. Caliber: .44-40. Thirteen-round magazine; Bbl: 24 inches. Overall length: 43 inches. Weight: 9 pounds. European walnut stock. Sights: Bead front, open adjustable rear. Brass receiver and buttplate. Introduced 1994.

1866 WINCHESTER REPLICA . . . . . NiB $525 Ex $475 Gd $400
Lever-action modeled after the original Model 1866 rifle. Caliber: .44-40. Thirteen-round magazine. Bbl: 24 inches, octagonal; overall length: 43 inches. Weight: 9 pounds. European walnut stock, brass receiver, butt plate and forend cap. Sights: Bead front, open adjustable rear.

1873 WINCHESTER REPLICA . . . . . NiB $475 Ex $410 Gd $350
Lever-action modeled after the original Model 1873 rifle. Caliber: .44-40, .45 Colt. Thirteen-round magazine. Bbl: 30 inches. Overall length: 43 inches. Weight: 8 pounds. European walnut stock. Sights: Bead front, open adjustable rear or globe front and tang rear. Color case-hardened steel receiver. Introduced 1994.
W/tang rear sight, globe front: . . . . .add $150

1873 SPORTING
MODEL REPLICA. . . . . NiB $600 Ex $515 Gd $475
Same as 1873 Winchester except with 30-inch bbl.
W/half-round, half-octagonal bbl., half magazine . . . . . . add $100

CATTLEMAN CARBINE . . . . NiB $300 Ex $260 Gd $200
Revolver with shoulder stock. Caliber: .44-40; six-round cylinder. Bbl: 18 inches. Overall length: 34 inches. Weight: 4 pounds. European walnut stock. Sights: Blade front, notch rear. Color case-hardened frame, remainder blued. Introduced 1994.

SHARPS SPORTING RIFLE . . . . NiB $800 Ex $725 Gd $500
Single-shot. Caliber: .45-70. Bbl: Tapered octagon, 32 inches. Overall length: 47 inches. Weight: 9 pounds. Checkered walnut stock. Sights: Blade front, open adjustable rear. Color case-hardened receiver and hammer; remainder blued. Introduced 1995.

CALICO LIGHT WEAPONS SYSTEMS — Bakersville, California

LIBERTY 50/100 SEMIAUTOMATIC RIFLE
Retarded blowback action. Caliber: 9mm. 50- or 100-round helical-feed magazine. 16.1-inch bbl. 34.5 inches overall. Weight: 7 lbs. Adjustable post front sight and aperture rear. Ambidextrous rotating safety. Glass-filled polymer or thumbhole-style wood stock. Made 1995 to date.
Model Liberty 50. . . . . NiB $749 Ex $596 Gd $341
Model Liberty 100. . . . . NiB $826 Ex $800 Gd $418

MODEL M-100 SEMIAUTOMATIC SERIES
Similar to the Liberty 100 Model except chambered for .22 LR. Weight: 5 lbs. 34.5 inches overall. Folding or glass-filled polymer stock and forearm. Made 1986 to date.
Model M-100 w/folding
stock (disc. 1994). NiB $443 Ex $306 Gd $163
Model M-100 FS w/fixed
stock (1996) . . . . NiB $617 Ex $418 Gd $290

MODEL M-105
SEMI-AUTOMATIC SPORTER . . . . . NiB $311 Ex $239 Gd $163
Similar to the Liberty 100 Model except fitted w/walnut buttstock and forearm. Made 1986 to date.

MODEL M-900 SEMIAUTOMATIC CARBINE
Caliber: 9mm Parabellum. 50- or 100-round magazine. 16.1-inch bbl. 28.5 inches overall. Weight: 3.7 lbs. Post front sight adj. for windage and elevation, fixed notch rear. Collapsible steel buttstock and glass-filled polymer grip. Matte black finish. Made 1989-94.
Model M-100 w/folding
stock (disc. 1994) . . . . NiB $545 Ex $418 Gd $265
Model M-100 FS w/fixed
stock (Intro. 1996) . . . . NiB $515 Ex $367 Gd $239

MODEL M-951 TACTICAL CARBINE
Similar to Model 900 except w/long compensator and adj. forward grip. Made 1990-94.
Model 951. . . . . NiB $515 Ex $367 Gd $270
Model 951-S . . . . NiB $545 Ex $311 Gd $290

CANADIAN MILITARY RIFLES — Quebec, Canada, Manufactured by Ross Rifle Co.

MODEL 1907 MARK II
ROSS MILITARY RIFLE . . . . NiB $337 Ex $235 Gd $205
Straight-pull bolt action. Caliber: .303 British. Five-round box magazine. 28-inch bbl. Weight: 8.5 lbs. Sights: adj. rear; blade front. Military-type full stock. Note: The Ross was originally issued as a Canadian service rifle in 1907. There were several variations; it was the official weapon at the start of WWI, but has been obsolete for many years. For Ross sporting rifle, see listing under Ross Rifle company.

CENTURY INTERNATIONAL ARMS, INC. — Boca Raton, Florida; (Formerly St. Albans, Vermont)

CENTURION M38/M96 BOLT-ACTION SPORTER
Sporterized Swedish M38/96 Mauser action. Caliber: 6.5x55mm. Five-round magazine. 24-inch bbl. 44 inches overall. Adj. rear sight. Blade front. Black synthetic or checkered European hardwood Monte Carlo stock. Holden Ironsighter see-through scope mount. Imported 1987 to date.
W/hardwood stock . . . . NiB $183 Ex $132 Gd $87
W/synthetic stock . . . . NiB $199 Ex $158 Gd $107

CENTURION M98 BOLT-ACTION SPORTER
Sporterized VZ24 or 98 Mauser action. Calibers: .270 Win., 7.62x39mm, .308 Win., .30-06. Five round magazine. 22-inch bbl. 44 inches overall. Weight: 7.5 lbs. W/Millet or Weaver scope base(s), rings and no iron sights. Classic or Monte Carlo laminated hardwood, black synthetic or checkered European hardwood stock. Imported 1992 to date.
M98 Action W/black
synthetic stock (w/o rings). . . . . NiB $234 Ex $183 Gd $126
M98 Action W/hardwood Stock (w/o rings). . . . NiB $204 Ex $158 Gd $97

(cont'd.) **CENTURION M98 BOLT-ACTION SPORTER**

VZ24 Action W/laminated Hardwood Stock (Elite) . . . . NiB $306 Ex $234 Gd $158
VZ24 Action W/black synthetic stock. . . . . NiB $292 Ex $234 Gd $161
W/Millet base and rings, add $25

CENTURION P-14 SPORTER

Sporterized P-14 action. Caliber: 7mm Rem. Mag., .300 Win. Mag. Five-round magazine. 24-inch bbl. 43.4 inches overall. Weight: 8.25 lbs. Weaver-type scope base. Walnut stained hardwood or fiberglass stock. Imported 1987 to date.

W/hardwood stock . . . . NiB $224 Ex $183 Gd $122
W/fiberglass stock. . . . . NiB $260 Ex $183 Gd $132

ENFIELD SPORTER 4 BOLT-ACTION RIFLE

Sporterized Lee-Enfield action. Caliber: .303 British. 10-round magazine. 25.25-inch bbl. 44.5 inches overall. Blade front sight, adj. aperture rear. Sporterized beechwood military stock or checkered walnut Monte Carlo stock. Blued finish. Imported 1987 to date.

W/sporterized military stock . . . . NiB $132 Ex $102 Gd $61
W/checkered walnut stock . . . . NiB $183 Ex $158 Gd $102

L1A1 FAL SPORTER . . . . .NiB $851 Ex $673 Gd $515

Sporterized L1A1 FAL semiautomatic. Caliber: .308 Win. 20.75-inch bbl. 41 inches overall. Weight: 9.75 lbs. Protected front post sight, adj. aperture rear. Matte blued finish. Black or camo Bell & Carlson thumbhole sporter stock w/rubber buttpad. Imported 1988-98.

M-14 SPORTER . . . . NiB $413 Ex $291 Gd $188

Sporterized M-14 gas operated semiautomatic action. Caliber: .308 Win. 10-round magazine. 22-inch bbl. 41 inches overall. Weight: 8.25 lbs. Blade front sight, adj. aperture rear sight. Parkerized finish. Walnut stock w/rubber recoil pad. Forged receiver. Imported 1991 to date.

TIGER DRAGUNOV . . . . NiB $3600 Ex $2656 Gd $1279

Russian SVD semiautomatic sniper rifle. Caliber: 7.62x54R. Five-round magazine. 21-inch bbl. 43 inches overall. Weight: 8.5 lbs. Blade front sight, open rear adj. for elevation. Blued finish. European laminated hardwood thumbhole stock. 4x range-finding scope w/lighted reticle and sunshade. Quick detachable scope mount. Imported 1994-95.

CHARTER ARMS CORPORATION — Stratford, Connecticut

AR-7 EXPLORER SURVIVAL RIFLE . . . . NiB $132 Ex $97 Gd $66

Same as Armalite AR-7, except w/black, instead of brown, "wood grain" plastic stock. See listing of that rifle for specifications. Made 1973-90.

CHIPMUNK RIFLES — Prospect, Oregon MFD. by Rogue Rifle Company (Formerly Oregon Arms Company and Chipmunk Manufacturing, Inc.)

BOLT-ACTION SINGLE-SHOT RIFLE

Calibers: .22 LR. or .22 WMR. 16.13-inch standard or 18.13-inch bull bbl. Weight: 2.5 lbs. (standard) or 4 lbs. (Bull bbl.) Peep sight rear; ramp front. Plain or checkered American walnut, laminated or black hardwood stock. Made 1982 to date.

(cont'd.) **BOLT-ACTION SINGLE-SHOT RIFLE**

Standard model w/plain walnut stock. . . . . NiB $173 Ex $117 Gd $71
Standard model w/black hardwood stock . . . . NiB $153 Ex $107 Gd $71
Standard model w/camouflage stock. . . . . NiB $183 Ex $137 Gd $86
Standard model w/laminated stock . . . . NiB $169 Ex $137 Gd $97
Deluxe grade w/checkered walnut stock. . . . . NiB $239 Ex $183 Gd $117
.22 WMR, add $20

CHURCHILL RIFLES — Mfd. in England. *Imported by Ellett Brothers, Inc., Chapin, SC (Previously by Kassnar Imports, Inc.)*

HIGHLANDER BOLT-ACTION RIFLE. . . . . NiB $461 Ex $370 Gd $255

Calibers: .243 Win., .25-06 Rem., .270 Win., .308 Win., .30-06, 7mm Rem. Mag., .300 Win. Mag. Four round magazine (standard); 3-round (magnum). Bbl. length: 22-inch (standard); 24-inch (magnum). 42.5 to 44.5 inches overall. Weight: 7.5 lbs. Adj. rear sight, blade front. Checkered European walnut pistol-grip stock. Imported 1986-91.

"ONE OF ONE THOUSAND" RIFLE
. . . . . NiB $2601 Ex $2081 Gd $943

Made for Interarms to commemorate that firm's 20th anniversary. Mauser-type action. Calibers: .270, 7mm Rem. Mag., .308, .30-06, .300 Win. Mag., .375 H&H Mag., .458 Win. Mag. Five round magazine (3-round in Magnum calibers). 24-inch bbl. Weight: 8 lbs. Classic-style French walnut stock w/cheekpiece, black forend tip, checkered pistol grip and forearm, swivel-mounted recoil pad w/cartridge trap, pistol-grip cap w/trap for extra front sight, barrel-mounted sling swivel. Limited issue of 1,000 rifles made in 1973. See illustration next page.

REGENT BOLT-ACTION RIFLE . . . . NiB $581 Ex $525 Gd $401

Calibers: .243 Win., .25-06 Rem., .270 Win., .308 Win., .30-06, 7mm Rem. Mag., .300 Win. Mag. Four round magazine. 22-inch round bbl. 42.5 inches overall. Weight: 7.5 lbs. Ramp front sight w/gold bead; adj. rear. Hand-checkered Monte Carlo-style stock of select European walnut; recoil pad. Made 1986-90. See illustration next page.

CIMARRON ARMS — Fredericksburg, Texas

1860 HENRY LEVER-ACTION REPLICA

Replica of 1860 Henry w/original Henry loading system.Calibers: .44-40, .44 Special, .45 Colt. 13-round magazine. 22-inch bbl. (carbine) or 24.25-inch bbl. (rifle). 43 inches overall (rifle). Weight: 9.5 lbs. (rifle). Bead front sight, open adj. rear. Brass receiver and buttplate. Smooth European walnut buttstock. Imported 1991 to date.

Carbine model. . . . . NiB $883 Ex $724 Gd $446
Rifle model . . . . NiB $909 Ex $652 Gd $471
Civil War model (U.S. issue martially marked). . . . . . NiB $909 Ex $744 Gd $497
W/A-engraving, add. $395
W/B-engraving, add. $495
W/C-engraving, add. $695

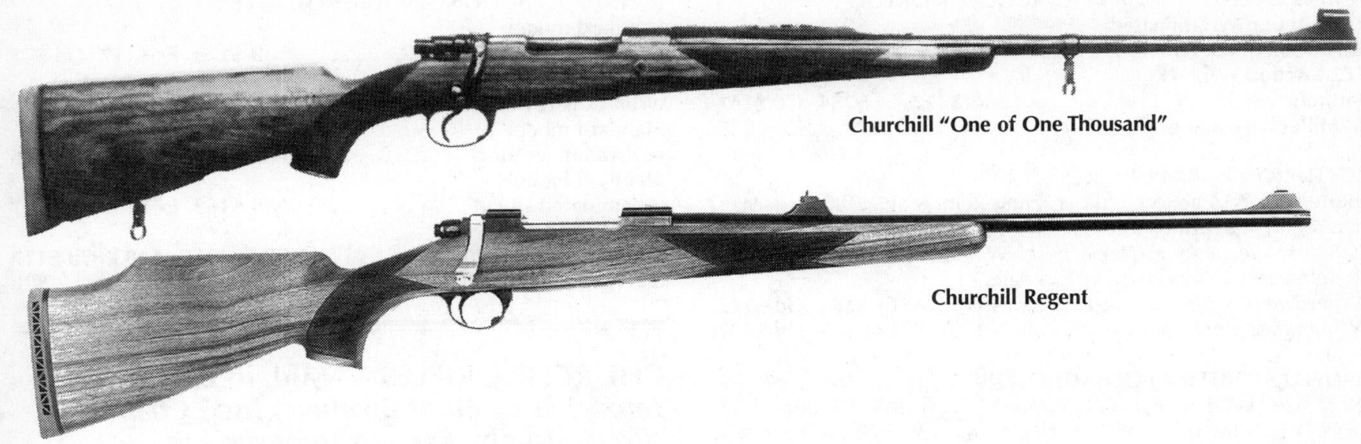

Churchill "One of One Thousand"

Churchill Regent

1866 YELLOWBOY LEVER-ACTION
Replica of 1866 Winchester. Calibers: .22 LR, 22WMR, .38 Special, .44-40, .45 Colt. 16-inch round bbl. (Trapper), 19-inch round bbl. (Carbine) or 24.25-inch ocatagonal bbl. (rifle). 43 inches overall (rifle). Weight: 9 lbs. (rifle). Bead front sight, open adj. rear. Brass receiver, buttplate and forend cap. Smooth European walnut stock. Imported 1991 to date.

Carbine .... **NiB $705 Ex $551 Gd $345**
Rifle .... **NiB $828 Ex $576 Gd $370**
Indian model (disc.) .... **NiB $679 Ex $551 Gd $345**
Trapper Model (.44-40 WCF only, disc.) ...... **NiB $551 Ex $422 Gd $268**
W/A-engraving, add **$425**
W/B-engraving, add. **$595**
W/C-engraving, add **$995**

1873 LEVER-ACTION
Replica of 1873 Winchester. Calibers: .22 LR. .22WMR, .357 Magnum, .44-40 or .45 Colt. 16-inch round bbl. (Trapper), 19-inch round bbl. (SRC), 20-inch octagonal bbl. (short rifle), 24.25-inch octagonal bbl. (sporting rifle) and 30-inch octagonal bbl. (express rifle). 43 inches overall (sporting rifle). Weight: 8 lbs. Fixed blade front sight, adj. semi-buckhorn rear or tang peep sight. Walnut stock and forend. Color case-hardened receiver. Imported 1989 to date.

Express Rifle .... **NiB $885 Ex $654 Gd $473**
Short Rifle (disc.) .... **NiB $860 Ex $602 Gd $412**
Sporting Rifle .... **NiB $731 Ex $576 Gd $391**
SRC Carbine .... **NiB $757 Ex $576 Gd $396**
Trapper (disc.) .... **NiB $623 Ex $499 Gd $209**
One of 1000 engraved model .... **NiB $2244 Ex $1832 Gd $1163**

1874 FALLING BLOCK SPORTING RIFLE
Replica of 1874 Sharps Sporting Rifle. Calibers: .45-65, .45-70, .45-90 or .45-120. 32- or 34-inch round or octagonal bbl. Weight: 9.5 to 10 lbs. Blade or globe front sight w/adj. open rear or sporting tang peep sight. Single or double set triggers. Checkered walnut stock and forend w/nose cap. Color case-hardened receiver. Imported 1997 to date.

1874 Sporting Rifle - Billy Dixon Model ... **NiB $1096 Ex $993 Gd $757**
1874 Sporting Rifle - Quigley Model ... **NiB $1508 Ex $1328 Gd $787**
Sharps Sporting No. 1 Rifle .... **NiB $1040 Ex $813 Gd $556**

CLERKE RECREATION PRODUCTS — Santa Monica, California

DELUXE HI-WALL .... **NiB $374 Ex $303 Gd $206**
Same as standard model, except w/adj. trigger, half-octagon bbl., select wood, stock w/cheekpiece and recoil pad. Made 1972-74.

HI-WALL
SINGLE-SHOT RIFLE .... **NiB $364 Ex $308 Gd $185**
Falling-block lever-action similar to Winchester 1885 High Wall S.S. Color casehardened investment-cast receiver. Calibers: .222 Rem., .22-250, .243 Rem., 6mm Rem., .25-06, .270 Win., 7mm Rem. Mag., .30-06, .45-70 Govt. 26-inch medium-weight bbl. Weight: 8 lbs. Furnished w/o sights. Checkered walnut pistol-grip stock and Schnabel forearm. Made 1972-74.

CLIFTON ARMS — Medina, Texas

SCOUT BOLT-ACTION RIFLE
Custom rifle built on the Dakota .76, Ruger .77 or Winchester .70 action. Shilen match-grade barrel cut and chambered to customer's specification. Clifton composite stock fitted and finished to customer's preference. Made 1992-97.

African
Scout .... **NiB $3655 Ex $2985 Gd $2311**
Pseudo
Scout .... **NiB $3526 Ex $2105 Gd $1312**
Standard
Scout .... **NiB $3500 Ex $2058 Gd $1286**
Super
Scout .... **NiB $3629 Ex $2908 Gd $1363**

COLT INDUSTRIES, FIREARMS DIVISION — Hartford, Connecticut

NOTE: *On Colt AR-15 Sporter models currently produced (i.e., Competition H-BAR, Sporter Match Target Lightweight, and Sporter Target Rifle), add $200 to pre-ban models made prior to 10-13-94.*

AR-15 A2 DELTA
MATCH H-BAR RIFLE .... **NiB $1663 Ex $1586 Gd $1354**
Similar to AR-15A2 Government Model except w/standard stock and heavy refined bbl. Furnished w/3-9x rubber armored scope and removeable cheekpiece. Made 1986-91.

AR-15 A2 GOVERNMENT
MODEL CARBINE .... **NiB $2209 Ex $1874 Gd $1045**
Caliber: .223 Rem., Five-round magazine. 16-inch bbl. w/flash suppressor. 35 inches overall. Weight: 5.8 lbs. Telescoping aluminum buttstock; sling swivels. Made 1985-91.

Colt AR-15 A2

Colt AR-15 A2 Delta Match H-BAR

Colt AR-15 A2 Government Model

Colt AR-15 Sporter Competition H-BAR

AR-15 A2 SPORTER II . . . . NiB $1303 Ex $1149 Gd $1041
Same general specifications as standard AR-15 Sporter except heavier bbl., improved pistol-grip. Weight 7.5 lbs.; optional 3x or 4x scope. Made 1985-89.

AR-15 COMPACT 9MM CARBINE . . . . NiB $1715 Ex $1458 Gd $1046
Semiautomatic. Caliber: 9mm NATO. 20-round detachable magazine. Bbl.: 16-inch round. Weight: 6.3 lbs. Adj. rear and front sights. Adj. buttstock. Ribbed round handguard. Made 1985-86.

Colt Stagecoach

Colteer 1-.22

Colteer .22 Autoloader

Coltsman Deluxe

Coltsman 1957 Standard

AR-15 SEMIAUTOMATIC SPORTER
Commercial version of U.S. M16 rifle. Gas-operated. Takedown. Caliber: .223 Rem. (5.56mm). 20-round magazine w/spacer to reduce capacity to 5 rounds. 20-inch bbl. w/flash suppressor. Sights: Rear peep w/windage adjustment in carrying handle; front adj. for windage. 3x scope and mount optional. Black molded buttstock of high-impact synthetic material, rubber buttplate. Barrel surrounded by handguard of black fiberglass w/heat-reflecting inner shield. Swivels, black web sling strap. Weight: w/o accessories, 6.3 lbs. Made 1964-94.
Standard Sporter .... NiB $1291 Ex $1035 Gd $707
W/adj. stock, redesigned forearm (disc. 1988), add $200
W/3x scope and mount, add............................... $100

AR-15 SPORTER COMPETITION H-BAR RIFLE .... NiB $1297 Ex $1035 Gd $654
Similar to AR-15 Sporter Target model except w/integral Weaver-type mounting system on a flat-top receiver. 20-inch bbl. w/counter-bored muzzle and 1:9 rifling twist. Made 1991 to date.

AR-15 SPORTER COMPETITION H-BAR (RS) .... NiB $1684 Ex $1349 Gd $829
Similar to AR-15 Sporter Competition H-BAR Model except "Range Selected" for accuracy w/3x9 rubber-clad scope w/mount. Carrying handle w/iron sights. Made 1992-94.

AR-15 SPORTER MATCH TARGET LIGHTWEIGHT
Calibers: .223 Rem., 7.62x39mm, 9mm. Five-round magazine. 16-inch bbl. (non-threaded after 1994). 34.5-35.5 inches overall. Weight: 7.1 lbs. Redesigned stock and shorter handguard. Made 1991 to date.
Standard LW Sporter (except 9mm) ..... NiB $1035 Ex $782 Gd $535
Standard LW Sporter, 9mm .... NiB $963 Ex $679 Gd $473
.22 LR conversion (disc. 1994), add $175

AR-15 SPORTER TARGET RIFLE
Caliber: .223 Rem. Five-round magazine. 20-inch bbl. w/flash suppressor (non-threaded after 1994). 39 inches overall. Weight: 7.5 lbs. Black composition stock, grip and handguard. Sights: post front; adj. aperture rear. Matte black finish. Made 1993 to date.
Sporter Target Rifle .... NiB $1143 Ex $963 Gd $628
.22 LR conversion (disc. 1994), add $200

LIGHTNING MAGAZINE RIFLE - LARGE FRAME
Similar to Medium Frame model except w/large frame to accommodate larger calibers: .38-56, .44-60, .45-60, .45-65, .45-85, or .50-95 Express. Standard 22-inch (carbine & baby carbine) or 28-inch round or octagonal bbl. (rifle). Note: Additional bbl. lengths optional. Weight: 8 to 10.5 lbs. Sights: Open rear; bead or blade front. Walnut stock and checkered forearm. Made 1887-94. (6,496 produced)
Rifle .... NiB $4220 Ex $3164 Gd $2263
Carbine .... NiB $8237 Ex $6280 Gd $4220
Baby Carbine .... NiB $10,393 Ex $8334 Gd $5700
.50-95 Express, add 35%

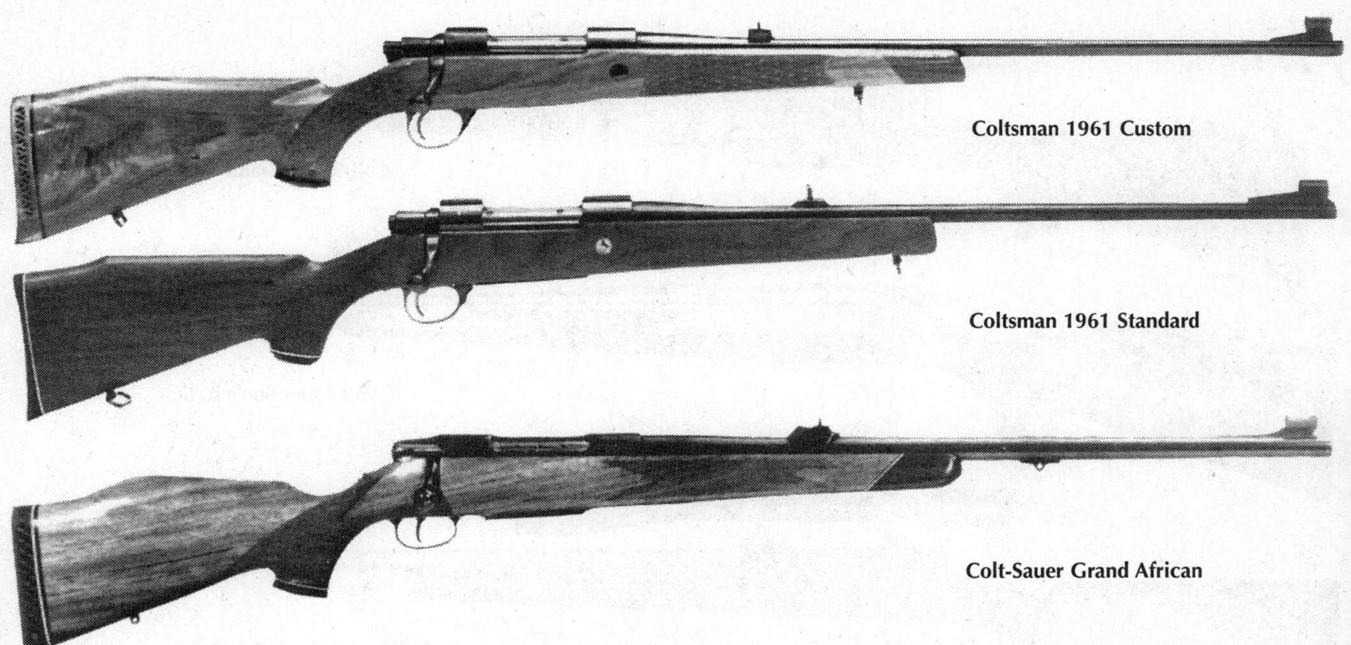
Coltsman 1961 Custom

Coltsman 1961 Standard

Colt-Sauer Grand African

LIGHTNING MAGAZINE RIFLE - MEDIUM FRAME
Slide-action w/12-round tubular magazine Carbine & Baby Carbine) or 15-round tubular magazine (rifle). Calibers: .32-20, .38-40, .44-40. Standard 20-inch (Carbine & Baby Carbine) or 26-inch round or octagonal bbl.(rifle). Note: Additional bbl. lengths optional. Weight: 5.5 lbs. (Baby Carbine), 6.25 lbs. (carbine) or 7 to 9 lbs. (rifle). Sights: Open rear; bead or blade front. Walnut stock and checkered forearm. Blue finish w/color casehardened hammer. Made 1884-1902. (89,777 produced)
Rifle .... NiB $2286 Ex $1719 Gd $1153
Carbine .... NiB $3625 Ex $2775 Gd $1900
Baby Carbine .... NiB $5170 Ex $4037 Gd $2801
Military model w/bayonet lug & sling swivels.......... NiB $5007 Ex $3603 Gd $2466

LIGHTNING MAGAZINE RIFLE - SMALL FRAME
Similar to Medium Frame model except w/smaller frame and chambered for .22 caliber only. Standard 24-inch round or octagonal bbl. w/half magazine. Note: Additional bbl. lengths optional. Weight: 6 lbs. Sights: Open rear; bead or blade front. Walnut stock and checkered forearm. Made 1884-1902. (89,912 produced)
Standard Rifle model............... NiB $1369 Ex $1040 Gd $710
W/Deluxe or optional features, add 20%

STAGECOACH .22 AUTOLOADER .... NiB $370 Ex $293 Gd $164
Same as Colteer .22 Autoloader except w/engraved receiver, saddle ring, 16.5-inch bbl. Weight: 4 lbs., 10 oz. Made 1965-75.

1-.22 SINGLE-SHOT BOLT-ACTION RIFLE................. NiB $319 Ex $242 Gd $164
Caliber: .22 LR. Long, Short. 20- or 22-inch bbl. Sights: Open rear; ramp front. Pistol-grip stock w/Monte Carlo comb. Weight: 5 lbs. Made 1957-67.

.22 AUTOLOADER .... NiB $319 Ex $242 Gd $164
Caliber: .22 LR. 15-round tubular magazine. 19.38-inch bbl. Sights: Open rear; hooded ramp front. Straight-grip stock, Western carbine-style forearm w/bbl. band. Weight: 4.75 lbs. Made 1964-75.

CUSTOM BOLT-ACTION SPORTING RIFLE.............. NiB $525 Ex $417 Gd $267
FN Mauser action, side safety, engraved floorplate. Calibers: .30-06, .300 H&H Mag. Five round box magazine. 24-inch bbl., rampfront sight. Fancy walnut stock. Monte Carlo comb, cheekpiece, pistol-grip, checkered, QD swivels. Weight: 7.25 lbs. Made 1957-61.

DELUXE RIFLE................ NiB $885 Ex $679 Gd $473
FN Mauser action. Same as Custom model, except plain floorplate, plainer wood and checkering. Made 1957-61. Value shown is for rifle as furnished by manufacturer w/o rear sight.

MODELS OF 1957 RIFLES
Sako medium action. Calibers: .243, .308. Weight: 6.75 lbs. Other specifications similar to those of models w/FN actions. Made 1957-61.
Custom .... NiB $834 Ex $628 Gd $422
Deluxe...................... NiB $834 Ex $654 Gd $422
Standard .... NiB $679 Ex $422 Gd $345

MODEL OF 1961, CUSTOM RIFLE..................... NiB $654 Ex $499 Gd $319
Sako action. Calibers: .222, .222 Mag., .223, .243, .264, .270, .308, .30-06, .300 H&H. 23-, 24-inch bbl. Sights: Folding leaf rear; hooded ramp front. Fancy French walnut stock w/Monte Carlo comb, rosewood forend tip and grip cap skip checkering, recoil pad, sling swivels. Weight: 6.5 - 7.5 lbs. Made 1963-65.

MODEL OF 1961, STANDARD RIFLE..... NiB $654 Ex $525 Gd $345
Same as Custom model except plainer, American walnut stock. Made 1963-65.

STANDARD RIFLE .... NiB $628 Ex $473 Gd $319
FN Mauser action. Same as Deluxe model except in .243, .30-06, .308, .300 Mag. and stock w/o cheekpiece, bbl. length 22 inches. Made 1957-61. Value shown is for rifle as furnished by manufacturer w/o rear sight.

COLT-SAUER DRILLINGS See Colt shotgun listings.

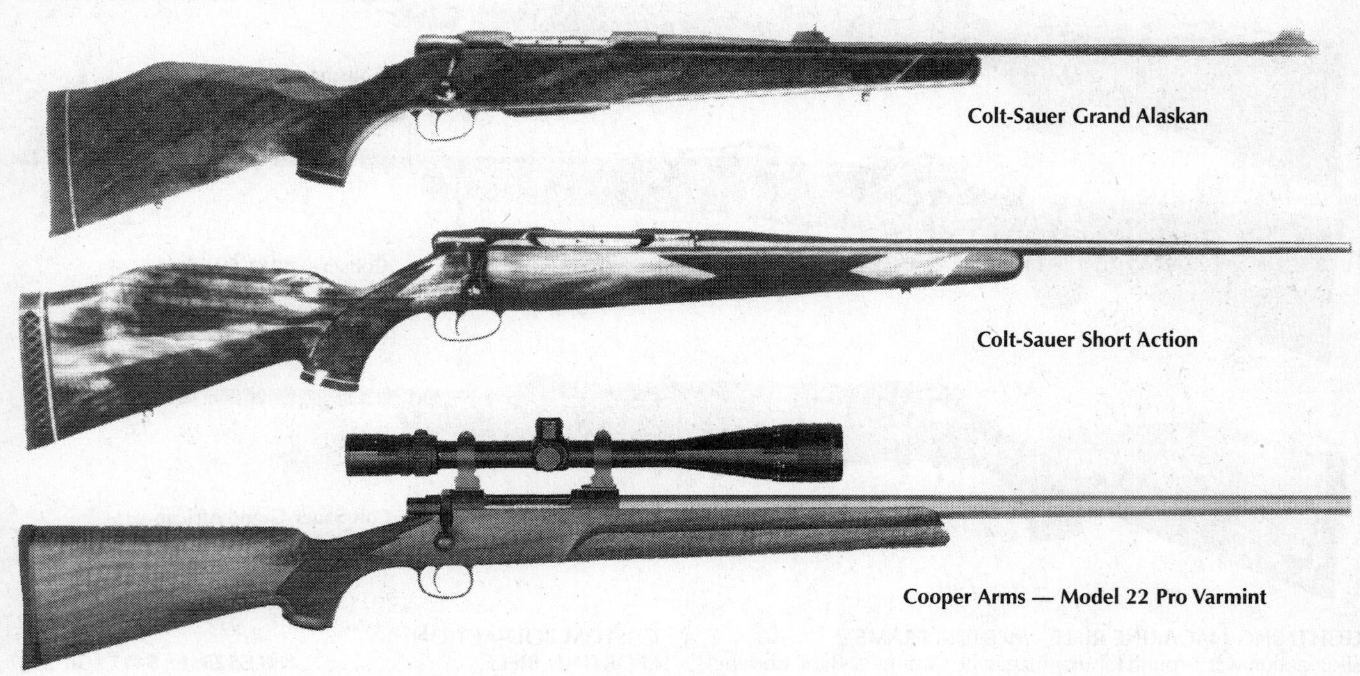

Colt-Sauer Grand Alaskan

Colt-Sauer Short Action

Cooper Arms — Model 22 Pro Varmint

GRAND AFRICAN . . . . NiB $1872 Ex $1460 Gd $971
Same specifications as standard model except .458 Win. Mag., weight: 9.5 lbs. Sights: Adj. leaf rear; hooded ramp front. Magnum-style stock of Bubinga. Made 1973-85. See illustration previous page.

GRAND ALASKAN . . . . NiB $1872 Ex $1280 Gd $842
Same specifications as standard model except .375 H&H, weight: 8.5 lbs. Sights: Adj. leaf rear; hooded ramp front. Magnum-style stock of walnut.

MAGNUM. . . . . NiB $1405 Ex $995 Gd $687
Same specifications as standard model except calibers 7mm Rem. Mag., .300 Win. Mag., .300 Weatherby. Weight: 8.5 lbs. Made 1973-85.

SHORT ACTION . . . . NiB $1254 Ex $971 Gd $662
Same specifications as standard model except shorter action chambered for the following calibers: .22-250, .243 Win., .308 Win. and similar length cartridges. Weight: 7.5 1bs.; 8.25 lbs. (.22-250). Drilled and tapped for scope mount. No front or rear open sights. Made 1973-88.

SPORTING RIFLE,
STANDARD MODEL . . . . NiB $1280 Ex $996 Gd $687
Sauer 80 non-rotating bolt action. Calibers: .25-06, .270 Win., .30-06. Three-round detachable box magazine. 24-inch bbl. Weight: 7.75 lbs., 8.5 lbs. (.25-06). Furnished w/o sights. American walnut stock w/Monte Carlo cheekpiece, checkered pistol grip and forearm, rosewood forend tip and pistol-grip cap, recoil pad. Made 1973-88.

COMMANDO CARBINES — Knoxville, Tennessee, (Formerly Volunteer Enterprises, Inc.)

MARK III SEMIAUTOMATIC CARBINE
Blow-back action, fires from closed bolt. Caliber: .45 ACP. 15- or 30-round magazine. 16.5-inch bbl. w/cooling sleeve and muzzle brake. Weight: 8 lbs. Sights: peep rear; blade front. "Tommy Gun" style stock and forearm or grip. Made l969-76.
W/horizontal forearm . . . . NiB $448 Ex $345 Gd $242

MARK 9
Same specifications as Mark III and Mark 45 except caliber 9mm Luger. Made 1976-81.
W/horizontal forearm . . . . NiB $473 Ex $381 Gd $262
W/vertical foregrip . . . . NiB $493 Ex $396 Gd $273

MARK 45
Same specifications as Mark III. Has redesigned trigger housing and magazines. Made 1976-88.
W/horizontal forearm . . . . NiB $473 Ex $412 Gd $267
W/vertical foregrip . . . . NiB $570 Ex $458 Gd $315

CONTINENTAL RIFLES — Manufactured in Belgium for Continental Arms, Corp., New York, N.Y.

DOUBLE RIFLE
Calibers: .270, .303 Sav., .30-40, .348 Win., .30-06, .375 H&H, .400 Jeffrey, .465, .470, .475 No. 2, .500, .600. Side-by-side. Anson-Deeley reinforced boxlock action w/triple bolting lever work. Two triggers. Nonautomatic safety. 24- or 26-inch bbls. Sights: Express rear; bead front. Checkered cheekpiece stock and forend. Weight: From 7 lbs., depending on caliber. Imported 1956-75.
Calibers: .270 to .348 Win. . . . . NiB $5218 Ex $4194 Gd $2884
Calibers: .375 H&H & larger . . . . NiB $6474 Ex $5198 Gd $3567

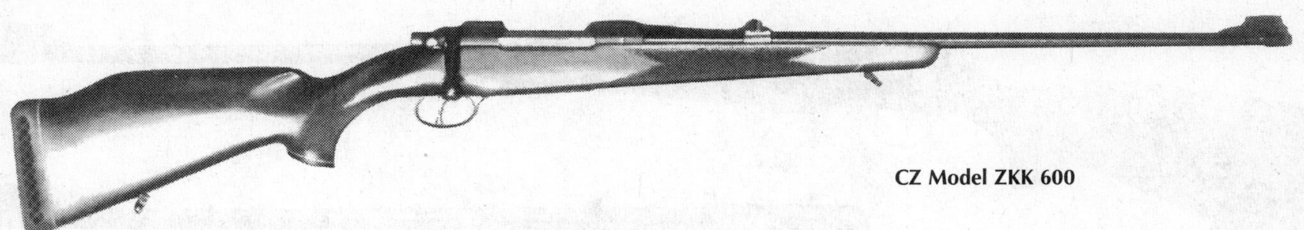
CZ Model ZKK 600

COOPER FIREARMS of MONTANA, INC. — (Previously COOPER ARMS), Stevensville, Montana

MODEL 21
Similar to Model 36C except in calibers .17 Rem., .17 Mach IV, .221 Fireball, .222, .223, 6x45, 6x47. 24-inch stainless or chrome-moly bbl. 43.5 inches overall. Weight: 8.75 lbs. Made 1994 to date.
21 Benchrest . . . . NiB $1925 Ex $1616 Gd $1045
21 Classic . . . . NiB $998 Ex $838 Gd $483
21 Custom Classic . . . . NiB $1771 Ex $1153 Gd $535
21 Western Classic . . . . NiB $1771 Ex $1153 Gd $535
21 Varminter . . . . NiB $973 Ex $767 Gd $483
21 Varmint Extreme. . . . . NiB $1771 Ex $1045 Gd $767

MODEL 22
Bolt-action, single-shot. Calibers: .22 BR. .22-250 Rem., .220 Swift, .243 Win., 6mm PPC, 6.5x55mm, 25-06 Rem., 7.62x39mm 26-inch bbl, 45.63 inches overall. Weight: 8 lbs., 12 oz. Single-stage trigger. AAA Claro walnut stock. Made 1996 to date.
22 Benchrest . . . . NiB $1822 Ex $1488 Gd $998
22 Classic . . . . NiB $1771 Ex $1215 Gd $638
22 Custom Classic. . . . . NiB $1256 Ex $1153 Gd $792
22 Western Classic . . . . NiB $1869 Ex $1251 Gd $844
22 Varminter . . . . NiB $1050 Ex $839 Gd $535
22 Pro-Varmint Extreme . . . . . . NiB $1761 Ex $1045 Gd $741
22 Black Jack. . . . . NiB $1761 Ex $1045 Gd $741

MODEL 36 RF/BR 50 . . . . NiB $1797 Ex $1153 Gd $767
Caliber: .22 LR. Bolt-action. Single-shot. 22-inch bbl. 40.5 inches overall. Weight: 6.8 lbs. No sights. Fully-adj. match-grade trigger. Stainless barrel. McMillan benchrest stock. Three mid-bolt locking lugs. Made 1994 to date.

MODEL 36 CF BOLT-ACTION RIFLE
Calibers: .17 CCM, .22 CCM, .22 Hornet. Four-round mag. 23.75 inch bbl. 42.5 inch overall. Weight: 7 lbs. Walnut or synthetic stock. Made 1992-94.
Marksman . . . . NiB $973 Ex $741 Gd $530
Sportsman . . . . NiB $870 Ex $664 Gd $458
Classic Grade . . . . NiB $1761 Ex $1045 Gd $767
Custom Grade . . . . NiB $1050 Ex $844 Gd $586
Custom Classic Grade. . . . . NiB $1771 Ex $1153 Gd $792

MODEL 36 RF BOLT-ACTION RIFLE
Similar to Model 36CF except in caliber .22 LR. Five round magazine. Weight: 6.5-7 lbs. Made 1992 to date.
BR-50 (22-inch stainless bbl.) . . . NiB $1359 Ex $1048 Gd $689
Custom Grade . . . . NiB $1050 Ex $824 Gd $561
Custom Classic Grade . . . . NiB $1153 Ex $844 Gd $586
Featherweight . . . . NiB $1115 Ex $896 Gd $615

MODEL 36 TRP-1 SERIES
Similar to Model 36RF except in target configuration w/ ISU or silhouette-style stock. Made 1991-93.
TRP-1 (ISU single-shot) . . . . NiB $947 Ex $767 Gd $458
TRP-1S (Silhouette) . . . . NiB $947 Ex $767 Gd $458

MODEL 38 SINGLE SHOT
Similar to Model 36CF except in calibers .17 or .22 CCM w/3-round magazine. Weight: 8 lbs. Walnut or synthetic stock. Made 1992-93.
Sporter Standard . . . . NiB $947 Ex $741 Gd $586
Classic Grade. . . . . NiB $1045 Ex $839 Gd $586
Custom Grade . . . . NiB $1179 Ex $998 Gd $586
Custom
Classic Grade . . . . NiB $1452 Ex $1153 Gd $767

MODEL 40 CLASSIC BOLT-ACTION RIFLE
Calibers: .17 CCM, .17 Ackley Hornet, .22 Hornet, .22K Hornet, .22 CCM, 4- or 5-round magazine. 23.75-inch bbl. Checkered oil-finished AAA Claro walnut stock. Made 1995-97.
Classic. . . . . NiB $1452 Ex $1153 Gd $767
Custom Classic . . . . NiB $1455 Ex $1251 Gd $844
Classic Varminter . . . . NiB $1565 Ex $1251 Gd $844

CUMBERLAND MOUNTAIN ARMS — Winchester, Tennessee

PLATEAU RIFLE
Falling block action w/underlever. Calibers: .40-65, and .45-70. 32-inch round bbl. 48 inches overall. Weight: 10.5 lbs. American walnut stock. Bead front sight, adj. buckhorn rear. Blued finish. Lacquer finish walnut stock w/crescent buttplate. Made 1995 to date.
Standard model. . . . . NiB $947 Ex $767 Gd $535
Deluxe model . . . . NiB $1359 Ex $1076 Gd $731

CZ RIFLES — Strankonice, Czechoslovakia (Currently Uhersky Brod and Brno, Czecho.) Mfd. by Ceska Zbrojovka-Nardoni Podnik (Formerly Bohmische Waffenfabrik A.G.)

See also listings under Brno Sporting Rifles and Springfield, Inc.

ZKK 600 BOLT-ACTION RIFLE
Calibers: .270 Win., 7x57, 7x64, .30-06. Five round magazine. 23.5- inch bbl. Weight: 7.5 lbs. Adj. folding-leaf rear sight, hooded ramp front. Pistol-grip walnut stock. Imported 1990 to date.
Standard model. . . . . NiB $552 Ex $444 Gd $305
Deluxe model . . . . NiB $641 Ex $515 Gd $354

ZKK 601 BOLT-ACTION RIFLE
Similar to Model ZKK 600 except w/short action in calibers .223 Rem., .243 Win., .308 Win. 43 inches overall. Weight: 6 lbs., 13 oz. Checkered walnut pistol-grip stock w/Monte Carlo cheekpiece. Imported 1990 to date.
Standard model. . . . . NiB $520 Ex $443 Gd $367
Deluxe model . . . . NiB $571 Ex $510 Gd $367

ZKK 602 BOLT-ACTION RIFLE
Similar to Model ZKK 600 except w/Magnum action in calibers .300 Win. Mag., 8x68S, .375 H&H, .458 Win. Mag. 25-inch bbl. 45.5 inches overall. Weight: 9.25 lbs. Imported 1990 to date.
Standard model. . . . . NiB $698 Ex $596 Gd $408
Deluxe model . . . . NiB $826 Ex $673 Gd $443

CA Model ZKM 452 LUX Model

CZ 511

CZ Model ZKM 527

CZ 550 LUX Model

ZKM 452 BOLT-ACTION REPEATING RIFLE
Calibers: .22 LR. or .22 WMR. Five, 6- or 10-round magazine. 25-inch bbl. 43.5 inches overall. Weight: 6 lbs. Adj. rear sight, hooded bead front. Oil-finished beechwood or checkered walnut stock w/Schnabel forend. Imported 1995 to date.
Standard model (22 LR)........... NiB $367 Ex $296 Gd $146
Deluxe model (22 LR)............ NiB $408 Ex $265 Gd $188
Varmint model (22 LR)........... NiB $341 Ex $265 Gd $188
.22 WMR, add $35

ZKM 527 BOLT-ACTION RIFLE
Calibers: .22 Hornet, .222 Rem., .223 Rem., 7.62x39mm. Five round magazine. 23.5-inch bbl. 42.5 inches overall. Weight: 6.75 lbs. Adj. rear sight, hooded ramp front. Grooved receiver. Adj. double-set triggers. Oil-finished beechwood or checkered walnut stock . Imported 1995 to date.
Standard model .... NiB $515 Ex $408 Gd $290
Classic model .... NiB $520 Ex $408 Gd $290
Carbine model (shorter configuration) .... NiB $545 Ex $413 Gd $290
Deluxe model .... NiB $602 Ex $510 Gd $316

ZKM 537 SPORTER BOLT-ACTION RIFLE
Calibers: .243 Win., .270 Win., 7x57mm, .308 Win., .30-06. Four or 5-round magazine. 19- or 23.5-inch bbl. 40.25 or 44.75 inches overall. Weight: 7 to 7.5 lbs. Adj. folding leaf rear sight, hooded ramp front. Shrouded bolt. Standard or Mannlicher-style checkered walnut stock. Imported 1992-94.
Standard model .... NiB $545 Ex $413 Gd $290
Mannlicher model .... NiB $775 Ex $520 Gd $367
Mountain Carbine model......... NiB $545 Ex $408 Gd $265

511 SEMI-AUTO RIFLE .... NiB $209 Ex $188 Gd $112
Caliber: .22 LR. 8-round magazine. 22- inch bbl., 38.6 inches overall. Weight: 5.39 lbs. Receiver top fitted for telescopic sight mounts. Walnut wood-lacquered checkering stock. Imported 1998 to date.

550 BOLT-ACTION SERIES
Calibers: .243 Win., 6.5x55mm, .270 Win., 7mm Mag., 7x57, 7x64, .30-06, .300 Win Mag., .375 H&H, .416 Rem., .416 Rigby, .458 Win. Mag., 9.3x62. Four or 5-round detachable magazine. 20.5- or 23.6-inch bbl. Weight: 7.25 to 8 lbs. No sights or Express sights on magnum models. Receiver drilled and tapped for scope mount. Standard or Mannlicher-style checkered walnut stock w/buttpad. Imported 1995 to date.
Standard .... NiB $478 Ex $392 Gd $265
Magnum .... NiB $596 Ex $474 Gd $316
Delux .... NiB $515 Ex $408 Gd $290
Mannlicher .... NiB $581 Ex $443 Gd $316
Calibers .416 Rem., .416 Rigby, .458 Win. Mag., add............ $70

CZECHOSLOVAKIAN MILITARY RIFLES — Brno, Czechoslovakia, Manufactured by Ceska Zbrojovka

MODEL 1924 (VZ24)
MAUSER MILITARY RIFLE........ NiB $263 Ex $202 Gd $135
Basically same as German Kar., 98k and F.N. (Belgian Model 1924.) Caliber: 7.9mm Mauser. Five round box magazine. 23.25-inch bbl. Weight: 8.5 lbs. Sights: Adj. rear; blade front w/guards. of Belgian-type military stock, full handguard. Mfd. 1924 thru WWII. Many of these rifles were made for export. As produced during the German occupation, this model was known as Gewehr 24t.

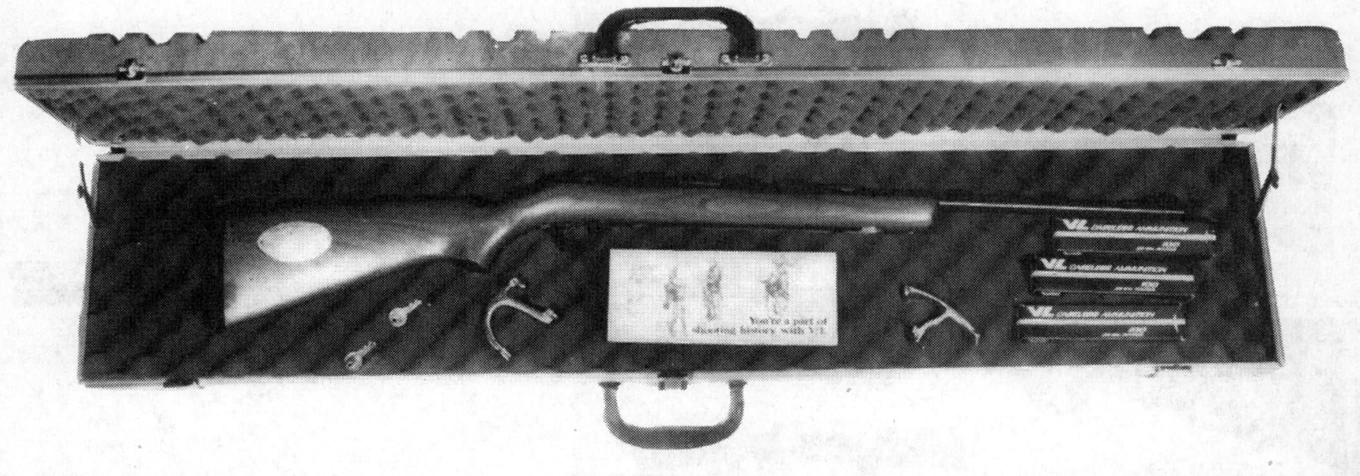

Daisy V/L Collector's Kit

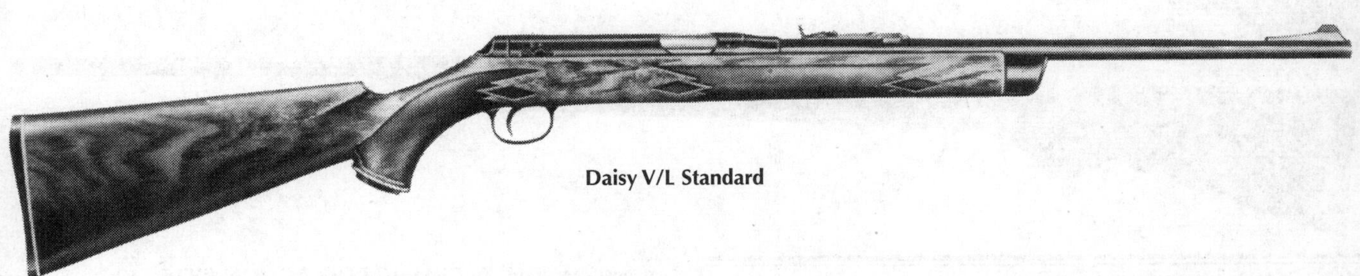

Daisy V/L Standard

MODEL 1933 (VZ33) MAUSER MILITARY CARBINE . . . . NiB $345 Ex $267 Gd $190
Modification of German M/98 action w/smaller receiver ring. Caliber: 7.9mm Mauser. 19.25-inch bbl. Weight: 7.5 lbs. Sights: Adj. rear; blade front w/guards. Military-type full stock. Mfd. 1933 thru WWII. A similar model, produced during the German occupation, was designated Gew. 33/40.

DAEWOO PRECISION INDUSTRIES — Manufactured in Korea (Previously Imported by Kimber of America; Daewoo Precision Industries; Nationwide Sports and KBI, Inc.)

DR200 SA SEMIAUTOMATIC SPORTER
Caliber: .223 Rem. (5.56mm). Six or 10-round magazine. 18.4-inch bbl. 39.25 inches overall. Weight: 9 lbs. Protected post front sight, fully-adj. aperture rear. Forged aluminum receiver w/rotating locking bolt assembly. Synthetic sporterized thumbhole stock. Imported 1994-96.
Sporter model . . . . NiB $679 Ex $525 Gd $396
Varmint model. . . . . NiB $576 Ex $525 Gd $293

DR300 SA SEMIAUTOMATIC SPORTER. . . . . NiB $602 Ex $515 Gd $345
Similar to Model Daewoo DR200 except chambered for 7.62x39mm. Imported 1994-96.

DAISY RIFLES — Rogers, Arkansas

Daisy V/L rifles carry the first and only commercial caseless cartridge system. These rifles are expected to appreciate considerably in future years. The cartridge, no longer made, is also a collector's item. Production was discontinued following BATF ruling the V/L model to be a firearm.

COLLECTOR'S KIT. . . . . NiB $438 Ex $355 Gd $248
Presentation-grade rifle w/gold plate inscribed w/owner's name and gun serial number mounted on the stock. Also includes a special gun case, pair of brass gun cradles for wall-hanging, 300 rounds of 22 V/L ammunition and a certificate signed by Daisy president Cass S. Hough. Approx. 1,000 manufactured 1968-69.

PRESENTATION GRADE . . . . NiB $319 Ex $252 Gd $218
Same specifications as standard model except w/walnut stock. Approx. 4,000 manufactured 1968-69.

STANDARD RIFLE . . . . NiB $252 Ex $200 Gd $144
Single-shot under-lever action. Caliber: .22 V/L (caseless cartridge, propellant ignited by jet of hot air). 18-inch bbl. Weight: 5 lbs. Sights: Adj. open rear, ramp w/blade front. Wood-grained Lustran stock (foam-filled). Approx. 19,000 manufactured 1968-69.

Dakota Model 10 Single-Shot Rifle

Dakota Arms Model 76 African Grade

Dakota Arms Model 76 Classic Grade

Dakota Arms Model 97 Hunter

DAKOTA ARMS, INC. — Sturgis, South Dakota

MODEL 10 SINGLE-SHOT RIFLE

Chambered for most commercially-loaded calibers. 23-inch bbl. 39.5 inches overall. Weight: 5.5 lbs. Top tang safety. No sights. Checkered pistol-grip buttstock and semi-beavertail forearm, QD swivels, rubber recoil pad. Made 1992 to date.

Standard calibers. . . . . NiB $3295 Ex $2878 Gd $1797
Magnum calibers. . . . . NiB $3779 Ex $3033 Gd $2054

MODEL 22 BOLT-ACTION SPORTER RIFLE . . . . NiB $1359 Ex $1101 Gd $730

Calibers: .22 LR. .22 Hornet. Five round magazine. 22-inch bbl. Weight: 6.5 lbs. Adj. trigger. Checkered classic-style Claro or English walnut stock w/black recoil pad. Made 1992 to date.

MODEL 76 AFRICAN BOLT-ACTION RIFLE. . . . . NiB $4284 Ex $3841 Gd $2399

Same general specifications as Model 76 Safari. Calibers: .404 Jeffery, .416 Rigby, .416 Dakota, .450 Dakota. 24-inch bbl. Weight: 8 lbs. Checkered select walnut stock w/two crossbolts. Made 1989 to date.

MODEL 76 ALPINE BOLT-ACTION RIFLE. . . . . NiB $2281 Ex $1616 Gd $1086

Same general specifications as Model 76 Classic except short action w/blind magazine. Calibers: .22-250, .243, 6mm Rem., .250-3000, 7mm-08, .308. 21-inch bbl. Weight: 7.5 lbs. Made 1989-93.

MODEL 76 CLASSIC BOLT-ACTION RIFLE. . . . . NiB $2930 Ex $2281 Gd $1565

Calibers: .257 Roberts, .270 Win., .280 Rem., .30-06, 7mm Rem. Mag., .300 Win. Mag., .338 Win. Mag., .375 H&H Mag., .458 Win. Mag. 21- or 23-inch bbl. Weight: 7.5 lbs. Receiver drilled and

(cont'd.) **MODEL 76 CLASSIC BOLT-ACTION RIFLE**

tapped for sights. Adj. trigger. Classic-style checkered walnut stock w/steel grip cap and solid recoil pad. Right- and left-hand models. Made 1988 to date.

MODEL 76 LONGBOW TACTICAL BOLT-ACTION RIFLE. . . . . NiB $4201 Ex $3218 Gd $2188

Calibers: .300 Dakota Mag., .330 Dakota Mag., .338 Lapua Mag. Blind magazine. Ported 28-inch bbl. 50 to 51 inches overall. Weight: 13.7 lbs. Black or oliver green fiberglass stock w/adj. cheekpiece and buttplate. Receiver drilled and tapped w/one-piece rail mount and no sights. Made 1997 to date.

MODEL 76 SAFARI BOLT-ACTION RIFLE. . . . . NiB $4227 Ex $3197 Gd $2116

Calibers: .300 Win. Mag., .338 Win. Mag., .375 H&H Mag. .458 Win. Mag. 23-inch bbl. w/bbl. band swivel. Weight: 8.5 lbs. Ramp front sight, standing leaf rear. Checkered fancy walnut stock w/ebony forend tip and solid recoil pad. Made 1988 to date.

MODEL 76 TRAVELER SERIES RIFLES

Threadless take-down action w/interchangeable bbl. capability based on the Dakota 76 design. Calibers: .257 through .458 Win (Standard-Classic & Safari) and .416 Dakota, .404 Jeffery, .416 Rigby, .338 Lapua and .450 Dakota Mag. (E/F Family-African Grade). 23- to 24- inch bbl. Weight: 7.5 to 9.5 lbs. Right or left-hand action. X grade (Classic) or XXX grade (Safari or African) oil finish English Bastogne or Claro walnut stock. Made 1999 to date.

Classic Grade. . . . . NiB $4304 Ex $3249 Gd $2188
Safari Grade . . . . NiB $4279 Ex $3274 Gd $2656
African Grade . . . . NiB $5431 Ex $4351 Gd $2969
Interchangeable bbl. assemblies
Classic Grade, add. $1150
Safari Grade, add. $1450
African Grade, add $1595

MODEL 76 VARMINT
BOLT-ACTION RIFLE . . . . NiB $2363 Ex $1848 Gd $1045
Similar to Model 76 Classic except single-shot action w/ heavy bbl. chambered for .17 Rem. to 6mm PPC. Weight: 13.7 lbs. Checkered walnut or synthetic stock. Receiver drilled and tapped for scope mounts and no sights. Made 1994-98.

MODEL 97 HUNTER BOLT-ACTION SERIES
Calibers: .22-250 Rem. to .330 Dakota Mag.(Lightweight), .25-06 to .375 Dakota Mag. (Long Range). 22-, 24- or 26-inch bbl. 43 to 46 inches overall. Weight: 6.16 lbs. to 7.7 lbs. Black composite fiberglass stock w/recoil pad. Fully adj. match trigger. Made 1997 to date.
Lightweight . . . . NiB $1869 Ex $1513 Gd $834
Long Range . . . . NiB $1630 Ex $1307 Gd $895

MODEL 97 VARMINT HUNTER
BOLT-ACTION RIFLE . . . . NiB $1668 Ex $1436 Gd $792
Similar to Model 97 Hunter except single-shot action w/ heavy bbl. chambered .22-250 Rem. to .308 Win. Checkered walnut stock. Receiver drilled and tapped for scope mounts and no sights. Made 1998 to date.

CHARLES DALY RIFLE — Harrisburg, Pennsylvania, *Imported by K.B.I., Inc., Harrisburg, PA, (Previously by Outdoor Sports Headquarters, Inc.)*

EMPIRE GRADE BOLT-ACTION RIFLE (RF)
Similar to Superior Grade except w/checkered California walnut stock w/rosewood grip cap and forearm cap. High polished blued finish and damascened bolt. Made 1998 to date.
Empire Grade (.22 LR). . . . . NiB $322 Ex $260 Gd $180
Empire Grade (.22WMR). . . . . NiB $348 Ex $280 Gd $194
Empire Grade (.22 Hornet) . . . . NiB $488 Ex $392 Gd $270

FIELD GRADE BOLT-ACTION RIFLE (RF)
Caliber: .22 LR. 16.25-, 17.5- or 22.63-inch bbl. 32 to 41 inches overall. Single-shot (True Youth) and 6- or 10-round magazine. Plain walnut-finished hardwood or checkered polymer stock. Blue or stainless finish. Imported 1998 to date.
Field Grade (Standard w/22.63-inch bbl.). . . . NiB $116 Ex $95 Gd $67
Field Grade (Youth w/17.5-inch bbl.) . . . . . . NiB $123 Ex $100 Gd $70
Field Grade (True Youth
w/16.25-inch bbl.) . . . . NiB $160 Ex $129 Gd $91
Field Grade (Polymer w/stainless action) . . . NiB $129 Ex $105 Gd $74

FIELD GRADE HUNTER BOLT-ACTION RIFLE
Calibers: .22 Hornet, .223 Rem., .243 Win., .270 Win., 7mm Rem. Mag. .308 Win., .30-06, .300 Win. Mag., .300 Rem. Ultra Mag., .338 Win. Mag. Three, 4-, or 5-round magazine. 22- or 24-inch bbl. w/o sights. Weight: 7.2 to 7.4 lbs. Checkered walnut or black polymer stock. Receiver drilled and tapped. Blue or stainless finish. Imported 1998 to date.
Field Grade Hunter (walnut stock) . . . . NiB $503 Ex $407 Gd $282
Field Grade Hunter (polymer stock) . . . . . . NiB $523 Ex $422 Gd $293
w/Left-hand model, add $35

HAMMERLESS DRILLING
See listing under Charles Daly shotguns.

HORNET RIFLE . . . . NiB $1227 Ex $984 Gd $674
Same as Herold Rifle. See listing of that rifle for specifications. imported during the 1930s

MAUSER 98
Calibers: .243 Win., .270 Win., 7mm Rem. Mag. .308 Win., .30-06, .300 Win. Mag., .375 H&H, or .458 Win. Mag. Three, 4-, or 5-round magazine. 23-inch bbl. 44.5 inches overall. Weight: 7.5 lbs. Checkered European walnut (Superior) or fiberglass/graphic (Field) stock w/recoil pad. Ramped front sight, adj. rear. Receiver drilled and tapped w/side saftey. Imported 1998 to date.
Field Grade (standard calibers). . . . . NiB $413 Ex $362 Gd $112
Field Grade (375 H&H
and 458 Win. Mag.) . . . . NiB $617 Ex $515 Gd $311
Superior Grade (standard calibers). . . . . . NiB $617 Ex $469 Gd $311
Superior Grade (magnum calibers). . . . . . NiB $845 Ex $719 Gd $558

MINI-MAUSER 98
Similar to Mauser 98 except w/19.25-inch bbl. chambered for .22 Hornet, .22-250 Rem., .223 Rem., or 7.62x39mm. Five round magazine. Imported 1998 to date.
Field Grade. NiB $367 Ex $316 Gd$199
Superior Grade . . . . NiB $479 Ex $392 Gd $214

SUPERIOR GRADE BOLT-ACTION RIFLE
Calibers: .22 LR. .22 WMR, .22 Hornet. 20.25- to 22.63-inch bbl. 40.5 to 41.25 inches overall. Five, 6-, or 10-round magazine. Ramped front sight, adj. rear w/grooved receiver. Checkered walnut stock. Made 1998 to date.
Superior Grade (.22 LR) . . . . NiB $159 Ex $128 Gd $77
Superior Grade (.22WMR) . . . . NiB $184 Ex $144 Gd $98
Superior Grade (.22 Hornet). . . . . . NiB $348 Ex $297 Gd $184

SEMIAUTOMATIC RIFLE
Caliber: .22 LR. 20.75-inch bbl. 40.5 inches overall. 10-round magazine. Ramped front sight, adj. rear w/grooved receiver. Plain walnut-finished hardwood stock (Field), checkered walnut (Superior), checkered polymer stock or checkered California walnut stock w/rosewood grip cap and forearm cap (Empire). Blue or stainless finish. Imported 1998 to date.
Field Grade . . . . NiB $118 Ex $98 Gd $62
Field Grade (Polymer
w/stainless action). . . . . NiB $130 Ex $108 Gd $67
Superior Grade . . . . NiB $184 Ex $159 Gd $98
Empire Grade . . . . NiB $302 Ex $235 Gd $159

EAGLE ARMS INC. — Geneseo, Illinois (Previously Coal Valley, Illinois)

In 1995, Eagle Arms Inc., became a division of ArmaLite and reintroduced that logo. For current ArmaLite production see models under that listing.

MODEL EA-15 CARBINE
Caliber: .223 Rem. (5.56mm). 30-round magazine. 16-inch bbl. and collapsible buttstock. Weight: 5.75 lbs. (E1); 6.25 lbs. (E2 w/heavy bbl. & National Match sights). Made 1989 to 94.
E1 Carbine. NiB $821 Ex $661 Gd $455
E2 Carbine. NiB $886 Ex $712 Gd $490

MODEL EA-15 GOLDEN
EAGLE MATCH RIFLE . . . . NiB $1145 Ex $892 Gd $583
Same general specifications as EA-15 Standard, except w/E2-style National Match sights. 20-inch Douglas Heavy Match bbl. NM trigger and bolt-carrier group. Weight: 12.75 lbs. Made 1991 to 94.

MODEL EA-15 SEMIAUTOMATIC RIFLE . . . . . NiB $836 Ex $661 Gd $434
Same as EA-15 Carbine except 20-inch bbl., 39 inches overall and weighs 7 lbs. Made 1989 to date.

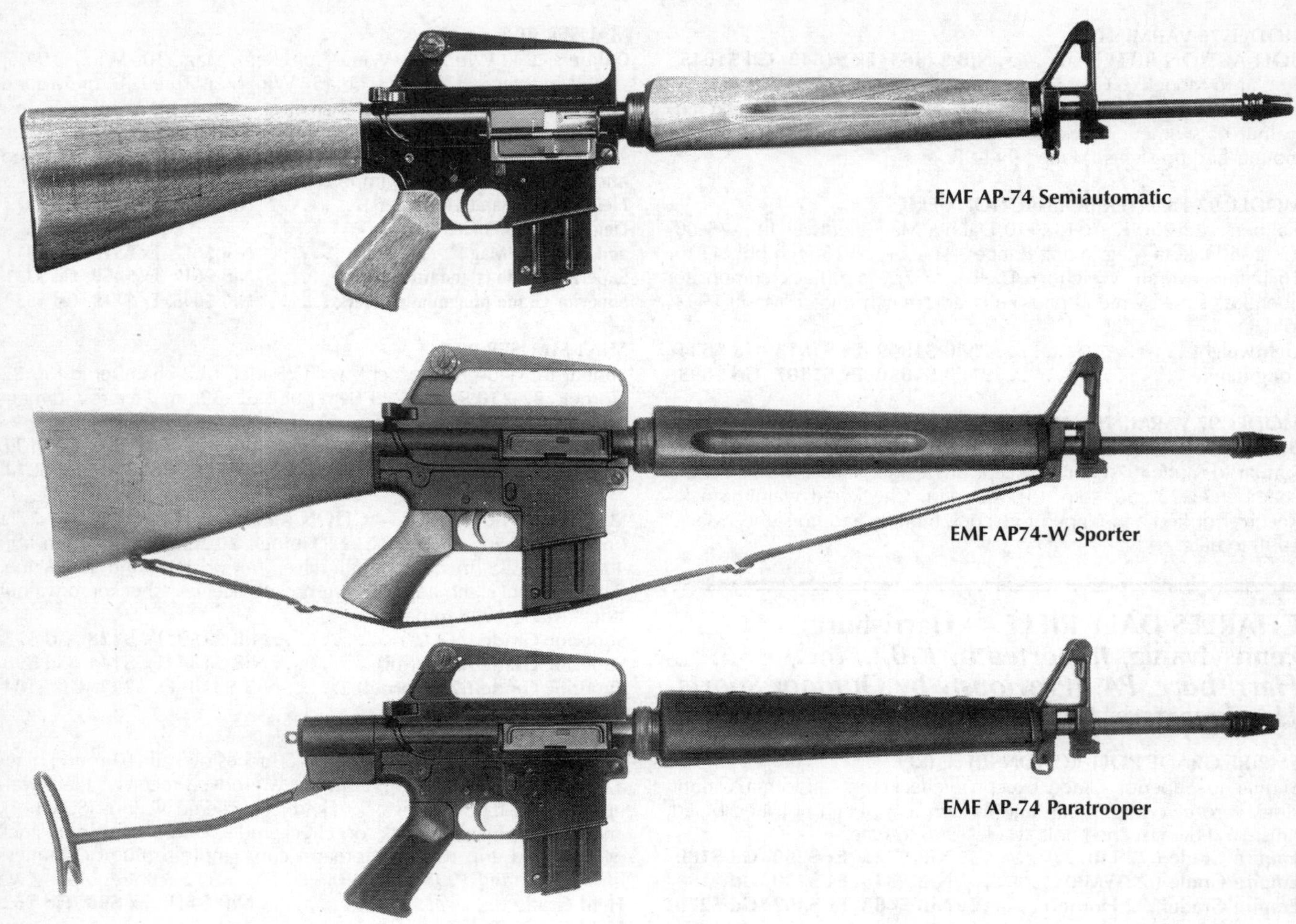

EMF AP-74 Semiautomatic

EMF AP74-W Sporter

EMF AP-74 Paratrooper

EMF COMPANY, INC. — Santa Ana, California

MODEL AP-74
SEMI-AUTOMATIC CARBINE . . . . . NiB $314 Ex $267 Gd $170
Calibers: .22 LR or .32 ACP, 15-round magazine. 20-inch bbl. w/flash reducer. 38 inches overall. Weight: 6.75 lbs. Protected pin front sight; protected rear peep sight. Lightweight plastic buttstock; ventilated snap-out forend. Importation. disc. 1989.

MODEL AP74-W
SPORTER CARBINE . . . . NiB $345 Ex $278 Gd $164
Sporterized version of AP-74 w/wood buttstock and forend. Importation disc. 1988.

MODEL AP74 PARATROOPER . . . . NiB $298 Ex $211 Gd $190
Same general specifications as Model AP74-W except w/folding tubular buttstock. Made in .22 LR. only. Importation disc. 1987.

MODEL 1860 HENRY RIFLE
Calibers: .44-40 and .45 LC. 24.25-inch bbl.; upper-half octagonal w/magazine tube in one-piece steel. 43.75-inches overall. Weight: 9.25 lbs. Varnished American walnut wood stock. Polished brass frame and brass buttplate. Original rifle was patented by B. Tyler Henry and produced by the New Haven Arms Company, when Oliver Winchester was president. Imported 1987 to date.
Deluxe model . . . . NiB $808 Ex $628 Gd $288
Engraved model . . . . NiB $1035 Ex $757 Gd $499

MODEL 1866
YELLOW BOY RIFLE . . . . NiB $602 Ex $520 Gd $309
Calibers: .44-40, .45 LC and .38 Special. Lever-action. Bbl: 24 inches, 43 inches overall. Bead front sight. Exact reproduction. Offered w/blued finish, walnut stock and brass frame.

MODEL 1866 YELLOW BOY CARBINE
Same features as 1866 Yellow Boy Rifle except carbine.
Standard carbine . . . . NiB $623 Ex $412 Gd $267
Engraved carbine . . . . NiB $628 Ex $499 Gd $293

MODEL 1873 SPORTING RIFLE
Calibers: .22 LR. .22 WMR, .357 Mag., .44-40 and .45 LC. 24.25-inch octagonal bbl. 43.25 inches overall. Weight: 8.16 lbs. Color casehardened frame w/blued steel magazine tube. Walnut stock and forend.
Standard Rifle . . . . NiB $782 Ex $628 Gd $396
Engraved Rifle . . . . NiB $911 Ex $602 Gd $412
Boy's Rifle
(Youth Model, .22 LR) . . . . NiB $618 Ex $499 Gd $319

MODEL 1873 SPORTING RIFLE CARBINE
Same features as 1873 sporting rifle except w/19-inch bbl. Overall length: 38.25 inches. Weight: 7.38 lbs. Color casehardened or blued frame.
Standard carbine . . . . NiB $782 Ex $628 Gd $396
Boy's carbine (Youth Model, .22 LR) . . . . . NiB $618 Ex $499 Gd $319

RIFLES

ERMA-WERKE — Dachau, Germany (Previously imported by Precision Sales International; Nygord Precision Products; Mandall's Shooting Supplies)

MODEL EG72
PUMP-ACTION REPEATER . . . . NiB $133 Ex $103 Gd $77
Visible hammer. Caliber: .22 LR. 15-round magazine. 18.5-inch bbl. Weight: 5.25 lbs. Sights: open rear; hooded ramp front. Receiver grooved for scope mounting. Straight-grip stock, grooved slide handle. Imported 1970-76.

MODEL EG73 . . . . NiB $276 Ex $241 Gd $133
Same as Model EG712 except chambered for .22 WMR w/12-round tubular magazine, 19.3-inch bbl. Imported 1973-97.

MODEL EG712 LEVER-ACTION
REPEATING CARBINE. . . . . NiB $271 Ex $241 Gd $127
Styled after Winchester Model 94. Caliber: .22 LR. Long, Short. Tubul33 magazine holds 15 LR, 17 Long, 21 Short. 18.5-inch bbl. Weight: 5.5 lbs. Sights: Open rear; hooded ramp front. Receiver grooved for scope mounting. Western carbine-style stock and forearm w/bbl. band. Imported 1976-97. Note: A similar carbine of Erma manufacture is marketed in U.S. as Ithaca Model 72 Saddle Gun.

MODEL EGM1. . . . . NiB $276 Ex $235 Gd $133
Same as Model EM1 except w/unslotted buttstock, ramp front sight, 5-round magazine standard. Imported 1970-95.

MODEL EM1 .22
SEMIAUTOMATIC CARBINE . . . . . . NiB $363 Ex $286 Gd $184
Styled after U.S. Carbine cal. 30 M1. Caliber: .22 LR. 10- or 15-round magazine. 18-inch bbl. Weight: 5.5 lbs. Carbine-type sights. Receiver grooved for scope mounting. Military stock/handguard. Imported 1966-97.

EUROPEAN AMERICAN ARMORY — Sharpes, Florida

MODEL HW 660 BOLT-ACTION
SINGLE-SHOT RIFLE. . . . . NiB $829 Ex $679 Gd $422
Caliber: .22 LR. 26.8-inch bbl., 45.7 inches overall. Weight: 10.8 lbs. Match-type aperture rear sight; Hooded ramp front. Stippled walnut stock. Imported 1992-96.

MODEL HW BOLT-ACTION
SINGLE-SHOT TARGET RIFLE . . . . . NiB $824 Ex $679 Gd $473
Same general specification as Model HW 660 except equipped w/ target stock. Imported 1995-96.

MODEL SABITTI SP1822
Caliber: .22 LR. 10-round detachable magazine. 18.5 inch bbl. 37.5 inches overall. Weight: 5.25 to 7.15 lbs. No sights. Hammer-forged heavy non-tapered bbl. Scope-mounted rail. Flush-mounted magazine release. Alloy receiver w/non-glare finish. Manual bolt lock. Wide claw extractor. Blowback action. Cross-trigger safety. Imported 1994-96.
Traditional Sporter model. . . . . NiB $210 Ex $170 Gd $118
Thumbhole Sporter
model (synthetic stock). . . . . NiB $332 Ex $267 Gd $185

FABRIQUE NATIONALE HERSTAL — Herstal & Liege, Belgium, (Formerly Fabrique Nationale d'Armes de Guerre)

MODELS 1924, 1934/30 AND
1930 MAUSER MILITARY RIFLES . . . . NiB $390 Ex $288 Gd $186
Similar to German Kar. 98k w/straight bolt handle. Calibers: 7mm, 7.65mm and 7.9mm Mauser. Five round box magazine. 23.5-inch bbl. Weight: 8.5 lbs. Sights: Adj. rear; blade front. Military stock of M/98 pattern w/slight modification. Model differences are minor. Also produced in a short carbine model w/17.25-inch bbl. Note: These rifles were manufactured under contract for Abyssinia, Argentina, Belgium, Bolivia, Brazil, Chile, China, Colombia, Ecuador, Iran, Luxembourg, Mexico, Peru, Turkey, Uruguay and Yugoslavia. Such arms usually bear the coat of arms of the country for which they were made together with the contractor's name and date of manufacture. Also sold commercially and exported to all parts of the world.

F.N. Model 1949

F.N. Model 1950 Mauser

F.N. Deluxe Mauser

F.N. Supreme Mauser

F.N. FAL Semiautomatic

MODEL 1949 SEMIAUTOMATIC MILITARY RIFLE . . . . **NiB $724 Ex $596 Gd $265**
Gas-operated. Calibers: 7mm, 7.65mm, 7.92mm, .30-06. 10-round box magazine, clip fed or loaded singly. 23.2-inch bbl. Weight: 9.5 lbs. Sights: Tangent rear-shielded post front. Pistol-grip stock, handguard. Note: Adopted by Belgium in 1949; also by Belgian Congo, Brazil, Colombia, Luxembourg, Netherlands, East Indies, and Venezuela. Approx. 160,000 were made.

MODEL 1950 MAUSER MILITARY RIFLE . . . . **NiB $469 Ex $316 Gd $239**
Same as previous F.N. models of Kar. 98k type except chambered for .30-06.

DELUXE MAUSER BOLT-ACTION SPORTING RIFLE . . . . **NiB $719 Ex $622 Gd $367**
American calibers: .220 Swift, .243 Win., .244 Rem., .250/3000, .257 Roberts, .270 Win., 7mm, .300 Sav., .308 Win. .30-06. European calibers: 7x57, 8x57JS, 8x60S, 9.3x62, 9.5x57, 10.75x68mm. Five round box magazine. 24-inch bbl. Weight: 7.5-8.25 lbs. American model is standard w/hooded ramp front sight and Tri-Range rear; Continental model w/two-leaf rear. Checkered stock w/cheekpiece, pistol-grip, swivels. Made 1947-63.

DELUXE MAUSER — PRESENTATION GRADE . . . . **NiB $1234 Ex $979 Gd $673**
Same as regular model except w/select grade stock; engraving on receiver, trigger guard, floorplate and bbl. breech. Disc. 1963.

FAL/FNC/LAR SEMIAUTOMATIC
Same as standard FAL military rifle except w/o provision for automatic firing. Gas-operated. Calibers: 7.62mm NATO (.308 Win.) or 5.56mm (.223 Rem.). 10- or 20-round box magazine. 25.5-inch bbl. (including flash hider). Weight: 9 lbs. Sights: Post front; aperture rear. Fixed wood or folding buttstock, pistol-grip, forearm/handguard w/carrying handle and sling swivels. Disc. 1988.

F.N. FAL/LAR model (Light Automatic Rifle) . . . . **NiB $2442 Ex $2111 Gd $1295**
F.N. FAL/HB model (heavy bbl.) . . . . . . **NiB $2762 Ex $2213 Gd $1511**
F.N. FAL/PARA (Paratrooper) . . . . **NiB $3386 Ex $2723 Gd $1703**
F.N. FNC Carbine model (.223 cal.) . . . . **NiB $2570 Ex $1846 Gd $1193**
F.N. FNC Carbine model w/flash suppresser (.223 cal.) . . . . **NiB $2672 Ex $1907 Gd $1244**

SUPREME MAUSER BOLT-ACTION SPORTING RIFLE . . . . **NiB $734 Ex $887 Gd $377**
Calibers: .243, .270, 7mm, .308, .30-06. Four round magazine in .243 and .308; 5-round in other calibers. 22-inch bbl. in .308; 24-inch in other calibers. Sights: Hooded ramp front, Tri-Range peep rear. Checkered stock w/ Monte Carlo cheekpiece, pistol-grip, swivels. Weight: 7.75 lbs. Made 1957-75.

SUPREME MAGNUM MAUSER . . . . **NiB $785 Ex $632 Gd $402**
Calibers: .264 Mag., 7mm Mag., .300 Win. Mag. Specifications same as for standard caliber model except 3-round magazine capacity.

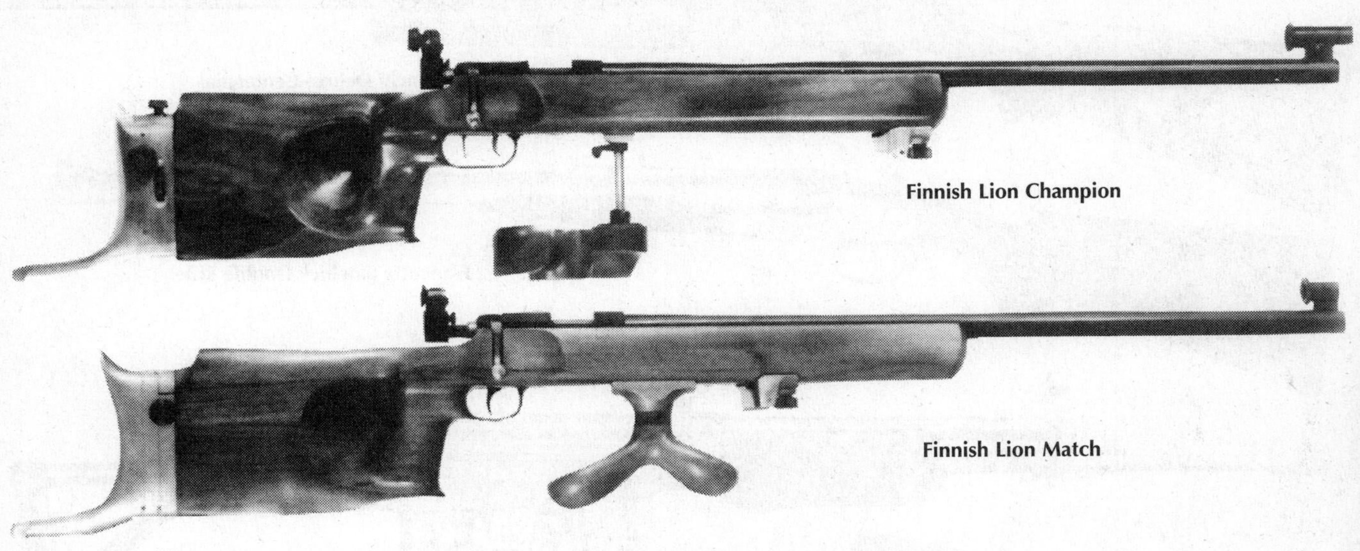
Finnish Lion Champion

Finnish Lion Match

FEATHER INDUSTRIES, INC. — Boulder, Colorado

See MITCHELL ARMS. For current production.

MODEL AT-9 SEMIAUTOMATIC RIFLE
Caliber: 9mm Parabellum. 10-, 25-, 32-, or 100-round magazine. 17-inch bbl. 35 inches overall (extended). Hooded post front sight, adj. aperture rear. Weight: 5 lbs. Telescoping wire stock w/composition pistol-grip and barrel-shroud handguard. Matte black finish. Made 1988-95.
Model AT-9 .... NiB $731 Ex $654 Gd $422
W/32-round magazine, add.......................... $75
W/100-round drum magazine, add.................. $250

MODEL AT-22 .... NiB $237 Ex $186 Gd $130
Caliber: .22 LR. 20-round magazine. 17-inch bbl. 35 inches overall (extended). Hooded post front sight; adj. aperture rear. Weight: 3.25 lbs. Telescoping wire stock w/composition pistol-grip and barrel shroud handguard. Matte black finish.

MODEL F2 SA CARBINE .... NiB $264 Ex $202 Gd $119
Similar to AT-22, except w/fixed Polymer stock and pistol-grip. Made 1992-95.

MODEL F9 SA CARBINE .... NiB $602 Ex $551 Gd $345
Similar to AT-9, except w/fixed Polymer stock and pistol-grip. Made 1992-95.

FINNISH LION RIFLES — Jyväkylylä, Finland Manufactured by Valmet Oy, Tourula Works

CHAMPION FREE RIFLE .... NiB $622 Ex $499 Gd $343
Bolt-action single-shot target rifle. Double-set trigger. Caliber: .22 LR. 28.75-inch heavy bbl. Weight: 16 lbs. Sights: Extension rear peep; aperture front. Walnut free-rifle stock w/full pistol-grip, thumbhole, beavertail forend, hook buttplate, palm rest, hand stop, swivel. Made 1965-72.

STANDARD ISU TARGET RIFLE .... NiB $370 Ex $293 Gd $164
Bolt-action, single-shot. Caliber: .22 LR. 27.5-inch bbl. Weight: 10.5 lbs. Sights: extension rear peep; aperture front. Walnut target stock w/full pistol-grip, checkered beavertail forearm, adj. buttplate, sling swivel. Made 1966-77.

MATCH RIFLE .... NiB $519 Ex $417 Gd $287
Bolt-action, single-shot. Caliber: .22 LR. 28.75-inch heavy bbl. Weight: 14.5 lbs. Sights: Extension rear peep; aperture front. Walnut free-rifle stock w/full pistol-grip, thumbhole, beavertail forearm, hook buttplate, palm rest, hand stop, swivel. Made 1937-72.

STANDARD TARGET RIFLE
Bolt-action, single-shot. Caliber: .22 LR. 27.5-inch bbl. 44.5 inches overall. Weight: 10.5 lbs. No sights; micrometer rear and globe front International-style sights available. Select walnut stock in target configuration. Currently in production.
Standard model .... NiB $757 Ex $623 Gd $396
Thumbhole stock model.................. NiB $814 Ex $654 Gd $448
Standard model .... NiB $370 Ex $267 Gd $164
Deluxe model .... NiB $396 Ex $319 Gd $216

LUIGI FRANCHI, S.P.A. — Brescia, Italy

CENTENNIAL AUTOMATIC RIFLE
Commemorates Franchi's 100th anniversary (1868-1968). Centennial seal engraved on receiver. Semiautomatic. Take-down. Caliber: .22 LR. 11-round magazine in buttstock. 21-inch bbl. Weight: 5.13 lbs. Sights: Open rear; gold bead front on ramp. Checkered walnut stock and forend. Deluxe model w/fully engraved receiver, premium grade wood. Made 1968.
Standard model............... NiB $367 Ex $275 Gd $188
Engraved model.............. NiB $433 Ex $341 Gd $234

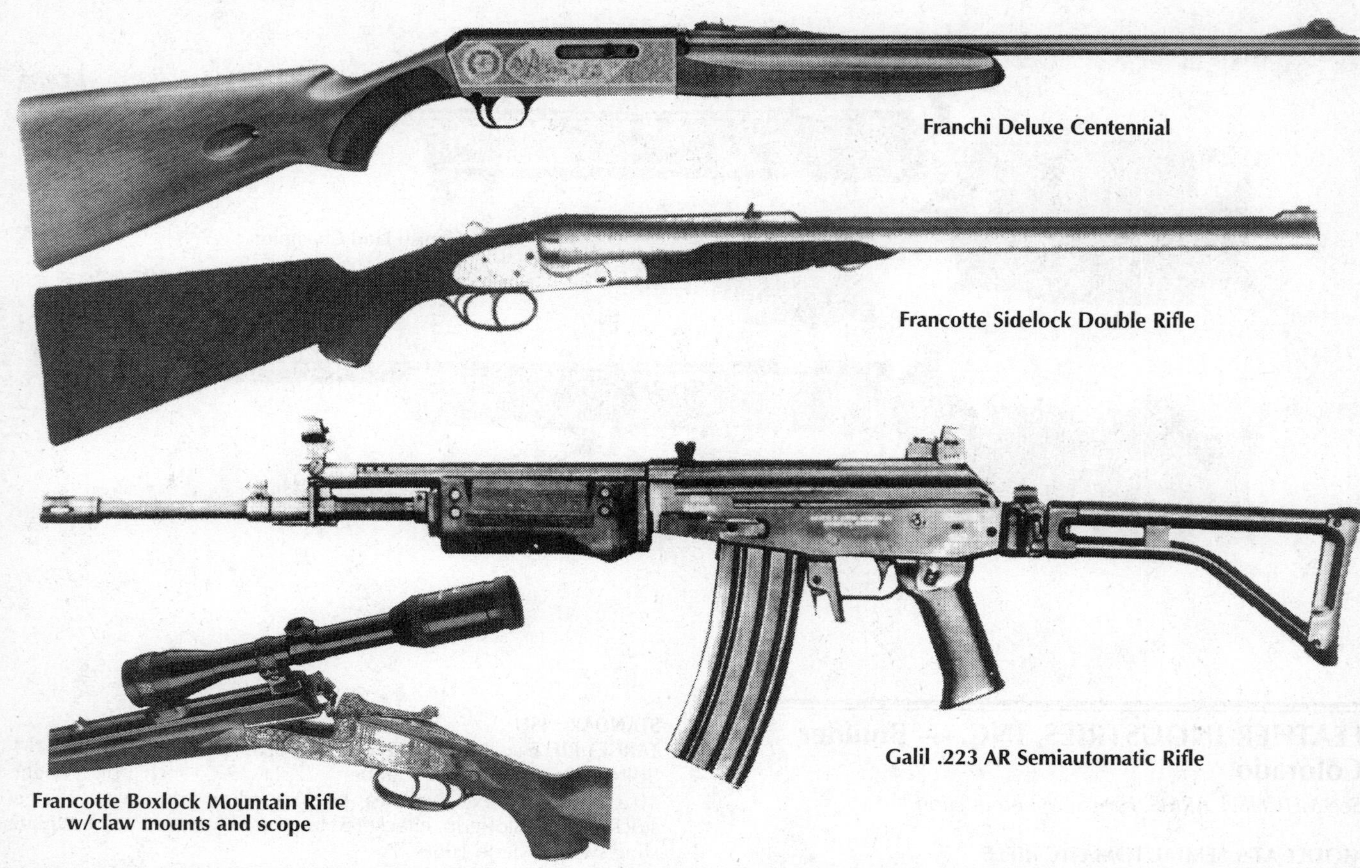

Franchi Deluxe Centennial

Francotte Sidelock Double Rifle

Galil .223 AR Semiautomatic Rifle

Francotte Boxlock Mountain Rifle w/claw mounts and scope

FRANCOTTE RIFLES — Leige, Belgium *Imported by Armes de Chasse, Hertford, NC (Previously by Abercrombie & Fitch)*

BOLT-ACTION RIFLE

Custom rifle built on Mauser style bolt action. Available in three action lengths. Calibers: .17 Bee to .505 Gibbs. Barrel length: 21- to 24.5-inches. Weight: 8 to 12 lbs. Stock dimensions, wood type and style to customer's specifications. Engraving, appointments and finish to customer's preference. Note: Deduct 25% for models w/o engraving.

Short action................ NiB $9450 Ex $7400 Gd $4550
Standard action............. NiB $7875 Ex $6050 Gd $3650
Magnum Francotte action..... NiB $13,750 Ex $10,800 Gd $7000

BOXLOCK MOUNTAIN RIFLE

Custom single-shot rifle built on Anson & Deeley style boxlock or Holland & Holland style sidelock action. 23- to 26-inch barrels chambered to customer's specification. Stock dimensions, wood type and style to customer's specifications. Engraving, appointments and finish to customer's preference. Note: Deduct 30% for models w/o engraving.

Boxlock................ NiB $13,900 Ex $11,700 Gd $7500
Sidelock............. NiB $22,438 Ex $17,950 Gd $12,206

DOUBLE RIFLE

Custom side-by-side rifle. Built on Francotte system boxlock or back-action sidelock. 23.5- to 26-inch barrels chambered to customer's specification. Stock dimensions, wood type and style to customer's specifications. Engraving, appointments and finish to customer's preference. Note: Deduct 30% for models w/o engraving.

Boxlock................ NiB $18,500 Ex $15,500 Gd $9500
Sidelock............. NiB $29,450 Ex $25,000 Gd $15,700

FRENCH MILITARY RIFLE — Saint Etienne, France

MODEL 1936
MAS MILITARY RIFLE .... NiB $159 Ex $118 Gd $67

Bolt-action. Caliber: 7.5mm MAS. Five-round box magazine. 22.5-inch bbl. Weight: 8.25 lbs. Sights: Adj. rear; blade front. Two-piece military-type stock. Bayonet carried in forend tube. Made 1936-1940 by Manufacture Francaise d'Armes et de Cycles de St. Etienne (MAS).

GALIL RIFLES — Manufactured by Israel Military Industries, Israel, Imported by UZI America Inc., North Haven, CT (Previously by Action Arms, Springfield Armory and Magnum Research, Inc.)

AR SEMIAUTOMATIC RIFLE

Calibers: .308 Win. (7.62 NATO), .223 Rem. (5.56mm). 25-round (.308) or 35-round (.223) magazine. 16-inch (.223) or 18.5-inch (.308) bbl. w/flash suppressor. Weight: 9.5 lbs. Folding aperture rear sight, post front. Folding metal stock w/carrying handle. Imported 1982-94. Currently select fire models available to law enforcement only.

Model .223 AR............. NiB $2290 Ex $1826 Gd $1054
Model .308 AR............. NiB $2290 Ex $1826 Gd $1054
Model .223 ARM............ NiB $2728 Ex $2084 Gd $1492
Model .308 ARM............ NiB $2728 Ex $2084 Gd $1492

SPORTER SEMIAUTOMATIC RIFLE. . . . . . NiB $1038 Ex $937 Gd $602
Same general specifications as AR Model except w/hardwood thumbhole stock and 5-round magazine. Weight: 8.5 lbs. Imported 1991-94.

GARCIA CORPORATION — Teaneck, New Jersey

BRONCO 22 SINGLE-SHOT RIFLE. . . . . NiB $105 Ex $85 Gd $60
Swing-out action. Takedown. Caliber: .22 LR. Long, Short. 16.5-inch bbl. Weight: 3 lbs. Sights: Open rear-blade front. One-piece stock and receiver, crackle finish. Intro. 1967. Discontinued.

GERMAN MILITARY RIFLES — Mfd. by Ludwig Loewe & Co., Berlin, other contractors and by German arsenals and various plants under German government control

MODEL 24T (GEW. 24T) MAUSER RIFLE . . . . NiB $525 Ex $370 Gd $242
Same general specifications as Czech Model 24 (VZ24) Mauser Rifle w/minor modification and laminated wood stock. Weight: 9.25 lbs. Made in Czechoslovakia during German occupation; adopted 1940.

MODEL 29/40 (GEW. 29/40)
MAUSER RIFLE . . . . NiB $370 Ex $267 Gd $164
Same general specifications as Kar. 98K w/minor differences. Made in Poland during German occupation; adopted 1940.

MODEL 33/40 (GEW. 33/40)
MAUSER RIFLE . . . . NiB $988 Ex $757 Gd $473
Same general specifications as Czech Model 33 (VZ33) Mauser Carbine w/minor modifications and laminated wood stock as found in war-time Model 98K carbines. Made in Czechoslovakia during German occupation; adopted 1940.

MODELS 41 AND 41-W (GEW. 41, GEW. 41-W)
SEMIAUTOMATIC MILITARY RIFLES
Gas-operated, muzzle cone system. Caliber: 7.9mm Mauser. Ten-round box magazine. 22.5-inch bbl. Weight: 10.25 lbs. Sights: Adj. leaf rear; blade front. Military-type stock w/semi-pistol grip, plastic handguard. Note: Model 41 lacks bolt release found on Model 41-W; otherwise, the models are the same. These early models were mfd. in Walther's Zella-Mehlis plant. Made c.1941-43.
Model 41 . . . . NiB $4230 Ex $3392 Gd $2321
Model 41-W . . . . NiB $3258 Ex $2615 Gd $1793

MODEL 43 (GEW. 43, KAR. 43)
SEMIAUTO MILITARY RIFLES. . . . . NiB $1244 Ex $998 Gd $685
Gas-operated, bbl. vented as in Russian Tokarev. Caliber: 7.9mm Mauser. 10-round detachable box magazine. 22- or 24-inch bbl. Weight: 9 lbs. Sights: Adj. rear; hooded front. Military-type stock w/semi-pistol-grip, wooden handguard. Note: These rifles are alike except for minor details, have characteristic late WWII mfg. short cuts: cast receiver and bolt cover, stamped steel parts, etc. Gew. 43 may have either 22- or 24-inch bbl. The former length was standardized in late 1944, when weapon designation was changed to "Kar. 43." Made 1943-45.

MODEL 1888 (GEW. 88) MAUSER-
MANNLICHER SERVICE RIFLE . . . . NiB $370 Ex $216 Gd $164
Bolt-action w/straight bolt handle. Caliber: 7.9mm Mauser (8x57mm). Five round Mannlicher box magazine. 29-inch bbl. w/jacket. Weight: 8.5 lbs. Fixed front sight, adj. rear. Military-type full stock. Mfd. by Ludwig Loewe & Co., Haenel, Schilling and other contractors.

MODEL 1888 (KAR. 88) MAUSER-
MANNLICHER CARBINE. . . . . NiB $265 Ex $214 Gd $192
Same general specifications as Gew. 88 except w/18-inch bbl., w/o jacket, flat turned-down bolt handle, weight: 6.75 lbs. Mfd. by Ludwig Loewe & Co., Haenel, Schilling and other contractors.

MODEL 1898 (GEW. 98)
MAUSER MILITARY RIFLE . . . . NiB $499 Ex $370 Gd $216
Bolt action with straight bolt handle. Caliber: 7.9mm Mauser (8x57mm). Five round box magazine. 29-inch stepped bbl. Weight: 9 lbs. Sights: Blade front; adj. rear. Military-type full stock w/rounded bottom pistol grip. Adopted 1898.

MODEL 1898A (KAR. 98A)
MAUSER CARBINE . . . . NiB $417 Ex $370 Gd $164
Same general specifications as Model 1898 (Gew.98) Rifle except has turned-down bolt handle, smaller receiver ring, light 23.5-inch-straight taper bbl., front sight guards, sling is attached to left side of stock, weight: 8 lbs. Note: Some of these carbines are marked "Kar. 98;" the true Kar. 98 is the earlier original M/98 carbine w/17-inch bbl. and is rarely encountered.

MODEL 1898B (KAR. 98B)
MAUSER CARBINE . . . . NiB $448 Ex $370 Gd $267
Same general specifications as Model 1898 (Gew.98) Rifle except has turned-down bolt handle and sling attached to left side of stock. This is post-WWI model.

MODEL 1898K (KAR. 98K)
MAUSER CARBINE . . . . NiB $448 Ex $370 Gd $267
Same general specifications as Model 1898 (Gew.98) Rifle except has turned-down bolt handle, 23.5-inch bbl., may have hooded front sight, sling attached to left side of stock, weighs about 8.5 lbs. Adopted in 1935, this was the standard German service rifle of WWII. Note: Late-war models had stamped sheet steel trigger guards and many of the Model 98K carbines made during WWII had laminated wood stocks These weigh .5 to .75 pound more than the previous Model 98K. Value shown is for earlier type.

MODEL VK 98
PEOPLE'S RIFLE ("VOLKSAEWEHR"). . NiB $232 Ex $186 Gd $129
Kar. 98K-type action. Caliber: 7.9mm. Single-shot or repeater (latter w/rough hole-in-the-stock 5-round "magazine" or fitted w/10-round clip of German Model 43 semiauto rifle). 20.9-inch bbl. Weight: 7 lbs. Fixed V-notch rear sight dovetailed into front receiver ring; front blade welded to bbl. Crude, unfinished, half-length stock w/o buttplate. Last ditch weapon made in 1945 for issue to German civilians. Note: Of value only as a military arms collector's item, this hastily-made rifle should be regarded as unsafe to shoot.

GÉVARM RIFLE — Saint Etienne, France Manufactured by Gevelot

E-1 AUTOLOADING RIFLE . . . . NiB $184 Ex $159 Gd $108
Caliber: .22 LR. Eight-round clip magazine. 19.5-inch bbl. Sights: Open rear; post front. Pistol-grip stock and forearm of French walnut.

GOLDEN EAGLE RIFLES — Houston, Texas Mfd. by Nikko Firearms Ltd., Tochigi, Japan

MODEL 7000 GRADE I AFRICAN . . . . . . NiB $679 Ex $525 Gd $417
Same as Grade I Big Game except: Caliber: .375 H&H Mag. and .458 Win. Mag. Two-round magazine in .458, weight: 8.75 lbs. in .375 and 10.5 lbs. in .458, furnished w/sights. Imported 1976-81.

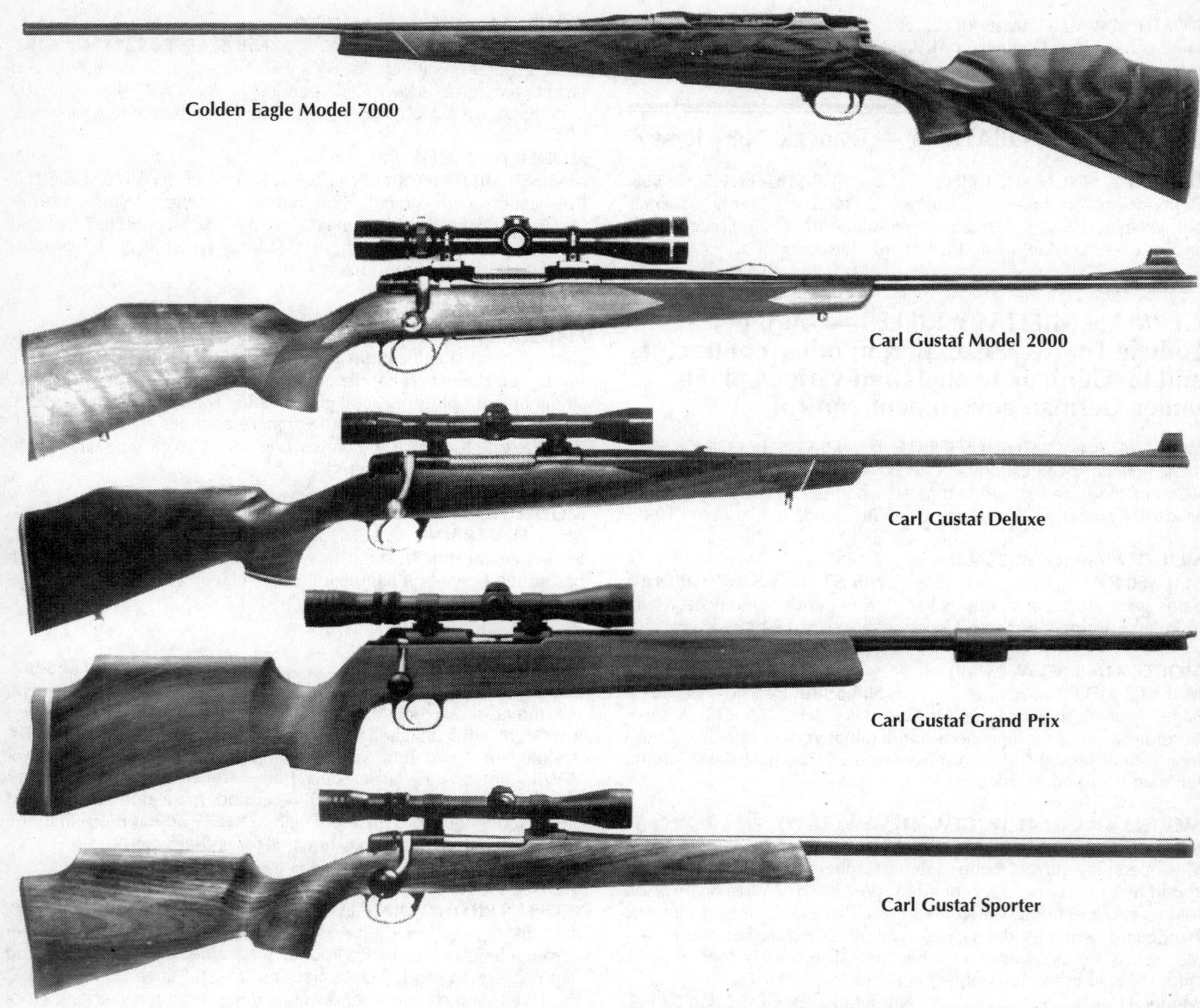
Golden Eagle Model 7000

Carl Gustaf Model 2000

Carl Gustaf Deluxe

Carl Gustaf Grand Prix

Carl Gustaf Sporter

MODEL 7000 BIG GAME SERIES
Bolt action. Calibers: .22-250, .243 Win., .25-06, .270 Win., Weatherby Mag., 7mm Rem. Mag., .30-06, .300 Weatherby Mag., .300 Win. Mag., .338 Win. Mag. Magazine capacity: 4 rounds in .22-250, 3 rounds in other calibers. 24- or 26-inch bbl. (26-inch only in 338). Weight: 7 lbs., .22-250; 8.75, lbs., other calibers. Furnished w/o sights. Fancy American walnut stock, skip checkered, contrasting wood forend tip and grip cap w/gold eagle head, recoil pad. Imported 1976-81.
Model 7000 Grade I . . . . NiB $711 Ex $571 Gd $392
Model 7000 Grade II. . . . . NiB $776 Ex $623 Gd $427

GREIFELT & CO. — Suhl, Germany

SPORT MODEL 22 HORNET
BOLT-ACTION RIFLE . . . . NiB $2205 Ex $1768 Gd $1210
Caliber: .22 Hornet. Five round box magazine. 22-inch Krupp steel bbl. Weight: 6 lbs. Sights: Two-leaf rear; ramp front. Walnut stock, checkered pistol-grip and forearm. Made before WWII.

CARL GUSTAF RIFLES — Eskilstuna, Sweden Mfd. by Carl Gustaf Stads Gevärsfaktori

MODEL 2000 BOLT-ACTION RIFLE
Calibers: .243, 6.5x55, 7x64, .270, .308 Win., .30-06, 7mm Rem. Mag., .300 Win. Mag. Three round magazine. 24-inch bbl. 44 inches overall. Weight: 7.5 lbs. Receiver drilled and tapped. Hooded ramp front sight, open rear. Adj. trigger. Checkered European walnut stock w/Monte Carlo cheekpiece and Wundhammer palmswell grip. Imported 1991-95
Model 2000
w/o sights . . . . NiB $1426 Ex $1144 Gd $783
Model 2000 w/sights. . . . . NiB $1626 Ex $1303 Gd $891
Model 2000 LUXE . . . . NiB $1762 Ex $1561 Gd $943

DELUXE. . . . . NiB $757 Ex $608 Gd $419
Same specifications as Monte Carlo Standard. Calibers: 6.5x55, 308 Win., .30-06, 9.3x62. Four round magazine in 9.3x62. Jeweled bolt. Engraved floorplate and trigger guard. Deluxe French walnut stock w/rosewood forend tip. Imported 1970-77.

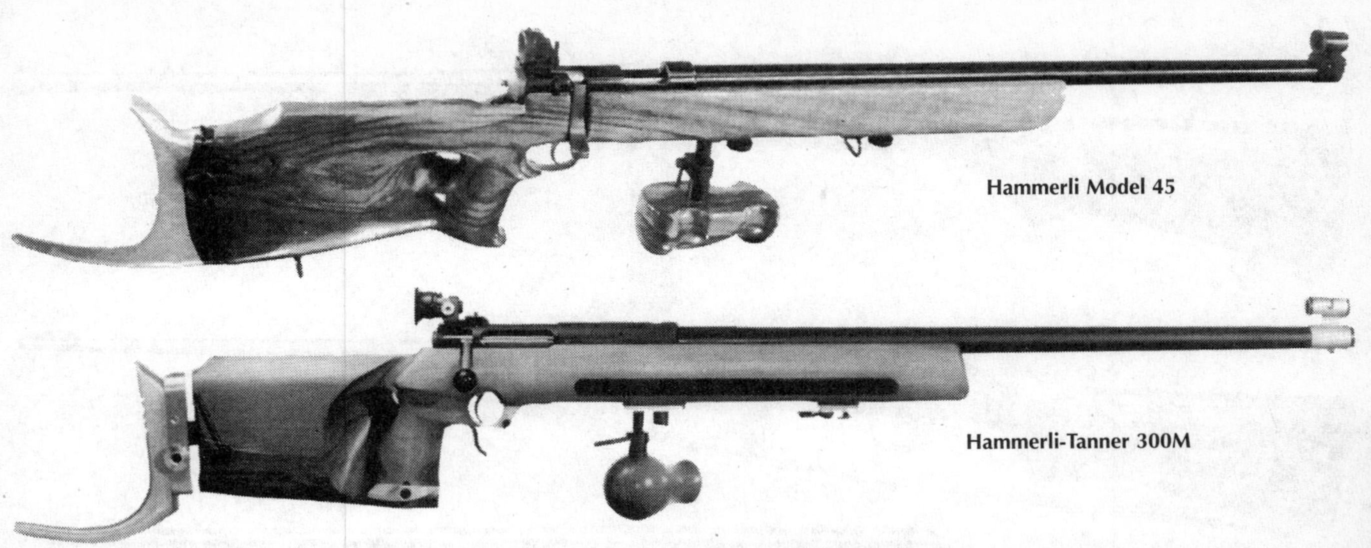
Hammerli Model 45

Hammerli-Tanner 300M

GRAND PRIX SINGLE-SHOT TARGET RIFLE . . . . NiB $623 Ex $520 Gd $350
Special bolt action with "world's shortest lock time." Single-stage trigger adjusts down to 18 oz. Caliber: .22 LR. 26.75-inch heavy bbl. w/adj. trim weight. Weight: 9.75 lbs. Furnished w/o sights. Target-type Monte Carlo stock of French walnut, adj. cork buttplate. Imported 1970-77.

MONTE CARLO STANDARD BOLT-ACTION SPORTING RIFLE . . . . NiB $473 Ex $417 Gd $370
Carl Gustaf 1900 action. Calibers: 6.5x55, 7x64, .270 Win., 7mm Rem. Mag., .308 Win., .30-06, 9.3x62. Five round magazine, except 4-round in 9.3x62 and 3-round in 7mm Rem. Mag. 23.5-inch bbl. Weight: 7 lbs. Sights: Folding leaf rear; hooded ramp front. French walnut Monte Carlo stock w/cheekpiece, checkered forearm and pistol grip, sling swivels. Also available in left-hand model. Imported1970-77.

SPECIAL. . . . . NiB $525 Ex $448 Gd $314
Also designated "Grade II" in U.S. and "Model 9000" in Canada. Same specifications as Monte Carlo Standard. Calibers: .22-250, .243 Win., .25-06, .270 Win., 7mm Rem. Mag., .308 Win., .30-06, .300 Win. Mag. Three round magazine in magnum calibers. Select wood stock w/rosewood forend tip. Left-hand model avail. Imported 1970-77.

SPORTER . . . . NiB $622 Ex $499 Gd $343
Also designated "Varmint-Target" in U.S. Fast bolt action w/large Bakelite bolt knob. Trigger pull adjusts down to 18 oz. Calibers: .222 Rem., .22-250, .243 Win., 6.5x55. Five round magazine except 6-round in .222 Rem. 26.75-inch heavy bbl. Weight: 9.5 lbs. Furnished w/o sights. Target-type Monte Carlo stock of French walnut. Imported 1970 to date.

STANDARD . . . . NiB $576 Ex $473 Gd $319
Same specifications as Monte Carlo Standard. Calibers: 6.5x55, 7x64, .270 Win., .308 Win., .30-06, 9.3x62. Classic-style stock w/o Monte Carlo. Imported 1970-77.

TROFÉ . . . . NiB $828 Ex $628 Gd $432
Also designated "Grade III" in U.S. and "Model 8000" in Canada. Same specifications as Monte Carlo Standard. Calibers: .22-250, .25-06, 6.5x55, .270 Win., 7mm Rem. Mag., .308 Win., .30-06, .300 Win. Mag. Three round magazine in magnum calibers. Furnished w/o sights. Fancy wood stock w/rosewood forend tip, high-gloss lacquer finish. Imported 1970-77.

C.G. HAENEL — Suhl, Germany

'88 MAUSER SPORTER . . . . NiB $551 Ex $427 Gd $319
Same general specifications as Haenel Mauser-Mannlicher except w/Mauser 5-round box magazine.

MAUSER-MANNLICHER BOLT-ACTION SPORTING RIFLE . . NiB $499 Ex $396 Gd $241
Mauser M/88-type action. Calibers: 7x57, 8x57, 9x57mm. Mannlicher clip-loading box magazine, 5-round. 22- or 24-inch half or full octagon bbl. w/raised matted rib. Double-set trigger. Weight: 7.5 lbs. Sights: Leaf-type open rear; ramp front. Sporting stock w/cheekpiece, checkered pistol-grip, raised side-panels, Schnabel tip, swivels.

HÄMMERLI AG JAGD-UND-SPORTWAFFEN-FABRIK —

Lenzburg, Switzerland, *Imported by Sigarms, Exetre, NH, (Previously by Hammerli USA; Mandall Shooting Supplies, Inc. & Beeman Precision Arms)*

MODEL 45 SMALLBORE BOLT-ACTION SINGLE-SHOT MATCH RIFLE . . . . NiB $690 Ex $576 Gd $370
Calibers: .22 LR. 22 Extra Long. 27.5-inch heavy bbl. Weight: 15.5 lbs. Sights: Micrometer peep rear; globe front. Free-rifle stock w/cheekpiece, full pistol-grip, thumbhole, beavertail forearm, palmrest, Swiss-type buttplate, swivels. Made 1945-57.

MODEL 54 SMALLBORE MATCH RIFLE . . . . NiB $700 Ex $576 Gd $345
Bolt-action, single-shot. Caliber: .22 LR. 27.5-inch heavy bbl. Weight: 15 lbs. Sights: Micrometer peep rear; globe front. Free-rifle stock w/cheekpiece, thumbhole, adj. hook buttplate, palm rest, swivel. Made 1954-57.

MODEL 503 FREE RIFLE . . . . NiB $705 Ex $576 Gd $345
Bolt-action, single-shot. Caliber: .22 LR. 27.5-inch heavy bbl. Weight: 15 lbs. Sights: Micrometer peep rear; globe front. Free-rifle stock w/cheekpiece, thumbhole, adj. hook buttplate, palm rest, swivel. Made 1957-62.

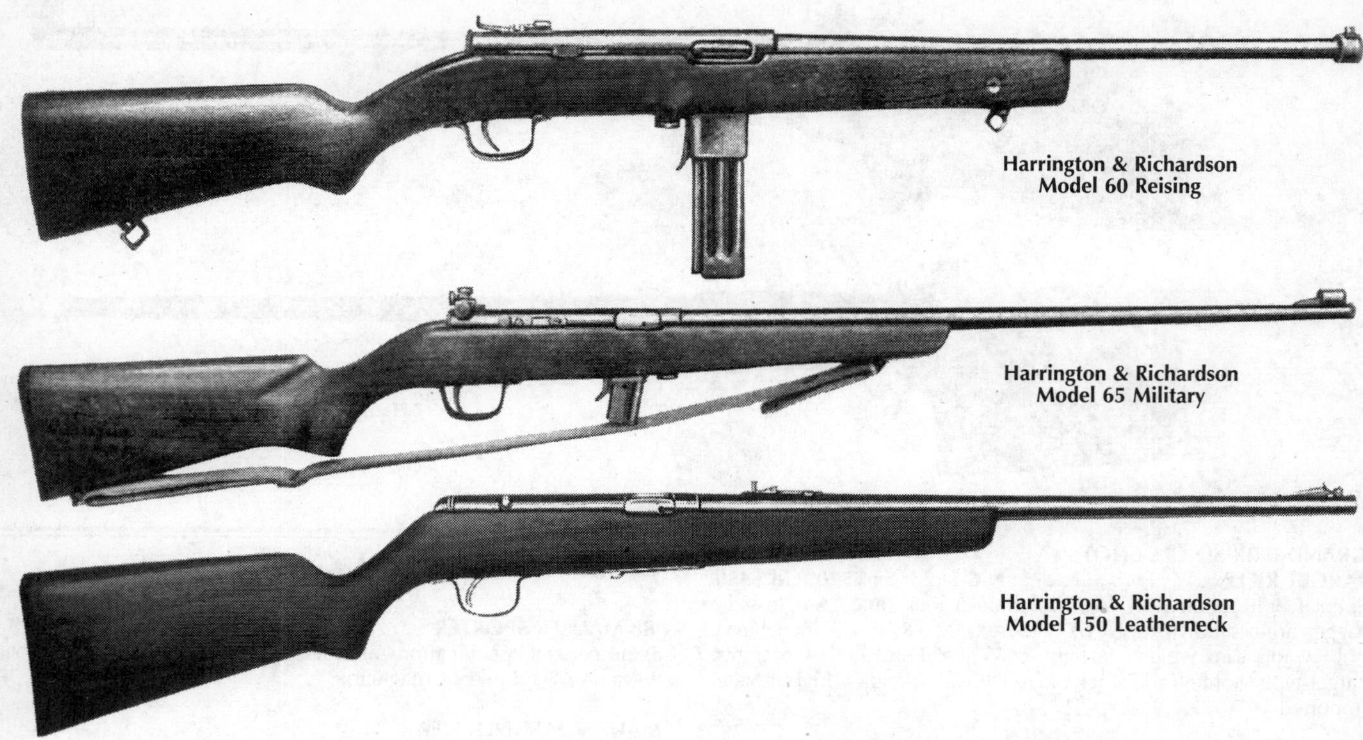

Harrington & Richardson Model 60 Reising

Harrington & Richardson Model 65 Military

Harrington & Richardson Model 150 Leatherneck

MODEL 506 SMALLBORE MATCH RIFLE .... NiB $705 Ex $576 Gd $370
Bolt-action, single-shot. Caliber: .22 LR. 26.75-inch heavy bbl. Weight: 16.5 lbs. Sights: Micrometer peep rear; globe front. Free-rifle stock w/cheekpiece, thumbhole adj. hook buttplate, palmrest, swivel. Made 1963-66.

MODEL OLYMPIA 300 METER BOLT-ACTION SINGLE-SHOT FREE RIFLE................ NiB $911 Ex $782 Gd $473
Calibers: .30-06, .300 H&H Magnum for U.S.A.; ordinarily produced in 7.5mm, other calibers available on special order. 29.5-inch heavy bbl. Double-pull or double-set trigger. Sights: Micrometer peep rear, globe front. Free-rifle stock w/cheekpiece, full pistol grip, thumbhole, beavertail forend, palmrest, Swiss-type buttplate, swivels. Made 1945-59.

TANNER 300 METER FREE RIFLE .... NiB $937 Ex $860 Gd $473
Bolt-action, single-shot. Caliber: 7.5mm standard, available in most popular centerfire calibers. 29.5-inch heavy bbl. Weight: 16.75 lbs. Sights: Micrometer peep rear; globe front. Free-rifle stock w/cheekpiece, thumbhole, adj. hook buttplate, palmrest, swivel. Intro. 1962. Disc. See Illustration previous page.

HARRINGTON & RICHARDSON, INC. — Gardner, Massachusetts (Now H&R 1871, INC., Gardner, Mass.)

Formerly Harrington & Richardson Arms Co. of Worcester, Mass. One of the oldest and most distinguished manufacturers of handguns, rifles and shotguns, H&R suspended operations on January 24, 1986. In 1987, New England Firearms was established as an independent company producing selected H&R models under the NEF logo. In 1991, H&R 1871, Inc. was formed from the residual of the parent company and that took over the New England Firearms facility. H&R 1871 produced firearms under both its logo and the NEF brand name until 1999, when the Marlin Firearms Company acquired the assets of H&R 1871.

MODEL 60 REISING SEMI-AUTOMATIC RIFLE .... NiB $525 Ex $499 Gd $242
Caliber: .45 Automatic. 12- and 20-round detachable box magazines. 18.25-inch bbl. Weight: 7.5 lbs. Sights: Open rear; blade front. Plain pistol-grip stock. Made 1944-46.

MODEL 65 MILITARY AUTOLOADING RIFLE .... NiB $319 Ex $257 Gd $149
Also called "General." Caliber: .22 LR. 10-round detachable box magazine. 23-inch heavy bbl. Weight: 9 lbs. Sights: Redfield 70 rear peep, blade front w/protecting "ears." Plain pistol-grip stock, "Garand" dimensions. Made 1944-46. Note: This model was used as a training rifle by the U.S. Marine Corps.

MODEL 150 LEATHERNECK AUTOLOADER............. NiB $111 Ex $90 Gd $70
Caliber: .22 LR. only. Five round detachable box magazine. 22-inch bbl. Weight: 7.25 lbs. Sights: Open rear; blade front, on ramp. Plain pistol-grip stock. Made 1949-53.

MODEL 151 .... NiB $162 Ex $96 Gd $80
Same as Model 150 except w/Redfield 70 rear peep sight.

MODEL 155 SINGLE-SHOT RIFLE.................. NiB $193 Ex $142 Gd $90
Model 158 action. Calibers: .44 Rem. Mag., .45-70 Govt. 24- or 28-inch bbl. (latter in .44 only). Weight: 7 or 7.5 lbs. Sights: Folding leaf rear; blade front. Straight-grip stock, forearm w/bbl. band, brass cleaning rod. Made 1972-82.

MODEL 157 SINGLE-SHOT RIFLE.................. NiB $193 Ex $111 Gd $80
Model 158 action. Calibers: .22 WMR, .22 Hornet, .30-30. 22-inch bbl. Weight: 6.25 lbs. Sights: Folding leaf rear; blade front. Pistol-grip stock, full-length forearm, swivels. Made 1976-86.

Harrington & Richardson Model 155

Harrington & Richardson Model 157

Harrington & Richardson Model 158 Topper Jet

Harrington & Richardson Model 158C w/extra shotgun barrel

MODEL 158 TOPPER JET SINGLE-SHOT COMBINATION RIFLE
Shotgun-type action w/visible hammer, side lever, auto ejector. Caliber: .22 Rem. Jet. 22-inch bbl. (interchanges with .30-30, .410 ga., 20 ga. bbls.). Weight: 5 lbs. Sights: Lyman folding adj. open rear; ramp front. Plain pistol-grip stock and forearm, recoil pad. Made 1963-67.
Rifle only . . . . NiB $160 Ex $135 Gd $88
Interchangeable bbl.
.30-30, shotgun . . . . NiB $57 Ex $47 Gd $32

MODEL 158C . . . . NiB $161 Ex $145 Gd $88
Same as Model 158 Topper Jet except calibers .22 Hornet, .30-30, .357 Mag., .357 Mag., .44 Mag. Straight-grip stock. Made 1963-86.

MODEL 163 MUSTANG SINGLE-SHOT RIFLE . . . . NiB $161 Ex $140 Gd $83
Same as Model 158 Topper except w/gold-plated hammer and trigger, straight-grip stock and contoured forearm. Made 1964-67.

MODEL 165 LEATHERNECK AUTOLOADER . . . NiB $135 Ex $119 Gd $83
Caliber: .22 LR. 10-round detachable box magazine. 23-inch bbl. Weight: 7.5 lbs. Sights: Redfield 70 rear peep; blade front, on ramp. Plain pistol-grip stock, swivels, web sling. Made 1945-61.

MODEL 171 . . . . NiB $368 Ex $317 Gd $204
Model 1873 Springfield Cavalry Carbine replica. Caliber: .45-70. 22-inch bbl. Weight: 7 lbs. Sights: Leaf rear; blade front. Plain walnut stock. Made 1972-81.

MODEL 171 DELUXE . . . . NiB $420 Ex $368 Gd $263
Same as Model 171 except engraved action and different sights. Made 1972-86. See illustration next page.

MODEL 172 . . . . NiB $700 Ex $650 Gd $495
Same as Model 171 Deluxe except silver-plated, w/fancy walnut stock, checkered, w/grip adapter; tang-mounted aperture sight. Made 1972-86.

MODEL 173 . . . . NiB $725 Ex $625 Gd $400
Model 1873 Springfield Officer's Model replica, same as 100th Anniversary Commemorative except w/o plaque on stock. Made 1972-86.

MODEL 174 . . . . NiB $422 Ex $370 Gd $267
Little Big Horn Commemorative Carbine. Same as Model 171 Deluxe except w/tang-mounted aperture sight, grip adapter. Made 1972-84.

MODEL 178 . . . . NiB $422 Ex $370 Gd $267
Model 1873 Springfield Infantry Rifle replica. Caliber: .45-70. 32-inch bbl. Weight: 8 lbs. 10 oz. Sights: Leaf rear; blade front. Full-length stock w/bbl. bands, swivels, ramrod. Made 1973-86.

MODEL 250 SPORTSTER BOLT-ACTION REPEATING RIFLE . . . . NiB $108 Ex $87 Gd $61
Caliber: .22 LR. Five-round detachable box magazine. 23-inch bbl. Weight: 6.5 lbs. Sights: Open rear; blade front, on ramp. Plain pistol-grip stock. Made 1948-61.

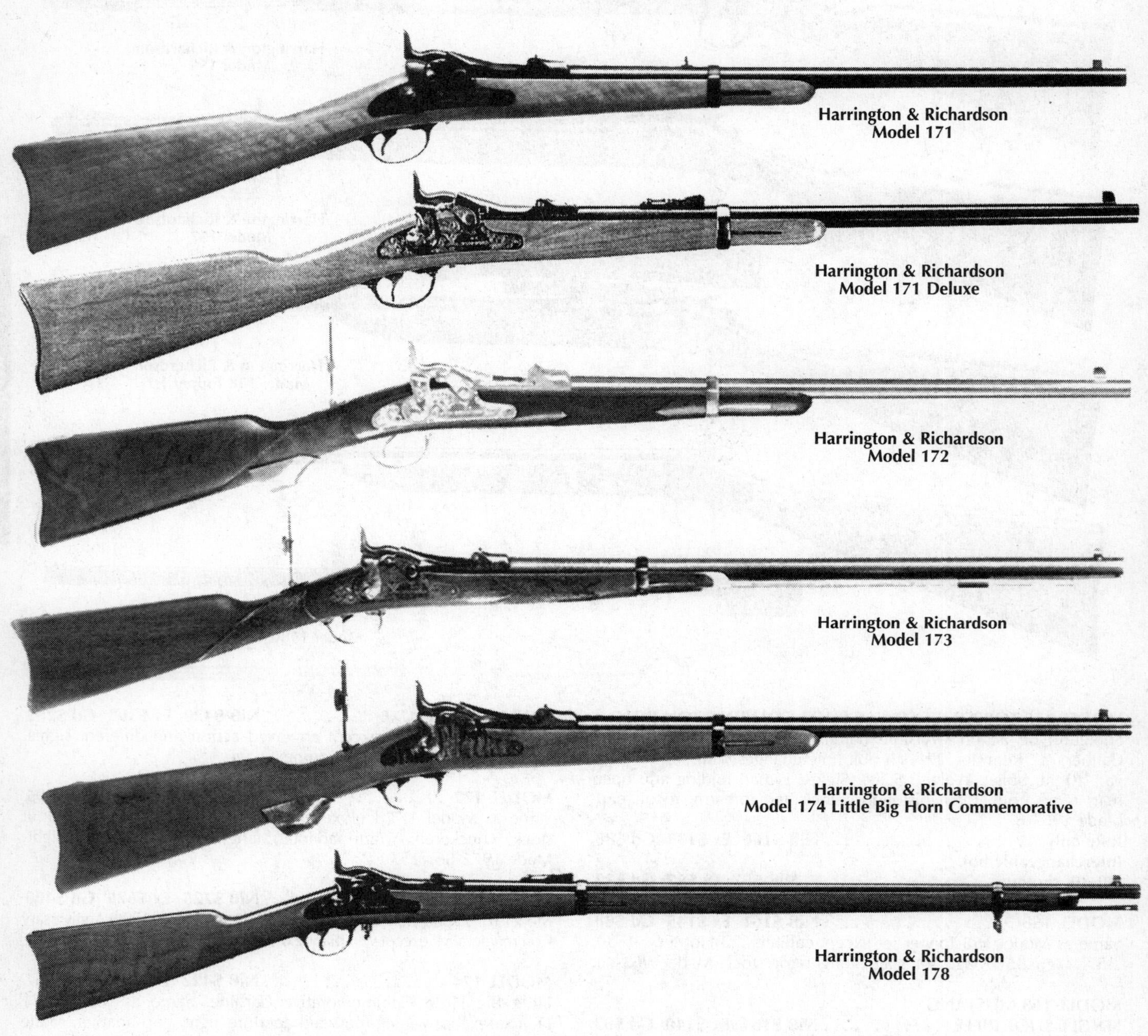

Harrington & Richardson Model 171

Harrington & Richardson Model 171 Deluxe

Harrington & Richardson Model 172

Harrington & Richardson Model 173

Harrington & Richardson Model 174 Little Big Horn Commemorative

Harrington & Richardson Model 178

MODEL 251 .... NiB $119 Ex $98 Gd $70
Same as Model 250 except w/Lyman No. 55H rear sight.

MODEL 265 "REG'LAR" BOLT-ACTION REPEATING RIFLE........ NiB $113 Ex $92 Gd $66
Caliber: .22 LR. 10-round detachable box magazine. 22-inch bbl. Weight: 6.5 lbs. Sights: Lyman No. 55 rear peep; blade front, on ramp. Plain pistol-grip stock. Made 1946-49.

MODEL 300 ULTRA BOLT-ACTION RIFLE............ NiB $535 Ex $458 Gd $252
Mauser-type action. Calibers: .22-250, .243 Win., .270 Win., .30-06, .308 Win., 7mm Rem. Mag., .300 Win. Mag. Three round magazine in 7mm and .300 Mag. calibers, 5-round in others. 22- or 24-inch bbl. Sights: Open rear; ramp front. Checkered stock w/rollover cheekpiece and full pistol grip, contrasting wood forearm tip and pistol grip, rubber buttplate, sling swivels. Weight: 7.25 lbs. Made 1965-82.

Harrington & Richardson Model 300

Harrington & Richardson Model 301 Carbine

Harrington & Richardson Model 317P

Harrington & Richardson Model 330

Harrington & Richardson Model 360 Ultra

Harrington & Richardson Model 370 Ultra Medalist

MODEL 301 CARBINE .... NiB $448 Ex $370 Gd $242
Same as Model 300 except w/18-inch bbl., Mannlicher-style stock, weighs 7.25 lbs.; not available in caliber .22-250. Made 1967-82.

MODEL 308 AUTOMATIC RIFLE... NiB $428 Ex $345 Gd $238
Original designation of the Model 360 Ultra. Made 1965-67.

MODEL 317 ULTRA WILDCAT BOLT-ACTION RIFLE............ NiB $623 Ex $576 Gd $345
Sako short action. Calibers: .17 Rem. 17/.223 (handload), .222 Rem., .223 Rem. Six round magazine. 20-inch bbl. No sights, receiver dovetailed for scope mounts. Checkered stock w/cheekpiece and full pistol grip, contrasting wood forearm tip and pistol-grip cap, rubber buttplate. Weight: 5.25 lbs. Made 1968-76.

(cont'd.) **MODEL 317 ULTRA WILDCAT BOLT-ACTION RIFLE**

MODEL 317P PRESENTATION GRADE .... NiB $735 Ex $606 Gd $426
Same as Model 317 except w/select grade fancy walnut stock w/basket weave carving on forearm and pistol-grip. Made 1968-76.

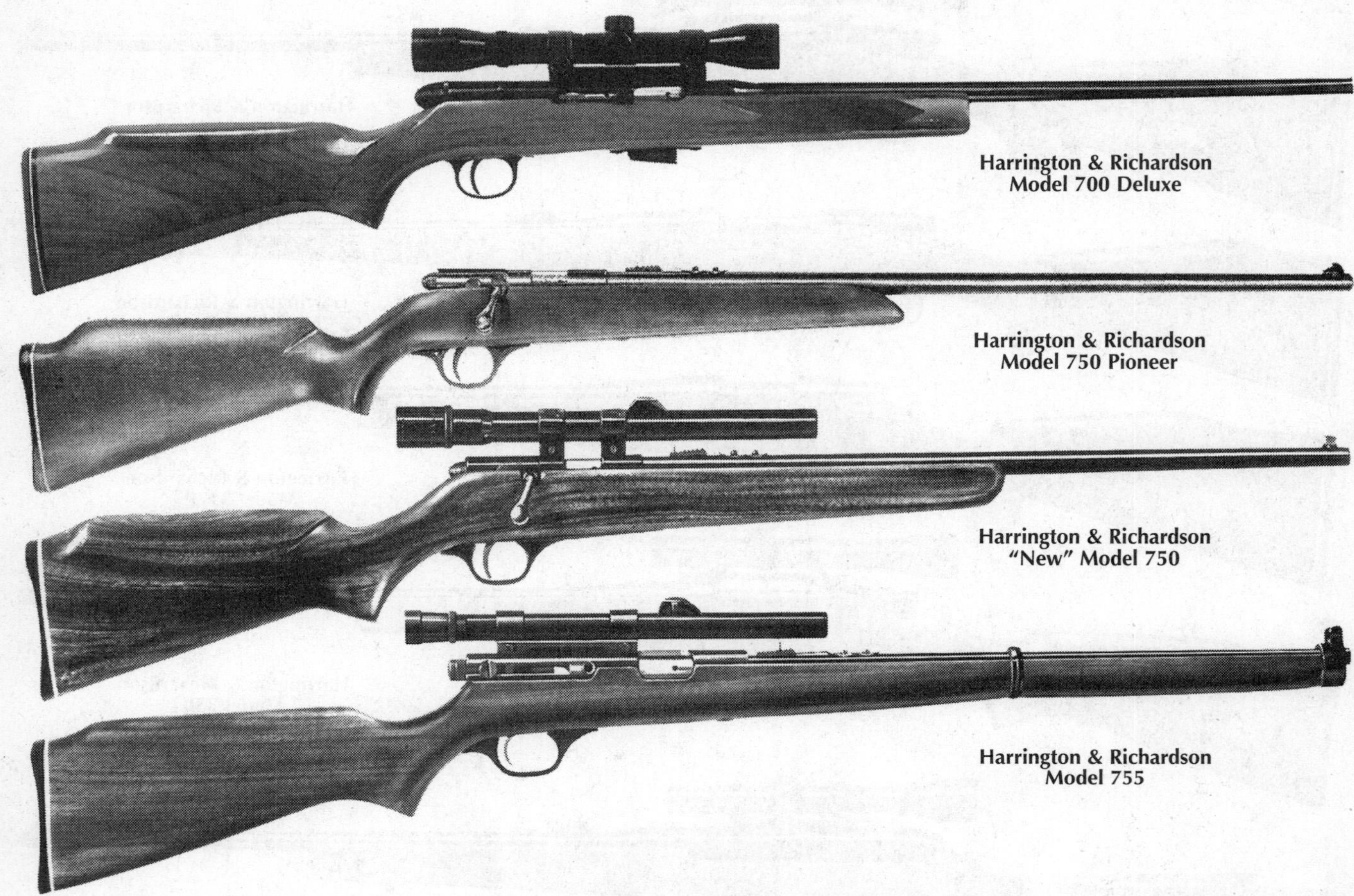

Harrington & Richardson Model 700 Deluxe

Harrington & Richardson Model 750 Pioneer

Harrington & Richardson "New" Model 750

Harrington & Richardson Model 755

MODEL 330 HUNTER'S RIFLE . . . . NiB $319 Ex $267 Gd $190
Similar to Model 300, but w/plainer stock. Calibers: .243 Win., .270 Win., .30-06, .308 Win., 7mm Rem. Mag., .300 Win. Mag. Weight: 7.13 lbs. Made 1967-72.

MODEL 333 . . . . NiB $267 Ex $242 Gd $139
Plainer version of Model 300 w/uncheckered walnut-finished hardwood stock. Calibers: 7mm Rem. Mag. and .30-06. 22-inch bbl. Weight: 7.25 lbs. No sights. Made in 1974.

MODEL 340 . . . . NiB $396 Ex $319 Gd $211
Mauser-type action. Calibers: .243 Win., .308 Win., .270 Win., .30-06, 7x57. 22-inch bbl. Weight: 7.25 lbs. Hand-checkered American walnut stock. Made 1982-84.

MODEL 360 ULTRA AUTOMATIC RIFLE . . . . . . NiB $427 Ex $345 Gd $242
Gas-operated semiautomatic. Calibers: .243 Win., .308 Win. Three round detachable box magazine. 22-inch bbl. Sights: Open rear; ramp front. Checkered stock w/rollover cheekpiece, full pistol grip, contrasting wood forearm tip and pistol-grip cap, rubber buttplate, sling swivels. Weight: 7.25 lbs. Made 1967-78.

MODEL 361 . . . . NiB $483 Ex $406 Gd $277
Same as Model 360 except w/full rollover cheekpiece for right- or left-hand shooters. Made 1970-73.

MODEL 365 ACE BOLT-ACTION SINGLE-SHOT RIFLE . . . . NiB $123 Ex $118 Gd $71
Caliber: .22 LR. 22-inch bbl. Weight: 6.5 lbs. Sights: Lyman No. 55 rear peep, blade front, on ramp. Plain pistol-grip stock. Made 1946-47.

MODEL 370 ULTRA MEDALIST . . . NiB $509 Ex $483 Gd $286
Varmint and target rifle based on Model 300. Calibers: .22-250, .243 Win., 6mm Rem. Three round magazine. 24-inch varmint weight bbl. No sights. Target-style stock w/semibeavertail forearm. Weight: 9.5 lbs. Made 1968-73.

MODEL 422 SLIDE-ACTION REPEATER . . . . NiB $139 Ex $108 Gd $87
Caliber: .22 LR. Long, Short. Tubular magazine holds 21 Short, 17 Long, 15 LR. 24-inch bbl. Weight: 6 lbs. Sights: Open rear; ramp front. Plain pistol-grip stock grooved slide handle. Made 1956-58.

MODEL 450 . . . . NiB $123 Ex $108 Gd $61
Same as Model 451 except w/o front and rear sights.

MODEL 451 MEDALIST BOLT-ACTION TARGET RIFLE . . . . . . NiB $190 Ex $164 Gd $92
Caliber: .22 LR. Five round detachable box magazine. 26-inch bbl. Weight: 10.5 lbs. Sights: Lyman No. 524F extension rear; Lyman No. 77 front, scope bases. Target stock w/full pistol-grip and forearm, swivels and sling. Made 1948-61.

Harrington & Richardson Model 760

Harrington & Richardson Model 866

Harrington & Richardson Model 1873 — 100th Anniversary

Harrington & Richardson Model 5200 Sporter

Harrington & Richardson Ultra Varmint

MODEL 465 TARGETEER SPECIAL BOLT-ACTION REPEATER .... NiB $175 Ex $139 Gd $92
Caliber: .22 LR. 10-round detachable box magazine. 25-inch bbl. Weight: 9 lbs. Sights: Lyman No. 57 rear peep; blade front, on ramp. Plain pistol-grip stock, swivels, web sling strap. Made 1946-47.

MODEL 700 AUTOLOADER ...... NiB $303 Ex $267 Gd $139
Caliber: .22 WMR. Five-round magazine. 22-inch bbl. Weight: 6.5 lbs. Sights: Folding leaf rear; blade front, on ramp. Monte Carlo-style stock of American walnut. Made 1977-86.

MODEL 700 DELUXE .... NiB $432 Ex $355 Gd $277
Same as Model 700 Standard except w/select custom polished and blued finish, select walnut stock, hand checkering, and no iron sights. Fitted w/H&R Model 432 4x scope. Made 1980-86.

MODEL 750 PIONEER BOLT-ACTION SINGLE-SHOT RIFLE .... NiB $103 Ex $82 Gd $61
Caliber: .22 LR. Long, Short. 22- or 24-inch bbl. Weight: 5 lbs. Sights: Open rear; bead front. Plain pistol-grip stock. Made 1954-81; redesigned 1982; discont. 1985.

MODEL 751 SINGLE-SHOT RIFLE .... NiB $87 Ex $67 Gd $46
Same as Model 750 except w/Mannlicher-style stock. Made 1971.

MODEL 755 SAHARA SINGLE-SHOT RIFLE .... NiB $87 Ex $67 Gd $46
Blow-back action, automatic ejection. Caliber: .22 LR. Long, Short. 18-inch bbl. Weight: 4 lbs. Sights: Open rear; military-type front. Mannlicher-style stock. Made 1963-71.

MODEL 760 SINGLE-SHOT .... NiB $103 Ex $82 Gd $61
Same as Model 755 except w/conventional sporter stock. Made 1965-70.

MODEL 765 PIONEER BOLT-ACTION SINGLE-SHOT RIFLE . . . . NiB $82 Ex $67 Gd $46
Caliber: .22 LR. Long, Short. 24-inch bbl. Weight: 5 lbs. Sights: Open rear; hooded bead front. Plain pistol-grip stock. Made 1948-54.

MODEL 800 LYNX AUTOLOADING RIFLE . . . . NiB $149 Ex $113 Gd $77
Caliber: .22 LR. Five or 10-round clip magazine. 22-inch bbl. Open sights. Weight: 6 lbs. Plain pistol-grip stock. Made 1958-60.

MODEL 852 FIELDSMAN BOLT-ACTION REPEATER . . . . NiB $123 Ex $67 Gd $72
Caliber: .22 LR. Long, Short. Tubular magazine holds 21 Short, 17 Long, 15 LR. 24-inch bbl. Weight: 5.5 lbs. Sights: Open rear; bead front. Plain pistol-grip stock. Made 1952-53.

MODEL 865 PLAINSMAN BOLT-ACTION REPEATER . . . . NiB $113 Ex $92 Gd $61
Caliber .22 LR. Long, Short. Five round detachable box magazine. 22- or 24-inch bbl. Weight: 5.25 lbs. Sights: Open rear, bead front. Plain pistol-grip stock. Made 1949-86.

MODEL 866 BOLT-ACTION REPEATER . . . . NiB $113 Ex $92 Gd $61
Same as Model 865, except w/Mannlicher-style stock. Made 1971.

MODEL 1873 100TH ANNIVERSARY (1871-1971) COMMEMORATIVE OFFICER'S SPRINGFIELD REPLICA . . . NiB $790 Ex $584 Gd $404
Model 1873 "trap door" single-shot action. Engraved breech block, receiver, hammer, lock, band and buttplate. Caliber: .45-70. 26-inch bbl. Sights: Peep rear; blade front. Checkered walnut stock w/anniversary plaque. Ramrod. Weight: 8 lbs. 10,000 made 1971.

MODEL 5200 SPORTER . . . . NiB $631 Ex $533 Gd $335
Turn-bolt repeater. Caliber: .22 LR. 24-inch bbl. Classic-style American walnut stock. Adj. trigger. Sights: Peep receiver; hooded ramp front. Weight: 6.5 lbs. Disc. 1983.

MODEL 5200 MATCH RIFLE. . . . . . NiB $430 Ex $425 Gd $327
Same action as 5200 Sporter. Caliber: .22 LR. 28-inch target weight bbl. Target stock of American walnut. Weight: 11 lbs. Made 1982-86.

CUSTER MEMORIAL ISSUE
Limited Edition Model 1873 Springfield Carbine replica, richly engraved and inlaid w/gold, fancy walnut stock, in mahogany display case. Made 1973.
Officers' Model
Limited to 25 pieces. . . . . NiB $5829 EX $4670 GD $3187
Enlisted Men's model,
limited to 243 pieces. . . . . NiB $3254 Ex $2610 Gd $1786

TARGETEER JR. BOLT-ACTION RIFLE . . . . NiB $164 Ex $138 Gd $102
Caliber: .22 LR. Five-round detachable box magazine. 20-inch bbl. Weight: 7 lbs. Sights: Redfield 70 rear peep; Lyman No. 17A front. Target stock, junior-size w/pistol grip, swivels and sling. Made 1948-51.

ULTRA SINGLE-SHOT RIFLE
Side-lever single-shot. Calibers: .22-250 Rem., .223 Rem., .25-06 Rem., .308 Win. 22- to 26-inch bbl. Weight: 7-8 lbs. Curly maple or laminated stock. Barrel-mounted scope mount, no sights. Made 1993 to date.
Ultra Hunter (.25-06, .308). . . . . . . NiB $206 Ex $139 Gd $113
Ultra Varmint. . . . . NiB $242 Ex $190 Gd $139

HARRIS GUNWORKS — Phoenix, Arizona (Formerly McMillan Gun Works)

SIGNATURE ALASKAN BOLT-ACTION RIFLE. . . . . NiB $3532 Ex $2811 Gd $1884
Same general specifications as Classic Sporter except w/match-grade bbl. Rings and mounts. Sights: Single-leaf rear, bbl. band front. Checkered Monte Carlo stock w/palmswell and solid recoil pad. Nickel finish. Calibers: LA (long): .270 Win., .280 Rem., .30-06, MA (Magnum): 7mm Rem. Mag., .300 Win. Mag., .300 Wby. Mag., .340 Wby. Mag., .358 Win., .375 H&H Mag. Made 1990 to date.

SIGNATURE CLASSIC SPORTER
The prototype for Harris' Signature Series, this bolt-action rifle is available in three lengths: SA (standard/ short) — from .22-250 to .350 Rem Mag.; LA (long) — .25-06 to .30-06; MA (Magnum) — 7mm STW to .416 Rem. Mag. Four-round or 3-round (Magnum) magazine. Bbl. lengths: 22, 24 or 26 inches. Weight: 7 lbs. (short action). No sights; rings and bases provided. Harris fiberglass stock, Fibergrain or wood stock optional. Stainless, matte black or black chrome sulfide finish. Available in right- and left-hand models. Made 1987 to date. Has pre-64 Model 70-style action for dangerous game.
Classic Sporter Standard . . . . . . NiB $2502 Ex $2193 Gd $1266
Classic Sporter Stainless . . . . . . NiB $2698 Ex $2219 Gd $1292
Talon Sporter. . . . . NiB $2708 Ex $1987 Gd $1369

SIGNATURE MOUNTAIN RIFLE. . . . . . NiB $3068 Ex $2708 Gd $1395
Same general specifications as Harris (McMillan) Classic Sporter except w/titanium action and graphite-reinforced fiberglass stock. Weight: 5.5 lbs. Calibers: .270 Win., .280 Rem., .30-06, 7mm Mag., .300 Win. Mag. Other calibers on special order. Made 1995 to date.

SIGNATURE SUPER VARMINTER . . . . . NiB $2502 Ex $2090 Gd $1266
Same general specifications as Harris (McMillan) Classic Sporter except w/heavy, contoured bbl., adj. trigger, fiberglass stock and field bipod. Calibers: .223, .22-250, .220 Swift, .244 Win., 6mm Rem., .25-06, 7mm-08, .308 Win., .350 Win. Mag. Made 1995 to date.

TALON SAFARI RIFLE
Same general specifications as Harris (McMillan) Classic Sporter except w/Harris Safari-grade action, match-grade bbl. and "Safari" fiberglass stock. Calibers: Magnum — .300 H&H Mag., .300 Win Mag., .300 Wby. Mag., .338 Win. Mag., .340 Wby. Mag., .375 H&H Mag., .404 Jeffrey, .416 Rem. Mag., .458 Win., Super Mag. — .300 Phoenix, .338 Lapua, .378 Wby. Mag., .416 Rigby, .416 Wby. Mag., .460 Wby. Mag. Matte black finish. Other calibers available on special order, and at a premium, but the "used gun" value remains the same. Imported 1989 to date.
Safari Magnum . . . . NiB $3789 Ex $2955 Gd $1935
Safari Super Magnum . . . . NiB $4195 Ex $3424 Gd $2437

HECKLER & KOCH, GMBH — Oberndorf/Neckar, Germany Imported by Heckler & Koch, Inc., Sterling, VA

MODEL 911 SEMIAUTO RIFLE. . . . . . . NiB $1822 Ex $1616 Gd $895
Caliber: .308 (7.62mm). Five-round magazine. 19.7-inch bull bbl. 42.4 inches overall. Sights: Hooded post front; adj. aperture rear. Weight: 11 lbs. Kevlar-reinforced fiberglass thumbhole-stock. Imported 1989-93.

MODEL HK91 A-2 SEMIAUTO . . . . . . NiB $2286 Ex $1977 Gd $1246
Delayed roller-locked blow-back action. Caliber: 7.62mmx51 NATO (308 Win.) 5- or 20-round box magazine. 19-inch bbl. Weight: W/o magazine, 9.37 lbs. Sights L "V" and aperture rear, post front. Plastic buttstock and forearm. Disc. 1991.

Heckler & Koch Model HK91 A-2

Heckler & Koch Model HK91 A-3

Heckler & Koch Model HK93 A-2

Heckler & Koch Model HK940 Carbine

MODEL HK91 A-3. . . . . NiB $2595 Ex $2337 Gd $1462
Same as Model HK91 A-2 except w/retractable metal buttstock, weighs 10.56 lbs. Disc. 1991.

MODEL HK93 SEMIAUTOMATIC
Delayed roller-locked blow-back action. Caliber: 5.56mm x 45 (.223 Rem.). 5- or 20-round magazine. 16.13-inch bbl. Weight: W/o magazine, 7.6 lbs. Sights: "V" and aperture rear; post front. Plastic buttstock and forearm. Disc. 1991.
HK93 A-2 . . . . NiB $2397 Ex $2234 Gd $1045
HK93 A-3 w/retractable stock. . . . . NiB $2440 Ex $2183 Gd $1925

MODEL HK94 SEMIAUTOMATIC CARBINE
Caliber: 9mm Para. 15-round magazine. 16-inch bbl. Weight: 6.75 lbs. Aperture rear sight, front post. Plastic buttstock and forend or retractable metal stock. Imported 1983-91.

(cont'd.) **MODEL HK94 SEMIAUTOMATIC CARBINE**
HK94-A2 w/standard stock. . . . . NiB $3120 Ex $3068 Gd $2605
HK94-A3 w/retractable stock . . . . NiB $4696 Ex $3764 Gd $2569

MODEL HK300
SEMIAUTOMATIC . . . . NiB $726 Ex $669 Gd $427
Caliber: .22 WMR. Five- or 15-round box magazine. 19.7-inch bbl. w/polygonal rifling. Weight: 5.75 lbs. Sights: V-notch rear; ramp front. High-luster polishing and bluing. European walnut stock w/cheekpiece, checkered forearm and pistol-grip. Disc. 1989.

MODEL HK630 SEMIAUTOMATIC. . . . . . NiB $1230 Ex $998 Gd $612
Caliber: .223 Rem. Four- or 10-round magazine. 24-inch bbl. Overall length: 42 inches. Weight: 7 lbs. Sights: Open rear; ramp front. European walnut stock w/Monte Carlo cheekpiece. Imported 1983-90.

Heckler & Koch
Model HK PSG-1

Heckler & Koch
Model SL-8

Heckler & Koch
Model USC Carbine

MODEL HK770 SEMIAUTOMATIC .... NiB $1900 Ex $1565 Gd $844
Caliber: .308 Win. Three- or 10-round magazine. Overall length: 44.5 inches. Weight: 8 lbs. Sights: Open rear; ramp front. European walnut stock w/Monte Carlo cheekpiece. Imported 1983-90.

MODEL HK940 SEMIAUTOMATIC .... NiB $2028 Ex $1822 Gd $973
Caliber: .30-06 Springfield. Three- or 10-round magazine. Overall length: 47 inches. Weight: 8.8 lbs. Sights: Open rear; ramp front. European walnut stock w/Monte Carlo cheekpiece. Imported 1983-90.

MODEL HK PSG-1
MARKSMAN'S RIFLE .... NiB $10,672 Ex $8547 Gd $5828
Caliber: .308 (7.62mm). Five- and 20-round magazine. 25.6-inch bbl. 47.5 inches overall. Hensoldt 6x42 telescopic sight. Weight: 17.8 lbs. Matte black composite stock w/pistol-grip. Imported 1988 to date.

MODEL SL8-1 RIFLE .... NiB $1668 Ex $1307 Gd $895
Caliber: .223 Win. Ten-round magazine. 20.80- inch bbl. 38.58 inches overall. Weight: 8.6 lbs. Gas-operated, short-stroke piston w/rotary locking bolt. Rear adjustable sight w/ambidextrous safety selector lever. Polymer receiver w/adjustable buttstock. Introduced 1999.

MODEL SR-9
SEMIAUTO RIFLE .... NiB $1822 Ex $1668 Gd $947
Caliber: .308 (7.62mm). Five round magazine. 19.7-inch bull bbl. 42.4 inches overall. Hooded post front sight; adj. aperture rear. Weight: 11 lbs. Kevlar-reinforced fiberglass thumbhole-stock w/wood grain finish. Imported 1989-93.

MODEL SR-9
TARGET RIFLE.................... NiB $2595 Ex $2028 Gd $1359
Same general specifications as standard SR-9 except w/ PSG-1 trigger group and adj. buttstock. Imported 1992-94.

MODEL USC
CARBINE RIFLE.................... NiB $1153 Ex $1045 Gd $689
Caliber: 45 ACP. 10-round magazine. 16- inch bbl., 35.43 inches overall. Weight: 6 lbs. Blow-back operating system. Polymer receiver w/integral grips. Rear adjustable sight w/ambidextrous safety selector lever. Introduced 1999.

HERCULES RIFLES

See listings under "W" for Montgomery Ward.

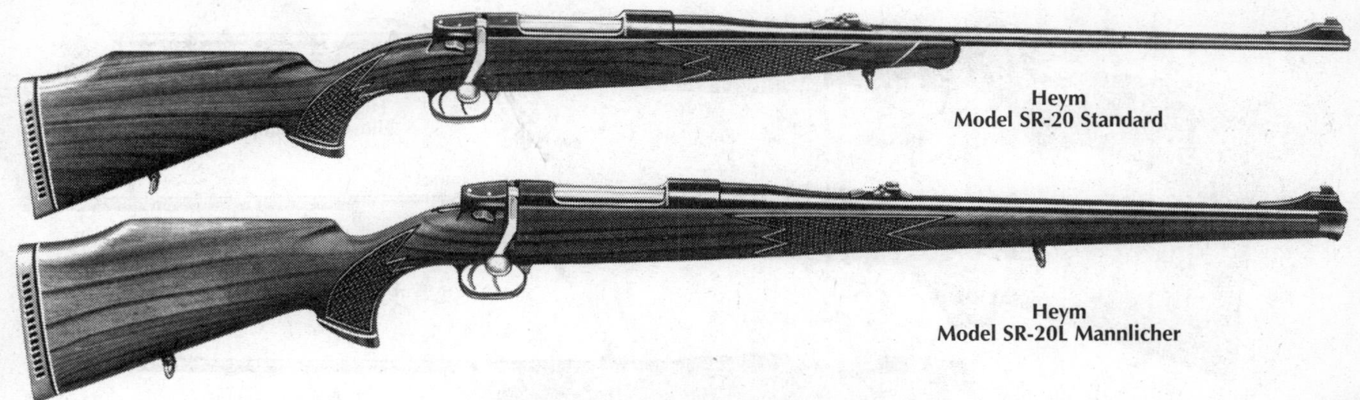

HEROLD RIFLE — Suhl,Germany Made by Franz Jaeger & Company

BOLT-ACTION REPEATING
SPORTING RIFLE. . . . . NiB $1297 Ex $1035 Gd $654
"Herold-Repetierbüchse." Miniature Mauser-type action w/unique 5-round box magazine on hinged floorplate. Double-set triggers. Caliber: .22 Hornet. 24-inch bbl. Sights: Leaf rear; ramp front. Weight: 7.75 lbs. Fancy checkered stock. Made before WWII. Note: These rifles were imported by Charles Daly and A.F. Stoeger Inc. of New York City and sold under their names.

HEYM RIFLES AMERICA, INC. — Mfd. By Heym, GmbH & Co JAGWAFFEN KD., Gleichamberg, Germany, *(Previously imported by Heym America, Inc.; Heckler & Koch; JagerSport, Ltd.)*

MODEL 55B O/U DOUBLE RIFLE
Kersten boxlock action w/double cross bolt and cocking indicators. Calibers: .308 Win., .30-06, .375 H&H, .458 Win. Mag., .470 N.E. 25-inch bbl. 42 inches overall. Weight: 8.25 lbs. Sights: fixed V-type rear; front ramp w/silver bead. Engraved receiver w/optional sidelocks, interchangeable bbls. and claw mounts. Checkered European walnut stock. Imported from Germany.
Model 55 (boxlock) . . . . NiB $7600 Ex $6200 Gd $5600
Model 55 (sidelock. . . . . NiB $12,038 Ex $9650 Gd $6594
W\Extra rifle bbls., add $5500
W/Extra shotgun bbls., add $2800

MODEL 88B DOUBLE RIFLE
Modified Anson & Deeley boxlock action w/standing gears, double underlocking lugs and Greener extension w/crossbolt. Calibers: 8x57 JRS, 9.3x74R, .30-06, .375 H&H, .458 Win. Mag., .470 Nitro Express, .500 Nitro Express. Other calibers available on special order. Weight: 8 to 10 lbs. Top tang safety and cocking indicators. Double triggers w/front set. Fixed or 3-leaf express rear sight, front ramp w/silver bead. Engraved receiver w/optional sidelocks. Checkered French walnut stock. Imported from Germany.
Model 88B Boxlock . . . . NiB $11,069 Ex $8875 Gd $6067
Model 88B/SS Sidelock. . . . . NiB $13,538 Ex $10,850 Gd $7410
Model 88B Safari (Magnum). . . . . . NiB $15,038 Ex $12,050 Gd $8226

EXPRESS BOLT-ACTION RIFLE
Same general specifications as Model SR-20 Safari except w/modified magnum Mauser action. Checkered AAA-grade European walnut stock w/cheekpiece, solid rubber recoil pad, rosewood forend tip and grip

***(cont'd.)* EXPRESS BOLT-ACTION RIFLE**
cap. Calibers: .338 Lapua Magnum, .375 H&H, .378 Wby. Mag., .416 Rigby .450 Ackley, .460 Wby. Mag., .500 A-Square, .500 Nitro Express, .600 Nitro Express. Other calibers available on special order, but no change in used gun value. Imported from Germany 1989-95.
Standard Express Magnum . . . . NiB $5288 Ex $4250 Gd $2922
600 Nitro Express. . . . . NiB $5600 Ex $4900 Gd $2900
Left-hand models, add $600

SR-20 BOLT-ACTION RIFLE
Calibers: .243 Win., .270 Win., .308 Win., .30-06, 7mm Rem. Mag., .300 Win. Mag., .375 H&H. Five round (standard) or 3-round (Magnum) magazine. Bbl. length: 20.5-inch (SR-20L); 24-inch (SR-20N); 26-inch (SR-20G). Weight: 7.75 lbs. Adj. rear sight, blade front. Checkered French walnut stock in Monte Carlo style (N&G Series) or full Mannlicher (L Series). Imported from Germany. Disc. 1992.
SR-20L. . . . . NiB $1980 Ex $1568 Gd $924
SR-20N . . . . NiB $2150 Ex $1743 Gd $1078
SR-20G . . . . NiB $2675 Ex $2108 Gd $1413

SR-20 CLASSIC BOLT-ACTION RIFLES
Same as SR-20 except w/.22-250 and .338 Win. Mag. plus metric calibers on request. 24-inch (standard) or 25-inch (Magnum) bbl. Checkered French walnut stock. Left-hand models. Imported from Germany since 1985; Sporter version 1989-93.
Classic (Standard) . . . . NiB $2255 Ex $1824 Gd $1272
Classic (Magnum) . . . . NiB $2495 Ex $2016 Gd $1302
Left-hand models, add. $300
Classic Sporter (Std.
w/22-inch bbl.) . . . . NiB $2409 Ex $1948 Gd $1357
Classic Sporter (Mag.
w/24-inch bbl.) . . . . NiB $2649 Ex $2139 Gd $1486

SR-20 ALPINE, SAFARI AND TROPHY SERIES
Same general specifications as Model SR-20 Classic Sporter except Alpine Series w/20-inch bbl., Mannlicher stock, chambered in standard calibers only; Safari Series w/24-inch bbl., 3-leaf express sights and magnum action in calibers .375 H & H, .404 Jeffrey, .425 Express, .458 Win. Mag.; Trophy Series w/Krupp-Special tapered octagon bbl. w/quarter rib and open sights, standard and Magnum calibers. Imported from Germany 1989-93.
Alpine Series . . . . NiB $2409 Ex $1948 Gd $1357
Safari Series. . . . . NiB $2456 Ex $1985 Gd $1381
Trophy Series (Stand. calibers) . . . . NiB $3113 Ex $2510 Gd $1739
Trophy Series
(Magnum calibers). . . . . NiB $3383 Ex $2726 Gd $1886

J.C. HIGGINS RIFLES

See Sears, Roebuck & Company.

High Standard Flite-King Pump

High Standard Hi-Power Deluxe

High Standard Sport-King Autoloading Carbine

High Standard Sport-King Deluxe Auto

High Standard Sport-King Field Auto

High Standard Sport-King Special Auto

HI-POINT FIREARMS — Dayton, Ohio

MODEL 995 CARBINE

Semiautomatic recoil-operated carbine. Calibers: 9mm Parabellum or 40 S&W. 10-round magazine. 16.5-inch bbl. 31.5 inches overall. Protected post front sight, aperture rear w/integral scope mount. Matte blue, chrome or Parkerized finish. Checkered polymer grip/frame. Made 1996 to date.

Model 995, 9mm (blue or Parkerized) . . . . . NiB $171 Ex $139 Gd $98
Model 995, .40 S&W (blue or Parkerized) . . . NiB $204 Ex $164 Gd $115
W/laser sights, add $35
W/chrome finish, add $15

HIGH STANDARD SPORTING FIREARMS — East Hartford, Connecticut, (Formerly High Standard Mfg. Co., Hamden, CT)

A long-standing producer of sporting arms, High Standard discontinued its operations in 1984.

FLITE-KING PUMP RIFLE . . . . NiB $164 Ex $113 Gd $72

Hammerless slide-action. Caliber: .22 LR. .22 Long, .22 Short. Tubular mag. holds 17 LR, 19 Long, or 24 Short. 24-inch bbl. Weight: 5.5 lbs. Sights: Partridge rear; bead front. Monte Carlo stock w/pistol grip, serrated semibeavertail forearm. Made 1962-75.

HI-POWER DELUXE RIFLE . . . . NiB $551 Ex $370 Gd $216

Mauser-type bolt action, sliding safety. Calibers: .270, .30-06. Four round magazine. 22-inch bbl. Weight: 7 lbs. Sights: Folding open rear; ramp front. Walnut stock w/checkered pistol-grip and forearm, Monte Carlo comb, QD swivels. Made 1962-66.

Holland & Holland
Best Quality Magazine

Holland & Holland
Royal Deluxe Double

Howa
Model 1500 Hunter

Howa
Model 1500 Lightning

HI-POWER FIELD BOLT-ACTION RIFLE. . . . . NiB $473 Ex $319 Gd $190
Same as Hi-Power Deluxe except w/plain field style stock. Made 1962-66.

**SPORT-KING AUTO-
LOADING CARBINE . . . . NiB $159 Ex $98 Gd $77**
Same as Sport-King Field Autoloader except w/18.25-inch bbl., Western-style straight-grip stock w/bbl. band, sling and swivels. Made 1964-73.

SPORT-KING DELUXE AUTOLOADER . . . . NiB $237 Ex $185 Gd $82
Same as Sport-King Special Autoloader except w/checkered stock. Made 1966-75.

SPORT-KING FIELD AUTOLOADER . . . . NiB $118 Ex $98 Gd $62
Calibers: .22 LR. .22 Long, .22 Short (high speed). Tubular magazine holds 15 LR, 17 Long, or 21 Short. 22.25-inch bbl. Weight: 5.5 lbs. Sights: Open rear; beaded post front. Plain pistol-grip stock. Made 1960-66.

SPORT-KING SPECIAL AUTOLOADER . . . . NiB $185 Ex $139 Gd $82
Same as Sport-King Field except stock w/Monte Carlo comb and semibeavertail forearm. Made 1960-66.

HOLLAND & HOLLAND, LTD. — London, England, *Imported by Holland & Holland, NY, NY*

**NO. 2 MODEL HAMMERLESS
EJECTOR DOUBLE RIFLE . . . . NiB $14,943 Ex $11,955 Gd $8131**
Same general specifications as Royal Model except plainer finish. Disc. 1960.

BEST QUALITY MAGAZINE RIFLE . . . . NiB $14,380 Ex $11,505 Gd $7825
Mauser or Enfield action. Calibers: .240 Apex, .300 H&H Mag., .375 H&H Magnum. Four round box magazine. 24-inch bbl. Weight: 7.25 lbs., 240 Apex; 8.25 lbs., .300 Mag. and .375 Mag. Sights: Folding leaf rear; hooded ramp front. Detachable French walnut stock w/cheekpiece, checkered pistol-grip and forearm, swivels. Currently mfd. Specifications given apply to most models.

DELUXE MAGAZINE RIFLE . . . . . . NiB $15,943 Ex $12,755 Gd $8675
Same specifications as Best Quality except w/exhibition-grade stock and special engraving. Currently mfd.

**ROYAL HAMMERLESS
EJECTOR RIFLE. . . . . NiB $40,630 Ex $32,505 Gd $22,105**
Sidelock. Calibers: .240 Apex, 7mm H&H Mag., .300 H&H Mag., .300 Win. Mag., .30-06, .375 H&H Mag., .458 Win. Mag., .465 H&H Mag. 24- to 28-inch bbls. Weight: From 7.5 lbs. Sights: Folding leaf rear, ramp front. Cheekpiece stock of select French walnut, checkered pistol-grip and forearm. Currently mfd. Same general specifications apply to prewar model.

ROYAL DELUXE DOUBLE RIFLE . . . . NiB $56,880 Ex $45,505 Gd $30,945
Formerly designated "Modele Deluxe." Same specifications as Royal Model except w/exhibition-grade stock and special engraving. Currently mfd.

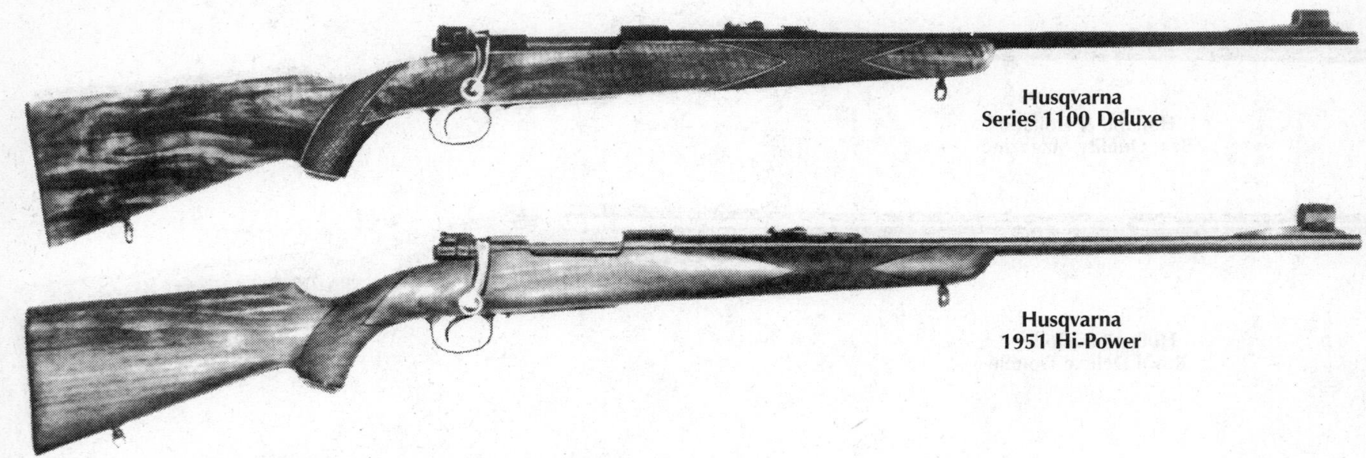

HOWA RIFLES — Mfg. By Howa Machinery Ltd., Shinkawa-Chonear, Nagoya 452, Japan, *Imported by Interarms, Alexandria, VA*

See also Mossberg (1500) Smith & Wesson (1500 & 1700) and Weatherby (Vanguard).

MODEL 1500 HUNTER
Similar to Trophy Model except w/standard walnut stock. No Monte Carlo cheekpiece or grip cap. Imported 1988-89.
Standard calibers .... NiB $473 Ex $422 Gd $293
Magnum calibers .... NiB $454 Ex $370 Gd $263
Stainless steel, add.................................. $85

MODEL 1500 LIGHTNING BOLT-ACTION RIFLE
Similar to Hunter Model except fitted w/black Bell & Carlson Carbelite stock w/checkered grip and forend. Weight: 7.5 lbs. Imported 1988-89.
Standard calibers .... NiB $437 Ex $350 Gd $211
Magnum calibers .... NiB $454 Ex $370 Gd $263

MODEL 1500 PCS BOLT-ACTION RIFLE
Similar to Hunter Model except in Police Counter Sniper configuration and chambered for .308 Win. only. Walnut or synthetic stock w/checkered grip and forend. Receiver drilled and tapped but w/o sights. Weight: 8.5 to 9.3 lbs. Imported 1999 to date.
PCS Model w/walnut stock ...... NiB $437 Ex $350 Gd $211
PCS Model w/synthetic stock ..... NiB $416 Ex $345 Gd $254
Stainless steel, add $85

MODEL 1500 REALTREE CAMO RIFLE .... NiB $499 Ex $422 Gd $293
Similar to Trophy Model except fitted w/Camo Bell & Carlson Carbelite stock w/checkered grip and forend. Weight: 8 lbs. Stock, action and barrel finished in Realtree camo. Available in standard calibers only. Imported 1993 to date.

MODEL 1500 TROPHY/VARMINT BOLT-ACTION RIFLE
Calibers: .22-250, .223, .243 Win., .270 Win., .308 Win., .30-06, 7mm Mag., .300 Win. Mag.,. .338 Win. Mag. 22-inch bbl. (standard); 24-inch bbl. (Magnum). 42.5 inches overall (standard). Weight: 7.5 lbs. Adj. rear sight hooded ramp front. Checkered walnut stock w/Monte Carlo cheekpiece. Varmint Model w/24-inch heavy bbl., weight of 9.5 lbs. in calibers .22-250, .223 and .308 only. Imported 1979-93.
Trophy Standard .... NiB $554 Ex $432 Gd $257
Trophy Magnum .... NiB $514 Ex $417 Gd $293
Varmint (Parkerized finish) .... NiB $422 Ex $340 Gd $235
Stainless steel, add $85

MODEL 1500 WOODGRAIN LIGHTNING RIFLE
Calibers: .243, .270, 7mm Rem. Mag., .30-06. Mag. Five round magazine 22-inch. 42 inches overall. Weight: 7.5 lbs. Receiver drilled and tapped for scope mount, no sights. Checkered woodgrain synthetic polymer stock. Imported 1993-94.
Standard calibers .... NiB $473 Ex $412 Gd $242
Magnum calibers .... NiB $539 Ex $437 Gd $308

H-S PRECISION — Rapid City, South Dakota

PRO-SERIES
Custom rifle built on Remington 700 bolt action. Calibers: .22 to .416, 24- or 26-inch bbl. w/fluted option. Aluminum bedding block system w/take-down option. Kevlar/carbon fiber stock to customer's specifications. Appointments and options to customer's preference. Made 1990 to date.
Sporter model..................... NiB $2054 Ex $1719 Gd $998
Pro-Hunter model (PHR)........... NiB $1726 Ex $1385 Gd $948
Long-Range Model .... NiB $1951 Ex $1642 Gd $921
Long-Range takedown model................. NiB $2274 Ex $1822 Gd $1246
Marksman model .... NiB $2054 Ex $1719 Gd $998
Marksman takedown model .... NiB $2379 Ex $1900 Gd $1256
Varmint takedown model (VTD).................... NiB $2028 Ex $1694 Gd $973
Left-hand models, add................................. $200

HUNGARIAN MILITARY RIFLES — Budapest, Hungary, Manufactured at Government Arsenal

MODEL 1935M MANNLICHER MILITARY RIFLE .... NiB $293 Ex $242 Gd $139
Caliber: 8x52mm Hungarian. Bolt action, straight handle. Five round projecting box magazine. 24-inch bbl. Weight: 9 lbs. Adj. leaf rear sight, hooded front blade. Two-piece military-type stock. Made 1935-40.

MODEL 1943M (GERMAN GEW 98/40) MANNLICHER MILITARY RIFLE .... NiB $345 Ex $267 Gd $164
Modification, during German occupation, of Model 1935M. Caliber: 7.9mm Mauser. Turned-down bolt handle and Mauser M/98-type box magazine; other differences are minor. Made 1940 to end of war in Europe.

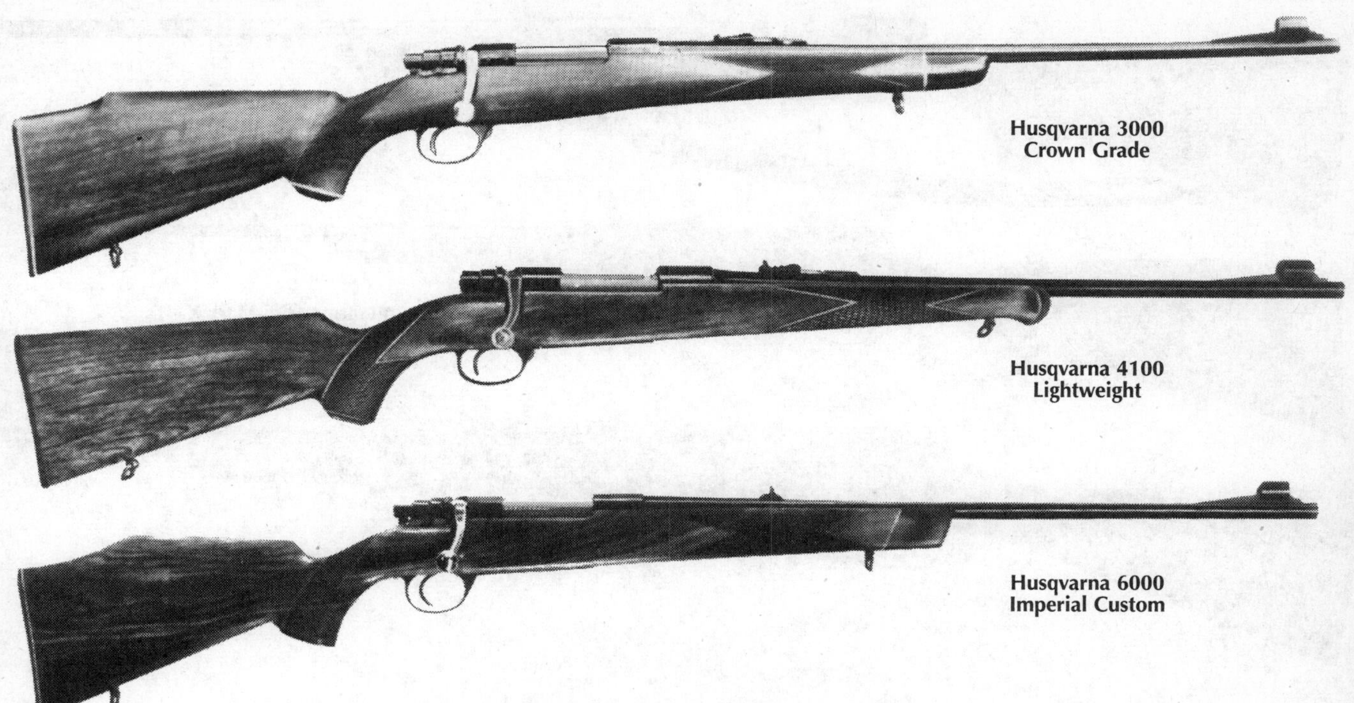

HUSQVARNA VAPENFABRIK A.B. — Husqvarna, Sweden

MODEL 456 LIGHTWEIGHT FULL-STOCK SPORTER .... NiB $525 Ex $422 Gd $293
Same as Series 4000/4100 except w/sporting style full stock w/slope-away cheekrest. Weight: 6.5 lbs. Made 1959-70.

SERIES 1000 SUPER GRADE ...... NiB $519 Ex $417 Gd $287
Same as 1951 Hi-Power except w/European walnut sporter stock w/Monte Carlo comb and cheekpiece. Made 1952-56.

SERIES 1100 DELUXE MODEL HI-POWER BOLT-ACTION SPORTING RIFLE .... NiB $525 Ex $422 Gd $290
Same as 1951 Hi-Power, except w/jeweled bolt, European walnut stock. Made 1952-56.

1950 HI-POWER SPORTING RIFLE ...... NiB $461 Ex $370 Gd $255
Mauser-type bolt action. Calibers: .220 Swift, .270 Win. .30-06 (see note below), 5-round box magazine. 23.75-inch bbl. Weight: 7.75 lbs. Sights: Open rear; hooded ramp front. Sporting stock of Arctic beech, checkered pistol grip and forearm, swivels. Note: Husqvarna sporters were first intro. in U.S. about 1948; earlier models were also available in calibers 6.5x55, 8x57 and 9.3x57. Made 1946-1951.

1951 HI-POWER RIFLE .... NiB $493 Ex $396 Gd $273
Same as 1950 Hi-Power except w/high-comb stock, low safety.

SERIES 3000 CROWN GRADE .... NiB $499 Ex $370 Gd $242
Same as Series 3100, except w/Monte Carlo comb stock.

SERIES 3100 CROWN GRADE .... NiB $499 Ex $370 Gd $242
HVA improved Mauser action. Calibers: .243, .270, 7mm, .30-06, .308 Win. Five round box magazine. 23.75-inch bbl. Weight: 7.75 lbs. Sights: Open rear; hooded ramp front. European walnut stock, checkered, cheekpiece, pistol-grip cap, black forend tip, swivels. Made 1954-72.

SERIES 4000 LIGHTWEIGHT RIFLE ..... NiB $499 Ex $370 Gd $242
Same as Series 4100 except w/Monte Carlo comb stock and no rear sight.

SERIES 4100 LIGHTWEIGHT RIFLE ...... NiB $494 Ex $370 Gd $216
HVA improved Mauser action. Calibers: .243, .270, 7mm, .30-06, .308 Win. Five round box magazine. 20.5-inch bbl. Weight: 6.25 lbs. Sights: Open rear; hooded ramp front. Lightweight walnut stock w/cheekpiece, pistol grip, Schnabel forend tip, checkered, swivels. Made 1954-72. See illustration previous page.

SERIES 6000 IMPERIAL CUSTOM GRADE . NiB $654 Ex $525 Gd $345
Same as Series 3100 except fancy-grade stock, 3-leaf folding rear sight, adj. trigger. Calibers: .243, .270, 7mm Rem. Mag. .308, .30-06. Made 1968-70. See illustration previous page.

SERIES 7000 IMPERIAL MONTE CARLO LIGHTWEIGHT... NiB $679 Ex $525 Gd $345
Same as Series 4000 Lightweight except fancy-grade stock, 3-leaf folding rear sight, adj. trigger. Calibers: .243, .270, .308, .30-06. Made 1968-70.

MODEL 8000 IMPERIAL GRADE RIFLE ... NiB $679 Ex $525 Gd $345
Same as Model 9000 except w/jeweled bolt, engraved floorplate, deluxe French walnut checkered stock, no sights. Made 1971-72.

MODEL 9000 CROWN GRADE RIFLE .... NiB $525 Ex $422 Gd $319
New design Husqvarna bolt action. Adj. trigger. Calibers: .270, 7mm Rem. Mag., .30-06, .300 Win. Mag. Five round box magazine, hinged floorplate. 23.75-inch bbl. Sights: Folding leaf rear; hooded ramp front. Checkered walnut stock w/Monte Carlo cheekpiece, rosewood forend tip and pistol-grip cap. Weight: 7 lbs. 3 oz. Made 1971-72.

SERIES P-3000 PRESENTATION RIFLE .... NiB $834 Ex $679 Gd $448
Same as Crown Grade Series 3000 except w/selected stock, engraved action, adj. trigger. Calibers: .243, .270, 7mm Rem. Mag., .30-06. Made 1968-70.

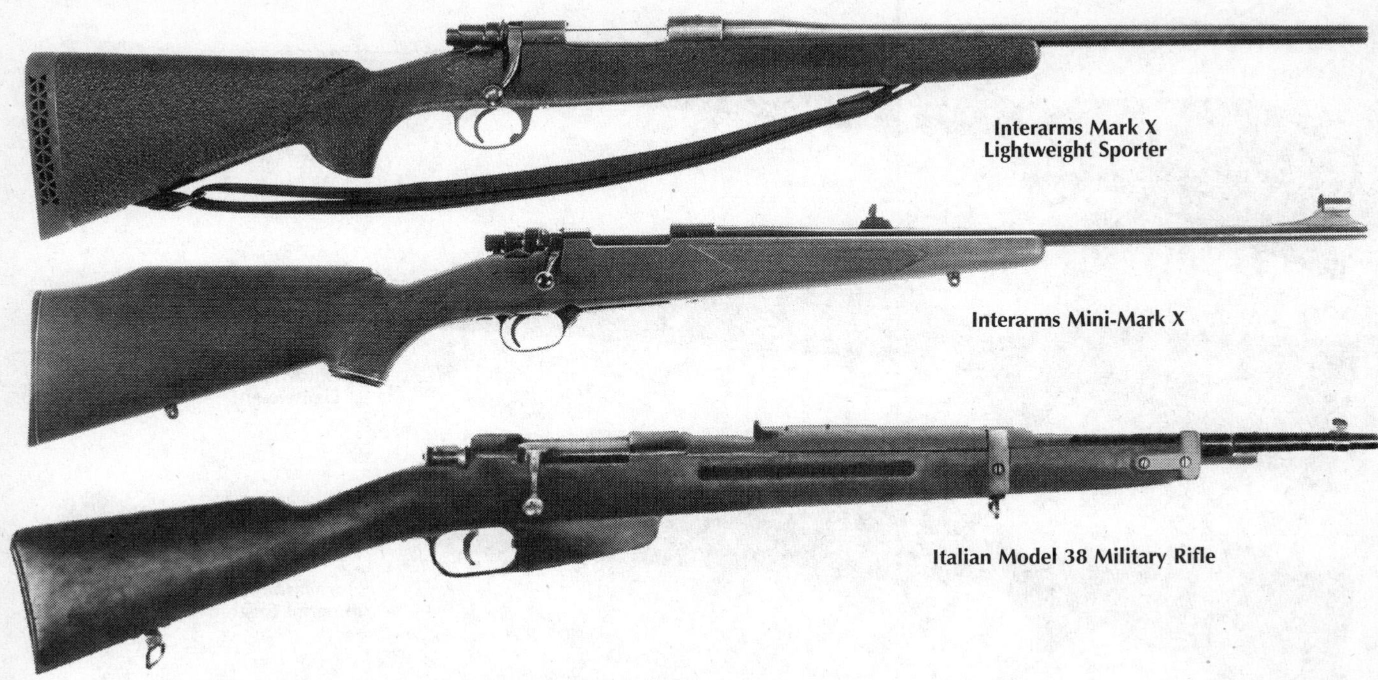

Interarms Mark X Lightweight Sporter

Interarms Mini-Mark X

Italian Model 38 Military Rifle

INTERARMS RIFLES — Alexandria, Virginia

The following Mark X rifles are manufactured by Zavodi Crvena Zastava, Belgrade, Yugoslavia.

MARK X ALASKAN . . . . NiB $494 Ex $367 Gd $265
Same specifications as Mark X Sporter, except chambered for .375 H&H Mag. and .458 Win. Mag. w/3-round magazine. Stock w/recoil-absorbing cross bolt and heavy duty recoil pad. Weighs 8.25 lbs. Made 1976-84.

MARK X BOLT-ACTION SPORTER SERIES
Mauser-type action. Calibers: .22-250, .243, .25-06, .270, 7x57, 7mm Rem. Mag., .308, .30-06, .300 Win. Mag. Five round magazine (3-round in magnum calibers). 24-inch bbl. Weight: 7.5 lbs. Sights: Adj. leaf rear; ramp front, w/hood. Classic-style stock of European walnut w/Monte Carlo comb and cheekpiece, checkered pistol grip and forearm, black forend tip, QD swivels. Made 1972-97.

Mark X Standard . . . . NiB $386 Ex $311 Gd $215
Mark X Camo (Realtree) . . . . NiB $488 Ex $392 Gd $270
American Field, std.
(rubber recoil pad) . . . . NiB $603 Ex $484 Gd $332
American Field, Magnum
(rubber recoil pad) . . . . NiB $641 Ex $515 Gd $354

MARK X CAVALIER . . . . NiB $392 Ex $316 Gd $214
Same specifications as Mark X Sporter except w/contemporary-style stock w/rollover cheekpiece, rosewood forend tip/grip cap, recoil pad. Intro. 1974; Disc.

MARK X CONTINENTAL
MANNLICHER STYLE CARBINE . . . . NiB $418 Ex $367 Gd $239
Same specifications as Mark X Sporter except straight European-style comb stock w/sculptured cheekpiece. Precise double-set triggers and classic "butterknife" bolt handle. French checkering. Weight: 7.25 lbs. Disc.

MARK X LIGHTWEIGHT SPORTER . . . . . . NiB $367 Ex $306 Gd $214
Calibers: .22-250 Rem., .270 Win., 7mm Rem. Mag., .30-06 or 7mm Mag. Four- or 5-round magazine. 20-inch bbl. Synthenic Carbolite stock Weight: 7 lbs. Imported 1988-90. (Reintroduced 1994-97.)

MARK X MARQUIS
MANNLICHER STYLE CARBINE . . . . NiB $450 Ex $362 Gd $250
Same specifications as Mark X Sporter except w/20-inch bbl., full-length Mannlicher-type stock w/metal forend/muzzle cap. Calibers: .270, 7x57, .308, .30-06. Imported 1976-84.

MINI-MARK X BOLT-ACTION
RIFLE. . . . . NiB $392 Ex $311 Gd $214
Miniature M98 Mauser action. Caliber: .223 Rem. Five round magazine. 20-inch bbl. 39.75 inches overall. Weight: 6.25 lbs. Adj. rear sight, hooded ramp front. Checkered hardwood stock. Imported 1987-94.

MARK X VISCOUNT . . . . NiB $392 Ex $316 Gd $214
Same specifications as Mark X Sporter except w/plainer field grade stock. Imported 1974-87.

AFRICAN SERIES . . . . NiB $647 Ex $561 Gd $367
Mauser-type bolt-action. Calibers: .375 H&H Mag., .458 Win. Mag. Three round magazine. 24-inch bbl. Weight: 8 lbs. Sights: 3-leaf express open rear, ramp front w/hood. English-style stock of European walnut, w/cheekpiece, black forend tip, checkered pistol grip and forearm, recoil pad, QD swivels. Imported 1974-96 by Whitworth Rifle Co., England.

ITALIAN MILITARY RIFLES
Manufactured by government plants at Brescia, Gardone, Terni and Turin, Italy

MODEL 38 MILITARY RIFLE . . . . NiB $107 Ex $97 Gd $56
Modification of Italian Model 1891 Mannlicher-Carcano Military Rifle w/turned-down bolt handle, detachable folding bayonet. Caliber: 7.35mm Italian Service (many arms of this model were later converted to the old 6.5mm caliber). Six round box magazine. 21.25-inch bbl. Weight: 7.5 lbs. Sights: Adj. rear-blade front. Military straight-grip stock. Adopted 1938.

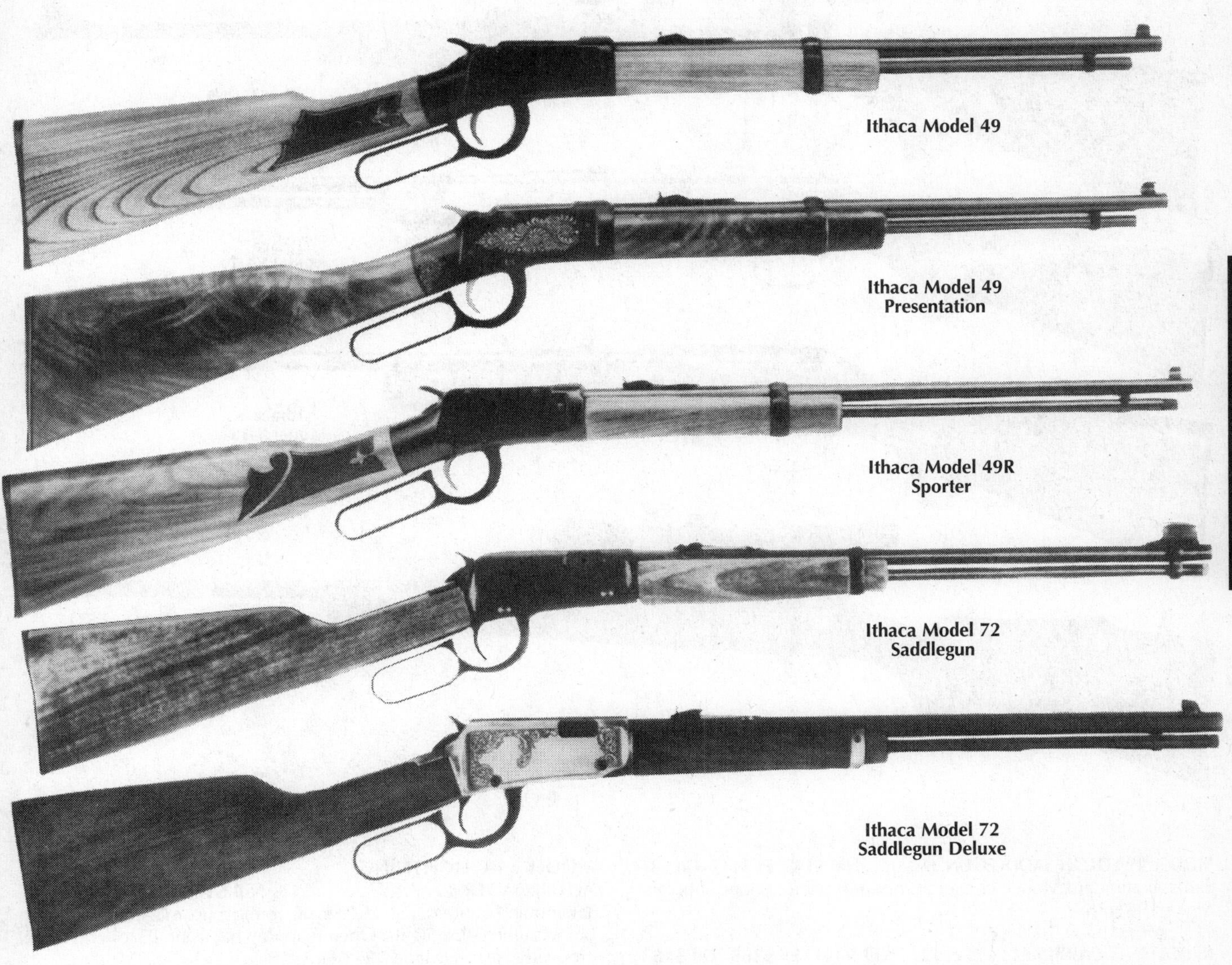

Ithaca Model 49

Ithaca Model 49 Presentation

Ithaca Model 49R Sporter

Ithaca Model 72 Saddlegun

Ithaca Model 72 Saddlegun Deluxe

ITHACA GUN COMPANY, INC. — King Ferry, New York, (Formerly Ithaca, NY)

MODEL 49 SADDLEGUN LEVER ACTION SINGLE-SHOT RIFLE .... NiB $158 Ex $143 Gd $71
Martini-type action. Hand-operated rebounding hammer. Caliber: .22 LR. Long, Short. 18-inch bbl. Open sights. Western carbine-style stock. Weight: 5.5 lbs. Made 1961-78.

MODEL 49 SADDLEGUN — DELUXE ..... NiB $188 Ex $137 Gd $86
Same as standard Model 49 except w/gold-plated hammer and trigger, figured walnut stock, sling swivels. Made 1962-75.

MODEL 49 SADDLEGUN — MAGNUM .. NiB $183 Ex $163 Gd $102
Same as standard Model 49 except chambered for .22 WMR cartridge. Made 1962-78.

MODEL 49 SADDLEGUN —PRESENTATION.................... NiB $306 Ex $290 Gd $132
Same as standard Model 49 Saddlegun except w/gold-plated hammer and trigger, engraved receiver, full fancy-figured walnut stock w/gold nameplate. Available in .22 LR or .22 WMR. Made 1962-74.

MODEL 49 SADDLEGUN — ST. LOUIS BICENTENNIAL..... NiB $306 Ex $290 Gd $132
Same as Model 49 Deluxe except w/commemorative inscription. 200 made in 1964. Top value is for rifle in new, unfired condition.

MODEL 49R SADDLEGUN REPEATING RIFLE .... NiB $280 Ex $260 Gd $112
Similar in appearance to Model 49 Single-Shot. Caliber: .22 LR. Long, Short. Tubular magazine holds 15 LR, 17 Long, 21 Short. 20-inch bbl. Weight: 5.5 lbs. Sights: Open rear-bead front. Western-style stock, checkered grip. Made 1968-71.

MODEL 49 YOUTH SADDLEGUN . . . . NiB $148 Ex $112 Gd $81
Same as standard Model 49 except shorter stock for young shooters. Made 1961-78.

REPEATING CARBINE . . . . NiB $341 Ex $265 Gd $163
Caliber: .22 LR. Long, Short. Tubular magazine holds 15 LR, 17 Long, 21 Short. 18.5-inch bbl. Weight: 5.5 lbs. Sights: Open rear; hooded ramp front. Receiver grooved for scope mounting. Western carbine stock and forearm of American walnut. Made 1973-78.

MODEL 72 SADDLEGUN — DELUXE . . . . NiB $392 Ex $316 Gd $204
Same as standard Model 72 except w/silver-finished and engraved receiver, octagon bbl., higher grade walnut stock and forearm. Made 1974-76.

MODEL LSA-65 BOLT ACTION STANDARD GRADE . . . . . NiB $443 Ex $392 Gd $265
Same as Model LSA-55 Standard Grade except calibers .25-06, .270, .30-06; 4-round magazine, 23-inch bbl., weight: 7 lbs. Made 1969-77.

MODEL LSA-65 DELUXE . . . . NiB $520 Ex $469 Gd $290
Same as Model LSA-65 Standard Grade except w/special features of Model LSA-55 Deluxe. Made 1969-77.

MODEL X5-C LIGHTNING AUTOLOADER . . . . NiB $188 Ex $137 Gd $86
Takedown. Caliber: .22 LR. Seven round clip magazine. 22-inch bbl. Weight: 6 lbs. Sights: Open rear; Ray-bar front. Pistol-grip stock, grooved forearm. Made 1958-64.

MODEL X5-T LIGHTNING AUTOLOADER TUBULAR REPEATING RIFLE . . . . NiB $188 Ex $137 Gd $86
Same as Model X5-C except w/16-round tubular magazine, stock w/plain forearm.

MODEL X-15 LIGHTNING AUTOLOADER . . . . NiB $174 Ex $153 Gd $86
Same general specifications as Model X5-C except forend is not grooved. Made 1964-67.

BSA CF-2 BOLT-ACTION REPEATING RIFLE . . . . NiB $316 Ex $290 Gd $183
Mauser-type action. Calibers: 7mm Rem. Mag., .300 Win. Mag. Three round magazine. 23.6-inch bbl. Weight: 8 lbs. Sights: Adj. rear; hooded ramp front. Checkered walnut stock w/Monte Carlo comb, rollover cheekpiece, rosewood forend tip, recoil pad, sling swivels. Imported 1976-77. Mfd. by BSA Guns Ltd., Birmingham, England.

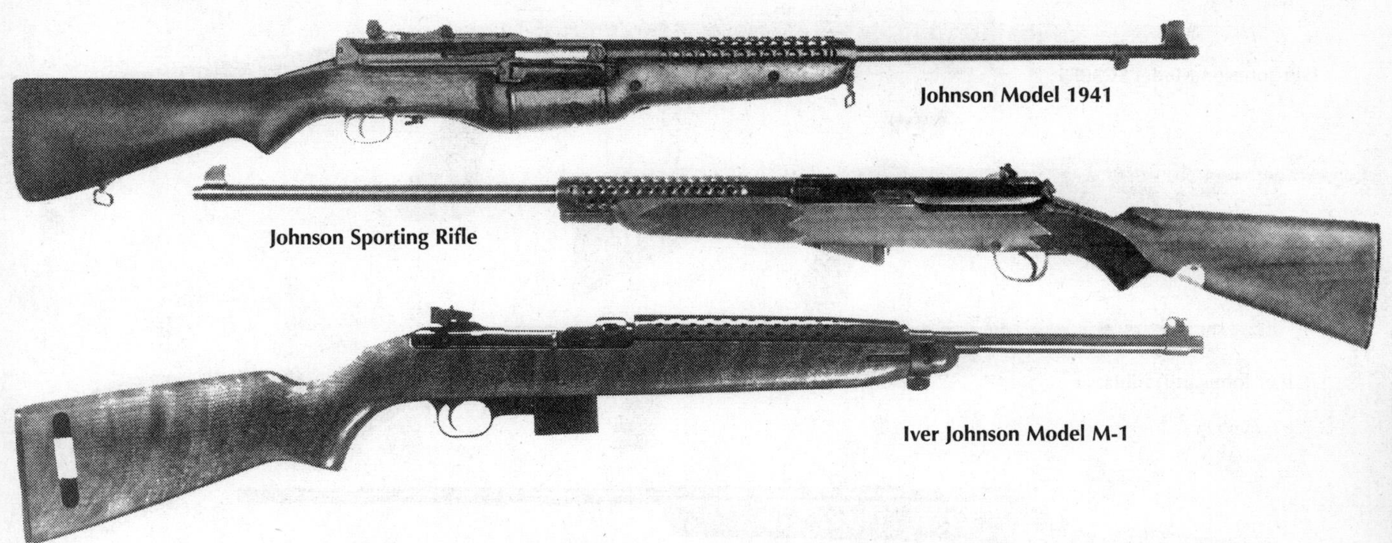

Johnson Model 1941

Johnson Sporting Rifle

Iver Johnson Model M-1

JAPANESE MILITARY RIFLES — Tokyo, Japan Manufactured by Government Plant

MODEL 38 ARISAKA SERVICE RIFLE . . . . . NiB $494 Ex $341 Gd $188
Mauser-type bolt action. Caliber: 6.5mm Japanese. Five round box magazine. Bbl. lengths: 25.38 and 31.25 inches. Weight: 9.25 lbs. w/long bbl. Sights: fixed front, adj. rear. Military-type full stock. Adopted in 1905, the 38th year of the Meiji reign hence, the designation "Model 38."

MODEL 38 ARISAKA CARBINE. . . . NiB $494 Ex $341 Gd $188
Same general specifications as Model 38 Rifle except w/19-inch bbl., heavy folding bayonet, weight 7.25 lbs.

MODEL 44 CAVALRY CARBINE . . . NiB $673 Ex $596 Gd $316
Same general specifications as Model 38 Rifle except w/19-inch bbl., heavy folding bayonet, weight 8.5 lbs. Adopted in 1911, the 44th year of the Meiji reign, hence the designation, "Model 44."

MODEL 99 SERVICE RIFLE . . . . NiB $398 Ex $214 Gd $163
Modified Model 38. Caliber: 7.7mm Japanese. Five round box magazine. 25.75-inch bbl. Weight: 8.75 lbs. Sights: Fixed front; adj. aperture rear; anti-aircraft sighting bars on some early models; fixed rear sight on some late WWII rifles. Military-type full stock, may have bipod. Takedown paratroop model was also made during WWII. Adopted in 1939, (Japanese year 2599) from which the designation "Model 99" is taken. Note: The last Model 99 rifles made were of poor quality; some with cast steel receivers. Value shown is for earlier type.

JARRETT CUSTOM RIFLES — Jackson, South Carolina

MODEL NO. 2 WALKABOUT
BOLT-ACTION RIFLE. . . . . NiB $3007 Ex $2656 Gd $1626
Custom lightweight rifle built on Remington M700 action. Jarrett match- grade barrel cut and chambered to customer's specification in short action calibers only. McMillan fiberglass stock pillar-bedded to action and finished to customer's preference.

MODEL NO. 3 CUSTOM
BOLT-ACTION RIFLE. . . . . NiB $2991 Ex $2502 Gd $1549
Custom rifle built on Remington M700 action. Jarrett match grade barrel cut and chambered to customer's specification. McMillan classic fiberglass stock pillar-bedded to action and finished to customer's preference. made 1989 to date.

MODEL NO. 4 PROFESSIONAL
HUNTER BOLT-ACTION RIFLE . . . . . NiB $6673 Ex $5592 Gd $4253
Custom magnum rifle built on Winchester M70 "controlled feed" action. Jarrett match grade barrel cut and chambered to customer's specification in magnum calibers only. Quarter rib w/iron sights and two Leupold scopes w/Q-D rings and mounts. McMillan classic fiberglass stock fitted and finished to customer's preference.

JOHNSON AUTOMATICS, INC. — Providence, Rhode Island

MODEL 1941 SEMIAUTO
MILITARY RIFLE . . . . NiB $2500 Ex $1575 Gd $1200
Short-recoil operated. Removable, air-cooled, 22-inch bbl. Caliber: .30-06, 7mm Mauser. 10-round rotary magazine. Two-piece wood stock, pistol grip, perforated metal radiator sleeve over rear half of bbl. Sights: Receiver peep; protected post front. Weight: 9.5 lbs. Note: The Johnson M/1941 was adopted by the Netherlands government in 1940-41 and the major portion of the production of this rifle, 1941-43, was on Dutch orders. A quantity was also bought by the U.S. government for use by Marine Corps parachute troops (1943) and for Lend Lease. All these rifles were caliber .30-06; the 7mm Johnson rifles were made for the South American government.

SPORTING RIFLE PROTOTYPE. . . . NiB $13,750 Ex $11,000 Gd $7480
Same general specifications as military rifle except fitted w/sporting stock, checkered grip and forend. Blade front sight; receiver peep sight. Less than a dozen made prior to World War II.

IVER JOHNSON ARMS, INC. — Jacksonville, Arkansas, (Formerly of Fitchburg, Massachusetts, and Middlesex, New Jersey)

LI'L CHAMP BOLT-ACTION RIFLE . . . . NiB $98 Ex $72 Gd $56
Caliber: .22 S. L. LR. Single-shot. 16.25-inch bbl. 32.5 inches overall. Weight: 3.25 lbs. Adj. rear sight, blade front. Synthetic composition stock. Made 1986-88.

Iver Johnson Model SC30FS

Iver Johnson Survival Semiautomatic Carbine

Iver Johnson Trailblazer

Iver Johnson Model XX (2X) Bolt-Action Rifle

MODEL M-1 SEMIAUTOMATIC CARBINE
Similar to U.S. M-1 Carbine. Calibers: 9mm Parabellum 30 U.S. Carbine. 15- or 30-round magazine. 18-inch bbl. 35.5 inches overall. Weight: 6.5 lbs. Sights: blade front, w/guards; adj. peep rear. Walnut, hardwood or collapsible wire stock. Parkerized finish.
Model M-1 (30 cal. w/hardwood). . . . . NiB $345 Ex $267 Gd $164
Model M-1 (30 cal. w/walnut) . . . . NiB $370 Ex $278 Gd $175
Model M-1 (30 cal. w/wire) . . . . NiB $422 Ex $345 Gd $180
Model M-1 (9mm w/hardwood) . . . . NiB $252 Ex $237 Gd $201
Model M-1 (9mm w/walnut). . . . . NiB $314 Ex $267 Gd $206
Model M-1 (9mm w/wire) . . . . NiB $370 Ex $309 Gd $195

MODEL PM.30
SEMIAUTOMATIC CARBINE . . . . . . NiB $350 Ex $267 Gd $164
Similar to U.S. Carbine, Cal. 30 M1. 18-inch bbl. Weight: 5.5 lbs. 15- or 30-round detachable magazine. Both hardwood and walnut stock.

MODEL SC30FS
SEMIAUTOMATIC CARBINE . . . . . . NiB $422 Ex $345 Gd $180
Similar to Survival Carbine except w/folding stock. Made 1983 to date.

SURVIVAL SEMIAUTOMATIC CARBINE . . NiB $396 Ex $370 Gd $190
Similar to Model PM.30 except in stainless steel. Made 1983 to date. W/folding high-impact plastic stock add $35.

TRAILBLAZER SEMIAUTO RIFLE . . . . NiB $134 Ex $118 Gd $98
Caliber: .22 LR. 18-inch bbl. Weight: 5.5 lbs. Sights: Open rear, blade front. Hardwood stock. Made 1983-85

MODEL X BOLT-ACTION RIFLE . . . . NiB $123 Ex $103 Gd $72
Takedown, Single-shot. Caliber: .22 Short, Long and LR. 22-inch bbl. Weight: 4 lbs. Sights: Open rear; blade front. Pistol-grip stock w/knob forend tip. Made 1928-32.

MODEL XX (2X) BOLT-ACTION RIFLE . . . . . NiB $134 Ex $98 Gd $77
Improved version of Model X w/heavier 24-inch bbl. larger stock (w/o knob tip), weight: 4.5 lbs. Made 1932-55.

MODEL 5100A1
BOLT-ACTION RIFLE . . . . NiB $5144 Ex $4115 Gd $2799
Single-shot long-range rifle w/removable bolt for breech loading. Caliber: 50BMG. Fluted 29-inch bbl. w/muzzle brake. 51.5 inches overall. Adj. composition stock w/folding bipod. Scope rings; no sights.

K.B.I., INC. — Harrisburg, Pennsylvania

See listing under Armscor; Charles Daly; FEG; Liberty and I.M.I.

SUPER CLASSIC
Calibers: .22 LR, .22 Mag., RF, .22 Hornet. Five- or 10-round capacity. Bolt and semiauto action. 22.6- or 20.75-inch bbl. 41.25 or 40.5 inches overall. Weight: 6.4 to 6.7 lbs. Blue finish. Oil-finished American walnut stock w/hardwood grip cap and forend tip. Checkered Monte Carlo comb and cheekpiece. High polish blued barreled action w/damascened bolt. Dovetailed receiver and iron sights. Recoil pad. QD swivel posts.
.22 Long Rifle (M-1500 SC). . . . . NiB $232 Ex $190 Gd $135
.22 Magnum Rimfire (M-1500 SC) . . . . NiB $258 Ex $211 Gd $150
.22 Hornet (M-1800-S) . . . . NiB $400 Ex $324 Gd $227
.22 Long Rifle Semiauto (M-2000 SC). . . . . NiB $258 Ex $211 Gd $150

K.D.F. INC. — Sequin, Texas

MODEL K15 BOLT-ACTION RIFLE
Calibers: (Standard) .22-250, .243 Win., 6mm Rem., .25-06, .270 Win., .280 Rem., 7mm Mag., .30-60; (Magnum) .300 Wby., .300 Win., .338 Win., .340 Wby., .375 H&H, .411 KDF, .416 Rem., .458 Win. Four round magazine (standard), 3-shot (magnum). 22-inch (standard) or 24-inch (magnum) bbl. 44.5 to 46.5 inches overall. Weight: 8 lbs. Sights optional. Kevlar composite or checkered walnut stock in Classic, European or thumbhole-style. Note: U.S. Manufacture limited to 25 prototypes and pre-production variations.
Standard model . . . . NiB $1802 Ex $1621 Gd $901
Magnum model . . . . NiB $1853 Ex $1467 Gd $952

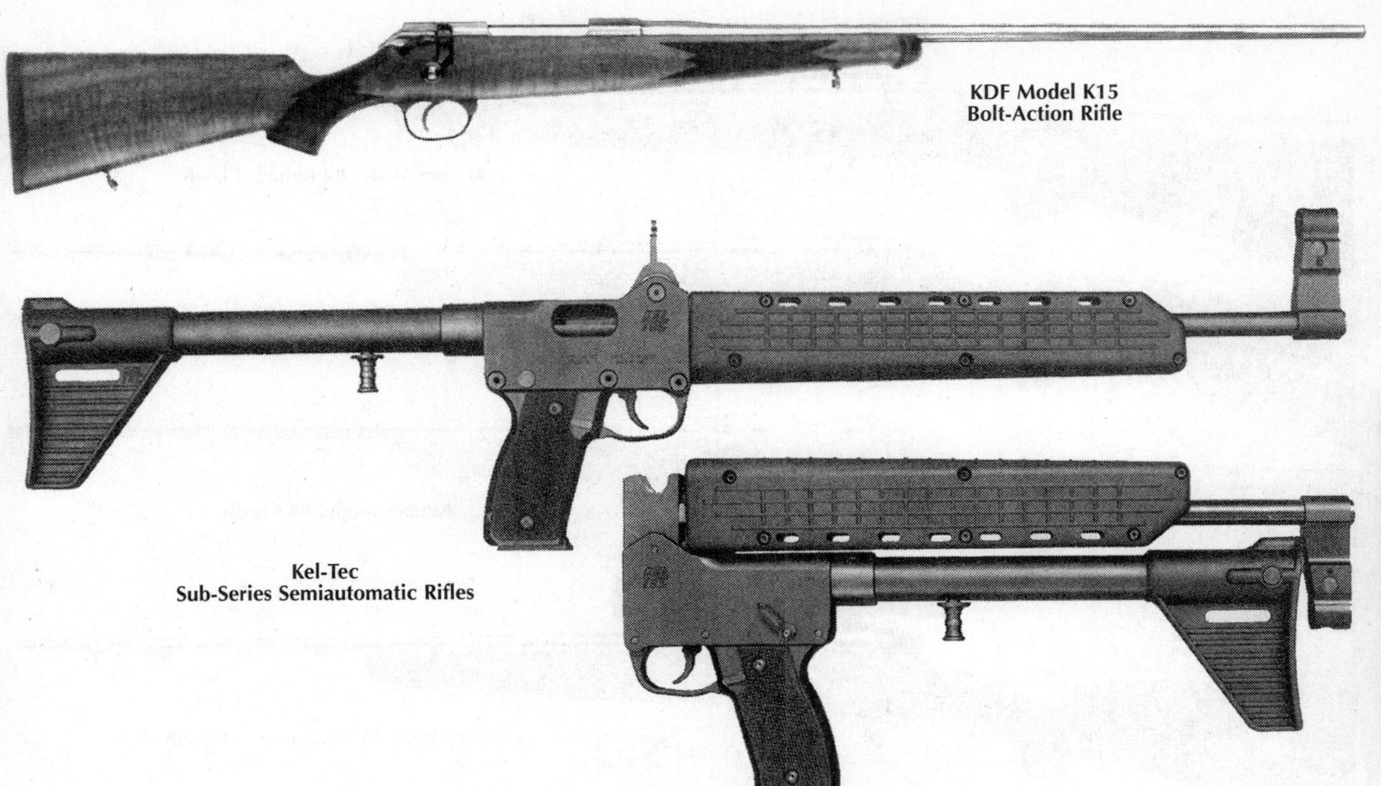
KDF Model K15
Bolt-Action Rifle

Kel-Tec
Sub-Series Semiautomatic Rifles

KEL-TEC CNC INDUSTRIES, INC. — Cocoa, Florida

SUB-SERIES SEMIAUTOMATIC RIFLES
Semiautomatic blow-back action w/pivoting bbl., takedown. 9mm Parabellum or 40 S&W. Interchangeable grip assembly accepts most double column, high capacity handgun magazines. 16.1-inch bbl. 31.5 inches overall. Weight: 4.6 lbs. Hooded post front sight, flip-up rear. Matte black finish. Tubular buttstock w/grooved polymer buttplate and vented handguard. Made 1997 to date.
Sub-9 Model (9mm). . . . . NiB $412 Ex $293 Gd $216
Sub-40 Model (40 S&W) . . . . NiB $499 Ex $412 Gd $267

KIMBER RIFLES — Mfd. By Kimber Manufacturing, Inc., Yonkers, NY (Formerly Kimber of America, Inc.; Kimber of Oregon, Inc.)

Note: From 1980-91, Kimber of Oregon produced Kimber firearms. A redesigned action designated by serialization with a "B" suffix was introduced 1986. Pre-1986 production is recognized as the "A" series but is not so marked. These early models in rare configurations and limited-run calibers command premium prices from collectors. Kimber of America, in Clackamas, Oregon, acquired the Kimber trademark and resumed manufactured of Kimber rifles. During this transition, Nationwide Sports Distributors, Inc. in Pennsylvania and Nevada became exclusive distributors of Kimber products. In 1997, Kimber Manufacturing acquired the trademark with manufacturing rights and expanded production to include a 1911-A1-style semiautomatic pistol, the Kimber Classic 45.
Rifle production resumed in late 1998 with the announcement of an all-new Kimber .22 rifle and a refined Model 84 in both single shot and repeater configurations.

MODEL 82 BOLT-ACTION RIFLE
Small action based on Kimber's "A" Model 82 rimfire receiver w/twin rear locking lugs. Calibers: .22 LR. .22 WRF, .22 Hornet, .218 Bee, .25-20. 5- or 10-round magazine (.22 LR); 5-round magazine (22WRF); 3-round magazine (.22 Hornet). .218 Bee and .25-20 are single-shot. 18- to 25-inch bbl. 37.63 to 42.5 inches overall. Weight: 6 lbs. (Light Sporter), 6.5 lbs. (Sporter), 7.5 lbs. (Varmint); 10.75 lbs. (Target). Right- and left-hand actions are available in distinctive stock styles.
Cascade (disc. 1987) . . . . NiB $891 Ex $814 Gd $531
Classic (disc. 1988) . . . . NiB $891 Ex $814 Gd $531
Continental . . . . NiB $1368 Ex $1097 Gd $751
Custom Classic
(disc. 1988) . . . . NiB $949 Ex $763 Gd $524
Mini Classic. . . . . NiB $602 Ex $485 Gd $334
Super America. . . . . NiB $1612 Ex $1020 Gd $762
Super Continental . . . . NiB $1551 Ex $1303 Gd $788
1990 Classifications
All-American Match . . . . NiB $917 Ex $788 Gd $557
Deluxe Grade
(disc. 1990) . . . . NiB $1303 Ex $1020 Gd $814
Hunter
(Laminated stock) . . . . NiB $840 Ex $685 Gd $454
Super America. . . . . NiB $1303 Ex $1041 Gd $687
Target
(Government Match) . . . . NiB $891 Ex $834 Gd $660

MODEL 82C CLASSIC BOLT-ACTION RIFLE
Caliber: .22 LR. Four- or 10-round magazine. 21-inch air-gauged bbl. 40.5 inches overall. Weight: 6.5 lbs. Receiver drilled and tapped for Warne scope mounts; no sights. Single-set trigger. Checkered Claro walnut stock w/red buttpad and polished steel grip cap. Reintroduced 1993.
Classic model . . . . NiB $866 Ex $727 Gd $428
Left-hand model, add. $75

Kimber Model 82 Rimfire Classic

Kimber Model 82C Rimfire Classic

Kimber Model 84 Classic

Kimber Model 89 Big Game 375 Caliber

Kimber Model 89 Big Game 375 H&H Caliber

Model 84 Bolt-Action Rifle

Classic (disc. 1988) Compact-medium action based on a scaled-down Mauser-type receiver, designed to accept small base centerfire cartridges. Calibers: .17 Rem., .221 Fireball, .222 Rem., .223 Rem. Five round magazine. Same general barrel and stock specifications as Model 82.

Classic (discontinued 1988) . . . . NiB $941 Ex $736 Gd $503
Continental . . . . NiB $1244 Ex $998 Gd $685
Custom Classic (disc. 1988) . . . . NiB $1121 Ex $901 Gd $618
Super America (disc. 1988). . . . . NiB $1276 Ex $1024 Gd $703
Super Continental (disc. 1988) . . . . NiB $1339 Ex $1076 Gd $738
l990 Classifications
Deluxe Grade (disc. 1990) . . . . NiB $1173 Ex $942 Gd $647
Hunter/Sporter (laminated stock). . . . . . . NiB $1044 Ex $839 Gd $577
Super America (disc. 1991). . . . . NiB $1301 Ex $1045 Gd $717
Super Varmint (disc. 1991) . . . . NiB $1339 Ex $1076 Gd $737
Ultra Varmint (disc. 1991) . . . . NiB $1250 Ex $1004 Gd $688

MODEL 89 BIG-GAME RIFLE

Large action combining the best features of the pre-64 Model 70 Winchester and the Mauser 98. Three action lengths are offered in three stock styles. Calibers: .257 Roberts, .25-06, 7x57, .270 Win., .280 Win., .30-06, 7mm Rem. Mag., .300 Win. Mag., .300 H&H, .338 Win., 35

***(cont'd.)* MODEL 89 BIG-GAME RIFLE**

Whelen, .375 H&H, .404 Jeffrey, .416 Rigby, .460 Wby., .505 Gibbs (.308 cartridge family to follow). Five round magazine (standard calibers); 3-round magazine (Magnum calibers). 22- to 24-inch bbl. 42 to 44 inches overall. Weight: 7.5 to 10.5 lbs. Model 89 African features express sights on contoured quarter rib, banded front sight. Barrel-mounted recoil lug w/integral receiver lug and twin recoil crosspins in stock.

BGR Long Action
Classic (disc. 1988). . . . . NiB $915 Ex $736 Gd $4507
Custom Classic (disc. 1988) . . . . NiB $1173 Ex $942 Gd $647
Super America. NiB $1430 Ex $1148 Gd $787
1990 Classifications
Deluxe Grade: Featherweight . . . . NiB $1693 Ex $1359 Gd $932
Medium. . . . . NiB $1731 Ex $1390 Gd $953
.375 H&H . . . . NiB $1821 Ex $1462 Gd $1002
Hunter Grade (laminated stock)
.270 and .30-06 . . . . NiB $1259 Ex $1013 Gd $700
.375 H&H . . . . NiB $1574 Ex $1266 Gd $873
Super America: Featherweight . . . . NiB $1960 Ex $1575 Gd $1083
Medium. . . . . NiB $2056 Ex $1652 Gd $1135
.375 H&H . . . . NiB $2610 Ex $2095 Gd $1435
African — All calibers. . . . . NiB $4664 Ex $3737 Gd $2553

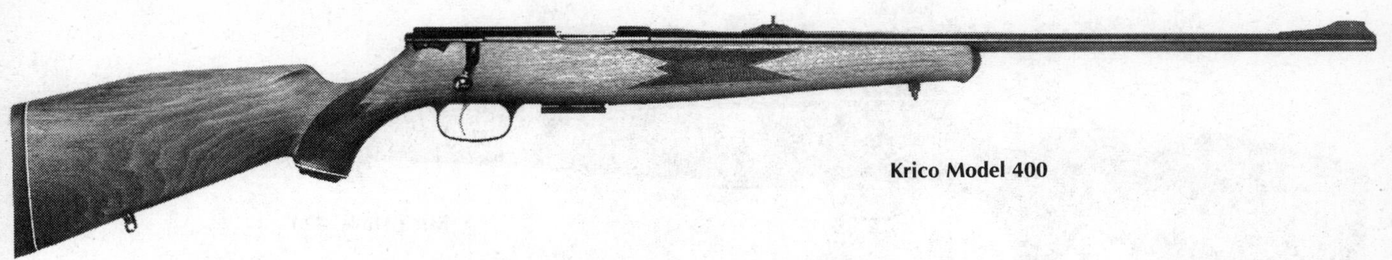

Krico Model 400

KNIGHT'S MANUFACTURING COMPANY — Vero Beach, Florida

SR-15 SEMIAUTOMATIC MATCH RIFLE .... NiB $1668 Ex $1410 Gd $947
AR-15 configuration. Caliber: .223 Rem. (5.56mm). Five- or 10-round magazine. 20-inch w/free-floating, match-grade bbl., 38 inches overall. Weight: 7.9 lbs. Integral Weaver-style rail. Two-stage target trigger. Matte black oxide finish. Black synthetic AR-15A2-style stock and forearm. Made 1997 to date.

SR-15 M-4 SEMIAUTOMATIC CARBINE
Similar to SR-15 rifle except w/16-inch bbl. Sights and mounts optional. Fixed synthetic or collapsible buttstock. Made 1997 to date.
Model SR-15 Carbine (w/collapsible stock)..... NiB $1389 Ex $1256 Gd $895
Model SR-15 Carbine (w/fixed stock)...... NiB $1389 Ex $1256 Gd $895

SR-15 M-5 SEMIAUTOMATIC RIFLE.... NiB $1523 Ex $1333 Gd $998
Caliber: .223 Rem. (5.56mm). Five- or 10-round magazine. 20-inch bbl. 38 inches overall. Weight: 7.6 lbs. Integral Weaver-style rail. Two-stage target trigger. Matte black oxide finish. Black synthetic AR-15A2-style stock and forearm. Made 1997 to date.

SR-25 MATCH RIFLE
Similar to SR-25 Sporter except w/free floating 20- or 24-inch match bbl. 39.5-43.5 inches overall. Weight: 9.25 and 10.75 lbs., respectively. Integral Weaver-style rail. Sights and mounts optional. 1 MOA guaranteed. Made 1993 to date.
Model SR-25 LW Match (w/20-inch bbl.)..... NiB $2764 Ex $2352 Gd $1503
Model SR-25 Match (w/24-inch bbl.)... NiB $2764 Ex $2352 Gd $1503
W/RAS (Rail Adapter System), add.......................... $300

SR-25 SEMIAUTOMATIC CARBINE
Similar to SR-25 Sporter except w/free floating 16-inch bbl. 35.75 inches overall. Weight: 7.75 lbs. Integral Weaver-style rail. Sights and mounts optional. Made 1995 to date.
Model SR-25 Carbine (w/o sights) .... NiB $2713 Ex $2455 Gd $1477
W/RAS (Rail Adapter System), add.......................... $300

SR-25 SEMIAUTOMATIC SPORTER RIFLE............. NiB $2816 Ex $2301 Gd $1580
AR-15 configuration. Caliber: .308 Win. (7.62 NATO). Five, 10- or 20-round magazine. 20-inch bbl. 39.5 inches overall. Weight: 8.75 lbs. Integral Weaver-style rail. Protected post front sight adjustable for elevation, detachable rear adjustable for windage. Two-stage target trigger. Matte black oxide finish. Black synthetic AR-15A2-style stock and forearm. Made 1993-97.

SR-50 SEMIAUTOMATIC LONG RANGE PRECISION RIFLE..... NiB $6589 Ex $5765 Gd $3396
Gas-operated semiautomatic action. Caliber: .50 BMG. 10-round magazine. 35.5-inch bbl. 58.5 inches overall. Weight: 31.75 lbs. Integral Weaver-style rail. Two-stage target trigger. Matte black oxide finish. Tubular-style stock. Made 1996 to date.

KONGSBERG RIFLES — Kongsberg, Norway

(Imported by Kongsberg America L.L.C., Fairfield, CT)

MODEL 393 CLASSIC SPORTER
Calibers: .22-250 Rem., .243 Win., 6.5x55, .270 Win., 7mm Rem. Mag., .30-06, .308 Win. .300 Win. Mag., .338 Win. Mag. Three- or 4-round rotary magazine. 23-inch bbl. (Standard) or 26-inch bbl. (magnum). Weight: 7.5 to 8 lbs. 44 to 47 inches overall. No sights w/ dovetailed receiver or optional hooded blade front sight, adjustable rear. Blue finish. Checkered European walnut stock w/rubber buttplate. Imported 1994-98.
Standard calibers .... NiB $921 Ex $792 Gd $513
Magnum calibers .... NiB $1200 Ex $988 Gd $716
Left-hand model, add $135
W/optional sights, add $50

MODEL 393 DELUXE SPORTER
Similar to Classic Model except w/deluxe European walnut stock. Imported 1994-98.
Standard calibers .... NiB $998 Ex $839 Gd $509
Magnum calibers............. NiB $1233 Ex $1014 Gd $734
Left-hand model, add............................ $135
W/optional sights, add $50

MODEL 393 THUMBHOLE SPORTER
Calibers: 22-250 Rem. or 308 Win. Four round rotary magazine. 23-inch heavy bbl. Weight: 8.5 lbs. 44 inches overall. No sights, dovetailed receiver. Blue finish. Stippled American walnut thumbhole stock w/adjustable cheekpiece. Imported 1993-98.
Right-hand model .... NiB $1410 Ex $1230 Gd $535
Left-hand model .... NiB $1698 Ex $1390 Gd $996

KRICO RIFLES — Stuttgart-Hedelfingen, Germany, Mfd. by Sportwaffenfabrik, Kriegeskorte GmbH, *Imported by Mandall Shooting Supplies, Scottsdale, AZ, (Previously by Beeman Precision Arms, Inc.)*

MODEL 260 SEMIAUTOMATIC RIFLE .... NiB $646 Ex $584 Gd $378
Caliber: .22 LR. 10-round magazine. 20-inch bbl. 38.9 inches overall. Weight: 6.6 lbs. Hooded blade front sight; adj. rear. Grooved receiver. Beech stock. Blued finish. Imported 1991 to date.

MODEL 300 BOLT-ACTION RIFLE
Calibers: .22 LR. .22 WMR, .22 Hornet. 19.6-inch bbl. (22 LR), 23.6-inch (22 Hornet). 38.5 inches overall. Weight: 6.3 lbs. Double-set triggers. Sights: Ramped blade front, adj. open rear. Checkered walnut-finished hardwood stock. Blued finish. Imported 1993 to date.
Model 300 Standard .... NiB $662 Ex $507 Gd $353
Model 300 Deluxe........................ NiB $688 Ex $533 Gd $378
Model 300 SA (Monte Carlo walnut stock) .... NiB $797 Ex $651 Gd $465
Model 300 Stutzen (full-length walnut stock) ..... NiB $919 Ex $790 Gd $533

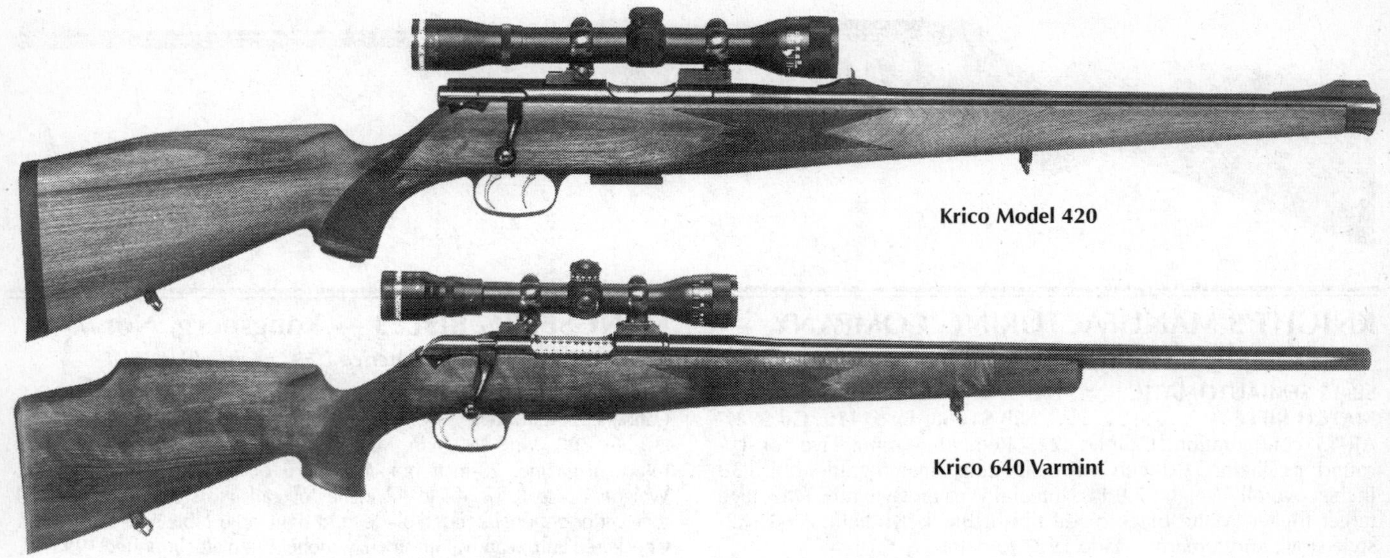
Krico Model 420

Krico 640 Varmint

MODEL 311 SMALL-BORE RIFLE
Bolt action. Caliber: .22 LR. Five or 10-round clip magazine. 22-inch bbl. Weight: 6 lbs. Single- or double-set trigger. Sights: Open rear; hooded ramp front; available w/factory-fitted Kaps 2.5x scope. Checkered stock w/cheekpiece, pistol-grip and swivels. Disc.
W/scope sight . . . . NiB $448 Ex $396 Gd $242
W/iron sights only . . . . NiB $370 Ex $267 Gd $216

MODEL 320 BOLT-ACTION SPORTER . . . . NiB $705 Ex $551 Gd $370
Caliber: .22 LR. Five round detachable box magazine. 19.5-inch bbl. 38.5 inches overall. Weight: 6 lbs. Adj. rear sight, blade ramp front. Checkered European walnut Mannlicher-style stock w/low comb and cheekpiece. Single or double-set triggers. Imported 1986-91.

MODEL 340 METALLIC SILHOUETTE BOLT-ACTION RIFLE . . . . NiB $721 Ex $602 Gd $412
Caliber: .22 LR. Five round magazine. 21-inch heavy, bull bbl. 39.5 inches overall. Weight: 7.5 lbs. No sights. Grooved receiver for scope mounts. European walnut stock in off-hand, match-style configuration. Match or double-set triggers. Imported 1983-86.

MODEL 360S BIATHLON RIFLE . . . . . . NiB $1355 Ex $1097 Gd $608
Caliber: .22 LR. Five 5-round magazines. 21.25-inch bbl. w/snow cap. 40.5 inches overall. Weight: 9.25 lbs. Straight-pull action. Match trigger w/17-oz. pull. Sights: Globe front, adj. match peep rear. Biathlon-style walnut stock w/high comb and adj. butt-plate. Imported 1991 to date.

MODEL 360 S2 BIATHLON RIFLE . . . . . NiB $1329 Ex $1046 Gd $582
Similar to Model 360S except w/pistol-grip activated action. Biathlon-style walnut stock w/black epoxy finish. Imported 1991 to date.

MODEL 400 BOLT-ACTION RIFLE . . . . NiB $879 Ex $705 Gd $483
Caliber: .22 Hornet. Five round detachable box magazine. 23.5-inch bbl. Weight: 6.75 lbs. Adj. open rear sight, ramp front. European walnut stock. Disc. 1990.

MODEL 420 BOLT-ACTION RIFLE . . . . NiB $911 Ex $731 Gd $499
Same as Model 400 except w/full-length Mannlicher-style stock and double-set triggers. Scope optional, extra. Disc. 1989.

MODEL 440 S BOLT-ACTION RIFLE . . . . . . NiB $854 Ex $685 Gd $468
Caliber: .22 Hornet. Detachable box magazine. 20-inch bbl. 36.5 inches overall. Weight: 7.5 lbs. No sights. French walnut stock w/ventilated forend. Disc. 1988.

MODEL 500 MATCH RIFLE . . . . NiB $3452 Ex $2769 Gd $1896
Caliber: .22 LR. Single-shot. 23.6-inch bbl. 42 inches overall. Weight: 9.4 lbs. Kricotronic electronic ignition system. Sights: Globe front; match micrometer aperture rear. Match-style European walnut stock w/adj. butt.

MODEL 600 BOLT-ACTION RIFLE . . . . . . NiB $1168 Ex $922 Gd $627
Same general specifications as Model 700 except w/short action. Calibers: .17 Rem., .222, .223, .22-250, .243, 5.6x50 Mag. and 308.

MODEL 620 BOLT-ACTION RIFLE . . . . . NiB $1220 Ex $1014 Gd $633
Same as Model 600 except w/short-action-chambered for .308 Win. only and full-length Mannlicher-style stock w/Schnabel forend tip. 20.75-inch bbl. Weight: 6.5 lbs. No longer imported.

MODEL 640 SUPER SNIPER BOLT-ACTION REPEATING RIFLE NiB $1425 Ex $1143 Gd $783
Calibers: .223 Rem., .308 Win. Three round magazine. 26-inch bbl. 44.25 inches overall. Weight: 9.5 lbs. No sights drilled and tapped for scope mounts. Single or double-set triggers. Select walnut stock w/adj. cheekpiece and recoil pad. Disc. 1989.

MODEL 640 VARMINT RIFLE . . . . NiB $911 Ex $782 Gd $473
Caliber: .222 Rem. Four round magazine. 23.75-inch bbl. Weight: 9.5 lbs. No sights. European walnut stock. No longer imported.

MODEL 700 BOLT-ACTION RIFLE
Calibers: .17 Rem., .222, .222 Rem. Mag., .223, .22-250, 5.6x50 Mag., .243, 5.6x57 RSW, 6x62, 6.5x55, 6.5x57, 6.5x68 .270 Win., 7x64, 7.5 Swiss, 7mm Mag., .30-06, .300 Win., 8x68S, 9.3x64. 24-inch (standard) or 26-inch (magnum) bbl. 44 inches overall (standard). Weight: 7.5 lbs. Adj. rear sight; hooded ramp front. Checkered European-style walnut stock w/Bavarian cheekpiece and rosewood Schnabel forend tip. Imported 1983 to date.
Model 700 . . . . NiB $1110 Ex $890 Gd $610
Model 700 Deluxe . . . . NiB $1168 Ex $937 Gd $642
Model 700 Deluxe S . . . . NiB $1425 Ex $1142 Gd $782
Model 700 Stutzen . . . . NiB $1239 Ex $993 Gd $680

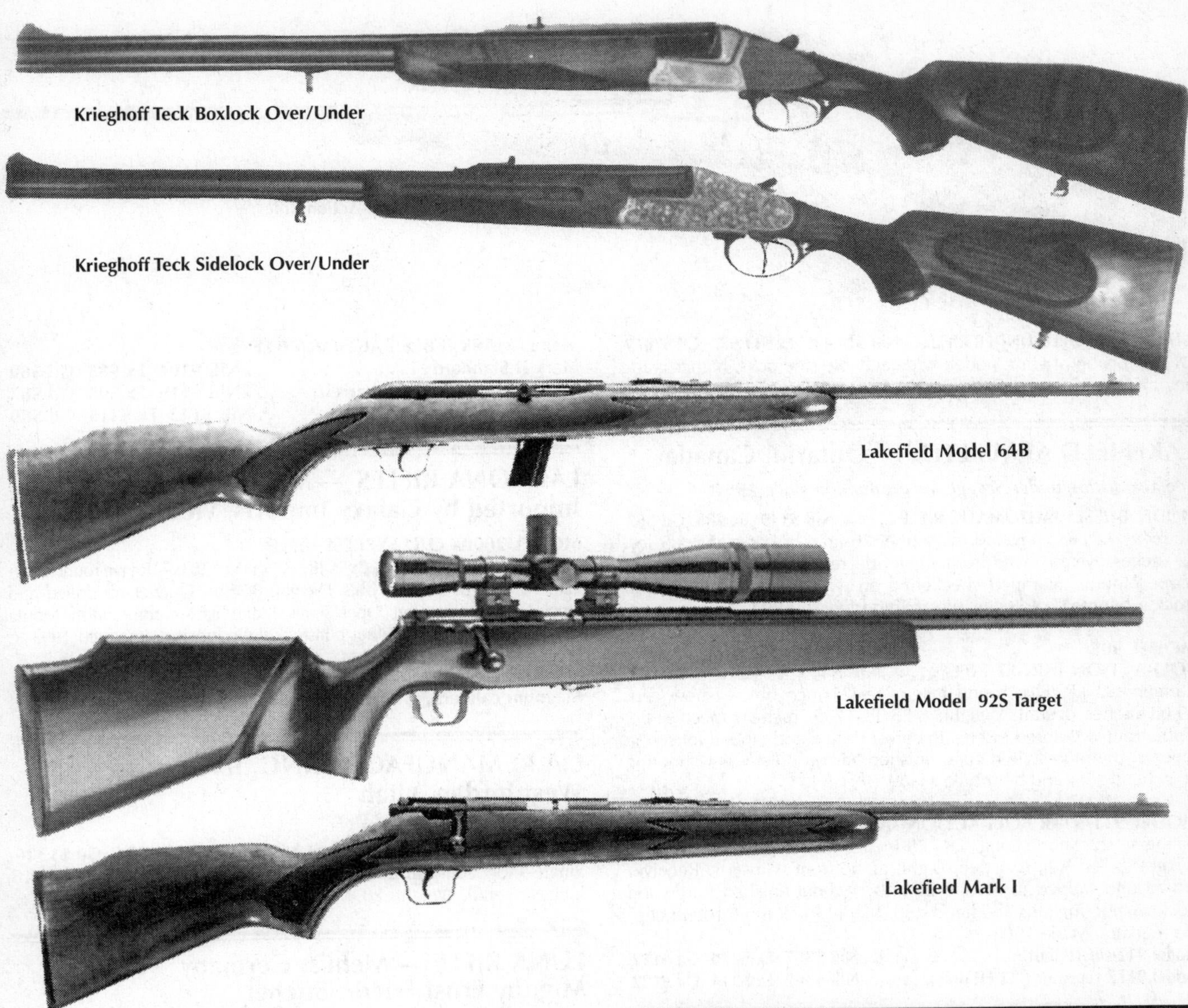

Kriegoff Teck Boxlock Over/Under

Krieghoff Teck Sidelock Over/Under

Lakefield Model 64B

Lakefield Model 92S Target

Lakefield Mark I

MODEL 720 BOLT-ACTION RIFLE
Same general specifications as Model 700 except in calibers .270 Win. and .30-06 w/full-length Mannlicher-style stock and Schnabel forend tip. 20.75-inch bbl. Weight: 6.75 lbs. Disc. importing 1990.
Sporter Model .... NiB $1163 Ex $932 Gd $637
Ltd. Edition .... NiB $2389 Ex $2070 Gd $1050

BOLT-ACTION SPORTING RIFLE .... NiB $628 Ex $576 Gd $396
Miniature Mauser action. Single- or double-set trigger. Calibers: .22 Hornet, .222 Rem. Four round clip magazine. 22-24- or 26-inch bbl. Weight: 6.25 lbs. Sights: Open rear; hooded ramp front. Checkered stock w/cheekpiece, pistol-grip, black forend tip, sling swivels. Imported 1956-62.

CARBINE .... NiB $679 Ex $551 Gd $370
Same as Krico Sporting Rifle except w/20- or 22-inch bbl., full-length Mannlicher-type stock.

SPECIAL VARMINT RIFLE .... NiB $679 Ex $551 Gd $370
Same as Krico Rifle except w/heavy bbl., no sights, weight: 7.25 lbs. Caliber: .222 Rem. only.

KRIEGHOFF RIFLES — Ulm (Donau), Germany, Mfd. by H. Krieghoff Jagd und Sportwaffenfabrik

See also Combination Guns under Krieghoff shotgun listings.

TECK OVER/UNDER RIFLE
Kersten action, double crossbolt, double underlugs. Boxlock. Calibers: 7x57r5, 7x64, 7x65r5, .30-30, .308 Win. .30-06, .300 Win. Mag., 9.3x74r5, .375 H&H Mag. .458 Win. Mag. 25-inch bbls. Weight: 8 to 9.5 lbs. Sights: Express rear; ramp front. Checkered walnut stock and forearm. Made 1967 to date.
Standard calibers .... NiB $9036 Ex $6667 Gd $5225
.375 H&H Mag.
(Disc. 1988)
.458 Win. Mag...................... NiB $9345 Ex $6976 Gd $6255

ULM OVER/
UNDER RIFLE .... NiB $14,729 Ex $10,609 Gd $6180
Same general specifications as Teck model except w/sidelocks w/leaf Arabesque engraving. Made 1963 to date.

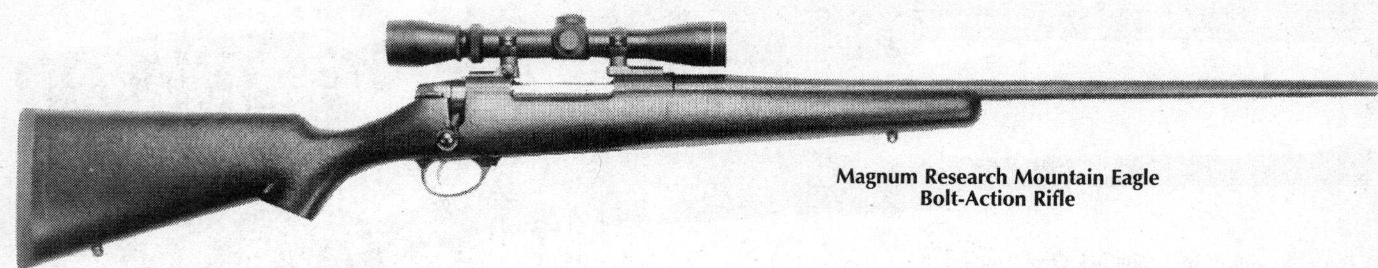

Magnum Research Mountain Eagle Bolt-Action Rifle

ULM-PRIMUS OVER/UNDER RIFLE. . . NiB $14,485 Ex $11,587 Gd $7879
Delux version of Ulm model, w/detachable sidelocks, higher grade engraving and stock wood. Made 1963 to date.

LAKEFIELD ARMS LTD. — Ontario, Canada

See also listing under Savage for production since 1994.

MODEL 64B SEMIAUTOMATIC RIFLE . . . . . . NiB $149 Ex $88 Gd $67
Caliber: .22 LR. 10-round magazine. 20-inch bbl. Weight: 5.5 lbs. 40 inches overall. Bead front sight, adj. rear. Grooved receiver for scope mounts. Stamped checkering on walnut-finished hardwood stock w/Monte Carlo cheekpiece. Imported 1990-94.

MODEL 90B
BOLT-ACTION TARGET RIFLE . . . . . NiB $443 Ex $316 Gd $189
Caliber: .22 LR. Five round magazine. 21-inch bbl. w/snow cap. 39.63 inches overall. Weight: 8.25 lbs. Adj. receiver peep sight; globe front w/colored inserts. Receiver drilled and tapped for scope mounts. Biathlon-style natural finished hardwood stock w/shooting rails, hand stop and butthook. Made 1991-94.

MODEL 91T/91TR BOLT-ACTION TARGET RIFLE
Calibers: .22 Short, Long, LR. 25-inch bbl. 43.63 inches overall. Weight: 8 lbs. Adj. rear peep sight; globe front w/inserts. Receiver drilled and tapped for scope mounts. Walnut-finished hardwood stock w/shooting rails and hand stop. Model 91TR is a 5-round clipfed repeater. Made 1991-94.
Model 91T single-shot. . . . . NiB $357 Ex $270 Gd $112
Model 91TR repeater (.22 LR only). . . . . . . NiB $367 Ex $214 Gd $122

MODEL 92S TARGET RIFLE . . . . NiB $297 Ex $239 Gd $166
Same general specifications as Model 90B except w/conventional target-style stock. 8 lbs. No sights, but drilled and tapped for scope mounts. Made 1993-95.

MODEL 93M BOLT ACTION . . . . NiB $149 Ex $120 Gd $84
Caliber: .22 WMR. Five round magazine. 20.75-inch bbl. 39.5 inches overall. Weight: 5.75 lbs. Bead front sight, adj. open rear. Receiver grooved for scope mount. Thumb-operated rotary safety. Checkered walnut-finished hardwood stock. Blued finish. Made 1995.

MARK I BOLT-ACTION RIFLE . . . . NiB $98 Ex $79 Gd $57
Calibers: .22 Short, Long, LR. Single-shot. 20.5-inch bbl. (19-inch Youth Model); available in smoothbore. Weight: 5.5 lbs. 39.5 inches overall. Bead front sight; adj. rear. Grooved receiver for scope mounts. Checkered walnut-finished hardwood stock w/Monte Carlo and pistol-grip. Blued finish. Made 1990-94.

MARK II BOLT-ACTION RIFLE
Same general specifications as Mark I except has repeating action w/10-round detachable box magazine. .22 LR. only. Made 1992-94.

(cont'd.) **MARK II BOLT-ACTION RIFLE**
Mark II Standard . . . . NiB $104 Ex $85 Gd $60
Mark II Youth (19-inch barrel). . . . . . . NiB $116 Ex $95 Gd $67
Mark II left-hand . . . . NiB $142 Ex $115 Gd $80

LAURONA RIFLES — Mfg. in Eibar, Spain Imported by Galaxy Imports, Victoria, TX

MODEL 2000X O/U EXPRESS RIFLE
Calibers: .30-06, 8x57 JRS, 8x75 JR, .375 H&H, 9.3x74R Five round magazine. 24-inch separated bbls. Weight: 8.5 lbs. Quarter rib drilled and tapped for scope mount. Open sights. Matte black chrome finish. Monte Carlo-style checkered walnut buttstock; tulip forearm. Imported 1993 to date.
Standard calibers. . . . . NiB $2930 Ex $2350 Gd $1609
Magnum calibers. . . . . NiB $3633 Ex $2911 Gd $1991

L.A.R. MANUFACTURING, INC. — West Jordan, Utah

BIG BOAR COMPETITOR
BOLT-ACTION RIFLE. . . . . NiB $2413 Ex $1936 Gd $1326
Single-shot, bull-pup action. Caliber: .50 BMG. 36-inch bbl. 45.5 inches overall. Weight: 28.4 lbs. Made 1994 to date.

LUNA RIFLE — Mehlis, Germany Mfg. by Ernst Friedr. Büchel

SINGLE-SHOT TARGET RIFLE . . . . NiB $1036 Ex $891 Gd $582
Falling block action. Calibers: .22 LR. .22 Hornet. 29-inch bbl. Weight: 8.25 lbs. Sights: Micrometer peep rear tang; open rear; ramp front. Cheekpiece stock w/full pistol-grip, semibeavertail forearm, checkered, swivels. Made before WWII.

MAGNUM RESEARCH, INC. — Minneapolis, Minnesota

MOUNTAIN EAGLE BOLT-ACTION RIFLE SERIES
Calibers: .222 Rem., .223 Rem., .270 Win., .280 Rem., 7mm Rem. Mag., 7mm STW, .30-06, .300 Win. Mag., .338 Win. Mag., .340 Wby. Mag., .375 H&H, .416 Rem. Mag. Five round (std.) or 4-round (Mag.). 24- or 26-inch bbl. 44 to 46 inches overall. Weight: 7.75 to 9.75 lbs. Receiver drilled and tapped for scope mount; no sights. Blued finish. Fiberglass composite stock. Made 1994 to date.
Standard model. . . . . NiB $1386 Ex $1125 Gd $636
Magnum model. . . . . NiB $1386 Ex $1125 Gd $636
Varmint model (Intro. 1996). . . . . NiB $1386 Ex $1125 Gd $636
Calibers .375 H&H, .416 Rem. Mag., add. $300

Mannlicher Model L Rifle

Mannlicher
Model M Carbine

Mannlicher Model M Professional

Mannlicher
Model M Rifle

MAGTECH — Las Vegas, Nevada
Mfg. by CBC, Brazil

MODEL MT 122.2/S BOLT-ACTION RIFLE . . NiB $120 Ex $100 Gd $59
Calibers: .22 Short, Long, Long Rifle. Six- or 10-round clip. Bolt action. 25-inch free-floating bbl. 43 inches overall. Weight: 6.5 lbs. Double locking bolt. Red cocking indicator. Safety lever. Brazilian hardwood finish. Double extractors. Beavertail forearm. Sling swivels. Imported 1994 to date.

MODEL MT 122.2/R BOLT-ACTION RIFLE. . . NiB $116 Ex $95 Gd $67
Same as Model MT 122.2/S except adj. rear sight and post front sight.

MODEL MT 122.2T BOLT-ACTION RIFLE . . NiB $123 Ex $100 Gd $70
Same as Model MT 122.2/S except w/adj. micrometer-type rear sight and ramp front sight.

MANNLICHER SPORTING RIFLES — Steyr, Austria, Mfg. by Steyr-Daimler-Puch, A.-G.

NOTE: *Certain Mannlicher-Schoenauer models were produced before WWII. Manufacture of sporting rifles and carbines was resumed at the Steyr-Daimler-Puch plant in Austria in 1950 during which time the Model 1950 rifles and carbines were introduced.*

In 1967, Steyr-Daimler-Puch introduced a series of sporting rifles with a bolt action that is a departure from the Mannlicher-Schoenauer system of earlier models. In the latter, the action is locked by lugs symmetrically arranged behind the bolt head as well as by placing the bolt handle ahead of the right flank of the receiver, the rear section of which is open on top for backward movement of the bolt handle. The current action, made in four lengths to accommodate different ranges of cartridges, has a closed-top receiver; the bolt locking lugs are located toward the rear of the bolt (behind the magazine). The Mannlicher-Schoenauer rotary magazine has been redesigned as a detachable box type made of Makrolon. Imported by Gun South, Inc. Trussville, AL

MODEL L CARBINE. . . . . NiB $1368 Ex $1097 Gd $751
Same general specifications as Model SL Carbine except w/type "L" action, weight: 6.2 lbs. Calibers same as for Model L Rifle. Imported 1968-96.

Mannlicher Model SL Rifle w/Single-Set Trigger

MODEL L RIFLE. . . . . NiB $1947 Ex $1406 Gd $840
Same general specifications as Model SL Rifle except w/type "L" action, weighs 6.3 lbs. Calibers: .22-250, 5.6x57 (disc. 1991), ..243 Win., 6mm Rem. .308 Win. Imported 1968-96.

MODEL L VARMINT RIFLE . . . . . NiB $1973 Ex $1448 Gd $830
Same general specifications as Model SL Varmint Rifle except w/type "L" action. Calibers: .22-250, .243 Win., .308 Win. Imported 1969-96.

MODEL LUXUS BOLT-ACTION RIFLE
Same general specifications as Models L and M except w/3-round detachable box magazine and single-set trigger. Full or half-stock w/low-luster oil or high-gloss lacquer finish. Disc. 1996.
Full stock. . . . . NiB $2022 Ex $1663 Gd $1203
Half stock . . . . NiB $2590 Ex $1822 Gd $823

MODEL M CARBINE
Same general specifications as Model SL Carbine except w/type "M" action, stock w/recoil pad, weighs 6.8 lbs. Left-hand version w/additional 6.5x55 and 9.3x62 calibers intro. 1977. Imported 1969-96.
Right-hand carbine . . . . NiB $2074 Ex $1462 Gd $792
Left-hand carbine . . . . NiB $2228 Ex $1868 Gd $1409

MODEL M PROFESSIONAL RIFLE . . . . . NiB $1977 Ex $1410 Gd $741
Same as standard Model M Rifle except w/synthetic (Cycolac) stock, weighs 7.5 lbs. Calibers: 6.5x55, 6.5x57, .270 Win., 7x57, 7x64, 7.5 Swiss, .30-06, 8x57JS, 9.3x62. Imported 1977-93.

MODEL M RIFLE
Same general specifications as Model SL Rifle except w/type "M" action, stock w/forend tip and recoil pad; weighs 6.9 lbs. Calibers: 6.5x57, .270 Win., 7x57, 7x64, .30-06, 8x57JS, 9.3x62. Made 1969 to date. Left-hand version also in calibers 6.5x55 and 7.5 Swiss. Imported 1977-96.
Right-hand rifle . . . . NiB $1565 Ex $1101 Gd $741
Left-hand rifle . . . . NiB $2228 Ex $1868 Gd $1409

MODEL S RIFLE. . . . . NiB $1565 Ex $1101 Gd $741
Same general specifications as Model SL Rifle except w/type "S" action, 4-round magazine, 25.63-inch bbl., stock w/forend tip and recoil pad, weighs 8.4 lbs. Calibers: 6.5x68, .257 Weatherby Mag., .264 Win. Mag., 7mm Rem. Mag., .300 Win. Mag., .300 H&H Mag., .308 Norma Mag., 8x68S, .338 Win. Mag., 9.3x64, .375 H&H Mag. Imported 1970-96.

MODEL SL CARBINE. . . . . NiB $1565 Ex $1101 Gd $741
Same general specifications as Model SL Rifle except w/20-inch bbl. and full-length stock, weight: 6 lbs. Imported 1968-96.

MODEL SL RIFLE. . . . . NiB $1565 Ex $1101 Gd $741
Steyr-Mannlicher SL bolt action. Calibers: .222 Rem., .222 Rem., .222 Rem. Mag., .223 Rem. Five round rotary magazine, detachable. 23.63-inch bbl. Weight: 6 lbs. Single- or double-set trigger (mechanisms interchangeable). Sights: Open rear; hooded ramp front. Half stock of European walnut w/Monte Carlo comb and cheekpiece, skip-checkered forearm and pistol grip, rubber buttpad, QD swivels. Imported 1967-96.

MODEL SL
VARMINT RIFLE . . . . NiB $1153 Ex $1127 Gd $767
Same general specifications as Model SL Rifle except caliber .222 Rem. only, w/25.63-inch heavy bbl., no sights, weighs 7.92 lbs. Imported 1969-96.

MODEL SSG MATCH TARGET RIFLE
Type "L" action. Caliber: .308 Win. (7.62x51 NATO). Five- or 10-round magazine, single-shot plug. 25.5-inch heavy bbl. Weight: 10.25 lbs. Single trigger. Sights: Micrometer peep rear; globe front. Target stock, European walnut or synthetic, w/full pistol-grip, wide forearm w/swivel rail, adj. rubber buttplate. Imported 1969 to date.
W/walnut stock. . . . . NiB $2286 Ex $1822 Gd $1155
W/synthetic stock . . . . NiB $1379 Ex $1045 Gd $618

MODEL S/T RIFLE. . . . . NiB $2075 Ex $1462 Gd $638
Same as Model S Rifle except w/heavy 25.63-inch bbl., weight: 9 lbs. Calibers: 9.3x64, .375 H&H Mag., .458 Win. Mag. Option of 23.63-inch bbl. in latter caliber. Imported 1975-96.

MODEL 1903
BOLT-ACTION
SPORTING CARBINE . . . . NiB $4037 Ex $3934 Gd $535
Caliber: 6.5x53mm (referred to in some European gun catalogs as 6.7x53mm, following the Austrian practice of designating calibers by bullet diameter). Five round rotary magazine. 450mm (17.7-inch) bbl. Weight: 6.5 lbs. Double-set trigger. Sights: Two-leaf rear; ramp front. Full-length sporting stock w/cheekpiece, pistol-grip, trap buttplate, swivels. Pre-WWII.

MODEL 1905 CARBINE . . . . NiB $1256 Ex $818 Gd $535
Same as Model 1903 except w/19.7-inch bbl.chambered 9x56mm and weight: 6.75 lbs. Pre-WWII.

MODEL 1908 CARBINE . . . . NiB $1359 Ex $1153 Gd $844
Same as Model 1905 except calibers 7x57mm and 8x56mm Pre-WWII.

MODEL 1910 CARBINE . . . . NiB $1565 Ex $1256 Gd $586
Same as Model 1905 except in 9.5x57mm. Pre-WWII.

MODEL 1924 CARBINE . . . . NiB $1668 Ex $1462 Gd $947
Same as Model 1905 except caliber .30-06 (7.62x63mm). Pre-WWII.

MODEL 1950
BOLT-ACTION
SPORTING RIFLE. . . . . NiB $1513 Ex $1359 Gd $483
Calibers: .257 Roberts, .270 Win., .30-06. Five round rotary magazine. 24-inch bbl. Weight: 7.25 lbs. Single trigger or double-set trigger. Redesigned low bolt handle, shotgun-type safety. Sights: Folding leaf open rear; hooded ramp front. Improved half-length stock w/cheekpiece, pistol grip, checkered, ebony forend tip, swivels. Made 1950-52.

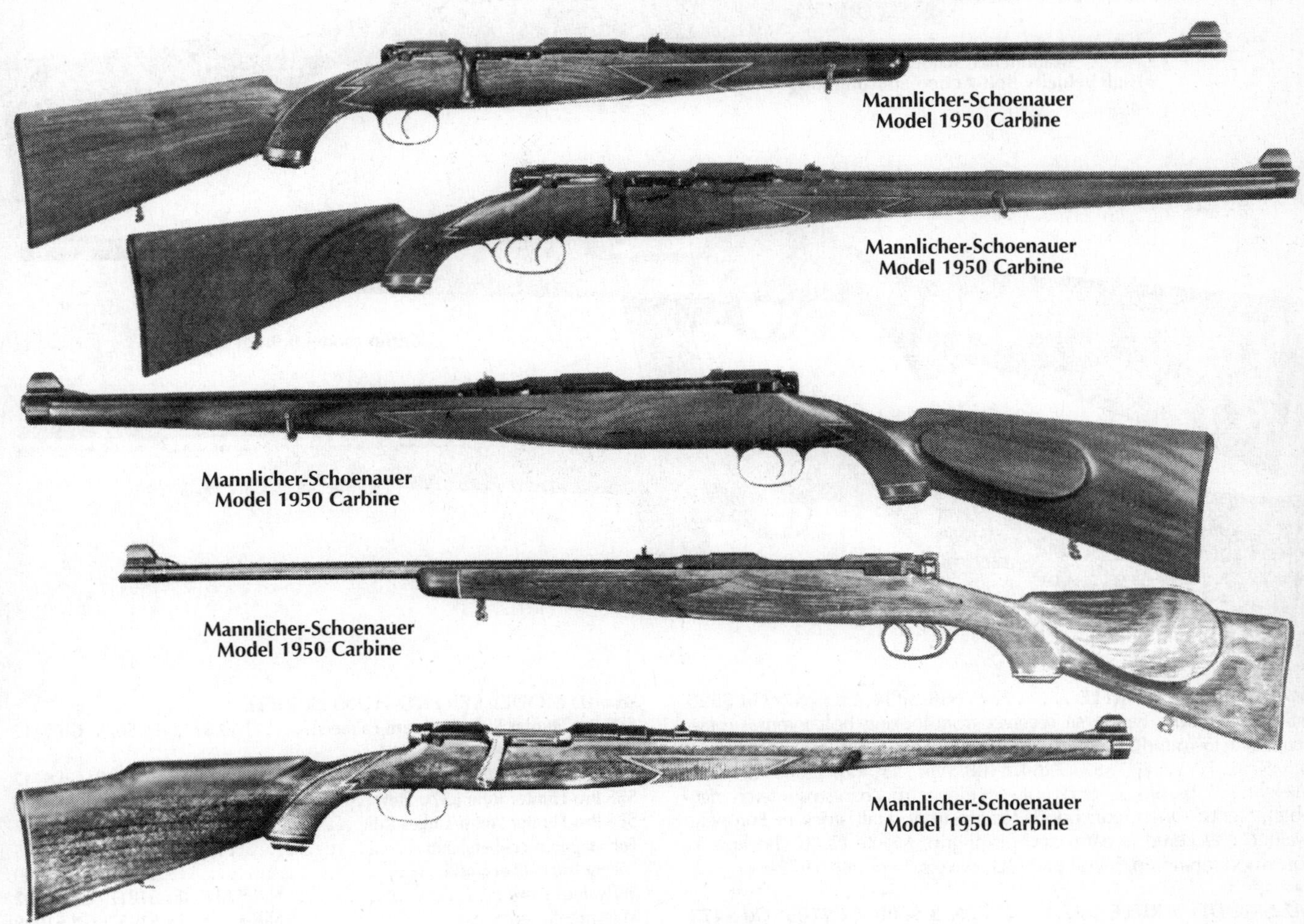
Mannlicher-Schoenauer Model 1950 Carbine

Mannlicher-Schoenauer Model 1950 Carbine

Mannlicher-Schoenauer Model 1950 Carbine

Mannlicher-Schoenauer Model 1950 Carbine

Mannlicher-Schoenauer Model 1950 Carbine

MODEL 1950 CARBINE .... NiB $1769 Ex $1460 Gd $893
Same general specifications as Model 1950 Rifle except w/20-inch bbl., full-length stock, weighs 7 lbs. Made 1950-52.

MODEL 1950 6.5 CARBINE .... NiB $1872 Ex $1666 Gd $935
Same as other Model 1950 Carbines except caliber 6.5x53mm, w/18.25-inch bbl., weighs 6.75 lbs. Made 1950-52.

MODEL 1952 IMPROVED CARBINE............... NiB $1975 Ex $1352 Gd $821
Same as Model 1950 Carbine except w/swept-back bolt handle, redesigned stock. Calibers: .257, .270, 7mm, .30-06. Made 1952-56.

MODEL 1952 IMPROVED 6.5 CARBINE................. NiB $1099 Ex $996 Gd $533
Same as Model 1952 Carbine except caliber 6.5x53mm, w/18.25-inch bbl. Made 1952-56.

MODEL 1952 IMPROVED SPORTING RIFLE............ NiB $1460 Ex $1254 Gd $790
Same as Model 1950 except w/swept-back bolt handle, redesigned stock. Calibers: .257, .270, .30-06, 9.3x62mm. Made 1952-56 and imported exclusively by Stoeger Arms Corp.

MODEL 1956 CUSTOM CARBINE .... NiB $911 Ex $731 Gd $499
Same general specifications as Models 1950 and 1952 Carbines except w/redesigned stock w/high comb. Drilled and tapped for scope mounts. Calibers: .243, 6.5mm, .257, .270, 7mm, .30-06, .308. Made 1956-60.

CARBINE, MODEL 1961-MCA . . NiB $2080 Ex $1925 Gd $535
Same as Model 1956 Carbine except w/universal Monte Carlo design stock. Calibers: .243 Win., 6.5mm, .270, .308, .30-06. Made 1961-71.

RIFLE, MODEL 1961-MCA ..... NiB $1720 Ex $1256 Gd $586
Same as Model 1956 Rifle except w/universal Monte Carlo design stock. Calibers: .243, .270, .30-06. Made 1961-71.

HIGH VELOCITY BOLT-ACTION SPORTING RIFLE. . . NiB $2183 Ex $1977 Gd $921
Calibers: 7x64 Brenneke, .30-06 (7.62x63), 8x60 Magnum, 9.3x62, 10.75x68mm. 23.6-inch bbl. Weight: 7.5 lbs. Sights: British-style 3-leaf open rear; ramp front. Half-length sporting stock w/cheekpiece, pistol grip, checkered, trap buttplate, swivels. Also produced in a takedown model. Pre-WWII. See illustration next page.

M72 MODEL L/M CARBINE ...... NiB $937 Ex $679 Gd $422
Same general specifications as M72 Model L/M Rifle except w/20-inch bbl. and full-length stock, weight: 7.2 lbs. Imported 1972 to date.

Mannlicher Schoenauer
High Velocity Bolt-Action Sporting Rifle

Marlin Model 9 9mm Carbine

Marlin Model 9N Nickel-Teflon

M72 MODEL L/M RIFLE . . . . NiB $834 Ex $757 Gd $525
M72 bolt-action, type L/M receiver front-locking bolt internal rotary magazine (5-round). Calibers: .22-250, 5.6x57, 6mm Rem., .243 Win., 6.5x57, .270 Win., 7x57, 7x64, .308 Win., .30-06. 23.63-inch bbl. Weight: 7.3 lbs. Single- or double-set trigger (mechanisms interchangeable). Sights: Open rear; hooded ramp front. Half stock of European walnut, checkered forearm and pistol-grip, Monte Carlo cheekpiece, rosewood forend tip, recoil pad QD swivels. Imported 1972-81.

M72 MODEL S RIFLE . . . . NiB $808 Ex $705 Gd $473
Same general specifications as M72 Model L/M Rifle except w/magnum action, 4-round magazine, 25.63-inch bbl., weighs 8.6 lbs. Calibers: 6.5x68, 7mm Rem. Mag., 8x68S, 9.3x64, .375 H&H Mag. Imported 1972-81.

M72 MODEL S/T RIFLE. . . . . NiB $1379 Ex $1070 Gd $714
Same as M72 Model S Rifle except w/heavy 25.63-inch bbl., weighs 9.3 lbs. Calibers: .300 Win. Mag. 9.3x64, .375 H&H Mag., .458 Win. Mag. Option of 23.63-inch bbl. in latter caliber. Imported 1975-81.

MODEL SBS FORESTER RIFLE
Calibers: .243 Win., .25-06 Rem., .270 Win., .6.5x55mm, 6.5x57mm, 7x64mm, 7mm-08 Rem., .30-06, .308 Win. 9.3x64mm. Four round detachable magazine. 23.6-inch bbl. 44.5 inches overall. Weight: 7.5 lbs. No sights w/drilled and tapped for Browning A-Bolt configuration. Checkered American walnut stock w/Monte Carlo cheekpiece and Pachmayr swivels. Polished or matte blue finish. Imported 1997 to date.
SBS Forester Rifle (standard calibers) . . . . . NiB $824 Ex $654 Gd $417
SBS Forester Mountain Rifle (20-inch bbl.) . . . . NiB $789 Ex $628 Gd $412
For magnum calibers, add. $25
For metric calibers, add $100

MODEL SBS PRO-HUNTER RIFLE
Similar to the Forester Model, except w/ASB black synthetic stock. Matte blue finish. Imported 1997 to date.

(cont'd.) **MODEL SBS PRO-HUNTER RIFLE**
SBS Pro-Hunter Rifle (standard calibers). . . . . . NiB $772 Ex $628 Gd $412
SBS Pro-Hunter Rifle
Mountain Rifle (20-inch bbl.) . . . . NiB $824 Ex $618 Gd $417
SBS Pro-Hunter Rifle (.376 Steyr) . . . . NiB $814 Ex $654 Gd $448
SBS Pro-Hunter Youth/Ladies Rifle . . . . NiB $824 Ex $654 Gd $417
For magnum calibers, add. $25
For metric calibers, add. $100
W/walnut stock . . . . NiB $2228 Ex $1817 Gd $1292
W/synthetic stock . . . . NiB $1791 Ex $1457 Gd $1030

MARLIN FIREARMS CO. — North Haven, Connecticut

MODEL 9 SEMIAUTOMATIC CARBINE
Calibers: 9mm Parabellum. 12-round magazine. 16.5-inch bbl. 35.5 inches overall. Weight: 6.75 lbs. Manual bolt hold-open. Sights: Hooded post front; adj. open rear. Walnut-finished hardwood stock w/rubber buttpad. Blued or nickel-Teflon finish. Made 1985 to date.
Model 9 . . . . NiB $360 Ex $242 Gd $118
Model 9N, Nickel-Teflon (disc. 1994). . . . . NiB $396 Ex $267 Gd $123

MODEL 15Y/15YN
Bolt-action, single-shot "Little Buckaroo" rifle. Caliber: .22 Short, Long or LR. 16.25-inch bbl. Weight: 4.25 lbs. Thumb safety. Ramp front sight; adj. open rear. One-piece walnut Monte Carlo stock w/full pistol-grip. Made 1984-88. Reintroduced in 1989 as Model 15YN.
Model 15Y. . . . . NiB $132 Ex $101 Gd $65
Model 15YN. .NiB $137 Ex $106 Gd $70

MODEL 18 BABY SLIDE-ACTION REPEATER . . . . NiB $309 Ex $293 Gd $164
Exposed hammer. Solid frame. Caliber: .22 LR, Long Short. Tubular magazine holds 14 Short cartridges. 20-inch bbl., round or octagon. Weight: 3.75 lbs. Sights: Open rear; bead front. Plain straight-grip stock and slide handle. Made 1906-09.

Marlin Model 15Y "Little Buckaroo"

Marlin Model 15YN

Marlin Model 20

Marlin Model 25M Bolt-Action Rifle

Marlin Model 25MB Midget Magnum

MODEL 20 SLIDE-ACTION REPEATING RIFLE . . . . NiB $314 Ex $298 Gd $164
Exposed hammer. Takedown. Caliber: .22 LR. Long, Short. Tubular magazine: Half-length holds 15 Short, 12 Long, 10 LR; full-length holds 25 Short, 20 Long, 18 LR. 24-inch octagon bbl. Weight: 5 lbs. Sights: Open rear; bead front. Plain straight-grip stock, grooved slide handle. Made 1907-22. Note: After 1920 was designated "Model 20-S."

MODEL 25 BOLT-ACTION RIFLE . . . . NiB $164 Ex $139 Gd $87
Caliber: .22 Short, Long or LR; 7-round clip. 22-inch bbl. Weight: 5.5 lbs. Ramp front sight, adj. open rear. One-piece walnut Monte Carlo stock w/full pistol-grip Mar-Shield finish. Made 1984-88.

MODEL 25 SLIDE-ACTION REPEATER . . . . NiB $443 Ex $299 Gd $170
Exposed hammer. Takedown. Caliber: .22 Short (also handles 22 CB caps). Tubular magazine holds 15 Short. 23-inch bbl. Weight: 4 lbs. Sights: Open rear; beaded front. Plain straight-grip stock and slide handle. Made 1909-10.

MODEL 25M BOLT ACTION W/SCOPE . . . . NiB $156 Ex $126 Gd $88
Caliber: .22 WMR. 7-round clip. 22-inch bbl. Weight: 6 lbs. Ramp front sight w/brass bead, adj. open rear. Walnut-finished stock w/Monte Carlo styling and full pistol-grip. Sling swivels. Made 1986-88.

MODEL 25MB MIDGET MAGNUM . . . . NiB $162 Ex $126 Gd $85
Bolt action. Caliber: .22 WMR. Seven round capacity.16.25-inch bbl. Weight: 4.75 lbs. Walnut-finished Monte Carlo-style stock w/full pistol grip and abbreviated forend. Sights: Ramp front w/brass bead, adj. open rear. Thumb safety. Made 1986-88.

MODEL 25MG/25MN/25N/25NC BOLT-ACTION RIFLE
Caliber: .22 WMR (Model 25MN) or .22 LR. (Model 25N). Seven round clip magazine. 22-inch bbl. 41 inches overall. Weight: 5.5 to 6 lbs. Adj. open rear sight, ramp front; receiver grooved for scope mounts. One piece walnut-finished hardwood Monte Carlo stock w/pistol grip. Made 1989 to date.
Marlin Model 25MG (Garden Gun) . . . . . . NiB $176 Ex $142 Gd $99
Marlin Model 25MN . . . . NiB $156 Ex $126 Gd $88
Marlin Model 25N . . . . NiB $143 Ex $116 Gd $81
Marlin Model 25NC (camouflage stock) . . . . NiB $176 Ex $142 Gd $99

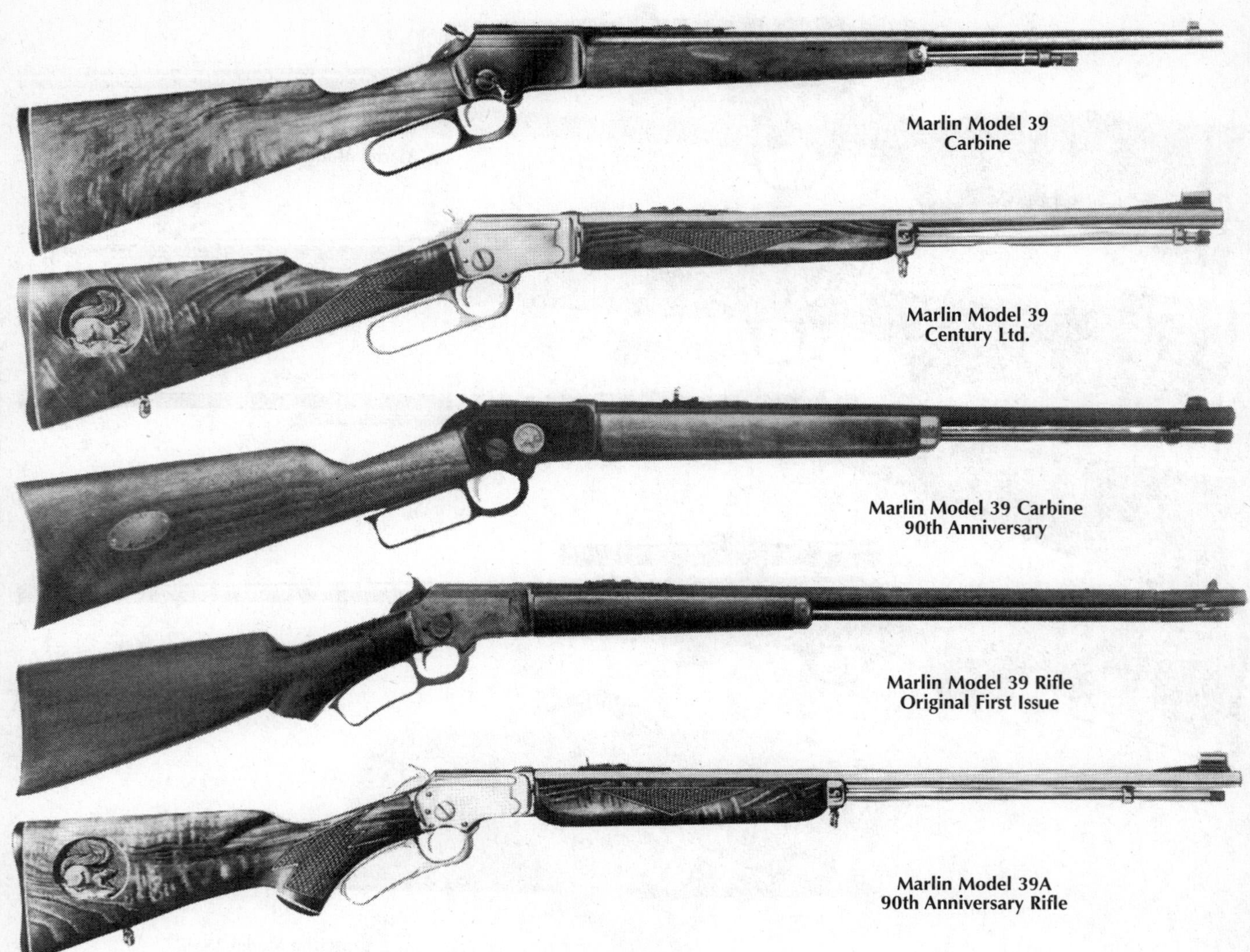
Marlin Model 39 Carbine

Marlin Model 39 Century Ltd.

Marlin Model 39 Carbine 90th Anniversary

Marlin Model 39 Rifle Original First Issue

Marlin Model 39A 90th Anniversary Rifle

MODEL 27 SLIDE-ACTION REPEATING RIFLE . . . . NiB $417 Ex $247 Gd $169
Exposed hammer. Takedown. Calibers: .25-20, .32-20. Magazine (tubular) holds 7 rounds. 24-inch octagon bbl. Weight: 5.75 lbs. Sights: Open rear; bead front. Plain, straight-grip stock, grooved slide handle. Made 1910-16.

MODEL 27S. . . . . NiB $324 Ex $229 Gd $144
Same as Model 27 except w/round bbl., also chambered for .25 Stevens rimfire Made 1920-32.

MODEL 29 SLIDE-ACTION REPEATER . . . . NiB $324 Ex $247 Gd $144
Similar to Model 20 w/23-inch round bbl., half magazine only, weight 5.75 lbs. Made 1913-16.

MODEL 30/30A AND 30AS LEVER-ACTION
Caliber: .30/30 Win. Six-round tubular magazine. 20-inch bbl. w/Micro-Groove rifling. 38.25 inches overall. Weight: 7 lbs. Brass bead front sight, adj. rear. Solid top receiver, offset hammer spur for scope use. Walnut-finished hardwood stock w/pistol-grip. Mar-Shield finish. Made 1964-2000.
Model 30/30A . . . . NiB $237 Ex $164 Gd $113
Model 30AS. . . . . NiB $237 Ex $164 Gd $113
Model 30AS w/4x scope, add $10

MODEL 32 SLIDE-ACTION REPEATER . . . . NiB $584 Ex $430 Gd $250
Hammerless. Takedown. Caliber: .22 LR. Long, Short. Tubular magazine holds 15 Short, 12 Long, 10 LR; full magazine, 25 Short, 20 Long, 18 LR. 24-inch octagon bbl. Weight: 5.5 lbs. Sights: Open rear; bead front. Plain pistol-grip stock, grooved slide handle. Made 1914-15.

MODEL 36 LEVER-ACTION REPEATING CARBINE
Calibers: .30-30, .32 Special. Seven-round tubular magazine. 20-inch bbl. Weight: 6.5 lbs. Sights: Open rear; bead front. Pistol-grip stock, semibeavertail forearm w/carbine bbl. band. Early production w/receiver, lever and hammer color casehardened and the remaining metal blued. Late production w/blued receiver. Made 1936-48. Note: In 1936, this was designated "Model 1936" and was so marked on the upper tang. In 1937, the model designation was shortened to "36". An "RC" serial number suffix identifies a "Regular/Carbine".
Model 1936 (CC receiver, w/long tang, w/o SN prefix) . . . . NiB $792 Ex $664 Gd $432
Model 1936 (CC receiver, w/short tang, w/o SN prefix) . . . . NiB $565 Ex $456 Gd $316
Model 1936 (CC receiver, w/SN prefix) . . . NiB $459 Ex $378 Gd $263
Model 36 (CC receiver, w/SN prefix) . . . . . NiB $436 Ex $353 Gd $246
Model 36 (blued receiver, w/SN prefix) . . . NiB $398 Ex $322 Gd $225

Marlin Model 39 — ADL

Marlin Model 39AS

MODEL 36 SPORTING CARBINE
Same as M36 carbine except w/6-round, (2/3 magazine) and weighs 6.25 lbs.
Model 1936 (CC receiver, w/long tang, w/o SN prefix) . . . . NiB $792 Ex $638 Gd $432
Model 1936 (CC receiver, w/short tang, w/o SN prefix) . . . . NiB $586 Ex $509 Gd $329
Model 1936 (CC receiver, w/SN prefix) . . . NiB $529 Ex $427 Gd $297
Model 36 (CC receiver, w/SN prefix) . . . . . NiB $483 Ex $391 Gd $272
Model 36 (blued receiver, w/SN prefix) . . . NiB $438 Ex $355 Gd $248

MODEL 36A/36A-DL LEVER-ACTION REPEATING RIFLE
Same as Model 36 Carbine except has 24-inch bbl. w/hooded front sight and 2/3 magazine holding 6 cartridges. Weight: 6.75 lbs. Note: An "A" serial number suffix identifies a Rifle while an "A-DL" suffix designates a Deluxe Model w/checkered stock, semibeavertail forearm, swivels and sling. Made 1936-48.
Model 1936 (CC receiver, w/long tang, w/o SN prefix) . . . . NiB $1208 Ex $1054 Gd $333
Model 1936 (CC receiver, w/short tang, w/o SN prefix) . . . . NiB $576 Ex $499 Gd $319
Model 1936 (CC receiver, w/SN prefix) . . . NiB $557 Ex $448 Gd $308
Model 36 (CC receiver, w/SN prefix) . . . . . NiB $493 Ex $396 Gd $273
Model 36 (blued receiver, w/SN prefix) . . . NiB $461 Ex $370 Gd $255
For ADL model, add 25%

MODEL 37 SLIDE-ACTION REPEATING RIFLE . . . . NiB $422 Ex $370 Gd $164
Similar to Model 29 except w/24-inch bbl. and full magazine. Weight: 5.25 lbs. Made 1913-16.

MODEL 38 SLIDE-ACTION REPEATING RIFLE . . . . NiB $370 Ex $267 Gd $164
Hammerless. Takedown. Caliber: .22 LR. Long, Short. 2/3 magazine (tubular) holds 15 Short, 12 Long, 10 LR. 24-inch octagon or round bbls. Weight: 5.5 lbs. Sights: Open rear; bead front. Plain shotgun-type pistol-grip buttstock w/hard rubber buttplate, grooved slide handle. Ivory bead front sight; adj. rear. About 20,000 Model 38 rifles were made between 1920-30.

MODEL 39 CARBINE . . . . NiB $267 Ex $190 Gd $139
Same as 39M except w/lightweight bbl., 3/4 magazine (capacity: 18 Short, 14 Long, 12 LR), slimmer forearm. Weight: 5.25 lbs. Made 1963-67.

MODEL 39 90TH ANNIVERSARY CARBINE . . . . NiB $1044 Ex $967 Gd $725
Carbine version of 90th Anniversary Model 39A. 500 made in 1960. Top value is for carbine in new, unfired condition.

MODEL 39 CENTURY LTD. . . . . NiB $473 Ex $319 Gd $206
Commemorative version of Model 39A. Receiver inlaid w/brass medallion, "Marlin Centennial 1870-1970." Square lever. 20-inch octagon bbl. Fancy walnut straight-grip stock and forearm; brass forend cap, buttplate, nameplate in buttstock. 35,388 made in 1970.

MODEL 39 LEVER-ACTION REPEATER . . . . NiB $2080 Ex $1925 Gd $1040
Takedown. Casehardened receiver. Caliber: .22 LR. Long, Short. Tubular magazine holds 25 Short, 20 Long, 18 LR. 24-inch octagon bbl. Weight: 5.75 lbs. Sights: Open rear; bead front. Plain pistol-grip stock and forearm. Made 1922-38.

MODEL 39A
General specifications same as Model 39 except w/blued receiver, round bbl., heavier stock w/semibeavertail forearm, weight 6.5 lbs. Made 1938-60.
Early model (no prefix) . . . . NiB $1207 Ex $969 Gd $664
Late model ("B" prefix) . . . . NiB $982 Ex $788 Gd $541

MODEL 39A 90TH ANNIVERSARY RIFLE . . . . NiB $1046 Ex $994 Gd $727
Commemorates Marlin's 90th anniversary. Same general specifications as Golden 39A except w/chrome-plated bbl. and action, stock and forearm of select walnut-finely checkered, carved figure of a squirrel on right side of buttstock. 500 made in 1960. Top value is for rifle in new, unfired condition.

MODEL 39A ARTICLE II RIFLE . . . . NiB $499 Ex $370 Gd $267
Commemorates National Rifle Association Centennial 1871-1971. "The Right to Bear Arms" medallion inlaid in receiver. Similar to Model 39A. Magazine capacity: 26 Short, 21 Long, 19 LR. 24-inch octagon bbl. Fancy walnut pistol-grip stock and forearm; brass forend cap, buttplate. 6,244. Made in 1971.

GOLDEN 39A/39AS RIFLE
Same as Model 39A except w/gold-plated trigger, hooded ramp front sight, sling swivels. Made 1960-87 (39A); Model 39AS 1988 to date.
Golden 39A. . . . . NiB $366 Ex $267 Gd $139
Golden 39AS (W/hammer block safety) . . NiB $247 Ex $150 Gd $123

MODEL 39A "MOUNTIE" LEVER-ACTION REPEATING RIFLE. . . . . . . NiB $370 Ex $319 Gd $190
Same as Model 39A except w/lighter, straight-grip stock, slimmer forearm. Weight: 6.25 lbs. Made 1953-60.

MODEL 39A OCTAGON. . . . . NiB $679 Ex $525 Gd $319
Same as Golden 39A except w/oct. bbl., plain bead front sight, slimmer stock and forearm, no pistol-grip cap or swivels. Made 1973. (2551 produced)

MODEL 39D . . . . NiB $242 Ex $195 Gd $139
Same as Model 39M except w/pistol-grip stock, forearm w/bbl. band. Made 1970-74.

39M ARTICLE II CARBINE. . . . . NiB $473 Ex $417 Gd $242
Same as 39A Article II Rifle except w/straight-grip buttstock, square lever, 20-inch octagon bbl., reduced magazine capacity. 3,824m, made in 1971.

GOLDEN 39M
Calibers: .22 Short, Long and LR. Tubular magazine holds 21 Short, 16 Long or 15 LR cartridges. 20-inch bbl. 36 inches overall. Weight: 6 lbs. Gold-plated trigger. Hooded ramp front sight, adj. folding semi-buckhorn rear. Two-piece, straight-grip American black walnut stock. Sling swivels. Mar-Shield finish. Made 1960-87.
Model Golden 39M. . . . . NiB $378 Ex $268 Gd $216
Model 39M Octagon (octagonal bbl. made 1973 only). NiB $448 Ex $417 Gd $319

MODEL 39M "MOUNTIE" CARBINE
Same as Model 39A "Mountie" Rifle except w/20-inch bbl. Weight: 6 lbs. 500 made in 1960. (For values See Marlin 39 90th Anniversary Carbine)

MODEL 39TDS CARBINE. . . . . NiB $319 Ex $216 Gd $139
Same general specifications as Model 39M except takedown style w/16.5-inch bbl. and reduced magazine capacity. 32.63 inches overall. Weight: 5.25 lbs. Made 1988-95.

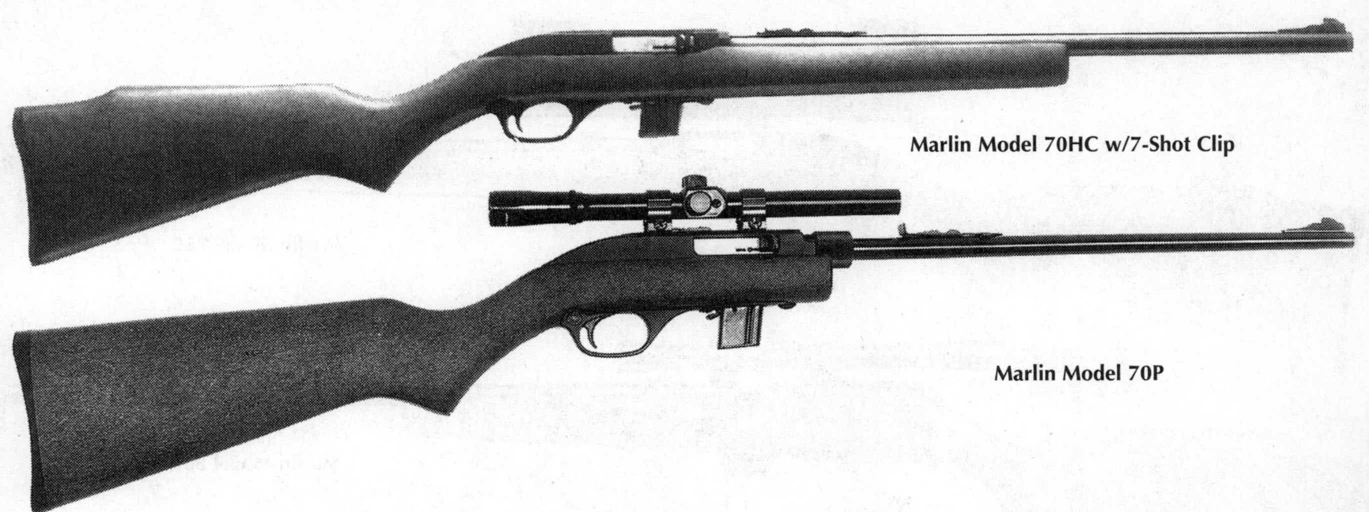

Marlin Model 70HC w/7-Shot Clip

Marlin Model 70P

MODEL 45 .... NiB $297 Ex $241 Gd $138
Semiautomatic action. Caliber: .45 Auto. Seven shot clip.16.5-inch bbl. 35.5 inches overall. Weight: 6.75 lbs. Manual bolt hold-open. Sights: Ramp front sight w/brass bead, adj. folding rear. Receiver drilled and tapped for scope mount. Walnut-finished hardwood stock. Made 1986 to date.

MODEL 49/49DL AUTOLOADING RIFLE
Same as Model 99C except w/two-piece stock, checkered after 1970. Made 1968-71. Model 49DL w/scrollwork on sides of receiver, checkered stock and forearm; made 1971-78.
Model 49..................... NiB $163 Ex $133 Gd $93
Model 49DL .... NiB $170 Ex $138 Gd $97

MODEL 50/50E AUTOLOADING RIFLE
Takedown. Cal: .22 LR. Six round detachable box mag. 22 inch bbl. Wt: 6 lbs. Sights: Open rear; bead front; Mdl. 50E w/peep rear sight, hooded front. Plain pistol-grip stock, forearm w/finger grooves. Made 1931-34.
Model 50..................... NiB $179 Ex $138 Gd $86
Model 50E.................... NiB $189 Ex $138 Gd $91

MODEL 56 LEVERMATIC RIFLE ... NiB $266 Ex $205 Gd $112
Same as Model 57 except clip-loading. Magazine holds eight rounds. Weight: 5.75 lbs. Made 1955-64.

MODEL 57 LEVERMATIC RIFLE ... NiB $266 Ex $205 Gd $112
Lever-action. Cal: .22 LR. 22 Long, 22 Short. Tubular mag. holds 19 LR, 21 Long, 27 Short. 22 inch bbl. Wt: 6.25 lbs. Sights: Open rear, adj. for windage and elevation; hooded ramp front. Monte Carlo-style stock w/pistol-grip. Made 1959-65.

MODEL 57M LEVERMATIC....... NiB $257 Ex $196 Gd $113
Same as Model 57 except chambered for 22 WMR cartridge, w/24-inch bbl., 15-round magazine. Made 1960-69.

MODEL 60 SEMIAUTOMATIC RIFLE .... NiB $112 Ex $86 Gd $60
Caliber: .22 LR. 14-round tubular magazine. 22-inch bbl. 40.5 inches overall. Weight: 5.5 lbs. Grooved receiver. Ramp front sight w/removable hood; adj. open rear. Anodized receiver w/blued bbl. Monte Carlo-style walnut-finished hardwood stock w/Mar-Shield finish. Made 1981 to date. Note: Marketed 1960-1980 under Glenfield promotion logo and w/slightly different stock configuration.

MODEL 60C SELF-LOADING RIFLE .... NiB $117 Ex $107 Gd $81
Cal: .22 LR. 14- round tubular mag. 22 inch Micro-Groove bbl., 40.5 inch overall. Wt: 5.5 lbs. Screw-adjustable open rear and ramp front sights. Aluminum receiver, grooved for scope mount. Hardwood Monte Carlo stock w/Mossy Oak "Break-Up" camouflage pattern. Made 1998 to date.

MODEL 60SS SEMIAUTOMATIC RIFLE
Same general specifications as Model 60 except w/stainless bbl. and magazine tube. Synthetic, uncheckered birch or laminated black/gray birch stock w/nickel-plated swivel studs. Made 1993 to date.
Model 60SB w/uncheckered
birch stock....................... NiB $215 Ex $163 Gd $102
Model 60SS w/laminated
birch stock....................... NiB $225 Ex $163 Gd $102
Model 60SSK w/fiberglass stock......... NiB $215 Ex $163 Gd $102

MODEL 62
LEVERMATIC RIFLE............. NiB $499 Ex $370 Gd $242
Lever-action. Calibers: .256 Magnum, .30 Carbine. Four round clip magazine. 23-inch bbl. Weight: 7 lbs. Sights: Open rear; hooded ramp front. Monte Carlo-style stock w/pistol-grip, swivels and sling. Made in .256 Magnum 1963-66; in .30 Carbine 1966-69.

MODEL 65 BOLT-ACTION
SINGLE-SHOT RIFLE............... NiB $99 Ex $68 Gd $47
Takedown. Caliber: .22 LR. Long, Short. 24-inch bbl. Weight: 5 lbs. Sights: Open rear; bead front. Plain pistol-grip stock w/grooved forearm. Made 1932-38. Model 65E is same as Model 65 except w/rear peep sight and hooded front sight.

MODEL 70HC SEMIAUTOMATIC
Caliber: .22 LR. Seven and 15-round magazine. 18-inch bbl. Weight: 5.5 lbs. 36.75 inches overall. Ramp front sight; adj. open rear. Grooved receiver for scope mounts. Walnut-finished hardwood stock w/Monte Carlo and pistol-grip. Made 1988-96.
Marlin model................. NiB $155 Ex $130 Gd $103
Glenfield model................. NiB $109 Ex $88 Gd $57

MODEL 70P
SEMIAUTOMATIC.............. NiB $160 Ex $135 Gd $78
"Papoose" takedown. Caliber: .22 LR. Seven round clip. 16.25-inch bbl. 35.25 inches overall. Weight: 3.75 lbs. Sights: Ramp front, adj. open rear. Side ejection, manual bolt hold-open. Cross-bolt safety. Walnut-finished hard-wood stock w/abbreviated forend, pistol-grip. Made 1984-94.

MODEL 70PSS
SELF-LOADING CARBINE .... NiB $171 Ex $135 Gd $83
"Papoose" takedown carbine. Caliber: .22 LR. Seven round clip. 16.25- inch bbl., 35.25 inches overall. Weight: 3.25 lbs. Ramp front and adjustable open rear sights. Automatic last-shot hold open (1996). Black fiberglass synthetic stock. Made 1995 to date.

Marlin Model 75C

Marlin Model 80C

Marlin Model 80DL

Marlin Model 81DL

MODEL 75C
SEMIAUTOMATIC . . . . **NiB $160 Ex $109 Gd $83**
Caliber: .22 LR. 13-round tubular magazine.18-inch bbl. 36.5 inches overall. Weight: 5 lbs. Side ejection. Cross-bolt safety. Sights: Ramp-mounted blade front; adj. open rear. Monte Carlo-style walnut-finished hardwood stock w/pistol-grip. Made 1975-92.

MODEL 80 BOLT-ACTION REPEATING RIFLE
Takedown. Caliber: .22 LR. Long, Short. Eight round detachable box magazine. 24-inch bbl. Weight: 6 lbs. Sights: Open rear; bead front. Plain pistol-grip stock. Made 1934-39. Model 80E, w/peep rear sight; hooded front, made 1934-40.
Model 80 Standard . . . . **NiB $130 Ex $99 Gd $68**
Model 80E . . . . **NiB $119 Ex $83 Gd $63**

MODEL 80C/80DL BOLT-ACTION REPEATER
Improved version of Model 80. Model 80C w/bead from sight, semibeavertail forearm; made 1940-70. Model 80DL w/peep rear sight; hooded blade front sight on ramp, swivels; made 1940-65.
Model 80C . . . . **NiB $130 Ex $99 Gd $68**
Model 80DL . . . . **NiB $119 Ex $83 Gd $68**

MODEL 81/81E BOLT-ACTION REPEATER
Takedown. .22 LR. Long, Short. Tubular magazine holds 24 Short, 20 Long, 18 LR. 24-inch bbl. Weight: 6.25 lbs. Sights: Open rear, bead front. Plain pistol-grip stock. Made 1937-40. Model 81E w/peep rear sight; hooded front w/ramp.
Model 81 . . . . **NiB $140 Ex $135 Gd $68**
Model 81E . . . . **NiB $160 Ex $109 Gd $99**

MODEL 81C/81DL BOLT-ACTION REPEATER
Improved version of Model 81 w/same general specifications. Model 81C w/bead front sight, semibeavertail forearm; made 1940-70. Model 81 DL w/peep rear sight, hooded front, swivels; disc. 1965.
Model 81C . . . . **NiB $160 Ex $135 Gd $68**
Model 81DL . . . . **NiB $176 Ex $140 Gd $83**

MODEL 88-C/88-DL AUTOLOADING
Takedown. Caliber: .22 LR. Tubular magazine in buttstock holds 14 cartridges. 24-inch bbl. Weight: 6.75 lbs. Sights: Open rear; hooded front. Plain pistol-grip stock. Made 1947-56. Model 88-DL w/received peep sight, checkered stock and sling swivels, made 1953-56.
Model 88-C . . . . **NiB $186 Ex $160 Gd $99**
Model 88-DL . . . . **NiB $191 Ex $171 Gd $104**

Marlin Model 93 Musket

Marlin Model 93 Lever Action

Marlin Model 94 Sporting Carbine

MODEL 89-C/89-DL AUTOLOADING RIFLE
Clip magazine version of Model 88-C. Seven round clip (12-round in later models); other specifications same. Made 1950-61. Model 89-DL w/receiver peep sight, sling swivels.
Model 89-C . . . . NiB $178 Ex $142 Gd $101
Model 89-DL . . . . NiB $183 Ex $162 Gd $106

MODEL 92 LEVER-ACTION REPEATING RIFLE
Calibers: .22 Short, Long, LR. .32 Short, Long (rimfire or centerfire by changing firing pin). Tubular magazines holding 25 Short, 20 Long, 18 LR (.22); or 17 Short, 14 Long (.32); 16-inch bbl. model w/shorter magazine holding 15 Short, 12 Long, 10 LR. Bbl. lengths: 16 (.22 cal. only) 24, 26, 28 inches. Weight: 5.5 lbs. w/24-inch bbl. Sights: open rear; blade front. Plain straight-grip stock and forearm. Made 1892-1916. Note: Originally designated "Model 1892."
Model 92 (.22 caliber). . . . . NiB $1874 Ex $1307 Gd $689
Model 92 (.32 caliber). . . . . NiB $1452 Ex $1153 Gd $823

MODEL 93/93SC CARBINE
Same as Standard Model 93 Rifle except in calibers .30-30 and .32 Special only. Model 93 w/7-round magazine. 20-inch round bbl., carbine sights, weight: 6.75 lbs. Model 93SC magazine capacity 5 rounds, weight 6.5 lbs.
Model 93 Carbine
(w/saddle ring) . . . . NiB $1565 Ex $1307 Gd $1024
Model 93 Carbine ("Bullseye"
w/o saddle ring) . . . . NiB $1050 Ex $937 Gd $586
Model 93SC Sporting Carbine. . . . . NiB $1668 Ex $1359 Gd $947

MODEL 93
LEVER-ACTION
REPEATING RIFLE . . . . NiB $2296 Ex $1884 Gd $1261
Solid frame or takedown. Calibers: .25-36 Marlin, .30-30, .32 Special, .32-40, .38-55. Tubular magazine holds 10 cartridges. 26-inch round or octagon bbl. standard; also made w/28-, 30- and 32-inch bbls. Weight: 7.25 lbs. Sights: Open rear; bead front. Plain straight-grip stock and forearm. Made 1893-1936. Note: Before 1915 designated "Model 1893."

MODEL 93 MUSKET . . . . NiB $4055 Ex $3015 Gd $1676
Same as Standard Model 93 except w/30-inch bbl., angular bayonet, ramrod under bbl., musket stock, full-length military-style forearm. Weight: 8 lbs. Made 1893-1915.

MODEL 94 LEVER-ACTION
REPEATING RIFLE . . . . NiB $2635 Ex $2090 Gd $1961
Solid frame or takedown. Calibers: .25-20, .32-20, .38-40, .44-40. 10-round tubular magazine. 24-inch round or octagon bbl. Weight: 7 lbs. Sights open rear; bead front. Plain straight-grip stock and forearm (also available w/pistol-grip stock). Made 1894-1934. Note: Before 1906 designated "Model 1894."

MODEL 94 LEVER-ACTION COWBOY SERIES
Calibers: .357 Mag., .44-40, .44 Mag., .45 LC. 10-round magazine. 24-inch tapered octagon bbl. Weight: 7.5 lbs. 41.5 inches overall. Marble carbine front sight, adjustable semi-buckhorn rear. Blue finish. Checkered, straight-grip American black walnut stock w/hard rubber buttplate. Made 1996 to date. Cowboy II introduced in 1997.
Cowboy model (.45 LC) . . . . NiB $525 Ex $396 Gd $267
Cowboy II model (.357 Mag.,
.44-40, .44 Mag) . . . . NiB $525 Ex $396 Gd $267

MODEL 97 LEVER-ACTION
REPEATING RIFLE . . . . NiB $2548 Ex $2064 Gd $1982
Takedown. Caliber: .22 LR. Long, Short. Tubular magazine; full length holds 25 Short, 20 Long, 18 LR; half length holds 16 Short, 12 Long and 10 LR. Bbl. lengths: 16, 24, 26, 28 inches. Weight: 6 lbs. Sights: Open rear; bead front. Plain, straight-grip stock and forearm (also avail. w/pistol-grip stock). Made 1897-1922. Note: Before 1905 designated "Model 1897."

MODEL 98 AUTOLOADING RIFLE. . . . . . . NiB $160 Ex $104 Gd $83
Solid frame. Caliber: .22 LR. Tubular magazine holds 15 cartridges. 22-inch bbl. Weight: 6.75 lbs. Sights: Open rear; hooded ramp front. Monte Carlo stock w/cheekpiece. Made 1950-61.

MODEL 99 AUTOLOADING RIFLE. . . . . . . NiB $160 Ex $104 Gd $83
Caliber: .22 LR. Tubular magazine holds 18 cartridges. 22-inch bbl. Weight: 5.5 lbs. Sights: Open rear; hooded ramp front. Plain pistol-grip stock. Made 1959-61.

MODEL 99C . . . . NiB $171 Ex $135 Gd $88
Same as Model 99 except w/gold-plated trigger, receiver grooved for tip-off scope mounts, Monte Carlo stock (checkered in later production). Made 1962-78.

MODEL 99DL . . . . NiB $215 Ex $189 Gd $107
Same as Model 99 except w/gold-plated trigger, jeweled breech bolt, Monte Carlo stock w/pistol-grip, swivels and sling. Made 1960-65.

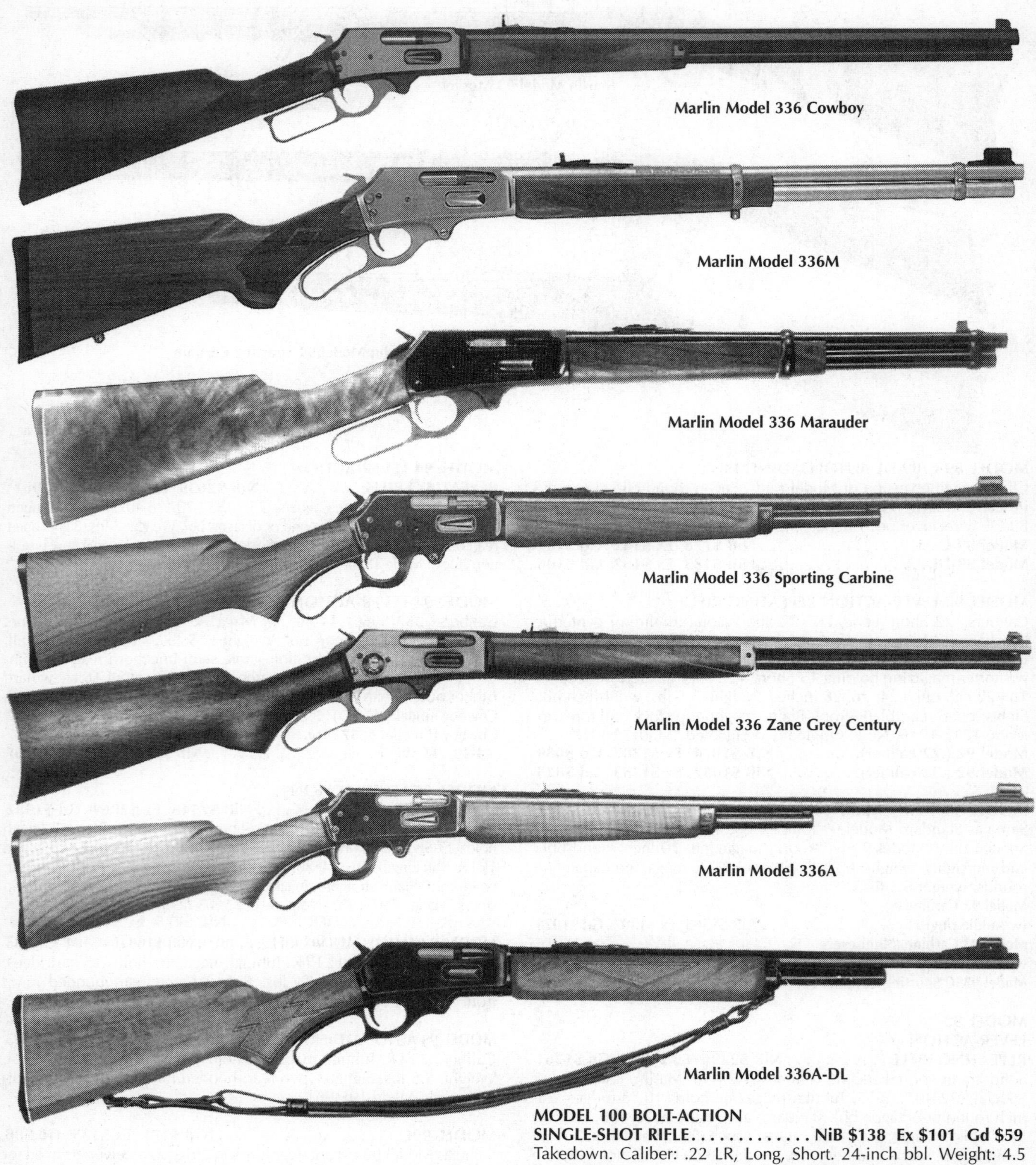
Marlin Model 336 Cowboy

Marlin Model 336M

Marlin Model 336 Marauder

Marlin Model 336 Sporting Carbine

Marlin Model 336 Zane Grey Century

Marlin Model 336A

Marlin Model 336A-DL

MODEL 99M1 CARBINE . . . . NiB $224 Ex $162 Gd $111
Same as Model 99C except styled after U.S. .30 M1 Carbine; 9-round tubular magazine, 18-inch bbl. Sights: Open rear; military-style ramp front; carbine stock w/handguard and bbl. band, sling swivels. Weight: 4.5 lbs. Made 1966-79.

MODEL 100 BOLT-ACTION SINGLE-SHOT RIFLE . . . . NiB $138 Ex $101 Gd $59
Takedown. Caliber: .22 LR, Long, Short. 24-inch bbl. Weight: 4.5 lbs. Sights: Open rear; bead front. Plain pistol-grip stock. Made 1936-60.

MODEL 100SB . . . . NiB $132 Ex $106 Gd $68
Same as Model 100 except smoothbore for use w/22 shot cartridges, shotgun sight. Made 1936-41.

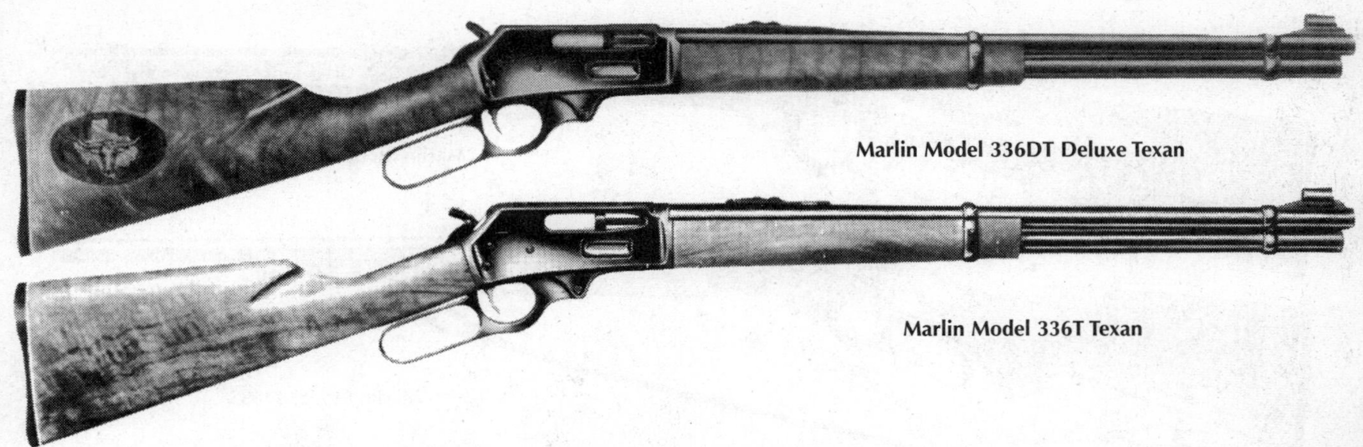
Marlin Model 336DT Deluxe Texan

Marlin Model 336T Texan

MODEL 100 TOM MIX SPECIAL. . . . . NiB $401 Ex $314 Gd $216
Same as Model 100 except w/peep rear sight; hooded front; sling. Made 1936-46.

MODEL 101 . . . . NiB $104 Ex $83 Gd $47
Improved version of Model 100 w/same general specifications, except w/stock w/beavertail forearm, weighs 5 lbs. Intro. 1951. Disc.

MODEL 101 DL. . . . . NiB $109 Ex $78 Gd $47
Same as Model 101 except has peep rear sight; hooded front, swivels. Disc.

MODEL 122 SINGLE-SHOT JUNIOR TARGET RIFLE . . . . NiB $83 Ex $57 Gd $42
Bolt action. Caliber: .22 LR, .22 Long, .22 Short. 22-inch bbl. Weight: 5 lbs. Sights: Open rear; hooded ramp front. Monte Carlo stock w/pistol-grip, swivels, sling. Made 1961-65.

MODEL 322 BOLT-ACTION VARMINT RIFLE . . . . NiB $578 Ex $527 Gd $316
Sako short Mauser action. Caliber: .222 Rem. Three round clip magazine. 24-inch medium weight bbl. Checkered stock. Sights: Two-position peep rear; hooded ramp front. Weight: 7.5 lbs. Made 1954-57.

MODEL 336A LEVER-ACTION RIFLE . . . . NiB $319 Ex $190 Gd $173
Improved version of Model 36A Rifle w/same general specifications except w/improved action w/round breech bolt. Calibers: .30-30, .32 Special (disc. 1963), .35 Rem. (intro. 1952). Made 1948-63; reintroduced 1973, disc. 1980.

MODEL 336A-DL . . . . NiB $553 Ex $475 Gd $295
Same as Model 336A Rifle except w/deluxe checkered stock and forearm, swivels and sling. Made 1948-63.

MODEL 336AS LEVER-ACTION RIFLE . . . . NiB $240 Ex $173 Gd $121
Similar to Model 30AS. Caliber: .30-30 Win., Six round tubular magazine. 20- inch Micro-Groove bbl. 38.25 inches overall. Weight: 7 lbs. Maine birch pistol grip stock w/swivel studs and hard rubber butt plate. Tapped for scope mount and receiver sight. Screw-adjustable open rear and ramp front sight. Checkered walnut finish. Made 1999 to date.

MODEL 336C LEVER-ACTION CARBINE . . . . NiB $291 Ex $235 Gd $160
Improved version of Model 36 Carbine w/same general specifications except w/improved action w/round breech bolt. Original calibers: .30-30 and .32 Win. Spec. Made 1948-83. Note: Caliber .35 Rem. intro. 1953. Caliber .32 Winchester Special disc. 1963.

MODEL 336 COWBOY LEVER-ACTION RIFLE . . . . NiB $578 Ex $424 Gd $295
Calibers: .30-30 Win., or .38-55 Win., 6- round tubular magazine. 24- inch tapered octagon bbl. 42.5 inches overall. Weight: 7.5 lbs. American black walnut checkering stock. Marble carbine front sight w/solid top receiver drilled and tapped for scope mount. Mar-Shield finish. Made 1998 to date.

MODEL 336CS W/SCOPE . . . . NiB $370 Ex $262 Gd $164
Lever-action w/hammer block safety. Caliber: .30/30 Win. or .35 Rem. Six round tubular magazine. 20-inch round bbl. w/Micro-Groove rifling. 38.5 inches overall. Weight: 7 lbs. Ramp front sight w/hood, adj. semi-buckhorn folding rear. Solid top receiver drilled and tapped for scope mount or receiver sight; offset hammer spur for scope use. American black walnut stock w/pistol-grip, fluted comb. Mar-Shield finish. Made 1984 to date.

MODEL 336DT DELUXE TEXAN. . . . . NiB $422 Ex $417 Gd $319
Same as Model 336T except w/select walnut stock and forearm, hand-carved longhorn steer and map of Texas on buttstock. Made 1962-64.

MODEL 336M LEVER-ACTION RIFLE. . . . . NiB $527 Ex $424 Gd $295
Calibers: .30-30 Win., 6- round tubular magazine. 20- inch stainless steel Micro Groove bbl., 38.5 inches overall. Weight: 7 lbs. American black walnut w/checkered pistol-grip stock. Adjustable folding semi-buckhorn rear and ramp front sight w/brass bead and removable Wide-Scan hood. Tapped for receiver sight and scope mount. Mar-Shield finish. Made 1999 to date.

MODEL 336 MARAUDER . . . . NiB $475 Ex $424 Gd $238
Same as Model 336 Texan Carbine except w/16.25-inch bbl., weight: 6.25 lbs. Made 1963-64.

MODEL 336-MICRO GROOVE ZIPPER . . . NiB $553 Ex $475 Gd $316
General specifications same as Model 336 Sporting Carbine except caliber .219 Zipper. Made 1955-61.

MODEL 336 OCTAGON . . . . NiB $527 Ex $460 Gd $197
Same as Model 336T except chambered for .30-30 only w/22-inch octagon bbl. Made 1973.

MODEL 336 SPORTING CARBINE. . . . . . . NiB $424 Ex $321 Gd $166
Same as Model 336A rifle except w/20-inch bbl., weight: 6.25 lbs. Made 1948-63.

MODEL 336T TEXAN CARBINE . . . . NiB $267 Ex $216 Gd $190
Same as Model 336 Carbine except w/straight-grip stock and is not available in caliber .32 Special. Made 1953-83. Caliber .44 Magnum made 1963-67.

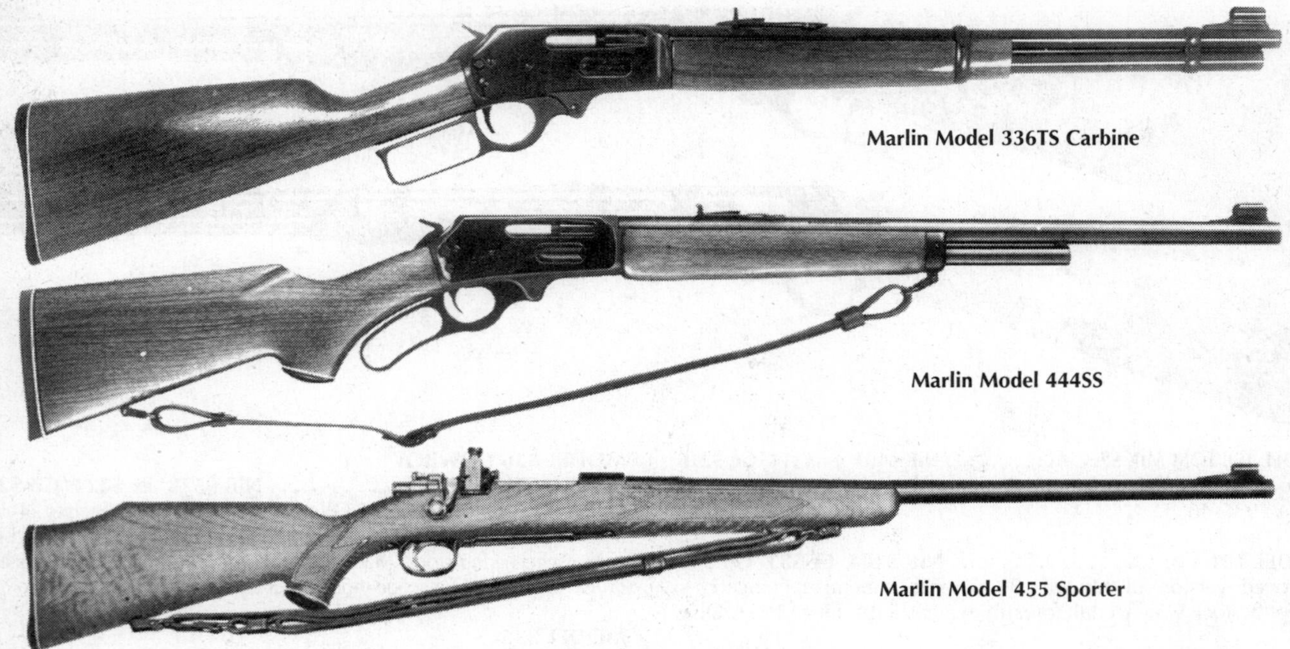

Marlin Model 336TS Carbine

Marlin Model 444SS

Marlin Model 455 Sporter

MODEL 336TS. . . . . NiB $345 Ex $293 Gd $139
Lever-action w/hammer-block safety. Caliber: .30-30 Win. Six round tubular magazine. 18.5-inch Micro-Groove bbl. 37 inches overall. Weight: 6.5 lbs. Ramp front sight, adj. semi-buckhorn folding rear. Straight-grip American black walnut stock. Made 1983-87.

MODEL 336 ZANE GREY CENTURY . . . . NiB $473 Ex $370 Gd $242
Similar to Model 336A except w/22-inch octagonal bbl., caliber .30-30, Zane Grey Centennial 1872-1972 medallion inlaid in receiver; select walnut stock w/classic pistol-grip and forearm; brass buttplate, forend cap. Weight: 7 lbs. 10,000 produced (numbered ZG1 through ZG10,000). Made 1972.

MODEL 444 LEVER-ACTION REPEATING RIFLE . . . . NiB $396 Ex $345 Gd $164
Action similar to Model 336. Caliber: .444 Marlin. Four round tubular magazine. 24-inch bbl. Weigh: 7.5 lbs. Sights: Open rear; hooded ramp front. Monte Carlo stock w/straight grip, recoil pad. Carbine-style forearm w/bbl. band. Swivels, sling. Made 1965-71.

MARLIN MODEL 444 SPORTER. . . . . NiB $401 Ex $370 Gd $175
Same as Model 444 Rifle except w/22-inch bbl., pistol-grip stock and forearm as on Model 336A, recoil pad, QD swivels and sling. Made 1972-83.

MODEL 444P (OUTFITTER) LEVER-ACTION RIFLE . . . . NiB $485 Ex $370 Gd $190
Caliber: .444 Marlin. Five round tubular magazine. 18.5-inch ported bbl., 37 inches overall. Weight: 6.75 lbs. Ramp front and adjustable folding rear sights. Black walnut straight grip stock w/cut checkering and Mar-Shield finish. Made 1998 to date.

MODEL 444SS. . . . . NiB $499 Ex $370 Gd $190
Same general specifications as Model 444 except w/hammer safety. Made 1984 to date.

MODEL 455 BOLT-ACTION SPORTER
FN Mauser action w/Sako trigger. Calibers: .30-06 or .308. Five round box magazine. 24-inch medium weight stainless-steel bbl. Monte Carlo stock w/cheekpiece, checkered pistol grip and forearm. Lyman No. 48 receiver sight; hooded ramp front. Weight: 8.5 lbs. Made 1957-59.

Model 455 (chambered for .30-06, 1079 produced) . . . . NiB $584 Ex $456 Gd $250
Model 455 (chambered for .308, 59 produced). . . . NiB $584 Ex $456 Gd $250

MODEL 780 BOLT-ACTION REPEATER SERIES
Caliber: .22 LR. Long, Short. Seven round clip magazine. 22-inch bbl. Weight: 5.5 to 6 lbs. Sights: Open rear; hooded ramp front. Receiver grooved for scope mounting. Monte Carlo stock w/checkered pistol-grip and forearm. Made 1971-88.

Model 780 Standard . . . . NiB $121 Ex $90 Gd $65
Model 781 (w/17-round tubular magazine) . . NiB $121 Ex $90 Gd $65
Model 782 (.22 WMR, w/swivels, sling) . . . . . NiB $121 Ex $90 Gd $65
Model 783 (w/12-round tubular magazine) . . NiB $121 Ex $90 Gd $65

MODEL 795 SELF-LOADING RIFLE . . . . NiB $137 Ex $111 Gd $90
Caliber: .22 LR. 10- round clip. 18- inch Micro-Groove bbl., 37 inches overall. Weight: 5 lbs. Screw-adjustable open rear and ramp front sight. Monte Carlo synthetic stock with checkering swivel studs. Made 1999 to date.

MODEL 880 BOLT-ACTION REPEATER SERIES
Caliber: .22 rimfire. Seven round magazine. 22-inch bbl. 41 inches overall. Weight: 5.5 to 6 lbs. Hooded ramp front sight; adj. folding rear. Grooved receiver for scope mounts. Checkered Monte Carlo-style walnut stock w/QD studs and rubber recoil pad. Made 1989-97.

Model 880 (.22 LR). . . . . NiB $195 Ex $144 Gd $87
Model 880SS (Stainless .22 LR). . . . . NiB $216 Ex $175 Gd $122
Model 880SQ (Squirrel .22 LR). . . . . NiB $229 Ex $185 Gd $129
Model 881 (w/7-round tubular magazine. . . NiB $200 Ex $149 Gd $87
Model 882 (.22 WMR) . . . . NiB $190 Ex $154 Gd $108
Model 882L (w/laminated hardwood stock) . . . . . . NiB $200 Ex $149 Gd $87
Model 882SS (Stainless w/fire sights) . . . . . NiB $236 Ex $190 Gd $133
Model 882SSV (Stainless .22 LR) . . . . NiB $236 Ex $190 Gd $133
Model 883 (.22 WMR w/12-round tubular magazine). . . . . NiB $195 Ex $144 Gd $87
Model 883N (w/nickel-Teflon finish) . . . . . NiB $232 Ex $189 Gd $136
Model 883SS (stainless w/laminated stock) . . . . NiB $251 Ex $170 Gd $148

Marlin Model 780

Marlin Model 781

Marlin Model 783

Marlin Model 882L

Marlin Model 883N

MODEL 922 MAGNUM SELF-LOADING RIFLE . . . . NiB $370 Ex $293 Gd $113
Similar to Model 9 except chambered for .22 WMR. Seven round magazine. 20.5-inch bbl. 39.5 inches overall. Weight: 6.5 lbs. American black walnut stock w/Monte Carlo. Blued finish. Made 1993 to date.

MODEL 980 .22 MAGNUM . . . . NiB $173 Ex $121 Gd $85
Bolt action. Caliber: .22 WMR. Eight round clip magazine. 24-inch bbl. Weight: 6 lbs. Sights: Open rear; hooded ramp front. Monte Carlo stock, swivels, sling. Made 1962-70.

MODEL 989 AUTOLOADING RIFLE. . . . . . . NiB $152 Ex $106 Gd $80
Caliber: .22 LR. Seven round clip magazine. 22-inch bbl. Weight: 5.5 lbs. Sights: Open rear; hooded ramp front. Monte Carlo walnut stock w/pistol grip. Made 1962-66.

MODEL 989M2 CARBINE . . . . NiB $152 Ex $101 Gd $77
Same as Model 99M1 except clip-loading, 7-round magazine. Made 1966-79.

MODEL 990 SEMIAUTOMATIC
Caliber: .22 LR. 17-round tubular magazine. 22-inch bbl. 40.75 inches overall. Weight: 5.5 lbs. Side ejection. Cross-bolt safety. Ramp front sight w/brass bead; adj. semi-buckhorn folding rear. Receiver grooved for scope mount. Monte Carlo-style American black walnut stock w/checkered pistol grip and forend. Made 1979-87.
Model 990 Semiautomatic . . . . NiB $152 Ex $121 Gd $80
Model 990L (w/14 rounds, laminated hardwood stock, QD studs, black recoil pad; 1992 to date). . . . . NiB $137 Ex $106 Gd $80

MODEL 995 SEMIAUTOMATIC .... NiB $173 Ex $132 Gd $85
Caliber: .22 LR. Seven round clip magazine.18-inch bbl. 36.75 inches overall. Weight: 5 lbs. Cross-bolt safety. Sights: Ramp front w/brass bead; adj. folding semi-buckhorn rear. Monte Carlo-style American black walnut stock w/checkered pistol grip and forend. Made 1979-94.

MODEL 1870-1970 CENTENNIAL MATCHED PAIR, MODELS 336 AND 39 .... NiB $1956 Ex $1621 Gd $1055
Presentation-grade rifles in luggage-style case. Matching serial numbers. Fancy walnut straight-grip buttstock and forearm brass buttplate and forend cap. Engraved receiver w/inlaid medallion; square lever. 20-inch octagon bbl. Model 336: .30-30, 7-round, 7 lbs. Model 39: .22 Short, Long, LR, tubular magazine holds 21 Short

***(cont'd.)* MODEL 1870-1970 CENTENNIAL MATCHED PAIR, MODELS 336 AND 39**
16 Long, 15 LR. 1,000 sets produced. Made 1970. Top value is for rifles in new, unfired condition. See illustration on page 283.

MODEL 1892 LEVER-ACTION RIFLE
See Marlin Model 92 listed previously under this section.

MODEL 1893 LEVER-ACTION RIFLE
See Marlin Model 93 listed previously under this section.

MODEL 1894 LEVER-ACTION RIFLE
See Marlin Model 94 Lever-Action Rifle listed previously under this section.

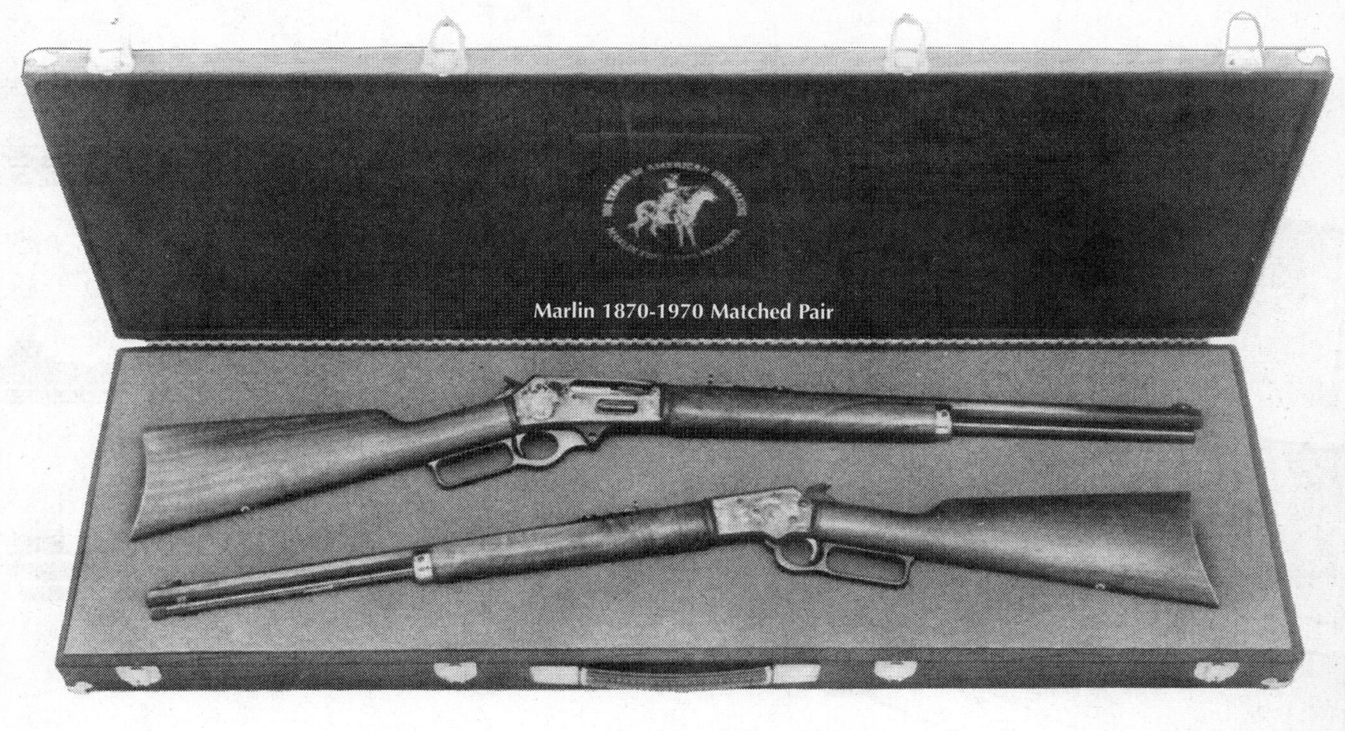

Marlin 1870-1970 Matched Pair

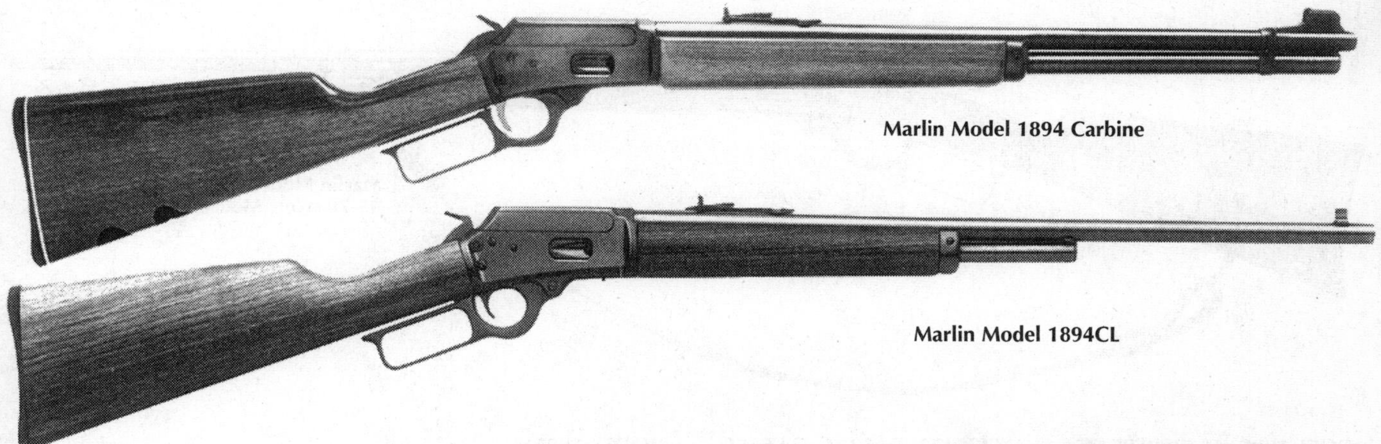

Marlin Model 1894 Carbine

Marlin Model 1894CL

MODEL 1894 CARBINE
Replica of original Model 94. Caliber: .44 Rem. 10-round magazine. 20-inch round bbl. Weight: 6 lbs. Sight: Open rear; ramp front. Straight-grip stock. Made 1969-84.
Standard Model
1894 Carbine .... **NiB $396 Ex $267 Gd $190**
Model 1894 Octagon
(made 1973) .... **NiB $422 Ex $345 Gd $195**
Model 1894 Sporter (w/22-inch bbl., made 1973) .... **NiB $396 Ex $267 Gd $242**

MODEL 1894CL CLASSIC .... **NiB $473 Ex $345 Gd $190**
Calibers: .218 Bee, .25-20 Win., .32-20 Win. Six round tubular magazine. 22-inch bbl. 38.75 inches overall. Weight: 6.25 lbs. Adj. semibuckhorn folding rear sight, brass bead front. Receiver tapped for scope mounts. Straight-grip American black walnut stock w/Mar-Shield finish. Made 1988-94.

MODEL 1894CS LEVER-ACTION .... **NiB $422 Ex $370 Gd $164**
Caliber: .357 Magnum, .38 Special. Nine round tubular magazine. 18.5-inch bbl. 36 inches overall. Weight: 6 lbs. Side ejection. Hammer block safety. Square finger lever. Bead front sight, adj. semi-buckhorn folding rear. Offset hammer spur for scope use. Two-piece straight grip American black walnut stock w/white buttplate spacer. Mar-Shield finish. Made 1984 to date.

MODEL 1894M LEVER-ACTION .... **NiB $319 Ex $267 Gd $164**
Caliber: .22 WMR.11-round tubular magazine. 20-inch bbl. Weight: 6.25 lbs. Sights: Ramp front w/brass bead and Wide-Scan hood; adj. semi-buckhorn folding rear. Offset hammer spur for scope use. Straight-grip American black walnut stock w/white buttplate spacer. Squared finger lever. Made 1986-88.

MODEL 1894S LEVER-ACTION .... **NiB $370 Ex $293 Gd $190**
Calibers: .41 Mag., .44 Rem. Mag., .44 S&W Special, .45 Colt.10-shot tubular magazine. 20-inch bbl.37.5 inches overall. Weight: 6 lbs. Sights and stock same as Model 1894M. Made 1984 to date.

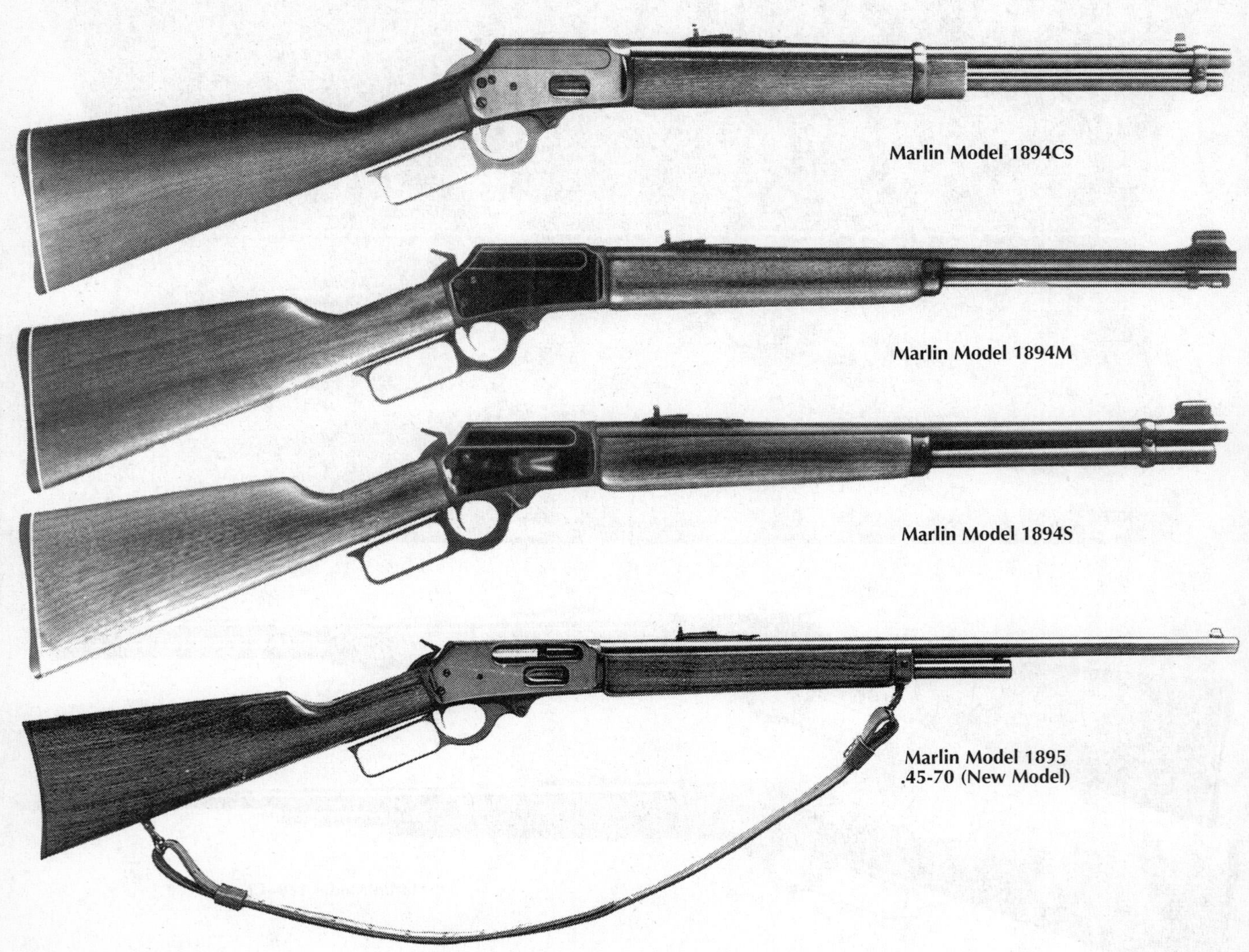

MODEL 1895 .45-70 REPEATER . . . NiB $433 Ex $324 Gd $169
Model 336-type action. Caliber: .45-70 Government. Four round magazine. 22-inch bbl. Weight: 7 lbs. Sights: Open rear; bead front. Straight-grip stock, forearm w/metal end cap, QD swivels, leather sling. Made 1972-79.

MODEL 1895
LEVER-ACTION REPEATER . . . . NiB $324 Ex $293 Gd $221
Solid frame or takedown. Calibers: .33 WCF, .38-56, .40-65, .40-70, .40-82, .45-70. Nine round tubular magazine. 24-inch round or octagongon bbl. standard (other lengths available). Weight: 8 lbs. Sights: Open rear; bead front. Plain stock and forearm (also available w/pistol-grip stock). Made 1895-1915.

MODEL 1895G (GUIDE GUN)
LEVER-ACTION RIFLE . . . . NiB $695 Ex $519 Gd $422
Caliber: .45-70 Govt., 4- round magazine. 18.5-inch ported bbl., 37 inches overall. Weight: 6.75 lbs. Ramp front and adjustable folding rear sights. Black walnut straight grip stock w/cut checkering and Mar-Shield finish. Made 1998 to date.

MODEL 1895M
LEVER-ACTION RIFLE . . . . NiB $615 Ex $530 Gd $490
Caliber: .450 Marlin. Four round tubular magazine., 18.5- inch ported bbl. w/Ballard-type rifling. 37 inches overall. Weight: 6.75 lbs. Genuine American black walnut straight-grip stock w/checkering. Ventilated recoil pad. Adjustable folding semi-buckhorn rear and ramp front sights. Mar-Shield finish. Made 1999 to date.

MODEL 1895SS
LEVER-ACTION. . . . . NiB $350 Ex $272 Gd $195
Caliber: .45-70 Govt. Four round tubular magazine. 22-inch bbl. w/Micro-Groove rifling. 40.5 inches overall. Weight: 7.5 lbs. Ramp front sight w/brass bead and Wide-Scan hood; adj. semi-buckhorn folding rear. Solid top receiver tapped for scope mount or receiver sight. Off-set hammer spur for scope use. Two-piece American black walnut stock w/fluted comb, pistol-grip, sling swivels. Made 1984 to date.

MODEL 1897 LEVER-ACTION RIFLE
See Marlin Model 97 listed previously under this section.

Marlin Model 1895G

Marlin Model 1895M

Marlin Model 1895SS

Marlin Model 1895 Rifle (Old Model — 1895-1915)

Marlin Model 1897 Cowboy

MODEL 1897 COWBOY LEVER-ACTION RIFLE . . . . NiB $628 Ex $525 Gd $293
Caliber: .22 LR., capacity: 19 LR, 21 L, or 26 S, tubular magazine. 24-inch tapered octagon bbl., 40 inches overall. Weight: 6.5 lbs. Marble front and adjustable rear sight, tapped for scope mount. Black walnut straight grip stock w/cut checkering and Mar-Shield finish. Made 1999 to date.

MODEL 1936 LEVER-ACTION CARBINE
See Marlin Model 36 listed previously under this section.

MODEL 2000 TARGET RIFLE
Bolt-action single-shot. Caliber: .22 LR. Optional 5-round adapter kit available. 22-inch bbl. 41 inches overall. Weight: 8 lbs. Globe front sight, adj. peep or aperture rear. two-stage target trigger. Textured composite Kevlar or black/gray laminated stock. Made 1991 to date.
Model 2000 (disc. 1995). . . . . NiB $499 Ex $427 Gd $267
Model 2000A w/Adj. comb (Made 1994 only) . . . . NiB $551 Ex $448 Gd $267
Model 2000L w/laminated stock (intro. 1996) . . . . NiB $581 Ex $473 Gd $337

MODEL 7000 . . . . NiB $220 Ex $178 Gd $123
Caliber: .22 LR. 10-round magazine. 18-inch bbl. Weight: 5.5 lbs. Synthetic stocks. No sights; receiver grooved for scope. Semi-auto. Side ejection. Manual bolt hold-open. Cross-bolt safety. Matte finish. Made 1997 to date.
Model 7000. . . . . NiB $240 Ex $188 Gd $137
Model 7000T. . . . . NiB $394 Ex $317 Gd $265

MODEL A-1 AUTOLOADING RIFLE . . . . NiB $188 Ex $111 Gd $85
Takedown. Caliber: .22 LR. Six round detachable box magazine. 24-inch bbl. Weight: 6 lbs. Open rear sight. Plain pistol-grip stock. Made 1935-46.

MODEL A-1C AUTOLOADING RIFLE. . . . . NiB $162 Ex $101 Gd $70
Improved version of Model A-1 w/same general specifications, stock w/semibeavertail forend. Made 1940-46.

MODEL A-1DL . . . . NiB $162 Ex $101 Gd $70
Same as Model A-1C except w/peep rear sight; hooded front, swivels.

MODEL A-1E . . . . **NiB $162 Ex $101 Gd $70**
Same as Model A-1 except w/peep rear sight; hooded front.

MODEL MR-7 BOLT-ACTION RIFLE
Calibers: .25-06 Rem., .270 Win., .280 Rem., .308 Win. or .30-06. Four round magazine. 22-inch bbl. w/ or w/o sights. 43.31 inches overall. Weight: 7.5 lbs. Checkered American walnut or birch stock w/recoil pad and sling-swivel studs. Jeweled bolt w/cocking indicator and 3-position safety. Made from 1996-99.
Model MR-7 . . . . **NiB $471 Ex $343 Gd $240**
Model MR7B w/birch stock (Intro. 1998) . . . . **NiB $142 Ex $137 Gd $106**
Open sights, add **$35**

MODEL 10 . . . . **NiB $111 Ex $90 Gd $64**
Same as Marlin Model 101 except w/walnut-finished hardwood stock. Made 1966-79. Note: Later production w/hot-iron-stamped wood pistol grip to simulate checkering/carving; plain forend.

MODEL 20 . . . . **NiB $111 Ex $90 Gd $64**
Same as Marlin Model 80/780 except w/bead front sight, walnut-finished hardwood stock. Made 1966-82. Note: Recent production has stamped pistol-grip to simulate checkering; plain forend.

MODEL 30 . . . . **NiB $162 Ex $101 Gd $70**
Same as Marlin Model 336C except chambered for .30-30 only, w/4-round magazine, plainer stock and forearm of walnut-finished hardwood. Made 1966-68.

MODEL 30A . . . . **NiB $240 Ex $162 Gd $111**
Same as Marlin Model 336C except chambered for .30-30 only, w/checkered stock of walnut-finished hardwood. Made 1969-83.

MODEL 36G . . . . **NiB $265 Ex $162 Gd $105**
Same as Marlin Model 336C except chambered for .30-30 only, w/5-round magazine, plainer stock. Made 1960-65.

MODEL 60 . . . . **NiB $85 Ex $59 Gd $44**
Same as Marlin Model 99C except w/walnut-finished hardwood stock. Made 1960-80.

MODEL 70 . . . . **NiB $90 Ex $70 Gd $49**
Same as Marlin Model 989M2 except w/walnut-finished hardwood stock; no handguard. Made 1966-69.

MODEL 80G . . . . **NiB $90 Ex $70 Gd $49**
Same as Marlin Model 80C except w/plain stock, bead front sight. Made 1960-65.

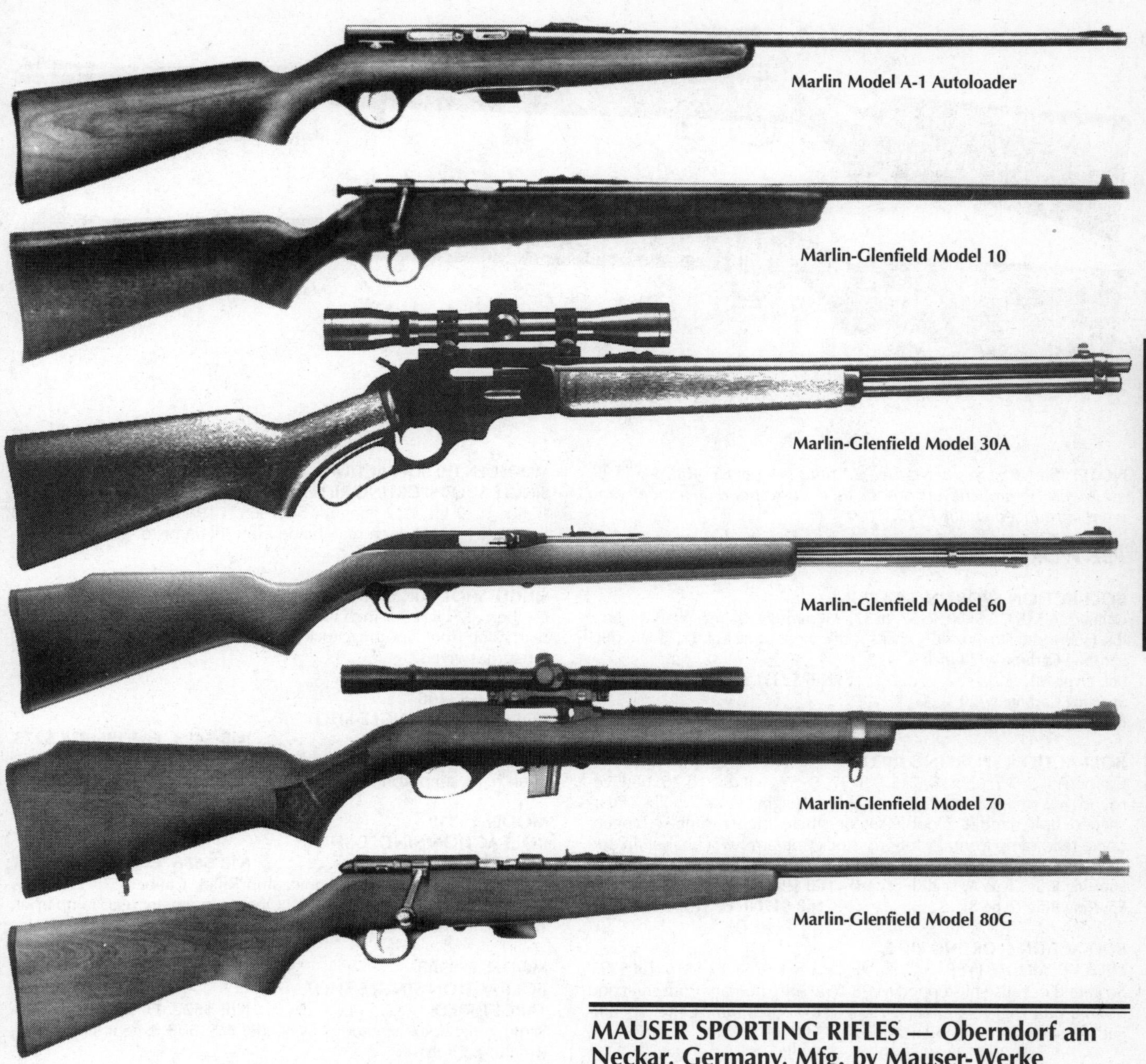
Marlin Model A-1 Autoloader

Marlin-Glenfield Model 10

Marlin-Glenfield Model 30A

Marlin-Glenfield Model 60

Marlin-Glenfield Model 70

Marlin-Glenfield Model 80G

MODEL 81G .... NiB $82 Ex $56 Gd $46
Same as Marlin Model 81C except w/plain stock, bead front sight. Made 1960-65.

MODEL 99G .... NiB $87 Ex $72 Gd $56
Same as Marlin Model 99C except w/plain stock, bead front sight. Made 1960-65.

MODEL 101G .... NiB $82 Ex $56 Gd $46
Same as Marlin Model 101 except w/plain stock. Made 1960-65.

MODEL 989G
AUTOLOADING RIFLE .... NiB $82 Ex $56 Gd $46
Same as Marlin Model 989 except w/plain stock, bead front sight. Made 1962-64.

MAUSER SPORTING RIFLES — Oberndorf am Neckar, Germany, Mfg. by Mauser-Werke GmbH, *Imported by Brolin Arms, Pomona, CA, (Previously by Gun South, Inc.; Gibbs Rifle Co.; Precision Imports, Inc. and KDF, Inc.)*

Before the end of WWI the name of the Mauser firm was "Waffenfabrik Mauser A.-G." Shortly after WWI it was changed to "Mauser-Werke A.-G." This information may be used to determine the age of genuine original Mauser sporting rifles made before WWII because all bear either of these firm names as well as the Mauser banner trademark.

The first four rifles listed were manufactured before WWI. Those that follow were produced between World Wars I and II. The early Mauser models can generally be identified by the pistol grip, which is rounded instead of capped, and the M/98 military-type magazine floorplate and catch. The later models have hinged magazine floorplates with lever or button release.

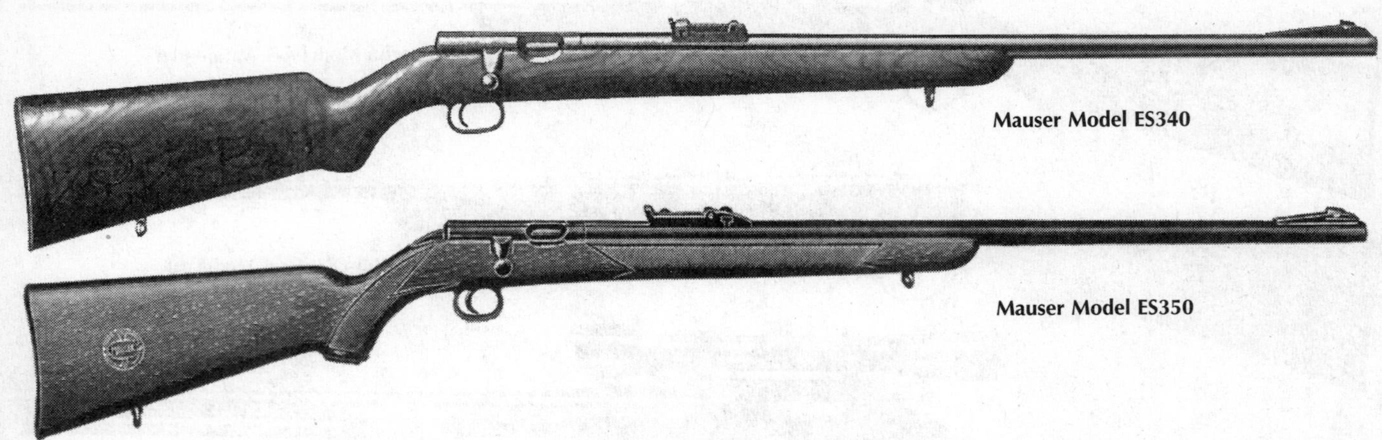
Mauser Model ES340

Mauser Model ES350

NOTE: *The "B" series of Mauser .22 rifles (Model ES340B, MS350B, etc.) were improved versions of their corresponding models and were introduced about 1935.*

PRE-WORLD WAR I MODELS

BOLT-ACTION SPORTING CARBINE
Calibers: 6.5x54, 6.5x58, 7x57, 8x57, 957mm. 19.75-inch bbl. Weight: 7 lbs. Full-stocked to muzzle. Other specifications same as for standard rifle.
Sporting Carbine w/20-inch bbl. (Type M)...................... NiB $2351 Ex $1889 Gd $1298
Sporting Carbine w/20 or 24-inch bbl. (Type S)............ NiB $2422 Ex $1945 Gd $1336

BOLT-ACTION SPORTING RIFLE
Calibers: 6.5x55, 6.5x58, 7x57, 8x57, 9x57, 9.3x62 10.75x68.Five-round box magazine, 23.5-inch bbl. Weight: 7 to 7.5 lbs. Pear-shaped bolt handle. Double-set or single trigger. Sights: Tangent curve rear; ramp front. Pistol-grip stock, forearm w/Schnabel tip and swivels.
Sporting Rifle (Type A, English export) . NiB $2496 Ex $2095 Gd $1438
Sporting Rifle (Type B) .... NiB $1708 Ex $1374 Gd $947

BOLT-ACTION SPORTING RIFLE, MILITARY MODEL TYPE C .... NiB $718 Ex $576 Gd $395
So called because of stepped M/98-type bbl., military front sight and double-pull trigger. Calibers: 7x57, 8x57, 9x57mm. Other specifications same as for standard rifle.

BOLT-ACTION SPORTING RIFLE SHORT MODEL TYPE K .... NiB $3695 Ex $2950 Gd $2021
Calibers: 6.5x54, 8x51mm. 19.75-inch bbl. Weight: 6.25 lbs. Other specifications same as for standard rifle.

PRE-WORLD WAR II MODELS

MODEL DSM34 BOLT-ACTION SINGLE-SHOT SPORTING RIFLE .... NiB $493 Ex $396 Gd $273
Also called "Sport-model." Caliber: .22 LR. 26-inch bbl. Weight: 7.75 lbs. Sights: Tangent curve open rear; Barleycorn front. M/98 military-type stock, swivels. Intro. c. 1935.

MODEL EL320 BOLT-ACTION SINGLE-SHOT SPORTING RIFLE .... NiB $473 Ex $381 Gd $262
Caliber: .22 LR. 23.5-inch bbl. Weight: 4.25 lbs. Sights: Adj. open rear; bead front. Sporting stock w/checkered pistol grip, swivels.

MODEL EN310 BOLT-ACTION SINGLE-SHOT SPORTING RIFLE .... NiB $428 Ex $345 Gd $238
Caliber: .22 LR. ("22 Lang fur Buchsen.") 19.75-inch bbl. Weight: 4 lbs. Sights: Fixed open rear, blade front. Plain pistol-grip stock.

MODEL ES340 BOLT-ACTION SINGLE-SHOT TARGET RIFLE .... NiB $493 Ex $396 Gd $273
Caliber: .22 LR. 25.5-inch bbl. Weight: 6.5 lbs. Sights: Tangent curve rear; ramp front. Sporting stock w/checkered pistol-grip and grooved forearm, swivels.

MODEL ES340B BOLT-ACTION SINGLE-SHOT TARGET RIFLE................. NiB $493 Ex $396 Gd $273
Caliber: .22 LR. 26.75-inch bbl. Weight: 8 lbs. Sights: Tangent curve open rear; ramp front. Plain pistol-grip stock, swivels.

MODEL ES350 BOLT-ACTION SINGLE-SHOT TARGET RIFLE................. NiB $686 Ex $551 Gd $378
"Meistershaftsbuchse" (Championship Rifle). Caliber: .22 LR. 27.5-inch bbl. Weight: 7.75 lbs. Sights: Open micrometer rear; ramp front. Target stock w/checkered pistol-grip and forearm, grip cap, swivels.

MODEL ES350B BOLT-ACTION SINGLE-SHOT TARGET RIFLE .... NiB $622 Ex $499 Gd $343
Same general specifications as Model MS350B except single-shot, weight: 8.25 lbs.

MODEL KKW BOLT-ACTION SINGLE-SHOT TARGET RIFLE........... NiB $493 Ex $396 Gd $273
Caliber: .22 LR. 26-inch bbl. Weight: 8.75 lbs. Sights: Tangent curve open rear; Barleycorn front. M/98 military-type stock, swivels. Note: This rifle has an improved design Mauser 22 action w/separate nonrotating bolt head. In addition to being produced for commercial sale, this model was used as a training rifle by the German armed forces; it was also made by Walther and Gustoff. Intro. just before WWII.

MODEL M410 BOLT-ACTION REPEATING SPORTING RIFLE .... NiB $884 Ex $710 Gd $488
Caliber: .22 LR. Five round detachable box magazine. 23.5-inch bbl. Weight: 5 lbs. Sights: Tangent curve open rear; ramp front. Sporting stock w/checkered pistol-grip, swivels.

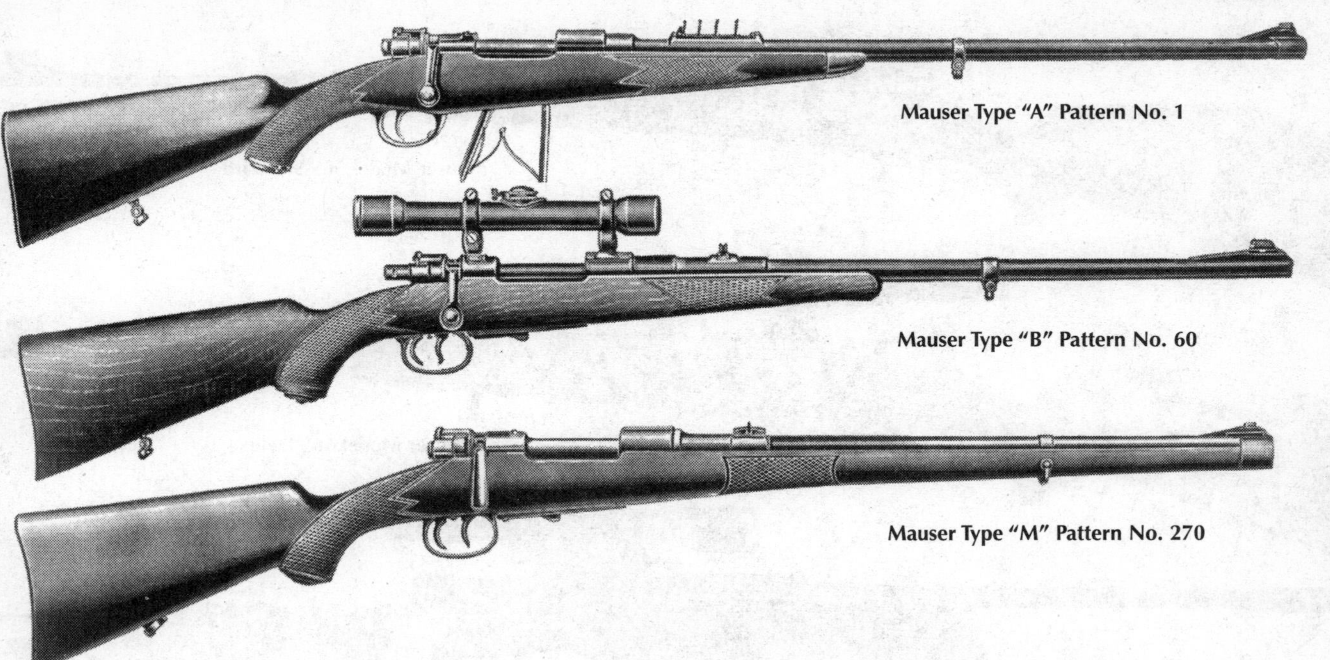
Mauser Type "A" Pattern No. 1

Mauser Type "B" Pattern No. 60

Mauser Type "M" Pattern No. 270

MODEL MM410B BOLT-ACTION REPEATING SPORTING RIFLE .... NiB $905 Ex $726 Gd $497
Caliber: .22 LR. Five round detachable box magazine. 23.5-inch bbl. Weight: 6.25 lbs. Sights: Tangent curve open rear; ramp front. Lightweight sporting stock w/checkered pistol-grip, swivels.

MODEL MS350B BOLT-ACTION REPEATING TARGET RIFLE............ NiB $905 Ex $726 Gd $497
Caliber: .22 LR. Five round detachable box magazine. Receiver and bbl. grooved for detachable rear sight or scope. 26.75-inch bbl. Weight: 8.5 lbs. Sights: Micrometer open rear; ramp front. Target stock w/checkered pistol grip and forearm, grip cap, sling swivels.

MODEL MS420 BOLT-ACTION REPEATING SPORTING RIFLE .... NiB $976 Ex $782 Gd $535
Caliber: .22 LR. Five round detachable box magazine. 25.5-inch bbl. Weight: 6.5 lbs. Sights: Tangent curve open rear; ramp front. Sporting stock w/checkered pistol grip, grooved forearm swivels.

MODEL MS420B BOLT-ACTION REPEATING TARGET RIFLE............ NiB $814 Ex $654 Gd $448
Caliber: .22 LR. Five round detachable box magazine. 26.75-inch bbl. Weight: 8 lbs. Sights: Tangent curve open rear; ramp front. Target stock w/checkered pistol grip, grooved forearm, swivels.

STANDARD MODEL RIFLE .... NiB $686 Ex $551 Gd $378
Refined version of German Service Kar. 98k. Straight bolt handle. Calibers: 7mm Mauser (7x57mm), 7.9mm Mauser (8x57mm). Five round box magazine. 23.5-inch bbl. Weight: 8.5 lbs. Sights: Blade front; adj. rear. Walnut stock of M/98 military-type. Note: These rifles were made for commercial sale and are of the high quality found in the Oberndorf Mauser sporters. They bear the Mauser trademark on the receiver ring.

TYPE "A" BOLT-ACTION SPORTING RIFLE............ NiB $2594 Ex $2080 Gd $1423
Special British Model. 7x57, 30-06 (7.62x63), 8x60, 9x57, 9.3x62mm. Five round box mag. 23.5-inch round bbl. Weight: 7.25 lbs. Mil.-type single trigger. Sights: Express rear; hooded ramp front. Circassian walnut sporting stock w/checkered pistol-grip and forearm, w/ or w/o cheekpiece, buffalo horn forend tip and grip cap, detachable swivels. Variations: Octagon bbl., double-set trigger, shotgun-type safety, folding peep rear sight, tangent curve rear sight, three-leaf rear sight.

TYPE "A" BOLT-ACTION SPORTING RIFLE, MAGNUM MODEL.......... NiB $2851 Ex $2286 Gd $1593
Same general specifications as standard Type "A" except w/Magnum action, weighs 7.5 to 8.5 lbs. Calibers: .280 Ross, .318 Westley Richards Express, 10.75x68mm, .404 Nitro Express.

TYPE "A" BOLT-ACTION SPORTING RIFLE, SHORT MODEL............. NiB $2336 Ex $1873 Gd $1283
Same as standard Type "A" except w/short action, 21.5-inch round bbl., weight 6 lbs. Calibers: .250-3000, 6.5x54, 8x51mm.

TYPE "B" BOLT-ACTION SPORTING RIFLE...................... NiB $1759 Ex $1410 Gd $966
Normal Model. Calibers: 7x57, .30-06 (7.62x63), 8x57, 8x60, 9x57, 9.3x62, 10.7568mm. Five round box magazine. 23.5-inch round bbl. Weight: 7.25 lbs. Double-set trigger. Sights: Three-leaf rear, ramp front. Fine walnut stock w/checkered pistol-grip, Schnabel forend tip, cheekpiece, grip cap, swivels. Variations: Octagon or half-octagon bbl., military-type single trigger, shotgun-type safety, folding peep rear sight, tangent curve rear sight, telescopic sight.

TYPE "K" BOLT-ACTION SPORTING RIFLE............ NiB $3710 Ex $2975 Gd $2036
Light Short Model. Same specifications as Normal Type "B" model except w/short action, 21.5-inch round bbl., weight: 6 lbs. Calibers: .250-3000, 6.5x54, 8x51mm.

TYPE "M" BOLT-ACTION SPORTING CARBINE .... NiB $2336 Ex $1874 Gd $1283
Calibers: 6.5x54, 7x57, .30-06 (7.62x63), 8x51, 8x60, 9x57mm. Five round box magazine. 19.75-inch round bbl. Weight: 6 to 6.75 lbs. Double-set trigger, flat bolt handle. Sights: Three-leaf rear; ramp front. Stocked to muzzle, cheekpiece, checkered pistol-grip and forearm, grip cap, steel forend cap, swivels. Variations: Military-type single trigger, shotgun-type trigger, shotgun-type safety, tangent curve rear sight, telescopic sight.

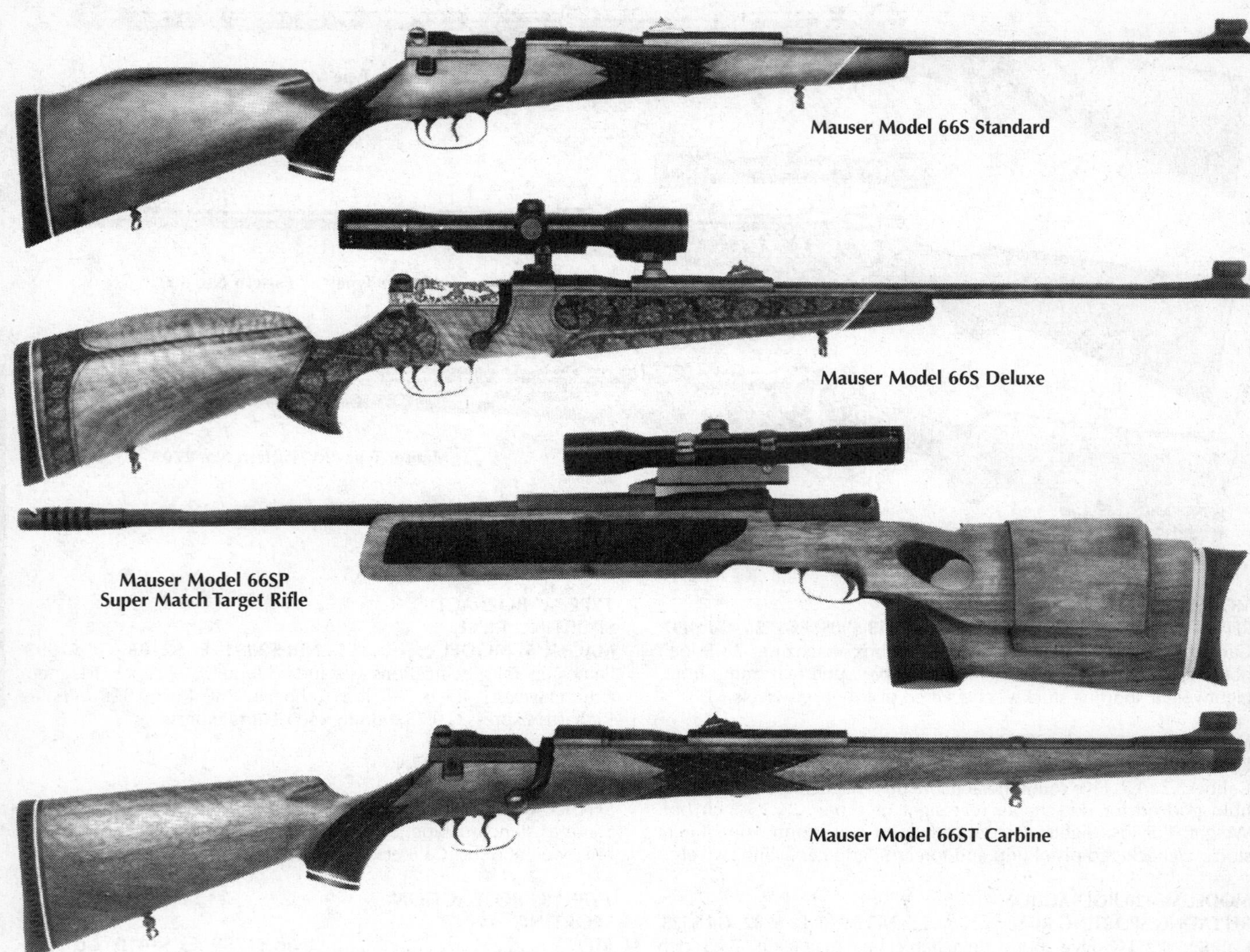
Mauser Model 66S Standard

Mauser Model 66S Deluxe

Mauser Model 66SP
Super Match Target Rifle

Mauser Model 66ST Carbine

TYPE "S" BOLT-ACTION
SPORTING CARBINE . . . . NiB $2415 Ex $2028 Gd $1282
Calibers: 6.5x54 7x57, 8x51, 8x60, 9x57mm. Five-round box magazine. 19.75-inch round bbl. Weight: 6 to 6.75 lbs. Double-set trigger. Sights: Three-leaf rear; ramp front. Stocked to muzzle, Schnabel forend tip, cheekpiece, checkered pistol-grip w/cap, swivels. Variations: Same as listed for Normal Model Type "B."

POST-WORLD WAR II MODELS

NOTE: *Production of original Mauser sporting rifles (66 series) resumed at the Oberndorf plant in 1965 by Mauser-Jagdwaffen GmbH, now Mauser-Werke Oberndorf GmbH. The Series 2000-3000-4000 rifles, however, were made for Mauser by Friedrich Wilhelm Heym Gewehrfabrik, Muennerstadt, West Germany.*

MODEL 66S BOLT-ACTION STANDARD SPORTING RIFLE
Telescopic short action. Bbls. interchangeable within cal. group. Single- or double-set trigger (interchangeable). Cal: .243 Win., 6.5x57, .270 Win., 7x64, .308 Win., .30-06. Three round mag. 23.6 inch bbl. (25.6inch in 7x64). Wt: 7.3 lbs. (7.5 lbs. in 7x64). Sights: Adj. open rear, hooded ramp front. Select Eur. walnut stock, Monte Carlo w/cheekpiece, rosewood forend tip and pistol-grip cap, skip checkering, recoil pad, sling swivels. Made 1965 to date, export to

(cont'd.) **MODEL 66S BOLT-ACTION STANDARD SPORTING RIFLE**
U.S. disc. 1974. Note: U.S.designation, 1971-73, was "Model 660."
Model 66S . . . . NiB $2389 Ex $2080 Gd $1050
W/extra bbl. assembly, add $550

MODEL 66S DELUXE SPORTER
Limited production special order. Model 66S rifles and carbines are available with /elaborate engraving, gold and silver inlays and carved select walnut stocks. Added value is upward of $4500.

MODEL 66S ULTRA
Same general specifications as Model 66S Standard except with 20.9-inch bbl., weight: 6.8 lbs.
Model 66S Ultra . . . . NiB $1627 Ex $1540 Gd $983
W/extra bbl. assembly, add $550

MODEL 66SG BIG GAME
Same general specifications as Model 66S Standard except w/25.6-inch bbl., weight 9.3 lbs. Calibers: .375 H&H Mag., .458 Win. Mag. Note: U.S. designation, 1971-73, was "Model 660 Safari."
Model 66SG . . . . NiB $3012 Ex $1956 Gd $1209
W/ extra bbl. assembly, add $550

Mauser Model 99

Mauser Model 201

Mauser Model 3000

Mauser Model 4000

MODEL 66SH HIGH PERFORMANCE . . NiB $1595 Ex $1420 Gd $995
Same general specifications as Model 66S Standard except w/25.6-inch bbl., weighs 7.5 lbs. (9.3 lbs. in 9.3x64). Calibers: 6.5x68, 7mm Rem. Mag., 7mm S.E.v. Hoffe, .300 Win. Mag., 8x68S, 9.3x64.

MODEL 66SP SUPER MATCH BOLT-ACTION TARGET RIFLE. . . . . NiB $4153 Ex $3535 Gd $1835
Telescopic short action. Adj. single-stage trigger. Caliber: .308 Win. (chambering for other cartridges available on special order). Three round magazine. 27.6-inch heavy bbl. w/muzzle brake, dovetail rib for special scope mount. Weight: 12 lbs. Target stock w/wide and deep forearm, full pistol-grip, thumbhole adj. cheekpiece, adj. rubber buttplate.

MODEL 66ST CARBINE
Same general specifications as Model 66S Standard except w/20.9-inch bbl., full-length stock, weight: 7 lbs.
Model 66ST . . . . NiB $6290 Ex $1507 Gd $1069
W/extra bbl. assembly, add $550

MODEL 83 BOLT-ACTION RIFLE . . . . . NiB $2425 Ex $2038 Gd $1266
Centerfire single-shot, bolt-action rifle for 300-meter competition. Caliber: .308 Win. 25.5-inch fluted bbl. Weight: 10.5 lbs. Adj. micrometer rear sight globe front. Fully adj. competition stock. Disc. 1988.

MODEL 96 . . . . NiB $686 Ex $551 Gd $378
Calibers: .25-06, .270 Win., 7x64, .308 Win., .30-06, 7mm Rem. Mag., .300 Win. Mag. 22-inch bbl.; magnums 24-inch. Weight: 6.25 lbs. No sights; drilled and tapped for scope. Walnut stock. Five-round top-loading magazine. 3-position safety.

MODEL 99 CLASSIC BOLT-ACTION RIFLE
Calibers: .243 Win., .25-06, .270 Win., .30-06, .308 Win., .257 Wby., .270 Wby., 7mm Rem. Mag., .300 Win., .300 Wby. .375 H&H. Four round magazine (standard), 3-round (Magnum). Bbl.: 24-inch (standard) or 26-inch (Magnum). 44 inches overall (standard). Weight: 8 lbs. No sights. Checkered European walnut stock w/rosewood grip cap available in Classic and Monte Carlo styles w/High-Luster or oil finish. Disc. importing 1994.
Standard Classic or Monte Carlo (oil finish). . . . . NiB $1174 Ex $973 Gd $638
Magnum Classic or Monte Carlo (oil finish). . . . . NiB $1264 Ex $1019 Gd $706
Standard Classic or Monte Carlo (H-L finish). . . . . NiB $1204 Ex $998 Gd $655
Magnum Classic or Monte Carlo (H-L finish). . . . . NiB $1250 Ex $1065 Gd $738

MODEL 107 BOLT-ACTION RIFLE . . . . . . NiB $380 Ex $277 Gd $174
Caliber: .22 LR. Mag. Five round magazine. 21.5-inch bbl. 40 inches overall. Weight: 5 lbs. Receiver drilled and tapped for rail scope mounts. Hooded front sight, adj. rear. Disc. importing 1994.

MODEL 201/201 LUXUS BOLT-ACTION RIFLE
Calibers: .22 LR. .22 Win. Mag. Five round magazine. 21-inch bbl. 40 inches overall. Weight: 6.5 lbs. Receiver drilled and tapped for scope mounts. Sights optional. Checkered walnut-stained beech stock w/Monte Carlo. Model 201 Luxus w/checkered European walnut stock QD swivels, rosewood forend and rubber recoil pad. Made 1989 to date. Disc. importing 1994.
Model 201 Standard . . . . NiB $736 Ex $684 Gd $396
Model 201 Magnum . . . . NiB $678 Ex $552 Gd $388
Model 201 Luxus Standard . . . . NiB $762 Ex $684 Gd $401
Model 201 Luxus Magnum . . . . NiB $871 Ex $709 Gd $504

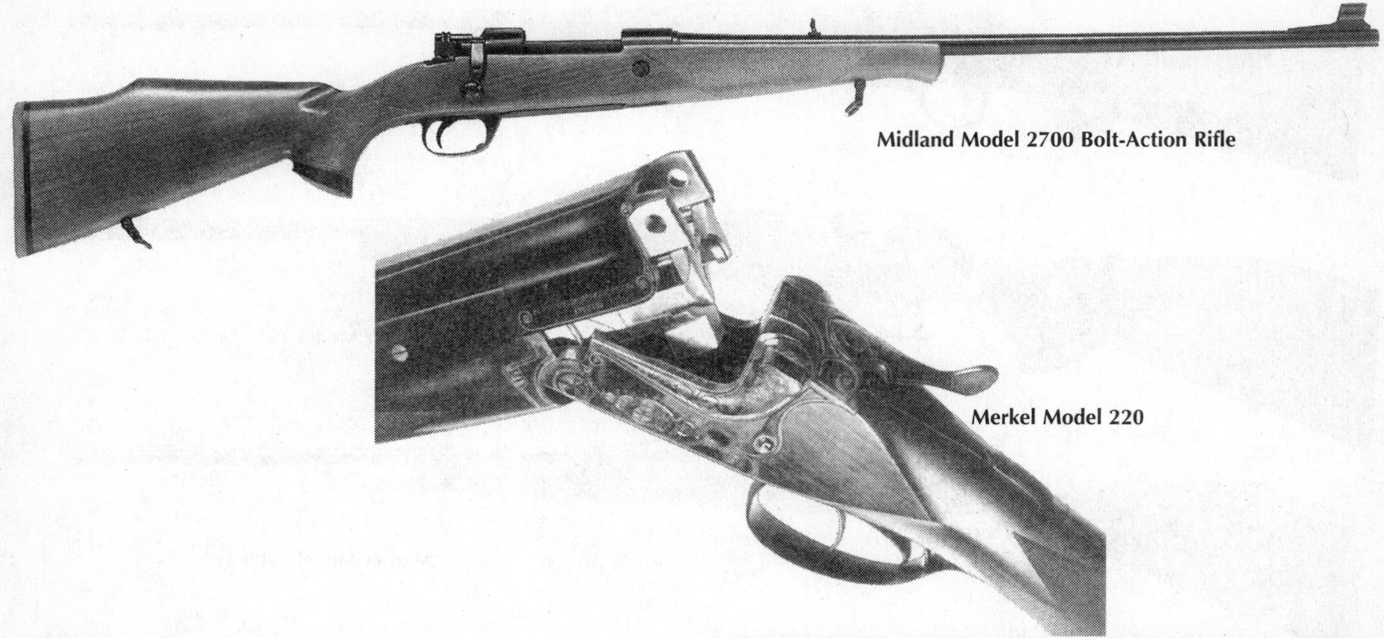

Midland Model 2700 Bolt-Action Rifle

Merkel Model 220

MODEL 2000 BOLT-ACTION SPORTING RIFLE. . . . . **NiB $597 Ex $499 Gd $319**
Modified Mauser-type action. Calibers: .270 Win., .308 Win., .30-06. Five-round magazine. 24-inch bbl. Weight: 7.5 lbs. Sights: Folding leaf rear; hooded ramp front. Checkered walnut stock w/Monte Carlo comb and cheekpiece, forend tip, sling swivels. Made 1969-71. Note: Model 2000 is similar in appearance to Model 3000.

MODEL 2000 CLASSIC BOLT-ACTION SPORTING RIFLE
Calibers: .22-250 Rem., .234 Win., .270 Win., 7mm Mag., .308 Win., .30-06, .300 Win. Mag. Three or 5-round magazine. 24-inch bbl. Weight: 7.5 lbs. Sights: Folding leaf rear; hooded ramp front. Checkered walnut stock w/Monte Carlo comb and cheekpiece, forend tip, sling swivels. Imported 1998. Note: The Model 2000 Classic is designed to interchange bbl. assemblies within a given caliber group.

Model 2000 Classic. . . . . **NiB $1597 Ex $1282 Gd $878**
Model 2000 Professional
w/Recoil Compensator . . . . **NiB $3223 Ex $2590 Gd $1768**
Model 2000 Sniper . . . . **NiB $1816 Ex $1457 Gd $997**
Model 2000 Varmint . . . . **NiB $1659 Ex $1410 Gd $966**
Extra bbl. assembly, add **$895**

MODEL 3000 BOLT-ACTION SPORTING RIFLE. . . . . **NiB $602 Ex $473 Gd $340**
Modified Mauser-type action. Calibers: .243 Win., .270 Win., .308 Win., .30-06. Five round magazine. 22-inch bbl. Weight: 7 lbs. No sights. Select European walnut stock, Monte Carlo style w/cheekpiece, rosewood forend tip and pistol-grip cap, skip checkering, recoil pad, sling swivels. Made 1971-74.

MODEL 3000 MAGNUM . . . . **NiB $602 Ex $525 Gd $422**
Same general specifications as standard Model 3000, except w/3-round magazine, 26-inch bbl., weight: 8 lbs. Calibers: 7mm Rem. Mag., .300 Win. Mag., .375 H&H Mag.

MODEL 4000 VARMINT RIFLE . . . . **NiB $525 Ex $422 Gd $309**
Same general specifications as standard Model 3000, except w/smaller action, folding leaf rear sight; hooded ramp front, rubber buttplate instead of recoil pad, weight 6.75 lbs. Calibers: .222 Rem., .223 Rem. 22-inch bbl. Select European walnut stock w/rosewood forend tip and pistol-grip cap. French checkering and sling swivels.

McMILLAN GUN WORKS — Phoenix, Arizona
Harris Gunworks

See Harris Gunworks.

GEBRÜDER MERKEL — Suhl, Germany

For Merkel combination guns and drillings, see listings under Merkel shotguns.

OVER/UNDER RIFLES ("BOCK-DOPPELBÜCHSEN")
Calibers: 5.6x35 Vierling, 6.5x58r5, 7x57r5, 8x57JR, 8x60R Magnum, 9.3x53r5, 9.3x72r5, 9.3x74r5, 10.3x60R as well as most of the British calibers for African and Indian big game. Various bbl. lengths, weights. In general, specifications correspond to those of Merkel over/under shotguns. Values of these over/under rifles (in calibers for which ammunition is obtainable) are about the same as those of comparable shotgun models currently manufactured. For more specific data, see Merkel shotgun models indicated below.

Model 220 . . . . **NiB $9000 Ex $8000 Gd $4000**
Model 220E . . . . **NiB $9575 Ex $8400 Gd $7400**
Model 221 . . . . **NiB $7438 Ex $5950 Gd $4046**
Model 221E . . . . **NiB $9813 Ex $7850 Gd $5338**
Model 320 . . . . **NiB $8125 Ex $6500 Gd $4420**
Model 320E . . . . **NiB $15,000 Ex $12,000 Gd $8160**
Model 321 . . . . **NiB $16,563 Ex $13,250 Gd $9010**
Model 321E . . . . **NiB $17,500 Ex $14,000 Gd $9520**
Model 322 . . . . **NiB $18,125 Ex $14,500 Gd $9860**
Model 323E . . . . **NiB $23,125 Ex $18,500 Gd $12,580**
Model 324 . . . . **NiB $26,875 Ex $21,500 Gd $14,620**

MEXICAN MILITARY RIFLE
Mfd. by Government Arsenal, Mexico, D.F.

MODEL 1936 MAUSER MILITARY RIFLE . . . NiB $211 Ex $159 Gd $85
Same as German Kar.98k w/minor variations and U.S. M/1903 Springfield-type knurled cocking piece.

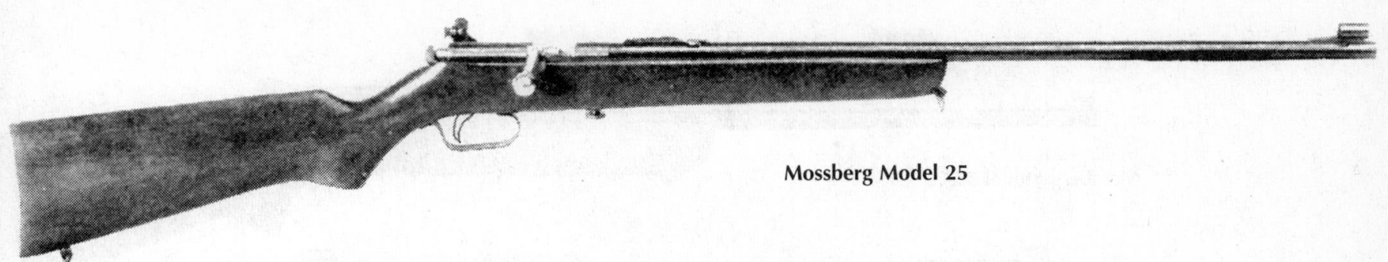

Mossberg Model 25

MIDLAND RIFLES — Mfg. by Gibbs Rifle Company, Inc., Martinsburg, WV

MODEL 2100 BOLT-ACTION RIFLE.............................. NiB $356 Ex $288 Gd $200
Calibers: .22-250, .243 Win., 6mm Rem., .270 Win., 6.5x55, 7x57, 7x64, .308 Win., and .30-06. Springfield 1903 action. Four-round magazine. 22-inch bbl. 43 inches overall. Weight: 7 lbs. Flip-up rear sight; hooded ramp front. Finely finished and checkered walnut stock w/pistol-grip cap and sling swivels. Steel recoil bar. Action drilled and tapped for scope mounts. Production disc.1997.

MODEL 2600 BOLT-ACTION RIFLE ...... NiB $375 Ex $303 Gd $180
Same general specifications as Model 2100 except no pistol-grip cap, and stock is walnut-finished hardwood. Made 1992-97.

MODEL 2700 BOLT-ACTION RIFLE ...... NiB $375 Ex $298 Gd $195
Same general specifications as Model 2100 except the weight of this rifle as been reduced by utilizing a tapered bbl., anodized aluminum trigger housing and lightened stock. Weight: 6.5 lbs. Disc.

MODEL 2800 LIGHTWEIGHT RIFLE ..... NiB $382 Ex $309 Gd $215
Same general specifications as Model 2100 except w/laminated birch stock. Made 1992-94 and 1996-97.

MITCHELL ARMS. INC. — Fountain Valley, California, (Formerly Santa Ana, CA)

MODEL 15/22 SEMIAUTOMATIC
High Standard-style action. Caliber: .22 LR. 15-round magazine (10-round after 10/13/94). 20.5-inch bbl. 37.5 inches overall. Weight: 6.25 lbs. Ramp front sight; adj. open rear. Blued finish. Mahogany stock; Monte Carlo-style American walnut stock on Deluxe model. Made 1994-96.
Model 15/22 SP (Special) w/plastic buttplate .... NiB $102 Ex $82 Gd $58
Model 15/22 Carbine .... NiB $140 Ex $113 Gd $78
Model 15/22D Deluxe .... NiB $166 Ex $134 Gd $93

MODEL 9300 SERIES BOLT-ACTION RIFLE
Calibers: .22 LR. .22 Mag. Five or 10-round magazine. 22.5-inch bbl. 40.75 inches overall. Weight: 6.5 lbs. Beaded ramp front sight; adj. open rear. Blued finish. American walnut stock. Made 1994-95.
Model 9302 (.22 LR, checkered, rosewood caps)............ NiB $248 Ex $201 Gd $140
Model 9302 (.22 Mag., checkered, rosewood caps)............ NiB $261 Ex $211 Gd $147
Model 9303 (.22 LR, plain stock) .... NiB $196 Ex $159 Gd $112
Model 9304 (.22 Mag., checkered, No rosewood caps).......... NiB $210 Ex $170 Gd $118
Model 9305 (.22 LR, special stock)........ NiB $171 Ex $139 Gd $98

AK-22 SEMIAUTOMATIC RIFLE .... NiB $248 Ex $201 Gd $140
Replica of AK-47 rifle. .22 LR. .22 WMR., 20-round magazine (.22 LR), 10-round (.22 WMR). 18-inch bbl. 36 inches overall. Weight: 6.5 lbs. Sights: Post front; open adj. rear. European walnut stock and forend. Matte black finish. Made 1985-94.

CAR-15 22 SEMIAUTOMATIC RIFLE..... NiB $248 Ex $201 Gd $140
Replica of AR-15 CAR rifle. Caliber: .22 LR. 15-round magazine.16.25-inch bbl. 32 inches overall. Sights: Adj. post front; adj. aperture rear. Telescoping buttstock and ventilated forend. Matte black finish. Made 1990-94.

GALIL 22 SEMIAUTOMATIC RIFLE...... NiB $293 Ex $242 Gd $154
Replica of Israeli Galil rifle. Calibers: .22 LR. .22 WMR., 20-round magazine (.22 LR), 10-round (.22 WMR). 18-inch bbl. 36 inches overall. Weight: 6.5 lbs. Sights: Adj. post front; rear adj. for windage. Folding metal stock w/European walnut grip and forend. Matte black finish. Made 1987-93.

M-16A 22 SEMIAUTOMATIC RIFLE ...... NiB $248 Ex $201 Gd $140
Replica of AR-15 rifle. Caliber: .22 LR. 15-round magazine. 20.5-inch bbl. 38.5 inches overall. Weight: 7 lbs. Sights: Adj. post front, adj. aperture rear. Black composite stock and forend. Matte black finish. Made 1990-94.

MAS 22 SEMIAUTOMATIC RIFLE........ NiB $293 Ex $237 Gd $164
Replica of French MAS bullpup rifle. Caliber: .22 LR. 20-round magazine. 18-inch bbl. 28 inches overall. Weight: 7.5 lbs. Sights: Adj. post front, folding aperture rear. European walnut buttstock and forend. Matte black finish. Made 1987-93.

PPS SEMIAUTOMATIC RIFLE
Caliber: .22 LR. 20-round magazine, 50-round drum. 16.5-inch bbl. 33.5 inches overall. Weight: 5.5 lbs. Sights: Blade front; adj. rear. European walnut stock w/ventilated bbl. shroud. Matte black finish. Made 1989-94.
Model PPS (20-round).......... NiB $267 Ex $216 Gd $150
Model PPS/50 (50-round drum) ... NiB $531 Ex $448 Gd $341

O.F. MOSSBERG & SONS, INC. — North Haven, Connecticut, (Formerly New Haven, CT)

MODEL 10 BOLT-ACTION SINGLE-SHOT RIFLE............ NiB $164 Ex $113 Gd $87
Takedown. Caliber: .22 LR, Long, Short. 22-inch bbl. Weight: 4 lbs. Sights: Open rear; bead front. Plain pistol-grip stock w/swivels, sling. Made 1933-35.

MODEL 14 BOLT-ACTION SINGLE-SHOT RIFLE............ NiB $175 Ex $113 Gd $87
Takedown. Caliber: .22 LR. Long, Short. 24-inch bbl. Weight: 5.25 lbs. Sights: Peep rear; hooded ramp front. Plain pistol-grip stock w/semi-beavertail forearm, 1.25-inch swivels. Made 1934-35.

MODEL 20 BOLT-ACTION SINGLE-SHOT RIFLE............ NiB $175 Ex $113 Gd $87
Takedown. Caliber: .22 LR. Long, Short. 24-inch bbl. Weight: 4.5 lbs. Sights: Open rear; bead front. Plain pistol-grip stock and forearm w/finger grooves, sling and swivels. Made 1933-35.

MODEL 25/25A BOLT-ACTION SINGLE-SHOT RIFLE
Takedown. Caliber: .22 LR. Long, Short. 24-inch bbl. Weight: 5 lbs. Sights: Peep rear; hooded ramp front. Plain pistol-grip stock w/semi-beavertail forearm. 1.25-inch swivels. Made 1935-36.
Model 25........................... NiB $175 Ex $113 Gd $82
Model 25A (Improved Model 25, 1936-38)..... NiB $185 Ex $113 Gd $87

RIFLES

Mossberg Model 35A

Mossberg Model L42A

Mossberg Model 42B

MODEL 26B/26C BOLT-ACTION SINGLE-SHOT
Takedown. Caliber: .22 LR. Long, Short. 26-inch bbl. Weight: 5.5 lbs. Sights; Rear, micrometer click peep or open; hooded ramp front. Plain pistol-grip stock swivels. Made 1938-41.
Model 26B . . . . NiB $185 Ex $144 Gd $87
Model 26C
(No rear sight/swivels) . . . . NiB $164 Ex $113 Gd $72

MODEL 30 BOLT-ACTION SINGLE-SHOT RIFLE . . . . NiB $144 Ex $113 Gd $82
Takedown. Caliber: .22 LR. Long, Short. 24-inch bbl. Weight: 4.5 lbs. Sights: Peep rear; bead front, on hooded ramp. Plain pistol-grip stock, forearm w/finger grooves. Made 1933-35.

MODEL 34 BOLT-ACTION SINGLE-SHOT RIFLE . . . . NiB $164 Ex $113 Gd $82
Takedown. Caliber: .22 LR. Long, Short. 24-inch bbl. Weight: 5.5 lbs. Sights: Peep rear; hooded ramp front. Plain pistol-grip stock w/semibeavertail forearm, 1.25-inch swivels. Made 1934-35.

MODEL 35 TARGET GRADE BOLT-ACTION SINGLE-SHOT RIFLE. . . . . . . NiB $345 Ex $237 Gd $94
Caliber: .22 LR. 26-inch heavy bbl. Weight: 8.25 lbs. Sights: Micrometer click rear peep; hooded ramp front. Large target stock w/full pistol grip, cheekpiece, full beavertail forearm, 1.25-inch swivels. Made 1935-37.

MODEL 35A BOLT-ACTION SINGLE-SHOT RIFLE . . . . NiB $345 Ex $236 Gd $92
Caliber: .22 LR. 26-inch heavy bbl. Weight: 8.25 lbs. Sights: Micrometer click peep rear; hooded front. Target stock w/cheekpiece full pistol grip and forearm, 1.25-inch sling swivels. Made 1937-38.

MODEL 35A-LS . . . . NiB $401 Ex $267 Gd $180
Caliber .22 LR. Same as Model 35A but w/Lyman No. 57 rear sight, 17A front. Target stock w/checkpiece, full pistol-grip and forearm.

MODEL 35B . . . . NiB $391 Ex $257 Gd $175
Same specifications as Model 44B except single-shot. Made 1938-40.

MODEL 40 BOLT-ACTION REPEATER. . . . . NiB $164 Ex $113 Gd $82
Takedown. Caliber: .22 LR. Long, Short, 16-round tubular magazine. 24-inch bbl. Weight: 5 lbs. Sights: Peep rear; bead front, on hooded ramp. Plain pistol-grip stock, forearm w/finger grooves. Made 1933-35.

MODEL 42 BOLT-ACTION REPEATER. . . . . NiB $164 Ex $113 Gd $82
Takedown. Caliber: .22 LR. Long, Short. Seven-round detachable box magazine. 24-inch bbl. Weight: 5 lbs. Sights: Receiver peep, open rear; hooded ramp front. Pistol-grip stock. 1.25-inch swivels. Made 1935-37.

MODEL 42A/L42A BOLT-ACTION REPEATERS
Takedown. Caliber: .22 LR. Long, Short. Seven-round detachable box magazine. 24-inch bbl. Weight: 5 lbs. Sights: Receiver peep, open rear; ramp front. Plain pistol-grip stock. Made 1937-38. Model L42A (left-hand action) made 1937-1941.
Model 42A. NiB $164 Ex $134 Gd $94
Model L42A. . . . . NiB $248 Ex $201 Gd $140

MODEL 42B/42C BOLT-ACTION REPEATERS
Takedown. Caliber: .22 LR. Long, Short. Five-round detachable box magazine. 24-inch bbl. Weight: 6 lbs. Sights: Micrometer click receiver peep, open rear hooded ramp front. Plain pistol-grip stock, swivels. Made 1938-41.
Model 42B. . . . . NiB $164 Ex $139 Gd $72
Model 42C (No rear peep sight) . . . . NiB $133 Ex $108 Gd $77

Mossberg Model 42C

Mossberg Model L-43

Mossberg Model 43B

Mossberg Model 44US

Mossberg Model L45A Left-Hand Model

Mossberg Model 45B

Mossberg Model L46A-LS

Mossberg Model 46B

MODEL 42M BOLT-ACTION REPEATER . . . . NiB $190 Ex $164 Gd $92
Caliber: .22 LR. Long, Short. Seven-round detachable box magazine. 23-inch bbl. Weight: 6.75 lbs. Sights: Microclick receiver peep, open rear; hooded ramp front. Two-piece Mannlicher-type stock w/cheekpiece and pistol-grip, swivels. Made 1940-50.

MODEL 43/L43 BOLT-ACTION REPEATERS . . . . NiB $428 Ex $345 Gd $238
Speedlock, adj. trigger pull. Caliber: .22 LR. Seven-round detachable box magazine. 26-inch heavy bbl. Weight: 8.25 lbs. Sights: Lyman No. 57 rear; selective aperture front. Target stock w/cheekpiece, full pistol-grip, beavertail forearm, adj. front swivel. Made 1937-38. Model L43 is same as Model 43 except w/left-hand action.

MODEL 43B . . . . NiB $370 Ex $267 Gd $108
Same as Model 44B except w/Lyman No. 57 receiver sight and No. 17A front sight. Made 1938-39.

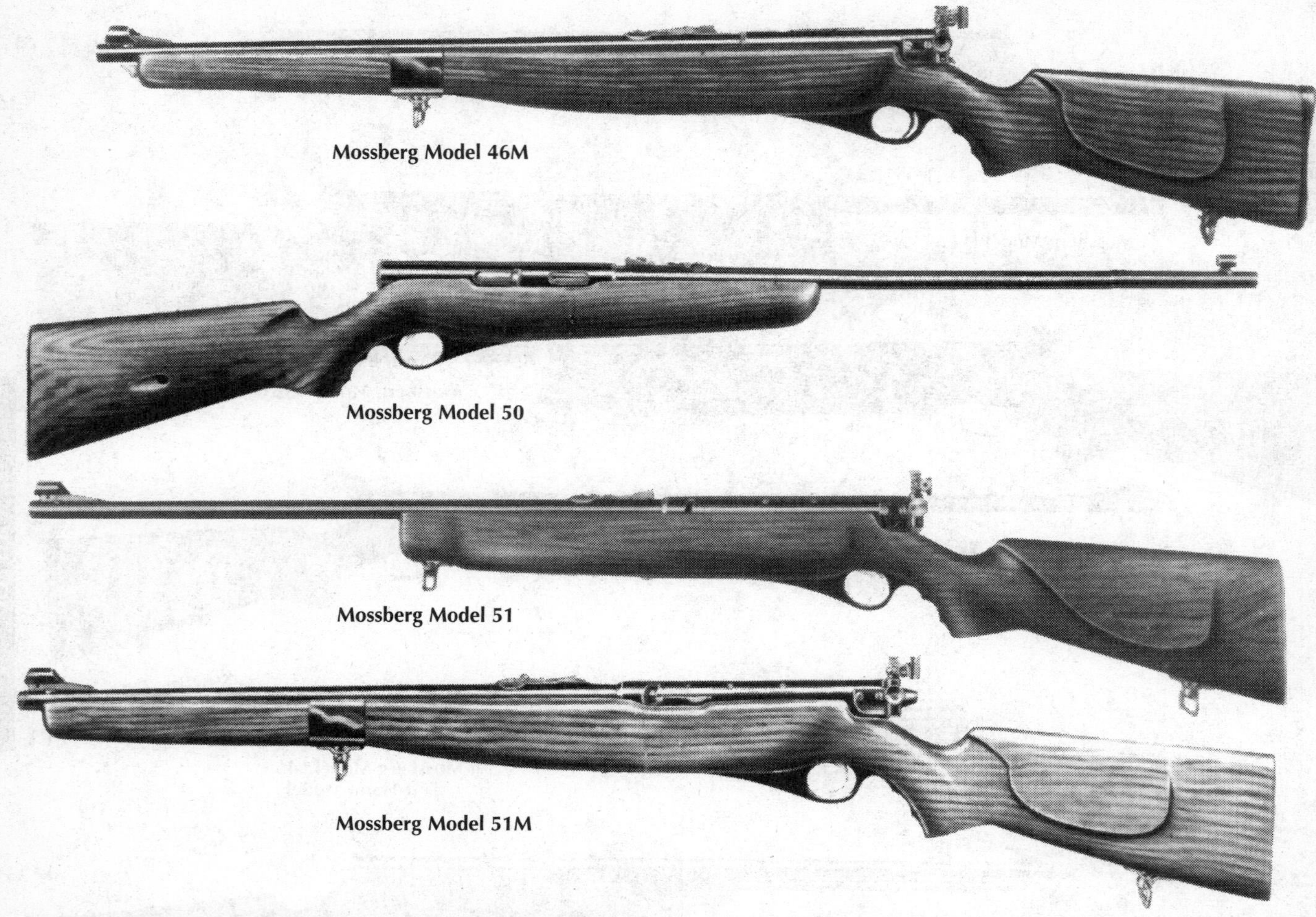

Mossberg Model 46M

Mossberg Model 50

Mossberg Model 51

Mossberg Model 51M

MODEL 44 BOLT-ACTION REPEATER. . . . . NiB $657 Ex $216 Gd $103
Takedown. Caliber: .22 LR. Long, Short. Tubular magazine holds 16 LR. 24-inch bbl. Weight: 6 lbs. Sights: Peep rear; hooded ramp front. Plain pistol-grip stock w/semi-beavertail forearm, 1.25-inch swivels. Made 1934-35. Note: Do not confuse this rifle w/later Models 44B and 44US, which are clip repeaters.

MODEL 44B BOLT-ACTION TARGET RIFLE . . . . NiB $288 Ex $216 Gd $113
Caliber: .22 LR. Seven-round detachable box magazine. Made 1938-41.

MODEL 44US BOLT-ACTION REPEATER
Caliber: .22 LR. Seven round detachable box magazine. 26-inch heavy bbl. Weight: 8.5 lbs. Sights: Micrometer click receiver peep, hooded front. Target stock, swivels. Made 1943-48. Note: This model was used as a training rifle by the U.S. Armed Forces during WWII.
Model 44US . . . . NiB $267 Ex $242 Gd $103
Model 44US (marked U.S. Property) . . . . . NiB $345 Ex $293 Gd $216

MODEL 45 BOLT-ACTION REPEATER. . . . . NiB $190 Ex $164 Gd $103
Takedown. Caliber: .22 LR. Long, Short. Tubular magazine holds 15 LR. 18 Long, 22 Short. 24-inch bbl. Weight: 6.75 lbs. Sights: Rear peep; hooded ramp front. Plain pistol-grip stock, 1.25-inch swivels. Made 1935-37.

MODEL 45A, L45A, 45AC BOLT-ACTION REPEATERS
Takedown. Caliber: .22 LR. Long, Short. Tubular magazine holds 15 LR, 18 Long, 22 Short. 24-inch bbl. Weight: 6.75 lbs. Sights: Receiver peep, open rear; hooded blade front sight mounted on ramp. Plain pistol-grip stock, 1.25-inch sling swivels. Made 1937-38. See illustration on previous page.

***(cont'd.)* MODEL 45A, L45A, 45AC BOLT-ACTION REPEATERS**
Model 45A . . . . NiB $190 Ex $154 Gd $108
Model L45A (Left-hand action). . . . . NiB $242 Ex $195 Gd $136
Model 45AC (No receiver peep sight). . . . . . NiB $175 Ex $134 Gd $92

MODEL 45B/45C BOLT-ACTION REPEATERS
Takedown. Caliber: .22 LR. Long, Short. Tubular magazine holds 15 LR, 18 Long, 22 Short. 24-inch bbl. Weight: 6.25 lbs. Open rear sight; hooded blade front sight mounted on ramp. Plain pistol-grip stock w/sling swivels. Made 1938-40.
Model 45B . . . . NiB $171 Ex $139 Gd $98
Model 45C (No sights, made 1935-37). . . . . NiB $152 Ex $123 Gd $87

MODEL 46 BOLT-ACTION REPEATER. . . . . NiB $190 Ex $195 Gd $103
Takedown. Caliber: .22 LR. Long, Short. Tubular magazine holds 15 LR, 18 Long, 22 Short. 26-inch bbl. Weight: 7.5 lbs. Sights: Micrometer click rear peep; hooded ramp front. Pistol-grip stock w/cheekpiece, full beavertail forearm, 1.25-inch swivels. Made 1935-37.

MODEL 46A, 46A-LS, L46A-LS BOLT-ACTION REPEATERS
Takedown. Caliber: .22 LR. Long, Short. Tubular magazine holds 15 LR, 18 Long, 22 Short. 26-inch bbl. Weight: 7.25 lbs. Sights: Micrometer click receiver peep, open rear; hooded ramp front. Pistol-grip stock w/cheekpiece and beavertail forearm, quick-detachable swivels. Made 1937-38.
Model 46A . . . . NiB $196 Ex $159 Gd $112
Mdl. 46A-LS (w/Lyman No. 57 receiver sight) . . . . NiB $261 Ex $211 Gd $147
Model L46A-LS (Left-hand action) . . . . NiB $376 Ex $304 Gd $210

Mossberg Model 140B

Mossberg Model 140K

Mossberg Model 144LS

Mossberg Model 146B

MODEL 46B BOLT-ACTION REPEATER . . . . NiB $156 Ex $126 Gd $88
Takedown. Caliber: .22 LR. Long, Short. Tubular magazine holds 15 LR, 18 Long, 22 Short. 26-inch bbl. Weight: 7 lbs. Sights: Micrometer click receiver peep, open rear, hooded front. Plain pistol-grip stock w/cheekpiece, swivels. Note: Postwar version of this model has full magazine holding 20 LR, 23 Long, 30 Short. Made 1938-50.

MODEL 46BT . . . . NiB $222 Ex $180 Gd $125
Same as Model 46B except w/heavier bbl. and stock. Weight: 7.75 lbs. Made 1938-39.

MODEL 46C . . . . NiB $216 Ex $164 Gd $103
Same as Model 46 except w/a heavier bbl. and stock than that model. Weight: 8.5 lbs. Made 1936-37.

MODEL 46M BOLT-ACTION REPEATER . . . . NiB $216 Ex $164 Gd $103
Caliber: .22 LR. Long, Short. Tubular magazine holds 22 Short, 18 Long, 15 LR. 23-inch bbl. Weight: 7 lbs. Sights: Microclick receiver peep, open rear; hooded ramp front. Two-piece Mannlicher-type stock w/cheekpiece and pistol-grip, swivels. Made 1940-52.

MODEL 50 AUTOLOADING RIFLE . . . . NiB $190 Ex $154 Gd $108
Same as Model 51 except w/plain stock w/o beavertail cheekpiece, swivels or receiver peep sight. Made 1939-42.

MODEL 51 AUTOLOADING RIFLE. . . . . . NiB $183 Ex $137 Gd $106
Takedown. Caliber: .22 LR. Fifteen-round tubular magazine in butt-stock. 24-inch bbl. Weight: 7.25 lbs. Sights: Micrometer click receiver peep, open rear; hooded ramp front. Cheekpiece stock w/full pistol grip and beavertail forearm, swivels. Made 1939 only.

MODEL 51M AUTOLOADING RIFLE . . . . . NiB $183 Ex $137 Gd $106
Caliber: .22 LR. Fifteen-round tubular magazine. 20-inch bbl. Weight: 7 lbs. Sights: Microclick receiver peep, open rear; hooded ramp front. Two-piece Mannlicher-type stock w/pistol-grip and cheekpiece, hard-rubber buttplate and sling swivels. Made 1939-46.

MODEL 140B SPORTER-TARGET RIFLE . . . NiB $183 Ex $137 Gd $106
Same as Model 140K except w/peep rear sight, hooded ramp front sight. Made 1957-58.

MODEL 140K BOLT-ACTION REPEATER . . . NiB $162 Ex $132 Gd $92
Caliber: .22 LR. .22 Long, .22 Short. Seven-round clip magazine. 24.5-inch bbl. Weight: 5.75 lbs. Sights: Open rear; bead front. Monte Carlo stock w/cheekpiece and pistol-grip, sling swivels. Made 1955-58.

MODEL 142-A BOLT-ACTION REPEATING CARBINE . . . . NiB $202 Ex $162 Gd $113
Caliber: .22 Short Long, LR. Seven-round detachable box magazine. 18-inch bbl. Weight: 6 lbs. Sights: Peep rear, military-type front. Monte Carlo stock w/pistol-grip, hinged forearm pulls down to form hand grip; sling swivels mounted on left side of stock. Made 1949-57.

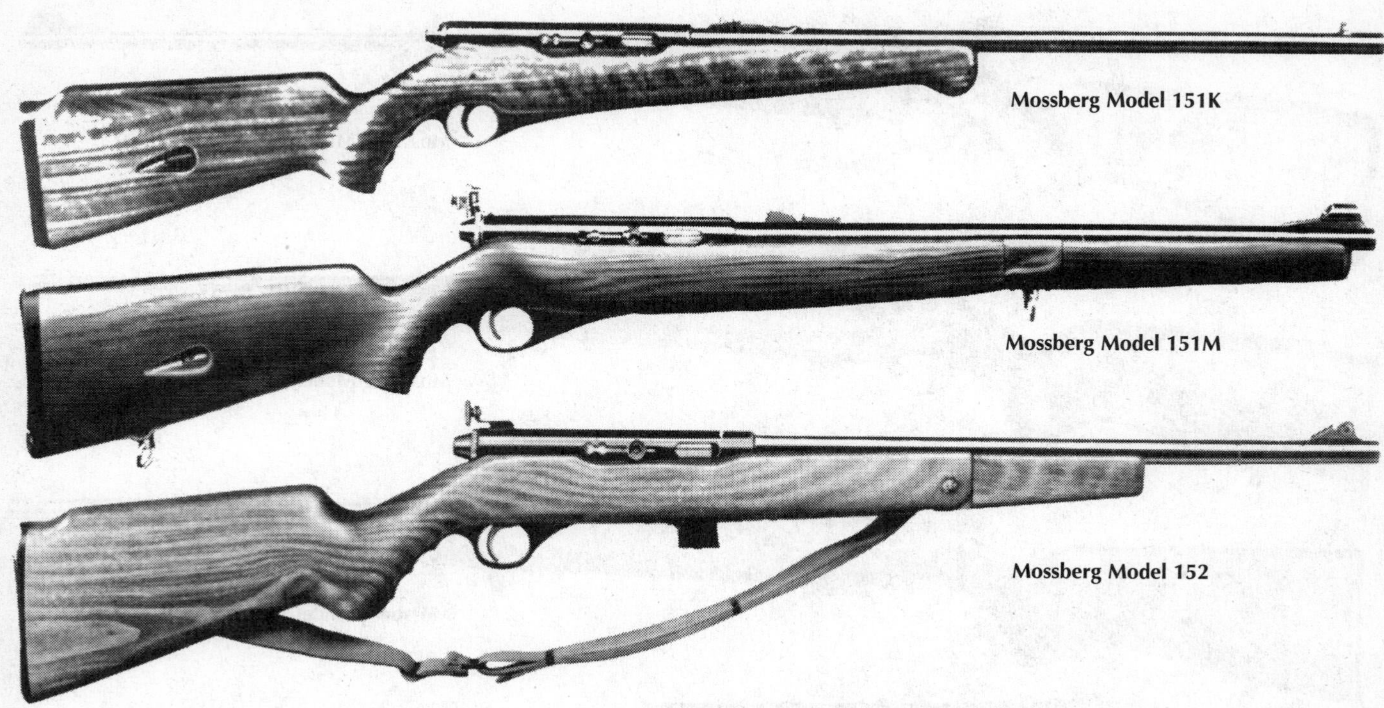

MODEL 142K . . . . **NiB $141 Ex $114 Gd $79**
Same as Model 142 except w/open rear sight. Made 1953-57.

MODEL 144 BOLT-ACTION TARGET RIFLE . . . . **NiB $422 Ex $345 Gd $190**
Caliber: .22 LR. Seven-round detachable box magazine. 26-inch heavy bbl. Weight: 8 lbs. Sights: Microclick receiver peep; hooded front. Pistol-grip target stock w/beavertail forearm, adj. hand stop, swivels. Made 1949-54. Note: This model designation was resumed c.1973 to replace Model 144LS, and then disc. again in 1985.

MODEL 144LS . . . . **NiB $473 Ex $412 Gd $180**
Same as Model 144 except w/Lyman No. 57MS or Mossberg S331 receiver sight and Lyman 17A front sight. Made 1954 to date. Note: Since 1973, this model has been marketed as Model 144.

MODEL 146B BOLT-ACTION REPEATER . . **NiB $214 Ex $162 Gd $111**
Takedown. Caliber: .22 LR. Long, Short. Tubular magazine holds 30 Short, 23 Long, 20 LR. 26-inch bbl. Weight: 7 lbs. Sights: Micrometer click rear peep, open rear; hooded front. Plain stock w/pistol-grip, Monte Carlo comb and cheekpiece, knob forend tip, swivels. Made 1949-54.

MODEL 151K . . . . **NiB $193 Ex $152 Gd $101**
Same as Model 151M except w/24-inch bbl., weight: 6 lbs., w/o peep sight, plain stock w/Monte Carlo comb and cheekpiece, pistol-grip knob, forend tip, w/o swivels. Made 1950-51.

MODEL 151M AUTOLOADING RIFLE . . . . **NiB $193 Ex $153 Gd $101**
Improved version of Model 51M w/same general specifications, complete action is instantly removable w/o use of tools. Made 1946-58.

MODEL 152 AUTOLOADING CARBINE . . **NiB $193 Ex $152 Gd $101**
Caliber: .22 LR. Seven-round detachable box magazine. 18-inch bbl. Weight: 5 lbs. Sights: Peep rear; military-type front. Monte Carlo stock w/pistol-grip, hinged forearm pulls down to form hand grip, sling mounted on swivels on left side of stock. Made 1948-57.

MODEL 152K . . . . **NiB $173 Ex $137 Gd $90**
Same as Model 152 except w/open instead of peep rear sight. Made 1950-57.

MODEL 320B BOY SCOUT TARGET RIFLE . . . . . **NiB $174 Ex $142 Gd $99**
Same as Model 340K except single-shot w/auto. safety. Made 1960-71.

MODEL 320K HAMMERLESS BOLT-ACTION SINGLE-SHOT . . . . . **NiB $134 Ex $108 Gd $75**
Same as Model 346K except single-shot, w/drop-in loading platform, automatic safety. Weight: 5.75 lbs. Made 1958-60.

MODEL 321B . . . . **NiB $153 Ex $123 Gd $85**
Same as Model 321K except w/receiver peep sight. Made 1972-75.

MODEL 321K BOLT-ACTION SINGLE-SHOT . . . . **NiB $159 Ex $129 Gd $89**
Same as Model 341 except single-shot. Made 1972-80.

MODEL 333 AUTOLOADING CARBINE . . **NiB $159 Ex $134 Gd $108**
Caliber: .22 LR. 15-round tubular magazine. 20-inch bbl. Weight: 6.25 lbs. Sights: Open rear; ramp front. Monte Carlo stock w/checkered pistol grip and forearm, bbl. band, swivels. Made 1972-73.

MODEL 340B TARGET SPORTER . . . . **NiB $193 Ex $162 Gd $111**
Same as Model 340K except w/peep rear sight, hooded ramp front sight. Made 1958-81.

MODEL 340K HAMMERLESS BOLT-ACTION REPEATER . . . . **NiB $162 Ex $137 Gd $111**
Same as Model 346K except clip type, 7-round magazine. Made 1958-71.

MODEL 340M . . . . **NiB $307 Ex $247 Gd $171**
Same as Model 340K except w/18.5-inch bbl., Mannlicher-style stock w/swivels and sling. Weight: 5.25 lbs. Made 1970-71.

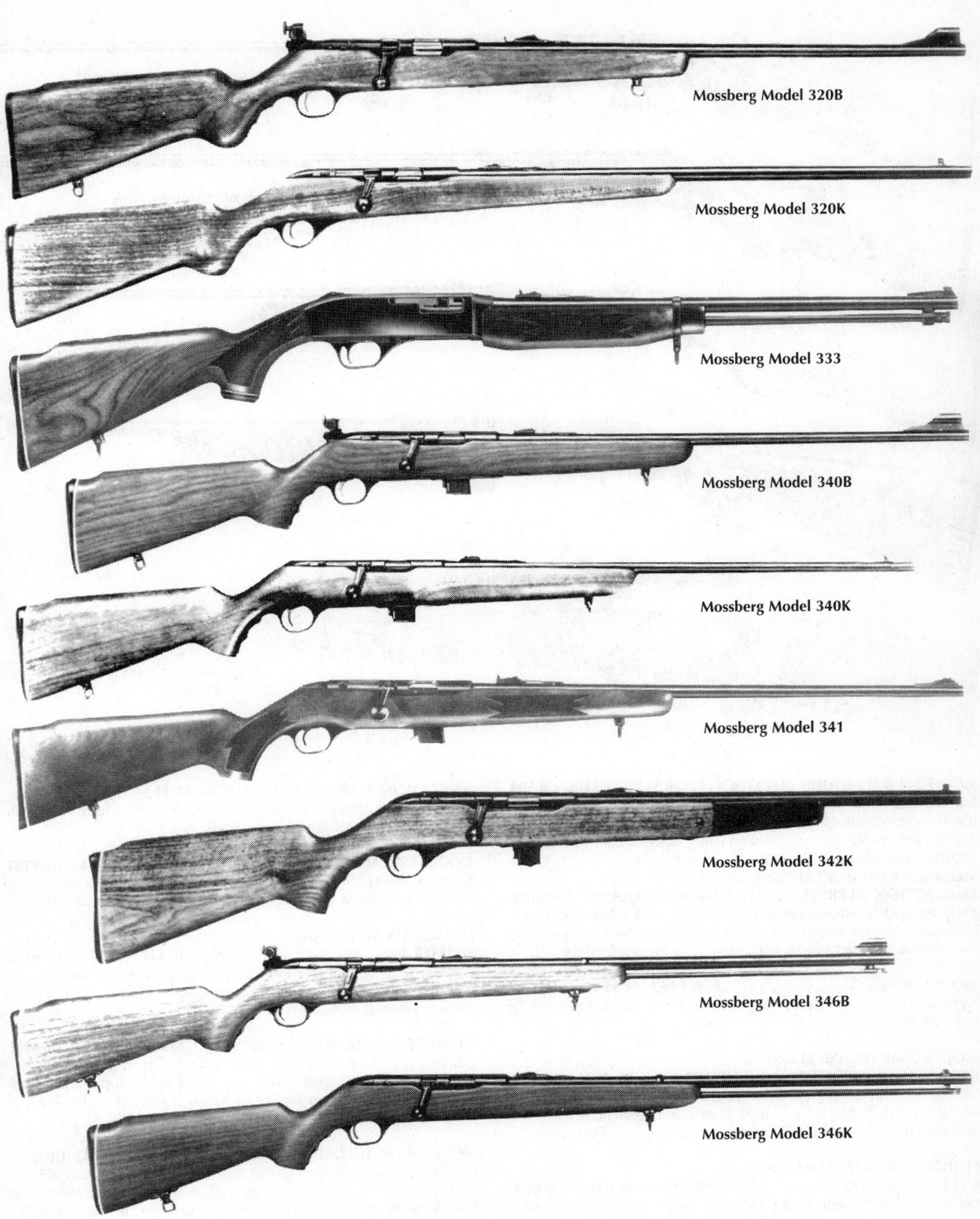
Mossberg Model 320B

Mossberg Model 320K

Mossberg Model 333

Mossberg Model 340B

Mossberg Model 340K

Mossberg Model 341

Mossberg Model 342K

Mossberg Model 346B

Mossberg Model 346K

MODEL 341 BOLT-ACTION REPEATER. . . . . NiB $137 Ex $106 Gd $80
Caliber: .22 Short. Long, LR. Seven-round clip magazine. 24-inch bbl. Weight: 6.5 lbs. Sights: Open rear, ramp front. Monte Carlo stock w/checkered pistol-grip and forearm, sling swivels. Made 1972-85.

MODEL 342K HAMMERLESS BOLT-ACTION CARBINE. . . . . NiB $162 Ex $137 Gd $101
Same as Model 340K except w/18-inch bbl., stock w/no cheekpiece, extension forend is hinged, pulls down to form hand grip; sling swivels and web strap on left side of stock. Weight: 5 lbs. Made 1958-74.

MODEL 346B . . . . NiB $162 Ex $137 Gd $101
Same as Model 346K except w/peep rear sight, hooded ramp front sight. Made 1958-67.

MODEL 346K HAMMERLESS BOLT-ACTION REPEATER . . . . NiB $146 Ex $126 Gd $88
Caliber: .22 Short. Long, LR. Tubular magazine holds 25 Short, 20 Long, 18 LR. 24-inch bbl. Weight: 6.5 lbs. Sights: Open rear; bead front. Walnut stock w/Monte Carlo comb, cheekpiece, pistol-grip, sling swivels. Made 1958-71.

MODEL 350K AUTOLOADING RIFLE — CLIP TYPE . . . . NiB $152 Ex $106 Gd $80
Caliber: .22 Short (High Speed), Long, LR. Seven-round clip magazine.

(cont'd.) **MODEL 350K AUTOLOADING RIFLE — CLIP TYPE**
23.5-inch bbl. Weight: 6 lbs. Sights: Open rear; bead front. Monte Carlo stock w/pistol-grip. Made 1958-71.

MODEL 351C AUTOLOADING CARBINE . NiB $173 Ex $142 Gd $101
Same as Model 351K except w/18.5-inch bbl., Western carbine-style stock w/barrel band and sling swivels. Weight: 5.5 lbs. Made 1965-71.

MODEL 351K AUTOLOADING SPORTER. . . . . NiB $173 Ex $142 Gd $101
Caliber: .22 LR. Fifteen-round tubular magazine in buttstock. 24-inch bbl. Weight: 6 lbs. Sights: Open rear; bead front. Monte Carlo stock w/pistol-grip. Made 1960-71.

MODEL 352K AUTOLOADING CARBINE. . . . . NiB $173 Ex $142 Gd $101
Caliber: .22 Short, Long, LR. Seven-round clip magazine. 18-inch bbl. Weight: 5 lbs. Sights: Open rear; bead front. Monte Carlo stock w/pistol grip; extension forend of Tenite is hinged, pulls down to form hand grip; sling swivels, web strap. Made 1958-71.

MODEL 353 AUTOLOADING CARBINE . . NiB $173 Ex $142 Gd $101
Caliber: .22 LR. Seven round clip magazine. 18-inch bbl. Weight: 5 lbs. Sights: Open rear; ramp front. Monte Carlo stock w/checkered pistol-grip and forearm; black Tenite extension forend pulls down to form hand grip. Made 1972-85.

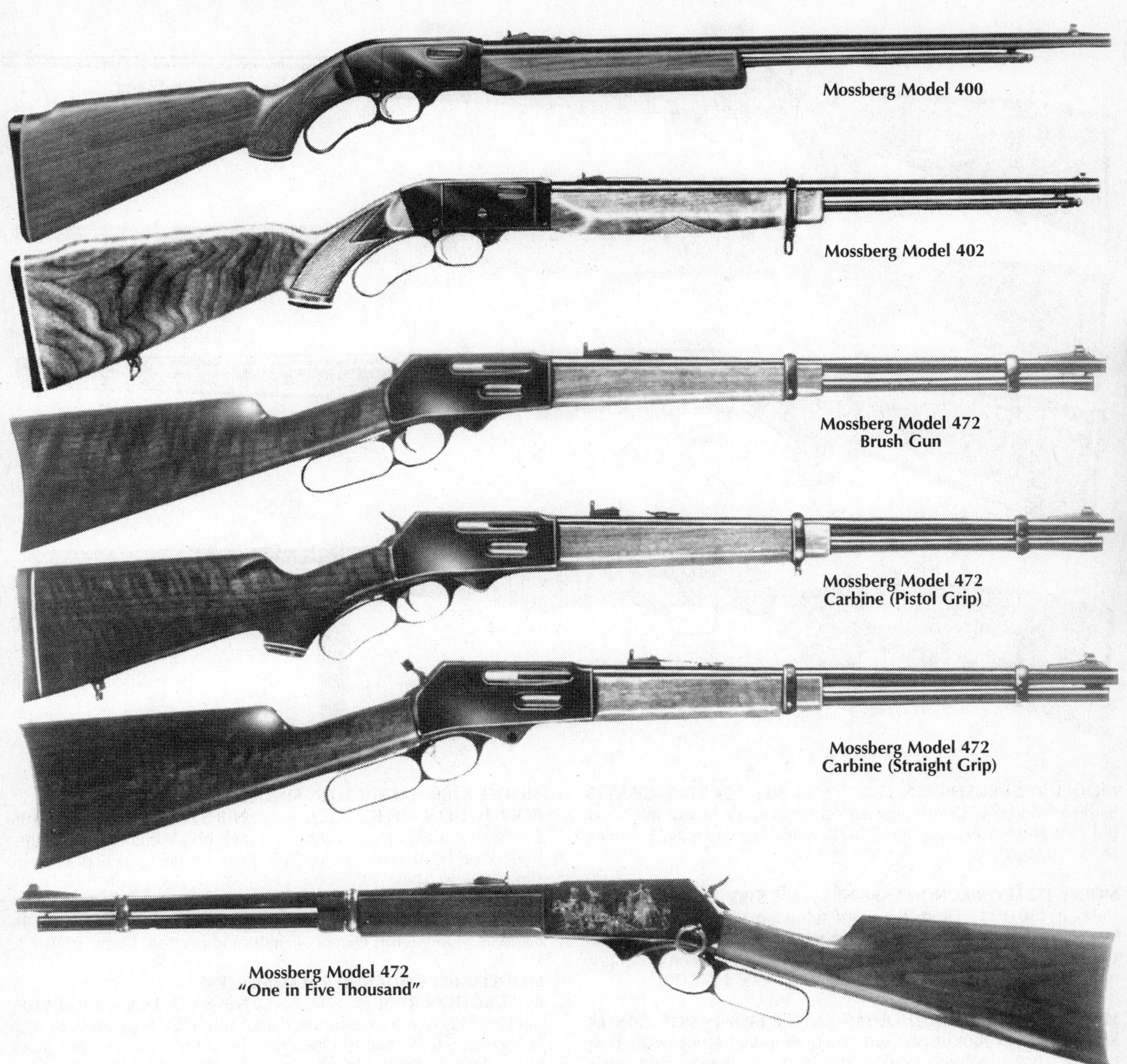
Mossberg Model 400

Mossberg Model 402

Mossberg Model 472 Brush Gun

Mossberg Model 472 Carbine (Pistol Grip)

Mossberg Model 472 Carbine (Straight Grip)

Mossberg Model 472 "One in Five Thousand"

MODEL 377 PLINKSTER AUTOLOADER . . NiB $195 Ex $154 Gd $108
Caliber: .22 LR. Fifteen-round tubular magazine. 20-inch bbl. Weight: 6.25 lbs. 4x scope sight. Thumbhole stock w/rollover cheekpiece, Monte Carlo comb, checkered forearm; molded of modified polystyrene foam in walnut-finish; sling swivel studs. Made 1977-79.

MODEL 380 SEMIAUTOMATIC RIFLE . . . . . NiB $164 Ex $134 Gd $94
Caliber: .22 LR. Fifteen-round buttstock magazine. 20-inch bbl. Weight: 5.5 lbs. Sights: Open rear; bead front. Made 1980-85.

MODEL 400 PALOMINO LEVER-ACTION. . . . . NiB $267 Ex $206 Gd $113
Hammerless. Caliber: .22 Short, Long, LR. Tubular magazine holds 20 Short, 17 Long, 15 LR. 24-inch bbl. Weight: 5.5 lbs. Sights: Open rear; bead front. Monte Carlo stock w/checkered pistol-grip; beavertail forearm. Made 1959-64.

MODEL 402 PALOMINO CARBINE . . . . . . NiB $267 Ex $216 Gd $190
Same as Model 400 except w/18.5-inch (1961-64) or 20-inch bbl. (1964-71), forearm w/bbl. band, swivels; magazine holds two fewer rounds. Weight: 4.75 lbs. Made 1961-71.

MODEL 430 AUTOLOADING RIFLE. . . . . . . NiB $156 Ex $126 Gd $88
Caliber: .22 LR. Eighteen-round tubular magazine. 24-inch bbl. Weight: 6.25 lbs. Sights: Open rear; bead front. Monte Carlo stock w/checkered pistol grip; checkered forearm. Made 1970-71.

MODEL 432 WESTERN-STYLE AUTO . . . . . . NiB $150 Ex $121 Gd $85
Same as Model 430 except w/plain straight-grip carbine-type stock and forearm, bbl. band, sling swivels. Magazine capacity: 15 cartridges. Weight: 6 lbs. Made 1970-71.

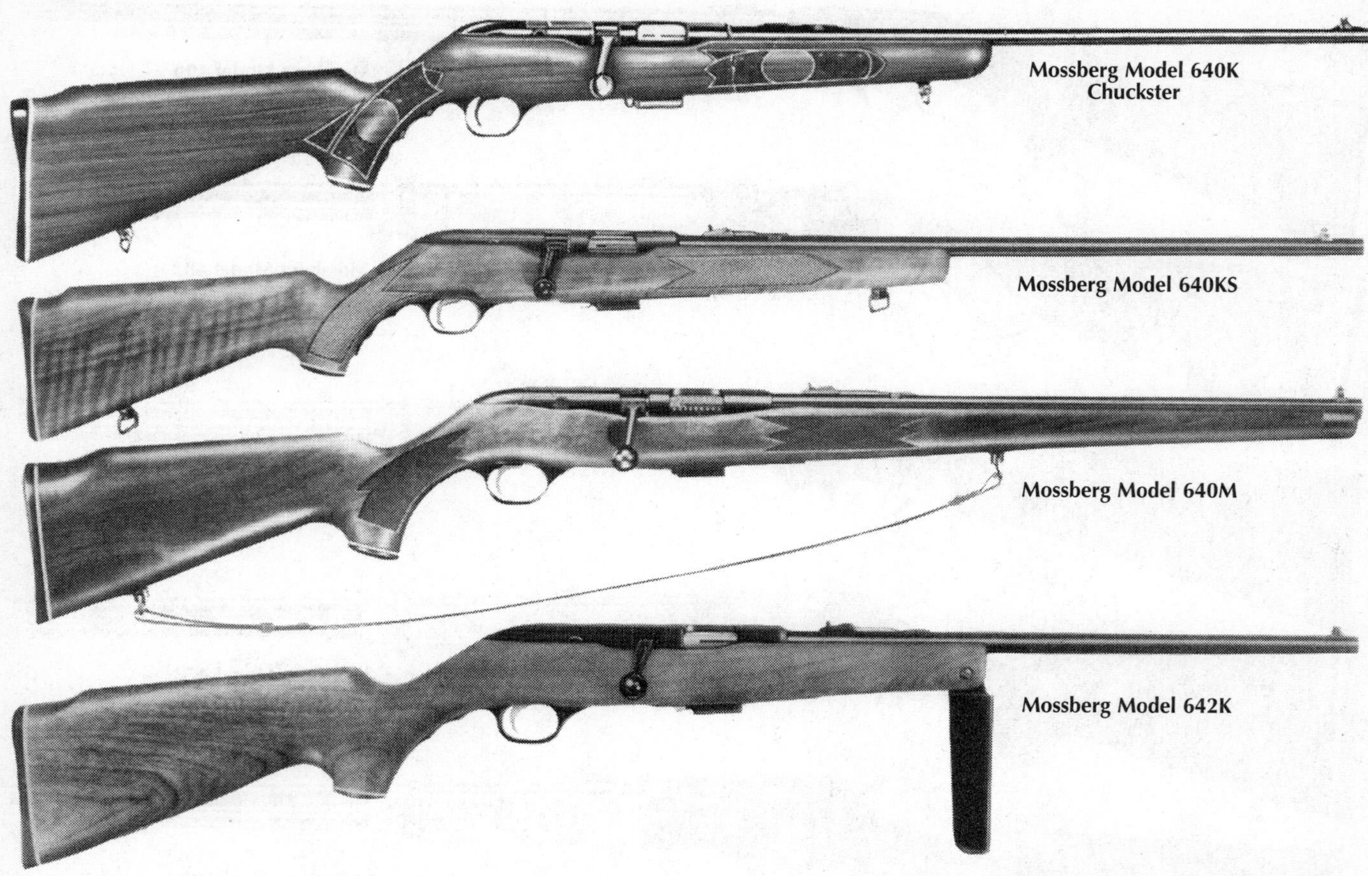

MODEL 472 BRUSH GUN . . . . NiB $216 Ex $190 Gd $113
Same as Model 472 Carbine w/straight-grip stock except w/18-inch bbl., weight: 6.5 lbs. Caliber: .30-30. Magazine capacity: 5 rounds. Made 1974-76.

MODEL 472 LEVER-ACTION CARBINE . . . NiB $195 Ex $164 Gd $113
Calibers: .30-30, .35 Rem. Six round tubular magazine. 20-inch bbl. Weight: 6.75 to 7 lbs. Sights: Open rear; ramp front. Pistol-grip or straight-grip stock, forearm w/bbl. band; sling swivels on pistol-grip model saddle ring on straight-grip model. Made 1972-79.

MODEL 472 ONE IN FIVE THOUSAND. . . NiB $458 Ex $329 Gd $164
Same as Model 472 Brush Gun except w/Indian scenes etched on receiver; brass buttplate, saddle ring and bbl. bands, gold-plated trigger, bright blued finish, select walnut stock and forearm. Limited edition of 5,000; serial numbered 1 to 5,000. Made in 1974.

MODEL 472 RIFLE. . . . . NiB $216 Ex $190 Gd $113
Same as Model 472 Carbine w/pistol-grip stock except w/24-inch bbl., 5-round magazine, weight: 7 lbs. Made 1974-76.

MODEL 479
Caliber: .30-30. Six-round tubular magazine. 20-inch bbl. Weight: 6.75 to 7 lbs. Sights: Open rear; ramp front. Made 1983-85.
Model 479 Rifle . . . . NiB $206 Ex $190 Gd $134
Model 479PCA
(Carbine w/20-inch bbl.). . . . . NiB $206 Ex $190 Gd $134
Model 479RR
(Roy Rogers, 5000 Ltd. Edition) . . . . NiB $345 Ex $293 Gd $134

MODEL 620K HAMMERLESS SINGLE-SHOT BOLT-ACTION RIFLE. . . . . NiB $173 Ex $152 Gd $106
Single shot. Caliber: .22 WMR. 24-inch bbl. Weight: 6 lbs. Sights: Open rear; bead front. Monte Carlo stock w/cheekpiece, pistol-grip, sling swivels. Made 1959-60.

MODEL 620K-A. . . . . NiB $169 Ex $137 Gd $96
Same as Model 640K except w/sight modification. Made 1960-68.

MODEL 640K CHUCKSTER HAMMERLESS BOLT-ACTION RIFLE. . . . . NiB $173 Ex $152 Gd $106
Caliber: .22 WMR. Five-round detachable clip magazine. 24-inch bbl. Weight: 6 lbs. Sights: Open rear; bead front. Monte Carlo stock w/cheekpiece, pistol grip, sling swivels. Made 1959-84.

MODEL 640KS . . . . NiB $214 Ex $162 Gd $111
Deluxe version of Model 640K w/select walnut stock hand checkering; gold-plated front sight, rear sight elevator, and trigger. Made 1960-64.

MODEL 640M. . . . . NiB $319 Ex $293 Gd $190
Similar to Model 640K except w/heavy receiver and jeweled bolt. 20-inch bbl., full length Mannlicher-style stock w/Monte Carlo comb and cheekpiece, swivels and leather sling. 40.75 inches overall. Weight: 6 lbs. Made 1971-73.

MODEL 642K CARBINE . . . . NiB $242 Ex $190 Gd $139
Caliber: .22 WMR. Five-round detachable clip magazine. 18-inch bbl. Weight: 5 lbs. 38.25 inches overall. Sights: Open rear; bead front. Monte Carlo walnut stock w/black Tenite forearm extension that pulls down to form hand grip. Made 1961-68.

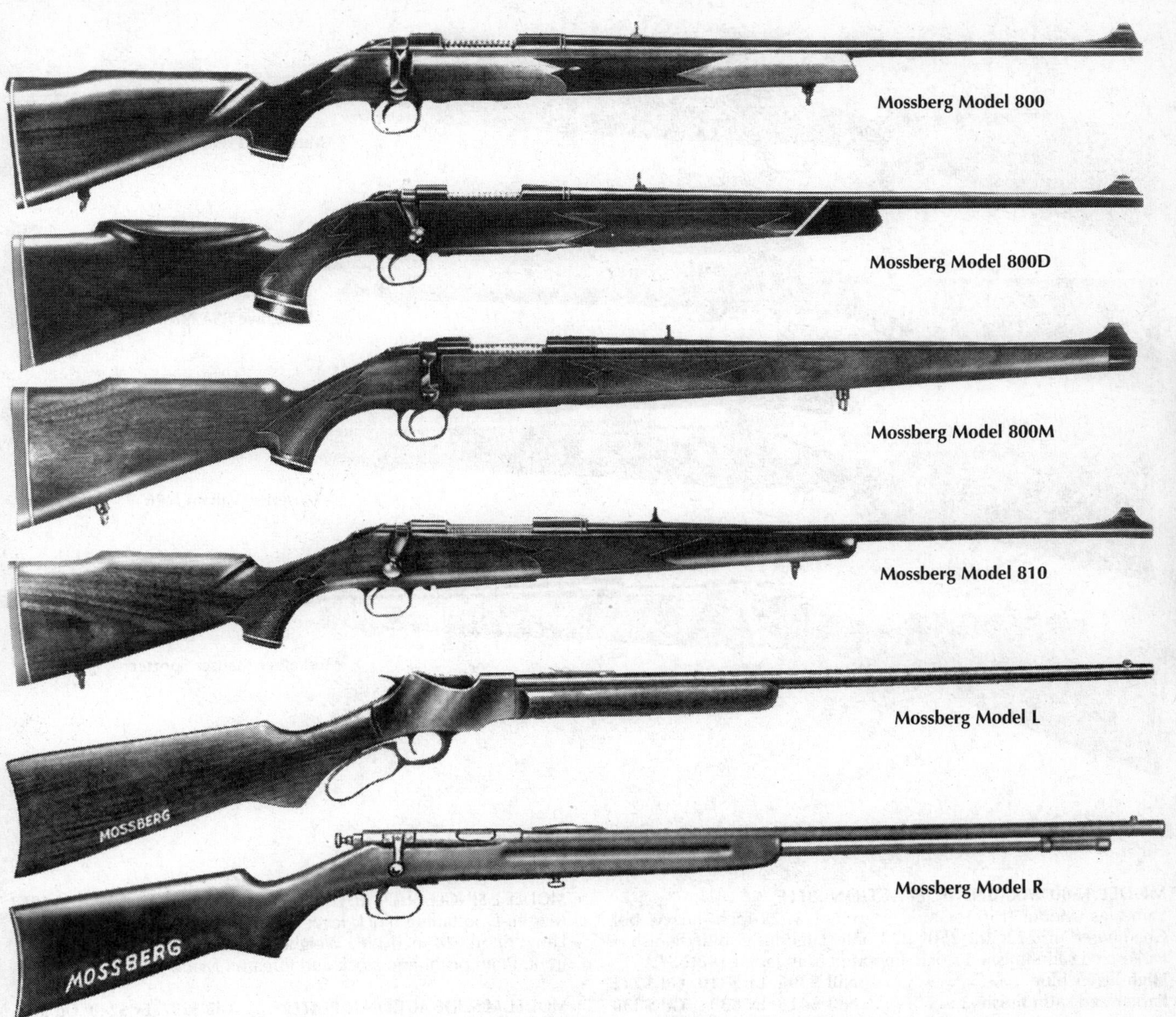

Mossberg Model 800

Mossberg Model 800D

Mossberg Model 800M

Mossberg Model 810

Mossberg Model L

Mossberg Model R

MODEL 800 BOLT-ACTION CENTERFIRE RIFLE .... NiB $236 Ex $190 Gd $133
.222 Rem., .22-250, .243 Win., .308 Win. Four-round mag., 3-round in .222. 22-inch bbl. Weight: 7.5 lbs. Sights: Folding leaf rear; ramp front. Monte Carlo stock w/cheekpiece, checkered pistol-grip and forearm, sling swivels. Made 1967-79.

MODEL 800D SUPER GRADE..... NiB $377 Ex $304 Gd $210
Deluxe version of Model 800 except w/stock w/rollover comb and cheekpiece, rosewood forend tip and pistol-grip cap. Weight: 6.75 lbs. Chambered for all calibers listed for the Model 800 except for .222 Rem. Sling swivels. Made 1970-73.

MODEL 800M................. NiB $293 Ex $267 Gd $164
Same as Model 800 except w/flat bolt handle, 20-inch bbl., Mannlicher-style stock. Weight: 6.5 lbs. Calibers: .22-250, .243 Win., .308 Win. Made 1969-72.

MODEL 800VT VARMINT/TARGET ...... NiB $242 Ex $190 Gd $139
Similar to Model 800 except w/24-inch heavy bbl., no sights. Weight: 9.5 lbs. Calibers: .222 Rem., .22-250, .243 Win. Made 1968-79.

MODEL 810 BOLT-ACTION CENTERFIRE RIFLE
Calibers: .270 Win., .30-06, 7mm Rem. Mag., .338 Win. Mag. Detachable box magazine (1970-75) or internal magazine w/hinged floorplate (1972 to date). Capacity: Four-round in .270 and .30-06, 3-round in Magnums. 22-inch bbl. in .270 and .30-06, 24-inch in Magnums. Weight: 7.5 to 8 lbs. Sights: Leaf rear; ramp front. Stock w/Monte Carlo comb and cheekpiece, checkered pistol-grip and forearm, grip cap, sling swivels. Made 1970-79.
Standard calibers.............. NiB $345 Ex $278 Gd $192
Magnum calibers.............. NiB $370 Ex $293 Gd $206

MODEL 1500 MOUNTAINEER GRADE I CENTERFIRE RIFLE...... NiB $396 Ex $319 Gd $242
Calibers: .223, .243, .270, .30-06, 7mm Mag. 22-inch or 24-inch (7mm Mag.) bbl. Weight: 7 lbs. 10 oz. Hardwood walnut-finished checkered stock. Sights: Hooded ramp front w/gold bead; fully adj. rear. Drilled and tapped for scope mounts. Sling swivel studs. Imported 1986-87.

Musgrave Premier NR5

Musgrave RSA NR1

Musgrave Valiant NR6

Musketeer Mauser Sporter

MODEL 1500 VARMINT BOLT-ACTION RIFLE
Same as Model 1500 Grade I except w/22-inch heavy bbl. Chambered in .222, .22-250, .223 only. High-luster blued finish or Parkerized satin finished stock. Imported from Japan 1986-87.
High-luster blue. . . . . NiB $396 Ex $319 Gd $242
Parkerized satin finish . . . . NiB $416 Ex $334 Gd $230

MODEL 1700LS CLASSIC HUNTER BOLT-ACTION RIFLE. . . . . NiB $448 Ex $370 Gd $242
Same as Model 1500 Grade I except w/checkered classic-style stock and Schnabel forend. Chambered in 243, 270, 30-06 only. Imported from Japan 1986-87.

MODEL B BOLT-ACTION RIFLE . . . . NiB $185 Ex $159 Gd $77
Takedown. Caliber: .22 LR. Long, Short. Single-shot. 22-inch bbl. Sights: Open rear; bead front. Plain pistol-grip stock. Made 1930-32.

MODEL K SLIDE-ACTION REPEATER . . . . . . NiB $190 Ex $134 Gd $87
Hammerless. Takedown. Caliber: .22 LR. Long, Short. Tubular magazine holds 20 Short, 16 Long, 14 LR. 22-inch bbl. Weight: 5 lbs. Sights: Open rear; bead front. Plain, straight-grip stock. Grooved slide handle. Made 1922-31.

MODELS L42A, L43, L45A, L46A-LS
See Models 42A, 43, 45A and 46A-LS respectively; "L" refers to a left-hand version of those rifles.

MODEL L SINGLE-SHOT RIFLE . . . . NiB $454 Ex $365 Gd $252
Martini-type falling-block lever-action. Takedown. Caliber: .22 LR, Long, Short. 24-inch bbl. Weight: 5 lbs. Sights: Open rear; bead front. Plain pistol-grip stock and forearm. Made 1929-32.

MODEL M SLIDE-ACTION REPEATER . . . . NiB $297 Ex $240 Gd $166
Specifications same as for Model K except w/24-inch octagon bbl., pistol-grip stock, weighs 5.5 lbs. Made 1928-31.

MODEL R BOLT-ACTION REPEATER . . . . . NiB $285 Ex $229 Gd $158
Takedown. Caliber: .22 LR, Long, Short. Tubular magazine. 24-inch bbl. Sights: Open rear; bead front. Plain pistol-grip stock. Made 1930-32.

MUSGRAVE RIFLES, MUSGRAVE MFRS. & DIST. (PTY) LTD. — Bloemfontein, South Africa

PREMIER NR5 BOLT-ACTION HUNTING RIFLE . . . . NiB $453 Ex $370 Gd $242
Calibers: .243 Win., .270 Win., .30-06, .308 Win., 7mm Rem. Mag. Five-round magazine. 25.5-inch bbl. Weight: 8.25 lbs. Furnished w/o sights, but drilled and tapped for scope mount. Select walnut Monte Carlo stock w/cheekpiece, checkered pistol-grip and forearm, contrasting pistol-grip cap and forend tip, recoil pad, swivel studs. Made 1971-76.

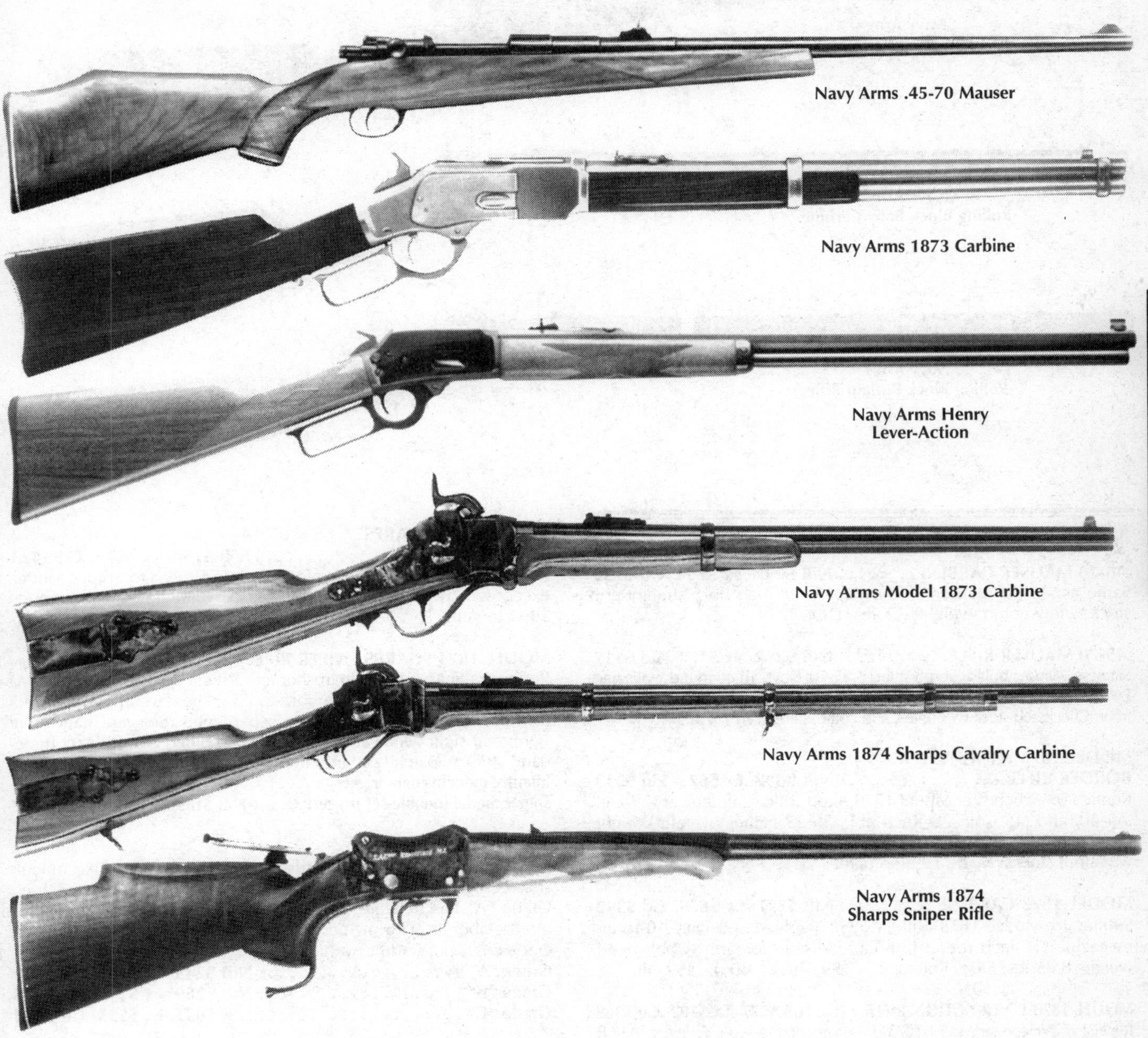

Navy Arms .45-70 Mauser

Navy Arms 1873 Carbine

Navy Arms Henry Lever-Action

Navy Arms Model 1873 Carbine

Navy Arms 1874 Sharps Cavalry Carbine

Navy Arms 1874 Sharps Sniper Rifle

RSA NR1 BOLT-ACTION SINGLE-SHOT TARGET RIFLE . . . . . NiB $454 Ex $365 Gd $252
Caliber: .308 Win. (7.62mm NATO). 26.4-inch heavy bbl. Weight: 10 lbs. Sights: Aperture receiver; tunnel front. Walnut target stock w/beavertail forearm, handguard, bbl. band, rubber buttplate, sling swivels. Made 1971-76.

VALIANT NR6 HUNTING RIFLE . . . NiB $417 Ex $319 Gd $211
Similar to Premier except w/24-inch bbl.; stock w/straight comb, skip French-style checkering, no grip cap or forend tip. Sights: Leaf rear; hooded ramp front bead sight. Weight: 7.7lbs. Made 1971-76.

MUSKETEER RIFLES — Washington, D.C. Mfd. by Firearms International Corp.

MAUSER SPORTER
FN Mauser bolt action. .243, .25-06, .270, .264 Mag., .308, .30-06, 7mm Mag., .300 Win. Mag. Magazine holds 5 standard, 3 Magnum cartridges. 24-inch bbl. Weight: 7.25 lbs. No sights. Monte Carlo stock w/checkered pistol-grip and forearm, swivels. Made 1963-72.
Standard Sporter . . . . NiB $396 Ex $345 Gd $211
Deluxe Sporter . . . . NiB $448 Ex $370 Gd $216
Standard Carbine. . . . . NiB $381 Ex $319 Gd $211

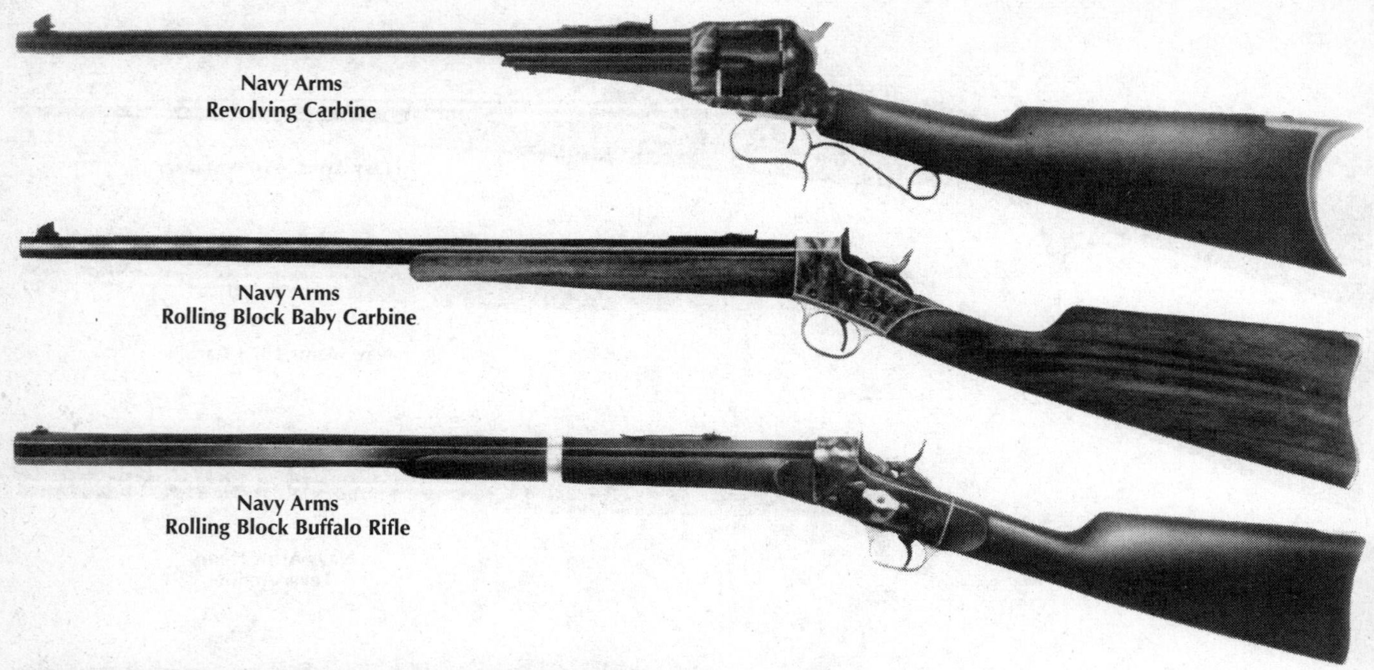

Navy Arms
Revolving Carbine

Navy Arms
Rolling Block Baby Carbine

Navy Arms
Rolling Block Buffalo Rifle

NAVY ARMS — Ridgefield, New Jersey

.45-70 MAUSER CARBINE. . . . . NiB $237 Ex $186 Gd $130
Same as .45-70 Mauser Rifle except w/18-inch bbl., straight-grip stock w/low comb, weight: 7.5 lbs. Disc.

.45-70 MAUSER RIFLE . . . . NiB $212 Ex $171 Gd $119
Siamese Mauser bolt action. Caliber: .45-70 Govt. Three-round magazine. 24- or 26-inch bbl. Weight: 8.5 lbs. w/26-inch bbl. Sights: Open rear; ramp front: Checkered stock w/Monte Carlo comb. Intoduced 1973. Disc.

MODEL 1873 WINCHESTER
BORDER RIFLE . . . . NiB $802 Ex $675 Gd $313
Replica of Winchester Model 1873 Short Rifle. Calibers: .357 Mag., .44-40, and .45 Colt. 20- inch bbl., 39.25 inches overall. Weight: 7.6 lbs. Blued full octagonal barrel, color casehardened receiver w/walnut stocks. Made 1999 to date.

MODEL 1873 CARBINE . . . . NiB $777 Ex $675 Gd $343
Similar to Model 1873 Rifle except w/blued receiver, 10-round magazine, 19-inch round bbl. carbine-style forearm w/bbl. band, weighs 6.75 lbs. Disc. Reissued in 1991 in .44-40 or .45 Colt.

MODEL 1873 LEVER-ACTION RIFLE . . . . . NiB $777 Ex $700 Gd $369
Replica of Winchester Model 1873. Casehardened receiver. Calibers: .22 LR. .357 Magnum, .44-40. 15-round magazine. 24-inch octagon bbl. Weight: 8 lbs. Sights: Open rear; blade front. Straight-grip stock, forearm w/end cap. Disc. Reissued in 1991 in .44-40 or .45 Colt w/12-round magazine. Disc. 1994.

MODEL 1873 TRAPPER'S . . . . NiB $602 Ex $494 Gd $357
Same as Model 1873 Carbine, except w/16.5-inch bbl., 8-round magazine, weighs 6.25 lbs. Disc.

MODEL 1873 SPORTING CARBINE/RIFLE
Replica of Winchester Model 1873 Sporting Rifle. Calibers: .357 Mag. (24.25-inch bbl. only), .44-40 and .45 Colt. 24.25-inch bbl. (Carbine) or 30-inch bbl. (Rifle). 48.75 to 53 inches overall. Weight: 8.14 to 9.3 lbs. Octagonal barrel, casehardened receiver and checkered walnut pistol-grip. Made 1992 to date.
Carbine model. . . . . NiB $883 Ex $754 Gd $397
Rifle model . . . . NiB $933 Ex $856 Gd $448

MODEL 1874 SHARPS
CAVALRY CARBINE. . . . . NiB $754 Ex $576 Gd $423
Replica of Sharps 1874 Cavalry Carbine. Similar to Sniper Model, except w/22-inch bbl. and carbine stock. Caliber: .45-70. Imported 1994 to date.

MODEL 1874 SHARPS SNIPER RIFLE
Replica of Sharps 1874 Sharpshooter's Rifle. Caliber: .45-70. Falling breech, single-shot. 30-inch bbl. 46.75 inches overall. Weight: 8.5 lbs. Double-set triggers. Color casehardened receiver. Blade front sight; rear sight w/elevation leaf. Polished blued bbl. Military three-band stock w/patch box. Imported 1994 to date.
Infantry model (single trigger) . . . . NiB $1142 Ex $1014 Gd $606
Sniper model (double set trigger) . . . . . . NiB $1652 Ex $1448 Gd $708

ENGRAVED MODELS
Yellowboy and Model 1873 rifles are available in deluxe models w/select walnut stocks and forearms and engraving in three grades. Grade "A" has delicate scrollwork in limited areas. Grade "B" is more elaborate with 40 percent coverage. Grade "C" has highest grade engraving. Add to value:
Grade "A" . . . . NiB $243 Ex $198 Gd $141
Grade "B" . . . . NiB $269 Ex $219 Gd $156
Grade "C" . . . . NiB $651 Ex $525 Gd $364

HENRY LEVER-ACTION RIFLE
Replica of the Winchester Model 1860 Henry Rifle. Caliber: .44-40. Twelve round magazine. 16.5-, 22- or 24.25-inch octagon bbl. Weight: 7.5 to 9 lbs. 35.4 to 43.25 inches overall. Sights: Blade front, adjustable ladder rear. European walnut straight grip buttstock w/bbl. and side stock swivels. Imported 1985 to date. Brass or steel receiver. Blued or color casehardened metal.
Carbine model w/22-inch bbl.,
introduced 1992) . . . . NiB $810 Ex $632 Gd $402
Military rifle model (w/brass frame) . . . . . . NiB $810 Ex $632 Gd $402
Trapper model (w/brass frame). . . . . NiB $810 Ex $632 Gd $402
Trapper model (w/iron frame). . . . . NiB $861 Ex $759 Gd $423
W/"A" engraving, add $300
W/"B" engraving, add. $500
W/"C" engraving, add. $900

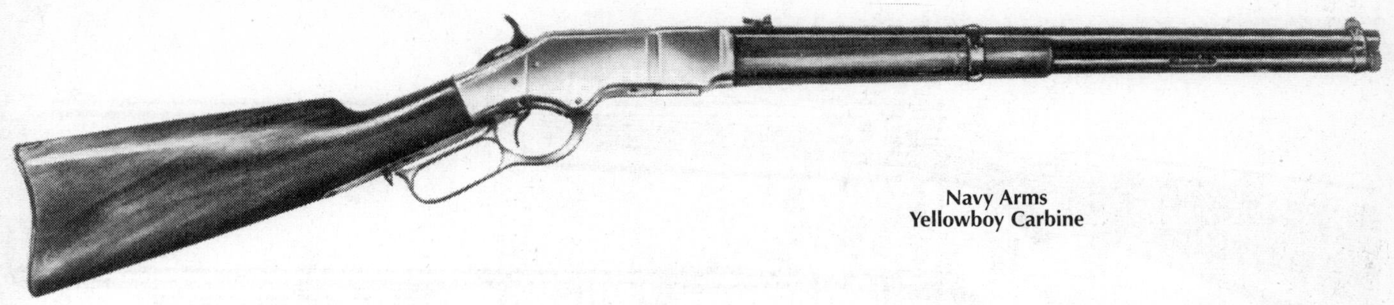

Navy Arms
Yellowboy Carbine

MARTINI TARGET RIFLE . . . . NiB $494 Ex $418 Gd $275
Martini single-shot action. Calibers: .444 Marlin, .45-70. 26- or 30-inch half-octagon or full-octagon bbl. Weight: 9 lbs. w/26-inch bbl. Sights: Creedmoor tang peep, open middle, blade front. Stock w/cheekpiece and pistol-grip, forearm w/Schnabel tip, both checkered. Intro. 1972. Disc.

REVOLVING CARBINE . . . . NiB $596 Ex $494 Gd $341
Action resembles that of Remington Model 1875 Revolver. Casehardened frame. Calibers: .357 Magnum, .44-40, .45 Colt. Six round cylinder. 20-inch bbl. Weight: 5 lbs. Sights: Open rear; blade front. Straight-grip stock brass trigger guard and buttplate. Intro. 1968. Disc.

ROLLING BLOCK BABY CARBINE . . . . NiB $231 Ex $186 Gd $129
Replica of small Remington Rolling Block single-shot action. Casehardened frame, brass trigger guard. Calibers: .22 LR. .22 Hornet, .357 Magnum, .44-40. 20-inch octagon or 22-inch round bbl. Weight: 5 lbs. Sights: Open rear; blade front. Straight-grip stock, plain forearm, brass buttplate. Imported 1968-81.

ROLLING BLOCK BUFFALO CARBINE. . . . NiB $402 Ex $367 Gd $316
Same as Buffalo Rifle except w/18-inch bbl., weigh: 10 lbs.

ROLLING BLOCK BUFFALO RIFLE. . . . . . . NiB $612 Ex $510 Gd $255
Replica Remington Rolling Block single-shot action. Casehardened frame, brass trigger guard. Calibers: .444 Marlin, .45-70, .50-70. 26- or 30-inch heavy half-octagon or full-octagon bbl. Weight: 11 to 12 lbs. Sights: Open rear; blade front. Straight-grip stock w/brass buttplate, forearm w/brass bbl. band. Made 1971 to date.

ROLLING BLOCK CREEDMOOR RIFLE
Same as Buffalo Rifle except calibers .45-70 and .50-70 only, 28- or 30-inch heavy half-octagon or full-octagon bbl., Creedmoor tang peep sight.
Target model . . . . NiB $811 Ex $586 Gd $316
Deluxe target model (disc. 1998) . . . . . NiB $1514 Ex $1234 Gd $1004

YELLOWBOY CARBINE. . . . . NiB $552 Ex $443 Gd $305
Similar to Yellowboy Rifle except w/19-inch bbl., 10-round magazine (14-round in 22 Long Rifle), carbine-style forearm. Weight: 6.75 lbs. Disc. Reissued 1991 in .44-40 only.

YELLOWBOY LEVER-ACTION REPEATER . . . . . NiB $647 Ex $520 Gd $316
Replica of Winchester Model 1866. Calibers: .38 Special, .44-40. 15-round magazine. 24-inch octagon bbl. Weight: 8 lbs. Sights: Folding leaf rear; blade front. Straight-grip stock, forearm w/end cap. Intro. 1966. Disc. Reissued 1991 in .44-40 only w/12-round magazine and adj. ladder-style rear sight.

YELLOWBOY TRAPPER'S MODEL. . . . . NiB $577 Ex $464 Gd $319
Same as Yellowboy Carbine except w/16.5-inch bbl., 8-round magazine, weighs 6.25 lbs. Disc.

NEW ENGLAND FIREARMS — Gardner, Massachusetts

In 1987, New England Firearms was established as an independent company producing selected H&R models under the NEF logo. In 1991, H&R 1871, Inc. was formed from the residual of the parent company and that took over the New England Firearms facility. H&R 1871 produced firearms under both its logo and the NEF brand name until 1999, when the Marlin Firearms Company acquired the assets of H&R 1871.

HANDI-RIFLE
Single-shot, break-open action w/side-lever release. Calibers: .22 Hornet, .22-250, .223, .243, .270, .30-30, .30-06, .45-70. 22-inch bbl. Weight: 7 lbs. Sights: Ramp front; folding rear. Drilled and tapped for scope mounts. Walnut-finished hardwood or synthetic stock. Blued finish. Made 1989 to date.
Calibers: .22-250, .243,
.270 and .30-06 . . . . NiB $212 Ex $151 Gd $105
Calibers: .22 Hornet, .223,
.30-30 and .45-70. . . . . NiB $212 Ex $151 Gd $105

NEWTON SPORTING RIFLES — Buffalo, New York

Mfd. by Newton Arms Co., Charles Newton Rifles Corp. and Buffalo Newton Rifle Co.

BUFFALO SPORTING RIFLE . . . . NiB $1307 Ex $1101 Gd $792
Same general specifications as Standard Model — Second Type. Made c. 1922-32 by Buffalo Newton Rifle Co.

MAUSER SPORTING RIFLE . . . . . NiB $1256 Ex $1143 Gd $741
Mauser (Oberndorf) action. Caliber: .256 Newton. Five round box magazine, hinged floorplate. Double-set triggers. 24-inch bbl. Open rear sight, ramp front sight. Sporting stock w/checkered pistol-grip. Weight: 7 lbs. Made c. 1914 by Newton Arms Co.

STANDARD MODEL
SPORTING RIFLE — FIRST TYPE . . . . . . NiB $1204 Ex $1024 Gd $628
Newton bolt action, interrupted screw-type breech-locking mechanism, double-set triggers. Calibers: .22, .256, .280, .30, ,33, ,35 Newton; ,30-06. 24-inch bbl. Sights: Open rear or cocking-piece peep; ramp front. Checkered pistol-grip stock. Weight: 7 to 8 lbs., depending on caliber. Made c. 1916-18 by Newton Arms Co.

STANDARD MODEL
SPORTING RIFLE
SECOND TYPE. . . . . NiB $967 Ex $777 Gd $535
Newton bolt action, improved design; distinguished by reversed-set trigger and 1917-Enfield-type bolt handle. Calibers: .256, .30, .35 Newton and .30-06. Five round box magazine. 24-inch bbl. Sights: Open rear; ramp front. Checkered pistol-grip stock. Weight: 7.75 to 8.25 lbs. Made c. 1921 by Charles Newton Rifle Corp.

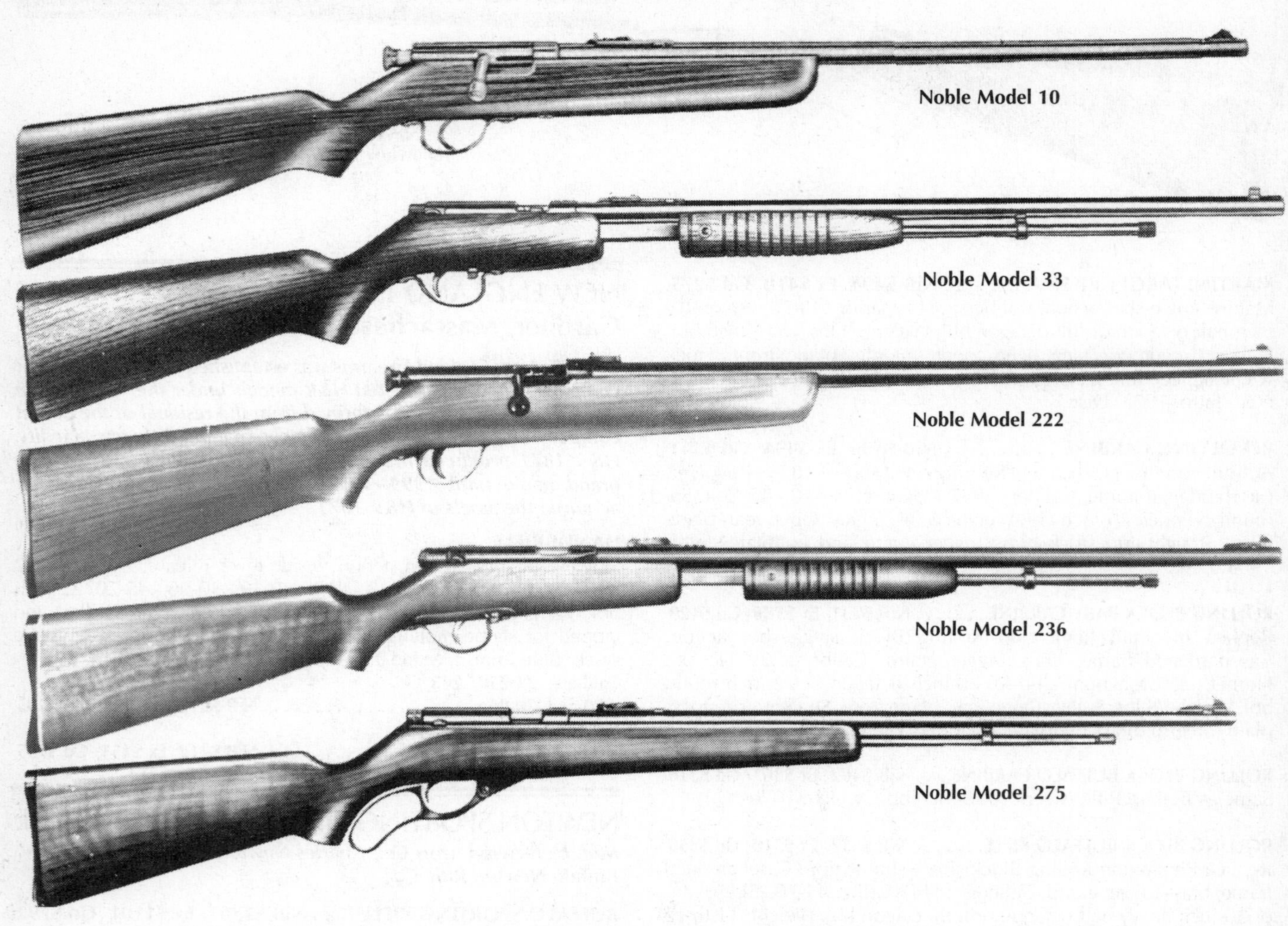

NIKKO FIREARMS, LTD. — Tochiga, Japan

See listings under Golden Eagle Rifles.

NOBLE MFG. CO. — Haydenville, Massachusetts

MODEL 10 BOLT-ACTION SINGLE-SHOT RIFLE . . . . **NiB $88 Ex $71 Gd $50**
Caliber: .22 LR. Long, Short. 24-inch bbl. Plain pistol-grip stock. Sights: Open rear, bead front. Weight: 4 lbs. Made 1955-58.

MODEL 20 BOLT-ACTION SINGLE-SHOT RIFLE . . . . **NiB $81 Ex $66 Gd $47**
Manually cocked. Caliber: .22 LR. Long, Short. 22-inch bbl. Weight: 5 lbs. Sights: Open rear; bead front. Walnut stock w/pistol grip. Made 1958-63.

MODEL 33 SLIDE-ACTION REPEATER . . . . . . **NiB $101 Ex $81 Gd $57**
Hammerless. Caliber: .22 LR. Long, Short. Tubular magazine holds 21 Short, 17 Long, 15 LR. 24-inch bbl. Weight: 6 lbs. Sights: Open rear; bead front. Tenite stock and slide handle. Made 1949-53.

MODEL 33A . . . . **NiB $88 Ex $71 Gd $50**
Same general specifications as Model 33 except w/wood stock and slide handle. Made 1953-55.

MODEL 222 BOLT-ACTION SINGLE-SHOT RIFLE . . . . **NiB $101 Ex $81 Gd $57**
Manually cocked. Caliber: .22 LR. Long, Short. Barrel integral w/receiver. Overall length: 38 inches. Weight: 5 lbs. Sights: Interchangeable V-notch and peep rear; ramp front. Scope mounting base. Pistol-grip stock. Made 1958-71.

MODEL 236 SLIDE-ACTION REPEATING RIFLE . . . . **NiB $113 Ex $92 Gd $64**
Hammerless. Caliber: .22 Short, Long, LR. Tubular magazine holds 21 Short, 17 Long, 15 LR. 24-inch bbl. Weight: 5.5 lbs. Sights: Open rear; ramp front. Pistol-grip stock, grooved slide handle. Made 1951 to date.

MODEL 275 LEVER-ACTION RIFLE . . . . . . **NiB $158 Ex $102 Gd $76**
Hammerless. Caliber: .22 Short, Long, LR. Tubular magazine holds 21 Short, 17 Long, 15 LR. 24-inch bbl. Weight: 5.5 lbs. Sights: Open rear; ramp front. Stock w/semipistol-grip. Made 1958-71.

Parker-Hale Model 81 Classic

Parker-Hale Model 87

NORINCO — Mfd. by Northern China Industries Corp., Beijing, China, *Imported by Century International Arms; Interarms; KBI and China Sports, Inc.*

MODEL 81S/AK SEMIAUTOMATIC RIFLE

Semiautomatic Kalashnikov style AK-47 action. Caliber: 7.62x39mm. Five, 30- or 40-round magazine. 17.5-inch bbl. 36.75 inches overall. Weight: 8.5 lbs. Hooded post front sight, 500 meters leaf rear sight. Oil-finished hardwood (military style) buttstock, pistol grip, forearn and handguard or folding metal stock. Black oxide finish. Imported 1988-89.

Model 81S (w/wood stock) . . . . NiB $1024 Ex $767 Gd $535
Model 81S-1 (w/under-folding metal stock) . . NiB $1173 Ex $942 Gd $647
Model 81S-5/56S-2 (w/side-folding metal stock) . . . . NiB $1044 Ex $839 Gd $577

MODEL 84S/AK SEMIAUTOMATIC RIFLE

Semiautomatic Kalashnikov style AK-47 action. Caliber: .223 (5.56mm). 30-round magazine. 16.25-inch bbl. 35.5 inches overall. Weight: 8.75 lbs. Hooded post front sight, 800 meters leaf rear sight. Oil-finished hardwood (military style) buttstock, pistol grip, forearn and handguard; sporterized composite fiberglass stock or folding metal stock. Black oxide finish. Imported 1988-89.

Model 84S (w/wood stock) . . . . NiB $577 Ex $465 Gd $332
Model 84S-1 (w/under-folding metal stock) . . . NiB $729 Ex $586 Gd $405
Model 84S-3 (w/fiberglass stock) . . . . NiB $696 Ex $561 Gd $388
Model 84S-5 (w/side-folding metal stock) . . . . NiB $1173 Ex $941 Gd $647

MODEL AK-47 THUMBHOLE SPORTER

Semiautomatic AK-47 sporterized variant. Calibers: .223 (5.56mm) or 7.62x39mm. Five round magazine. 16.25-inch bbl. or 23.25-inch bbl. 35.5 or 42.5 inches overall. Weight: 8.5 to 10.3 lbs. Adj. post front sight, open adj. rear. Forged receiver w/black oxide finish. Walnut-finished thumbhole stock w/recoil pad. Imported 1991-93

Model AK-47 Sporter (5.56mm) . . . . NiB $519 Ex $417 Gd $287
Model AK-47 Sporter (7.62x39mm) . . . . . . NiB $493 Ex $396 Gd $273

MODEL MAK 90/91 SPORT

Similar to Model AK-47 Thumbhole Sporter except w/minor modifications implemented to meet importation requirements. Imported 1994-95.

Model Mak 90 (w/16.25-inch bbl.) . . . . NiB $499 Ex $422 Gd $293
Model Mak 91 (w/23.25-inch bbl.) . . . . NiB $499 Ex $422 Gd $293

OLYMPIC ARMS — Olympia, Washington

PCR SERIES

Gas-operated semi-auto action. Calibers: .17 Rem., .223, 7.62x39, 6x45, 6PPC or 9mm, .40 S&W, 4.5ACP (in carbine version only). Ten-round magazine. 16-, 20- or 24-inch bbl. Weight: 7 to 10.2 lbs. Black composite stocks. Post front, rear adj. sights; scope ready flat-top. Barrel fluting. William set trigger. Made 1994 to date.

PCR-1/Ultra Match . . . . NiB $1007 Ex $893 Gd $533
PCR-2/MultiMatch ML-1 . . . . NiB $1042 Ex $837 Gd $575
PCR-3/MultiMatch ML-2 . . . . NiB $1099 Ex $893 Gd $584
PCR-4/AR-15 Match . . . . NiB $1253 Ex $1006 Gd $690
PCR-5/CAR-15 (.223 Rem.) . . . . NiB $1007 Ex $739 Gd $456
PCR-5/CAR-15 (9mm, 40S&W, 45ACP) . . . . NiB $842 Ex $734 Gd $481
PCR-5/CAR-15 (.223 Rem.) . . . . NiB $784 Ex $631 Gd $435
PCR-6/A-2 (7.62x39mm) . . . . NiB $822 Ex $662 Gd $456

PARKER-HALE LIMITED — Birmingham, England

MODEL 81 AFRICAN . . . . NiB $921 Ex $741 Gd $483

Same general specifications as Model 81 Classic except in caliber .375 H&H only. Sights: African Express rear; hooded blade front. Barrel-band swivel. All-steel trigger guard. Checkered European walnut stock w/pistol grip and recoil pad. Engraved receiver. Imported 1986-91.

MODEL 81 CLASSIC BOLT-ACTION RIFLE . . . . NiB $762 Ex $586 Gd $380

Calibers: .22-250, .243 Win., .270 Win., 6mm Rem., 6.5x55, 7x57, 7x64, .308 Win., .30-06, .300 Win. Mag., 7mm Rem. Mag. Four round magazine. 24-inch bbl. Weight: 7.75 lbs. Sights: Adj. open rear, hooded ramp front. Checkered pistol-grip stock of European walnut. Imported 1984-91.

MODEL 85 SNIPER RIFLE . . . . . . NiB $1827 Ex $1493 Gd $900

Caliber: .308 Win. Ten or 20-round M-14-type magazine. 24.25-inch bbl. 45 inches overall. Weight: 12.5 lbs. Blade front sight, folding aperture rear. McMillan fiberglass stock w/detachable bipod. Imported 1989-91.

Parker-Hale Model 1100 Lightweight

Parker-Hale Model 1200 Super Clip

MODEL 87 BOLT-ACTION REPEATING TARGET RIFLE . . . . . NiB $1436 Ex $1153 Gd $689
Calibers: .243 Win., 6.5x55, .308 Win., .30-06 Springfield, .300 Win. Mag. Five-round detachable box magazine. 26-inch bbl. 45 inches overall. Weight: 10 lbs. No sights; grooved for target-style scope mounts. Stippled walnut stock w/adj. buttplate. Sling swivel studs. Parkerized finish. Folding bipod. Imported 1988-91.

MODEL 1000 STANDARD RIFLE . . . . NiB $422 Ex $345 Gd $211
Calibers: .22-250, .243 Win., .270 Win., 6mm Rem., .308 Win., .30-06. Four-round magazine. Bolt action. 22-inch or 24-inch (22-250) bbl. 43 inches overall. 7.25 lbs. Checkered walnut Monte Carlo-style stock w/satin finish. Imported 1984-88.

MODEL 1100 LIGHTWEIGHT BOLT-ACTION RIFLE . . . . NiB $499 Ex $422 Gd $288
Same general specifications as Model 1000 Standard except w/22-inch lightweight profile bbl., hollow bolt handle, alloy trigger guard and floorplate, 6.5 lbs., Schnabel forend. Imported 1984-91.

MODEL 1100M AFRICAN MAGNUM RIFLE . . . . NiB $834 Ex $689 Gd $458
Same as Model 1000 Standard except w/24-inch bbl. in calibers .404 Jeffery, .458 Win. Mag. Weight: 9.5 lbs. Sights: Adj. rear; hooded post front. Imported 1984-91.

MODEL 1200 SUPER CLIP BOLT-ACTION RIFLE . . . . NiB $566 Ex $473 Gd $293
Same as Model 1200 Super except w/detachable box magazine in calibers .243 Win., 6mm Rem., .270 Win. .30-06 and .308 Win., .300 Win. Mag., 7mm Rem. Mag. Imported 1984-91.

MODEL 1200 SUPER BOLT-ACTION SPORTING RIFLE. . . . . NiB $566 Ex $473 Gd $293
Mauser-type bolt action. Calibers: .22-250, .243 Win., 6mm Rem., .25-06, .270 Win., .30-06, .308 Win. Four round magazine. 24-inch bbl. Weight: 7.25 lbs. Sights: Folding open rear, hooded ramp front. European walnut stock w/rollover Monte Carlo cheekpiece, rosewood forend tip and pistol-grip cap, skip checkering, recoil pad, sling swivels. Imported 1968-91.

MODEL 1200 SUPER MAGNUM . . . . NiB $608 Ex $489 Gd $309
Same general specifications as 1200 Super except calibers 7mm Rem. Mag. and .300 Win. Mag., 3-round magazine. Imported 1988-91.

MODEL 1200P PRESENTATION . . . . NiB $519 Ex $417 Gd $287
Same general specifications as 1200 Super except w/scroll-engraved action, trigger guard and floorplate, no sights. QD swivels. Calibers: .243 Win. and .30-06. Imported 1969-75.

MODEL 1200V VARMINT . . . . NiB $551 Ex $448 Gd $391
Same general specifications as 1200 Super, except w/24-inch heavy bbl., no sights, weight: 9.5 lbs. Calibers: .22-250, 6mm Rem., .25-06, .243 Win. Imported 1969-89.

MODEL 1300C SCOUT . . . . NiB $737 Ex $634 Gd $505
Calibers: .243, .308 Win. 10-round magazine. 20-inch bbl. w/muzzle brake. 41 inches overall. Weight: 8.5 lbs. No sights, drilled and tapped for scope. Checkered laminated birch stock w/QD swivels. Imported 1991.

MODEL 2100 MIDLAND BOLT-ACTION RIFLE . . . . NiB $347 Ex $290 Gd $192
Calibers: .22-250, .243 Win., 6mm Rem., .270 Win., 6.5x55, 7x57, 7x64, .308 Win, .30-06. Four-round box magazine. 22-inch or 24-inch (22-250) bbl. 43-inches overall. Weight: 7 lbs. Sights: Adj. folding rear; hooded ramp front. Checkered European walnut Monte Carlo stock w/pistol-grip. Imported 1984-91.

MODEL 2700 LIGHTWEIGHT . . . . NiB $372 Ex $295 Gd $192
Same general specifications as Model 2100 Midland except w/tapered lightweight bbl. and aluminum trigger guard. Weight: 6.5 lbs. Imported 1991.

MODEL 2800 MIDLAND . . . . NiB $321 Ex $269 Gd $26
Same general specifications as model 2100 except w/laminated birch stock. Imported 1991.

PEDERSEN CUSTOM GUNS — North Haven, Connecticut, Division of O.F. Mossberg & Sons, Inc.

MODEL 3000 GRADE I BOLT-ACTION RIFLE . . . . NiB $1044 Ex $839 Gd $577
Richly engraved w/silver inlays, full-fancy American black walnut stock. Mossberg Model 810 action. Calibers: .270 Win., .30-06, 7mm Rem. Mag., .338 Win. Mag. Three-round magazine, hinged floorplate. 22-inch bbl. in .270 and .30-06, 24-inch in Magnums. Weight: 7 to 8 lbs. Sights: Open rear; hooded ramp front. Monte Carlo stock w/roll-over cheekpiece, wraparound hand checkering on pistol grip and forearm, rosewood pistol-grip cap and forend tip, recoil pad or steel buttplate w/trap, detachable swivels. Imported 1973-75.

MODEL 3000 GRADE II . . . . NiB $776 Ex $623 Gd $427
Same as Model 3000 Grade I except less elaborate engraving, no inlays, fancy grade walnut stock w/recoil pad. Imported 1973-75.

MODEL 3000 GRADE III. . . . . NiB $647 Ex $520 Gd $357
Same as Model 3000 Grade I except no engraving or inlays, select grade walnut stock w/recoil pad. Imported 1973-74.

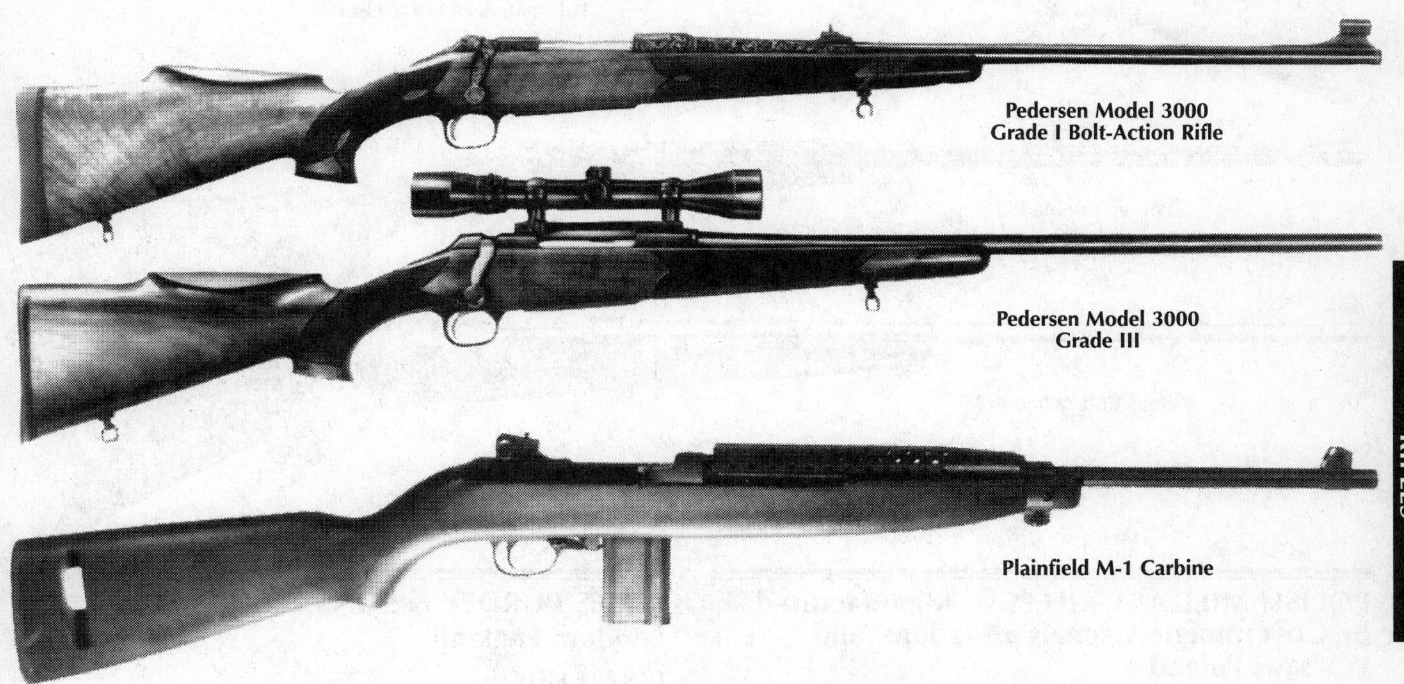
Pedersen Model 3000 Grade I Bolt-Action Rifle

Pedersen Model 3000 Grade III

Plainfield M-1 Carbine

MODEL 4700 CUSTOM DELUXE LEVER-ACTION RIFLE.......... NiB $261 Ex $211 Gd $147
Mossberg Model .472 action. Calibers: .30-30, 35 Rem. Five-round tubular magazine. 24-inch bbl. Weight: 7.5 lbs. Sights: Open rear, hooded ramp front. Hand-finished black walnut stock and beavertail forearm, barrel band swivels. Imported 1975.

J.C. PENNEY CO., INC. — Dallas,Texas

Firearms sold under the J.C. Penney label were mfd. by Marlin, High Standard, Stevens, Savage and Springfield.

MODEL 2025 BOLT-ACTION REPEATER...... NiB $76 Ex $46 Gd $41
Takedown. Caliber: .22 RF. Eight round detachable box magazine. 24-inch bbl. Weight: 6 lbs. Sights: Open rear; bead front. Plain pistol-grip stock. Mfd. by Marlin.

MODEL 2035 BOLT-ACTION REPEATER...... NiB $76 Ex $46 Gd $41
Takedown. Caliber: .22 RF. Eight round detachable box magazine. 24-inch bbl. Weight: 6 lbs. Sights: Open rear; bead front. Plain pistol-grip stock. Mfd. by Marlin.

MODEL 2935 LEVER-ACTION RIFLE ...... NiB $183 Ex $148 Gd $97
Same general specifications as Marlin Model 336.

MODEL 6400 BOLT-ACTION CENTERFIRE RIFLE .... NiB $168 Ex $132 Gd $87
Same general specifications as Savage Model 340.

MODEL 6660 AUTOLOADING RIFLE.................... NiB $81 Ex $66 Gd $56
Caliber: .22 RF. Tubular magazine. 22-inch bbl. Weight: 5.5 lbs. Sights: Open rear; hooded ramp front. Plain pistol-grip stock. Mfd. by Marlin.

PLAINFIELD MACHINE COMPANY — Dunellen, New Jersey

M-1 CARBINE .... NiB $183 Ex $138 Gd $102
Same as U.S. Carbine, Cal. .30, M-1 except also available in caliber 5.7mm (.22 caliber w/necked-down .30 Carbine cartridge case). Current production w/ventilated metal handguard and barrel band w/o bayonet lug; earlier models have standard military-type fittings. Made 1960-77.

M-1 CARBINE, COMMANDO MODEL............... NiB $189 Ex $158 Gd $112
Same as M-1 Carbine except w/paratrooper-type stock w/telescoping wire shoulderpiece. Made 1960-77.

M-1 CARBINE, MILITARY SPORTER...... NiB $183 Ex $153 Gd $117
Same as M-1 Carbine except w/unslotted buttstock and wood handguard. Made 1960-77.

M-1 DELUXE SPORTER .... NiB $189 Ex $158 Gd $112
Same as M-1 Carbine except w/Monte Carlo sporting stock Made 1960-73.

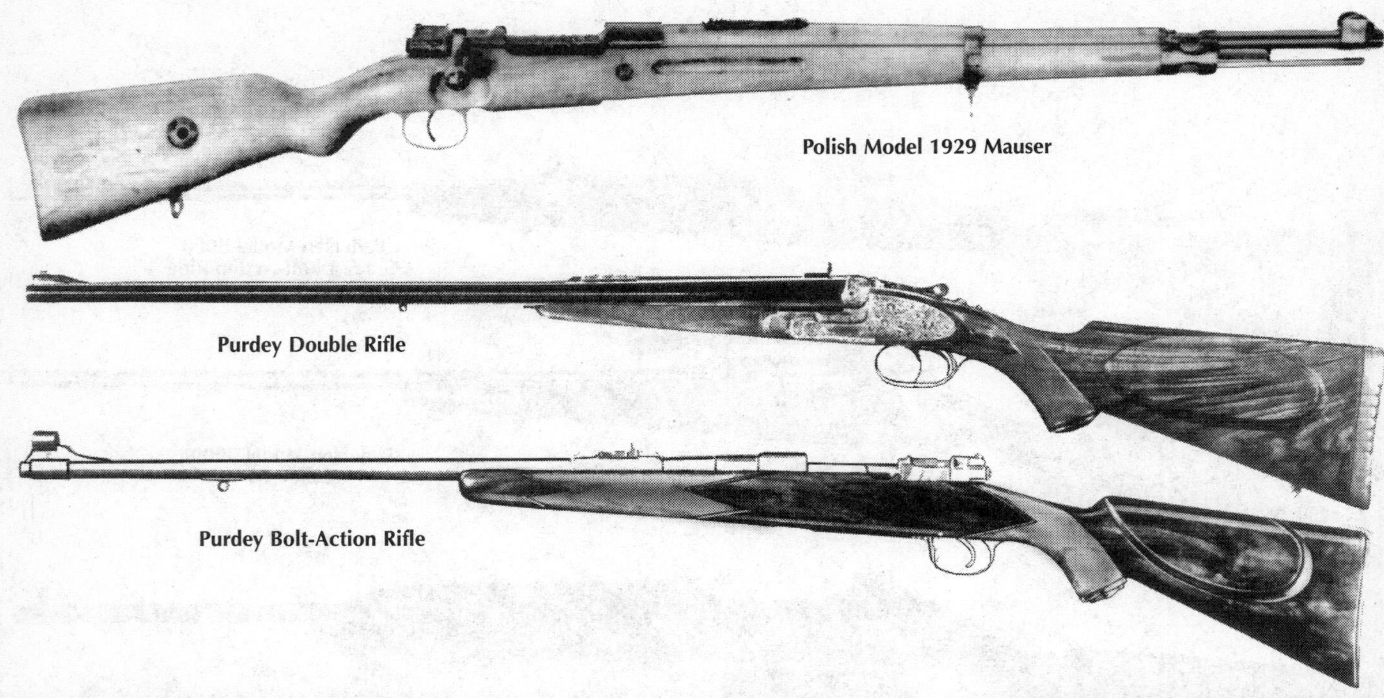

Polish Model 1929 Mauser

Purdey Double Rifle

Purdey Bolt-Action Rifle

POLISH MILITARY RIFLES — Manufactured by Government Arsenals at Radom and Warsaw, Poland

MODEL 1898 (KARABIN 98, K98)
MAUSER MILITARY CARBINE.......... Nib $285 Ex $188 Gd $137
Same as German Kar. 98A except for minor details. First manufactured during early 1920s.

MODEL 1898 (KARABIN 98, WZ98A)
MAUSER MILITARY RIFLE............. NiB $265 Ex $158 Gd $122
Same as German Kar. 98 used in WWI except for minor details. Manufacture began c. 1921.

MODEL 1929 (KARABIN 29, WZ29)
MAUSER MILITARY RIFLE............. NiB $285 Ex $188 Gd $137
Same as Czech Model 24, mfd. 1929 thru WWII except for minor details. A similar model produced during German occupation was designated Gew. 29/40.

WILLIAM POWELL & SON LTD. — Birmingham, England

DOUBLE-BARREL RIFLE........ NiB $31,250 Ex $25,000 Gd $17,000
Boxlock. Made to order in any caliber during the time that rifle was manufactured. Bbls.: Made to order in any legal length, but 26 inches recommended. Highest grade French walnut buttstock and forearm w/fine checkering. Metal is elaborately engraved. Imported by Stoeger 1938-51.

BOLT-ACTION RIFLE......... NiB $2650 Ex $2125 Gd $1453
Mauser-type bolt action. Calibers: 6x54 through .375 H&H Magnum. Three and 4-shot magazine, depending upon chambering. 24-inch bbl. Weight: 7.5 to 8.75 lbs. Sights: Folding leaf rear; hooded ramp front. Cheekpiece stock, checkered forearm and pistol grip, swivels. Imported by Stoeger 1938-51.

JAMES PURDEY & SONS LTD. — London, England

DOUBLE RIFLE
Sidelock action, hammerless, ejectors. Almost any caliber is available but the following are the most popular: .375 Flanged Magnum Nitro Express, .500/465 Nitro Express .470 Nitro Express, .577 Nitro Express. 25.5-inch bbls. (25-inch in .375). Weight: 9.5 to 12.75 lbs. Sights: Folding leaf rear; ramp front. Cheekpiece stock, checkered forearm and pistol-grip, recoil pad, swivels. Currently manufactured to individual measurements and specifications; same general specifications apply to pre-WWII model.
H&H calibers................ NiB $69,375 Ex $55,500 Gd $37,740
NE calibers.................. NiB $85,000 Ex $55,500 Gd $37,774

BOLT-ACTION RIFLE.......... NiB $22,000 Ex $19,000 Gd $12,000
Mauser-type bolt action. Calibers: 7x57, .300 H&H Magnum, .375 H&H Magnum, 10.75x73. Three round magazine. 24-inch bbl. Weight: 7.5 to 8.75 lbs. Sights: Folding leaf rear; hooded ramp front. Cheekpiece stock, checkered forearm and pistol-grip, swivels. Currently manufactured; same general specifications apply to pre-WWII model.

RAPTOR ARMS COMPANY, INC. — Newport, New Hampshire

BOLT-ACTION RIFLE
Calibers: .243 Win., .270 Win., .30-06 or .308 Win. Four round magazine. 22-inch sporter or heavy bbl. Weight: 7.3 to 8 lbs. 42.5 inches overall. No sights w/drilled and tapped receiver or optional blade front, adjustable rear. Blue, stainless or "Taloncote" rust-resistant finish. Checkered black synthetic stock w/Monte Carlo cheepiece and vented recoil pad. Imported 1997 to date.
Raptor Sporter model................ NiB $261 Ex $211 Gd $147
Raptor Deluxe Peregrine model (Disc. 1998).... NiB $313 Ex $435 Gd $175
Raptor heavy barrel model............ NiB $299 Ex $242 Gd $168
Raptor stainless barrel model.......... NiB $325 Ex $247 Gd $182

Remington No. 7
Target and Sporting Rifle

REMINGTON ARMS COMPANY — Ilion, New York

To facilitate locating Remington firearms, models are grouped into four categories: Single-shot rifles, bolt-action repeating rifles, slide-action (pump) rifles, and semiautomatic rifles. For a complete listing, please refer to the index.

SINGLE-SHOT RIFLES

NO. 1 SPORTING RIFLE .... NiB $1915 Ex $1658 Gd 1035
Single-Shot, rolling-block action. Calibers: .40-50, .40-70, .44-77, .50-45, .50-70 Gov't. centerfire and .44 Long, .44 Extra Long, .45-70, .46 Long, .46 Extra Long, .50-70 rimfire. Bbl. lengths: 28- or 30-inch part octagon. Weight: 5 to 7.5 lbs. Sights: Folding leaf rear sight; sporting front, dovetail bases. Plain walnut straight stock; flanged-top, semicarbine buttplate. Plain walnut forend with thin, rounded front end. Made 1868 to 1902.

NO. 1 1/2 SPORTING RIFLE.... NiB $3625 Ex $3110 Gd $689
Single-Shot, rolling-block action. Calibers: .22 Short, Long, or Extra Long. 25 Stevens, .32, and .38 rimfire cartridges. .32-20, .38-40 and .44-40 centerfire. Bbl. lengths: 24-, 26-, 28- or 30-inch part octagon. Remaining features similar to Remington No. 1. Made from 1869 to 1902.

NO. 2 SPORTING RIFLE
Single-shot, rolling-block action. Calibers: .22, .25, .32, .38, .44 rimfire or centerfire. Bbl. lengths: 24, 26, 28 or 30 inches. Weight: 5 to 6 lbs. Sights: Open rear; bead front. Straight-grip sporting stock and knobtip forearm of walnut. Made 1873-1910.
Calibers: .22, .25, .32 .... NiB $834 Ex $628 Gd $293
Calibers: .38, .44............... NiB $885 Ex $654 Gd $319

NO. 3 CREEDMOOR AND SCHUETZEN RIFLES
.... NiB to $32,187 Ex to $25,7500 Gd to $17,510
Produced in a variety of styles and calibers, these are collector's items and bring far higher prices than the sporting types. The Schuetzen Special, which has an under-lever action, is especially rare — perhaps fewer than 100 have been made.

NO. 3 HIGH POWER RIFLE
Single-shot, Hepburn falling-block action w/side lever. Calibers: .30-30, .30-40, .32 Special, .32-40, .38-55, .38-72 (high-power cartridges). Bbl. lengths: 26-, 28-, 30-inch. Weight: About 8 lbs. Open sporting sights. Checkered pistol-grip stock and forearm. Made 1893-1907.
Calibers: .30-30, .30-40, .32 Special, .32-40 .... NiB $2080 Ex $1565 Gd $998
Calibers: .38-55, .38-72 .... NiB $2274 Ex $1822 Gd $1246

NO. 3 SPORTING RIFLE....... NiB $2595 Ex $2080 Gd 1045
Single-shot, Hepburn falling-block action w/side lever. Calibers: .22 WCF, .22 Extra Long, .25-20 Stevens, .25-21 Stevens, .25-25 Stevens, .32 WCF, .32-40 Ballard & Marlin, .32-40 Rem., .38 WCF, .38-40 Rem., .38-50 Rem., .38-55 Ballard & Marlin, .40-60 Ballard & Marlin, .40-60 WCF, .40-65 Rem. Straight, .40-82 WCF, .45-70 Gov., .45-90 WCF, also was supplied on special order in bottle-necked .40-50, .40-70, .40-90, .44-77, .44-90, .44-105, .50-70 Gov., .50-90 Sharps Straight. Bbl. lengths: 26-inch (22, 25, 32 cal. only), 28-inch, 30-inch; half-octagon or full-octagon. Weight: 8 to 10 lbs. Sights: Open rear; blade front. Checkered pistol-grip stock and forearm. Made 1880 to c. 1911.

NO. 4 SINGLE-SHOT RIFLE .... NiB $911 Ex $679 Gd $422
Rolling-block action. Solid frame or takedown. Calibers: .22 Short and Long, .22 LR. .25 Stevens R.F., .32 Short and Long R.F. 22.5-inch octagon bbl., 24-inch available in .32 caliber only. Weight: About 4.5 lbs. Sights: Open rear; blade front. Plain walnut stock and forearm. Made 1890-1933.

NO. 4S MILITARY MODEL 22 SINGLE-SHOT RIFLE .... NiB $885 Ex $757 Gd $525
Rolling-block action. Calibers: .22 Short only, .22 LR. only. 28-inch bbl. Weight: About 5 lbs. Sights: Military-type rear; blade front. Military-type stock w/handguard, stacking swivel, sling. Has a bayonet stud on the barrel; bayonet and scabbard were regularly supplied. Note: At one time the Military Model was the official rifle of the Boy Scouts of America and was called the Boy Scout Rifle. Made 1913-33.

NO. 5 SPECIAL SINGLE-SHOT RIFLE
Single-shot, rolling-block action. Calibers: 7mm Mauser, .30-30, .30-40 Krag, .303 British, .32-40, .32 Special, .38-55 (high-power cartridges). Bbl. lengths: 24, 26 and 28 inches. Weight: About 7 lbs. Open sporting sights. Plain straight-grip stock and forearm. Made 1902-18. Note: Models 1897 and 1902 Military Rifles, intended for the export market, are almost identical with the No. 5, except for 30-inch bbl. full military stock and weight (about 8.5 lbs.); a carbine was also supplied. The military rifles were produced in caliber 8mm Lebel for France, 7.62mm Russian for Russia and 7mm Mauser for the Central and South American government trade. At one time, Remington also offered these military models to retail buyers.
Sporting model .... NiB $847 Ex $679 Gd $465
Military model.................. NiB $622 Ex $499 Gd $343

NO. 6 TAKEDOWN RIFLE........ NiB $551 Ex $391 Gd $216
Single-shot, rolling-block action. Calibers: .22 Short, .22 Long, .22 LR, .32 Short/Long RF. 20-inch bbl. Weight: Avg. 4 lbs. Sights: Open front and rear; tang peep. Plain straight-grip stock, forearm. Made 1901-33.

NO. 7 TARGET AND SPORTING RIFLE ....NiB $2531 Ex $2028 Gd $1386
Single-shot. Rolling-block Army Pistol frame. Calibers: .22 Short, .22 LR. 25-10 Stevens R.F. (other calibers as available in No. 2 Rifle were supplied on special order). Half-octagon bbls.: 24-, 26-, 28-inch. Weight: About 6 lbs. Sights: Lyman combination rear; Beach combination front. Fancy walnut stock and forearm, Swiss buttplate available as an extra. Made 1903-11.

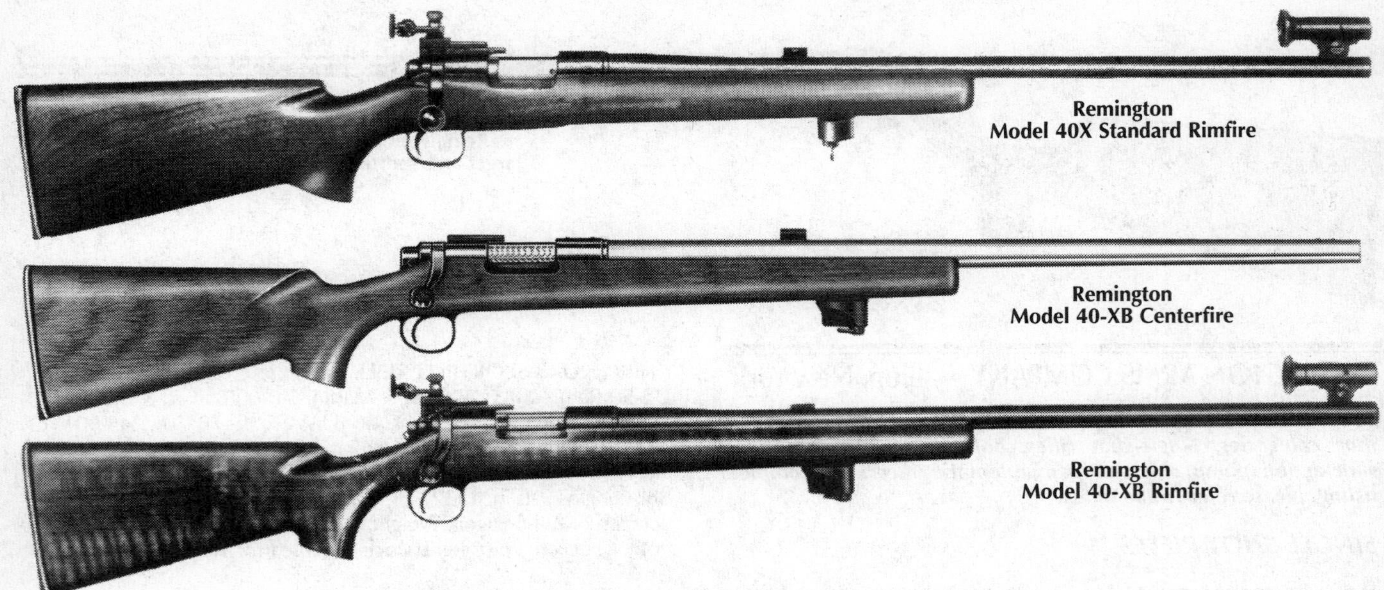

MODEL 33 BOLT-ACTION SINGLE-SHOT RIFLE . . . . NiB $211 Ex $149 Gd $103
Takedown. Caliber: .22 Short, Long, LR. 24-inch bbl. Weight: About 4.5 lbs. Sights: Open rear, bead front. Plain, pistol-grip stock, forearm with grasping grooves. Made 1931-36.

MODEL 33 NRA JUNIOR TARGET RIFLE . . . . NiB $314 Ex $262 Gd $108
Same as Model 33 Standard except has Lyman peep rear sight, Partridge-type front sight, 0.88-inch sling and swivels, weighs about 5 lbs.

MODEL 40X CENTERFIRE RIFLE . . . . NiB $1246 Ex $782 Gd $345
Specifications same as for Model 40X Rimfire (heavy weight). Calibers: .222 Rem., .222 Rem. Mag., 7.62mm NATO, .30-06 (others were available on special order). Made 1961-64. Value shown is for rifle w/o sights.

MODEL 40X HEAVYWEIGHT BOLT-ACTION TARGET RIFLE (RIMFIRE)
Caliber: .22 LR. Single shot. Action similar to Model 722. Click adj. trigger. 28-inch heavy bbl. Redfield Olympic sights. Scope bases. High-comb target stock bedding device, adj. swivel, rubber buttplate. Weight: 12.75 lbs. Made 1955-1964.
With sights. . . . . NiB $1132 Ex $1035 Gd $499
Without sights . . . . NiB $1133 Ex $932 Gd $396

MODEL 40-X SPORTER . . . . NiB $1620 Ex $1297 Gd $885
Same general specifications as Model 700 C Custom (see that listing in this section) except in caliber .22 LR. Made 1972-77.

MODEL 40X STANDARD BARREL
Same as Model 40X Heavyweight except has lighter bbl. Weight: 10.75 lbs.
With sights. NiB $731 Ex $566 Gd $216
Without sights . . . . NiB $824 Ex $679 Gd $309

MODEL 40-XB CENTERFIRE MATCH RIFLE . . NiB $1246 Ex $782 Gd $391
Bolt-action, single-shot. Calibers: .222 Rem., .222 Rem. Mag., .223 Rem., .22-250, 6x47mm, 6mm Rem., .243 Win., .25-06, 7mm Rem. Mag., .30-06, .308 Win. (7.62mm NATO), .30-338, (7.62mm NATO), .30-338, .300 Win. Mag. 27 25-inch standard or heavy bbl. Target stock w/adj. front swivel block on guide rail, rubber buttplate. Weight w/o sights: Standard bbl., 9.25 lbs.; heavy bbl., 11.25 lbs. Value shown is for rifle without sights. Made 1964 to date.

MODEL 40-XB RANGEMASTER CENTERFIRE
Single-shot target rifle with same basic specifications as Model 40-XB Centerfire Match. Additional calibers in .220 Swift, 6mm BR Rem. and 7mm BR Rem., and stainless bbl. only. American walnut or Kevlar (weighs 1 lb. less) target stock with forend stop. Discontinued 1994.
Model 40-XB right-hand model. . . . . NiB $1034 Ex $828 Gd $567
Model 40-XB left-hand model. . . . . NiB $1105 Ex $885 Gd $605
For 2-oz. trigger, add $100
Model 40-XB KS (Kevlar stock, R.H.) . . . . NiB $1163 Ex $932 Gd $637
Model 40-XB KS (Kevlar stock, L.H.). . . . . NiB $1105 Ex $885 Gd $605
For 2-oz. trigger, add $100
For Repeater model, add. $100

MODEL 40-XB RANGEMASTER RIMFIRE MATCH RIFLE . . . . NiB $834 Ex $721 Gd $345
Bolt-action, single-shot. Caliber: .22 LR. 28-inch standard or heavy bbl. Target stock with adj. front swivel block on guide rail, rubber buttplate. Weight w/o sights: Standard bbl., 10 lbs.; heavy bbl., 11.25 lbs. Value shown is for rifle without sights. Made 1964-74.

MODEL 40-XB VARMINT SPECIAL RIFLE . . . . NiB $1251 Ex $787 Gd $396
Same general specifications as Model 40-XB Repeater except has synthetic stock (Kevlar). Made 1987-94.

MODEL 40-XBBR BENCH REST RIFLE
Bolt action, single shot. Calibers: .222 Rem., .222 Rem. Mag., .223 Rem., 6x47mm, .308 Win. (7.62mm NATO). 20- or 26-inch unblued stainless-steel bbl. Supplied w/o sights. Weight: With 20-inch bbl., 9.25 lbs., with 26-inch bbl.,12 lbs. (Heavy Varmint class; 7.25 lbs. w/Kevlar stock (Light Varmint class). Made 1969 to date.
Model 40-XBBR (discontinued). . . . . NiB $910 Ex $731 Gd $497
Model 40-XBBR KS (Kevlar stock) . . . . . . NiB $1168 Ex $937 Gd $643

Remington Model 40-XB Varmint Special

Remington Model 40-XBR

Remington Model 40-XC

Remington Model 40-XR Custom Sporter Grade II

Remington Model 40-XR Rimfire Position Rifle

MODEL 40-XC NATIONAL MATCH COURSE RIFLE
Bolt-action repeater. Caliber: .308 Win. (7.62mm NATO). Five round magazine, clip slot in receiver. 24-inch bbl. Supplied w/o sights. Weight: 11 lbs. Thumb groove stock w/adj. hand stop and sling swivel, adj. buttplate. Made 1974 to date.
Mdl. 40-XC (wood stock) (disc.) . . . . NiB $906 Ex $679 Gd $448
Mdl. 40-XC KS (Kevlar stk. disc. 1994) . . . NiB $1340 Ex $937 Gd $602

MODEL 40-XR CUSTOM SPORTER RIFLE
Caliber: .22 RF. 24-inch contoured bbl. Supplied w/o sights. Made in four grades of checkering, engraving and other custom features. Made 1987 to date.
Grade I . . . . NiB $1143 Ex $963 Gd $731
Grade II. . . . . NiB $2085 Ex $1729 Gd $1060
Grade III . . . . NiB $3017 Ex $2244 Gd $1163
Grade IV . . . . NiB $5051 Ex $4871 Gd $2708

MODEL 40-XR RIMFIRE POSITION RIFLE
Bolt action, single shot. Caliber: .22 LR. 24-inch heavy bbl. Supplied w/o sights. Weight: 10 lbs. Position-style stock w/thumb groove, adj. hand stop and sling swivel on guide rail, adj. buttplate. Made 1974 to date.
Model 40-XR. . . . . NiB $1143 Ex $963 Gd $551
Model 40-XR KS (Kevlar stock) . . . . NiB $1246 Ex $1035 Gd $628

MODEL 41A TARGETMASTER BOLT-ACTION SINGLE-SHOT RIFLE. . . . . NiB $211 Ex $159 Gd $103
Takedown. Caliber: .22 Short, Long, LR. 27-inch bbl. Weight: About 5.5 lbs. Sights: Open rear; bead front. Plain pistol-grip stock. Made 1936-40.

MODEL 41AS . . . . NiB $211 Ex $159 Gd $103
Same as Model 41A except chambered for .22 Remington Special (.22 W.R.F.).

MODEL 41P . . . . NiB $211 Ex $159 Gd $103
Same as Model 41A except has peep rear sight, hooded front sight.

MODEL 41SB . . . . NiB $190 Ex $134 Gd $108
Same as Model 41A except smoothbore for use with shot cartridges.

MODEL 510A TARGETMASTER BOLT-ACTION SINGLE-SHOT RIFLE. . . . . . NiB $166 Ex $134 Gd $93
Takedown. Caliber: 22 Short, Long, LR. 25-inch bbl. Weight: About 5.5 lbs. Sights: Open rear; bead front. Plain pistol-grip stock. Made 1939-62.

MODEL 510P . . . . NiB $178 Ex $144 Gd $101
Same as Model 510A except has peep rear sight, Partridge front on ramp.

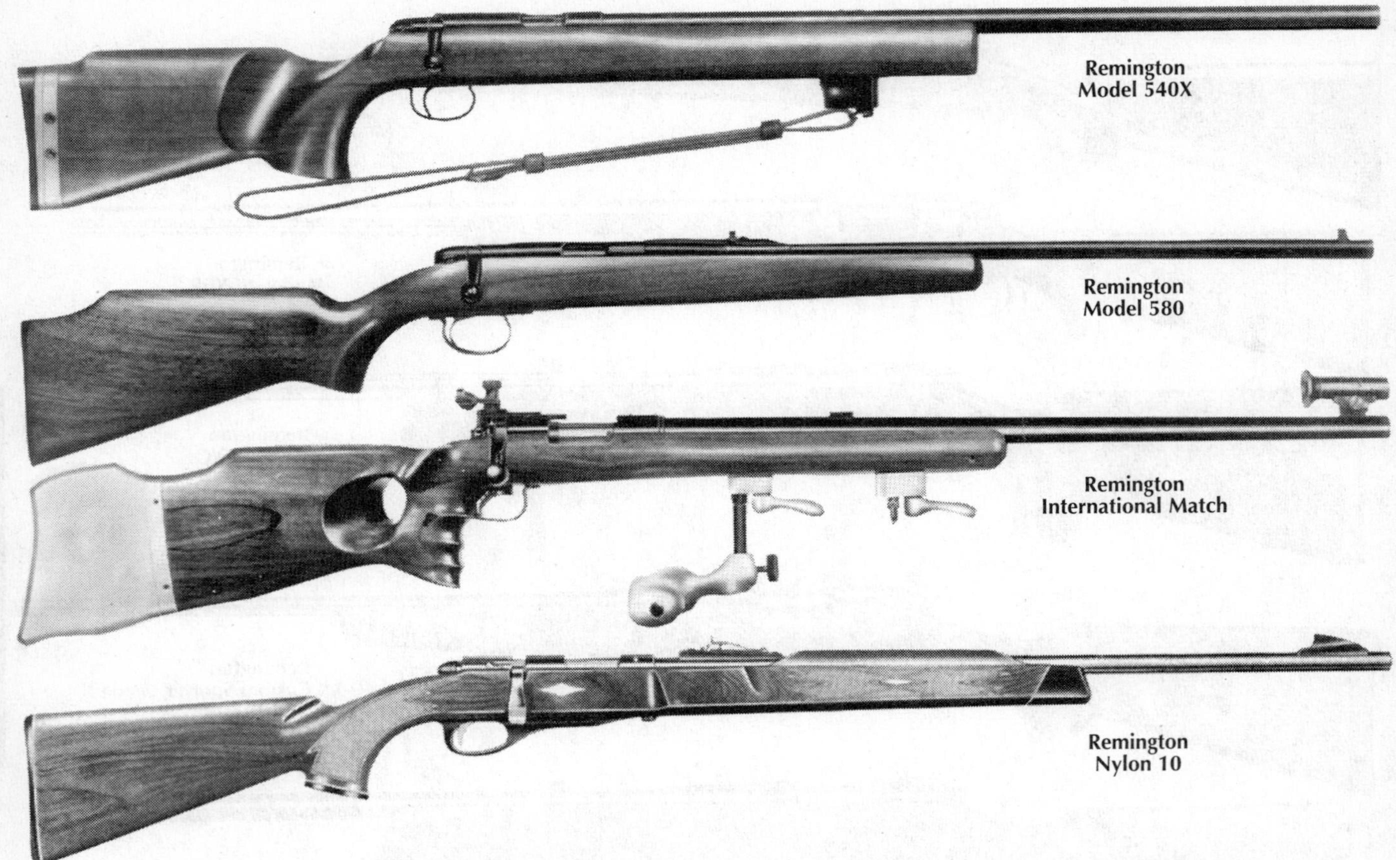

MODEL 510SB .... **NiB $314 Ex $211 Gd $159**
Same as Model 510A except smoothbore for use with shot cartridges, shotgun bead front sight, no rear sight.

MODEL 510X BOLT-ACTION SINGLE-SHOT RIFLE .... **NiB $211 Ex $159 Gd $98**
Same as Model 510A except improved sights. Mfd.1964-66.

MODEL 514 BOLT-ACTION SINGLE-SHOT .... **NiB $159 Ex $134 Gd $98**
Takedown. Caliber: .22 Short, Long, LR. 24-inch bbl. Weight: 4.75 lbs. Sights: Open rear; bead front. Plain pistol-grip stock. Made 1948-71.

MODEL 514BC BOY'S CARBINE .... **NiB $170 Ex $139 Gd $103**
Same as Model 514 except has 21-inch bbl., 1-inch shorter stock. Made 1961-71.

MODEL 514P .... **NiB $170 Ex $139 Gd $103**
Same as Model 514 except has receiver peep sight.

MODEL 540-X RIMFIRE TARGET RIFLE ... **NiB $345 Ex $267 Gd $113**
Bolt-action, single-shot. Caliber: .22 R. 26-inch heavy bbl. Supplied w/o sights. Weight: About 8 lbs. Target stock w/Monte Carlo cheekpiece and thumb groove, guide rail for hand stop and swivel, adj. buttplate. Made 1969-74.

MODEL 540-XR POSITION RIFLE .... **NiB $370 Ex $293 Gd $163**
Bolt-action, single-shot. Caliber: .22 LR. 26-inch medium-weight bbl. Supplied w/o sights. Weight: 8 lbs., 13 oz. Position-style stock w/thumb groove, guide rail for hand stop and swivel, adj. buttplate. Made 1974-84.

MODEL 540-XRJR .... **NiB $370 Ex $293 Gd $164**
Same as Model 540-XR except 1.75-inch shorter stock. Made 1974-84.

MODEL 580 BOLT-ACTION SINGLE-SHOT .... **NiB $159 Ex $129 Gd $89**
Caliber: .22 Short, Long, LR. 24-inch bbl. Weight: 4.75 lbs. Sights: Bead front; U-notch rear. Monte Carlo stock. Made 1967-78.

MODEL 580BR BOY'S RIFLE .... **NiB $173 Ex $139 Gd $96**
Same as Model 580 except w/1-inch shorter stock. Made 1971-78.

MODEL 580SB SMOOTH BORE ... **NiB $231 Ex $185 Gd $128**
Same as Model 580 except smooth bore for .22 Long Rifle shot cartridges. Made 1967-78.

INTERNATIONAL FREE RIFLE ..... **NiB $988 Ex $731 Gd $422**
Same as Model 40-XB rimfire and centerfire except has free rifle-type stock with adj. buttplate and hook, adj. palm rest, movable front sling swivel, 2-oz. trigger. Weight: About 15 lbs. Made 1964-74. Value shown is for rifle with professionally finished stock, no sights.

INTERNATIONAL MATCH FREE RIFLE ... **NiB $1045 Ex $916 Gd $504**
Calibers: .22 LR, .222 Rem., .222 Rem. Mag., 7.62mm NATO, .30-06 (others were available on special order). Model 40X-type bolt-action, single-shot. 2-oz. adj. trigger. 28-inch heavy bbl. Weight: About 15.5 lbs. Free rifle-style stock with thumbhole (furnished semifinished by mfr.); interchangeable and adj. rubber buttplate and hook buttplate, adj. palm rest, sling swivel. Made 1961-64. Value shown is for rifle with professionally-finished stock, no sights.

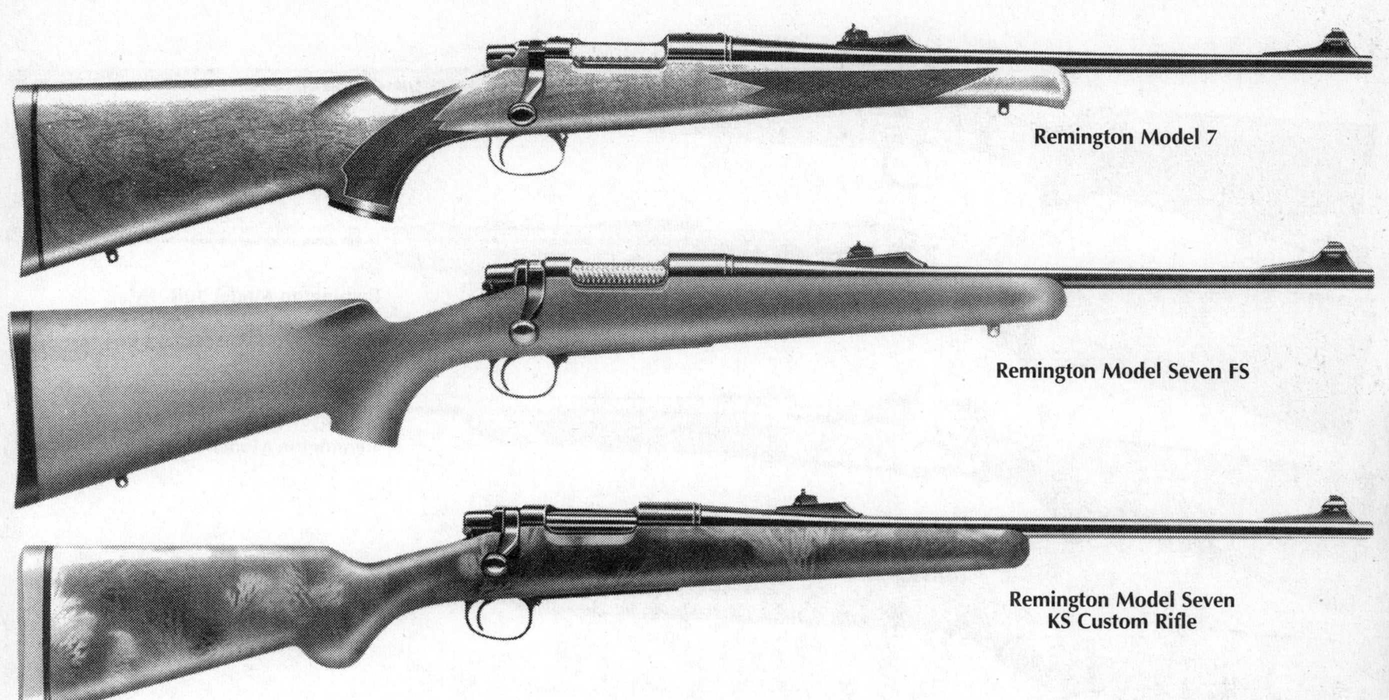

Remington Model 7

Remington Model Seven FS

Remington Model Seven KS Custom Rifle

NYLON 10 BOLT-ACTION SINGLE-SHOT RIFLE . . . . NiB $159 Ex $134 Gd $103
Caliber: .22 Short, Long, LR. 19.13-inch bbl. Weight: 4.25 lbs. Open rear sight; ramped blade front. Receiver grooved for scope mount. Brown nylon stock. Made 1962-1966.

BOLT-ACTION REPEATING RIFLES

MODEL SEVEN (7) CF BOLT-ACTION RIFLE
Calibers: .17 Rem., .222 Rem., .223 Rem., .243 Win., 6mm Rem., 7mm-08 Rem., .308 Win. Magazine capacity: 5-round in .17 Rem., .222 Rem., .223 Rem., 4-round in other calibers. 18.5-inch bbl. Weight: 6.5 lbs. Walnut stock checkering, and recoil pad. Made 1983 to date. .223 Rem. added in 1984.
Standard calibers except
.17 Rem. & .222 Rem.. . . . . NiB $473 Ex $396 Gd $267
Caliber .17 Rem & .222 Rem.. . . . . NiB $499 Ex $417 Gd $278

MODEL SEVEN (7) FS RIFLE. . . . . NiB $557 Ex $448 Gd $308
Calibers: .243, 7mm-08 Rem., .308 Win. 18.5-inch bbl. 37.5 inches overall. Weight: 5.25 lbs. Hand layup fiberglass stock, reinforced with DuPont Kevlar at points of bedding and stress. Made 1987-90.

MODEL SEVEN (7) KS RIFLE . . . . . . NiB $808 Ex $654 Gd $422
Calibers: .223 Rem., 7mm-08, .308, .35 Rem. and .350 Rem. Mag. 20-inch bbl. Custom-made in Remington's Custom Shop with Kevlar stock. Made 1987 to date.

MODEL SEVEN (7) LS RIFLE . . . . . . NiB $525 Ex $448 Gd $267
Calibers: .223 Rem., .243 Win., .260 Rem., 7mm-08 and 308 Win. 20-inch matte bbl. Laminated hardwood stock w/matte brown finish. Weight: 6.5 lbs. Made 2000 to date.

MODEL SEVEN (7) LSS RIFLE . . . . . NiB $576 Ex $448 Gd $293
Similar to Model 7 LS except stainless bbl. w/o sights. Calibers: .22-250 Rem., .243 Win. or 7mm-08. Made 2000 to date.

MODEL SEVEN (7) MS CUSTOM RIFLE . . . NiB $998 Ex $870 Gd $509
Similar to the standard Model 7 except fitted with a laminated full Mannlicher-style stock. Weight: 6.75 lbs. Calibers: .222 Rem., .22-250, .243, 6mm Rem.,7mm-08, .308, .350 Rem. Additional calibers available on special order. Made 1993 to date.

MODEL SEVEN (7) SS RIFLE . . . . . . NiB $551 Ex $422 Gd $293
Same as Model 7 except 20-inch stainless bbl., receiver and bolt; black synthetic stock. Calibers: .243, 7mm-08 or .308. Made 1994 to date.

MODEL SEVEN (7) YOUTH RIFLE. . . . . NiB $370 Ex $319 Gd $242
Similar to the standard Model 7 except fitted with hardwood stock with a 12.19-inch pull. Calibers: .243, 6mm, 7mm-08 only. Made 1993 to date.

MODEL 30A BOLT-ACTION EXPRESS RIFLE. . . . . NiB $583 Ex $468 Gd $322
Standard Grade. Modified M/1917 Enfield Action. Calibers: .25, .30, .32 and .35 Rem., 7mm Mauser, .30-06. Five round box magazine. 22-inch bbl. Weight: About 7.25 lbs. Sights: Open rear; bead front. Walnut stock w/checkered pistol grip and forearm. Made 1921-40. Note: Early Model 30s had a slender forend with Schnabel tip, military-type double-pull trigger.

MODEL 30R CARBINE . . . . NiB $596 Ex $499 Gd $376
Same as Model 30A except has 20-inch bbl., plain stock weighs about 7 lbs.

MODEL 30S SPORTING RIFLE . . . . NiB $716 Ex $576 Gd $397
Special Grade. Same action as Model 30A. Calibers: .257 Roberts, 7mm Mauser, .30-06. Five round box magazine. 24-inch bbl. Weight: About 8 lbs. Lyman No. 48 Receiver sight, bead front sight. Special high comb stock with long, full forearm, checkered. Made 1930-40.

MODEL 34 BOLT-ACTION REPEATER. . . . NiB $162 Ex $136 Gd $101
Takedown. Caliber: .22 Short, Long, LR. Tubular magazine holds 22 Short, 17 Long or 15 LR. 24-inch bbl. Weight: 5.25 lbs. Sights: Open rear; bead front. Plain, pistol-grip stock, forearm w/grasping grooves. Made 1932-36.

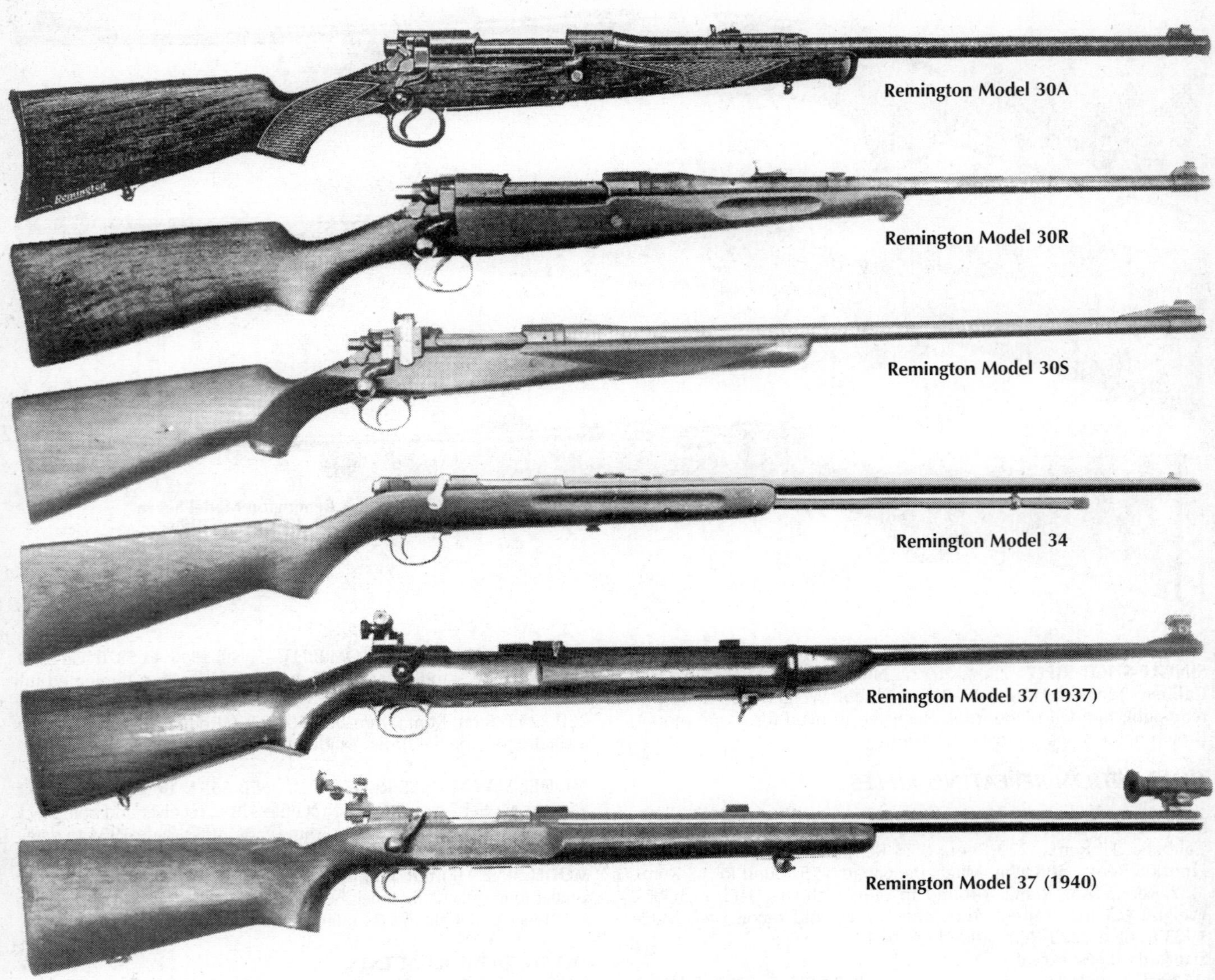
Remington Model 30A

Remington Model 30R

Remington Model 30S

Remington Model 34

Remington Model 37 (1937)

Remington Model 37 (1940)

MODEL 34 NRA TARGET RIFLE . . . . NiB $422 Ex $345 Gd $216
Same as Model 34 Standard except has Lyman peep rear sight, Partridge-type front sight, .88-inch sling and swivels, weight: About 5.75 lbs.

MODEL 37 RANGEMASTER BOLT-ACTION TARGET RIFLE (I)
Model of 1937. Caliber: .22 LR. Five round box magazine, single shot adapter also supplied as standard equipment. 28-inch heavy bbl. Weight: About 12 lbs. Remington front and rear sights, scope bases. Target stock, swivels, sling. Note: Original 1937 model had a stock with outside bbl. band similar in appearance to that of the old-style Winchester Model 52, forearm design was modified and bbl. band eliminated in 1938. Made 1937-40.
With factory sights . . . . NiB $576 Ex $448 Gd $319
Without sights . . . . NiB $499 Ex $422 Gd $242

MODEL 37 RANGEMASTER BOLT-ACTION TARGET RIFLE (II)
Model of 1940. Same as Model of 1937 except has "Miracle" trigger mechanism and Randle-design stock with high comb, full pistol-grip and wide beavertail forend. Made 1940-54.
With factory sights . . . . NiB $719 Ex $576 Gd $395
Without sights . . . . NiB $519 Ex $417 Gd $287

MODEL 40-XB
CENTERFIRE REPEATER. . . . . NiB $1095 Ex $880 Gd $605
Same as Model 40-XB Centerfire except 5-round repeater. Calibers: .222 Rem., .222 Rem. Mag., .223 Rem., .22-250, 6x47mm, 6mm Rem., .243 Win., .308 Win. (7.62mm NATO). Heavy bbl. only. Discontinued.

MODEL 78 SPORTSMAN
BOLT-ACTION RIFLE . . . . NiB $297 Ex $240 Gd $668
Similar to Model 700 ADL except with straight-comb walnut-finished hardwood stock in calibers .223 Rem., .243 Win, .270 Win., .30-06 Springfield and .308 Win. 22-inch bbl. Weight: 7 lbs. Adj. sights. Made 1984-91.

MODEL 341A SPORTSMASTER
BOLT-ACTION REPEATER . . . . NiB $182 Ex $144 Gd $100
Takedown. Caliber: .22 Short, Long, LR. Tubular magazine holds 22 Short, 17 Long, 15 LR. 27-inch bbl. Weight: About 6 lbs. Sights: Open rear; bead front. Plain pistol-grip stock. Made 1936-40.

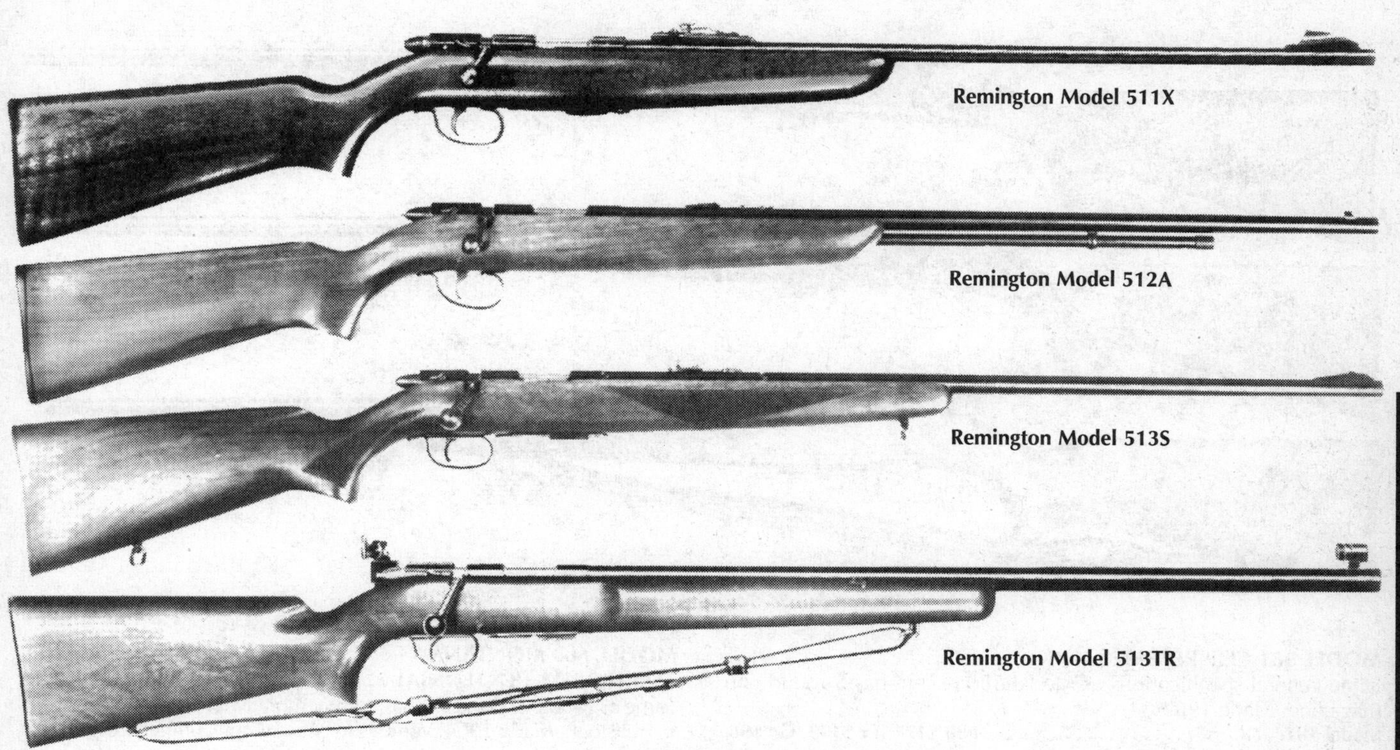

MODEL 341P .... NiB $210 Ex $170 Gd $118
Same as Model 341A except has peep rear sight, hooded front sight.

MODEL 341SB .... NiB $216 Ex $242 Gd $164
Same as Model 341A except smoothbore for use with shot cartridges.

MODEL 511A SCOREMASTER BOLT-ACTION BOX MAGAZINE REPEATER .... NiB $196 Ex $159 Gd $112
Takedown. Caliber: 22 Short, Long, LR. Six round detachable box magazine. 25-inch bbl. Weight: About 5.5 lbs. Sights: Open rear; bead front. Plain pistol-grip stock. Made 1939-62.

MODEL 511P .... NiB $204 Ex $164 Gd $115
Same as Model 511A except has peep rear sight, Partridge-type blade front on ramp.

MODEL 511X BOLT-ACTION REPEATER .. NiB $210 Ex $170 Gd $118
Clip type. Same as Model 511A except improved sights. Made 1964-66.

MODEL 512A SPORTSMASTER BOLT-ACTION REPEATER .... NiB $184 Ex $149 Gd $105
Takedown. Caliber: .22 Short, Long, LR. Tubular magazine holds 22 Short, 17 Long, 15 LR. 25-inch bbl. Weight: About 5.75 lbs. Sights: Open rear; bead front. Plain pistol-grip stock w/semibeavertail forend. Made 1940-62.

MODEL 512P .... NiB $236 Ex $190 Gd $133
Same as Model 512A except has peep rear sight, blade front, on ramp.

MODEL 512X BOLT-ACTION REPEATER .. NiB $247 Ex $200 Gd $140
Tubular magazine type. Same as Model 512A except has improved sights. Made 1964-66.

MODEL 513S BOLT-ACTION RIFLE ...... NiB $525 Ex $473 Gd $293
Caliber: .22 LR. Six round detachable box magazine. 27-inch bbl. Weight: About 6.75 lbs. Marble open rear sight, Partridge-type front. Checkered sporter stock. Made 1941-56.

MODEL 513TR MATCHMASTER BOLT-ACTION TARGET RIFLE ..... NiB $351 Ex $283 Gd $195
Caliber: .22 LR. Six round detachable box magazine. 27-inch bbl. Weight: About 9 lbs. Sights: Redfield No. 75 rear; globe front. Target stock. Sling and swivels. Made 1941-69.

MODEL 521TL JUNIOR TARGET BOLT-ACTION REPEATER .... NiB $313 Ex $252 Gd $175
Takedown. Caliber: .22 LR. Six round detachable box magazine. 25-inch bbl. Weight: About 7 lbs. Sights: Lyman No. 57RS rear; dovetailed blade front. Target stock. Sling and swivels. Made 1947-69.

MODEL 522 VIPER .... NiB $164 Ex $113 Gd $87
Calibers: .22 LR. 10-round magazine. 20-inch bbl. 40 inches overall. Weight: 4.63 lbs. Checkered black PET resin stock with beavertail forend. Dupont high-tech synthetic lightweight receiver. Matte black finish on all exposed metal. Made 1993 to date.

MODEL 541-S CUSTOM SPORTER....... NiB $719 Ex $576 Gd $395
Bolt-action repeater. Scroll engraving on receiver and trigger guard. Caliber: .22 Short, Long, LR. Five round clip magazine. 24-inch bbl. Weight: 5.5 lbs. Supplied w/o sights. Checkered walnut stock w/rosewood-finished forend tip, pistol-grip cap and buttplate. Made 1972-84.

MODEL 541-T BOLT-ACTION RIFLE
Caliber: .22 RF. Clip-fed, Five round. 24-inch bbl. Weight: 5.88 lbs. Checkered walnut stock. Made 1986 to date; heavy bbl. model intro. 1993.
Model 541-T Standard .... NiB $422 Ex $293 Gd $175
Model 541-T-HB heavy bbl........ NiB $448 Ex $319 Gd $231

Remington Model 521TL

Remington Model 541-S

Remington Model 581-S

MODEL 581 CLIP REPEATER
Same general specifications as Model 580 except has 5-round clip magazine. Made 1967-84.
Model 581 . . . . NiB $171 Ex $139 Gd $98
Model 581 left hand (made 1969-1984) . . . . NiB $204 Ex $164 Gd $115

MODEL 581-S BOLT-ACTION RIFLE . . . . . NiB $190 Ex $164 Gd $113
Caliber: .22 RF. Clip-fed, 5-round. 24-inch bbl. Weight: 4.75 lbs. Plain walnut-colored stock. Made 1987-92.

MODEL 582 TUBULAR REPEATER . . . . NiB $178 Ex $144 Gd $101
Same general specifications as Model 580 except has tubular magazine holding 20 Short,15 Long,14 LR. Weight: About 5 lbs. Made 1967-84.

MODEL 591 BOLT-ACTION CLIP REPEATER . . . . NiB $261 Ex $211 Gd $147
Caliber: 5mm Rimfire Magnum. Four round clip magazine. 24-inch bbl. Weight: 5 lbs. Sights: Bead front; U-notch rear. Monte Carlo stock. Made 1970-73.

MODEL 592 TUBULAR REPEATER . . . . NiB $196 Ex $159 Gd $112
Same as Model 591 except has tubular magazine holding 10 rounds, weight: 5.5 lbs. Made 1970-73.

MODEL 600 BOLT-ACTION CARBINE
Calibers: .222 Rem., .223 Rem., .243 Win., 6mm Rem., .308 Win., 35 Rem., 5-round magazine (6-round in .222 Rem.) 18.5-inch bbl. with ventilated rib. Weight: 6 lbs. Sights: Open rear; blade ramp front. Monte Carlo stock w/pistol-grip. Made 1964-67.
.222 Rem. . . . . NiB $846 Ex $769 Gd $460
.223 Rem . . . . NiB $1374 Ex $1147 Gd $757
.35 Rem. . . . . NiB $826 Ex $666 Gd $460
Standard calibers . . . . NiB $660 Ex $532 Gd $369

MODEL 600 MAGNUM . . . . NiB $1046 Ex $841 Gd $579
Same as Model 600 except calibers 6.5mm Mag. and .350 Rem. Mag., 4-round magazine, special Magnum-type bbl. with bracket for scope back-up, laminated walnut and beech stock w/recoil pad. QD swivels and sling; weight: About 6.5 lbs. Made 1965-67.

MODEL 600 MONTANA TERRITORIAL CENTENNIAL $784
Same as Model 600 except has commemorative medallion embedded in buttstock. Made 1964. Value is for rifle in new, unfired condition.

MODEL 660 STP
Calibers: .222 Rem., 6mm Rem., .243 Win., .308 Win., 5-round magazine. (6-round in .222 Rem.) 20-inch bbl. Weight: 6.5 lbs. Sights: Open rear; bead front on ramp. Monte Carlo stock, checkered, black pistol-grip cap and forend tip. Made 1968-71.
.222 Rem . . . . NiB $636 Ex $512 Gd $352
Other calibers . . . . NiB $592 Ex $475 Gd $327

MODEL 660 MAGNUM . . . . NiB $887 Ex $707 Gd $578
Same as Model 660 except calibers 6.5mm Rem. Mag. and .350 Rem. Mag., 4-round magazine, laminated walnut-and-beech stock with recoil pad. QD swivels and sling. Made 1968-71.

MODEL 700 ADL CENTERFIRE RIFLE . . . . . NiB $396 Ex $314 Gd $210
Calibers: .22-250, .222 Rem., .25-06, 6mm Rem., .243 Win., .270 Win., .30-06, .308 Win., 7mm Rem. Mag. Magazine capacity: 6-round in .222 Rem.; 4-round in 7mm Rem. Mag. Five round in other calibers. Bbl. lengths: 24-inch in .22-250, .222 Rem., .25-06, 7mm Rem. Mag.; 22-inch in other calibers. Weight: 7 lbs. standard; 7.5 lbs. in 7mm Rem. Mag. Sights: Ramp front; sliding ramp open rear. Monte Carlo stock w/cheekpiece, skip checkering, recoil pad on Magnum. Laminated stock also avail. Made 1962-93.

MODEL 700 APR BOLT-ACTION RIFLE . . NiB $1244 Ex $998 Gd $685
Acronym for African Plains Rifle. Calibers: 7mm Rem. Mag., 7mm STW, 300 Win. Mag., 300 Wby. Mag., 300 Rem. Ultra Mag., 338 Win. Mag., 375 H&H. Three round magazine. 26-inch bbl. on a magnum action. 46.5 inches overall. Weight: 7.75 lbs. Matte blue finish. Checkered classic-style laminated wood stock w/black magnum recoil pad. Made 1994 to date.

MODEL 700 AS BOLT-ACTION RIFLE
Similar to the Model 700 BDL except with nonreflective matte black metal finish, including the bolt body. Weight: 6.5 lbs. Straight comb synthetic stock made of Arylon, a fiberglass-reinforced thermoplastic resin with nonreflective matte finish. Made 1988-92.
Standard caliber . . . . NiB $480 Ex $386 Gd $265
Magnum caliber . . . . NiB $519 Ex $417 Gd $287

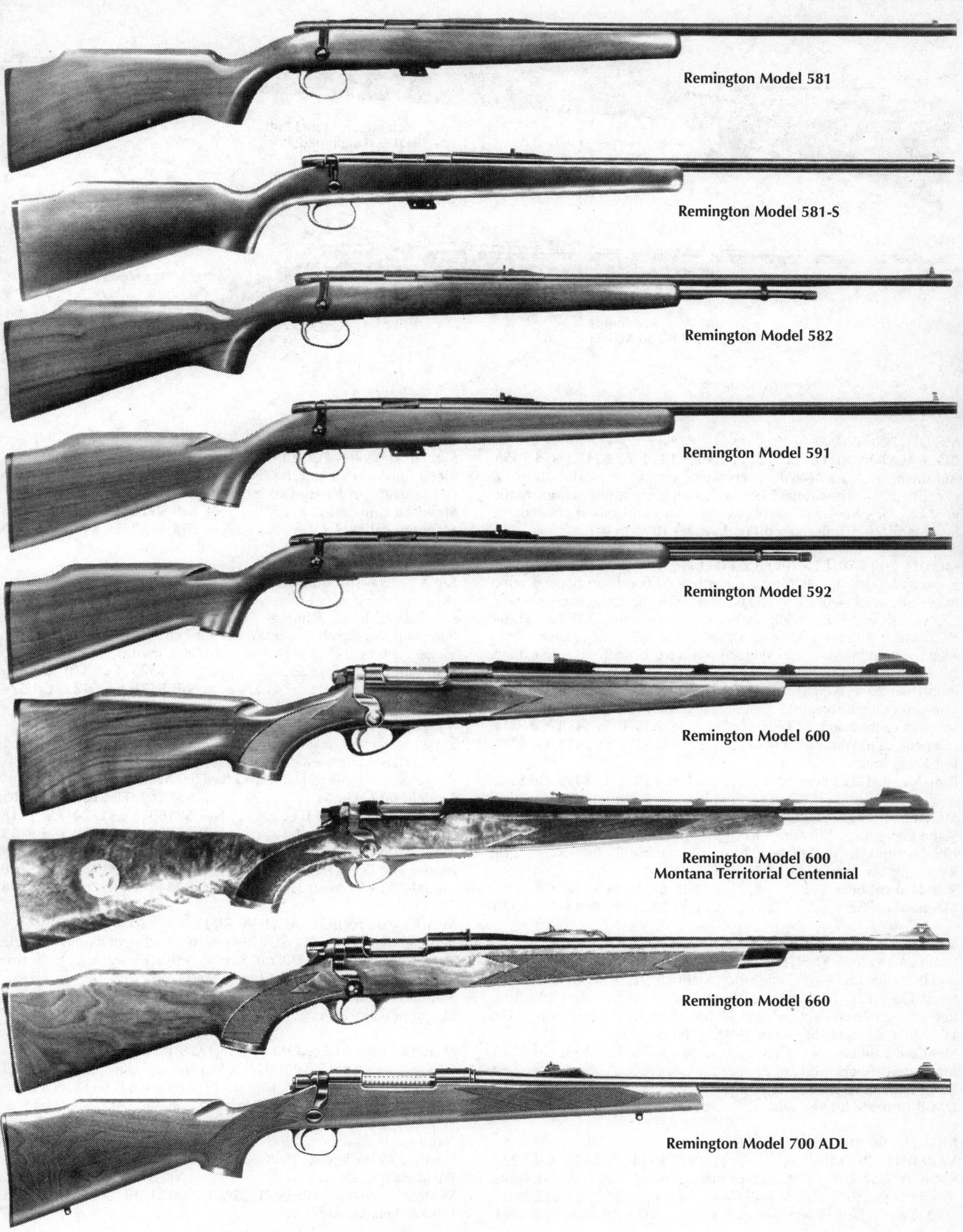
Remington Model 581

Remington Model 581-S

Remington Model 582

Remington Model 591

Remington Model 592

Remington Model 600

Remington Model 600
Montana Territorial Centennial

Remington Model 660

Remington Model 700 ADL

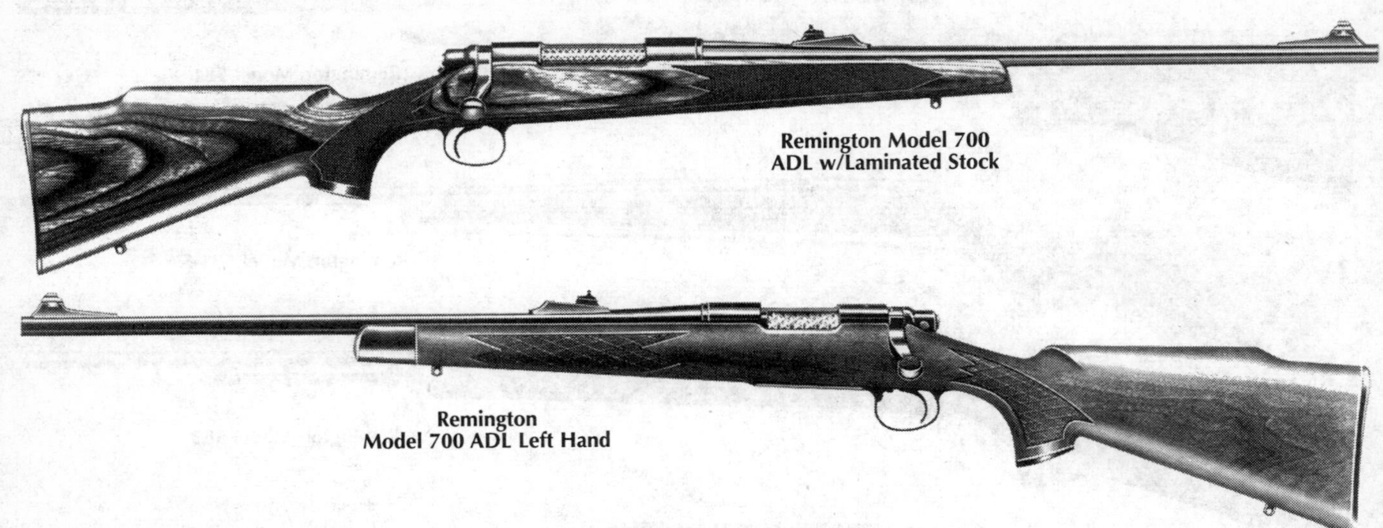

Remington Model 700 ADL w/Laminated Stock

Remington Model 700 ADL Left Hand

MODEL 700 AWR
BOLT-ACTION RIFLE . . . . NiB $1359 Ex $1153 Gd $998
Acronym for Alaskan Wilderness Rifle, similar to Model 700 APR except w/24-inch stainless bbl. and black chromed action. Matte gray or black Kevlar stock w/straight comb and raised cheekpiece fitted w/black magnum recoil pad. Made 1994 to date.

MODEL 700 BDL CENTERFIRE RIFLE
Same as Model 700 ADL except has hinged floorplate hooded ramp front sight, stock w/black forend tip and pistol-grip cap, cut checkering, QD swivels and sling. Additional calibers: .17 Rem., .223 Rem., .264 Win. Mag., 7mm-08, .280, .300 Sav., .300 Win. Mag., 8mm Rem. Mag., .338 Win. Mag., .35 Whelen. All have 24-inch bbls. Magnums have 4-round magazine, recoil pad, weighs 7.5 lbs; .17 Rem. has 6-round magazine, weighs 7 lbs. Made 1962 to date. Made 1973 to date.
Standard calibers except .17 Rem.. . . . . . . NiB $505 Ex $407 Gd $280
Magnum calibers and .17 Rem. . . . . NiB $570 Ex $458 Gd $315
Left-hand, .270 Win. and .30-06. . . . . NiB $519 Ex $417 Gd $287
Left-hand, 7mm
Rem. Mag and .222 Rem. . . . . NiB $576 Ex $499 Gd $422

MODEL 700 BDL EUROPEAN RIFLE
Same general specifications as Model 700 BDL, except has oil-finished walnut stock. Calibers: .243, .270, 7mm-08, 7mm Mag., .280 Rem., .30-06. Made 1993-95.
Standard calibers. . . . . NiB $525 Ex $422 Gd $293
Magnum calibers. . . . . NiB $525 Ex $483 Gd $370

MODEL 700 BDL SS BOLT-ACTION RIFLE
Same as Model 700 BDL except w/24-inch stainless bbl., receiver and bolt plus black synthetic stock. Calibers: .223 Rem., .243 Win., 6mm Rem., .25-06 Rem., .270 Win. .280 Rem., 7mm-08, 7mm Rem. Mag., 7mm Wby. Mag., .30-06, .300 Win., .308 Win., .338 Win. Mag. .375 H&H. Made 1992 to date.
Standard calibers. . . . . NiB $576 Ex $499 Gd $298
Magnum calibers, add $80
DM (detachable magazine), add $40
DM-B (muzzle brake), add $90

MODEL 700 BDL
VARMINT SPECIAL . . . . NiB $525 Ex $422 Gd $288
Same as Model 700 BDL except has 24-inch heavy bbl., no sights, weighs 9 lbs. (8.75 lbs. in 308 Win.). Calibers: .22-250, .222 Rem., .223 Rem., .25-06, 6mm Rem., .243 Win., .308 Win. Made 1967-94.

REMINGTON MODEL 700 CS BOLT-ACTION RIFLE
Similar to Model 700 BDL except with nonreflective matte black metal finish, including the bolt body. Straight comb synthetic stock camouflaged in Mossy Oak Bottomland pattern. Made 1992-94.
Standard calibers. . . . . NiB $519 Ex $417 Gd $287
Magnum calibers. . . . . NiB $557 Ex $448 Gd $308

MODEL 700 CLASSIC
Same general specifications as Model 700 BDL except has "Classic" stock of high-quality walnut with full-pattern cut-checkering, special satin wood finish; Schnabel forend. Brown rubber buttpad. Hinged floorplate. No sights. Weight: 7 lbs. Also chambered for "Classic" cartridges such as .257 Roberts and .250-3000. Intro. 1981.
Standard calibers. . . . . NiB $525 Ex $370 Gd $267
Magnum calibers. . . . . NiB $576 Ex $422 Gd $288

MODEL 700 CUSTOM BOLT-ACTION RIFLE
Same general specifications as Model 700 BDL except custom-built; available in choice of grades, each with higher quality wood, different checkering patterns, engraving, high-gloss blued finish. Introduced in 1965.
Model 700 C Grade I . . . . NiB $1249 Ex $1003 Gd $690
Model 700 C Grade II . . . . NiB $2150 Ex $1724 Gd $1181
Model 700 C Grade III . . . . NiB $2794 Ex $2239 Gd $1531
Model 700 C Grade IV . . . . NiB $5111 Ex $4093 Gd $2792
Model 700 D Peerless . . . . NiB $1985 Ex $1462 Gd $1002
Model 700 F Premier. . . . . NiB $3444 Ex $2760 Gd $1884

MODEL 700 FS BOLT-ACTION RIFLE
Similar to Model 700 ADL except with straight comb fiberglass stock reinforced with DuPont Kevlar, finished in gray or gray camo with Old English-style recoil pad. Made 1987-89.
Standard calibers. . . . . NiB $587 Ex $525 Gd $319
Magnum calibers. . . . . NiB $628 Ex $525 Gd $370

MODEL 700 KS CUSTOM MOUNTAIN RIFLE
Similar to standard Model 700 MTN Rifle, except with custom Kevlar reinforced resin synthetic stock with standard or wood-grain finish. Calibers: .270 Win., .280 Rem., 7mm Rem Mag., .30-06, .300 Win. Mag., .300 Wby. Mag., 8mm Rem. Mag., .338 Win. Mag., .35 Whelen, .375 H&H. Four round magazine. 24-inch bbl. Weight: 6.75 lbs. Made 1986 to date.
Standard KS stock (disc. 1993) . . . . NiB $1079 Ex $899 Gd $487
Wood-grain KS stock. . . . . NiB $1002 Ex $771 Gd $532
SS Model Stainless Synthetic (1995-97) . NiB $1215 Ex $1018 Gd $766
Left-hand model, add $75

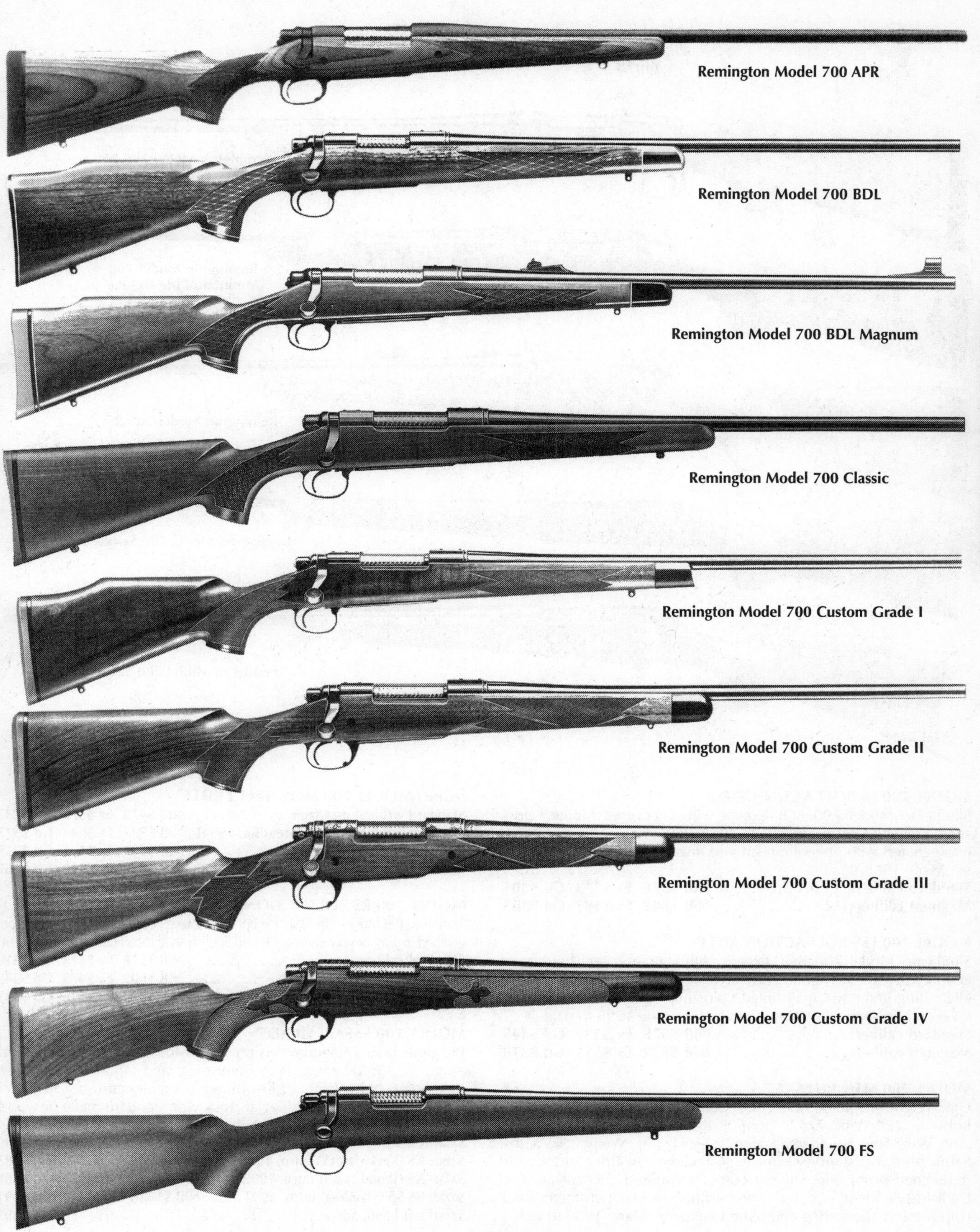

Remington Model 700 APR

Remington Model 700 BDL

Remington Model 700 BDL Magnum

Remington Model 700 Classic

Remington Model 700 Custom Grade I

Remington Model 700 Custom Grade II

Remington Model 700 Custom Grade III

Remington Model 700 Custom Grade IV

Remington Model 700 FS

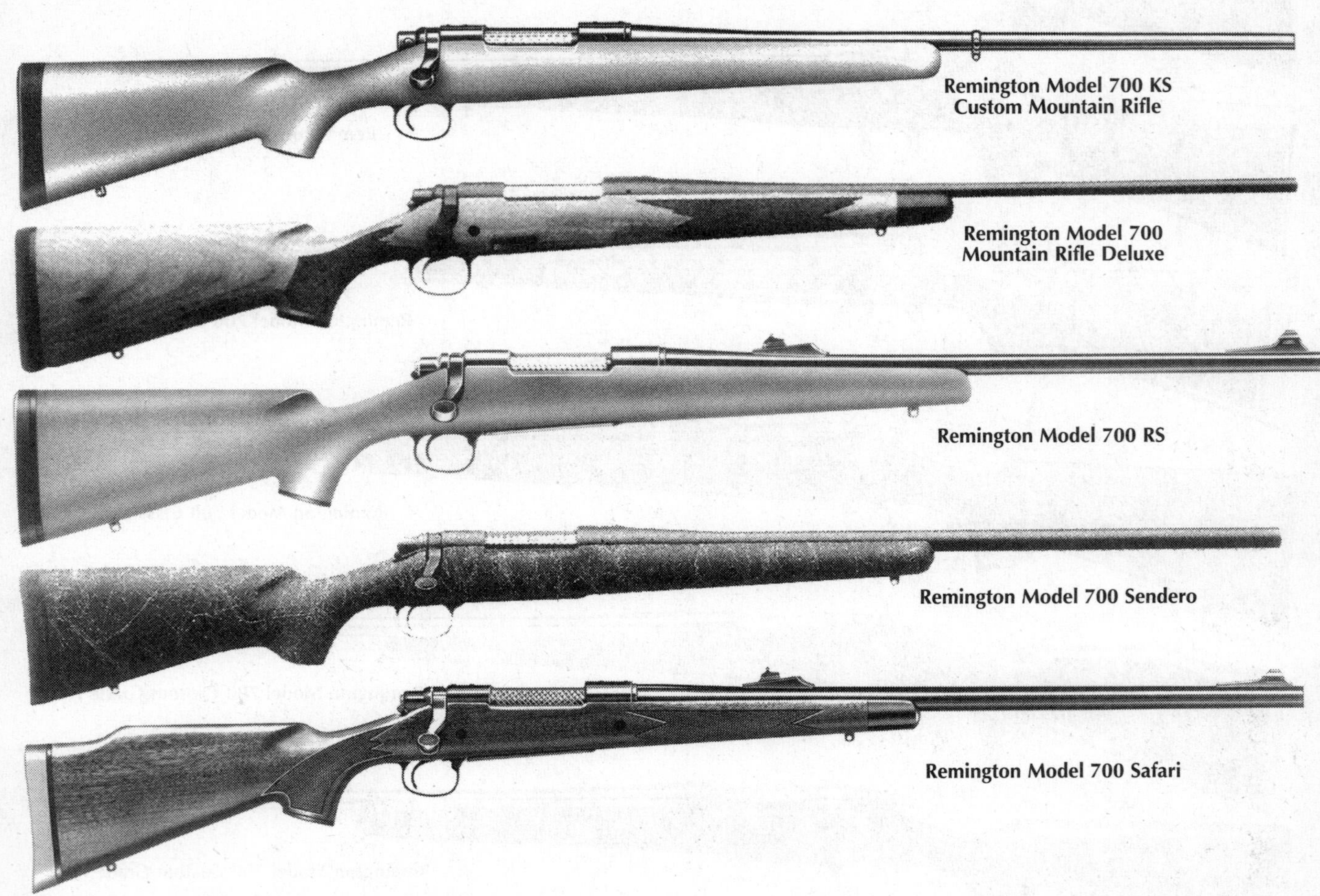

MODEL 700 LS BOLT-ACTION RIFLE

Similar to Model 700 ADL except with checkered Monte Carlo-style laminated wood stock with alternating grain and wood color, impregnated with phenolic resin and finished with a low satin luster. Made 1988-93

Standard calibers . . . . NiB $576 Ex $473 Gd $301
Magnum calibers . . . . NiB $602 Ex $483 Gd $345

MODEL 700 LSS BOLT-ACTION RIFLE

Similar to Model 700 BDL except with stainless steel barrel and action. Checkered Monte Carlo-style laminated wood stock with alternating grain and gray tinted color impregnated with phenolic resin and finished with a low satin luster. Made 1996 to date.

Standard calibers . . . . NiB $576 Ex $499 Gd $345
Magnum calibers . . . . NiB $628 Ex $551 Gd $370

MODEL 700 MTN RIFLE

Lightweight version of Model 700. Calibers: .243 Win., .25-06, .257 Roberts, .270 Win., 7x57, 7mm-08 Rem., .280 Rem., .30-06 and .308 Win. Four round magazine. 22-inch bbl. Weight: 6.75 lbs. Satin blue or stainless finish. Checkered walnut stock and redesigned pistol grip, straight comb, contoured cheekpiece, Old English-style recoil pad and satin oil finish or black synthetic stock with pressed checkering and blind magazine. Made 1986 to date.

(*cont'd.*) **MODEL 700 MOUNTAIN RIFLE**

Standard w/blind magazine . . . . NiB $473 Ex $370 Gd $232
Standard w/hinged floorplate (disc. 1994) . NiB $533 Ex $443 Gd $327
DM Model (New 1995). . . . . NiB $587 Ex $473 Gd $319
SS Model stainless synthetic (disc. 1993) . . NiB $484 Ex $370 Gd $267

MODEL 700 RS BOLT-ACTION RIFLE

Similar to the Model 700 BDL except with straight comb DuPont Rynite stock finished in gray or gray camo with Old English style recoil pad. made 1987-90.

Standard calibers . . . . NiB $576 Ex $473 Gd $319
Magnum calibers. NiB $602 Ex $473 Gd $345
.280 Rem. calibers (Limited production). . . NiB $719 Ex $576 Gd $395

MODEL 700 SAFARI GRADE

Big game heavy magnum version of the Model 700 BDL. 8mm Rem. Mag., .375 H&H Mag., .416 Rem. Mag. and .458 Win. Mag. 24-inch heavy bbl. Weight: 9 lbs. Blued or stainless finish. Checkered walnut stock in synthetic/Kevlar stock with standard matte or wood-grain finish with old English style recoil pad. made 1962 to date.

Safari Classic/Monte Carlo . . . . NiB $1076 Ex $947 Gd $509
Safari KS (Kevlar stock) intro. 1989 . . . . NiB $1250 Ex $1045 Gd $783
Safari KS (Wood-grain) intro. 1992. . . . . . NiB $1166 Ex $947 Gd $667
Safari KS SS (Stainless) intro. 1993 . . . . . NiB $1450 Ex $1204 Gd $891
Safari left-hand, add $95

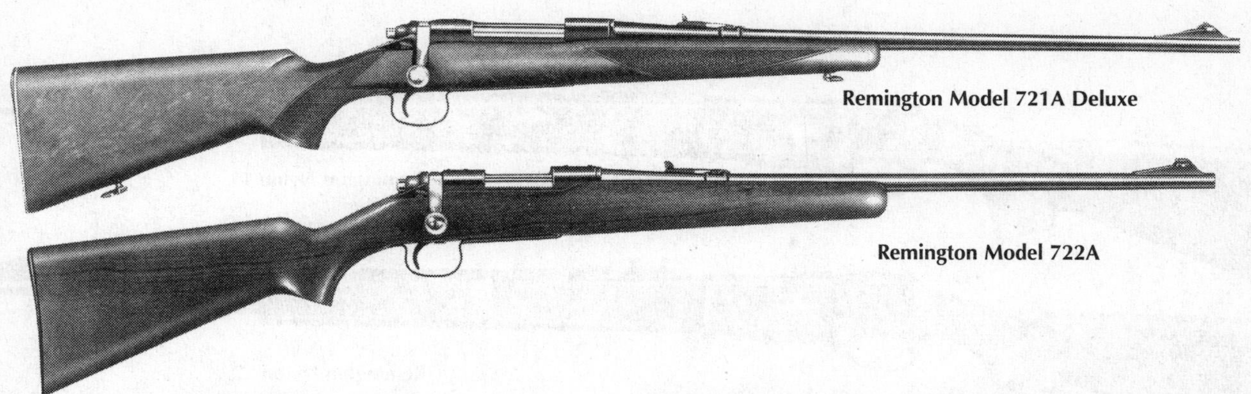

Remington Model 721A Deluxe

Remington Model 722A

MODEL 700 SENDERO BOLT-ACTION RIFLE

Same as Model 700 VS except chambered in long action and magnum .25-06 Rem., .270 Win., .280 Rem., 7mm Rem. Mag., .300 Win. Made 1994 to date.

Standard calibers............... NiB $679 Ex $576 Gd $345
Magnum calibers, add........................... $30
SF Model (stainless fluted), add.................... $115

MODEL 700 VLS (VARMINT LAMINATED STOCK) BOLT-ACTION RIFLE................. NiB $602 Ex $473 Gd $319

Same as Model 700 BDL Varmint Special except with 26-inch polished blue barrel. Laminated wood stock with alternating grain and wood color impregnated with phenolic resin and finished with a satin luster. Calibers: .222 Rem., .223 Rem., .22-250 Rem., .243 Win., 7mm-08 Rem., .308 Win. Weight: 9.4 lbs. Made 1995 to date.

MODEL 700 VS BOLT-ACTION RIFLE

Same as Model 700 BDL Varmint Special except w/26-inch matte blue or fluted stainless barrel. Textured black or gray synthetic stock reinforced with Kevlar, fiberglass and graphite with full length aluminum bedding block. Calibers: .22-250 Rem., .220 Swift, .223 Rem., .308 Win. Made 1992 to date.

Model 700 VS...................... NiB $679 Ex $499 Gd $370
Model 700 VS SF (fluted barrel)......... NiB $725 Ex $597 Gd $434
Model 700 VS SF/SF-P
(Fluted & ported barrel).............. NiB $892 Ex $757 Gd $584

MODEL 720A BOLT-ACTION HIGH POWER.............. NiB $1331 Ex $1151 Gd $996

Modified M/1917 Enfield action. .257 Roberts, .270 Win., .30-06. Five round box magazine. 22-inch bbl. Weight: About 8 lbs. Sights: Open rear; bead front, on ramp. Pistol-grip stock, checkered. Model 720R has 20-inch bbl.; Model 720S has 24-inch bbl. Made 1941.

MODEL 721A STANDARD GRADE BOLT-ACTION HIGH-POWER RIFLE..... NiB $422 Ex $370 Gd $309

Calibers: .270 Win., .30-06. Four round box magazine. 24-inch bbl. Weight: About 7.25 lbs. Sights: Open rear; bead front, on ramp. Plain sporting stock. Made 1948-62.

MODEL 721A MAGNUM STANDARD GRADE............ NiB $576 Ex $448 Gd $370

Caliber: .264 Win. Mag. or .300 H&H Mag. Same as standard model except has 26-inch bbl. Three round magazine and recoil pad. Weight: 8.25 lbs.

MODEL 721ADL/BDL DELUXE

Same as Model 721A Standard or Magnum except has deluxe checkered stock and/or select wood.

Model 721ADL Deluxe Grade.......... NiB $654 Ex $576 Gd $448
Model 721ADL .300 Magnum Deluxe.... NiB $776 Ex $654 Gd $497
Model 721BDL Deluxe Special Grade.... NiB $661 Ex $551 Gd $410
Model 721BDL .300 Magnum Deluxe..... NiB $734 Ex $618 Gd $469

MODEL 722A STANDARD GRADE SPORTER

Same as Model 721A bolt-action except shorter action. .222 Rem. mag., .243 Win., .257 Roberts, .308 Win., .300 Savage. Four or 5-round magazine. Weight: 7-8 lbs. .222 Rem. introduced 1950; .244 Rem. introduced 1955. Made 1948-62.

.222 Rem.................... NiB $428 Ex $345 Gd $238
.244 Rem.................... NiB $390 Ex $314 Gd $218
.222 Rem. Mag. & .243 Win....... NiB $493 Ex $396 Gd $273
Other Calibers................. NiB $422 Ex $345 Gd $216

MODEL 722ADL DELUXE GRADE

Same as Model 722A except has deluxe checkered stock.

Standard calibers............... NiB $576 Ex $473 Gd $319
.222 Rem. Deluxe Grade......... NiB $628 Ex $525 Gd $396
.244 Rem. Deluxe Grade......... NiB $731 Ex $654 Gd $396

MODEL 722BDL DELUXE SPECIAL GRADE

Same as Model 722ADL except select wood.

Standard calibers............... NiB $576 Ex $525 Gd $422
.222 Rem. Deluxe Special Grade... NiB $576 Ex $525 Gd $422
.224 Rem. Deluxe Special Grade... NiB $628 Ex $520 Gd $396

MODEL 725 KODIAK MAGNUM RIFLE............ NiB $4130 Ex $3409 Gd $2070

Similar to Model 725ADL. Calibers: .375 H&H Mag., .458 Win. Mag. Three round magazine. 26-inch bbl. with recoil reducer built into muzzle. Weight: About 9 lbs. Deluxe, reinforced Monte Carlo stock with recoil pad, black forend tip swivels, sling. Fewer than 100 made in 1961.

MODEL 725ADL BOLT-ACTION REPEATING RIFLE

Calibers: .222, .243, .244, .270, .280, .30-06. Four round box mag. (5-round in 222). 22-inch bbl. (24-inch in .222). Weight: About 7 lbs. Sights: Open rear, hooded ramp front. Monte Carlo comb stock w/pistol-grip, checkered, swivels. Made 1958-61.

.222 Rem., .243 Win., .244 Rem... NiB $756 Ex $607 Gd $418
.270 Win....................... NiB $766 Ex $581 Gd $375
.280 Win....................... NiB $839 Ex $710 Gd $427
.30-06........................ NiB $607 Ex $478 Gd $375

MODEL 788 CENTERFIRE BOLT-ACTION

Calibers: .222 Rem., .22-250, .223 Rem., 6mm Rem., .243 Win., 7mm-08 Rem., .308 Win., .30-30, .44 Rem. Mag. Three round clip magazine (4-round in .222 and .223 Rem.). 24-inch bbl. in .22s, 22-inch in other calibers. Weight: 7.5 lbs. with 24-inch bbl.; 7.25 lbs. with 22-inch bbl. Sights: Blade front on ramp; U-notch rear. Plain Monte Carlo stock. Made 1967-84.

.22-250, .223 Rem., 6mm Rem.,
.243 Win., .308 Win................. NiB $394 Ex $291 Gd $204
.30-30 Win........................ NiB $457 Ex $374 Gd $267
7mm-08 Rem........................ NiB $459 Ex $368 Gd $253
.44 Mag........................... NiB $503 Ex $405 Gd $278
Left-hand (6mm Rem. and
.308 Win. 1972-79).................. NiB $404 Ex $333 Gd $239

RIFLES

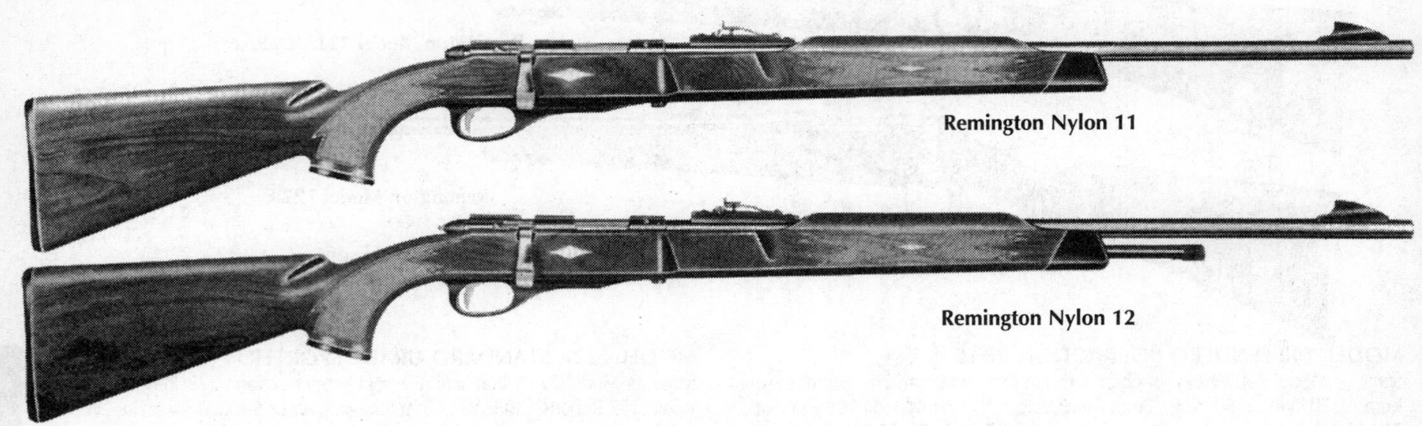
Remington Nylon 11

Remington Nylon 12

NYLON 11 BOLT-ACTION REPEATER . . . . **NiB $267 Ex $164 Gd $103**
Clip type. Caliber: .22 Short, Long, LR. Six- or 10-round clip mag. 19.63-inch bbl. Weight: 4.5 lbs. Sights: Open rear; blade front. Nylon stock. Made 1962-66.

NYLON 12 BOLT-ACTION REPEATER . . . . **NiB $267 Ex $164 Gd $103**
Same as Nylon 11 except has tubular magazine holding 22 Short, 17 Long, 15 LR. Made 1962-66.

SLIDE- AND LEVER-ACTION RIFLES

MODEL SIX (6) SLIDE-ACTION REPEATER . . . . **NiB $428 Ex $345 Gd $238**
Hammerless. Calibers: 6mm Rem., .243 Win., .270 Win. 7mm Express Rem., .30-06, .308 Win. 22-inch bbl. Weight: 7.5 lbs. Checkered Monte Carlo stock and forearm. Made 1981-88.

MODEL SIX (6) SLIDE-ACTION REPEATER, PEERLESS GRADE . . . . **NiB $1822 Ex $1565 Gd $947**
Same as Model Six Standard except has engraved receiver. Made 1981-88.

MODEL SIX (6) SLIDE-ACTION REPEATER, PREMIUM GRADES
Same as Model Six Standard except has engraved receiver with gold inlay. Made 1981-88.
Peerless D Grade . . . . **NiB $1837 Ex $1631 Gd $988**
Premier F Grade . . . . **NiB $4220 Ex $3382 Gd $2311**
Premier Gold F Grade . . . . **NiB $5951 Ex $4768 Gd $3254**

MODEL 12A, 12B, 12C, 12CS SLIDE-ACTION REPEATERS
Standard Grade. Hammerless. Takedown. Caliber: .22 Short, Long or LR. Tubular magazine holds 15 Short, 12 Long or 10 LR cartridges. 22- or 24-inch round or octagonal bbl. Open rear sight, bead front. Plain, half-pistol-grip stock and grooved slide handle of walnut. Made 1909-36.
Model 12A . . . . **NiB $525 Ex $319 Gd $216**
Model 12B (22 Short only w/octagon bbl.) . . . . **NiB $654 Ex $499 Gd $319**
Model 12C (w/24-inch octagon bbl.) . . . . **NiB $551 Ex $473 Gd $293**
Model 12CS (22 WRF w/24-inch octagon bbl.) . . . . **NiB $525 Ex $396 Gd $267**

MODEL 14A HIGH POWER SLIDE-ACTION REPEATING RIFLE . . . . **NiB $561 Ex $422 Gd $370**
Standard grade. Hammerless. Takedown. Calibers: .25, .30, .32 and .35 Rem. Five round tubular magazine. 22-inch bbl. Weight: About 6.75 lbs. Sights: Open rear; bead front. Plain half-pistol-grip stock and grooved slide handle of walnut. Made 1912-35.

MODEL 14R CARBINE . . . . **NiB $890 Ex $710 Gd $427**
Same as Model 14R except has 18.5-inch bbl., straight-grip stock, weight: About 6 lbs.

MODEL 14.5 CARBINE . . . . **NiB $890 Ex $684 Gd $401**
Same as Model 14A Rifle except has 9-round magazine, 18.5-inch bbl.

MODEL 14.5 RIFLE . . . . **NiB $993 Ex $710 Gd $478**
Similar to Model 14A except calibers: .38-40 and .44-40, 11-round full magazine, 22.5-inch bbl. Made 1912 to early 1920's.

MODEL 25A SLIDE-ACTION REPEATER . . . . **NiB $890 Ex $530 Gd $401**
Standard Grade. Hammerless. Takedown. Calibers: .25-20, .32-20. 10-round tubular magazine. 24-inch bbl. Weight: About 5.5 lbs. Sights: Open rear; bead front. Plain, pistol-grip stock, grooved slide handle. Made 1923-36.

MODEL 25R CARBINE . . . . **NiB $942 Ex $556 Gd $427**
Same as Model 25A except has 18-inch bbl. Six round magazine, straight-grip stock, weight: About 4.5 lbs.

MODEL 121A FIELDMASTER SLIDE-ACTION REPEATER . . . . **NiB $576 Ex $422 Gd $267**
Standard Grade. Hammerless. Takedown. Caliber: .22 Short, Long, LR. Tubular magazine holds 20 Short, 15 Long or 14 LR cartridges. 24-inch round bbl. Weight: 6 lbs. Plain, pistol-grip stock and grooved semi-beavertail slide handle. Made 1936-54.

MODEL 121S . . . . **NiB $557 Ex $448 Gd $308**
Same as Model 121A except chambered for .22 Remington Special (.22 W.R.F.). Magazine holds 12 rounds. Disc.

MODEL 121SB . . . . **NiB $648 Ex $520 Gd $357**
Same as Model 121A except smoothbore. Disc.

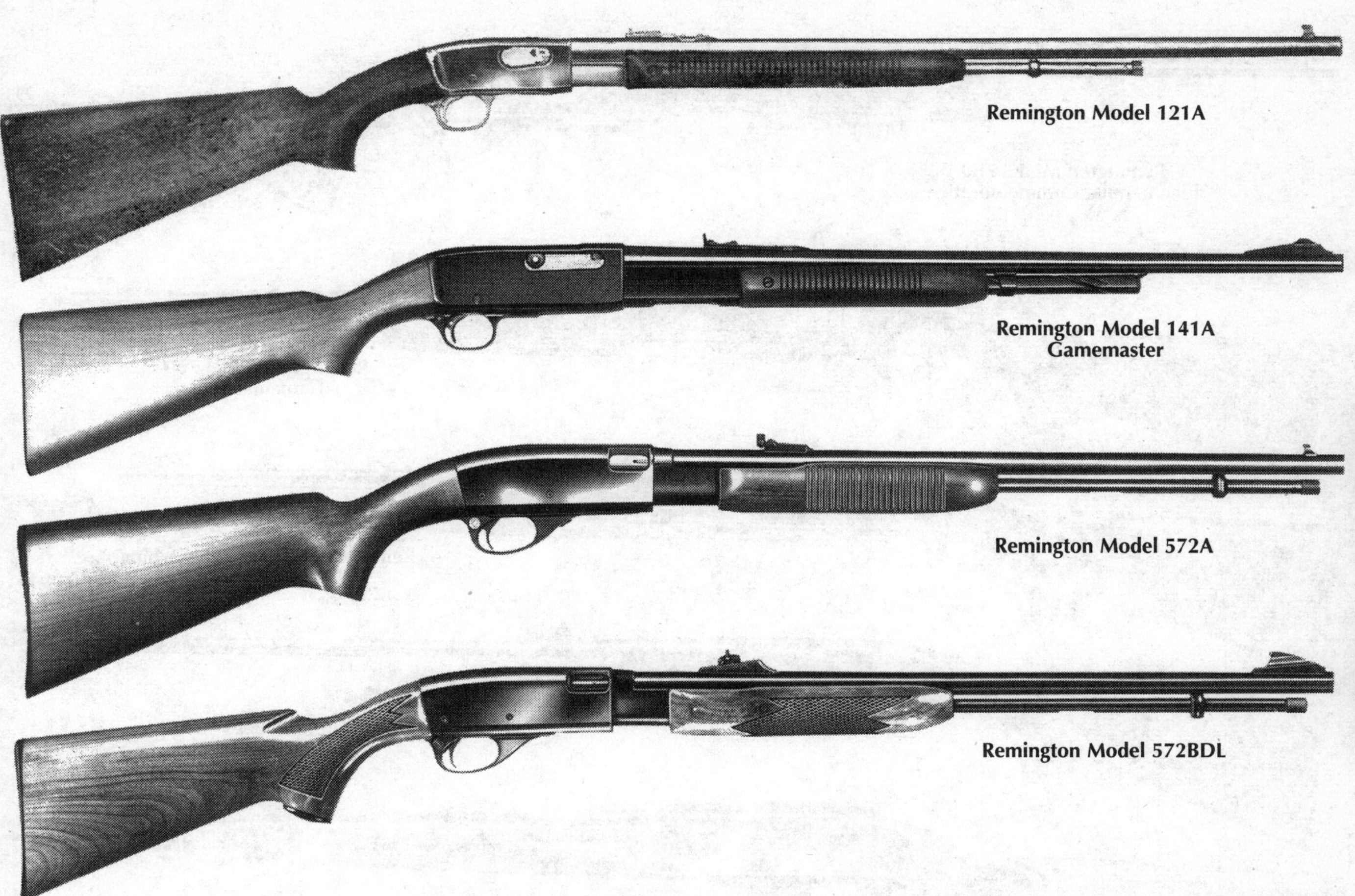

MODEL 141A GAMEMASTER
SLIDE-ACTION REPEATER. . . . . NiB $422 Ex $293 Gd $206
Standard Grade. Hammerless. Takedown. Calibers: .30, .32 and .35 Rem. Five round tubular magazine. 24-inch bbl. Weight: About 7.75 lbs. Sights: Open rear; bead front, on ramp. Plain, pistol-grip stock, semibeavertail forend (slide-handle). Made 1936-50.

MODEL 572A FIELDMASTER
SLIDE-ACTION REPEATER. . . . . NiB $267 Ex $139 Gd $103
Hammerless. Caliber: .22 Short, Long, LR. Tubular magazine holds 20 Short, 17 Long, 15 LR. 23-inch bbl. Weight: About 5.5 lbs. Sights: Open rear; ramp front. Pistol-grip stock, grooved forearm. Made 1955-88.

MODEL 572BDL DELUXE . . . . NiB $319 Ex $216 Gd $113
Same as Model 572A except has blade ramp front sight, sliding ramp rear; checkered stock and forearm. Made 1966 to date.

MODEL 572SB SMOOTH BORE . . . NiB $332 Ex $267 Gd $185
Same as Model 572A except smoothbore for .22 LR shot cartridges. Made 1961 to date.

MODEL 760 BICENTENNIAL
COMMEMORATIVE. . . . . NiB $731 Ex $525 Gd $396
Same as Model 760 except has commemorative inscription on receiver. Made 1976.

MODEL 760 CARBINE . . . . NiB $576 Ex $458 Gd $216
Same as Model 760 Rifle except made in calibers .270 Win., .280 Rem., .30-06 and .308 Win. only, has 18.5-inch bbl., weight: 7.25 lbs. Made 1961-80.

MODEL 760 GAMEMASTER
STANDARD GRADE SLIDE-ACTION REPEATING RIFLE
Hammerless. Calibers: .223 Rem., 6mm Rem., .243 Win., .257 Roberts, .270 Win. .280 Rem., .30-06, .300 Sav., .308 Win., .35 Rem. 22-inch bbl. Weight: About 7.5 lbs. Sights: Open rear; bead front, on ramp. Plain pistol-grip stock, grooved slide handle on early models; current production has checkered stock and slide handle. Made 1952-80.
.222 Rem. NiB $1230 Ex $947 Gd $586
.223 Rem. . . . . NiB $1410 Ex $1039 Gd $638
.257 Roberts . . . . NiB $937 Ex $715 Gd $432
Other calibers . . . . NiB $895 Ex $741 Gd $252

MODEL 760ADL
DELUXE GRADE. NiB $499 Ex $396 Gd $267
Same as Model 760 except has deluxe checkered stock, standard or high comb, grip cap, sling swivels. Made 1953-63.

MODEL 760BDL
CUSTOM DELUXE . . . . NiB $480 Ex $386 Gd $255
Same as Model 760 Rifle except made in calibers .270, .30-06 and .308 only, has Monte Carlo cheekpiece stock forearm with black tip, basket-weave checkering. Available also in left-hand model. Made 1953-80.

MODEL 760D
PEERLESS GRADE . . . . NiB $1303 Ex $1046 Gd $788
Same as Model 760 except scroll engraved, fancy wood. Made 1953-80.

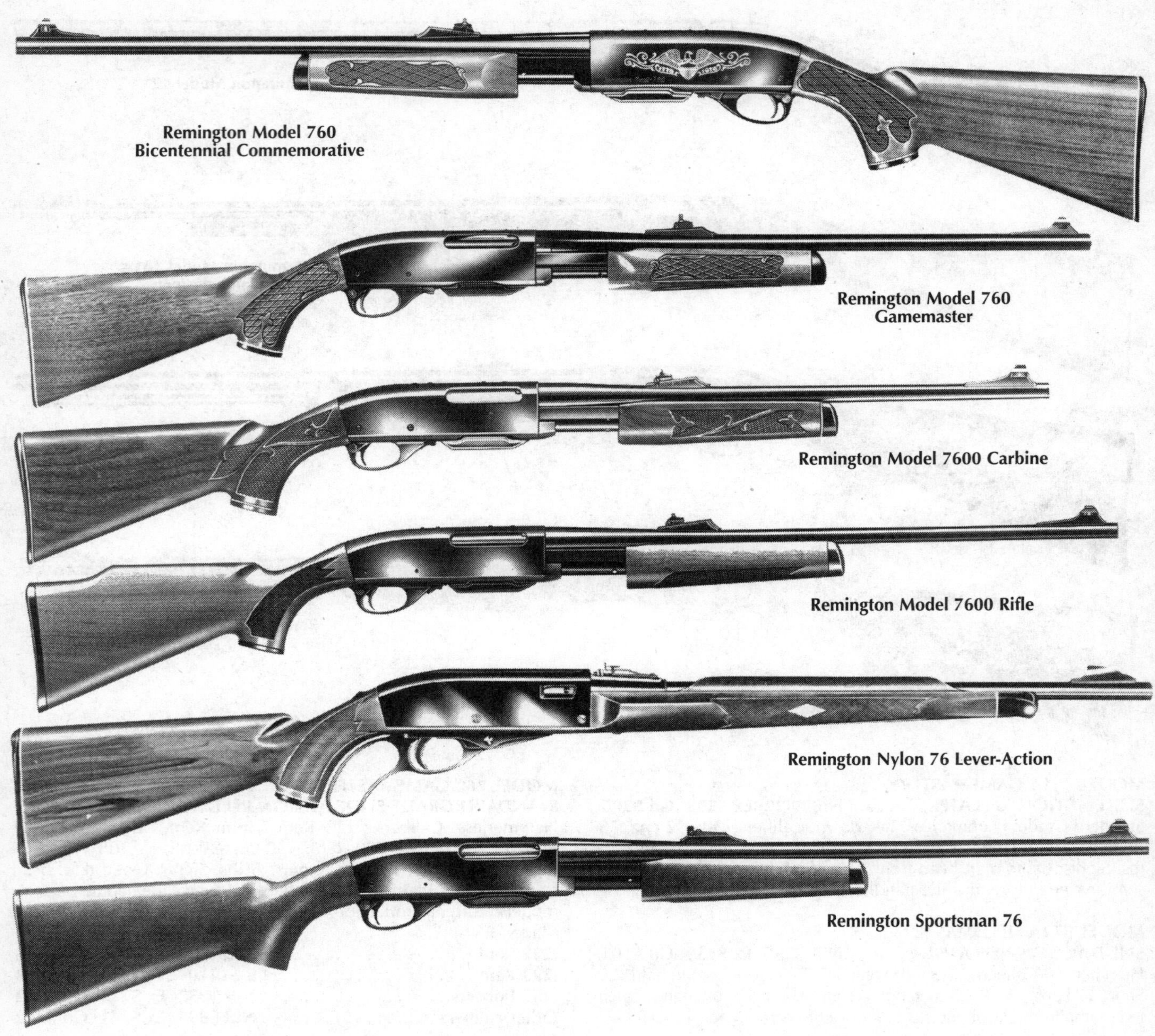
Remington Model 760 Bicentennial Commemorative

Remington Model 760 Gamemaster

Remington Model 7600 Carbine

Remington Model 7600 Rifle

Remington Nylon 76 Lever-Action

Remington Sportsman 76

MODEL 760F PREMIER GRADE
Same as Model 760 except extensively engraved with game scenes and scroll, finest grade wood. Also available with receiver inlaid with gold; adds 50 percent to value. Made 1953-80.
Premier F Grade . . . . NiB $2541 Ex $2038 Gd $1396
Premier Gold F Grade . . . . NiB $5946 Ex $4763 Gd $3249

MODEL 7600 SLIDE-ACTION CARBINE . . . . NiB $525 Ex $345 Gd $242
Same general specifications as Model 7600 Rifle except has 18.5-inch bbl. and weighs 7.25 lbs. Made 1987 to date.

MODEL 7600 SLIDE-ACTION RIFLE . . . . . . NiB $499 Ex $401 Gd $242
Similar to Model Six except has lower grade finishes. Made 1981 to date.

MODEL 7600 SPECIAL PURPOSE . . . . NiB $473 Ex $370 Gd $216
Same general specification as the Model 7600, except chambered only in .270 or .30-06. Special Purpose matte black finish on all exposed metal. American walnut stock with SP nonglare finish.

NYLON 76 LEVER-ACTION REPEATER . . . . NiB $319 Ex $267 Gd $164
Short-throw lever action. Caliber: .22 LR. 14-round buttstock tubular magazine. Weight: 4 lbs. Black or brown nylon stock and forend. Made 1962-64. Remington's only lever-action rifle.

SPORTSMAN 76 SLIDE-ACTION RIFLE . . . NiB $309 Ex $242 Gd $164
Caliber: .30-06, 4-round magazine. 22-inch bbl. Weight: 7.5 lbs. Open rear sight; front blade mounted on ramp. Uncheckered hardwood stock and forend. Made 1985-87.

SEMIAUTOMATIC RIFLES

MODEL FOUR (4) AUTOLOADING RIFLE
Hammerless. Calibers: 6mm Rem., .243 Win., .270 Win. 7mm Express Rem., .30-06, .308 Win. 22-inch bbl. Weight: 7.5 lbs. Sights: Open rear; bead front, on ramp. Monte Carlo checkered stock and forearm. Made 1981-88.
Standard . . . . NiB $731 Ex $602 Gd $267
Peerless Grade (Engr. receiver) . . . . NiB $2090 Ex $1884 Gd $802
Premier Grade (Engr. receiver) . . . . NiB $3829 Ex $3068 Gd $2096
Prem. Gr. (Engr. rec., gold inlay). . . . . NiB $6274 Ex $5025 Gd $3427

MODEL FOUR DIAMOND ANNIVERSARY LTD. EDITION $1040
Same as Model Four Standard except has engraved receiver w/inscription, checkered high-grade walnut stock and forend. Only 1,500 produced. Made 1981 only. (Value for new condition)

MODEL 8A AUTOLOADING RIFLE . . . . . . NiB $782 Ex $628 Gd $875
Standard Grade. Takedown. Calibers: .25, .30, .32 and .35 Rem. Five-round, clip-loaded magazine. 22-inch bbl. Weight: 7.75 lbs. Sights: Adj. and dovetailed open rear; dovetailed bead front. Half-moon metal buttplate on plain straight-grip walnut stock; plain walnut forearm with thin curved end. Made 1906-1936.

MODEL 16 AUTOLOADING RIFLE. . . . . . . NiB $422 Ex $319 Gd $190
Takedown. Closely resembles the Winchester Model 03 semiautomatic rifle. Calibers: .22 Short, .22 LR, 22 Rem. Auto. 15-round tubular magazine in buttstock. 22-inch bbl. Weight: 5.75 lbs. Sights: Open rear; dovetailed bead front. Plain straight-grip stock and forearm. Made 1914-1928. Note: In 1918 this model was discontinued in all calibers except .22 Rem. Auto; specifications are for that model.

MODEL 24A AUTOLOADING RIFLE . . . . . NiB $422 Ex $293 Gd $190
Standard Grade. Takedown. Calibers: .22 Short only, .22 LR. only. Tubular magazine in buttstock, holds 15 Short or 10 LR. 21-inch bbl. Weight: About 5 lbs. Sights: Dovetailed adj. open rear; dovetailed bead front. Plain walnut straight-grip buttstock; plain walnut forearm. Made 1922-35.

MODEL 81A WOODSMASTER AUTOLOADER . . . . NiB $551 Ex $422 Gd $242
Standard Grade. Takedown. Calibers: .30, .32 and .35 Rem., .300 Sav. Five round box magazine (not detachable). 22-inch bbl. Weight: 8.25 lbs. Sights: Open rear; bead front. Plain walnut pistol-grip stock, forearm. Made 1936-50.

MODEL 241A SPEEDMASTER AUTOLOADER . . . . NiB $319 Ex $267 Gd $164
Standard Grade. Takedown. Calibers: .22 Short only, .22 LR. only. Tubular magazine in buttstock, holds 15 Short or 10 LR. 24-inch bbl. Weight: About 6 lbs. Sights: Open rear, bead front. Plain walnut stock and forearm. Made 1935-51.

MODEL 550A AUTOLOADER . . . . . . NiB $242 Ex $164 Gd $87
Has "Power Piston" or floating chamber, which permits interchangeable use of 22 Short, Long or LR cartridges. Tubular magazine holds 22 Short, 17 Long, 15 LR. 24-inch bbl. Weight: About 6.25 lbs. Sights: Open rear; bead front. Plain, one-piece pistol-grip stock. Made 1941-71.

MODEL 550P . . . . NiB $242 Ex $164 Gd $87
Same as Model 550A except has peep rear sight, blade front, on ramp.

MODEL 550-2G . . . . NiB $319 Ex $242 Gd $139
"Gallery Special." Same as Model 550A except has 22-inch bbl., screweye for counter chain and fired shell deflector.

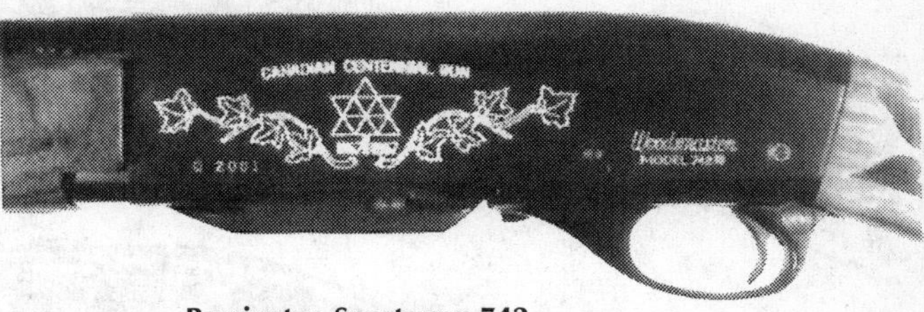

Remington Sportsman 742 Canadian Centennial

MODEL 552A SPEEDMASTER AUTOLOADER . . . . NiB $242 Ex $164 Gd $87
Caliber: .22 Short, Long, LR. Tubular magazine holds 20 Short, 17 Long, 15 LR. 25-inch bbl. Weight: About 5.5 lbs. Sights: Open rear; bead front. Pistol-grip stock, semi-beavertail forearm. Made 1957-88.

MODEL 552BDL DELUXE . . . . NiB $309 Ex $206 Gd $139
Same as Model 552A except has checkered walnut stock and forearm. Made 1966 to date.

MODEL 552C CARBINE . . . . NiB $267 Ex $164 Gd $113
Same as Model 552A except has 21-inch bbl. Made 1961-77.

MODEL 552GS GALLERY SPECIAL. . . . . . NiB $309 Ex $206 Gd $139
Same as Model 552A except chambered for .22 Short only. Made 1957-77.

MODEL 740A WOODSMASTER AUTOLOADER
Standard Grade. Gas-operated. Calibers: .30-06 or .308. Four round detachable box magazine. 22-inch bbl. Weight: About 7.5 lbs. Plain pistol-grip stock, semibeavertail forend with finger grooves. Sights: Open rear; ramp front. Made 1955-60.
Rifle model . . . . NiB $396 Ex $319 Gd $206
Carbine model. . . . . NiB $448 Ex $370 Gd $242

MODEL 740ADL/BDL DELUXE
Same as Model 740A except has deluxe checkered stock, standard or high comb, grip cap, sling swivels. Model 740 BDL also has select wood. Made 1955-60.
Model 740 ADL Deluxe Grade . . . . NiB $602 Ex $473 Gd $242
Model 740 BDL Deluxe Special Grade . . . NiB $679 Ex $525 Gd $370

MODEL 742 BICENTENNIAL COMMEMORATIVE. $731
Same as Model 742 Woodsmaster rifle except has commemorative inscription on receiver. Made 1976. (Value for new condition)

MODEL 742 CANADIAN CENTENNIAL $731
Same as Model 742 rifle except has commemorative inscription on receiver. Made 1967. Value is for rifle in new, unfired condition.

MODEL 742 CARBINE . . . . NiB $679 Ex $473 Gd $206
Same as Model 742 Woodsmaster Rifle except made in calibers .30-06 and .308 only, has 18.5-inch bbl., weight 6.75 lbs. Made 1961-80.

MODEL 742 WOODSMASTER AUTOMATIC BIG GAME RIFLE . . . . NiB $618 Ex $422 Gd $211
Gas-operated semiautomatic. Calibers: 6mm Rem., .243 Win., .280 Rem., .30-06, .308 Win. Four round clip magazine. 22-inch bbl. Weight: 7.5 lbs. Sights: Open rear; bead front, on ramp. Checkered pistol-grip stock and forearm. Made 1960-80.

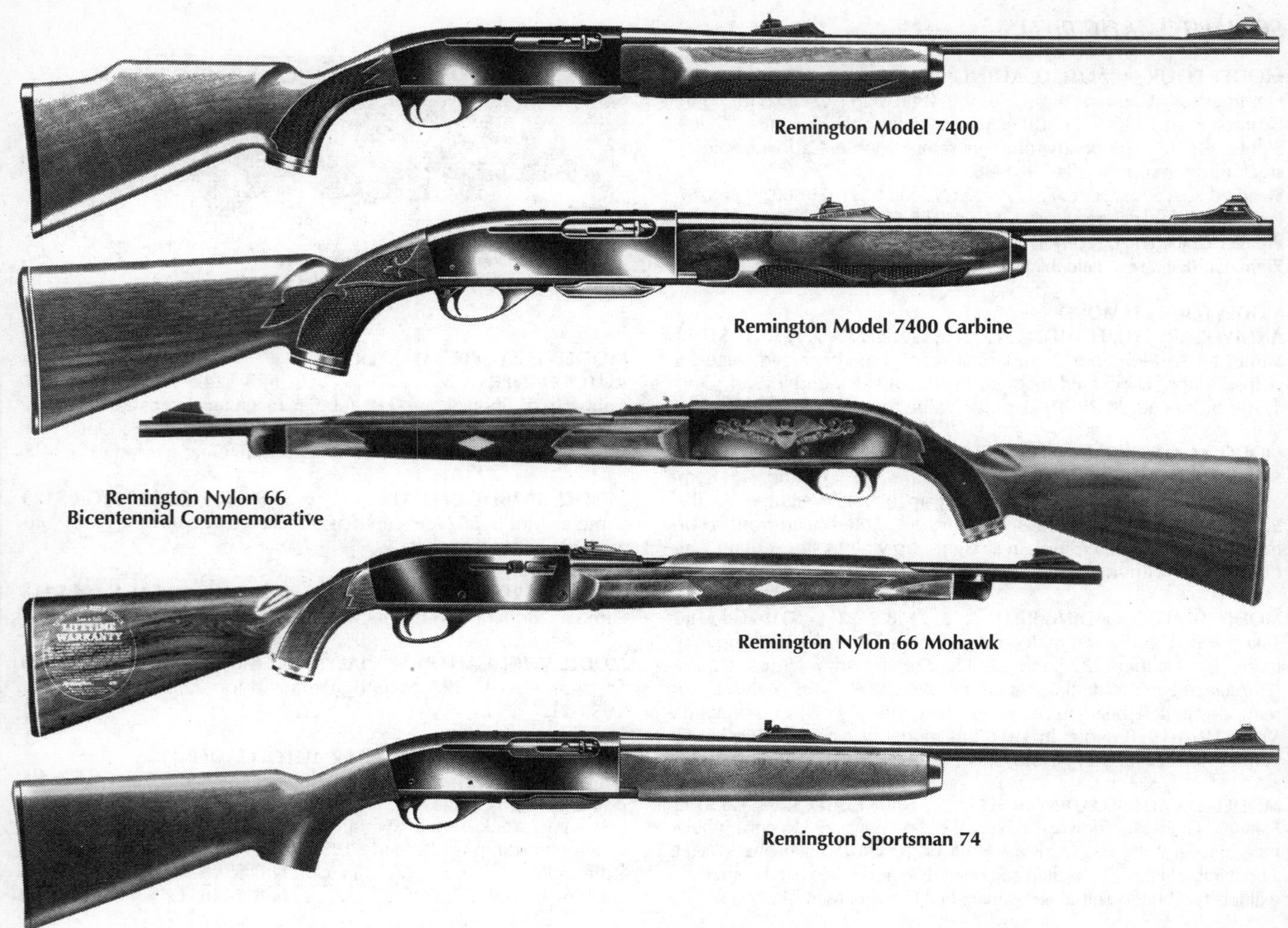

Remington Model 7400

Remington Model 7400 Carbine

Remington Nylon 66 Bicentennial Commemorative

Remington Nylon 66 Mohawk

Remington Sportsman 74

MODEL 742BDL CUSTOM DELUXE. . . . . . NiB $576 Ex $473 Gd $242
Same as Model 742 Rifle except made in calibers .30-06 and .308 only, has Monte Carlo cheekpiece stock, forearm with black tip, basket-weave checkering. Available in left-hand model. Made 1966-80.

MODEL 742D PEERLESS GRADE . . . . NiB $1799 Ex $1490 Gd $949
Same as Model 742 except scroll engraved, fancy wood. Made 1961-80.

MODEL 742F PREMIER GRADE
Same as Model 742 except extensively engraved with game scenes and scroll, finest grade wood. Also available with receiver inlaid with gold; adds 50 percent to value. Made 1961-1980.
Premier F Grade . . . . NiB $3835 Ex $3074 Gd $2102
Premier Gold F Grade . . . . NiB $5952 Ex $4769 Gd $3255

MODEL 7400 AUTOLOADER
Similar to Model Four w/lower grade finishes. Made 1981 to date.
Model 7400 Standard . . . . NiB $448 Ex $370 Gd $211
Model 7400 HG
(High gloss finish) . . . . NiB $454 Ex $365 Gd $252

MODEL 7400 CARBINE . . . . NiB $448 Ex $319 Gd $242
Caliber: .30-06 only. Similar to the Model 7400 rifle except has 18.5-inch bbl. and weight: 7.25 lbs. Made 1988 to date.

MODEL 7400 SPECIAL PURPOSE. . . . . NiB $448 Ex $345 Gd $216
Same general specification as the Model 7400 except chambered only in .270 or .30-06. Special Purpose matte black finish on metal. American walnut stock with SP nonglare finish. Made 1993-95.

NYLON 66 APACHE BLACK . . . . . . NiB $214 Ex $137 Gd $101
Same as Nylon 66 Mohawk Brown except bbl. and receiver cover chrome-plated, black stock. Made 1962-84.

NYLON 66 BICENTENNIAL
COMMEMORATIVE . . . . NiB $240 Ex $162 Gd $111
Same as Nylon 66 except has commemorative inscription on receiver. Made 1976.

NYLON 66MB AUTOLOADING RIFLE . . . . NiB $214 Ex $137 Gd $101
Similar to the early production Nylon 66 Black Apache except with blued bbl. and receiver cover. Made 1978-87.

NYLON 66 MOHAWK
BROWN AUTOLOADER . . . . NiB $162 Ex $111 Gd $96
Caliber: .22 LR. Tubular magazine in buttstock holds14 rounds. 19.5-inch bbl. Weight: About 4 lbs. Sights: Open rear; blade front. Brown nylon stock and forearm. Made 1959-87.

NYLON 77 CLIP REPEATER. . . . . . . NiB $188 Ex $137 Gd $101
Same as Nylon 66 except has 5-round clip magazine. Made 1970-71.

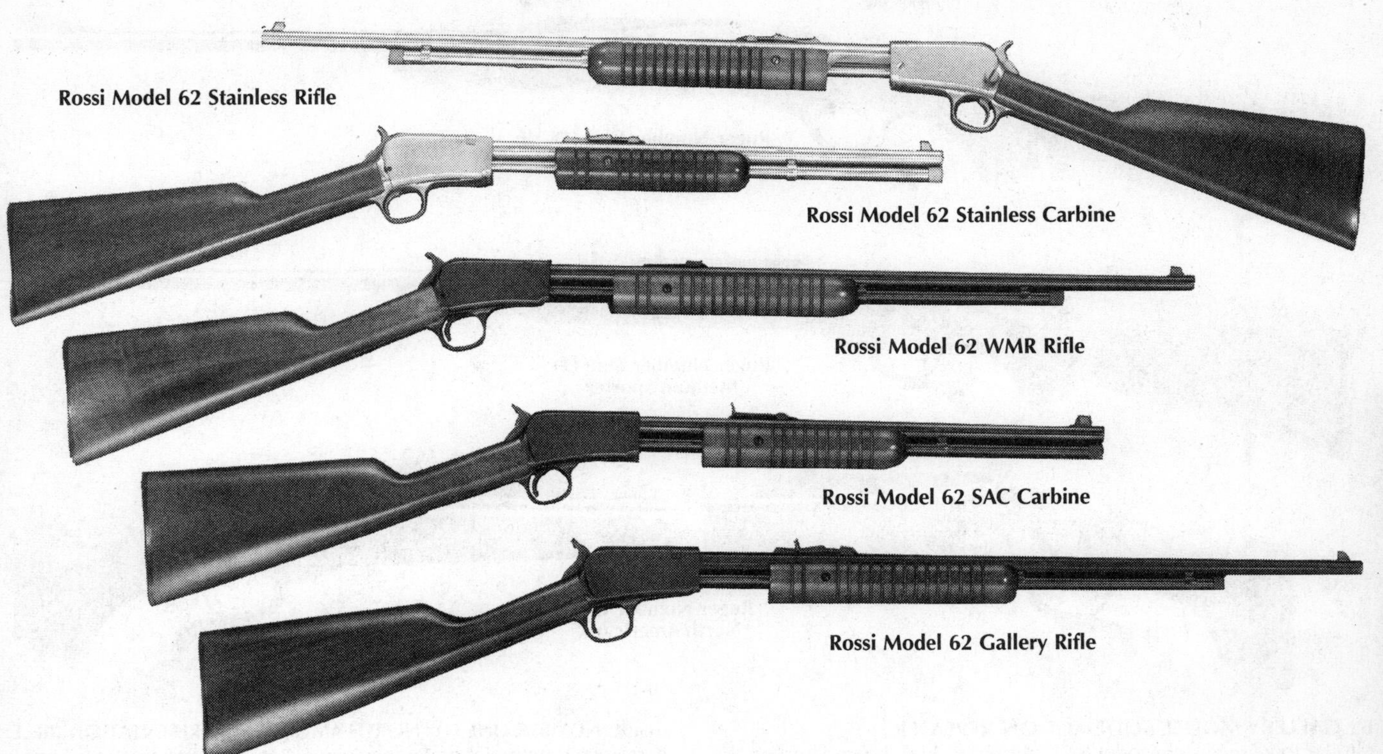
Rossi Model 62 Stainless Rifle

Rossi Model 62 Stainless Carbine

Rossi Model 62 WMR Rifle

Rossi Model 62 SAC Carbine

Rossi Model 62 Gallery Rifle

SPORTSMAN 74 AUTOLOADING RIFLE..... NiB $343 Ex $245 Gd $162
Caliber: .30-06, 4-round magazine. 22-inch bbl. Uncheckered buttstock and forend. Open rear sight; ramped blade front sight. Made 1985-88.

JOHN RIGBY & CO. — London, England

MODEL 275 MAGAZINE SPORTING RIFLE NiB $6250 Ex $5000+ Gd $3400
Mauser action. Caliber: .275 High Velocity or 7x57mm; 5-round box magazine. 25-inch bbl. Weight: about 7.5 lbs. Sights: Folding leaf rear; bead front. Sporting stock w/half-pistol-grip, checkered. Specifications given are those of current model; however, in general, they apply also to prewar model.

MODEL 275 LIGHTWEIGHT
MAGAZINE RIFLE................. NiB $5000 Ex $4000 Gd $2720
Same as standard .275 rifle except has 21-inch bbl. Weight: 6.75 lbs.

MODEL 350 MAGNUM
MAGAZINE SPORTING RIFLE .... NiB $4375 Ex $3500 Gd $2380
Mauser action. Caliber: .350 Magnum. Five round box magazine. 24-inch bbl. Weight: About 7.75 lbs. Sights: Folding leaf rear; bead front. Sporting stock with full pistol-grip, checkered. Currently mfd.

MODEL 416 BIG GAME
MAGAZINE SPORTING RIFLE .... NiB $7500 Ex $6000 Gd $4080
Mauser action. Caliber: .416 Big Game. Four round box magazine. 24-inch bbl. Weight: 9 to 9.25 lbs. Sights: Folding leaf rear; bead front. Sporting stock with full pistol-grip, checkered. Currently mfd.

BEST QUALITY HAMMERLESS
EJECTOR DOUBLE RIFLE....... NiB $48,750 Ex $39,000 Gd $26,520
Sidelocks. Calibers: .275 Magnum, .350 Magnum, .470 Nitro Express. 24- to 28-inch bbls. Weight: 7.5 to 10.5 lbs. Sights: Folding leaf rear; bead front. Checkered pistol-grip stock and forearm.

SECOND QUALITY HAMMERLESS
EJECTOR DOUBLE RIFLE...... NiB $21,875 Ex $17,500 Gd $11,900
Same general specifications as Best Quality double rifle except boxlock.

THIRD QUALITY HAMMERLESS
EJECTOR DOUBLE RIFLE.......... NiB $12,375 Ex $9900 Gd $6732
Same as Second Quality double rifle except plainer finish and not of as high quality.

ROSS RIFLE CO. — Quebec, Canada

MODEL 1910 BOLT-ACTION
SPORTING RIFLE.............. NiB $633 Ex $216 Gd $195
Straight-pull bolt-action with interrupted screw-type lugs. Calibers: .280 Ross, .303 British. Four round or 5-round magazine. Bbl. lengths: 22, 24, 26 inches. Sights: Two-leaf open rear; bead front. Checkered sporting stock. Weight: About 7 lbs. Made c. 1910 to end of World War I. Note: Most firearm authorities agree that this and other Ross models with interrupted screw-type lugs are unsafe to fire.

ROSSI RIFLES — Sao Leopoldo, Brazil Manufactured by Amadeo Rossi, S.A.

62 GALLERY MODEL SAC CARBINE
Same as standard Gallery Model except in .22 LR only with 16.25-inch bbl.; weight 5.5 lbs. Imported 1975-98.
Blued finish .... NiB $201 Ex $164 Gd $103
Nickel finish .... NiB $216 Ex $175 Gd $128
Stainless....................... NiB $267 Ex $195 Gd $134

62 GALLERY MODEL MAGNUM .... NiB $206 Ex $175 Gd $113
Same as standard Gallery Model except chambered for .22 WMR, 10-shot magazine. Imported 1975-98.

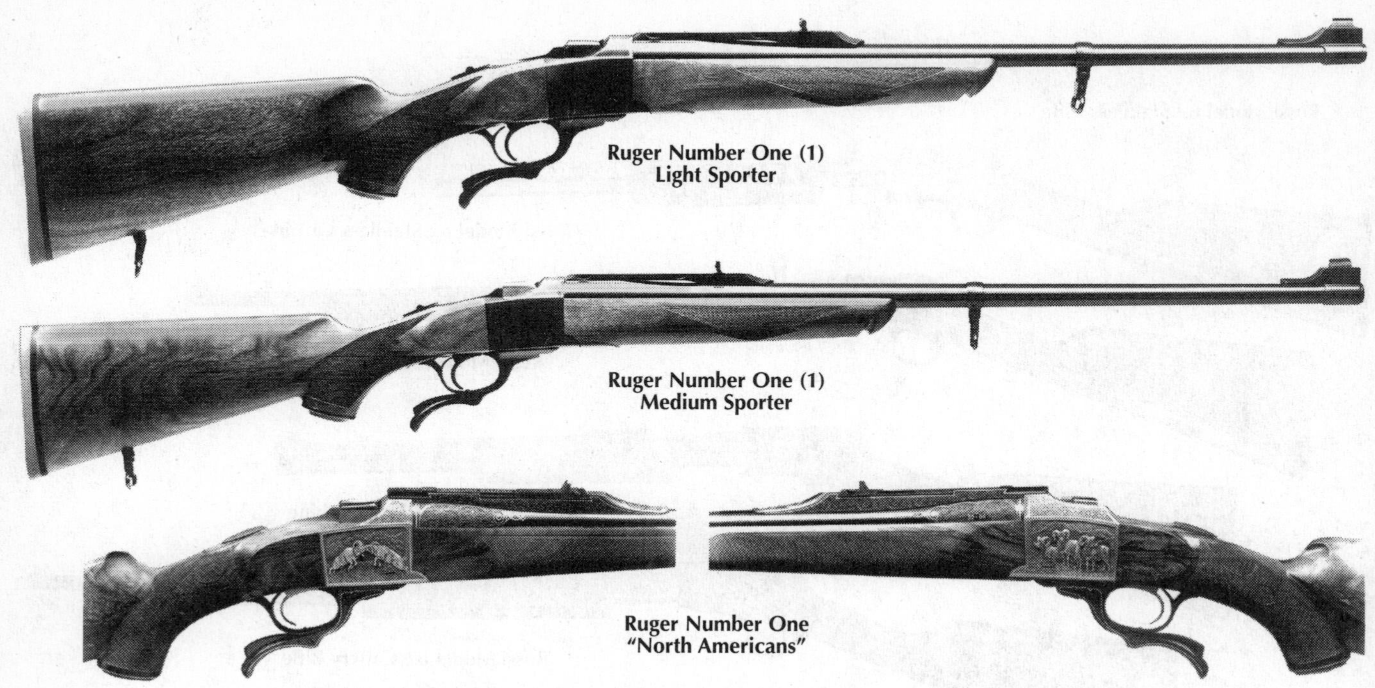

Ruger Number One (1)
Light Sporter

Ruger Number One (1)
Medium Sporter

Ruger Number One
"North Americans"

62 GALLERY MODEL SLIDE-ACTION REPEATER
Similar to Winchester Model 62. Calibers: .22 LR. Long, Short or .22 WMR. Tubular magazine holds 13 LR, 16 Long, 20 Short. 23-inch bbl. 39.25 inches overall. Weight: 5.75 lbs. Sights: Open rear; bead front. Straight-grip stock, grooved slide handle. Blued, nickel or stainless finish. Imported 1970-98. Values same as SAC Model.

LEVER-ACTION 65/92 CARBINE
Similar to Winchester Model 92. Caliber: .38 Special/.357 Mag., .44 Mag., .44-40, .45 LC. 8- or 10-round magazine. 16-, 20- or 24-inch round or half-octagonal bbl. Weight: 5.5 to 6 lbs. 33.5- to 41.5-inches overall. Satin blue, chrome or stainless finish. Brazilian hardwood buttstock and forearm. Made 1978-98.
Model M92 SRC .45LC . . . . NiB $370 Ex $293 Gd $206
Model M92 SRC .38/357, .44 Mag . . . . . . NiB $370 Ex $293 Gd $206
Model M92 w/octagon bbl . . . . NiB $396 Ex $216 Gd $211
Model M92 LL Lever . . . . NiB $370 Ex $242 Gd $190
Engraved, add $75
Chrome, add $25
Stainless, add $75

RUGER RIFLES — Southport, Connecticut Manufactured by Sturm, Ruger & Co.

NUMBER ONE (1) LIGHT SPORTER. . . . . . NiB $679 Ex $551 Gd $267
Same as No.1 Standard except has 22-inch bbl., folding leaf rear sight on quarter-rib and ramp front sight, Henry pattern forearm. Made 1966 to date.

NUMBER ONE (1) MEDIUM SPORTER . . . NiB $628 Ex $499 Gd $293
Same as No. 1 Light Sporter except has 26-inch bbl. 22-inch in 45-70); weight: 8 lbs (7.25 lbs. in .45-70). Calibers: 7mm Rem. Mag., .300 Win. Mag., .45-70. Made 1966 to date.

NUMBER ONE (1) "NORTH AMERICANS" PRESENTATION RIFLE $52,570
Same general specifications as the Ruger No. 1 Standard except highly customized with elaborate engravings, carvings, fine-line checkering and gold inlays. A series of 21 is planned, each rifle depicting a North American big-game animal, chambered in the caliber appropriate to the game. Stock is of Northern California English walnut. Comes in trunk-style Huey case with Leupold scope and other accessories.

NUMBER ONE (1) RSI INTERNATIONAL SINGLE-SHOT RIFLE. . . . . NiB $628 Ex $473 Gd $309
Similar to the No. 1 Light Sporter except with lightweight 20-inch bbl. and full Mannlicher-style forend, in calibers .243 Win., .270 Win., 7x57mm, .30-06. Weight: 7.25 lbs.

NUMBER ONE (1) SPECIAL VARMINTER . . . . NiB $628 Ex $473 Gd $309
Same as No. 1 Standard except has heavy 24-inch bbl. with target scope bases, no quarter-rib. Weight: 9 lbs. Calibers: .22-250, .25-06, 7mm Rem. Mag., .300 Win. Mag. Made 1966 to date.

NUMBER ONE (1) STANDARD RIFLE. NiB $618 Ex $448 Gd $293
Falling-block single-shot action with Farquharson-type lever. Calibers: .22-250, .243 Win., 6mm Rem., .25-06, .270 Win., .30-06, 7mm Rem. Mag., .300 Win. Mag. 26-inch bbl. Weight: 8 lbs. No sights, has quarter-rib for scope mounting. Checkered pistol-grip buttstock and semi-beavertail forearm, QD swivels, rubber buttplate. Made 1966 to date.

NUMBER ONE (1) TROPICAL RIFLE. . . . . . NiB $679 Ex $546 Gd $319
Same as No. 1 Light Sporter except has heavy 24-inch bbl.; calibers are .375 H&H .404 Jeffery, .416 Rigby, and .458 Win. Mag. Weight: 8.25 to 9 lbs. Made 1966 to date.

NUMBER THREE (3) SINGLE-SHOT CARBINE . . . . NiB $473 Ex $422 Gd $242
Falling-block action with American-style lever. Calibers: .22 Hornet .223 Rem., .30-40 Krag, .357 Win., .44 Mag., .45-70. 22-inch bbl. Weight: 6 lbs. Sights: Folding leaf rear; gold bead front. Carbine-style stock w/curved buttplate, forearm with bbl. band. Made 1972-87.

Ruger Number One "North Americans" Presentation Set

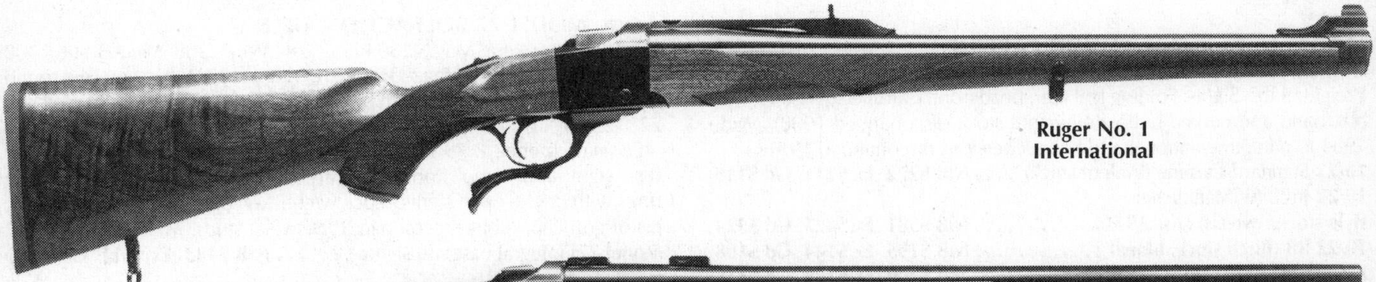

Ruger No. 1
International

Ruger No. 1
Special Varminter

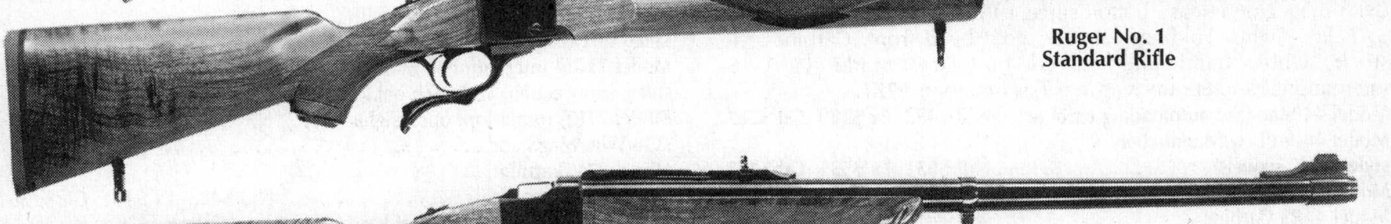

Ruger No. 1
Standard Rifle

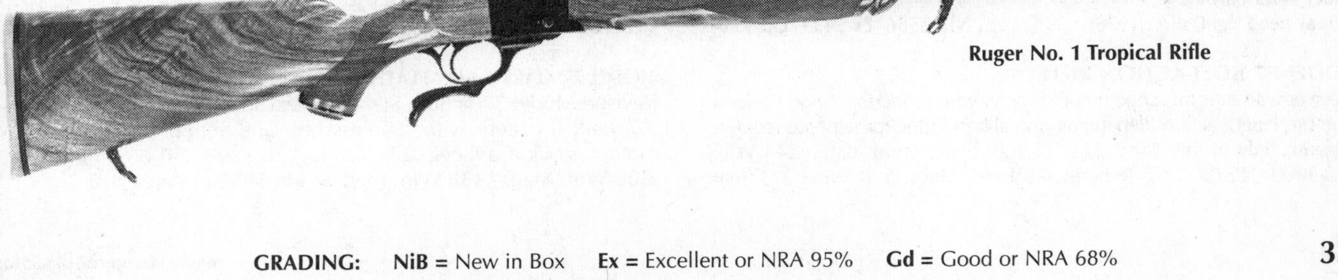

Ruger No. 1 Tropical Rifle

Ruger No. 3 Single-Shot Carbine

Ruger Model 10/22 Standard Rifle

Ruger Model 10/22 Deluxe Rifle

Ruger Model 44 Autoloading Carbine

MODEL 10/22 AUTOLOADING CARBINE

Caliber: .22 LR. Detachable 10-round rotary magazine. 18.5-inch bbl. Weight: 5 lbs. Sights: Folding leaf rear; bead front. Carbine-style stock with bbl. band and curved buttplate (walnut stock discontinued 1980). Made 1964 to date. International and Sporter versions discontinued 1971.

10/22 Standard Carbine (Walnut stock) .... NiB $272 Ex $211 Gd $118
10/22 Int'l. (w/Mannlicher style stock, swivels) Disc.1971 .... NiB $581 Ex $427 Gd $324
10/22 RB (Birch stock, blued) .... NiB $195 Ex $144 Gd $108
K10/22 RB (Birch stock, stainless) .... NiB $200 Ex $169 Gd $118
10/22 Sporter (MC stock, flat buttplate, swivels) Disc.1971 .... NiB $200 Ex $169 Gd $118
10/22 SP Deluxe Sporter (made since 1966).... NiB $253 Ex $205 Gd $145
10/22 RBI Int'l. (blued); made since 1994 ... NiB $241 Ex $193 Gd $138
10/22 RBI Int'l. (stainless); made since 1995 .... NiB $266 Ex $216 Gd $152

MODEL 44 AUTOLOADING CARBINE

Gas-operated. Caliber: .44 Magnum. Four round tubular magazine (with magazine release button since 1967). 18.5-inch bbl. Weight: 5.75 lbs. Sights: Folding leaf rear; gold bead front. Carbine-style stock w/bbl. band and curved buttplate. Made 1961-86. International and Sporter versions discontinued 1971.

Model 44 Standard autoloading carbine... NiB $483 Ex $380 Gd $267
Model 44 Int'l (w/Mannlicher-style stock, swivels) .... NiB $631 Ex $535 Gd $432
Mdl. 44 Sporter (MC stk. w/fingergroove)... NiB $638 Ex $689 Gd $483
Model 44RS Carbine (w/rear peep sight, disc. 1978) .... NiB $586 Ex $432 Gd $324

MODEL 77 BOLT-ACTION RIFLE

Receiver with integral scope mount base or with round top. Short stroke or magnum length action (depending on caliber) in the former type receiver, magnum only in the latter. .22-250, .220 Swift, 6mm Rem., .243 Win., .250-3000, .25-06, .257 Roberts, 6.5 Rem. Mag., .270 Win., 7x57mm,

(cont'd.) MODEL 77 BOLT-ACTION RIFLE

7mm-08 7mm Rem. Mag., .280 Rem., .284 Win., .308 Win., .30-06, .300 Win. Mag. .338 Win. Mag., .350 Rem. Mag., .458 Win. Mag. Five round magazine standard, 4-round in .220 Swift, 3-round in magnum calibers. 22 24- or 26-inch bbl. (depending on caliber). Weight: About 7 lbs.; .458 Mag. model, 8.75 lbs. Round-top model furnished w/folding leaf rear sight and ramp front; integral base model furnished w/scope rings,with or w/o open sights. Stock w/checkered pistol grip and forearm, pistol-grip cap, rubber recoil pad, QD swivel studs. Made 1968-92.

Model 77, integral base, no sights .... NiB $483 Ex $411 Gd $226
6.5 Rem. Mag., add $75
.284 Win., add $30
.338 Win. Mag., add $50
.350 Rem. Mag., 6.5 Rem. Mag., add $75
Model 77RL Ultra Light, no sights,....... NiB $483 Ex $380 Gd $252
Model 77RL Ultra Light, open sights,..... NiB $494 Ex $401 Gd $277
Model 77RS, integral base, open sights ... NiB $490 Ex $395 Gd $275
.338 Win. Mag., .458 Win. Mag., with standard stock, add $75
Model 77RSC, .458 Win. Mag. with fancy Circassian walnut stock, add $525
Model 77RSI International, Mannlicher stock, short action, 18.5-inch bbl., 7 lbs..... NiB $483 Ex $380 Gd $252
Model 77ST, round top, open sights ...... NiB $494 Ex $391 Gd $308
.338 Win. Mag., add $50
Model 77V, Varmint, integral base, no sights .... NiB $483 Ex $411 Gd $226
Model 77NV, Varmint, integral base, no sights, stainless steel barrel, laminated wood stock....... NiB $509 Ex $422 Gd $277

MODEL 77 MARK II ALL-WEATHER RIFLE ... NiB $483 Ex $380 Gd $252

Revised Model 77 action. Same general specifications as Model M-77 Mark II except with stainless bbl. and action. Zytel injection-molded stock. Calibers: .223, .243, .270, .308, .30-06, 7mm Mag., .300 Win. Mag., .338 Win. Mag. Made 1990 to date.

Ruger Model 77 Round Top Receiver

Ruger Model 77 Ultra-Light Carbine

Ruger Model 77 International Carbine

Ruger Model 77 Varmint Rifle

Ruger Model 77 Mark II All-Weather Rifle

MODEL 77 MARK II BOLT-ACTION RIFLE

Revised Model 77 action. Same general specifications as Model M-77 except with new 3-position safety and fixed blade ejector system. Calibers .22 PPC, .223 Rem., 6mm PPC, 6.5x55 Swedish, .375 H&H, .404 Jeffery and .416 Rigby also available. Weight: 6 to 10.25 lbs. Made 1989 to date.

Model 77 MKIIR, integral base, no sights . . NiB $473 Ex $370 Gd $242
Left-hand Model 77LR MKII, add $25
Model 77RL MKII, Ultra Light, no sights. . . NiB $473 Ex $401 Gd $216
Model 77RLS MKII, Ultra Light, open sights . . . . NiB $473 Ex $412 Gd $267
Model 77RS MKII, integral base, open sights . . . NiB $480 Ex $386 Gd $265
Model 77RS MKII, Express, with fancy French walnut stock, integral base, open sights . NiB $1261 Ex $1029 Gd $694
Model 77RSI MKII, International, Mannlicher . . . . NiB $519 Ex $417 Gd $287
Model 77RSM MKII magnum, with fancy Circassian walnut stock, integral base, open sights. . . . . NiB $1354 Ex $1045 Gd $736
Model 77VT (VBZ or VTM) MKII Varmint/Target stainless steel action, laminated wood stock. . . . . NiB $499 Ex $412 Gd $267

MODEL 77/.22 HORNET BOLT-ACTION RIFLE

Mini-Sporter built on the 77/.22 action in caliber .22 Hornet. Six round rotary magazine. 20- inch bbl. 40 inches overall. Weight: 6 lbs. Receiver machined for Ruger rings (included). Beaded front sight and open adj. rear, or no sights. Blued or stainless finish. Checkered American walnut stock. Made 1994 to date.

***(cont'd.)* MODEL 77/.22 HORNET BOLT-ACTION RIFLE**

Model 77/.22RH (rings, no sights) . . . . . . NiB $345 Ex $319 Gd $216
Model 77/.22RSH (rings & sights). . . . . NiB $370 Ex $319 Gd $216
Model 77/.22VHZ (S/S w/ laminated wood stock) . . . . NiB $396 Ex $370 Gd $242

MODEL 77/.22 RIMFIRE BOLT-ACTION RIFLE

Calibers: .22 LR. or .22 WMR. 10-shot (.22 LR) or 9-shot (.22 WMR) rotary magazine. 20-inch bbl. 39.75 inches overall. Weight: 5.75 lbs. Integral scope bases; with or w/o sights. Checkered American walnut or Zytel injection-molded stock. Stainless or blued finish. Made 1983 to date. (Blued); stainless. Introduced 1989.

77/.22 R, rings, no sights, walnut stock . . . . . NiB $364 Ex $293 Gd $203
77/.22 RS, rings, sights, walnut. . . . . NiB $370 Ex $293 Gd $216
77/.22 RP, rings, no sights, synthetic stock . . . . NiB $299 Ex $242 Gd $168
77/.22 RSP, rings, sights, synthetic stock . . . . . NiB $325 Ex $262 Gd $182
K77/.22 RP, S/S rings, no sights, synthetic . . . . NiB $377 Ex $304 Gd $210
K77/.22 RSP, S/S, rings, sights, synthetic . . . . . NiB $390 Ex $314 Gd $217
77/.22 RM, .22 WMR, rings, no sights, walnut . . . . NiB $370 Ex $293 Gd $206
77/.22 RSM, .22 WMR, rings, sights, walnut . . . NiB $396 Ex $309 Gd $216
K77/.22 RSMP, .22 WMR, S/S, rings, sights, synthetic. . . . . NiB $390 Ex $314 Gd $217
K77/.22 RMP, .22 WMR, S/S, no sights, synthetic . . . . NiB $364 Ex $293 Gd $203
K77/.22 VBZ, .22 WMR, no sights, laminated. (1993) . . . . NiB $390 Ex $314 Gd $217

Ruger Model 77 Mark II

Ruger Model 77/.22 Rimfire

Ruger Model 77/.22 All Weather

Ruger Model 77/.44 All Weather

MODEL 77/.44 BOLT-ACTION
Short-action, carbine-style M77 similar to the 77/.22RH. Chambered .44 Rem. Mag. Four round rotary magazine. 18.5-inch bbl. 38.25 inches overall. Weight: 6 lbs. Gold bead front sight, folding adjustable rear w/integral scope base and Ruger rings. Blue or stainless finish. Synthetic or checkered American walnut stock w/rubber buttpad and swivels. Made 1997 to date.
Model 77/.44 blued. . . . . NiB $499 Ex $370 Gd $242
Model 77/.44 stainless. . . . . NiB $515 Ex $381 Gd $247

MODEL 96 LEVER ACTION CARBINE
Caliber: .22 LR. .22 Mag., .44 Mag. Detachable 10-, 9- or 4-round magazine. 18.5-inch bbl. Weight: 5.25 lbs. Front gold bead sights. Drilled and tapped for scope. American hardwood stock. Made 1996 to date.
.22 Long Rifle . . . . NiB $267 Ex $216 Gd $144
.22 Magnum . . . . NiB $278 Ex $242 Gd $154
.44 Magnum . . . . NiB $454 Ex $365 Gd $252

MINI-14 SEMIAUTOMATIC RIFLE
Gas-operated. Caliber: .223 Rem. (5.56mm). 5-, 10- or 20-round box magazine. 18.5-inch bbl. Weight: About 6.5 lbs. Sights: Peep rear; blade front mounted on removable barrel band. Pistol-grip stock w/curved buttplate, handguard. Made 1976 to date.
Mini-14/5 blued . . . . NiB $551 Ex $515 Gd $319
K-Mini-14/5 stainless steel . . . . NiB $576 Ex $525 Gd $370

(*cont'd.*) MINI-14 SEMIAUTOMATIC RIFLE
Mini-14/5F blued, folding stock . . . . NiB $736 Ex $623 Gd $427
K-Mini-14/5F stainless, folding stock . . . . . NiB $762 Ex $633 Gd $453
Mini-14 Ranch Rifle,
scope model, 6.25 lbs. . . . . NiB $581 Ex $530 Gd $324
K-Mini-1H Ranch Rifle,
scope model, stainless. . . . . NiB $607 Ex $556 Gd $349

MINI-THIRTY (30) AUTOLOADER
Caliber: 7.62 x 39mm. 5-round detachable magazine. 18.5-inch bbl. 37.25 inches overall. Weight: 7 lbs. 3 oz. Designed for use with telescopic sights. Walnut stained stock. Sights: Peep rear; blade front mounted on bbl. band. Blued or stainless finish. Made 1986 to date.
Blued . . . . NiB $576 Ex $525 Gd $309
Stainless. . . . . NiB $602 Ex $576 Gd $319

PC SERIES SEMIAUTOMATIC CARBINES
Calibers: 9mm Parabellum or .40 S&W. 10-round magazine. 15.25-inch bbl. Weight: 6.25 lbs. Integral Ruger scope mounts with or without sights. Optional blade front sight, adjustable open rear. Matte black oxide finish. Matte black Zytel stock w/checkered pistol-grip and forearm. Made 1997 to date.
Model PC9 (w/o sights). . . . . NiB $447 Ex $396 Gd $242
Model PC40 (w/o sights). . . . . NiB $473 Ex $422 Gd $267
W/adjustable sights, add $40

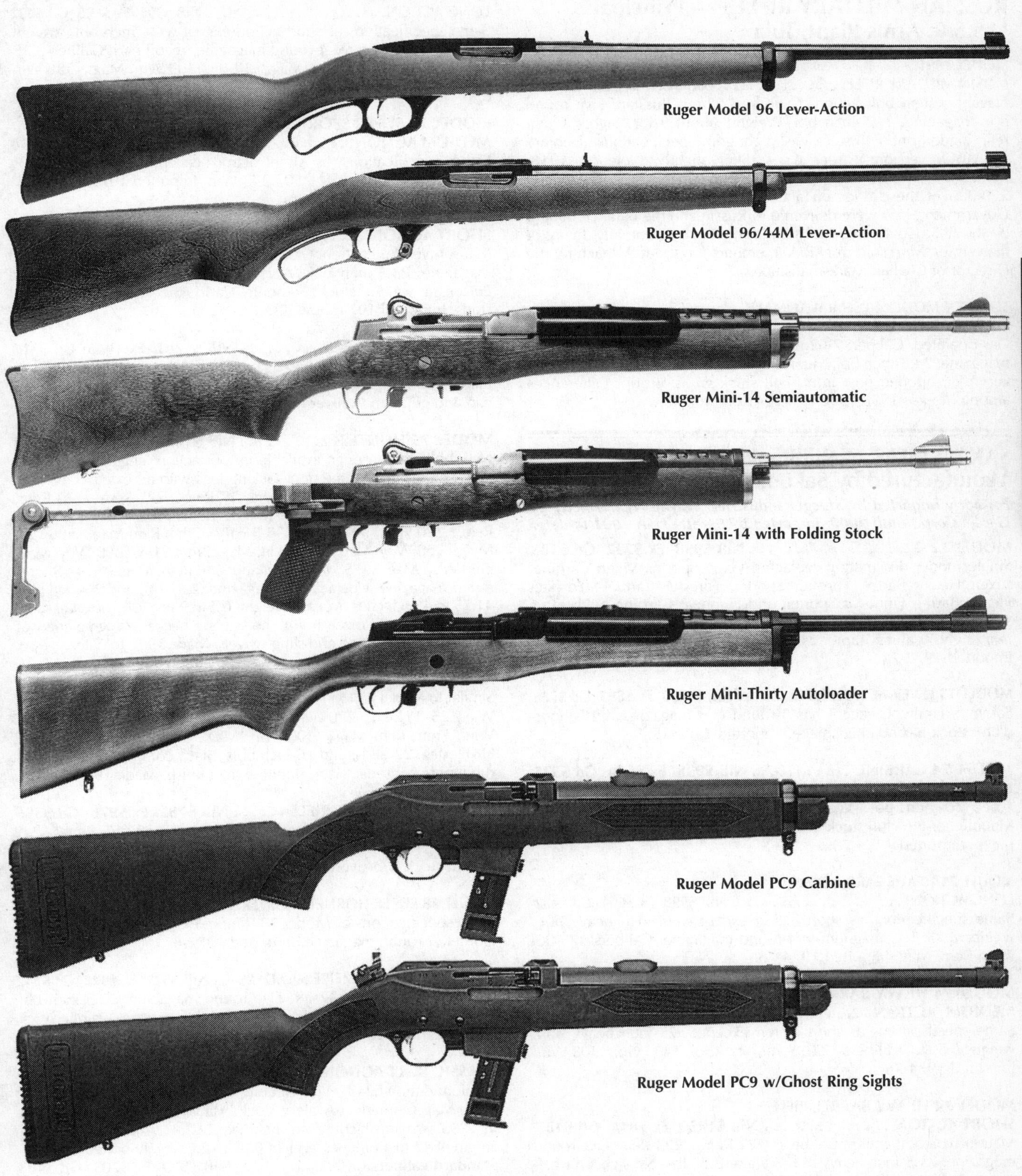
Ruger Model 96 Lever-Action

Ruger Model 96/44M Lever-Action

Ruger Mini-14 Semiautomatic

Ruger Mini-14 with Folding Stock

Ruger Mini-Thirty Autoloader

Ruger Model PC9 Carbine

Ruger Model PC9 w/Ghost Ring Sights

RUSSIAN MILITARY RIFLES — Principal U.S.S.R. Arms Plant, Tula

MODEL 1891
MOSIN MILITARY RIFLE. . . . . NiB $422 Ex $113 Gd $67
Nagant system bolt action. Caliber: 7.62mm Russian. Five round box magazine. 31.5-inch bbl. Weight: About 9 lbs. Sights: Open rear; blade front. Full stock w/straight grip. Specifications given are for WWII version; earlier types differ slightly. Note: In 1916, Remington Arms Co. and New England Westinghouse Co. produced 250,000 of these rifles on a contract from the Imperial Russian Government. Few were delivered to Russia and the balance bought by the U.S. Government for training in 1918. Eventually, many of these rifles were sold to N.R.A. members for about $3 each by the Director of Civilian Marksmanship.

TOKAREV MODEL 40 SEMIAUTOMATIC
MILITARY RIFLE . . . . NiB $787 Ex $377 Gd $223
Gas-operated. Caliber: 7.62mm Russian. 10-round detachable box magazine. 24.5-inch bbl. Muzzle brake. Weight: About 9 lbs. Sights: Leaf rear, hooded post front. Full stock w/pistol grip. Differences among Models 1938,1940 and 1941 are minor.

SAKO RIFLES — Riihimaki, Finland Manufactured by Sako L.T.D.

Formerly imported by Stoeger Industries, Wayne NJ (formerly by Garcia Corp.) until 2000. Imported by Beretta USA 2001 to date.

MODEL 72 . . . . NiB $998 Ex $792 Gd $586
Single model designation replacing Vixen Sporter, Vixen Carbine, Vixen Heavy Barrel, Forester Sporter, Forester Carbine, Forester Heavy Barrel, Finnbear Sporter, and Finnbear Carbine, with same specifications, except all but heavy barrel models fitted with open rear sight. Values same as for corresponding earlier models. Imported 1972-74.

MODEL 73 LEVER-ACTION RIFLE . . . . . . NiB $1050 Ex $895 Gd $586
Same as Finnwolf except has 3-round clip magazine, flush floorplate; stock has no cheekpiece. Imported 1973-75.

MODEL 74 CARBINE . . . . NiB $998 Ex $664 Gd $525
Long Mauser-type bolt action. Caliber: .30-06. Five round magazine. 20-inch bbl. Weight: 7.5 lbs. No sights. Checkered Mannlicher-type full stock of European walnut, Monte Carlo cheekpiece. Imported 1974-78.

MODEL 74 HEAVY BARREL RIFLE,
LONG ACTION. . . . . NiB $998 Ex $664 Gd $432
Same specifications as short action except w/24-inch heavy bbl., weighs 8.75 lbs.; magnum w/4-round magazine. Calibers: .25-06, 7mm Rem. Mag. Imported 1974-78.

MODEL 74 HEAVY BARREL RIFLE,
MEDIUM ACTION . . . . NiB $998 Ex $664 Gd $432
Same specifications as short action except w/23-inch heavy bbl., weighs 8.5 lbs. Calibers: .220 Swift, .22-250, .243 Win., .308 Win. Imported 1974-78.

MODEL 74 HEAVY BARREL RIFLE,
SHORT ACTION . . . . NiB $1050 Ex $844 Gd $483
Mauser-type bolt action. Calibers: .222 Rem., .223 Rem. Five round magazine. 23.5-inch heavy bbl. Weight: 8.25 lbs. No sights. Target-style checkered European walnut stock w/beavertail forearm. Imported 1974-78.

MODEL 74 SUPER SPORTER,
LONG ACTION. . . . . NiB $998 Ex $698 Gd $432
Same specifications as short action except w/24-inch bbl., weight: 8 lbs.; magnums have 4-round magazine, recoil pad. Calibers: .25-06, .270 Win. 7mm Rem. Mag., .30-06, .300 Win. Mag., .338 Win. Mag., .375 H&H Mag. Imported 1974-78.

MODEL 74 SUPER SPORTER,
MEDIUM ACTION. . . . . NiB $1024 Ex $715 Gd $458
Same specifications as short action except weight: 7.25 lbs. Calibers: .220 Swift, .22-250, .243 Win. Imported 1974-78.

MODEL 74 SUPER SPORTER,
SHORT ACTION . . . . NiB $1024 Ex $689 Gd $432
Mauser-type bolt action. Calibers: .222 Rem., .223 Rem. Five round magazine. 23.5-inch bbl. Weight: 6.5 lbs. No sights. Checkered European walnut stock w/Monte Carlo cheekpiece, QD swivel studs. Imported 1974, now disc.

MODEL 75 DELUXE . . . . NiB $1301 Ex 1045 Gd $717
Same specifications as Sako 75 Hunter Model except w/hinged floor plate, deluxe high gloss checkered walnut stock w/rosewood forend cap and grip cap w/silver inlay. Imported 1998 to date.

MODEL 75 HUNTER. . . . . NiB $1024 Ex $757 Gd $535
New bolt action design available in four action lengths fitted with a new bolt featuring three front locking lugs with an external extractor positioned under the bolt. Calibers: .17 Rem., .222 Rem., .223 Rem., (I); .22-250 Rem., .243 Win., 7mm-08 Rem., .308 Win., (III); .25-06 Rem., .270 Win., .280 Rem., .30-06, (IV); 7mm Rem Mag., .300 Win. Mag., .300 Wby. Mag., .338 Win. Mag. 7mm STW, .300 Wby. Mag., .340 Wby. Mag., .375 H&H Mag. and .416 Rem. Mag.,(V). 4-, 5- or 6-round magazine w/detachable magazine. 22-, 24-, and 26-inch bbls. 41.75 to 45.6 inches over all. Weight: 6.3 to 9 lbs. Sako dovetail scope base integral with receiver with no sights. Checkered high-grade walnut stock w/recoil pad and sling swivels. Made 1997 to date.

MODEL 75 STAINLESS SYNTHETIC . . . . . NiB $1082 Ex $870 Gd $598
Similar to Model 75 Hunter except chambered for .22-250 Rem., .243 Win., .25-06 Rem., .270 Win., 7mm-08 Rem., 7mm STW, .30-06, .308 Win., 7mm Rem Mag., .300 Win. Mag., .338 Win. Mag. or .375 H&H Mag. 22-, 24-, and 26-inch bbls. Black composite stock w/soft rubber grips inserts. Matte stainless steel finish. Made 1997 to date.

MODEL 75 VARMINT RIFLE . . . . . . NiB $782 Ex $576 Gd $396
Similar to Model 75 Hunter except chambered .17 Rem., .222 Rem., .223 Rem. and .22-250 Rem. 24-inch bbl. Matte lacquered walnut stock w/beavertail forearm. Made 1998 to date.

MODEL 78 SUPER HORNET SPORTER. . . . NiB $576 Ex $448 Gd $293
Same specifications as Model 78 Rimfire except chambered for .22 Hornet, 4-round magazine. Imported 1977-87.

MODEL 78 SUPER RIMFIRE SPORTER . . . . NiB $525 Ex $422 Gd $242
Bolt action. Caliber: .22 LR. Five round magazine. 22.5-inch bbl. Weight, 6.75 lbs. No sights. Checkered European walnut stock, Monte Carlo cheekpiece. Imported 1977-86.

CLASSIC BOLT-ACTION RIFLE
Medium Action (.243. Win.) or Long Action (.270 Win. .30-06, 7mm Rem. Mag.). American walnut stock. Made 1980-86. Reintroduced in 1993 w/matte lacquer finish stock, 22- or 24-inch bbl., overall length of 42 to 44 inches, weight 6.88 to 7.25lbs. Imported 1992-97.
Standard calibers. . . . . NiB $879 Ex $705 Gd $483
Magnum caliber . . . . NiB $943 Ex $757 Gd $518
Left-hand models. . . . . NiB $956 Ex $767 Gd $525

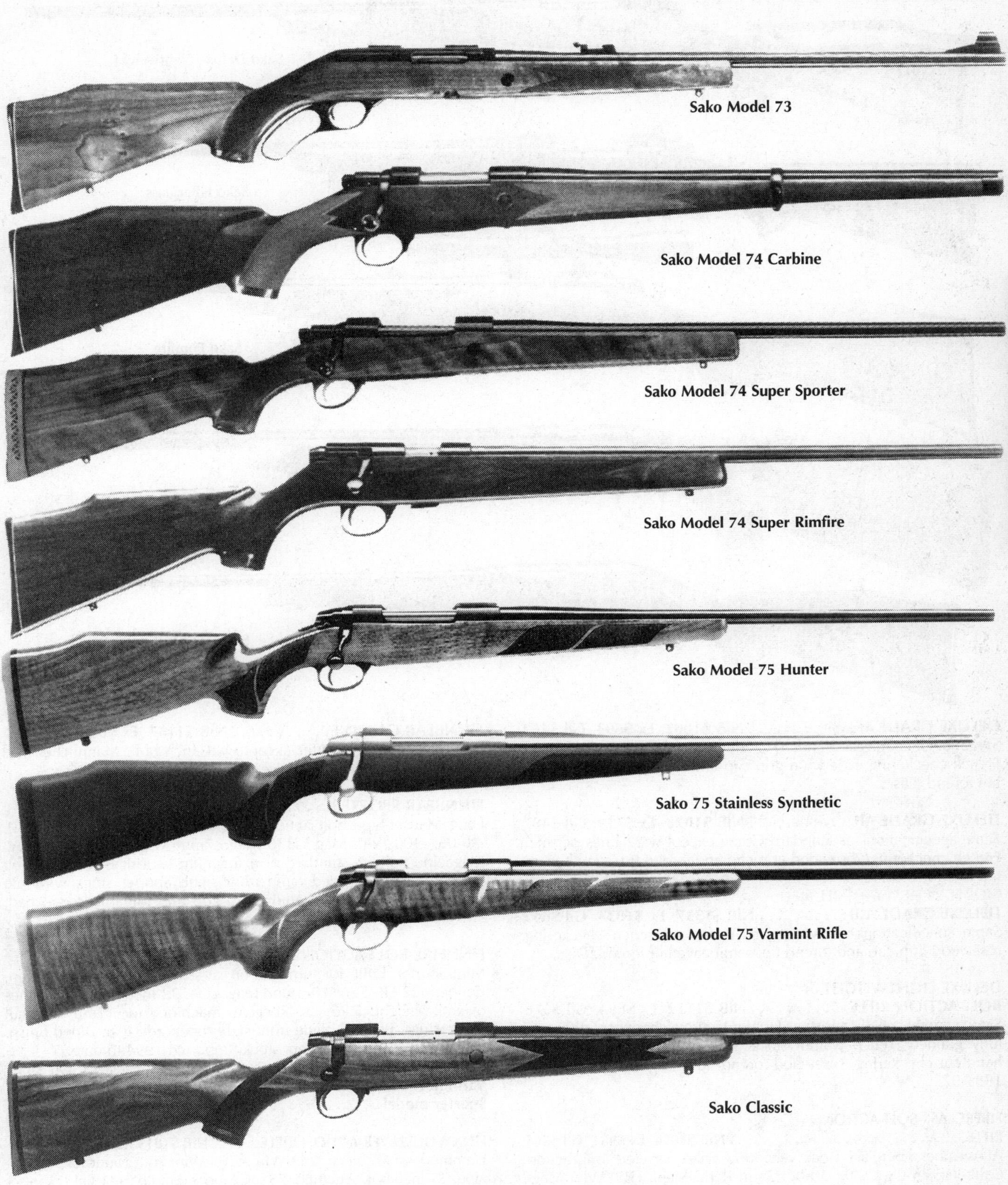

Sako Model 73

Sako Model 74 Carbine

Sako Model 74 Super Sporter

Sako Model 74 Super Rimfire

Sako Model 75 Hunter

Sako 75 Stainless Synthetic

Sako Model 75 Varmint Rifle

Sako Classic

Sako Deluxe Lightweight

Sako Fiberglass

Sako Finnfire

Sako Finnfire Heavy Barrel

Sako Finnwolf

DELUXE GRADE AI . . . . NiB $1002 Ex $693 Gd $462
Same specifications as Standard Grade except w/22 lines to the inch French checkering, rosewood grip cap and forend tip, semibeavertail forend. Disc.

DELUXE GRADE AII . . . . NiB $1028 Ex $719 Gd $487
Same specifications as Standard Grade except w/22 lines per inch French checkering, rosewood grip cap and forend tip, semi beavertail forend. Disc.

DELUXE GRADE AIII . . . . NiB $1337 Ex $1033 Gd $642
Same specifications as w/standard except w/French checkering, rosewood grip cap and forend tip, semibeavertail forend. Disc.

DELUXE LIGHTWEIGHT BOLT-ACTION RIFLE . . . . NiB $1112 Ex $894 Gd $616
Same general specifications as Hunter Lightweight except w/beautifully grained French walnut stock; superb high-gloss finish, fine hand-cut checkering, rosewood forend tip and grip cap. Imported 1985-97.

FIBERCLASS BOLT-ACTION RIFLE . . . . NiB $1054 Ex $951 Gd $565
All-weather fiberglass stock version of Sako barreled long action. Calibers: .25-06, .270, .30-06, 7mm Rem. Mag., .300 Win. Mag., .338 Win. Mag., .375 H&H Mag. Bbl. length: 22.5 inches. Overall length: 44.25 inches. Weight: 7.25 lbs. Imported 1984-96.

FINNBEAR CARBINE . . . . NiB $1157 Ex $848 Gd $513
Same as Finnbear Sporter except w/20-inch bbl., Mannlicher-type full stock. Imported 1971. Disc.

FINNBEAR SPORTER . . . . NiB $1105 Ex $848 Gd $513
Long Mauser-type bolt action. Calibers: .25-06, .264 Mag. .270, .30-06, .300 Win. Mag., .338 Mag., 7mm Mag., .375 H&H Mag. Magazine holds 5 standard or 4 magnum cartridges. 24-inch bbl. Weight: 7 lbs. Hooded ramp front sight. Sporter stock w/Monte Carlo cheekpiece, checkered pistol-grip and forearm, recoil pad, swivels. Imported 1961-71.

FINNFIRE BOLT-ACTION RIFLE
Mini-Sporter built for rimfires on a scaled-down Sako design. Caliber: .22 LR. 5- or 10-round magazine. 22-inch bbl. 39.5 inches overall. Weight: 5.25 lbs. Receiver machined for 11mm dovetail scope rings. Beaded blade front sight, open adj. rear. Blued finish. Checkered European walnut stock. Imported 1994 to date.
Hunter model . . . . NiB $736 Ex $623 Gd $453
Varmint model. . . . . NiB $834 Ex $633 Gd $478
Sporter model . . . . NiB $948 Ex $762 Gd $523

FINNWOLF LEVER-ACTION RIFLE . . . . . . NiB $1013 Ex $813 Gd $558
Hammerless. Calibers: .243 Win., .308 Win. Four round clip magazine. 23-inch bbl. Weight: 6.75 lbs. Hooded ramp front sight. Sporter stock w/Monte Carlo cheekpiece, checkered pistol-grip and forearm, swivels (available w/right- or left-hand stock). Imported 1963-72.

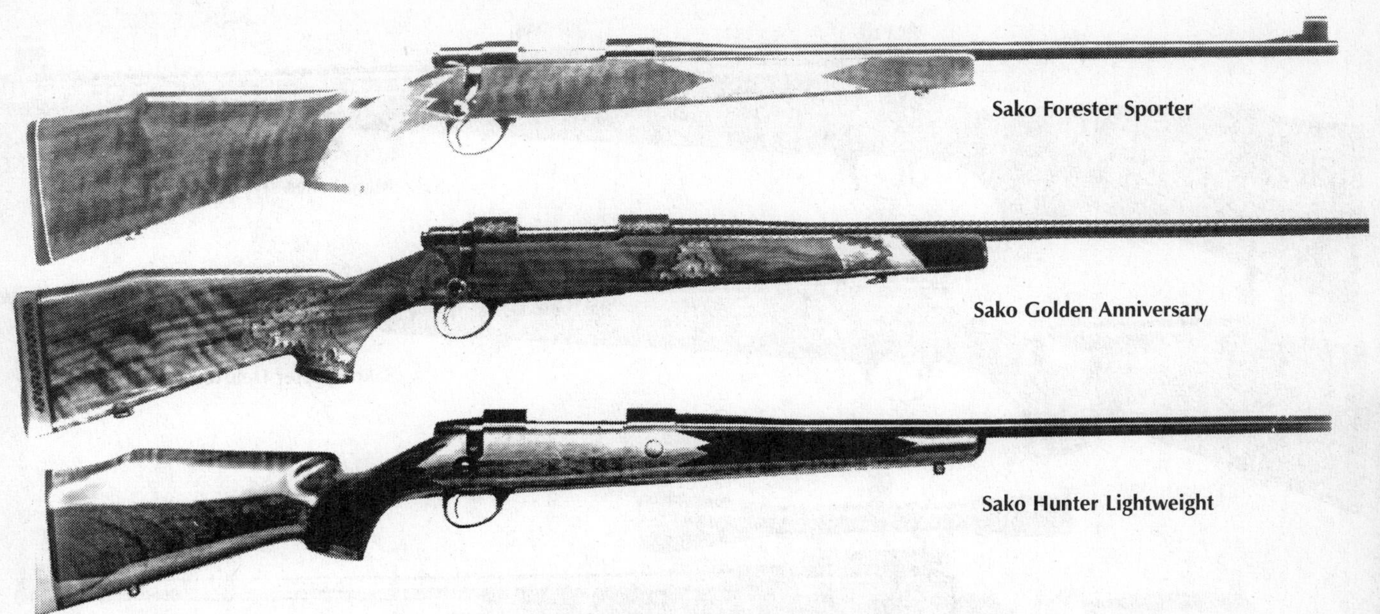

FINSPORT 2700 .... **NiB $890 Ex $736 Gd $478**
Bolt-action centerfire rifle. Calibers: .270, .30-06, 7mm Rem. Mag., .300 Win. Mag. Bbl. length: 24 inches. Weight: 8 lbs. Imported 1984-86.

FORESTER CARBINE .... **NiB $1096 Ex $968 Gd $504**
Same as Forester Sporter except w/20-inch bbl., Mannlicher-type full stock. Imported 1958-71.

FORESTER HEAVY BARREL ...... **NiB $1045 Ex $942 Gd $453**
Same as Forester Sporter except w/24-inch heavy bbl. Weight 7.5 lbs. Imported 1958-71.

FORESTER SPORTER .... **NiB $1148 Ex $968 Gd $478**
Medium-length Mauser-type bolt action. Calibers: .22-250, .243 Win., .308 Win. Five round magazine. 23-inch bbl. Weight: 6.5 lbs. Hooded ramp front sight. Sporter stock w/Monte Carlo cheekpiece, checkered pistol grip and forearm, swivels. Imported 1957-71.

GOLDEN ANNIVERSARY MODEL .... **NiB $2688 Ex $2054 Gd $1369**
Special presentation-grade rifle issued in 1973 to commemorate Sako's 50th anniversary. 1,000 (numbered 1 to 1,000) made. Same specifications as Deluxe Sporter: Long action, 7mm Rem. Mag. receiver, trigger guard and floorplate decorated w/gold oak leaf and acorn motif. Stock of select European walnut, checkering bordered w/hand-carved oak leaf pattern.

HIGH-POWER MAUSER SPORTING RIFLE...... **NiB $1060 Ex $957 Gd $751**
FN Mauser action. Calibers: .270, .30-06. Five round magazine. 24-inch bbl. Sights: Open rear leaf; Partridge front; hooded ramp. Checkered stock w/Monte Carlo comb and cheekpiece. Weight: 7.5 lbs. Imported 1950-57.

HUNTER LIGHTWEIGHT BOLT-ACTION RIFLE
5- or 6-round magazine. Bbl. length: 21.5 inches, AI; 22 inches, AII; 22.5 inches, AIII. Overall length: 42.25-44.5 inches. Weight: 5.75 lbs., AI; 6.75 lbs. AII; 7.25 lbs., AIII. Monte Carlo-style European walnut stock, oil finished. Hand-checkered pistol-grip and forend. Imported 1985-97. Left-hand version intro. 1987.
AI (Short Action) .17 Rem. .... **NiB $1019 Ex $737 Gd $530**
.222 Rem., .223 Rem. .... **NiB $993 Ex $762 Gd $530**
AII (medium action)
.22-250 Rem., .243 Win., .308 Win. ...... **NiB $890 Ex $736 Gd $478**

(cont'd.) **HUNTER LIGHTWEIGHT BOLT-ACTION RIFLE**
AII1 (long action) .25-06 Rem.,
.270 Win., .30-06 .... **NiB $948 Ex $762 Gd $523**
.338 Win. Mag. .... **NiB $1085 Ex $885 Gd $630**
.375 H&H Mag. .... **NiB $1182 Ex $963 Gd $682**
Left-hand model (standard cal.) .... **NiB $1212 Ex $973 Gd $666**
Magnum calibers.................. **NiB $1470 Ex $1194 Gd $842**

LAMINATED STOCK BOLT-ACTION RIFLES
Similar in style and specifications to Hunter Grade except w/stock of resin-bonded hardwood veneers. Available 18 calibers in AI (Short), AII (Medium) or AV action, left-hand version in 10 calibers, AV only. Imported 1987-95.
Short or medium action .... **NiB $993 Ex $813 Gd $530**
Long action/Magnum .... **NiB $1019 Ex $839 Gd $556**

MAGNUM MAUSER .... **NiB $1466 Ex $1157 Gd $822**
Similar specifications as Standard Model except w/recoil pad and redesigned longer AIII action to handle longer magnum cartridges. Calibers: .300 H&H Magnum, .375 H&H Magnum, standard at time of introduction. Disc.

MANNLICHER-STYLE CARBINE
Similar to Hunter Model except w/full Mannlicher-style stock and 18.5-inch bbl. Weighs 7.5 lbs. Chambered in .243, .25-06, .270, .308, .30-06, 7mm Rem. Mag., .300 Win. Mag., .338 Win. Mag., .375 H&H. Intro. in 1977. Disc.
Standard calibers .... **NiB $1208 Ex $925 Gd $590**
Magnum calibers (except .375)......... **NiB $1234 Ex $951 Gd $632**
.375 H&H .... **NiB $1250 Ex $977 Gd $668**

SAFARI GRADE .... **NiB $2425 Ex $1863 Gd $1034**
Classic bolt-action. Calibers: .300 Win. Mag., .338 Win. Mag., .375 H&H. Oil-finished European walnut stock w/hand-checkering. Barrel band swivel, express-type sight rib; satin or matte blue finish. Imported 1980-96.

SPORTER DELUXE............. **NiB $1204 Ex $921 Gd $586**
Same as Vixen, Forester, Finnbear and Model 74 except w/fancy French walnut stock w/skip checkering, rosewood forend tip and pistol-grip cap, recoil pad, inlaid trigger guard and floorplate. Disc.

Sako Mannlicher-Style Carbine

Sako Sporter Deluxe

Sako TRG-21 Target Rifle

STANDARD GRADE AI . . . . NiB $996 Ex $713 Gd $378
Short bolt-action. Calibers: .17 Rem., .222 Rem., .223 Rem. Five round magazine. 23.5-inch bbl. Weight: 6.5 lbs. No sights. Checkered European walnut stock w/Monte Carlo cheekpiece, QD swivel studs. Imported 1978-85.

STANDARD GRADE AII. . . . . NiB $1007 Ex $729 Gd $404
Medium bolt-action. Calibers: .22-250 Rem., .243 Win., .308 Win. 23.5-inch bbl. in .22-250; 23-inch bbl. in other calibers. Five round magazine. Weight: 7.25 lbs. Checkered European walnut stock w/Monte Carlo cheekpiece, QD swivel studs. Imported 1978-85.

STANDARD GRADE AIII . . . . NiB $1043 Ex $765 Gd $456
Long bolt action. Calibers: .25-06 Rem., .270 Win., .30-06, 7mm Rem. Mag., .300 Win. Mag., .338 Win. Mag., .375 H&H. 24-inch bbl. 4-round magazine. Weight: 8 lbs. Imported 1978-84.

SUPER DELUXE RIFLE . . . . NiB $2335 Ex $2052 Gd $1202
Available in AI, AII, AIII calibers. Select European walnut stock, hand-checkered, deep oak leaf hand-engraved design. Disc.

TRG-BOLT-ACTION TARGET RIFLE
Caliber: .308 Win., .330 Win. or .338 Lapua Mag. Detachable 10-round magazine. 25.75- or 27.2-inch bbl. Weight: 10.5 to 11 lbs. Blued action w/stainless barrel. Adjustable two-stage trigger. modular reinforced polyurethane target stock w/adj. cheekpiece and buttplate. Options: Muzzle break; detachable bipod; QD sling swivels and scope mounts w/1-inch or 30mm rings. Imported 1993 to date.

(cont'd.) **TRG-BOLT-ACTION TARGET RIFLE**
TRG-21 .308 Win . . . . NiB $2600 Ex $2075 Gd $1415
TRG-22 .308 Win. . . . . NiB $2665 Ex $2136 Gd $1461
TRG-41 .338 Lapua. . . . . NiB $3109 Ex $2492 Gd $1703
TRG-42 .300 Win. or .338 Lapua . . . . . NiB $3180 Ex $2557 Gd $1741

TRG-S BOLT-ACTION RIFLE
Calibers: .243, 7mm-08, .270, .30-06, 7mm Rem. Mag., .300 Win. Mag., .338 Win. Mag. Five shot magazine (standard calibers), 4-shot (magnum), 22- or 24-inch bbl. 45.5 inches overall. Weight: 7.75 lbs. No sights. Reinforced polyurethane stock w/Monte Carlo. Intro. in 1993.
Standard calibers. . . . . NiB $736 Ex $659 Gd $401
Magnum calibers. . . . . NiB $781 Ex $628 Gd $432

VIXEN CARBINE . . . . NiB $1103 Ex $975 Gd $846
Same as Vixen Sporter except w/20-inch bbl., Mannlicher-type full stock. Imported 1947-71.

VIXEN HEAVY BARREL . . . . NiB $1052 Ex $846 Gd $470
Same as Vixen Sporter except calibers .222 Rem., .222 Rem. Mag., .223 Rem., heavy bbl., target-style stock w/beavertail forearm. Weight: 7.5 lbs. Imported 1947-71.

VIXEN SPORTER . . . . NiB $1103 Ex $1000 Gd $485
Short Mauser-type bolt-action. Cals.: .218 Bee, .22 Hornet, .222 Rem., .222 Rem. Mag., .223 Rem. Five round magazine. 23.5-inch bbl. Weight: 6.5 lbs. Hooded ramp front sight. Sporter stock w/Monte Carlo cheekpiece, checkered pistol-grip and forearm, swivels. Imported 1946-71.

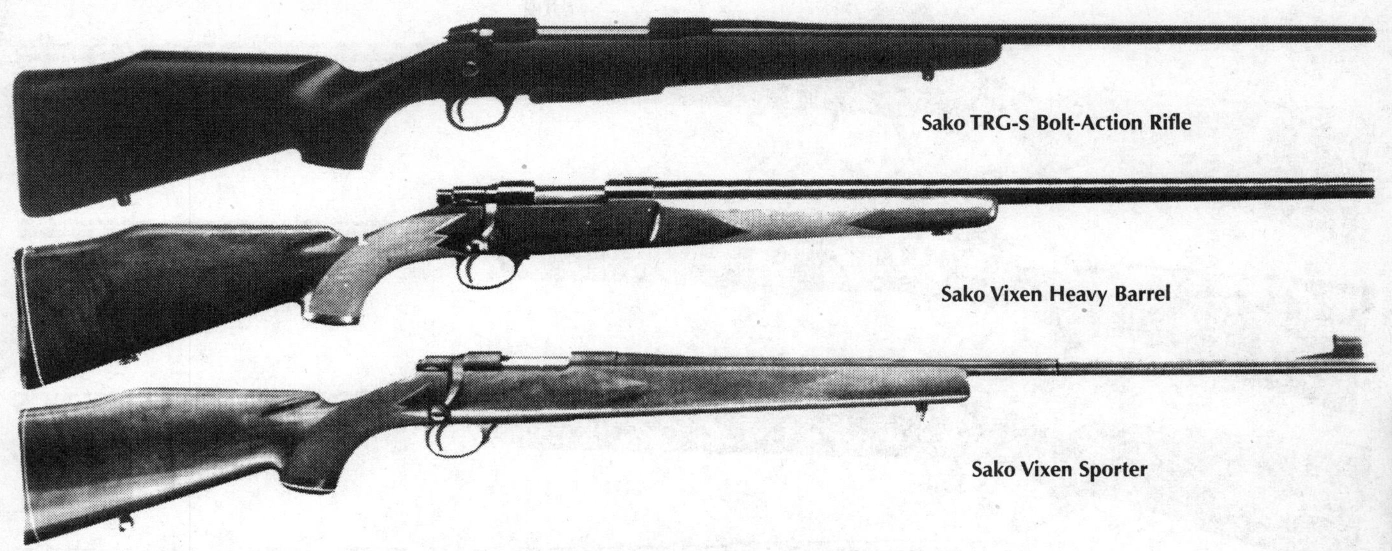
Sako TRG-S Bolt-Action Rifle

Sako Vixen Heavy Barrel

Sako Vixen Sporter

J. P. SAUER & SOHN — Eckernforde, Germany, (Formerly Suhl, Germany), Imported by Sigarms Exeter, NH , (Previously by Paul Company Inc. and G.U. Inc.)

MAUSER BOLT-ACTION SPORTING RIFLE .... **NiB $1287 Ex $1020 Gd $695**
Calibers: 7x57 and 8x57mm most common, but these rifles were produced in a variety of calibers including most of the popular Continental calibers as well as our .30-06. Five round box magazine. 22- or 24-inch Krupp steel bbl., half-octagon w/raised matted rib. Double-set trigger. Weight: 7.5 lbs. Sights: Three-leaf open rear; ramp front. Sporting stock w/cheekpiece, checkered pistol grip, raised side-panels, Schnabel tip, swivels. Also made w/20-inch bbl. and full-length stock. Mfd. before WWII.

MODEL S-90 BOLT-ACTION RIFLES
Calibers: .243 Win., .308 Win. (Short action); .25-06, .270 Win., .30-06 (Medium action); 7mm Rem. Mag., .300 Win. Mag., .300 Wby., .338 Win., .375 H&H (Magnum action). Four round (standard) or 3-round magazine (magnum). Bbl. length: 20-inch (Stutzen), 24-inch. Weight: 7.6 to 10.75 lbs. Adjustable (Supreme) checkered Monte Carlo style stock. contrasting forend and pistol grip cap w/high-gloss finish or European (Lux) checkered Classic-style European walnut stock w/satin oil finish. Imported 1983-89.
S-90 Standard .... **NiB $1050 Ex $921 Gd $509**
S-90 Lux .... **NiB $1256 Ex $998 Gd $535**
S-90 Safari .... **NiB $1230 Ex $973 Gd $535**
S-90 Stutzen .... **NiB $1050 Ex $921 Gd $509**
S-90 Supreme .... **NiB $1359 Ex $1101 Gd $741**
Grade I engraving, add **$600**
Grade II engraving, add **$800**
Grade III engraving add **$1000**
Grade IV engraving, add **$1500**

MODEL 200 BOLT-ACTION RIFLES
Calibers: .243 Win., .25-06, .270 Win., 7mm Rem Mag., .30-06, .308 Win., .300 Win. Mag., Detachable box magazine. 24-inch (American) or 26-inch (European) interchangeable bbl. Standard (steel) or lightweight (alloy) action. Weight: 6.6 to 7.75 lbs. 44 inches overall. Stock options: American Model w/checkered Monte Carlo style 2-piece stock contrasting forend and pistol grip cap w/high gloss finish and no sights. European walnut stock w/Schnabel forend, satin oil finish and iron sights. Contemporary Model w/synthetic carbon fiber stock. Imported 1986-93.
Standard model .... **NiB $1282 Ex $972 Gd $612**

(cont'd.) **MODEL 200 BOLT-ACTION RIFLES**
Lightweight model .... **NiB $1055 Ex $926 Gd $514**
Contemporary model .... **NiB $1178 Ex $978 Gd $566**
American model .... **NiB $1261 Ex $1003 Gd $566**
European model .... **NiB $1287 Ex $1029 Gd $591**
Left-hand model, add **$125**
Magnum calibers, add **$115**
Interchangeable barrel assembly, add **$295**

MODEL 202 BOLT-ACTION RIFLES
Calibers: .243 Win., 6.5x55, 6.5x57, 6.6x68, .25-06, .270 Win., .280 7x64, .308, .30-06, Springfield, 7mm Rem. Mag., .300 Win. Mag., .300 Wby. Mag., 8x68S, .338 Win. Mag., .375 H&H Mag. Removable 3-round box magazine. 23.6- and 26-inch interchangable bbl. 44.3 and 46 inches overall. Modular receiver drilled and tapped for scope bases. Adjustable two-stage trigger w/dual release safety. Weight: 7.7 to 8.4 lbs. Stock options: Checkered Monte Carlo-style select American walnut two-piece stock; Euro-classic French walnut two-piece stock w/semi Schnabel forend and satin oil finish; Super Grade Claro walnut two-piece stock fitted w/rosewood forend and grip cap w/high-gloss epoxy finish. Imported 1994 to date.
Standard model .... **NiB $1209 Ex $772 Gd $514**
Euro-Classic model .... **NiB $1251 Ex $797 Gd $514**
Super Grade model .... **NiB $1261 Ex $823 Gd $540**
Left-hand model, add **$150**
Magnum calibers, add **$125**
Interchangeable barrel assembly, add **$295**

SAVAGE INDUSTRIES — Westfield, Massachusetts, (Formerly Chicopee Falls, MA and Utica, NY)

MODEL 3 BOLT-ACTION SINGLE-SHOT RIFLE .... **NiB $162 Ex $137 Gd $85**
Takedown. Caliber: .22 Short, Long, LR. 26-inch bbl. on prewar rifles, postwar production w/24-inch bbl. Weight: 5 lbs. Sights: Open rear; bead front. Plain pistol-grip stock. Made 1933-52.

MODEL 3S .... **NiB $198 Ex $162 Gd $101**
Same as Model 3 except w/peep rear sight, hooded front. Made 1933-42.

MODEL 3ST .... **NiB $204 Ex $188 Gd $106**
Same as Model 3S except fitted w/swivels and sling. Made 1933-42.

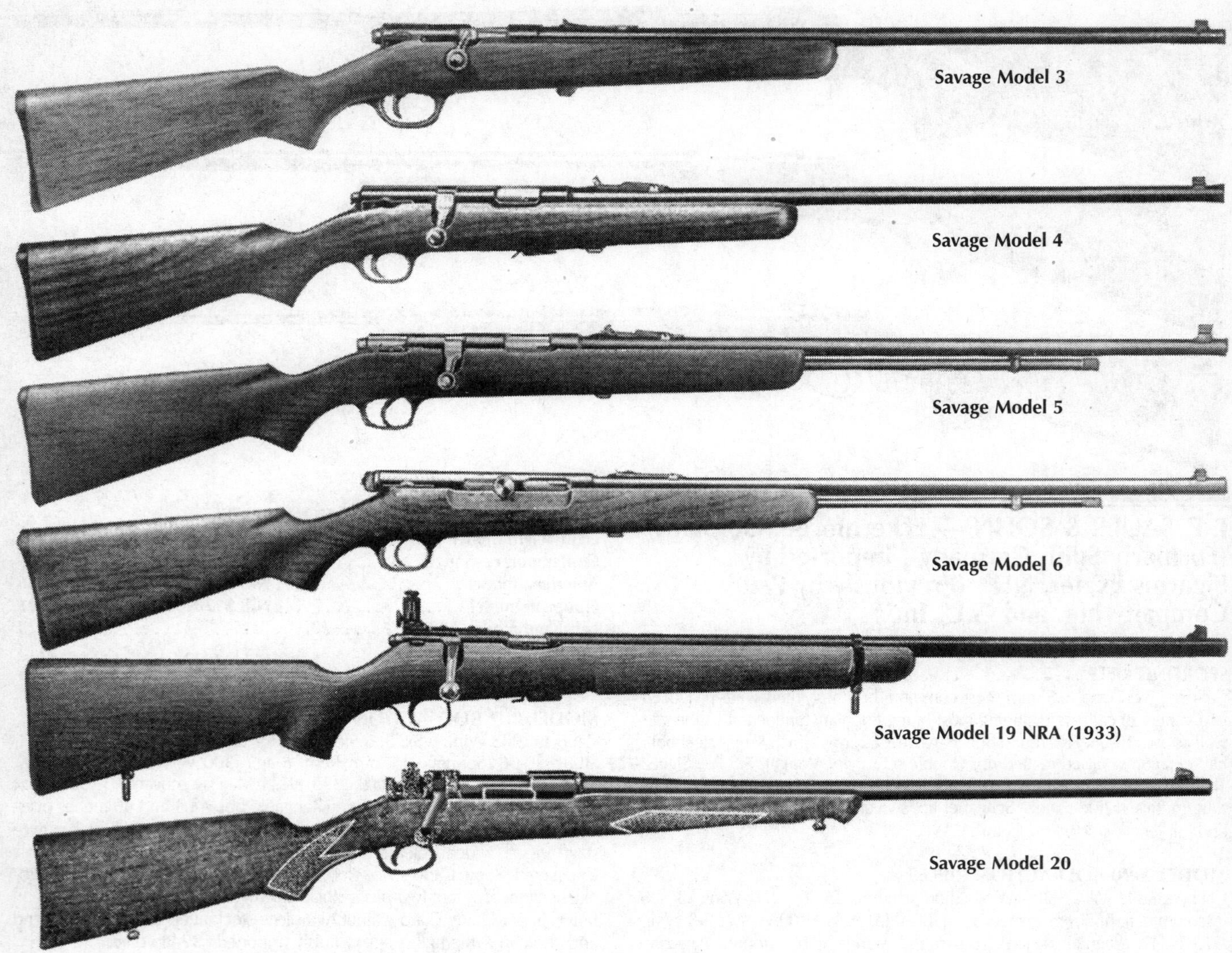
Savage Model 3

Savage Model 4

Savage Model 5

Savage Model 6

Savage Model 19 NRA (1933)

Savage Model 20

MODEL 4 BOLT-ACTION REPEATER. . . . . NiB $188 Ex $147 Gd $106
Takedown. Caliber: .22 Short, Long, LR. Five round detachable box magazine. 24-inch bbl. Weight: 5.5 lbs. Sights: Open rear; bead front. Checkered pistol-grip stock on prewar models, early production had grooved forearm; postwar rifles have plain stocks. Made 1933-65.

MODEL 4M . . . . NiB $162 Ex $96 Gd $80
Same as Model 4 except chambered for .22 Rimfire Magnum. Made 1961-65.

MODEL 4S. NiB $204 Ex $106 Gd $85
Same as Model 4 except w/peep rear sight, hooded front. Made 1933-42.

MODEL 5 BOLT-ACTION REPEATER . . . . NiB $188 Ex $106 Gd $85
Same as Model 4 except w/tubular magazine (holds 21 Short, 17 Long, 15 LR), weight: 6 lbs. Made 1936-61.

MODEL 5S. . . . . NiB $188 Ex $152 Gd $106
Same as Model 5 except w/peep rear sight, hooded front. Made 1936-42.

MODEL 6 AUTOLOADING RIFLE. . . . . . . NiB $188 Ex $162 Gd $111
Takedown. Caliber: .22 Short, Long, LR. Tubular magazine holds 21 Short, 17 Long, 15 LR. 24-inch bbl. Weight: 6 lbs. Sights: Open rear; bead front. Checkered pistol-grip stock on prewar models, postwar rifles have plain stocks. Made 1938-68.

MODEL 6S. . . . . NiB $204 Ex $173 Gd $116
Same as Model 6 except w/peep rear sight, bead front. Made 1938-42.

MODEL 7 AUTOLOADING RIFLE. . . . . . . NiB $214 Ex $188 Gd $121
Same general specifications as Model 6 except w/5-round detachable box magazine. Made 1939-51.

MODEL 7S. . . . . NiB $193 Ex $132 Gd $111
Same as Model 7 except w/peep rear sight, hooded front. Made 1938-42.

MODEL 19 BOLT-ACTION TARGET RIFLE. . . . NiB $370 Ex $267 Gd $164
Model of 1933. Speed lock. Caliber: .22-LR. Five round detachable box magazine. 25-inch bbl. Weight: 8 lbs. Adj. rear peep sight, blade front on early models, later production equipped w/extension rear sight, hooded front. Target stock w/full pistol-grip and beavertail forearm. Made 1933-46.

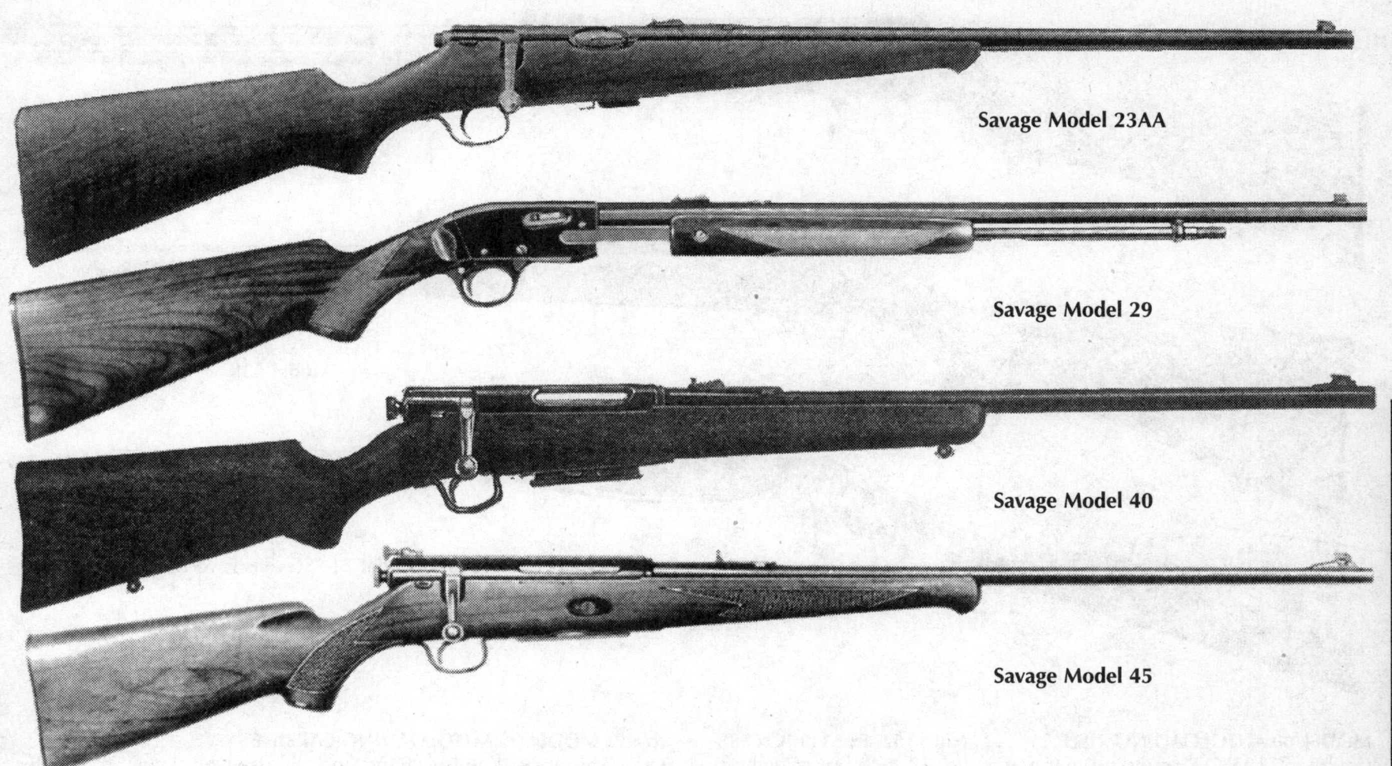
Savage Model 23AA

Savage Model 29

Savage Model 40

Savage Model 45

MODEL 19 NRA BOLT-ACTION MATCH RIFLE . . . . NiB $530 Ex $478 Gd $247
Model of 1919. Caliber: .22 LR. Five round detachable box magazine. 25-inch bbl. Weight: 7lbs. Sights: Adj. rear peep; blade front. Full military stock w/pistol-grip. Made 1919-33.

MODEL 19H . . . . NiB $607 Ex $504 Gd $324
Same as standard Model 19 (1933) except chambered for .22 Hornet, w/Model 23D-type bolt mechanism, loading port and magazine. Made 1933-42.

MODEL 19L. . . . . NiB $370 Ex $267 Gd $164
Same as standard Model 19 (1933) except equipped w/Lyman No. 48Y receiver sight, 17A front sight. Made 1933-42.

MODEL 19M . . . . NiB $478 Ex $427 Gd $195
Same as standard Model 19 (1933) except w/heavy 28-inch bbl. w/scope bases, weight: 9.25 lbs. Made 1933-42.

MODEL 20-1926 HI-POWER . . . . NiB $478 Ex $375 Gd $272
Same as Model 1920 except w/24-inch medium weight bbl., improved stock, Lyman 54 rear peep sight, weight: 7 lbs. Made 1926-29.

MODEL 23A BOLT-ACTION SPORTING RIFLE. . . . . NiB $257 Ex $180 Gd $144
Caliber: 22 LR. Five round detachable box magazine. 23-inch bbl. Weight: 6 lbs. Sights: Open rear, blade or bead front. Plain pistol-grip stock w/slender forearm and Schnabel tip. Made 1923-33.

MODEL 23AA . . . . NiB $314 Ex $267 Gd $175
Model of 1933. Improved version of Model 23A w/same general specifications except w/speed lock, improved stock, weighs 6.5 lbs. Made 1933-42.

MODEL 23B . . . . NiB $293 Ex $190 Gd $139
Same as Model 23A except caliber .25-20, 25-inch bbl. Model of 1933 w/improved stock w/full forearm instead of slender forearm w/Schnabel found on earlier production. Weight: 6.5 lbs. Made 1923-42.

MODEL 23C . . . . NiB $319 Ex $237 Gd $144
Same as Model 23B except caliber .32-20. Made 1923-42.

MODEL 23D . . . . NiB $396 Ex $267 Gd $190
Same as Model 23B except caliber .22 Hornet. Made 1933-47.

MODEL 25 SLIDE-ACTION REPEATER . . . . NiB $530 Ex $375 Gd $221
Takedown. Hammerless. Caliber: .22 Short, Long, LR. Tubular magazine holds 20 Short, 17 Long, 15 LR. 24-inch octagon bbl. Weight: 5.75 lbs. Sights: Open rear; blade front. Plain pistol-grip stock, grooved slide handle. Made 1925-29.

MODEL 29 SLIDE-ACTION REPEATER . . . . NiB $453 Ex $324 Gd $221
Takedown. Hammerless. Caliber: .22 Short, Long, LR. Tubular magazine holds 20 Short, 17 Long, 15 LR. 24-inch bbl., octagon on prewar, round on postwar production. Weight: 5.5 lbs. Sights: Open rear; bead front. Stock w/checkered pistol grip and slide handle on prewar, plain stock and grooved forearm on postwar production. Made 1929-67.

MODEL 40 BOLT-ACTION SPORTING RIFLE. . . . . NiB $396 Ex $242 Gd $195
Standard Grade. Calibers: .250-3000, .300 Sav., .30-30, .30-06. Four round detachable box magazine. 22-inch bbl. in calibers .250-3000 and .30-30; 24-inch in .300 Sav. and .30-06. Weight: 7.5 lbs. Sights: Open rear; bead front, on ramp. Plain pistol-grip stock w/tapered forearm and Schnabel tip. Made 1928-40.

MODEL 45 SUPER SPORTER. . . . . NiB $556 Ex $422 Gd $272
Special Grade. Same as Model 40 except w/checkered pistol-grip and forearm, Lyman No. 40 receiver sight. Made 1928-40.

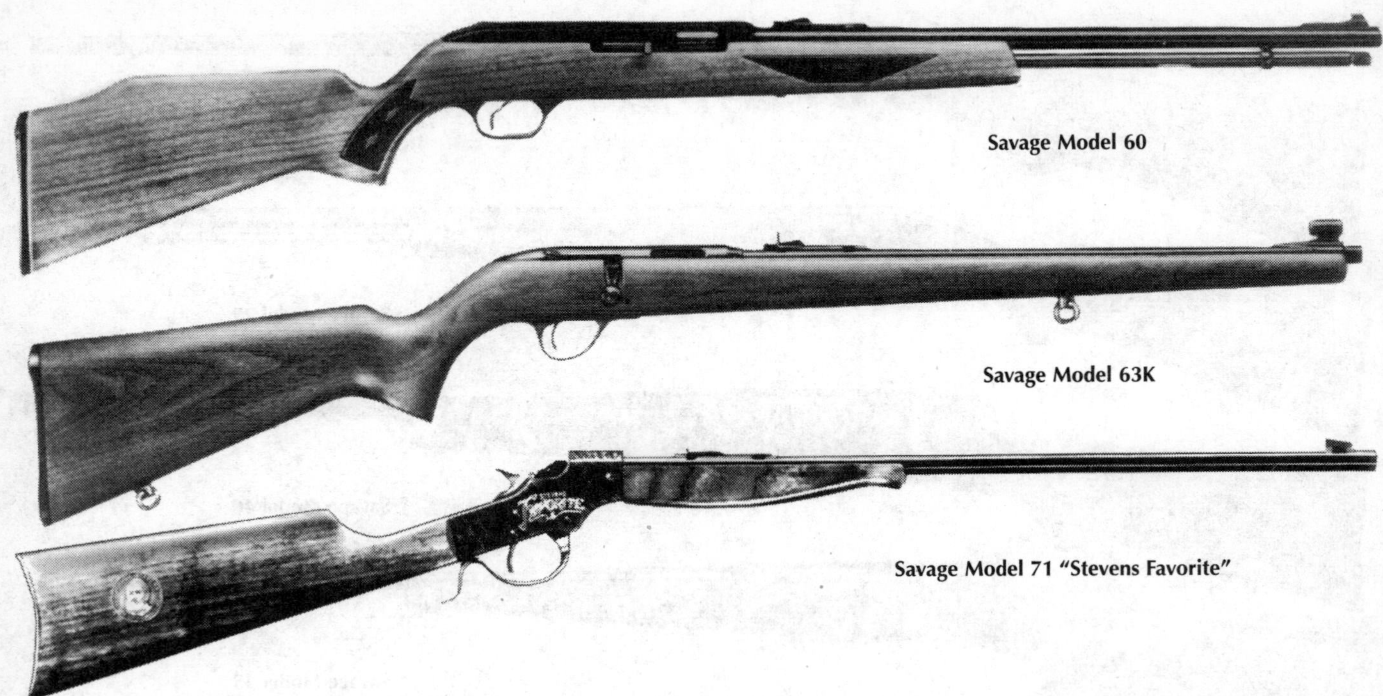

Savage Model 60

Savage Model 63K

Savage Model 71 "Stevens Favorite"

MODEL 60 AUTOLOADING RIFLE....... NiB $162 Ex $111 Gd $88
Caliber: .22 LR. 15-round tubular magazine. 20-inch bbl. Weight: 6 lbs. Sights: Open rear, ramp front. Monte Carlo stock of walnut w/checkered pistol-grip and forearm. Made 1969-72.

MODEL 63K KEY LOCK BOLT-ACTION SINGLE-SHOT RIFLE............. NiB $111 Ex $80 Gd $59
Trigger locked w/key. Caliber: .22 Short, Long, LR. 18-inch bbl. Weight: 4 lbs. Sights: Open rear; hooded ramp front. Full-length stock w/pistol grip, swivels. Made 1970-72.

MODEL 63KM.................. NiB $126 Ex $85 Gd $70
Same as Model 63K except chambered for .22 WMR. Made 1970-72.

MODEL 64F AUTOLOADING RIFLE........ NiB $111 Ex $85 Gd $70
Same general specifications as Model 64G except w/black graphite/polymer stock. Weight: 5 lbs. Made 1997 to date.

MODEL 64G AUTOLOADING RIFLE ...... NiB $121 Ex $101 Gd $80
Caliber: 22 LR. 10-round magazine. 20-inch bbl. Weight: 5.5 lbs. 40 inches overall. Sights: Adj. open rear; bead front. Grooved receiver for scope mounts. Stamped checkering on walnut-finished hardwood stock w/Monte Carlo cheekpiece. Made 1996 to date.

MODEL 71 "STEVENS FAVORITE" SINGLE-SHOT LEVER-ACTION RIFLE..... NiB $265 Ex $188 Gd $137
Replica of original Stevens Favorite issued as a tribute to Joshua Stevens, "Father of .22 Hunting." Caliber: .22 LR. 22-inch full-octagon bbl. Brass-plated hammer and lever. Sights: Open rear; brass blade front. Weight: 4.5 lbs. Plain straight-grip buttstock and Schnabel forend; brass commemorative medallion inlaid in buttstock, brass crescent-shaped buttplate. 10,000 produced. Made in 1971 only. Top value is for new, unfired gun.

MODEL 90 AUTO-LOADING CARBINE........................... NiB $162 Ex $132 Gd $92
Similar to Model 60 except w/16.5-inch bbl. w/folding leaf rear sight, bead front. 10-round tubular magazine. Uncheckered, carbine-style walnut stock w/bbl. Band and sling swivels. Weight: 5.75 lbs. Made 1969-72.

MODEL 93G BOLT-ACTION RIFLE....... NiB $162 Ex $137 Gd $101
Caliber: .22 Win Mag. 5-round magazine. 20.75-inch bbl. 39.5 inches overall. Weight: 5.75 lbs. Sights: Adj. open rear; bead front. Grooved receiver for scope mounts. Stamped checkering on walnut-finished hardwood stock w/Monte Carlo cheekpiece. Made 1996 to date.

MODEL 93F BOLT-ACTION RIFLE .... NiB $137 Ex $90 Gd $85
Same general specifications as Model 93G except w/black graphite/polymer stock. Weight: 5.2 lbs. Made 1997 to date.

NOTE: MODEL 99 LEVER-ACTION REPEATER
Introduced in 1899, this model has been produced in a variety of styles and calibers. Original designation "Model 1899" was changed to "Model 99" c.1920. Earlier rifles and carbines — similar to Models 99A, 99B and 99H — were supplied in calibers .25-35, .30-30, .303 Sav., .32-40 and .38-55. Post-WWII Models 99A, 99C, 99CD, 99DE, 99DL, 99F and 99PE have top tang safety other 99s have slide safety on right side of trigger guard. Models 99C and 99CD have detachable box magazine instead of traditional Model 99 rotary magazine.

MODEL 99A (I)................. NiB $895 Ex $689 Gd $303
Hammerless. Solid frame. Calibers: .30-30, .300 Sav., .303 Sav. Five-round rotary magazine. 24-inch bbl. Weight: 7.25 lbs. Sights: Open rear; bead front, on ramp. Plain straight-grip stock, tapered forearm. Made 1920-36.

MODEL 99A (II) .... NiB $844 Ex $792 Gd $483
Current model. Similar to original Model 99A except w/top tang safety, 22-inch bbl., folding leaf rear sight, no crescent buttplate. Calibers: .243 Win., .250 Sav., .300 Sav., .308 Win. Made 1971-82.

MODEL 99B .... NiB $1045 Ex $839 Gd $509
Takedown. Otherwise same as Model 99A except weight: 7.5 lbs. Made 1920-36.

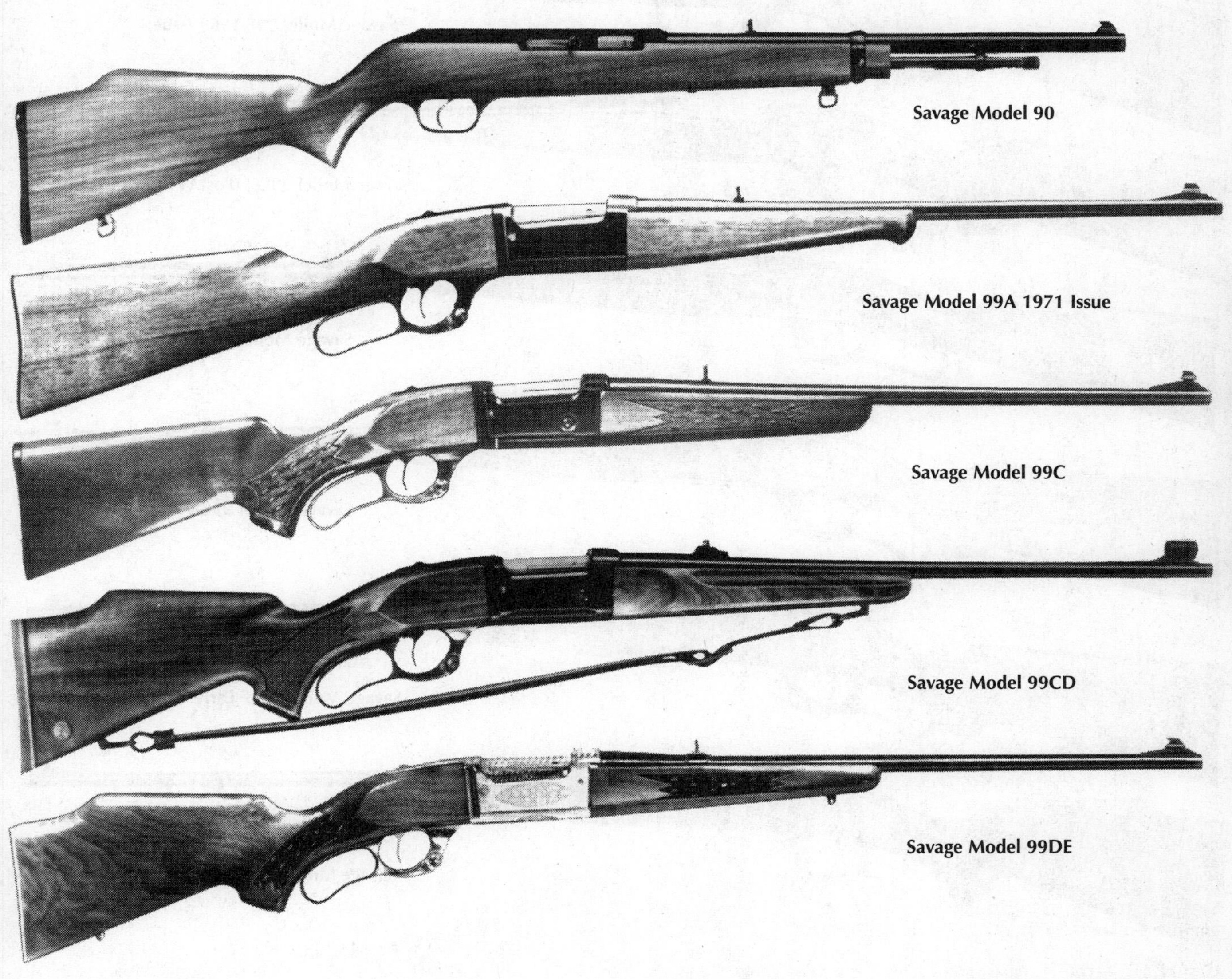

Savage Model 90

Savage Model 99A 1971 Issue

Savage Model 99C

Savage Model 99CD

Savage Model 99DE

MODEL 99C .... NiB $1045 Ex $947 Gd $329
Current model. Same as Model 99F except w/clip magazine instead of rotary. Calibers: .243 Win., .284 Win., .308 Win. Four round detachable magazine holds one round less in .284. Weight: 6.75 lbs. Made 1965 to date.

MODEL 99CD .... NiB $633 Ex $556 Gd $324
Deluxe version of Model 99C. Calibers: .243 Win., .250 Sav., .308 Win. Hooded ramp front sight. Weight: 8.25 lbs. Stock w/Monte Carlo comb and cheekpiece, checkered pistol-grip, grooved fore-arm, swivels and sling. Made 1975 to 81.

MODEL 99DE CITATION GRADE........ NiB $890 Ex $607 Gd $427
Same as Model 99PE except w/less elaborate engraving. Made 1968-70.

MODEL 99DL DELUXE .... NiB $427 Ex $324 Gd $221
Postwar model. Calibers: .243 Win., .308 Win. Same as Model 99F, except w/high comb Monte Carlo stock, sling swivels. Weight: 6.75 lbs. Made 1960-73.

MODEL 99E CARBINE (I) .... NiB $787 Ex $633 Gd $350
Pre-WWII type. Solid frame. Calibers: .22 Hi-Power, .250/3000, .30/30, .300 Sav., .303 Sav. w/22-inch bbl.; .300 Sav. 24-inch. Weight: 7 lbs. Other specifications same as Model 99A. Made 1920-36.

MODEL 99E CARBINE (II)........ NiB $417 Ex $283 Gd $169
Current model. Solid frame. Calibers: .250 Sav., .243 Win., .300 Sav., .308 Win. 20- or 22-inch bbl. Checkered pistol-grip stock and forearm. Made 1960-89.

Savage Model 99E 1969 Issue

Savage Model 99EG (Post WWII)

Savage Model 99F

Savage Model 99G

Savage Model 99PE Early Issue

Savage Model 99PE Late Issue

MODEL 99EG (I) . . . . NiB $823 Ex $689 Gd $406
Pre-WWII type. Solid frame. Plain pistol-grip stock and forearm. Otherwise same as Model G. Made 1936-41.

MODEL 99EG (II) . . . . NiB $638 Ex $432 Gd $329
Post-WWII type. Same as prewar model except w/checkered stock and forearm. Calibers: .250 Sav., .300 Sav., .308 Win. (intro. 1955), .243 Win., and .358 Win. Made 1946-60.

MODEL 99F FEATHERWEIGHT (I) . . . . NiB $895 Ex $638 Gd $447
Pre-WWII type. Takedown. Specifications same as Model 99E, except weight: 6.5 lbs. Made 1920-42.

MODEL 99F FEATHERWEIGHT (II). . . . . NiB $581 Ex $375 Gd $221
Postwar model. Solid frame. Calibers: .243 Win., .300 Sav., .308 Win. 22-inch bbl. Checkered pistol-grip stock and forearm. Weight: 6.5 lbs. Made 1955-73.

MODEL 99G . . . . NiB $895 Ex $6338 Gd $447
Takedown. Checkered pistol-grip stock and forearm. Weight: 7.25 lbs. Other specifications same as Model 99E. Made 1920-42.

MODEL 99H CARBINE . . . . NiB $834 Ex $525 Gd $370
Solid frame. Calibers: .250/3000, .30/30, .303 Sav. 20-inch special weight bbl. Walnut carbine stock w/metal buttplate; walnut forearm w/bbl. band. Weight: 6.5 lbs. Open rear sights; ramped blade front sight. Other specifications same as Model 99A. Made 1931-42.

MODEL 99K . . . . NiB $2301 Ex $1966 Gd $1055
Deluxe version of Model G w/similar specifications except w/fancy stock and engraving on receiver and bbl. Lyman peep rear sight and folding middle. Made 1931-42.

MODEL 99PE PRESENTATION GRADE . . . NiB $1879 Ex $1621 Gd $746
Same as Model 99DL except w/engraved receiver (game scenes on sides), tang and lever, fancy walnut Monte Carlo stock and forearm w/hand checkering, QD swivels. Calibers: .243, .284, .308. Made 1968-70.

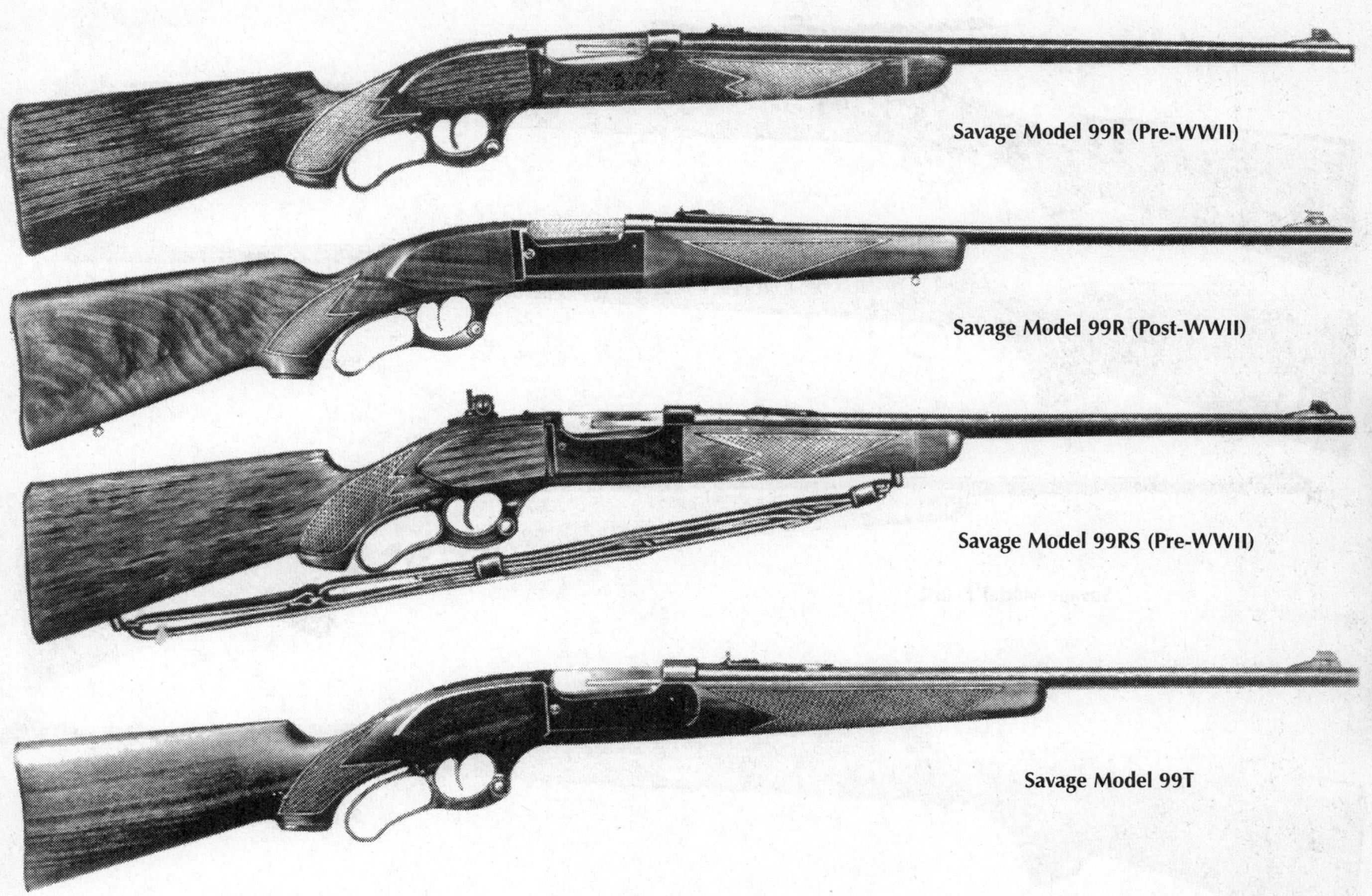

Savage Model 99R (Pre-WWII)

Savage Model 99R (Post-WWII)

Savage Model 99RS (Pre-WWII)

Savage Model 99T

MODEL 99R (I) . . . . NiB $890 Ex $633 Gd $453
Pre-WWII type. Solid frame. Calibers: .250-3000 (22-inch bbl.), .300 Sav. (24-inch bbl.). Weight: 7.5 lbs. Special large pistol-grip stock and forearm, checkered. General specifications same as other Model 99 rifles. Made 1936-42.

MODEL 99R (II) . . . . NiB $818 Ex $427 Gd $298
Post-WWII type. Same as prewar mod except w/24-inch bbl. only, w/screw eyes for sling swivels. Calibers: .250 Sav., .300 Sav., .308 Win., .243 Win. and .358 Win. Made 1946-60.

MODEL 99RS (I) . . . . NiB $813 Ex $556 Gd $427
Pre-WWII type. Same as prewar Model 99R except equipped w/Lyman rear peep sight and folding middle sight, quick detachable swivels and sling. Made 1936-42.

MODEL 99RS (II). . . . . NiB $813 Ex $530 Gd $401
Post-WWII type. Same as postwar Model 99RS except equipped w/Redfield 70LH receiver sight, blank in middle sight slot. Made 1946-58.

MODEL 99T . . . . NiB $818 Ex $453 Gd $339
Featherweight. Solid frame. Calibers: .22 Hi-Power, .30/30, .303 Sav. w/20-inch bbl.; .300 Sav. w/22-inch bbl. Checkered pistol-grip stock and beavertail forearm. Weight: 7 lbs. General specifications same as other Model 99 rifles. Made 1936-42.

MODEL 99-358 . . . . NiB $576 Ex $422 Gd $319
Similar to current Model 99A except caliber .358 Win. has grooved forearm, recoil pad, swivel studs. Made 1977-80.

MODEL 110 SPORTER BOLT-ACTION RIFLE. . . . . NiB $226 Ex $164 Gd $113
Calibers: .243, .270, .308, .30-06. Four round box magazine. 22-inch bbl. Weight: About 6.75 lbs. Sights: Open rear; ramp front. Standard sporter stock with checkered pistol-grip. Made 1958-63.

MODEL 110B BOLT-ACTION RIFLE
Same as Model 110E except with checkered select walnut Monte Carlo-style stock (early models) or brown laminated stock (late models). Calibers: .243 Win., .270 Win. .30-06, 7mm Rem. Mag., .338 Win. Mag. Made 1976 to date.
Early model . . . . NiB $332 Ex $267 Gd $185
Laminated stock model. . . . . NiB $351 Ex $283 Gd $195

MODEL 110BL . . . . NiB $390 Ex $314 Gd $217
Same as Model 110B except has left-hand action.

MODEL 110C
Calibers: .22-250, .243, .25-06, .270, .308, .30-06, 7mm Rem. Mag., .300 Win. Mag. Four round detachable clip magazine (3-round in Magnum calibers). 22-inch bbl. (24-inch in .22-250 Magnum calibers). Weight: 6.75 lbs., Magnum, 7.75 to 8 lbs. Sights: Open rear; ramp front. Checkered Monte Carlo-style walnut stock (Magnum has recoil pad). Made 1966-88.
Standard calibers . . . . NiB $612 Ex $375 Gd $195
Magnum calibers . . . . NiB $659 Ex $401 Gd $221

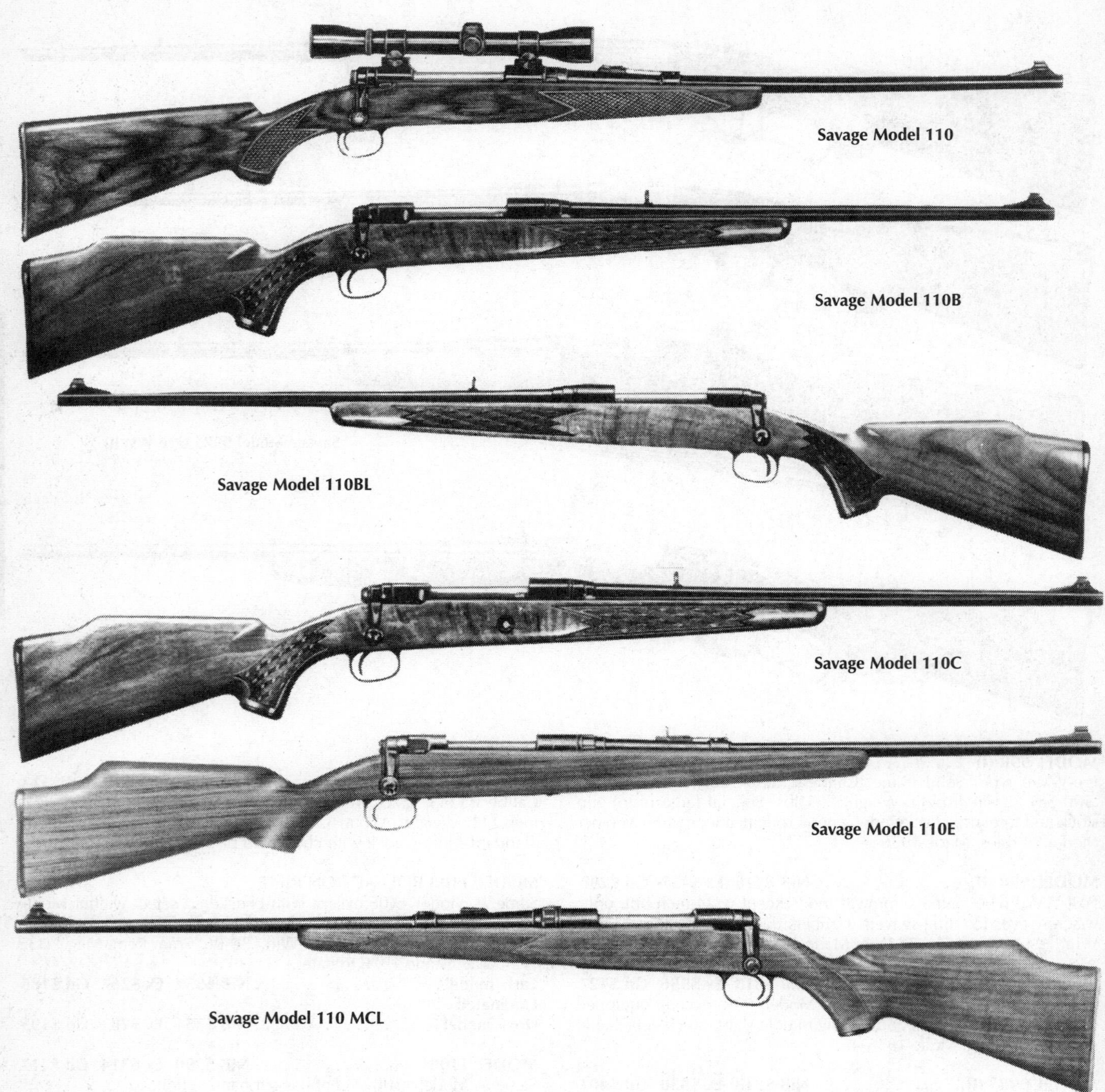
Savage Model 110

Savage Model 110B

Savage Model 110BL

Savage Model 110C

Savage Model 110E

Savage Model 110 MCL

MODEL 110CL
Same as Model 110C except has left-hand action. (Available only in .243 Win., .30-06, .270 Win. and 7mm Mag.) Made 1963-66.
Standard calibers. . . . . NiB $370 Ex $293 Gd $206
Magnum calibers. . . . . NiB $396 Ex $298 Gd $216

MODEL 110CY
YOUTH/LADIES RIFLE . . . . NiB $370 Ex $319 Gd $190
Same as Model 110G except with walnut-finished hardwood stock with 12.5-inch pull. Calibers: .243 Win. and .300 Savage. Made 1991 to date.

MODEL 110D
Similar to Model 110C except has internal magazine with hinged floorplate. Calibers: .243 Win., .270 Win., .30-06, 7mm Rem. Mag., .300 Win. Mag. Made 1972-88.
Standard calibers. . . . . NiB $370 Ex $299 Gd $209
Magnum calibers. . . . . NiB $396 Ex $320 Gd $223

MODEL 110DL
Same as Model 110D except has left-hand action. Discontinued.
Standard calibers. . . . . NiB $434 Ex $351 Gd $244
Magnum calibers. . . . . NiB $467 Ex $376 Gd $261

Savage Model 110P

Savage Model 110PE

MODEL 110E. . . . . NiB $309 Ex $216 Gd $164
Calibers: .22-250, .223 Rem., .243 Win., .270 Win., .308, 7mm Rem. Mag., .30-06. Four round box magazine (3-round in Magnum). 20- or 22-inch bbl. (24-inch stainless steel in Magnum). Weight: 6.75 lbs.; Magnum, 7.75 lbs. Sights: Open rear; ramp front. Plain Monte Carlo stock on early production; current models have checkered stocks of walnut-finished hardwood (Magnum has recoil pad). Made 1963-89.

MODEL 110EL. . . . . NiB $325 Ex $262 Gd $182
Same as Model 110E except has left-hand action made in .30-06 and 7mm Rem. Mag. only. Made 1969-73.

MODEL 110F/110K BOLT-ACTION RIFLE
Same as Model 110E except Model 110F has black Rynite synthetic stock, swivel studs; made 1988-93. Model 110K has laminated camouflage stock; made 1986-88.
Model 110F, adj. sights . . . . NiB $364 Ex $293 Gd $203
Model 110FNS, no sights . . . . NiB $377 Ex $304 Gd $210
Model 110K, standard calibers . . . . NiB $390 Ex $314 Gd $217
Model 110K, magnum calibers . . . . NiB $442 Ex $355 Gd $245

MODEL 110FM SIERRA ULTRA LIGHT. . . . NiB $370 Ex $293 Gd $195
Calibers: .243 Win., .270 Win., .30-06, .308 Win. Five round magazine. 20-inch bbl. 41.5 inches overall. Weight: 6.25 lbs. No sights w/drilled and tapped receiver. Black graphite/fiberglass composition stock. Non-glare matte blue finish. Made 1996 to date.

MODEL 110FP POLICE RIFLE . . . . . NiB $407 Ex $309 Gd $206
Calibers: .223, .308 Win. Four round magazine. 24-inch bbl. 45.5 inches overall. Weight: 9 lbs. Black Rynite composite stock. Matte blue finish. Made 1990 to date.

MODEL 110G BOLT-ACTION RIFLE
Calibers: .223, .22-250, .243 Win., .270, 7mm Rem. Mag., .308 Win., .30-06, .300 Win. Mag. Five round (standard) or 4-round magazine (magnum). 22- or 24-inch bbl. 42.38 overall (standard). Weight: 6.75 to 7.5 lbs. Ramp front sight, adj. rear. Checkered walnut-finished hardwood stock with rubber recoil pad. Made 1989-93.
Model 110G, standard calibers. . . . . NiB $370 Ex $267 Gd $164
Model 110G, magnum calibers. . . . . NiB $396 Ex $293 Gd $206
Model 110GLNS, left-hand, no sights . . . . . NiB $402 Ex $324 Gd $223

MODEL 110GV VARMINT RIFLE . . . . NiB $370 Ex $293 Gd $190
Similar to the Model 110G except fitted with medium-weight varmint bbl. with no sights. Receiver drilled and tapped for scope mounts. Calibers .22-250 and .223 only. Made 1989-93.

MODEL 110M MAGNUM
Same as Model 110MC except calibers: 7mm Rem. Mag. .264, .300 and .338 Win. 24-inch bbl. Stock with recoil pad. Weight: 7.75 to 8 lbs. Made 1963-69.
Model 110M Magnum . . . . NiB $422 Ex $406 Gd $226
Model 110ML Magnum. . . . . NiB $447 Ex $432 Gd $406

MODEL 110MC
Same as Model 110 except has Monte Carlo-style stock. Calibers: .22-250, .243 Win., .270, .308, .30-06. 24-inch bbl. in .22-250. Made 1959-69.
Model 110MC. . . . . NiB $242 Ex $190 Gd $123
Model 110MCL . . . . NiB $248 Ex $201 Gd $140

MODEL 110P PREMIER GRADE
Calibers: .243 Win., 7mm Rem. Mag., .30-06. Four round magazine (3-round in Magnum). 22-inch bbl. (24-inch stainless steel in Magnum). Weight: 7 lbs.; Magnum, 7.75 lbs. Sights: Open rear folding leaf; ramp front. French walnut stock w/Monte Carlo comb and cheekpiece, rosewood forend tip and pistol-grip cap, skip checkering, sling swivels (Magnum has recoil pad). Made 1964-70.
Calibers .243 Win. and .30-06. . . . . NiB $473 Ex $345 Gd $242
Caliber 7mm Rem. Mag. . . . . NiB $489 Ex $370 Gd $267

MODEL 110PE PRESENTATION GRADE
Same as Model 110P except has engraved receiver, floorplate and trigger guard, stock of choice grade French walnut. Made 1968-70.
Calibers .243 Win. and .30-06. . . . . NiB $727 Ex $584 Gd $403
Caliber 7mm Rem. Mag. . . . . NiB $784 Ex $631 Gd $435

MODEL 110PEL PRESENTATION GRADE
Same as Model 110PE except has left-hand action.
Calibers .243 Win. and .30-06. . . . . NiB $784 Ex $631 Gd $435
Caliber 7mm Rem. Mag. . . . . NiB $856 Ex $687 Gd $473

MODEL 110PL PREMIER GRADE
Same as Model 110P except has left-hand action.
Calibers .243 Win. and .30-06. . . . . NiB $507 Ex $378 Gd $250
Caliber 7mm Rem. Mag. . . . . NiB $528 Ex $378 Gd $272

MODEL 110S/110V
Same as Model 110E except Model 110S in .308 Win. only; discontinued 1985. Model 110V in .22-250 and .223 Rem. w/heavy 2-inch barrel, 47 inches overall, weight: 9 lbs. Discontinued. 1989.
Model 110S . . . . NiB $369 Ex $298 Gd $208
Model 110V. . . . . NiB $395 Ex $318 Gd $222

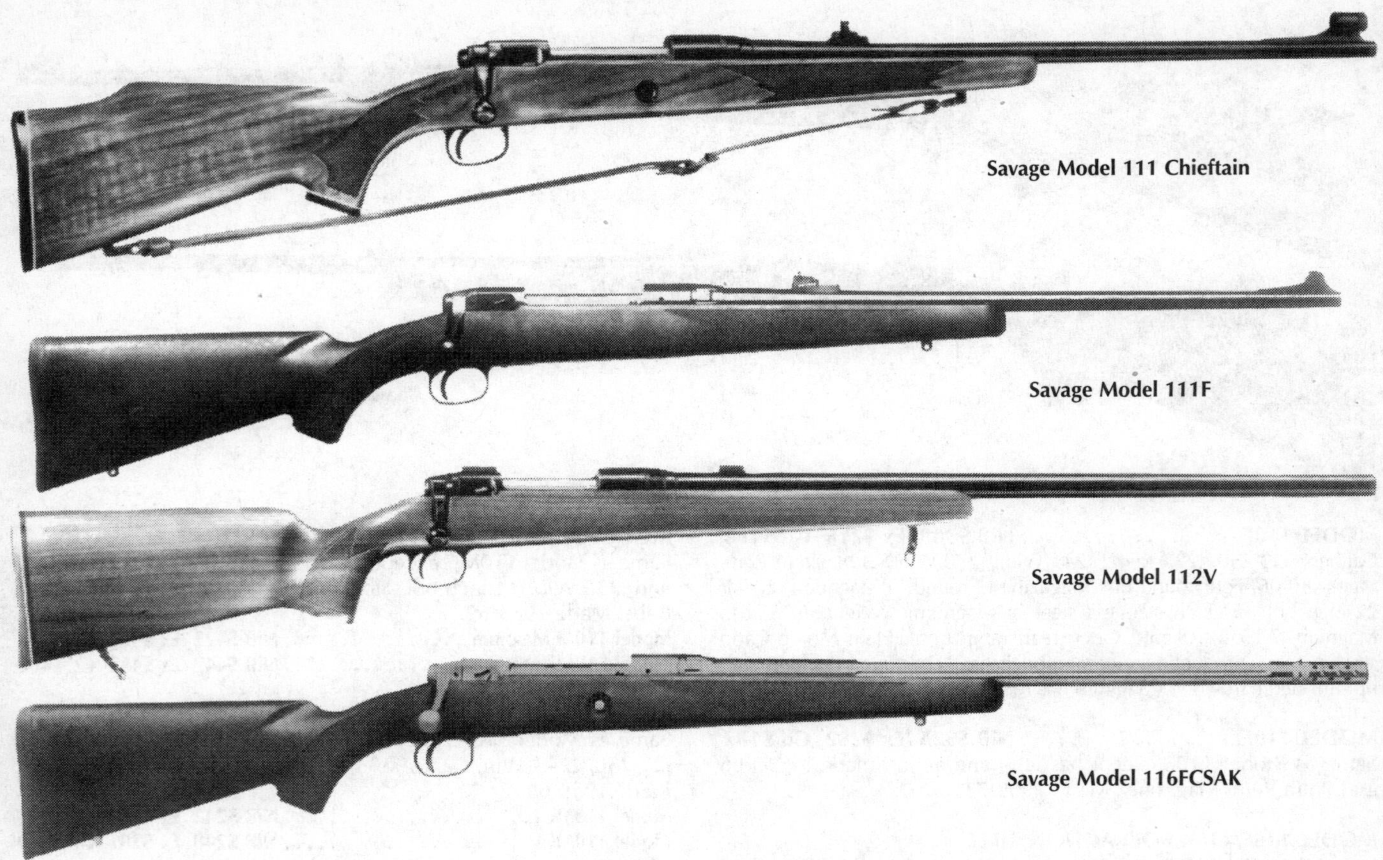

MODEL 111 CHIEFTAIN BOLT-ACTION RIFLE
Calibers: .243 Win., .270 Win., 7x57mm, 7mm Rem. Mag. .30-06. 4-round clip magazine (3-round in Magnum). 22-inch bbl. (24-inch in Magnum). Weight: 7.5 lbs., 8.25 lbs. Magnum. Sights: Leaf rear; hooded ramp front. Select walnut stock w/Monte Carlo comb and cheekpiece, checkered, pistol-grip cap, QD swivels and sling. Made 1974-79.
Standard calibers . . . . NiB $427 Ex $350 Gd $221
Magnum calibers . . . . NiB $480 Ex $391 Gd $278

MODELS 111F, 111FC, 111FNS CLASSIC HUNTERS
Similar to the Model 111G except with graphite/fiberglass composite stock. Weight: 6.25 lbs. Made 1994 to date.
Model 111F (Box mag., right/left hand) . . . NiB $375 Ex $247 Gd $195
Model 111FC (Detachable magazine) . . . . . NiB $453 Ex $324 Gd $221
Model 111FNS (Box mag., no sights, R/L hand) . . . . NiB $350 Ex $283 Gd $198

MODELS 111G, 111GC, 111GNS CLASSIC HUNTERS
Calibers: .22-250 Rem., .223 Rem., .243 Win., .25-06 Rem. .250 Sav., .270 Win., 7mm-08 Rem., 7mm Rem. Mag., .30-06, .300 Sav., .300 Win. Mag., .308 Win., .338 Win. 22- or 24-inch bbl. Weight: 7 lbs. Ramp front sight, adj. open rear. Walnut-finished hardwood stock. Blued finish. Made 1994 to date.
Model 111G (Box mag., right/left hand) . . . NiB $375 Ex $298 Gd $169
Model 111GC (Detachable mag., R/L hand) . . . . NiB $396 Ex $303 Gd $180
Model 111GNS (Box mag., no sights) . . . . . NiB $355 Ex $272 Gd $144

MODEL 112BV,112BVSS HEAVY VARMINT RIFLES
Similar to the Model 110G except fitted with 26-inch heavy bbl. Laminated wood stock with high comb. .22-250 and .223 only.

***(cont'd.)* MODEL 112BV,112BVSS HEAVY VARMINT RIFLES**
Model 112BV (Made 1993-94) . . . . NiB $586 Ex $432 Gd $319
Model 112BVSS (Fluted stainless bbl.; made since 1994) . . . . NiB $612 Ex $458 Gd $355

MODEL 112FV,112FVS,112FVSS VARMINT RIFLES
Similar to the Model 110G except fitted with 26-inch heavy bbl. and Dupont Rynite stock. Calibers: .22-250, .223 and .220 Swift (112FVS only). Blued or stainless finish. Made 1991 to date.
Model 112FV (blued) . . . . NiB $374 Ex $303 Gd $213
Model 112FV-S (blued, single round), disc. 1993 . . . . NiB $406 Ex $380 Gd $236
Model 112FVSS (stainless) . . . . NiB $535 Ex $458 Gd $277
Model 112 FVSS-S (stainless, single round). NiB $561 Ex $483 Gd $303

MODEL 112V VARMINT RIFLE . . . . NiB $426 Ex $344 Gd $240
Bolt action, single shot. Caliber: .220 Swift, .222 Rem., .223 Rem., .22-250, .243 Win., .25-06. 26-inch heavy bbl. with scope bases. Supplied w/o sights. Weight: 9.25 lbs. Select walnut stock in varmint style w/checkered pistol-grip, high comb, QD sling swivels. Made 1975-79.

MODEL 114C, 114CE, 114CU RIFLES
Calibers: .270 Win., 7mm Rem. Mag., .30-06, .300 Win. Mag. 22- or 24-inch bbl. Weight: 7 lbs. Detachable 3- or 4-round magazine. Ramp front sight; adjustable, open rear; (114CU has no sights). Checkered select walnut stock w/oil finish, red butt pad. Schnabel forend and skip-line checkering (114CE). High-luster blued finish. Made 1991 to date.
Model 114C (Classic) . . . . NiB $509 Ex $432 Gd $257
Model 114CE (Classic European) . . . . NiB $514 Ex $432 Gd $262
Model 114CU (Classic Ultra) . . . . NiB $530 Ex $406 Gd $277

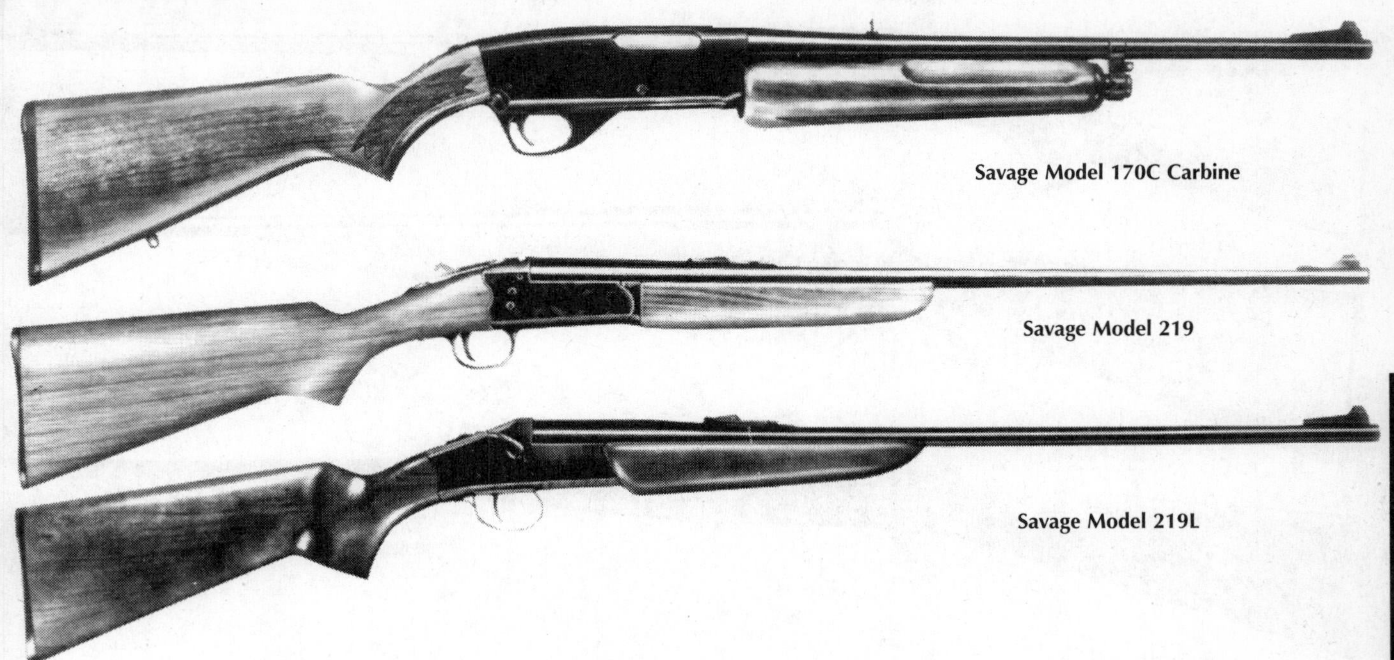
Savage Model 170C Carbine

Savage Model 219

Savage Model 219L

MODELS 116FSAK, 116FCSAK BOLT-ACTION RIFLES
Similar to the Model 116FSK except in calibers .270 Win., .30-06, 7mm Mag., .300 Win. Mag., .338 Win. Mag. Fluted 22-inch stainless bbl. w/adj. muzzle brake. Weight: 6.5 lbs. Made 1994 to date.
Model 116FSAK .... NiB $530 Ex $478 Gd $298
Model 116FCSAK (detachable mag.)..... NiB $581 Ex $484 Gd $324

MODELS 116FSC, 116FSS BOLT-ACTION RIFLES
Improved Model 110 with satin stainless action and bbl. Calibers: .223, .243, .270, .30-06, 7mm Rem. Mag., .300 Win. Mag., .338 Win. Mag. 22- or 24-inch bbl. Four or 5-round capacity. Weight: About 7.5 lbs. Black Rynite stock w/recoil pad and swivel studs. Receiver drilled and tapped for scope mounts, no sights. Made 1991 to date.
Model 116FSS...................... NiB $556 Ex $488 Gd $298
Model 116FSC, detachable magazine..... NiB $581 Ex $501 Gd $325

MODEL 116FSK KODIAK RIFLE......... NiB $607 Ex $427 Gd $324
Similar to the Model 116FSS except with 22-inch bbl. chambered for 338 Win. Mag. only. "Shock Suppressor" recoil reducer. Made 1993 to date.

MODEL 116SE, 116US RIFLES
Calibers: .270 Win., 7mm Rem Mag., .30-06, .300 Win. Mag. (116US); .300 Win. Mag., .338 Win. mag., .425 Express, .458 Win. Mag. (116SE). 24-inch stainless barrel (with muzzle brake 116SE only). 45.5 inches overall. Weight: 7.2 to 8.5 lbs. Three round magazine. 3-leaf Express sights 116SE only. Checkered Classic style select walnut stock with ebony forend tip. Stainless finish. Made 1994 to date.
Model 116SE (Safari Express) ..... NiB $916 Ex $710 Gd $478
Model 116US (Ultra Stainless) .... NiB $681 Ex $530 Gd $350

MODEL 170 PUMP-ACTION CENTERFIRE RIFLE .... NiB $257 Ex $206 Gd $139
Calibers: .30-30, .35 Rem. Three round tubular magazine. 22-inch bbl. Weight: 6.75 lbs. Sights: Folding leaf rear; ramp front. Select walnut stock w/checkered pistol-grip Monte Carlo comb, grooved slide handle. Made 1970-81.

MODEL 170C CARBINE .... NiB $293 Ex $211 Gd $139
Same as Model 170 Rifle except has 18.5-inch bbl., straight comb stock, weight: 6 lbs.; caliber .30-30 only. Made 1974-81.

MODEL 219 SINGLE-SHOT RIFLE
Hammerless. Takedown. Shotgun-type action with top lever. Calibers: .22 Hornet, .25-20, .32-20, .30-30. 26-inch bbl. Weight: about 6 lbs. Sights: Open rear; bead front. Plain pistol-grip stock and forearm. Made 1938-65.
Model 219......................... NiB $267 Ex $190 Gd $134
Model 219L (w/side lever, made 1965-67) . NiB $190 Ex $139 Gd $103

MODEL 221-229 UTILITY GUNS
Same as Model 219 except in various calibers, supplied in combination with an interchangeable shotgun bbl. All versions discontinued.
Model 221 (.30-30,12-ga. 30-inch bbl.)... NiB $190 Ex $154 Gd $108
Model 222 (.30-30,16-ga. 28-inch bbl.) .... NiB $171 Ex $139 Gd $98
Model 223 (.30-30, 20-ga. 28-inch bbl.).... NiB $152 Ex $123 Gd $87
Model 227 (.22 Hornet, 12-ga. 30-inch bbl.)... NiB $204 Ex $164 Gd $115
Model 228 (.22 Hornet, 16-ga. 28-inch bbl.) . NiB $196 Ex $159 Gd $112
Model 229 (.22 Hornet, 20-ga. 28-inch bbl.) . NiB $190 Ex $154 Gd $108

MODEL 340 BOLT-ACTION REPEATER
Calibers: .22 Hornet, .222 Rem., .223 Rem., .225 Win., .30-30. Clip magazine; 4-round capacity (3-round in 30-30). Bbl. lengths: Originally 20-inch in .30-30, 22-inch in .22 Hornet; later 22-inch in .30-30, 24-inch in other calibers. Weight: 6.5 to 7.5 lbs. depending on caliber and vintage. Sights: Open rear (folding leaf on recent production); ramp front. Early models had plain pistol-grip stock, checkered since 1965. Made 1950-85. (Note: Those rifles produced between 1947-1950 were .22 Hornet Stevens Model .322 and .30-30 Model .325. The Savage model, however, was designated Model .340 for all calibers.)
Pre-1965 with plain stock .... NiB $319 Ex $206 Gd $139
Current model................. NiB $216 Ex $175 Gd $122
Savage Model 340C Carbine...... NiB $319 Ex $206 Gd $139

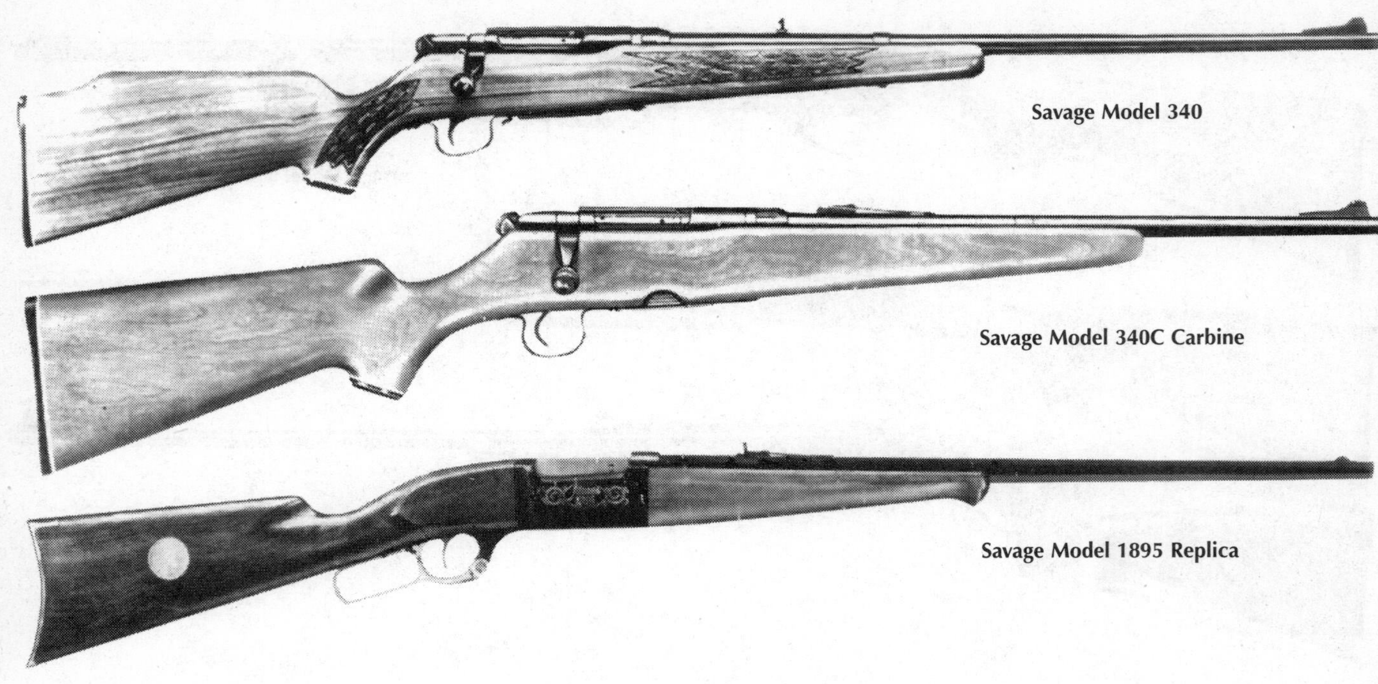
Savage Model 340

Savage Model 340C Carbine

Savage Model 1895 Replica

MODEL 340S DELUXE .... NiB $370 Ex $267 Gd $154
Same as Model 340 except has checkered stock, screw eyes for sling, peep rear sight, hooded front. Made 1955-60.

MODEL 342 .... NiB $360 Ex $267 Gd $164
Designation, 1950 to 1955, of Model 340 .22 Hornet.

MODEL 342S DELUXE .... NiB $396 Ex $293 Gd $164
Designation, 1950 to 1955, of Model 340S .22 Hornet.

ANNIVERSARY MODEL
1895 LEVER-ACTION .... NiB $1570 Ex $1364 Gd $1055
Replica of Savage Model 1895 Hammerless Lever-Action Rifle issued to commemorate the 75th anniversary (1895-1970) of Savage Arms. Caliber: .308 Win. Five round rotary magazine. 24-inch full-octagon bbl. Engraved receiver. Brass-plated lever. Sights: Open rear; brass blade front. Plain straight-grip buttstock, Schnabel-type forend; brass medallion inlaid in buttstock, brass crescent-shaped buttplate. 9,999 produced. Made in 1970 only. Top value is for new, unfired specimen.

MODEL 1903 SLIDE-ACTION
REPEATER .... NiB $396 Ex $267 Gd $206
Hammerless. Takedown. Caliber: .22 Short, Long, LR. Detachable box magazine. 24-inch octagon bbl. Weight: About 5 lbs. Sights: Open rear; bead front. Pistol-grip stock, grooved slide handle. Made 1903-21.

MODEL 1904 BOLT-ACTION
SINGLE-SHOT RIFLE .... NiB $164 Ex $113 Gd $61
Takedown. .22 Short, Long, LR. 18-inch bbl. Weight: About 3 lbs. Sights: Open rear; bead front. Plain, straight-grip, one-piece stock. Made 1904-17.

MODEL 1905 BOLT-ACTION
SINGLE-SHOT RIFLE .... NiB $164 Ex $113 Gd $61
Takedown. .22 Short, Long, LR. 22-inch bbl. Weight: About 5 lbs. Sights: Open rear; bead front. Plain, straight-grip one-piece stock. Made 1905-19.

MODEL 1909 SLIDE-ACTION
REPEATER .... NiB $390 Ex $269 Gd $192
Hammerless. Takedown. Similar to Model 1903 except has 20-inch round bbl., plain stock and forearm, weight: about 4.75 lbs. Made 1909-15.

MODEL 1912
AUTOLOADING RIFLE .... NiB $507 Ex $317 Gd $172
Takedown. Caliber: 22 LR. only. Seven round detachable box magazine. 20-inch bbl., plain stock and forearm. Made 1912-16.

MODEL 1914 SLIDE-ACTION
REPEATER .... NiB $393 Ex $269 Gd $192
Hammerless. Takedown. Caliber: .22 Short, Long, LR, Tubular magazine holds 20 Short, 17 Long, 15 LR. 24-inch octagon bbl. Weight: About 5.75 lbs. Sights: Open rear; bead front. Plain pistol-grip stock, grooved slide handle. Made 1914-24.

MODEL 1920 HI-POWER BOLT-ACTION RIFLE
Short Mauser-type action. Calibers: .250/3000, .300 Sav. Five round box magazine. 22-inch bbl. in .250 cal.; 24-inch in .300 cal. Weight: About 6 lbs. Sights: Open rear; bead front. Checkered pistol-grip stock w/slender forearm and Schnabel tip. Made 1920-26.
Model 1920
Hi-Power
(.250-3000 Sav.)...................... NiB $586 Ex $406 Gd $252
Model 1920
Hi-Power
(.300 Sav.).......................... NiB $535 Ex $355 Gd $226

NOTE: *In 1965, Savage began the importation of rifles manufactured by J. G. Anschutz GmbH, Ulm, West Germany. Models designated "Savage/Anschutz" are listed in this section, those marketed in the U.S. under the "Anschutz" name are included in that firm's listings. Anschutz rifles are now distributed in the U.S. by Precision Sales Int'l., Westfield, Mass. See "Anschutz" for detailed specifications.*

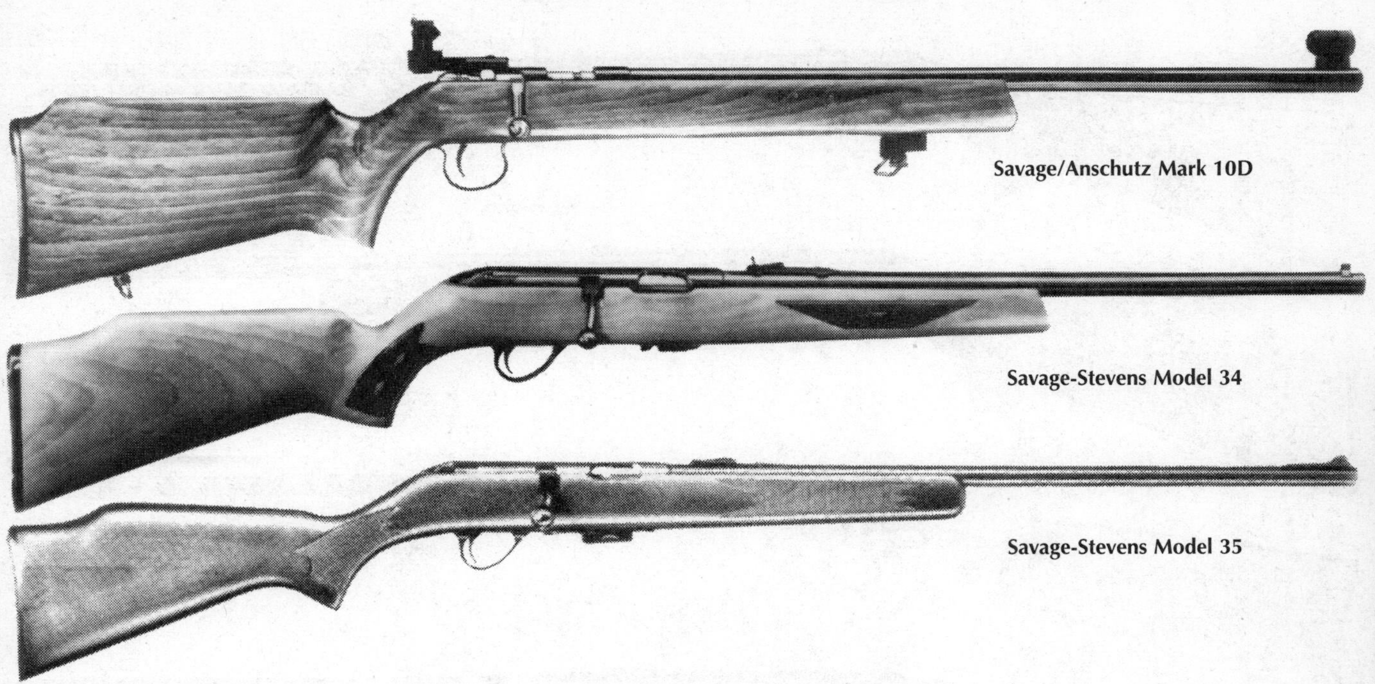

Savage/Anschutz Mark 10D

Savage-Stevens Model 34

Savage-Stevens Model 35

MARK 10 BOLT-ACTION TARGET RIFLE. . . . . NiB $473 Ex $314 Gd $216
Single shot. Caliber: .22 LR. 26-inch bbl. Weight: 8.5 lbs. Sights: Anschutz micrometer rear; globe front. Target stock w/full pistol-grip and cheekpiece, adj. hand stop and swivel. Made 1967-72.

MARK 10D . . . . NiB $499 Ex $319 Gd $216
Same as Mark 10 except has redesigned stock with Monte Carlo comb, different rear sight. Weight: 7.75 lbs. Made 1972.

MODEL 54 CUSTOM SPORTER. . . . . NiB $715 Ex $586 Gd $329
Same as Anschutz Model 1422D.

MODEL 54M. . . . . NiB $870 Ex $612 Gd $380
Same as Anschutz Model 1522D.

MODEL 64 BOLT-ACTION TARGET RIFLE. . . . . NiB $586 Ex $432 Gd $277
Same as Anschutz Model 1403.

MODEL 153 BOLT-ACTION SPORTER . . . . NiB $638 Ex $432 Gd $303
Caliber: .222 Rem. Three round clip magazine. 24-inch bbl. Sights: Folding leaf open rear; hooded ramp front. Weight: 6.75 lbs. French walnut stock w/cheekpiece, skip checkering, rosewood forend tip and grip cap, swivels. Made 1964-67.

MODEL 153S. . . . . NiB $715 Ex $509 Gd $329
Same as Model 153 except has double-set trigger. Made 1965-67.

MODEL 164 CUSTOM SPORTER. . . . . NiB $535 Ex $380 Gd $226
Same as Anschutz Model 1416.

MODEL 164M. . . . . NiB $612 Ex $406 Gd $252
Same as Anschutz Model 1516.

MODEL 184 SPORTER . . . . NiB $586 Ex $432 Gd $226
Same as Anschutz Model 1441.

NOTE: *Since J. Stevens Arms (see also separate listing) is a division of Savage Industries, certain Savage models carry the "Stevens" name.*

MODEL 34 BOLT-ACTION REPEATER . . . . NiB $154 Ex $98 Gd $61
Caliber: .22 Short, Long, LR. 20-inch bbl. Weight: 4.75 lbs. Sights: Open rear; bead front. Plain pistol-grip stock. Made 1965-80.

MODEL 34M. . . . . NiB $139 Ex $103 Gd $72
Same as Model 34 except chambered for 22 WMR. Made 1969-73.

MODEL 35 . . . . NiB $139 Ex $103 Gd $72
Bolt-action repeater. Caliber: 22 LR. Six round clip magazine. 22-inch bbl. Weight: About 5 lbs. Sights: Open rear; ramp front. Monte Carlo stock w/checkered pistol grip and forearm. Made 1982 to date.

MODEL 35M. . . . . NiB $164 Ex $113 Gd $77
Same as Model 35 except chambered for 22 WMR. Made 1982 to date.

MODEL 46 BOLT-ACTION RIFLE. . . . . NiB $149 Ex $103 Gd $72
Caliber: .22 Short, Long, LR. Tubular magazine holds 22 Short, 17 Long, 15 LR. 20-inch bbl. Weight: 5 lbs. Plain pistol-grip stock on early production; later models have Monte Carlo stock w/checkering. Made 1969-73.

MODEL 65 BOLT-ACTION RIFLE. . . . . NiB $164 Ex $113 Gd $72
Caliber: .22 Short, Long, LR. Five round clip magazine. 20-inch bbl. Weight: 5 lbs. Sights: Open rear; ramp front. Monte Carlo stock w/checkered pistol grip and forearm. Made 1969-73.

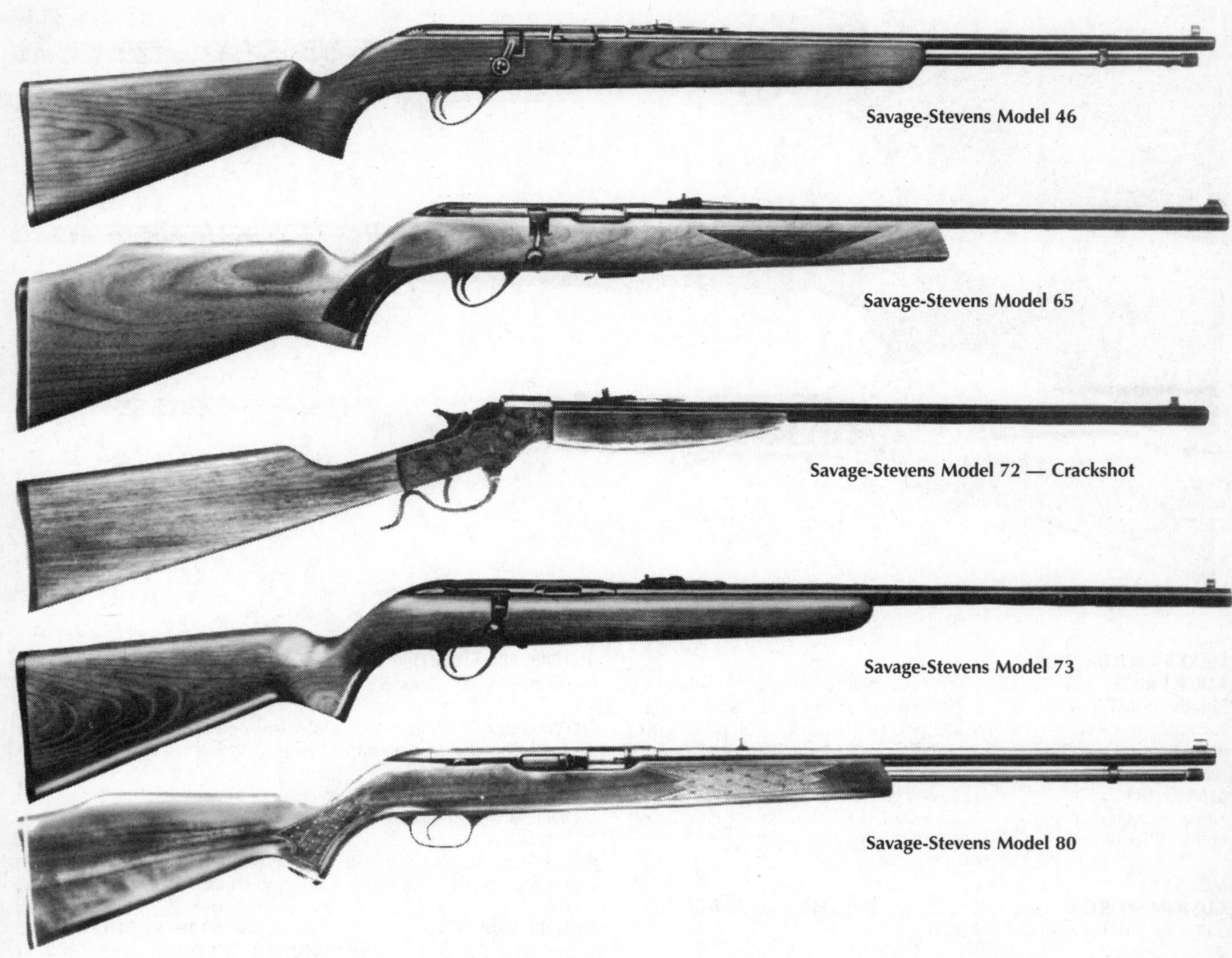

Savage-Stevens Model 46

Savage-Stevens Model 65

Savage-Stevens Model 72 — Crackshot

Savage-Stevens Model 73

Savage-Stevens Model 80

MODEL 65M . . . . NiB $164 Ex $123 Gd $82
Same as Model 65 except chambered for .22 WMR, has 22-inch bbl., weighs 5.25 lbs. Made 1969-81.

NOTE: *The Model 72 is a "Favorite"-type single-shot unlike the smaller, original "Crackshot" made by Stevens from 1913-39.*

MODEL 72 CRACKSHOT SINGLE-SHOT LEVER-ACTION RIFLE . . . . NiB $267 Ex $216 Gd $139
Falling-block action. Casehardened frame. Caliber: .22 Short, Long, LR. 22-inch octagon bbl. Weight: 4.5lbs. Sights: Open rear; bead front. Plain straight-grip stock and forend of walnut. Made 1972 to date.

MODEL 73 BOLT-ACTION SINGLE-SHOT . . . NiB $113 Ex $92 Gd $72
Caliber: .22 Short, Long, LR. 20-inch bbl. Weight: 4.75 lbs. Sights: Open rear; bead front. Plain pistol-grip stock. Made 1965-80.

MODEL 73Y YOUTH MODEL . . . . NiB $118 Ex $98 Gd $72
Same as Model 73 except has 18-inch bbl., 1.5-inch shorter butt-stock, weight: 4.5 lbs. Made 1965-80.

MODEL 74 LITTLE FAVORITE . . . . NiB $185 Ex $173 Gd $103
Same as Model 72 Crackshot except has black-finished frame, 22-inch round bbl., walnut-finished hardwood stock. Weight: 4.75 lbs. Made 1972-74.

MODEL 80 AUTOLOADING RIFLE . . . . NiB $164 Ex $134 Gd $94
Caliber: 22 LR. 15-round tubular magazine. 20-inch bbl. Weight: 6 lbs. Sights: Open rear, bead front. Monte Carlo stock of walnut w/checkered pistol-grip and forearm. Made 1976 to date. (Note: This rifle is essentially the same as the Model 60 of 1969-72 except for a different style of checkering, side instead of top safety and plain bead instead of ramp front sight.)

MODEL 88 AUTOLOADING RIFLE . . . . NiB $175 Ex $164 Gd $103
Similar to Model 60 except has walnut-finished hardwood stock, plain bead front sight. Weight: 5.75 lbs. Made 1969-72.

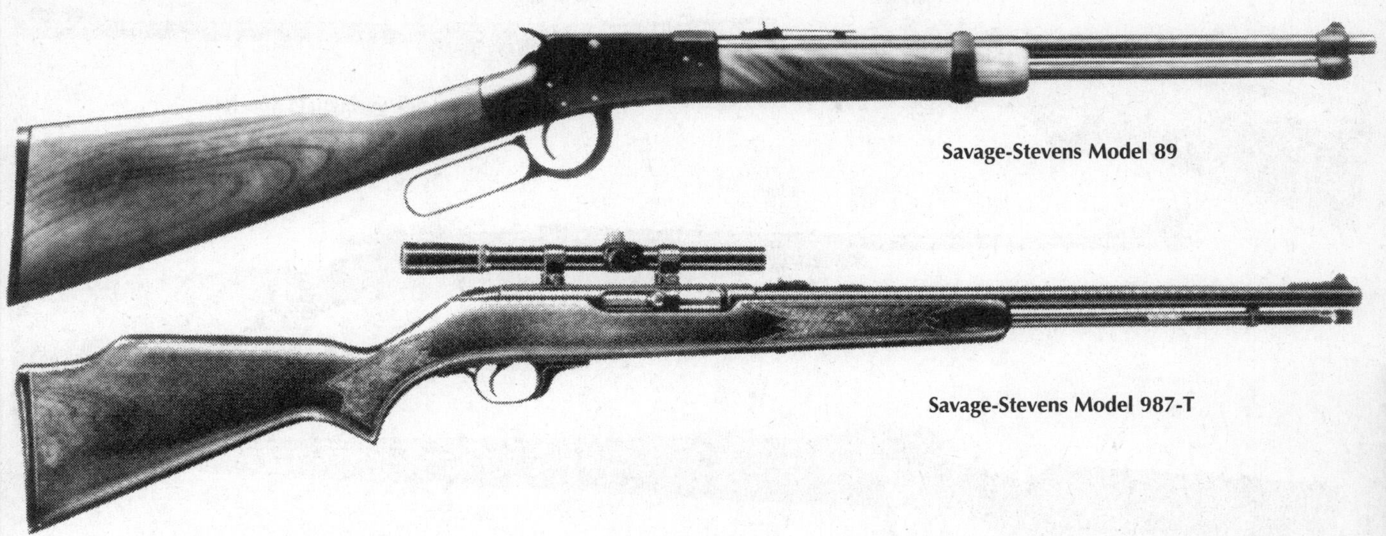
Savage-Stevens Model 89

Savage-Stevens Model 987-T

MODEL 89 SINGLE-SHOT LEVER-ACTION CARBINE .... NiB $102 Ex $87 Gd $61
Martini-type action. Caliber: .22 Short, Long, LR. 18.5-inch bbl. Weight: 5 lbs. Sights: Open rear; bead front. Western-style carbine stock w/straight grip, forearm with bbl. band. Made 1976-89.

MODEL 987-T AUTOLOADING RIFLE .... NiB $164 Ex $134 Gd $94
Caliber: .22 LR. 15-round tubular magazine. 20-inch bbl. Weight: 6 lbs. Sights: Open rear; ramp front. Monte Carlo stock w/checkered pistol grip and forearm. Made 1981-89.

"STEVENS FAVORITE"
See Savage Model 71.

V.C. SCHILLING — Suhl, Germany

MAUSER-MANNLICHER BOLT ACTION SPORTING RIFLE .. NiB $857 Ex $689 Gd $475
Same general specifications as given for the Haenel Mauser-Mannlicher Sporter. See separate listing.

'88 MAUSER SPORTER .... NiB $824 Ex $664 Gd $458
Same general specifications as Haenel '88 Mauser Sporter. See separate listing.

SCHULTZ & LARSEN GEVAERFABRIK — Otterup, Denmark

MATCH RIFLE NO. 47........... NiB $741 Ex $689 Gd $509
Caliber: .22 LR. Bolt-action, single-shot, set trigger. 28.5-inch heavy bbl. Weight: 14 lbs. Sights: Micrometer receiver, globe front. Free-rifle stock w/cheekpiece, thumbhole, adj. Schuetzen-type buttplate, swivels, palmrest.

FREE RIFLE MODEL 54 .... NiB $998 Ex $818 Gd $535
Calibers: 6.5x55mm or any standard American centerfire caliber. Schultz & Larsen M54 bolt-action, single-shot, set trigger. 27.5-inch heavy bbl. Weight: 15.5 lbs. Sights: Micrometer receiver; globe front. Free-rifle stock w/cheekpiece, thumbhole, adj. Schuetzen-type buttplate, swivels, palm rest.

MODEL 54J SPORTING RIFLE............... NiB $705 Ex $576 Gd $370
Calibers: .270 Win., .30-06, 7x61 Sharpe & Hart. Schultz & Larsen bolt action. Three-round magazine. 24-inch bbl. in .270 and .30-06, 26-inch in 7x61 S&H. Checkered stock w/Monte Carlo comb and cheekpiece. Value shown is for rifle less sights.

SEARS, ROEBUCK & COMPANY — Chicago, Illinois

The most encountered brands or model designations used by Sears are J. C. Higgins and Ted Williams. Firearms sold under these designations have been mfd. by various firms including Winchester, Marlin, Savage, Mossberg, etc.

MODEL 2C BOLT-ACTION RIFLE.............. NiB $110 Ex $90 Gd $69
Caliber: .22RF. Seven round clip mag. 21-inch bbl. Weight: 5 lbs. Sights: Open rear; ramp front. Plain Monte Carlo stock. Mfd. by Win.

MODEL 42 BOLT-ACTION REPEATER .... NiB $1 Ex $90 Gd $63
Takedown. Caliber: .22RF. Eight round detachable box magazine. 24-inch bbl. Weight: 6 lbs. Sights: Open rear; bead front. Plain pistol-grip stock. Mfd. by Marlin.

MODEL 42DL BOLT-ACTION REPEATER .... NiB $110 Ex $90 Gd $69
Same general specifications as Model 42 except fancier grade w/peep sight, hooded front sight and swivels.

MODEL 44DL LEVER-ACTION RIFLE .... NiB $186 Ex $146 Gd $100
Caliber: .22RF. Tubular magazine holds 19 LR cartridges. 22-inch bbl. Weight: 6.25 lbs. Sights: Open rear; hooded ramp front. Monte Carlo-style stock w/pistol grip. Mfd. by Marlin.

MODEL 53 BOLT-ACTION RIFLE .... NiB $237 Ex $161 Gd $120
Calibers: .243, .270, .308, .30-06. Four-round magazine. 22-inch bbl. Weight: 6.75 lbs. Sights: Open rear; ramp front. Standard sporter stock w/pistol-grip, checkered. Mfd. by Savage.

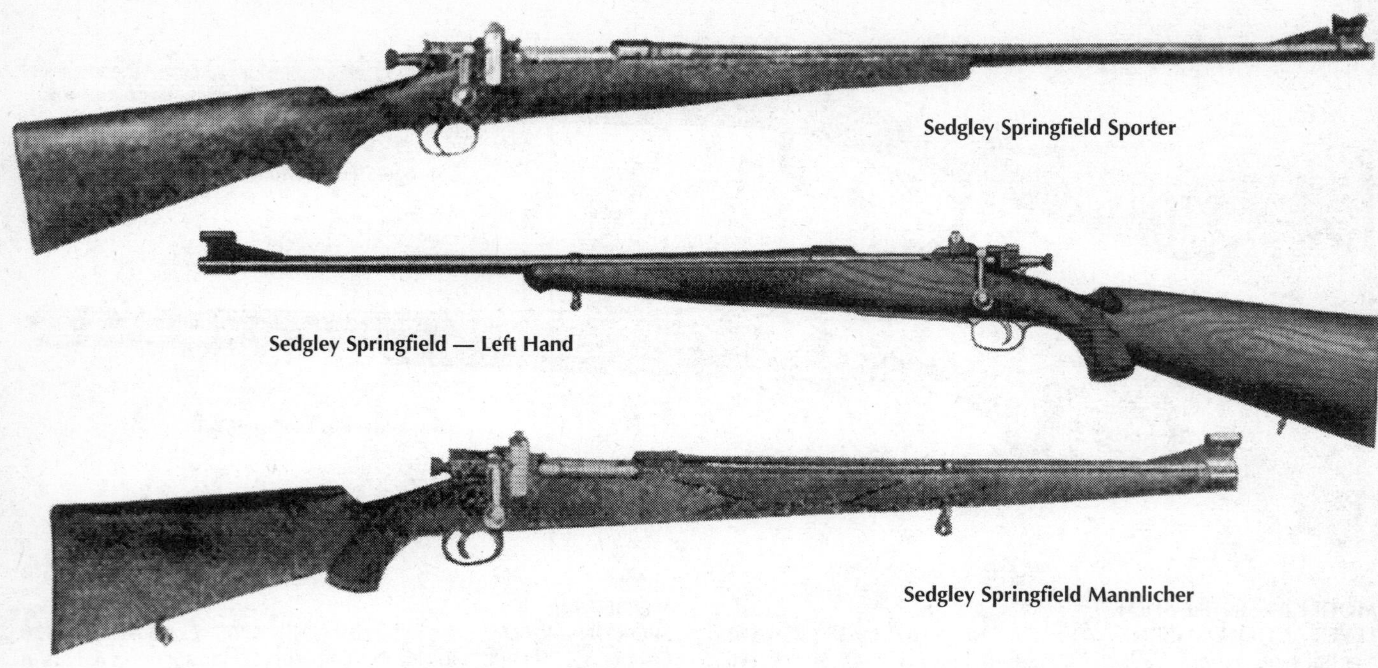

Sedgley Springfield Sporter

Sedgley Springfield — Left Hand

Sedgley Springfield Mannlicher

MODEL 54 LEVER-ACTION RIFLE............................ NiB $188 Ex $163 Gd $112
Similar general specifications as Winchester Model 94 carbine. Made in .30-30 caliber only. Mfd. by Winchester.

MODEL 103 SERIES BOLT-ACTION REPEATER................ NiB $194 Ex $86 Gd $66
Same general specifications as Model 103.2 w/minor changes. Mfd. by Marlin.

MODEL 103.2 BOLT-ACTION REPEATER....................... NiB $112 Ex $86 Gd $66
Takedown. Caliber: .22RF. Eight-round detachable box magazine. 24-inch bbl. Weight: 6 lbs. Sights: Open rear; bead front. Plain pistol-grip stock. Mfd. by Marlin.

R. F. SEDGLEY, INC. — Philadelphia, Pennsylvania

SPRINGFIELD SPORTER .... NiB $1339 Ex $1056 Gd $541
Springfield '03 bolt action. Calibers: .220 Swift, .218 Bee, .22-3000, R, .22-4000, .22 Hornet, .25-35, .250-3000, .257 Roberts, .270 Win., 7mm, .30-06. 24-inch bbl. Weight: 7.5 lbs. Sights: Lyman No. 48 receiver; bead front on matted ramp. Checkered walnut stock, grip cap, sling swivels. Disc. 1941.

SPRINGFIELD LEFT-HAND SPORTER... NiB $1519 Ex $1252 Gd $824
Bolt-action reversed for left-handed shooter; otherwise the same as standard Sedgley Springfield Sporter. Disc. 1941.

SEDGLEY SPRINGFIELD MANNLICHER-TYPE SPORTER........ NiB $1622 Ex $1339 Gd $953
Same as standard Sedgley Springfield Sporter except w/20-inch bbl., Mannlicher-type full stock w/cheekpiece, weight: 7.75 lbs. Disc. 1941.

SHILEN RIFLES, INC. — Ennis, Texas

DGA BENCHREST RIFLE....... NiB $1516 Ex $1133 Gd $850
DGA single-shot bolt-action. Calibers as listed for Sporter. 26-inch medium-heavy or heavy bbl. Weight: From 10.5 lbs. No sights. Fiberglass or walnut stock, classic or thumbhole pattern. Currently manufactured.

DGA SPORTER .... NiB $1571 Ex $1051 Gd $737
DGA bolt action. Calibers: .17 Rem., .222 Rem., .223 Rem. .22-250, .220 Swift, 6mm Rem., .243 Win., .250 Sav., .257 Roberts, .284 Win., .308 Win., .358 Win. Three round blind magazine. 24-inch bbl. Average weight: 7.5 lbs. No sights. Select Claro walnut stock w/cheekpiece, pistol grip, sling swivel studs. Currently manufactured.

DGA VARMINTER............ NiB $1463 Ex $1107 Gd $762
Same as Sporter except w/25-inch medium-heavy bbl. Weight: 9 lbs.

SHILOH RIFLE MFG. Co. — Big Timber, Montana (Formerly Shiloh Products)

SHARPS MODEL 1874 BUSINESS RIFLE.... NiB $1107 Ex $1030 Gd $644
Replica of 1874 Sharps similar to No. 3 Sporting Rifle. .32-40, .38-55, .40-50 BN, .40-70 BN, .40-90 BN, .45-70 ST, .45-90 ST, .50-70 ST, .50-100 ST. 28-inch round heavy bbl. Blade front sight, buckhorn rear. Double-set triggers. Straight-grip walnut stock w/steel crescent buttplate. Made 1986 to date.

SHARPS MODEL 1874 LONG RANGE EXPRESS RIFLE....... NiB $1674 Ex $1622 Gd $1051
Replica of 1874 Sharps w/single-shot falling breech action. .32-40, .38-55, .40-50 BN, .40-70 BN, .40-90 BN, .45-70 ST, .45-90 ST, .45-110 ST, .50-70 ST, .50-90 ST, .50-110 ST. 34-inch tapered octagon bbl. 51 inches overall. Weight: 10.75 lbs. Globe front sight, sporting tang peep rear. Walnut buttstock w/pistol-grip and Schnabel-style forend. Color casehardened action w/double-set triggers Made 1986 to date.

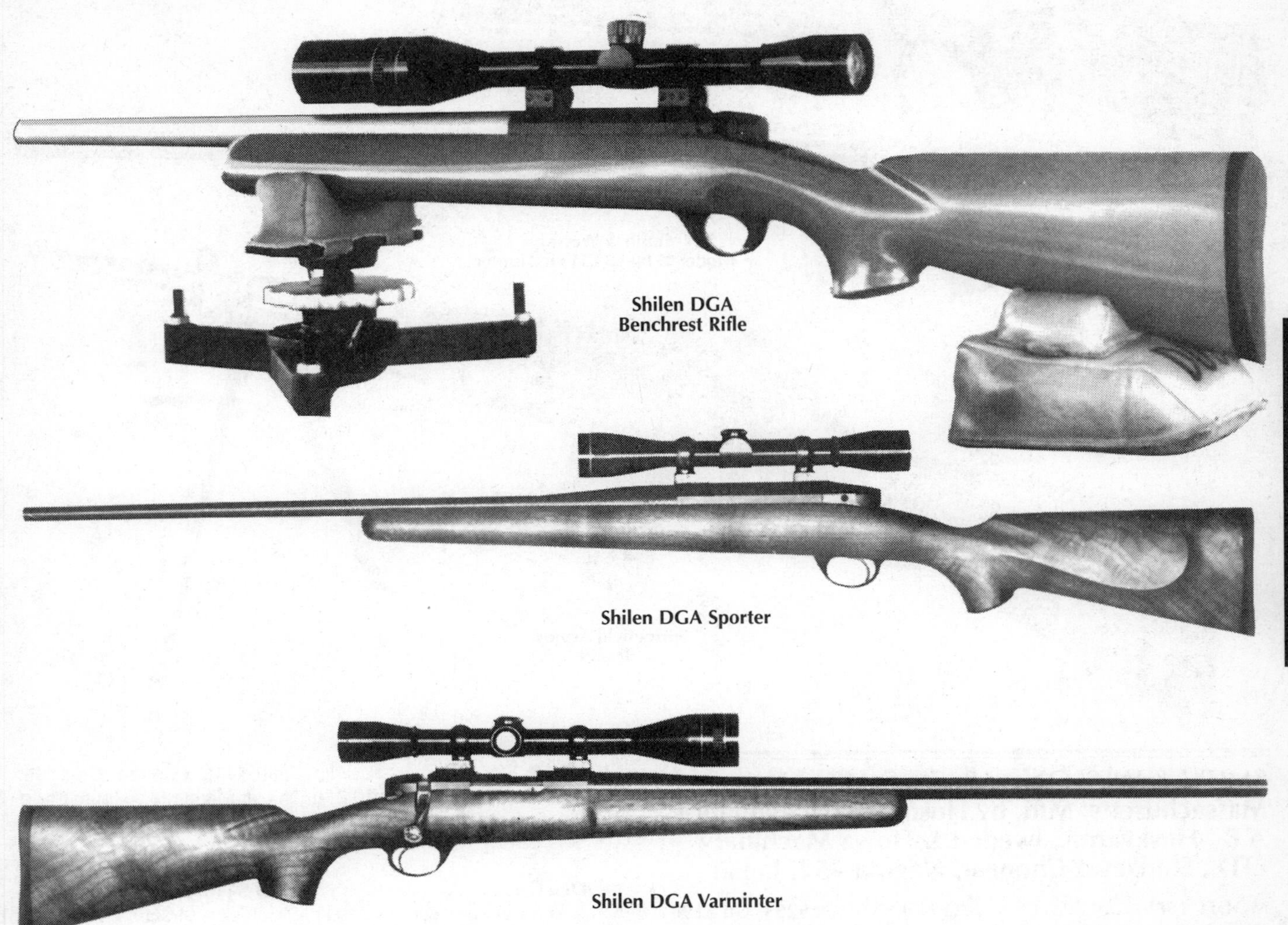
Shilen DGA Benchrest Rifle

Shilen DGA Sporter

Shilen DGA Varminter

SHARPS MODEL 1874 SADDLE RIFLE . . NiB $1151 Ex $1043 Gd $636
Similar to 1874 Express Rifle except w/30-inch bbl., blade front sight and buckhorn rear. Made 1986 to date.

SHARPS MODEL 1874
SPORTING RIFLE NO. 1 . . . . NiB $1244 Ex $1043 Gd $644
Similar to 1874 Express Rifle except w/30-inch bbl., blade front sight and buckhorn rear. Made 1986 to date.

SHARPS MODEL 1874
SPORTING RIFLE NO. 3 . . . . NiB $1048 Ex $919 Gd $610
Similar to 1874 Sporting Rifle No. 1 except w/straight-grip stock w/steel crescent buttplate. Made 1986 to date.

SHARPS MODEL 1874 MONTANA ROUGHRIDER
Similar to 1874 Sporting Rifle No. 1 except w/24- to 34-inch half-octagon or full-octagon bbl. Standard or deluxe walnut stock w/pistol-grip or military-style buttstock. Made 1989 to date.
Standard model . . . . NiB $1043 Ex $636 Gd $559
Deluxe model . . . . NiB $1177 Ex $893 Gd $533

SIG SWISS INDUSTRIAL COMPANY — Neuhausen-Rhine Falls, Switzerland

AMT SEMIAUTOMATIC RIFLE . . . . NiB $4191 Ex $4139 Gd $2826
.308 Win.(7.62 NATO). Five, 10, or 20-round magazine. 18.5-inch bbl. w/flash suppressor. Weight: 9.5 lbs. Sights: Adj. aperture rear, post front. Walnut buttstock and forend w/synthetic pistol grip. Imported 1980-88.

AMT SPORTING RIFLE . . . . NiB $3907 Ex $2877 Gd $2100
Semiautomatic version of SG510-4 automatic assault rifle based on Swiss Army SIGW57. Roller-delayed blowback action. Caliber: 7.62x51mm NATO (.308 Win.). Five, 10- and 20-round magazines. 19-inch bbl. Weight: 10 lbs. Sights, aperture rear, post front. Wood buttstock and forearm, folding bipod. Imported 1960-88.

PE57 SEMIAUTOMATIC RIFLE . . . . NiB $5189 Ex $4160 Gd $2844
Caliber: 7.5 Swiss. 24-round magazine. 23.75-inch bbl. Weight: 12.5 lbs. Sights: Adj. aperture rear; post front. High-impact synthetic stock. Imported from Switzerland during the 1980s.

Smith & Wesson
Model 1500DL

Smith & Wesson
Model 1700 LS Classic Hunter

Springfield Armory
BM-59

SMITH & WESSON — Springfield, Massachusetts, Mfd. by Husqvarna, Vapenfabrik A.B., Huskvarna, Sweden & Howa Machinery LTD., Shinkawa-Chonear, Nagota 452, Japan

MODEL 1500 . . . . NiB $370 Ex $293 Gd $190
Bolt-action. .243 Win., .270 Win., .30-06, 7mm Rem. Mag. 22-inch bbl. (24-inch in 7mm Rem. Mag.). Weight: 7.5 lbs. American walnut stock w/Monte Carlo comb and cheekpiece, cut checkering. Sights: Open rear, hooded ramp, gold beadfront. This model was also imported by Mossberg (see separate listings); Imported 1979-84.

MODEL 1500DL DELUXE . . . . NiB $370 Ex $293 Gd $195
Same as standard model, except w/o sights; w/engine-turned bolt, decorative scroll on floorplate, French checkering. Imported 1983-84.

MODEL 1700 LS "CLASSIC HUNTER" . . . . NiB $422 Ex $370 Gd $216
Bolt action. Calibers: .243 Win., .270 Win., .30-06, 5-round magazine. 22-inch bbl. Weight: 7.5 lbs. Solid recoil pad, no sights, Schnabel forend, checkered walnut stock. Imported 1983-84.

MODEL A BOLT-ACTION RIFLE . . . . NiB $499 Ex $370 Gd $257
Similar to Husqvarna Model 9000 Crown Grade. Mauser-type bolt action. Calibers: .22-250, .243 Win., .270 Win., .308 Win., .30-06, 7mm Rem. Mag., .300 Win. Mag. Five round magazine except 3-round capacity in latter two calibers. 23.75-inch bbl. Weight: 7 lbs. Sights: Folding leaf rear; hooded ramp front. Checkered walnut stock w/Monte Carlo cheekpiece, rosewood forend tip and pistol-grip cap, swivels. Made 1969-72.

MODEL B . . . . NiB $448 Ex $324 Gd $190
Same as Model A except w/20.25-inch extra-light bbl., Monte Carlo cheekpiece w/Schnabel-style forearm, weight: 6 lbs., 10 oz. Calibers: .243 Win., .30-06.

MODEL C . . . . NiB $448 Ex $329 Gd $190
Same as Model B except w/cheekpiece stock w/straight comb.

MODEL D . . . . NiB $576 Ex $422 Gd $293
Same as Model C except w/full-length Mannlicher-style forearm.

MODEL E. NiB $576 Ex $422 Gd $293
Same as Model B except w/full-length Mannlicher-style forearm.

SPRINGFIELD, INC. — Colona, Illinois (Formerly Springfield Armory of Geneseo, Ill.)

This is a private firm not to be confused with the former U.S. Government facility in Springfield, Mass.

BM-59 SEMIAUTOMATIC RIFLE
Gas-operated. Caliber: .308 Win. (7.62mm NATO). 20-round detachable box magazine. 19.3-inch bbl. w/flash suppressor. About 43 inches overall. Weight: 9.25 lbs. Adj. military aperture rear sight, square post front; direct and indirect grenade launcher sights. European walnut stock w/handguard or folding buttstock (Alpine Paratrooper). Made 1981-90.

Standard model . . . . NiB $2079 Ex $1668 Gd $1143
Paratrooper model . . . . NiB $2085 Ex $1699 Gd $1338

Springfield Armory
SAR-8 Sporter Rifle

M-1 GARAND SEMIAUTOMATIC RIFLE
Gas-operated. Calibers: .308 Win. (7.62 NATO), .30-06. Eight round stripper clip. 24-inch bbl. 43.5 inches overall. Weight: 9.5 lbs. Adj. aperture rear sight, military square blade front. Standard "Issue-grade" walnut stock or folding buttstock. Made 1979-90.
Standard model . . . . NiB $941 Ex $715 Gd $483
National match . . . . NiB $947 Ex $741 Gd $535
Ultra match . . . . NiB $998 Ex $895 Gd $586
Sniper model . . . . NiB $998 Ex $895 Gd $586
Tanker model. . . . . NiB $792 Ex $689 Gd $406
Paratrooper w/folding stock . . . . . NiB $1024 Ex $792 Gd $561

MATCH M1A
Same as Standard M1A except w/National Match-grade bbl. w/modified flash suppressor, National Match sights, turned trigger pull, gas system assembly in one unit, modified mainspring guide glass-bedded walnut stock. Super Match M1A w/premium-grade heavy bbl. (weighs 10 lbs).
Match M1A . . . . NiB $1565 Ex $1349 Gd $844
Super Match M1A . . . . NiB $1771 Ex $1359 Gd $973

STANDARD M1A SEMIAUTOMATIC
Gas-operated. Similar to U.S. M14 service rifle except w/o provision for automatic firing. Caliber: 7.65mm NATO (.308 Win.). Five, 10- or 20-round detachable box magazine. 25.13-inch bbl w/flash suppressor. Weight: 9 lbs. Sights: Adj. aperture rear; blade front. Fiberglass, birch or walnut stock, fiberglass handguard, sling swivels. Made 1974 to date.
W/fiberglass or birch stock . . . . . . NiB $1071 Ex $818 Gd $535
W/walnut stock . . . . NiB $1216 Ex $1003 Gd $732

M-6 SCOUT RIFLE/SHOTGUN COMBO
Similar to (14-inch) short-barrel Survival Gun provided as backup weapon to U.S. combat pilots. Calibers: .22 LR/.410 and .22 Hornet/.410. 18.5-inch bbl. 32 inches overall. Weight: 4 lbs. Parkerized or stainless steel finish. Folding detachable stock w/storage for fifteen .22 LR cartridges and four .410 shells. Drilled and tapped for scope mounts. Intro. 1982 and imported from Czech Republic 1995 to date.
First Issue (no trigger guard). . . . NiB $1980 Ex $1524 Gd $1050
Second Issue (w/trigger guard) . . NiB $1670 Ex $1310 Gd $950

SAR-8 SPORTER RIFLE
Similar to H&K 911 semiautomatic rifle. Calibers: .308 Win., (7.62x51) NATO. Detachable 5- 10- or 20-round magazine. 18- or 20-inch bbl. 38.25 or 45.3 inches overall. Weight: 8.7 to 9.5 lbs. Protected front post and rotary adj. rear sight. Delayed roller-locked blow-back action w/fluted chamber. Kevlar-reinforced fiberglass thumb-hole style wood stock. Imported 1990 to date.
SAR-8 w/wood stock (disc. 1994). . . . . . NiB $1357 Ex $1101 Gd $788
SAR-8 w/thumb-hole stock . . . . NiB $1076 Ex $895 Gd $612

SAR-48, SAR-4800
Similar to Browning FN FAL/LAR semiautomatic rifle. Calibers: .233 Rem. (5.56x45) and 3.08 Win. (7.62x51) NATO. Detachable 5- 10- or 20-round magazine. 18- or 21-inch chrome-lined bbl. 38.25 or 45.3 inches overall. Weight: 9.5 to 13.25 lbs. Protected post front and adj. rear sight. Forged receiver and bolt w/adj. gas system. Pistol-grip or thumb-hole style; synthetic or wood stock. Imported 1985; reintroduced 1995.
SAR-48 w/pistol-grip stock
(disc. 1989). . . . . NiB $1204 Ex $1024 Gd $612
SAR-48 w/wood stock (disc. 1989). . . . NiB $2377 Ex $1925 Gd $1349
SAR-48 w/folding stock (disc. 1989). . . NiB $2671 Ex $2157 Gd $1500
SAR-48 w/thumb-hole stock . . . . NiB $1231 Ex $993 Gd $688

SQUIRES BINGHAM CO., INC. — Makati, Rizal, Philippines

MODEL 14D DELUXE BOLT-ACTION REPEATING RIFLE . . . . NiB $112 Ex $86 Gd $61
Caliber: .22 LR. Five round box magazine. 24-inch bbl. Sights: V-notch rear; hooded ramp front. Receiver grooved for scope mounting. Pulong Dalaga stock w/contrasting forend tip and grip cap, checkered forearm and pistol-grip. Weight: 6 lbs. Disc.

MODEL 15 . . . . NiB $137 Ex $92 Gd $86
Same as Model 14D except chambered for .22 WMR. Importation. Disc.

MODEL M16 SEMIAUTOMATIC RIFLE. . . . NiB $132 Ex $137 Gd $102
Styled after U.S. M16 military rifle. Caliber: .22 LR. 15-round box magazine. 19.5-inch bbl. w/muzzle brake/flash hider. Rear sight in carrying handle, post front on high ramp. Black-painted mahogany buttstock and forearm. Weight: 6.5 lbs. Importation. Disc.

MODEL M20D DELUXE . . . . NiB $214 Ex $188 Gd $107
Caliber: .22 LR. 15-round box magazine. 19.5-inch bbl. w/muzzle brake/flash hider. Sights: V-notch rear; blade front. Receiver grooved for scope mounting. Pulong Dalaga stock w/contrasting forend tip and grip cap, checkered forearm/pistol-grip. Weight: 6 lbs. Importation. Disc.

STANDARD ARMS COMPANY — Wilmington, Delaware

MODEL G AUTOMATIC RIFLE . . . . NiB $633 Ex $324 Gd $216
Gas-operated. Autoloading. Hammerless. Takedown. .25-35, .30-30, .25 Rem., .30 Rem., .35 Rem. Magazine capacity: 4 rounds in .35 Rem., 5 rounds in other calibers. 22.38-inch bbl. Weight: 7.75 lbs. Sights: Open sporting rear; ivory bead front. Shotgun-type stock. Made c. 1910. Note: This was the first gas-operated rifle manufactured in the U.S. While essentially an autoloader, the gas port can be closed and the rifle may be operated as a slide-action repeater.

Star
Rolling Block Carbine

MODEL M HAND-OPERATED RIFLE ..... NiB $319 Ex $293 Gd $164
Slide-action repeater w/same general specifications as Model G except lacks autoloading feature. Weight: 7 lbs.

STAR — Eibar, Spain
Mfd. by Bonifacio Echeverria, S.A.

ROLLING BLOCK CARBINE ...... NiB $216 Ex $175 Gd $122
Single-shot action similar to Remington Rolling Block. .30-30, .357 Mag., .44 Mag. 20-inch bbl. Weight: 6 lbs. Sights: Folding leaf rear; ramp front. Walnut straight-grip stock w/crescent buttplate, forearm w/bbl. band. Imported 1973-75.

STERLING — Imported by Lanchester U.S.A., Inc., Dallas, Texas

MARK 6 SEMIAUTOMATIC CARBINE..... NiB $787 Ex $607 Gd $422
Caliber: 9mm Para 34-round magazine. Bbl.: 16.1 inches. Weight: 7.5 lbs. Flip-type rear peep sight, ramp front. Folding metal skeleton stock. Made 1983-94.

J. STEVENS ARMS CO. — Chicopee Falls, Massachusetts, Div. of Savage Industries, Westfield, Mass.

J. Stevens Arms eventually became a division of Savage Industries. Consequently, the "Stevens" brand name is used for some rifles by Savage; see separate Savage-Stevens listings under Savage.

NO. 12 MARKSMAN SINGLE-SHOT RIFLE. . NiB $214 Ex $163 Gd $86
Lever-action, tip-up. Takedown. Calibers: .22 LR, .25 R.F., .32 R.F. 22-inch bbl. Plain straight-grip stock, small tapered forearm.

NO. 14 LITTLE SCOUT
SINGLE-SHOT RIFLE.................. NiB $214 Ex $107 Gd $61
Caliber: .22 RF. 18-inch bbl. One-piece slab stock readily distinguishes it from the No. 14X that follows. Made 1906-1910.

NO. 14.5 LITTLE SCOUT
SINGLE-SHOT RIFLE .... NiB $214 Ex $112 Gd $86
Rolling block. Takedown. Caliber: .22 LR. 18- or 20-inch bbl. Weight: 2.75 lbs. Sights: open rear; blade front. Plain straight-grip stock, small tapered forearm.

MODEL 15 .... NiB $188 Ex $112 Gd $102
Same as Stevens-Springfield Model 15 except w/24-inch bbl., weight: 5 lbs., w/redesigned stock. Made 1948-65.

MODEL 15Y YOUTH'S RIFLE ...... NiB $163 Ex $107 Gd $92
Same as Model 15 except w/21-inch bbl., short buttstock, weight: 4.75 lbs. Made 1958-65.

NO. 44 IDEAL
SINGLE-SHOT RIFLE.................. NiB $771 Ex $619 Gd $425
Rolling block. Lever-action. Takedown. Calibers: .22 LR. .25 R.F., .32 R.F., .25-20 S.S., .32-20, .32-40, .38-40, .38-55, .44-40. Bbl. lengths: 24-inch, 26-inch (round, half-octagon, full-octagon). Weight: 7 lbs w/26-inch round bbl. Sights: Open rear; Rocky Mountain front. Plain straight-grip stock and forearm. Made 1894-32.

NO. 44.5 IDEAL SINGLE-SHOT RIFLE .... NiB $969 Ex $777 Gd $532
Falling-block. Lever-action rifle. Aside from the new design action intro. 1903, specifications of this model are the same as those of Model 44. Model 44X disc. 1916.

NOS. 45 TO 54 IDEAL SINGLE-SHOT RIFLES
These are higher-grade models, differing from the standard No. 44 and 44.5 chiefly in finish, engraving, set triggers, levers, bbls., stock, etc. The Schuetzen types (including the Stevens-Pope models) are in this series. Model Nos. 45 to 54 were intro. 1896 and originally had the No. 44-type rolling-block action, which was superseded in 1903 by the No. 44.5-type falling-block action. These models were all disc. about 1916. Generally speaking, the 45-54 series rifles, particularly the Stevens Pope and higher grade Schuetzen models are collector's items, bringing much higher prices than the ordinary No. 44 and 44.5.

MODEL 66 BOLT-ACTION
REPEATING RIFLE............... NiB $188 Ex $112 Gd $97
Takedown. Caliber: .22 Short, Long, LR. Tubular magazine holds 13 LR, 15 Long, 19 Short. 24-inch bbl. Weight: 5 lbs. Sights: Open rear, bead front. Plain pistol-grip stock w/grooved forearm. Made 1931-35.

NO. 70 VISIBLE LOADING
SLIDE-ACTION .... NiB $316 Ex $265 Gd $112
Exposed hammer. Caliber: .22 LR., Long, Short. Tubular magazine holds 11 LR., 13 Long, 15 Short. 22-inch bbl. Weight: 4.5 lbs. Sights: Open rear; bead front. Plain straight-grip stock, grooved slide handle. Made 1907-34. Note: Nos. 702, 71, 712, 72, 722 essentially the same as No. 70, differing chiefly in bbl. length or sight tooling.

MODEL 87 AUTOLOADING RIFLE...... NiB $188 Ex $137 Gd $102
Takedown. Caliber: .22 LR. 15-round tubular magazine. 24-inch bbl. (20-inch on current model). Weight: 6 lbs. Sights: Open rear, bead front. Pistol-grip stock. Made 1938 to date. Note: This model originally bore the "Springfield" brand name, disc. in 1948.

MODEL 322 HI-POWER
BOLT-ACTION CARBINE......... NiB $316 Ex $265 Gd $137
Caliber: .22 Hornet. 4-round detachable magazine. 21-inch bbl. Weight: 6.75 lbs. Sights: Open rear; ramp front. Pistol-grip stock. Made 1947-50 (See Savage models 340, 342.)

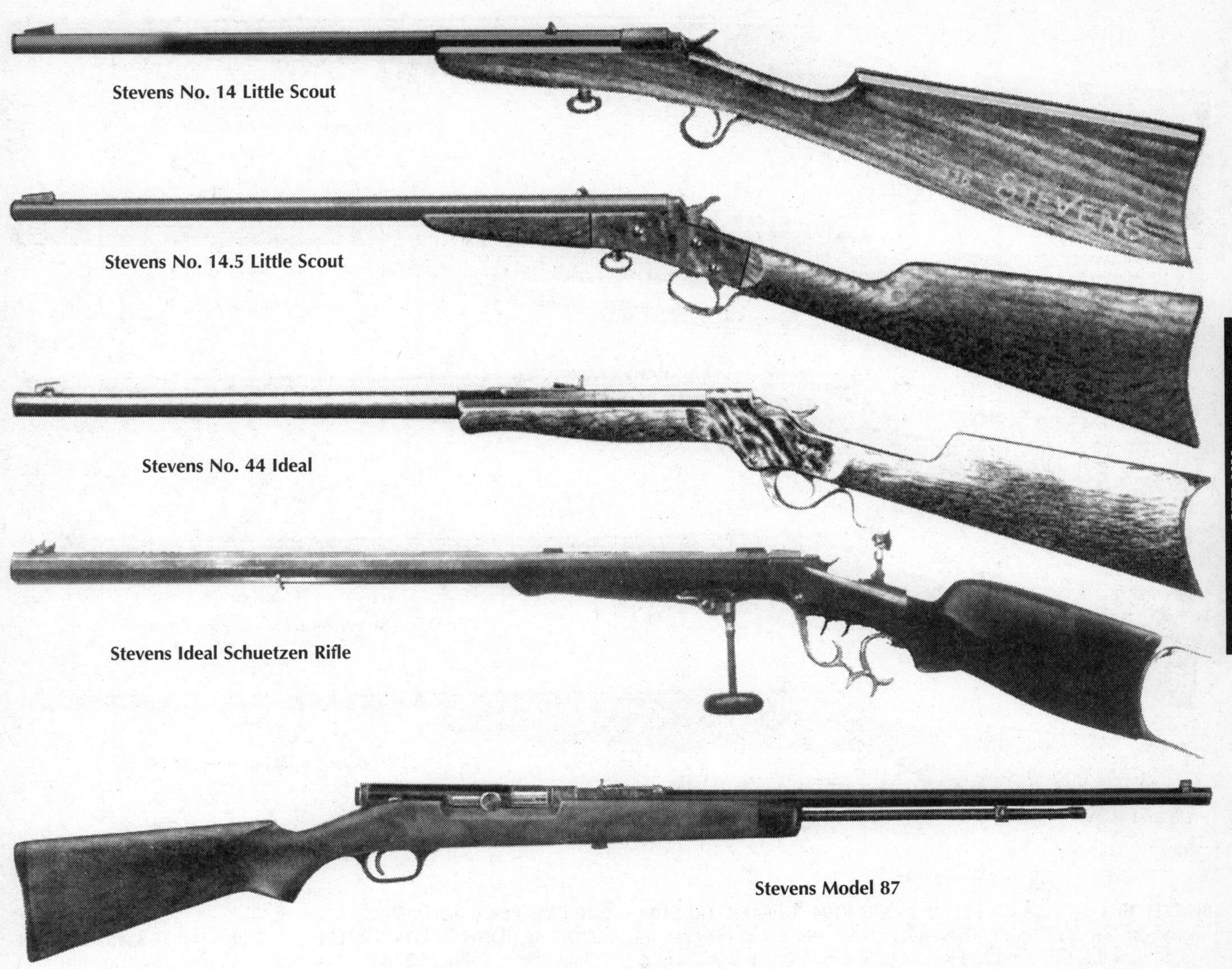
Stevens No. 14 Little Scout

Stevens No. 14.5 Little Scout

Stevens No. 44 Ideal

Stevens Ideal Schuetzen Rifle

Stevens Model 87

6MODEL 322-S . . . . NiB $367 Ex $290 Gd $163
Same as Model 325 except w/peep rear sight. (See Savage models 340S, 342S.)

MODEL 325 HI-POWER BOLT-ACTION CARBINE . . . . NiB $316 Ex $265 Gd $137
Caliber: .30-30. Three round detachable box magazine. 21-inch bbl. Weight: 6.75 lbs. Sights: Open rear; bead front. Plain pistol-grip stock. Made 1947-50. (See Savage Model 340.)

MODEL 325-S . . . . NiB $657 Ex $290 Gd $163
Same as Model 325 except w/peep rear sight. (See Savage Model 340S.)

NO. 414 ARMORY MODEL SINGLE-SHOT RIFLE . . . . NiB $520 Ex $443 Gd $290
No. 44-type lever-action. Calibers: .22 LR only, .22 Short only. 26-inch bbl. Weight: 8 lbs. Sights: Lyman receiver peep; blade front. Plain straight-grip stock, military-type forearm, swivels. Made 1912-32.

MODEL 416 BOLT-ACTION TARGET RIFLE . . . . NiB $342 Ex $239 Gd $194
Caliber: .22 LR. Five round detachable box magazine. 26-inch heavy bbl. Weight: 9.5 lbs. Sights: Receiver peep; hooded front. Target stock, swivels, sling. Made 1937-49.

NO. 419 JUNIOR TARGET MODEL BOLT-ACTION SINGLE-SHOT RIFLE . . . . . . NiB $367 Ex $265 Gd $188
Takedown. Caliber: .22 LR. 26-inch bbl. Weight: 5.5 lbs. Sights: Lyman No. 55 rear peep; blade front. Plain junior target stock w/pistol grip and grooved forearm, swivels, sling. Made 1932-36.

BUCKHORN MODEL 053 BOLT-ACTION SINGLE-SHOT RIFLE . . . . NiB $149 Ex $120 Gd $84
Takedown. Calibers: .22 Short, Long, LR., .22 WRF. .25 Stevens R.F. 24-inch bbl. Weight: 5.5 lbs. Sights: Receiver peep; open middle; hooded front. Sporting stock w/pistol-grip and black forend tip. Made 1935-48.

BUCKHORN MODEL 53 . . . . NiB $192 Ex $161 Gd $100
Same as Buckhorn Model 053 except w/open rear sight and plain bead front sight.

Stevens No. 414 Armory

Stevens Model 416

Stevens Buckhorn Model 53

Stevens Buckhorn Model 055

Stevens Buckhorn Model 56

BUCKHORN 055. . . . . NiB $194 Ex $163 Gd $102
Takedown. Same as Model 056 except in single-shot configuration. Weight: 5.5 lbs. Caliber: .22 LR., Long, Short. 24-inch bbl. Weight: 6 lbs. Sights: Receiver peep, open middle, hooded front. Made 1935-48.

BUCKHORN MODEL 056
BOLT-ACTION . . . . NiB $199 Ex $163 Gd $107
Takedown. Caliber: .22 LR., Long, Short. Five round detachable box magazine. 24-inch bbl. Weight: 6 lbs. Sights: Receiver peep, open middle, hooded front. Sporting stock w/pistol grip and black forend tip. Made 1935-48.

BUCKHORN
MODEL 56 . . . . NiB $188 Ex $137 Gd $102
Same as Buckhorn Model 056 except w/open rear sight and plain bead front sight.

BUCKHORN NO. 057. . . . . NiB $173 Ex $112 Gd $86
Same as Buckhorn Model 076 except w/5-round detachable box magazine. Made 1939-48.

BUCKHORN NO. 57. . . . . NiB $173 Ex $112 Gd $86
Same as Buckhorn Model 76 except w/5-round detachable box magazine. Made 1939-48.

BUCKHORN MODEL 066
BOLT-ACTION REPEATING RIFLE . . . . . . NiB $241 Ex $190 Gd $1014
Takedown. Caliber: .22 LR, Long, Short. Tubular magazine holds 21 Short, 17 Long, 15 LR. 24-inch bbl. Weight: 6 lbs. Sights: Receiver peep; open middle; hooded front. Sporting stock w/pistol grip and black forend tip. Made 1935-48.

BUCKHORN MODEL 66. . . . . NiB $173 Ex $112 Gd $86
Same as Buckhorn Model 066 except w/open rear sight, plain bead front sight.

BUCKHORN NO. 076
AUTOLOADING RIFLE . . . . NiB $188 Ex $163 Gd $107
Takedown. Caliber: .22 LR. 15-round tubular magazine. 24-inch bbl. Weight: 6 lbs. Sights: Receiver peep; open middle; hooded front. Sporting stock w/pistol grip, black forend tip. Made 1938-48.

BUCKHORN NO. 76. . . . . NiB $188 Ex $163 Gd $102
Same as Buckhorn No. 076 except w/open rear sight, plain bead front sight.

CRACKSHOT NO. 26
SINGLE-SHOT RIFLE . . . . NiB $265 Ex $1209 Gd $137
Lever-action. Takedown. Calibers: .22 LR, .32 R.F. 18-inch or 22-inch bbl. Weight: 3.25 lbs. Sights: Open rear; blade front. Plain straight-grip stock, small tapered forearm. Made 1913-39.

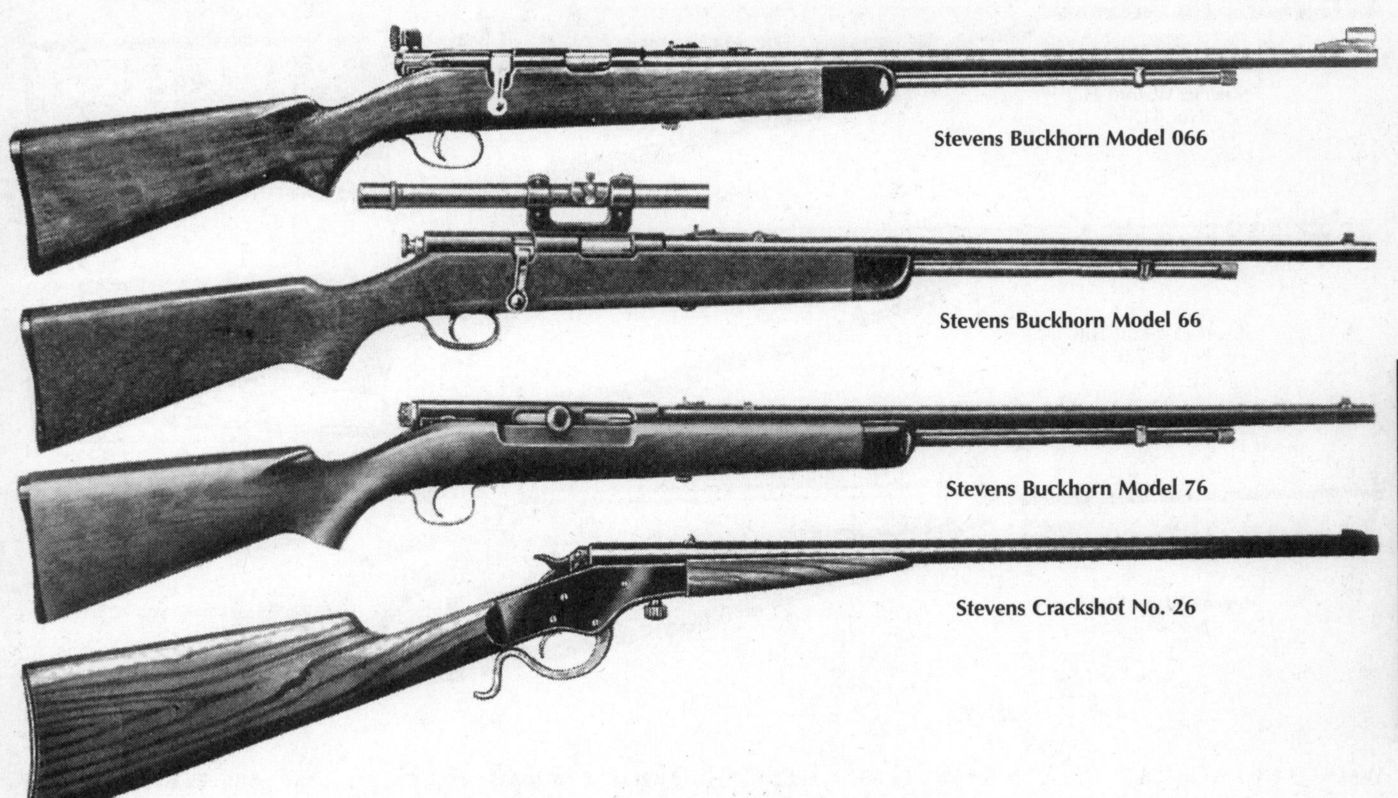
Stevens Buckhorn Model 066

Stevens Buckhorn Model 66

Stevens Buckhorn Model 76

Stevens Crackshot No. 26

CRACKSHOT NO. 26.5 . . . . NiB $306 Ex $188 Gd $163
Same as Crackshot No. 26 except w/smoothbore bbl. for shot cartridges.

FAVORITE NO. 17
SINGLE-SHOT RIFLE . . . . NiB $290 Ex $188 Gd $137
Lever-action. Takedown. Calibers: .22 LR, .25 R.F., .32 R.F. 24-inch round bbl; other lengths were available. Weight: 4.5 lbs. Sights: Open rear; Rocky Mountain front. Plain straight-grip stock, small tapered forearm. Made 1894-1935.

FAVORITE NO. 18. . . . . NiB $367 Ex $265 Gd $137
Same as Favorite No. 17 except w/Vernier peep rear sight, leaf middle sight, Beach combination front sight.

FAVORITE NO. 19. . . . . NiB $392 Ex $290 Gd $163
Same as Favorite No. 17 except w/Lyman combination rear sight, leaf middle sight, Lyman front sight.

FAVORITE NO. 20. . . . . NiB $367 Ex $290 Gd $188
Same as Favorite No. 17 except w/smoothbore barrel.

FAVORITE NO. 27. . . . . NiB $392 Ex $290 Gd $1204
Same as Favorite No. 17 except w/octagon bbl.

FAVORITE NO. 28. . . . . NiB $367 Ex $265 Gd $188
Same as Favorite No. 18 except w/octagon bbl.

FAVORITE NO. 29. . . . . NiB $392 Ex $265 Gd $188
Same as Favorite No. 19 except w/octagon bbl.

WALNUT HILL NO. 417-0
SINGLE-SHOT TARGET RIFLE . . . . NiB $912 Ex $708 Gd $453
Lever-action. Calibers: .22 LR only, .22 Short only, .22 Hornet. 28-inch heavy bbl. (extra heavy 29-inch bbl. also available). Weight: 10.5 lbs. Sights: Lyman No. 52L extension rear; 17A front, scope bases mounted on bbl. Target stock w/full pistol-grip, beavertail forearm, bbl. band, swivels, sling. Made 1932-47.

WALNUT HILL NO. 417-1 . . . . NiB $938 Ex $912 Gd $530
Same as No. 417-0 except w/Lyman No. 48L receiver sight.

WALNUT HILL NO. 417-2 . . . . NiB $989 Ex $912 Gd $555
Same as No. 417-0 except w/Lyman No. 144 tang sight.

WALNUT HILL NO. 417-3 . . . . NiB $928 Ex $785 Gd $428
Same as No. 417-0 except w/o sights.

WALNUT HILL NO. 417.5
SINGLE-SHOT RIFLE . . . . NiB $938 Ex $861 Gd $479
Lever-action. Calibers: .22 LR, .22 WMR, .25 R.F., .22 Hornet. 28-inch bbl. Weight: 8.5 lbs. Sights: Lyman No. 144 tang peep, folding middle; bead front. Sporting stock w/pistol-grip, semi-beavertail forearm, swivels, sling. Made 1932-40.

WALNUT HILL NO. 418
SINGLE-SHOT RIFLE . . . . NiB $571 Ex $418 Gd $341
Lever-action. Takedown. Calibers: .22 LR only, .22 Short only. 26-inch bbl. Weight: 6.5 lbs. Sights: Lyman No. 144 tang peep; blade front. Pistol-grip stock, semi-beavertail forearm, swivels, sling. Made 1932-40.

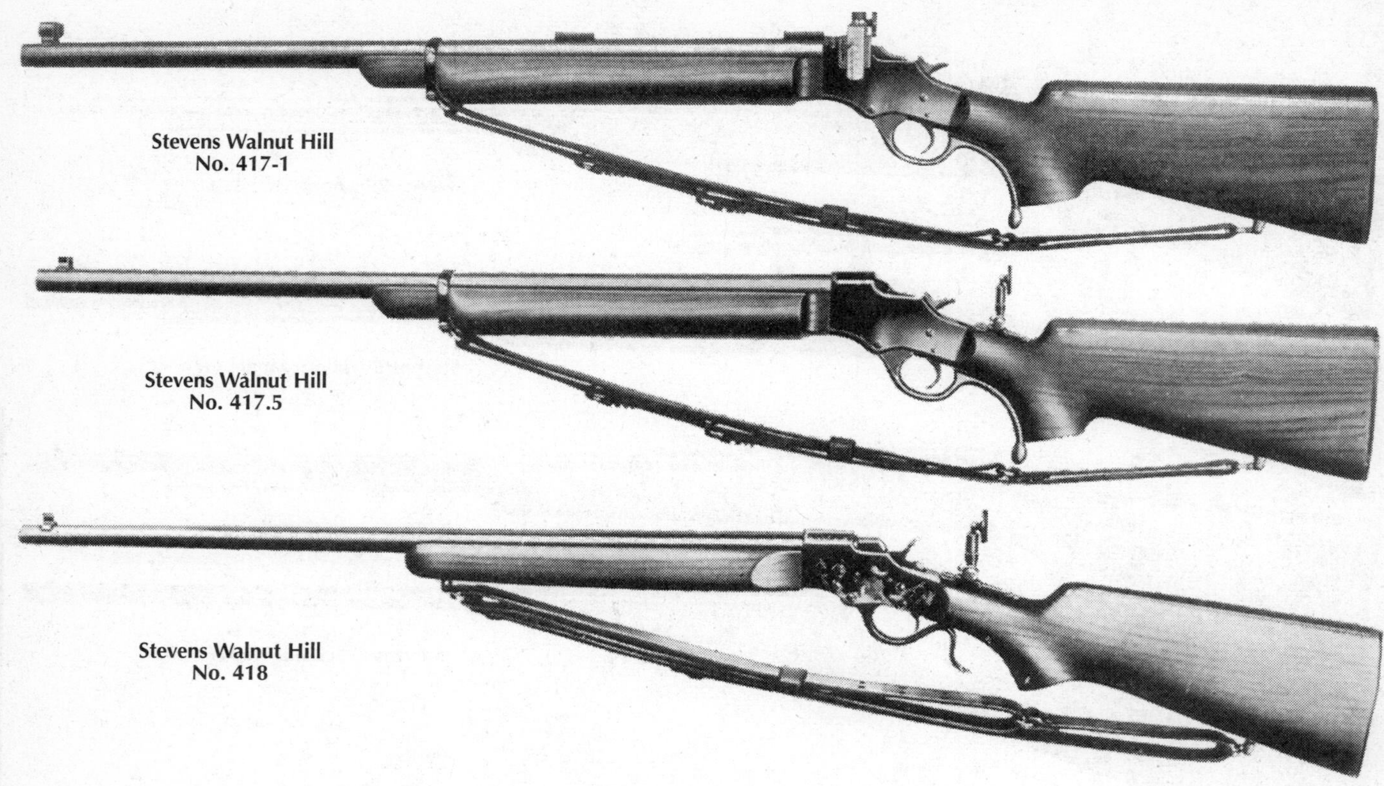

Stevens Walnut Hill No. 417-1

Stevens Walnut Hill No. 417.5

Stevens Walnut Hill No. 418

WALNUT HILL NO. 418.5 . . . . NiB $647 Ex $571 Gd $408
Same as No. 418 except also available in calibers .22 WRF and .25 Stevens R.F., w/Lyman No. 2A tang peep sight, bead front sight.

MODEL 15 SINGLE-SHOT BOLT-ACTION RIFLE. . . . . NiB $161 Ex $110 Gd $84
Takedown. Caliber: .22 LR, Long, Short. 22-inch bbl. Weight: 4 lbs. Sights: Open rear, bead front. Plain pistol-grip stock. Made 1937-48.

MODEL 82 BOLT-ACTION SINGLE-SHOT RIFLE . . . . NiB $132 Ex $115 Gd $84
Takedown. Caliber: .22 LR, Long, Short. 22-inch bbl. Weight: 4 lbs. Sights: Open rear; gold bead front. Plain pistol-grip stock w/grooved forearm. Made 1935-39.

MODEL 83 BOLT-ACTION SINGLE-SHOT RIFLE . . . . NiB $161 Ex $100 Gd $79
Takedown. Calibers: .22 LR, Long, Short; .22 WRF, .25 Stevens R.F. 24-inch bbl. Weight: 4.5 lbs. Sights: Peep rear; open middle; hooded front. Plain pistol-grip stock w/grooved forearm. Made 1935-39.

MODEL 84 . . . . NiB $184 Ex $161 Gd $102
Same as Model 86 except w/5-round detachable box magazine. Pre-1948 rifles of this model were designated Springfield Model 84, later known as Stevens Model 84. Made 1940-65.

MODEL 84-S (084) . . . . NiB $184 Ex $161 Gd $105
Same as Model 84 except w/peep rear sight and hooded front sight. Pre-1948 rifles of this model were designated Springfield Model 084, later known as Stevens Model 84-S. Disc.

MODEL 85 . . . . NiB $202 Ex $120 Gd $90
Same as Stevens Model 87 except w/5-round detachable box magazine. Made 1939 to date. Pre-1948 rifles of this model were designated Springfield Model 85, currently known as Stevens Model 85. Earlier models command slight premiums.

MODEL 85-S (085) . . . . NiB $186 Ex $135 Gd $100
Same as Model 85 except w/peep rear sight and hooded front sight. Pre-1948 models were designated Springfield Model 085; also known as Stevens Model 85-S.

MODEL 86 BOLT-ACTION. . . . . NiB $186 Ex $135 Gd $100
Takedown. Caliber: .22 LR, Long, Short. Tubular magazine holds 15 LR, 17 Long, 21 Short. 24-inch bbl. Weight: 6 lbs. Sights: Open rear, gold bead front. Pistol-grip stock, black forend tip on later production. Made 1935-65. Note: The Springfield brand name was disc. in 1948.

MODEL 86-S (086) . . . . NiB $194 Ex $161 Gd $110
Same as Model 86 except w/peep rear sight and hooded front sight. Pre-1948 rifles of this model were designated as Springfield Model 086, later known as Stevens Model 86-S. Disc.

MODEL 87-S (087) . . . . NiB $202 Ex $186 Gd $115
Same as Stevens Model 87 except w/peep rear sight and hooded front sight. Pre-1948 rifles of this model were designated as Springfield Model 087, later known as Stevens Model 87-S. Disc.

STEYR-DAIMLER-PUCH A.-G. — Steyr, Austria

See also listings under Mannlicher.

AUG-SA SEMIAUTOMATIC RIFLE. . . . . NiB $3891 Ex $3110 Gd $2133
Gas-operated. Caliber: .223 Rem. (5.56mm). Thirty or 40-round magazine. 20-inch bbl. standard; optional 16-inch or 24-inch heavy bbl. w/folding bipod. 31 inches overall. Weight: 8.5 lbs. Sights: Integral 1.5x scope and mount. Green high-impact synthetic stock w/folding vertical grip.

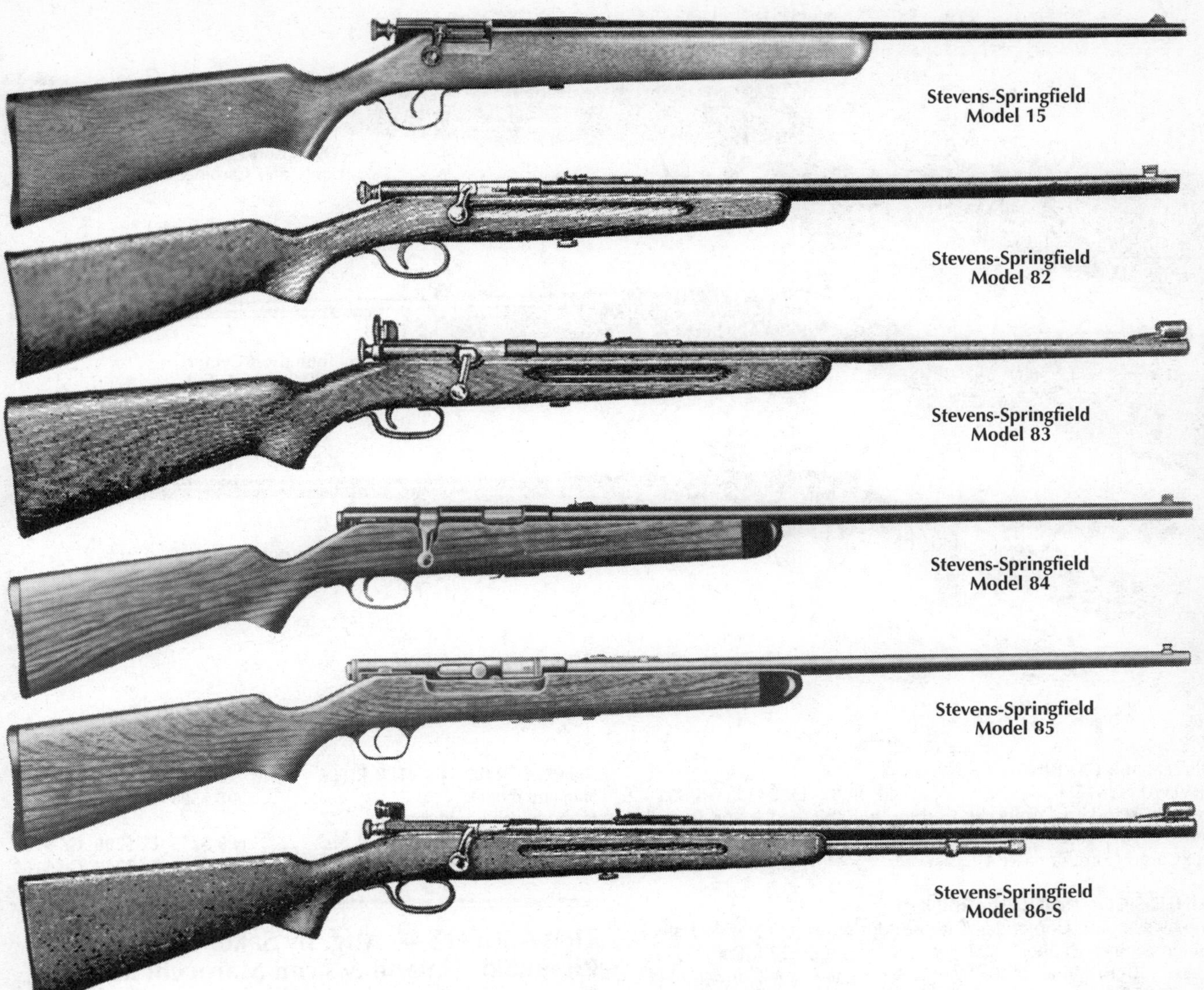

SMALL BORE CARBINE.......... NiB $557 Ex $448 Gd $308
Bolt-action repeater. Caliber: .22 LR. Five round detachable box magazine. 19.5-inch bbl. Sights: Leaf rear; hooded bead front. Mannlicher-type stock, checkered, swivels. Made 1953-67.

STOEGER RIFLE — Mfd. by Franz Jaeger & Co., Suhl, Germany; dist. in the U.S. by A. F. Stoeger, Inc., New York, N.Y.

HORNET RIFLE............... NiB $1307 Ex $921 Gd $586
Same specifications as Herold Rifle, designed and built on a Miniature Mauser-type action. See listing under Herold Bolt-Action Repeating Sporting Rifle for additional specifications. Imported during the 1930s.

SURVIVAL ARMS — Orange, CT

AR-7 EXPLORER .... NiB $153 Ex $112 Gd $71
Caliber: .22 LR. Eight round magazine. Weight: 3 lbs. Polymer stocks. Drift adj. sights. Disassembles into five separate elements, allowing

(cont'd.) **AR-7 EXPLORER**
barrel, action and magazine to fit into buttstock; assembles quickly w/o tools. Choice of camo, silvertone or black matte finishes. Made 1992-95.

THOMPSON/CENTER ARMS — Rochester, New Hampshire

CONTENDER CARBINE
Calibers: .22 LR, .22 Hornet, .222 Rem., .223 Rem., 7mm T.C.U., 7x30 Waters, .30-30 Win., .35 Rem., .44 Mag., .357 Rem. Max. and .410 bore. 21-inch interchangeable bbls. 35 inches overall. Adj. iron sights. Checkered American walnut or Rynite stock and forend. Made 1985 to date.

Standard model (rifle calibers) .... NiB $432 Ex $329 Gd $252
Standard model (.410 bore) .... NiB $492 Ex $401 Gd $286
Rynite stock model (rifle calibers) .... NiB $555 Ex $483 Gd $393
Rynite stock model (.410 bore).......... NiB $580 Ex $504 Gd $407
Extra bbls. (rifle calibers) .... NiB $276 Ex $231 Gd $173
Extra bbls. (.410 bore)................ NiB $292 Ex $241 Gd $178
Youth model (all calibers and .410 bore) .... NiB $380 Ex $303 Gd $200

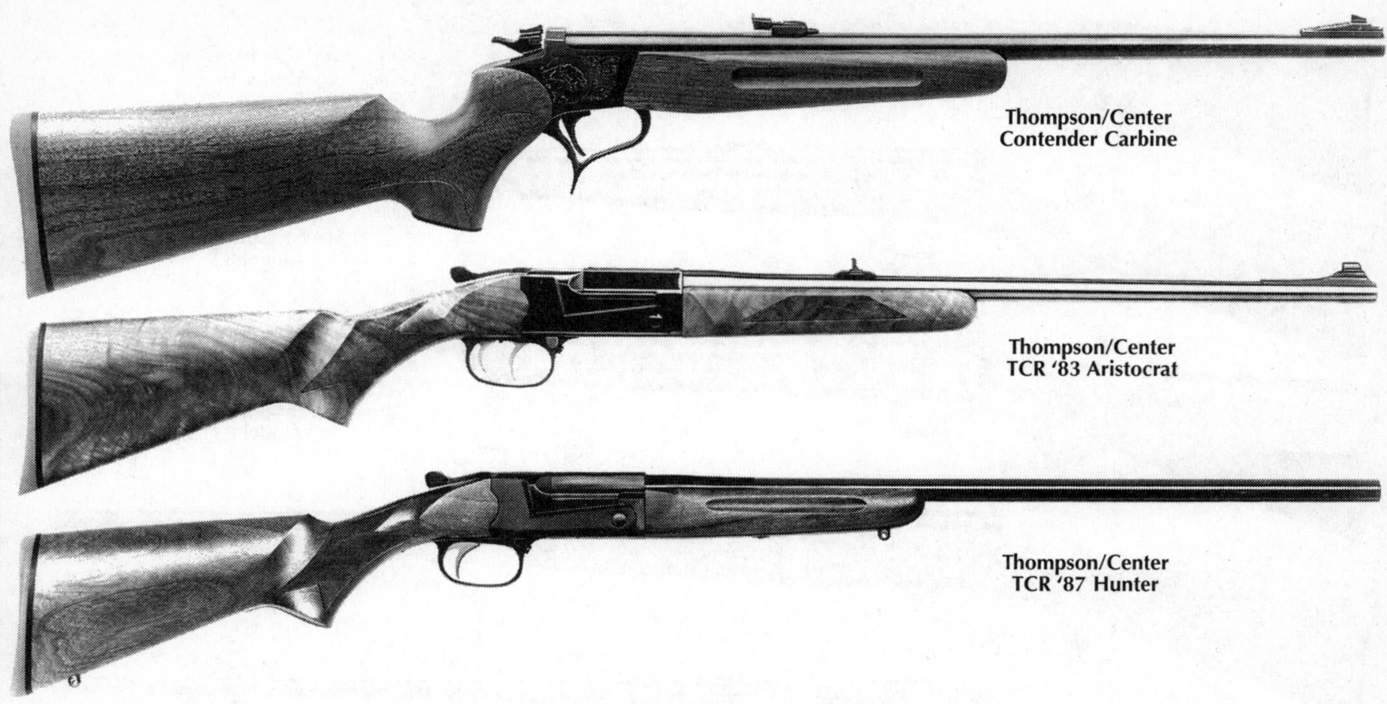

Thompson/Center
Contender Carbine

Thompson/Center
TCR '83 Aristocrat

Thompson/Center
TCR '87 Hunter

CONTENDER CARBINE
SURVIVAL SYSTEM. . . . . NiB $602 Ex $422 Gd $319
Similar to standard Contender Carbine w/Rynite stock and forend. Comes w/two 16.25-inch bbls. chambered in .223 and .45/.410 bore. Camo Cordura case.

STAINLESS CONTENDER CARBINE
Same as standard Contender Carbine Model, except stainless steel w/blued sights. Calibers: .22 LR, .22 Hornet, .223 Rem., 7-30 Waters, .30-30 Win., .410. Walnut or Rynite stock and forend. Made 1993 to date.
Walnut stock model. . . . . NiB $473 Ex $396 Gd $267
Rynite stock model . . . . NiB $448 Ex $370 Gd $257
Youth stock model. . . . . NiB $422 Ex $345 Gd $242
Extra bbls. (rifle calibers). . . . . NiB $236 Ex $190 Gd $133

TCR '83 ARISTOCRAT MODEL
Break frame, overlever action. Calibers: .223 Rem., .22/250 Rem., .243 Win., 7mm Rem. Mag., .30-06 Springfield. Interchangeable bbls.: 23 inches in length. Weight: 6 lbs., 14 oz. American walnut stock and forearm, checkered, black rubber recoil pad, cheekpiece. Made 1983-87.
TCR '83 Standard model . . . . NiB $448 Ex $396 Gd $216
TCR '83 Aristocrat. . . . . NiB $520 Ex $370 Gd $242
Extra bbls. (rifle calibers). . . . . NiB $236 Ex $190 Gd $133

TCR '87 HUNTER RIFLE
Similar to TCR '83 except in calibers .22 Hornet, ..222 Rem., 223 Rem., .22-250 Rem., .243 Win., .270 Win., 7mm-08, .308 Win., .30-06, .32-40 Win. Also 12-ga. slug and 10- and 12-ga. field bbls. 23-inch standard or 25.88-inch heavy bbl. interchangeable. 39.5 to 43.38 inches overall. Weight: 6 lbs., 14 oz. to 7.5 lbs. Iron sights optional. Checkered American black walnut buttstock w/fluted end. Disc. 1993.

(cont'd.) **TCR '87 HUNTER RIFLE**
Standard model. . . . . NiB $525 Ex $422 Gd $242
Extra bbl. (rifle calibers and
10- or 12-ga. Field) . . . . NiB $255 Ex $206 Gd $143
Extra bbl. (12-ga. slug) . . . . NiB $299 Ex $242 Gd $168

TIKKA RIFLES — Mfg. by Sako, Ltd. of Riihimaki, Finland & Armi Marocchi in Italy

Imported by Beretta USA

Note: *Tikka New Generation, Battue and Continental series bolt action rifles are being manufactured by Sako, Ltd., in Finland. Tikka O/U rifles (previously Valmet) are being manufactured in Italy by Armi Marocchi. For earlier importation see additional listings under Ithaca LSA and Valmet 412S models.*

MODEL 412S DOUBLE RIFLE
Calibers: .308 Win., .30-06, 9.3x74R. 24-inch bbl. w/quarter rib machined for scope mounts; automatic ejectors (9.3x74R only). 40 inches overall. Weight: 8.5 lbs. Ramp front and folding adj. rear sight. Barrel selector on trigger and cocking indicators in tang. European walnut buttstock and forearm. Model 412S was replaced by the 512S version in 1994. Imported 1989-93.
Model 412S
(disc. 1993). . . . . NiB $1452 Ex $1050 Gd $792
Extra barrel assembly
(O/U shotgun), add. $650
Extra barrel assembly
(O/U Combo), add $775
Extra barrel assembly
(O/U rifle), add. $995

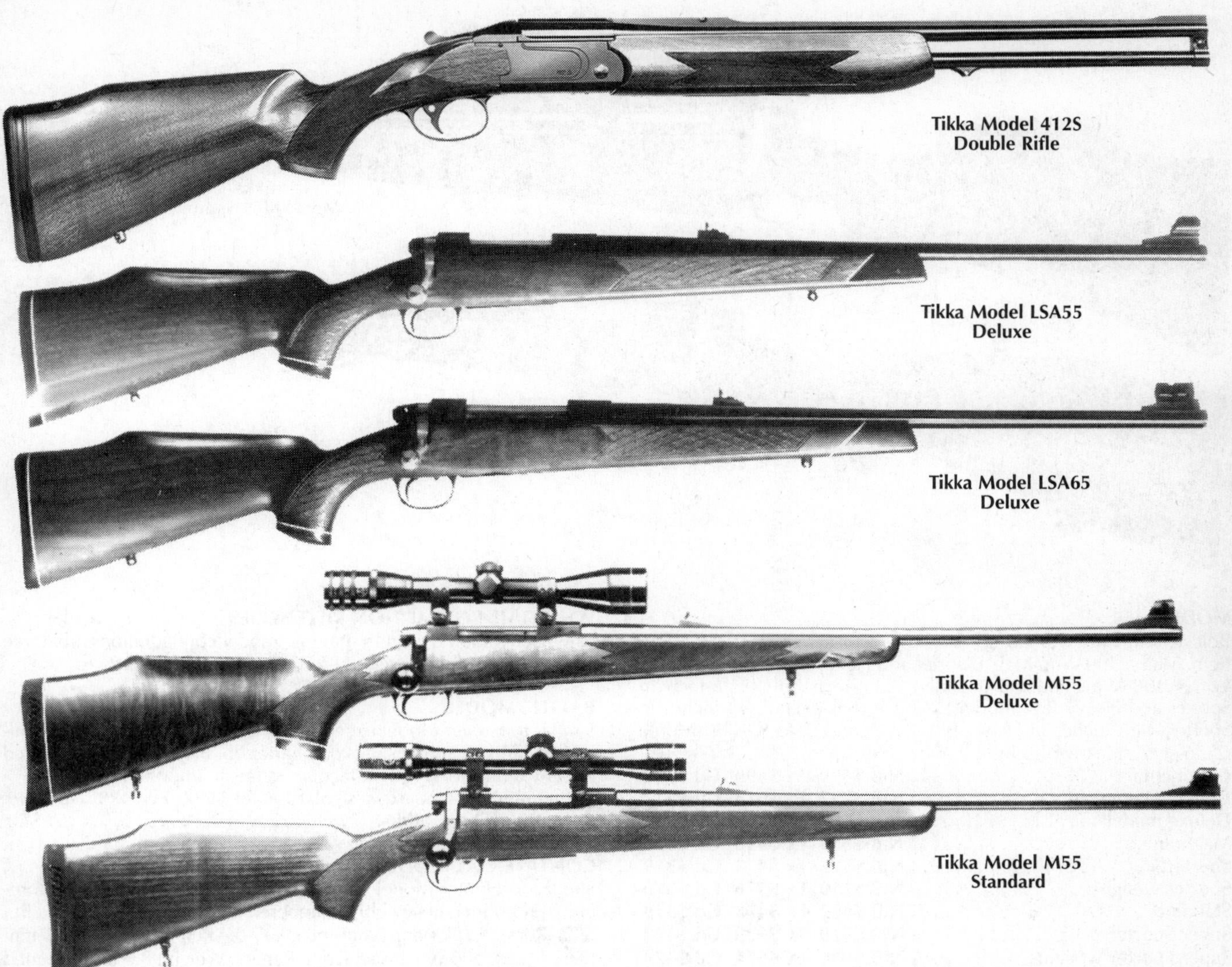
Tikka Model 412S Double Rifle

Tikka Model LSA55 Deluxe

Tikka Model LSA65 Deluxe

Tikka Model M55 Deluxe

Tikka Model M55 Standard

MODEL 512S DOUBLE RIFLE
Formerly Valmet 412S. In 1994, following the joint venture of 1989, the model designation was changed to 512S. Imported 1994 to date.
Model 512S....................... NiB $1462 Ex $1333 Gd $973
Extra barrel assembly
(O/U rifle), add.. $755

LSA55 DELUXE .... NiB $525 Ex $473 Gd $396
Same as LSA55 Standard except w/rollover cheekpiece, rosewood grip cap and forend tip, skip checkering, high-luster blue. Imported 1965-88.

LSA55 SPORTER .... NiB $518 Ex $417 Gd $287
Same as LSA55 except has 22.8-inch heavy bbl. w/o sights, special stock w/beavertail forearm, not available in 6mm Rem. Weighs 9 lbs. Imported 1965-88.

LSA55 STANDARD
BOLT-ACTION REPEATER .... NiB $473 Ex $345 Gd $216
Mauser-type action. Calibers: .222 Rem., .22-250, 6mm Rem. Mag., .243 Win., .308 Win. Three round clip magazine. 22.8-inch bbl. Weight: 6.8 lbs. Sights: Folding leaf rear; hooded ramp front. Checkered walnut stock w/Monte Carlo cheekpiece, swivels. Made 1965-88.

LSA65 DELUXE .... NiB $551 Ex $473 Gd $319
Same as LSA65 Standard except w/special features of LSA55 Deluxe. Imported 1970-88.

LSA65 STANDARD .... NiB $448 Ex $345 Gd $216
Same as LSA55 Standard except calibers: .25-06, 6.5x55 .270 Win., .30-06. Five round magazine, 22-inch bbl., weight: 7.5 lbs. Imported 1970-88.

MODEL M 55
Bolt action. Calibers: .222 Rem., .22-250 Rem., .223 Rem. .243 Win., .308 Win. (6mm Rem. and 17 Rem. available in Standard and Deluxe models only). 23.2-inch bbl. (24.8-inch in Sporter and Heavy Barrel models). 42.8 inches overall (44 inches in Sporter and Heavy Barrel models). Weight: 7.25 to 9 lbs. Monte Carlo-style stock w/pistol-grip. Sling swivels. Imported 1965-88.
Continental .... NiB $679 Ex $499 Gd $350
Deluxe model .... NiB $721 Ex $504 Gd $370
Sporter.................... NiB $654 Ex $525 Gd $345
Sporter w/sights .... NiB $679 Ex $499 Gd $349
Standard .... NiB $602 Ex $473 Gd $319
Super Sporter .... NiB $757 Ex $618 Gd $370
Super Sporter w/sights ..... NiB $824 Ex $396 Gd $422
Trapper .... NiB $690 Ex $473 Gd $345

Tikka
Model M65 Sporter

Tikka
Model M65 Wild Boar

MODEL M65
Bolt action. Calibers: .25-06, .270 Win., .308 Win., .30-06, 7mm Rem. Mag., .300 Win. Mag. (Sporter and Heavy Bbl. models in .270 Win., .308 Win. and .30-06 only). 22.4-inch bbl. (24.8-inch in Sporter and Heavy Bbl. models). 43.2 inches overall (44 inches in Sporter, 44.8 inches in Heavy Bbl.). Weight: 7.5 to 9.9 lbs. Monte Carlo-style stock w/pistol-grip. Disc. 1989.
Continental . . . . NiB $679 Ex $499 Gd $360
Deluxe Magnum . . . . NiB $757 Ex $618 Gd $417
Deluxe model . . . . NiB $705 Ex $499 Gd $345
Magnum . . . . NiB $654 Ex $448 Gd $370
Sporter. . . . . NiB $525 Ex $473 Gd $319
Sporter w/sights . . . . NiB $710 Ex $576 Gd $370
Standard . . . . NiB $602 Ex $473 Gd $319
Super Sporter . . . . NiB $829 Ex $628 Gd $422
Super Sporter w/sights . . . . NiB $834 Ex $624 Gd $473
Super Sporter Master. . . . . NiB $1050 Ex $850 Gd $535

MODEL M65 WILDBOAR . . . . NiB $705 Ex $576 Gd $412
Same general specifications as Model M 65 except 20.8-inch bbl., overall length of 41.6 inches, weight: of 7.5 lbs. Disc. 1989.

NEW GENERATION RIFLES
Short-throw bolt available in three action lengths. Calibers: .22-250 Rem., .223 Rem., .243 Win., .308 Win., (medium action) .25-06 Rem., .270 Win., .30.06, (Long Action) 7mm Rem. Mag., .300 Win. Mag., .338 Win. Mag., (Magnum Action). 22- to 26-inch bbl. 42.25 to 46 inches overall. Weight: 7.2 to 8.5 lbs. Available w/o sights or w/hooded front and open rear sight on quarter rib. Quick-release 3- or 5-round detachable magazine w/recessed side release. Barrel selector on trigger and cocking indicators in tang. European walnut buttstock and forearm matte lacquer finish. Imported 1989-94.
Standard calibers. . . . . NiB $782 Ex $618 Gd $396
Magnum calibers. . . . . NiB $808 Ex $628 Gd $422

PREMIUM GRADE RIFLE
Similar to New Generation rifles except w/hand-checkered deluxe wood stock w/roll-over check-piece and rosewood grip cap and forend tip. High polished blued finish. Imported 1989-94.
Standard calibers. . . . . NiB $829 Ex $679 Gd $422
Magnum calibers. . . . . NiB $911 Ex $679 Gd $499

WHITETAIL BOLT-ACTION RIFLE SERIES
New Generation design in multiple model configurations and three action lengths chambered .22-250 to .338 Win. Mag.

BATTUE MODEL
Similar to Hunter Model except designed for snapshooting w/hooded front and open rear sights on quarter rib. Blued finish. Checkered select walnut stock w/matt lacquered finish. Imported 1991-97.
Battue model (standard w/sights) . . NiB $597 Ex $473 Gd $319
Magnum calibers, add $40

CONTINENTAL MODEL
Similar to Hunter Model except w/prone-style stock w/wider forearm and 26-inch heavy bbl. chambered for 17 Rem., .22-250 Rem., .223 Rem., .308 Win. (Varmint); .25-06 Rem., .270 Win., 7mm Rem. Mag., .300 Win. Mag. (Long Range). Weight: 8.6 lbs. Imported 1991 to date.
Continental Long-Range model . . . . NiB $705 Ex $499 Gd $350
Continental Varmint model . . . . NiB $654 Ex $499 Gd $345
Magnum calibers, add $40

SPORTER MODEL . . . . NiB $885 Ex $705 Gd $551
Similar to Hunter Model except 23.5-inch bbl. Five round detachable mazigine. Chambered .22-250 Rem., .223 Rem., .308 Win. Weight: 8.6 lbs. Adjustable buttplate and cheekpiece w/stippled pistol grip and forend. Imported 1998 to date.

WHITETAIL HUNTER MODEL
Calibers: .22-250 Rem., .223 Rem., .243 Win., .25-06 Rem., .270 Win., 7mm Rem. Mag., .308 Win .30.06, .300 Win. Mag., .338 Win. Mag. Three or 5-round detachable box magazine. 20.5- to 24.5-inch bbl. with no sights. 42 to 44.5 inches overall. Weight: 7 to 7.5 lbs. Adj. single-stage or single-set trigger. Blued or stainless finish. All-Weather synthetic or checkered select walnut stock w/matt lacquered finish. Imported 1991 to date.
Standard model . . . . NiB $602 Ex $473 Gd $319
Deluxe model . . . . NiB $731 Ex $576 Gd $396
Synthetic model. . . . . NiB $705 Ex $473 Gd $345
Stainless model . . . . NiB $710 Ex $520 Gd $345
Magnum calibers, add $40
Left-hand model, add. $70

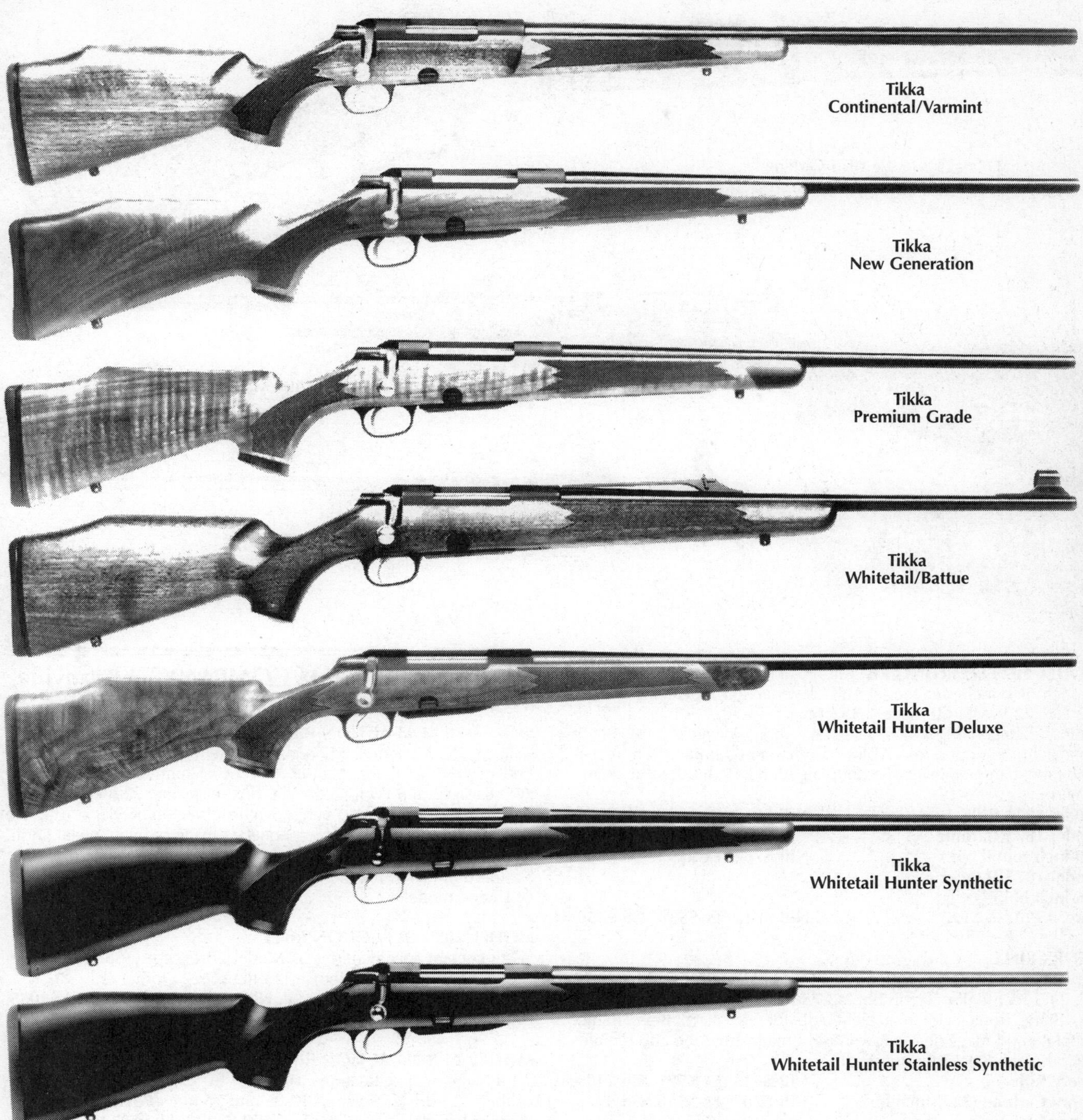

UBERTI RIFLES — Lakeville, Connecticut Mfd. By Aldo Uberti, Ponte Zanano, Italy *Imported by Stoeger Industries, Accokeek, MD*

MODEL 1866 SPORTING RIFLE

Replica of Winchester Model 1866 lever-action repeater. Calibers: .22 LR, .22 WMR, .38 Spec., .44-40, .45 LC. 24.25-inch octagonal bbl. 43.25 inches overall. Weight: 8.25 lbs. Blade front sight,rear elevation leaf. Brass frame and buttplate. Bbl., magazine tube, other metal parts blued. Walnut buttstock and forearm.

Model 1866 Rifle. . . . . NiB $787 Ex $607 Gd $324
Model 1866 Carbine
(19-inch round bbl.) . . . . NiB $679 Ex $556 Gd $350
Model 1866 Trapper
(16-inch bbl.)
Disc. 1989. . . . . NiB $607 Ex $478 Gd $345
Model 1866
Rimfire
(Indian Rifle) . . . . NiB $556 Ex $453 Gd $324
Model 1866 Rimfire
(Indian Carbine) . . . . NiB $530 Ex $432 Gd $319

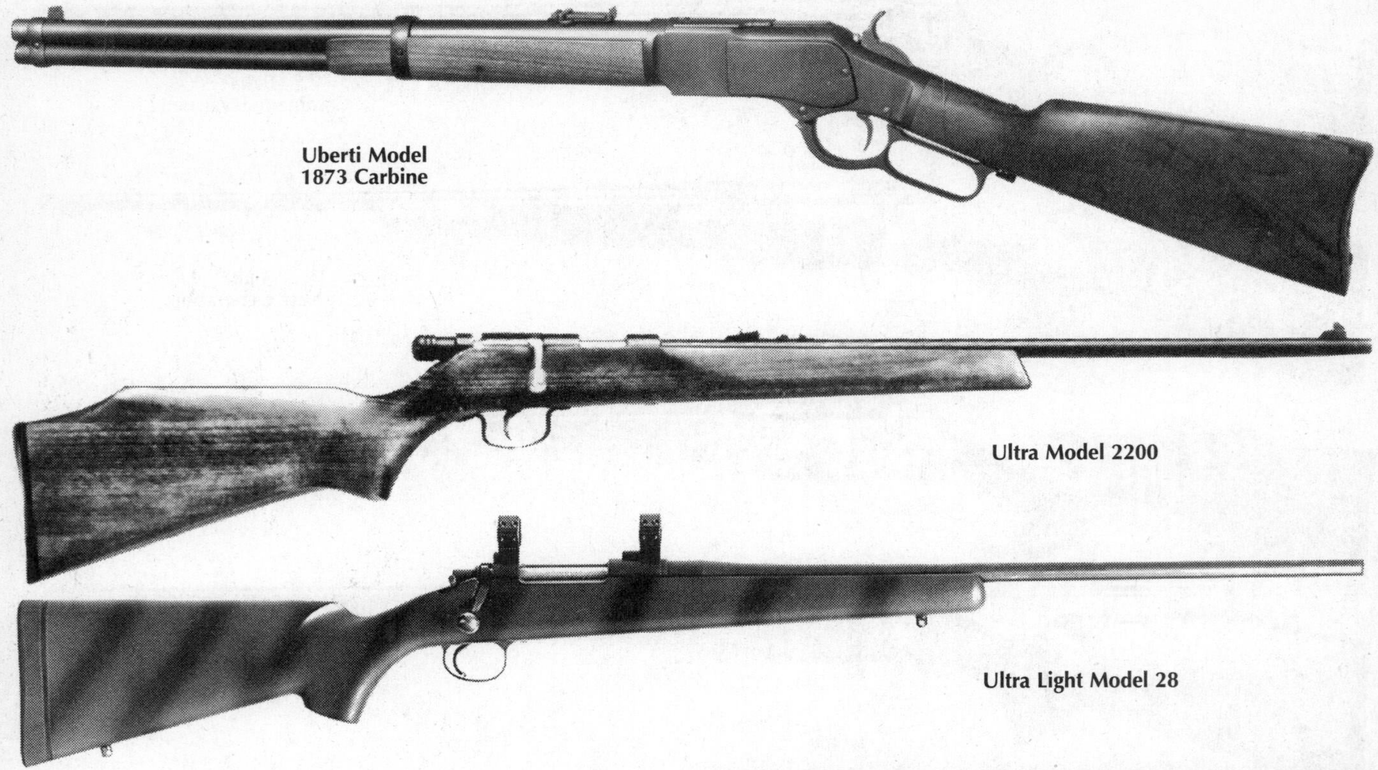

Uberti Model 1873 Carbine

Ultra Model 2200

Ultra Light Model 28

MODEL 1873 SPORTING RIFLE

Replica of Winchester Model 1873 lever-action repeater. Calibers: .22 LR, .22 WMR, .38 Spec., .357 Mag., .44-40, .45 LC. 24.25- or 30-inch octagonal bbl. 43.25 inches overall. Weight: 8 lbs. Blade front sight; adj. open rear. Color case-hardened frame. Bbl., magazine tube, hammer, lever and buttplate blued. Walnut buttstock and forearm.

Model 1873 Rifle. . . . . NiB $865 Ex $623 Gd $375
Model 1873 Carbine
(19-inch round bbl.) . . . . NiB $762 Ex $592 Gd $365
Model 1873 Trapper
(16-inch bbl.)
Disc. 1990. . . . . NiB $710 Ex $530 Gd $350

HENRY RIFLE

Replica of Henry lever-action repeating rifle. Calibers: .44-40, .45 LC. 24.5-inch half-octagon bbl. 43.75 inches overall. Weight: 9.25 lbs. Blade front sight; rear sight adj. for elevation. Brass frame, buttplate and magazine follower. Bbl., magazine tube and remaining parts blued. Walnut buttstock.

Henry Rifle . . . . NiB $813 Ex $581 Gd $401
Henry Carbine (22.5-inch bbl.) . . . . NiB $787 Ex $556 Gd $375
Henry Trapper
(16- or 18-inch bbl.) . . . . NiB $736 Ex $592 Gd $407
Steel frame, add. $85

ULTRA-HI PRODUCTS COMPANY — Hawthorne, New Jersey

MODEL 2200 SINGLE-SHOT
BOLT-ACTION RIFLE. . . . . NiB $164 Ex $123 Gd $87

Caliber: .22 LR, Long, Short. .23-inch bbl. Weight: 5 lbs. Sights: Open rear; blade front. Monte Carlo stock w/pistol grip. Made in Japan. Intro. 1977; Disc.

ULTRA LIGHT ARMS COMPANY — Granville, West Virginia

MODEL 20 BOLT-ACTION RIFLE

Calibers: .22-250 Rem., .243 Win., 6mm Rem., .250-3000 Savage, .257 Roberts, .257 Ack., 7mm Mauser, 7mm Ack., 7mm-08 Rem., .284 Win., .300 Savage, .308 Win., .358 Win. Box magazine. 22-inch ultra light bbl. Weight: 4.75 lbs. No sights. Synthetic stock of Kevlar or graphite finished, seven different colors. Nonglare matte or bright metal finish. Medium-length action available L.H. models. Made 1985 to date.

Standard model . . . . NiB $2317 Ex $1930 Gd $1050
Left-hand model . . . . NiB $2091 Ex $1699 Gd $1196

MODEL 20S BOLT-ACTION RIFLE

Same general specifications as Model 20 except w/short action in calibers 17 Rem., .222 Rem., .223 Rem., .22 Hornet only.

Standard model . . . . NiB $2332 Ex $1956 Gd $1055
Left-hand model . . . . NiB $2182 Ex $1771 Gd $1246

MODEL 24 BOLT-ACTION RIFLE

Same general specifications as Model 20 except w/long action in calibers .25-06, .270 Win., .30-06 and 7mm Express only.

Standard model . . . . NiB $2420 Ex $1972 Gd $1050
Left-hand model . . . . NiB $2124 Ex $1724 Gd $1214

MODEL 28 BOLT-ACTION RIFLE . . . . . NiB $2600 Ex $1869 Gd $1158

Same general specifications as Model 20 except w/long magnum action in calibers .264 Win. Mag., 7mm Rem. Mag., .300 Win. Mag., .338 Win. Mag. only. Offered w/recoil arrester. Left-hand model available.

MODEL 40 BOLT-ACTION RIFLE

Similar to Model 28 except in calibers .300 Wby. and .416 Rigby. Weight: 5.5 lbs. Made 1994 to date.

Standard model . . . . NiB $2600 Ex $1869 Gd $1158
Left-hand, model . . . . NiB $2568 Ex $2080 Gd $1456

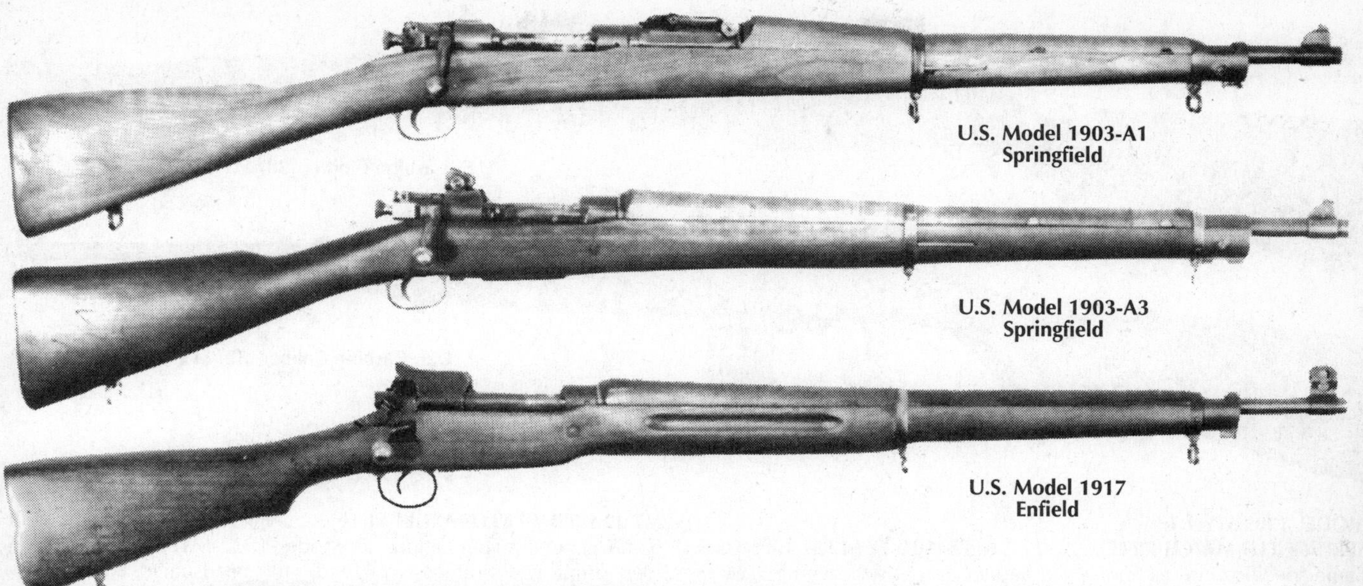

U.S. Model 1903-A1 Springfield

U.S. Model 1903-A3 Springfield

U.S. Model 1917 Enfield

UNIQUE RIFLE — Hendaye, France Mfd. by Manufacture d'Armes des Pyrénées Francaises

T66 MATCH RIFLE. . . . . NiB $499 Ex $422 Gd $293
Single-shot bolt-action rifle. Caliber: .22 LR. 25.5-inch bbl. Weight: 10.5 lbs. Sights: Micrometer aperture rear; globe front. French walnut target stock w/Monte Carlo comb, bull pistol-grip, wide and deep forearm, stippled grip surfaces, adj. swivel on accessory track, adj. rubber buttplate. Made 1966. Disc.

U.S. MILITARY RIFLES — Mfd. by Springfield Armory, Remington Arms Co., Winchester Repeating Arms Co., Inland Mfg. Div. of G.M.C., and other contractors. See notes.

Unless otherwise indicated, the following U.S. military rifles were mfg. at Springfield Armory, Springfield, Mass.

MODEL 1898
KRAG-JORGENSEN CARBINE . . NiB $1966 Ex $1760 Gd $1013
Same general specifications as Model 1898 Rifle except w/22-inch bbl., weight: 8 lbs., carbine-type stock. Note: The foregoing specifications apply, in general, to Carbine models 1896 and 1899, which differed from Model 1898 only in minor details.

MODEL 1898
KRAG-JORGENSEN MILITARY RIFLE . . NiB $1966 Ex $1660 Gd $1013
Bolt action. Caliber: .30-40 Krag. Five round hinged box magazine. 30-inch bbl. Weight: 9 lbs. Sights: Adj. rear; blade front. Military-type stock, straight grip. Note: The foregoing specifications apply, in general, to Rifle models 1892 and 1896, which differed from Model 1898.

MODEL 1903 MARK I SPRINGFIELD . . . NiB $1940 Ex $1734 Gd $833
Same as Standard Model 1903 except altered to permit use of the Pedersen Device. This device, officially designated "U.S. Automatic Pistol Model 1918," converted the M/1903 to a semiautomatic weapon firing a .30 caliber cartridge similar to .32 automatic pistol ammunition. Mark I rifles have a slot milled in the left side of the receiver to serve as an ejection port when the Pedersen Device was in use; these rifles were also fitted w/a special sear and cut-off. Some 65,000 of these devices were manufactured and, presumably, a like number of M/1903 rifles were converted to handle them. During the early 1930s, all Pedersen Devices were ordered destroyed and the Mark I rifles were reconverted by replacement of the special sear and cut-off w/standard components. Some 20-odd specimens are known to have escaped destruction and are in government museums and private collections. Probably more are extant. Rarely is a Pedersen Device offered for sale, so a current value cannot be assigned. However, many of the altered rifles were bought by members of the National Rifle Association through the Director of Civilian Marksmanship. Value shown is for the Mark I rifle w/o the Pedersen Device.

MODEL 1903 NATIONAL
MATCH SPRINGFIELD . . . . NiB $1604 Ex $1451 Gd $853
Same general specifications as Standard Model 1903 except specially selected w/star-gauged bbl., Type C pistol-grip U.S. Model 1903 National Match Springfield (Con't) stock, polished bolt assembly; early types have headless firing pin assembly and reversed safety lock. Produced especially for target shooting.

MODEL 1903 SPRINGFIELD MILITARY RIFLE
Modified Mauser-type bolt action. Caliber: .30-06. Five round box magazine. 23.79-inch bbl. Weight: 8.75 lbs. Sights: Adj. rear; blade front. Military-type stock straight grip. Note: M/1903 rifles of Springfield manufacture w/serial numbers under 800,000 (1903-1918) have casehardened receivers; those between 800,000 and 1,275,767 (1918-1927) were double heat-treated; rifles numbered over 1,275,767 have nickle steel bolts and receivers. Rock Island production from No. 1 to 285,507 have case-hardened receivers. Improved heat treatment was adopted in May 1918 with No. 285,207; about three months later, with No. 319,921, the use of nickel steel was begun, but the production of some double-heat-treated carbon-steel receivers and bolts continued. Made 1903-30 at Springfield Armory during WWI, M/1903 rifles were also made at Rock Island Arsenal, Rock Island, Ill.
W/case-hardened receiver. . . . . NiB $5250 Ex $4477 Gd $2005
W/double heat-treated receiver . . . NiB $4168 Ex $3447 Gd $1439
W/nickel steel receiver . . . . NiB $1593 Ex $1387 Gd $872

MODEL 1903 SPRINGFIELD SPORTER. . NiB $1316 Ex $1060 Gd $733
Same general specifications as National Match except w/sporting design stock, Lyman No. 48 receiver sight.

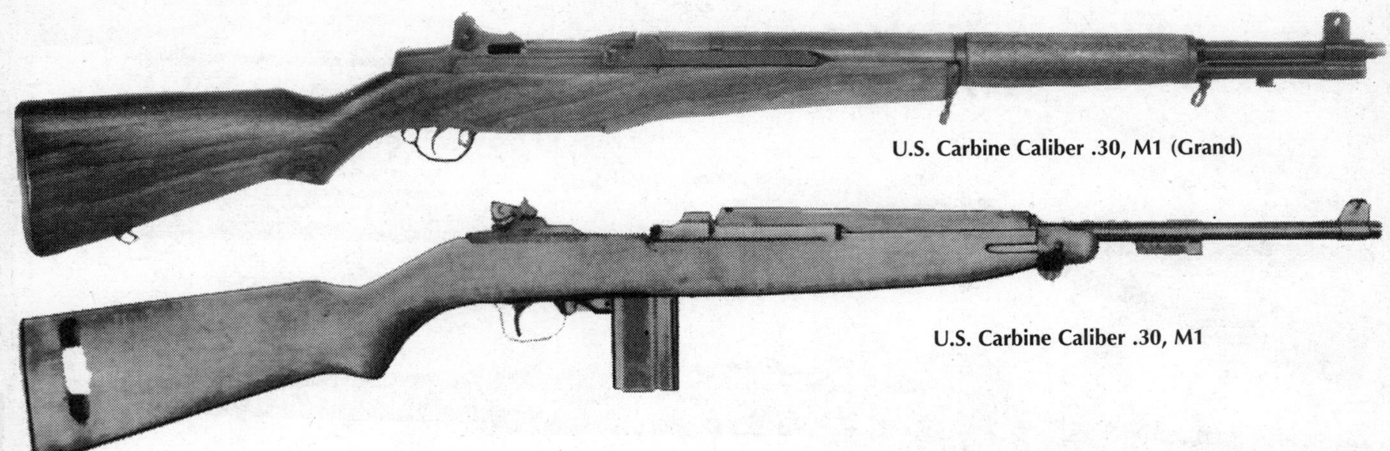

U.S. Carbine Caliber .30, M1 (Grand)

U.S. Carbine Caliber .30, M1

MODEL 1903 STYLE T
SPRINGFIELD MATCH RIFLE . . . . NiB $1501 Ex $1204 Gd $825
Same specifications as Springfield Sporter except w/heavy bbl. (26-, 28- or 30-inch), scope bases, globe front sight, weight: 12.5 lbs. w/26-inch bbl.

MODEL 1903 TYPE A
SPRINGFIELD FREE RIFLE . . . . . . NiB $1791 Ex $1436 Gd $983
Same as Style T except made w/28-inch bbl. only, w/Swiss buttplate, weight: 13.25 lbs.

MODEL 1903 TYPE B
SPRINGFIELD FREE RIFLE . . . . . NiB $2374 Ex $1905 Gd $1303
Same as Type A, except w/cheekpiece stock, palm rest, Woodie double-set triggers, Garand fast firing pin, weight: 14.75 lbs.

MODEL 1903-A1 SPRINGFIELD
Same general specifications as Model 1903 except may have Type C pistol-grip stock adopted in 1930. The last Springfields produced at the Springfield Armory were of this type; final serial number was 1,532,878, made in 1939. Note: Late in 1941, Remington Arms Co., Ilion, N.Y., began production, under government contract, of Springfield rifles of this type w/a few minor modifications. These rifles are numbered 3,000,001-3,348,085 and were manufactured before the adoption of Model 1903-A3.
Springfield manufacture . . . . NiB $1302 Ex $1148 Gd $633
Remington manufacture . . . . NiB $852 Ex $714 Gd $470

MODEL 1903-A3 SPRINGFIELD . . . . NiB $1565 Ex $1359 Gd $355
Same general specifications as Model 1903-A1, except modified to permit increased production and lower cost; may have either straight-grip or pistol-grip stock, bolt is not interchangeable w/earlier types, w/receiver peep sight, many parts are stamped sheet steel, including the trigger guard and magazine assembly. Quality of these rifles, lower than that of other 1903 Springfields, reflects the emergency conditions under which they were produced. Mfd. during WWII by Remington Arms Co. and L. C. Smith Corona Typewriters, Inc.

MODEL 1922-M1 22
SPRINGFIELD TARGET RIFLE . . . . NiB $1153 Ex $927 Gd $639
Modified Model 1903. Caliber: .22 LR. Five round detachable box magazine. 24.5-inch bbl. Weight: 9 lbs. Sights: Lyman No. 48C receiver, blade front. Sporting-type stock similar to that of Model 1903 Springfield Sporter. Issued 1927. Note: The earlier Model 1922, which is seldom encountered, differs from the foregoing chiefly in the bolt mechanism and magazine.

M2 22 SPRINGFIELD TARGET RIFLE . . . . NiB $1246 Ex $968 Gd $530
Same general specifications as Model 1922-M1 except w/speedlock, improved bolt assembly adj. for headspace. Note: These improvements were later incorporated in many rifles of the preceding models (M1922, M1922MI) and arms so converted were marked "M1922M2" or "M1922MII."

NOTE: *The WWII-vintaqe .30-caliber U.S. Carbine was mfd. by Inland Mfg. Div. of G.M.C., Dayton, OH; Winchester Repeating Arms Co., New Haven, CT, and other contractors: International Business Machines Corp., Poughkeepsie, NY; National Postal Meter Co., Rochester, NY; Quality Hardware & Machine Co., and Rock-Ola Co., Chicago, IL; Saginaw Steering Gear Div. of G.M.C., Saginaw, M1; Standard Products Co., Port Clinton, OH; Underwood-Elliott-Fisher Co., Hartford, CT.*

CALIBER .30, M1
(GARAND) MIL. RIFLE . . . . . . NiB $1302 Ex $1096 Gd $1019
Clip-fed, gas-operated, air-cooled semiautomatic. Uses a clip containing 8 rounds. 24-inch bbl. Weight: W/o bayonet, 9.5 lbs. Sights: Adj. peep rear; blade front w/guards. Pistol-grip stock, handguards. Made 1937-57. Note: Garand rifles have also been produced by Winchester Repeating Arms Co., Harrington & Richardson Arms Co., and International Harvester Co. Deduct 25% for arsenal-assembled mismatches.

CALIBER .30, M1,
NATIONAL MATCH . . . . NiB $2183 Ex $1616 Gd $638
Accurized target version of the Garand. Glass-bedded stock; match grade bbl., sights, gas cylinder. "NM" stamped on bbl. forward of handguard.

NOTE: *The U.S. Model 1917 Enfield was mfd. 1917-18 by Remington Arms Co. of Delaware (later Midvale Steel & Ordnance Co., Eddystone, PA); Remington Arms Co., Ilion, NY; Winchester Repeating Arms Co., New Haven, CT.*

MODEL 1917 ENFIELD MILITARY RIFLE . . NiB $829 Ex $705 Gd $267
Modified Mauser-type bolt action. Caliber: .30-06. Five round box magazine. 26-inch bbl. Weight: 9.25 lbs. Sights: Adj. rear; blade front w/guards. Military-type stock w/semi-pistol-grip. This design originated in Great Britain as the, "Pattern 14" and was mfd. in caliber .303 for the British Government in three U.S. plants. In 1917, the U.S. Government contracted w/these firms to produce the same rifle in caliber .30-06; over two million of these Model 1917 Enfields were mfd. While no more were produced after WWI, the U.S. supplied over a million of them to Great Britain during WWII.

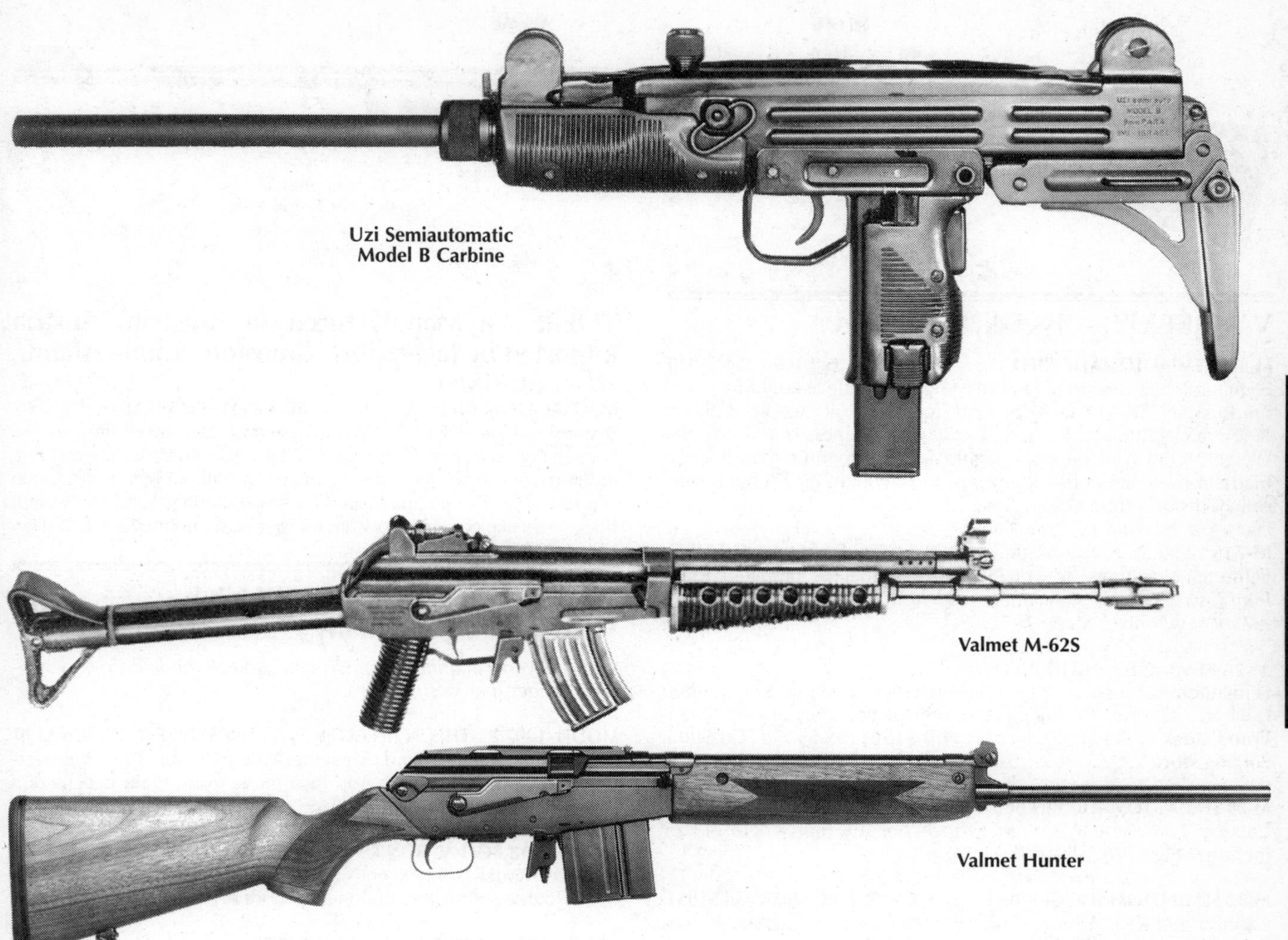
Uzi Semiautomatic Model B Carbine

Valmet M-62S

Valmet Hunter

CARBINE, CALIBER 30, M1 . . . . NiB $756 Ex $608 Gd $419
Gas-operated (short-stroke piston), semiautomatic. 15- or 30-round detachable box magazine. 18-inch bbl. Weight: 5.5 lbs. Sights: adj. rear; blade front sight w/guards. Pistol-grip stock w/handguard, side-mounted web sling. Made 1942-45. In 1963, 150,000 surplus M1 Carbines were sold at $20 each to members of the National Rifle Assn. by the Dept. of the Army. Note: For Winchester and Rock-Ola, add 30%; for Irwin Pedersen, add 80%. Quality Hardware did not complete its production run. Guns produced by other manufacturers were marked "Unquality" & command premium prices.

U.S. REPEATING ARMS CO.

See Winchester Rifle listings.

UNIVERSAL SPORTING GOODS, INC. — Miami, Florida

DELUXE CARBINE. . . . . NiB $341 Ex $290 Gd $163
Same as standard model except also available in caliber .256, w/deluxe walnut Monte Carlo stock and handguard. Made 1965 to date.

STANDARD M-1 CARBINE . . . . NiB $239 Ex $188 Gd $137
Same as U.S. Carbine, Cal. .30, M1 except may have either wood or metal handguard, bbl. band w/ or w/o bayonet lug; 5-round magazine standard. Made 1964 to date.

UZI CARBINE — Mfd. by Israel Military Industries, Israel

SEMIAUTOMATIC MODEL B CARBINE
Calibers: 9mm Parabellum, .41 Action Express, .45 ACP. 20- to 50-round magazine. 16.1-inch bbl. Weight: 8.4 lbs. Metal folding stock. Front post-type sight, open rear, both adj. Imported by Action Arms 1983-89. NFA (Selective Fire) models imported by UZI America, INC., 1994 to date.
Model B Carbine (9mm or .45 ACP) . . . . NiB $1330 Ex $1108 Gd $722
Model B Carbine (.41 AE) . . . . NiB $1563 Ex $1258 Gd $914
Centerfire conversion unit, add $250
Rimfire conversion unit, add. $175

SEMIAUTOMATIC MINI CARBINE . . . . NiB $2550 Ex $2087 Gd $1469
Similar to Uzi Model B except with 19.75-inch bbl.and chambered 9mm Parabellum only. 20-round magazine. Weight: 7.2 lbs. Imported 1989.

Vickers Jubilee
Single-Shot Target Rifle

VALMET OY — Jyväskylä, Finland

M-62S SEMIAUTOMATIC RIFLE . . . . . . NiB $1856 Ex $1490 Gd $1020
Semiautomatic version of Finnish M-62 automatic assault rifle based on Russian AK-47. Gas-operated rotating bolt action. Caliber: 7.62mmX39 Russian. 15- and 30-round magazines. 16.63-inch bbl. Weight: 8 lbs. w/metal stock. Sights: Tangent aperture rear; hooded blade front w/luminous flip-up post for low-light use. Tubular steel or wood stock. Intro. 1962. Disc.

M-71S . . . . NiB $1876 Ex $1644 Gd $923
Same specifications as M-62S except caliber 5.56mmx45 (.223 Rem.), w/open rear sight, reinforced resin or wood stock, weight: 7.75 lbs. w/former. Made 1971-89.

M-76 SEMIAUTOMATIC RIFLE
Semiautomatic assault rifle. Gas-operated, rotating bolt action. Caliber: 223 Rem. 15- and 30-round magazines. Made 1984-89.
Wood stock . . . . NiB $1561 Ex $1253 Gd $905
Folding stock . . . . NiB $1947 Ex $1562 Gd $1070

M-78 SEMIAUTOMATIC RIFLE . . . . NiB $1761 Ex $1412 Gd $973
Caliber: 7.62x51 (NATO). 24.13-inch bbl. Overall length: 43.25 inches. Weight: 10.5 lbs.

M-82 SEMIAUTOMATIC CARBINE . . . . NiB $2605 Ex $2038 Gd $1034
Caliber: .223 Rem. 15- or 30-round magazine. 17-inch bbl. 27 inches overall. Weight: 7.75 lbs.

MODEL 412 S DOUBLE RIFLE . . . . NiB $1378 Ex $1117 Gd $761
Boxlock. Manual or automatic extraction. Calibers: .243, .308, .30-06, .375 Win., 9.3x74R. Bbls.: 24-inch over/under. Weight: 8.63 lbs. American walnut checkered stock and forend.

HUNTER SEMIAUTOMATIC RIFLE . . . . NiB $996 Ex $790 Gd $533
Similar to M-78 except in calibers .223 Rem. (5.56mm), .243 Win., .308 Win. (7.62 NATO) and .30-06. Five , 9- or 15-round magazine. 20.5-inch plain bbl. 42 inches overall. Weight: 8 lbs. Sights: Adj. combination scope mount/rear; blade front, mounted on gas tube. Checkered European walnut buttstock and extended checkered forend and handguard. Imported 1986-89.

VICKERS LTD. — Crayford, Kent, England

JUBILEE MODEL SINGLE-SHOT-
TARGET RIFLE . . . . NiB $448 Ex $345 Gd $216
Round-receiver Martini-type action. Caliber: .22 LR. 28-inch heavy bbl. Weight: 9.5 lbs. Sights: Parker-Hale No. 2 front; Perfection rear peep. One-piece target stock w/full forearm and pistol-grip. Made before WWII.

EMPIRE MODEL . . . . NiB $499 Ex $370 Gd $242
Similar to Jubilee Model except w/27- or 30-inch bbl., straight-grip stock, weight: 9.25 lbs. w/30-inch bbl. Made before WWII.

VOERE — Manufactured in Kufstein, Austria Imported by JagerSport, Cranston, Rhode Island

VEC-91 LIGHTNING
BOLT-ACTION RIFLE . . . . NiB $2531 Ex $2028 Gd $1386
Features unique electronic ignition system to activate or fire caseless ammunition. Calibers: .5.56 UCC (.222 Cal.), 6mm UCC caseless. Five round magazine. 20-inch bbl. 39 inches overall. Weight: 6 lbs. Open adj. rear sight. Drilled and tapped for scope mounts. European walnut stock w/cheekpiece. Twin forward locking lugs. Imported 1992 to date.

VOERE, VOELTER & COMPANY — Vaehrenbach, Germany

Mauser-Werke acquired Voere in 1987 and all models are now marketed under new designations.

MODEL 1007 BIATHLON REPEATER . . . . . NiB $370 Ex $293 Gd $190
Caliber: 22 LR. Five round magazine. 19.5-inch bbl. 39 inches overall. Weight: 5.5 lb. Sights: Adj. rear, blade front. Plain beechwood stock. Imported 1984-86.

MODEL 1013 BOLT-ACTION REPEATER . . . . . NiB $685 Ex $479 Gd $325
Same as Model 1007 except w/military-style stock in 22 WMR caliber. Double-set triggers optional. Imported 1984-86 by KDF, Inc.

MODEL 2107 BOLT-ACTION REPEATER
Caliber: 22 LR. Five or 8-round magazine. 19.5-inch bbl. 41 inches overall. Weight: 6 lbs. Sights: Adj. rear sight, hooded front. European hardwood Monte Carlo-style stock. Imported 1986 by KDF, Inc.
Standard model . . . . NiB $370 Ex $242 Gd $164
Deluxe model . . . . NiB $422 Ex $293 Gd $216

WALTHER RIFLES — Mfd. by the German firms of Waffenfabrik Walther and Carl Walther Sportwaffenfabrik

The following Walther rifles were mfd. before WWII by Waffenfabrik Walther, Zella-Mehlis (Thür.), Germany.

MODEL 1 AUTOLOADING
RIFLE (LIGHT) . . . . NiB $734 Ex $636 Gd $378
Similar to Standard Model 2 but w/20-inch bbl., lighter stock, weight: 4.5 lbs.

MODEL 2 AUTOLOADING RIFLE . . . . NiB $713 Ex $584 Gd $353
Bolt-action, may be used as autoloader, manually operated repeater or single-shot. Caliber: .22 LR. Five or 9-round detachable box magazine. 24.5-inch bbl. Weight: 7 lbs. Sights: Tangent-curve rear; ramp front. Sporting stock w/checkered pistol grip, grooved forearm, swivels. Disc.

Walther Model 1

Walther Model 2

Walther Model GX-1

Walther Model KKM-S

Walther Model U.I.T. Super Match

OLYMPIC BOLT-ACTION MATCH RIFLE . . . . NiB $1211 Ex $972 Gd $668
Single-shot. Caliber: .22 LR. 26-inch heavy bbl. Weight: 13 lbs. Sights: Micrometer extension rear; interchangeable front. Target stock w/checkered pistol-grip, thumbhole, full beavertail forearm covered w/corrugated rubber, palm rest, adj. Swiss-type buttplate, swivels. Disc.

MODEL V BOLT-ACTION SINGLE-SHOT RIFLE . . . . NiB $576 Ex $412 Gd $293
Caliber: .22 LR. 26-inch bbl. Weight: 7 lbs. Sights: Open rear; ramp front. Plain pistol-grip stock w/grooved forearm. Disc.

MODEL V MEISTERBÜCHSE (CHAMPION) . . . . NiB $654 Ex $473 Gd $314
Same as standard Model V except w/micrometer open rear sight and checkered pistol-grip. Disc.

POST WWII MODELS
The Walther rifles listed below have been manufactured since WWII by Carl Walther Sportwaffenfabrik, Ulm (Donau), Germany.

MODEL GX-1 FREE RIFLE . . . . . . NiB $1949 Ex $1434 Gd $816
Bolt-action, single-shot. Caliber: .22 LR. 25.5-inch heavy bbl. Weight: 15.9 lbs. Sights: Micrometer aperture rear; globe front. Thumbhole stock w/adj. cheekpiece and buttplate w/removable hook, accessory rail. Left-hand stock available. Accessories furnished include hand stop and sling swivel, palm rest, counterweight assembly.

MODEL KKJ SPORTER. . . . . NiB $1254 Ex $1022 Gd $528
Bolt action. Caliber: .22 LR. Five round box magazine. 22.5-inch bbl. Weight: 5.5 lbs. Sights: Open rear; hooded ramp front. Stock w/cheekpiece, checkered pistol-grip and forearm, sling swivels. Disc.

MODEL KKJ-HO . . . . NiB $1511 Ex $1305 Gd $971
Same as Model KKJ except chambered for .22 Hornet. Disc.

MODEL KKJ-MA . . . . NiB $1305 Ex $1151 Gd $523
Same as Model KKJ except chambered for .22 WMR. Disc.

MODEL KKM INTERNATIONAL MATCH RIFLE . . . . NiB $971 Ex $790 Gd $533
Bolt-action, single-shot. Caliber: .22 LR. 28-inch heavy bbl. Weight: 15.5 lbs. Sights: Micrometer aperture rear; globe front. Thumbhole stock w/high comb, adj. hook buttplate, accessory rail. Left-hand stock available. Disc.

MODEL KKM-S . . . . NiB $1022 Ex $842 Gd $559
Same specifications as Model KKM, except w/adj. cheekpiece. Disc.

MOVING TARGET MATCH RIFLE . . . . NiB $968 Ex $710 Gd $458
Bolt-action, single-shot. Caliber: .22 LR. 23.6-inch bbl. w/weight. Weight: 8.6 lbs. Supplied w/o sights. Thumbhole stock w/adj. cheekpiece and buttplate. Left-hand stock available.

PRONE 400 TARGET RIFLE . . . . NiB $813 Ex $659 Gd $427
Bolt-action, single-shot. Caliber: .22 LR. 25.5-inch heavy bbl. Weight: 10.25 lbs. Supplied w/o sights. Prone stock w/adj. cheekpiece and buttplate, accessory rail. Left-hand stock available. Disc.

MODEL SSV VARMINT RIFLE . . . . . NiB $757 Ex $633 Gd $427
Bolt-action, single-shot. Calibers: .22 LR, .22 Hornet. 25.5-inch bbl. Weight: 6.75 lbs. Supplied w/o sights. Monte Carlo stock w/high cheekpiece, full pistol grip and forearm. Disc.

MODEL U.L.T. SPECIAL MATCH RIFLE . . . . . NiB $1302 Ex $968 Gd $684
Bolt-action, single-shot. Caliber: .22 LR. 25.5-inch bbl. Weight: 10.2 lbs. Sights: Micrometer aperture rear; globe front. Target stock w/high comb, adj. buttplate, accessory rail. Left-hand stock avail. Disc. 1993.

MODEL U.L.T. SUPER MATCH RIFLE . . . . NiB $1328 Ex $993 Gd $710
Bolt-action, single-shot. Caliber: .22 LR. 25.5-inch heavy bbl. Weight: 10.2 lbs. Micrometer aperture rear; globe front. Target stock w/support for off-hand shooting, high comb, adj. buttplate and swivel. Left-hand stock available. Disc. 1993.

MONTGOMERY WARD — Chicago, Illinois Western Field and Hercules Models

Firearms under the "private label" names of Western Field and Hercules are manufactured by such firms as Mossberg, Stevens, Marlin, and Savage for distribution and sale by Montgomery Ward.

MODEL 14M-497B WESTERN FIELD BOLT-ACTION RIFLE . . . . NiB $110 Ex $90 Gd $63
Caliber: .22 RF. Seven round detachable box magazine. 24-inch bbl. Weight: 5 lbs. Sights: Receiver peep; open rear; hooded ramp front. Pistol-grip stock. Mfg. by Mossberg.

MODEL M771 WESTERN FIELD LEVER-ACTION RIFLE . . . . NiB $161 Ex $135 Gd $105
Calibers: .30-30, .35 Rem. Six round tubular magazine. 20-inch bbl. Weight: 6.75 lbs. Sights: Open rear; ramp front. Pistol-grip or straight stock, forearm w/barrel band. Mfg. by Mossberg.

MODEL M772 WESTERN FIELD LEVER-ACTION RIFLE . . . . NiB $186 Ex $161 Gd $110
Calibers: .30-30, .35 Rem. Six round tubular magazine. 20-inch bbl. Weight: 6.75 lbs. Sights: Open rear; ramp front. Pistol-grip or straight stock, forearm w/bbl. band. Mfg. by Mossberg.

MODEL M775 BOLT-ACTION RIFLE . . . . NiB $120 Ex $105 Gd $79
Calibers: .222 Rem., .22-250, .243 Win., .308 Win. Four round magazine. Weight: 7.5 lbs. Sights: Folding leaf rear; ramp front. Monte Carlo stock w/cheekpiece, pistol-grip. Mfg by Mossberg.

MODEL M776 BOLT-ACTION RIFLE . . . . NiB $212 Ex $186 Gd $135
Calibers: .222 Rem., .22-250, .243 Win., .308 Win. Four round magazine. Weight: 7.5 lbs. Sights: Folding leaf rear; ramp front. Monte Carlo stock w/cheekpiece, pistol-grip. Mfg. by Mossberg.

MODEL M778 LEVER-ACTION . . . . NiB $207 Ex $161 Gd $110
Calibers: .30-30, .35 Rem. Six round tubular magazine. 20-inch bbl. Weight: 6.75 lbs. Sights: Open rear; ramp front. Pistol-grip or straight stock, forearm w/bbl. band. Mfg. by Mossberg.

MODEL M780 BOLT-ACTION RIFLE . . . . NiB $212 Ex $186 Gd $135
Calibers: .222 Rem., .22-250, .243 Win., .308 Win. Four round magazine. Weight: 7.5 lbs. Sights: Folding leaf rear; ramp front. Monte Carlo stock w/cheekpiece, pistol grip. Mfg. by Mossberg.

MODEL M782 BOLT-ACTION RIFLE . . . . NiB $212 Ex $186 Gd $135
Same general specifications as Model M780.

MODEL M808 . . . . NiB $112 Ex $95 Gd $68
Takedown. Caliber: .22RF. Fifteen round tubular magazine. Bbls.: 20- and 24-inch. Weight: 6 lbs. Sights: Open rear; bead front. Pistol-grip stock. Mfg. by Stevens.

MODEL M832 BOLT-ACTION RIFLE . . . . . . NiB $120 Ex $100 Gd $69
Caliber: .22 RF. Seven round clip magazine. 24-inch bbl. Weight: 6.5 lbs. Sights: Open rear; ramp front. Mfg. by Mossberg.

MODEL M836 . . . . NiB $125 Ex $100 Gd $79
Takedown. Caliber: .22RF. Fifteen round tubular magazine. Bbls.: 20- and 24-inch. Weight: 6 lbs. Sights: Open rear; bead front. Pistol-grip stock. Mfg. by Stevens.

MODEL M865 LEVER-ACTION CARBINE . . . NiB $151 Ex $110 Gd $95
Hammerless. Caliber: .22RF. Tubular magazine. Made w/both 18.5-inch and 20-inch bbls., forearm w/bbl. band, swivels. Weight: 5 lbs. Mfg. by Mossberg.

MODEL M894 AUTO-LOADING CARBINE . . . . NiB $135 Ex $110 Gd $84
Caliber: .22 RF. Fifteen round tubular magazine. 20-inch bbl. Weight: 6 lbs. Sights: Open rear; ramp front. Monte Carlo stock w/pistol-grip. Mfg. by Mossberg.

MODEL M-SD57 . . . . NiB $120 Ex $100 Gd $69
Takedown. Caliber: .22RF. 15-round tubular magazine. Bbls.: 20- and 24-inch. Weight: 6 lbs. Sights: Open rear; bead front. Pistol-grip stock. Mfg. by Stevens.

WEATHERBY, INC. — Atascadero, CA (Formerly South Gate, CA)

CROWN CUSTOM RIFLE . . . . . NiB $5941 Ex $4061 Gd $2104
Calibers: .240, .30-06, .257, .270, 7mm, .300, and .340. Bbl.: Made to order. Super fancy walnut stock. Also available w/engraved barreled action including gold animal overlay.

Weatherby Mark V Classicmark I

Weatherby Crown Custom

Weatherby Fiberguard

Weatherby Fibermark

DELUXE .378 MAGNUM RIFLE . . . . . . NiB $2722 Ex $1975 Gd $1341
Same general specifications as Deluxe Magnum in other calibers except caliber .378 W. M. Schultz & Larsen action; 26-inch bbl. Disc. 1958.

DELUXE MAGNUM RIFLE. . . . . NiB $1983 Ex $1473 Gd $1061
Calibers: .220 Rocket, .257 Weatherby Mag., .270 W.M. 7mm W.M., .300 W.M., .375 W.M. Specially processed FN Mauser action. 24-inch bbl. (26-inch in .375 cal.). Monte Carlo-style stock w/cheekpiece, black forend tip, grip cap, checkered pistol-grip and forearm, quick-detachable sling swivels. Value shown is for rifle w/o sights. Disc. 1958.

DELUXE RIFLE. . . . . NiB $1421 Ex $1087 Gd $778
Same general specifications as Deluxe Magnum except chambered for standard calibers such as .270, .30-06, etc. Disc. 1958.

FIBERGUARD RIFLE . . . . NiB $715 Ex $586 Gd $406
Same general specifications as Vanguard except for fiberglass stock and matte metal finish. Disc, 1988.

FIBERMARK RIFLE. . . . . NiB $1257 Ex $927 Gd $618
Same general specifications as Mark V except w/molded fiberglass stock, finished in a nonglare black wrinkle finish. The metal is finished in a non-glare matte finish. Disc. 1993.

MARK V ACCUMARK BOLT-ACTION REPEATING
Weatherby Mark V magnum action. Calibers: .257 Wby., .270 Wby., 7mm Rem. Mag., 7mm Wby., 7mm STW, .300 Win. Mag., .300 Wby.

(cont'd.) **MARK V ACCUMARK BOLT ACTION REPEATING**
Mag., .30-338 Wby., .30-378 Wby. and .340 Wby. 26- or 28-inch stainless bbl. w/black oxide flutes. 46.5 or 48.5 inches overall. Weight: 8 to 8.5 lbs. No sights, drilled and tapped for scope. Stainless finish w/blued receiver. H-S Precision black synthetic stock w/aluminum bedding plate, recoil pad and sling swivels. Imported 1996 to date.

Mark V Accumark (.30-338
& .30-378 Wby. Mag.). . . . . NiB $1372 Ex $1101 Gd $755
Mark V Accumark (All other calibers). . . . NiB $1173 Ex $942 Gd $647
Mark V Left-Action, add $75

MARK V ACCUMARK
LIGHT WEIGHT RIFLE. . . . . NiB $1271 Ex $1076 Gd $638
Similar to the Mark V Accumark except w/LightWeight Mark V action designed for standard calibers w/sixlocking lugs rather than nine. 24-inch stainless bbl. Weight: 5.75 lbs. Gray or black Monte Carlo-style composite Kevlar/fiberglass stock w/Pachmayr "Decelerator" pad. No sights. Imported 1997 to date.

MARK V CLASSICMARK I RIFLE
Same general specifications as Mark V except w/checkered select American Claro walnut stock w/oil finish and presentation recoil pad. Satin metal finish. Imported 1992-93.
Calibers .240 to .300 Wby. . . . . . . NiB $1127 Ex $792 Gd $483
Caliber .340 Wby. . . . . NiB $1148 Ex $818 Gd $483
Caliber .378 Wby. . . . . NiB $1333 Ex $818 Gd $483
Caliber .416 Wby. . . . . NiB $1204 Ex $870 Gd $483
Caliber .460 Wby. . . . . NiB $1307 Ex $947 Gd $509

Weatherby Mark V Deluxe

Weatherby Mark V Euromark

Weatherby Mark V Lazermark

Weatherby Mark V Safari Grade

MARK V CLASSICMARK LL RIFLE
Same general specifications as Classicmark I except w/checkered select American walnut stock w/oil finish steel grip cap and Old English recoil pad. Satin metal finish. Right-hand only. Imported 1992-93.

Calibers .240 to .340 Wby.
(26-inch bbl.) . . . . NiB $1410 Ex $1101 Gd $741
Caliber .378 Wby. . . . . NiB $1462 Ex $1127 Gd $792
Caliber .416 Wby. . . . . NiB $1591 Ex $1354 Gd $942
Caliber .460 Wby. . . . . NiB $1642 Ex $1385 Gd $973

MARK V DELUXE RIFLE. . . . . NiB $1045 Ex $767 Gd $514
Similar to Mark V Sporter except w/Lightweight Mark V action designed for standard calibers w/sixlocking lugs rather than nine, 4- or 5-round magazine. 24-inch bbl. 44 inches overall. Weight: 6.75 lbs. Checkered Monte Carlo American walnut stock w/rosewood forend and pistol grip and diamond inlay. Imported 1997 to date.

WEATHERBY MARK V DELUXE BOLT-ACTION SPORTING RIFLE
Mark V action, right or left hand. Calibers: .22-250, .30-06- .224 Weatherby Varmintmaster; .240, .257, .270, 7mm, .300, .340, .375, .378, .416, .460 Weatherby Magnums. Box magazine holds 2 to 5 cartridges depending on caliber. 24- or 26-inch bbl. Weight: 6.5 to 10.5 lbs. Monte Carlo-style stock w/cheekpiece, skip checkering, forend tip, pistol-grip cap, recoil pad, QD swivels. Values shown are for rifles w/o sights. Made in Germany 1958-69; in Japan 1970-94. Values shown for Japanese production.

Calibers .22-250, .224 . . . . NiB $1076 Ex $828 Gd $576
Caliber .375 H&H Magnum . . . . NiB $1153 Ex $973 Gd $664
Caliber .378 Weatherby Magnum . . . . . . NiB $1333 Ex $1050 Gd $818
Caliber .416 Weatherby Magnum . . . . . . NiB $1410 Ex $1101 Gd $741
Caliber .460 Weatherby Magnum . . . . . . NiB $1822 Ex $1328 Gd $998

MARK V EUROMARK BOLT-ACTION RIFLE
Same general specifications as other Mark V rifles except w/hand-rubbed, satin oil finish Claro walnut stock and nonglare special process blue matte barreled action. Left-hand models available. Imported 1986-93. Reintroduced 1995.

Caliber .378 Wby. Mag. . . . . NiB $1406 Ex $1097 Gd $737
Caliber .416 Wby. Mag. . . . . NiB $1509 Ex $1175 Gd $840
Caliber .460 Wby Mag. . . . . NiB $1795 Ex $1383 Gd $996
Other calibers . . . . NiB $968 Ex $731 Gd $478

MARK V LAZERMARK RIFLE
Same general specifications as Mark V except w/laser-carved stock.

Caliber .378 Wby. Mag. . . . . NiB $1898 Ex $1487 Gd $837
Caliber .416 Wby. Mag. . . . . NiB $1898 Ex $1486 Gd $837
Caliber .460 Wby. Mag. . . . . . . NiB $2234 Ex $1565 Gd $1024
Other calibers . . . . NiB $1352 Ex $1043 Gd $662

MARK V SAFARI GRADE RIFLE. . . . . . . NiB $2203 Ex $1766 Gd $1208
Same general specifications as Mark V except extra capacity magazine, bbl. sling swivel, and express rear sight typical "Safari" style.

MARK V SPORTER RIFLE
Sporter version of Mark V Magnum w/low-luster metal finish. Checkered Carlo walnut stock w/o grip cap or forend tip. No sights. Imported 1993 to date.

Calibers .257 to .300 Wby. . . . . NiB $978 Ex $813 Gd $427
.340 Weatherby . . . . NiB $1040 Ex $659 Gd $453
.375 H&H . . . . NiB $1071 Ex $762 Gd $556

MARK V LIGHTWEIGHT SPORTER RIFLE. . NiB $942 Ex $762 Gd $427
Similar to Mark V Sporter except w/Lightweight Mark V action designed for standard calibers w/six locking lugs rather than nine. Imported 1997 to date.

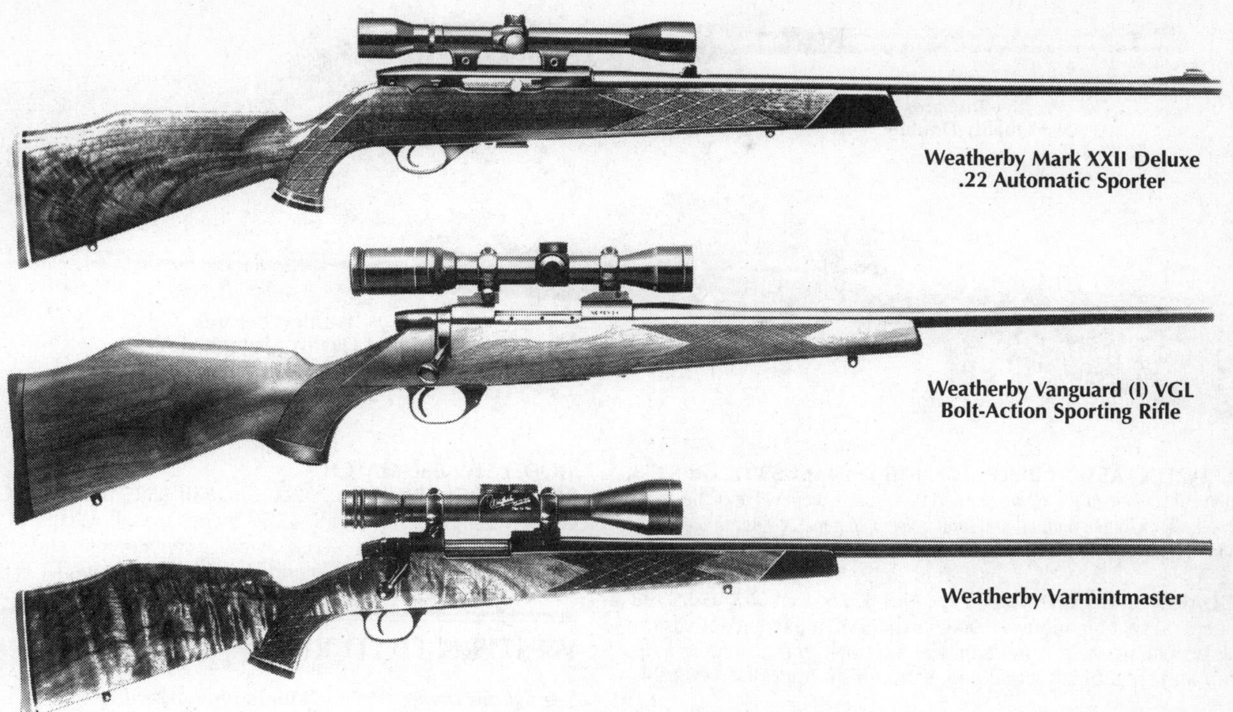

Weatherby Mark XXII Deluxe .22 Automatic Sporter

Weatherby Vanguard (I) VGL Bolt-Action Sporting Rifle

Weatherby Varmintmaster

MARK V STAINLESS RIFLE
Similar to the Mark V Magnum except in 400-series stainless steel w/bead-blasted matte finish. Weight: 8 lbs. Monte Carlo synthetic stock w/aluminum bedding block. Imported 1995 to date.
Mark V Stainless (.30-.378 Wby.). . NiB $1173 Ex $956 Gd $503
Mark V Stainless (.375 H&H.) . . . . NiB $1173 Ex $956 Gd $503
All other calibers. . . . . NiB $1018 Ex $730 Gd $503
W/fluted bbl., add. $100

MARK V (LW) STAINLESS RIFLE . . . . NiB $808 Ex $623 Gd $417
Similar to the Mark V (standard calibers) except in 400-series stainless steel w/bead-blasted matte finish. Five round magazine. 24-inch bbl. 44 inches overall. Weight: 6.5 lbs. Monte Carlo synthetic stock w/aluminum bedding block. Imported 1995 to date.

MARK V SLS RIFLE
Acronym for Stainless Laminated Sporter. Similar to the Mark V Magnum Sporter, except w/stainless 400-series action and 24- or 26-inch stainless bbl. Laminated wood stock. Weight: 8.5 lbs. Black oxide bead-blasted matte blue finish. Imported 1997 to date.
Mark V SLS (.340 Wby.). . . . . NiB $1175 Ex $958 Gd $505
All other calibers. . . . . NiB $1020 Ex $732 Gd $505

MARK V SYNTHETIC RIFLE
Similar to the Mark V Magnum except w/Monte Carlo synthetic stock w/aluminum bedding block. 24- or 26-inch standard tapper or fluted bbl. Weight: 7.75 to 8 lbs. Matte blue finish. Imported 1995 to date.
Mark V Synthetic (.340 Wby.) . . . . NiB $1020 Ex $732 Gd $479
Mark V Synthetic (.30-378 Wby.) . . . . . . NiB $1041 Ex $711 Gd $479
All other calibers . . . . NiB $757 Ex $576 Gd $396
W/fluted bbl., add. $100

MARK V ULTRA LIGHT WEIGHT RIFLE
Similar to the Mark V Magnum except w/skeletonized bolt handle. 24- or 26-inch fluted stainless bbl. chambered .257 Wby., .270 Wby., 7mm Rem. Mag., 7mm Wby., .300 Win. Mag., .300 Wby. Monte Carlo synthetic stock w/aluminum bedding block. Weight: 6.75 lbs. Imported 1998 to date.

(cont'd.) **MARK V ULTRA LIGHT WEIGHT RIFLE**
Mark V Ultra Lightweight
(standard calibers). . . . . NiB $1900 Ex $1462 Gd $767
Mark V Ultra Lightweight
(Weatherby calibers) . . . . NiB $1925 Ex $1513 Gd $792
Mark V Ultra Lightweight
(Left-hand action), add $100

MARK XXII DELUXE .22 AUTOMATIC
SPORTER, CLIP-FED MODEL . . . . NiB $520 Ex $473 Gd $345
Semiautomatic w/single-shot selector. Caliber: .22 LR. Five and 10-round clip magazines. 24-inch bbl. Weight: 6 lbs. Sights: Folding leaf open rear; ramp front. Monte Carlo-type stock w/cheekpiece, pistol-grip, forend tip, grip cap, skip checkering, QD swivels. Intro. 1964. Made in Italy 1964-69; in Japan, 1970-1981; in the U.S., 1982-90.

MARK XXII, TUBULAR
MAGAZINE MODEL . . . . NiB $417 Ex $340 Gd $210
Same as Mark XXII, clip-fed model except w/15-round tubular magazine. Made in Japan 1973-81; in the U.S.,1982-90.

VANGUARD (I) BOLT-ACTION SPORTING RIFLE
Mauser-type action. Calibers: .243 Win., .25-06, .270 Win., 7mm Rem. Mag., .30-06, .300 Win. Mag. Five round magazine; (3-round in Magnum calibers). 24-inch bbl. Weight: 7 lbs. 14 oz. No sights. Monte Carlo-type stock w/cheekpiece, rosewood forend tip and pistol-grip cap, checkering, rubber buttpad, QD swivels. Imported 1970-84.
Vanguard Standard . . . . NiB $473 Ex $396 Gd $242
Vanguard VGL (w/shorter
20-inch bbl., plain checkered
stock matte finish, 6.5 lbs. . . . . NiB $448 Ex $370 Gd $247
Vanguard VGS (w/24-inch
bbl., plain checkered stock,
matte finish. . . . . NiB $499 Ex $381 Gd $267
Vanguard VGX
(w/higher grade finish) . . . . NiB $551 Ex $448 Gd $293

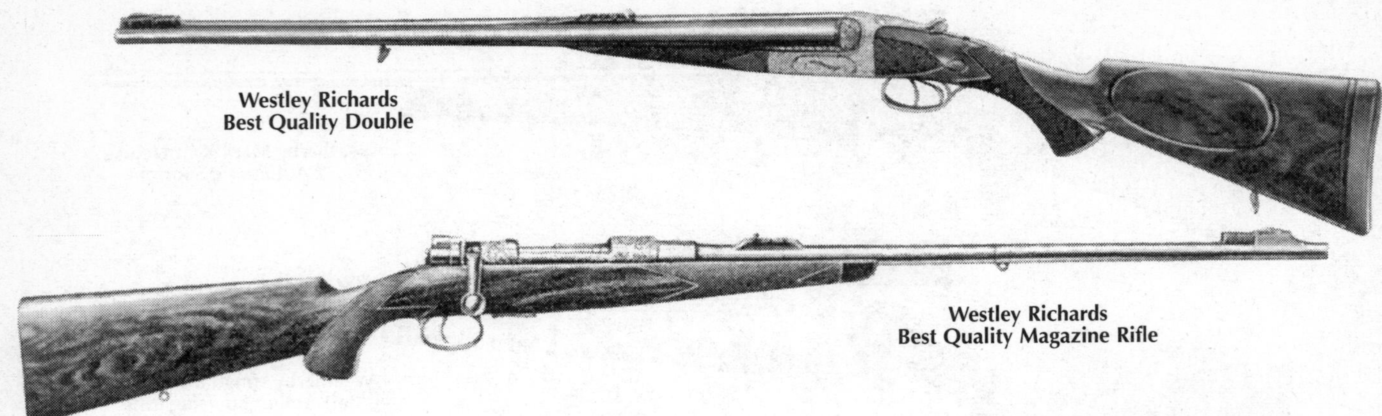

Westley Richards
Best Quality Double

Westley Richards
Best Quality Magazine Rifle

VANGUARD CLASSIC I RIFLE. . . . . NiB $504 Ex $391 Gd $273
Same general specifications as Vanguard VGX Deluxe except w/hand-checkered classic-style stock, black buttpad and satin finish. Calibers .223 Rem., .243 Win. .270 Win., 7mm-08, 7mm Rem. Mag., .30-06 and .308 Win. Imported 1989-94.

VANGUARD CLASSIC II RIFLE . . . . NiB $726 Ex $602 Gd $396
Same general specifications as Vanguard VGX Deluxe except custom checkered classic-style American walnut stock w/black forend tip, grip cap and solid black recoil pad, satin finish. Imported 1989-94.

VANGUARD VGX DELUXE . . . . NiB $654 Ex $520 Gd $370
Calibers: .22-250 Rem., .243 Rem., .270 Wby. Mag., .270 Win., 7mm Rem. Mag., .30-06, .300 Win. Mag., .300 Wby. Mag., .338 Win. Mag. Three or 5-round capacity. 24-inch bbl. About 44 inches overall. Weight: 7 to 8.5 lbs. Custom checkered American walnut stock w/Monte Carlo and recoil pad. Rosewood forend tip and pistol-grip cap. High-luster finish. Disc. 1994.

VARMINTMASTER BOLT-ACTION RIFLE. . NiB $1872 Ex $1455 Gd $790
Calibers: .224 Wby., .22-250, 4-round magazine. 26-inch bbl. 45 inches overall. Weight: 7.75 lbs. Checkered walnut stock. No sights. Disc.

WEATHERMARK RIFLE
Same gen. specs. as Classicmark except w/checkered blk. Weathermark composite stock. Mark V bolt act. Cal: .240, .257, .270, .300, .340, .378, .416 and .460 Weatherby Mag.; plus .270 Win., 7mm Rem. Mag., .30-06 and .375 H&H Mag. Wt: 8 to 10 lbs. Right-hand only. Imp. 1992-94.
Calibers .257 to .300 Wby. . . . . NiB $726 Ex $551 Gd $370
Caliber .340 Weatherby. . . . . NiB $757 Ex $576 Gd $381
Caliber .375 H&H . . . . NiB $988 Ex $679 Gd $473
Other non-Wby. calibers . . . . NiB $725 Ex $520 Gd $370

WEATHERMARK ALASKAN RIFLE. . . . . NiB $808 Ex $654 Gd $448
Same general specifications as Weathermark except w/nonglare electroless nickel finish. Right-hand only. Imported 1992-94.

WEIHRAUCH — Melrichstadt, West Germany
Imported by European American Armory, Sharpes, FL.

MODEL HW 60 TARGET RIFLE. . . . NiB $653 Ex $575 Gd $369
Single-shot. Caliber: .22 LR. 26.75-inch bbl. Walnut stock. Adj. buttplate and trigger. Hooded ramp front sight. Push button safety. Imported 1995-97.

MODEL HW 66 BOLT-ACTION RIFLE . . . . NiB $601 Ex $514 Gd $318
Caliber: .22 Hornet. 22.75-inch bbl. 41.75 inches overall. Weight: 6.5 lbs. Walnut stock w/cheekpiece. Hooded blade ramp front sight. Checkered pistol grip and forend. Imported 1989-90.

MODEL HW 660 MATCH
BOLT-ACTION RIFLE. . . . . NiB $885 Ex $757 Gd $422
Caliber: .22 LR. 26-inch bbl. 45.33 inches overall. Weight: 10.75 lbs. Walnut or laminated stock w/adj. cheekpiece and buttplate. Checkered pistol grip and forend. Adj. trigger. Imported 1991 to date.

WESTERN FIELD RIFLES

See listings under "W" for Montgomery Ward.

WESTLEY RICHARDS & CO., LTD. — London, England

BEST QUALITY
DOUBLE RIFLE. . . . . NiB $34,375 Ex $27,500 Gd $18,700
Boxlock, hammerless, ejector. Hand-detachable locks. Calibers: .30-06, .318 Accelerated Express, .375 Mag., .425 Mag. Express, .465 Nitro Express, .470 Nitro Express. 25-inch bbls. Weight: 8.5 to 11 lbs. Sights: leaf rear; hooded front. French walnut stock w/cheekpiece, checkered pistol grip and forend.

BEST QUALITY MAGAZINE RIFLE
Mauser or Magnum Mauser action. Calibers: 7mm High Velocity, .30-06, .318 Accelerated Express, .375 Mag., .404 Nitro Express, .425 Mag. Bbl. lengths: 24-inch; 7mm, 22-inch; .425 caliber, 25-inch. Weight 7.25 to 9.25 lbs. Sights: Leaf rear; hooded front.
Standard action . . . . NiB $8688 Ex $6950 Gd $4726
Magnum action . . . . NiB $12,813 Ex $10,250 Gd $6970

WICHITA ARMS — Wichita, Kansas

MODEL WCR CLASSIC BOLT-ACTION RIFLE
Single-shot. Calibers: .17 Rem through .308 Win. 21-inch octagon bbl. Hand-checkered walnut stock. Drilled and tapped for scope w/no sights. Right or left-hand action w/Canjar trigger. Non-glare blued finish. Made 1978 to date.
Right-hand model . . . . NiB $3392 Ex $2620 Gd $1693
Left-hand model . . . . NiB $3309 Ex $2692 Gd $1903

MODEL WSR SILHOUETTE BOLT-ACTION RIFLE
Single-shot, bolt action, chambered in most standard calibers. Right or left-hand action w/fluted bolt. Drilled and tapped for scope mount with no sights. 24-inch bbl. Canjar trigger. Metallic gray Fiberthane stock w/vented rubber recoil pad. Made 1983-95.
Right-hand model . . . . NiB $2568 Ex $1873 Gd $1281
Left-hand model . . . . NiB $2511 Ex $2053 Gd $1468

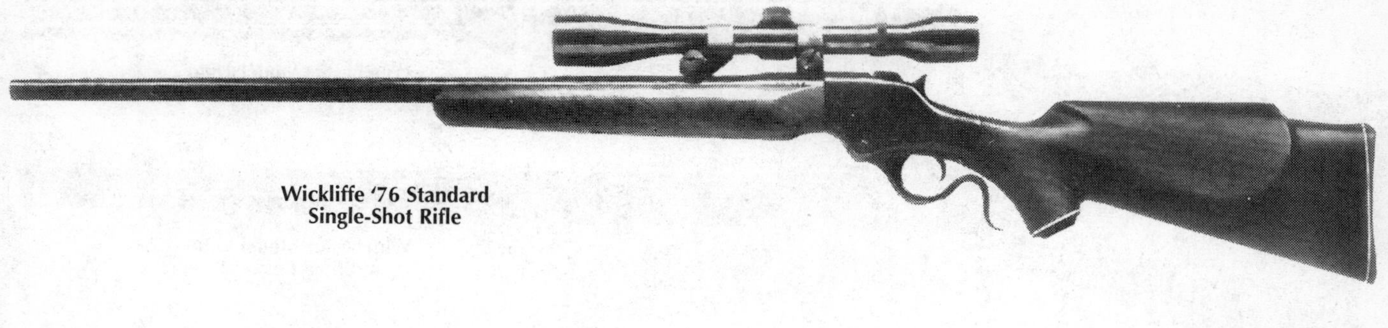

Wickliffe '76 Standard
Single-Shot Rifle

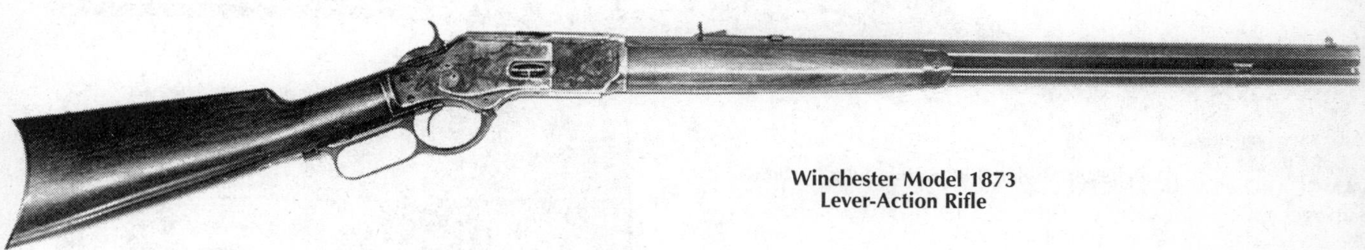

Winchester Model 1873
Lever-Action Rifle

MODEL WMR STAINLESS
MAGNUM BOLT-ACTION RIFLE .... **NiB $2085 Ex $1771 Gd $1050**
Single-shot or w/blind magazine action chambered .270 Win. through .458 Win. Mag. Drilled and tapped for scope with no sights. Fully adj. trigger. 22- or 24-inch bbl. Hand-checkered select walnut stock. Made 1980-84.

MODEL WVR VARMINT RIFLE
Calibers: .17 Rem through .308 Win. Three round magazine. Right or left-hand action w/jeweled bolt. 21-inch bbl. w/o sights. Drilled and tapped for scope. Hand-checkered American walnut pistol-grip stock. Made 1978 to date.
Right-hand model .... **NiB $2600 Ex $1869 Gd $1158**
Left-hand model .... **NiB $2555 Ex $2085 Gd $1483**

WICKLIFFE RIFLES — Wickliffe, Ohio Mfd. by Triple S Development Co., Inc.

'76 COMMEMORATIVE
MODEL.............................. **NiB $1256 Ex $998 Gd $818**
Limited edition of 100. Same as Deluxe Model except w/filled etching on receiver sidewalls, U.S. silver dollar inlaid in stock, 26-inch bbl. only, comes in presentation case. Made in 1976 only.

'76 DELUXE MODEL............ **NiB $521 Ex $419 Gd $289**
Same as Standard Model except w/22-inch bbl. in .30-06 only; high-luster blued finish, fancy-grade figured American walnut stock w/nickel silver grip cap.

'76 STANDARD MODEL
SINGLE-SHOT RIFLE............ **NiB $444 Ex $357 Gd $247**
Falling-block action. Calibers: .22 Hornet, .223 Rem., .22-250, .243 Win., .25-06, .308 Win., .30-06, .45-70. 22-inch lightweight bbl. (.243 and .308 only) or 26-inch heavy sporter bbl. Weight: 6.75 or 8.5 lbs., depending on bbl. No sights. Select American walnut Monte Carlo stock w/right or left cheekpiece and pistol-grip, semi-beavertail forearm. Intro. 1976. Disc.

STINGER MODEL .... **NiB $461 Ex $370 Gd $255**
Falling block, single-shot. Calibers: .22 Hornet and .223 Rem. .22-inch bbl. w/no sights. American walnut Monte Carlo stock w/continental-type forend. Made 1979-80.

TRADITIONALIST MODEL .... **NiB $463 Ex $360 Gd $252**
Falling block single-shot. Calibers: .30-06, .45-70. 24-inch bbl. w/open sights. Hand-checkered. American walnut classic-style buttstock and forearm. Made 1979-80.

WILKINSON ARMS CO. — Covina, California

TERRY CARBINE .... **NiB $499 Ex $386 Gd $267**
Caliber: 9mm Para. Semiautomatic. Thirty round magazine. 16-inch bbl. 30 inches overall. Weight: 6 lbs. Dovetailed receiver for scope mounting. Bolt-type safety. Ejection port w/automatic trap door. Blowback action. Fires from closed bolt. Made 1975 to date.

TED WILLIAMS RIFLES

See Sears, Roebuck and Company.

WINCHESTER RIFLES — Winchester Repeating Arms Company, New Haven, Connecticut

EARLY MODELS 1873 – 1918

NOTE: *Most Winchester rifles manufactured prior to 1918 used the date of approximate manufacture as the model number. For example, the Model 1894 repeating rifle was manufactured from 1894 to 1937. When Winchester started using two-digit model numbers after 1918, the "18" was dropped and the rifle was then called the Model 94. The Model 1892 was called the Model 92, etc.*

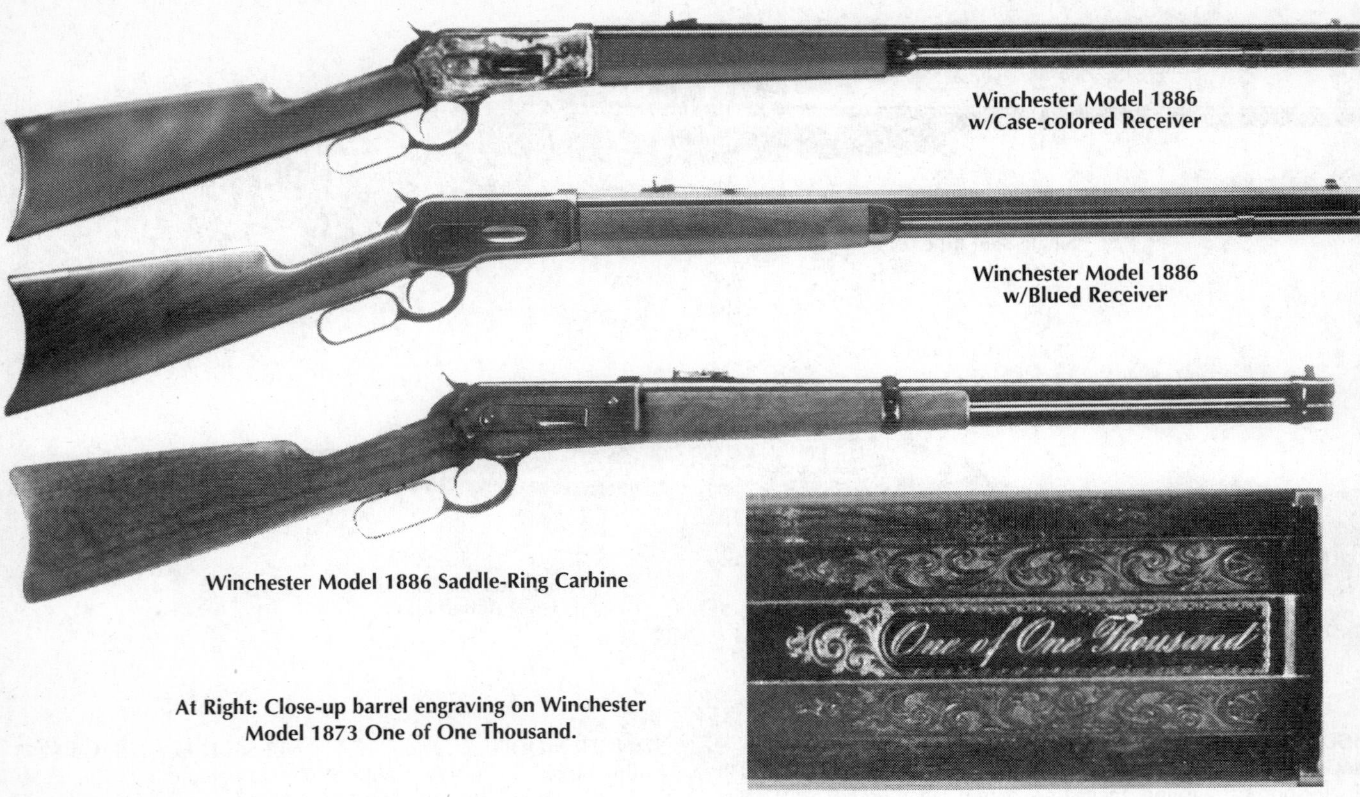

Winchester Model 1886 w/Case-colored Receiver

Winchester Model 1886 w/Blued Receiver

Winchester Model 1886 Saddle-Ring Carbine

At Right: Close-up barrel engraving on Winchester Model 1873 One of One Thousand.

MODEL 1873 LEVER-ACTION CARBINE . . . . NiB $9658 Ex $7739 Gd $5284
Same as Standard Model 1873 Rifle except w/20-inch bbl., 12-round magazine, weight: 7.25 lbs.

MODEL 1873 LEVER-ACTION RIFLE . . . . NiB $9009 Ex $7218 Gd $4928
Calibers: .32-20, .38-40, .44-40; a few were chambered for .22 rimfire. Fifteen round magazine, also made w/6-round half magazine. 24-inch bbl. (round, half-octagon, octagon). Weight: 8.5 lbs. Sights: Open rear; bead or blade front. Plain straight-grip stock and forearm. Made 1873-1924. 720,610 rifles of this model were mfd.

MODEL 1873 — ONE OF ONE THOUSAND . . . . NiB $195,700+ Ex $82,400+ Gd $51,500+
During the late 1870s, Winchester offered Model 1873 rifles of superior accuracy and extra finish, designated "One of One Thousand" grade, at $100. These rifles are marked "1 of 1000" or "One of One Thousand." Only 136 of this model are known to have been manufactured. This is one of the rarest of shoulder arms and, because so few have been sold in recent years, it is extremely difficult to assign a value; however, an "excellent" specimen would probably bring a price upward of $200,000.

MODEL 1873 SPECIAL SPORTING RIFLE . . . . NiB $10,300 Ex $8755 Gd $5150
Same as Standard Model 1873 Rifle except this type has receiver casehardened in colors, pistol-grip stock of select walnut, octagon bbl. only.

MODEL 1885 SINGLE-SHOT RIFLE
Designed by John M. Browning, this falling-block, lever-action rifle was manufactured from 1885 to 1920 in a variety of models and chambered for most of the popular cartridges of the period — both rimfire and centerfire — from .22 to .50 caliber. There are two basic styles of frames, low-wall and high-wall. The low-wall was chambered only for the lower-powered cartridges, while the high-wall was supplied in all calibers and made in three basic types. The standard model for No. 3 and heavier barrels is the type commonly encountered; the thin-walled version was supplied with No. 1 and No. 2 light barrels and the thick-walled action in the heavier calibers. Made in both solid frame and takedown versions. Barrels were available in five weights ranging from the lightweight No. 1 to the extra-heavy No. 5 in round, half-octagon and full-octagon styles. Many other variations were also offered.

MODEL 1885 HIGH-WALL SPORTING RIFLE. . . . . NiB $3705 Ex $2057 Gd $1645
Solid frame or takedown. No. 3, 30-inch bbl., standard. Weight: 9.5 lbs. Standard trigger and lever. Open rear sights; blade front sight. Plain stock and forend.

MODEL 1885 LOW-WALL SPORTING RIFLE. . . . . NiB $1682 Ex $1358 Gd $931
Solid frame. No. 1, 28-inch round or octagon bbl. Weight: 7 lbs. Open rear sight; blade front sight. Plain stock and forend.

MODEL 1885 SCHUETZEN RIFLE . . . . NiB $5699 Ex $4603 Gd $3119
Solid frame or takedown. High-wall action. Schuetzen double-set trigger. Spur finger lever. No. 3, 30-inch octagon bbl. Weight: 12 lbs. Vernier rear peep sight; wind-gauge front sight. Fancy walnut Schuetzen stock with checkered pistol-grip and forend. Schuetzen buttplate; adj. palm rest.

MODEL 1885 SPECIAL SPORTING RIFLE . . . . NiB $2600 Ex $2085 Gd $1467
Same general specifications as the standard high-wall model except with checkered fancy walnut stock and forend.

Winchester Model 1890

Winchester Model 1892

MODEL 1885 SINGLE-SHOT MUSKET .... **NiB $1297 Ex $1041 Gd $713**
Solid frame. Low-wall. .22 Short and Long Rifle. 28-inch round bbl. Weight: 8.6 lbs. Lyman rear peep sight; blade front sight. Military-type stock and forend. Note: The U.S. Government purchased a large quantity of these muskets during World War I for training purposes.

MODEL 1885 SINGLE-SHOT "WINDER" MUSKET .... **NiB $989 Ex $825 Gd $526**
Solid frame or takedown. High-wall. Plain trigger. 28-inch round bbl. Weight: 8.5 lbs. Musket rear sight; blade front sight. Military-type stock and forend w/bbl. band and sling stud/rings.

MODEL 1886 LEVER-ACTION RIFLE
Solid frame or takedown. .33 Win., .38-56, .38-70, .40-65, .40-70, .40-82, .45-70, .45-90, .50-100, .50-110. The .33 Win. and .45-70 were the last calibers in which this model was supplied. Eight round tubular magaine; also 4-round half-magazine. 26-inch bbl. (round, half-octagon, octagon). Weight: 7.5 lbs. Sights: Open rear; bead or blade front. Plain straight-grip stock and forend or standard models. Made 1886-1935.
Standard model .... **NiB $5161 Ex $4143 Gd $2842**
Takedown model .... **NiB $6378 Ex $5117 Gd $3504**
Deluxe model (pistol-grip and high-quality walnut) .... **NiB $10,375 Ex $9850 Gd $6255**

MODEL 1886 SADDLE-RING CARBINE .... **NiB $12,425 Ex $9939 Gd $6759**
Same as standard rifle except with 22-inch bbl., carbine buttstock and forend. Carbine rear sight. Saddle ring on left side of receiver.

MODEL 1890 SLIDE-ACTION RIFLE
Visible hammer. Calibers: .22 Short, Long, LR; .22 WRF (not interchangeable). Tubular magazine holds 15 Short, 12 Long, 11 LR; 12 WRF. 24-inch octagon bbl. Weight: 5.75 lbs. Sights: Open rear; bead front. Plain straight-grip stock, grooved slide handle. Originally solid frame; after No. 15,499, all rifles of this model were takedown-type. Fancy checkered pistol-grip stock, nickel-steel bbl. supplied at extra cost, which can also increase the value by 100% or more. Made 1890-1932.
Blue WRF .... **NiB $1935 Ex $1575 Gd $1008**
Blue (.22 LR) .... **NiB $1987 Ex $1935 Gd $1034**
Color casehardened receiver .... **NiB $6363 Ex $5102 Gd $3489**

MODEL 1892 LEVER-ACTION RIFLE .... **NiB $2475 Ex $1987 Gd $1363**
Solid frame or takedown. Calibers: .25-20, .32-20, .38-40, .44-40. Thirteen round tubular magazine; also 7-round half-magazine. 24-inch bbl. (round, octagon, half-octagon). Weight: from 6.75 lbs. up. Sights: Open rear; bead front. Plain straight-grip stock and forend. Pistol-grip fancy walnut stocks were available at extra cost and also doubles the value of the current value for standard models.

MODEL 1892 SADDLE-RING CARBINE .... **NiB $2599 Ex $2290 Gd $1672**
Same general specifications as the Model 1892 rifle except carbine buttstock, forend and sights. 20-inch bbl. Saddle ring on left side of receiver.

MODEL 1894 LEVER-ACTION RIFLE .... **NiB $1945 Ex $1560 Gd $1068**
Solid frame or takedown. .25-35, .30-30, .32-40, .32 Special, .38-55. Seven round tubular magazine or 4-round half-magazine. 26-inch bbl. (round, octagon, half-octagon). Weight: about 7.35 lbs. Sights: Open rear; bead front. Plain straight-grip stock and forearm on standard model; crescent-shaped or shotgun-style buttplate. Made 1894-1937. See also Winchester Model 94 for later variations of this model.

MODEL 1894 LEVER-ACTION DELUXE. NiB $2402 Ex $1925 Gd $1316
Same general specifications as the standard rifle except checkered pistol-grip buttstock and forend using high-grade walnut. Engraved versions are considerably higher in value.

MODEL 1894 SADDLE-RING CARBINE .... **NiB $1565 Ex $1457 Gd $998**
Same general specifications as the Model 1894 standard rifle except 20-inch bbl., carbine buttstock, forend, and sights. Saddle ring on left side of receiver. Weight: about 6.5 lbs.

MODEL 1894 STANDARD CARBINE . . . NiB $1301 Ex $1045 Gd $717
Same general specifications as Saddle-Ringle Carbine except shotgun type buttstock and plate, no saddle ring, standard open rear sight. Sometimes called "Eastern Carbine." See also Winchester Model 94 carbine.

1895 LEVER-ACTION CARBINE .... **NiB $2802 Ex $2247 Gd $1539**
Same as Model 95 Standard Rifle except has 22-inch bbl., carbine-style buttstock and forend, weight: About 8 lbs., calibers .30-40 Krag, .30-03, .30-06 and .303, solid frame only.

1895 LEVER-ACTION RIFLE . . . . NiB $3120 Ex $1935 Gd $1060
Calibers: .30-40 Krag, .30-03, .30-60, .303 British, 7.62mm Russian, .35 Win., .38-72, .40-72, .405 Win. Four round box magazine except .30-40 and .303, which have 5-round magazines. Bbl. lengths: 24-, 26-, 28-inches (round, half-octagon, octagon). Weight: About 8.5 lbs. Sights: Open rear; bead or blade front. Plain straight-grip stock and forend (standard). Both solid frame and takedown models were made from1897-1931.

MODEL (1897) LEE BOLT-ACTION RIFLE
Straight-pull bolt-action. .236 U.S. Navy, 5-round box magazine, clip loaded. 24- and 28-inch bbl. Weight: 7.5 to 8.5 lbs. Sights: Folding leaf rear sight on musket; open sporting sight on sporting rifle.
Musket model .... **NiB $1823 Ex $1669 Gd $1025**
Sporting rifle .... **NiB $1926 Ex $1720 Gd $1025**

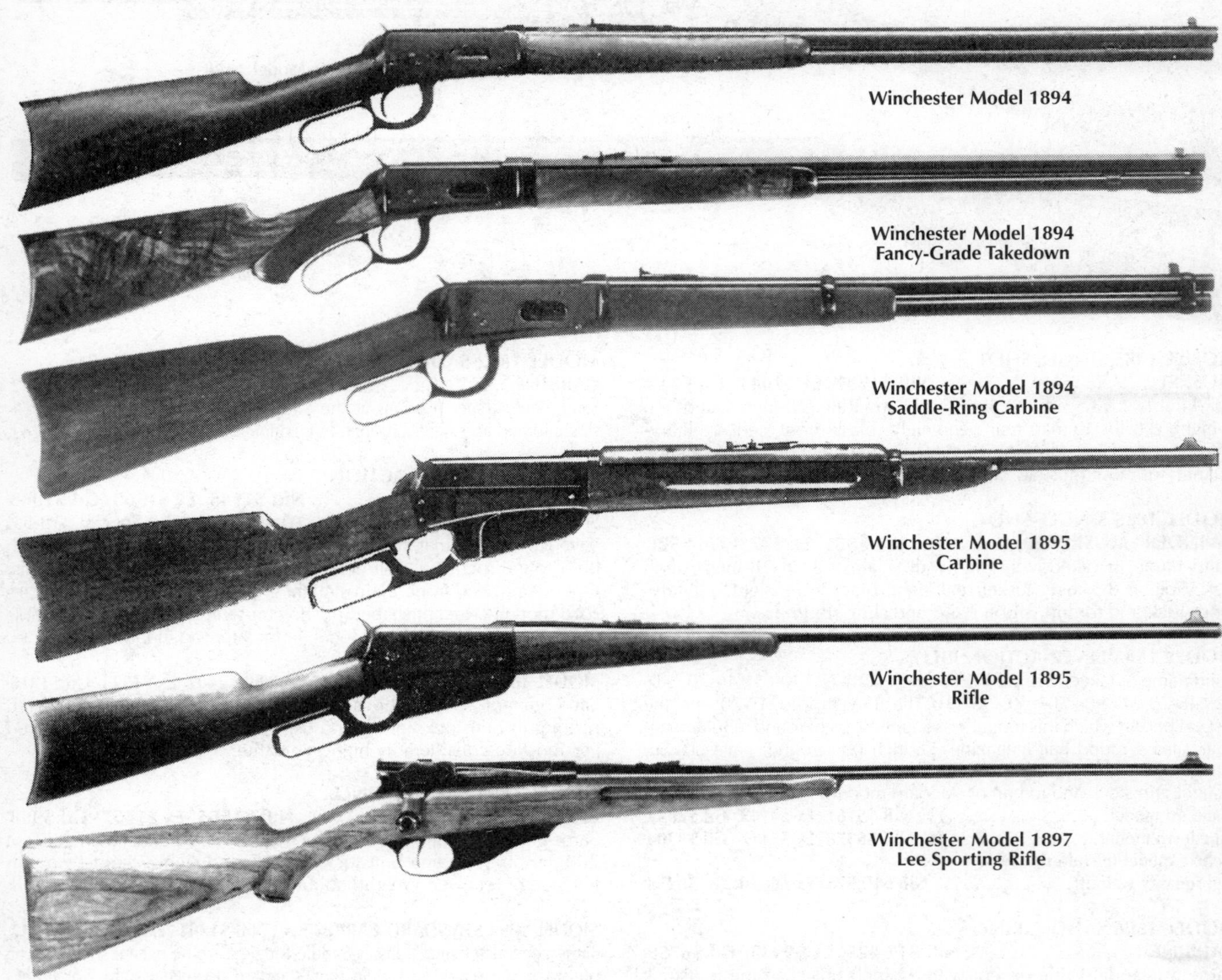

MODEL 1900 BOLT-ACTION SINGLE-SHOT RIFLE .... NiB $557 Ex $448 Gd $308
Takedown. Caliber: .22 Short and Long. 18-inch bbl. Weight: 2.75 lbs. Open rear sight; blade front sight. One-piece, straight-grip stock. Made from 1899 to 1902.

MODEL 1902 BOLT-ACTION SINGLE-SHOT RIFLE .... NiB $422 Ex $319 Gd $216
Takedown. Basically the same as Model 1900 with minor improvements. Calibers: .22 Short and Long, .22 Extra Long, .22 LR. Weight: 3 lbs. Made 1902-1931.

MODEL 1903 SELF-LOADING RIFLE .... NiB $1018 Ex $786 Gd $503
Takedown. Caliber: .22 WRA. Ten round tubular magazine in buttstock. 20-inch bbl. Weight: 5.75 lbs. Sights: Open rear; bead front. Plain straight-grip stock and forearm (fancy grade illustrated). Made 1903-36.

MODEL (1904) 99 THUMB-TRIGGER BOLT-ACTION SINGLE-SHOT RIFLE .... NiB $776 Ex $623 Gd $427

***(cond't)* MODEL (1904) 99**
Takedown. Same as Model 1902 except fired by pressing a button behind the cocking piece. Made 1904-23.

MODEL 1904 BOLT-ACTION SINGLE-SHOT RIFLE .... NiB $422 Ex $319 Gd $216
Similar to Model 1902. Takedown. Caliber: 22 Short, Long Extra Long, LR. 21-inch bbl. Weight: 4 lbs. Made 1904-31.

MODEL 1905 SELF-LOADING RIFLE........... NiB $762 Ex $530 Gd $453
Takedown. Calibers: .32 Win. S. and L., .35 Win. S. and L. Five or 10-round detachable box magazine. 22-inch bbl. Weight: 7.5 lbs. Sights: Open rear; bead front. Plain pistol-grip stock and forearm. Made 1905-20.

MODEL 1906 SLIDE-ACTION REPEATER ..... NiB $839 Ex $787 Gd $530
Takedown. Visible hammer. Caliber: .22 Short, Long, LR. Tubular magazine holds 20 Short, 16 Long or 14 LR. 20-inch bbl. Weight: 5 lbs. Sights: Open rear; bead front. Straight-grip stock and grooved forearm. Made 1906-32.

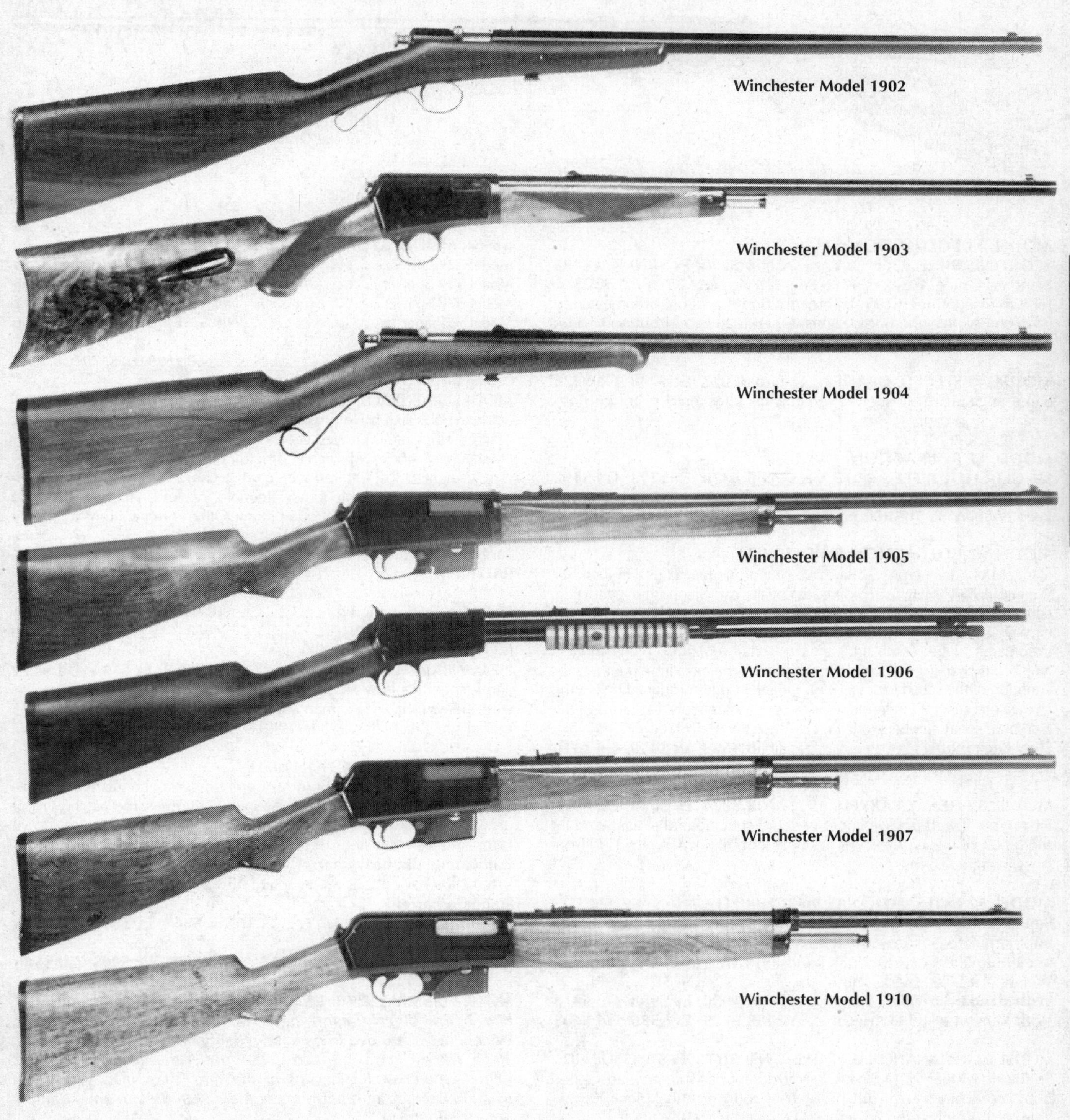
Winchester Model 1902

Winchester Model 1903

Winchester Model 1904

Winchester Model 1905

Winchester Model 1906

Winchester Model 1907

Winchester Model 1910

MODEL 1907 SELF-LOADING RIFLE . . . . . NiB $653 Ex $525 Gd $362
Takedown. Caliber: .351 Win. S. and L. Five or 10-round detachable box magazine. 20-inch bbl. Weight: 7.75 lbs. Sights: Open rear; bead front. Plain pistol-grip stock and forearm. Made 1907-57.

MODEL 1910 SELF-LOADING RIFLE . . . . . NiB $781 Ex $628 Gd $432
Takedown. Caliber: .401 Win. S. and L. Four round detachable box magazine. 20-inch bbl. Weight: 8.5 lbs. Sights: Open rear; bead front. Plain pistol-grip stock and forearm. Made 1910-36.

Winchester Model 43
Special Grade

MODEL 43 BOLT-ACTION SPORTING RIFLE. . . . . NiB $790 Ex $630 Gd $424
Standard Grade. Calibers: .218 Bee, .22 Hornet, .25-20, .32-20 (latter two discontinued 1950). Three round detachable box magazine. 24-inch bbl. Weight: 6 lbs. Sights: Open rear, bead front on hooded ramp. Plain pistol-grip stock with swivels. Made 1949-57.

MODEL 43 SPECIAL GRADE. . . . . NiB $1027 Ex $790 Gd $528
Same as Standard Model 43 except has checkered pistol-grip and forearm, grip cap.

MODEL 47 BOLT-ACTION SINGLE-SHOT RIFLE. . . . . NiB $370 Ex $293 Gd $190
Caliber: .22 Short, Long, LR. 25-inch bbl. Weight: 5.5 lbs. Sights: Peep or open rear; bead front. Plain pistol-grip stock. Made 1949-54.

MODEL 52 BOLT-ACTION TARGET RIFLE
Standard bbl. First type. .22 LR. Five round box magazine. 28-inch bbl. Weight: 8.75 lbs. Sights: Folding leaf peep rear; blade front sight; standard sights various other combinations available. Scope bases. Semi-military-type target stock w/pistol grip; original model has grasping grooves in forearm; higher comb and semi-beavertail forearm on later models. Numerous changes were made in this model; the most important was the adoption of the speed lock in 1929. Model 52 rifles produced before this change are generally referred to as "slow lock" models. Last arms of this type bore serial numbers followed by the letter "A." Made 1919-37.
Slow Lock model. . . . . NiB $559 Ex $450 Gd $310
Speed Lock model. . . . . NiB $753 Ex $604 Gd $415

MODEL 52 HEAVY BARREL . . . . . . NiB $824 Ex $664 Gd $458
First type speed lock. Same general specifications as Standard Model 52 of this type except has heavier bbl., Lyman No. 17G front sight, weight: 10 lbs.

MODEL 52 INTERNATIONAL MATCH RIFLE
Similar to Model 52-D Heavy Barrel except has special lead-lapped bbl., laminated "free rifle"-style stock with high comb, thumbhole, hook buttplate, accessory rail, handstop/swivel assembly, palm rest. Weight: 13.5 lbs. Made 1969-78.
With standard trigger . . . . NiB $1050 Ex $998 Gd $818
With Kenyon or I.S.U. trigger . . . . . NiB $729 Ex $586 Gd $405

MODEL 52 INTERNATIONAL PRONE . . NiB $1076 Ex $1045 Gd $823
Similar to Model 52-D Heavy Barrel except has special lead-lapped bbl., prone stock with full pistol-grip, rollover cheekpiece removable for bore-cleaning. Weight 11.5 lbs. Made 1975-80.

MODEL 52 SPORTING RIFLE
First type. Same as Standard Model 52 of this type except has lightweight 24-inch bbl., Lyman No. 48 receiver sight and gold bead front sight on hooded ramp, deluxe checkered sporting stock with cheekpiece, black forend tip, etc. Weight: 7.75 lbs. Made 1934-58. Reintroduced 1993.

***(cont'd.)* MODEL 52 SPORTING RIFLE**
Model 52 Sporter . . . . NiB $2551 Ex $2048 Gd $1406
Model 52A Sporter . . . . NiB $3649 Ex $2919 Gd $1998
Model 52B Sporter . . . . NiB $2866 Ex $2301 Gd $1577
Model 52C Sporter . . . . NiB $3581 Ex $2862 Gd $1966
Model 52 C Sporter (1993 BAC re-issue) . . . . NiB $689 Ex $530 Gd $360

MODEL 52-B BOLT-ACTION RIFLE
Standard bbl. Extensively redesigned action. Supplied with choice of "Target" stock, an improved version of the previous Model 52 stock, or "Marksman" stock with high comb, full pistol grip and beavertail forearm. Weight: 9 lbs. Offered with a wide choice of target sight combinations (Lyman, Marble-Goss, Redfield, Vaver, Winchester), value shown is for rifle less sight equipment. Other specifications as shown for first type. Made 1935-47. Reintroduced 1997.
Target model . . . . NiB $844 Ex $689 Gd $973
BAC model (1997 BAC re-issue). . . . . NiB $658 Ex $530 Gd $367
USRAC Sporting model . . . . NiB $689 Ex $531 Gd $380

MODEL 52-B BULL GUN HEAVY BARREL. . . . . NiB $889 Ex $715 Gd $493
Same specifications as Standard Model 52-B except Bull Gun has extra heavy bbl., Marksman stock only, weight: 12 lbs. Heavy Bbl. model weight: 11 lbs. Made 1940-47.

MODEL 52-C BOLT-ACTION RIFLE
Improved action with "Micro-Motion" trigger mechanism and new-type "Marksman" stock. General specifications same as shown for previous models. Made 1947-61, Bull Gun from 1952. Value shown is for rifle less sights.
Bull Gun (extra heavy barrel, Wt. 12 lbs.) . . . . NiB $1050 Ex $844 Gd $586
Standard barrel (Wt. 9.75 lbs.). . . . . NiB $844 Ex $689 Gd $576
Target model (heavy barrel) . . . . NiB $895 Ex $995 Gd $586

NOTE: *Following WWI, Winchester had financial difficulties and, like many other firearm firms of the day, failed. However, Winchester continued to operate in the hands of receivers. Then, in 1931, The Western Cartridge Co. — under the leadership of John Olin — purchased all assets of the firm. After that, Winchester leaped ahead of all other firms of the day in firearm and ammunition development.*
The first sporting firearm to come out of the Winchester plant after WWI was the Model 20 shotgun, but this was quickly followed by the famous Model 52 bolt-action rifle. This was also a time when Winchester dropped the four-digit model numbers and began using two-digit numbers instead. This model-numbering procedure, with one exception (Model 677), continued for the next several years.

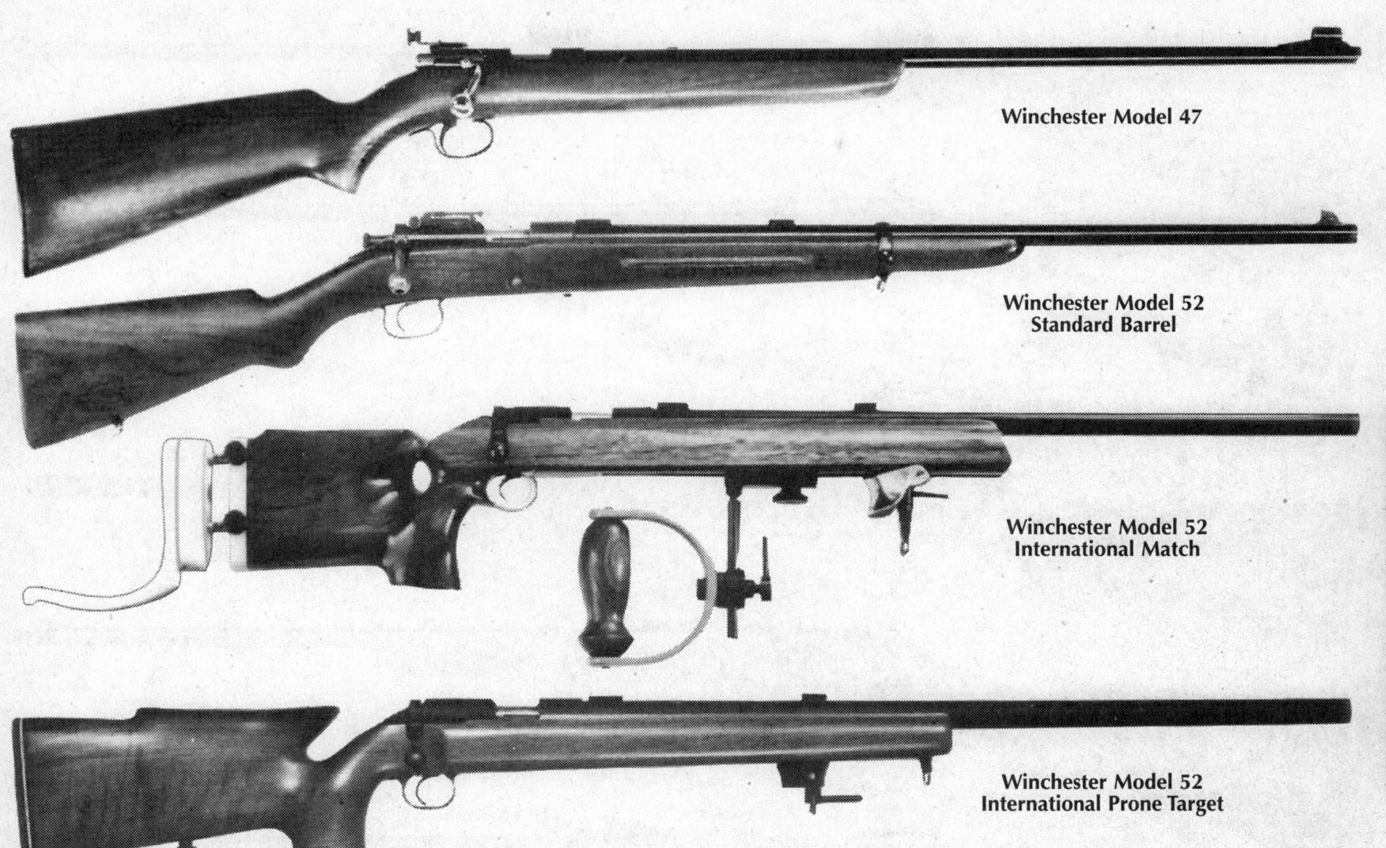

Winchester Model 47

Winchester Model 52
Standard Barrel

Winchester Model 52
International Match

Winchester Model 52
International Prone Target

MODEL 52-D BOLT-ACTION TARGET RIFLE . . . . NiB $830 Ex $786 Gd $423
Redesigned Model 52 action, Single-Shot. Caliber: .22 LR. 28-inch standard or heavy bbl., free-floating, with blocks for standard target scopes. Weight: With standard bbl., 9.75 lbs., with heavy barrel, 11 lbs. Restyled Marksman stock with accessory channel and forend stop, rubber buttplate. Made 1961-78. Value shown is for rifle without sights.

MODEL 53 LEVER-ACTION REPEATER . . . . NiB $2204 Ex $1767 Gd $1209
Modification of Model 92. Solid frame or takedown. Calibers: .25-20, .32-20, .44-40. Six round tubular half-magazine in solid frame model. Seven round in takedown. 22-inch nickel steel bbl. Weight: 5.5 to 6.5 lbs. Sights: Open rear; bead front. Redesigned straight-grip stock and forearm. Made 1924-32.

MODEL 54 BOLT-ACTION HIGH POWER SPORTING RIFLE (I) . . . . . . NiB $942 Ex $839 Gd $581
First type. Calibers: .270 Win., 7x57mm, .30-30, .30-06, 7.65x53mm, 9x57mm. Five round box magazine. 24-inch bbl. Weight: 7.75 lbs. Sights: Open rear; bead front. Checkered stock w/pistol grip, tapered forearm w/Schnabel tip. This type has two-piece firing pin. Made 1925-30.

MODEL 54 BOLT-ACTION HIGH POWER SPORTING RIFLE (II) . . . . . NiB $993 Ex $865 Gd $530
Standard Grade. Improved type with speed lock and one-piece firing pin. Calibers: .22 Hornet, .220 Swift, .250/3000, .257 Roberts, .270 Win., 7x57mm, .30-06. Five round box magazine. 24-inch bbl., 26-inch in cal. .220 Swift. Weight: About 8 lbs. Sights: Open rear, bead front on ramp. NRA-type stock w/checkered pistol-grip and forearm. Made 1930-36. Add $200 for .22 Hornet caliber.

MODEL 54 CARBINE (I) . . . . NiB $1052 Ex $846 Gd $563
First type. Same as Model 54 rifle except has 20-inch bbl., plain lightweight stock with grasping grooves in forearm. Weight: 7.25 lbs.

MODEL 54 CARBINE (II). . . . . NiB $1052 Ex $897 Gd $588
Improved type. Same as Model 54 Standard Grade Sporting Rifle of this type except has 20-inch bbl. Weight: About 7.5 lbs. This model may have either NRA-type stock or the lightweight stock found on the first-type Model 54 Carbine.

MODEL 54 NATIONAL MATCH RIFLE . . . . NiB $1084 Ex $872 Gd $600
Same as Standard Model 54 except has Lyman sights, scope bases, Marksman-type target stock, weighs 9.5 lbs. Same calibers as Standard Model.

MODEL 54 SNIPER'S MATCH RIFLE . . . . NiB $1571 Ex $1309 Gd $537
Similar to the earlier Model 54 Sniper's Rifle except has Marksman-type target stock, scope bases, weight: 12.5 lbs. Available in same calibers as Model 54 Standard Grade.

MODEL 54 SNIPER'S RIFLE. . . . . . NiB $1181 Ex $949 Gd $640
Same as Standard Model 54 except has heavy 26-inch bbl., Lyman No. 48 rear peep sight and blade front sight semi-military stock, weight: 11.75 pounds, cal. .30-06 only.

MODEL 54 SUPER GRADE . . . . . NiB $1567 Ex $1309 Gd $846
Same as Standard Model 54 Sporter except has deluxe stock with cheekpiece, black forend tip, pistol-grip cap, quick detachable swivels, 1-inch sling strap.

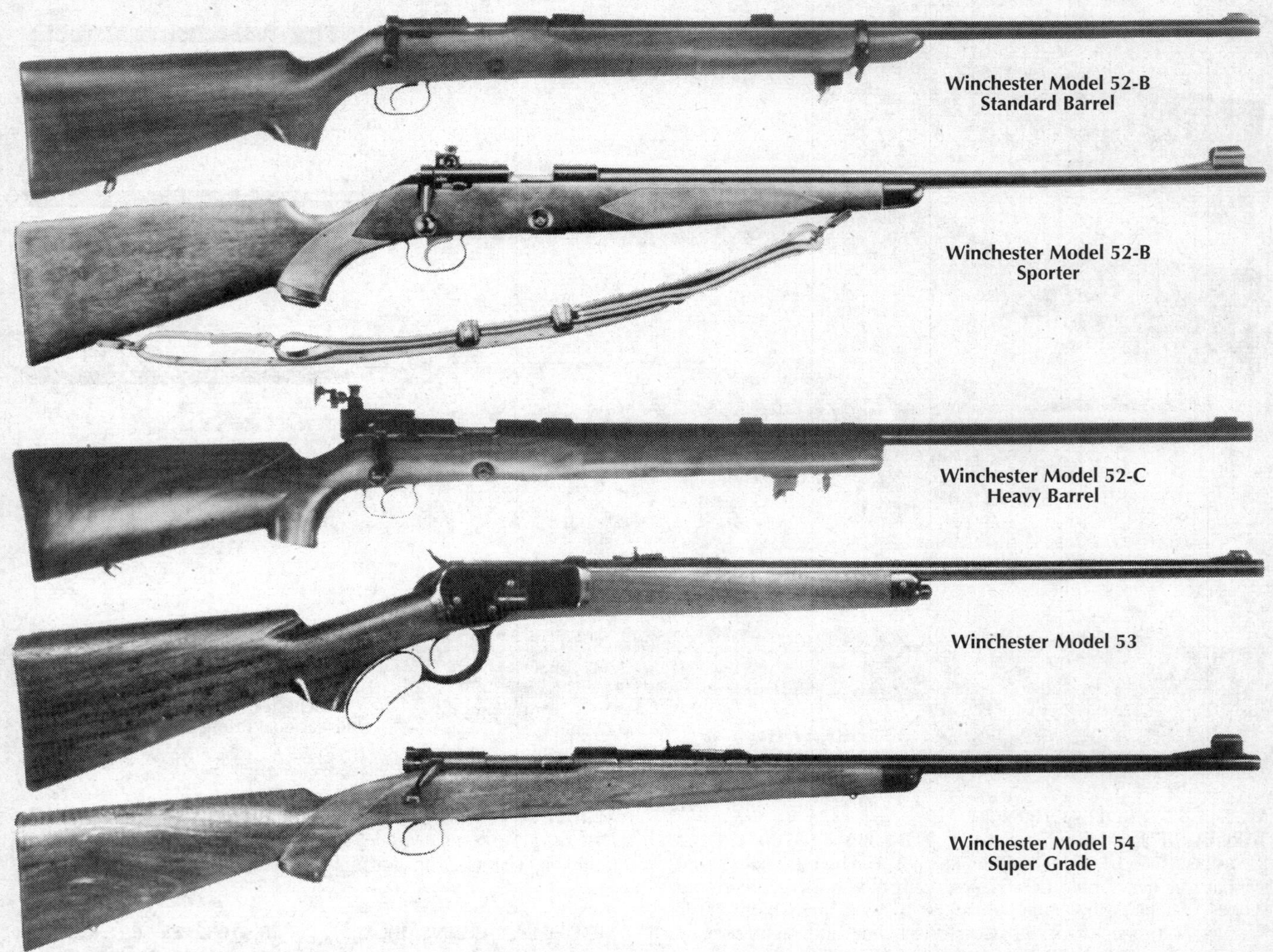

MODEL 54 TARGET RIFLE....... NiB $1084 Ex $872 Gd $600
Same as Standard Model 54 except has 24-inch medium-weight bbl. (26-inch in cal. .220 Swift), Lyman sights, scope bases, Marksman-type target stock, weight: 10.5 lbs., same calibers as Standard Model.

MODEL 55 "AUTOMATIC" SINGLE-SHOT.................. NiB $331 Ex $254 Gd $176
Caliber: .22 Short, Long, LR. 22-inch bbl. Sights: Open rear, bead front. One-piece walnut stock. Weight: About 5.5 lbs. Made 1958-60.

MODEL 55 LEVER-ACTION REPEATER
Modification of Model 94. Solid frame or takedown. Calibers: .25-35, .30-30, .32 Win. Special. Three round tubular half magazine. 24-inch nickel steel bbl. Weight: About 7 lbs. Sights: Open rear; bead front. Made 1924-32.
Standard model (straight grip) .... NiB $1246 Ex $1000 Gd $687
Deluxe model (pistol grip) .... NiB $3235 Ex $2592 Gd $1770

MODEL 56 BOLT-ACTION SPORTING RIFLE............. NiB $1261 Ex $1047 Gd $614
Solid frame. Caliber: .22 LR., .22 Short. Five or 10-round detachable box magazine. 22-inch bbl. Weight: 4.75 lbs. Sights: Open rear; bead front. Plain pistol-grip with Schnabel forend. Made 1926-29.

MODEL 57 BOLT-ACTION RIFLE
Solid frame. Same as Model 56 except available (until 1929) in .22 Short as well as LR with 5- or 10-round magazine. Has semi-military style target stock, bbl. band on forend, swivels and web sling, Lyman peep rear sight, weight: 5 lbs. Mfd. 1926-36.
Sporter model .... NiB $717 Ex $588 Gd $434
Target model .... NiB $666 Ex $614 Gd $460

MODEL 58 BOLT-ACTION SINGLE-SHOT...................... NiB $440 Ex $357 Gd $250
Similar to Model 52. Takedown. Caliber. .22 Short, Long LR. 18-inch bbl. Weight: 3 lbs. Sights, Open rear; blade front. Plain, flat, straight-grip hardwood stock. Not serial numbered. Made 1928-31.

MODEL 59 BOLT-ACTION SINGLE-SHOT...................... NiB $563 Ex $434 Gd $305
Improved version of Model 58, has 23-inch bbl., redesigned stock w/pistol grip, weight: 4.5 lbs. Made 1930.

MODEL 60, 60A BOLT-ACTION SINGLE-SHOT
Redesign of Model 59. Caliber: .22 Short, Long, LR. 23-inch bbl. (27-inch after 1933). Weight: 4.25 lbs. Sights: Open rear, blade front. Plain pistol-grip stock. Made 1930-34 (60), 1932-39 (60A).
Model 60.................... NiB $331 Ex $228 Gd $166
Model 60A.................. NiB $408 Ex $238 Gd $176

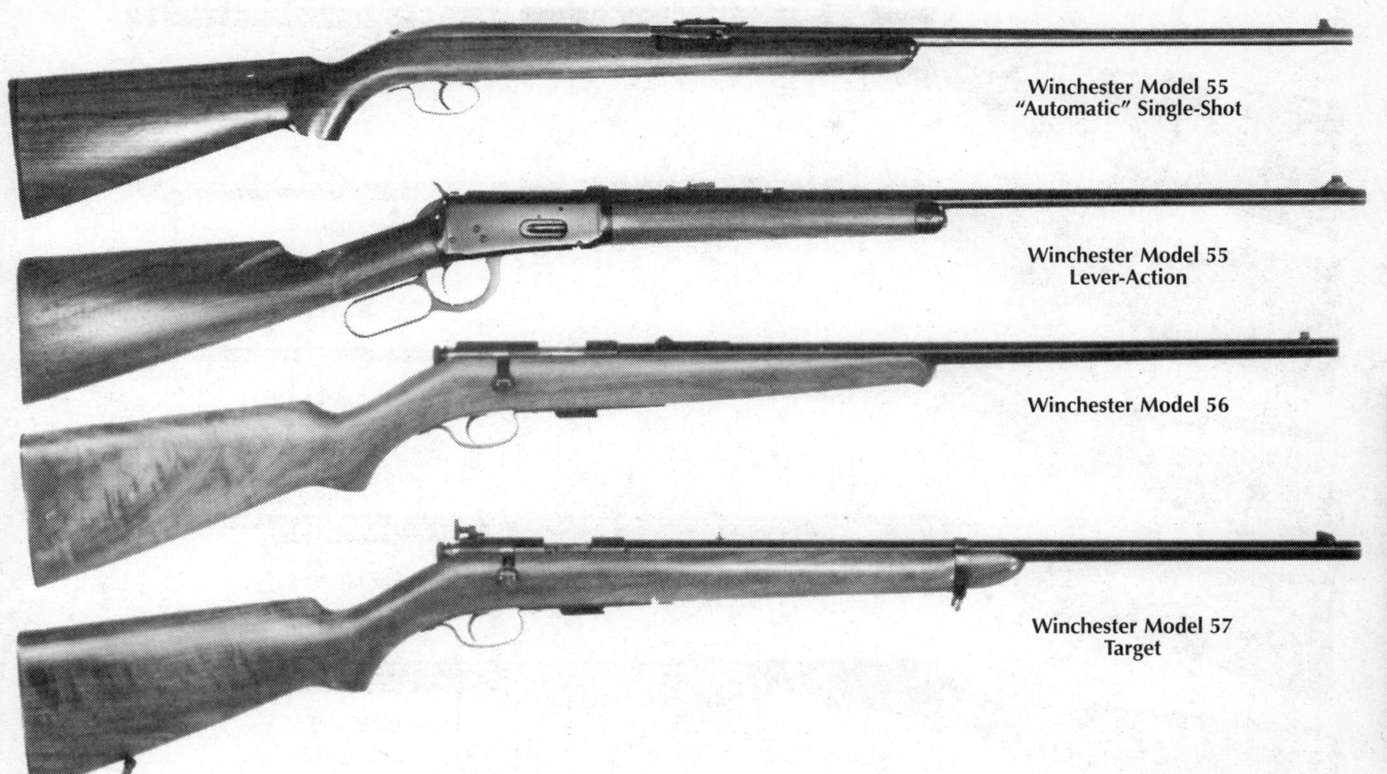

Winchester Model 55 "Automatic" Single-Shot

Winchester Model 55 Lever-Action

Winchester Model 56

Winchester Model 57 Target

MODEL 60A TARGET RIFLE . . . . . . NiB $473 Ex $396 Gd $267
Essentially the same as Model 60 except has Lyman peep rear sight and square top front sight, semi-military target stock and web sling, weight: 5.5 lbs. Made 1932-39.

MODEL 61 HAMMERLESS SLIDE-ACTION REPEATER
Takedown. Caliber: .22 Short, Long, LR. Tubular magazine holds 20 Short, 16 Long, 14 LR. 24-inch round bbl. Weight: 5.5 lbs. Sights: Open rear; bead front. Plain pistol-grip stock, grooved semi-beavertail slide handle. Also available with 24-inch full-octagon bbl. and only calibers .22 Short, .22 LR or .22 WRF. Note: Octagon barrel model discontinued 1943-44; assembled 1948.
Model 61 (round barrel) . . . . NiB $781 Ex $628 Gd $432
Model 61 (grooved receiver) . . . . . . NiB $981 Ex $787 Gd $540
Model 61 (octagon barrel) . . . . . NiB $1683 Ex $1349 Gd $922

MODEL 61 MAGNUM . . . . NiB $968 Ex $787 Gd $504
Same as Standard Model 61 except chambered for .22 WMR; magazine holds 12 rounds. Made 1960-63.

MODEL 62 VISIBLE HAMMER. . . . . NiB $654 Ex $525 Gd $370
Modernized version of Model 1890. Caliber: .22 Short, Long, LR. 23-inch bbl. Weight: 5.5 lbs. Plain straight-grip stock, grooved semi-beavertail slide handle. Also available in Gallery Model chambered for .22 Short only. Made 1932-1959. Note: Pre-WWII model (small forearm) commands 25% higher price.

MODEL 63 SELF-LOADING RIFLE
Takedown. Caliber: .22 LR High Speed only. Ten round tubular magazine in buttstock. 23-inch bbl. Weight: 5.5 lbs. Sights: Open rear, bead front. Plain pistol-grip stock and forearm. Originally available with 20-inch bbl. as well as 23-inch. Made 1933-59. Reintroduced 1997.
Model 63 w/23-inch bbl. . . . . NiB $913 Ex $734 Gd $505
Model 63 w/20-inch bbl. . . . . NiB $1370 Ex $1099 Gd $753

(cont'd.) **MODEL 63 SELF-LOADING RIFLE**
Model 63 grooved receiver) . . . . NiB $1260 Ex $1012 Gd $694
Model 63 Grade I (1997 BAC reissue) . . . . NiB $745 Ex $601 Gd $414
Model 63 High Grade (1997 BAC reissue). . . NiB $1331 Ex $1043 Gd $687

MODEL 64 DELUXE DEER RIFLE . . . . . . NiB $1299 Ex $1043 Gd $715
Same as Standard Model 64 calibers .30-30 and .32 Win. Special, except has checkered pistol-grip and semi-beavertail forearm, swivels and sling, weighs 7.75 lbs. Made 1933-56.

MODEL 64 LEVER-ACTION REPEATER
Standard Grade. Improved version of Models 94 and 55. Solid frame. Calibers: .25-35, .30-30, .32 Win. Special. Five round tubular two-thirds magazine. 20- or 24-inch bbl. Weight: About 7 lbs. Sights: Open rear; bead front on ramp w/sight cover. Plain pistol-grip stock and forearm. Made 1933-56. Production resumed in 1972 (caliber .30-30, 24-inch bbl.). Discontinued 1974.
Original model . . . . NiB $864 Ex $735 Gd $555
1972-74 model . . . . NiB $683 Ex $504 Gd $374

MODEL 64 .219 ZIPPER . . . . . . NiB $2462 Ex $1974 Gd $1350
Same as Standard Grade Model 64 except has 26-inch bbl., peep rear sight. Made 1937-47.

MODEL 65 LEVER-ACTION REPEATER . . . . NiB $2591 Ex $2077 Gd $1420
Improved version of Model 53. Solid frame. Calibers: .25-20 and .32-20. Six round tubular half-magazine. 22-inch bbl. Weight: 6.5 lbs. Sights: Open rear, bead front on ramp base. Plain pistol-grip stock and forearm. made 1933-47.

MODEL 65 .218 BEE . . . . NiB $2791 Ex $2236 Gd $1528
Same as Standard Model 65 except has 24-inch bbl., peep rear sight. Made 1938-47.

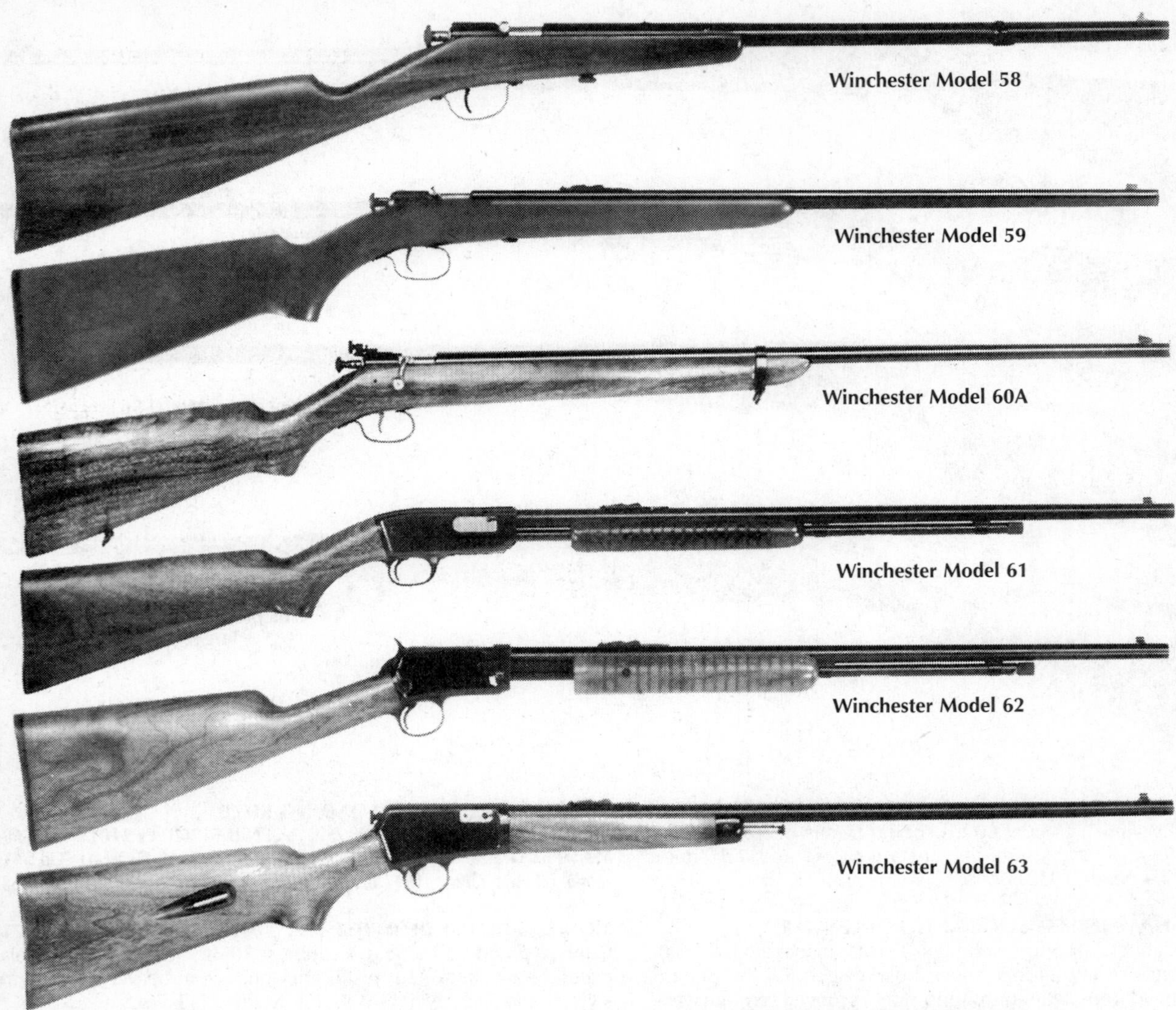

MODEL 67 BOLT-ACTION SINGLE-SHOT RIFLE. . . . . NiB $214 Ex $188 Gd $111
Takedown. Calibers: .22 Short, Long, LR, .22 LR round (smoothbore), .22 WRF. 27-inch bbl. Weight: 5 lbs. Sights: Open rear, bead front. Plain pistol-grip stock (original model had grasping grooves in forearm). Made 1934-63.

MODEL 67 BOY'S RIFLE . . . . NiB $240 Ex $188 Gd $121
Same as Standard Model 6 except has shorter stock, 20-inch bbl., weighs 4.25 lbs.

MODEL 68 BOLT-ACTION SINGLE-SHOT . . . . NiB $265 Ex $188 Gd $147
Same as Model 67 except has rear peep sight. Made 1934-1946.

MODEL 69 BOLT-ACTION RIFLE . . NiB $378 Ex $291 Gd $162
Takedown. Caliber: .22 S, L, LR. Five or 10-round box magazine. 25-inch bbl. Weight: 5.5 lbs. Peep or open rear sight. Plain pistol-grip stock. Rifle cocks on closing motion of the bolt. Made 1935-37.

MODEL 69A BOLT-ACTION RIFLE
Same as the Model 69 except cocking mechanism was changed to cock the rifle by the opening motion of the bolt. Made 1937-63. Note: Models with grooved receivers command 20% higher prices.
Model 69A standard. . . . . NiB $428 Ex $345 Gd $238

Cont'd) **MODEL 69A BOLT-ACTION RIFLE**
Match Mdl. w/Lyman No. 57E W receiver sight . . . . NiB $519 Ex $417 Gd $287
(Target Model w/Winchester peep rear sight, swivels, sling. . . . . NiB $626 Ex $503 Gd $347

MODEL 70
Introduced in 1937, the Model 70 Bolt-Action Repeating Rifle was offered in several styles and calibers. Only minor design changes were made over a period of 27 years and more than 500,000 of these rifles were sold. The original model was dubbed "The Rifleman's Rifle." In 1964, the original Model 70 was superseded by a revised version with redesigned action, improved bolt, swaged (free-floating) barrel, restyled stock. This model again underwent major changes in 1972. Most visible: New stock with contrasting forend tip and grip cap, cut checkering (instead of impressed as in predecessor) knurled bolt handle. The action was machined from a solid block of steel with barrels made from chrome molybdenum steel. Other changes in the design and style of the Model 70 continued. The XTR models were added in 1978 along with the Model 70A, the latter omitting the white liners, forend caps and floor plates. In 1981, an XTR Featherweight Model was added to the line, beginning with serial number G1,440,000. This version featured lighter barrels, fancy-checkered stocks with Schnabel forend. After U.S. Repeating Arms took over the Winchester plant, the Model 70 went through even more changes as described under that section of Winchester rifles.

Winchester Model 64
Deer Rifle

Winchester Model 64
Standard

Winchester Model 64
1972-74 Type

Winchester Model 65

Winchester Model 67

Winchester Model 68

Winchester Model 69

Winchester Model 69 Match

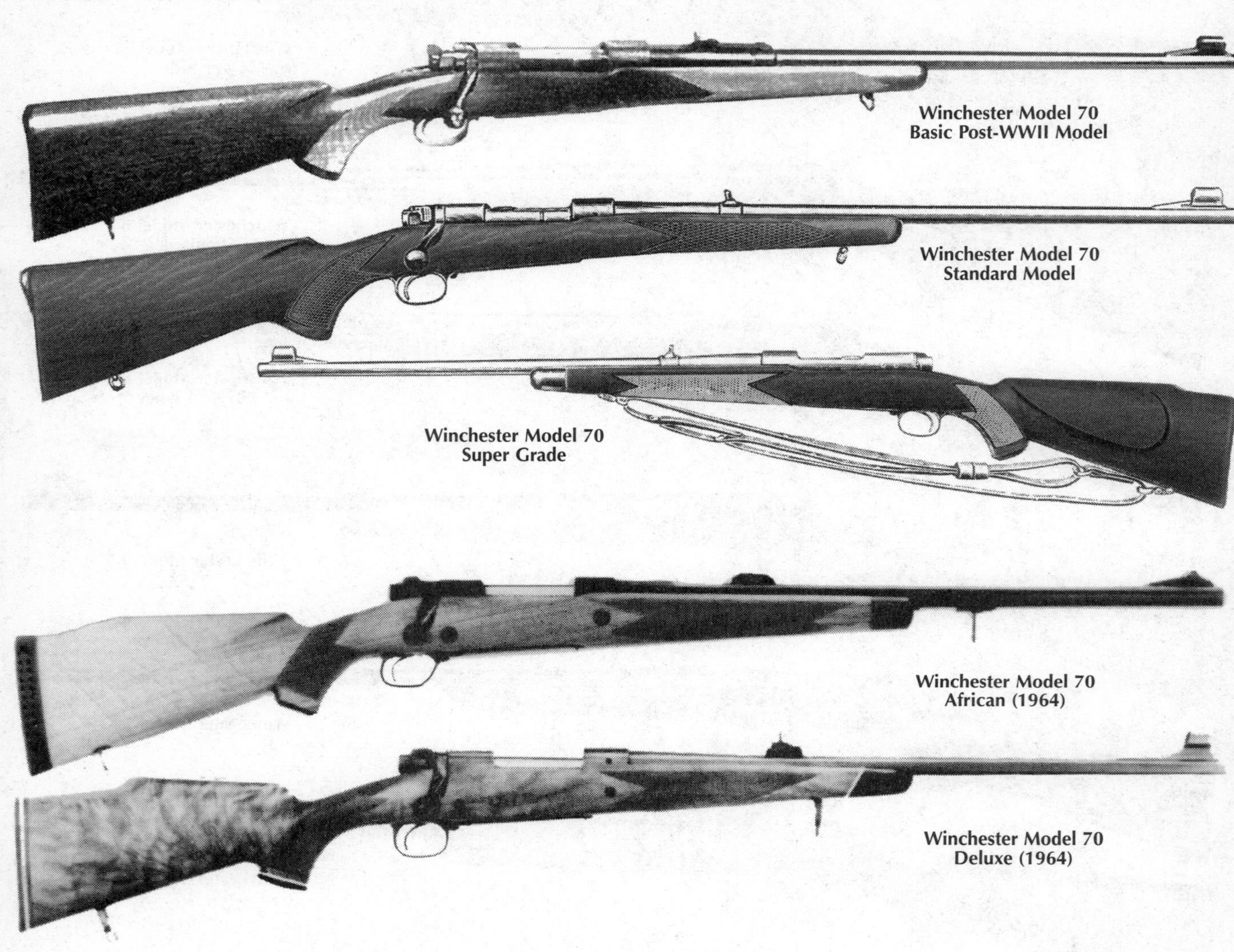

PRE-1964 MODEL 70

MODEL 70
AFRICAN RIFLE . . . . NiB $5220 Ex $4653 Gd $2645
Same general specifications as Super Grade Model 70 except w/25-inch bbl., 3-round magazine, Monte Carlo stock w/recoil pad. Weight: 9.5 lbs. Caliber: .458 Winchester Magnum. Made 1956–63.

MODEL 70 ALASKAN
Same as Standard Model 70 except calibers .338 Win. Mag., .375 H&H Mag.; 3-round magazine in .338, 4-round in .375 caliber; 25-inch bbl.; stock w/recoil pad. Weight: 8 lbs. in .338; 8.75 lbs. in .375 caliber. Made 1960–63.
.338 Win.
Magnum . . . . NiB $1821 Ex $1462 Gd $1002
.375 H&H . . . . NiB $2336 Ex $1874 Gd $1283

MODEL 70 BULL GUN . . . . . . NiB $4150 Ex $3635 Gd $2090
Same as Standard Model 70 except w/heavy 28-inch bbl., scope bases, Marksman stock, weighs 13.25 lbs., caliber .300 H&H Magnum and .30-06 only. Disc. 1963.

MODEL 70 FEATHERWEIGHT SPORTER
Same as Standard Model 70 except w/redesigned stock and 22-inch bbl., aluminum trigger guard, floorplate and buttplate. Calibers: .243 Win., .264 Win. Mag., .270 Win., .308 Win., .30-06, .358 Win. Weight: 6.5 lbs. Made 1952–63.
.243 Win.. . . . . NiB $1044 Ex $838 Gd $577
.264 Win.. . . . . NiB $1559 Ex $1251 Gd $857
.270 Win.. . . . . NiB $1301 Ex $1045 Gd $717
.30-06 Springfield . . . . NiB $986 Ex $792 Gd $545
.308 Win.. NiB $915 Ex $736 Gd $507
.358 Win.. . . . . NiB $2213 Ex $1776 Gd $1218

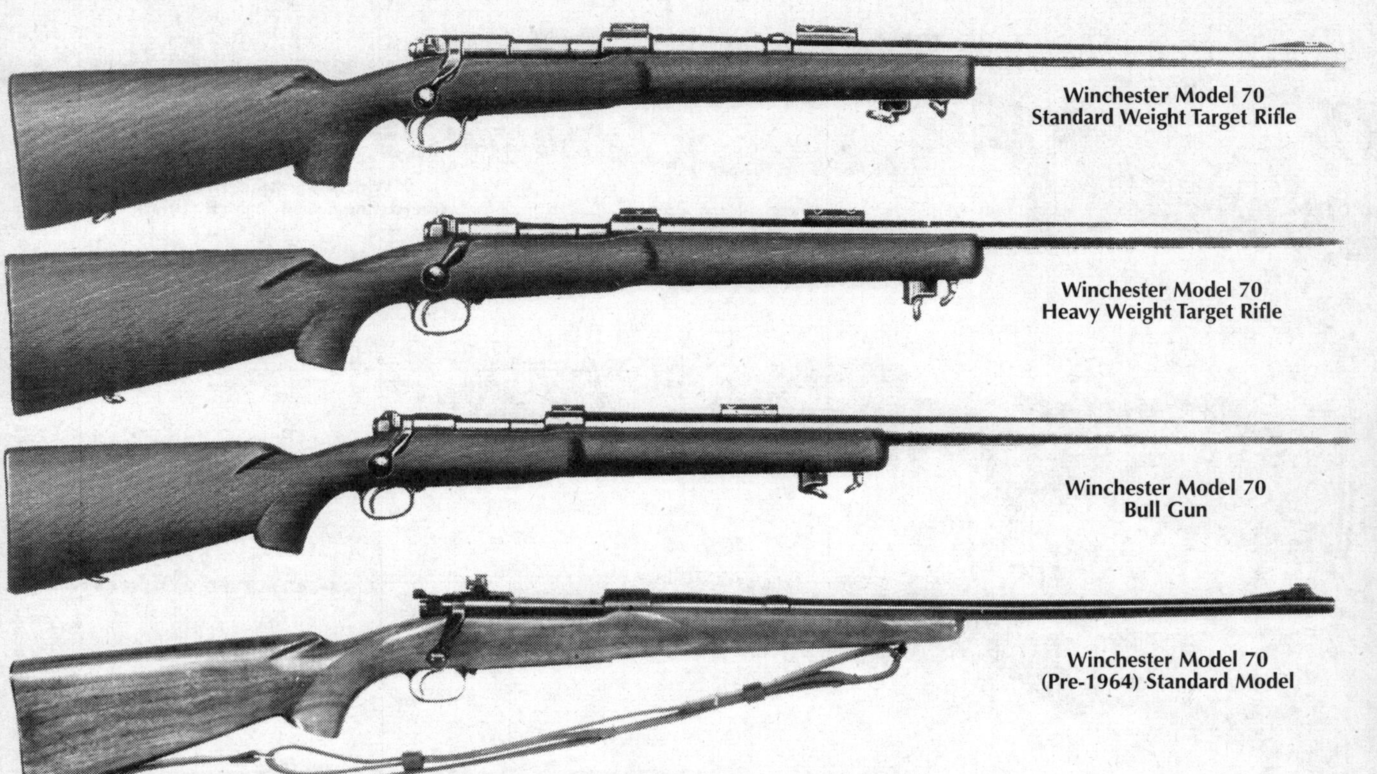
Winchester Model 70
Standard Weight Target Rifle

Winchester Model 70
Heavy Weight Target Rifle

Winchester Model 70
Bull Gun

Winchester Model 70
(Pre-1964) Standard Model

MODEL 70 NATIONAL
MATCH RIFLE . . . . NiB $2085 Ex $1750 Gd $1467
Same as Standard Model 70 except w/scope bases, Marksman-type target stock, weight: 9.5 lbs. caliber .30-06 only. Disc. 1960.

MODEL 70 STANDARD GRADE
Calibers: .22 Hornet, .220 Swift, .243 Win., .250-3000, .257 Roberts, .270 Win., 7x57mm, .30-06, .308 Win., .300 H&H Mag., .375 H&H Mag. Five round box magazine (4-round in Magnum calibers). 24-inch bbl. standard; 26-inch in .220 Swift and .300 Mag.; 25-inch in .375 Mag.; at one time a 20-inch bbl. was available. Sights: Open rear; hooded ramp front. Checkered walnut stock; Monte Carlo comb standard on later production. Weight: From 7.75 lbs. depending on caliber and bbl. length. Made 1937–63.
.22 Hornet (1937-58) . . . . NiB $2011 Ex $1621 Gd $1111
.220 Swift (1937-63). . . . . NiB $1430 Ex $1148 Gd $787
.243 Win. (1955-63) . . . . NiB $1173 Ex $942 Gd $687
.250-3000 Sav. (1937-49) . . . . NiB $2593 Ex $2080 Gd $1423
.257 Roberts (1937-59). . . . . NiB $1816 Ex $1457 Gd $997
.264 Win. Mag. (1959-63) limited. . . . . . NiB $1301 Ex $1045 Gd $717
.270 Win. (1937-63) . . . . NiB $1044 Ex $838 Gd $577
7x57mm Mauser (1937-49) . . . . NiB $2856 Ex $2291 Gd $1568
7.65 Argentine (1937 only) limited . . . . Very Rare
.30-06 Springfield (1937-63). . . . . NiB $857 Ex $689 Gd $475
.308 Win. (1952-63) special order. . . . . Very Rare
.300 H&H (1937-63). . . . . NiB $1501 Ex $1204 Gd $825
.300 Sav. (1944-50) limited . . . . Rare
.300 Win. Mag. (1962-63). . . . . NiB $1950 Ex $1565 Gd $1073
.338 Win. Mag. (1959-63)
special order only . . . . NiB $1859 Ex $1493 Gd $1023
.35 Rem. (1941-47) limited . . . . Very Rare
.358 Win. (1955-58) . . . . Very Rare
.375 H&H (1937-63). . . . . NiB $2336 Ex $1874 Gd $1283
.458 Win. Mag. (1956-63)
Super Grade only . . . . NiB $4669 Ex $3743 Gd $2558
9x57 Mauser (1937 only) limited. . . . . Very Rare

MODEL 70 SUPER GRADE
Same as Standard Grade Model 70 except w/deluxe stock w/cheekpiece, black forend tip, pistol-grip cap, quick detachable swivels, sling. Disc. 1960. Prices for Super Grade models also reflect rarity in both production and caliber. Values are generally twice that of standard models of similar configuration.

MODEL 70 SUPER GRADE FEATHERWEIGHT
Same as Standard Grade Featherweight except w/deluxe stock w/cheekpiece, black forend tip, pistol-grip cap, quick detachable swivels, sling. Disc. 1960. Note: SG-FWs are very rare, but unless properly documented will not command premium prices. Prices for authenticated Super Grades Featherweight models are generally 4 to 5 times that of a standard production Featherweight model w/similar chambering.

MODEL 70 TARGET RIFLE
Same as Standard Model 70 except w/24-inch medium-weight bbl., scope bases, Marksman stock, weight 10.5 lbs. Originally offered in all of the Model 70 calibers, this rifle was available later in calibers .243 Win. and .30-06. Disc. 1963. Values are generally twice that of standard models of similar configuration.

MODEL 70 TARGET
HEAVY WEIGHT . . . . NiB $3748 Ex $1889 Gd $1250
Same general specifications as Standard Model 70 except w/either 24- or 26-inch heavy weight bbl. weight: 10.5 lbs. No checkering. .243 and .30-06 calibers.

MODEL 70 TARGET
BULL BARREL . . . . NiB $4166 Ex $2312 Gd $1709
Same general specifications as Standard Model 70 except 28-inch heavy weight bbl. and chambered for either .30-06 or .300 H&H Mag. Drilled and tapped for front sight base. Receiver slotted for clip loading. Weight: 13.25 lbs.

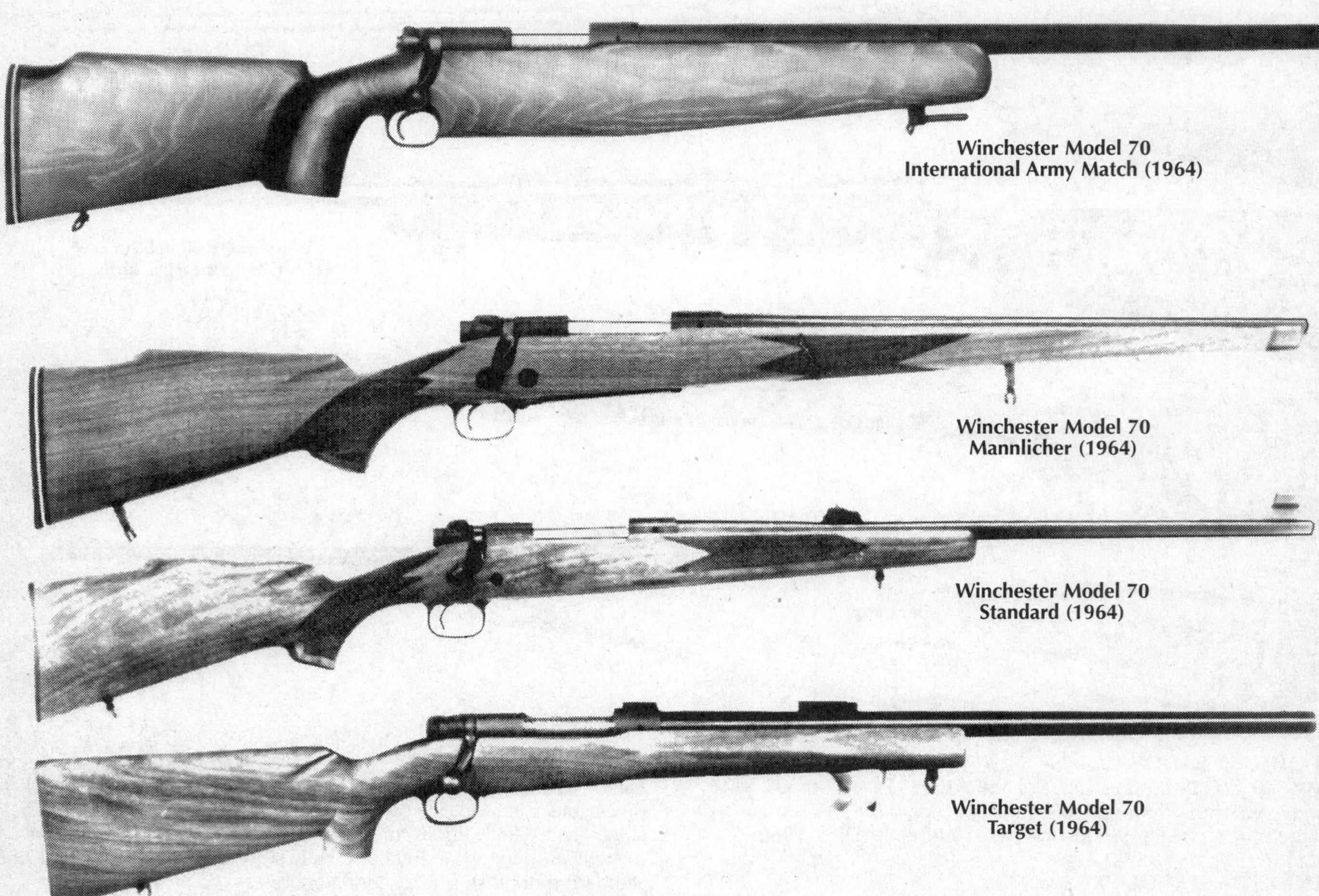

Winchester Model 70
International Army Match (1964)

Winchester Model 70
Mannlicher (1964)

Winchester Model 70
Standard (1964)

Winchester Model 70
Target (1964)

MODEL 70
VARMINT RIFLE . . . . NiB $1258 Ex $1181 Gd $1026
Same general specifications as Standard Model 70 except w/26-inch heavy bbl., scope bases, special varminter stock. Calibers: .220 Swift, .243 Win. Made 1956–63.

MODEL 70
WESTERNER . . . . NiB $1206 Ex $1047 Gd $923
Same as Standard Model 70 except calibers .264 Win. Mag., .300 Win. Mag.; 3-round magazine; 26-inch bbl. in former caliber, 24-inch in latter. Weight: 8.25 lbs. Made 1960–63.

1964-TYPE MODEL 70

MODEL 70 AFRICAN . . . . NiB $1155 Ex $717 Gd $532
Caliber: .458 Win. Mag. Three round magazine. 22-inch bbl. Weight: 8.5 lbs. Special "African" sights. Monte Carlo stock w/ebony forend tip, hand-checkering, twin stock-reinforcing bolts, recoil pad, QD swivels. Made 1964–71.

MODEL 70 DELUXE . . . . NiB $1047 Ex $769 Gd $460
Calibers: .243, .270 Win., .30-06, .300 Win. Mag. Five round box magazine (3-round in Magnum). 22-inch bbl. (24-inch in Magnum). Weight: 7.5 lbs. Sights: Open rear; hooded ramp front. Monte Carlo stock w/ebony forend tip, hand-checkering, QD swivels, recoil pad on Magnum. Made 1964–71.

MODEL 70 INTERNATIONAL
ARMY MATCH RIFLE. . . . . NiB $998 Ex $834 Gd $612
Caliber: .308 Win. (7.62 NATO). Five round box magazine. 24-inch heavy barrel. Externally adj. trigger. Weight: 11 lbs. ISU stock w/military oil finish, forearm rail for standard accessories, vertically adj. buttplate. Made in 1971. Value shown is for rifle w/o sights.

MODEL 70 MAGNUM
Calibers: 7mm Rem. Mag.; .264, .300, .338 Win. Mag.; .375 H&H Mag. Three round magazine. 24-inch bbl. Weight: 7.75 to 8.5 lbs. Sights: Open rear; hooded ramp front. Monte Carlo stock w/cheekpiece, checkering, twin stock-reinforcing bolts, recoil pad, swivels. Made 1964–71.
Caliber .375 H&H Mag. . . . . NiB $728 Ex $586 Gd $405
Other calibers . . . . NiB $493 Ex $396 Gd $273

MODEL 70 MANNLICHER . . . . NiB $737 Ex $634 Gd $531
Calibers: .243, .270, .308 Win., .30-06. Five round box magazine. 19-inch bbl. Sights: open rear; hooded ramp front. Weight: 7.5 lbs. Mannlicher-style stock w/Monte Carlo comb and cheekpiece, checkering, steel forend cap, QD sling swivels. Made 1969–71.

MODEL 70 STANDARD. . . . . NiB $448 Ex $370 Gd $247
Calibers: .22-250, .222 Rem., .225, .243, .270, .308 Win., .30-06. Five round box magazine. 22-inch bbl. Weight: 7.5 lbs. Sights: Open rear; hooded ramp front. Monte Carlo stock w/cheekpiece, checkering, swivels. Made 1964–71.

Winchester Model 70 African (1972)

MODEL 70 TARGET............. NiB $691 Ex $556 Gd $383
Calibers: .308 Win. (7.62 NATO) and .30-06. Five round box magazine. 24-inch heavy bbl. Blocks for target scope. No factory sights installed, but drilled and tapped for front and rear sights. Weight: 10.25 lbs. High-comb Marksman-style stock, aluminum hand stop, swivels. Straight-grain, one-piece stock w/sling swivels, but no checkering. Made 1964–71.

MODEL 70 VARMINT........... NiB $494 Ex $396 Gd $298
Same as Model 70 Standard except w/24-inch target weight bbl., blocks for target scope. No factory sights installed, but drilled and tapped for front and rear sights. Available in calibers .22-250, .222 Rem., and .243 Win. only. Weight: 9.75 lbs. Made 1964–71.

1972-TYPE MODEL 70

MODEL 70 AFRICAN .... NiB $786 Ex $633 Gd $437
Similar to Model 70 Magnum except w/22-inch bbl. caliber .458 Win. Mag. w/special African open rear sight, reinforced stock w/ebony forend tip, detachable swivels and sling; front sling swivel stud attached to bbl. Weight: 8.5 lbs. Made 1972-92.

MODEL 70 CLASSIC SM
Similar to Model 70 Classic Sporter except w/checkered black composite stock and matte metal finish. Made 1994-96.
Model 70 Classic SM............ NiB $499 Ex $422 Gd $272
Caliber .375 H&H.............. NiB $607 Ex $478 Gd $324
W/BOSS, add.. $100
W/open sights, add $40

MODEL 70 CLASSIC SPORTER
Similar to Model 70 Sporter except w/pre-64-style action w/controlled round feeding, classic-style stock. Optional open sights. Made 1994 to date.
Standard model................ NiB $458 Ex $386 Gd $128
W/BOSS, add.. $100
W/open sights, add $40

MODEL 70 CLASSIC SPORTER STAINLESS
Similar to Model 70 Classic Sporter except w/matte stainless steel finish. Weight: 7.5 lbs. No sights. Made 1994 to date.
Standard model................ NiB $648 Ex $556 Gd $268
Magnum model................. NiB $710 Ex $581 Gd $350
W/BOSS, add.. $100

MODEL 70 CUSTOM SHARPSHOOTER
Calibers: .22-250, .223, .308 Win., .300 Win. Mag. 24- or 26-inch bbl. 44.5 inches overall (24-inch bbl.). Weight: 11 lbs. Custom-fitted, hand-honed action. McMillan A-2 target-style stock. Matte blue or stainless finish. Made 1992-96.
Model 70 Custom
Sharpshooter (blued)............... NiB $1858 Ex $1420 Gd $931
Model 70 Custom
Sharpshooter (stainless) .... NiB $1934 Ex $1472 Gd $983

MODEL 70 CUSTOM SPORTING SHARPSHOOTER
Similar to Custom Sharpshooter Model except w/sporter-style gray composite stock. Stainless 24- or 26-inch bbl. w/blued receiver. Calibers: .270, 7mm STW, .300 Win. Mag. Made 1993 to date.
Model 70 Custom Sharpshooter
blued (disc. 1995).................. NiB $1858 Ex $1420 Gd $931
Model 70 Custom Sharpshooter, stainless . NiB $1935 Ex $1472 Gd $983

MODEL 70 GOLDEN 50TH ANNIVERSARY EDITION
BOLT-ACTION RIFLE............................. $1055
Caliber: .300 Win. Three round magazine. 24-inch bbl. 44.5 inches overall. Weight: 7.75 lbs. Checkered American walnut stock. Hand-engraved American scroll pattern on bbl., receiver, magazine cover, trigger guard and pistol-grip cap. Sights: Adj. rear; hooded front ramp. Inscription on bbl. reads "The Rifleman's Rifle 1937–1987." Only 500 made 1986–87. (Value for guns in new condition)

MODEL 70 FEATHERWEIGHT CLASSIC...... NiB $562 Ex $453 Gd $313
Similar to Model 70 XTR Featherweight except w/controlled-round feeding system. Calibers: .270, .280 and .30-06. Made 1992 to date.

MODEL 70 INTERNATIONAL
ARMY MATCH..................... NiB $947 Ex $818 Gd $535
Caliber: .308 Win. (7.62mm NATO). Five round magazine, clip slot in receiver bridge. 24-inch heavy barrel. Weight: 11 lbs. No sights, but drilled and tapped for front and rear iron sights, and/or scope mounts. ISU target stock. Intro. 1973; disc.

MODEL 70 LIGHTWEIGHT....... NiB $607 Ex $375 Gd $159
Calibers: .22-250 and .223 Rem.; .243, .270 and .308 Win.; .30-06 Springfield. Five round mag. capacity (6-round .223 Rem.). 22-inch barrel. 42 to 42.5 inches overall. Weight: 6 to 6.25 lbs. Checkered classic straight stock. Sling swivel studs. Made 1986-95.

MODEL 70 MAGNUM
Same as Model 70 except w/3-round magazine, 24-inch bbl., reinforced stock w/recoil pad. Weight: 7.75 lbs. (except 8.5 lbs. in .375 H&H Mag.). Calibers: .264 Win. Mag., 7mm Rem. Mag., .300 Win. Mag., .338 Win. Mag., .375 H&H Mag. Made 1972-80.
.375 H&H Magnum............. NiB $684 Ex $515 Gd $315
Other magnum calibers.......... NiB $581 Ex $390 Gd $310

MODEL 70 STANDARD.......... NiB $433 Ex $350 Gd $243
Same as Model 70A except w/5-round magazine, Monte Carlo stock w/cheekpiece, black forend tip and pistol-grip cap w/white spacers, checkered pistol grip and forearm, detachable sling swivels. Same calibers plus .225 Win. Made 1972-80.

MODEL 70 STANDARD CARBINE .... NiB $440 Ex $355 Gd $245
Same general specifications as Standard Model 70 except 19-inch bbl. and weight: 7.25 lbs. Shallow recoil pad. Walnut stock and forend w/traditional Model 70 checkering. Swivel studs. No sights, but drilled and tapped for scope mount.

Winchester Model 70 Featherweight

Winchester Model 70 Golden 50th Anniversary

Winchester Model 70 Featherweight Classic

Winchester Model 70 Lightweight

Winchester Model 70 Magnum

Winchester Model 70 Carbine

MODEL 70 SPORTER DBM
Same general specifications as Model 70 Sporter SSM except w/detachable box magazine. Calibers: .22-250 (disc. 1994), .223 (disc. 1994), .243 (disc. 1994), .270, 7mm Rem. Mag., .308 (disc. 1994), .30-06, .300 Win. Mag. Made 1992-94.
Model 70 DBM .... NiB $499 Ex $417 Gd $267
Model 70 DBM-S (w/iron sights) .... NiB $519 Ex $417 Gd $287

MODEL 70 STAINLESS SPORTER SSM .... NiB $519 Ex $417 Gd $287
Same general specifications as Model 70 XTR Sporter except w/checkered black composite stock and matte finished receiver, bbl. and other metal parts. Calibers: .270, 7mm Rem. Mag., .30-06, .300 Win. Mag., .338 Win. Mag. Weight: 7.75 lbs. Made 1992-94.

MODEL 70 CLASSIC SUPER GRADE ..... NiB $841 Ex $764 Gd $424
Calibers: .270, 7mm Rem. Mag., .30-06, .300 Win. Mag., .338 Win. Mag. Five round magazine (standard), 3-round (magnum). 24-inch bbl. 44.5 inches overall. Weight: 7.75 lbs. Checkered walnut stock w/sculptured cheekpiece and tapered forend. Scope bases and rings, no sights. Controlled-round feeding system. Made 1990 to date.

MODEL 70 TARGET............. NiB $865 Ex $788 Gd $427
Calibers: .30-06 and .308 Win. (7.62mm NATO). Five round magazine. 26-inch heavy bbl. Weight: 10.5 lbs. No sights, but drilled and tapped for scope mount and open sights. High-comb Marksman-style target stock, aluminum hand stop and swivels. Intro. 1972. Disc.

MODEL 70 ULTRA MATCH....... NiB $893 Ex $816 Gd $456
Similar to Model 70 Target but custom grade w/26-inch heavy bbl. w/deep counterbore, glass bedding, externally adj. trigger. Intro. 1972. Disc.

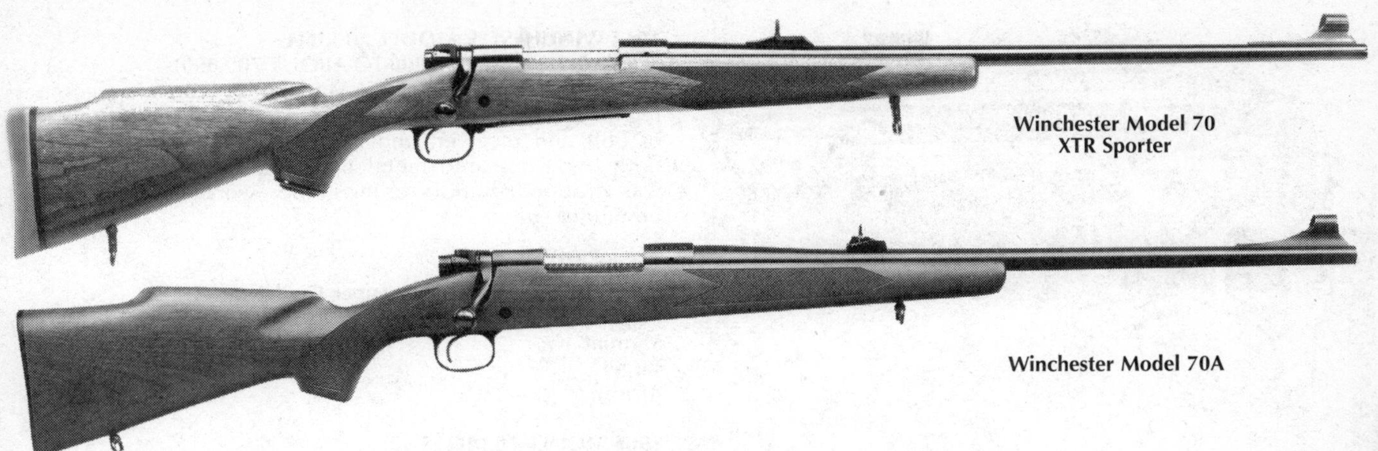

Winchester Model 70 XTR Sporter

Winchester Model 70A

MODEL 70 VARMINT (HEAVY BARREL)
Same as Model 70 Standard except w/medium-heavy, counter-bored 26-inch bbl., no sights, stock w/less drop. Weight: 9 lbs. Calibers: .22-250 Rem., .223 Rem., .243 Win., .308 Win. Made 1972-93. Model 70 SHB, in .308 Win. only w/black synthetic stock and matte blue receiver/bbl. Made 1992-93.
Model 70 Varmint . . . . NiB $684 Ex $556 Gd $303
Model 70 SHB (synthetic heavy barrel) . . . NiB $489 Ex $401 Gd $272

MODEL 70 WIN-CAM RIFLE . . . . . . NiB $475 Ex $372 Gd $218
Caliber: .270 Win. and .30-06 Springfield. 24-inch barrel. Camouflage one-piece laminated stock. Recoil pad. Drilled and tapped for scope. Made 1986 to date.

MODEL 70 WINLITE BOLT-ACTION RIFLE . . . . . NiB $659 Ex $478 Gd $355
Calibers: .270 Win., .280 Rem., .30-06 Springfield, 7mm Rem., .300 Win. Mag., and .338 Win. Mag. Five round magazine; 3-round for Magnum calibers. 22-inch bbl.; 24-inch for Magnum calibers. 42.5 inches overall; 44.5, Magnum calibers. Weight: 6.25 to 7 lbs. Fiberglass stock w/rubber recoil pad, sling swivel studs. Made 1986-90.

MODEL 70 WIN-TUFF BOLT-ACTION RIFLE
Calibers: .22-250, .223, .243, .270, .308 and .30-06 Springfield. 22-inch bbl. Weight: 6.25–7 lbs. Laminated dye-shaded brown wood stock w/recoil pad. Barrel drilled and tapped for scope. Swivel studs. FWT Model made 1986–94. LW Model intro. 1992.
Featherweight model . . . . NiB $530 Ex $401 Gd $283
Lightweight model (Made 1992–93) . . . . . . NiB $475 Ex $362 Gd $249

MODEL 70 XTR FEATHERWEIGHT . . . . NiB $495 Ex $398 Gd $275
Similar to Standard Win. Model 70 except lightweight American walnut stock w/classic Schnabel forend, checkered. 22-inch bbl., hooded blade front sight, folding leaf rear sight. Stainless-steel magazine follower. Weight: 6.75 lbs. Made 1984-94.

MODEL 70 XTR SPORTER RIFLE . . . . NiB $530 Ex $401 Gd $272
Calibers: .264 Win. Mag., 7mm Rem. Mag., .300 Win. Mag., .200 Weatherby Mag., and .338 Win. Mag. Three round magazine. 24-inch barrel. 44.5 inches overall. Weight: 7.75 lbs. Walnut Monte Carlo stock. Rubber buttpad. Receiver tapped and drilled for scope mounting. Made 1986-94.

MODEL 70 XTR SPORTER MAGNUM . . . . NiB $530 Ex $401 Gd $282
Calibers: .264 Win. Mag., 7mm Rem. Mag., .300 Win. Mag., .338 Win. Mag. Three round magazine. 24-inch bbl. 44.5 inches overall. Weight: 7.75 lbs. No sights furnished, optional adj. folding leaf rear; hooded ramp. Receiver drilled and tapped for scope. Checkered American walnut Monte Carlo-style stock w/satin finish. Made 1986-94.

MODEL 70 XTR SPORTER VARMINT . . . . NiB $486 Ex $398 Gd $2569
Same general specifications as Model 70 XTR Sporter, except in calibers .223, .22-250, .243 only. Checkered American walnut Monte Carlo-style stock w/cheekpiece. Made 1986-94.

MODEL 70A . . . . NiB $381 Ex $293 Gd $211
Calibers: .222 Rem., .22-250, .243 Win., .25-06, .270 Win., .30-06, .308 Win. Four round magazine. 22-inch bbl. (except 24- or 26-inch in 25-06). Weight: 7.5 lbs. Sights: Open rear; hooded ramp front. Monte Carlo stock w/checkered pistol grip and forearm, sling swivels. Made 1972-78.

MODEL 70A MAGNUM . . . . NiB $396 Ex $293 Gd $216
Same as Model 70A except w/3-round magazine, 24-inch bbl., recoil pad. Weight: 7.75 lbs. Calibers: .264 Win. Mag., 7mm Rem. Mag., .300 Win. Mag. Made 1972-78

MODEL 70 ULTIMATE CLASSIC BOLT-ACTION RIFLE
Calibers: .25-06 Rem., .264 Win., .270 Win., .270 Wby. Mag., .280 Rem., 7mm Rem. Mag., 7mm STW, .30-06, Mag., .300 Win. Mag., .300 Wby. Mag., .300 H&H Mag., .338 Win. Mag., .340 Wby. Mag., .35 Whelen, .375 H&H Mag., .416 Rem. Mag. and .458 Win. Mag. Three, 4- or 5-round magazine. 22- 24- 26-inch stainless bbl. in various configurations including: full-fluted tapered round, half round and half octagonal or tapered full octagonal. Weight: 7.75 to 9.25 lbs. Checkered fancy walnut stock. Made 1995 to date.
Model 70 Ultimate Classic . . . . NiB $2399 Ex $1935 Gd $1034
For Mag. calibers (.375 H&H, .416 and .458), add. $250

MODEL 70 LAMINATED STAINLESS BOLT-ACTION RIFLE . . . . NiB $890 Ex $762 Gd $422
Calibers: .270 Win., .30-06 Spfld., 7mm Rem. Mag., .300 Win. Mag., and .338 Win. Mag. Five round magazine. 24-inch bbl. 44.75 inches overall. Weight: 8 to 8.525 lbs. Gray/Black laminated stock. Made 1998 to date.

MODEL 70 CHARACTERISTICS

MODEL 70 FIRST MODEL (SERIAL NUMBERS 1 – 80,000)
First manufactured in 1936; first sold in 1937. Receiver drilled for Lyman No. 57W or No. 48WJS receiver peep sights. Also drilled and tapped for Lyman or Fecker scope sight block. Weight w/24-inch bbl. in all calibers except .375 H&H Mag.: 8.25 lbs. 9 lbs. in H&H Mag. Early type safety located on bolt top. Production of this model ended in 1942 near serial number 80,000 due to World War II.

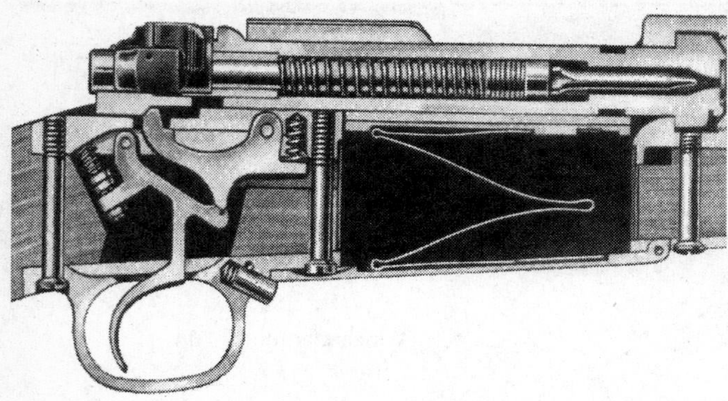

Cross-sectional view of the pre-1964 Winchester Model 70's speed lock action. This action cocks on the opening movement of the bolt with polished, smooth-functioning cams and guide lug, insuring fast and smooth operation.

MODEL 70 SECOND MODEL (SERIAL NUMBERS 80,000 – 350,000)
All civilian production of Winchester Model 70 rifles halted during World War II. Production resumed in 1947 w/improved safety and integral front-sight ramp. Serial numbers started at around 80,000. This model type was produced until 1954, ending around serial number 350,000.

MODEL 70 THIRD MODEL (SERIAL NUMBERS 350,000 – 400,000)
This variety was manufactured from 1954 to 1960 and retained many features of the Second Model except that a folding rear sight replaced the earlier type and front-sight ramps were brazed onto the bbl. rather than being an integral part of the bbl. The Model 70 Featherweight Rifle was intro. in 1954 in .308 WCF caliber. It was fitted w/light 22-inch bbl. and was also available w/either a Monte Carlo or Standard stock. The .243 Win. cartridge was added in 1955 in all grades of the Winchester Model 70 except the National Match and Bull Gun models. The .358 Win. cartridge was also intro. in 1955, along w/new Varmint Model chambered in .243 caliber only.

MODEL 70 FOURTH MODEL (SERIAL NUMBERS 400,000 – 500,000)
Different markings were inscribed on the barrels of these models and new magnum calibers were added; that is, .264 Win Mag., .338 Win. Mag, and .458 Win. Mag. All bbls. of this variation were about 0.13 inch shorter than previous ones. The .22 Hornet and .257 Roberts were disc. in 1962; the .358 Win. caliber in 1963.

MODEL 70 FIFTH MODEL (SERIAL NUMBERS 500,000 TO ABOUT 570,000)
These rifles may be recognized by slightly smaller checkering patterns and slightly smaller lightweight stocks. Featherweight bbls. were marked "Featherweight." Webbed recoil pads were furnished on magnum calibers.

POST-1964 MODEL 70 RIFLES

In 1964, the Winchester-Western Division of Olin Industries claimed that they were losing money on every Model 70 they produced. Both labor and material costs had increased to a level that could no longer be ignored. Other models followed suit. Consequently, sweeping changes were made to the entire Winchester line. Many of the older, less popular models were discontinued. Models that were to remain in production were modified for lower production costs.

1964 WINCHESTER MODEL 70 RIFLES SERIAL NUMBERS 570,000 TO ABOUT 700,000)
The first version of the "New Model 70s" utilized a free-floating barrel, swaged rifle bore, new stock and sights, new type of bolt and receiver, and a different finish throughout on both the wood and metal parts. The featherweight grade was dropped, but six other grades were available in this new line:

Standard
Deluxe (Replaced Previous Super Grade)
Magnum
Varmint
Target
African

1966 MODEL 70 RIFLES (SERIAL NUMBERS 700,000-G TO ABOUT 1,005,000)
In general, this group of Model 70s had fancier wood checkering, cross-bolt stock reinforcement, improved wood finish and improved action. One cross-bolt reinforcement was used on standard guns. Magnum calibers, however, used an additional forward cross-bolt and red recoil pad. The free-floating barrel clearance forward of the breech taper was reduced in thickness. Impressed checkering was used on the Deluxe models until 1968. Hand checkering was once again used on Deluxe and Carbine models in 1969; the big, red "W" was removed from all grip caps. A new, red safety-indicator and undercut cheekpiece was introduced in 1971.

1972 MODEL 70 RIFLES (SERIAL NUMBERS G1,005,000 TO ABOUT G1,360,000)
Both the barrels and receivers for this variety of Model 70s were made from chrome molybdenum (C-M) steel. The barrels were tapered w/spiral rifling, ranging in length from 22 to 24 inches. Calibers .222 Rem., .225 Win. .22-250, .243 Win., .25-06, .270, .308 Win., .30-06 and .458 WM used the 22-inch length, while the following calibers used the 24-inch length: .222 Rem., .22-250, .243 Win., .264 Win. Mag., 7mm Mag., .300 and .375 H&H Mag. The .225 Win caliber was dropped in 1973; Mannlicher stocks were also disc. in 1973. The receiver for this variety of Model 70s was machined from a block of C-M steel. A new improved anti-bind bolt was introduced along with a new type of ejector. Other improvements included hand-cut checkering, pistol-grip stocks with pistol-grip and dark forend caps. An improved satin wood finish was also utilized.

1978 MODEL 70 RIFLES (SERIAL NUMBERS BEGAN AROUND G1,360,000)
This variety of Model 70 was similar to the 1972 version except that a new XTR style was added which featured high-luster wood and metal finishes, fine-cut checkering, and similar embellishments. All Model 70 rifles made during this period used the XTR style; no standard models were available. In 1981, beginning with serial number G1,440,000 (approximately), a Featherweight version of the Model 70 XTR was introduced. The receiver was identical to the 1978 XTR, but lighter barrels were fitted. Stocks were changed to a lighter design with larger scroll checkering patterns and a Schnabel forend with no Monte Carlo comb. A satin sheen stock finish on the featherweight version replaced the high-luster finish used on the other XTR models. A new-style red buttplate with thick, black rubber liner was used on the Featherweight models. The grip cap was also redesigned for this model.

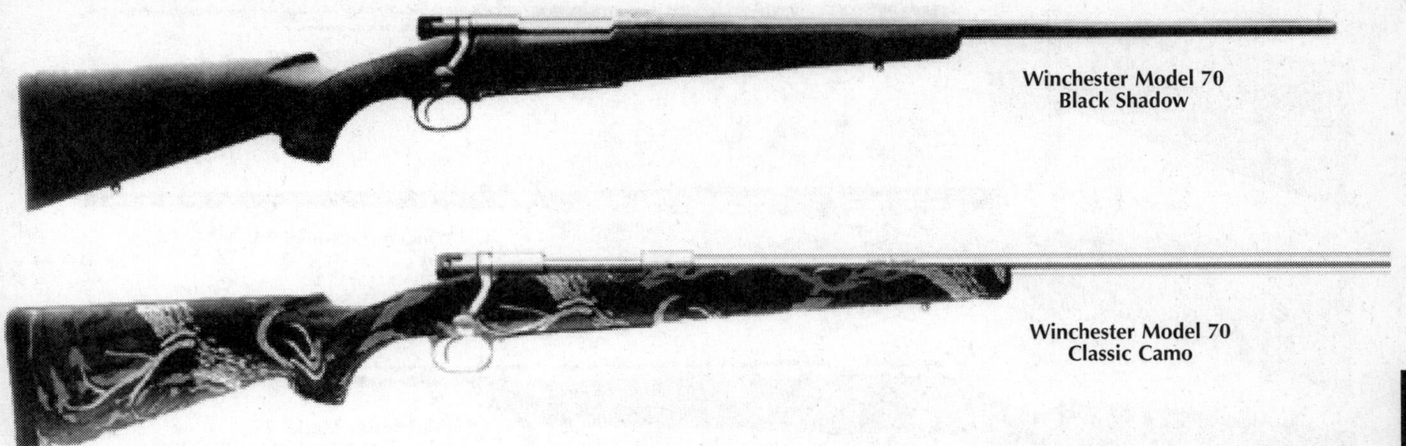
Winchester Model 70 Black Shadow

Winchester Model 70 Classic Camo

U.S. REPEATING ARMS MODEL 70 — 1982 TO DATE

In the early 1980s, negotiations began between Olin Industries and an employee-based corporation. The result of these negotiations ended with Olin selling all tools, machinery, supplies, etc. at the New Haven plant to the newly-formed corporation which was eventually named U.S. Repeating Arms Company. Furthermore, U.S. Repeating Arms Company purchased the right to use the Winchester name and logo. Winchester Model 70s went through very few changes the first two years after the transistion. However, in 1984, the Featherweight Model 70 XTR rifles were offered in a new short action for .22-250 Rem., .223 Rem., .243 Win. and .308 Win. calibers, in addition to their standard action which was used for the longer cartridges. A new Model 70 lightweight carbine was also introduced this same year. Two additional models were introduced in 1985 — the Model 70 Lightweight Mini-Carbine Short Action and the Model 70 XTR Sporter Varmint. The Model 70 Winlite appeared in the 1986 "Winchester" catalog, along with two economy versions of the Model 70 — the Winchester Ranger and the Ranger Youth Carbine. Five or six different versions of the Winchester Model 70 had been sufficient for 28 years (1937 - 1964). Now, changes in design and the addition of new models each year seemed to be necessary to keep the rifle alive. New models were added, old models dropped, changed in design, etc., on a regular basis. The trend continues. Still, the Winchester Model 70 Bolt-Action Repeating Rifle — in any of its variations — is the most popular bolt-action rifle ever built.

MODEL 70 BLACK SHADOW. . . . . NiB $407 Ex $319 Gd $242
Calibers: .243 Win., .270 Win., .300 Win. Mag., .308 Win., .338 Win. Mag., .30-06 Spfld., 7mm STW., 7mm Rem. Mag. and 7mm-08 Rem. Three, 4- or 5-round magazine. 20- 24- 25- or 26-inch bbls. 39.5 to 46.75 inches overall.Weight: 6.5 to 8.25 lbs. Composite, Walnut or Gray/Black laminated stocks. Made 1998 to date.

MODEL 70 CLASSIC CAMO BOLT-ACTION RIFLE. . . . . . NiB $867 Ex $789 Gd $429
Calibers: .270 Win., 30-06 Spfld., 7mm Rem. Mag., .300 Win. Mag. Three or 5-round magazine. 24- or 26-inch bbl. 44.75 to 46.75 inches overall. Weight; 7.25 to 7.5 lbs. Mossy Oak finish and composite stock. Made 1998 to date.

MODEL 70 CLASSIC COMPACT BOLT-ACTION RIFLE. . . NiB $524 Ex $422 Gd $292
Calibers: .243 Win., .308 Win., and 7mm-08 Rem. Three round magazine. 20-inch bbl., 39.5 inches overall. Weight: 6.5 lbs. Walnut stock. Made 1998 to date.

MODEL 70 CLASSIC LAREDO RANGE HUNTER BOLT-ACTION RIFLE
Calibers: 7mm STW, 7mm Rem. mag., .300 Win. Mag. Three round magazine. 26-inch bbl. 46.75 inches overall. Weight: 9.5 lbs. Composite stock. Made 1996 to date.
Classic Laredo. . . . . NiB $687 Ex $559 Gd $425
Classic Laredo Fluted (Made 1998 to date). . . . . NiB $713 Ex $584 Gd $404
Bossâ Classic Laredo. . . . . NiB $694 Ex $559 Gd $386

MODEL 70 COYOTE . . . . NiB $576 Ex $478 Gd $298
Calibers: .22-250 Rem., .223 Rem., and .243 Win. Five or 6-round magazine. 24- inch bbl., 44 inches overall. Weight: 9 lbs. Medium-heavy stainless steel barrel w/laminated stock. Reverse taper forend. Made 1999 to date.

MODEL 70 RANGER COMPACT RIFLE. . . . . NiB $396 Ex $304 Gd $190
Calibers: .22-250 Rem., .223 Rem., .243 Win., 7mm-08 Rem., Mag., and .308 Win. Five or 6-round magazine. 20- or 22-inch bbl. 41 inches overall. Weight: 6.5 lbs. Adjustable TRUGLO front and rear fiber optic sights. Push-feed action. Made 1999 to date.

MODEL 70 STEALTH RIFLE . . . . NiB $710 Ex $618 Gd $348
Varminter style bolt-action rifle. Calibers: .22-250 Rem., .223 Rem., and .308 Win. Five or 6-round magazine. 26- inch bbl. 46 inches overall. Weight: 10.75 lbs. Black synthetic stock w/Pillar Plus Accu Block and full-length aluminum bedding block. Matte blue finish. Made 1999 to date.

MODEL 71 LEVER-ACTION REPEATER
Solid frame. Caliber: .348 Win. Four round tubular magazine. 20- or 24-inch bbl. Weight: 8 lbs. Sights: Open or peep rear; bead front on ramp w/hood. Walnut stock. Made 1935–57.
Special Grade (checkered pistol-grip and forearm, grip cap, quick-detachable swivels and sling . . . . NiB $1954 Ex $1568 Gd $1027
Special Grade Carbine (20-inch bbl.; disc. 1940) . . . . NiB $2470 Ex $1982 Gd $1358
Standard Grade (lacks checkering, grip cap, sling and swivels) . . . . NiB $1156 Ex $1001 Gd $564
Standard Grade Carbine (20-inch bbl.; disc. 1940) . . . . NiB $2090 Ex $1678 Gd $1055

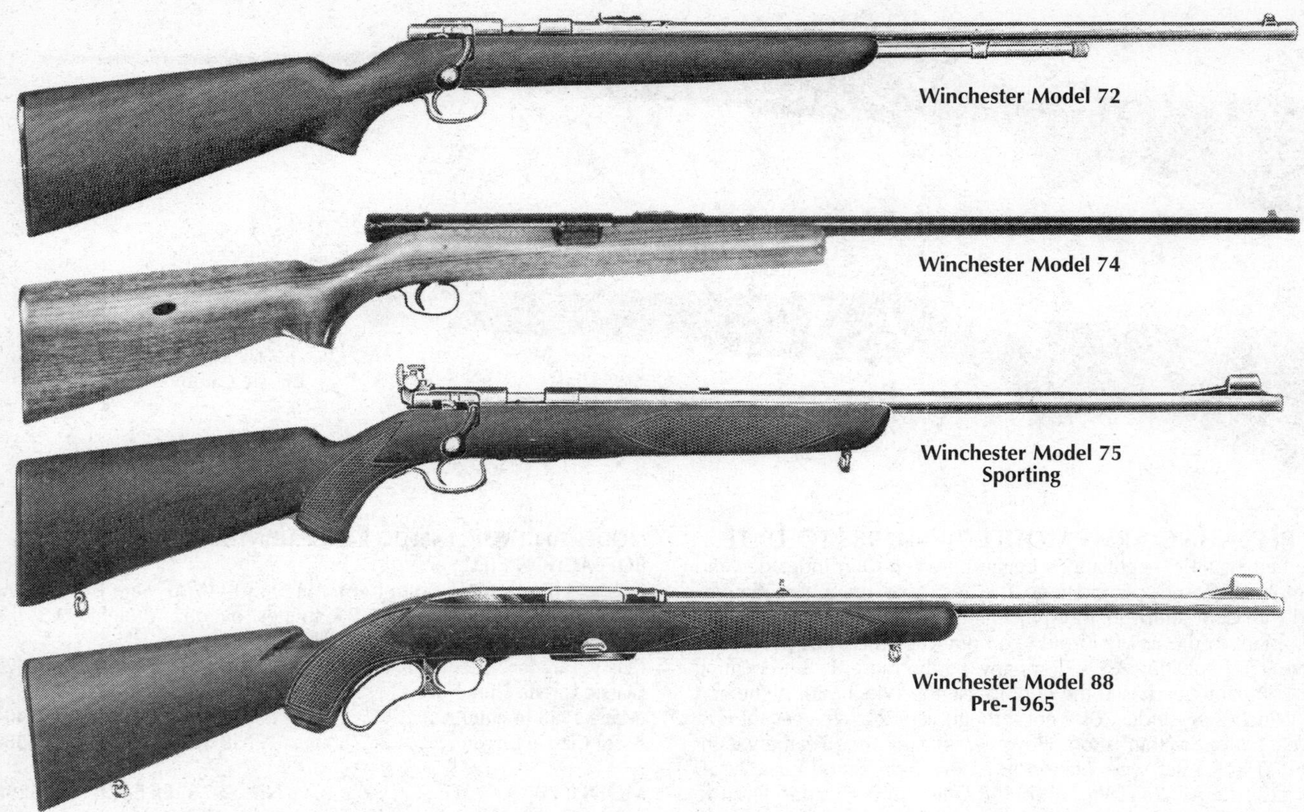

MODEL 72 BOLT-ACTION REPEATER. . . . . NiB $475 Ex $347 Gd $218
Tubular magazine. Takedown. Caliber: .22 Short, Long, LR. Magazine holds 20 Short, 16 Long or 15 LR. 25-inch bbl. Weight: 5.75 lbs. Sights: Peep or open rear; bead front. Plain pistol-grip stock. Made 1938–59.

MODEL 73 LEVER-ACTION REPEATER
See Model 1873 rifles, carbines, "One of One Thousand" and other variations of this model at the beginning of Winchester Rifle Section. Note: The Winchester Model 1873 was the first lever-action repeating rifle bearing the Winchester name.

MODEL 74 SELF-LOADING RIFLE . . . . NiB $293 Ex $242 Gd $164
Takedown. Calibers: .22 Short only, .22 LR only. Tubular magazine in buttstock holds 20 Short, 14 LR. 24-inch bbl. Weight: 6.25 lbs. Sights: Open rear; bead front. Plain pistol-grip stock, one-piece. Made 1939–55.

MODEL 75 SPORTING RIFLE . . . . . NiB $838 Ex $741 Gd $432
Same as Model 75 Target except has 24-inch bbl., checkered sporter stock, open rear sight; bead front on hooded ramp, weight: 5.5 lbs.

MODEL 75 TARGET RIFLE. . . . . NiB $581 Ex $427 Gd $272
Caliber: .22 LR. 5- or 10-round box magazine. 28-inch bbl. Weight: 8.75 lbs. Target sights (Lyman, Redfield or Winchester). Target stock w/pistol grip and semi-beavertail forearm, swivels and sling. Made 1938–59.

MODEL 77 SEMIAUTOMATIC RIFLE,
CLIP TYPE . . . . NiB $293 Ex $242 Gd $154
Solid frame. Caliber: .22 LR. Eight round clip magazine. 22-inch bbl. Weight: About 5.5 lbs. Sights: Open rear; bead front. Plain, one-piece pistol-grip stock. Made 1955–63.

MODEL 77,
TUBULAR MAGAZINE . . . . NiB $293 Ex $242 Gd $164
Same as Model 77. Clip type except has tubular magazine holding 15 rounds. Made 1955–63.

MODEL 86 CARBINE AND RIFLE
See Model 1886 at beginning of Winchester Rifle section.

MODEL 88 CARBINE
Same as Model 88 Rifle except has 19-inch bbl., plain carbine-style stock and forearm with bbl. band. Weight: 7 lbs. Made 1968-73.
88 Carbine. NiB $659 Ex $525 Gd $350
.284 Win.. . . . . NiB $1359 Ex $1256 Gd $947

MODEL 88 LEVER-ACTION RIFLE
Hammerless. Calibers: .243 Win., .284 Win., .308 Win., .358 Win. Four round box magazine. Three round in pre-1963 models and in .284. 22-inch bbl. Weight: About 7.25 lbs. One-piece walnut stock with pistol-grip, swivels (1965 and later models have basket-weave ornamentation instead of checkering). Made 1955–1973. Note: .243 and .358 introduced 1956, later discontinued 1964; .284 introduced 1963.
Model 88 (checkered stock) . . . . NiB $684 Ex $530 Gd $360
Model 88 (basketweave stock) . . . . NiB $581 Ex $478 Gd $330
.284 Win. . . . . NiB $1115 Ex $895 Gd $615
.358 Win. . . . . NiB $1301 Ex $1045 Gd $717

MODEL 92 LEVER-ACTION RIFLE
Similar to the original Model 1892. Calibers: .357 Mag., .44-40, .44 Mag., .45 LC. Ten round magazine. 24-inch round bbl. Weight: 6.25 lbs. 41.25 inches overall. Bead front sight, adjustable buckhorn rear. Etched receiver and gold trigger. Blue finish. Smooth straight-grip walnut stock and forewarn w/ metal grip cap. Made 1997 to date.
Standard Rifle . . . . NiB $590 Ex $473 Gd $325
Short Rifle w/20-inch bbl. (.44 Mag. only) . . . . NiB $570 Ex $458 Gd $315

Winchester Model 70 Coyote

Winchester Model 70 Ranger Compact

Winchester Model 70 Stealth

Winchester Model 94 Traditional

MODEL 94
ANTIQUE CARBINE . . . . NiB $293 Ex $267 Gd $190
Same as standard Post-64 Model 94 Carbine except has decorative scrollwork and casehardened receiver, brass-plated loading gate, saddle ring; caliber .30-30 only. Made 1964–84.

MODEL 94 CARBINE
Same as Model 1894 Rifle except 20-inch round bbl., 6-round full-length magazine. Weight: About 6.5 lbs. Originally made in calibers .25-35, .30-30, .32 Special and .38-55. Original version discontinued 1964. See 1894 Models at beginning of Winchester Rifle Section.
Pre-World War II
(under No. 1,300,000) . . . . NiB $1306 Ex $1050 Gd $722
Postwar, pre-1964
(under No. 2,700,000) . . . . NiB $718 Ex $576 Gd $395

MODEL 94
CLASSIC CARBINE . . . . NiB $401 Ex $293 Gd $242
Same as Canadian Centennial '67 Commemorative Carbine except without commemorative details; has scroll-engraved receiver, gold-plated loading gate. Made 1968–70.

MODEL 94
CLASSIC RIFLE . . . . NiB $381 Ex $267 Gd $242
Same as Model 67 Rifle except without commemorative details; has scroll-engraved receiver, gold-plated loading gate. Made 1968–70.

MODEL 94
DELUXE CARBINE. . . . . NiB $377 Ex $304 Gd $210
Caliber: .30-30 Win. Six round magazine. 20-inch bbl. 37.75 inches overall. Weight: 6.5 lbs. Semi-fancy American walnut stock with rubber buttpad, long forearm and specially cut checkering. Engraved with "Deluxe" script. Made 1987 to date.

MODEL 94 LONG BARREL RIFLE. . . . . NiB $345 Ex $293 Gd $164
Caliber: .30-30 Win. Seven round magazine. 24-inch bbl. 41.75 inches overall. Weight: 7 lbs. American walnut stock. Blade front sight. Made 1987 to date.

MODEL 94 TRAPPER. . . . . NiB $345 Ex $267 Gd $175
Same as Winchester Model 94 Carbine except 16-inch bbl. and weight: 6 lbs., 2 oz. Made 1980 to date.

MODEL 94 WIN-TUFF RIFLE . . . . . NiB $319 Ex $242 Gd $175
Caliber: .30-30 Win. Six round magazine. 20-inch bbl. 37.75 inches overall. Weight: 6.5 lbs. Brown laminated wood stock. Made 1987 to date.

MODEL 94 WRANGLER CARBINE
Same as standard Model 94 Carbine except has 16-inch bbl., engraved receiver and chambered for .32 Special & .38-55 Win.
Wrangler, Top
Eject (disc.1984). NiB $345 Ex $267 Gd $190
Wrangler II,
Angle Eject (disc. 1985) . . . . NiB $293 Ex $206 Gd $164

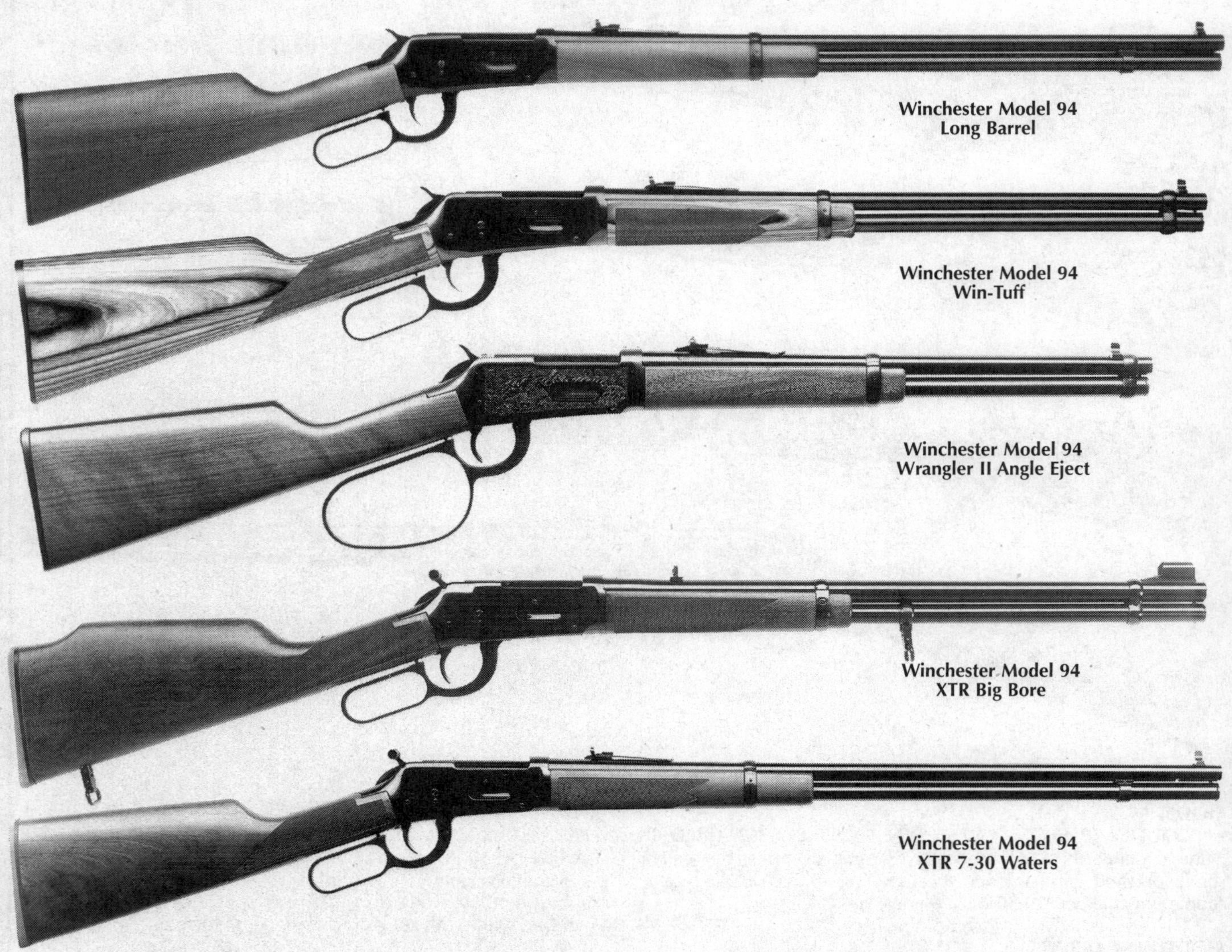

Winchester Model 94
Long Barrel

Winchester Model 94
Win-Tuff

Winchester Model 94
Wrangler II Angle Eject

Winchester Model 94
XTR Big Bore

Winchester Model 94
XTR 7-30 Waters

MODEL 94 XTR BIG BORE....... NiB $376 Ex $273 Gd $175
Modified Model 94 action for added strength. Caliber: .375 Win. 20-inch bbl. Rubber buttpad. Checkered stock and forearm. Weight: 6.5 lbs. Made 1978 to date.

MODEL 94 XTR
LEVER-ACTION RIFLE........... NiB $319 Ex $216 Gd $154
Same general specifications as standard Angle Eject M94 except chambered .30-30 and 7-30 Waters and has 20- or 24-inch bbl. Weight: 7 lbs. Made 1985 to date by U.S. Repeating Arms.

MODEL 94 COMMEMORATIVES

MODEL 94 ANTLERED GAME..... NiB $691 Ex $556 Gd $383
Standard Model 94 action. Gold-colored medallion inlaid in stock. Antique gold-plated receiver, lever tang and bbl. bands. Medallion and receiver engraved with elk, moose, deer and caribou. 20.5-inch bbl. Curved steel buttplate. In .30-30 caliber. 19,999 made in 1978.

MODEL 94 BICENTENNIAL
'76 CARBINE.................. NiB $844 Ex $715 Gd $525
Same as Standard Model 94 Carbine except caliber .30-30 Win. only; antique silver-finished, engraved receiver; stock and forearm of fancy walnut, checkered, Bicentennial medallion embedded in buttstock, curved buttplate. 20,000 made in 1976.

MODEL 94 BUFFALO BILL COMMEMORATIVE
Same as Centennial '66 Rifle except receiver is black-chromed, scroll-engraved and bears name "Buffalo Bill"; hammer, trigger, loading gate, saddle ring, forearm cap, and buttplate are nickel-plated; Buffalo Bill Memorial Assn. commemorative medallion embedded in buttstock; "Buffalo Bill Commemorative" inscribed on bbl., facsimile signature "W.F. Cody, Chief of Scouts" on tang. Carbine has 20-inch bbl., 6-round magazine, 7-lb. weight. 112,923 made in 1968.

Carbine .... NiB $595 Ex $478 Gd $330
Rifle.......................... NiB $627 Ex $504 Gd $348
Matched carbine rifle set....... NiB $1425 Ex $1148 Gd $787

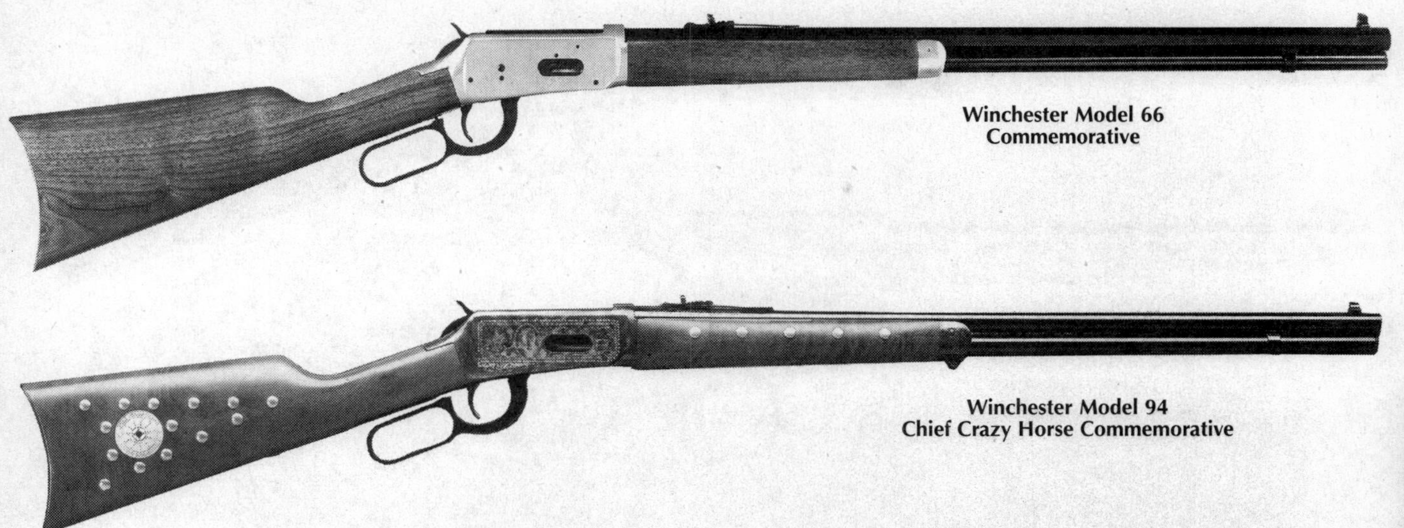

Winchester Model 66 Commemorative

Winchester Model 94 Chief Crazy Horse Commemorative

CANADIAN CENTENNIAL '67 COMMEMORATIVE
Same as Centennial '66 Rifle except receiver engraved with maple leaves and forearm cap is black-chromed, buttplate is blued, commemorative inscription in gold on barrel and top tang: "Canadian Centennial 1867–1967." Carbine has 20-inch bbl., 6-round magazine, weight: 7 lbs., 90,398 made in 1967.
Carbine . . . . NiB $595 Ex $478 Gd $330
Rifle. . . . . NiB $627 Ex $504 Gd $348
Matched carbine/rifle set . . . . . . NiB $1372 Ex $1101 Gd $755

CENTENNIAL '66 COMMEMORATIVE
Commemorates Winchester's 100th anniversary. Standard Model 94 action. Caliber: .30-30. Full-length magazine holds 8 rounds. 26-inch octagon bbl. Weight: 8 lbs. Gold-plated receiver and forearm cap. Sights: Open rear; post front. Saddle ring. Walnut buttstock and forearm with high-gloss finish, solid brass buttplate. Commemorative inscription on bbl. and top tang of receiver. 100,478 made in 1966.
Carbine . . . . NiB $595 Ex $478 Gd $330
Rifle. . . . . NiB $627 Ex $504 Gd $348
Matched carbine/
rifle set . . . . NiB $1430 Ex $1148 Gd $787

MODEL 94 CHEYENNE
COMMEMORATIVE. . . . . NiB $1038 Ex $870 Gd $714
Available in Canada only. Same as Standard Model 94 Carbine except chambered for .44-40. 11,225 made in 1977.

MODEL 94
CHIEF CRAZY HORSE
COMMEMORATIVE. . . . . NiB $724 Ex $581 Gd $400
Cailber: .38-55, 7-round tubular magazine. 24-inch bbl., 41.75 inches overall. Walnut stock with medallion of the United Sioux Tribes; buttstock and forend also decorated with brass tacks. Engraved receiver. Open rear sights; bead front sight. 19,999 made in 1983.

MODEL 94 COLT COMMEMORATIVE
CARBINE SET. . . . . NiB $3901 Ex $3120 Gd $2143
Standard Model 94 action. Caliber: .44-40 Win. 20-inch bbl. Weight: 6.25 lbs. Features the horse-and-rider trademark and distinctive WC monogram in gold etching on left side of receiver. Sold in set with Colt Single Action Revolver chambered for same caliber. See illustration next page.

MODEL 94 COWBOY COMMEMORATIVE CARBINE
Same as Standard Model 94 Carbine except caliber .30-30 only; nickel-plated receiver, tangs, lever, bbl. bands; engraved receiver, "Cowboy Commemorative" on bbl., commemorative medallion embedded in buttstock; curved buttplate. 20,915 made in 1970. Nickel-silver medallion inlaid in stock. Antique silver-plated receiver engraved with scenes of the old frontier. Checkered walnut stock and forearm. 19,999 made in 1970.
Cowboy
Carbine . . . . NiB $595 Ex $478 Gd $330
Cowboy
Carbine
(1 of 300) . . . . NiB $3773 Ex $3027 Gd $2073

MODEL 94 GOLDEN SPIKE COMMEMORATIVE
CARBINE. NiB $524 Ex $422 Gd $292
Same as Standard Model 94 Carbine except caliber .30-30 only; gold-plated receiver, tangs and bbl. bands; engraved receiver, commemorative medallion embedded in stock. 64,758 made in 1969.

MODEL 94 ILLINOIS
SESQUICENTENNIAL
COMMEMORATIVE CARBINE. . . . . NiB $524 Ex $422 Gd $292
Same as Standard Model 94 Carbine except caliber .30-30 only; gold-plated buttplate, trigger, loading gate, and saddle ring; receiver engraved with profile of Lincoln, commemorative inscription on receiver, bbl.; souvenir medallion embedded in stock. 31,124 made in 1968.

MODEL 94 LEGENDARY
FRONTIERSMEN
COMMEMORATIVE. . . . . NiB $691 Ex $556 Gd $383
Standard Model 94 action. Caliber: .39-55. 24-inch round bbl. Nickel-silver medallion inlaid in stock. Antique silver-plated receiver engraved with scenes of the old frontier. Checkered walnut stock and forearm. 19,999 made in 1979.

MODEL 94
LEGENDARY LAWMEN
COMMEMORATIVE. . . . . NiB $691 Ex $556 Gd $383
Same as Standard Model 94 Carbine except .30-30 Win. only; antique silver-plated receiver engraved with action law-enforcement scenes. 16-inch Trapper bbl., antique silver-plated bbl. bands. 19,999 made in 1978.

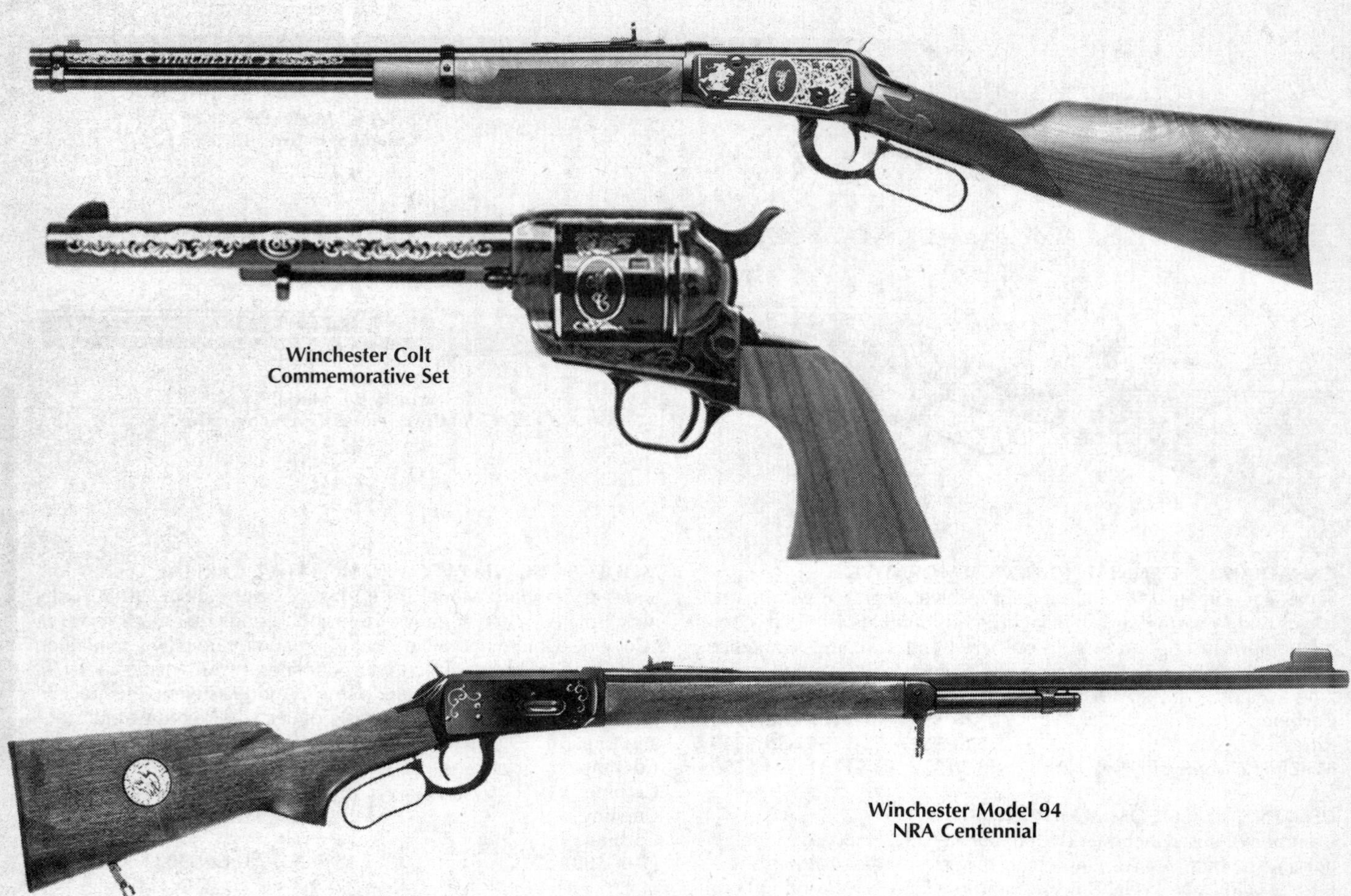

Winchester Colt Commemorative Set

Winchester Model 94 NRA Centennial

MODEL 94 LONE STAR COMMEMORATIVE
Same as Theodore Roosevelt Rifle except yellow-gold plating; "Lone Star" engraving on receiver and bbl., commemorative medallion embedded in buttstock. 30,669 made in 1970.
Rifle or carbine . . . . NiB $595 Ex $478 Gd $330
Matched carbine/rifle set . . . . . . NiB $1430 Ex $1148 Gd $788

MODEL 94 NRA
CENTENNIAL MUSKET . . . . NiB $562 Ex $453 Gd $313
Commemorates 100th anniversary of National Rifle Association of America. Standard Model 94 action. Caliber: .30-30. Seven round magazine. 26-inch bbl. Sights: Military folding rear; blade front. Black chrome-finished receiver engraved "NRA 1871–1971" plus scrollwork. Barrel inscribed "NRA Centennial Musket." Musket-style buttstock and full-length forearm; commemorative medallion embedded in buttstock. Weight: 7.13 lbs. Made in 1971.

MODEL 94 NRA
CENTENNIAL RIFLE . . . . NiB $595 Ex $478 Gd $330
Same as Model 94 Rifle except has commemorative details as in NRA Centennial Musket (barrel inscribed "NRA Centennial Rifle"); caliber .30-30, 24-inch bbl., QD sling swivels. Made in 1971.

MODEL 94 NRA
CENTENNIAL MATCHED SET . . . NiB $1246 Ex $1000 Gd $687
Rifle and musket were offered in sets with consecutive serial numbers. Note: Production figures not available. These rifles offered in Winchester's 1972 catalog.

MODEL 94
NEBRASKA CENTENNIAL
COMMEMORATIVE CARBINE . . . . NiB $1765 Ex $1391 Gd $972
Same as Standard Model 94 Carbine except caliber .30-30 only; gold-plated hammer, loading gate, bbl. band, and buttplate; souvenir medallion embedded in stock, commemorative inscription on bbl. 2,500 made in 1966.

MODEL 94 THEODORE ROOSEVELT
COMMEMORATIVE RIFLE/CARBINE
Standard Model 94 action. Caliber: .30-30. Rifle has 6-round half-magazine, 26-inch octagon bbl., weight: 7.5-lb. Carbine has 6-round full magazine, 20-inch bbl., weight: 7-lb. White gold-plated receiver, upper tang, and forend cap; receiver engraved with American Eagle, "26th President 1901–1909," and Roosevelt's signature. Commemorative medallion embedded in buttstock. Saddle ring. Half pistol-grip, contoured lever. 49,505 made in 1969.
Carbine . . . . NiB $562 Ex $453 Gd $313
Rifle. . . . . NiB $595 Ex $478 Gd $330
Matched set. . . . . NiB $1376 Ex $1115 Gd $759

MODEL 94
TEXAS RANGER
ASSOCIATION CARBINE . . . . . NiB $3376 Ex $2708 Gd $1853
Same as Texas Ranger Commemorative Model 94 except special edition of 150 carbines, numbered 1 through 150, with hand-checkered full-fancy walnut stock and forearm. Sold only through Texas Ranger Association. Made in 1973.

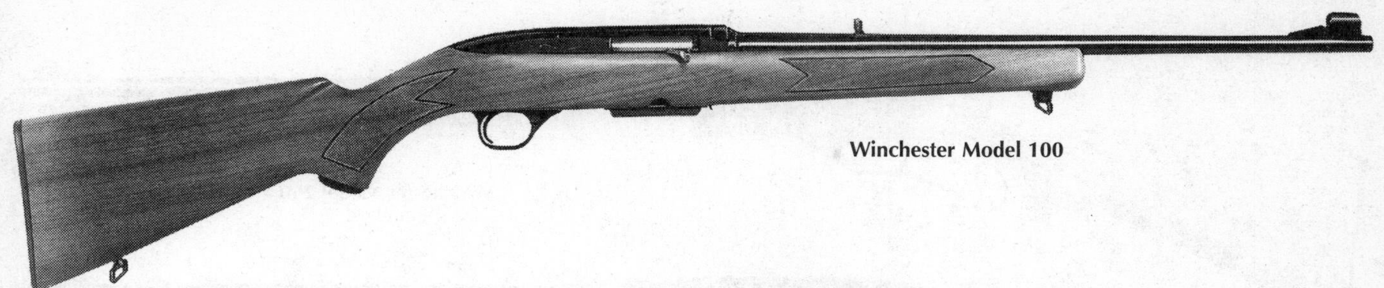
Winchester Model 100

MODEL 94 TEXAS RANGER COMMEMORATIVE CARBINE. . . . . NiB $977 Ex $785 Gd $540
Same as Standard Model 94 Carbine except caliber .30-30 Win. only, stock and forearm of semi-fancy walnut, replica of Texas Ranger star embedded in buttstock, curved buttplate. 5,000 made in 1973.

MODEL 94 TRAPPER
Same as Winchester Model 94 Carbine except w/16-inch bbl. and weighs 6 lbs. 2 oz. Angle Eject introduced in 1985 also chambered for .357 Mag., .44 Mag. and .45 LC. Made 1980 to date.
94 Trapper, Top Eject (disc. 1984). . . . . NiB $345 Ex $267 Gd $190
94 Trapper, Angle Eject (.30-30) . . . . NiB $319 Ex $211 Gd $139
.357 Mag., .44 Mag. or .45 LC., add. $25

MODEL 94 JOHN WAYNE COMMEMORATIVE CARBINE. . . NiB $1249 Ex $1003 Gd $690
Standard Model 94 action. Caliber: .32-40. 18.5-inch bbl. Receiver is pewter-plated with engraving of Indian attack and cattle drive scenes. Oversized bow on lever. Nickel-silver medallion in buttstock bears a bas-relief portrait of Wayne. Selected American walnut stock with deep-cut checkering. Introduced by U.S. Repeating Arms in 1981.

MODEL 94 WELLS FARGO & CO. COMMEMORATIVE CARBINE. . . . . NiB $691 Ex $556 Gd $383
Same as Standard Model 94 Carbine except .30-30 Win. only; antique silver-finished, engraved receiver; stock and forearm of fancy walnut, checkered, curved buttplate. Nickel-silver stagecoach medallion (inscribed "Wells Fargo & Co. —1852–1977—125 Years") embedded in buttstock. 20,000 made in 1977.

MODEL 94 O. F. WINCHESTER COMMEMORATIVE RIFLE. . . . . NiB $953 Ex $767 Gd $527
Standard Model 94 action. Caliber: .38-55. 24-inch octagonal bbl. Receiver is satin gold-plated with distinctive engravings. Stock and forearm semi-fancy American walnut with high grade checkering.

MODEL 94 WRANGLER CARBINE
Same as standard Model 94 Carbine except w/16-inch bbl., engraved receiver and chambered for .32 Special and .38-55 Win. Angle Eject introduced in 1985 as Wrangler II, also chambered for .30-30 Win., .44 Mag. and .45 LC. Made 1980-86. Re-introduced in 1992.
94 Wrangler, Top Eject (disc. 1984) . . . . . . NiB $298 Ex $242 Gd $164
94 Wrangler II, Angle Eject (.30-30) . . . . . . NiB $293 Ex $216 Gd $154
.44 Mag. or .45 LC., add. $25

MODEL 94 WYOMING DIAMOND JUBILEE COMMEMORATIVE CARBINE . . . . NiB $1945 Ex $1560 Gd $1068
Same as Standard Model 94 Carbine except caliber .30-30 Win. only, receiver engraved and casehardened in colors, brass saddle ring and loading gate, souvenir medallion embedded in buttstock, commemorative inscription on bbl. 1,500 made in 1964.

MODEL 94 ALASKAN PURCHASE CENTENNIAL COMMEMORATIVE CARBINE . . . . NiB $2074 Ex $1663 Gd $1138
Same as Wyoming issue except different medallion and inscription. 1,501 made in 1967.

MODEL 94 XTR BIG BORE
Modified Model 94 action for added strength. Calibers: .307 Win., .356 Win., .375 Win. or .444 Marlin. 20-inch bbl. Six round magazine. Rubber buttpad. Checkered stock and forearm. Weight: 6.5 lbs. Made 1978 to date.
94 XTR BB, Top Eject (disc. 1984). . . . . NiB $376 Ex $267 Gd $164
94 XTR BB, Angle Eject (intro. 1985) . . . . . NiB $293 Ex $211 Gd $164
.356 Win. or .375 Win., add $150

MODEL 94 XTR LEVER-ACTION RIFLE
Same general specifications as standard M94 and Angle Eject M94 except chambered for .30-30 Win. and 7-30 Waters and has 20- or 24-inch bbl. Weight: 6.5 to 7 lbs. Made 1978-88 by U.S. Repeating Arms.
94 XTR Top Eject (disc. 1984) . . . . NiB $345 Ex $252 Gd $164
94 XTR Angle Eject (.30-30) . . . . NiB $314 Ex $242 Gd $149
94 XTR Deluxe Angle Eject (.30-30) . . . . . . NiB $396 Ex $314 Gd $206
7-30 Waters, add. $80

MODEL 100 AUTOLOADING RIFLE. . . . . . NiB $576 Ex $448 Gd $293
Gas-operated semiautomatic. Calibers: .243, .284, .308 Win. Four round clip magazine (3-round in .284). 22-inch bbl. Weight: 7.25 lbs. Sights: Open rear; hooded ramp front. One-piece stock w/pistol grip, basket-weave checkering, grip cap, sling swivels. Made 1961–73.

MODEL 100 CARBINE . . . . NiB $633 Ex $504 Gd $324
Same as Model 100 Rifle except has 19-inch bbl., plain carbine-style stock and forearm with bbl. band. Weight: 7 lbs. Made 1967–73.

MODEL 121 DELUXE . . . . NiB $171 Ex $139 Gd $98
Same as Model 121 Standard except has ramp front sight, stock with fluted comb and sling swivels. Made 1967–73.

MODEL 121 STANDARD BOLT-ACTION SINGLE SHOT. . . . . . NiB $164 Ex $134 Gd $94
Caliber: .22 Short, Long, LR. 20.75-inch bbl. Weight: 5 lbs. Sights: Open rear; bead front. Monte Carlo-style stock. Made 1967–73.

MODEL 121 YOUTH. . . . . NiB $164 Ex $134 Gd $103
Same as Model 121 Standard except has 1.25-inch shorter stock. Made 1967–73.

MODEL 131 BOLT-ACTION REPEATER. . . . NiB $184 Ex $149 Gd $105
Caliber: .22 Short, Long or LR. Seven round clip magazine. 20.75-inch bbl. Weight: 5 lbs. Sights: Open rear; ramp front. Plain Monte Carlo stock. Made 1967–73.

MODEL 135 . . . . NiB $171 Ex $139 Gd $98
Same as Model 131 except chambered for .22 WMR cartridge. Magazine holds 5 rounds. Made in 1967.

MODEL 141 BOLT-ACTION TUBULAR REPEATER. . . . . NiB $206 Ex $164 Gd $108
Same as Model 131 except has tubular magazine in buttstock; holds 19 Short, 15 Long, 13 LR. Made 1967–73.

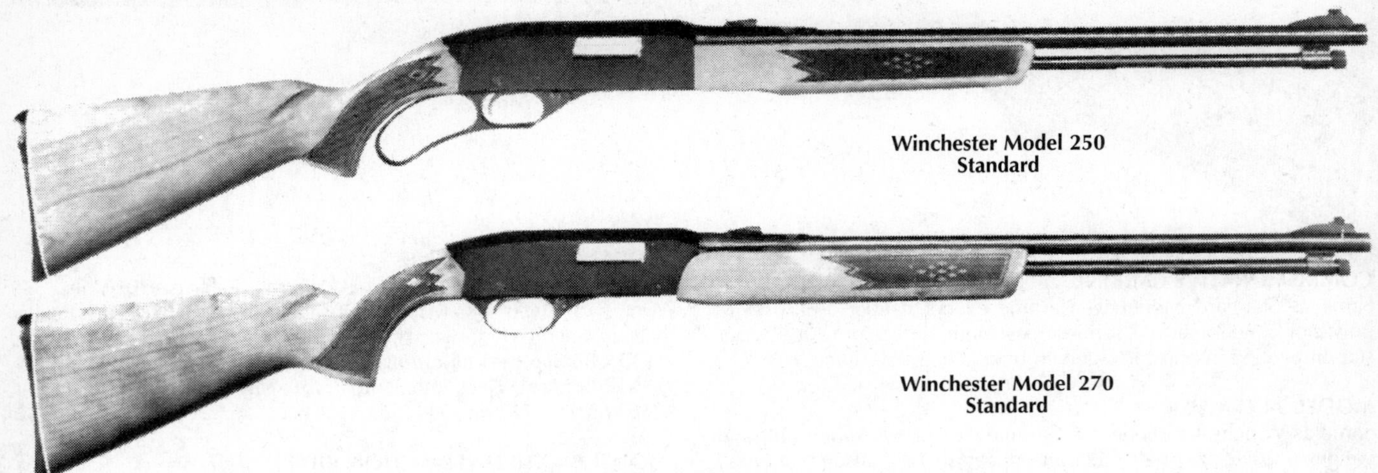

Winchester Model 250 Standard

Winchester Model 270 Standard

MODEL 145 . . . . NiB $195 Ex $164 Gd $108
Same as Model 141 except chambered for .22 WMR; magazine holds 9 rounds. Made in 1967.

MODEL 150 LEVER-ACTION CARBINE . . . . NiB $164 Ex $139 Gd $87
Same as Model 250 except has straight loop lever, plain carbine-style straight-grip stock and forearm with bbl. band. Made 1967–73.

MODEL 190 CARBINE . . . . NiB $164 Ex $139 Gd $87
Same as Model 190 rifle except has carbine-style forearm with bbl. band. Made 1967–73.

MODEL 190 SEMIAUTOMATIC RIFLE . . . . NiB $144 Ex $113 Gd $77
Same as current Model 290 except has plain stock and forearm. Made 1966–78.

MODEL 250 DELUXE RIFLE . . . . . . NiB $242 Ex $190 Gd $113
Same as Model 250 Standard Rifle except has fancy walnut Monte Carlo stock and forearm, sling swivels. Made 1965–71.

MODEL 250 STANDARD LEVER-ACTION RIFLE . . . . NiB $164 Ex $134 Gd $94
Hammerless. Caliber: .22 Short, Long or LR. Tubular magazine holds 21 Short, 17 Long, 15 LR. 20.5-inch bbl. Sights: Open rear; ramp front. Weight: About 5 lbs. Plain stock and forearm on early production; later model has checkering. Made 1963–73.

MODEL 255 DELUXE RIFLE . . . . NiB $242 Ex $206 Gd $92
Same as Model 250 Deluxe Rifle except chambered for .22 WMR cartridge. Magazine holds 11 rounds. Made 1965–73.

MODEL 255 STANDARD RIFLE. . . . NiB $204 Ex $155 Gd $115
Same as Model 250 Standard Rifle except chambered for .22 WMR cartridge. Magazine holds 11 rounds. Made 1964–70.

MODEL 270 DELUXE RIFLE . . . . . . NiB $210 Ex $164 Gd $103
Same as Model 270 Standard Rifle except has fancy walnut Monte Carlo stock and forearm. Made 1965–73.

MODEL 270 STANDARD SLIDE-ACTION RIFLE . . . . NiB $143 Ex $113 Gd $82
Hammerless. Caliber: .22 Short, Long or LR. Tubular magazine holds 21 Short, 17 Long, 15 LR. 20.5-inch bbl. Sights: Open rear; ramp front. Weight: About 5 lbs. Early production had plain walnut stock and forearm (slide handle); latter also furnished in plastic (Cycolac); last model has checkering. Made 1963–73.

MODEL 275 DELUXE RIFLE . . . . . . NiB $242 Ex $190 Gd $113
Same as Model 270 Deluxe Rifle except chambered for .22 WMR cartridge. Tubular magazine holds 11 rounds. Made 1965–70.

MODEL 275 STANDARD RIFLE . . . . NiB $175 Ex $139 Gd 103
Same as Model 270 Standard Rifle except chambered for .22 WMR cartridge. Magazine holds 11 rounds. Made 1964–70.

MODEL 290 DELUXE RIFLE . . . . NiB $242 Ex $206 Gd $92
Same as Model 290 Standard Rifle except has fancy walnut Monte Carlo stock and forearm. Made 1965–73.

MODEL 290 STANDARD SEMIAUTOMATIC RIFLE
Caliber: .22 Long or LR. Tubular magazine holds 17 Long, 15 LR. 20.5-inch bbl. Sights: Open rear; ramp front. Weight: About 5 lbs. Plain stock and forearm on early production; current model has checkering. Made 1963–77.
W/plain stock/forearm . . . . NiB $242 Ex $206 Gd $92
W/checkered stock/forearm . . . . NiB $267 Ex $216 Gd $108

MODEL 310 BOLT-ACTION SINGLE SHOT . . . . NiB $267 Ex $211 Gd $149
Caliber: .22 Short, Long, LR. 22-inch bbl. Weight: 5.63 lbs. Sights: Open rear; ramp front. Monte Carlo stock w/checkered pistol-grip and forearm, sling swivels. Made 1972–75.

MODEL 320 BOLT-ACTION REPEATER. . . . . NiB $309 Ex $267 Gd $164
Same as Model 310 except has 5-round clip magazine. Made 1972–74.

MODEL 490 SEMIAUTOMATIC RIFLE . . . . NiB $2309 Ex $242 Gd $164
Caliber: .22 LR. Five round clip magazine. 22-inch bbl. Weight: 6 lbs. Sights: Folding leaf rear; hooded ramp front. One-piece walnut stock w/checkered pistol grip and forearm. Made 1975–77.

MODEL 670 BOLT-ACTION SPORTING RIFLE. . . . . NiB $370 Ex $267 Gd $195
Calibers: .225 Win., .243 Win., .270 Win., .30-06, .308 Win. Four round magazine. 22-inch bbl. Weight: 7 lbs. Sights: Open rear; ramp front. Monte Carlo stock w/checkered pistol-grip and forearm. Made 1967–73.

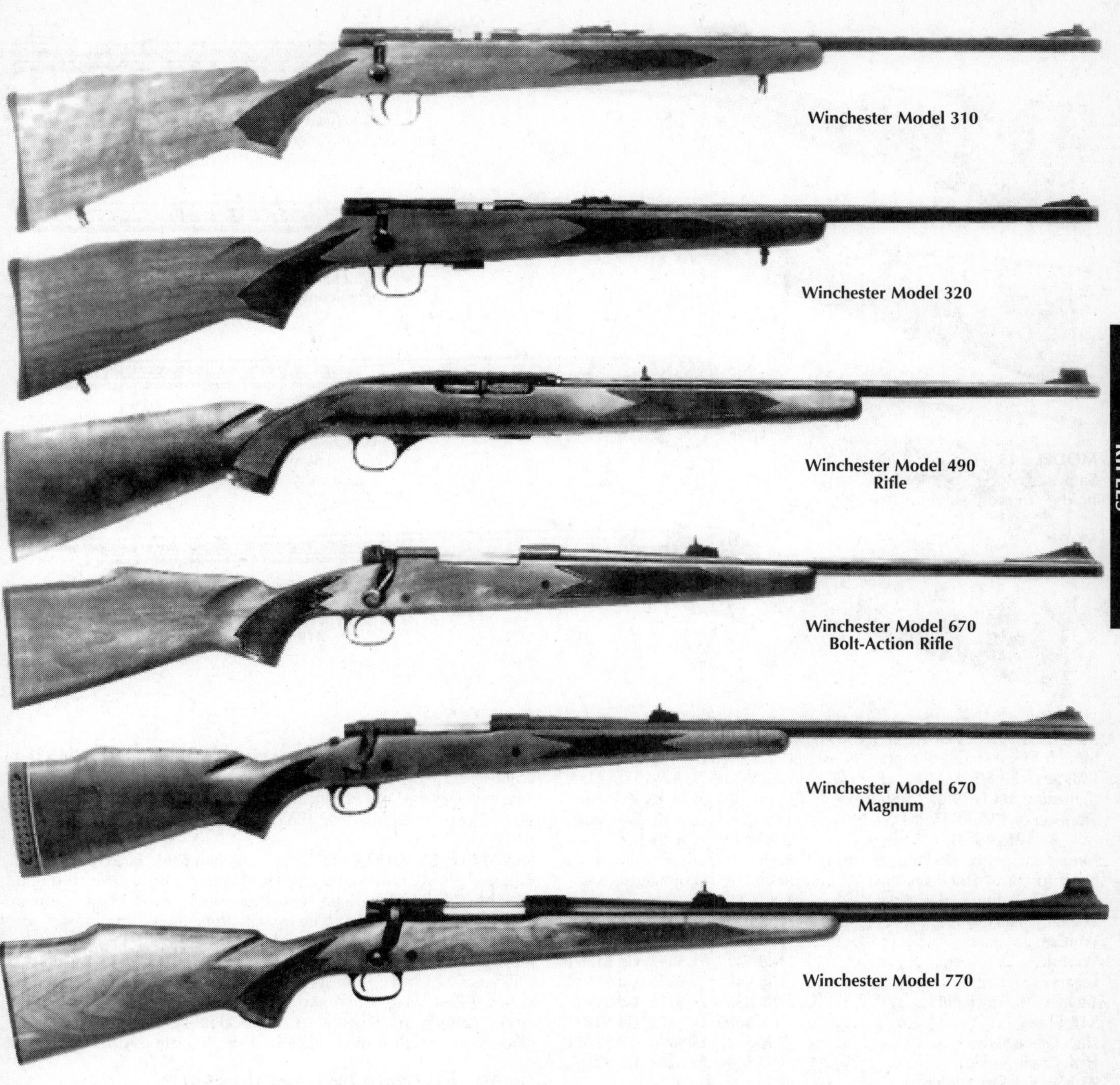

Winchester Model 310

Winchester Model 320

Winchester Model 490 Rifle

Winchester Model 670 Bolt-Action Rifle

Winchester Model 670 Magnum

Winchester Model 770

MODEL 670 CARBINE .... NiB $370 Ex $298 Gd $201
Same as Model 670 Rifle except has 19-inch bbl. Weight: 6.75 lbs. Calibers: .243 Win., .270 Win., .30-06. Made 1967–70.

MODEL 670 MAGNUM .... NiB $417 Ex $293 Gd $231
Same as Model 670 Rifle except has 24-inch bbl., reinforced stock with recoil pad with slightly different checkering pattern. Weight: 7.25 lbs. Calibers: .264 Win. Mag., 7mm Rem. Mag., .300 Win. Mag. Open rear sight; ramp front sight with hood. Made 1967–70.

MODEL 770 BOLT-ACTION SPORTING RIFLE. .... NiB $396 Ex $293 Gd $216
Model 70-type action. Calibers: .22-250, .222 Rem., .243, .270 Win., .30-06. Four round box magazine. 22-inch bbl. Sights: Open rear; hooded ramp front. Weight: 7.13 lbs. Monte Carlo stock, checkered pistol-grip and forend; sling swivels. Made 1969–71.

MODEL 770 MAGNUM .... NiB $422 Ex $345 Gd $267
Same as Standard Model 770 except 24-inch bbl., weight: 7.25 lbs., recoil pad. Calibers: 7mm Rem. Mag., .264 and .300 Win. Mag. Made 1969–71.

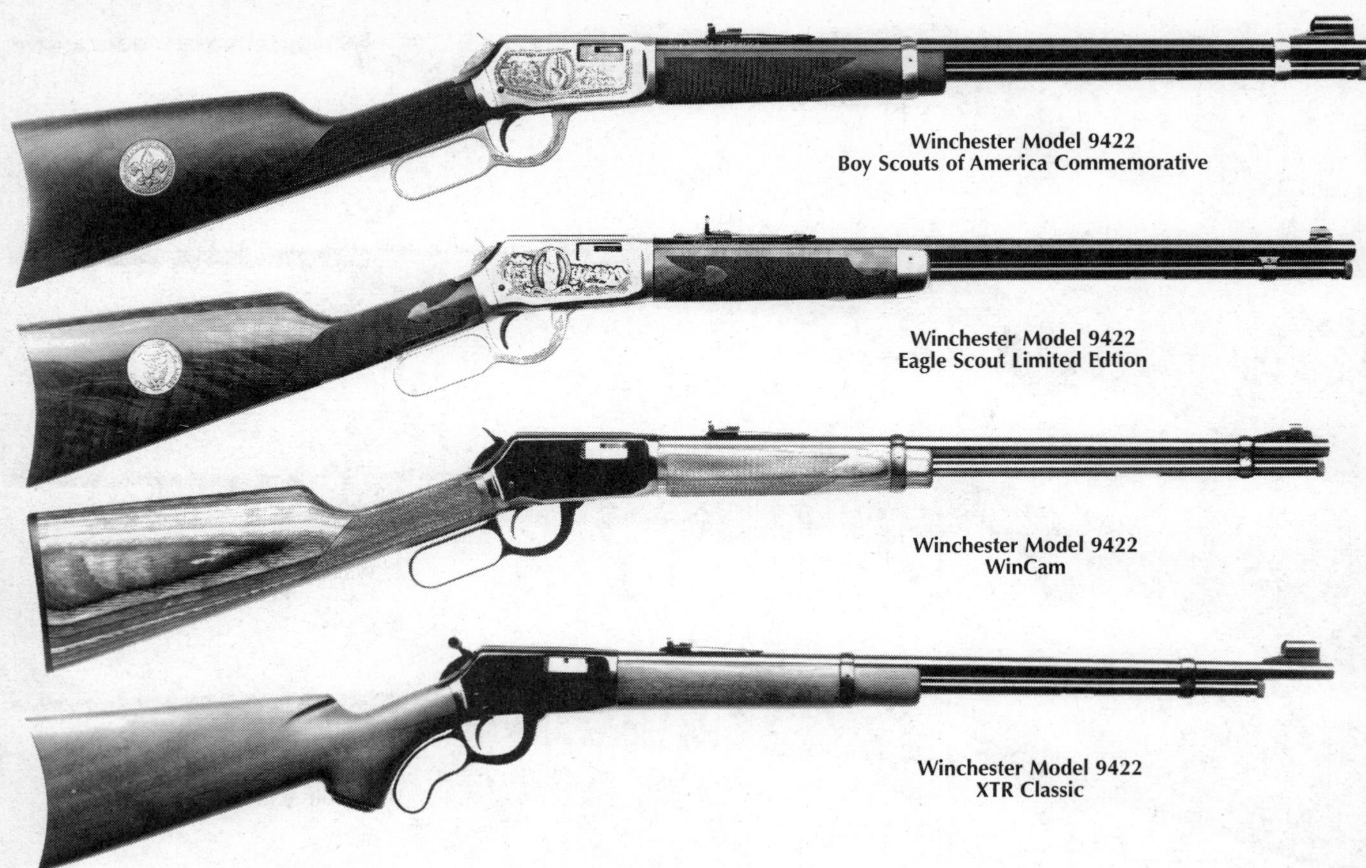
Winchester Model 9422
Boy Scouts of America Commemorative

Winchester Model 9422
Eagle Scout Limited Edtion

Winchester Model 9422
WinCam

Winchester Model 9422
XTR Classic

MODEL 9422 LEVER-ACTION RIMFIRE RIFLES
Similar to the standard Model 94 except chambered for .22 Rimfire. Calibers: .22 Short, Long, LR. (9422) or .22 WMR (9422M). Tubular magazine holds 21 or 15 Short.17 or 12 Long, 15 or 11 LR (9422 or Trapper) or 11 or 8 WRM (9422M or Trapper M). 16.5- or 20.5 inch bbl. 33.125- to 37.125 inches overall. Weight: 5.75 to 6.25 lbs. Open rear sight; hooded ramp front. Carbine-style stock and barrel-band forearm. Stock options: Walnut (Standard), laminated brown (WinTuff), laminated green (WinCam). Made 1972 to date.
Walnut (Standard) .... NiB $365 Ex $293 Gd $190
WinCam .... NiB $370 Ex $298 Gd $195
WinTuff............................ NiB $313 Ex $252 Gd $175
Legacy............................. NiB $401 Ex $345 Gd $190
Trapper (16.5-inch bbl.) .... NiB $355 Ex $278 Gd $190
XTR Classic .... NiB $499 Ex $473 Gd $319
High Grade Series I.................. NiB $437 Ex $370 Gd $237
High Grade Series II .... NiB $396 Ex $293 Gd $216
25th Anniversary Edition
Grade I(1of 2500).................... NiB $571 Ex $478 Gd $375
25th Anniversary Edition
High Grade (1of 250) .... NiB $1251 Ex $1024 Gd $715
Boy Scout
Commemorative (1of 15,000)........... NiB $684 Ex $571 Gd $375
Eagle Scout
Commemorative (1of 1000) .... NiB $3507 Ex $2812 Gd $1925
22 WRM, add 10%

DOUBLE XPRESS RIFLE....... NiB $2855 Ex $2290 Gd $1567
Over/under double rifle. Caliber: .30-06. 23.5-inch bbl. Weight: 8.5 lbs. Made for Olin Corp. by Olin-Kodensha in Japan. Introduced 1982.

RANGER YOUTH
BOLT-ACTION CARBINE......... NiB $370 Ex $267 Gd $164
Calibers: .223 (discontinued 1989), .243 Win., and .308 Win. Four and 5-round magazine. Bbl.: 20-inch. Weight: 5.75 lbs. American hardwood stock. Open rear sight. Made 1985 to date by U.S. Repeating Arms.

RANGER LEVER-ACTION CARBINE ...... NiB $261 Ex $210 Gd $147
Caliber: .30-30. Five round tubular magazine. Bbl.: 20-inch round. Weight: 6.5 lbs. American hardwood stock. Economy version of Model 94. Made 1985 to date by U.S. Repeating Arms.

RANGER BOLT-ACTION CARBINE.......... NiB $345 Ex $278 Gd $192
Calibers: .223 Rem., .243 Win., .270, .30-06, 7mm Rem. (discontinued 1985), Mag. Three and 4-round magazine. Bbl.: 24-inch in 7mm; 22-inch in .270 and .30-06. Open sights. American hardwood stock. Made 1985 to date by U.S. Repeating Arms.

MODEL 1892 GRADE I LEVER-ACTION RIFLE
Similar to the original Model 1892. Calibers: .357 Mag., .44-40, .44 Mag., .45 LC. 10-round magazine. 24-inch round bbl. Weight: 6.25 lbs. 41.25 inches overall. Bead front sight, adjustable buckhorn rear. Etched receiver and gold trigger. Blue finish. Smooth straight-grip walnut stock and forearm w/ metal grip cap. Made 1997 to date.
Standard Rifle .... NiB $700 Ex $612 Gd $350
Short Rifle w/20-inch bbl.
(.44 Mag. only) .... NiB $575 Ex $463 Gd $320

MODEL 1892 GRADE
II LEVER-ACTION RIFLE .... NiB $1179 Ex $1023 Gd $632
Similar to the Grade I Model 1892 except w/gold appointments and receiver game scene. Chambered .45 LC only. Limited production of 1,000 in 1997.

Winslow Commander Grade

Winslow Crown Grade

Winslow Regent Grade
Bushmaster Stock

WINSLOW ARMS COMPANY — Camden, South Carolina

BOLT-ACTION SPORTING RIFLE
Action: FN Supreme Mauser, Mark X Mauser, Remington 700 and 788, Sako, Winchester 70. Standard calibers: .17-222, .17-223, .222 Rem., .22-250, .243 Win., 6mm Rem., .25-06, .257 Roberts, .270 Win., 7x57, .280 Rem., .284 Win., .308 Win., .30-06, .358 Win. Magnum calibers: .17-222 Mag., .257 Wby., .264 Win., .270 Wby., 7mm Rem., 7mm Wby., .300 H&H, .300 Wby., .300 Win., .308 Norma, 8mm Rem., .338 Win., .358 Norma, .375 H&H, .375 Wby., .458 Win. Three-round magazine in standard calibers, 2-round in magnum. 24-inch barrel in standard calibers, 26-inch in magnum. Weight: With 24-inch bbl., 7 to 7.5 lbs.; with 26-inch bbl., 8 to 9 lbs. No sights. Stocks: "Bushmaster" with slender pistol-grip and beavertail forearm, "Plainsmaster" with full curl pistol-grip and flat forearm; both styles have Monte Carlo cheekpiece. Values shown are for basic rifle in each grade; extras such as special fancy wood, more elaborate carving, inlays and engraving can increase these figures considerably. Made 1962–89.
Commander Grade . . . . **NiB $530 Ex $504 Gd $360**
Regal Grade . . . . **NiB $648 Ex $623 Gd $427**

(cont'd.) **BOLT-ACTION SPORTING RIFLE**
Regent Grade . . . . **NiB $787 Ex $684 Gd $499**
Regimental Grade . . . . **NiB $935 Ex $762 Gd $643**
Crown Grade . . . . **NiB $1467 Ex $1261 Gd $803**
Royal Grade . . . . **NiB $1673 Ex $1467 Gd $1106**
Imperial Grade . . . . **NiB $3640 Ex $3125 Gd $2301**
Emperor Grade . . . . **NiB $6665 Ex $5941 Gd $4185**

ZEPHYR DOUBLE RIFLES Manufactured by Victor Sarasqueta Company — Eibar, Spain

DOUBLE RIFLE . . . . **NiB $20,625 Ex $16,500 Gd $11,225**
Boxlock. Calibers: Available in practically every caliber from .22 Hornet to .505 Gibbs. Bbls.: 22 to 28 inches standard, but any lengths were available on special order. Weight: 7 lbs. for the smaller calibers up to 12 or more lbs. for the larger calibers. Imported by Stoeger from about 1938 to 1951.

Twenty-Eighth Edition
GUN TRADER'S GUIDE

Shotguns

American Arms
Bristol (Sterling) Over/Under

American Arms
Derby Hammerless Double

American Arms
Gentry/York Hammerless Double

American Arms
Silver Over/Under

American Arms
Camper Special

ALDENS SHOTGUN — Chicago, Illinois

MODEL 670 CHIEFTAIN SLIDE ACTION . . NiB $233 Ex $199 Gd $134
Hammerless. Gauges: 12, 20 and others. Three round tubular magazine. Bbl.: 26- to 30-inch; various chokes. Weight: 6.25 to 7.5 lbs. depending on bbl. length and ga. Walnut-finished hardwood stock.

AMERICAN ARMS — N. Kansas City, Missouri

See also Franchi Shotguns.

BRISTOL (STERLING) O/U . . . . NiB $740 Ex $592 Gd $414
Boxlock w/Greener crossbolt and engraved sideplates. Single selective trigger. Selective automatic ejectors. Gauges: 12, 20; 3-inch chambers. 26-, 28-, 30-, or 32-inch vent-rib bbls. w/screw-in choke tubes (Improved Cylinder/Modified/Full). Weight: 7 lbs. Antique-silver receiver w/game scene or scroll engraving. Checkered full pistol-grip-style buttstock and forearm w/high-gloss finish. Imported 1986-88 with the model designation Bristol; redesignated Sterling 1989-90.

BRITTANY HAMMERLESS DOUBLE . . . . . . NiB $735 Ex $602 Gd $414
Boxlock w/engraved case-colored receiver. Single selective trigger. Selective automatic ejectors. Gauges: 12, 20. 3-inch chambers. Bbls.: 25- or 27-inch w/screw-in choke tubes (IC/M/F). Weight: 6.5 lbs. (20 ga.). Checkered English-style walnut stock w/semi-beavertail forearm or pistol-grip stock w/high-gloss finish. Imported 1989 to date.

CAMPER SPECIAL . . . . NiB $118 Ex $97 Gd $69
Similar to the Single Barrel except takedown model w/21-inch bbl., M choke and pistol-grip stock. Made in 1989 only.

COMBO . . . . NiB $208 Ex $168 Gd $117
Similar to the Single-Barrel model except available w/interchangeable rifle and shotgun bbls. .22 LR/20-ga. shotgun or .22 Hornet/12-ga. shotgun. Rifle bbl. has adj. rear sights; blade-type front sight. Made in 1989.

DERBY HAMMERLESS DOUBLE
Sidelock w/engraved sideplates. Single non-selective or double triggers. Selective automatic ejectors. Gauges: 12, 20, 28 and .410. 3 inch chambers. Bbls.: 26-inch (IC/M) or 28-inch (M/F). Weight: 6 lbs. (20 ga.). Checkered English-style walnut stock and splinter forearm w/hand-rubbed oil finish. Engraved frame/sideplates w/antique silver finish. Imported 1986-94.
12 or 20 ga.. . . . . NiB $928 Ex $800 Gd $494
28 or .410 ga. (disc. 1991) . . . . NiB $992 Ex $800 Gd $555

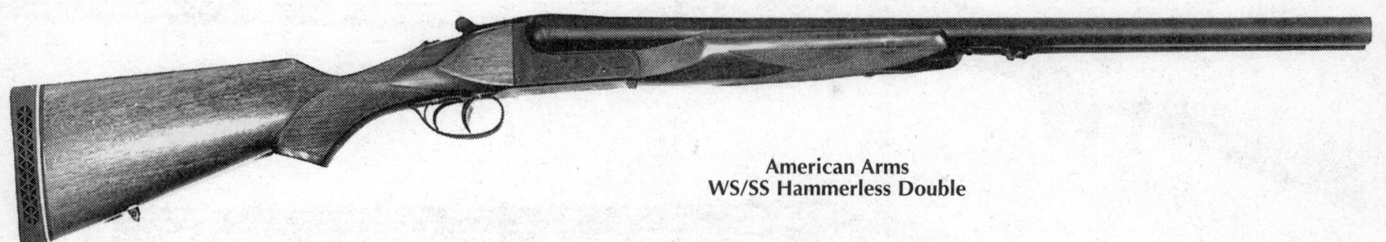

American Arms
WS/SS Hammerless Double

F.S. SERIES O/U
Greener crossbolt in Trap and Skeet configuration. Single selective trigger. Selective automatic ejectors. 12 gauge only. 26-, 28-, 30-, or 32-inch separated bbls. Weight: 6.5 to 7.25 lbs. Black or chrome receiver. Checkered walnut buttstock and forearm. Imported 1986-87.
Model F.S. 200 Boxlock. . . . . NiB $734 Ex $591 Gd $413
Model F.S. 300 Boxlock. . . . . NiB $872 Ex $719 Gd $515
Model F.S. 400 Sidelock . . . . NiB $1228 Ex $1019 Gd $718
Model F.S. 500 Sidelock . . . . NiB $1228 Ex $1024 Gd $718

GENTRY/YORK HAMMERLESS DOUBLE
Chrome, coin-silver or color casehardened boxlock receiver w/scroll engraving. Double triggers. Extractors. Gauges: 12, 16, 20, 28, .410. 3-inch chambers (16 and 28 have 2.75-inch). Bbls.: 26-inch (IC/M) or 28-inch (M/F, 12, 16 and 20). Weight: 6.75 lbs. (12 ga.). Checkered walnut buttstock w/pistol-grip and beavertail forearm; both w/semi-gloss oil finish. Imported as York from 1986-88, redesignated Gentry 1989 to date.
Gentry 12, or 16 or 20 ga. . . . . .NiB $666 Ex $487 Gd $334
Gentry 28 or .410 ga. . . . . .NiB $727 Ex $589 Gd $426
York 12, 16 or 20 ga. (disc. 1988) . . . . . .NiB $532 Ex $431 Gd $302
York 28 or .410 ga. (disc. 1988) . . . . .NiB $634 Ex $513 Gd $357

GRULLA #2 HAMMERLESS DOUBLE
True sidelock w/engraved detachable sideplates. Double triggers. Extractors and cocking indicators. Gauges: 12, 20, .410 w/3-inch chambers; 28 w/2.75-inch. 26-inch bbl. Imported 1989 to date.
Standard model . . . . NiB $3281 Ex $2645 Gd $1831
Two-bbl. set (disc. 1995) . . . . . . NiB $4244 Ex $3415 Gd $2354

SILVER I O/U
Boxlock. Single selective trigger. Extractors. Gauges: 12, 20 and .410 w/3-inch chambers; 28 w/2.75 inch. Bbls.: 26-inch (IC/M), 28-inch (M/F, 12 and 20 ga. only). Weight: 6.75 lbs. (12 ga.). Checkered walnut stock and forearm. Antique-silver receiver w/scroll engraving. Imported 1987 to date.
12 or 20 ga. .NiB $561 EX. $458 Gd $306
28 or .410 ga. . . . . .NIB $599 EX $484 Gd $337

SILVER II O/U
Similar to Model Silver I except w/selective automatic ejectors and 26-inch bbls. w/screw-in tubes (12 and 20 ga.). Fixed chokes (28 and .410). Made 1987 to date.
12 or 20 ga . . . . NiB $699 Ex $566 Gd $394
28 or .410 ga. . . . . NiB $763 Ex $617 Gd $429
Upland Lite II . . . . NiB $845 Ex $683 Gd $476
Two-bbl. set. . . . . NiB $1087 Ex $877 Gd $607

SILVER LITE O/U
Similar to Model Silver II except w/blued, engraved alloy receiver. Available in 12 and 20 ga. only. Imported from 1990-92.
Standard Model. . . . . NiB $719 Ex $591 Gd $438
Two-bbl. Set . . . . NiB $1115 Ex $897 Gd $620

SILVER SKEET/TRAP. . . . . NiB $859 Ex $693 Gd $482
Similar to the Silver II Model except has 28-inch (Skeet) or 30-inch (Trap) ported bbls. w/target-style rib and mid-bead sight. Imported 1992-94.

SILVER SPORTING O/U . . . . NiB $872 Ex $734 Gd $489
Boxlock. Single selective trigger. Selective automatic ejectors. Gauges: 12, 2.75-inch chambers. 28-inch bbls.w/Franchoke tubes (SK, IC, M and F). Weight: 7.5 lbs. Checkered walnut stock and forearm. Special broadway rib and vented side ribs. Engraved receiver w/chrome-nickel finish. Imported from 1990 to date.

SINGLE-SHOT SHOTGUN
Break-open action. Gauges: 10 (3.5), 12, 20, .410, 3-inch chamber. Weight: about 6.5 lbs. Bead front sight. Walnut-finished hardwood stock w/checkered grip and forend. Made from 1988 to 1990.
10 ga. (3.5-inch) . . . . NiB $144 Ex $118 Gd $85
12, 20 or .410 ga. . . . . NiB $124 Ex $103 Gd $75
Multi-choke bbl., add $30

SLUGGER SINGLE-SHOT SHOTGUN. . . . . NiB $137 Ex $113 Gd $82
Similar to the Single-Shot model except in 12 and 20 ga. only w/24-inch slug bbl. Rifle-type sights and recoil pad. Made from 1989 to 1990.

TS/OU 12 SHOTGUN. . . . . NiB $744 Ex $617 Gd $428
Turkey Special. Boxlock. Single selective trigger. Selective automatic ejectors. Gauge: 12, 3.5-inch chambers. Bbls.: 24-inch O/U w/screw-in choke tubes (IC, M, F). Weight: 6 lbs. 15 oz. Checkered European walnut stock and beavertail forearm. Matte blue metal finish. Imported 1987 to date.

TS/SS 10 HAMMERLESS DOUBLE . . . . . . NiB $699 Ex $566 Gd $414
Turkey Special. Same general specifications as Model WS/ SS 10, except w/26-inch side-by-side bbls., screw-in choke tubes (F/F) and chambered for 10-ga. 3.5-inch shells. Weight: 10 lbs., 13 oz. Imported 1987 to 1993.

TS/SS 12 HAMMERLESS DOUBLE . . . . . . NiB $642 Ex $540 Gd $362
Same general specifications as Model WS/SS 10 except in 12 ga. w/26-inch side-by-side bbls. and 3 screw-in choke tubes (IC/M/F). Weight: 7 lbs., 6 oz. Imported 1987 to date.

WS/OU 12 SHOTGUN . . . . NiB $678 Ex $540 Gd $372
Waterfowl Special. Boxlock. Single selective trigger. Selective automatic ejectors. Gauge: 12; 3.5-inch chambers. Bbls.: 28-inch O/U w/screw-in tubes (IC/M/F). Weight: 7 lbs. Checkered European walnut stock and beavertail forearm. Matte blue metal finish. Imported 1987 to date.

WS/SS 10 HAMMERLESS DOUBLE. . . . . . NiB $744 Ex $617 Gd $418
Waterfowl Special. Boxlock. Double triggers. Extractors. Gauge: 10; 3.5-inch chambers. Bbls.: 32-inch side/side choked F/F. Weight: About 11 lbs. Checkered walnut stock and beavertail forearm w/satin finish. Parkerized metal finish. Imported from 1987 to 1995.

WT/OU 10 Shotgun .... NiB $955 Ex $777 Gd $537
Same general specifications as Model WS/OU 12 except chambered for 10-ga. 3.5-inch shells. Extractors. Satin wood finish and matte blue metal. Imported 1987 to date.

ARMALITE, INC. — Costa Mesa, California

AR-17 GOLDEN GUN........... NiB $718 Ex $540 Gd $418
Recoil-operated semiautomatic. High-test aluminum bbl. and receiver housing. 12 ga. only. Two round capacity. 24-inch bbl. w/interchangeable choke tubes: IC/M/F. Weight: 5.6 lbs. Polycarbonate stock and forearm recoil pad. Gold-anodized finish standard, also made w/black finish. Made 1964-65. Fewer than 2,000 produced.

ARMSCOR (Arms Corp.) — Manila, Philippines, *Imported until 1991 by Armscor Precision, San Mateo, CA; 1991-95 by Ruko Products, Inc., Buffalo NY: Currently imported by K.B.I., Harrisburg, PA*

MODEL M-30 FIELD PUMP SHOTGUN
Double slide-action bars w/damascened bolt. Gauge: 12 only w/3-inch chamber. Bbl.: 28-inch w/fixed chokes or choke tubes. Weight: 7.6 lbs. Walnut or walnut finished hardwood stock.
Model M30-F (w/hard-
wood stock and fixed chokes) ..... NiB $242 Ex $191 Gd $104
Model M-30F (w/hard-
wood stock and choke tubes) ..... NiB $267 Ex $196 Gd $109
Model M-30F/IC (w/walnut
stock and choke tubes) .... NiB $277 Ex $201 Gd $114

MODEL M-30 RIOT PUMP
Double-action slide bar w/damascened bolt. Gauge: 12 only w/3-inch chamber. Bbls: 18.5 and 20-inch w/IC bore. Five or 7-round magazine. Weight: 7 lbs, 2 ozs. Walnut finished hardwood stock.

(cont'd.) **MODEL M-30 RIOT PUMP**
Model M-30R6 (5-round magazine) ...... NiB $189 Ex $163 Gd $110
Model M-30R8 (7-round magazine) ...... NiB $199 Ex $173 Gd $112

MODEL M-30 SPECIAL COMBO
Simlar to Special Purpose Model except has detachable synthetic stock that removes to convert to pistol-grip configuration.
Model M-30C (disc. 1995) .... NiB $224 Ex $189 Gd $132
Model M-30RP (disc. 1995) ..... NiB $233 Ex $189 Gd $131

MODEL M-30 SPECIAL PURPOSE
Double-action slide bar w/damascened bolt. Seven round magazine. Gauge: 12 only w/3-inch chamber. 20-inch bbl. w/cylinder choke. Iron sights (DG Model) or venter handguard (SAS Model). Weight: 7.5 lbs. Walnut finished hardwood stock.
Model M-30DG (Deer Gun) .... NiB $222 Ex $180 Gd $126
Model M-30SAS (Special Air Services) .... NiB $248 Ex $201 Gd $141

ARMSPORT, INC. — Miami, Florida

1000 SERIES HAMMERLESS DOUBLES
Side-by-side w/engraved receiver, double triggers and extractors. Gauges: 10 (3.5), 12, 20, .410- 3-inch chambers. Model 1033: 10 ga., 32-inch bbl. Model 1050/51: 12 ga., 28-inch bbl., M/F choke. Model 1052/53: 20 ga., 26-inch bbl., I/M choke. Model 1054/57: .410 ga., 26-inch bbl., I/M. Model 1055: 28 ga., Weight: 5.75 to 7.25 lbs. European walnut buttstock and forend. Made in Italy. Importation disc. 1993.
Model 1033 (10 ga. disc. 1989) ...... NiB $761 Ex $615 Gd $426
Model 1050 (12 ga. disc. 1993) ...... NiB $677 Ex $628 Gd $407
Model 1051 (12 ga. disc. 1985) ...... NiB $439 Ex $356 Gd $251
Model 1052 (20 ga. disc. 1985) ...... NiB $411 Ex $334 Gd $235
Model 1053 (20 ga. disc. 1993) ...... NiB $720 Ex $581 Gd $403
Model 1054 (.410 disc. 1992)........ NiB $797 Ex $643 Gd $445
Model 1055 (28 ga. disc. 1992) ...... NiB $481 Ex $390 Gd $274
Model 1057 (.410 disc. 1985)........ NiB $517 Ex $419 Gd $292

MODEL 1125 SINGLE-SHOT SHOTGUN ...... NiB $100 Ex $85 Gd $59
Bottom-opening lever. Gauges: 12, 20. 3-inch chambers. Bead front sight. Plain stock and forend. Imported 1987-89.

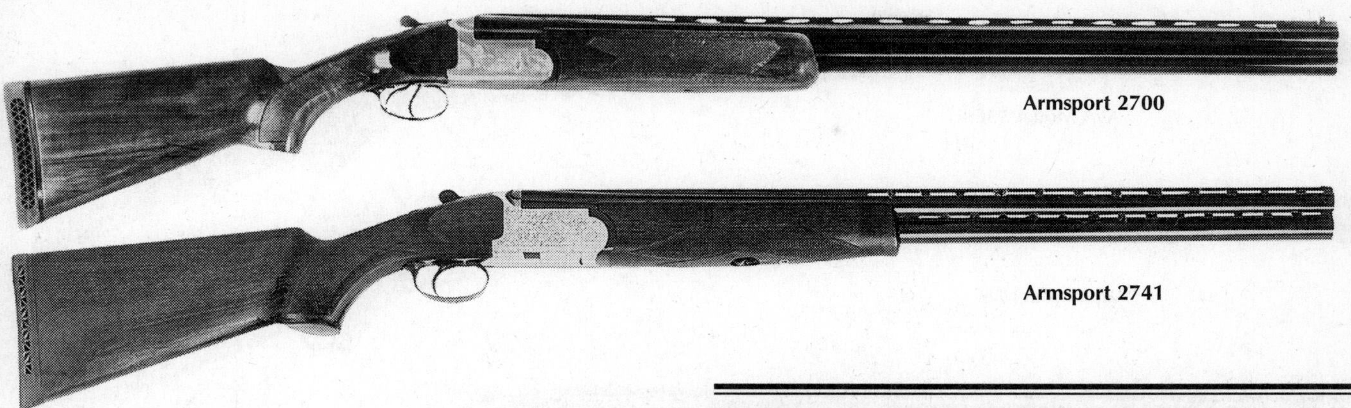
Armsport 2700

Armsport 2741

MODEL 2700 GOOSE GUN
Similar to the 2700 Standard Model except 10 ga. w/3.5-inch chambers. Double triggers w/28-inch bbl. choked IC/M or 32-inch bbl., F/F. 12mm wide vent rib. Weight: 9.5 lbs. Canada geese engraved on receiver. Antiqued silver-finished action. Checkered European walnut stock w/rubber recoil pad. Imported from Italy 1986 to 1993.
W/fixed chokes .... NiB $1017 Ex $813 Gd $548
W/choke tubes .... NiB $1299 Ex $889 Gd $609

MODEL 2700 OVER/UNDER SERIES
Hammerless, takedown shotgun w/engraved receiver. Selective single or double triggers. Gauges: 10, 12, 20, 28 and .410. Bbl.: 26-or 28-inch w/fixed chokes or choke tubes. Weight: 8 lbs. Checkered European walnut buttstock and forend. Made in Italy. Importation disc. 1993.
Model 2701 12 ga. (disc. 1985) .... NiB $524 Ex $423 Gd $294
Model 2702 12 ga.................... NiB $562 Ex $454 Gd $315
Model 2703 20 ga. (disc. 1985) .... NiB $549 Ex $443 Gd $308
Model 2704 20 ga.................... NiB $594 Ex $479 Gd $332
Model 2705 (.410, DT, fixed chokes) ..... NiB $694 Ex $561 Gd $389
Model 2730/31 (Boss-style action, SST Choke tubes) .... NiB $784 Ex $635 Gd $438
Model 2733/35 (Boss-style action, extractors).................. NiB $727 Ex $586 Gd $406
Model 2741 (Boss-style action, ejectors) .... NiB $631 Ex $510 Gd $354
Model 2742 Sporting Clays (12 ga./choke tubes)................. NiB $758 Ex $612 Gd $424
Model 2744 Sporting Clays (20 ga./choke tubes)................. NiB $771 Ex $622 Gd $431
Model 2750 Sporting Clays (12 ga./sideplates).................... NiB $822 Ex $663 Gd $459
Model 2751 Sporting Clays (20 ga./sideplates).................... NiB $854 Ex $688 Gd $467

MODEL 2755 SLIDE-ACTION SHOTGUN
Gauge: 12 w/3-inch chamber. Tubular magazine. Bbls.: 28- or 30-inch w/fixed choke or choke tubes. Weight: 7 lbs. European walnut stock. Made in Italy 1986-87.
Standard model, fixed choke...... NiB $350 Ex $299 Gd $191
Standard model, choke tubes ..... NiB $528 Ex $416 Gd $293
Police model, 20-inch bbl......... NiB $319 Ex $273 Gd $181

MODEL 2900 TRI-BARREL (TRILLING) SHOTGUN
Boxlock. Double triggers w/top-tang bbl. selector. Extractors. Gauge: 12; 3-inch chambers. Bbls.: 28-inch (IC, M and F). Weight: 7.75 lbs. Checkered European walnut stock and forearm. Engraved silver receiver. Imported 1986-87 and 1990-93.
Model 2900 (fixed chokes) .... NiB $2146 Ex $1733 Gd $1202
Model 2900 (choke tubes)..... NiB $2874 Ex $2314 Gd $1598
Deluxe grades, add $500

ARRIETA, S.L. — Elgoibar, Spain
Imported by New England Arms Corp., Wingshooting Adventures Quality Arms, Griffin & Howe and Orvis.

Custom double-barreled shotguns with frames scaled to individual gauges. Standard guages are 12 and 16 gauge. Add: 5% for small gauges (20, 24, 28, 32 and .410 bore) on currently manufactured models; $900 for single trigger (most actions); 5% for matched pairs; 10% for rounded action on standard models; extra bbls., add $1375 to $2000 per set.

MODEL 557 STANDARD
Gauges: 12, 16 or 20. Demi-Bloc steel barrels, detachable engraved sidelocks, double triggers, ejectors **NiB $3125 Ex $1625 Gd $975**

MODEL 570 LIEJA
Gauges: 12, 16 or 20. Non-detachable sidelocks.
.... NiB $3875 Ex $1950 Gd $1150

MODEL 578 VICTORIA
Gauges: 12, 16 or 20. Similar to Model 570 but with fine English scrollwork.................. **NiB $4175 Ex $2200 Gd $1215**

LIGERA MODEL
Available in all gauges. Lightweight 12 ga. has 2-inch chambers, lightweight or standard action. Includes unique frame engraving and Turkish wood upgrade. Wt. appox. 6 pounds
.... NiB $5425 Ex $4050 Gd $2900

MODEL 590 REGINA
Gauges: 12, 16 or 20. Similar to Model 570 but has more elaborate engraving. .... **NiB $3375 Ex $3000 Gd $2075**

MODEL 595 PRINCIPE
Available in all gauges, sidelock, engraved hunting scenes, ejectors,double triggers........... **NiB $5375 Ex $4135 Gd $3225**

MODEL 600 IMPERIAL
Gauges: 12, 16 or 20. Self-opening action, very ornate engraving throughout. .... **NiB $4575 Ex $3700 Gd $2375**

MODEL 601 IMPERIAL TYRO
Available in all gauges, sidelock, nickel plating, ejectors,single selective trigger, border engraving. **NiB $6615 Ex $3790 Gd $3015**

MODEL 801
Available in all gauges, detachable sidelocks, ejectors,coin-wash finish, Churchill-style engraving. **NiB $8210 Ex $6760 Gd $5485**
With self-opening action (models 801 through 875) ... add $900

SHOTGUNS

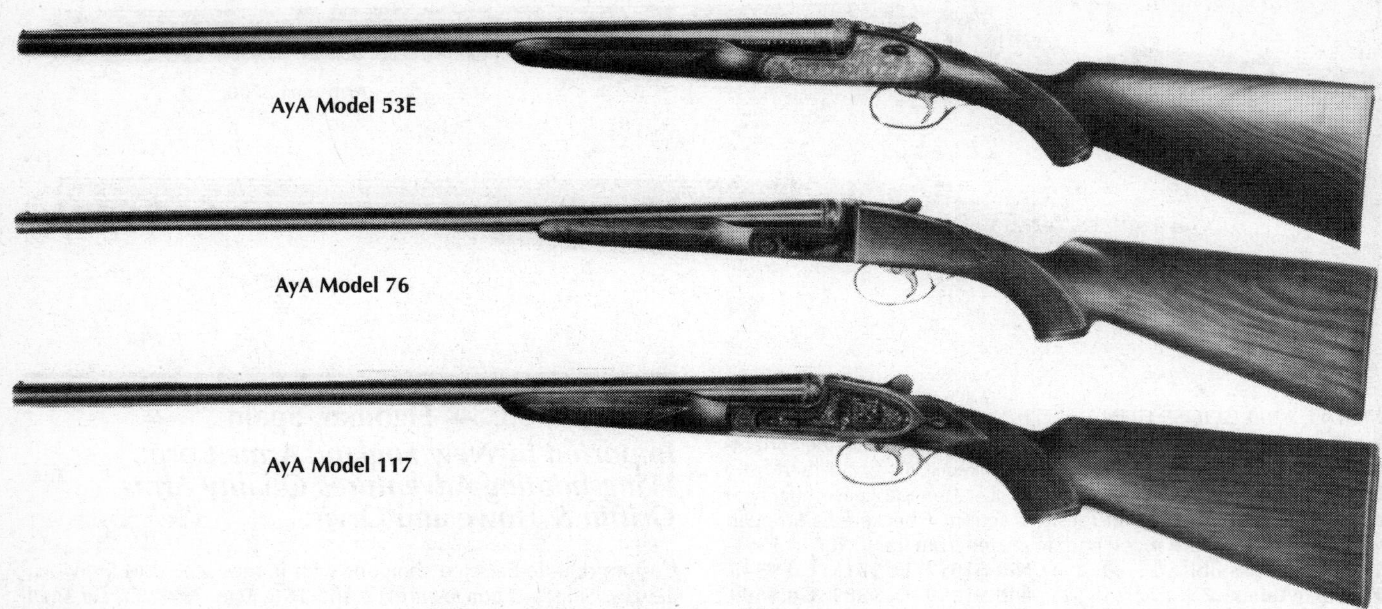

MODEL 802
Gauges: 12, 16 or 20. Similar to Model 801 except with non-detachable sidelocks, finest Holland-style engraving. . . . . NiB $8460 Ex $6985 Gd $5435

BOSS ROUND BODY
Available in all gauges, Boss pattern best quality engraving, wood upgrade.. NiB $9735 Ex $7460 Gd $6205

MODEL 803
Available in all gauges. Similar to Model 801 except finest Purdey-style engraving. . . . . NiB $6455 Ex $5075 Gd $3775

MODEL 871
Available in all gauges. Rounded frame sidelock action with Demi-Bloc barrels, scroll engraving, ejectors,double triggers. . . . . NiB $4740 Ex $3990 Gd $2440

MODEL 871 EXTRA FINISH
Similar to Model 871 except with standard game scene engraving with woodcock and ruffed grouse.NiB $5980 Ex $4555 Gd $3755

RENAISSANCE MODEL
Available in all gauges. Best quality sidelock, custom engraving, wood upgrade, manufactured in Spain in made in Italy. Prices range from $8,000 to $17,000 depending on engraving and wood options.

MODEL 872
Available in all gauges, rounded frame sidelock action, Demi-Bloc barrels, elaborate scroll engraving with third lever fastener. . . . . NiB $11,275 Ex $9225 Gd $6100

MODEL 873
Available in all gauges. Sidelock, gold line engraved action, ejectors, single selective trigger. . . . . NiB $7775 Ex $4895 Gd $3575

MODEL 874
Available in all gauges. Sidelock, gold line engraved action, Demi-Bloc barrels.. . . . . NiB $8350 Ex $6090 Gd $4875

MODEL 875
Available in all gauges. Custom model built to individual specifications only, elaborate engraving, gold inlays . . . . NiB $14,000 Ex $11,975 Gd $9600

MODEL 931
Available in all gauges. Self-opening action, elaborate engraving, H&H selective ejectors. . . . NiB $14,995 Ex $12,595 Gd $9650

ASTRA SHOTGUNS — Guernica, Spain Manufactured by Unceta y Compania

MODEL 650 O/U SHOTGUN
Hammerless, takedown w/double triggers. 12 ga. w/.75-inch chambers. Bbls.: 28-inch (M/F or SK/SK); 30-inch (M/F). Weight: 6.75 lbs. Checkered European walnut·buttstock and forend.
W/extractors . . . . **NiB $594 Ex $467 Gd $339**
W/ejectors . . . . **NiB $722 Ex $584 Gd $390**

MODEL 750 O/U SHOTGUN
Similar to the Model 650 except w/selective single trigger and ejectors. Made in field, skeet and trap configurations since 1980.
Field model w/extractors. . . . . **NiB $671 Ex $543 Gd $380**
Field model w/ejectors . . . . **NiB $792 Ex $640 Gd $446**
Trap or Skeet . . . . **NiB $919 Ex $742 Gd $515**

AYA (Aguirre Y Aranzabal) — Eibar, Spain (Previously Mfd. by Diarm, *Imported by Armes De Chasse, Hertford, NC*

MODEL 1 HAMMERLESS DOUBLE
A Holland & Holland sidelock similar to the Model 2 except in 12 and 20 ga. only, w/special engraving and exhibition-grade wood. Weight: 5-8 lbs., depending on ga. Imported by Diarm until 1987, since 1992 by Armes de Chasse.
Model 1 Standard . . . . **NiB $6643 Ex $3232 Gd $1989**
Model 1 Deluxe. . . . . **NiB $8125 Ex $3757 Gd $2197**

AyA Matador II

AyA Model XXV Boxlock

MODEL 2
HAMMERLESS DOUBLE
Sidelock action w/selective single or double triggers automatic ejectors and safety. Gauges: 12, 20, 28, (2.75-inch chambers); .410 (3-inch chambers). Bbls.: 26- or 28-inch w/various fixed choke combinations. Weight: 7 lbs. (12 ga.). English-style straight walnut buttstock and splinter forend. Imported by Diarm until 1987, since 1992 by Armes de Chasse.
12 or 20 ga. w/double triggers . NiB $3111 Ex $1608 Gd $1244
12 or 20 ga. w/single trigger . . . NiB $3168 Ex $2440 Gd $1343
28 or .410 ga. w/double triggers NiB $3194 Ex $2445 Gd $1374
28 or .410 ga. w/single trigger . NiB $3220 Ex $2579 Gd $1374
Extra set of bbls., add $1325

MODEL 4
HAMMERLESS DOUBLE
Lightweight Anson & Deely boxlock, scalloped frame. Gauges: 12, 16, 20, 28, and .410. Bbls.: 25- to 28-inch w/concave rib. Importation disc. 1987 and resumed in 1992 by Armes de Chasse.
12 ga. . . . . NiB $1264 Ex $1211 Gd $587
16 ga. (early importation) . . . . NiB $685 Ex $561 Gd $403
20 ga. . . . . NiB $951 Ex $769 Gd $535
28 ga. . . . . NiB $1081 Ex $847 Gd $509
.410 ga. . . . . NiB $1086 Ex $847 Gd $535
Deluxe grades, add $500

MODEL 37 SUPER
O/U SHOTGUN . . . . NiB $3474 Ex $2799 Gd $1936
Sidelock. automatic ejectors. Selective single trigger. Made in all gauges, bbl. lengths and chokes. Vent rib bbls. Elaborately engraved. Checkered stock (w/straight or pistol grip) and forend. Disc. 1995.

MODEL 37 SUPER A
O/U SHOTGUN . . . . NiB $6099 Ex $4904 Gd $3375
Similar to the Standard Model 37 Super except has nickel steel frame and is fitted w/detachable sidelocks engraved w/game scenes. Importation disc. 1987 and resumed 1992 by Armes de Chasse.

MODEL 53E. . . . . NiB $2406 Ex $1939 Gd $1342
Same general specifications as Model 117 except more elaborate engraving and select figured wood. Importation disc. 1987 and resumed in 1992 by Armes de Chasse.

MODEL 56 HAMMERLESS DOUBLE
Pigeon weight Holland & Holland sidelock w/Purdey-style third lug and sideclips. Gauges: 12, 16, 20. Receiver has fine-line scroll and rosette engraving; gold-plated locks. Importation disc. 1987 and resumed 1992 by Armes de Chasse.

(cont'd.) **MODEL 56 HAMMERLESS DOUBLE**
12 ga. NiB $7514 Ex $3614 Gd $3042
16 ga. (early importation) . . . . . NiB $6890 Ex $2470 Gd $1721
20 ga. (early importation). . . . . NiB $7670 Ex $3744 Gd $2314

MODEL 76 HAMMERLESS DOUBLE . . NiB $846 Ex $702 Gd $419
Anson & Deeley boxlock. Auto ejectors. Selective single trigger. Gauges: 12, 20 (3-inch). Bbls.: 26-, 28-, 30-inch (latter in 12 ga. only), any standard choke combination. Checkered pistol-grip stock/beavertail forend. Disc.

MODEL 76—.410 GA.. . . . . NiB $870 Ex $700 Gd $484
Same general specifications as 12 and 20 ga. Model 76 except chambered for 3-inch shells in .410, has extractors, double triggers, 26-inch bbls. only, English-style stock w/straight grip and small forend. Disc.

MODEL 117 HAMMERLESS DOUBLE. . NiB $975 Ex $787 Gd $546
Holland & Holland-type sidelocks, hand-detachable. Engraved action. Automatic ejectors. Selective single trigger. Gauges: 12, 20 (3-inch). Bbls.: 26-, 27-, 28-, 30-inch; 27- and 30-inch in 12 ga. only; any standard choke combination. Checkered pistol-grip stock and beavertail forend of select walnut. Manufactured in 1985.

BOLERO . . . . NiB $510 Ex $420 Gd $300
Same general specifications as Matador except non-selective single trigger and extractors. Gauges: 12 16, 20, 20 Magnum (3-inch), .410 (3-inch). Note: This model, prior to 1956, was designated F. I. Model 400 by the importer. Made 1955-63.

CONTENTO OVER/UNDER SHOTGUN
Boxlock w/Woodward side lugs and double internal bolts. Gauge: 12 (2.75-inch chambers). Bbls.: 26-, 28-inch field; 30-, 32-inch trap; fixed chokes as required or screw-in choke tubes. Hand-checkered European walnut stock and forend. Single selective trigger and automatic ejectors.
M.K.2. . . . . NiB $973 Ex $785 Gd $544
M.K.3. NiB $1685 Ex $1357 Gd $938
W/Interchangeable single bbl., add. $400

MATADOR
HAMMERLESS DOUBLE . . . . NiB $488 Ex $390 Gd $1265
Anson & Deeley boxlock. Selective automatic ejectors. Selective single trigger. Gauges: 12, 16, 20, 20 Magnum (3-inch). Bbls: 26-, 28-, 30-inches; any standard choke combination. Weight: 6.5 to 7.5 lbs., depending on ga. and bbl. length. Checkered pistol-grip stock and beavertail forend. Note: This model, prior to 1956, was designated F. I. Model 400E by the U. S. importer, Firearms Int'l. Corp. of Washington, D.C. Made 1955-63.

MATADOR II.................. NiB $582 Ex $472 Gd $331
Improved version of Matador w/same general specifications except has vent-rib bbls. Made 1964-69.

MATADOR III .... NiB $842 Ex $680 Gd $472
Same general specifications as AyA Matador II. Made 1970-85.

MODEL XXV BOXLOCK
Anson & Deeley boxlock w/double locking lugs. Gauges: 12 and 20. 25-inch chopper lump, satin blued bbls. w/Churchill rib. Weight: 5 to 7 lbs. Double triggers. Automatic safety and ejectors. Color-casehardened receiver w/Continental-style scroll and floral engraving. European walnut stock. Imported 1979-86 and 1991 to date.
12 or 20 ga.................. NiB $2678 Ex $1529 Gd $910
Extra set of bbls., add $1050

MODEL XXV SIDELOCK
Holland & Holland-type sidelock. Gauges: 12, 20, 28 and .410; 25-, 26-, 27- 28-, 29-, and 32-inch bbls. Chopper lump, satin blued bbls. w/Churchill rib. Weight: 5 to 7 lbs. Double triggers standard or selective or non-selective single trigger optional. Automatic safety and ejectors. Cocking indicators. Color-casehardened or coin-silver-finished receiver w/Continental-style scroll and floral engraving. Select European walnut stock w/hand-cut checkering and oil finish. Imported 1979-86 and 1991 to date.
12 or 20 ga................. NiB $3822 Ex $1898 Gd $1113
28 ga. (disc. 1997)........... NiB $2359 Ex $1882 Gd $1319
.410 ga. (disc. 1997) .... NiB $2695 Ex $2170 Gd $1501
Single trigger, add $75
Single selective trigger, add.......................... $120
Extra set of bbls., add $1700

BAIKAL SHOTGUNS — Izhevsk and Tula, Russia

MODEL IJ-18M SINGLE SHOT .... NiB $75 Ex $62 Gd $46
Hammerless w/cocking indicator. Automatic ejector. Manual safety. Gauges: 12 , 20, 16 w/2.75-inch chamber or .410 w/3-inch chamber. Bbls.: 26-, 28-inch w/fixed chokes (IC, M, F). Weight: 5.5 to 6 lbs. Made in Russia.

MODEL IJ-27 FIELD O/U .... NiB $374 Ex $298 Gd $211
Boxlock. Double triggers w/extractors. 12 ga.; 2.75-inch chambers. Bbls.: 26-inch, IC/M; 28-inch, M/F w/fixed chokes. Weight: 6.75 lbs. Made in Russia.

MODEL IJ-43 FIELD SIDE-BY-SIDE
Side-by-side; boxlock. Double triggers; extractors. 12 or 20 ga. w/2.75-inch chambers. Bbls: 20-inch cylinder bbl and 26-or 28-inch modified full bbl. Weight: 6.75 to 7 lbs. Checkered walnut stock, forend. Blued, engraved receiver. Imported 1994-96.
Model IJ-43 Field w/20-inch bbls.... NiB $246 Ex $199 Gd $139
Model IJ-43 Field
w/26- or 28-inch bbls .... NiB $220 Ex $178 Gd $124

IZH-43 SERIES SIDE-BY-SIDE
Boxlock. Gauges: 12, 16, 20 or .410 w/2.75- or 3-inch chambers. Bbls.: 20-, 24-, 26- or 28-inch w/fixed chokes or choke tubes. Single selective or double triggers. Weight: 6.75 lbs. Checkered hardwood (standard on Hunter II Model) or walnut stock and forend (standard on Hunter Model). Blued, engraved receiver. Imported 1994 to date.
Model IZH-43Hunter
(12 ga. w/walnut stock).......... NiB $352 Ex $306 Gd $148
Model IZH-43 Hunter
(20, 16 or .410 ga.)............. NiB $355 Ex $285 Gd $199

***(cont'd.)* IZH-43 SERIES SIDE-BY-SIDE**
Model IZH-43 Hunter II
(12 ga. w/external hammers) ..... NiB $366 Ex $296 Gd $206
Model IZH-43 Hunter II
(12 ga. hammerless) .... NiB $238 Ex $194 Gd $136
Model IZH-43 Hunter II
(20, 16 or .410 ga.)............ NiB $250 Ex $204 Gd $144
Hunter II w/walnut stock, add $35
Hunter II w/single selective trigger, add $45

MODEL IJ-27 O/U
Boxlock. Single selective trigger w/automatic ejectors or double triggers w/extractors. Gauges: 12 or 20 w/2.75-inch chambers. Bbls.: 26-inch or 28-inch w/fixed chokes. Weight: 7 lbs. Checkered European hardwood stock and forearm. Made in Russia.
Model IJ-27 (w/double
triggers and extractors.)......... NiB $352 Ex $296 Gd $148
Model IJ-27
(single selective
trigger and ejectors) .... NiB $372 Ex $311 Gd $148

BAKER SHOTGUNS — Batavia, New York Made 1903-1933 by Baker Gun Company

BATAVIA LEADER HAMMERLESS DOUBLE
Sidelock. Plain extractors or automatic ejectors. Double triggers. Gauges: 12, 16, 20. Bbls.: 26- to 32-inch; any standard boring. Weight: About 7.75 lbs. (12 ga. w/30-inch bbls.). Checkered pistol-grip stock and forearm.
W/plain extractors .... NiB $843 Ex $385 Gd $292
W/automatic ejectors .... NiB $874 Ex $462 Gd $292

BATAVIA EJECTOR .... NiB $1112 Ex $849 Gd $586
Same general specifications as the Batavia Leader except higher quality and finer finish throughout; has Damascus or homotensile steel bbls., checkered pistol-grip stock and forearm of select walnut; automatic ejectors standard; 12 and 16 ga. only. Deduct 60% for Damascus bbls.

BATAVIA SPECIAL............. NiB $525 Ex $319 Gd $216
Same general specifications as the Batavia Leader except 12 and 16 ga. only; extractors, homotensile steel bbls.

BLACK BEAUTY
Same general specifications as the Batavia Leader except higher quality and finer finish throughout; has line engraving, special steel bbls., select walnut stock w/straight, full or half-pistol-grip.
Black Beauty w/plain extractors ... NiB $577 Ex $345 Gd $268
Black Beauty Special
w/plain extractors............. NiB $1040 Ex $659 Gd $427
Black Beauty Special
w/automatic ejectors.......... NiB $1097 Ex $788 Gd $530

GRADE R
High-grade gun w/same general specifications as the Batavia Leader except has fine Damascus or Krupp fluid steel bbls., engraving in line, scroll and game scene designs, checkered stock and forearm of fancy European walnut; 12 and 16 ga. only. Deduct 60% for Damascus bbls.
Non-ejector................ NiB $1406 Ex $1024 Gd $685
W/automatic ejectors .... NiB $1406 Ex $1024 Gd $685

GRADE S
Same general specifications as the Batavia Leader except higher quality and finer finish throughout; has Flui-tempered steel bbls., line and scroll engraving, checkered stock w/half-pistol-grip and

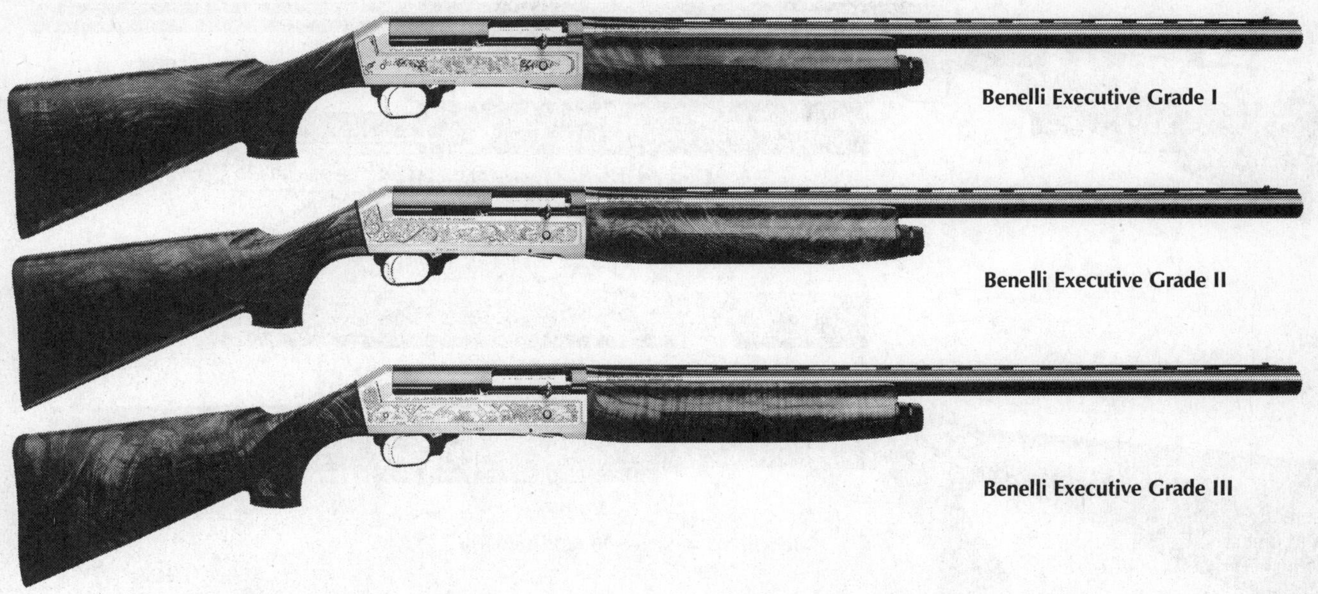

Benelli Executive Grade I

Benelli Executive Grade II

Benelli Executive Grade III

(cont'd.) **GRADE S**
forearm of semi-fancy imported walnut; 10, 12 and 16 ga.
Non-ejector . . . . NiB $1110 Ex $801 Gd $543
W/automatic ejectors . . . . NiB $1419 Ex $1037 Gd $698

PARAGON, EXPERT AND DELUXE GRADES
Made to order only, these are the higher grades of Baker hammerless sidelock double-bbl. shotguns. After 1909, the Paragon Grade, as well as the Expert and Deluxe intro. that year, had a crossbolt in addition to the regular Baker system taper wedge fastening. There are early Paragon guns w/Damascus bbls. and some are non-ejector, but this grade was also produced w/automatic ejectors and w/the finest fluid steel bbls., in lengths to 34 inches, standard on Expert and Deluxe guns.
Differences among the three models are in overall quality, finish, engraving and grade of fancy figured walnut in the stock and forearm; Expert and Deluxe wood may be carved as well as checkered. Choice of straight, full or half-pistol grip was offered. A single trigger was available in the two higher grades. The Paragon was available in 10 ga (Damascus bbls. only), and the other two models were regularly produced in 12, 16 and 20 ga.
Paragon grade, non-ejector . . . . NiB $1826 Ex $1467 Gd $1007
Paragon grade,
Automatic ejectors . . . . NiB $2084 Ex $1673 Gd $1115
Expert grade . . . . NiB $3043 Ex $2402 Gd $1645
Deluxe grade . . . . NiB $4223 Ex $3386 Gd $2314
For single trigger, add $250

BELKNAP SHOTGUNS — Louisville, Kentucky

MODEL B-68 SINGLE-SHOT SHOTGUN . NiB $133 Ex $108 Gd $77
Takedown. Visible hammer. Automatic ejector. Gauges: 12, 16, 20 and .410. Bbls.: 26-inch to 36-inch; F choke. Weight: 6 lbs. Plain pistol-grip stock and forearm.

MODEL B-63 SINGLE-SHOT SHOTGUN . . . . NiB $119 Ex $98 Gd $70
Takedown. Visible hammer. Automatic ejector. Gauges: 12, 20 and .410. Bbls.: 26- to 36-inch, F choke. Weight: Average 6 lbs. Plain pistol-grip stock and forearm.

MODEL B-63E SINGLE-SHOT SHOTGUN . . . . NiB $119 Ex $98 Gd $70
Same general specifications as Model B-68 except has side lever opening instead of top lever.

MODEL B-64 SLIDE-ACTION SHOTGUN . . . . NiB $246 Ex $190 Gd $133
Hammerless. Gauges: 12, 16, 20 and .410. Three round tubular magazine. Various bbl. lengths and chokes from 26-inch to 30-inch. Weight: 6.25 to 7.5 lbs. Walnut-finished hardwood stock.

MODEL B-65C AUTOLOADING SHOTGUN . . . . NiB $389 Ex $316 Gd $220
Browning-type lightweight alloy receiver. 12 ga. only. Four round tubular magazine. Bbl.: plain, 28-inch. Weight: About 8.25 lbs. Disc. 1949.

BENELLI SHOTGUNS — Urbino, Italy *Imported by Benelli USA, Accokeek, MD*

MODEL 121 M1 MILITARY/POLICE AUTOLOADING SHOTGUN . . . . NiB $498 Ex $430 Gd $290
Gauge: 12. Seven round magazine. 19.75-inch bbl. 39.75 inches overall. Cylinder choke, 2.75-inch chamber. Weight: 7.4 lbs. Matte black finish and European hardwood stock. Post front sight, fixed buckhorn rear sight. Imported in 1985.

BLACK EAGLE AUTOLOADING SHOTGUN
Two-piece aluminum and steel receiver. Ga: 12; 3-inch chamber. Four round magazine. Screw-in choke tubes (SK, IC, M, IM, F). Bbls.: Ventilated rib; 21, 24, 26 or 28 inches w/bead front sight; 24-inch rifled slug. 42.5 to 49.5 inches overall. Weight: 7.25 lbs. (28-inch bbl.). Matte black lower receiver w/blued upper receiver and bbl. Checkered walnut stock w/high-gloss finish and drop adjustment. Imported from 1989-90 and 1997-98.
Limited edition . . . . NiB $1840 Ex $1580 Gd $1060
Competition model . . . . NiB $1086 Ex $842 Gd $488
Slug model (disc. 1992) . . . . NiB $774 Ex $540 Gd $384
Standard model (disc. 1992) . . . . NiB $878 Ex $696 Gd $426

SHOTGUNS

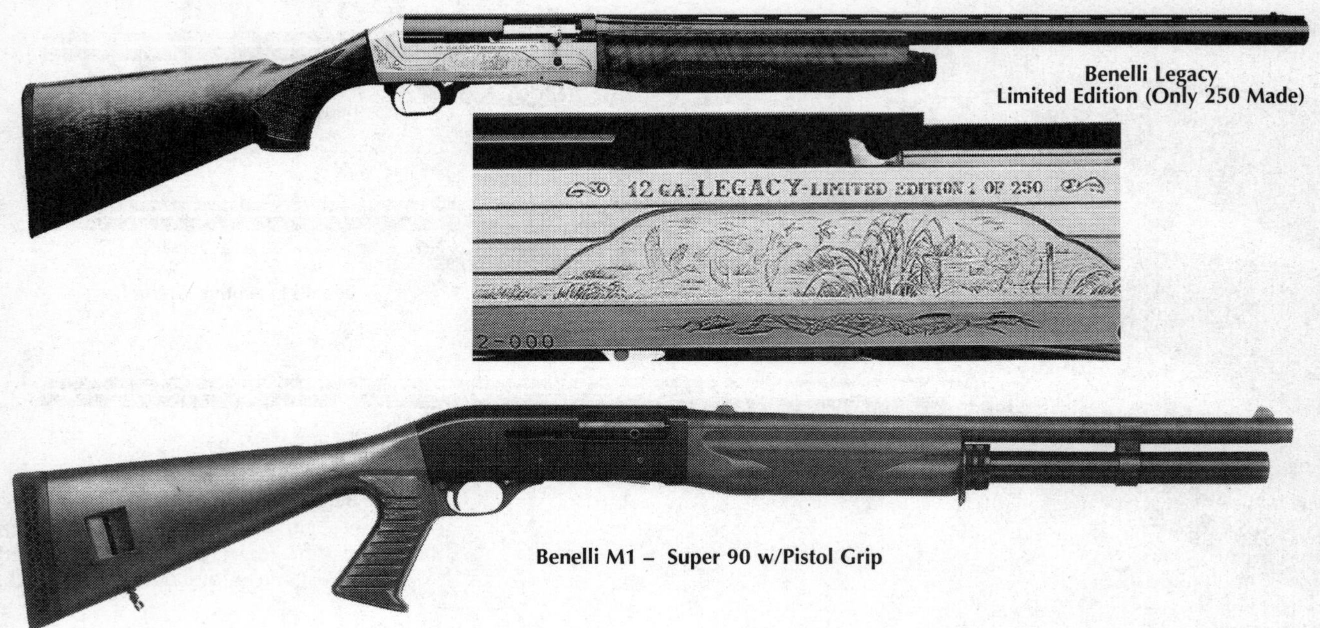

Benelli Legacy
Limited Edition (Only 250 Made)

Benelli M1 – Super 90 w/Pistol Grip

BLACK EAGLE EXECUTIVE
Custom Black Eagle Series. Montefeltro-style rotating bolt w/three locking lugs. All-steel lower receiver engraved, gold inlay by Bottega Incisione di Cesare Giovanelli. 12 ga. only. 21-, 24-, 26-, or 28-inch vent-rib bbl. w/5 screw-in choke tubes (Type I) or fixed chokes. Custom deluxe walnut stock and forend. Built to customer specifications on special order.
Executive Grade I . . . . NiB $3919 Ex $3140 Gd $2143
Executive Grade II. . . . . NiB $4251 Ex $3405 Gd $2323
Executive Grade III . . . . NiB $4998 Ex $4003 Gd $2730

LEGACY AUTOLOADING SHOTGUN
Gauges: 12 and 20 ga. w/3-inch chambers. 24- 26- or 28-inch bbl. 47.63 to 49.62 inches overall. Weight: 5.8 to 7.5 lbs. Four round magazine. Five screw-in choke tubes. Lower alloy receiver and upper steel reciever cover. Features Benelli's inertia recoil operating system. Imported 1998 to date. See illustration next page.
Legacy model . . . . NiB $1190 Ex $956 Gd $800
Legacy model Limited edition . . . NiB $1788 Ex $1502 Gd $904

M1 SUPER 90
AUTO-LOADING SHOTGUN . . . . . NiB $846 Ex $716 Gd $430
Gauge: 12. Seven round magazine. Cylinder choke. 19.75-inch bbl. 39.75 inches overall. Weight: 7 lbs., 4 oz. to 7 lbs., 10 oz. Matte black finish. Stock and forend made of fiberglass-reinforced polymer. Sights: Post front, fixed buckhorn rear, drift adj. Introduced 1985; when the model line expanded in 1989, this configuration was discontinued.

M1 SUPER 90 DEFENSE AUTOLOADER. . . . . . NiB $976 Ex $768 Gd $404
Same general specifications as Model Super 90 except w/pistol-grip stock. Available w/Ghost-Ring sight option. Imported 1986-98.

M1 SUPER 90
ENTRY AUTOLOADER. . . . . NiB $846 Ex $716 Gd $392
Same gen. specifications as Model Super 90 except w/5-round magazine. 14-inch bbl. 35.5 inches overall. Weight: 6.5 lbs. Standard or pistol-grip stock. Imported 1992 to date. *Special permit required for under 18 inch bbl. firearms.*

M1 SUPER 90 FIELD
Inertia-recoil semiautomatic shotgun. Gauge: 12; 3-inch chamber. Three round magazine. Bbl.: 21, 24, 26 or 28 inches. 42.5 to 49.5 inches overall. Choke: SK, IC, M, IM, F. Matte receiver. Standard polymer stock or satin walnut (26- or 28-inch bbl. only). Bead front sight. Imported from 1990 to date.
W/Realtree camo . . . . NiB $744 Ex $614 Gd $380
W/polymer stock . . . . NiB $630 Ex $456 Gd $328
W/walnut stock . . . . NiB $666 Ex $484 Gd $354

M1 SUPER 90 SLUG AUTOLOADER
Same general specifications as M1 Super 90 Field except w/5-round magazine. 18.5-inch bbl. Cylinder bore. 39.75 inches overall. Weight: 6.5 lbs. Polymer standard stock. Rifle or Ghost-Ring sights. Imported 1986-98.
W/rifle sights . . . . NiB $692 Ex $536 Gd $432
W/ghost-ring sights . . . . NiB $744 Ex $562 Gd $432
W/Realtree camo finish, add $100

M1 SUPER 90 SPORTING
SPECIAL AUTOLOADER . . . . NiB $796 Ex $692 Gd $406
Same general specifications as M1 Super 90 Field except w/18.5-inch bbl. 39.75 inches overall. Weight: 6.5 lbs. Ghost-ring sights. Polymer stock. Imported 1994-98.

M1 SUPER 90 TACTICAL AUTOLOADER
Same general specifications as M1 Super 90 Field except w/18.5-inch bbl. Five round magazine. IC, M, or F choke. 39.75 inches overall. Weight: 6.5 lbs. Rifle or Ghost-Ring sights. Polymer pistol-grip or standard stock. Imported1994 to date.
W/rifle sights . . . . NiB $796 Ex $692 Gd $406
W/ghost-ring sights . . . . NiB $842 Ex $687 Gd $489
W/pistol-grip stock, add $25

M3 SUPER 90 PUMP/AUTOLOADER
Inertia-recoil semiautomatic and/or pump action. Gauge: 12. Seven round magazine. Cylinder choke. 19.75-inch bbl. 41 inches overall (31 inches folded). Weight: 7 to 7.5 lbs. Matte black finish. Stock: standard synthetic, pistol-grip or folding tubular steel. Standard rifle or Ghost-Ring sights. Imported 1989 to date. Caution:

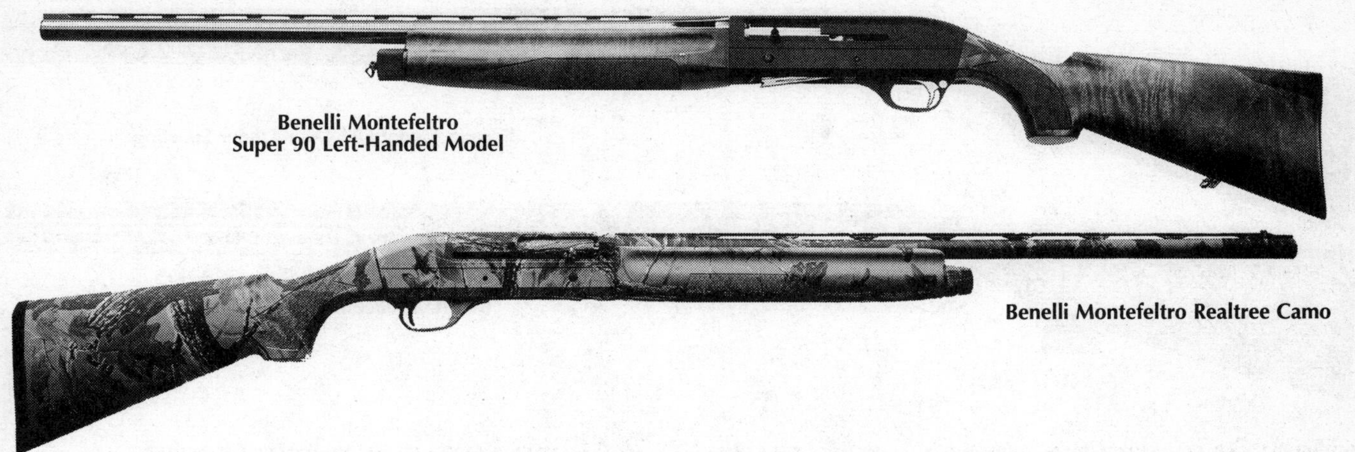

Benelli Montefeltro
Super 90 Left-Handed Model

Benelli Montefeltro Realtree Camo

(cont'd.) **M3 SUPER 90 PUMP/AUTOLOADER**
Increasing the magazine capacity to more than 5 rounds in M3 shotguns w/pistol-grip stocks violates provisions of the 1994 Crime Bill. This model may be used legally only by the military and law-enforcement agencies.
Standard model . . . . NiB $869 Ex $723 Gd $427
Pistol-grip model . . . . NiB $992 Ex $796 Gd $546
W/folding stock . . . . NiB $1054 Ex $847 Gd $583
W/laser sight . . . . NiB $1314 Ex $1055 Gd $724
For ghost ring sights, add $50

MONTEFELTRO/SUPER 90 SEMIAUTOMATIC
Gauges: 12 or 20 gauge w/3-inch chamber. 21- 24- 26- or 28-inch bbl. 43.7 to 49.5 inches overall. Weight: 5.3 to 7.5 lbs. Four round magazine. Five screw-in choke tubes (C, IC, M, IM, F). High gloss or satin walnut or Realtree Camo stock. Blued metal finish. Imported 1987 to date.
Standard Hunter model . . . . NiB $875 Ex $731 Gd $433
Slug model (disc. 1992). . . . . NiB $698 Ex $542 Gd $334
Turkey model . . . . NiB $698 Ex $620 Gd $334
Uplander model . . . . NiB $698 Ex $542 Gd $334
Limited Edition (1995-96) . . . . . NiB $1892 Ex $1522 Gd $1040
20 ga. w/Realtree camo . . . . NiB $716 Ex $594 Gd $411
20 ga. Youth Model w/short stock, add $40
Left-hand model, add $25

SL 121V SEMIAUTO (SL-80 SERIES) . . . NiB $557 Ex $323 Gd $271
Recoil-operated semiautomaticw/split receiver design. Gauge: 12. Five round capacity. 26-, 28- or 30-inch ventilated rib bbl. (26-inch choked M, IM, IC, 28-inch, F, M, IM; 30-inch, F choke - Mag.). Straight walnut stock w/hand-checkered pistol grip and forend. Importation disc. in 1985.

SL 121V SLUG SHOTGUN
(SL-80 SERIES) . . . . NiB $567 Ex $349 Gd $281
Same general specifications as Benelli SL 121V except designed for rifled slugs and equipped w/rifle sights. Disc. in 1985.

SL 123V SEMIAUTO (SL-80 SERIES) . . . NiB $479 Ex $385 Gd $266
Gauge: 12. 26- and 28-inch bbls. 26-inch choked IM, M, IC; 28-inch choked F, IM, M. Disc. in 1985.

SL 201 SEMIAUTOMATIC
(SL-80 SERIES) . . . . NiB $427 Ex $344 Gd $238
Gauge: 20. 26-inch bbl. Mod. choke. Weight: 5 lbs., 10 oz. Ventilated rib. Disc. in 1985.

SPORT AUTOLOADING SHOTGUN . . NiB $996 Ex $800 Gd $550
Similar to the Black Eagle Competition model except has one-piece matte- finished alloy receiver w/inscribed red Benelli logo. 26 or 28 inches bbl. w/2 inchangable carbon fiber vent ribs. Oil-finished checkered walnut stock w/adjustable buttpad and buttstock. Imported 1997 to date.

SUPER BLACK EAGLE AUTOLOADING SHOTGUN
Same general specifications as Black Eagle except w/3.5-inch chamber that accepts 2.75-, 3- and 3.5-inch shells. Two round magazine (3.5-inch), 3-round magazine (2.75- or 3-inch). High-gloss, satin finish or camo stock. Realtree camo, matte black or blued metal finish. Imported 1991 to date.
Standard model . . . . NiB $1057 Ex $850 Gd $586
Realtree camo . . . . NiB $1187 Ex $954 Gd $656
Custom slug model . . . . NiB $999 Ex $803 Gd $553
Limited edition . . . . NiB $1885 Ex $1505 Gd $1031
W/wood stock, add $25
Left-hand model, add. $30

BERETTA USA CORP. — Accokeek, Maryland Mfd. by Fabbrica D'Armi Pietro Beretta S.p.A. in Gardone Val Trompia (Brescia), Italy *Imported by Beretta USA (Previously by Garcia Corp.)*

MODEL 57E O/U
Same general specifications as Golden Snipe, but higher quality throughout. Imported 1955-67.
W/non-selective single trigger . . . NiB $1058 Ex $933 Gd $517
W/selective single trigger . . . . NiB $1095 Ex $881 Gd $606

MODEL 409PB
HAMMERLESS DOUBLE . . . . NiB $1016 Ex $694 Gd $429
Boxlock. Double triggers. Plain extractors. Gauges: 12, 16, 20, 28. Bbls.: 27.5-, 28.5- and 30-inch, IC/M choke or M/F choke. Weight: from 5.5 to 7.75 lbs., depending on ga. and bbl. length. Straight or pistol-grip stock and beavertail forearm, checkered. Imported 1934-64.

MODEL 410E
Same general specifications as Model 409PB except has automatic ejectors and is of higher quality throughout. Imported 1934-64.
Model 410E (12 ga.) . . . . NiB $1331 Ex $1175 Gd $759
Model 410E (20 ga.) . . . . NiB $1819 Ex $1461 Gd $1003
Model 410E (28 ga.) . . . . NiB $4581 Ex $3671 Gd $2506

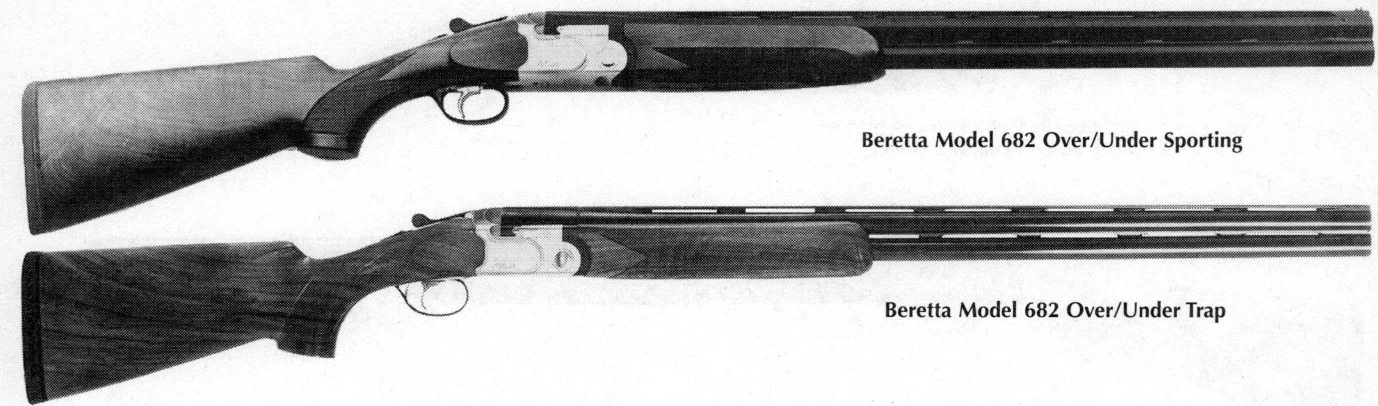

Beretta Model 682 Over/Under Sporting

Beretta Model 682 Over/Under Trap

MODEL 410 10-GA. MAGNUM . NiB $1264 Ex $1016 Gd $700
Same as Model 410E except heavier construction. Plain extractors. Double triggers. 10-ga. Magnum, 3.5-inch chambers. 32-inch bbls., both F choke. Weight: about 10 lbs. Checkered pistol-grip stock and forearm, recoil pad. Imported 1934-84.

MODEL 411E
Same general specifications as Model 409PB except has sideplates, automatic ejectors and is of higher quality throughout. Imported 1934-64.
Model 411E (12 ga.) . . . . NiB $1972 Ex $1583 Gd $1086
Model 411E (20 ga.) . . . . NiB $2564 Ex $2056 Gd $1407
Model 411E (28 ga.) . . . . NiB $4714 Ex $3779 Gd $2583

MODEL 424 HAMMERLESS DOUBLE . . . . NiB $1442 Ex $1157 Gd $793
Boxlock. Light border engraving. Plain extractors. Gauges: 12, 20; chambers 2.75-inch in former, 3-inch in latter. Bbls.: 28-inch M/F choke, 26-inch IC/M choke. Weight: 5 lbs. 14 oz. to 6 lbs. 10 oz., depending on ga. and bbl. length. English-style straight-grip stock and forearm, checkered. Imported 1977-84.

MODEL 426E. . . . . NiB $1942 Ex $1474 Gd $1032
Same as Model 424 except action body is finely engraved, silver pigeon inlaid in top lever; has selective automatic ejectors and selective single trigger, stock and forearm of select European walnut. Imported 1977-84.

MODEL 450 SERIES HAMMERLESS DOUBLES
Custom English-style sidelock. Single, non-selective trigger or double triggers. Manual safety. Selective automatic ejectors. Gauge: 12; 2.75- or 3-inch chambers. Bbls.: 26, 28 or 30 inches choked to customers' specifications. Weight: 6.75 lbs. Checkered high-grade walnut stock. Receiver w/coin-silver finish. Imported 1948 to date.
Model 450 EL (disc. 1982). . . . . NiB $7774 Ex $6241 Gd $4279
Model 450 EELL (disc. 1982). . . NiB $8236 Ex $6610 Gd $4520
Model 451 (disc. 1987) . . . . NiB $6734 Ex $5409 Gd $3714
Model 451 E (disc. 1989) . . . . . NiB $7383 Ex $5929 Gd $4067
Model 451 EL (disc. 1985) . . . . . NiB $12,936 Ex $10,348 Gd $7037
Model 451 EELL (disc. 1990) . . . NiB $14,202 Ex $11,362 Gd $7726
Model 452 (Intro. 1990) . . . . . NiB $20,750 Ex $18,200 Gd $12,376
Model 452 EELL (intro. 1992) . . NiB $30,226 Ex $24,180 Gd $16,442
Extra set of bbls., add 30%

MODEL 470 SERIES HAMMERLESS DOUBLE
Gauge: 12 and 20 ga. w/3-inch chambers. 26- or 28-inch bbl. Weight: 5.9 to 6.5 lbs. Low profile, improved box lock action w/single selective trigger. Selected walnut, checkered stock and forend. Metal front bead sight. Scroll-engraved receiver w/gold inlay and silver chrome finish. Imported 1999 to date.

(cont'd.) **MODEL 470 SERIES HAMMERLESS DOUBLE**
Model 470 Silver Hawk 12 ga. . . . . . NiB $2436 Ex $1954 Gd $1339
Model 470 Silver Hawk 20 ga. . . . . . NiB $2624 Ex $2105 Gd $1441
Model 470 EL Silver Hawk 12 ga. . . . NiB $4059 Ex $3850 Gd $2214
Model 470 EL Silver Hawk 20 ga. . . . NiB $4227 Ex $3975 Gd $2316
Model 470 EELL (Jubilee II) 12 ga. . . . NiB $8024 Ex $6025 Gd $4411
Model 470 EELL (Jubilee II) 20 ga. . . . NiB $8486 Ex $6808 Gd $4661
Extra set of bbls., add. 30%

MODEL 625 S/S HAMMERLESS DOUBLE
Boxlock. Gauges: 12 or 20. Bbls.: 26-, 28- or 30-inch w/fixed choke combinations. Single selective or double triggers w/extractors. Checkered English-style buttstock and forend. Imported 1984-87.
W/double triggers . . . . NiB $986 Ex $798 Gd $557
W/single selective trigger . . . . NiB $1150 Ex $928 Gd $645
20 ga., add. $150

MODEL 626 S/S HAMMERLESS DOUBLE
Field Grade side-by-side. Boxlock action w/single selective trigger, extractors and automatic safety. Gauges: 12 (2.75-inch chambers); 20 (3-inch chambers). Bbls.: 26- or 28-inch w/Mobilchoke or various fixed-choke combinations. Weight: 6.75 lbs. (12 ga.). Bright chrome finish. Checkered European walnut buttstock and forend in straight English style. Imported 1985-94.
Model 626 Field (disc. 1988). . . . NiB $1240 Ex $1032 Gd $538
Model 626 Onyx . . . . NiB $1370 Ex $1110 Gd $818
Model 626 Onyx (3.5-inch Magnum, disc. 1993). . . . . NiB $1468 Ex $1183 Gd $819
20 ga., add. $200

MODEL 627 S/S HAMMERLESS DOUBLE
Same as Model 626 S/S except w/engraved sideplates and pistol-grip or straight English-style stock. Imported 1985-94.
Model 627 EL Field . . . . NiB $2549 Ex $2035 Gd $1405
Model 627 EL Sport. . . . . NiB $2570 Ex $2092 Gd $1443
Model 627 EELL. . . . . NiB $4550 Ex $3632 Gd $2504

MODEL 682 O/U SHOTGUN
Hammerless takedown w/single selective trigger. Gauges: 12, 20, 28, .410. Bbls.: 26- to 34-inch w/fixed chokes or Mobilchoke tubes. Checkered European walnut buttstock/forend in various grades and configurations. Imported 1984 to date.
Model 682 Comp Skeet . . . . . . NiB $1979 Ex $1590 Gd $1093
Model 682 Comp Skeet Deluxe. . . . . NiB $2889 Ex $2318 Gd $1588
Mdl. 682 Comp Super Skeet . . . . NiB $2369 Ex $1902 Gd $1305
Mdl. 682 Comp Skeet 2-bbl. set (disc. 1989) . . . . NiB $4848 Ex $3887 Gd $2658
Mdl. 682 Comp Skeet 4 bbl. Set (disc. 1996) . . . . NiB $5570 Ex $4464 Gd $3050

Beretta Model 687EL

Beretta Model 687EEL

(*cont'd.*) **MODEL 682 O/U SHOTGUN**

Mdl. 682 Sporting Continental .... NiB $1979 Ex $1590 Gd $1093
Mdl. 682 Sporting Combo .... NiB $3101 Ex $2479 Gd $1697
Mdl. 682 Sporting Gold .... NiB $1849 Ex $1486 Gd $1122
Mdl. 682 Sporting Super Sport .... NiB $1217 Ex $1621 Gd $1113
Mdl. 682 Comp Trap Gold X .... NiB $1979 Ex $1590 Gd $1093
Mdl. 682 Comp Trap Top Sgle. (1986-95) .. NiB $1921 Ex $1543 Gd $1029
Mdl. 682 Comp Trap Live Pig. (1990-98) ... NiB $2546 Ex $2046 Gd $1405
Mdl. 682 Comp Mono/ComboTrp. Gld. X .. NiB $2750 Ex $2280 Gd $1564
Mdl. 682 Comp Mono Trap (1985-88) ...... NiB $1719 Ex $1382 Gd $951
Mdl. 682 Super Trap Gold X (1991-95) .... NiB $2051 Ex $1647 Gd $1121
Mdl. 682 Sup. Trap
Combo Gld. X (1991-97) .... NiB $2889 Ex $2318 Gd $1588
Mdl. 682 Super Trap
Top Sgle. Gld. X (1991-95) .... NiB $2109 Ex $1694 Gd $1163
Mdl. 682 Sup. Trap Unsingle (1992-94) .... NiB $1979 Ex $1590 Gd $1095

MODEL 686 O/U SHOTGUN

Low-profile improved boxlock action. Single selective trigger. Selective automatic ejectors. Gauges: 12, 20, 28 w/3.5- 3- or 2.75-inch chambers, depending upon ga. Bbls.: 26-, 28-, 30-inch w/fixed chokes or Mobilchoke tubes. Weight: 5.75 to 7.5 lbs. Checkered American walnut stock and forearm of various qualities, depending upon model. Receiver finishes also vary, but all have blued bbls. Sideplates to simulate sidelock action on EL models. Imported 1988 to date.

Model 686 Field Onyx .... NiB $1336 Ex $993 Gd $572
Mdl. 686 (3.5-inch Mag., disc.
1993 & reintro.1996) .... NiB $1404 Ex $1014 Gd $676
Model 686 EL Gold Perdiz (1992-97) .... NiB $1684 Ex $1347 Gd $916
Model 686 Essential (1994-96) .... NiB $930 Ex $744 Gd $505
Model 686 Silver Essential (1997-98) .... NiB $1036 Ex $829 Gd $564
Model 686 Sil. Pig. Onyx (intro. 1996) .... NiB $1359 Ex $1087 Gd $738
Mdl. 686 Sil. Perdiz Onyx (disc. 1996) ...... NiB $1322 Ex $1058 Gd $719
Model 686 Sil. Pig./Perdiz Onyx Combo ..... NiB $1894 Ex $1515 Gd $823
Model 686 L Silver Perdiz (disc. 1994) ...... NiB $1072 Ex $858 Gd $583
Model 686 Skeet Silver Pigeon (1996-98) ..... NiB $1137 Ex $909 Gd $619
Model 686 Skeet Silver Perdiz (1994-96) .... NiB $1358 Ex $1087 Gd $738
Model 686 Skeet Sil. Pig./Perdiz Combo ..... NiB $1358 Ex $1087 Gd $738
Model 686 Sporting Special (1987-93) ...... NiB $1565 Ex $1252 Gd $852
Model 686 Sporting English (1991-92) .... NiB $1644 Ex $1316 Gd $894
Model 686 Sporting Onyx
w/fixed chokes (1991-92) .... NiB $1565 Ex $1252 Gd $852
Model 686 Sporting Onyx
w/tubes (intro. 1992) .... NiB $1179 Ex $943 Gd $644
Mdl. 686 Sporting Onyx Gld. (disc. 1993) ... NiB $1709 Ex $1367 Gd $930
Mdl. 686 Sporting Sil. Pig. (intro. 1996) ..... NiB $1393 Ex $1115 Gd $758
Model 686 Sporting Sil. Perdiz (1993-96) .... NiB $1358 Ex $1087 Gd $738
Mdl. 686 Sporting Coll. Sport (1996-97) .... NiB $1036 Ex $829 Gd $564
Model 686 Sporting Combo .... NiB $2423 Ex $1939 Gd $1319
Model 686 Trap International (1994-95) .... NiB $1019 Ex $821 Gd $567
Model 686 Trap Silver Pigeon (intro. 1997)... NiB $1098 Ex $884 Gd $609
Model 686 Trap Top Mono (intro. 1998) .... NiB $1134 Ex $922 Gd $628
Model 686 Ultralight Onyx (intro. 1992) ... NiB $1449 Ex $1164 Gd $800
Mdl. 686 Ultralight Del. Onyx (intro. 1998) .... NiB $1814 Ex $1456 Gd $998

MODEL 687 O/U SHOTGUN

Same as Model 686 except w/decorative sideplates and varying grades of engraving and game-scene motifs.

Model 687 L Onyx (disc. 1991) .... NiB $1348 Ex $1084 Gd $745
Model 687 L Onyx Gold Field (1988-89) .. NiB $1528 Ex $1227 Gd $842
Model 687 L Onyx Silver Pigeon .... NiB $1956 Ex $1570 Gd $1075
Model 687 EL Onyx (disc. 1990) .... NiB $2656 Ex $2134 Gd $1467
Model 687 EL Gold Pigeon .... NiB $3042 Ex $2440 Gd $1677
Model 687 EL Gold Pigeon Sm. Fr. ..... NiB $2825 Ex $2277 Gd $1563
Mdl. 687 EL Gld. Pig. Sporting (Int. 1993) .... NiB $4186 Ex $3358 Gd $2299
Model 687 EELL Diamond Pigeon ...... NiB $4186 Ex $3358 Gd $2299
Mdl. 687 EELL Diamond Pig. Skeet ...... NiB $4044 Ex $3244 Gd $2212
Mdl. 687 EELL Diam. Pig. Sporting ...... NiB $4265 Ex $3422 Gd $2341
Mdl. 687 EELL Diam. Pig. X Trap .... NiB $3729 Ex $2992 Gd $2050
Mdl. 687 EELL Diam. Pig. Mono Trap .... NiB $3817 Ex $3079 Gd $2108
Mdl. 687 EELL Diam. Pig. Trap Combo ... NiB $5188 Ex $4159 Gd $2844
Model 687 EELL Field Combo .... NiB $4330 Ex $3473 Gd $2377
Model 687 EELL Skeet 4-bbl. set .... NiB $7125 Ex $5709 Gd $3897
Model 687 EELL Gallery Special .... NiB $6618 Ex $5303 Gd $3518
Model 687 EELL Gallery Special Combo . NiB $7983 Ex $6396 Gd $4354
Model 687 EELL Gallery Special pairs . NiB $15,730 Ex $12,584 Gd $8557
Model 687 Sporting English (1991-92) ... NiB $2121 Ex $1706 Gd $1174
Mdl. 687 Sporting Sil. Pig. (intro. 1996) . NiB $1898 Ex $1528 Gd $1055
Mdl. 687 Sporting Sil. Perdiz (1993-96) .. NiB $1977 Ex $1591 Gd $1190

MODEL 1200 SERIES SEMIAUTOLOADING SHOTGUN

Short recoil action. Gauge: 12; 2.75- or 3-inch chamber. Six round magazine. 24-, 26- or 28-inch vent-rib bbl. w/fixed chokes or Mobilchoke tubes. Weight: 7.25 lbs. Matte black finish. Adj. technopolymer stock and forend. Imported 1988 to date.

Model 1200 w/fixed choke (disc. 1989) ...... NiB $562 Ex $453 Gd $312
Model 1200 Riot (disc. 1989) .... NiB $576 Ex $460 Gd $321
Model 1201 w/Mobilchoke (disc. 1994) ...... NiB $591 Ex $476 Gd $329
Model 1201 Riot .... NiB $634 Ex $511 Gd $352
W/Pistol-grip stock, add $72
W/Tritium sights, add $56

MODEL A-301 AUTOLOADING SHOTGUN.......
.... NiB $463 Ex $374 Gd $259

Field Gun. Gas-operated. Scroll-decorated receiver. Gauge: 12 or 20; 2.75-inch chamber in former, 3-inch in latter. Three round magazine. Bbl.: Ventilated rib; 28-inch F or M choke, 26-inch IC. Weight: 6 lbs., 5 oz. – 6 lbs., 14 oz., depending on gauge and bbl. length. Checkered pistol-grip stock/forearm. Imported 1977-82.

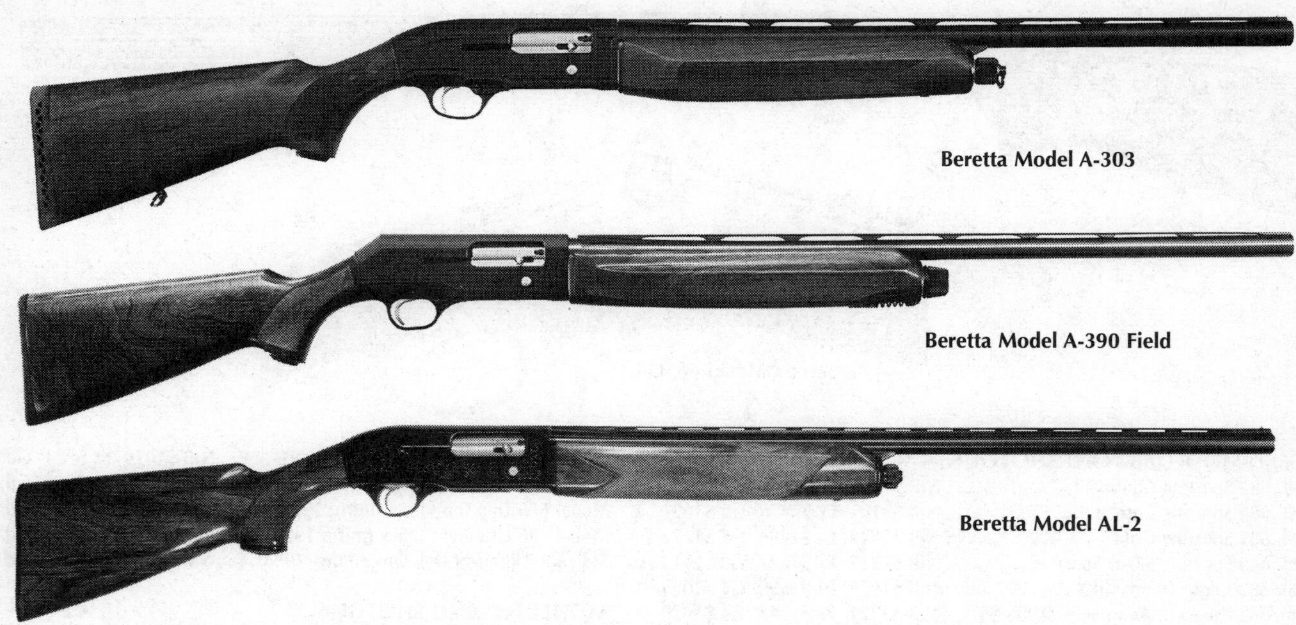
Beretta Model A-303

Beretta Model A-390 Field

Beretta Model AL-2

MODEL A-301 MAGNUM. . . . . NiB $481 Ex $388 Gd $270
Same as Model A-301 Field Gun except chambered for 12 ga. Three inch Magnum shells, 30-inch F choke bbl. only, stock w/recoil pad. Weight: 7.25 lbs.

MODEL A-301 SKEET GUN. . . . . . . NiB $507 Ex $409 Gd $284
Same as Model A-301 Field Gun except 26-inch bbl. SK choke only, skeet-style stock, gold-plated trigger.

MODEL A-301 SLUG GUN . . . . NiB $475 Ex $383 Gd $267
Same as Model A-301 Field Gun except has plain 22-inch bbl., slug choke, w/rifle sights. Weight: 6 lbs., 14 oz.

MODEL A-301 TRAP GUN . . . . NiB $507 Ex $409 Gd $284
Same as Model A-301 Field Gun except has 30-inch bbl. in F choke only, checkered Monte Carlo stock w/recoil pad, gold-plated trigger. Blued bbl. and receiver. Weight: 7 lbs., 10 oz. Imported 1978-82.

MODEL A-302 SEMIAUTOLOADING SHOTGUN
Similar to gas-operated Model 301. Hammerless, takedown shotgun w/tubular magazine and Mag-Action that handles both 2.75- and 3-inch Magnum shells. Gauge: 12 or 20; 2.75- or 3-inch Mag. chambers. Bbl.: Vent or plain; 22-inch/Slug (12 ga.); 26-inch/IC (12 or 20) 28-inch/M (20 ga.), 28-inch/Multi-choke (12 or 20 ga.) 30-inch/F (12 ga.). Weight: 6.5 lbs., 20 ga.; 7.25.lbs., 12 ga. Blued/ black finish. Checkered European walnut, pistol-grip stock and forend. Imported 1983 to c. 1987.
Standard model w/fixed choke . . . . NiB $481 Ex $388 Gd $270
Standard model w/multi-choke . . . . NiB $533 Ex $430 Gd $299

MODEL A-302 SUPER LUSSO . . NiB $2354 Ex $2320 Gd $1418
A custom A-302 in presentation grade w/hand-engraved receiver and custom select walnut stock.

MODEL A-303 SEMIAUTOLOADER
Similar to Model 302, except w/target specifications in Trap, Skeet and Youth configurations, and weighs 6.5 to 8 lbs. Imported 1983-96.
Field and Upland models. . . . . NiB $562 Ex $531 Gd $492
Skeet and Trap (disc. 1994) . . . . . . NiB $692 Ex $557 Gd $384
Slug model (disc. 1992). . . . . NiB $757 Ex $609 Gd $419

***(cont'd.)* MODEL A-303 SEMIAUTOLOADER**
Sporting Clays . . . . NiB $779 Ex $637 Gd $439
Super Skeet . . . . NiB $1149 Ex $923 Gd $635
Super Trap . . . . NiB $1092 Ex $878 Gd $613
Waterfowl/Turkey (disc. 1992) . . . . NiB $727 Ex $585 Gd $415
Mobil choke, add. $50

MODEL A-303 YOUTH GUN . . . . . NiB $696 Ex $488 Gd $280
Locked-breech, gas-operated action. Ga: 12 and 20; 2-round magazine. Bbls.: 24, 26, 28, 30 or 32-inches, vent rib. Weight: 7 lbs. (12 ga.), 6 lbs. (20 ga.). Crossbolt safety. Length of pull shortened to 12.5 inches. Imported 1988-96.

MODEL A-390 SEMIAUTOMATIC SHOTGUN
Gas-operated, self-regulating action designed to handle any size load. Gauges: 12 or 20 w/ 3-inch chamber. Three round magazine. Bbl.: 24, 26, 28 or 30 inches w/vent rib and Mobilchoke tubes. Weight: 7.5 lbs. Select walnut stock w/adj. comb. Blued or matte black finish. Imported 1992-96. Superseded by AL-390 series.
Standard model/Slug model . . . . . . NiB $586 Ex $472 Gd $328
Field model/Silver Mallard . . . . NiB $598 Ex $481 Gd $335
Deluxe model/Gold Mallard . . . . . . NiB $650 Ex $524 Gd $363
Turkey/Waterfowl model (matte finish) . . . NiB $612 Ex $493 Gd $335
For 20 ga., add $35

MODEL A-390 TARGET
Similar to the Model 390 Field except w/2.75-inch chamber. Skeet: 28-inch ported bbl. w/wide vent rib and fixed choke (SK). Trap: 30- or 32-inch w/Mobilchoke tubes. Weight: 7.5 lbs. Fully adj. buttstock. Imported from 1993-96.
Sport Trap model . . . . NiB $598 Ex $483 Gd $335
Sport Skeet model . . . . NiB $586 Ex $472 Gd $328
Sporting Clays model (unported). . . NiB $606 Ex $488 Gd $338
Super Trap model (ported). . . . . NiB $794 Ex $639 Gd $441
Super Skeet model (ported). . . . . . . NiB $780 Ex $628 Gd $434
W/ported bbl., add $85
20 ga., add. $35

MODEL AL-1 FIELD GUN . . . . NiB $468 Ex $379 Gd $264
Same as Model AL-2 gas-operated Field Gun except has bbl. w/o rib, no engraving on receiver. Imported 1971-73.

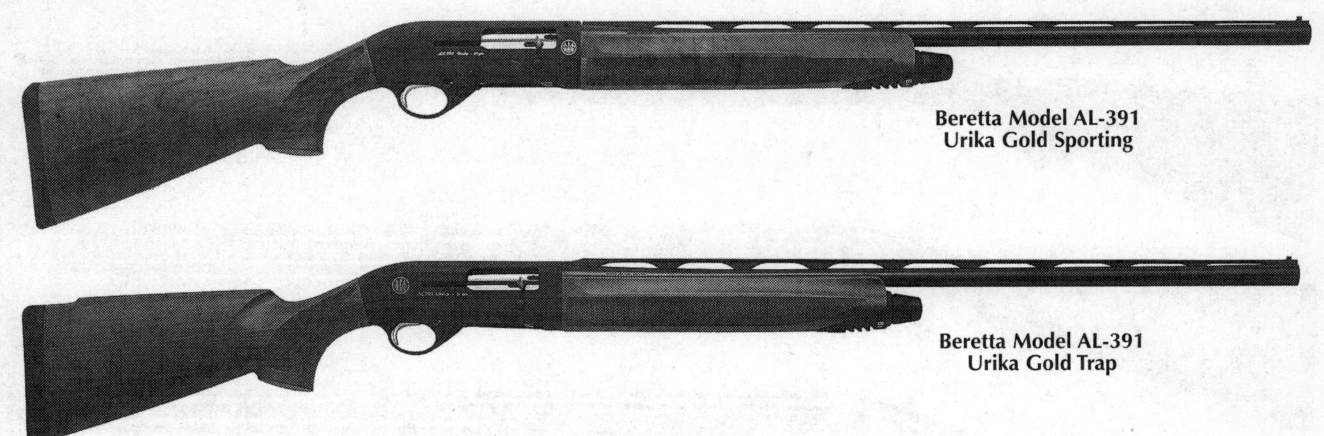
Beretta Model AL-391 Urika Gold Sporting

Beretta Model AL-391 Urika Gold Trap

MODEL AL-2 AUTOLOADING SHOTGUN
Field Gun. Gas-operated. Engraved receiver (1968 version, 12 ga. only, had no engraving). Gauge: 12 or 20. 2.75-inch chamber. Three round magazine. Bbls.: Vent rib; 30-inch F choke, 28-inch F or M choke, 26-inch IC. Weight: 6.5 to 7.25 lbs, depending on ga. and bbl. length. Checkered pistol-grip stock and forearm. Imported 1968-75.
W/Plain receiver . . . . NiB $400 Ex $326 Gd $232
W/Engraved receiver . . . . NiB $544 Ex $441 Gd $310

MODEL AL-2 MAGNUM . . . . NiB $492 Ex $399 Gd $281
Same as Model AL-2 Field Gun except chambered for 12 ga. 3-inch Magnum shells; 30-inch F or 28-inch M choke bbl. only. Weight: About 8 lbs. Imported 1973-75.

MODEL AL-2 SKEET GUN . . . . NiB $466 Ex $378 Gd $267
Same as Model AL-2 Field Gun except has wide rib, 26-inch bbl. in SK choke only, checkered pistol-grip stock and beavertail forearm. Imported 1973-75.

MODEL AL-2 TRAP GUN . . . . NiB $452 Ex $368 Gd $260
Same as Model AL-2 Field Gun except has wide rib, 30 inch bbl. in F choke only, beavertail forearm. Monte Carlo stock w/recoil pad. Weight: About 7.75 lbs. Imported 1973-75.

MODEL AL-3
Similar to corresponding AL-2 models in design and general specifications. Imported 1975-76.
Field model . . . . NiB $466 Ex $378 Gd $267
Magnum model . . . . NiB $478 Ex $389 Gd $274
Skeet model . . . . NiB $486 Ex $394 Gd $278
Trap model . . . . NiB $440 Ex $358 Gd $253

MODEL AL-3 DELUXE TRAP GUN . . . . NiB $927 Ex $749 Gd $517
Same as standard Model AL-3 Trap Gun except has fully-engraved receiver, gold-plated trigger and safety, stock and forearm of premium-grade European walnut, gold monogram escutcheon inlaid in buttstock. Imported 1975-76.

AL390 FIELD SHOTGUN
Lightweight version of A-390 series. Gauges: 12 or 20 ga. 22- 24-, 26-, 28-, or 30-inch bbl., 41.7 to 47.6 inches overall. Weight: 6.4 to 7.5 lbs. Imported 1997 to date.
Mdl. AL390 Field/Sil. Mallard (12 or 20 ga.) . . . NiB $706 Ex $571 Gd $397
Mdl. AL390 Field/Sil. Mallard Yth. (20 ga.) . . . . NiB $714 Ex $577 Gd $400
Model AL390 Field/Slug (12 ga. only) . . . . NiB $690 Ex $558 Gd $388
Model AL390 Silver Mallard camouflage . . NiB $768 Ex $621 Gd $428
Model AL390 Silver Mallard synthetic . . . . NiB $722 Ex $583 Gd $406
Model AL390 Gold Mallard (12 or 20 ga.) . NiB $800 Ex $646 Gd $448
Model AL390 NWTF Spec. camouflage . . . NiB $956 Ex $771 Gd $533
Model AL390 NWTF Spec. synthetic . . . . . NiB $769 Ex $621 Gd $430
Mdl. AL390 NWTF Spec. Yth. . . . . NiB $818 Ex $470 Gd $309

AL390 SPORT SPORTING SHOTGUN
Similar to Model AL-390 Sport Skeet. Gauges: 12 or 20 ga., 28- or 30-inch bbls. Weight: 6.8 to 8 lbs. Imported 1997 to date.
Model AL390 Sport Sporting . . . . NiB $712 Ex $583 Gd $406
Model AL390 Sport Sporting Collection . . . . . . NiB $667 Ex $611 Gd $430
Mdl. AL390 Sport Sporting
Yth. (20 ga. only) . . . . NiB $690 Ex $558 Gd $388
Model AL390 Sport Gold Sporting . . . . NiB $956 Ex $771 Gd $533
Mdl. AL390 EELL Sport
Diamond Sporting. . . . . NiB $3488 Ex $2803 Gd $1927
W/Ported bbl., add $75

AL390 SPORT SKEET SHOTGUN
Gauges: 12 ga. only. 26- or 28-inch bbl. w/3-round mqagazine. Weight: 7.6 to 8 lbs. Matte finish wood and metal. Imported 1997 to date.
Model AL390 Sport Skeet . . . . NiB $731 Ex $589 Gd $409
Mdl. AL390 Sport Super Skeet (Semi-Auto) . . . . NiB $991 Ex $797 Gd $550
W/ported bbl., add $95

BERETTA AL390 SPORT TRAP SHOTGUN
Gauges: 12 ga. only. 30- or 32-inch bbl. w/3-round chamber. Weight: 7.8 to 8.25 lbs. Matte finish wood and metal. Black recoil rubber pad. Imported 1997 to date.
Model AL390 Sport Trap . . . . NiB $731 Ex $589 Gd $409
Model AL390 Sport Super Trap . . . NiB $1039 Ex $836 Gd $576
Multi-choke bbl. (30″ only), add $40
Ported bbl., add $95

AL391 URIKA AUTOLOADING SHOTGUN
Gauge: 12 and 20 ga. w/3-inch chambers. 28- 30- or 32-inch bbl. Weight: 6.6 to 7.7 lbs. Self-compensating gas valve. Adjustable synthetic and walnut stocks w/ five interchangeable chokes. Imported 2000 to date.
Model AL391 Urika. . . . . NiB $842 Ex $689 Gd $470
Model AL391 Urika synthetic . . . . NiB $860 Ex $694 Gd $480
Model AL391 Urika camo
w/Realtree Hardwoods . . . . NiB $947 Ex $763 Gd $527
Model AL391 Urika
Gold w/black receiver . . . . NiB $992 Ex $799 Gd $551
Model AL391 Urika Gold
w/silver receiver, lightweight . . . . NiB $1071 Ex $862 Gd $595
Model AL391 Urika Youth. . . . . NiB $850 Ex $686 Gd $466
Model AL391 Urika Sporting . . . . NiB $966 Ex $778 Gd $538
Model AL391 Urika Gold
Sporting w/black receiver. . . . . NiB $1036 Ex $834 Gd $575
Model AL391 Urika
Gold Sporting w/silver receiver . . . . NiB $1107 Ex $890 Gd $614
Model AL391 Urika Trap. . . . . NiB $974 Ex $785 Gd $542
Model AL391 Gold Trap . . . . NiB $1071 Ex $862 Gd $595
Model AL391 Parallel Target . . . . NiB $946 Ex $762 Gd $527

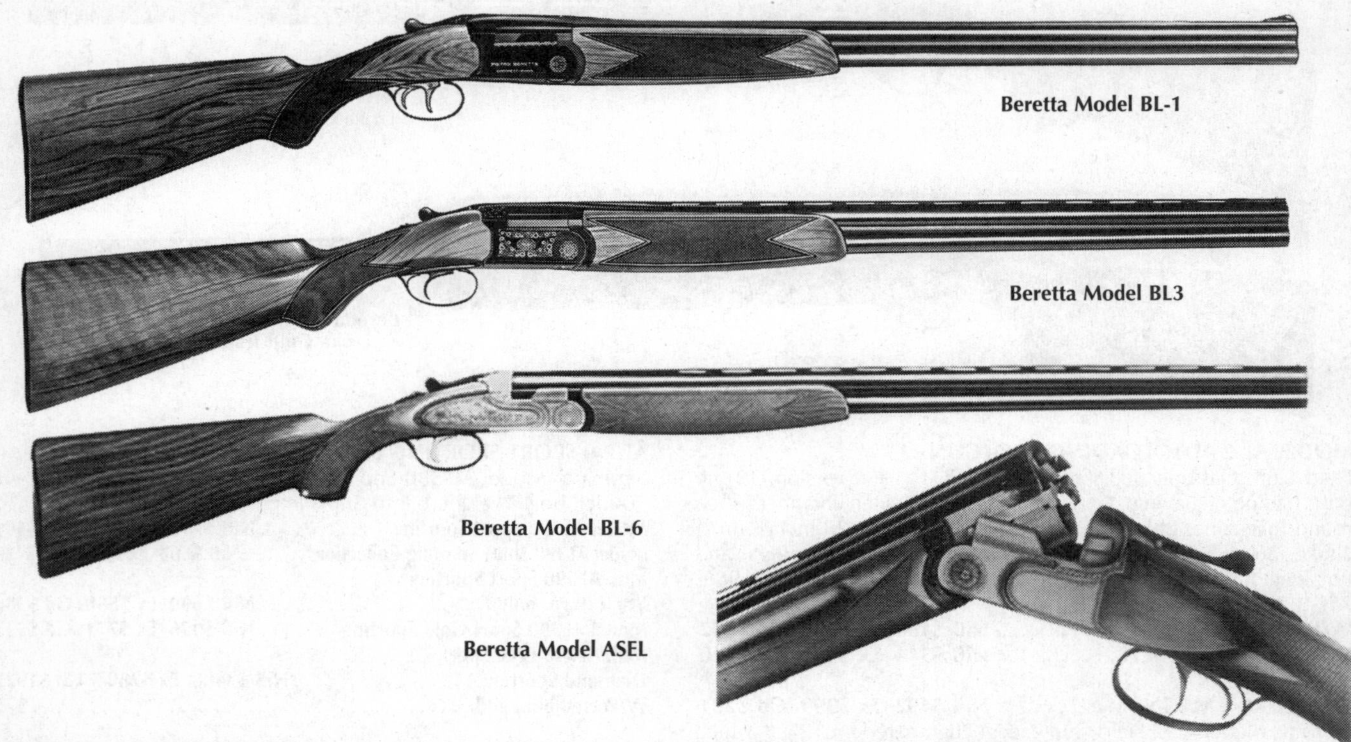

Beretta Model BL-1

Beretta Model BL3

Beretta Model BL-6

Beretta Model ASEL

MODEL ASE 90 O/U SHOTGUN
Competition-style receiver w/coin-silver finish and gold inlay featuring drop-out trigger group. Gauge: 12; 2.75-inch chamber. Bbls.: 28- or 30-inch w/fixed or Mobilchoke tubes; vent rib. Weight: 8.5 lbs. (30-inch bbl.). Checkered high-grade walnut stock. Imported 1992 to date.
Pigeon, Skeet, Trap models . . . . NiB $7720 Ex $6203 Gd $4251
Sporting Clays model. . . . . NiB $7908 Ex $6349 Gd $4354
Trap Combo model. . . . . NiB $12,140 Ex $9734 Gd $6656
Deluxe (introduced 1996) . . . . NiB $14,090 Ex $11,294 Gd $7716

MODEL ASE SERIES O/U SHOTGUN
Boxlock. Single non-selective trigger. Selective automatic ejectors. gauges: 12 and 20. Bbls. 26-, 28-, 30-inch; IC and M choke or M and F choke. Weight: about 5.75-7 lbs. Checkered pistol-grip stock and forearm. Receiver w/various grades of engraving. Imported 1947-64.
Model ASE (light scroll engraving). . . . . . . NiB $2185 Ex $1758 Gd $1211
Model ASEL (half coverage engraving) . . . . NiB $3122 Ex $2508 Gd $1716
Model ASEELL (full coverage engraving) . . . NiB $4759 Ex $3817 Gd $2612
For 20 ga. models, add 95%

MODEL BL-1/BL-2 O/U
Boxlock. Plain extractors. Double triggers.12 gauge, 2.75-inch chambers only. Bbls.: 30-and 28-inch M/F choke, 26-inch IC/M choke. Weight: 6.75-7 lbs., depending on bbl. length. Checkered pistol-grip stock and forearm. Imported 1968-73.
Model BL-1. . . . . NiB $416 Ex $328 Gd $228
Model BL-2 (single selective trigger) . . . . NiB $504 Ex $406 Gd $281

MODEL BL-2/S . . . . NiB $520 Ex $420 Gd $292
Similar to Model BL-1, except has selective "Speed-Trigger," vent-rib bbls., 2.75- or 3-inch chambers. Weight: 7-7.5 lbs. Imported 1974-76.

MODEL BL-3 . . . . NiB $742 Ex $597 Gd $412
Same as Model BL-1, except has deluxe engraved receiver, selective single trigger, vent-rib bbls., 12 or 20 ga., 2.75-inch or 3-inch chambers in former, 3-inch in latter. Weight: 6-7.5 lbs. depending on ga. and bbl. length. Imported 1968-76.

MODELS BL-4, BL-5 AND BL-6
Higher grade versions of Model BL-3 w/more elaborate engraving and fancier wood; Model BL-6 has sideplates. Selective automatic ejectors standard. Imported 1968-76.
Model BL-4 . . . . NiB $905 Ex $729 Gd $504
Model BL-5 . . . . NiB $1191 Ex $958 Gd $660
Model BL-6 (1973-76) . . . . NiB $1489 Ex $1197 Gd $823

SERIES BL SKEET GUNS
Models BL-3, BL-4, BL-5 and BL-6 w/standard features of their respective grades plus wider rib and skeet-style stock, 26-inch bbls. SK choked. Weight: 6-7.25 lbs. depending on ga.
Model BL-3 skeet gun . . . . NiB $807 Ex $651 Gd $451
Model BL-4 skeet gun . . . . NiB $931 Ex $750 Gd $519
Model BL-5 skeet gun . . . . NiB $1229 Ex $989 Gd $701
Model BL-6 skeet gun . . . . NiB $1659 Ex $1332 Gd $914

SERIES BL TRAP GUNS
Models BL-3, BL-4, BL-5 and BL-6 w/standard features of their respective grades plus wider rib and Monte Carlo stock w/recoil pad; 30-inch bbls., improved M/F or both F choke. Weight: About 7.5 lbs.
Model BL-3 trap gun . . . . NiB $713 Ex $583 Gd $406
Model BL-4 trap gun . . . . NiB $801 Ex $646 Gd $448
Model BL-5 trap gun . . . . NiB $1229 Ex $989 Gd $681
Model BL-6 trap gun . . . . NiB $1581 Ex $1270 Gd $873

MODEL FS-1 FOLDING SINGLE . . . . NiB $244 Ex $166 Gd $114
Formerly "Companion." Folds to length of bbl. Hammerless. Underlever. Gauge: 12, 16, 20, 28 or .410. Bbl.: 30-inch in 12 ga., 28-inch in 16 and 20 ga.; 26-inch in 28 and .410 ga.; all F choke. Checkered semipistol-grip stock/forearm. Weight: 4.5-5.5 lbs. depending on ga. Disc. 1971.

GOLDEN SNIPE O/U
Same as Silver Snipe (see page 430) except has automatic ejectors, vent rib is standard feature. Imported 1959-67.
W/non-selective single trigger . . . . NiB $1059 Ex $904 Gd $492
W/selective single trigger, add $100

Beretta Model GR-2

Beretta FS-1 Folding

Beretta Mark II Trap

Beretta S58 Trap

MODEL GR-2 HAMMERLESS DOUBLE . . . NiB $991 Ex $797 Gd $550
Boxlock. Plain extractors. Double triggers. Gauges: 12, 20; 2.75-inch chambers in former, 3-inch in latter. Bbls.: Vent rib; 30-inch M/F choke (12 ga. only); 28-inch M/F choke, 26-inch IC/M choke. Weight: 6.5 to 7.5 lbs. depending on ga. and bbl. length. Checkered pistol-grip stock and forearm. Imported 1968-76.

MODEL GR-3 . . . . NiB $1121 Ex $901 Gd $620
Same as Model GR-2 except has selective single trigger chambered for 12-ga. Three inch or 2.75-inch shells. Magnum model has 30-inch M/F choke bbl., recoil pad. Weight: about 8 lbs. Imported 1968-76.

MODEL GR-4 . . . . NiB $1527 Ex $1226 Gd $841
Same as Model GR-2 except has automatic ejectors and selective single trigger, higher grade engraving and wood. 12 ga., 2.75-inch chambers only. Imported 1968-76.

GRADE 100 O/U
SHOTGUN . . . . NiB $1968 Ex $1579 Gd $1082
Sidelock. Double triggers. Automatic ejectors. 12 ga. only. Bbls.: 26-, 28-, 30-inch, any standard boring. Weight: About 7.5 lbs. Checkered stock and forend, straight or pistol grip. Disc.

GRADE 200 . . . . NiB $2579 Ex $2072 Gd $1423
Same general specifications as Grade 100 except higher quality; bores and action parts hard chrome plated. Disc.

MARK II SINGLE-BARREL TRAP GUN . . . . NiB $604 Ex $486 Gd $336
Boxlock action similar to that of Series "BL" over-and-unders. Engraved receiver. Automatic ejector. 12 ga. only. 32- or 34-inch bbl. w/wide vent rib. Weight: About 8.5 lbs. Monte Carlo stock w/pistol grip and recoil pad, beavertail forearm. Imported 1972-76.

MODEL S55B O/U
SHOTGUN . . . . NiB $642 Ex $590 Gd $460
Boxlock. Plain extractors. Selective single trigger. Gauges: 12, 20; 2.75- or 3-inch chambers in former, 3-inch in latter. Bbls. vent rib; 30-inch M/F choke or both F choke in 12-ga. Three inch Magnum only; 28-inch M/F choke; 26 inch IC/M choke. Weight: 6.5 to 7.5 lbs. depending on ga. and bbl. length. Checkered pistol-grip stock and forearm. Introduced in 1977. Disc.

MODEL S56E. . . . . NiB $902 Ex $642 Gd $434
Same as Model S55B except has scroll-engraved receiver selective automatic ejectors. Introduced in 1977. Disc.

MODEL S58 SKEET GUN . . . . NiB $850 Ex $600 Gd $434
Same as Model S56E except has 26-inch bbls. of Boehler Antinit Anticorro steel, SK choked, w/wide vent rib; skeet-style stock and forearm. Weight: 7.5 lbs. Introduced in 1977.

MODEL S58 TRAP GUN . . . . NiB $845 Ex $460 Gd $434
Same as Model S58 Skeet Gun except has 30-inch bbls. bored IM/F Trap, Monte Carlo stock w/recoil pad. Weight: 7 lbs. 10 oz. Introduced in 1977. Disc.

SILVER HAWK FEATHERWEIGHT
HAMMERLESS DOUBLE-BARREL SHOTGUN
Boxlock. Double triggers or non-selective single trigger. Plain extractor. Gauges: 12, 16, 20, 28, 12 Mag. Bbls.: 26- to 32-inch w/high matted rib, all standard choke combinations. Weight: 7 lbs. (12 ga. w/26-inch bbls.). Checkered walnut stock w/beavertail forearm. Disc. 1967.
W/double triggers . . . . NiB $692 Ex $512 Gd $330
For non-selective single trigger, add $65

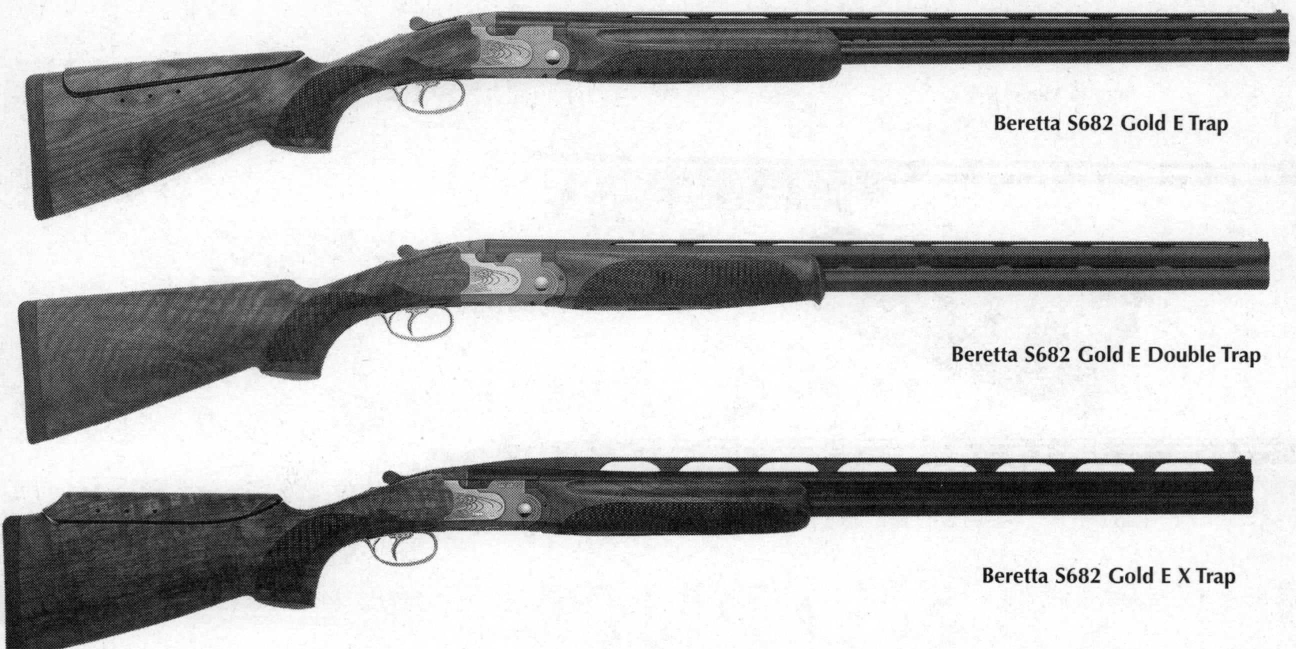

Beretta S682 Gold E Trap

Beretta S682 Gold E Double Trap

Beretta S682 Gold E X Trap

SILVER SNIPE O/U SHOTGUN

Boxlock. Non-selective or selective single trigger. Plain extractor. Gauges: 12, 20, 12 Mag., 20 Mag. Bbls.: 26-, 28-, 30-inch; plain or vent rib; chokes IC/M, M/F, SK number 1 and number 2, F/F. Weight: From about 6 lbs. in 20 ga. to 8.5 lbs. in 12 ga. (Trap gun). Checkered walnut pistol-grip stock and forearm. Imported 1955-67.

W/plain bbl., non-selective trigger .... NiB $792 Ex $714 Gd $356
W/vent rib bbl., non-selective single trigger .... NiB $818 Ex $740 Gd $402
For selective single trigger, add $65

MODEL SL-2 PIGEON SERIES PUMP GUN

Hammerless. Takedown.12 ga. only. Three round magazine. Bbls.: Vent rib; 30-inch F choke, 28-inch M, 26-inch IC. Weight: 7-7.25 lbs., depending on bbl. length. Receiver w/various grades of engraving. Checkered pistol-grip stock and forearm. Imported 1968-71.

Model SL-2 .... NiB $432 Ex $350 Gd $245
Silver Pigeon .... NiB $357 Ex $289 Gd $203
Gold Pigeon.................... NiB $544 Ex $439 Gd $305
Ruby Pigeon.................... NiB $694 Ex $559 Gd $386

"SO" SERIES SHOTGUNS

Jubilee Series introduced in 1998. The Beretta Boxlock is made with mechanical works from a single block of hot forged, high- resistance steel. The gun is richly engraved in scroll and game scenes. All engraving is signed by master engravers. High-quality finishing on the inside with high polishing of all internal points. Sidelock. Selective automatic ejectors. Selective single trigger or double triggers. 12 ga. only, 2.75- or 3-inch chambers. Bbls.: Vent rib (wide type on skeet and trap guns); 26-, 27-, 29-, 30-inch; any combination of standard chokes. Weight: 7 to 7.75 lbs., depending on bbl. length, style of stock and density of wood. Stock and forearm of select walnut, finely checkered; straight or pistol-grip, field, skeet and trap guns have appropriate styles of stock and forearm. Models differ chiefly in quality of wood and grade of engraving. Models SO-3EL, SO-3EELL, SO4 and SO-5 have hand-detachable locks. "SO-4" is used to designate skeet and trap models derived from Model SO-3EL, but with less elaborate engraving. Models SO3EL and SO-3EELL are similar to the earlier SO-4 and SO-5, respectively. Imported 1933 to date.

(*cont'd.*) "SO" SERIES SHOTGUNS

Jubilee O/U 410-28-20-12 .... NiB to $17,933 Ex to 14,347 Gd to 9756
Jubilee II Side-by-side .... NiB to $19,441 Ex to $14,637 Gd to $9953
Mdl. SO-2 .... NiB to $8573 Ex to $4570 Gd to $3107
Mdl. SO-3 .... NiB to $7143 Ex to $6629 Gd to $4508
Mdl. SO-3EL .... NiB to $9145 Ex to $7773 Gd to $5286
Mdl. SO-3EELL............ NiB to $10,861 Ex to $11,434 Gd to $7775
Mdl. SO-4 Field, Skeet or Trap gun .... NiB to $9147 Ex to $8313 Gd to $6220
Model SO-5 Sporting, Skt. or Trp. .... NiB to $11,830 Ex to $9880 Gd to $7768
W/extra bbl. set, add 25%

MODELS SO-6 AND SO-9 PREMIUM GRADE SHOTGUNS

High-grade over/unders in the SO series. Gauges: 12 ga. only (SO-6); 12, 20, 28 and .410 (SO-9). Fixed or Mobilchoke (12 ga. only). Sidelock action. Silver or casehardened receiver (SO-6); English custom hand-engraved scroll or game scenes (SO-9). Supplied w/leather case and accessories. Imported from about 1990 to date.

SO-6 O/U .... NiB to $7996 Ex to $6812 Gd to $4632
SO-6 EELL O/U .... NiB to $5714 Ex to $8730 Gd to $5937
SO-9 O/U .... to $48,667
SO-9 EELL special engraver.......................... to $93,600
W/extra bbl. set, add.................................. 25%

MODEL SO6/SO-7 S/S DOUBLES

Side-by-side shotgun w/same general specifications as SO Series over/unders except higher grade w/more elaborate engraving, fancier wood.

SO-6 SxS (imported 1948-82) .... to $6,937
SO-7 SxS (imported 1948-90) .... to $8,856

MODEL TR-1 SINGLE-SHOT TRAP GUN...... NiB $367 Ex $298 Gd $208

Hammerless. Underlever action. Engraved frame.12 ga. only. 32-inch bbl. w/vent rib. Weight: About 8.25 lbs. Monte Carlo stock w/pistol grip and recoil pad, beavertail forearm. Imported 1968-71.

MODEL TR-2 .... NiB $411 Ex $332 Gd $231

Same as Model TR-1 except has extended ventilated rib. Imported 1969-73.

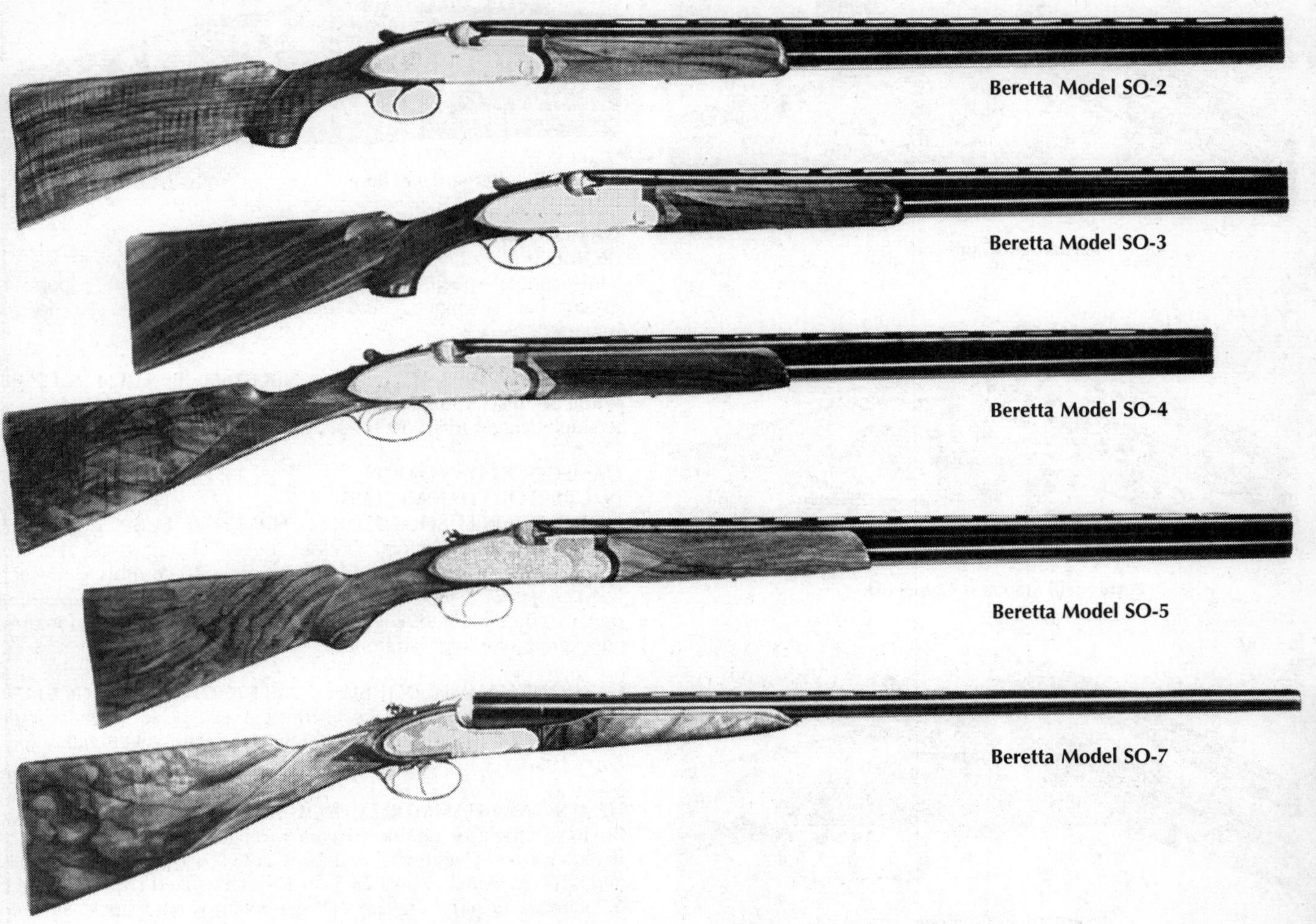
Beretta Model SO-2

Beretta Model SO-3

Beretta Model SO-4

Beretta Model SO-5

Beretta Model SO-7

VICTORIA PINTAIL (ES100) SEMIAUTOLOADER

Short Montefeltro-type recoil action. Gauge: 12 w/3-inch chamber. Bbl.: 24-inch slug, 24-, 26- or 28-inch vent rib w/Mobilchoke tubes. Weight: 7 lbs. to 7 lbs., 5 oz. Checkered synthetic or walnut buttstock and forend. Matte finish on both metal and stock. Imported 1993 to date.

Field model w/synthetic stock (intro. 1998) .... NiB $634 Ex $513 Gd $357
Field model w/walnut stock (disc. 1998)...... NiB $592 Ex $478 Gd $334
Rifled slug model w/synthetic stock (intro. 1998) .... NiB $777 Ex $627 Gd $435
Standard slug model w/walnut stock (disc. 1998) .... NiB $563 Ex $456 Gd $318
Wetland Camo model (intro. 2000) ...... NiB $734 Ex $583 Gd $412

VINCENZO BERNARDELLI — Gardone V.T. (Brescia), Italy

Previously imported by Armsport, Miami, FL (formerly by Magnum Research, Inc., Quality Arms, Stoeger Industries, Inc. & Action Arms, LTD).

115 SERIES O/U SHOTGUNS

Boxlock w/single trigger and ejectors. 12 ga. only. 25.5-, 26.75-, and 29.5-inch bbls. Concave top and vented middle rib. Anatomical grip stock. Blued or coin-silver finish w/various grades of engraving. Imported 1985-97.

***(cont'd.)* 115 SERIES O/U SHOTGUNS**

Hunting Model 115 (disc. 1990)...... NiB $1885 Ex $1515 Gd $1042
Hunting Model 115E (disc. 1990)..... NiB $5604 Ex $4489 Gd $3063
Hunting Model 115L (disc. 1990)..... NiB $3108 Ex $2494 Gd $1706
Hunting Model 115S (disc. 1990) .... NiB $2643 Ex $2123 Gd $1453
Target Model 115 (disc. 1992)....... NiB $2108 Ex $1693 Gd $1161
Target Model 115E (disc. 1992) ...... NiB $6330 Ex $5070 Gd $3463
Target Model 115L (disc. 1992) ...... NiB $3934 Ex $3156 Gd $2158
Target Model 115S (disc. 1992) ...... NiB $2827 Ex $2270 Gd $1555
Trap/Skeet Model 115S (imported 1996-97) .... NiB $2892 Ex $2321 Gd $1591
Sporting Clays Model 115S (imported 1995-97)................ NiB $4257 Ex $3414 Gd $2333

BRESCIA HAMMER DOUBLE............ NiB $1003 Ex $807 Gd $557

Back-action sidelock. Plain extractors. Double triggers. Gauges: 12, 20. Bbls.: 27.5 or 29.5-inch M/F choke in 12 ga. 25.5-inch IC/M choke in 20 ga.. Weight: From 5.75 to 7 lbs., depending on ga. and bbl. length. English-style stock and forearm, checkered. No longer imported.

ELIO .... NiB $1191 Ex $958 Gd $660

Lightweight game gun, 12 ga. only, w/same general specifications as Standard Gamecock (S. Uberto 1) except weight: About 6 to 6.25 lbs.; has automatic ejectors, fine English-pattern scroll engraving. No longer imported. See illustration next page.

Bernardelli Gamecock

Bernardelli Standard Gamecock

Bernardelli Gardone

Bernardelli Italia

Bernardelli Roma 6

Bernardelli Elio

GAMECOCK, PREMIER (ROME 3)

Same general specifications as Standard Gamecock (S. Uberto 1) except has sideplates, auto ejectors, single trigger. No longer imported.

Roma 3 (disc. 1989, Reintroduced 1993-97) . . . . NiB $1650 Ex $1324 Gd $908
Roma 3E (disc. 1950) Roma 3M w/single trigger (disc. 1997) . . . NiB $1838 Ex $1475 Gd $1011

GAMECOCK, STANDARD (S. UBERTO 1) HAMMERLESS DOUBLE-BARREL SHOTGUN . . . . NiB $1149 Ex $925 Gd $637

Boxlock. Plain extractors. Double triggers. Gauges: 12, 16, 20; 2.75-inch chambers in 12 and 16, 3-inch in 20 ga. Bbls. 25.5-inch IC/M choke; 27.5-inch M/F choke. Weight: 5.75-6.5 lbs., depending on ga. and bbl. length. English-style straight-grip stock and forearm, checkered. No longer imported.

GARDONE HAMMER DOUBLE . . . NiB $2602 Ex $2097 Gd $1470

Same general specifications as Brescia except for higher grade engraving and wood, but not as high as the Italia. Half-cock safety. Disc. 1956.

HEMINGWAY HAMMERLESS DOUBLE

Boxlock. Single or double triggers w/hinged front. Selective automatic ejectors. Gauges: 12 and 20 w/2.75- or 3-inch chambers, 16 and 28 w/2.75-inch. Bbls.: 23.5- to 28-inch w/fixed chokes. Weight: 6.25 lbs. Checkered English-style European walnut stock. Silvered and engraved receiver.

Standard model . . . . NiB $2097 Ex $1692 Gd $1175
Deluxe model w/sideplates (disc. 1993) . . . . . . NiB $2440 Ex $1963 Gd $1359
For single trigger, add $100

ITALIA . . . . NiB $3424 Ex $2739 Gd $1862

Same general specifications as Brescia except higher grade engraving and wood. Disc. 1986.

ROMA 4 AND ROMA 6

Same as Premier Gamecock (Rome 3) except higher grade engraving and wood, double triggers. Disc. 1997.

Roma 4 (disc. 1989) . . . . NiB $1336 Ex $1077 Gd $746
Roma 4E (disc. 1997) . . . . NiB $1668 Ex $1342 Gd $926
Roma 6 (disc. 1989) . . . . NiB $1374 Ex $1108 Gd $767
Roma 6E (disc. 1997) . . . . NiB $2064 Ex $1656 Gd $1144

ROMA 7, 8, AND 9

Side-by-side. Anson & Deeley boxlock; hammerless. Ejectors; double triggers. 12 ga. Barrels: 27.5-or 29.5-inch. M/F chokes. Fancy hand-checkered European walnut straight or pistol-grip stock, forearm. Elaborately engraved, silver-finished sideplates. Imported 1994-97.

Roma 7 . . . . NiB $2453 Ex $1972 Gd $1356
Roma 8 . . . . NiB $2974 Ex $2388 Gd $1639
Roma 9 . . . . NiB $3682 Ex $2955 Gd $2025

S. UBERTO 2 . . . . NiB $1445 Ex $1160 Gd $796
Same as Standard Gamecock (S. Uberto 1) except higher grade engraving and wood. Currently imported.

S. UBERTO F.S.
Same as Standard Gamecock except w/higher grade engraving, wood and has auto-ejectors. Disc. 1989, reintroduced 1993-97.
Model FS . . . . NiB $1788 Ex $1430 Gd $972
Model V.B. Incisio . . . . NiB $2037 Ex $1630 Gd $1108
W/single trigger, add $75

HOLLAND V.B. SERIES SHOTGUNS
Holland & Holland-type sidelock action. Auto-ejectors. Double triggers. 12 ga. only. Bbl. length or choke to custom specification. Silver-finish receiver (Liscio) or engraved coin finish receiver (Incisio). Extra-select wood and game scene engraving (Lusso). Checkered stock (straight or pistol-grip). Imported 1992-97.
Model V.B. Liscio. . . . . NiB $6234 Ex $4987 Gd $3391
Model V.B. Incisio . . . . NiB $7736 Ex $6188 Gd $4208
Model V.B. Lusso . . . . NiB $9223 Ex $7379 Gd $5018
Model V.B. Extra. . . . . NiB $10,726 Ex $8580 Gd $5834
Model V.B. Gold. . . . . NiB $37,636 Ex $30,108 Gd $20,473
Engraving Pattern No. 4, add. $950
Engraving Pattern No. 12, add. $4450
Engraving Pattern No. 20, add $8750
Single trigger, add. $595

Bernardelli Uberto 2

Bernardelli Uberto F.S.

BOSS & COMPANY — London, England

HAMMERLESS DOUBLE-BARREL SHOTGUN . . . . NiB $62,676 Ex $50,000 Gd $32,800
Sidelock. Automatic ejectors. Double triggers, non-selective or selective single trigger. Made in all gauges, bbl. lengths and chokes. Checkered stock and forend, straight or pistol-grip.

HAMMERLESS O/U SHOTGUN . . . . NiB $109,683 Ex $80,500 Gd $40,000
Sidelock. Automatic ejectors. Selective single trigger. Made in all gauges, bbl. lengths and chokes. Checkered stock and forend, straight or pistol-grip. Disc.

Bernardelli V.B. Holland Liscio

BREDA MECCANICA BRESCIANA — Brescia, Italy, *formerly ERNESTO BREDA, Milan, Italy*

AUTOLOADING SHOTGUN
Recoil-operated.12 ga, 2.75-inch chamber. Four round tubular magazine. Bbls.: 25.5- and 27.5-inch, plain, matted or vent rib, IC, M or F choke; current model has 26-inch vent-rib bbl. w/interchangeable choke tubes. Weight: About 7.25 lbs. Checkered straight or pistol-grip stock and forearm. Disc. 1988.
W/plain bbl. . . . . NiB $481 Ex $390 Gd $272
W/raised matted rib bbl. . . . . NiB $533 Ex $431 Gd $301
W/vent rib bbl. . . . . NiB $559 Ex $451 Gd $314
W/vent rib, interchangeable choke tubes. . . . . NiB $578 Ex $467 Gd $325

MAGNUM
Same general specifications as standard model except chambered for 12-ga. 3-inch Magnum, 3-round magazine; latest model has 29-inch vent-rib bbl. Disc. 1988.
W/plain bbl. NiB $605 Ex $479 Gd $325
W/vent rib bbl. . . . . NiB $618 Ex $513 Gd $357

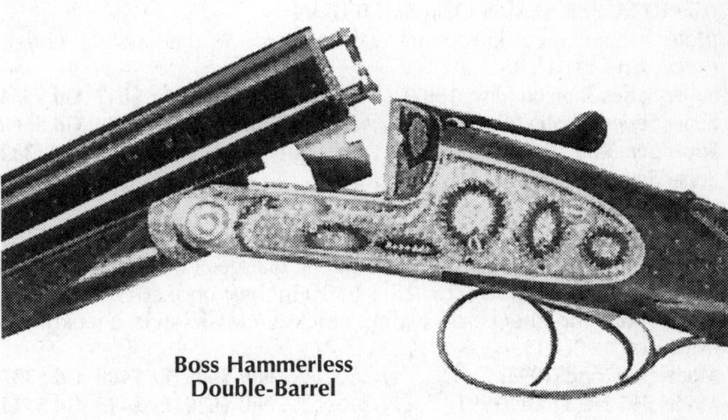
Boss Hammerless Double-Barrel

BRETTON SHOTGUNS — St. Etienne (Cedex1), France

BABY STANDARD SPRINT O/U .... NiB $1053 Ex $945 Gd $595
Inline sliding breech action. 12 or 20 gauge w/2.75-inch chambers. 27.5-inch separated bbls. w/vent rib and choke tubes. Weight: 4.8 to 5 lbs. Engraved alloy receiver. Checkered walnut buttstock and forearm w/satin oil finish. Imported 1992 to date.

SPRINT DELUXE O/U.................... NiB $950 Ex 826 Gd $538
Similar to the Standard Model except w/engraved coin-finished receiver and chambered 12, 16 and 20 ga. Discontinued 1994.

FAIR PLAY O/U............... NiB $1006 Ex $847 Gd $517
Lightweight action similar to the Sprint Model except w/hinged action that pivots open and is chambered 12 or 20 gauge only.

BRNO SHOTGUNS — Brno and Uherski Brod, Czech Republic, (formerly Czechoslovakia)

500 O/U SHOTGUN .... NiB $903 Ex $775 Gd $466
Hammerless boxlock w/double triggers and ejectors.12 ga. w/2.75-inch chambers. 27.5-inch bbls.. choked M/F. 44 inches overall. Weight: 7 lbs. Etched receiver. Checkered walnut stock w/classic style cheekplece. Imported 1987-91.

500 SERIES O/U COMBINATION GUNS
Similar to the 500 Series over/under shotgun, except w/lower . bbl. chambered in rifle calibers and set trigger option. Imported 1987-95.
Model 502 12/222, 12/243 (disc. 1991)..... NiB $1101 Ex $887 Gd $612
Model 502 12/308, 12/30.06 (disc. 1991) ... NiB $1148 Ex $924 Gd $637
Model 571 12/6x65R (disc. 1993) .... NiB $993 Ex $801 Gd $553
Model 572 12/7x65R (imported since 1992).... NiB $1070 Ex $862 Gd $594
Model 584 12/7x57R (imported since 1992)..... NiB $1101 Ex $887 Gd $612
Sport Series 4-bbl. set (disc. 1991) .... NiB $2918 Ex $2346 Gd $1614

CZ 581 SOLO O/U SHOTGUN........... NiB $834 Ex $671 Gd $463
Hammerless boxlock w/double triggers, ejectors and automatic safety. 12 ga. w/2.75- or 3-inch chambers. 28-inch bbls. choked M/F. Weight: 7.5 lbs. Checkered walnut stock. Disc. 1996.

SUPER SERIES O/U SHOTGUN
Hammerless sidelock w/selective single or double triggers and ejectors. 12 ga. w/2.75- or 3-inch chambers. 27.5-inch bbls. choked M/F. 44.5 inches overall. Weight: 7.25 lbs. Etched or engraved side
***(cont'd.)* SUPER SERIES O/U SHOTGUN**
plates. Checkered European walnut stock w/classic-style cheekpiece. Imported 1987-91.
Super Series Shotgun (disc. 1992).......... NiB $1052 Ex $847 Gd $584
Super Series Combo (disc. 1992) .... NiB $1230 Ex $989 Gd $660
Super Ser. 3-bbl. set (disc. 1990)......... NiB $2426 Ex $1946 Gd $1332
Super Series engraving, add $1250

ZH 300 SERIES O/U SHOTGUNS
Hammerless boxlock w/double triggers. Gauge: 12 or 16 w/2.75- or 3-inch chambers. Bbls.: 26, 27.5 or 30 inches; choked M/F. Weight: 7 lbs. Skip-line checkered walnut stock w/classic-style cheekpiece. Imported 1986-93.
Model 300 (disc. 1993) .... NiB $605 Ex $488 Gd $337
Model 301 Field (disc. 1991) .... NiB $620 Ex $499 Gd $345
Model 302 Skeet (disc. 1992) .... NiB $691 Ex $556 Gd $384
Model 303 Trap (disc. 1992) .... NiB $718 Ex $578 Gd $399

ZH 300 SERIES O/U COMBINATION GUNS
Similar to the 300 Series over/under shotgun except lower bbl. chambered in rifle calibers.
Model 300 Combo
8-bbl. Set (disc. 1991) .... NiB $3441 Ex $2773 Gd $1918
Model 304 12 ga./7x57R (disc. 1995) .... NiB $706 Ex $571 Gd $398
Model 305 12 ga./5.6x52R (disc. 1993) ...... NiB $796 Ex $643 Gd $447
Model 306 12 ga./5.6x50R (disc. 1993) ...... NiB $834 Ex $674 Gd $468
Model 307 12 ga./.22 Hornet
(Imported since 1995) .... NiB $739 Ex $597 Gd $415
Model 324 16 ga./7x57R (disc. 1987 .... NiB $771 Ex $622 Gd $433

ZP 149 HAMMERLESS DOUBLE
Sidelock action w/double triggers, automatic ejectors and automatic safety.12 ga. w/2.75- or 3-inch chambers. 28.5-inch bbls. choked M/F. Weight: 7.25 lbs. Checkered walnut buttstock w/cheekpiece.
Standard model .... NiB $642 Ex $519 Gd $463
Engraved model .... NiB $700 Ex $566 Gd $495

BROLIN ARMS, INC. — Pomona, California

ARMS HAWK PUMP SHOTGUN, FIELD SERIES
Slide-action. Gauge: 12 ga. w/3-inch chamber. 24-, 26-, 28- or 30-inch bbl. 44 and 50 inches overall. Weight: 7.3 to 7.6 lbs. Cross-bolt safety. Vent rib bbl. w/screw-in choke tube and bead sights. Non-reflective metal finish. Synthetic or oil-finished wood stock w/swivel studs. Made 1997-98.
Synthetic stock model .... NiB $237 Ex $193 Gd $135
Wood stock model.............. NiB $224 Ex $182 Gd $128

ARMS HAWK PUMP SHOTGUN COMBO MODEL
Similar to the Field Model except w/extra 18.5- or 22-inch bbl. w/bead or rifle sight. Made 1997-98.
Synthetic stock model .... NiB $259 Ex $209 Gd $146
Wood stock model.............. NiB $246 Ex $198 Gd $139

ARMS HAWK PUMP SHOTGUN LAWMAN MODEL
Similar to the Field Model except has 18.5-inch bbl. w/cylinder bore fixed choke. Weight: 7 lbs. Dual operating bars. Bead, rifle or ghost ring sights. Black synthetic or wood stock. Matte chrome or satin nickel finish. Made 1997-99.
Synthetic stock model .... NiB $220 Ex $178 Gd $124
Wood stock model .... NiB $208 Ex $168 Gd $117
Rifle sights, add.. $20
Ghost ring sights, add...................................... $35
Satin nickel finish (disc. 1997), add $25

ARMS HAWK SLUG MODEL
Similar to the Field Model except has 18.5- or 22-inch bbl. w/IC fixed choke or 4-inch extended rifled choke. Rifle or ghost ring sights or optional cantilevered scope mount. Black synthetic or wood stock. Matte blued finish. Made 1998-99.
Synthetic stock model .... NiB $220 Ex $178 Gd $124
Wood stock model .... NiB $208 Ex $168 Gd $117
W/rifled bbl., add $20
W/cantilevered scope mount, add $35

ARMS HAWK TURKEY SPECIAL
Similar to the Field Model except has 22-inch vent-rib bbl. w/extended extra-full choke. Rifle or ghost ring sights or optional cantilevered scope mount. Black synthetic or wood stock. Matte blued finish. Made 1998-99.
Synthetic stock model .... NiB $214 Ex $173 Gd $121
Wood stock model .... NiB $202 Ex $163 Gd $114
W/cantilevered
scope mount, add $25

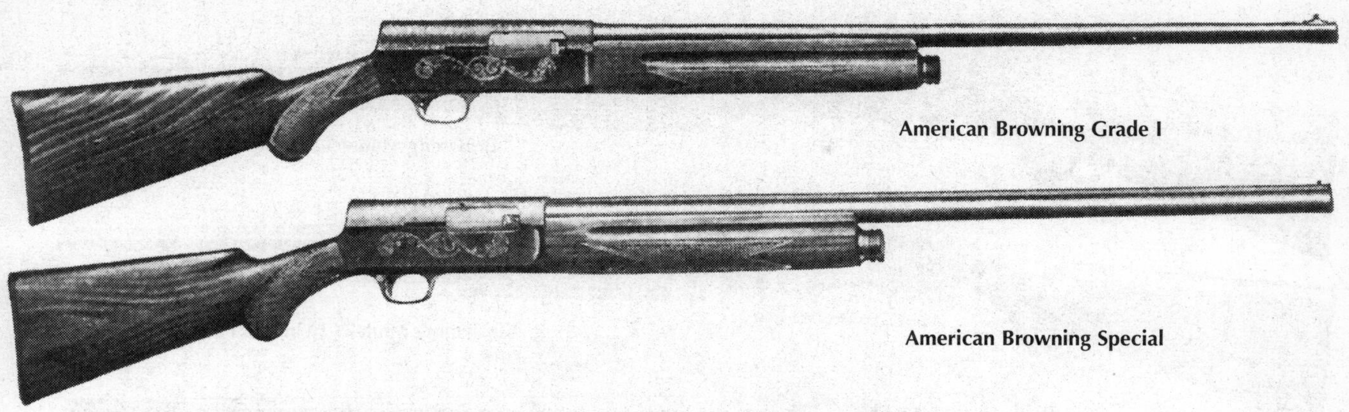
American Browning Grade I

American Browning Special

BROWNING SHOTGUNS — Morgan (formerly Ogden), Utah

AMERICAN BROWNING SHOTGUNS

Designated "American" Browning because they were produced in Ilion, New York, the following Remington-made Brownings are almost identical to the Remington Model 11A and Sportsman and the Browning Auto-5. They are the only Browning shotguns manufactured in the U.S. during the 20th century and were made for Browning Arms when production was suspended in Belgium because of WW II.

NOTE: *Fabrique Nationale Herstal (formerly Fabrique Nationale d'Armes de Guerre) of Herstal, Belgium, is the longtime manufacturer of Browning shotguns dating back to 1900. Miroku Firearms Mfg. Co. of Tokyo, Japan, bought into the Browning company and has, since the early 1970s, undertaken some of the production. The following shotguns were manufactured for Browning by these two firms.*

GRADE I AUTOLOADER (AUTO-5)

Recoil-operated autoloader. Similar to the Remington Model 11A except w/different style engraving and identified w/the Browning logo. Gauges: 12, 16 or 20. Plain 26- to 32-inch bbl. w/any standard boring. Two or four shell tubular magazine w/magazine cut-off. Weight: About 6.88 lbs. (20 ga.) to 8 lbs. (12 ga.). Checkered pistol-grip stock and forearm. Made 1940-49.

(*cont'd.*) GRADE I AUTOLOADER (AUTO-5)
American Browning Grade I
Auto-5, 12 or 16 ga. . . . . NiB $717 Ex $614 Gd $280
20 ga., add. 20%

SPECIAL 441

Same general specifications as Grade I except supplied w/raised matted rib or vent rib. Disc. 1949.

W/raised matted rib . . . . NiB $795 Ex $692 Gd $357
W/vent rib . . . . NiB $820 Ex $717 Gd $357
20 ga., add. 20%

SPECIAL SKEET MODEL . . . . NiB $698 Ex $563 Gd $390

Same general specifications as Grade I except has 26-inch bbl. w/vent rib and Cutts Compensator. Disc. 1949.

UTILITY FIELD GUN. . . . . NiB $537 Ex $331 Gd $228

Same general specifications as Grade I except has 28-inch plain bbl. w/Poly Choke. Disc. 1949.

MODEL 12 PUMP SHOTGUN

Special limited edition Winchester Model 12. Gauge: 20 or 28. Five-round tubular magazine. 26-inch bbl., M choke. 45 inches overall. Weight: about 7 lbs. Grade I has blued receiver, checkered walnut stock w/matte finish. Grade V has engraved receiver, checkered deluxe walnut stock w/high-gloss finish. Made 1988-92. See illustration next page.

Grade I,
20 ga. (8600) . . . . NiB $602 Ex $486 Gd $337
Grade I, 28 ga. . . . . NiB $634 Ex $511 Gd $355
Grade V,
20 ga (4000) . . . . NiB $1055 Ex $850 Gd $587
Grade V, 28 ga . . . . NiB $1020 Ex $820 Gd $565

MODEL 42 LIMITED EDITION SHOTGUN

Special limited edition Winchester Model 42 pump shotgun. Same general specifications as Model 12 except w/smaller frame in .410 ga. and 3-inch chamber. Made 1991-93.

Grade I
(6000 produced) . . . . NiB $660 Ex $532 Gd $369
Grade V
(6000 produced) . . . . NiB $1055 Ex $840 Gd $588

2000 BUCK SPECIAL. . . . . NiB $428 Ex $346 Gd $242

Same as Field Model except has 24-inch plain bbl. Bored for rifled slug and buckshot, fitted w/rifle sights (open rear, ramp front). 12 ga., 2.75-inch or 3-inch chamber; 20 ga., 2.75-inch chamber. Weight: 12 ga., 7 lbs., 8 oz.; 20 ga., 6 lbs., 10 oz. Made 1974-81 by FN.

2000 GAS AUTOMATIC SHOTGUN, FIELD MODEL

Gas-operated. Gauge: 12 or 20. 2.75-inch chamber. Four-round magazine. Bbl.: 26-, 28-, 30-inch, any standard choke plain matted bbl. (12 ga. only) or vent rib. Weight: 6 lbs. 11 oz.-7 lbs. 12 oz. depending on ga. and bbl. length. Checkered pistol-grip stock/forearm. Made 1974-81 by FN; Assembled in Port gal.

W/plain
matted bbl. . . . . NiB $592 Ex $360 Gd $257
W/vent rib bbl. . . . . NiB $602 Ex $386 Gd $262

2000 MAGNUM MODEL . . . . NiB $602 Ex $386 Gd $262

Same as Field Model except chambered for 3-inch shells, three-round magazine. Bbl.: 26- (20 ga. only), 28-, 30- or 32-inch (latter two 12 ga. only); any standard choke; vent rib. Weight: 6 lbs., 11 oz.-7 lbs., 13 oz. depending on ga. and bbl. Made 1974-81 by FN.

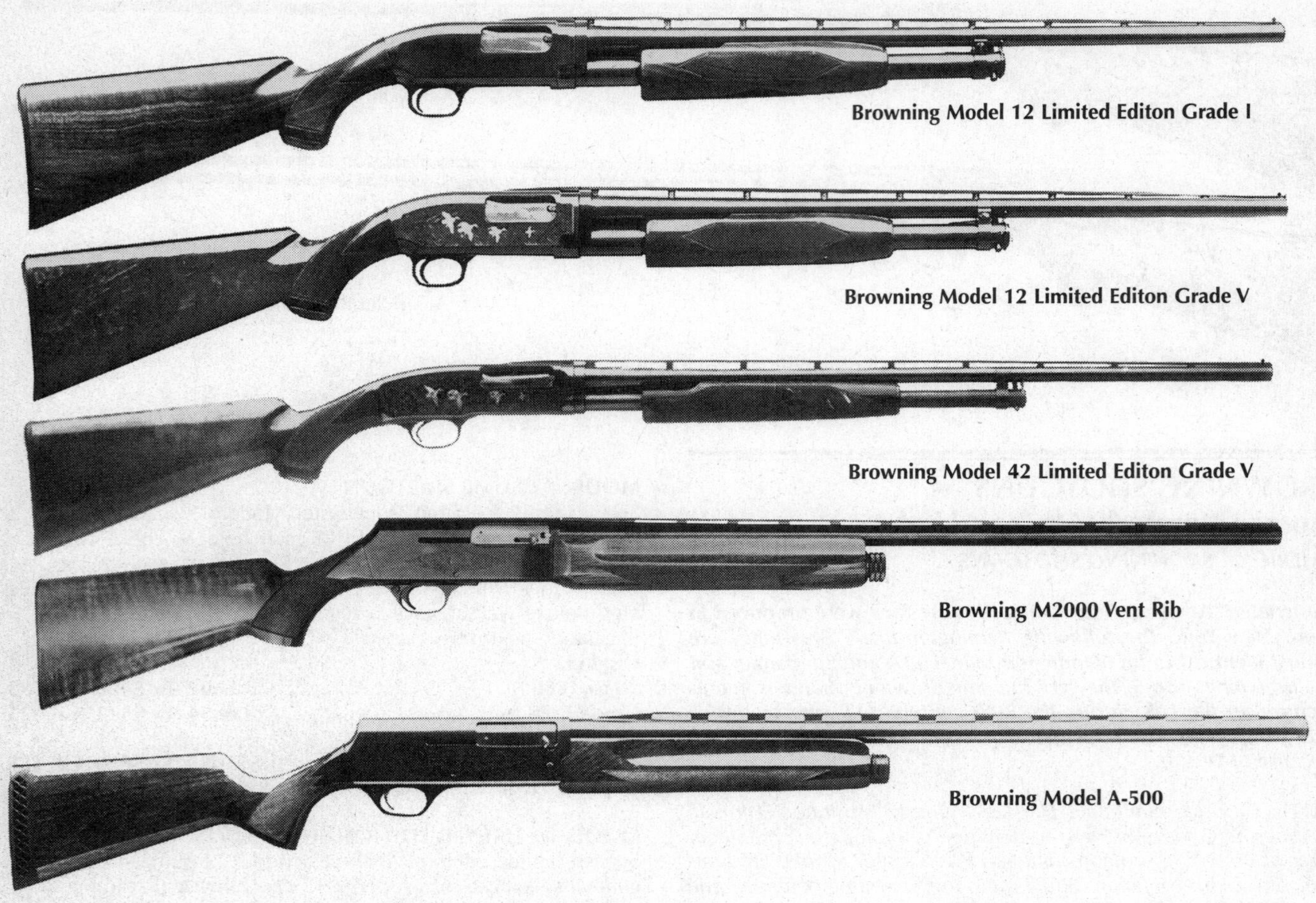

2000 SKEET MODEL . . . . NiB $464 Ex $375 Gd $262
Same as Field Model except has skeet-style stock w/recoil pad, 26-inch vent-rib bbl., SK choke. 12 or 20 ga., 2.75-inch chamber. Weight: 8 lbs., 1 oz. (12 ga.); 6 lbs., 12 oz. (20 ga.) Made 1974-81 by FN.

2000 TRAP MODEL. . . . . NiB $464 Ex $375 Gd $262
Same as Field Model except has Monte Carlo stock w/recoil pad, 30- or 32-inch bbl. w/high-post vent rib and receiver extension, M/I/F chokes. 12 ga., 2.75-inch chamber. Weight: About 8 lbs., 5 oz. Made 1974-81 by FN.

A-500G GAS-OPERATED SEMIAUTOMATIC
Same general specifications as Browning Model A-500R except gas-operated. Made 1990-93.
Buck Special . . . . NiB $588 Ex $478 Gd $338
Hunting model . . . . NiB $601 Ex $489 Gd $345

A-500G SPORTING CLAYS . . . . NiB $601 Ex $489 Gd $345
Same general specifications as Model A-500G except has matte blued receiver w/"Sporting Clays" logo. 28- or 30-inch bbl. w/Invector choke tubes. Made 1992-93.

A-500R SEMIAUTOMATIC
Recoil-operated. Gauge: 12. 26- to 30-inch vent-rib bbls. 24-inch Buck Special. Invector choke tube system. 2.75- or 3-inch Magnum cartridges. Weight: 7 lbs., 3 oz.-8 lbs., 2 oz. Cross-bolt safety. Gold-plated trigger. Scroll-engraved receiver. Gloss-finished walnut stock

(*cont'd.*) **A-500R SEMIAUTOMATIC**
and forend. Made by FN from 1987-93.
Hunting model . . . . NiB $593 Ex $478 Gd $332
Buck Special . . . . NiB $632 Ex $509 Gd $353

A-BOLT SERIES SHOTGUN
Bolt-action repeating single-barrel shotgun. 12 ga. only w/3-inch chambers, 2-round magazine. 22- or 23-inch rifled bbl., w/or w/o a rifled invector tube. Receiver drilled and tapped for scope mounts. Bbl. w/ or w/o open sights. Checkered walnut or graphite/fiberglass composite stock. Matte black metal finish. Imported 1995-98.
Stalker model w/
composite stock . . . . NiB $426 Ex $344 Gd $240
Hunter model w/walnut stock . . . . NiB $406 Ex $329 Gd $230
W/rifled bbl., add $95
W/open sights, add $25

AUTOLOADING SHOTGUNS, GRADES II, III AND IV
These higher grade models differ from the Standard or Grade I in general quality, grade of wood, checkering, engraving, etc., otherwise specifications are the same. Grade IV guns, sometimes called Midas Grade, are inlaid w/yellow and green gold. Disc. in 1940.
Grade II, plan bbl. . . . . NiB $1434 Ex $1232 Gd $849
Grade III, plain bbl. . . . . NiB $2773 Ex $2413 Gd $1655
Grade IV, plain bbl.. . . . . NiB $4138 Ex $3855 Gd $3665
For raised matte rib bbl., add 15%
For vent rib bbl., add. 30%

Browning Model A-Bolt Hunter

Browning Model A-Bolt Stalker

Browning Automatic-5 Gold Classic

Browning Automatic-5 Buck Special

Browning Automatic-5 Classic

AUTOMATIC-5, LIGHT 20
Same general specifications as Standard Model except lightweight and 20 ga. Bbl.: 26- or 28-inch; plain or vent rib. Weight: About 6.25-6.5 lbs. depending on bbl. Made 1958-76 by FN, since then by Miroku.
FN manuf., plain bbl.. . . . . NiB $688 Ex $555 Gd $385
FN manuf., vent-rib bbl. . . . . NiB $901 Ex $823 Gd $488
Miroku manuf., vent rib,fixed choke . . NiB $823 Ex $638 Gd $334
Miroku manuf., vent rib, invectors . . . NiB $875 Ex $695 Gd $385

AUTOMATIC-5, BUCK SPECIAL MODELS
Same as Light 12, Magnum 12, Light 20, Magnum 20, in respective gauges, except 24-inch plain bbl. bored for rifled slug and buckshot, fitted w/rifle sights (open rear, ramp front). Weight: 6.13-8.25 lbs. depending on ga. Made 1964-76 by FN, since then by Miroku.
FN manuf., w/plain bbl. . . . . NiB $901 Ex $638 Gd $375
Miroku manuf., ... NiB $772 Ex $591 Gd $360
W/3-inch mag. rec., add 10%

AUTOMATIC-5 CLASSIC. . . . . NiB $1153 Ex $901 Gd $798
Gauge: 12. 5-round capacity. 28-inch vent rib bbl./M choke. 2.75-

***(cont'd.)* AUTOMATIC-5 CLASSIC**
inch chamber. Engraved silver-gray receiver. Gold-plated trigger. Crossbolt safety. High-grade, hand-checkered select American walnut stock w/rounded pistol grip. 5,000 issued; made in Japan in 1984, engraved in Belgium.

AUTOMATIC-5 GOLD CLASSIC. . . . . . NiB $4014 Ex $3344 Gd $2469
Same general specifications as Automatic-5 Classic except engraved receiver inlaid w/gold. Pearl border on stock and forend plus fine-line hand-checkering. Each gun numbered "1 of Five Hundred," etc. 500 issued in 1984; made in Belgium.

AUTOMATIC-5, LIGHT 12
12 ga. only. Same general specifications as Standard Model except lightweight (about 7.25 lbs.), has gold-plated trigger. Guns w/rib have striped matting on top of bbl. Fixed chokes or Invector tubes. Made 1948-76 by FN, since then by Miroku.
FN manuf., plain bbl. . . . . NiB $623 Ex $506 Gd $358
FN manuf., raised matte rib . . . . . . NiB $713 Ex $609 Gd $491
FN manuf., ventilated rib . . . . NiB $919 Ex $790 Gd $506
Miroku manuf., vent rib, fixed choke . . NiB $623 Ex $506 Gd $358
Miroku manuf., vent rib, invectors . . . NiB $841 Ex $656 Gd $403

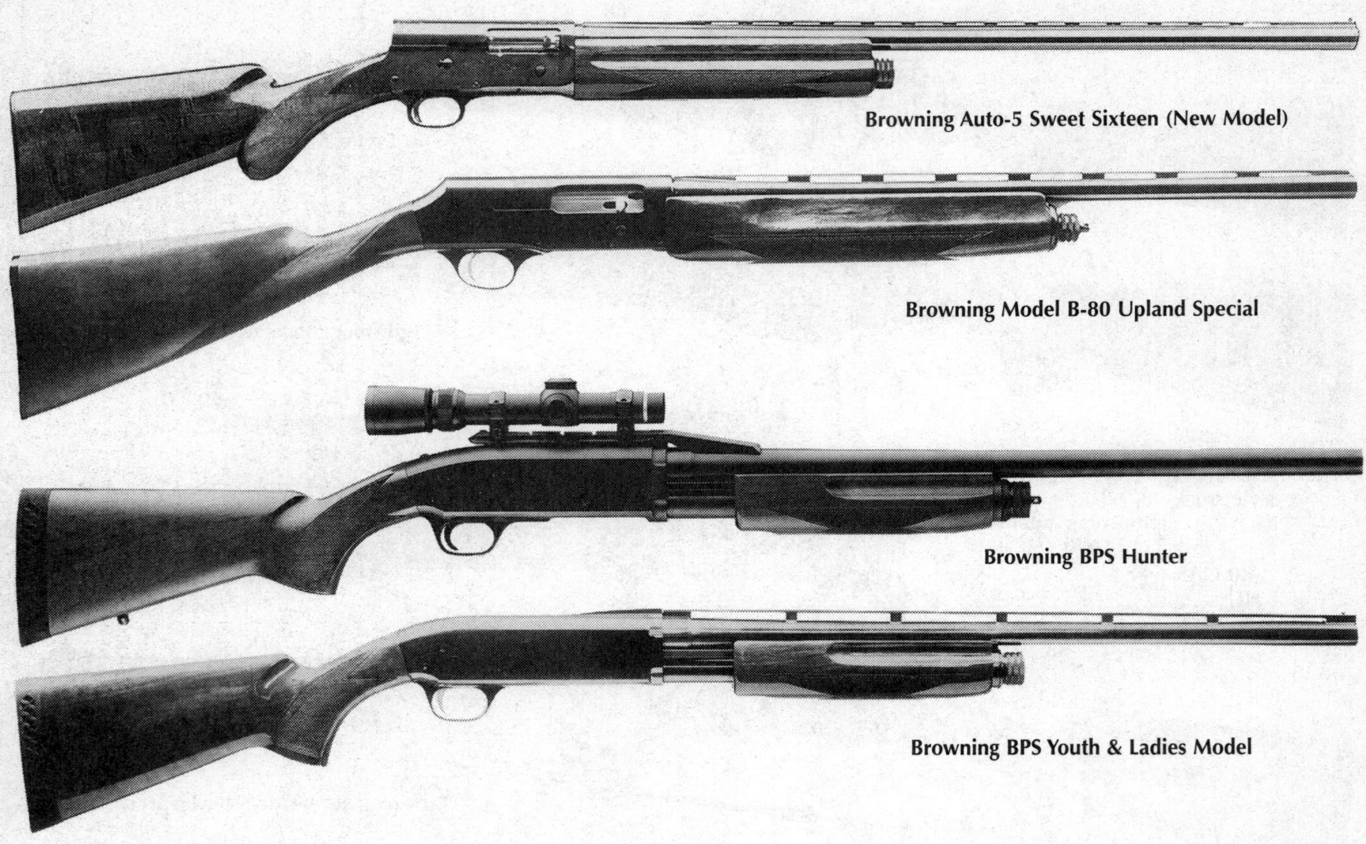

Browning Auto-5 Sweet Sixteen (New Model)

Browning Model B-80 Upland Special

Browning BPS Hunter

Browning BPS Youth & Ladies Model

AUTOMATIC-5, MAGNUM 12 GAUGE

Same general specifications as Standard Model. Chambered for 3-inch Magnum 12-ga. shells. Bbl.: 28-inch M/F, 30- or 32-inch F/F, plain or vent rib. Weight: 8.5-9 lbs. depending on bbl. Buttstock has recoil pad. Made 1958-76 by FN, since then by Miroku. Fixed chokes or Invector tubes.

FN manuf., plain bbl. . . . . NiB $822 Ex $663 Gd $461
FN manuf., vent rib bbl. . . . . NiB $888 Ex $717 Gd $497
Miroku manuf., vent rib, fixed chokes . . NiB $674 Ex $545 Gd $380
Miroku manuf., vent rib, invectors . . . . NiB $762 Ex $616 Gd $429

AUTOMATIC-5, MAGNUM 20 GAUGE

Same general specifications as Standard Model except chambered for 3-inch Magnum 20-ga. shell. Bbl.: 26- or 28-inch, plain or vent rib. Weight: 7 lbs., 5 oz.-7 lbs., 7 oz. depending on bbl. Made 1967-76 by FN, since then by Miroku.

FN manuf., plain bbl. . . . . NiB $815 Ex $658 Gd $457
FN manuf., vent rib bbl. . . . . NiB $859 Ex $679 Gd $480
Miroku manuf., vent rib, invectors . NiB $679 Ex $549 Gd $382

AUTOMATIC-5, SKEET MODEL

12 ga. only. Same general specifications as Light 12. Bbl.: 26-or 28-inch, plain or vent rib, SK choke. Weight: 7 lbs., 5 oz.-7 lbs., 10 oz. depending on bbl. Made by FN prior to 1976, since then by Miroku.

FN manuf., plain bbl. . . . . NiB $762 Ex $616 Gd $429
FN manuf., vent rib bbl. . . . . NiB $807 Ex $651 Gd $452
Miroku manuf., vent rib bbl. . . . . . NiB $615 Ex $498 Gd $348

AUTOMATIC-5 STALKER

Same general specifications as Automatic-5 Light and Magnum models except w/matte blue finish and black graphite fiberglass stock and forearm. Made 1992 to date.

Light model . . . . NiB $826 Ex $707 Gd $474
Magnum model . . . . NiB $875 Ex $706 Gd $489

AUTOMATIC-5, STANDARD (GRADE I)

Recoil-operated. Gauge: 12 or 16 (16-gauge guns made prior to WW II were chambered for 2-inch shells; standard 16 disc. 1964). Four shell magazine in 5-round model, prewar guns were also available in 3-round model. Bbls.: 26- to 32-inch; plain, raised matted or vent rib; choice of standard chokes. Weight: About 8 lbs., in 12 ga., 7.5 lbs., in 16 ga. Checkered pistol-grip stock and forearm. (Note: Browning Special, disc. about 1940.) Made 1900-73 by FN.

Grade I, plain bbl. . . . . NiB $666 Ex $538 Gd $376
Grade I or Browning Special,
Raised matted rib . . . . NiB $842 Ex $680 Gd $471
Grade I or Browning Special, vent rib . . . . NiB $866 Ex $700 Gd $485

AUTOMATIC-5, SWEET 16

16 ga. Same general specifications as Standard Model except lightweight (about 6.75 lbs.), has gold plated trigger. Guns w/rib have striped matting on top of bbl. Made 1937-76 by FN.

W/plain bbl. . . . . $NiB $754 Ex $609 Gd $423
W/raised matted or ventilated rib . . . . NiB $826 Ex $667 Gd $474

AUTO-5,
SWEET SIXTEEN NEW MODEL . . . . NiB $922 Ex $744 Gd $515

Reissue of popular 16-gauge Hunting Model w/5-round capacity, 2.75-inch chamber, scroll-engraved blued receiver, high-gloss French walnut stock w/rounded pistol grip. 26- or 28-inch vent-rib bbl. F choke tube. Weight: 7 lbs., 5 oz. Reintro. 1987-93.

Browning BPS Waterfowl – Mossy Oak Shadow Grass

Browning BPS Stalker

AUTOMATIC-5, TRAP MODEL . . . . NiB $906 Ex $699 Gd $442
12 ga. only. Same general specifications as Standard Model except has trap-style stock, 30-inch vent-rib bbl. F choke. Weight: 8.5 lbs. Disc. 1971.

MODEL B-80 GAS-OPERATED AUTOMATIC . . . . NiB $539 Ex $437 Gd $307
Gauge: 12 or 20; 2.75-inch chamber. Four round magazine. Bbl.: 26-, 28- or 30-inch, any standard choke, vent-rib bbl. w/fixed chokes or Invector tubes. Weight: 6 lbs., 12 oz.-8 lbs., 1 oz. depending on ga. and bbl. Checkered pistol-grip stock and forearm. Made 1981-87.

MODEL B-80 PLUS . . . . NiB $590 Ex $478 Gd $335
Same general specifications as Browning Model B-80 except chambered for 3-inch shotshells. Made in 1988 only.

MODEL B-80 SUPERLIGHT . . . . NiB $539 Ex $437 Gd $307
Same as Standard Model except weighs 1 lb. less.

MODEL B-80 UPLAND SPECIAL . . NiB $551 Ex $447 Gd $313
Gauge: 12 or 20. 22-inch vent-rib bbl. Invector choke tube system. 2.75-inch chambers. 42 inches overall. Weight: 5 lbs., 7 oz. (20 ga.); 6 lbs., 10 oz. (12 ga.). German nickel silver sight bead. Crossbolt safety. Checkered walnut straight-grip stock and forend. Disc. 1988.

BPS GAME GUN DEER SPECIAL . . . NiB $481 Ex $390 Gd $275
Same general specifications as Standard BPS model except has 20.5-inch bbl. w/adj. rifle-style sights. Solid scope mounting system. Checkered walnut stock w/sling swivel studs. Made from 1992 to date.

BPS GAME GUN TURKEY SPECIAL . . . . . . NiB $494 Ex $401 Gd $282
Same general specifications as Standard BPS model except w/matte blue metal finish and satin-finished stock. Chambered for 12 ga. 3-inch only. 20.5-inch bbl. w/extra full invector choke system. Receiver drilled and tapped for scope. Made 1992 to date.

BPS PIGEON GRADE . . . . NiB $642 Ex $519 Gd $363
Same general specifications as Standard BPS model except w/select grade walnut stock and gold-trimmed receiver. Available in 12 ga. only w/26- or 28-inch vent-rib bbl. Made 1992 to date.

BPS PUMP INVECTOR STALKER
Same general specifications as BPS Pump Shotgun except in 10 and 12 ga. w/Invector choke system, 22-, 26-, 28- or 30-inch bbls.; matte blue metal finish w/matte black stock. Made 1987 to date.
12 ga. model (3-inch) . . . . NiB $462 Ex $375 Gd $265
10- & 12 ga. model (3.5-inch) . . . . NiB $628 Ex $509 Gd $355

BPS PUMP SHOTGUN
Takedown. Gauges: 10, 12 (3.5-inch chamber); 12, 20 and .410 (3-inch) and 28 ga. chambered 2.75-inch. Bbls.: 22-, 24-, 26-, 28-, 30-, or 32-inch; fixed choke or Invector tubes. Weight: 7.5 lbs. (w/28-inch bbl.). Checkered select walnut pistol-grip stock and semi-beavertail forearm, recoil pad. Introduced in 1977. Made by Miroku.
Model BPS Magnum Hunter . . . . NiB $642 Ex $519 Gd $363
Model BPS Magnum Stalker . . . . NiB $622 Ex $504 Gd $352
Model BPS Magnum Camo . . . . NiB $699 Ex $566 Gd $395
Model BPS Hunter . . . . NiB $539 Ex $437 Gd $307
Model BPS Upland . . . . NiB $539 Ex $437 Gd $307
Model BPS Stalker (26- 28- or 30-inch bbl.) . . . NiB $519 Ex $421 Gd $296
Model BPS Stalker 24-inch bbl . . . . NiB $545 Ex $442 Gd $310
Model BPS Game Gun—Turkey Special . . . . . . NiB $577 Ex $468 Gd $328
Model BPS Game Gun—fully rifled bbl. . . . . . . NiB $648 Ex $524 Gd $366
Model BPS Hunter 20 ga. . . . . NiB $539 Ex $437 Gd $307
Model BPS Upland 20 ga. . . . . NiB $539 Ex $437 Gd $307
Model BPS Micro . . . . NiB $539 Ex $437 Gd $307
Model BPS Hunter 28 ga. . . . . NiB $571 Ex $463 Gd $325
Model BPS Bore Hunter .410 . . . . NiB $571 Ex $463 Gd $325
Model BPS Buck Spec. (10 or 12 ga., 3.5-inch) . . . . NiB $610 Ex $494 Gd $345
Model BPS Buck Spec. (12 or 20 ga.) . . . . NiB $436 Ex $354 Gd $250
Model BPS Waterfowl
(10 or 12 ga., 3.5-inch) . . . . NiB $668 Ex $540 Gd $377
W/fixed choke, deduct $50

BPS YOUTH AND LADIES' MODEL
Lightweight (6 lbs., 11 oz.) version of BPS Pump Shotgun in 20 ga. w/22-inch bbl. and floating vent rib, F choke (invector) tube. Made 1986 to date.
Standard Invector model (disc. 1994) . . . . NiB $405 Ex $329 Gd $232
Invector Plus model . . . . NiB $443 Ex $360 Gd $253

BSA 10 SEMIAUTOMATIC SHOTGUN
Gas-operated short-stroke action. 10 ga.; 3.5-inch chamber. Five round magazine. Bbls.: 26-, 28-or 30-inches w/Invector tubes and vent rib. Weight: 10.5 lbs. Checkered select walnut buttstock and forend. Blued finish. Made 1993 to date. Note: Although intro. as the BSA 10, this model is now marketed as the Gold Series. See separate listing for pricing.

B-SS SIDE-BY-SIDE
Boxlock. Automatic ejectors. Non-selective single trigger (early production) or selective-single trigger (late production). Gauges: 12 or 20 w/3-inch chambers. Bbls.: 26-, 28-, or 30-inches; IC/M, M/F, or F/F chokes; matte solid rib. Weight: 7 to 7.5 lbs. Checkered straight-grip stock and beavertail forearm. Made 1972-88 by Miroku.
Standard model (early/NSST) . . . . NiB $572 Ex $463 Gd $323
Standard model (late/SST) . . . . NiB $663 Ex $535 Gd $372
Grade II (antique silver receiver) . . . . NiB $1120 Ex $901 Gd $620
20 ga. models, add $100

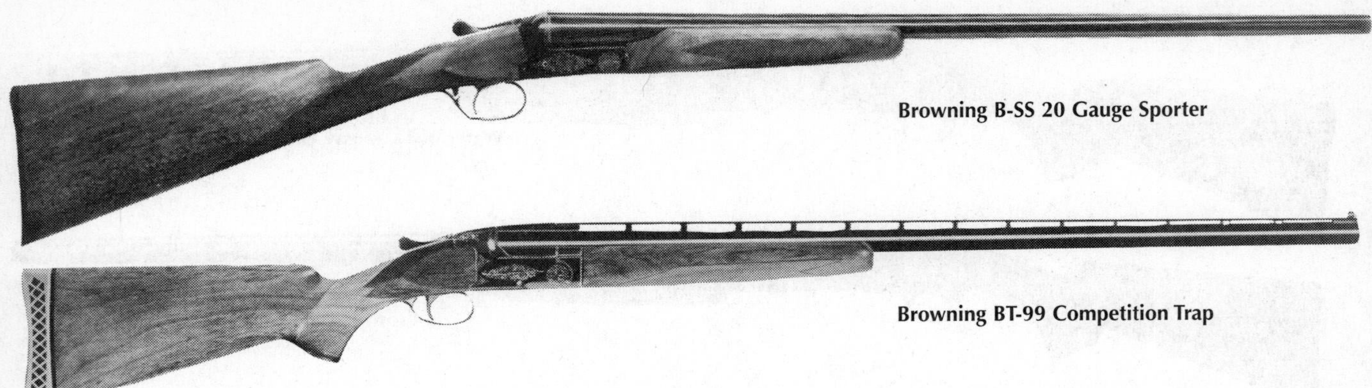

Browning B-SS 20 Gauge Sporter

Browning BT-99 Competition Trap

B-SS SIDE-BY-SIDE SIDELOCK

Same general specifications as B-SS boxlock models except sidelock version available in 26- or 28-inch bbl. lengths. 26-inch choked IC/M; 28-inch, M/F. Double triggers. Satin-grayed receiver engraved w/rosettes and scrolls. German nickel-silver sight bead. Weight: 6.25 lbs. to 6 lbs., 11 oz. 12 ga. made in 1983; 20 ga. Made in 1984. Disc. 1988.

12 ga. model . . . . NiB $952 Ex $725 Gd $1009
20 ga. model . . . . NiB $2508 Ex $2015 Gd $1385

B-SS S/S 20 GAUGE SPORTER . . . . NiB $773 Ex $624 Gd $434

Same as standard B-SS 20 ga. except has selective single trigger, straight-grip stock. Introduced 1977. Disc. 1987.

BT-99 GRADE I SINGLE BBL. TRAP . . . . . . NiB $829 Ex $670 Gd $465

Boxlock. Automatic ejector. 12 ga. only. 32- or 34-inch vent rib bbl., M, IM or F choke. Weight: About 8 lbs. Checkered pistol-grip stock and beavertail forearm, recoil pad. Made 1971-76 by Miroku.

BT-99 MAX

Boxlock. 12 ga. only w/ejector selector and no safety. 32- or 34-inch ported bbl. w/high post vent rib. Checkered select walnut buttstock and finger-grooved forend w/high luster finish. Engraved receiver w/blued or stainless metal finish. Made 1995-96.

Blued . . . . NiB $1207 Ex $971 Gd $671
Stainless. NiB $1809 Ex $1445 Gd $992

BT-99 PLUS

Similar to the BT-99 Competition except w/Browning Recoil Reduction System. Made 1989-95.

Grade I . . . . NiB $1183 Ex $952 Gd $657
Pigeon grade . . . . NiB $1349 Ex $1086 Gd $738
Signature grade . . . . NiB $1311 Ex $1055 Gd $727
Stainless model . . . . NiB $1440 Ex $1158 Gd $797
Golden Clays . . . . NiB $2484 Ex $2305 Gd $2047

BT-99 PLUS MICRO. . . . . NiB $1219 Ex $991 Gd $676

Same general specifications as BT-99 Plus except scaled down for smaller shooters. 30-inch bbl. w/adj. rib and Browning's recoil reducer system. Made 1991 to date.

BT-100 COMPETITION TRAP SPECIAL

Same as BT-99 except has super-high wide rib and standard Monte Carlo or fully adj. stock. Available w/adj. choke or Invector Plus tubes w/optional porting. Made 1976-94.

Grade I w/fixed
choke (disc. 1992). . . . . NiB $902 Ex $751 Gd $505
Grade I w/Invectors . . . . NiB $1120 Ex $901 Gd $620
Grade I stainless (disc. 1994) . . . . NiB $1178 Ex $947 Gd $652
Grade I Pigeon Grade (disc. 1994) . . . . . NiB $1087 Ex $875 Gd $603

BT-100 SINGLE-SHOT TRAP

Similar to the BT-99 Max, except w/additional stock options and removable trigger group. Made 1995 to date.

Model BT-100 Grade I blued. . . . . NiB $1441 Ex $1158 Gd $795
Model BT-100 stainless . . . . NiB $1667 Ex $1338 Gd $918
Model BT-100 satin. . . . . NiB $1344 Ex $1081 Gd $743
Model BT-100 w/adj. comb, add. $250
Thumbhole stock, add. $295
Replacement trigger assembly, add. $495
Fixed choke, deduct $65

CITORI HUNTING O/U MODELS

Boxlock. Gauges: 12, 16 (disc. 1989), 20, 28 (disc. 1992) and .410 bore (disc. 1989). Bbl. lengths: 24-, 26-, 28-, or 30-inch w/vent rib. Chambered 2.75-, 3- or 3.5-inch mag. Chokes: IC/M, M/F (Fixed Chokes); Standard Invector, or Invector plus choke systems. Overall length ranges from 41-47 inches. 2.75-, 3- or 3-inch Mag. loads, depending on ga. Weight: 5.75 lbs. to 7 lbs. 13 oz. Single selective, gold-plated trigger. Medium raised German nickel-silver sight bead. Checkered, rounded pistol-grip walnut stock w/beavertail forend. Invector Chokes and Invector Plus became standard in 1988 and 1995, respectively. Made from 1973 to date by Miroku.

Grade I (disc. 1994) . . . . NiB $824 Ex $664 Gd $458
Grade I - 3.5-inch Mag.(1989 to date) . . . NiB $1108 Ex $890 Gd $612
Grade II (disc. 1983). . . . . NiB $1018 Ex $818 Gd $563
Grade III (1985-95) . . . . NiB $1173 Ex $942 Gd $647
Grade V (disc. 1984). . . . . NiB $1630 Ex $1308 Gd $896
Grade VI (1985-95). . . . . NiB $1816 Ex $1457 Gd $997
Model Sporting Hunter
(12 and 20 ga.; 1998 to date). . . . . NiB $986 Ex $793 Gd $545
Model Satin Hunter
(12 ga. only; 1998 to date). . . . . NiB $889 Ex $715 Gd $493
Mdls. w/o Inv. choke syst., deduct $120
For 3.5-inch Mag., add $90
For disc. ga 16, 28 and .410, add 15%

CITORI LIGHTNING O/U MODELS

Same general specifications as the Citori Hunting models except w/classic Browning rounded pistol-grip stock. Made from 1988 to date by Miroku.

Grade I . . . . NiB $852 Ex $687 Gd $476
Grade III . . . . NiB $1270 Ex $1022 Gd $704
Grade VI . . . . NiB $1824 Ex $1465 Gd $1005
Gran Lightning model . . . . NiB $1347 Ex $1084 Gd $743
Feather Model (alloy receiver) . . . . NiB $1026 Ex $826 Gd $571
Feather Combo model (2-bbl. set) . . . . NiB $2422 Ex $1946 Gd $1336
Privilege Mdl. (engraved w/sideplates) . . . . NiB $4669 Ex $3743 Gd $2558
Micro model, add 10%
Models w/o Invector
choke system, deduct $120
28 and .410 ga., add 15%

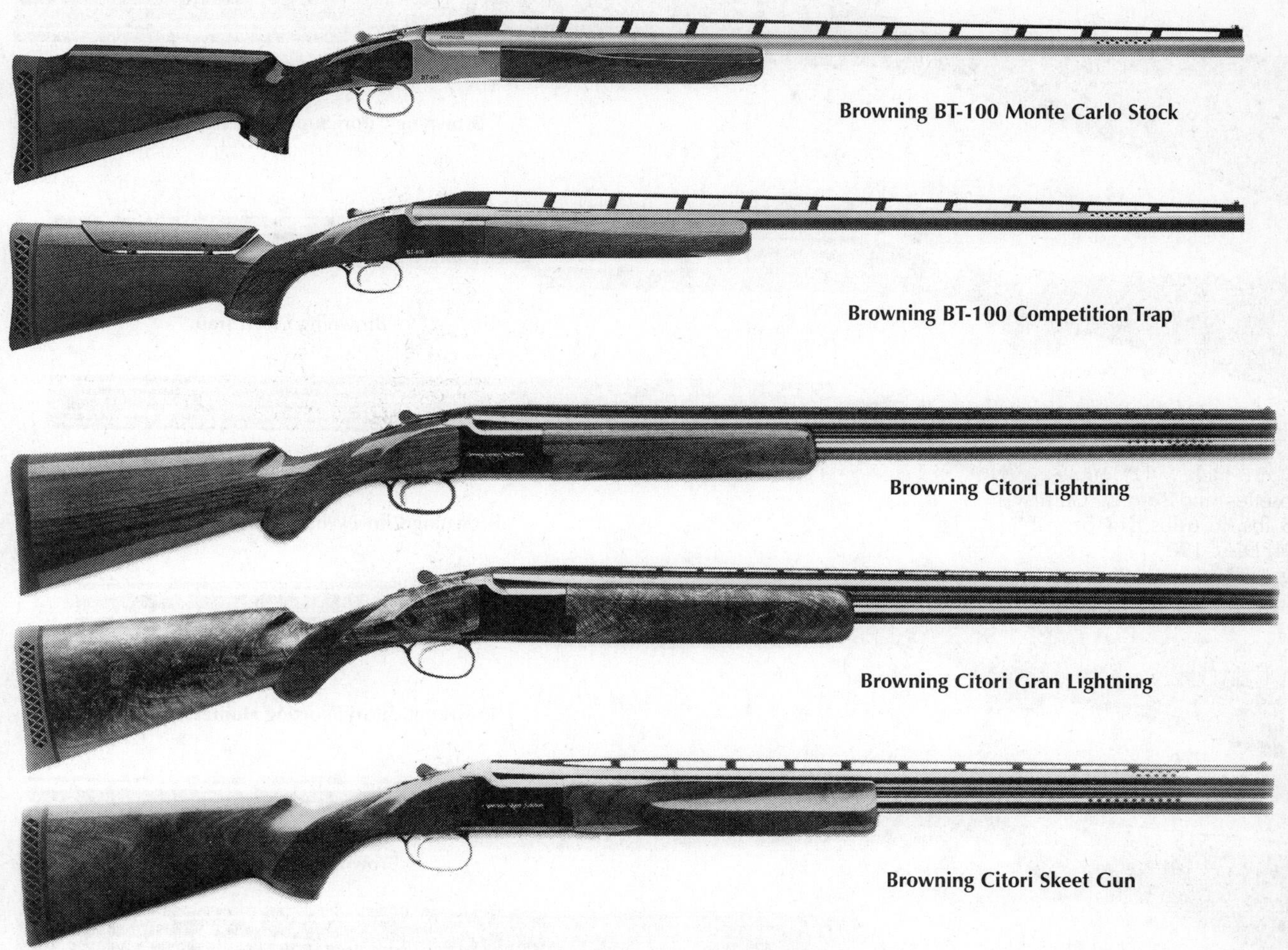

Browning BT-100 Monte Carlo Stock

Browning BT-100 Competition Trap

Browning Citori Lightning

Browning Citori Gran Lightning

Browning Citori Skeet Gun

CITORI SKEET GUN
Same as Hunting model except has skeet-style stock and forearm, 26- or 28-inch bbls., both bored SK choke. Available w/either standard vent rib or special target-type, high-post, wide vent rib. Weight (w/26-inch bbls.): 12 ga., 8 lbs., 20 ga., 7 lbs. Made 1974 to date by Miroku.

Grade I . . . . NiB $1467 Ex $1008 Gd $596
Grade II . . . . NiB $1125 Ex $906 Gd $625
Grade III . . . . NiB $1311 Ex $1055 Gd $727
Grade VI (disc. 1995) . . . . . . NiB $1955 Ex $1570 Gd $1078
Golden Clays. . . . . NiB $2155 Ex $1730 Gd $1186
28 and .410 ga., add 15%
3-bbl. Set, Grade I (disc. 1996). . . . . . NiB $2354 Ex $1903 Gd $1326
3-bbl. Set, Grade III (disc. 1996) . . . . NiB $2540 Ex $2052 Gd $1418
3-bbl. Set, Grade VI (disc. 1994). . . . . NiB $2869 Ex $2314 Gd $1606
3-bbl. Set, Golden Clays (disc. 1995) . . . . . NiB $3699 Ex $2879 Gd $2058
4-bbl. Set, Grade I . . . . NiB $3395 Ex $2736 Gd $1892
4-bbl. Set, Grade III . . . . NiB $3770 Ex $3035 Gd $2096
4-bbl. Set, Grade VI (disc. 1994). . . . . NiB $3699 Ex $3185 Gd $2239
4-bbl. Set, Golden Clays (disc. 1995) . . NiB $4671 Ex $3757 Gd $2586

CITORI SPORTING CLAYS
Similar to the standard Citori Lightning model except Classic-style stock with rounded pistol-grip. 30-inch back-bored bbls. with Invector Plus tubes. Receiver with "Lightning Sporting Clays Edition" logo. Made 1989 to date.

(cont'd.) **CITORI SPORTING CLAYS**
GTI model (disc. 1995). . . . . NiB $1328 Ex $942 Gd $607
GTI Golden Clays model (1993-94) . . . NiB $1991 Ex $1606 Gd $1114
Lightning model (intro. 1989). . . . . NiB $1179 Ex $957 Gd $672
Lightning Golden Clays (1993-98) . . . . NiB $2062 Ex $1662 Gd $1152
Lightning Pigeon Grade (1993-94) . . . . . NiB $1257 Ex $1019 Gd $714
Micro Citori Lightning model
(w/low rib) . . . . NiB $1393 Ex $942 Gd $622
Special Sporting model (intro. 1989) . . . . NiB $1425 Ex $967 Gd $646
Special Sporting
Golden Clays (1993-98) . . . . NiB $2381 Ex $1903 Gd $1318
Special Sporting Pigeon Gr. (1993-94) . . NiB $1289 Ex $1044 Gd $730
Ultra mdl. (intro. 1995-previously GTI) . NiB $1321 Ex $1069 Gd $748
Ultra Golden Clays (intro. 1995) . . . . . NiB $2386 Ex $1924 Gd $1333
Model 325 (1993-94) . . . . NiB $1266 Ex $1028 Gd $723
Model 325 Golden Clays (1993-94) . . . NiB $2038 Ex $1646 Gd $1143
Model 425 Grade I (intro. 1995) . . . . . . NiB $1356 Ex $1100 Gd $772
Model 425 Golden Clays (intro. 1995) . . . . NiB $2386 Ex $1924 Gd $1333
Model 425 WSSF (intro. 1995) . . . . NiB $1299 Ex $1054 Gd $740
Model 802 Sporter (ES)
Extended Swing (intro. 1996 . . . . NiB $1427 Ex $1157 Gd $810
For 2 bbl. set add $850
For adjustable stock, add $200
For high rib, add $85
For ported barrels, add $65

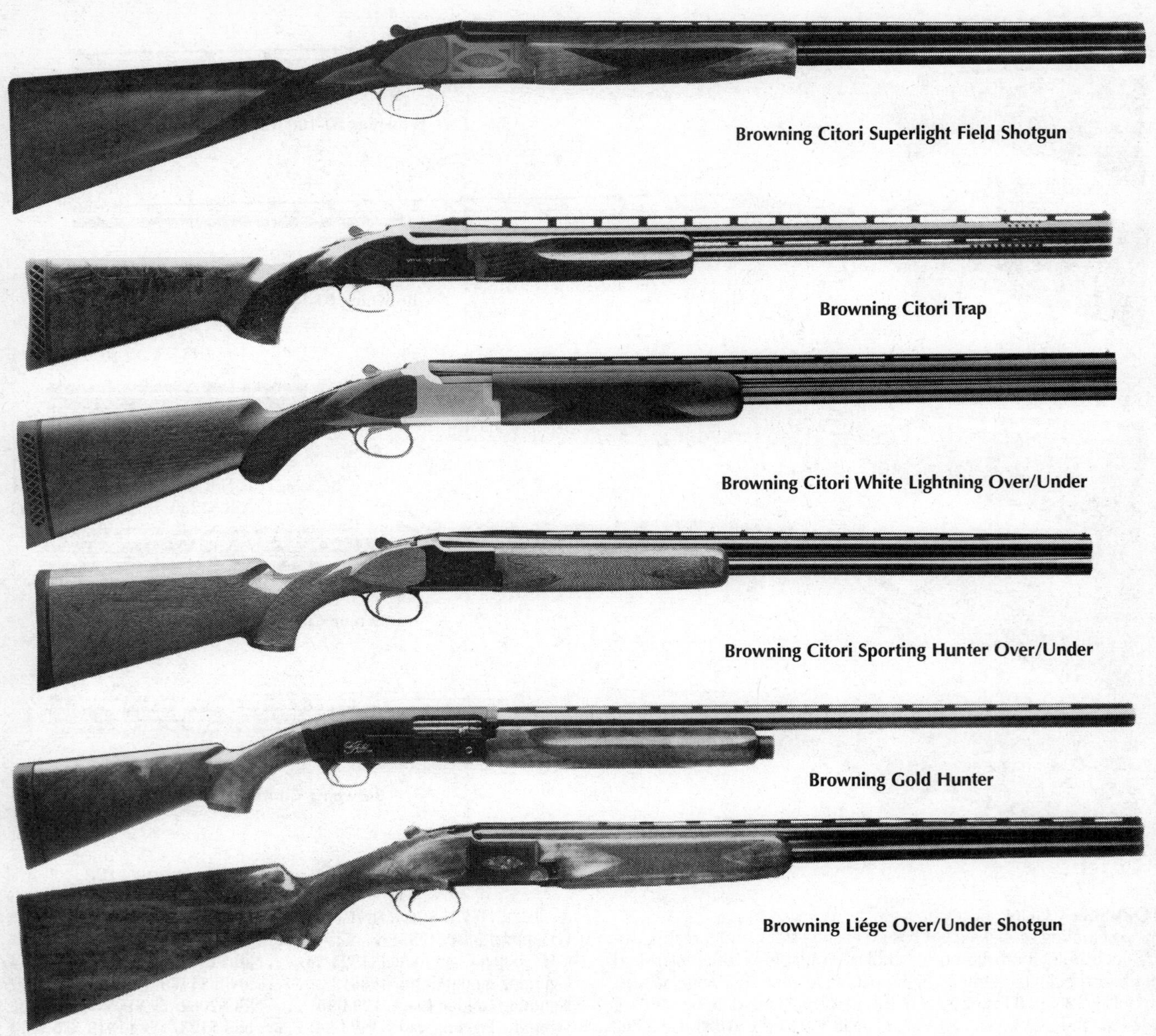
Browning Citori Superlight Field Shotgun

Browning Citori Trap

Browning Citori White Lightning Over/Under

Browning Citori Sporting Hunter Over/Under

Browning Gold Hunter

Browning Liége Over/Under Shotgun

CITORI SUPERLIGHT O/U FIELD SHOTGUNS
Similar to the Citori Hunting model except w/straight-grip stock and Schnabel forend tip. Made by Miroku 1982 to date.

Grade I	**NiB $1277**	**Ex $1025**	**Gd $704**
Grade III	**NiB $1687**	**Ex $1353**	**Gd $932**
Grade V (disc. 1985)	**NiB $2188**	**Ex $1754**	**Gd $1200**
Grade VI	**NiB $2537**	**Ex $2036**	**Gd $1399**
Models w/o Invector choke system, deduct			**$120**
28 and .410 ga., add			**15%**

CITORI TRAP GUN
Same as Hunting model except 12 ga. only, has Monte Carlo or fully adjustable stock and beavertail forend, trap-style recoil pad; 20- or 32-inch bbls.; M/F, IM/F, or F/F. Available with either standard vent rib or special target-type, high-post, wide vent rib. Weight: 8 lbs. Made from 1974 to date by Miroku.

(*cont'd.*) **CITORI TRAP GUN**

Grade I Trap	**NiB $1429**	**Ex $1153**	**Gd $800**
Grade I Trap Pigeon grade (disc. 1994)	**NiB $1715**	**Ex $1381**	**Gd $1014**
Grade I Trap Signature grade (disc. 1994)	**NiB $1681**	**Ex $1354**	**Gd $936**
Grade I Plus Trap (disc. 1994)	**NiB $1764**	**Ex $1421**	**Gd $982**
Grade I Plus Trap w/ported bbls. (disc. 1994)	**NiB $1881**	**Ex $1514**	**Gd $1046**
Grade I Plus Trap Combo (disc. 1994)	**NiB $4065**	**Ex $3270**	**Gd $2252**
Grade I Plus Trap Golden Clays (disc. 1994)	**NiB $1764**	**Ex $1421**	**Gd $982**
Grade II w/HP rib (disc. 1984)	**NiB $1547**	**Ex $1247**	**Gd $864**
Grade III Trap	**NiB $1881**	**Ex $1515**	**Gd $1046**
Grade V Trap (disc. 1984)	**NiB $2066**	**Ex $1666**	**Gd $1154**
Grade VI Trap (disc. 1994)	**NiB $2384**	**Ex $1916**	**Gd $1319**
Grade VI Trap Golden Clays (disc. 1994)	**NiB $2886**	**Ex $2318**	**Gd $1592**

CITORI UPLAND SPECIAL O/U SHOTGUN
A shortened version of the Hunting model fitted with 24-inch bbls. and straight-grip stock.
Upland Special 12, 20 ga. models....... NiB $1155 Ex $928 Gd $639
Upland Spec. 16 ga. mdl. (disc. 1989) .. NiB $1356 Ex $1089 Gd $749
Models w/o Inv. choke sys., deduct $120

CITORI WHITE LIGHTNING O/U SHOTGUN
Similar to the standard Citori Lightning model except w/silver nitride receiver w/scroll and rosette engraving. Satin wood finish w/round pistol grip. Made 1998 to date.
12, 20 ga. models................ NiB $1356 Ex $1089 Gd $749
28, .410 ga. models (Intro. 2000)...... NiB $1472 Ex $1183 Gd $812

CITORI WHITE UPLAND SPECIAL...... NiB $1188 Ex $955 Gd $657
Similar to the standard Citori Upland model except w/silver nitride receiver w/scroll and rosette engraving. Satin wood finish w/round pistol grip. Made 2000 to date.

DOUBLE AUTOMATIC (STEEL RECEIVER)
Short recoil system. Takedown. 12 ga. only. Two round capacity. Bbls.: 26-, 28-, 30-inches; any standard choke. Checkered pistol-grip stock and forend. Weight: About 7.75 lbs. Made 1955-1961.
With plain bbl. .... NiB $623 Ex $504 Gd $350
With recessed-rib bbl............. NiB $785 Ex $633 Gd $438

GOLD DEER HUNTER AUTOLOADING SHOTGUN
Similar to the Standard Gold Hunter model except chambered 12 ga. only. 22-inch bbl. W/rifled bore or smooth bore w/5-inch rifled invector tube. Cantilevered scope mount. Made 1997 to date.
Gold Deer Hunter (w/standard finish) ... NiB $788 Ex $6036 Gd $451
Field model (w/Mossy Oak finish) .... NiB $666 Ex $538 Gd $375

GOLD HUNTER SERIES
Self-cleaning, gas-operated, short-stroke action. Gauges: 10 or 12 (3.5-inch chamber); 12 or 20 (3-inch chamber). 26-, 28-, or 30-inch bbl. w/Invector or Invector Plus choke tubes. Checkered walnut stock. Polished or matte black metal finish. Made 1994 to date.
Gold Hunter (Light 10 ga. 3.5-inch w/wal. St.) .... NiB $864 Ex $713 Gd $494
Gold Hunter (12 ga. 3.5-inch).......... NiB $832 Ex $672 Gd $438
Gold Hunter (12 or 20 ga. 3-inch) .... NiB $540 Ex $437 Gd $305
Gld. Hunter Clas. Mdl. (12 or 20 Ga. 3-inch) ..... NiB $572 Ex $463 Gd $323
Gld. Hunter High Gr.
Classic (12 or 20 ga. 3-inch)........... NiB $1157 Ex $931 Gd $643
Gold Deer Hunter
(12 ga. w/22-inch bbl.)................ NiB $605 Ex $489 Gd $340
Gold Turkey Hunter Camo
(12 ga. w/24-inch bbl.)................ NiB $559 Ex $452 Gd $315
Gold Waterfowl Hunter
Camo (12 ga. w/24-inch bbl.)........... NiB $540 Ex $437 Gd $305

GOLD STALKER SERIES
Self-cleaning, gas-operated, short-stroke action. Gauges: 10 or 12 (3.5-inch chamber); 12 or 20 (3-inch chamber). 26-, 28-, or 30-inch bbl. w/Invector or Invector Plus choke tubes. Graphite/fiberglass composite stock. Polished or matte black metal finish. Made 1998 to date.
Gold Stalker (Light 10 ga.
3.5-inch w/composite stock)............ NiB $867 Ex $699 Gd $485
Gold Stalker (12 ga. 3.5-inch) .... NiB $796 Ex $643 Gd $447
Gold Stalker (12 or 20 ga. 3-inch) .... NiB $534 Ex $432 Gd $302
Gold Stalker Classic
Model (12 or 20 ga. 3-inch) .... NiB $540 Ex $437 Gd $305
Gold Deer Stalker
(12 ga. w/22-inch bbl.)................ NiB $605 Ex $489 Gd $340
Gold Turkey Stalker Camo
(12 ga. w/24-inch bbl.)................ NiB $559 Ex $452 Gd $315

Browning Over/Under Gold Classic

(cont'd.) **GOLD STALKER SERIES**
Gold Waterfowl Stalker
Camo (12 Ga. w/24-inch bbl.) .... NiB $931 Ex $514 Gd $442

GOLD SPORTING SERIES
Similar to Gold Hunter Series except w/2.75-inch chamber and 28- or 30-inch ported bbl. w/Invector Plus chokes. Made 1999 to date.
Gold Sporting Clays (standard).......... NiB $816 Ex $700 Gd $551
Gold Sporting Clays (youth or ladies)..... NiB $834 Ex $715 Gd $561
Gold Sporting Clays w/Eng. nick. rec.... NiB $1260 Ex $1055 Gd $793

LIEGE O/U SHOTGUN (B26/27)
Boxlock. Automatic ejectors. Non-selective single trigger. 12 ga. only. Bbls.: 26.5-, 28-, or 30-inch; 2.75-inch chambers in 26.5- and 28-inch, 3-inch in 30-inch, IC/M, M/F, or F/F chokes; vent rib. Weight: 7 lbs., 4 oz.to 7 lbs., 14 oz., depending on bbls. Checkered pistol-grip stock and forearm. Made 1973-75 by FN.
Liège (B-26 BAC production) .... NiB $911 Ex $735 Gd $509
Liège (B-27 FN prod.) Stand. Game Mdl. .. NiB $881 Ex $711 Gd $492
Deluxe Game model.................. NiB $992 Ex $799 Gd $553
Grand Delux Game model .... NiB $1207 Ex $971 Gd $671
Deluxe Skeet model .... NiB $1029 Ex $829 Gd $573
Deluxe Trap model .... NiB $1014 Ex $817 Gd $565
COL Commemorative model .... NiB $1437 Ex $1155 Gd $794

LIGHT SPORTING 802ES ...... NiB $1311 Ex $1055 Gd $727
Over/under. Invector-plus choke tubes. 12 ga. only with 28-inch bbl. Weight: 7 lbs., 5 oz.

LIGHTNING SPORTING CLAYS
Similar to the standard Citori Lightning model except Classic-style stock with rounded pistol grip. 30-inch back-bored bbls. with Invector Plus tubes. Receiver with "Lightning Sporting Clays Edition" logo. Made 1989 to date.
Standard model .... NiB $1159 Ex $906 Gd $620
Pigeon grade .... NiB $1221 Ex $983 Gd $678

O/U CLASSIC .... NiB $2170 Ex $1745 Gd $1201
Gauge: 20, 2.75-inch chambers. 26-inch blued bbls. choked IC/M. Gold-plated, single selective trigger. Manual, top-tang-mounted safety. Engraved receiver. High grade, select American walnut straight-grip stock with Schnabel forend. Fine-line checkering with pearl borders. High-gloss finish. 5,000 issued in 1986; made in Japan, engraved in Belgium.

O/U GOLD CLASSIC.............. NiB $5239 Ex $4290 Gd $2894
Same general specifications as Over/Under Classic except more elaborate engravings, enhanced in gold, including profile of John M. Browning. Fine oil finish. 500 issued; made in 1986 in Belgium.

RECOILLESS TRAP SHOTGUN
The action and bbl. are driven forward when firing to achieve 72 percent less recoil. 12 ga, 2.75-inch chamber. 30-inch bbl. with Invector Plus tubes; adjustable vent rib. 51.63 inches overall. Weight: 9 lbs. Adj. checkered walnut buttstock and forend. Blued finish. Made from 1993-96.

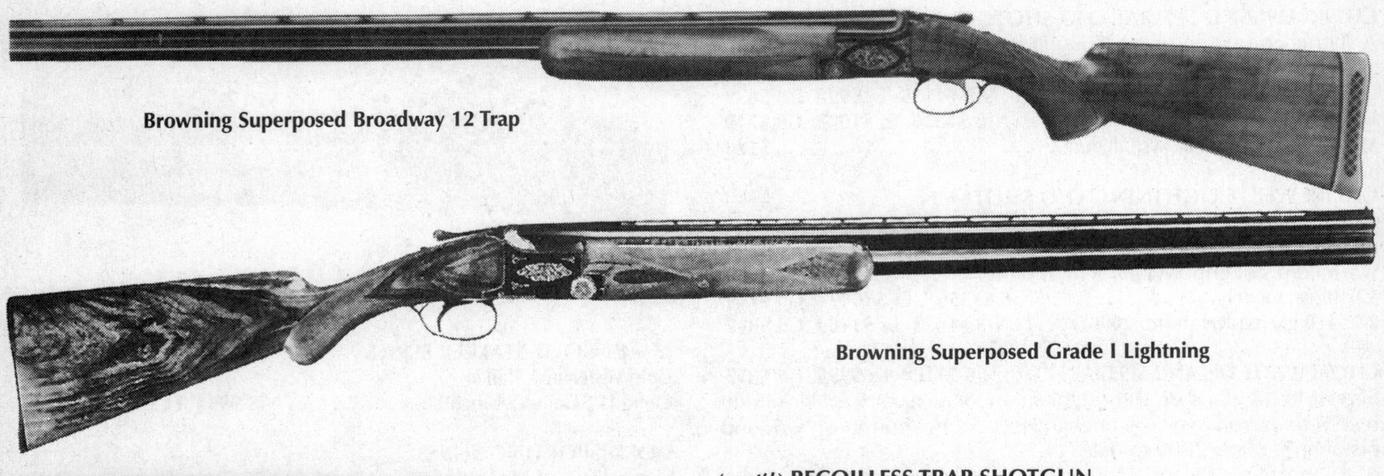

Browning Superposed Broadway 12 Trap

Browning Superposed Grade I Lightning

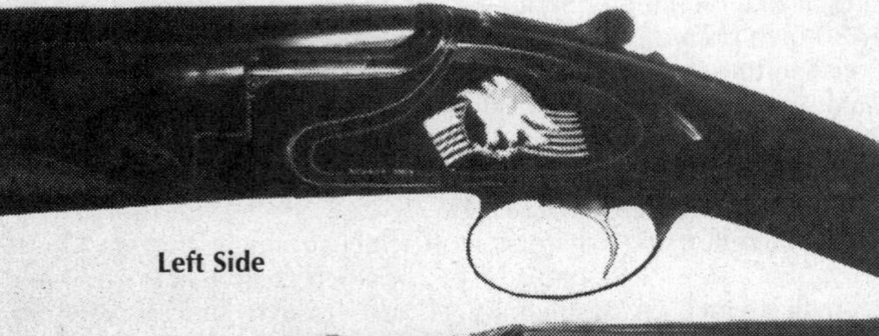

Left Side

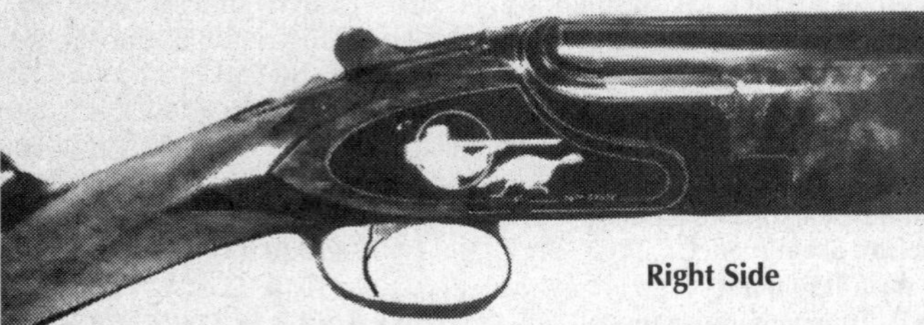

Right Side

Browning Superposed Bicentennial

Browning Superposed Grade IV Diana (Postwar)

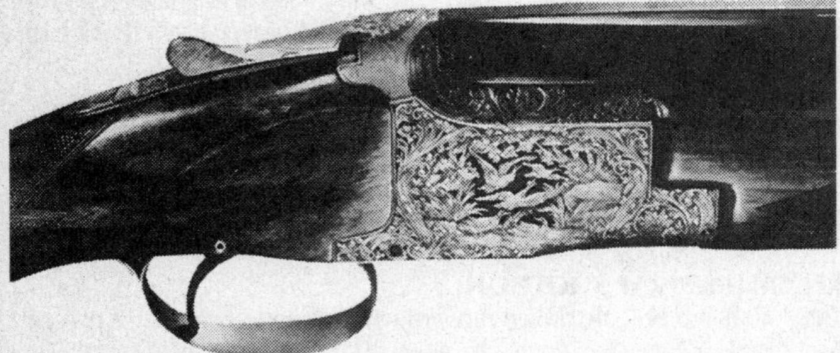

Browning Superposed Grade V Midas (Postwar)

(*cont'd.*) RECOILLESS TRAP SHOTGUN

Standard model. . . . . NiB $910 Ex $736 Gd $514
Micro model (27-inch bbl.) . . . . NiB $936 Ex $757 Gd $528
Signature model (27-inch bbl.) . . . . NiB $1350 Ex $1089 Gd $786

SUPERPOSED BICENTENNIAL
COMMEMORATIVE . . . . NiB $13,197 Ex $10,558 Gd $7180
Special limited edition issued to commemorate U.S. Bicentennial. 51 guns, one for each state in the Union plus one for Washington, D.C. Receiver with sideplates has engraved and gold-inlaid hunter and wild turkey on right side, U.S. flag and bald eagle on left side, together with state markings inlaid in gold, on blued background. Checkered straight-grip stock and Schnabel-style forearm of highly-figured American walnut. Velvet-lined wood presentation case. Made in 1976 by FN. Value shown is for gun in new, unfired condition. See illustration next page.

SUPERPOSED
BROADWAY 12 TRAP . . . . NiB $2006 Ex $1614 Gd $1110
Same as Standard Trap Gun except has 30- or 32-inch bbls. with wider Broadway rib. Disc. 1976.

SUPERPOSED SHOTGUNS, HUNTING MODELS
Over/under boxlock. Selective automatic ejectors. Selective single trigger; earlier models (worth 25% less) supplied w/double triggers, twin selective triggers or non-selective single trigger. Gauges: 12, 20 (intro. 1949, 3-inch chambers in later production), 28, .410 (latter two ga. intro. 1960). Bbls.: 26.5-, 28-, 30-, 32-inch, raised matted or vent rib, prewar Lightning Model made w/ribbed bbl., postwar version supplied only w/vent rib; any combination of standard chokes. Weight (w/26.5-inch vent-rib bbls.): Standard 12, 7 lbs., 11 oz., Lightning 12, 7 lbs., 6 oz.; Standard 20, 6 lbs., 8 oz.; Lightning 20, 6 lbs., 4 oz.; Lightning 28, 6 lbs., 7 oz.; Lightning .410, 6 lbs., 10 oz. Checkered pistol-grip stock/forearm.
Higher grades (Pigeon, Pointer, Diana, Midas, Grade VI) differ from standard Grade I models in overall quality, engraving, wood and checkering; otherwise, specifications are the same. Midas Grade and Grade VI guns are richly gold inlaid. Made by FN 1928-1976. Prewar models may be considered as disc. in 1940 when Belgium was occupied by Germany. Grade VI offered 1955-1960. Pointer Grade disc. in 1966, Grade I Standard in 1973, Pigeon Grade in 1974. Lightning Grade I, Diana and Midas Grades were not offered after 1976.
Grade I standard weight . . . . NiB $1735 Ex $1396 Gd $964
Grade I Lightning . . . . NiB $2114 Ex $1703 Gd $1177
Grade I Lightning, prewar,
matted bbl., no rib . . . . NiB $3056 Ex $2433 Gd $1674
Grade II—Pigeon. . . . . NiB $3176 Ex $2553 Gd $1758

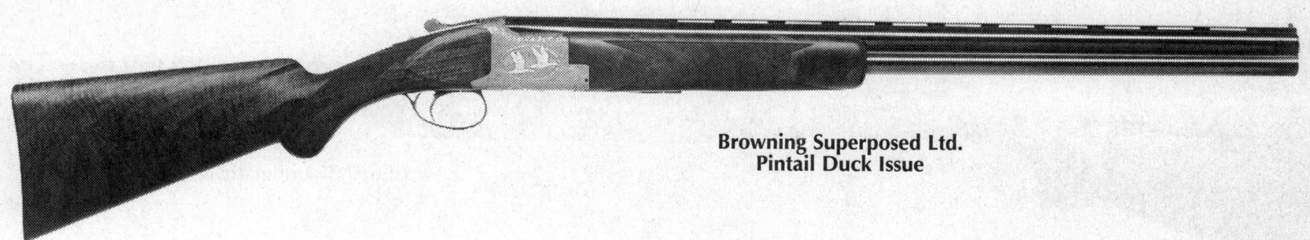

Browning Superposed Ltd.
Pintail Duck Issue

(*cont'd.*) **SUPERPOSED SHOTGUNS**
Grade III—Pointer........... NiB $3091 Ex $2485 Gd $1711
Grade IV—Diana............ NiB $3792 Ex $3047 Gd $2093
Grade V—Midas .... NiB $9400 Ex $7533 Gd $5143
Grade VI .... NiB $6368 Ex $5107 Gd $3494
Add for 20 ga. 20%
Add for 28 ga. 75%
Add for .410. .... 45%
Values shown are for models w/ventilated rib.
If gun has raised matted rib, deduct 10%

SUPERPOSED LIGHTNING AND SUPERLIGHT MODELS (REISSUE B-25)
Reissue of popular 12-and 20-ga. Superposed shotguns. Lightning models available in 26.5- and 28-inch bbl. lengths w/2.75- or 3-inch chambering, full pistol grip. Superlight models available in 26.5-inch bbl. lengths w/2.75-inch chambering only, and straight-grip stock w/Schnabel forend. Both have hand-engraved receivers, fine-line checkering, gold-plated single selective trigger, automatic selective ejectors, manual safety. Weight: 6 to 7.5 lbs. Reintroduced 1985.
Grade I, Standand .... NiB $1718 Ex $1464 Gd $1037
Grade II, Pigeon .... NiB $3164 Ex $2527 Gd $1758
Grade III, Pointer .... NiB $3936 Ex $3165 Gd $2178
Grade IV, Diana............. NiB $4323 Ex $3474 Gd $2388
Grade V, Midas .... NiB $5610 Ex $4504 Gd $3088
W/extra bbls., add 45%

SUPERPOSED MAGNUM ...... NiB $1660 Ex $1338 Gd $926
Same as Grade I except chambered for 12-ga. 3-inch shells, 30-inch vent-rib bbls., stock w/recoil pad. Weight: About 8.25 lbs. Disc. 1976.

SUPERPOSED LTD. BLACK DUCK ISSUE .... NiB $7301 Ex $5879 Gd $4013
Gauge: 12. Superposed Lightning action. 28-inch vent-rib bbls. Choked M/F. 2.75-inch chambers. Weight: 7 lbs., 6 oz. Gold-inlaid receiver and trigger guard engraved w/black duck scenes. Gold-plated, single selective trigger. Top-tang mounted manual safety. Automatic, selective ejectors. Front and center ivory sights. High-grade, hand-checkered, hand-oiled select walnut stock and forend. 500 issued in 1983.

SUPERPOSED LTD. MALLARD DUCK ISSUE ...... NiB $7495 Ex $6014 Gd $4118
Same general specifications as Ltd. Black Duck issue except mallard duck scenes engraved on receiver and trigger guard, dark French walnut stock w/rounded pistol-grip. 500 issued in 1981.

SUPERPOSED LTD. PINTAIL DUCK ISSUE........ NiB $7681 Ex $6163 Gd $4220
Same general specifications as Ltd. Black Duck issue except pintail duck scenes engraved on receiver and trigger guard. Stock is of dark French walnut w/rounded pistol-grip. 500 issued in 1982.

SUPERPOSED, PRESENTATION GRADES
Custom versions of Super-Light, Lightning Hunting, Trap and Skeet

(*cont'd.*) **SUPERPOSED, PRESENTATION GRADES**
Models, w/same general specifications as those of standard guns, but of higher overall quality. The four Presentation grades differ in receiver finish (grayed or blued), engraving gold inlays, wood and checkering. Presentation 4 has sideplates. Made by FN, these models were Intro. in 1977.
Presentation 1 .... NiB $3140 Ex $2523 Gd $1734
Presentation 1, gold-inlaid..... NiB $3597 Ex $2888 Gd $1982
Presentation 2 .... NiB $4041 Ex $3244 Gd $2224
Presentation 2, gold-inlaid..... NiB $4756 Ex $3812 Gd $2612
Presentation 3, gold-inlaid..... NiB $6139 Ex $4923 Gd $3365
Presentation 4 .... NiB $6874 Ex $5510 Gd $3765
Presentation 4, gold-inlaid..... NiB $8876 Ex $7112 Gd $4554

SUPERPOSED SKEET GUNS, GRADE I
Same as standard Lightning 12, 20, 28 and .410 Hunting models, except has skeet-style stock and forearm, 26.5- or 28-inch vent-rib bbls. w/SK choke. Available also in All Gauge Skeet Set: Lightning 12 w/one removable forearm and three extra sets of bbls. in 20, 28 and .410 ga. in fitted luggage case. Disc. 1976. (For higher grades see listings for comparable Hunting models)
12 or 20 ga................. NiB $1895 Ex $1522 Gd $1044
28 or .410 ga. .... NiB $2344 Ex $1882 Gd $1291
All ga. skeet set .... NiB $5972 Ex $4788 Gd $3219

SUPERPOSED SUPER LIGHT MODEL .... NiB $1862 Ex $1496 Gd $1026
Ultralight field gun version of Standard Lightning Model has classic straight-grip stock and slimmer forearm. Available only in 12 and 20 gauges (2.75-inch chambers), w/26.5-inch vent-rib bbls. Weight: 6.5 lbs., (12 ga.); 6 lbs., (20 ga.). Made 1967-76.

SUPERPOSED TRAP GUN..... NiB $1927 Ex $1547 Gd $1061
Same as Grade I except has trap-style stock, beavertail forearm, 30-inch vent-rib bbls., 12 ga. only. Disc. 1976. (For higher grades see listings for comparable hunting models)

TWELVETTE DOUBLE AUTOMATIC
Lightweight version of Double Automatic w/same general specifications except aluminum receiver. Bbl. w/plain matted top or vent rib. Weight: 6.75 to 7 lbs., depending on bbl. Receiver is finished in black w/gold engraving; 1956-1961 receivers were also anodized in gray, brown and green w/silver engraving. Made 1955-71
W/plain bbl. .... NiB $561 Ex $452 Gd $312
W/vent rib bbl. .... NiB $690 Ex $555 Gd $383

CENTURY INTERNATIONAL ARMS INC. — St. Albans, VT

CENTURION .... NiB $355 Ex $287 Gd $201
O/U boxlock action with double triggers and extractors. 12 ga. w/2.75-inch chamber. Bbls: 28-inch choked modified/full with ventilated rib. Weight: 7-1/4 lbs. Checkered European walnut buttstock and forend. Polished blue finish. Imported 1993 to date.

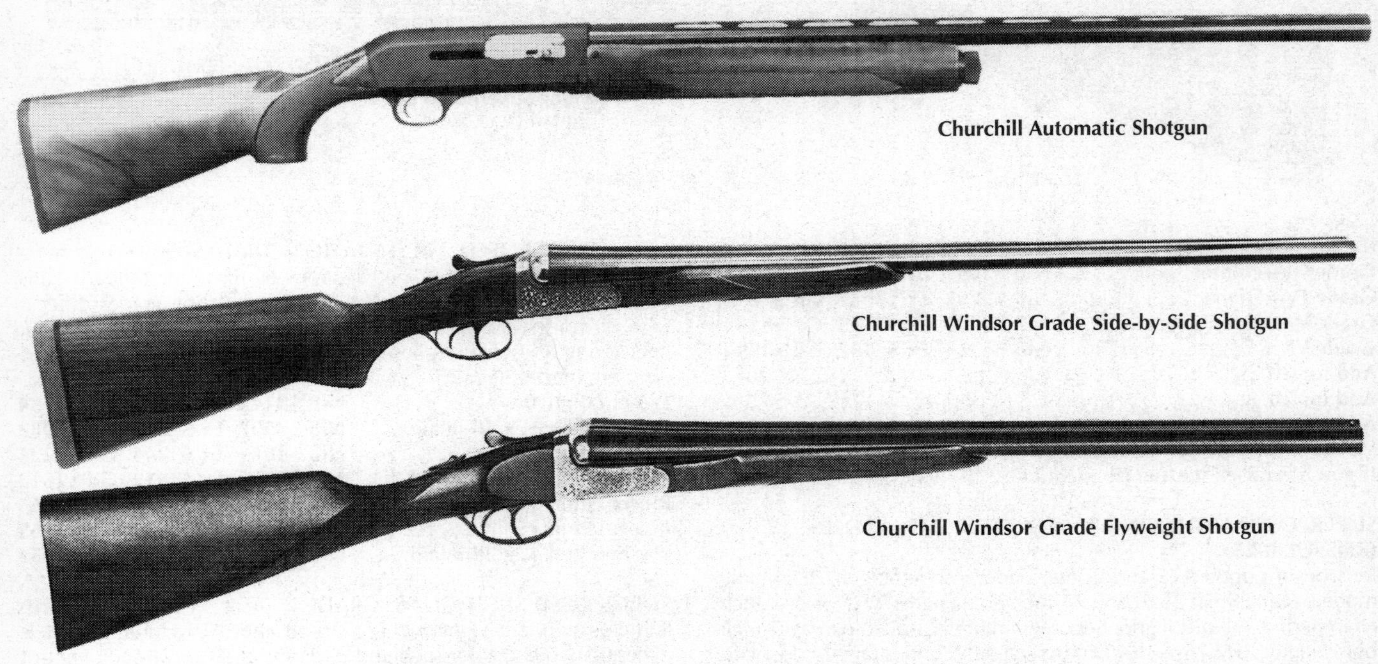

Churchill Automatic Shotgun

Churchill Windsor Grade Side-by-Side Shotgun

Churchill Windsor Grade Flyweight Shotgun

CHURCHILL SHOTGUNS — Italy and Spain Imported by Ellett Brothers, Inc., Chapin, SC; previously by Kassnar Imports, Inc., Harrisburg, PA

AUTOMATIC SHOTGUN

Gas-operated. Gauge: 12, 2.75- or 3-inch chambers. Five round magazine w/cutoff. Bbl.: 24-, 25-, 26-, 28-inch w/ICT choke tubes. Checkered walnut stock w/satin finish. Imported from Italy 1990-94.

Standard model . . . . NiB $534 Ex $431 Gd $300
Turkey model . . . . NiB $560 Ex $452 Gd $313

MONARCH O/U SHOTGUN

Hammerless, takedown w/engraved receiver. Selective single or double triggers. Gauges: 12, 20, 28, .410; 3-inch chambers. Bbls.: 25- or 26-inch (IC/M); 28-inch (M/F). Weight: 6.5-7.5 lbs. Checkered European walnut buttstock and forend. Made in Italy 1986-93.

W/double triggers . . . . NiB $489 Ex $402 Gd $280
W/single trigger. . . . . NiB $556 Ex $448 Gd $311

REGENT O/U SHOTGUNS

Gauges: 12 or 20; 2.75-inch chambers. 27-inch bbls. w/interchangeable choke tubes and wide vent rib. Single selective trigger, selective automatic ejectors. Checkered pistol-grip stock in fancy walnut. Imported from Italy 1984-88 and 1990-94.

Regent V(disc. 1988). . . . . NiB $1013 Ex $807 Gd $557
Regent VII w/
sideplates (disc. 1994) . . . . NiB $1136 Ex $914 Gd $631

REGENT SKEET . . . . NiB $837 Ex $675 Gd $467

12 or 20 ga. w/2.75-inch chambers. Selective automatic ejectors, single-selective trigger. 26-inch over/under bbls. w/vent rib. Weight: 7 lbs. Made in Italy 1984-88.

REGENT TRAP . . . . NiB $851 Ex $685 Gd $465

12-ga. competition shotgun w/2.75-inch chambers. 30-inch over/under bbls. choked IM/F, vent side ribs. Weight: 8 lbs. Selective automatic ejectors, single selective trigger. Checkered Monte Carlo stock w/Supercushion recoil pad. Made in Italy 1984-88.

SPORTING CLAYS O/U . . . . NiB $889 Ex $717 Gd $495

Same general specifications as Windsor IV except in 12 ga. only w/28-inch ported bbls. and choke tubes. Selective automatic ejectors. Weight: 7.5 lbs. Made from 1992-94.

WINDSOR O/U SHOTGUNS

Hammerless, boxlock w/engraved receiver, selective single trigger. Extractors or ejectors. Gauges: 12, 20, 28 or .410; 3-inch chambers. Bbls.: 24 to 30 inches w/fixed chokes or choke tubes. Weight: 6 lbs., 3 oz. (Flyweight) to 7 lbs., 10 oz. (12 ga.). Checkered straight (Flyweight) or pistol-grip stock and forend of European walnut. Imported from Italy 1984-93.

Windsor III w/fixed chokes. . . . . NiB $673 Ex $543 Gd $377
Windsor III w/choke tubes . . . . NiB $837 Ex $674 Gd $467
Windsor IV w/fixed
chokes (disc. 1993). . . . . NiB $782 Ex $630 Gd $436
Windsor IV w/choke tubes . . . . NiB $782 Ex $565 Gd $288

WINDSOR SIDE-BY-SIDE SHOTGUNS

Boxlock action w/double triggers, ejectors or extractors and automatic safety. Gauges: 10, (3.5-inch chambers); 12, 20, 28, .410 (3-inch chambers), 16 (2.75-inch chambers). Bbls.: 23 to 32 inches w/various fixed choke or choke tube combinations. Weight: 5 lbs., 12 oz. (Flyweight) to 11.5 lbs. (10 ga.). European walnut buttstock and forend. Imported from Spain 1984-90.

Windsor I 10 ga. . . . . NiB $755 Ex $609 Gd $423
Windsor I 12 thru .410 ga. . . . . NiB $580 Ex $469 Gd $327
Windsor II 12 or 20 ga.. . . . . NiB $545 Ex $441 Gd $308
Windsor VI 12 or 20 ga. . . . . NiB $785 Ex $633 Gd $438

E.J. CHURCHILL, LTD. — Surrey (previously London), England

The E.J. Churchill shotguns listed below are no longer imported.

PREMIERE QUALITY HAMMERLESS DOUBLE
Sidelock. Automatic ejectors. Double triggers or selective single trigger. Gauges: 12, 16, 20, 28. Bbls.: 25-, 28- 30-, 32-inch; any degree of boring. Weight: 5-8 lbs. depending on ga. and bbl. length. Checkered stock and forend, straight or pistol-grip.
W/double triggers............... NiB $17,898 Ex $14,508 Gd $10,400
W/selective single trigger, add................................ 10%

FIELD MODEL HAMMERLESS DOUBLE
Sidelock Hammerless ejector gun w/same general specifications as Premiere Model but of lower quality.
W/double triggers .... NiB $10,050 Ex $7970 Gd $6930
W/selective single trigger, add 10%

PREMIERE QUALITY O/U SHOTGUN
Sidelock. Automatic ejectors. Double triggers or selective single trigger. Gauges: 12, 16, 20, 28. Bbls.: 25-, 28-, 30-, 32-inch, any degree of boring. Weight: 5-8 lbs. depending on ga. and bbl. length. Checkered stock and forend, straight or pistol-grip.
W/double triggers............... NiB $20,150 Ex $16,120 Gd $10,961
W/selective single trigger, add................................ 10%
Raised vent rib, add... 15%

UTILITY MODEL HAMMERLESS DOUBLE-BARREL
Anson & Deeley boxlock action. Double triggers or single trigger. Gauges: 12, 16, 20, 28, .410. Bbls.: 25-, 28-, 30-, 32-inch, any degree of boring. Weight: 4.5-8 lbs. depending on ga. and bbl. length. Checkered stock and forend, straight or pistol-grip.
W/double triggers .... NiB $6650 Ex $4830 Gd $3530
W/selective single trigger, add 10%

XXV PREMIERE
HAMMERLESS DOUBLE ... NiB $17,226 Ex $13,780 Gd $9370
Sidelock. Assisted opening. Automatic ejectors. Double triggers. Gauges: 12, 20. 25-inch bbls. w/narrow, quick-sighting rib; any standard choke combination. English-style straight-grip stock and forearm, checkered.

XXV IMPERIAL .... NiB $14,332 Ex $11,466 Gd $7797
Similar to XXV Premiere but no assisted opening feature.

XXV HERCULES .... NiB $10,004 Ex $8002 Gd $5442
Boxlock, otherwise specifications same as for XXV Premiere.

XXV REGAL................ NiB $5661 Ex $4555 Gd $3141
Similar to XXV Hercules but w/o assisted opening feature. Gauges: 12, 20, 28, .410.

CLASSIC DOUBLES — Tochigi, Japan

Imported by Classic Doubles International, St. Louis, MO, and previously by Olin as Winchester Models 101 and 23.

MODEL 101 O/U SHOTGUN
Boxlock. Engraved receiver w/single selective trigger, auto ejectors and combination bbl. selector and safety. Gauges: 12, 20, 28 or .410, 2.75-, 3-inch chambers, 25.5- 28- or 30-inch vent-rib bbls. Weight: 6.25 – 7.75 lbs. Checkered French walnut stock. Imported 1987-90.

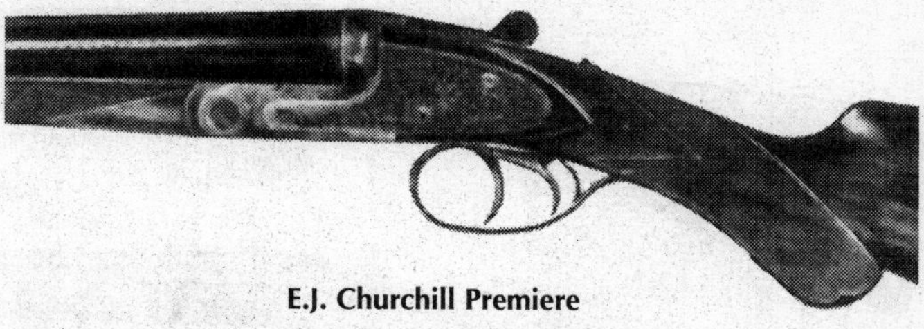
E.J. Churchill Premiere

(cont'd.) **MODEL 101 O/U SHOTGUN**
Classic I Field .... NiB $1618 Ex $1306 Gd $910
Classic II Field.................... NiB $1820 Ex $1468 Gd $1019
Classic Sporter .... NiB $1950 Ex $1572 Gd $1089
Classic Sporter combo .... NiB $3146 Ex $2534 Gd $1752
Classic Trap .... NiB $1592 Ex $1286 Gd $895
Classic Trap Single................ NiB $1618 Ex $1307 Gd $910
Classic Trap combo .... NiB $2361 Ex $1905 Gd $1323
Classic Skeet .... NiB $1691 Ex $1365 Gd $949
Classic Skeet
2-bbl. set......................... NiB $2549 Ex $2056 Gd $1426
Classic Skeet
4-bbl. set......................... NiB $4341 Ex $3495 Gd $2413
ClassicWaterfowler................ NiB $1359 Ex $1100 Gd $769
For Grade II (28 ga.), add $750
For Grade II (.410 ga.), add $250

MODEL 201 SIDE-BY-SIDE SHOTGUN
Boxlock. Single selective trigger, automatic safety and selective ejectors. Gauges: 12 or 20; 3-inch chambers. 26- or 28-inch vent-rib bbl., fixed chokes or internal tubes. Weight: 6 to 7 lbs. Checkered French walnut stock and forearm. Imported 1987-90.
Field model....................... NiB $1610 Ex $1297 Gd $897
Skeet model .... NiB $1896 Ex $1526 Gd $1053
With internal choke tubes, add............................ $100

MODEL 201
SMALL BORE SET .... NiB $4814 Ex $3879 Gd $2683
Same general specifications as the Classic Model 201 except w/smaller frame, in 28 ga. (IC/M) and .410 (F/M). Weight: 6-6.5 lbs. Imported 1987-90.

COGSWELL & HARRISON, LTD. — London, England

AMBASSADOR HAMMERLESS
DOUBLE-BARREL SHOTGUN .... NiB $5890 Ex $5292 Gd $3394
Boxlock. Sideplates w/game scene or rose scroll engraving. Automatic ejectors. Double triggers. Gauges: 12, 16, 20. Bbls.: 26-28-, 30-inch; any choke combination. Checkered straight-grip stock and forearm. Disc.

SHOTGUNS

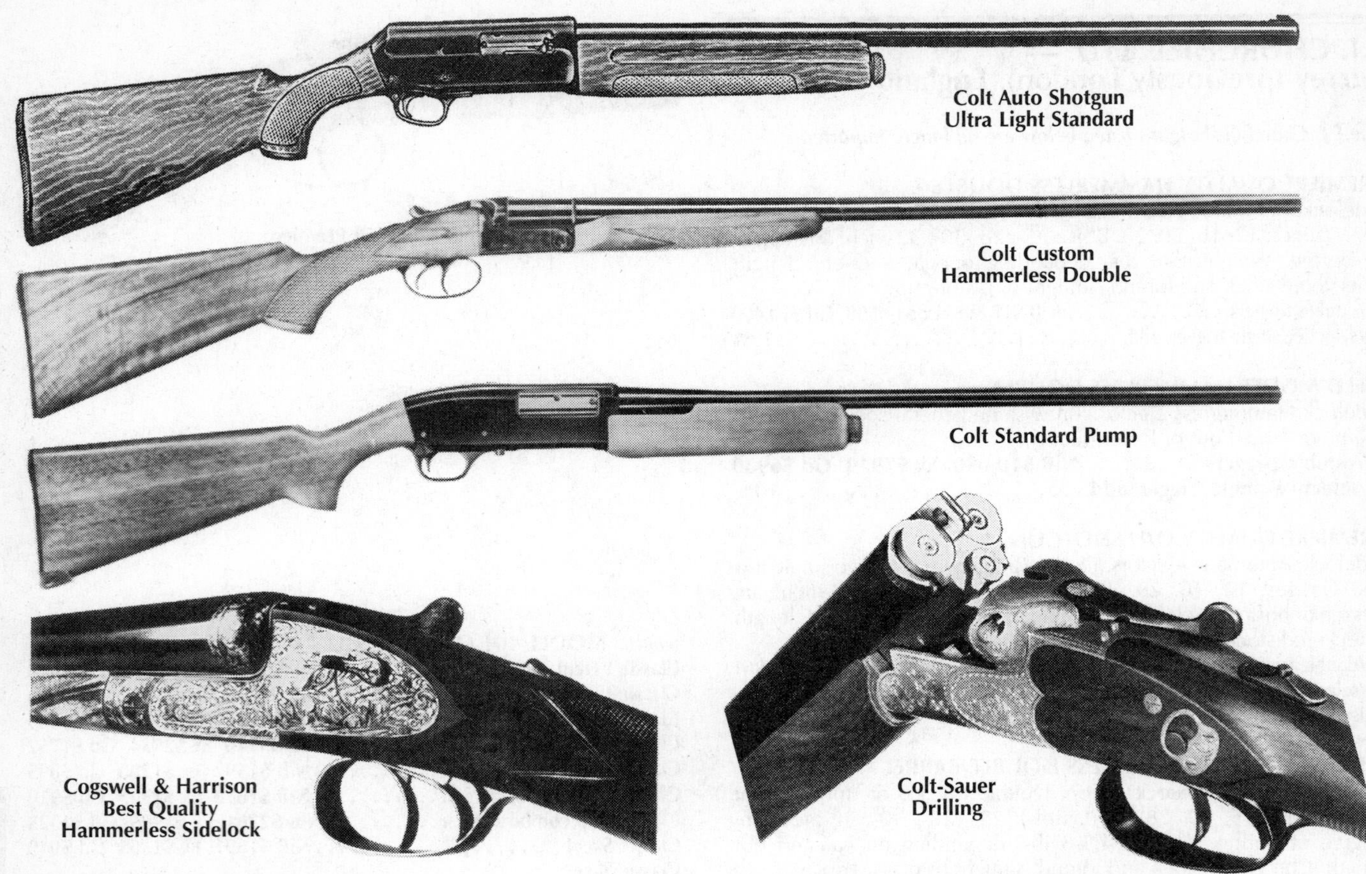
Colt Auto Shotgun Ultra Light Standard

Colt Custom Hammerless Double

Colt Standard Pump

Cogswell & Harrison Best Quality Hammerless Sidelock

Colt-Sauer Drilling

AVANT TOUT SERIES HAMMERLESS DOUBLE-BARREL SHOTGUNS

Boxlock. Sideplates (except Avant Tout III Grade). Automatic ejectors. Double triggers or single trigger (selective or non-selective). Gauges: 12, 16, 20. Bbls.: 25-, 27.5-, 30-inch, any choke combination. Checkered stock and forend, straight grip standard. Made in three models (Avant Tout I or Konor, Avant Tout II or Sandhurst, Avant Tout III or Rex) which differ chiefly in overall quality of engraving, grade of wood, checkering, etc. General specifications are the same. Disc.

Avant Tout I .... NiB $3604 Ex $2903 Gd $2006
Avant Tout II........................ NiB $3156 Ex $2544 Gd $1762
Avant Tout III .... NiB $2434 Ex $1967 Gd $1370
Single trigger, non-selective, add.............................. $225
Single trigger, selective, add $395

BEST QUALITY HAMMERLESS SIDELOCK DOUBLE-BARREL SHOTGUN

Hand-detachable locks. Automatic ejectors. Double triggers or single trigger (selective or non-selective). Gauges: 12, 16, 20. Bbls.: 25-, 26-, 28-, 30-inch, any choke combination. Checkered stock and forend, straight grip standard.

Victor model...................... NiB $10,123 Ex $8141 Gd $5602
Primic model (disc.).................. NiB $7066 Ex $5695 Gd $3939
Single trigger, non-selective, add $225
Single trigger, selective, add $395

HUNTIC MODEL HAMMERLESS DOUBLE

Sidelock. Automatic ejectors. Double triggers or single trigger (selective or non-selective). Gauges: 12, 16, 20. Bbls.: 25-, 27.5-, 30-inch; any choke combination. Checkered stock and forend, straight grip standard. Disc.

(cont'd.) **HUNTIC MODEL HAMMERLESS DOUBLE**
W/double triggers .... NiB $4412 Ex $3570 Gd $2488
Single trigger, non-selective, add.............................. $225
Single trigger, selective, add $350

MARKOR HAMMERLESS DOUBLE

Boxlock. Non-ejector or ejector. Double triggers. Gauges: 12, 16, 20. Bbls.: 27.5 or 30-inch; any choke combination. Checkered stock and forend, straight grip standard. Disc.

Non-ejector .... NiB $1826 Ex $1474 Gd $1025
Ejector model .... NiB $2225 Ex $1795 Gd $1246

REGENCY HAMMERLESS DOUBLE...... NiB $3069 Ex $2472 Gd $1707

Anson & Deeley boxlock action. Automatic ejectors. Double triggers. Gauges: 12, 16, 20. Bbls.: 26-, 28-, 30-inch, any choke combination. Checkered straight-grip stock and forearm. Introduced in 1970 to commemorate the firm's bicentennial, this model has deep scroll engraving and the name "Regency" inlaid in gold on the rib. Disc.

COLT INDUSTRIES — Hartford, Connecticut

Auto Shotguns were made by Franchi and are similar to corresponding models of that manufacturer.

AUTO SHOTGUN — ULTRA LIGHT STANDARD

Recoil-operated. Takedown. Alloy receiver. Gauges: 12, 20. Mag. holds 4 rounds. Bbls.: plain, solid or vent rib, chrome-lined; 26-inch IC or M choke, 28-inch M or F choke, 30-inch F choke, 32-inch F choke. Weight: 12 ga., about 6.25 lbs. Checkered pistol-grip stock and forearm. Made 1964-66.

W/plain bbl. .... NiB $505 Ex $407 Gd $282
W/solid rib bbl.................. NiB $375 Ex $303 Gd $211
W/vent rib bbl. .... NiB $401 Ex $324 Gd $226

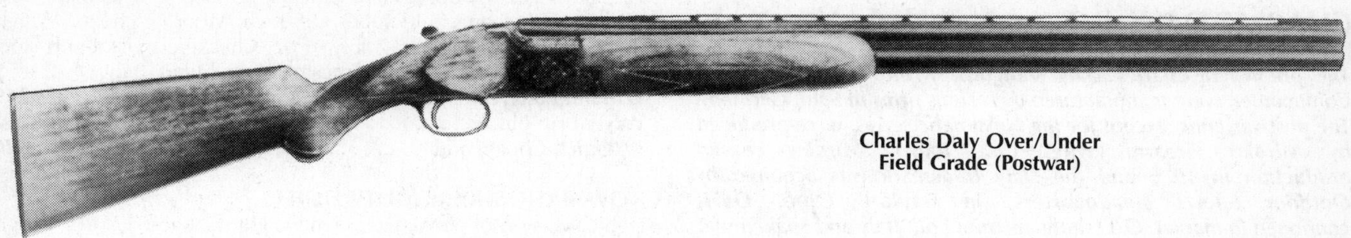

Charles Daly Over/Under
Field Grade (Postwar)

AUTO SHOTGUN — MAGNUM CUSTOM
Same as Magnum except has engraved receiver, select walnut stock and forearm. Made 1964-66.
W/Solid-rib bbl. . . . . **NiB $572 Ex $462 Gd $321**
W/ventilated rib bbl. . . . . **NiB $638 Ex $514 Gd $356**

AUTO SHOTGUN — ULTRA LIGHT CUSTOM
Same as Standard Auto except has engraved receiver, select walnut stock and forearm. Made 1964-66.
W/solid-rib bbl. . . . . **NiB $476 Ex $384 Gd $268**
W/ventilated-rib bbl. . . . . **NiB $508 Ex $410 Gd $285**

AUTO SHOTGUN — MAGNUM
Same as Standard Auto except steel receiver,chambered for 3-inch Magnum shells, 30- and 32-inch bbls. in 12 ga., 28-inch in 20 ga. Weight: 12 ga., about 8.25 lbs. Made 1964-66.
W/plain bbl. . . . . **NiB $456 Ex $368 Gd $257**
W/solid-rib bbl. . . . . **NiB $508 Ex $410 Gd $285**
W/ventilated rib bbl. . . . . **NiB $534 Ex $431 Gd $300**

CUSTOM HAMMERLESS DOUBLE . . . . **NiB $794 Ex $639 Gd $441**
Boxlock. Double triggers. Auto ejectors. Gauges: 12 Mag., 16. Bbls.: 26-inch IC/M; 28-inch M/F; 30-inch F/F. Weight: 12 ga., about 7.5 lbs. Checkered pistol-grip stock and beavertail forearm. Made in 1961.

STANDARD PUMP SHOTGUN . . . . **NiB $365 Ex $296 Gd $207**
Takedown. Gauges: 12, 16, 20. Magazine holds 4 rounds. Bbls.: 26-inch IC; 28-inch M or F choke; 30-inch F choke. Weight: About 6 lbs. Plain pistol-grip stock and forearm. Made 1961-65 by Manufrance.

CUSTOM PUMP . . . . **NiB $400 Ex $324 Gd $226**
Same as Standard Pump shotgun except has checkered stock, vent-rib bbl. Weight: About 6.5 lbs. Made 1961-63 by Manufrance.

SAUER DRILLING . . . . **NiB $3131 Ex $2523 Gd $1747**
Three-bbl. combination gun. Boxlock. Set rifle trigger. Tang bbl. selector, automatic rear sight positioner. 12 ga. over .30-06 or .243 rifle bbl. 25-inch bbls., F and M choke. Weight: About 8 lbs. Folding leaf rear sight, blade front w/brass bead. Checkered pistol-grip stock and beavertail forearm, recoil pad. Made 1974 to date by J. P. Sauer & Sohn, Eckernförde, Germany.

CONNECTICUT VALLEY CLASSICS — Westport, Connecticut

SPORTER O/U
Gauge: 12; 3-inch chamber. Bbls.: 28-, 30- or 32-inch w/ screw-in tubes. Weight: 7.75 lbs. Engraved stainless or nitrided receiver; blued bbls. Checkered American black walnut buttstock and forend w/low-luster satin finish. Made from 1993 to date.
Classic Sporter . . . . **NiB $2159 Ex $1744 Gd $1213**
Stainless Classic Sporter . . . . . . **NiB $2549 Ex $2056 Gd $1426**

FIELD O/U
Similar to the standard Classic Sporter over/under model except w/30-inch bbls. only and non-reflective matte blued finish on both bbls. and receiver for Waterfowler; other grades w/different degrees of embellishment; Grade I the lowest and Grade III the highest. Made 1993 to date.
Grade I . . . . **NiB $2414 Ex $2115 Gd $1465**
Grade II . . . . **NiB $2794 Ex $2252 Gd $1559**
Grade III . . . . **NiB $3164 Ex $2550 Gd $1762**
Waterfowler . . . . **NiB $2508 Ex $2024 Gd $1404**

CONNENTO/VENTUR — Formerly imported by Ventura, Seal Beach, California

Model 51 . . . . **NiB $525 Ex $325 Gd $250**
Gauge: 12, 16, 20, 28 and .410. Double-barrel, box-lock action. Barrels: 26, 28, 30 and 32 inches; various chokes; extractors; and double triggers. Checkered walnut stock. Introduced in 1980, discontinued 1985.

Model 52 . . . . **NiB $525 Ex $350 Gd $250**
Same as Model 51 except in 10 gauge.

Model 53 . . . . **NiB $565 Ex $375 Gd $275**
Same as Model 51 except with scalloped receiver, automatic ejectors and optional single selective trigger. Discontinued in 1985.
W/single trigger, add **25%**

Model 62 . . . . **NiB $975 Ex $775 Gd $600**
Holland & Holland-design sidelock shotgun with various barrel lengths and chokes; automatic ejectors; cocking indicators. Floral engraved receiver, checkered walnut stock. Discontinued in 1982.

Model 64 . . . . **NiB $1200 Ex $895 Gd $725**
Same as Model 62 except deluxe finish. Discontinued.

Grade I . . . . **NiB $1150 Ex $825 Gd $700**
Gauge: 12. Over/under shotgun. Barrels: 32 inches; screw-in choke tubes; high ventilated rib; automatic ejectors; single selective trigger standard. Checkered Monte Carlo walnut stock.

Mark II . . . . **NiB $1400 Ex $1095 Gd $925**
Same as Mark I model but with an extra single barrel and fitted leather case.
Mark III . . . . **NiB $1650 Ex $1300 Gd $925**
Same as Mark I model but with finely figured walnut stock and engraved metal.

Mark III Combo . . . . **NiB $3000 Ex $2450 Gd $1825**
Same as Mark III model but with extra single barrel and fitted leather case.

CHARLES DALY, INC. — New York, New York

The pre-WWII Charles Daly shotguns, w/the exception of the Commander, were manufactured by various firms in Suhl, Germany. The postwar guns, except for the Novamatic series, were produced by Miroku Firearms Mfg. Co., Tokyo. Miroku ceased production in 1976 and the Daly trademark was acquired by Outdoor Sports Headquarters, in Dayton, Ohio. OSHI continued to market O/U shotguns from both Italy and Spain under the Daly logo. Automatic models were produced in Japan for distribution in the USA. In 1996, KBI, Inc. in Harrisburg, PA acquired the Daly trademark and currently imports firearms under that logo.

COMMANDER O/U SHOTGUN

Daly-pattern Anson & Deeley system boxlock action. Automatic ejectors. Double triggers or Miller selective single trigger. Gauges: 12, 16, 20, 28, .410. Bbls.: 26- to 30-inch, IC/M or M/F choke. Weight: 5.25 to 7.25 lbs. depending on ga. and bbl. length. Checkered stock and forend, straight or pistol grip. The two models, 100 and 200, differ in general quality, grade of wood, checkering, engraving, etc.; otherwise specs are the same. Made in Belgium c. 1939.

Model 100 .... NiB $541 Ex $437 Gd $312
Model 200 .... NiB $708 Ex $572 Gd $397
Miller single trigger, add $100

HAMMERLESS DOUBLE-BARREL SHOTGUN

Daly-pattern Anson & Deeley system boxlock action. Automatic ejectors except "Superior Quality" is non-ejector. Double triggers. Gauges: 10, 12, 16, 20, 28, .410. Bbls.: 26- to 32-inch, any combination of chokes. Weight: from 4 to 8.5 lbs. depending on ga. and bbl. length. Checkered pistol-grip stock and forend. The four grades—Regent Diamond, Diamond, Empire, Superior—differ in general quality, grade of wood, checkering, engraving, etc.; otherwise specifications are the same. Disc. about 1933.

Diamond quality............... NiB $11,376 Ex $9100 Gd $6188
Empire quality.................... NiB $5526 Ex $4420 Gd $3006
Regent Diamond quality .... NiB $13,650 Ex $10,920 Gd $7426
Superior quality .... NiB $1236 Ex $988 Gd $672

HAMMERLESS DRILLING

Daly pattern Anson & Deeley system boxlock action. Plain extractors. Double triggers, front single set for rifle bbl. Gauges: 12, 16, 20, .25-20, .25-35, .30-30 rifle bbl. Supplied in various bbl. lengths and weights. Checkered pistol-grip stock and forend. Auto rear sight operated by rifle bbl. selector. The three grades — Regent Diamond, Diamond, Superior—differ in general quality, grade of wood, checkering, engraving, etc.; otherwise, specifications are the same. Disc. about 1933.

Diamond quality .... NiB $6351 Ex $5115 Gd $3504
Regent Diamond quality ... NiB $13,326 Ex $10,661 Gd $7249
Superior quality .... NiB $3464 Ex $2789 Gd $1926

HAMMERLESS DOUBLE EMPIRE GRADE .... NiB $1000 Ex $855 Gd $666

Boxlock. Plain extractors. Non-selective single trigger. Gauges: 12, 16, 20; 3-inch chambers in 12 and 20, 2.75-inch in 16 ga. Bbls.: vent rib; 26-, 28-, 30-inch (latter in 12 ga. only); IC/M, M/F, F/F. Weight: 6 to 7.75 lbs., depending on ga. and bbls. Checkered pistol-grip stock and beavertail forearm. Made 1968-71.

1974 WILDLIFE COMMEMORATIVE .... NiB $2314 Ex $1873 Gd $1309

Limited issue of 500 guns. Similar to Diamond Grade over/under. 12-ga. trap and skeet models only. Duck scene engraved on right side of receiver, fine scroll on left side. Made in 1974.

NOVAMATIC LIGHTWEIGHT AUTOLOADER

Same as Breda. Recoil-operated. Takedown.12 ga., 2.75-inch chamber. *(cont'd)* **NOVAMATIC LIGHTWEIGHT AUTOLOADER** Four round tubular magazine. Bbls.: Plain vent rib; 26-inch IC or Quick-Choke w/three interchangeable tubes, 28-inch M or F choke. Weight (w/26-inch vent-rib bbl.): 7 lbs., 6 oz. Checkered pistol-grip stock and forearm. Made 1968 by Ernesto Breda, Milan, Italy.

W/plain bbl. .... NiB $441 Ex $357 Gd $249
W/vent rib bbl. .... NiB $475 Ex $383 Gd $267
W/Quick-Choke, add $20

NOVAMATIC SUPER LIGHTWEIGHT

Lighter version of Novamatic Lightweight. Gauges: 12, 20. Weight (w/26-inch vent-rib bbl.): 12 ga., 6 lbs., 10 oz., 20 ga., 6 lbs. SK choke available in 26-inch vent-rib bbl. 28-inch bbls. in 12 ga. only. Quick-Choke in 20 ga. w/plain bbl. Made 1968 by Ernesto Breda, Milan, Italy.

12 ga., plain bbl. .... NiB $403 Ex $326 Gd $228
12 ga., vent rib bbl. .... NiB $441 Ex $357 Gd $249
20 ga., plain bbl. .... NiB $409 Ex $331 Gd $231
20 ga., plain bbl. w/Quick-Choke .... NiB $441 Ex $357 Gd $249
20 ga., vent rib bbl. .... NiB $467 Ex $378 Gd $264

NOVAMATIC SUPER LIGHTWEIGHT 20 GA. MAGNUM..................... NiB $467 Ex $378 Gd $263

Same as Novamatic Super Lightweight 2, except 3-inch chamber, has 3-round magazine, 28-inch vent-rib bbl., F choke.

NOVAMATIC 12 GA. MAGNUM..................... NiB $475 Ex $383 Gd $267

Same as Novamatic Lightweight, except chambered for 12-ga. Magnum 3-inch shell. Has 3-round magazine, 30-inch vent rib bbl., F choke, and stock w/recoil pad. Weight: 7.75 lbs.

Post-War Charles Daly shotguns were imported by Sloan's Sporting Goods trading as Charles Daly in New York. In 1976, Outdoor Sports Headquarters acquired the Daly trademark and continued to import European-made shotguns under that logo. In 1996, KBI, Inc., in Harrisburg, PA, acquired the Daly trademark and currently imports firearms under that logo.

NOVAMATIC TRAP GUN .... NiB $507 Ex $409 Gd $284

Same as Novamatic Lightweight except has 30-inch vent rib bbl., F choke and Monte Carlo stock w/recoil pad. Weight: 7.75 lbs.

O/U SHOTGUNS (PREWAR)

Daly-pattern Anson & Deeley-system boxlock action. Sideplates. Auto ejectors. Double triggers. Gauges: 12, 16, 20. Supplied in various bbl. lengths and weights. Checkered pistol-grip stock and forend. The two grades — Diamond and Empire — differ in general quality, grade of wood, checkering, engraving, etc.; otherwise specifications are the same. Disc. about 1933.

Diamond Quality .... NiB $5859 Ex $4716 Gd $3254
Empire Quality .... NiB $4501 Ex $3629 Gd $2514

O/U SHOTGUNS (POSTWAR)

Boxlock. Auto ejectors or selective auto/manual ejection. Selective single trigger. Gauges: 12, 12 Magnum (3-inch chambers), 20 (3-inch chambers), 28, .410. Bbls.: Vent rib; 26-, 28-, 30-inch; standard choke combinations. Weight: 6 to 8 lbs. depending on ga. and bbls. Select walnut stock w/pistol grip, fluted forearm checkered; Monte Carlo comb on trap guns; recoil pad on 12-ga. mag. and trap models. The various grades differ in quality of engraving and wood. Made 1963-76.

Diamond grade .... NiB $1385 Ex $1126 Gd $795
Field grade .... NiB $807 Ex $663 Gd $480
Superior grade.............. NiB $1033 Ex $845 Gd $604
Venture grade .... NiB $773 Ex $637 Gd $462

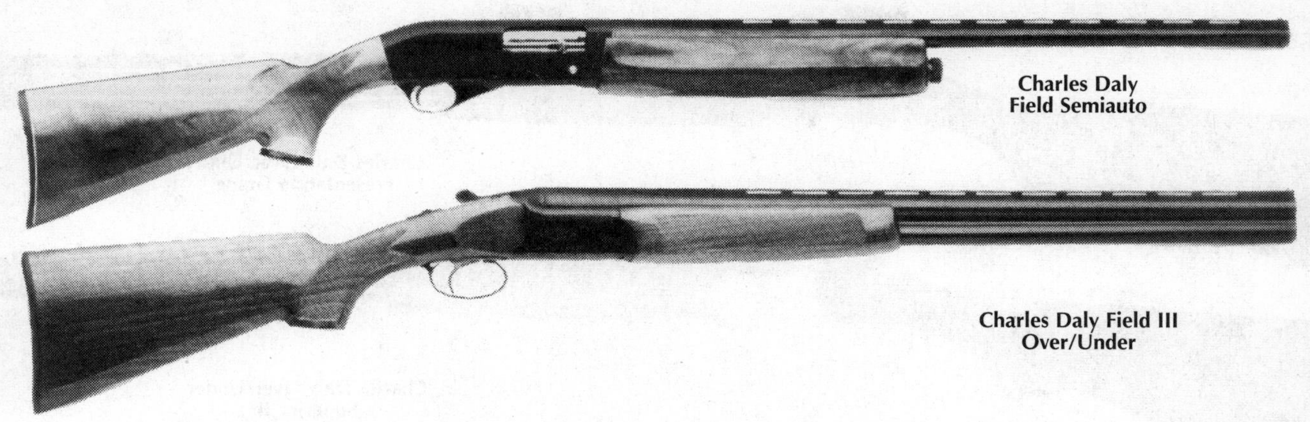

SEXTUPLE MODEL SINGLE-BARREL TRAP GUN
Daly-pattern Anson & Deeley system boxlock action. Six locking bolts. Auto ejector. 12 ga. only. Bbls.: 30-, 32-, 34-inch, vent rib. Weight: 7.5 to 8.25 lbs. Checkered pistol-grip stock and forend. The two models made Empire and Regent Diamond differ in general quality, grade of wood, checkering, engraving, etc., otherwise specifications are the same. Disc. about 1933.
Regent Diamond quality (Linder) . . . . NiB $612 Ex $502 Gd $361
Empire quality (Linder) . . . . NiB $5044 Ex $4057 Gd $2794
Regent Diamond quality (Sauer) . . . . . . NiB $3614 Ex $2913 Gd $2016
Empire quality (Sauer) . . . . NiB $2704 Ex $2185 Gd $1521

SINGLE-SHOT TRAP GUN
Daly-pattern Anson & Deeley system boxlock action. Auto ejector. 12 ga. only. Bbls.: 30-, 32-, 34-inch, vent rib. Weight: 7.5 to 8.25 lbs. Checkered pistol-grip stock and forend. This model was made in Empire Quality only. Disc. about 1933.
Empire grade (Linder) . . . . NiB $4466 Ex $3594 Gd $2479
Empire grade (Sauer) . . . . NiB $2256 Ex $1826 Gd $1277

SUPERIOR GRADE SINGLE-SHOT TRAP . . NiB $850 Ex $695 Gd $497
Boxlock. Automatic ejector. 12 ga. only. 32- or 34-inch vent-rib bbl., F choke. Weight: About 8 lbs. Monte Carlo stock w/pistol grip and recoil pad, beavertail forearm, checkered. Made 1968-76.

DIAMOND GRADE O/U
Boxlock. Single selective trigger. Selective automatic ejectors. Gauges: 12 and 20, 3-inch chambers (2.75 target grade). Bbls.: 26, 27- or 30-inch w/fixed chokes or screw-in tubes. Weight: 7 lbs. Checkered European walnut stock and forearm w/oil finish. Engraved antique silver receiver and blued bbls. Made 1984-90.
Standard model . . . . NiB $892 Ex $729 Gd $522
Skeet model . . . . NiB $967 Ex $789 Gd $563
Trap model . . . . NiB $1028 Ex $838 Gd $596

DIAMOND GTX DL HUNTER O/U SERIES
Sidelock. Single selective trigger and selective auto ejectors. Gauges: 12, 20, 28 ga. or .410 bore. 26-, 28- and 30-inch bbls w/3-inch chambers (2.75-inch 28 ga.). Choke tubes (12 and 20 ga.), Fixed chokes (28 and 410). Weight: 5-8 lbs. Checkered European walnut stock w/hand-rubbed oil finish and recoil pad. Made 1997 to date.
Diamond GTX DL Hunter . . . . NiB $9916 Ex $7952 Gd $5439
Diamond GTX EDL Hunter . . . . NiB $12,122 Ex $9698 Gd $6595
Diamond GTX Sporting (12 or 20 ga.) . . . . . NiB $5539 Ex $4448 Gd $3052
Diamond GTX Skeet (12 or 20 ga.) . . . . NiB $5149 Ex $4136 Gd $2840
Diamond GTX Trap (12 ga. only) . . . . . NiB $5351 Ex $4297 Gd $2949

EMPIRE DL HUNTER O/U . . . . . NiB $1260 Ex $1078 Gd $688
Boxlock. Ejectors. Single selective trigger. Gauges:12, 20, 28 ga. and .410 bore. 26- or 28- inch bbls. w/3-inch chambers (2.75-inch 28 ga.). Choke tubes (12 and 20 ga.), Fixed chokes (28 and .410). Engraved coin-silver receiver w/game scene. Imported 1997 to date.

EMPIRE EDL HUNTER SERIES
Similar to Empire DL Hunter except engraved sideplates. Made 1998 to date.
Empire EDL Hunter . . . . NiB $1266 Ex $1026 Gd $718
Empire Sporting . . . . NiB $1234 Ex $1000 Gd $700
Empire Skeet . . . . NiB $1202 Ex $974 Gd $683
Empire Trap . . . . NiB $1266 Ex $1026 Gd $718
28 ga., add $95
.410 ga, add $120
Multi-chokes w/Monte
Carlo stock, add $125

DSS HAMMERLESS DOUBLE . . . . . NiB $722 Ex $586 Gd $411
Boxlock. Single selective trigger. Selective automatic ejectors. Gauges: 12 and 20; 3-inch chambers. 26-inch bbls. w/screw-in choke tubes. Weight: 6.75 lbs. Checkered walnut pistol-grip stock and semi-beavertail forearm w/recoil pad. Engraved antique silver receiver and blued bbls. Made from 1990 to date.

FIELD GRADE O/U . . . . NiB $540 Ex $440 Gd $312
Boxlock. Single selective trigger. Extractors. Gauges: 12 and 20; 3-inch chambers. Bbls.: 26-inch, IC/M; 28-inch, M/F. Weight: 6.75 lbs. (12 ga.). Checkered walnut stock and forearm w/semi-gloss finish and recoil pad. Engraved color-casehardened receiver and blued bbls. Made from 1989 to date.

FIELD SEMIAUTO SHOTGUN. . . . . NiB $424 Ex $347 Gd $249
Recoil-operated. Takedown. 12-ga. and 12-ga. Magnum. Bbls.: 27- and 30-inch; vent rib. Made 1982-88.

FIELD III O/U SHOTGUN . . . . NiB $554 Ex $451 Gd $320
Boxlock. Plain extractors. Non-selective single trigger. Gauges: 12 or 20. Bbls.: vent rib; 26- and 28-inch; IC/M, M/F. Weight: 6 to 7.75 lbs. depending on ga. and bbls. Chrome-molybdenum steel bbls. Checkered pistol-grip stock and forearm. Made from 1982 to date.

LUX O/U . . . . NiB $795 Ex $645 Gd $454
Similar to the Field Grade except w/selective automatic ejectors and choke tubes. Gauges: 12, 20, 28 and .410. Receiver w/antique silver finish and blued bbls. Made from 1989 to date.

SHOTGUNS

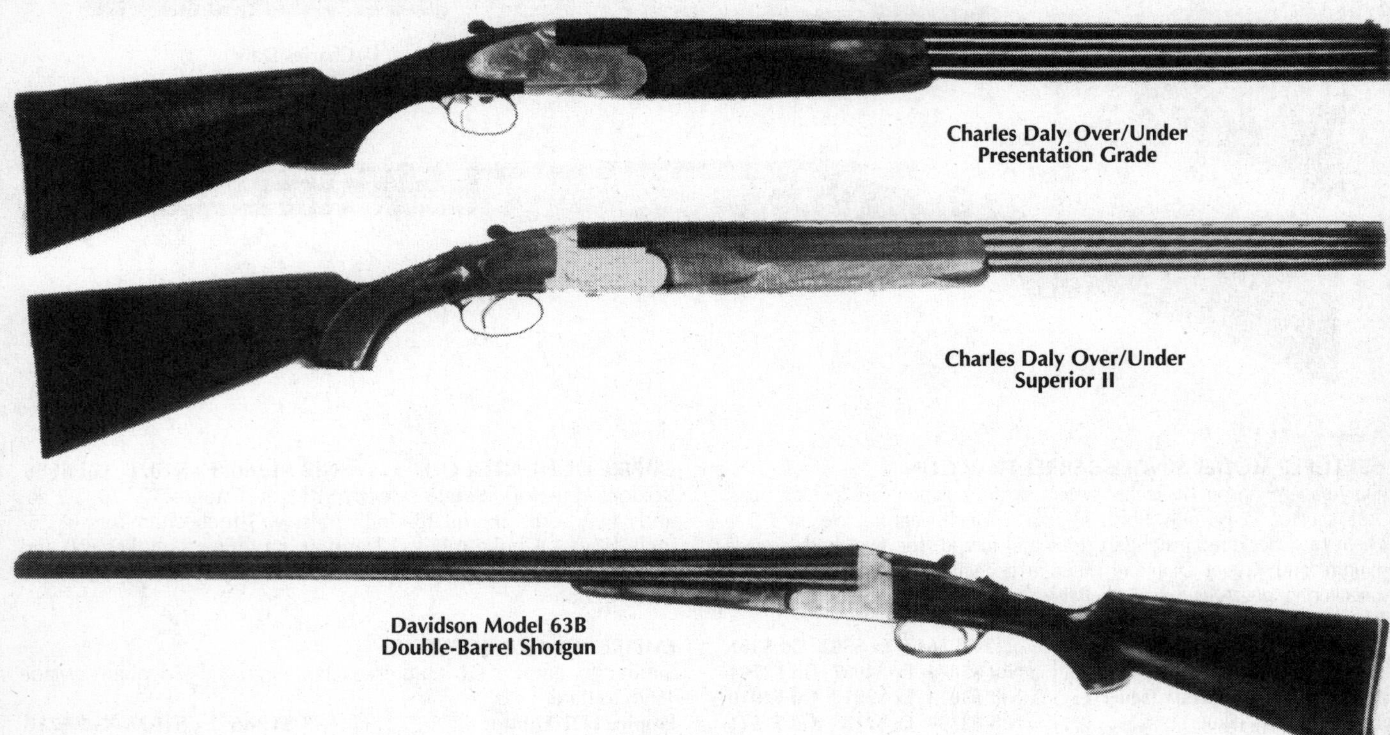
Charles Daly Over/Under
Presentation Grade

Charles Daly Over/Under
Superior II

Davidson Model 63B
Double-Barrel Shotgun

MULTI-XII SELF-LOADING SHOTGUN...... NiB $523 Ex $420 Gd $289
Similar to the gas-operated field semiauto except w/new Multi-Action gas system designed to shoot all loads w/o adjustment. 12 ga. w/3-inch chamber. 27-inch bbl. w/Invector choke tubes, vent rib. Made in Japan from 1987 to date.

O/U
PRESENTATION GRADE........NiB $1117 Ex $898 Gd $617
Purdey boxlock w/double cross-bolt. Gauges: 12 or 20. Engraved receiver w/single selective trigger and auto-ejectors. 27-inch chrome-molybdenum steel, rectified, honed and internally chromed, vent-rib bbls. Hand-checkered deluxe European walnut stock. Made 1982-86.

O/U
Superior II Shotgun............. NiB $953 Ex $766 Gd $527
Boxlock. Plain extractors. Non-selective single trigger. Gauges: 12 or 20. Bbls.: chrome-molybdenum vent rib 26-, 28-, 30-inch, latter in magnum only, assorted chokes. Silver engraved receiver. Checkered pistol-grip stock and forearm. Made from 1982 to date.

SPORTING CLAYS O/U .... NiB $832 Ex $669 Gd $461
Similar to the Field Grade except in 12 ga. only w/ported bbls. and internal choke tubes. Made from 1990 to date.

DAKOTA ARMS, INC. — Sturgis, South Dakota

CLASSIC FIELD GRADE
S/S SHOTGUN .... NiB $7883 Ex $6246 Gd $4151
Boxlock. Gauge: 20 ga. 27-inch bbl. w/fixed chokes. Double triggers. Selective ejectors. Color-casehardened receiver. Weight: 6 lbs. Checkered English walnut stock and splinter forearm w/hand-rubbed oil finish. Made 1996 to date.

PREMIUM GRADE
S/S SHOTGUN .... NiB $14,456 Ex $10,608 Gd $6760
Similar to Classic Field Grade model except w/50% engraving coverage. Exhibition grade English walnut stock. Made 1996 to date.

AMERICAN LEGEND
S/S SHOTGUN .... NiB $17,290 Ex $14,040 Gd $9880
Limited edition built to customer's specifications. Gauge: 20 ga. 27-inch bbl. Double triggers. Selective ejectors. Fully engraved, coin-silver finished receiver w/gold inlays. Weight: 6 lbs. Hand checkered special-selection English walnut stock and forearm. Made 1996 to date.

DARNE S.A. — Saint-Etienne, France

HAMMERLESS DOUBLE-BARREL SHOTGUNS
Sliding-breech action w/fixed bbls. Auto ejectors. Double triggers. Gauges: 12, 16, 20, 28; also 12 and 20 Magnum w/3-inch chambers. Bbls.: 27.5-inch standard, 25.5- to 31.5-inch lengths available; any standard choke combination. Weight: 5.5 to 7 lbs. depending on ga. and bbl. length. Checkered straight-grip or pistol-grip stock and forearm. The various models differ in grade of engraving and wood. Manufactured 1881-1979.

Model R11
(Bird Hunter) .... NiB $1640 Ex $1484 Gd $808
Model R15
(Pheasant Hunter)................ NiB $2443 Ex $1944 Gd $1286
Model R16
(Magnum) .... NiB $3775 Ex $3151 Gd $2007
Model V19
(Quail Hunter) .... NiB $4840 Ex $4320 Gd $3800
Model V22 .... NiB $5426 Ex $4580 Gd $2562
Model V Hors Série No. 1........... NiB $6815 Ex $5905 Gd $4740

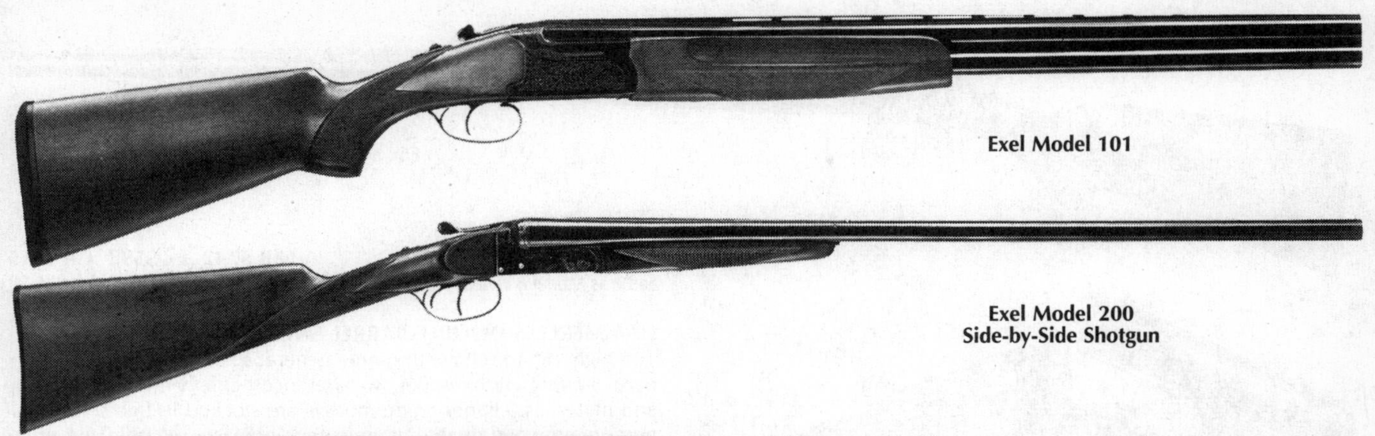
Exel Model 101

Exel Model 200
Side-by-Side Shotgun

DAVIDSON GUNS — Mfd. by Fabrica de Armas ILJA, Eibar, Spain; distributed by Davidson Firearms Co., Greensboro, North Carolina

MODEL 63B DOUBLE-BARREL SHOTGUN . . . . NiB $380 Ex $307 Gd $213
Anson & Deeley boxlock action. Frame engraved and nickel plated. Plain extractors. Auto safety. Double triggers. Gauges: 12, 16, 20, 28, .410. Bbl. lengths: 25 (.410 only), 26, 28, 30 inches (latter 12 ga. only). Chokes: IC/ M, M/F, F/F. Weight: 5 lbs., 11 oz. (.410) to 7 lbs. (12 ga.). Checkered pistol-grip stock and forearm of European walnut. Made 1963. Disc.

MODEL 63B MAGNUM
Similar to standard Model 63B except chambered for 10 ga. 3.5-inch, 12 and 20 ga. 3-inch Magnum shells; 10 ga. has 32-inch bbls., choked F/F. Weight: 10 lb., 10 oz. Made from 1963. Disc.
12-and 20 ga. magnum . . . . NiB $441 Ex $356 Gd $247
10 ga. magnum. . . . . NiB $518 Ex $417 Gd $288

MODEL 69SL DOUBLE-BARREL SHOTGUN. . . . . NiB $646 Ex $539 Gd $404
Sidelock action w/detachable sideplates, engraved and nickel plated. Plain extractors. Auto safety. Double triggers. 12 and 20 ga. Bbls.: 26-inch IC/M, 28-inch M/F. Weight: 12 ga., 7 lbs., 20 ga., 6.5 lbs. Pistol-grip stock and forearm of European walnut, checkered. Made 1963-76.

MODEL 73 STAGECOACH HAMMER DOUBLE . . . . NiB $352 Ex $284 Gd $198
Sidelock action w/detachable sideplates and exposed hammers. Plain extractors. Double triggers. Gauges: 12, 20, 3-inch chambers. 20-inch bbls, M/F chokes. Weight: 7 lbs., 12 ga.; 6.5 lbs., 20 ga. Checkered pistol-grip stock and forearm. Made from 1976. Disc.

EXEL ARMS OF AMERICA — Gardner, Massachusetts

SERIES 100 O/U SHOTGUN
Gauge: 12. Single selective trigger. Selective auto ejectors. Hand-checkered European walnut stock w/full pistol grip, tulip forend. Black metal finish. Chambered for 2.75-inch shells (Model 103 for 3-inch). Weight: 6. 88 to 7.88 lbs. Disc 1988.
Model 101, 26-inch bbl., IC/M . . . . NiB $492 Ex $397 Gd $274
Model 102, 28-inch bbl., IC/IM . . . . NiB $498 Ex $402 Gd $277
Model 103, 30-inch bbl., M/F . . . . NiB $518 Ex $417 Gd $288
Model 104, 28-inch bbl., IC/IM . . . . NiB $569 Ex $458 Gd $316
Model 105, 28-inch bbl., 5 choke tubes . . . . . . NiB $722 Ex $581 Gd $401
Model 106, 28-inch bbl., 5 choke tubes . . . . . . NiB $868 Ex $693 Gd $479
Model 107 Trap, 30-inch bbl., Full or 5 tubes . . . . . NiB $932 Ex $729 Gd $600

SERIES 200 SIDE-BY-SIDE SHOTGUN . . . . NiB $524 Ex $423 Gd $294
Gauges: 12, 20, 28 and .410. Bbls.: 26-, 27- and 28-inch; various choke combinations. Weight: 7 lbs. average. American or European-style stock and forend. Made 1985 to 87.

SERIES 300 O/U SHOTGUN . . . . NiB $594 Ex $479 Gd $332
Gauge: 12. Bbls.: 26-, 28- and 29-inch. Non-glare black-chrome matte finish. Weight: 7 lbs. average. Selective auto ejectors, engraved receiver. Hand-checkered European walnut stock and forend. Made 1985-86.

FABARM SHOTGUNS — Brescia, Italy

Currently imported by Heckler & Koch, Inc., of Sterling, VA (previously by Ithaca Acquisition Corp., St. Lawrence Sales, Inc. and Beeman Precision Arms, Inc.)

See Current listings under "Heckler & Koch."

FIAS — Fabrica Italiana Armi Sabatti Gardone Val Trompia, Italy

GRADE I O/U
Boxlock. Single selective trigger. Gauges: 12, 20, 28, .410; 3-inch chambers. Bbls.: 26-inch IC/M; 28-inch M/F; screw-in choke tubes. Weight: 6.5 to 7.5 lbs. Checkered European walnut stock and forearm. Engraved receiver and blued finish.
12 ga. model . . . . NiB $498 Ex $402 Gd $280
20 ga. model . . . . NiB $562 Ex $453 Gd $315
28 and .410 ga. models . . . . NiB $722 Ex $581 Gd $402

FOX SHOTGUNS — Made by A. H. Fox Gun Co., Philadelphia, PA, 1903 to 1930, and since then by Savage Arms, originally of Utica, NY, now of Westfield, MA. In 1993, Connecticut Manufacturing Co. of New Britain, CT, reintroduced selected models.

Values shown are for 12 and 16 ga. doubles made by A. H. Fox. Twenty gauge guns often are valued up to 75% higher. Savage-made Fox models generally bring prices 25% lower. With the exception of Model B, production of Fox shotguns was discontinued about 1942.

SHOTGUNS

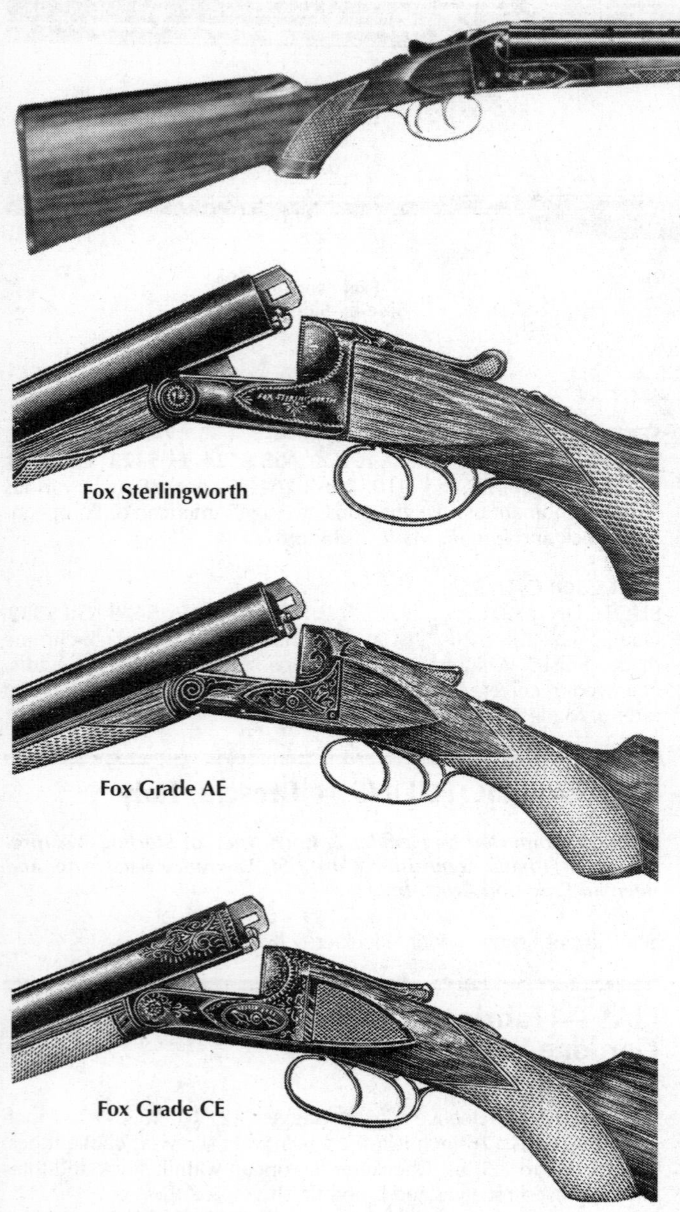
Fox Model B

Fox Sterlingworth

Fox Grade AE

Fox Grade CE

MODEL B HAMMERLESS DOUBLE ...... NiB $320 Ex $260 Gd $183
Boxlock. Double triggers. Plain extractor. Gauges: 12, 16, 20, .410. 24- to 30-inch bbls., vent rib on current production; chokes: M/F, C/M, F/F (.410 only). Weight: About 7.5 lbs., 12 ga. Checkered pistol-grip stock and forend. Made about 1940-85.

MODEL B-ST .... NiB $498 Ex $402 Gd $280
Same as Model B except has non-selective single trigger. Made 1955-66.

MODEL B-DE .... NiB $526 Ex $425 Gd $295
Same as Model B-ST except frame finished in satin chrome, select walnut buttstock w/checkered pistol grip and beavertail forearm. Made 1965-66.

MODEL B-DL .... NiB $584 Ex $471 Gd $327
Same as Model B-ST except frame finished in satin chrome, select walnut buttstock w/checkered pistol grip side panels, beavertail forearm. Made 1962-66.

MODEL B-SE.................. NiB $742 Ex $598 Gd $415
Same as Model B except has selective ejectors and single trigger. Made 1966-89.

HAMMERLESS DOUBLE-BARREL SHOTGUNS
The higher grades have the same general specifications as the standard Sterlingworth model, w/differences chiefly in workmanship and materials. Higher grade models are stocked in fine select walnut; quantity and quality of engraving increases w/grade and price. Except for Grade A, all other grades have auto ejectors.
Grade A .... NiB $2984 Ex $2382 Gd $1650
Grade AE .... NiB $3398 Ex $2737 Gd $1891
Grade BE .... NiB $4679 Ex $3762 Gd $2589
Grade CE .... NiB $5915 Ex $4751 Gd $3261
Grade DE .... NiB $11,394 Ex $10,428 Gd $10,803
Grade FE .... NiB $21,357 Ex $17,085 Gd $11,618
Grade XE .... NiB $7552 Ex $6066 Gd $3890
Kautzky selective single trigger, add.......................... $350
Ventilated rib, add $450
Beavertail forearm, add $275
20 ga., add 60%

SINGLE-BARREL TRAP GUNS
Boxlock. Auto ejector.12 ga. only. 30- or 32-inch vent-rib bbl. Weight: 7.5 to 8 lbs. Trap-style stock and forearm of select walnut, checkered, recoil pad optional. The four grades differ chiefly in quality of wood and engraving; Grade M guns, built to order, have finest Circassian walnut. Stock and receiver are elaborately engraved and inlaid w/gold. Disc. 1942. Note: In 1932, the Fox Trap Gun was redesigned and those manufactured after that date have a stock w/full pistol grip and Monte Carlo comb; at the same time frame was changed to permit the rib line to extend across it to the rear.
Grade JE .... NiB $5167 Ex $4158 Gd $2868
Grade KE .... NiB $5862 Ex $4715 Gd $3245
Grade LE .... NiB $8198 Ex $6519 Gd $4484
Grade ME .... NiB $14,611 Ex $11,689 Gd $7948

"SKEETER" DOUBLE-BARREL SHOTGUN
.... NiB $4699 Ex $3782 Gd $2609
Boxlock. Gauge: 12 or 20. Bbls.: 28 inches w/full-length vent rib. Weight: Approx. 7 lbs. Buttstock and beavertail forend of select American walnut, finely checkered. Soft rubber recoil pad and ivory bead sights. Made in early 1930s.

STERLINGWORTH DELUXE
Same general specifications as Sterlingworth except 32-inch bbl. also available, recoil pad, ivory bead sights.
W/plain extractors............ NiB $1699 Ex $1369 Gd $947
W/automatic ejectors .... NiB $2144 Ex $1737 Gd $1217
20 ga., add.. 45%

STERLINGWORTH HAMMERLESS DOUBLE
Boxlock. Double triggers (Fox-Kautzky selective single trigger extra). Plain extractors (auto ejectors extra). Gauges: 12,16, 20. Bbl. lengths: 26-, 28-, 30-inch; chokes F/F, M/F, C/M (any combination of C to F choke borings was available at no extra cost). Weight: 12 ga., 6.88 to 8.25 lbs.; 16 ga., 6 to 7 lbs.; 20 ga., 5.75 to 6.75 lbs. Checkered pistol-grip stock and forearm.
W/plain extractors .... NiB $1570 Ex $1265 Gd $875
W/automatic ejectors .... NiB $1990 Ex $1601 Gd $1102
Selective single trigger, add 25%

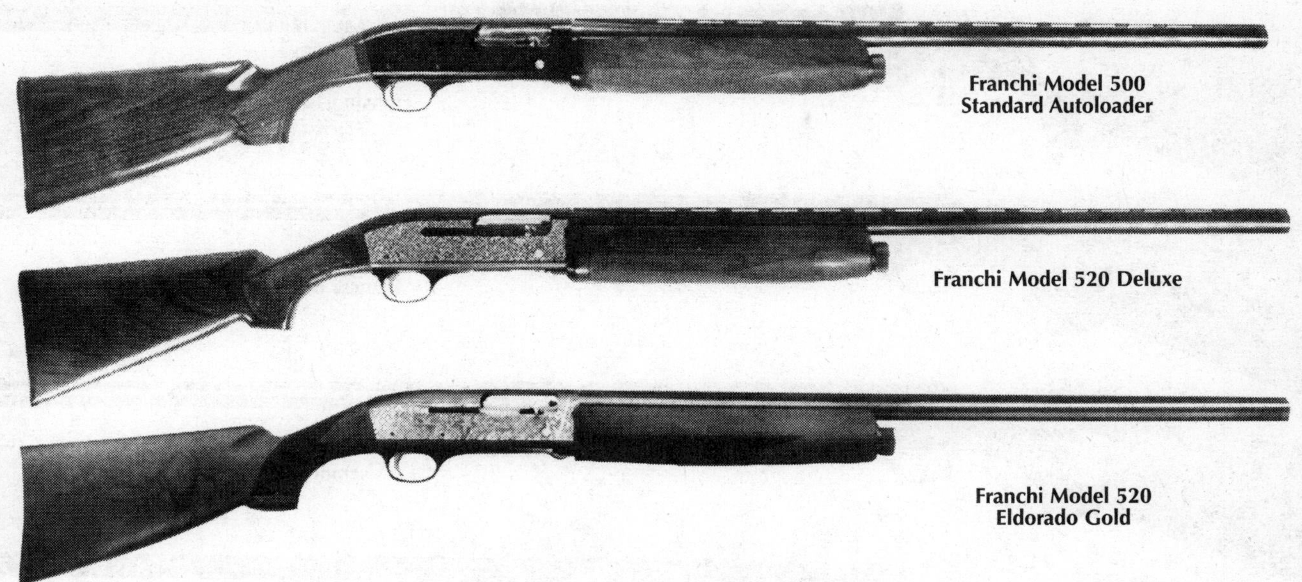

Franchi Model 500 Standard Autoloader

Franchi Model 520 Deluxe

Franchi Model 520 Eldorado Gold

STERLINGWORTH SKEET AND UPLAND GAME GUN
Same general specifications as the standard Sterlingworth except has 26- or 28-inch bbls. w/skeet boring only, straight-grip stock. Weight: 7 lbs. (12 ga.).
W/plain extractors. . . . . NiB $2364 Ex $1908 Gd $1324
W/automatic ejectors . . . . NiB $2820 Ex $2273 Gd $1572
20 ga., add 45%

SUPER HE GRADE. . . . . NiB $5457 Ex $4392 Gd $3031
Long-range gun made in 12 ga. only (chambered for 3-inch shells on order), 30- or 32-inch full choke bbls., auto ejectors standard. Weight: 8.75 to 9.75 lbs. General specifications same as standard Sterlingworth.

CMC HAMMERLESS DOUBLE-BARREL SHOTGUNS
High-grade doubles similar to the original Fox models. 20 ga. only. 26- 28- or 30-inch bbls. Double triggers automatic safety and ejectors. Weight: 5.5 to 7 lbs. Custom Circassian walnut stock w/hand-rubbed oil finish. Custom stock configuration: straight, semi- or full pistol-grip stock w/traditional pad, hard rubber plate checkered or skeleton butt; Schnabel, splinter or beavertail forend. Made 1993 to date.
CE grade . . . . NiB $8124 Ex $6525 Gd $4479
XE grade . . . . NiB $8588 Ex $6900 Gd $4740
DE grade . . . . NiB $12,344 Ex $9875 Gd $6715
FE grade . . . . NiB $16,563 Ex $13,250 Gd $9010
Exhibition grade . . . . NiB $23,744 Ex $18,995 Gd $12,917

LUIGI FRANCHI S.P.A. — Brescia, Italy

MODEL 48/AL ULTRA LIGHT SHOTGUN
Recoil-operated, takedown, hammerless shotgun w/tubular magazine. Gauges: 12 or 20 (2.75-inch); 12-ga. Magnum (3-inch chamber). Bbls.: 24- to 32-inch w/various choke combinations. Weight: 5 lbs., 2 oz. (20 ga.) to 6.25 lbs. (12 ga.). Checkered pistol-grip walnut stock and forend w/high-gloss finish.
Standard model . . . . NiB $556 Ex $463 Gd $344
Hunter or magnum models . . . . . . NiB $594 Ex $493 Gd $365

MODEL 500 STANDARD AUTOLOADER . . . . NiB $462 Ex $381 Gd $278
Gas-operated. 12 gauge. Four round magazine. Bbls.: 26-, 28-inch; vent rib; IC, M, IM, F chokes. Weight: About 7 lbs. Checkered pistol-grip stock and forearm. Made 1976-80.

MODEL 520 DELUXE . . . . NiB $507 Ex $417 Gd $303
Same as Model 500 except higher grade w/engraved receiver. Made 1975-79.

MODEL 520 ELDORADO GOLD . . . . NiB $1020 Ex $827 Gd $582
Same as Model 520 except custom grade w/engraved and gold-inlaid receiver, finer quality wood. Intro. 1977.

MODEL 610VS SEMIAUTOMATIC SHOTGUN
Gas-operated Variopress system adjustable to function w/2.75- or 3-inch shells. 12 gauge. Four round magazine. 26- or 28-inch vent rib bbls. w/Franchoke tubes. Weight: 7 lbs., 2 oz. 47.5 inches overall. Alloy receiver w/four-lug rotating bolt and loaded chamber indicator. Checkered European walnut buttstock and forearm w/satin finish. Imported 1997-98.
Standard SV model . . . . NiB $634 Ex $519 Gd $372
Engraved SVL model . . . . NiB $691 Ex $565 Gd $404

MODEL 612 VARIOPRESS AUTOLOADING SHOTGUN
Gauge: 12 ga. Only. 24- to 28-inch bbl. 45 to 49-inches overall. Weight: 6.8 to 7 lbs. Five round magazine. Bead type sights with C, IC, M chokes. Blued, matte or Advantage camo finish. Imported 1999 to date.
Model 612 satin walnut
stock w/blued finish. . . . . NiB $484 Ex $394 Gd $280
Model 612 synthetic
stock w/matte finish. . . . . NiB $515 Ex $419 Gd $297
Model 612 Advantage stock and finish . . . . NiB $579 Ex $470 Gd $332
Model 612 Defense . . . . NiB $461 Ex $368 Gd $262
Model 612 Sporting . . . . NiB $804 Ex $615 Gd $458

MODEL 620 VARIOPRESS AUTOLOADING SHOTGUN
Gauge: 20 ga. Only. 24- 26- or 28-inch bbl. 45 to 49-inches overall. Weight: 5.9 to 6.1 lbs. Five round magazine. Bead type sights with C, IC, M chokes. Satin walnut or Advantage camo stock. Imported 1999 to date.
Model 620 satin walnut
stock w/matte finish . . . . NiB $482 Ex $392 Gd $278
Model 620 Advantage
camo stock and finish . . . . NiB $577 Ex $468 Gd $330
Model 620 Youth (short stock). . . . . NiB $488 Ex $397 Gd $281

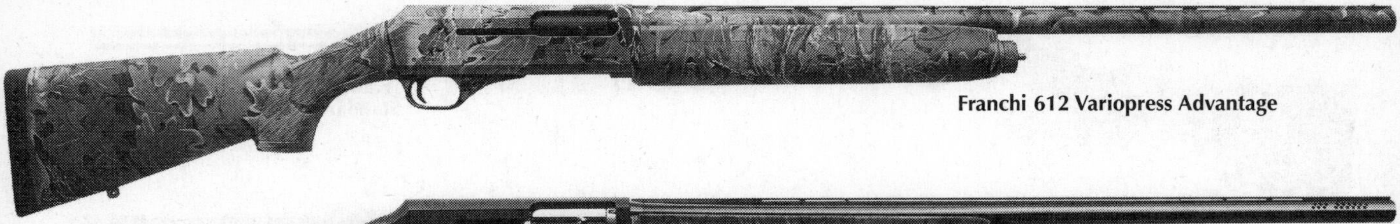

Franchi 612 Variopress Advantage

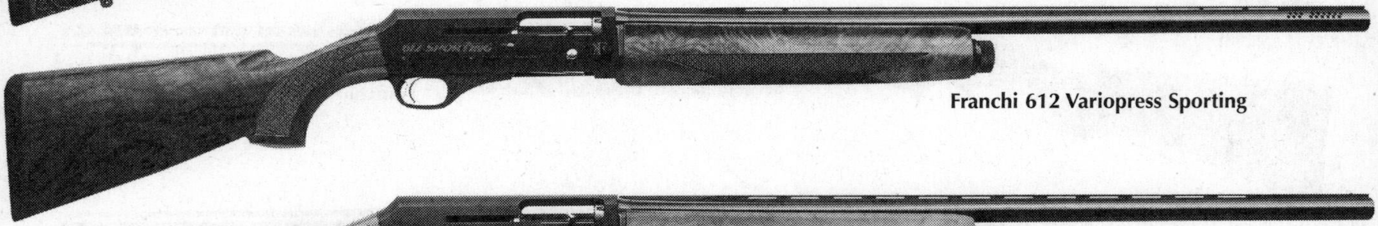

Franchi 612 Variopress Sporting

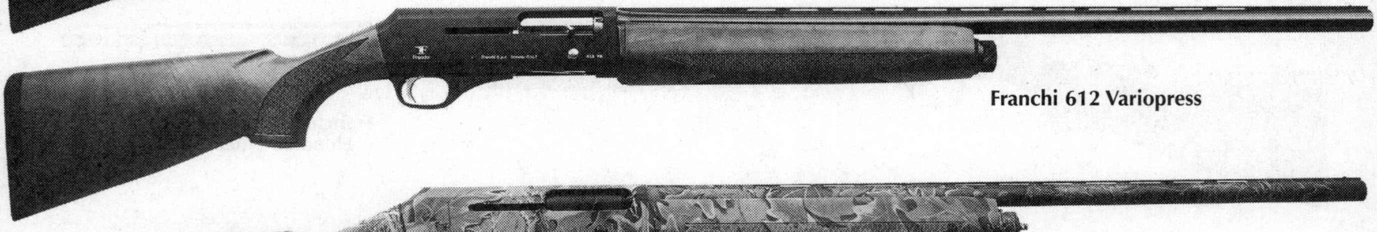

Franchi 612 Variopress

Franchi 620 Variopress Advantage

Franchi 620 Variopress

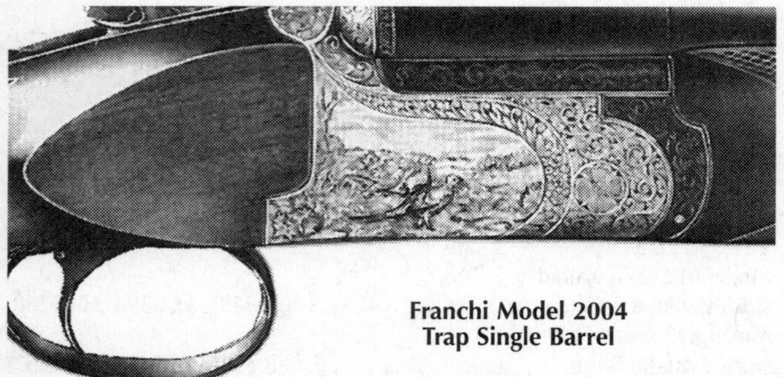

Franchi Model 2004 Trap Single Barrel

MODEL 2003 TRAP O/U . . . . NiB $1292 Ex $1185 Gd $884
Boxlock. Auto ejectors. Selective single trigger. 12 ga. Bbls.: 30-, 32-inch IM/F, F/F, high-vent rib. Weight (w/30-inch bbl.): 8.25 lbs. Checkered walnut beavertail forearm and stock w/straight or Monte Carlo comb, recoil pad. Luggage-type carrying case. Introduced 1976. Disc.

MODEL 2004 TRAP SINGLE BARREL . . . NiB $1325 Ex $1073 Gd $751
Same as Model 2003 except single bbl., 32- or 34-inch. Full choke. Weight (w/32-inch bbl.): 8.25 lbs. Introduced 1976. Disc.

MODEL 2005 COMBINATION TRAP . . NiB $1900 Ex $1534 Gd $1065
Model 2004/2005 type gun w/two sets of bbls., single and over/under. Introduced 1976. Disc.

MODEL 2005/3 COMBINATION TRAP . . . . . NiB $2669 Ex $2160 Gd $1509
Model 2004/2005 type gun w/three sets of bbls., any combination of single and over/under. Introduced 1976. Disc.

MODEL 3000/2 COMBINATION TRAP . . . . . NiB $3013 Ex $2440 Gd $1708
Boxlock. Automatic ejectors. Selective single trigger. 12 ga. only. Bbls.: 32-inch over/under choked F/IM, 34-inch underbarrel M choke; high vent rib. Weight (w/32-inch bbls.): 8 lbs., 6 oz. Choice of six different castoff buttstocks. Introduced 1979. Disc.

AIRONE HAMMERLESS DOUBLE . . . . . NiB $1247 Ex $1012 Gd $712
Boxlock. Anson & Deeley system action. Auto ejectors. Double triggers. 12 ga. Various bbl. lengths, chokes, weights. Checkered straight-grip stock and forearm. Made 1940-50.

ALCIONE O/U SHOTGUN
Hammerless, takedown shotgun w/engraved receiver. Selective single trigger and ejectors. 12 ga. w/3-inch chambers. Bbls.: 26-inch (IC/M, 28-inch (M/F). Weight: 6.75 lbs. Checkered French walnut buttstock and forend. Imported from Italy 1982-89.
Standard model . . . . NiB $697 Ex $563 Gd $391
SL model
(disc. 1986) . . . . NiB $1181 Ex $953 Gd $661

ALCIONE FIELD (97-12 IBS) O/U
Similar to the Standard Alcione model except w/nickel-finished receiver. 26- or 28-inch bbls. w/Franchoke tubes. Imported 1998 to date.
Standard Field model . . . . NiB $896 Ex $723 Gd $503
SL Field model
(w/sideplates, disc.) . . . . NiB $1092 Ex $881 Gd $612

ALCIONE SPORT (SL IBS) O/U. . . . . NiB $1074 Ex $871 Gd $612
Similar to the Alcione Field model except chambered for 2.75 or 3-inch shells. Ported 29-inch bbls. w/target vent rib and Franchoke tubes.

ALCIONE 2000 SX O/U SHOTGUN. . . . NiB $1546 Ex $1248 Gd $868
Similar to the Standard Alcione model except w/silver finished receiver and gold inlays. 28-inch bbls. w/Franchoke tubes. Weight: 7.25 lbs. Imported 1996-97.

ARISTOCRAT FIELD MODEL O/U . . . . NiB $611 Ex $492 Gd $340
Boxlock. Selective auto ejectors. Selective single trigger. 12 ga. Bbls.: 26-inch IC/M; 28- and 30-inch M/F choke, vent rib. Weight (w/26-inch bbls.): 7 lbs. Checkered pistol-grip stock and forearm. Made 1960-69.

ARISTOCRAT DELUXE AND SUPREME GRADES
Available in Field, Skeet and Trap models w/the same general specifications as standard guns of these types. Deluxe and Supreme Grades are of higher quality, w/stock and forearm of select walnut, elaborate relief engraving on receiver, trigger guard, tang and top lever. Supreme game birds inlaid in gold. Made 1960-66.
Deluxe grade . . . . NiB $1116 Ex $904 Gd $632
Supreme grade . . . . NiB $1580 Ex $1275 Gd $885

ARISTOCRAT IMPERIAL AND MONTE CARLO GRADES
Custom guns made in Field, Skeet and Trap models w/the same general specifications as standard for these types. Imperial and Monte Carlo grades are of highest quality w/stock and forearm of select walnut, fine engraving — elaborate on the latter grade. Made 1967-69.
Imperial grade . . . . NiB $2899 Ex $2339 Gd $1623
Monte Carlo grade . . . . NiB $4046 Ex $3257 Gd $2247

ARISTOCRAT MAGNUM MODEL. . . . . . . NiB $701 Ex $567 Gd $397
Same as Field Model except chambered for 3-inch shells, has 32-inch bbls. choked F/F; stock has recoil pad. Weight: About 8 lbs. Made 1962-65.

ARISTOCRAT SILVER KING. . . . . . . NiB $804 Ex $650 Gd $453
Available in Field, Magnum, Meet and Trap models w/the same general specifications as standard guns of these types. Silver King has stock and forearm of select walnut more elaborately engraved silver-finished receiver. Made 1962-69.

ARISTOCRAT SKEET MODEL . . . . . NiB $764 Ex $618 Gd $432
Same general specifications as Field Model except made only w/26-inch vent-rib bbls. w/SK chokes No. 1 and No. 2, skeet-style stock and forearm. Weight: About 7.5 lbs. Later production had wider (10mm) rib. Made 1960-69.

ARISTOCRAT TRAP MODEL . . . . . . NiB $771 Ex $623 Gd $435
Same general specifications as Field Model except made only w/30-inch vent-rib bbls., M/F choke, trap-style stock w/recoil pad, beavertail forearm. Later production had Monte Carlo comb, 10mm rib. Made 1960-69.

ASTORE HAMMERLESS DOUBLE. . . . . . . NiB $1054 Ex $851 Gd $592
Boxlock. Anson & Deeley system action. Plain extractors. Double triggers. 12 ga. Various bbl. lengths, chokes, weights. Checkered straight-grip stock and forearm. Made 1937-60.

ASTORE II . . . . NiB $1309 Ex $1055 Gd $731
Similar to Astore S but not as high grade. Furnished w/either plain extractors or auto ejectors, double triggers, pistol-grip stock. Bbls.: 27-inch IC/IM; 28-inch M/F chokes. Currently manufactured for Franchi in Spain.

Franchi Astore 5

ASTORE 5 . . . . NiB $2184 Ex $1772 Gd $1245
Same as Astore except has higher grade wood, fine engraving. automatic ejectors, single trigger, 28-inch bbl. M/F or IM/F chokes are standard on current production. Disc.

STANDARD MODEL AUTOLOADER
Recoil operated. Light alloy receiver. Gauges: 12, 20. Four round magazine. Bbls.: 26-, 28-, 30-inch; plain, solid or vent rib, IC/ M, F chokes. Weight: 12 ga., about 6.25 lbs. 20 ga., 5.13 lbs. Checkered pistol-grip stock and forearm. Made 1950 to date.
W/plain bbl. . . . . NiB $513 Ex $356 Gd $286
W/solid rib . . . . NiB $462 Ex $379 Gd $268
W/vent rib. NiB $494 Ex $402 Gd $285

CROWN, DIAMOND AND IMPERIAL GRADE
Same general specifications as Standard Model except these are custom guns of the highest quality. Crown Grade has hunting scene engraving, Diamond Grade has silver-inlaid scroll engraving; Imperial Grade has elaborately engraved hunting scenes w/figures inlaid in gold. Stock and forearm of fancy walnut. Made 1954-75.
Crown grade . . . . NiB $1719 Ex $1389 Gd $957
Diamond grade . . . . NiB $2229 Ex $1797 Gd $1244
Imperial grade . . . . NiB $2810 Ex $2261 Gd $1559

STANDARD MODEL MAGNUM
Same general specifications as Standard model except has 3-inch chamber, 32-inch (12 ga.) or 28-inch (20 ga.) F choke bbl., recoil pad. Weight: 12 ga., 8.25 lbs.; 20 ga., 6 lbs. Formerly designated "Superange Model." Made 1954-88.
W/plain bbl. . . . . NiB $510 Ex $414 Gd $293
W/vent rib . . . . NiB $536 Ex $436 Gd $307

DYNAMIC-12
Same general specifications and appearance as Standard Model, except 12 ga. only, has heavier steel receiver. Weight: About 7.25 lbs. Made 1965-72.
W/plain bbl. . . . . NiB $411 Ex $336 Gd $240
W/vent rib. NiB $449 Ex $366 Gd $260

DYNAMIC-12 SLUG GUN . . . . NiB $462 Ex $377 Gd $267
Same as standard gun except 12 ga. only, has heavier steel receiver. Made 1965-72.

DYNAMIC-12 SKEET GUN . . . . NiB $563 Ex $457 Gd $323
Same general specifications and appearance as Standard model except has heavier steel receiver, made only in 12 ga. w/26-inch vent-rib bbl., SK choke, stock and forearm of extra fancy walnut. Made 1965-72.

ELDORADO MODEL . . . . NiB $590 Ex $479 Gd $337
Same general specifications as Standard model except highest grade w/gold-filled engraving, stock and forearm of select walnut, furnished w/vent-rib bbl. only. Made 1954-75.

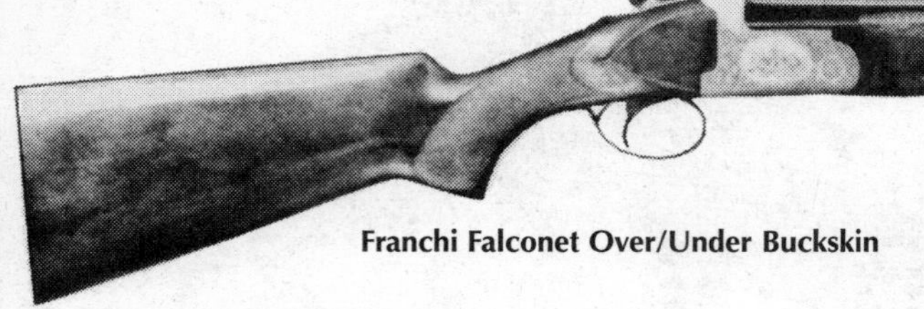
Franchi Falconet Over/Under Buckskin

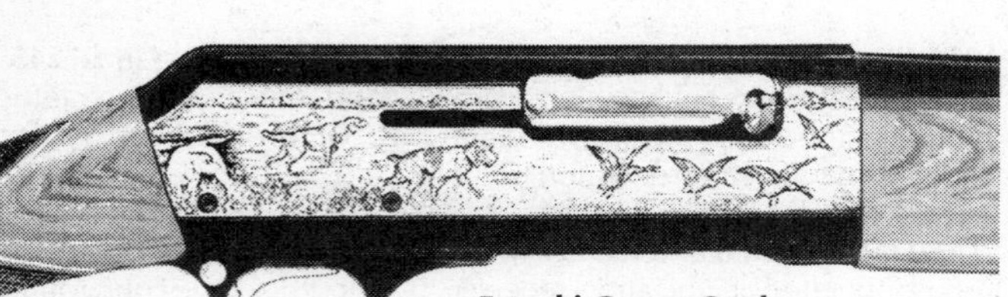
Franchi Crown Grade

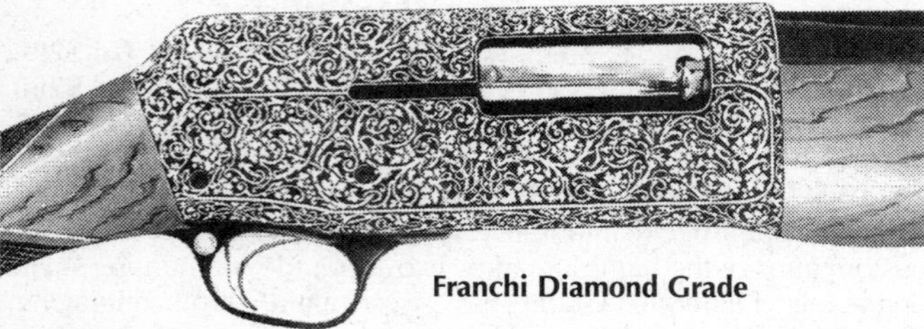
Franchi Diamond Grade

Franchi Eldorado

FALCONET INTERNATIONAL SKEET MODEL... NiB $1180 Ex $956 Gd $669
Similar to Standard Skeet model but higher grade. Made 1970-74.

FALCONET INTERNATIONAL TRAP MODEL . . . . NiB $1203 Ex $975 Gd $682
Similar to Standard model but higher grade; w/straight or Monte Carlo comb stock. Made 1970-74.

FALCONET O/U FIELD MODELS
Boxlock. Auto ejectors. Selective single trigger. Gauges: 12, 16, 20, 28, .410. Bbls.: 24-, 26-, 28-, 30-inch; vent rib. Chokes: C/IC, IC/M, M/F. Weight: from about 6 lbs. Engraved lightweight alloy receiver, light-colored in Buckskin model, blued in Ebony model, pickled silver in Silver model. Checkered walnut stock and forearm. Made 1968-75.
Buckskin or Ebony model . . . . NiB $732 Ex $593 Gd $415
Silver model . . . . NiB $809 Ex $655 Gd $457

FALCONET STANDARD SKEET MODEL . . . . NiB $1007 Ex $813 Gd $565
Same general specifications as Field models except made only w/26-inch bbls. w/SK chokes No. 1 and No. 2, wide vent rib, color-casehardened receiver skeet-style stock and forearm. Weight: 12 ga., about 7.75 lbs. Made 1970-74.

FALCONET STANDARD TRAP MODEL . . . . . NiB $1018 Ex $826 Gd $581
Same general specifications as Field models except made only in 12 ga. w/30-inch bbls., choked M/F, wide vent rib, color-casehardened receiver, Monte Carlo trap style stock and forearm, recoil pad. Weight: About 8 lbs. Made 1970-74.

HAMMERLESS SIDELOCK DOUBLES
Hand-detachable locks. Self-opening action. Auto ejectors. Double triggers or single trigger. Gauges: 12,16, 20. Bbl. lengths, chokes, weights according to customer's specifications. Checkered stock and forend, straight or pistol grip. Made in six grades — Condor, Imperiale, Imperiale S, Imperiale Montecarlo No. 5, Imperiale Montecarlo No.11, Imperiale Montecarlo Extra — which differ chiefly in overall quality, engraving, grade of wood, checkering, etc.; general specifications are the same. Only the Imperiale Montecarlo Extra Grade is currently manufactured.
Condor grade. . . . . NiB $8537 Ex $6851 Gd $4695
Imperiale, Imperiale S grades . . . . NiB $11,982 Ex $9585 Gd $6518
Imperiale Monte Carlo grades No. 5, 11 . . . . NiB $16,862 Ex $13,489 Gd $9173
Imperiale Monte Carlo Extra grade . . . . . NiB $19,613 Ex $15,690 Gd $10,669

HUNTER MODEL
Same general specifications as Standard Model except higher grade w/engraved receiver; furnished w/ribbed bbl. only. Made 1950 to 90.
W/solid rib . . . . NiB $453 Ex $366 Gd $255
W/vent rib . . . . NiB $486 Ex $392 Gd $272

HUNTER MODEL MAGNUM. . . . . NiB $551 Ex $445 Gd $311
Same as Standard Model Magnum except higher grade w/engraved receiver, vent rib bbl. only. Formerly designated "Wildfowler Model." Made 1954-73.

PEREGRINE MODEL 400 . . . . NiB $755 Ex $611 Gd $427
Same general specifications as Model 451 except has steel receiver. Weight (w/26.5-inch bbl.): 6 lbs., 15 oz. Made 1975-78.

PEREGRINE MODEL 451 O/U . . . . NiB $755 Ex $553 Gd $387
Boxlock. Lightweight alloy receiver. Automatic ejectors. Selective single trigger. 12 ga. Bbls.: 26.5-, 28-inch; choked C/IC, IC/M, M/F; vent rib. Weight (w/26.5-inch bbls.): 6 lbs., 1 oz. Checkered pistol-grip stock and forearm. Made 1975-78.

PG-80 GAS-OPERATED SEMIAUTOMATIC SHOTGUN
Gas-operated, takedown, hammerless shotgun w/tubular magazine. 12 ga. w/2.75-inch chamber. Five round magazine. Bbls.: 24 to 30 inches w/vent rib. Weight: 7.5 lbs. Gold-plated trigger. Checkered pistol-grip stock and forend of European walnut. Imported from Italy 1985-90.
Prestige model . . . . NiB $598 Ex $485 Gd $339
Elite model . . . . NiB $665 Ex $538 Gd $376

SKEET GUN. NiB $541 Ex $439 Gd $307
Same general specifications and appearance as Standard Model except made only w/26-inch vent-rib bbl., SK choke. Stock and forearm of extra fancy walnut. Made 1972-74.

SLUG GUN . . . . NiB $393 Ex $314 Gd $213
Same as Standard Model except has 22-inch plain bbl., Cyl. bore, folding leaf open rear sight, gold bead front sight. Made 1960 to date.

Franchi Hunter Model w/Ventilated Rib

Franchi Black Magic 48/AL Semiautomatic

Franchi LAW-12

Franchi SPAS-12

Franchi Sporting 2000

TURKEY GUN . . . . NiB $493 Ex $397 Gd $275
Same as Standard Model Magnum except higher grade w/turkey scene engraved receiver, 12 ga. only, 36-inch matted-rib bbl., Extra Full choke. Made 1963-65.

BLACK MAGIC 48/AL SEMIAUTOMATIC
Similar to the Franchi Model 48/AL except w/Franchoke screw-in tubes and matte black receiver w/Black Magic logo. Gauge: 12 or 20, 2.75-inch chamber. Bbls.: 24-, 26-, 28-inch w/vent rib; 24-inch rifled slug w/sights. Weight: 5.2 lbs. (20 ga.). Checkered walnut buttstock and forend. Blued finish.
Standard model . . . . NiB $569 Ex $458 Gd $316
Slug bbl. model . . . . NiB $611 Ex $491 Gd $338

FALCONET 2000 O/U . . . . NiB $1320 Ex $1672 Gd $729
Boxlock. Single selective trigger. Selective automatic ejectors. Gauge: 12, 2.75-inch chambers. Bbls.: 26-inch w/Franchoke tubes; IC/M/F. Weight: 6 lbs. Checkered walnut stock and forearm. Engraved silver receiver w/gold-plated game scene. Imported from 1992-93.

LAW-12 SHOTGUN. . . . . NiB $593 Ex $478 Gd $330
Similar to the SPAS-12 Model except gas-operated semiautomatic

(cont'd.) LAW-12 SHOTGUN
action only, ambidextrous safety, decocking lever and adj. sights. Made 1983-94.

SPAS-12 SHOTGUN
Selective operating system functions as a gas-operated semi-automatic or pump action. Gauge: 12, 2.75-inch chamber. Seven round magazine. Bbl.: 21.5 inches w/cylinder bore and muzzle protector or optional screw-in choke tubes, matte finish. 41 inches overall w/fixed stock. Weight: 8.75 lbs. Blade front sight, aperture rear sight. Folding or black nylon buttstock w/pistol grip and forend, non-reflective anodized finish. Made 1983-94.
Fixed stock model . . . . NiB $916 Ex $739 Gd $512
Folding stock model . . . . NiB $1044 Ex $841 Gd $582
Optional choke tubes, add $125

SPORTING 2000 O/U. . . . . NiB $1402 Ex $1136 Gd $794
Similar to the Franchi Falconet 2000. Boxlock. Single selective trigger. Selective automatic ejectors. Gauge: 12; 2.75-inch chambers. Ported (1992-93) or unported 28-inch bbls., w/vent rib. Weight: 7.75 lbs. Blued receiver. Bead front sight. Checkered walnut stock and forearm; plastic composition buttplate. Imported from 1992-93 and 1997 to date.

Francotte Model 8446

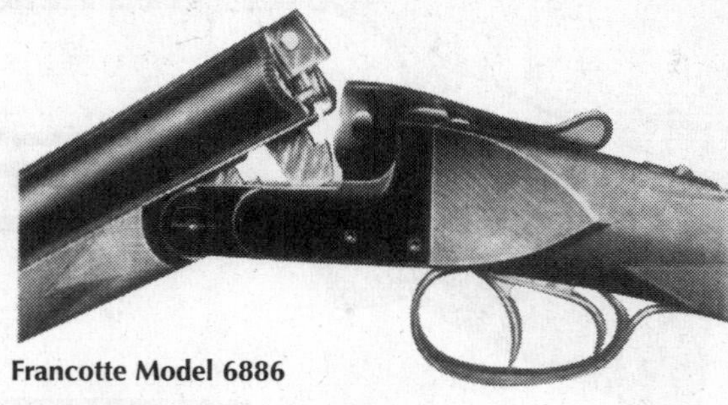

Francotte Model 6886

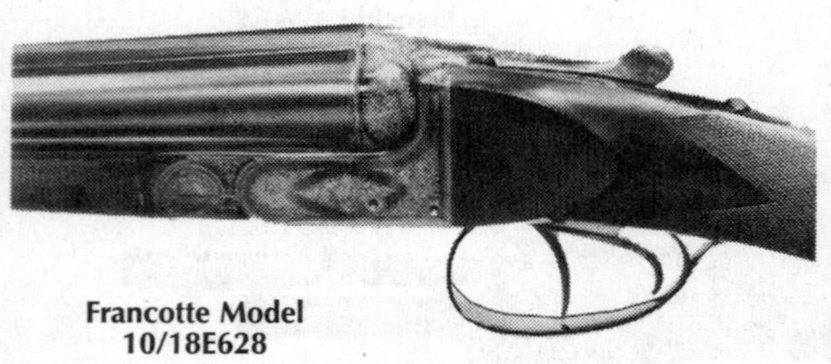

Francotte Model 10/18E628

Francotte Model 9261

AUGUSTE FRANCOTTE & CIE., S.A. — Liège, Belgium

Francotte shotguns for many years were distributed in the U.S. by Abercrombie & Fitch of New York City. This firm has used a series of model designations for Francotte guns which do not correspond to those of the manufacturer. Because so many Francotte owners refer to their guns by the A & F model names and numbers, the A & F series is included in a listing separate from that of the standard Francotte numbers.

BOXLOCK HAMMERLESS DOUBLES

Anson & Deeley system. Side clips. Greener crossbolt on models 6886, 8446, 4996 and 9261; square crossbolt on Model 6930, Greener-Scott crossbolt on Model 8457, Purdey bolt on Models 11/18E and 10/18E/628. Auto ejectors. Double triggers. Made in all standard gauges, barrel lengths, chokes, weights. Checkered stock and forend, straight or pistol-grip. The eight models listed vary chiefly in fastenings as described above, finish and engraving, etc.; general specifications are the same. Disc.

Model 6886 . . . . NiB $3539 Ex $2863 Gd $1998
Model 8446 (Francotte Special),
6930, 4996 . . . . NiB $3979 Ex $3215 Gd $2138
Model 8457,
9261 (Francotte Original), 11/18E . . . . NiB $5084 Ex $4125 Gd $2845
Model 10/18E/628 . . . . NiB $6416 Ex $5168 Gd $3571

BOXLOCK HAMMERLESS DOUBLES — A & F SERIES

Boxlock, Anson & Deeley type. Crossbolt. Sideplate on all except Knockabout Model. Side clips. Auto ejectors. Double triggers. Gauges: 12, 16, 20, 28, .410. Bbls.: 26- to 32-inch in 12 ga., 26- and 28-inch in other ga.; any boring. Weight: 4.75 to 8 lbs.

(cont'd.) **BOXLOCK HAMMERLESS DOUBLES — A & F SERIES**

depending on ga. and bbl. length. Checkered stock and forend; straight, half or full pistol grip. The seven grades (No. 45 Eagle Grade, No. 30, No. 25, No. 20, No. 14, Jubilee Model, Knockabout Model) differ chiefly in overall quality, engraving, grade of wood, checkering, etc.; general specifications are the same. Disc.

Jubilee model
No. 14 . . . . NiB $2261 Ex $1843 Gd $1307
Jubilee model
No. 18 . . . . NiB $2918 Ex $2368 Gd $1665
Jubilee model
No. 20 . . . . NiB $3677 Ex $2975 Gd $2077
Jubilee model
No. 25 . . . . NiB $3951 Ex $3194 Gd $2226

(cont'd.) **BOXLOCK HAMMERLESS DOUBLES — A & F SERIES**

Jubilee model
No. 30 . . . . NiB $5949 Ex $4797 Gd $3324
Eagle grade
No. 45 . . . . NiB $8225 Ex $6620 Gd $4566
Knockabout model . . . . NiB $2619 Ex $2128 Gd $1500

BOXLOCK HAMMERLESS DOUBLES (SIDEPLATES)

Anson & Deeley system. Reinforced frame w/side clips. Purdey-type bolt except on Model 8455, which has Greener crossbolt. Auto ejectors. Double triggers. Made in all standard gauges, bbl. lengths, chokes, weights. Checkered stock and forend, straight or pistol grip. Models 10594, 8455 and 6982 are of equal quality, differing chiefly in style of engraving; Model 9/40E/38321 is a higher grade gun in all details and has fine English-style engraving. Present models quoted and built to customer specifications.

Models 10594, 8455, 6982 . . . . NiB $5141 Ex $4148 Gd $2877
Model 9/40E/38321 . . . . NiB $6232 Ex $5020 Gd $3470

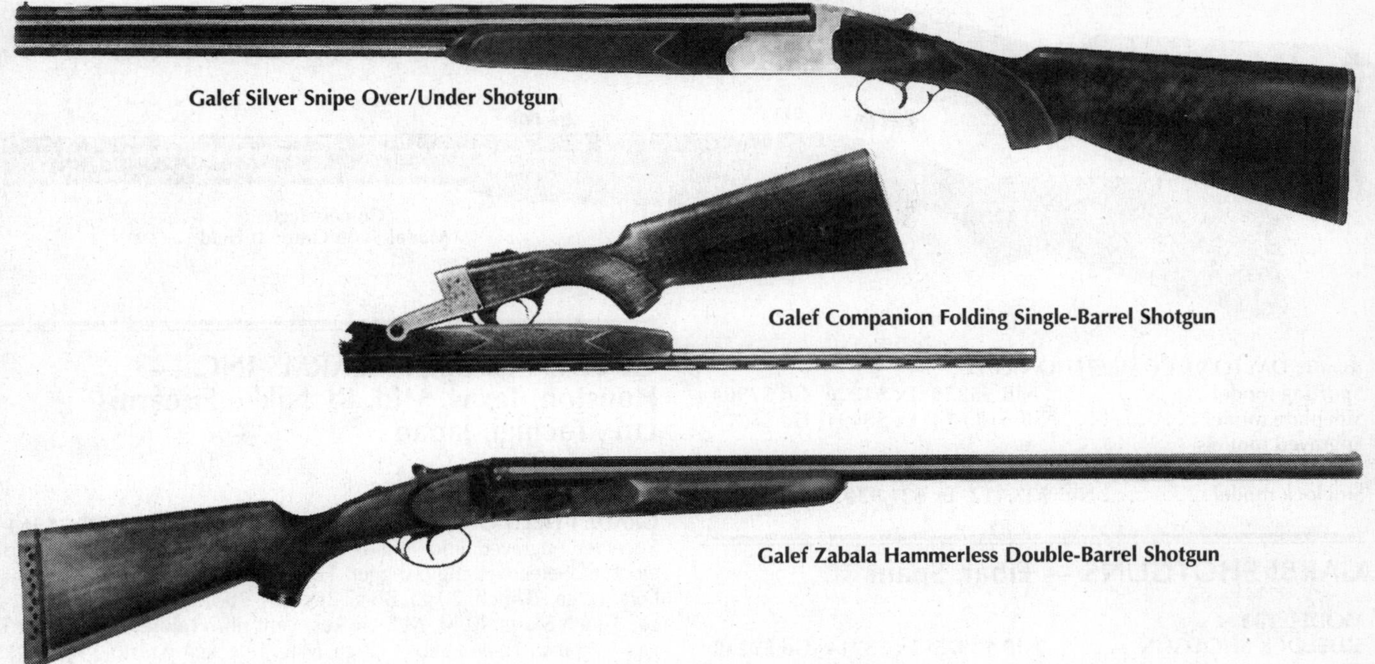
Galef Silver Snipe Over/Under Shotgun

Galef Companion Folding Single-Barrel Shotgun

Galef Zabala Hammerless Double-Barrel Shotgun

FINE O/U SHOTGUN $9296
Model 9/40.SE. Boxlock, Anson & Deeley system. Auto ejectors. Double triggers. Made in all standard gauges; bbl. length, boring to order. Weight: About 6.75 lbs. 12 ga. Checkered stock and forend, straight or pistol grip. Currently manufactured to customer specifications.

FINE SIDELOCK
HAMMERLESS DOUBLE .... NiB $24,544 Ex $19,635 Gd $13,352
Model 120.HE/328. Automatic ejectors. Double triggers. Made in all standard ga.; bbl. length, boring, weight to order. Checkered stock and forend, straight or pistol-grip. Currently manufactured to customer specifications.

HALF-FINE O/U SHOTGUN .... NiB $10,104 Ex $8083 Gd $5447
Model SOB.E/11082. Boxlock, Anson & Deeley system. Auto ejectors. Double triggers. Made in all standard gauges; barrel length, boring to order. Checkered stock and forend, straight or pistol grip. Note: This model is similar to No. 9/40.SE except general quality lower. Disc.

GALEF SHOTGUNS — Manufactured for J. L. Galef & Son, Inc., New York, New York, by M. A. V. I., Gardone F. T., Italy, by Zabala Hermanos, Eiquetta, Spain, and by Antonio Zoli, Gardone V. T., Italy

SILVER SNIPE OVER/UNDER SHOTGUN .... NiB $551 Ex $438 Gd $305
Boxlock. Plain extractors. Single trigger. Gauges: 12, 20; 3-inch chambers. Bbls: 26-, 28-, 30-inch (latter in 12 ga. only); IC/M, M/F chokes; vent rib. Weight: 12 ga. w/28-inch bbls., 6.5 lbs. Checkered walnut pistol-grip stock and forearm. Introduced by Antonio Zoli in 1968. Disc. See illustration previous page.

GOLDEN SNIPE .... NiB $620 Ex $501 Gd $349
Same as Silver Snipe, except has selective automatic ejectors. Made by Antonio Zoli 1968 to date.

MONTE CARLO TRAP
SINGLE-BARREL SHOTGUN.............. NiB $264 Ex $214 Gd $151
Hammerless. Underlever. Plain extractor. 12 ga. 32-inch bbl., F choke, vent rib.

***(cont'd.)* MONTE CARLO TRAP SINGLE-BARREL SHOTGUN**
Weight: About 8.25 lbs. Checkered pistol-grip stock w/Monte Carlo comb and recoil pad, beavertail forearm. Introduced by M. A. V. I. in 1968. Disc.

SILVER HAWK HAMMERLESS DOUBLE..... NiB $527 Ex $426 Gd $297
Boxlock. Plain extractors. Double triggers. Gauges: 12, 20; 3-inch chambers. Bbls.: 26-, 28-, 30-inch (latter in 12 ga. only); IC/M, M/F chokes. Weight: 12 ga. w/26-inch bbls., 6 lbs. 6 oz. Checkered walnut pistol-grip stock and beavertail forearm. Made by Antonio Zoli 1968-72.

COMPANION FOLDING SINGLE-BARREL SHOTGUN
Hammerless. Underlever. Gauges: 12 Mag., 16, 20 Mag., 28, .410. Bbls.: 26-inch (.410 only), 28-inch (12, 16, 20, 28), 30-inch (12-ga. only); F choke; plain or vent rib. Weight: 4.5 lbs. for .410 to 5 lbs., 9 oz. for 12 ga. Checkered pistol-grip stock and forearm. Made by M. A. V. I. from 1968 to date.
W/plain bbl. .... NiB $136 Ex $111 Gd $79
W/ventilated rib .... NiB $176 Ex $144 Gd $101

ZABALA HAMMERLESS DOUBLE-BARREL SHOTGUN
Boxlock. Plain extractors. Double triggers. Gauges: 10 Mag., 12 Mag., 16, 20 Mag., 28, .410. Bbls.: 22-, 26-, 28-, 30-, 32-inch; IC/IC, IC/M, M/F chokes. Weight: 12 ga. w/28-inch bbls., 7.75 lbs. Checkered walnut pistol-grip stock and beavertail forearm, recoil pad. Made by Zabala from 1972 to date. See illustration previous page.
10 ga. .... NiB $297 Ex $239 Gd $166
Other ga. .... NiB $220 Ex $178 Gd $124

GAMBA — Gardone V. T. (Brescia), Italy

DAYTONA COMPETITION O/U
Boxlock w/Boss-style locking system. Anatomical single trigger; optional adj., single-selective release trigger. Selective automatic ejectors. Gauge: 12 or 20; 2.75- or 3-inch chambers. Bbls.: 26.75-, 28-, 30- or 32-inch choked SK/SK, IM/F or M/F. Weight: 7.5 to 8.5 lbs. Black or chrome receiver w/blued bbls. Checkered select walnut stock and forearm w/oil finish. Imported by Heckler & Koch until 1992.
American Trap model................. NiB $5514 Ex $4430 Gd $3043
Pigeon, Skeet, Trap models .... NiB $6336 Ex $5088 Gd $3491

SHOTGUNS

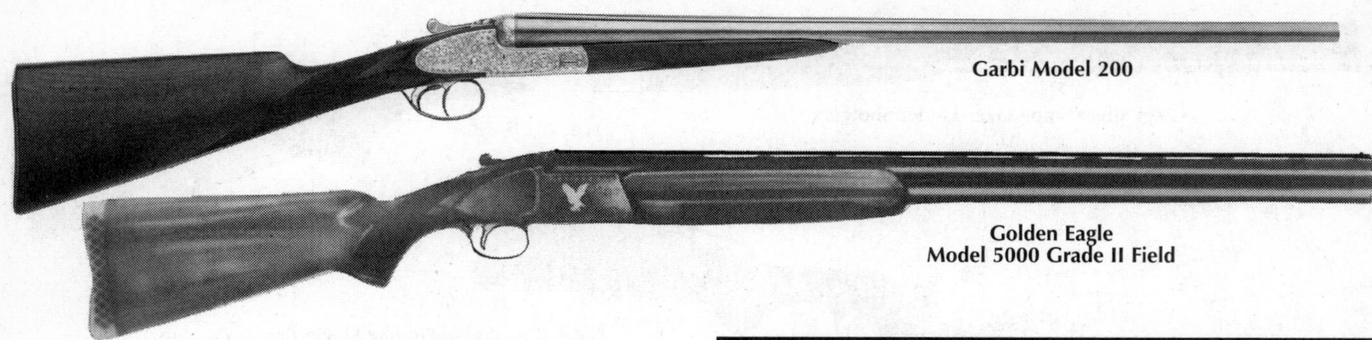
Garbi Model 200

Golden Eagle Model 5000 Grade II Field

(cont'd.) DAYTONA COMPETITION O/U
Sporting model . . . . NiB $5259 Ex $4226 Gd $2904
Sideplate model . . . . NiB $10,614 Ex $8491 Gd $5774
Engraved models
. . . . NiB to $12,750 Ex to $10,200 Gd to $6936
Sidelock model. . . . . NiB $27,412 Ex $21,930 Gd $14,912

GARBI SHOTGUNS — Eibar, Spain

MODEL 100
SIDELOCK SHOTGUN . . . . NiB $3975 Ex $3214 Gd $2240
Gauges: 12, 16, 20 and 28. Bbls.: 25-, 28-, 30-inch. Action: Holland & Holland pattern sidelock; automatic ejectors and double trigger. Weight: 5 lbs., 6 oz. to 7 lbs. 7 oz. English-style straight grip stock w/fine-line hand-checkered butt; classic forend. Made 1985 to date.

MODEL 101
SIDELOCK SHOTGUN . . . . NiB $5009 Ex $4041 Gd $2802
Same general specifications as Model 100 except the sidelocks are handcrafted w/hand-engraved receiver; select walnut straight-grip stock.

MODEL 102
SIDELOCK SHOTGUN . . . . NiB $5352 Ex $4315 Gd $2989
Similar to the Model 101 except w/large scroll engraving. Made 1985-93.

MODEL 103 HAMMERLESS DOUBLE
Similar to Model 100 except w/Purdey-type, higher grade engraving.
Model 103A Standard . . . . NiB $5429 Ex $4377 Gd $3031
Model 103A Royal Deluxe . . . NiB $10,005 Ex $8043 Gd $5532
Model 103B. . . . . NiB $8119 Ex $6534 Gd $4505
Model 103B Royal Deluxe . . . . NiB $14,018 Ex $11,214 Gd $7625

MODEL 200
HAMMERLESS DOUBLE . . . . . . NiB $8042 Ex $6471 Gd $4464
Similar to Model 100 except w/double heavy-duty locks. Continental-style floral and scroll engraving. Checkered deluxe walnut stock and forearm.

GARCIA CORPORATION — Teaneck, New Jersey

BRONCO 22/.410 O/U COMBO . . . NiB $132 Ex $108 Gd $77
Swing-out action. Takedown. 18.5-inch bbls.; .22 LR over, .410 ga. under. Weight: 4.5 lbs. One-piece stock and receiver, crackle finish. Intro. In 1976. Disc.

BRONCO .410 SINGLE SHOT. . . . . . . NiB $107 Ex $87 Gd $63
Swing-out action. Takedown. .410 ga. 18.5-inch bbl. Weight: 3.5 lbs. One-piece stock and receiver, crackle finish. Intro. In 1967. Disc.

GOLDEN EAGLE FIREARMS INC. — Houston, Texas, Mfd. By Nikko Firearms Ltd., Tochigi, Japan

EAGLE MODEL 5000
GRADE I FIELD O/U. . . . . NiB $911 Ex $825 Gd $564
Receiver engraved and inlaid w/gold eagle head. Boxlock. Auto ejectors. Selective single trigger. 12, 20 ga.; 2.75- or 3-inch chambers, 12 ga., 3-inch, 20 ga. Bbls.: 26-, 28-, 30-inch (latter only in 12-ga. 3-inch Mag.); IC/M, M/F chokes; vent rib. Weight: 6.25 lbs., 20 ga.; 7.25 lbs., 12 ga.; 8 lbs., 12-ga. Mag. Checkered pistol-grip stock and semi-beavertail forearm. Imported 1975-82. Note: Guns marketed 1975-76 under the Nikko brand name have white receivers; since 1976 are blued.

EAGLE MODEL 5000
GRADE I SKEET. . . . . NiB $1011 Ex $809 Gd $564
Same as Field model except has 26- or 28-inch bbls. w/wide (11 mm) vent rib, SK choked. Imported 1975-82.

EAGLE MODEL 5000
GRADE I TRAP . . . . NiB $958 Ex $775 Gd $541
Same as Field model except has 30-, or 32-inch bbls. w/wide (11 mm) vent rib (M/F, IM/F, F/F chokes), trap-style stock w/recoil pad. Imported 1975-82.

EAGLE MODEL 5000
GRADE II FIELD . . . . NiB $1043 Ex $843 Gd $587
Same as Grade I Field model except higher grade w/fancier wood, more elaborate engraving and "screaming eagle" inlaid in gold. Imported 1975-82.

EAGLE MODEL 5000
GRADE II SKEET . . . . NiB $1079 Ex $873 Gd $610
Same as Grade I Skeet model except higher grade w/fancier wood, more elaborate engraving and "screaming eagle" inlaid in gold; inertia trigger, vent side ribs. Imported 1975-82.

EAGLE MODEL 5000
GRADE II TRAP. . . . . NiB $1096 Ex $887 Gd $619
Same as Grade I Trap model except higher grade w/fancier wood, more elaborate engraving and "screaming eagle" inlaid in gold; inertia trigger, vent side ribs. Imported 1975-82.

EAGLE MODEL 5000
GRADE III GRANDEE . . . . NiB $2852 Ex $2303 Gd $1601
Best grade, available in Field, Skeet and Trap models w/same general specifications as lower grades. Has sideplates w/game scene engraving, scroll on frame and bbls., fancy wood (Monte Carlo comb, full pistol-grip and recoil pad on Trap model). Made 1976-82.

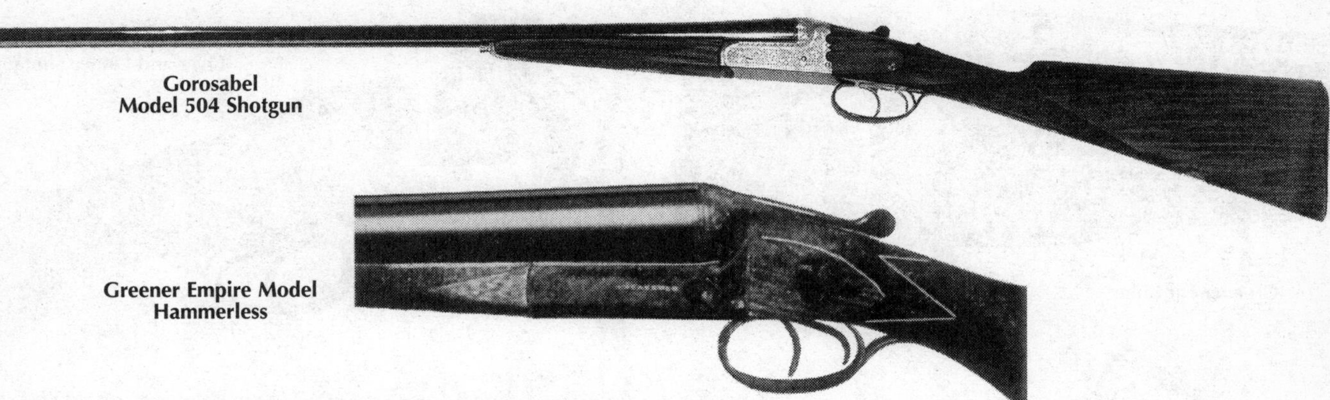

Gorosabel Model 504 Shotgun

Greener Empire Model Hammerless

GOROSABEL SHOTGUNS — Spain

MODEL 503 SHOTGUN . . . . NiB $935 Ex $758 Gd $531
Gauges: 12, 16, 20 and .410. Action: Anson & Deely-style boxlock. Bbls.: 26-, 27-, and 28-inch. Select European walnut, English or pistol grip, sliver or beavertail forend, hand-checkering. Scalloped frame and scroll engraving. Intro. 1985; disc..

MODEL 504 SHOTGUN . . . . NiB $1006 Ex $814 Gd $569
Gauge: 12 or 20. Action: Holland & Holland-style sidelock. Bbl.: 26-, 27-, or 28-inch. Select European walnut, English or pistol grip, sliver or beavertail forend, hand-checkering. Holland-style large scroll engraving. Inro. 1985; disc..

MODEL 505 SHOTGUN . . . . NiB $1381 Ex $1114 Gd $773
Gauge: 12 or 20. Action: Holland & Holland-style sidelock. Bbls.: 26-, 27-, or 28-inch. Select European walnut, English or pistol grip, silver or beavertail forend, hand-checkering. Purdey-style fine scroll and rose engraving. Intro. 1985; disc..

STEPHEN GRANT — London, England

BEST QUALITY SELF-OPENER DOUBLE-BARREL SHOTGUN . . . . NiB $15,313 Ex $12,250 Gd $8330
Sidelock, self-opener. Gauges: 12, 16 and 20. Bbls.: 25 to 30 inches standard. Highest-grade English or European walnut straight-grip buttstock and forearm w/Greener type lever. Imported by Stoeger in the 1950s.

BEST QUALITY SIDE-LEVER DOUBLE-BARREL SHOTGUN . . . . NiB $13,125 Ex $10,500 Gd $7140
Sidelock, self-lever. Gauges: 12, 16 and 20. Bbls.: 25 to 30 inches standard. Highest-grade English or European walnut straight-grip buttstock and forearm w/Greener type lever. Imported by Stoeger in the 1950s.

W. W. GREENER, LTD. — Birmingham, England

EMPIRE MODEL HAMMERLESS DOUBLES
Boxlock. Non-ejector or w/automatic ejectors. Double triggers. 12 ga. only (2.75-inch or 3-inch chamber). Bbls.: 28- to 32-inch; any choke combination. Weight: from 7.25 to 7.75 lbs. depending on bbl. length. Checkered stock and forend, straight- or half-pistol grip. Also furnished in "Empire Deluxe Grade," this model has same general specs, but deluxe finish.
Empire model, non-ejector . . . . NiB $2111 Ex $1711 Gd $1201
Empire model, ejector . . . . NiB $2298 Ex $1861 Gd $1303
Empire Deluxe model, non-ejector . . . NiB $2143 Ex $1738 Gd $1218
Empire Deluxe model, ejector . . . . NiB $2426 Ex $1964 Gd $1373

FAR-KILLER MODEL GRADE FH35 HAMMERLESS DOUBLE-BARREL SHOTGUN
Boxlock. Non-ejector or w/automatic ejectors. Double triggers. Gauges: 12 (2.75-inch or 3-inch), 10, 8. Bbls.: 28-, 30- or 32-inch. Weight: 7.5 to 9 lbs. in 12 ga. Checkered stock, forend; straight or half-pistol grip. See illustration next page.
Non-ejector, 12 ga. . . . . NiB $3021 Ex $2456 Gd $1733
Ejector, 12 ga. . . . . NiB $3614 Ex $2930 Gd $2054
Non-ejector, 10 or 8 ga. . . . . . . NiB $3086 Ex $2507 Gd $1768
Ejector, 10 or 8 ga. . . . . NiB $4013 Ex $3249 Gd $2271

G. P. (GENERAL PURPOSE) SINGLE BARREL . . . . NiB $478 Ex $387 Gd $272
Greener Improved Martini Lever Action. Takedown. Ejector. 12 ga. only. Bbl. lengths: 26-, 30-, 32-inch. M or F choke. Weight: 6.25 to 6.75 lbs. depending on bbl. length. Checkered straight-grip stock and forearm.

HAMMERLESS EJECTOR DOUBLE-BARREL SHOTGUNS
Boxlock. Auto ejectors. Double triggers, non-selective or selective single trigger. Gauges: 12, 16, 20, 28, .410 (two latter gauges not supplied in Grades DH40 and DH35). Bbls.: 26-, 28-, 30-inch; any choke combination. Weight: From 4.75 to 8 lbs. Depending on ga. and bbl. length. Checkered stock and forend, straight- or half-pistol grip. The Royal, Crown, Sovereign and Jubilee Models differ in quality, engraving, grade of wood, checkering, etc. General specifications are the same.
Royal Model Grade DH75 . . . . . NiB $4824 Ex $3898 Gd $2713
Crown Model Grade DH55 . . . . NiB $3614 Ex $2930 Gd $2054
Sovereign Model Grade DH40 . . . . NiB $3202 Ex $2600 Gd $1831
Jubilee Model Grade DH35 . . . . NiB $2687 Ex $2188 Gd $1549
W/selective single trigger, add. $330
W/non-selective single trigger, add $250

GREIFELT & COMPANY — Suhl, Germany

GRADE NO. 1 O/U SHOTGUN
Anson & Deeley boxlock, Kersten fastening. Auto ejectors. Double triggers or single trigger. Elaborately engraved. Gauges: 12, 16, 20, 28, .410. Bbls.: 26- to 32-inch, any combination of chokes, vent or solid matted rib. Weight: 4.25 to 8.25 lbs. depending on ga. and bbl. length. Straight- or pistol-grip stock, Purdey-type forend, both checkered. Manufactured prior to World War II.
W/solid matted-rib bbl., except .410 & 28 ga. . . . . NiB $3650 Ex $2956 Gd $2068
W/solid matted-rib bbl., .410 & 28 ga . . . . NiB $4526 Ex $3656 Gd $2544
W/ventilated rib, add $395
W/single trigger, add $425

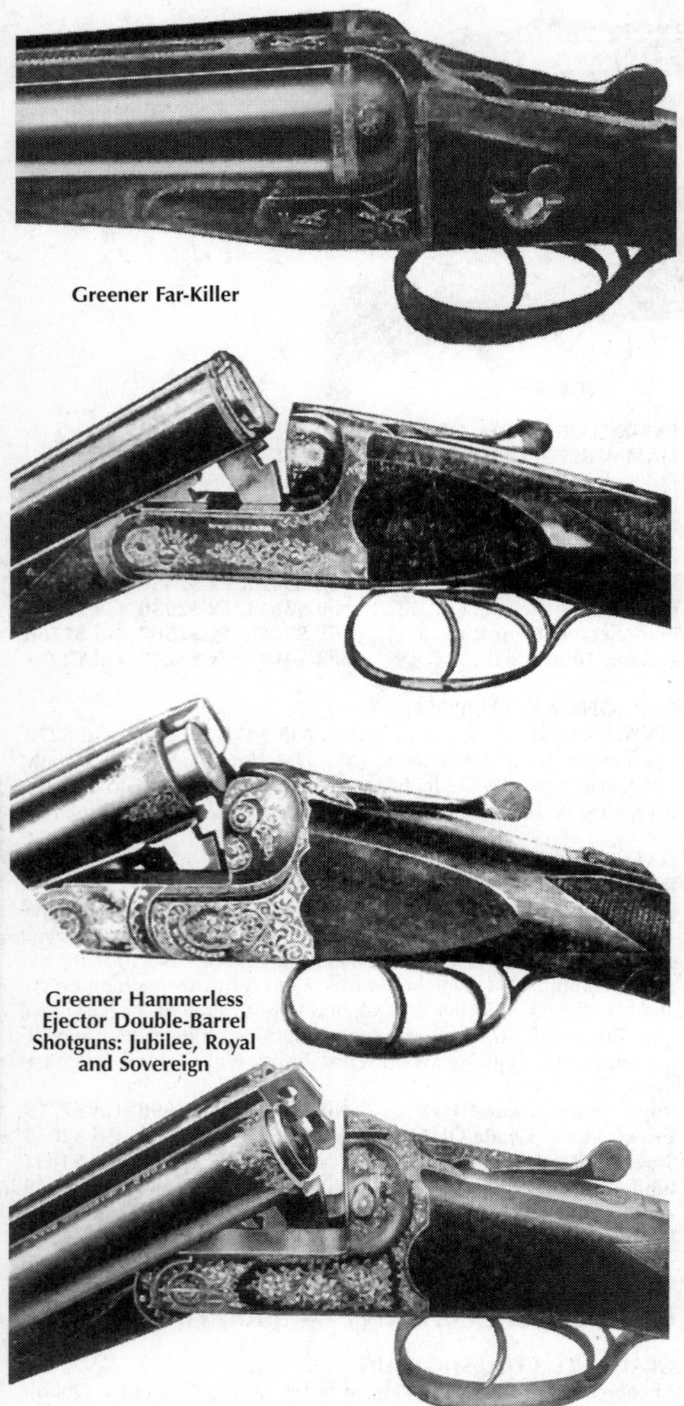
Greener Far-Killer

Greener Hammerless Ejector Double-Barrel Shotguns: Jubilee, Royal and Sovereign

GRADE NO. 3 O/U SHOTGUN
Same general specifications as Grade No. 1 except less fancy engraving. Manufactured prior to World War II.
W/solid matted-rib bbl., except .410 & 28 ga. . . . . NiB $2955 Ex $2400 Gd $1690
W/solid matted-rib bbl., .410 & 28 ga. . . . . NiB $3482 Ex $2822 Gd $1976
W/ventilated rib, add $395
W/single trigger, add. $425

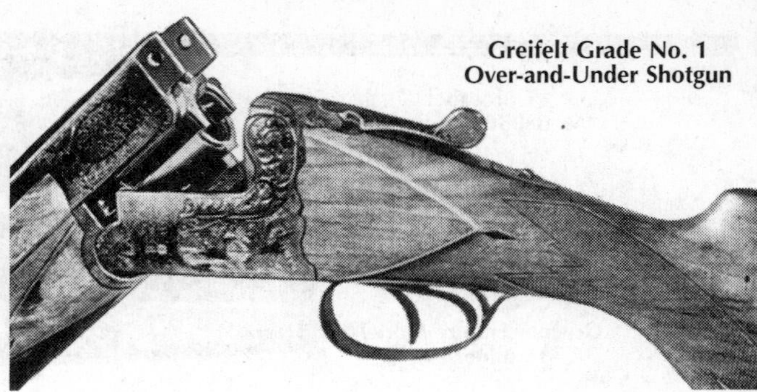
Greifelt Grade No. 1 Over-and-Under Shotgun

MODEL 22 HAMMERLESS DOUBLE. . . NiB $2012 Ex $1630 Gd $1139
Anson & Deeley boxlock. Plain extractors. Double triggers. Gauges: 12 and 16. Bbls.: 28- or 30-inch, M/F choke. Checkered stock and forend, pistol grip and cheekpiece standard, English-style stock also supplied. Manufactured since World War II.

MODEL 22E
HAMMERLESS DOUBLE . . . . . . NiB $2738 Ex $2229 Gd $1578
Same as Model 22 except has automatic ejectors.

MODEL 103
HAMMLERLESS DOUBLE . . . . . NiB $1948 Ex $1578 Gd $1105
Anson & Deeley boxlock. Plain extractors. Double triggers. Gauges: 12 and 16. Bbls.: 28- or 30-inch, M and F choke. Checkered stock and forend, pistol grip and cheekpiece standard, English-style stock also supplied. Manufactured since World War II.

MODEL 103E
HAMMERLESS DOUBLE . . . . . . NiB $2064 Ex $1671 Gd $1168
Same as Model 103 except has automatic ejectors.

MODEL 143E O/U SHOTGUN
General specifications same as pre-war Grade No. 1 Over-and-Under, except this model is not supplied in 28 and .410 ga. or w/32-inch bbls. Model 143E is not as high quality as the Grade No. 1 gun. Mfd. Since World War II.
W/raised matted rib, double triggers . . . . NiB $2439 Ex $1988 Gd $1409
W/ventilated rib, selective single trigger. . . . . NiB $2925 Ex $2400 Gd $1690

HAMMERLESS DRILLING (THREE-BARREL COMBINATION GUN) . . . . . . NiB $3718 Ex $2996 Gd $2072
Boxlock. Plain extractors. Double triggers, front single set for rifle bbl. Gauges: 12, 16, 20; rifle bbl. in any caliber adapted to this type of gun. 26-inch bbls. Weight: About 7.5 lbs. Auto rear sight operated by rifle bbl. selector. Checkered stock and forearm, pistol-grip and cheekpiece standard. Manufactured prior to WW II. Note: Value shown is for guns chambered for cartridges readily obtainable. If rifle bbl. is an odd foreign caliber, value will be considerably less.

O/U COMBINATION GUN
Similar in design to this maker's over-and-under shotguns. Gauges: 12, 16, 20, 28, .410; rifle bbl. in any caliber adapted to this type of gun. Bbls.: 24- or 26-inch, solid matted rib. Weight: From 4.75 to 7.25 lbs. Folding rear sight. Manufactured prior to WWII. Note: Values shown are for gauges other than .410 w/rifle bbl. Chambered for a cartridge readily obtainable; if in an odd foreign caliber, value will be considerably less. .410 ga. increases in value by about 50%.
W/non-automatic ejector . . . . . NiB $6114 Ex $4931 Gd $3417
W/automatic ejector . . . . NiB $6858 Ex $5605 Gd $3675

HARRINGTON & RICHARDSON ARMS COMPANY — Gardner, Massachusetts, Now H&R 1871, Inc.

Formerly Harrington & Richardson Arms Co. of Worcester, Mass. One of the oldest and most distinguished manufacturers of handguns, rifles and shotguns, H&R suspended operations on January 24, 1986. In 1987, New England Firearms was established as an independent company producing selected H&R models under the NEF logo. In 1991, H&R 1871, Inc. was formed from the residual of the parent company and then took over the New England Firearms facility. H&R 1871 produced firearms under both their logo and the NEF brand name until 1999, when the Marlin Firearms Company acquired the assets of H&R 1871.

NO. 3 HAMMERLESS SINGLE-SHOT SHOTGUN .... NiB $124 Ex $88 Gd $63
Takedown. Automatic ejector. Gauges: 12, 16, 20, .410. Bbls.: plain, 26- to 32-inch, F choke. Weight: 6.5 to 7.25 lbs. depending on ga. and bbl. length. Plain pistol-grip stock and forend. Disc. 1942.

NO. 5 STANDARD LIGHTWEIGHT HAMMER SINGLE................ NiB $145 Ex $94 Gd $68
Takedown. Auto ejector. Gauges: 24, 28, .410. Bbls.: 26- or 28-inch, F choke. Weight: About 4 to 4.75 lbs. Plain pistol-grip stock/forend. Disc. 1942.

NO. 6 HEAVY BREECH SINGLE-SHOT HAMMER SHOTGUN............. NiB $145 Ex $94 Gd $68
Takedown. Automatic ejector. Gauges: 10, 12, 16, 20. Bbls.: Plain, 28- to 36-inch, F choke. Weight: About 7 to 7.25 lbs. Plain stock and forend. Disc. 1942.

NO. 7 OR 9 BAY STATE SINGLE-SHOT HAMMER SHOTGUN............. NiB $145 Ex $94 Gd $68
Takedown. Automatic ejector. Gauges: 12, 16, 20, .410. Bbls.: Plain 26- to 32-inch, F choke. Weight: 5.5 to 6.5 lbs. depending on ga. and bbl. length. Plain pistol-grip stock and forend. Disc. 1942.

NO. 8 STANDARD SINGLE-SHOT HAMMER SHOTGUN............ NiB $165 Ex $104 Gd $73
Takedown. Automatic ejector. Gauges: 12, 16, 20, 24, 28, .410. Bbl.: plain, 26- to 32-inch, F choke. Weight: 5.5 to 6.5 lbs. depending on ga. and bbl. length. Plain pistol-grip stock and forend. Made 1908-42.

MODEL 348 GAMESTER BOLT-ACTION SHOTGUN .... NiB $124 Ex $88 Gd $63
Takedown. 12 and 16 ga. Two round tubular magazine, 28-inch bbl, F choke. Plain pistol-grip stock. Weight: About 7.5 lbs. Made 1949-54.

MODEL 349 GAMESTER DELUXE.... NiB $165 Ex $94 Gd $68
Same as Model 348 except has 26-inch bbl. W/adj. choke device, recoil pad. Made 1953-55.

MODEL 351 HUNTSMAN BOLT-ACTION SHOTGUN .... NiB $171 Ex $139 Gd $99
Takedown. 12 and 16 ga. Two round tubular magazine. Pushbutton safety. 26-inch bbl. w/H&R variable choke. Weight: About 6.75 lbs. Monte Carlo stock w/recoil pad. Made 1956-58.

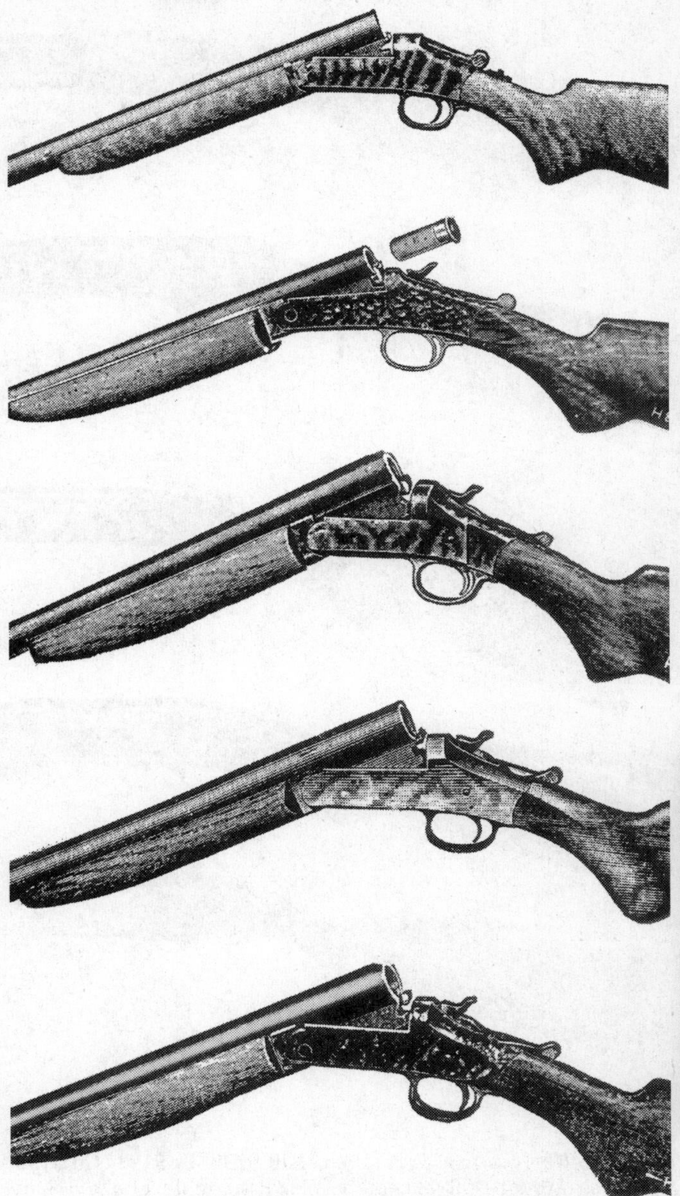

Harrington & Richardson No. 3, 5, 6, 7 and 8 Shotguns

MODEL 400 PUMP............. NiB $235 Ex $190 Gd $133
Hammerless. Gauges: 12, 16, 20. Tubular magazine holds 4 shells. 28-inch bbl., F choke. Weight: About 7.25 lbs. Plain pistol-grip stock (recoil pad in 12 and 16 ga.), grooved slide handle. Made 1955-67.

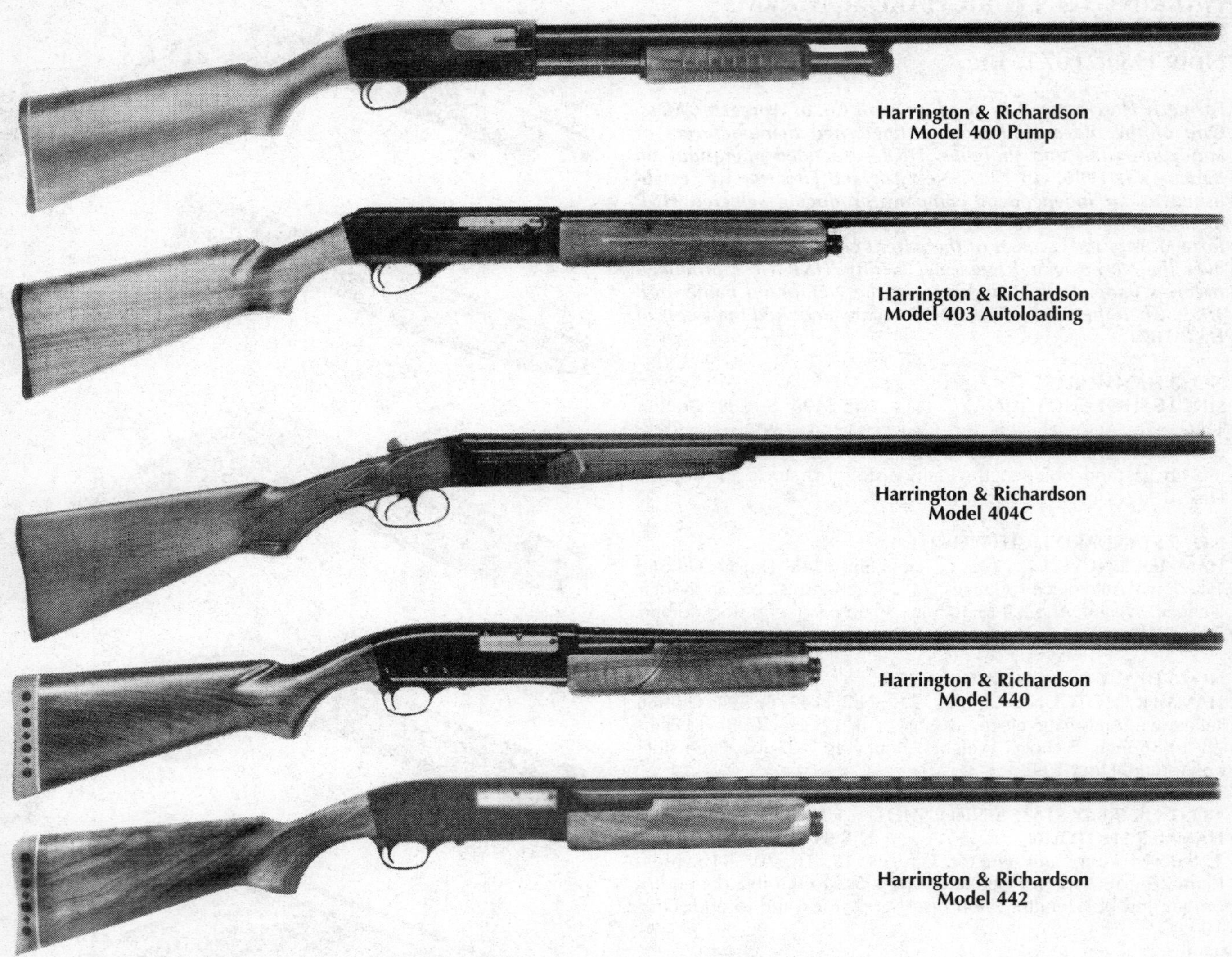

Harrington & Richardson
Model 400 Pump

Harrington & Richardson
Model 403 Autoloading

Harrington & Richardson
Model 404C

Harrington & Richardson
Model 440

Harrington & Richardson
Model 442

MODEL 401 .... NiB $238 Ex $193 Gd $136
Same as Model 400 except has H&R variable choke. Made 1956-63.

MODEL 402 .... NiB $241 Ex $204 Gd $144
Similar to Model 400 except .410 ga., weight: About 5.5 lbs. Made 1959-67.

MODEL 403 AUTOLOADING SHOTGUN .... NiB $257 Ex $209 Gd $147
Takedown. .410 ga. Tubular magazine holds four shells. 26-inch bbl., F choke. Weight: About 5.75 lbs. Plain pistol-grip stock and forearm. Made in 1964.

MODEL 404/404C.............. NiB $302 Ex $245 Gd $171
Boxlock. Plain extractors. Double triggers. Gauges: 12, 20, .410. Bbls.: 28-inch in 12 ga. (M/F choke), 26-inch in 20 ga. (IC/M and .410 (F/F). Weight: 5.5 to 7.25 lbs. Plain walnut-finished hardwood stock and forend on Model 404; 404C checkered. Made in Brazil by Amadeo Rossi 1969-1972.

MODEL 440 PUMP............ NiB $200 Ex $163 Gd $116
Hammerless. Gauges: 12, 16, 20. 2.75-inch chamber in 16 ga., 3-inch in 12 and 20 ga. Three round magazine. Bbls.: 26-, 28-, 30-inch; IC, M, F choke. Weight: 6.25 lbs. Plain pistol-grip stock and slide handle, recoil pad. Made 1968-73.

MODEL 442 .... NiB $251 Ex $204 Gd $144
Same as Model 440 except has vent rib bbl., checkered stock and forearm, weight: 6.75 lbs. Made 1969-73.

ULTRA SLUG SERIES........... NiB $213 Ex $173 Gd $122
Singel shot 12 or 20 ga w/3-inch chamber w/heavy-wall 24-inch fully rifled bbl. w/scope . Weight: 9 lbs. Walnut-stained Monte Carlo stock, sling swivels, black nylon sling. Made 1995 to date.

MODEL 1212 FIELD .... NiB $359 Ex $290 Gd $204
Boxlock. Plain extractors. Selective single trigger. 12 ga., 2.75-inch chambers. 28-inch bbls., IC/IM, vent rib. Weight: 7 lbs. Checkered walnut pistol-gip stock and fluted forearm. Made 1976-80 by Lanber Arms S. A., Zaldibar (Vizcaya), Spain.

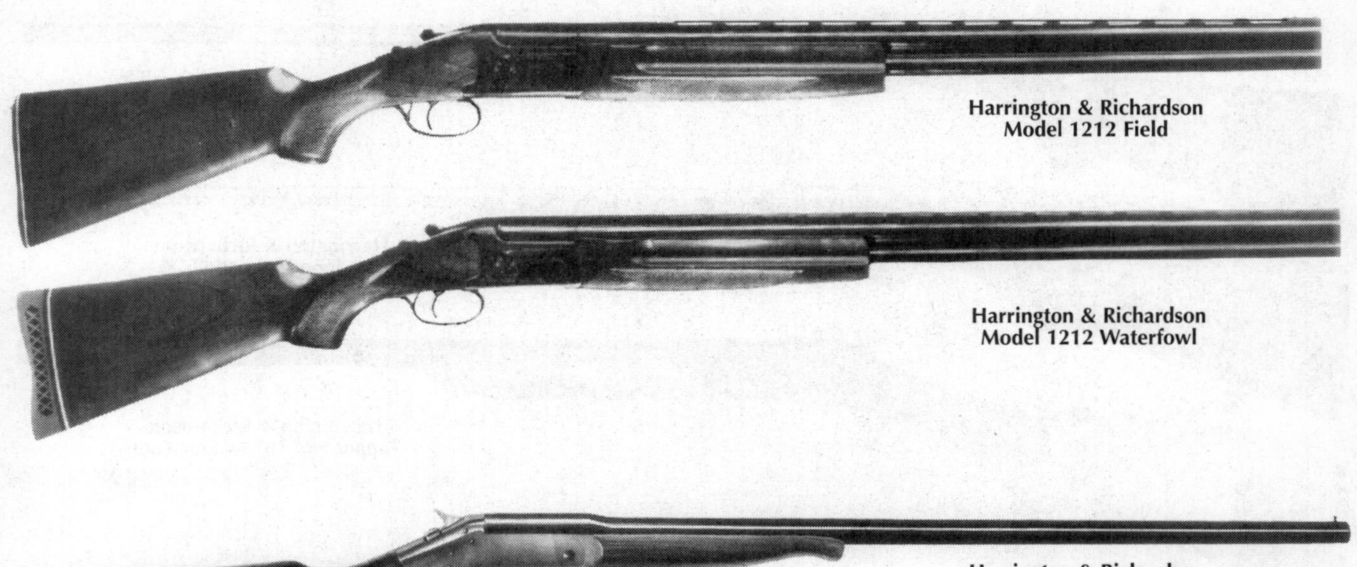

Harrington & Richardson
Model 1212 Field

Harrington & Richardson
Model 1212 Waterfowl

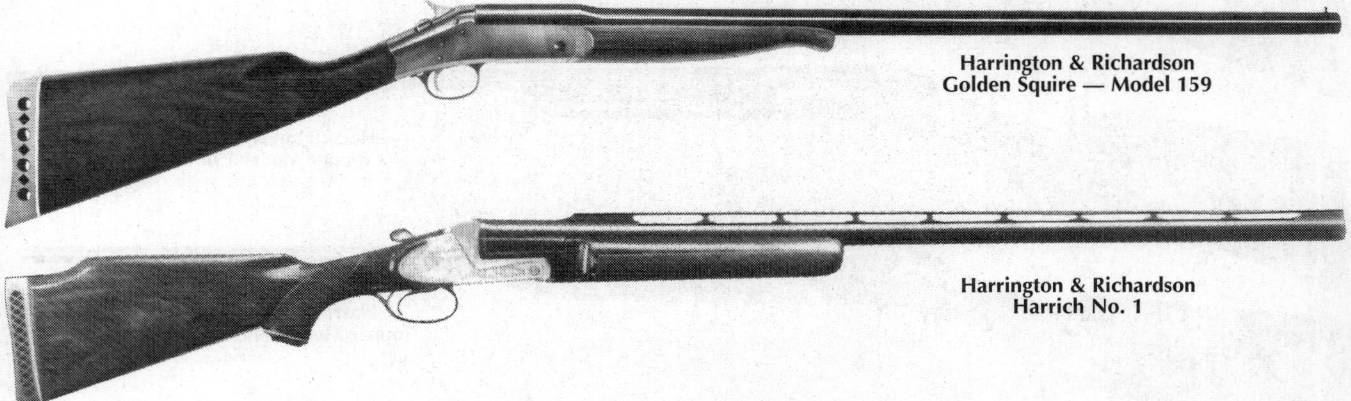

Harrington & Richardson
Golden Squire — Model 159

Harrington & Richardson
Harrich No. 1

MODEL 1212
WATERFOWL GUN............. NiB $392 Ex $318 Gd $222
Same as Field Gun except chambered for 12-ga, 3-inch mag. shells, has 30-inch bbls., M/F chokes, stock and recoil pad, weight: 7.5 lbs. Made 1976-1980.

MODEL 1908
SINGLE-SHOT SHOTGUN .... NiB $169 Ex $113 Gd $77
Takedown. Automatic ejector. Gauges: 12, 16, 24 and 28. Bbls.: 26- to 32-inch, F choke. Weight: 5.25 to 6.5 lbs. depending on ga. and bbl. length. Casehardened receiver. Plain pistol-grip stock. Bead front sight. Made 1908-1934.

MODEL 1908 .410 (12MM)
SINGLE-SHOT SHOTGUN .... NiB $159 Ex $130 Gd $94
Same general specifications as standard Model 1908 except chambered for .410 or 12mm shot cartridge w/bbl. milled down at receiver to give a more pleasing contour.

MODEL 1915 SINGLE-SHOT SHOTGUN
Takedown. Both non-auto and auto-ejectors available. Gauges: 24, 28, .410, 14mm and 12mm. Bbls.: 26- or 28-inch, F choke. Weight: 4 to 4.75 lbs. depending on ga. and bbl. length. Plain black walnut stock w/semi pistol-grip.
24 ga. .... NiB $226 Ex $196 Gd $130
28, .410 ga................... NiB $188 Ex $154 Gd $110

FOLDING GUN .... NiB $188 Ex $154 Gd $110
Single bbl. hammer shotgun hinged at the front of the frame, the bbl. folds down against the stock. Light Frame model: gauges — 28, 14mm, .410; 22-inch bbl.; weighs about 4.5 lbs. Heavy Frame model: gauges — 12, 16, 20, 28, .410; 26-inch bbl.; weighs from 5.75 to 6.5 lbs. Plain pistol-grip stock and forend. Disc. 1942.

GOLDEN SQUIRE MODEL 159
SINGLE-BARREL
HAMMER SHOTGUN............ NiB $143 Ex $118 Gd $85
Hammerless. Side lever. Automatic ejection. Gauges: 12, 20. Bbls: 30-inch in 12 ga., 28-inch in 20 ga., both F choke. Weight: About 6.5 lbs. Straight-grip stock w/recoil pad, forearm w/Schnabel. Made 1964-66.

GOLDEN SQUIRE JR. MODEL 459.. NiB $153 Ex $133 Gd $96
Same as Model 159 except gauges 20 and .410, 26-inch bbl., youth stock. Made in 1964.

HARRICH NO. 1 SINGLE-BARREL
TRAP GUN .... NiB $1585 Ex $1280 Gd $889
Anson & Deeley-type locking system w/Kersten top locks and double underlocking lugs. Sideplates engraved w/hunting scenes. 12 ga. Bbls.: 32-, 34-inch; F choke; high vent rib. Weight: 8.5 lbs. Checkered Monte Carlo stock w/pistol-grip and recoil pad, beavertail forearm, of select walnut. Made in Ferlach, Austria, 1971-75.

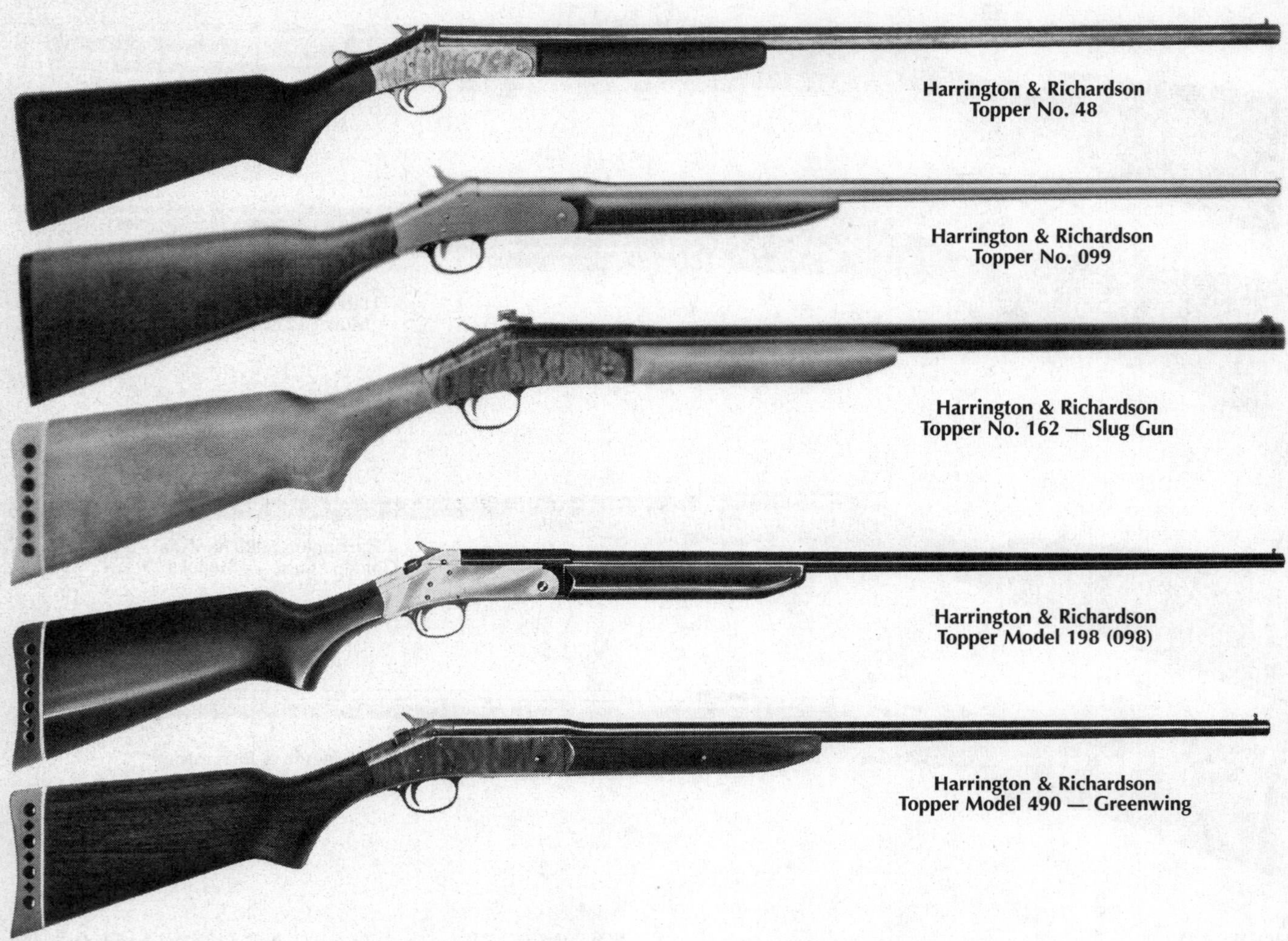

Harrington & Richardson Topper No. 48

Harrington & Richardson Topper No. 099

Harrington & Richardson Topper No. 162 — Slug Gun

Harrington & Richardson Topper Model 198 (098)

Harrington & Richardson Topper Model 490 — Greenwing

"TOP RIB" SINGLE-BARREL SHOTGUN . . . . NiB $231 Ex $195 Gd $150
Takedown. Auto ejector. Gauges: 12, 16 and 20. Bbls.: 28- to 30-inch, F choke w/full-length matted top rib. Weight: 6.5 to 7 lbs. depending on ga. and bbl. length. Black walnut pistol-grip stock (capped) and forend; both checkered. Flexible rubber buttplate. Made during 1930s.

TOPPER NO. 48 SINGLE-BARREL HAMMER SHOTGUN . . . . NiB $185 Ex $153 Gd $110
Similar to old Model 8 Standard. Takedown. Top lever. Auto ejector. Gauges: 12, 16, 20, .410. Bbls.: plain; 26- to 30-inch; M or F choke. Weight: 5.5 to 6.5 lbs. depending on ga. and bbl. length. Plain pistol-grip stock and forend. Made 1946-57.

TOPPER MODEL 099 DELUXE . . . . . NiB $146 Ex $119 Gd $84
Same as Model 158 except has matte nickel finish, semipistol grip walnut-finished American hardwood stock; semibeavertail forearm; 12, 16, 20, and .410 ga. Made 1982-86.

TOPPER MODEL 148 SINGLE-SHOT HAMMER SHOTGUN . . . . NiB $153 Ex $124 Gd $88
Takedown. Side lever. Auto-ejection. Gauges: 12, 16, 20, .410.

(*cont'd.*) TOPPER MODEL 148
Bbls.: 12 ga.,30-, 32- and 36-inch; 16 ga., 28- and 30-inch; 20 and .410 ga., 28-inch; F choke. Weight: 5 to 6.5 lbs. Plain pistol-grip stock and forend, recoil pad. Made 1958-61.

TOPPER MODEL 158 (058) SINGLE-SHOT HAMMER SHOTGUN . . . . NiB $159 Ex $129 Gd $92
Takedown. Side lever. Automatic ejection. Gauges: 12, 20, .410 (2.75-inch and 3-inch shells); 16 (2.75-inch). bbl. length and choke combinations: 12 ga., 36-inch/F, 32-inch/F, 30-inch/F, 28-inch/F or M; .410, 28-inch/F. Weight: about 5.5 lbs. Plain pistol-grip stock and forend, recoil pad. Made 1962-81. Note: Designation changed to 058 in 1974.

TOPPER MODEL 162 SLUG GUN. . NiB $205 Ex $166 Gd $117
Same as Topper Model 158 except has 24-inch bbl., Cyl. bore, w/rifle sights. Made 1968-86.

TOPPER MODEL 176 10 GA. MAGNUM . . . . NiB $197 Ex $160 Gd $113
Similar to Model 158, but has 36-inch heavy bbl. chambered for 3.5-inch 10- ga. Mag. shells, weight: 10 lbs.; stock w/Monte Carlo comb and recoil pad, longer and fuller forearm. Made 1977-86.

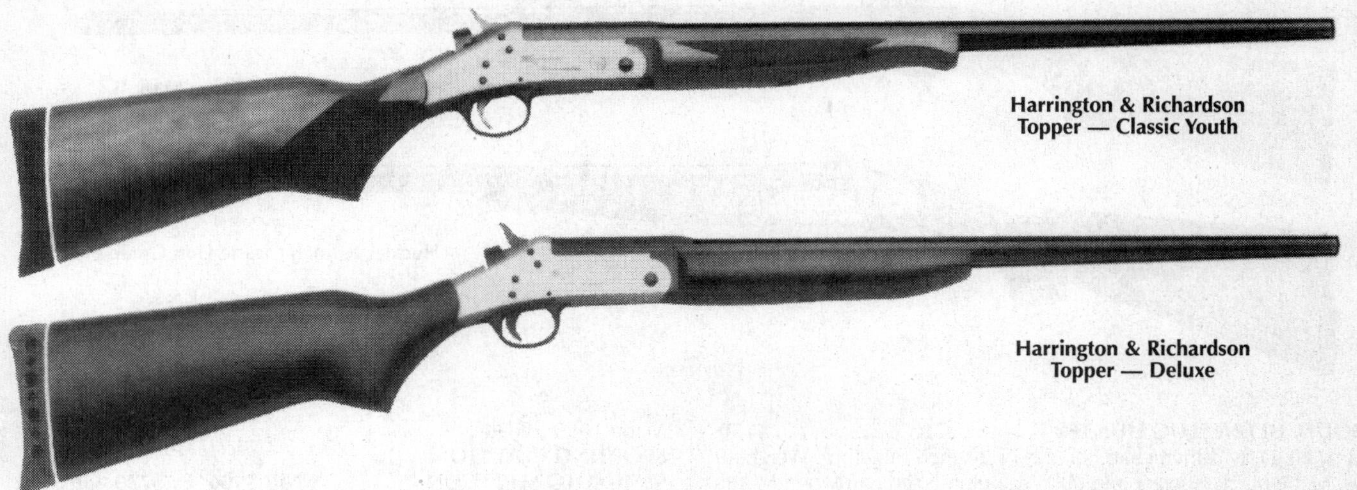

Harrington & Richardson
Topper — Classic Youth

Harrington & Richardson
Topper — Deluxe

TOPPER MODEL 188 DELUXE ..... NiB $171 Ex $139 Gd $99
Same as standard Topper Model 148 except has chromed frame, stock and forend in black, red, yellow, blue, green, pink, or purple colored finish. .410 ga. only. Made 1958-61.

TOPPER MODEL 198 (098) DELUXE ..... NiB $178 Ex $145 Gd $102
Same as Model 158 except has chrome-plated frame, black finished stock and forend; 12, 20 and .410 ga. Made 1962-81. Note: Designation changed to 098 in 1974.

TOPPER JR. MODEL 480 .... NiB $165 Ex $109 Gd $83
Similar to No. 48 Topper except has youth-size stock, 26-inch bbl, .410 ga. only. Made 1958-61.

TOPPER NO. 488 DELUXE .... NiB $166 Ex $135 Gd $96
Same as standard No. 48 Topper except chrome-plated frame, black lacquered stock and forend, recoil pad. Disc. 1957.

TOPPER MODEL 490 .... NiB $159 Ex $129 Gd $92
Same as Model 158 except has youth-size stock (3 inches shorter), 26-inch bbl.; 20 and 28 ga. (M choke), .410 (F). Made 1962-86.

TOPPER MODEL 490 GREENWING...... NiB $178 Ex $145 Gd $102
Same as the Model 490 except has a special high-polished finish. Made 1981-86.

TOPPER JR. MODEL 580.......... NiB $139 Ex $114 Gd $81
Same as Model 480 except has colored stocks as on Model 188. Made 1958-61.

TOPPER MODEL 590 .... NiB $147 Ex $119 Gd $84
Same as Model 490 except has chrome-plated frame, black finished stock and forend. Made 1962-63.

The following models are manufactured and distributed by the reorganized company of H&R 1871, Inc.

MODEL 098 TOPPER CLASSIC YOUTH ..... NiB $133 Ex 109 Gd $78
Same as Topper Junior except also available in 28 ga. and has checkered American black walnut stock/forend w/satin finish and recoil pad. Made 1991 to date.

MODEL 098 TOPPER DELUXE ..... NiB $133 Ex $109 Gd $78
Same as Model 098 Single Shot Hammer except in 12 ga., 3-inch chamber only. 28-inch bbl.; Mod. choke tube. Made 1992 to date.

**MODEL 098 TOPPER
DELUXE RIFLED SLUG GUN ...... NiB $165 Ex $134 Gd $95**
Same as Topper Deluxe Shotgun except has compensated 24-inch rifled slug bbl. Nickel plated receiver and blued bbl. Black finished hardwood stock. Made 1996 to date.

**MODEL 098 TOPPER HAMMER
SINGLE-SHOT SHOTGUN .... NiB $114 Ex $94 Gd $67**
Side lever. Automatic ejector. Gauges: 12, 20 and .410; 3-inch chamber. Bbls.: 28-inch, (12 ga./M); 26-inch, (20 ga./M); 26-inch (.410/F). Weight: 5 to 6 lbs. Satin nickel receiver, blued bbl. Plain pistol-grip stock and semibeavertail forend w/black finish. Re-Intro. 1992.

MODEL 098 TOPPER JUNIOR ...... NiB $120 Ex $99 Gd $71
Same as Model 098 except has youth-size stock and 22-inch bbl. 20 or .410 ga. only. Made 1991 to date.

MODEL .410 TAMER SHOTGUN ... NiB $133 Ex $109 Gd $78
Takedown. Topper-style single-shot, side lever action w/auto ejector. Gauge: .410; 3-inch chamber. 19.5-inch bbl. 33 inches overall. Weight: 5.75 lbs. Black polymer thumbhole stock designed to hold 4 extra shotshells. Matte nickel finish. Made 1994 to date.

MODEL N. W. T. F. TURKEY MAG
Same as Model 098 Single-Shot Hammer except has 24-inch bbl. chambered 10 or 12 ga. w/3.5-inch chamber w/screw-in choke tube. Weight: 6 lbs. American hardwood stock, Mossy Oak camo finish. Made 1991-96.
NWTF 10 ga. Turkey Mag (Made 1996) .... NiB $155 Ex $126 Gd $90
NWTF 12 ga. Turkey Mag (Made 1991-95).. NiB $138 Ex $113 Gd $80

**MODEL N. W. T. F.
YOUTH TURKEY GUN............ NiB $152 Ex $124 Gd $87**
Same as Model N.W.T.F. Turkey Mag except has 22-inch bbl. chambered in 20 ga. w/3-inch chamber and fixed full choke. Realtree camo finish. Made 1994-95.

**MODEL SB1-920
ULTRA SLUG HUNTER.......... NiB $201 Ex $163 Gd $115**
Special 12 ga. action w/12 ga. bbl. blank underbored to 20 ga. to form a fully rifled slug bbl. Gauge: 20 w/3 inch chamber. 24-inch bbl. Weight: 8.5 lbs. Satin nickel receiver, blued bbl. Walnut finished hardwood Monte Carlo stock. Made 1996-98.

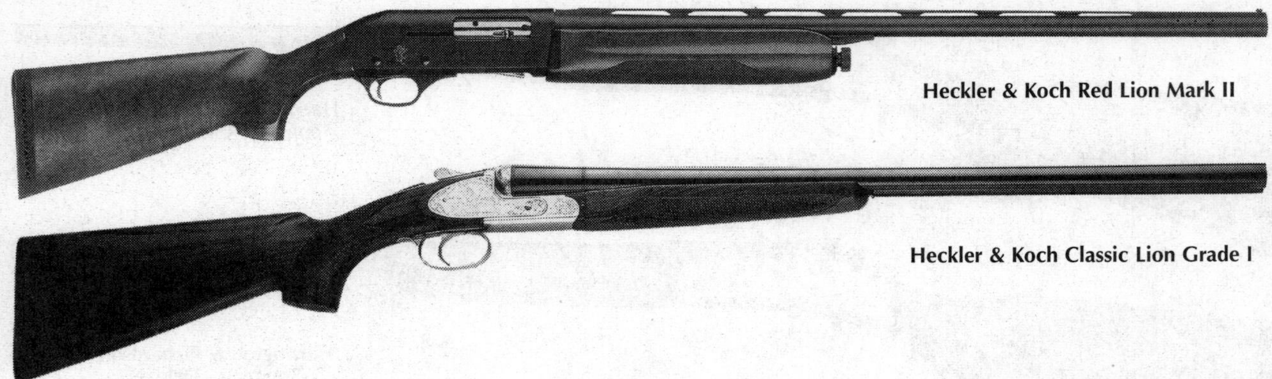

MODEL ULTRA SLUG HUNTER $150
12 or 20 ga. w/3-inch chamber. 22- or 24-inch rifled bbl. Weight: 9 lbs. Matte black receiver and bbl. Walnut finished hardwood Monte Carlo stock. Made 1997 to date.

MODEL ULTRA SLUG HUNTER DELUXE ..... NiB $210 Ex $170 Gd $119
Similar to Ultra Slug Hunter model except with compensated bbl. Made 1997 to date.

HECKLER & KOCH FABARM SHOTGUNS — Oberndorf/Neckar, West Germany, and Sterling, Virginia

CLASSIC LION SIDE-BY-SIDE SHOTGUN
12 ga. only. 28- or 30-inch non-ported Tribor bbl. w/3-inch chamber. 46.5 to 48.5-inches overall. Weight: 7 to 7.2 lbs. Five choke tubes; C, IC, M, IM, F. Traditional boxlock design. Oil-finished walnut forearms and stocks w/diamond-cut checkering. Imported 1999 to date.
Classic Lion Grade I .... NiB $1346 Ex $1084 Gd $748
Classic Lion Grade II........ NiB $2024 Ex $1617 Gd $1110

CAMO LION SEMI-AUTO SHOTGUN .... NiB $887 Ex $759 Gd $479
12 ga. Only. 24 to 28-inches Tribor bbl. 44.25-48.25-inches overall. Weight: 7-7.2 lbs. 3 inch chamber w/5 choke tubes - C, IC, M, IM, F. Two round mag. Camo covered walnut stock w/rear front bar sights. Imp. 1999 to date.

MAX LION O/U SHOTGUN.... NiB $1763 Ex $1513 Gd $850
12 or 20 ga. 26- 28- or 30-inch TriBore system bbls. 42.5-47.25-inches overall. Weight: 6.8-7.8 lbs. 3-inch chamber w/5 choke tubes - C, IC, M, IM, F. Single selective adj. trigger and auto ejectors. Side plates w/high-grade stock and rubber recoil pad. Made 1999 to date.

RED LION MARK II SEMI-AUTO SHOTGUN .... NiB $779 Ex $627 Gd $433
12 ga. Only. 24- 26- or 28-inch TriBore system bbls. 44.25 to 48.25-inches overall. Weight: 7 to 7.2 lbs. 3-inch chamber w/five choke tubes- C, IC, M, IM, F. Two round magazine. Matte finish w/walnut wood stock. Rubber vented recoil pad w/leather cover. Made 1999 to date.

SILVER LION O/U SHOTGUN......... NiB $1182 Ex $953 Gd $661
12 or 20 ga. 26- 28- or 30-inch TriBore system bbls. 43.25-47.25 inchesoverall. 3-inch chamber w/5 choke tubes - C, IC, M, IM, F. Single selective trig. and auto ejectors. Wal. stock w/rubber recoil pad. Made 1999 to date.

SPORTING CLAY LION SEMI-AUTO SHOTGUN .... NiB $906 Ex $729 Gd $502
12 ga. only. 28- or 30-inch bbl. w/3-inch chamber and ported Tribore system barrel. Matte finish w/gold plated trigger and carrier release button. Made 1999 to date.

HERCULES SHOTGUNS

See Listings under "W" for Montgomery Ward.

HEYM SHOTGUNS — Münnerstadt, Germany

MODEL 22S "SAFETY" SHOTGUN/ RIFLE COMBINATION .... NiB $3359 Ex $2706 Gd $1871
16 and 20 ga. Cal: .22 Mag., .22 Hornet, .222 Rem., .222 Rem. Mag., 5.6x50R Mag., 6.5x57R, 7x57R, .243 Win. 24-inch bbls. 40 inches overall. Weight: About 5.5 lbs. Single-set trigger. Left-side bbl. selector. Integral dovetail base for scope mounting. Arabesque engraving. Walnut stock. Disc. 1993.

MODEL 55 BF SHOTGUN/ RIFLE COMBO .... NiB $7261 Ex $5843 Gd $4030
12, 16 and 20 ga. Calibers: 5.6x50R Mag., 6.5x57R, 7x57R, 7x65R, .243 Win., .308 Win., .30-06. 25-inch bbls., 42 inches overall. Weight: About 6.75 lbs. Black satin-finished, corrosion-resistant bbls. of Krupp special steel. Hand-checkered walnut stock w/long pistol-grip. Hand-engraved leaf scroll. German cheekpiece. Disc. 1988.

J. C. HIGGINS SHOTGUNS

See Sears, Roebuck & Company.

HUGLU HUNTING FIREARMS — Huglu, Turkey, Imported by Turkish Firearms Corp.

MODEL 101 B 12 AT-DT COMBO O/U TRAP .... NiB $2224 Ex $1717 Gd $1297
Over/Under boxlock. 12 ga. w/3-inch chambers. Combination 30- or 32-inch top single & O/U bbls. w/fixed chokes or choke tubes. Weight: 8 lbs. Automatic ejectors or extractors. Single selective trigger. Manual safety. Circassian walnut Monte Carlo trap stock w/palm-swell grip and recoil pad. Silvered frame w/engraving. Imported 1993-97.

Heym Model 22S
"Safety" Shotgun/Rifle Combination Gun

Heym Model 55
BF Shotgun/Rifle

MODEL 101 B 12 ST O/U TRAP. . . . NiB $1446 Ex $1172 Gd $820
Same as Model 101 AT-DT except in 32-inch O/U configuration only. Imported 1994-96.

MODEL 103 B 12 ST O/U
Boxlock. Gauges: 12, 16, 20, 28 or .410. 28-inch bbls. w/fixed chokes. Engraved action w/inlaid game scene and dummy sideplates. Double triggers, extractors and manual safety. Weight: 7.5 lbs. Circassian walnut stock. Imported 1995-96.
Model 103B w/extractors . . . . NiB $1078 Ex $877 Gd $620
28 and .410, add $100

MODEL 103 C 12 ST O/U
Same general specs as Model 103 B 12 S except w/extractors or ejectors. 12 or 20 ga. w/3-inch chambers. Black receiver w/50% engraving coverage. Imported 1995-97.
Model 103C w/extractors . . . . NiB $1088 Ex $885 Gd $626
Model 103C w/ejectors. . . . . NiB $1343 Ex 1089 Gd $765

MODEL 103 D 12 ST O/U
Same gen. specs as Mdl. 103 B 12 ST except stand. boxlock. Ext. or eject. 12 or 20 ga. w/3-inch chambers. 80% engraving coverage. Imp. 1995-97.
Model 103D w/extractors . . . . . . NiB $1044 Ex $846 Gd $594
Model 103D w/ejectors. . . . . NiB $1299 Ex $1050 Gd $732

MODEL 103 F 12 ST O/U
Same as Model 103 B except extractors or ejectors. 12 or 20 ga. only. 100% engraving coverage. Imported 1996-97.
Model 103F w/extractors . . . . NiB $1158 Ex $941 Gd $664
Model 103F w/ejectors . . . . NiB $1413 Ex $1145 Gd $802

MODEL 104 A 12 ST O/U
Boxlock. Gauges: 12, 20, 28 or .410. 28-inch bbls. w/fixed chokes or choke tubes. Silvered, engraved receiver w/15% engraving coverage. Double triggers, manual safety and extractors or ejectors. Weight: 7.5 lbs. Circassian walnut stock w/field dimensions. Imported 1995-97.
Model 104A w/extractors . . . . . .NiB $1027 Ex $835 Gd $590
Model 104A w/ejectors. . . . . NiB $1282 Ex $1039 Gd $729

(cont'd.) **MODEL 104 A 12 ST O/U**
28 and .410, add $100
W/Choke Tubes, add $50

MODEL 200 SERIES DOUBLE
Boxlock. Gauges: 12, 20, 28, or .410 w/3-inch chambers. 28-inch bbls. w/fixed chokes. Silvered, engraved receiver. Extractors, manual safety, single selective trigger or double triggers. Weight: 7.5 lbs. Circassion walnut stock. Imported 1995-97.
Model 200 (w/15% engraving coverage, SST) . . . . NiB $1058 Ex $860 Gd $608
Model 201 (w/30% engraving coverage, SST). . . . . . . NiB $1344 Ex $1090 Gd $765
Model 202 (w/Greener cross bolt, DT). . . . . NiB $1127 Ex $916 Gd $647
28 and .410, add $100

HIGH STANDARD SPORTING ARMS — East Hartford, Connecticut, Formerly High Standard Mfg. Corp. of Hamden, Conn.

In 1966, High Standard introduced new series of Flite-King Pumps and Supermatic autoloaders, both readily identifiable by the damascened bolt and restyled checkering. To avoid confusion, these models are designated "Series II" in this text. This is not an official factory designation. Operation of this firm was discontinued in 1984.

FLITE-KING FIELD PUMP—12 GA. . . . . NiB $289 Ex $234 Gd $164
Hammerless. Magazine holds five rounds. Bbls.: 26-inch IC, 28-inch M or F, 30-inch F choke. Weight: 7.25 lbs. Plain pistol-grip stock and slide handle. Made 1960-66.

FLITE-KING BRUSH—12 GA. . . . . . NiB $219 Ex $199 Gd $168
Same as Flite-King Field 12 except has 18- or 20-inch bbl. (cylinder bore) w/rifle sights. Made 1962-64.

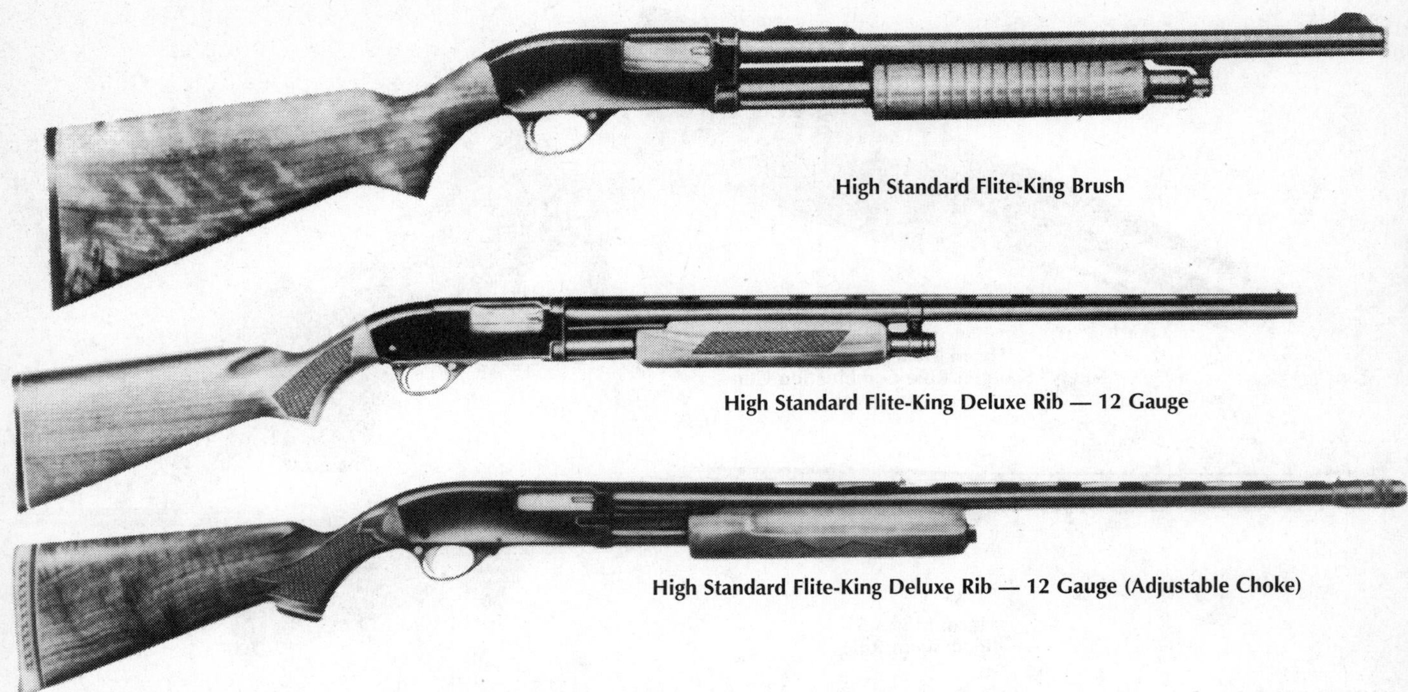

High Standard Flite-King Brush

High Standard Flite-King Deluxe Rib — 12 Gauge

High Standard Flite-King Deluxe Rib — 12 Gauge (Adjustable Choke)

FLITE-KING BRUSH DELUXE ..... NiB $285 Ex $250 Gd $168
Same as Flite-King Brush except has adj. peep rear sight, checkered pistol grip, recoil pad, fluted slide handle, swivels and sling. Not available w/18-inch bbl. Made 1964-66.

FLITE-KING BRUSH (SERIES II).... NiB $275 Ex $223 Gd $156
Same as Flite-King Deluxe 12 (II) except has 20-inch bbl., cylinder bore, w/rifle sights. Weight: 7 lbs. Made 1966-75.

FLITE-KING BRUSH DELUXE (II) .. NiB $318 Ex $256 Gd $176
Same as Flite-King Brush (II) except has adj. peep rear sight, swivels and sling. Made 1966-75.

FLITE-KING DELUXE 12 GA. (SERIES II)
Hammerless. Five round magazine. 27-inch plain bbls.w/adj. choke. 26-inch IC, 28-inch M or F. 30-inch F choke. Weight: About 7.25 lbs. Checkered pistol-grip stock and forearm, recoil pad. Made 1966-75.
W/adj. choke .... NiB $318 Ex $258 Gd $180
W/O adj. choke .... NiB $290 Ex $235 Gd $164

FLITE-KING DELUXE
20, 28, .410 GA. (SERIES II) ...... NiB $286 Ex $232 Gd $163
Same as Flite-King Deluxe 12 (II) except chambered for 20 and .410 ga. 3-inch shell, 28 ga. 2.75-inch shell w/20- or 28-inch plain bbl. Weight: About 6 lbs. Made 1966-75.

FLITE-KING DELUXE RIB 12 GA...... NiB $348 Ex $281 Gd $195
Same as Flite-King Field 12 except vent rib bbl. (28-inch M or F. 30-inch F). Checkered stock and forearm. Made 1961-66.

FLITE-KING DELUXE RIB 12 GA. (II)
Same as Flite-King Deluxe 12 (II) except has vent rib bbl., available in 27-inch w/adj. choke, 28-inch M or F, 30-inch F choke. Made 1966-75.
W/adj. choke .... NiB $362 Ex $301 Gd $209
W/O adj. choke................ NiB $348 Ex $281 Gd $196

FLITE-KING DELUXE RIB 20 GA. .... NIB $335 EX $271 GD $189
Same as Flite-King Field 20 except vent-rib bbl. (28 inch M or F), checkered stock and slide handle. Made 1962-66.

FLITE-KING DELUXE RIB 20, 28, .410 GA. (SERIES II)
Same as Flite-King Deluxe 20, 28, .410 (II) except 20 ga. available w/27-inch adj. choke, 28-inch M or F choke. Weight: about 6.25 lbs. Made 1966-75.
W/adj. choke.................. NiB $391 Ex $316 Gd $220
W/O adj. choke................ NiB $366 Ex $296 Gd $206

FLITE-KING DELUXE SKEET GUN
12 GA. (SERIES II).............. NiB $340 Ex $275 Gd $191
Same as Flite-King Deluxe Rib 12 (II) except available only w/26-inch vent rib bbl., SK choke, recoil pad optional. Made 1966-75.

FLITE-KING DELUXE SKEET GUN
20, 28, .410 GA. (SERIES II)...... NIB $391 EX $316 GD $220
Same as Flite-King Deluxe Rib 20, 28, .410 (II) except available only w/26-inch vent-rib bbl., SK choke. Made 1966-75.

FLITE-KING DELUXE
TRAP GUN (II) .... NIB $324 EX $262 GD $182
Same as Flite-King Deluxe Rib 12 (II) except available only w/30-inch vent-rib bbl., F choke; trap-style stock. Made 1966-75.

FLITE-KING FIELD PUMP 20 GA. .... NIB $264 EX $214 GD $151
Hammerless. Chambered for 3-inch Magnum shells, also handles 2.75-inch. Magazine holds four rounds. Bbls.: 26-inch IC, 28-inch M or F choke. Weight: About 6 lbs. Plain pistol-grip stock and slide handle. Made 1961-66.

FLITE-KING PUMP SHOTGUNS 16 GA.
Same general specifications as Flite-King 12 except not available in Brush, Skeet and Trap Models or 30-inch bbl. Values same as for 12-ga. guns. Made 1961-65.

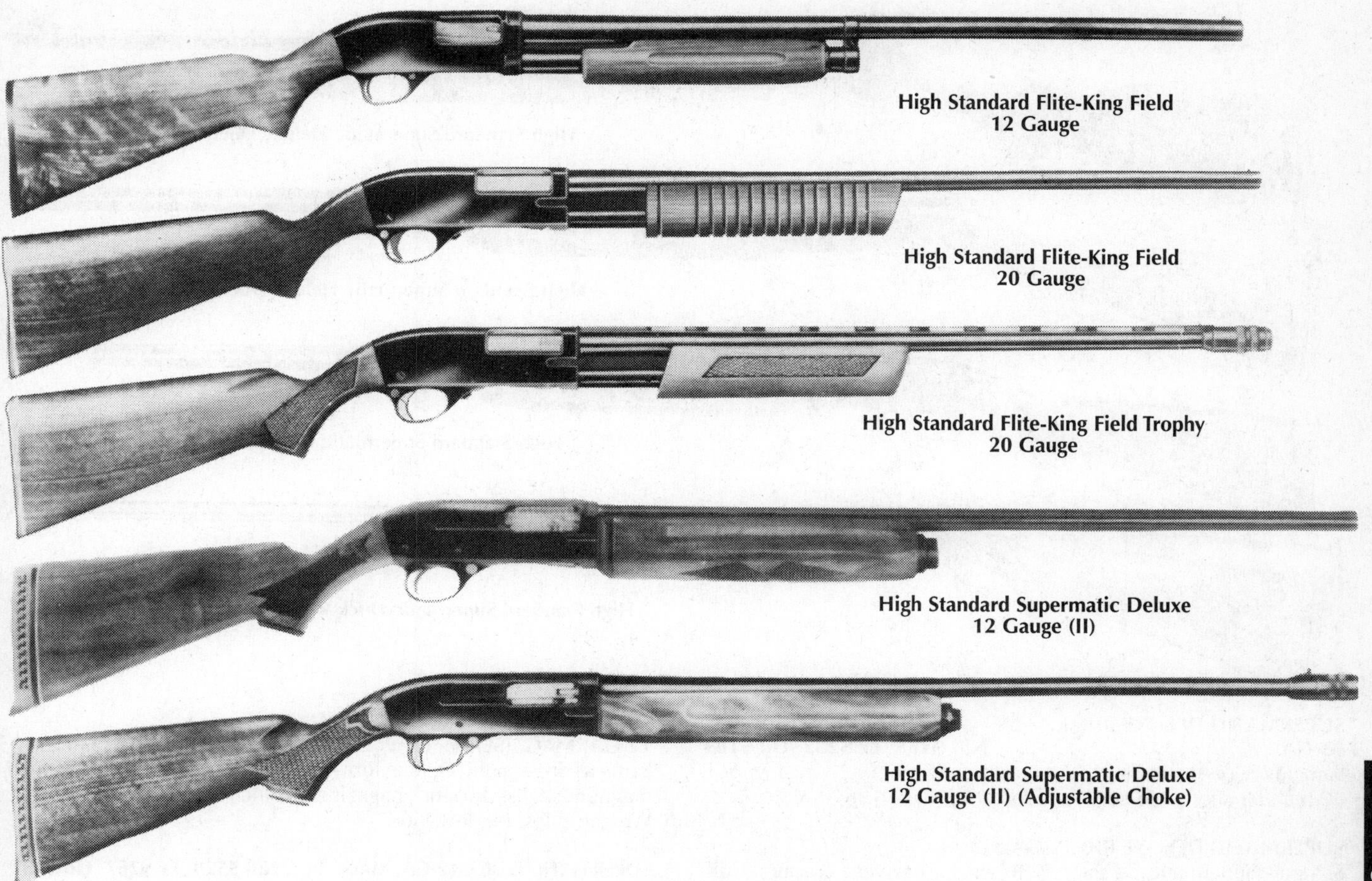

High Standard Flite-King Field
12 Gauge

High Standard Flite-King Field
20 Gauge

High Standard Flite-King Field Trophy
20 Gauge

High Standard Supermatic Deluxe
12 Gauge (II)

High Standard Supermatic Deluxe
12 Gauge (II) (Adjustable Choke)

FLITE-KING PUMP SHOTGUNS (.410 GA.)
Same general specifications as Flite-King 20 except not available in Special and Trophy Models, or w/other than 26-inch choke bbl. Values same as for 20 ga. guns. Made 1962-66.

FLITE-KING SKEET
12 GA. . . . . NiB $377 Ex $306 Gd $214
Same as Flite-King Deluxe Rib except 26-inch vent rib bbl., w/SK choke. Made 1962-66.

FLITE-KING SPECIAL 12 GA. . . . . . NiB $280 Ex $228 Gd $161
Same as Flite-King Field 12 except has 27-inch bbl. w/adj. choke. Made 1960-66.

FLITE-KING SPECIAL 20 GA. . . . . . NiB $286 Ex $233 Gd $165
Same as Flite-King Field 20 except has 27-inch bbl. w/adj. choke. Made 1961-66.

FLITE-KING TRAP 12 GA. . . . . NiB $377 Ex $306 Gd $214
Same as Flite-King Deluxe Rib 12 except 30-inch vent rib bbl., F choke, special trap stock w/recoil pad. Made 1962-66.

FLITE-KING TROPHY 12 GA. . . . . . NiB $353 Ex $286 Gd $201
Same as Flite-King Deluxe Rib 12 except has 27-inch vent rib bbl. w/adj. choke. Made 1960-66.

FLITE-KING TROPHY
20 GA. . . . . NiB $377 Ex $306 Gd $214
Same as Flite-King Deluxe Rib 20 except has 27-inch vent rib bbl. w/adj. choke. Made 1962-66.

SUPERMATIC DEER GUN . . . . NiB $371 Ex $301 Gd $211
Same as Supermatic Field 12 except has 22-inch bbl. (cylinder bore) w/rifle sights, checkered stock and forearm, recoil pad. Weight: 7.75 lbs. Made in 1965.

SUPERMATIC DELUXE 12 GA. (SERIES II)
Gas-operated autoloader. Four round magazine. Bbls.: Plain; 27-inch w/adj. choke (disc. about 1970); 26-inch IC, 28-inch M or F. 30-inch F choke. Weight: About 7.5 lbs. Checkered pistol-grip stock and forearm, recoil pad. Made 1966-75.
W/adj. choke . . . . NiB $396 Ex $321 Gd $225
W/O adj. choke . . . . NiB $325 Ex $270 Gd $200

SUPERMATIC DELUXE 20 GA. (SERIES II)
Same as Supermatic Deluxe 12 (II) except chambered for 20 ga. Three inch shell; bbls. available in 27-inch w/adj. choke (disc. about 1970), 26-inch IC, 28-inch M or F choke. Weight: About 7 lbs. Made 1966-75.
W/adj. choke . . . . NiB $294 Ex $239 Gd $169
W/O adj. choke . . . . NiB $345 Ex $280 Gd $196

SUPERMATIC DELUXE DEER GUN (II) NiB $434 Ex $351 Gd $245
Same as Supermatic Deluxe 12 (II) except has 22-inch bbl., cylinder bore, w/rifle sights. Weight: 7.75 lbs. Made 1966-74.

SUPERMATIC DELUXE DUCK
12 GA. MAGNUM (SERIES II) . . . . . NiB $305 Ex $249 Gd $179
Same as Supermatic Deluxe 12 (II) except chambered for 3-inch magnum shells, 3-round magazine, 30-inch plain bbl., F choke. Weight: 8 lbs. Made 1966-74.

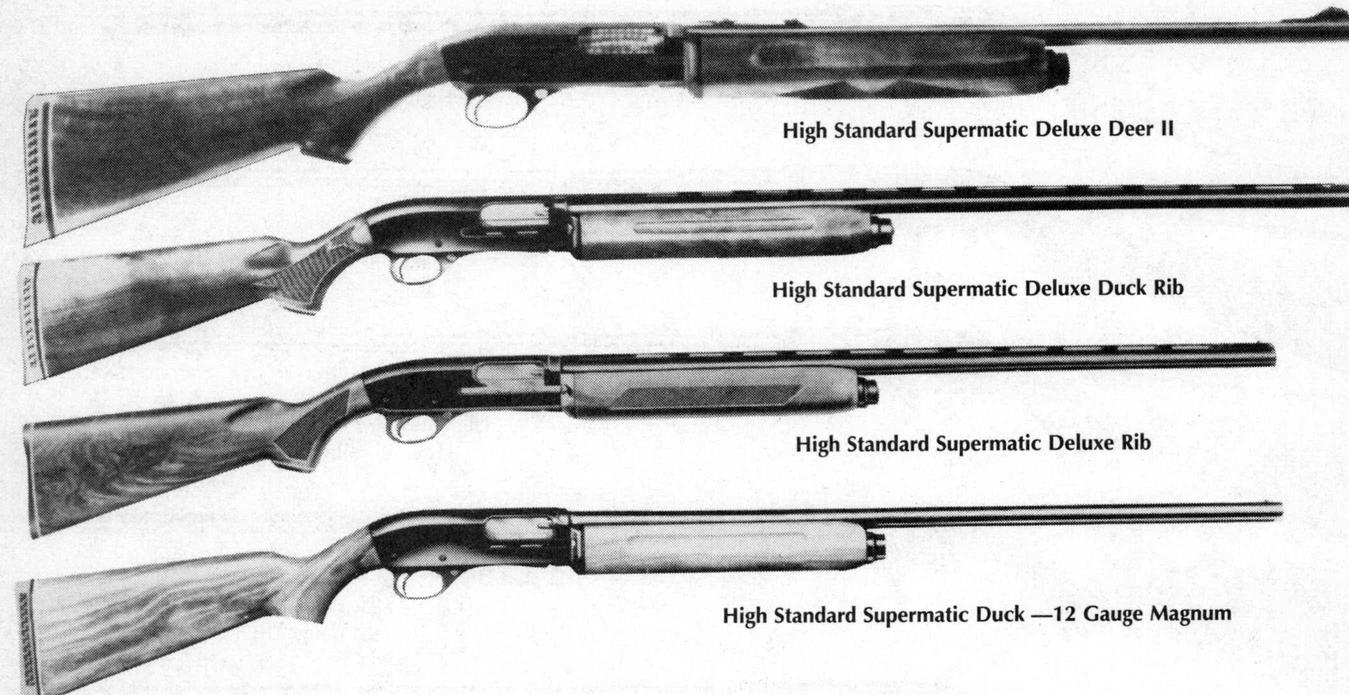

High Standard Supermatic Deluxe Deer II

High Standard Supermatic Deluxe Duck Rib

High Standard Supermatic Deluxe Rib

High Standard Supermatic Duck —12 Gauge Magnum

SUPERMATIC DELUXE RIB 12 GA.. . . . . NiB $286 Ex $232 Gd $163
Same as Supermatic Field 12 except vent rib bbl. (28-inch M or F, 30-inch F), checkered stock and forearm. Made 1961-66.

SUPERMATIC DELUXE RIB 12 GA. (II)
Same as Supermatic Deluxe 12 (II) except has vent rib bbl.; available in 27-inch w/adj. choke, 28-inch M or F, 30-inch F choke. Made 1966-75.
W/adj. choke . . . . NiB $358 Ex $290 Gd $204
W/O adj. choke . . . . NiB $326 Ex $265 Gd $186

SUPERMATIC DELUXE RIB 20 GA.. . . . . NiB $358 Ex $290 Gd $204
Same as Supermatic Field 20 except vent rib bbl. (28-inch M or F), checkered stock and forearm. Made 1963-66.

SUPERMATIC DELUXE RIB 20 GA. (II)
Same as Supermatic Deluxe 20 (II) except has vent rib bbl. Made 1966-75.
W/adj. choke . . . . NiB $329 Ex $267 Gd $187
W/O adj. choke . . . . NiB $305 Ex $247 Gd $175

SUPERMATIC DELUXE SKEET GUN 12 GA. (SERIES II) . . . . NiB $329 Ex $267 Gd $187
Same as Supermatic Deluxe Rib 12 (II) except available only w/26-inch vent rib bbl., SK choke. Made 1966-75.

SUPERMATIC DELUXE SKEET GUN 20 GA. (SERIES II) . . . . NiB $340 Ex $276 Gd $194
Same as Supermatic Deluxe Rib 20 (II) except available only w/26-inch vent rib bbl., SK choke. Made 1966-75.

SUPERMATIC DELUXE TRAP GUN (SERIES II) . . . . NiB $353 Ex $286 Gd $201
Same as Supermatic Deluxe Rib 12 (II) except available only w/30-inch vent rib bbl., full choke; trap-style stock. Made 1966-75.

SUPERMATIC DELUXE DUCK RIB 12 GA. MAG. (SERIES II) . . . . NiB $329 Ex $267 Gd $187
Same as Supermatic Deluxe Rib 12 (II) except chambered for 3-inch magnum shells, 3-round magazine; 30-inch vent rib bbl., F choke. Weight: 8 lbs. Made 1966-75.

SUPERMATIC DUCK 12 GA. MAG. . . . . NiB $329 Ex $267 Gd $187
Same as Supermatic Field 12 except chambered for 3-inch Magnum shell, 30-inch F choke bbl., recoil pad. Made 1961-66.

SUPERMATIC TROPHY 12 GA. . . . . NiB $280 Ex $228 Gd $161
Same as Supermatic Deluxe Rib 12 except has 27-inch vent-rib bbl. w/adj. choke. Made 1961-66.

SUPERMATIC DUCK RIB 12 GA. MAG.. . . . . NiB $353 Ex $286 Gd $201
Same as Supermatic Duck 12 Magnum except has vent rib bbl., checkered stock and forearm. Made 1961-66.

SUPERMATIC FIELD AUTOLOADING SHOTGUN 12 GA. . . . . NiB $377 Ex $306 Gd $214
Gas-operated. Magazine holds four rounds. Bbls.: 26-inch IC, 28-inch M or F choke, 30-inch F choke. Weight: About 7.5 lbs. Plain pistol-grip stock and forearm. Made 1960-66.

SUPERMATIC FIELD AUTOLOADING SHOTGUN 20 GA.. . . . . NiB $294 Ex $239 Gd $169
Gas-operated. Chambered for 3-inch mag. shells, also handles 2.75-inch. Magazine holds three rounds. Bbls.: 26-inch IC, 28-inch M or F choke. Weight: About 7 lbs. Plain pistol-grip stock and forearm. Made 1963-66.

SUPERMATIC SHADOW AUTOMATIC . . . NiB $422 Ex $341 Gd $238
Gas-operated. Ga.: 12, 20, 2.75- or 3-inch chamber in 12 ga., 3-inch in 20 ga. Mag. holds four 2.75-inch shells, three 3-inch. Bbls.: Full-size airflow rib; 26-inch (IC or SK choke), 28-inch (M, IM or F), 30-inch (trap or F choke), 12-ga. 3-inch Mag. available only in 30-inch F choke; 20 ga. not available in 30-inch. Weight: 12 ga., 7 lbs. Checkered walnut stock and forearm. Made 1974-75 by Caspoll Int'l., Inc., Tokyo.

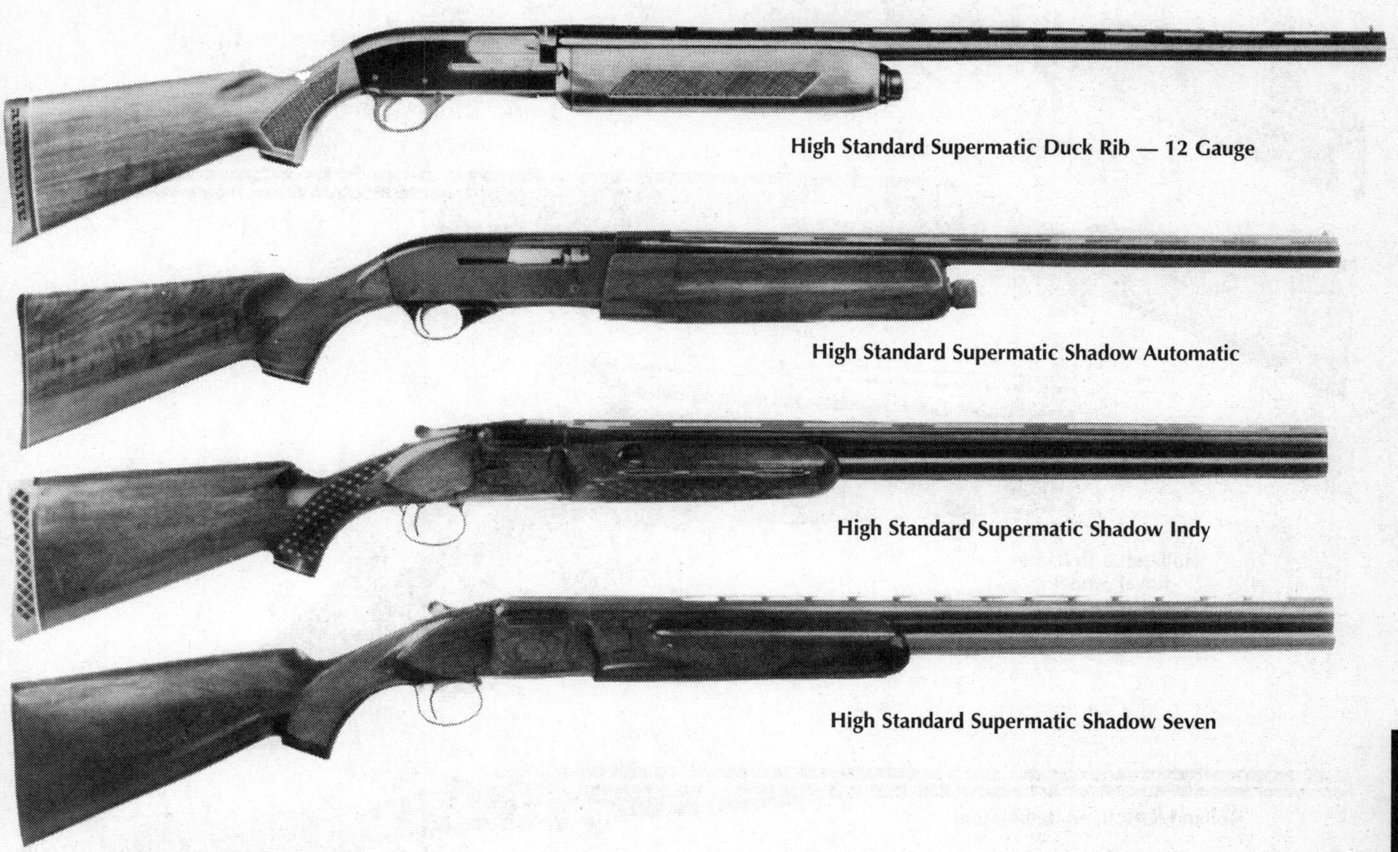

High Standard Supermatic Duck Rib — 12 Gauge

High Standard Supermatic Shadow Automatic

High Standard Supermatic Shadow Indy

High Standard Supermatic Shadow Seven

SUPERMATIC SHADOW INDY O/U.................... NiB 1079 Ex $876 Gd $617
Boxlock. Fully engraved receiver. Selective auto ejectors. Selective single trigger. 12 ga. 2.75-inch chambers. Bbls.: Full-size airflow rib; 27.5 inch both SK choke, 29.75-inch IM/F or F/F. Weight: W/29.75-inch bbls., 8 lbs. 2 oz. Pistol-grip stock w/recoil pad, ventilated forearm, skip checkering. Made 1974-75 by Caspoll Int'l., Inc., Tokyo.

SUPERMATIC SHADOW SEVEN ... NiB $910 Ex $737 Gd $516
Same general specifications as Shadow Indy except has conventional vent rib, less elaborate engraving, standard checkering forearm is not vented, no recoil pad. 27.5-inch bbls.; also available in IC/M, M/F choke. Made 1974-75.

SUPERMATIC SKEET 12 GA....... NiB $292 Ex $237 Gd $167
Same as Supermatic Deluxe Rib 12 except 26-inch vent-rib bbl. w/SK choke. Made 1962-66.

SUPERMATIC SKEET 20 GA....... NiB $312 Ex $253 Gd $177
Same as Supermatic Deluxe Rib 20 except 26-inch vent-rib bbl. w/SK choke. Made 1964-66.

SUPERMATIC SPECIAL 12 GA..... NiB $261 Ex $212 Gd $150
Same as Supermatic Field 12 except has 27-inch bbl. w/adj. choke. Made 1960-66.

SUPERMATIC SPECIAL 20 GA..... NiB $286 Ex $232 Gd $164
Same as Supermatic Field 20 except has 27-inch bbl. w/adj. choke. Made 1963-66.

SUPERMATIC TRAP 12 GA........ NiB $292 Ex $237 Gd $167
Same as Supermatic Deluxe Rib 12 except 30-inch vent rib bbl., F choke, special trap stock w/recoil pad. Made 1962-66.

SUPERMATIC TROPHY 20 GA..... NiB $305 Ex $247 Gd $174
Same as Supermatic Deluxe Rib 20 except has 27-inch vent rib bbl. w/adj. choke. Made 1963-66.

HOLLAND & HOLLAND, LTD. — *London England*

BADMINTON MODEL HAMMERLESS DOUBLE-BARREL SHOTGUN. ORIGINALLY NO. 2 GRADE
General specifications same as Royal Model except without self-opening action. Made as a game gun or pigeon and wildfowl gun. Introduced in 1902. Disc.
W/double triggers .... NiB $10,856 Ex $8684 Gd $5905
W/single trigger .... NiB $12,416 Ex $9932 Gd $6754
20 ga., add 25%
28 ga., add 40%
.410, add 65%

CENTENARY MODEL HAMMERLESS DOUBLE-BARREL SHOTGUN
Lightweight (5.5 lbs.). 12 ga. game gun designed for 2-inch shell. Made in four grades—Model Deluxe, Royal, Badminton, Dominion. Values same as shown for standard guns in those grades. Disc. 1962.

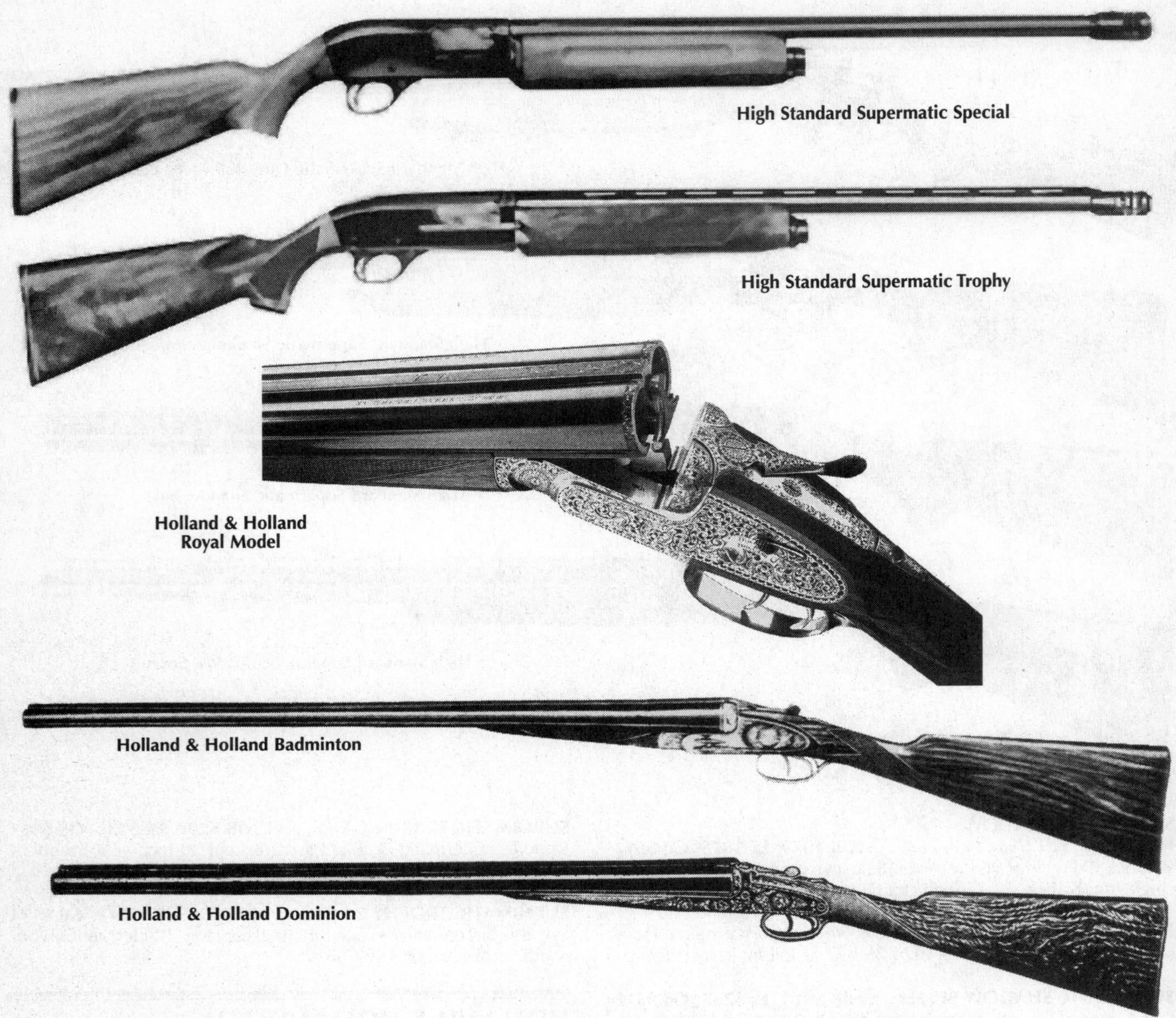

High Standard Supermatic Special

High Standard Supermatic Trophy

Holland & Holland Royal Model

Holland & Holland Badminton

Holland & Holland Dominion

DOMINION MODEL HAMMERLESS DOUBLE-BBL. SHOTGUN . . . . NiB $6608 Ex $5326 Gd $3686
Game Gun. Sidelock. Auto ejectors. Double triggers. Gauges: 12, 16, 20. bbls. 25- to 30-inch, any standard boring. Checkered stock and forend, straight grip standard. Disc. 1967.

MODEL DELUXE HAMMERLESS DOUBLE
Same as Royal Model except has special engraving and exhibition grade stock and forearm. Currently manufactured.
W/double triggers . . . . . . NiB $59,150 Ex $47,320 Gd $32,178
W/single trigger . . . . NiB $64,675 Ex $51,740 Gd $35,183

NORTHWOOD MODEL HAMMERLESS DOUBLE-BARREL SHOTGUN . . NiB $6884 Ex $5507 Gd $3745
Anson & Deeley system boxlock. Auto ejectors. Double triggers. Gauges: 12, 16, 20, 28 in Game Model; 28 ga. not offered in Pigeon Model; Wildfowl Model in 12 ga. only (3-inch chambers available). Bbls.: 28-inch standard in Game and Pigeon Models, 30-inch in Wildfowl Model; other lengths, any standard choke combination

***(cont'd)* NORTHWOOD MODEL HAMMERLESS DOUBLE-BARREL SHOTGUN**
available. Weight: From 5 to 7.75 lbs. depending on ga. and bbls. Checkered straight-grip or pistol-grip stock and forearm. Disc.

RIVIERA MODEL PIGEON GUN . . . . NiB $15,014 Ex $12,012 Gd $8168
Same as Badminton Model but supplied w/two sets of bbls., double triggers. Disc. 1967.

ROYAL MODEL HAMMERLESS DOUBLE
Self-opening. Sidelocks hand-detachable. Auto ejectors. Double triggers or single trigger. Gauges: 12, 16, 20, 28 .410. Built to customer's specifications as to bbl. length, chokes, etc. Made as a Game Gun or Pigeon and Wildfowl Gun, the latter having treble-grip action and side clips. Checkered stock and forend, straight grip standard. Made from 1885 to date.
W/double triggers . . . . . . NiB $58,826 Ex $47,060 Gd $32,000
W/single trigger . . . . NiB $63,376 Ex $50,700 Gd $34,476

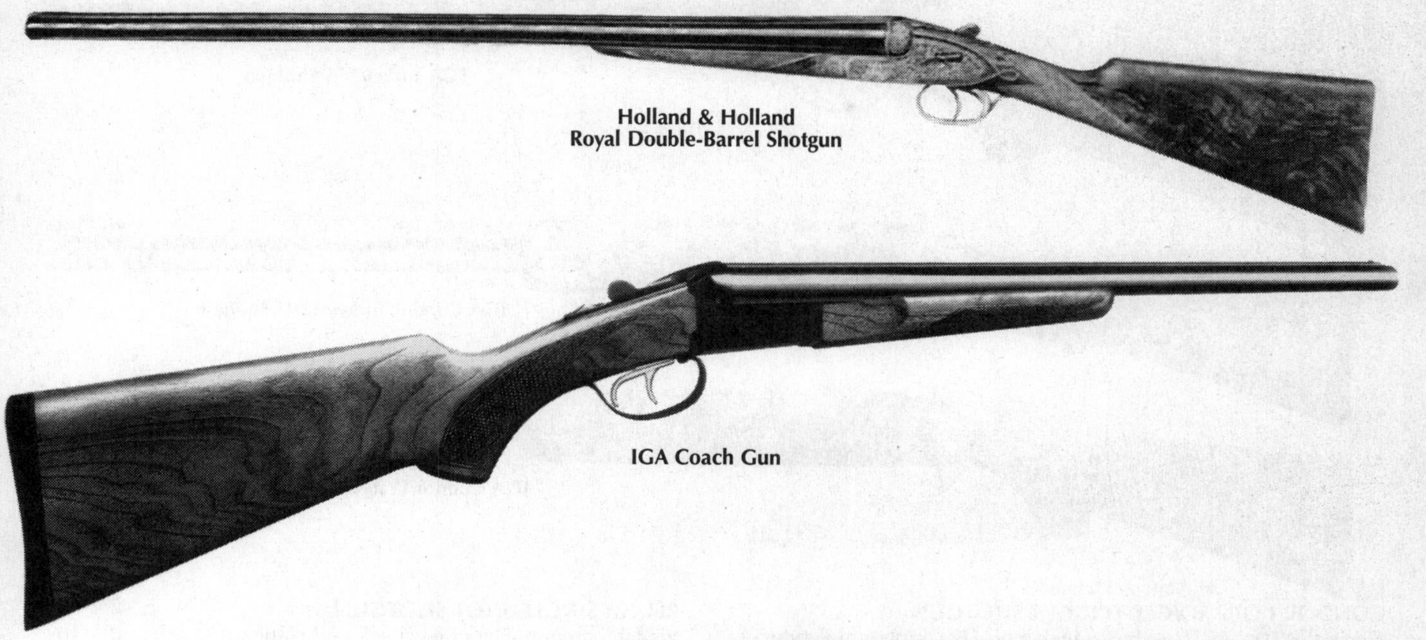
Holland & Holland
Royal Double-Barrel Shotgun

IGA Coach Gun

ROYAL MODEL O/U
Sidelocks, hand-detachable. Auto-ejectors. Double triggers or single trigger. 12 ga. Built to customer's specifications as to bbl. length, chokes, etc. Made as a Game Gun or Pigeon and Wildfowl Gun. Checkered stock and forend, straight grip standard. Note: In 1951 Holland & Holland introduced its New Model Under/Over w/an improved, narrower action body. Disc. 1960.

New model (double triggers) .... NiB $38,026 Ex $30,420 Gd $20,686
New model (single trigger) .... NiB $39,650 Ex $31,720 Gd $21,570
Old model (double triggers) .... NiB $32,436 Ex $25,948 Gd $17,645
Old model (single trigger) .... NiB $34,450 Ex $27,560 Gd $18,741

SINGLE-SHOT SUPER TRAP GUN
Anson & Deeley system boxlock. Auto-ejector. No safety. 12 ga. Bbls.: Wide vent rib, 30- or 32-inch, w/Extra Full choke. Weight: About 8.75 lbs. Monte Carlo stock w/pistol grip and recoil pad, full beavertail forearm. Models differ in grade of engraving and wood. Disc.

Standard grade .... NiB $5726 Ex $4620 Gd $3206
Deluxe grade .... NiB $8976 Ex $7220 Gd $4974
Exhibition grade .... NiB $10,726 Ex $8580 Gd $5834

SPORTING O/U .... NiB $27,950 Ex $22,360 Gd $15,205
Blitz action. Auto ejectors; single selective trigger. Gauges: 12 or 20 w/2.75-inch chambers. Barrels: 28- to 32-inch w/screw-in choke tubes. Hand-checkered European walnut straight-grip or pistol grip stock, forearm. Made 1993 to date.

HOLLAND & HOLLAND SPORTING O/U DELUXE .... NiB $36,336 Ex $29,068 Gd $19,766
Same general specs as Sporting O/U except better engraving and select wood. Made 1993 to date.

HUNTER ARMS COMPANY — Fulton, New York

HUNFULTON HAMMERLESS DOUBLE-BARREL. SHOTGUN
Boxlock. Plain extractors. Double triggers or non-selective single trigger. Gauges: 12 16, 20. Bbls.: 26- to 32-inch various choke combinations. Weight: about 7 lbs. Checkered pistol-grip stock and forearm. Disc. 1948.

W/double triggers .... NiB $453 Ex $374 Gd $273
W/single trigger .... NiB $726 Ex $539 Gd $422

SPECIAL HAMMERLESS DOUBLE-BARREL. SHOTGUN
Boxlock. Plain extractors. Double triggers or non-selective single trigger. Gauges: 12,16, 20. Bbls.: 26- to 30-inch various choke combinations. Weight: 6.5 to 7.25 lbs. depending on bbl. length and ga. Checkered full pistol-grip stock and forearm. Disc. 1948.

W/double triggers .... NiB $662 Ex $541 Gd $387
W/single trigger .... NiB $806 Ex $657 Gd $465

IGA SHOTGUNS — Veranopolis, Brazil
Imported by Stoeger Industries, Inc. Accokeek, Maryland

COACH GUN
Side-by-side double. Gauges: 12, 20 and .410. 20-inch bbls. w/3-inch chambers. Fixed chokes (standard model) or screw-in tubes (deluxe model). Weight: 6.5 lbs. Double triggers. Ejector and automatic safety. Blued or nickel finish. Hand-rubbed oil-finished pistol grip stock and forend w/hand checkering (hardwood on standard model or Brazilian walnut (deluxe). Imported 1983 to date.

Standard Coach Gun (blued finish).... NiB $291 Ex $237 Gd $168
Standard Coach Gun (nickel finish) ... NiB $353 Ex $286 Gd $201
Standard Coach Gun (engraved stock) .... NiB $377 Ex $306 Gd $214
Deluxe Coach Gun (intro. 1997)... NiB $413 Ex $334 Gd $237
Choke tubes, add.................................. $20

SHOTGUNS

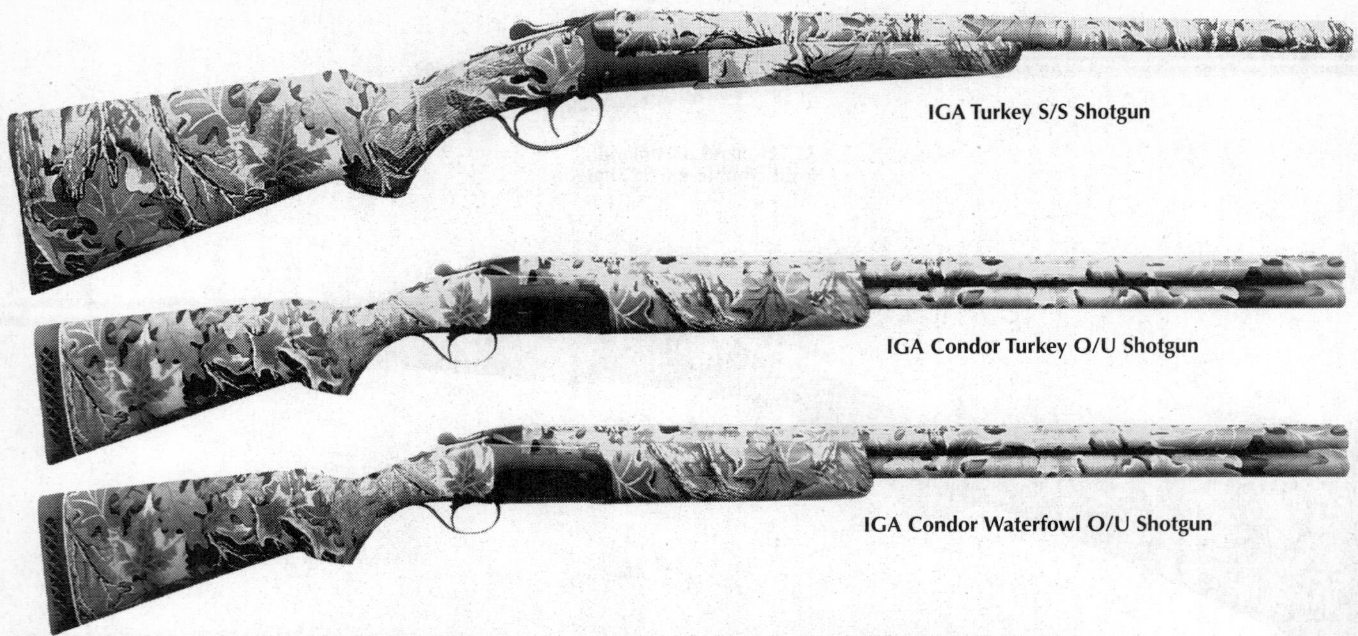

IGA Turkey S/S Shotgun

IGA Condor Turkey O/U Shotgun

IGA Condor Waterfowl O/U Shotgun

CONDOR I O/U SINGLE-TRIGGER SHOTGUN
Gauges: 12 or 20. 26- or 28-inch bbls. of chrome-molybdenum steel. Chokes: Fixed — M/F or IC/M; screw-in choke tubes (12 and 20 ga.). Three inch chambers. Weight: 6.75 to 7 lbs. Sighting rib w/anti-glare surface. Hand-checkered hardwood pistol-grip stock and forend. Imported 1983 to date.
W/fixed chokes . . . . NiB $377 Ex $306 Gd $214
W/screw-in tubes . . . . NiB $426 Ex $344 Gd $240

CONDOR II O/U DOUBLE-TRIGGER SHOTGUN . . . . NiB $371 Ex $300 Gd $211
Same general specifications as the Condor I O/U except w/double triggers and fixed chokes only; 26-inch bbls., IC/M; 28-inch bbls., M/F.

CONDOR SUPREME . . . . NiB $565 Ex $456 Gd $317
Same general specifications as Condor I except upgraded w/fine-checkered Brazilian walnut buttstock and forend, a matte-laquered finish, and a massive monoblock that joins the bbls. in a solid one-piece assembly at the breech end. Bbls. w/recessed interchangeable choke tubes formulated for use w/steel shot. Automatic ejectors. Imported 1996 to date.

CONDOR TURKEY MODEL O/U SHOTGUN . . . . NiB $655 Ex $528 Gd $366
12 gauge only. 26-inch vent-rib bbls. w/3-inch chambers fitted w/recessed interchangeable choke tubes. Weight: 8 lbs. Mechanical single trigger. Ejectors and automatic safety. Advantage camouflage on stock and bbls. Made 1997 to date.

CONDOR WATERFOWL MODEL . . . . . NiB $669 Ex $539 Gd $373
Similar to Condor Turkey-Advantage camo model except w/30-inch bbls. Made 1998 to date.

DELUXE HUNTER CLAY SHOTGUN
Same general specifications and values as IGA Condor Supreme. Imported 1997 to date.

ERA 2000 O/U SHOTGUN . . . . NiB $488 Ex $394 Gd $274
Gauge: 12 w/3-inch chambers. 26- or 28-inch bbls. of chrome-molybdenum steel w/screw-in choke tubes. Extractors. Manual safety. (Mechanical triggers.) Weight: 7 lbs. Checkered Brazilian hardwood stock w/oil finish. Imported 1992-95.

REUNA SINGLE-SHOT SHOTGUN
Visible hammer. Under-lever release. Gauges: 12, 20 and .410; 3-inch chambers. 26- or 28-inch bbls. w/fixed chokes or screw-in choke tubes (12 ga. only). Extractors. Weight: 5.25 to 6.5 lbs. Plain Brazilian hardwood stock and semi-beavertail forend. Imported 1992 to date.
W/fixed choke . . . . NiB $118 Ex $97 Gd $69
W/choke tubes . . . . NiB $195 Ex $158 Gd $111

UPLANDER SIDE-BY-SIDE SHOTGUN
Gauges: 12, 20, 28 and .410. 26- or 28-inch bbls. of chrome-molybdenum steel. Various fixed-choke combinations; screw-in choke tubes (12 and 20 ga.). Three inch chambers (2.75-inch in 28 ga.). Weight: 6.25 to 7 lbs. Double triggers. Automatic safety. Matte-finished solid sighting rib. Hand checkered pistol-grip or straight stock and forend w/hand-rubbed, oil-finish. Imported 1983 to date.
Upland w/fixed chokes . . . . NiB $312 Ex $253 Gd $177
Upland w/screw-in tubes . . . . NiB $371 Ex $303 Gd $210
English model (straight grip) . . . . . . NiB $361 Ex $291 Gd $204
Ladies model . . . . NiB $371 Ex $302 Gd $210
Supreme model . . . . NiB $494 Ex $396 Gd $276
Youth model . . . . NiB $336 Ex $272 Gd $190

UPLANDER TURKEY MODEL S/S DOUBLE . . . . NiB $485 Ex $391 Gd $271
12 gauge only. 24-inch solid rib bbls. w/3-inch chambers choked F&F. Weight: 6.75 lbs. Double triggers. Automatic safety. Advantage camouflage on stock and bbls. Made 1997 to date.

ITHACA GUN COMPANY — King Ferry (formerly Ithaca), New York. Now Ithaca Acquisition Corp./Ithaca Gun Co.

MODEL 37 BICENTENNIAL COMMEMORATIVE. . . . . NiB $693 Ex $463 Gd $325
Limited to issue of 1976. Similar to Model 37 Supreme except has special Bicentennial design etched on receiver, full-fancy walnut stock and slide handle. Serial numbers U.S.A. 0001 to U.S.A. 1976. Originally issued w/presentation case w/cast-pewter belt buckle. Made in 1976. Best value is for gun in new, unfired condition.

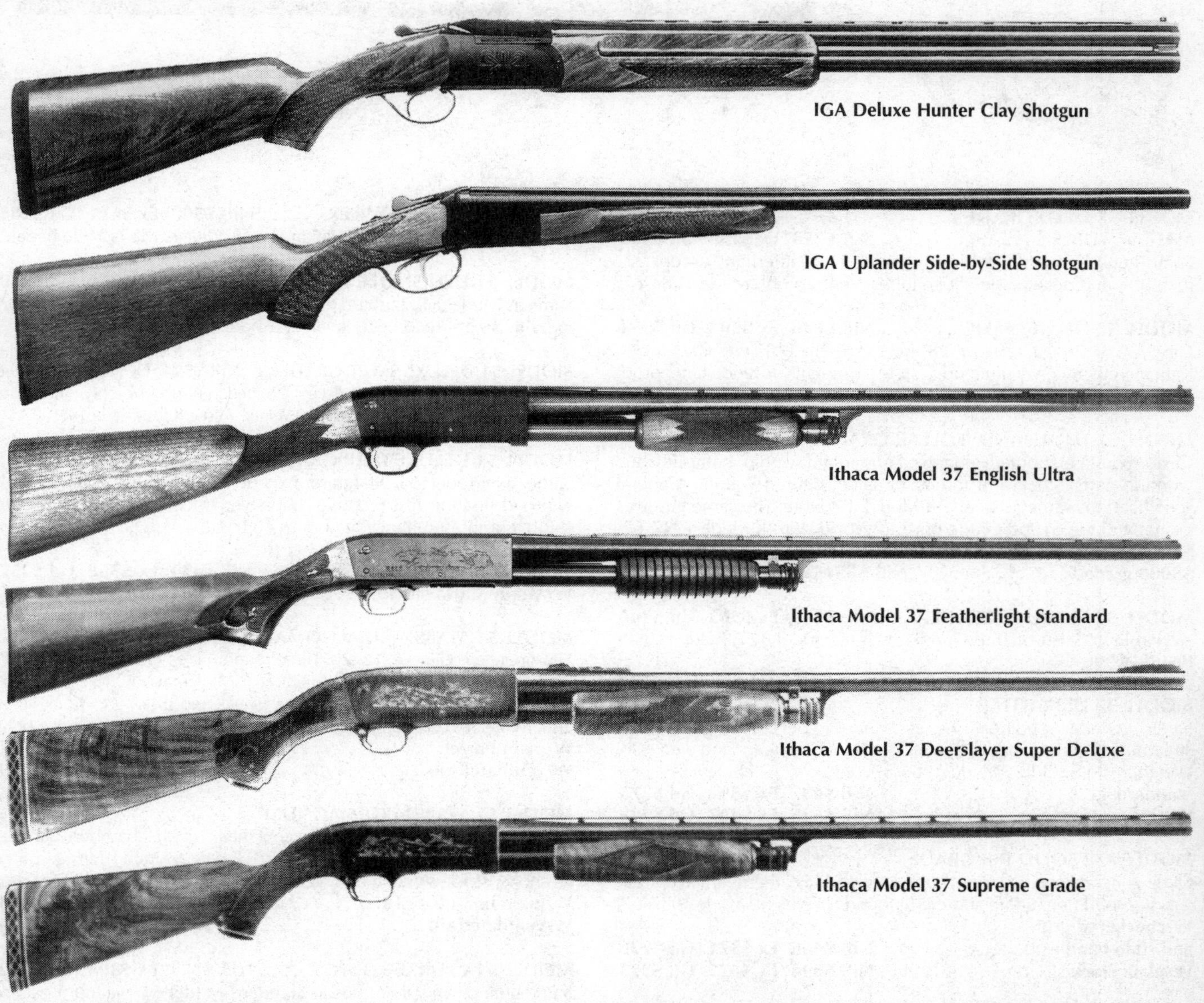
IGA Deluxe Hunter Clay Shotgun

IGA Uplander Side-by-Side Shotgun

Ithaca Model 37 English Ultra

Ithaca Model 37 Featherlight Standard

Ithaca Model 37 Deerslayer Super Deluxe

Ithaca Model 37 Supreme Grade

MODEL 37 DEERSLAYER DELUXE
Formerly "Model 87 Deerslayer Deluxe" reintroduced under the original Model 37 designation w/the same specifications. Available w/smooth bore or rifled bbl. Reintroduced 1996.
Deluxe model (smoothbore) . . . . . . NiB $468 Ex $378 Gd $264
Deluxe model (rifled bbl.) . . . . NiB $522 Ex $421 Gd $292

MODEL 37 DEERSLAYER II . . . . NiB $555 Ex $448 Gd $312
Gauges: 12 or 20 ga. Five round capacity. 20- or 25-inch rifled bbl. Weight: 7 lbs. Monte Carlo checkered walnut stock and forearm. Receiver drilled and tapped for scope mount. Made 1996 to date.

MODEL 37 DEERSLAYER STANDARD . . . . NiB $339 Ex $275 Gd $193
Same as Model 37 Standard except has 20- or 26-inch bbl. bored for rifled slugs, rifle-type open rear sight and ramp front sight. Weight: 5.75 to 6.5 lbs. depending on ga. and bbl. length. Made 1959-86.

MODEL 37 DEERSLAYER
SUPER DELUXE . . . . NiB $434 Ex $351 Gd $245
Formerly "Deluxe Deerslayer." Same as Model 37 Standard Deerslayer except has stock and slide handle of fancy walnut. Made from 1962-86.

MODEL 37 ENGLISH ULTRA . . . . . NiB $495 Ex $399 Gd $278
Same general specifications as Model 37 Ultralite except straight buttstock, 25-inch Hot Forged vent-rib bbl. Made 1984-87.

MODEL 37 FEATHERLIGHT STANDARD GRADE
SLIDE-ACTION REPEATING SHOTGUN
Adaptation of the earlier Remington Model 17, a Browning design patented in 1915. Hammerless. Takedown. Gauges: 12, 16 (disc. 1973), 20. Four round magazine. Bbl. lengths: 26-, 28-, 30-inch (the latter in 12 ga. only); standard chokes. Weight: From 5.75 to 7.5 lbs. depending on ga. and bbl. length. Checkered pistol-grip stock and slide handle. Some guns made in the 1950s and 1960s have grooved slide handle; plain or checkered pistol-grip. Made 1937-84.
Standard w/checkered pistol-grip . . NiB $303 Ex $245 Gd $172
W/plain stock . . . . NiB $271 Ex $220 Gd $155
Mdl 37D Deluxe (1954-77) . . . . NiB $379 Ex $306 Gd $214
Mdl 37DV Deluxe vent rib (1962-84) . . . NiB $434 Ex $351 Gd $245
Mdl 37R Deluxe
solid rib (1955-61). . . . . NiB $367 Ex $296 Gd $207
Mdl 37V Standard
vent rib (1962-84) . . . . NiB $354 Ex $286 Gd $200

Ithaca Model 51
Deluxe Trap

MODEL 37 FIELD GRADE MAG. W/TUBES . . . . NiB $353 Ex $285 Gd $200
Same general specifications as Model 37 Featherlight except 32-inch bbl. and detachable choke tubes. Vent rib bbl. Made 1984-87.

MODEL 37 NEW CLASSIC . . . . NiB $630 Ex $508 Gd $354
Ggs: 12 or 20 ga. 20- or 28-inch vent rib bbl. w/choke tubes. Knuckle-cut receiver and orig. style "ring-tail" forend. Lim. prod. 1998 to date.

MODEL 37 THOUSAND DOLLAR GRADE
Custom built, elaborately engraved and inlaid w/gold, hand-finished working parts, stock and forend of select figured walnut. General specifications same as standard Model 37. Note: The same gun was designated the $1000 Grade prior to World War II. Made 1937-67.
$1000 grade . . . . NiB $6821 Ex $5475 Gd $3774
$5000 grade . . . . NiB $6515 Ex $5240 Gd $3608

MODEL 37 SUPREME GRADE. . . . . NiB $699 Ex $565 Gd $394
Available in Skeet or Trap Gun, similar to Model 37T. Made 1967-86 and 1996-97.

MODEL 37 ULTRALITE
Same general specifications as Model 37 Featherlight except streamlined forend, gold trigger, Sid Bell grip cap and vent rib. Weight: 5 to 5.75 lbs. Made 1984-87.
Standard . . . . NiB $487 Ex $394 Gd $275
W/choke tubes . . . . NiB $528 Ex $427 Gd $298

MODEL 37R SOLID RIB GRADE
Same general specifications as the Model 37 Featherlight except has a raised solid rib, adding about .25 pounds of weight. Made 1937-67.
W/checkered grip and slide handle . . . . NiB $400 Ex $324 Gd $226
W/plain stock . . . . NiB $394 Ex $421 Gd $223

MODEL 37S SKEET GRADE. . . . . . . NiB $562 Ex $453 Gd $315
Same general specifications as the Model 37 Featherlight except has vent rib and large extension-type forend; weight: About .5 lb. more. Made 1937-55.

MODEL 37T TARGET GRADE . . . . . NiB $523 Ex $422 Gd $292
Same general specifications as Model 37 Featherlight except has vent-rib bbl., checkered stock and slide handle of fancy walnut (choice of skeet- or trap-style stock). Note: This model replaced Model 37S Skeet and Model 37T Trap. Made 1955-61.

MODEL 37T TRAP GRADE . . . . NiB $562 Ex $453 Gd $315
Same gen. specs. as Mdl. 37S except has straighter trap-style stock of select walnut, recoil pad; weight: About .5 lb. more. Made 1937-55.

MODEL 37 TURKEYSLAYER
Gauges: 12 ga. (Standard) or 20 ga. (youth). Slide action. 22-inch bbl. Extended choke tube. Weight: 7 lbs. Advantage camouflage or Realtree pattern. Made 1996 to date.
Standard model . . . . NiB $488 Ex $394 Gd $274
Youth model(intro. 1998) . . . . NiB $522 Ex $421 Gd $292

MODEL 37 WATERFOWLER . . . . . . NiB $508 Ex $411 Gd $285
12 ga. only w/28-inch bbl. Wetlands camouflage. Made 1998 to date.

MODEL 51 DEERSLAYER. . . . . NiB $388 Ex $314 Gd $220
Same as Model 51 Standard except has 24-inch plain bbl. w/slug boring, rifle sights, recoil pad. Weight: About 7.25 lbs. Made 1972-84.

MODEL 51 DELUXE SKEET GRADE . . . NiB $524 Ex $423 Gd $294
Same as Model 51 Standard except 26-inch vent-rib bbl. only, SK choke, skeet-style stock, semi-fancy wood. Weight: About 8 lbs. Made 1970-87.

MODEL 51 DELUXE TRAP GRADE
Same as Model 51 Standard except 12 ga. only, 30-inch bbl. w/broad floating rib, F choke, trap-style stock w/straight or Monte Carlo comb, semifancy wood, recoil pad. Weight: About 8 lbs. Made 1970-87.
W/straight stock . . . . NiB $454 Ex $368 Gd $257
W/Monte Carlo stock . . . . NiB $481 Ex $389 Gd $271

MODEL 51 STANDARD AUTOMATIC SHOTGUN
Gas-operated. Gauges: 12, 20. Three round. Bbls.: Plain or vent rib, 30-inch F choke (12 ga. only), 28-inch F or M, 26-inch IC. Weight: 7.25-7.75 lbs. depending on ga. and bbl. Checkered pistol-grip stock, forearm. Made 1970-80. Still avail. in 12 and 20 ga., 28-inch M choke only.
W/plain barrel. . . . . NiB $312 Ex $253 Gd $177
W/ventilated rib . . . . NiB $369 Ex $298 Gd $209

MODEL 51 STANDARD MAGNUM
Same as Model 51 Standard except has 3-inch chamber, handles Magnum shells only; 30-inch bbl. in 12 ga., 28-inch in 20 ga., F or M choke, stock w/recoil pad. Weight: 7.75-8 lbs. Made 1972 to date.
W/plain bbl. (disc. 1976) . . . . NiB $285 Ex $227 Gd $173
W/ventilated rib . . . . NiB $351 Ex $284 Gd $199

MODEL 51A TURKEY GUN. . . . . . . NiB $375 Ex $304 Gd $212
Same general specifications as standard Model 51 Magnum except 26-inch bbl. and matte finish. Disc. 1986.

MODEL 66 LONG TOM . . . . NiB $137 Ex $112 Gd $79
Same as Model 66 Standard except has 36-inch F choke bbl., 12 ga. only, checkered stock and recoil pad standard. Made 1969-74.

MODEL 66 STANDARD SUPER SINGLE LEVER
Single shot. Hand-cocked hammer. Gauges: 12 (disc. 1974), 20, .410, 3-inch chambers. Bbls.: 12 ga., 30-inch F choke, 28-inch F or M; 20 ga., 28-inch F or M; .410, 26-inch F. Weight: About 7 lbs. Plain or checkered straight-grip stock, plain forend. Made 1963-78.
Standard model . . . . NiB $169 Ex $138 Gd $97
Vent rib model (20 ga., checkered stock, recoil pad, 1969-74) . . . . . . NiB $195 Ex $158 Gd $111
Youth model (20 & .410 ga., 26-inch bbl., shorter stock, recoil pad, 1965-78). . . . . NiB $169 Ex $137 Gd $97

MODEL 66RS BUCKBUSTER. . . . . . NiB $202 Ex $163 Gd $114
Same as Model 66 Standard except has 22-inch bbl. cylinder bore w/rifle sights, later version has recoil pad. Originally offered in 12 and 20 ga.; the former was disc. in 1970. Made 1967-78.

Ithaca Model 66RS Buckbuster

Previously issued as the Ithaca Model 37, the Model 87 guns listed below were made available through the Ithaca Acquisition Corp. From 1986-95. Production of the Model 37 resumed under the original logo in 1996.

MODEL 87 DEERSLAYER SHOTGUN
Gauges: 12 or 20, 3-inch chamber. Bbls.: 18.5-, 20- or 25-inch (w/special or rifled bore). Weight: 6 to 6.75 lbs. Ramp blade front sight, adj. rear. Receiver grooved for scope. Checkered American walnut pistol-grip stock and forearm. Made 1988-96.
Basic model .... NiB $371 Ex $301 Gd $211
Basic Field Combo (w/extra 28-inch bbl.)
.... NiB $422 Ex $341 Gd $238
Deluxe model .... NiB $396 Ex $321 Gd $225
Deluxe Combo (w/extra 28-inch bbl.)
.... NiB $498 Ex $402 Gd $280
DSPS (8-round model) .... NiB $377 Ex $306 Gd $214
Field model .... NiB $326 Ex $265 Gd $183
Monte Carlo model .... NiB $345 Ex $280 Gd $196
Ultra model (disc. 1991) .... NiB $467 Ex $377 Gd $263

MODEL 87 DEERSLAYER II
RIFLED SHOTGUN .... NiB $434 Ex $351 Gd $245
Similar to Standard Deerslayer except w/solid frame construction and 25-inch rifled bbl. Monte Carlo stock. Made 1988-96.

MODEL 87 ULTRALITE
FIELD PUMP SHOTGUN......... NiB $415 Ex $335 Gd $235
Gauges: 12 and 20; 2.75-inch chambers. 25-inch bbl. w/choke tube. Weight: 5 to 6 lbs. Made 1988-90.

MODEL 87 FIELD GRADE
Gauge: 12 or 20.; 3-inch chamber. Five round magazine. Fixed chokes or screw-in choke tubes (IC, M, F). Bbls.: 18.5-inch (M&P); 20- and 25-inch (Combo); 26-, 28-, 30-inch vent rib. Weight: 5 to 7 lbs. Made from 1988-96.
Basic field model (disc. 1993)..... NiB $390 Ex $316 Gd $221
Camo model .... NiB $422 Ex $341 Gd $238
Deluxe model .... NiB $453 Ex $367 Gd $256
Deluxe Combo model .... NiB $460 Ex $372 Gd $260
English model .... NiB $396 Ex $321 Gd $225
Hand grip model
(w/polymer pistol-grip) .... NiB $434 Ex $352 Gd $245
M&P model (disc. 1995) .... NiB $377 Ex $306 Gd $214
Supreme model .... NiB $594 Ex $479 Gd $332
Turkey model.................. NiB $396 Ex $321 Gd $225
Ultra Deluxe model (disc. 1992)... NiB $485 Ex $392 Gd $273

HAMMERLESS DOUBLE-BARREL SHOTGUNS
Boxlock. Plain extractors, auto ejectors standard on the "E" grades. Double triggers, non-selective or selective single trigger extra. Gauges: Magnum 10, 12; 12, 16, 20, 28, .410. Bbls.: 26- to 32-inch, any standard boring. Weight: 5.75 (.410) to 10.5 lbs. (Magnum 10).

(cont'd.) **HAMMERLESS DOUBLE-BARREL SHOTGUNS**
Checkered pistol-grip stock and forearm standard. Higher grades differ from Field Grade in quality of workmanship, grade of wood, checkering, engraving, etc.; general specifications are the same. Ithaca doubles made before 1925 (serial number 425,000) the rotary bolt and a stronger frame were adopted. Values shown are for this latter type; earlier models valued about 50% lower. Smaller gauge guns may command up to 75% higher. Disc. 1948.
Field grade.................. NiB $898 Ex $724 Gd $501
No. 1 grade .... NiB $958 Ex $772 Gd $636
No. 2 grade .... NiB $1436 Ex $1157 Gd $800
No. 3 grade .... NiB $1819 Ex $1463 Gd $1008
No. 4E grade (ejector)........ NiB $3239 Ex $2501 Gd $1789
No. 5E grade (ejector)........ NiB $7658 Ex $3488 Gd $4198
No. 7E grade (ejector) $12,750
$2000 (pre-war $1000) grade
ejector and selective single trigger standard $9129

Extras:
Magnum 10 or 12 ga.
(in other than the four highest grades), add.............. 20%
Automatic ejectors (grades No. 1, 2, 3, w/ejectors designated No. 1E, 2E, 3E), add.............................. $200
Selective single trigger, add........................ $250
Non-selective single trigger, add $175
Beavertail forend (Field No. 1 or 2), add................ $150
Beavertail forend (No. 3 or 4), add $175
Beavertail forend (No. 5, 7 or $2000 grade), add $250
Ventilated rib (No. 4, 5, 7 or $2000 grade), add.......... $250
Ventilated rib (lower grades), add $175

LSA-55 TURKEY GUN .... NiB $694 Ex $561 Gd $389
Over/under shotgun/rifle combination. Boxlock. Exposed hammer. Plain extractor. Single trigger. 12 ga./222 Rem. 24.5-inch ribbed bbls. (rifle bbl. has muzzle brake). Weight: About 7 lbs. Folding leaf rear sight, bead front sight. Checkered Monte Carlo stock and forearm. Made 1970-77 by Oy Tikkakoski AB, Finland.

MAG-10 AUTOMATIC SHOTGUN
Gas-operated. 10 ga. 3.5-inch Magnum. Three round capacity. 32-inch plain (Standard Grade only) or vent-rib bbl. F choke. Weight: 11 lbs., plain bbl.; 11.5 lbs., vent rib. Standard grade has plain stock and forearm. Deluxe and Supreme Grades have checkering, semi-fancy and fancy wood respectively, and stud swivel. All have recoil pad. Deluxe and Supreme grades made 1974-1982. Standard Grade intro. in 1977. All grades disc. 1986.
Camo model .... NiB $745 Ex $601 Gd $417
Deluxe grade................. NiB $781 Ex $630 Gd $436
Roadblocker .... NiB $805 Ex $649 Gd $450
Standard grade, plain barrel ...... NiB $650 Ex $533 Gd $371
Standard grade, ventilated rib..... NiB $691 Ex $557 Gd $387
Standard grade, w/tubes .... NiB $781 Ex $630 Gd $436
Supreme grade................. NiB $902 Ex $727 Gd $502

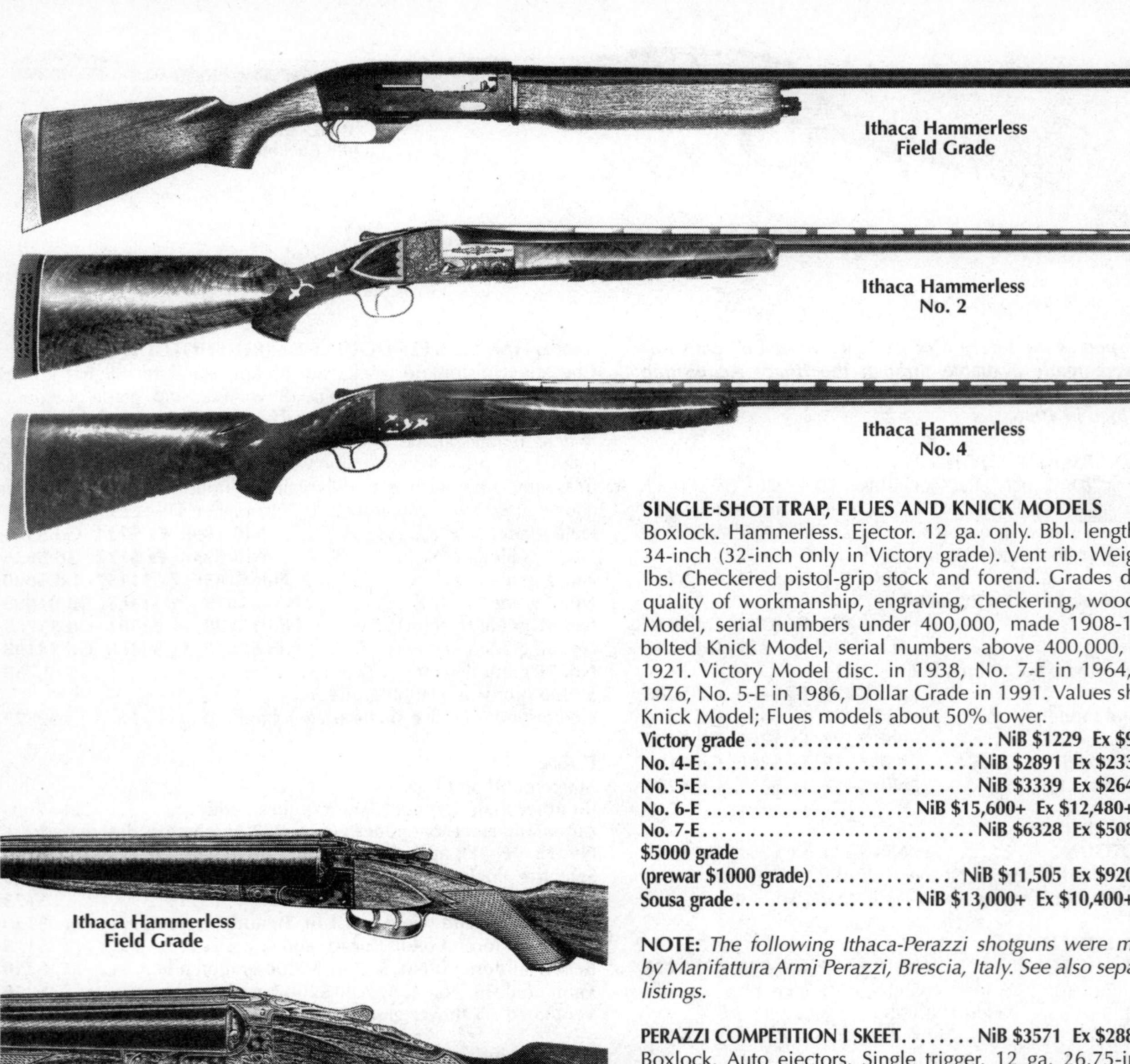

Ithaca Hammerless Field Grade

Ithaca Hammerless No. 2

Ithaca Hammerless No. 4

Ithaca Hammerless Field Grade

Ithaca Model 5-E

Ithaca Single-Shot Trap "Dollar Grade"

SINGLE-SHOT TRAP, FLUES AND KNICK MODELS
Boxlock. Hammerless. Ejector. 12 ga. only. Bbl. lengths: 30-, 32-, 34-inch (32-inch only in Victory grade). Vent rib. Weight: About 8 lbs. Checkered pistol-grip stock and forend. Grades differ only in quality of workmanship, engraving, checkering, wood, etc. Flues Model, serial numbers under 400,000, made 1908-1921. Triple-bolted Knick Model, serial numbers above 400,000, made since 1921. Victory Model disc. in 1938, No. 7-E in 1964, No. 4-E in 1976, No. 5-E in 1986, Dollar Grade in 1991. Values shown are for Knick Model; Flues models about 50% lower.
Victory grade . . . . NiB $1229 Ex $996 Gd $698
No. 4-E. . . . . NiB $2891 Ex $2331 Gd $1615
No. 5-E. . . . . NiB $3339 Ex $2640 Gd $1860
No. 6-E . . . . NiB $15,600+ Ex $12,480+ Gd $8486+
No. 7-E. . . . . NiB $6328 Ex $5082 Gd $3486
$5000 grade
(prewar $1000 grade). . . . . NiB $11,505 Ex $9204 Gd $6259
Sousa grade. . . . . NiB $13,000+ Ex $10,400+ Gd $7072+

NOTE: *The following Ithaca-Perazzi shotguns were manufactured by Manifattura Armi Perazzi, Brescia, Italy. See also separate Perazzi listings.*

PERAZZI COMPETITION I SKEET. . . . . . . NiB $3571 Ex $2881 Gd $2070
Boxlock. Auto ejectors. Single trigger. 12 ga. 26.75-inch vent-rib bbls. SK choke w/integral muzzle brake. Weight: About 7.75 lbs. Checkered skeet-style pistol-grip buttstock and forearm; recoil pad. Made 1969-74.

PERAZZI COMPETITION TRAP I O/U . . . . NiB $3701 Ex $2881 Gd $2070
Boxlock. Auto ejectors. Single trigger. 12 ga. 30- or 32-inch vent-rib bbls. IM/F choke. Weight: About 8.5 lbs. Checkered pistol-grip stock, forearm; recoil pad. Made 1969-74.

PERAZZI COMPETITION I
TRAP SINGLE BARREL. . . . . NiB $2661 Ex $2153 Gd $1504
Boxlock. Auto ejection. 12 ga. 32- or 34-inch bbl., vent rib, F choke. Weight: 8.5 lbs. Checkered Monte Carlo stock and beavertail forearm, recoil pad. Made 1973-78.

PERAZZI COMPETITION IV
TRAP GUN. . . . . NiB $3239 Ex $2616 Gd $1819
Boxlock. Auto ejection. 12 ga. 32- or 34-inch bbl. With high, wide vent rib, four interchangeable choke tubes (Extra Full, F, IM, M). Weight: About 8.75 lbs. Checkered Monte Carlo stock and beavertail forearm, recoil pad. Fitted case. Made 1977-78.

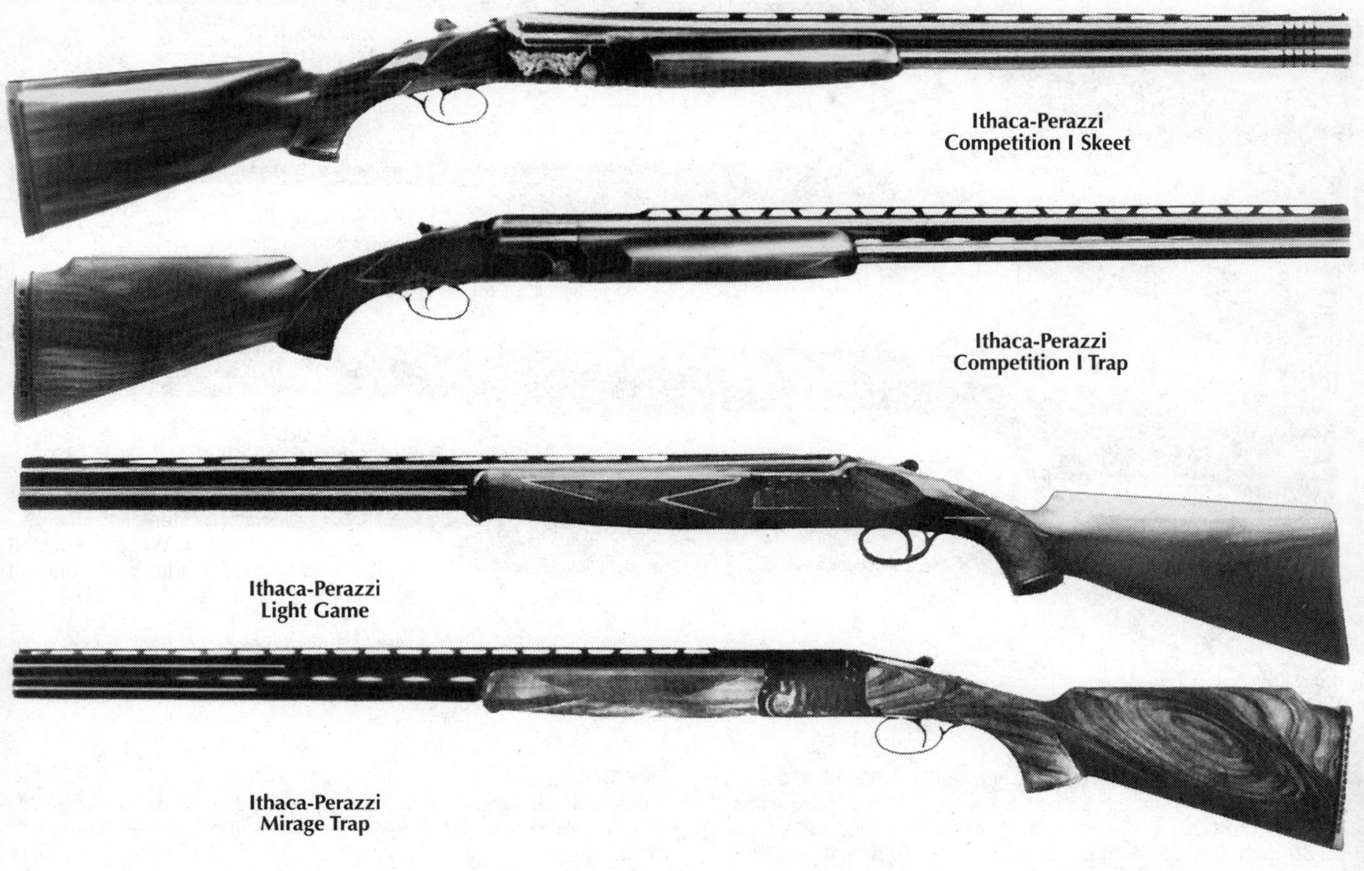

Ithaca-Perazzi Competition I Skeet

Ithaca-Perazzi Competition I Trap

Ithaca-Perazzi Light Game

Ithaca-Perazzi Mirage Trap

PERAZZI LIGHT GAME O/U FIELD
. . . . . NiB $3995 Ex $3205 Gd $2194
Boxlock. Auto ejectors. Single trigger. 12 ga. 27.5-inch vent rib bbls., M/F or IC/M choke. Weight: 6.75 lbs. Checkered field-style stock and forearm. Made 1972-74.

PERAZZI MIRAGE LIVE BIRD . . NiB $4481 Ex $3592 Gd $2457
Same as Mirage Trap except has 28-inch bbls., M and Extra Full choke, special stock and forearm for live bird shooting. Weight: About 8 lbs. Made 1973-78.

PERAZZI MIRAGE SKEET . . . . . . NiB $3797 Ex $3046 Gd $2086
Same as Mirage Trap except has 28-inch bbls. w/integral muzzle brakes, SK choke, skeet-stype stock and forearm. Weight: About 8 lbs. Made 1973-78.

PERAZZI MIRAGE TRAP . . . . . . NiB $3934 Ex $3096 Gd $2159
Same general specifications as MX-8 Trap except has tapered rib. Made 1973-78.

PERAZZI MT-6 SKEET . . . . NiB $3934 Ex $3096 Gd $2120
Same as MT-6 Trap except has 28-inch bbls. w/two skeet choke tubes instead of Extra Full and F, skeet-style stock and forearm. Weight: About 8 lbs. Made 1976-78.

PERAZZI MT-6 TRAP COMBO . . . . NiB $4951 Ex $3969 Gd $2714
MT-6 w/extra single under bbl. w/high-rise aluminum vent rib, 32- or 34-inch; seven interchanageable choke tubes (IC through Extra Full). Fitted case. Made 1977-78.

PERAZZI MT-6
TRAP O/U . . . . NiB $3449 Ex $2768 Gd $1896
Boxlock. Auto selective ejectors. Non-selective single trigger. 12 ga. Barrels separated, wide vent rib, 30-or 32-inch, five interchangeable choke tubes (Extra full, F, IM, M, IC). Weight: About 8.5 lbs. Checkered pistol-grip stock/forearm, recoil pad. Fitted case. Made 1976-78.

PERAZZI MX
8 TRAP COMBO . . . . NiB $5435 Ex $4357 Gd $2977
MX-8 w/extra single bbl., vent rib, 32- or 34-inch, F choke, forearm; two trigger groups included. Made 1973-78.

PERAZZI MX-8 TRAP
O/U . . . . NiB $3995 Ex $3204 Gd $2194
Boxlock. Auto selective ejectors. Non-selective single trigger. 12 ga. Bbls.: High vent rib; 30- or 32-inch, IM/F choke. Weight: 8.25 to 8.5 lbs. Checkered Monte Carlo stock and forearm, recoil pad. Made 1969-78.

PERAZZI SINGLE-BARREL
TRAP GUN . . . . NiB $2664 Ex $2138 Gd $1466
Boxlock. Auto ejection. 12 ga. 34-inch vent rib bbl., F choke. Weight: Abaout 8.5 lbs. Checkered pistol-grip stock, forearm; recoil pad. Made 1971-72.

The following Ithaca-SKB shotguns, manufactured by SKB Arms Company, Tokyo, Japan, were distributed in the U.S. by Ithaca Gun Company from 1966-1976. See also listings under SKB.

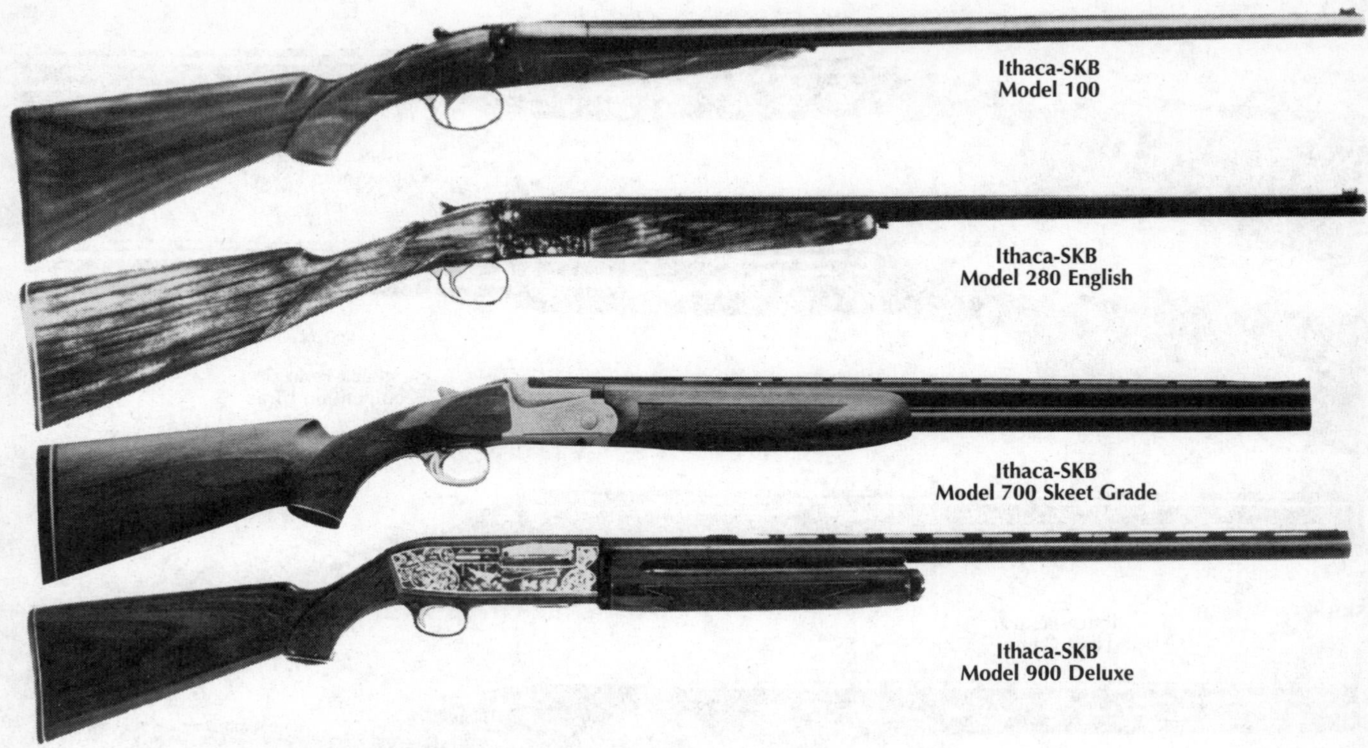
Ithaca-SKB Model 100

Ithaca-SKB Model 280 English

Ithaca-SKB Model 700 Skeet Grade

Ithaca-SKB Model 900 Deluxe

SKB MODEL 100 SIDE-BY-SIDE. . . . NiB $550 Ex $445 Gd $311
Boxlock. Plain extractors. Selective single trigger. Auto safety. Gauges: 12 and 20; 2.75-inch and 3-inch chambers respectively. Bbls.: 30-inch, F/F (12 ga. only); 28-inch, F/M; 26-inch, IC/M (12 ga. only); 25-inch, IC/M (20 ga. only). Weight: 12 ga., about 7 lbs.; 20 ga., about 6 lbs. Checkered stock and forend. Made 1966-76.

SKB MODEL 150 FIELD GRADE . . . NiB $581 Ex $470 Gd $328
Same as Model 100 except has fancier scroll engraving, beavertail forearm. Made 1972-74.

SKB 200E FIELD GRADE S/S . . . . . . NiB $812 Ex $655 Gd $453
Same as Model 100 except auto selective ejectors, engraved and silver-plated frame, gold-plated nameplate and trigger, beavertail forearm. Made 1966-76.

SKB MODEL 200E SKEET GUN . . . . NiB $884 Ex $713 Gd $496
Same as Model 200E Field Grade except 26-inch (12 ga.) and 25-inch (20 ga./2.75-inch chambers) bbls., SK choke; nonautomatic safety and recoil pad. Made 1966-76.

SKB MODEL 280 ENGLISH . . . . . . NiB $1033 Ex $835 Gd $581
Same as Model 200E except has scrolled game scene engraving on frame, English-style straight-grip stock; 30-inch bbls. not available; special quail gun in 20 ga. has 25-inch bbls., both bored IC. Made 1971-76.

SKB MODEL 300 STANDARD AUTOMATIC SHOTGUN
Recoil-operated. Gauges: 12, 20 (3-inch). Five round capacity. Bbls.: plain or vent rib; 30-inch F choke (12 ga. only), 28-inch F or M, 26-inch IC. Weight: about 7 lbs. Checkered pistol-grip stock and forearm. Made 1968-72.
W/plain barrel. . . . . NiB $324 Ex $262 Gd $184
W/ventilated rib . . . . NiB $362 Ex $294 Gd $205

SKB MODEL 500 FIELD GRADE O/U . . . . NiB $572 Ex $462 Gd $321
Boxlock. Auto selective ejectors. Selective single trigger. Non-automatic safety. Gauges: 12 and 20; 2.75-inch and 3-inch chambers respectively. Vent-rib bbls.: 30-inch M/F (12 ga. only); 28-inch M/F; 26-inch IC/M. Weight: 12 ga., about 7.5 lbs; 20 ga., about 6.5 lbs. Checkered stock and forearm. Made 1966-76.

SKB MODEL 500 MAGNUM. . . . . . NiB $668 Ex $538 Gd $373
Same as Model 500 Field Grade except chambered for 3-inch 12 ga. shells, has 30-inch bbls., IM/F choke. Weight: About 8 lbs. Made 1973-76.

SKB MODEL 600 DOUBLES GUN . . . . NiB $782 Ex $630 Gd $436
Same as Model 600 Trap Grade except specially choked for 21-yard first target, 30-yard second. Made 1973-75.

SKB MODEL 600 FIELD GRADE . . . NiB $738 Ex $595 Gd $411
Same as Model 500 except has silver-plated frame, higher grade wood. Made 1969-76.

SKB MODEL 600 MAGNUM. . . . . . NiB $766 Ex $617 Gd $427
Same as Model 600 Field Grade except chambered for 3-inch 12 ga. shells; has 30-inch bbls., IM/F choke. Weight: 8.5 lbs. Made 1969-72.

SKB MODEL 600 SKEET GRADE
Same as Model 500 except also available in 28 and .410 ga., has silver-plated frame, higher grade wood, recoil pad, 26- or 28-inch bbls. (28-inch only in 28 and .410), SK choke. Weight: 7 to 7.75 lbs. depending on ga. and bbl. length. Made 1966-76.
12 or 20 ga. . . . . NiB $898 Ex $754 Gd $571
28 or .410 ga. . . . . NiB $994 Ex $832 Gd $624

SKB MODEL 600 SKEET SET . . . . NiB $2110 Ex $1695 Gd $1164
Model 600 Skeet Grade w/matched set of 20, 28 and .410 ga. bbls., 28-inch, fitted case. Made 1970-76.

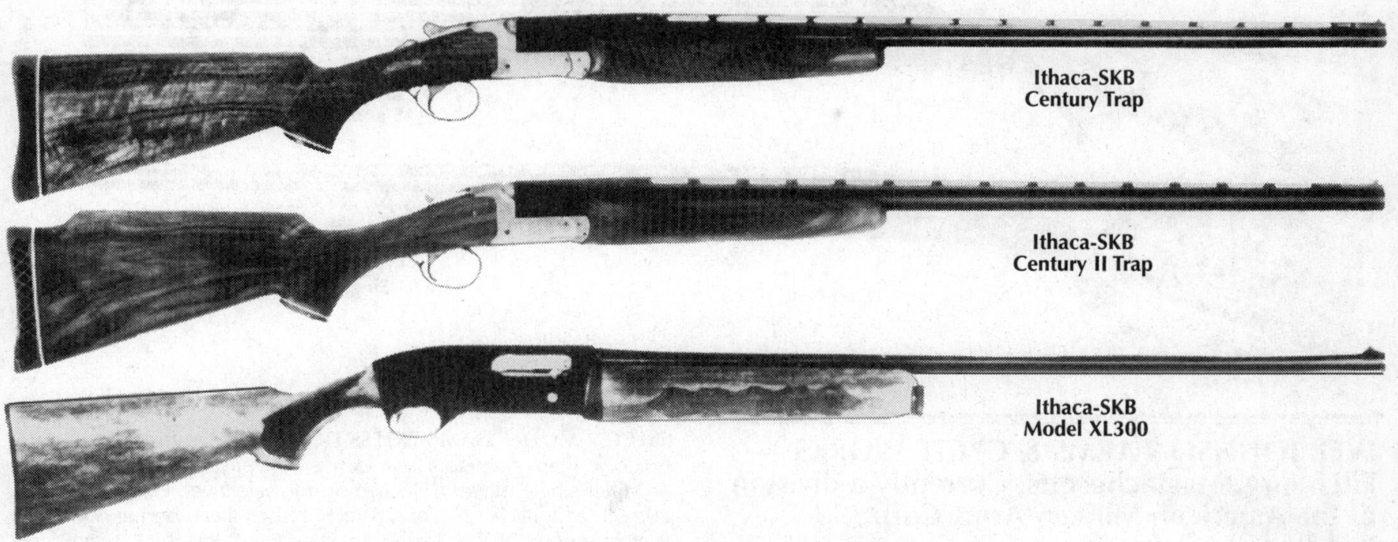

SKB MODEL 600
TRAP GRADE O/U . . . . NiB $717 Ex $577 Gd $399
Same as Model 500 except 12 ga. only, has silver-plated frame, 30- or 32-inch bbls. choked F/F or F/IM, choice of Monte Carlo or straight stock of higher grade wood, recoil pad. Weight: About 8 lbs. Made 1966-76.

SKB MODEL 680 ENGLISH . . . . NiB $754 Ex $608 Gd $419
Same as Model 600 Field Grade except has intricate scroll engraving, English-style straight-grip stock and forearm of extra-fine walnut; 30-inch bbls. not available. Made 1973-76.

SKB MODEL 700
SKEET COMBO SET . . . . NiB $3356 Ex $2696 Gd $1852
Model 700 Skeet Grade w/matched set of 20, 28 and .410 ga. bbls., 28-inch fitted case. Made 1970-71.

SKB MODEL 700 SKEET GRADE . . . NiB $979 Ex $769 Gd $458
Same as Model 600 Skeet Grade except not available in 28 and .410 ga., has more elaborate scroll engraving, extra-wide rib, higher grade wood. Made 1969-75.

SKB MODEL 700 TRAP GRADE. . . . NiB $942 Ex $759 Gd $524
Same as Model 600 Trap Grade except has more elaborate scroll engraving, extra-wide rib, higher grade wood. Made 1969-75.

SKB MODEL 700
DOUBLES GUN . . . . NiB $1083 Ex $847 Gd $600
Same as Model 700 Trap Grade except choked for 21-yard first target, 30-yard second target. Made 1973-75.

SKB MODEL 900
DELUXE AUTOMATIC . . . . NiB $430 Ex $348 Gd $243
Same as Model 30 except has game scene etched and gold-filled on receiver, vent rib standard. Made 1968-72.

SKB MODEL 900 SLUG GUN . . . . . NiB $390 Ex $316 Gd $222
Same as Model 900 Deluxe except has 24-inch plain bbl. w/slug boring, rifle sights. Weight: About 6.5 lbs. Made 1970-72.

SKB CENTURY SINGLE-SHOT
TRAP GUN . . . . NiB $843 Ex $680 Gd $470
Boxlock. Auto ejector. 12 ga. Bbls.: 32- or 34-inch, vent rib, F choke.

***(cont'd)* SKB CENTURY SINGLE-SHOT**
Weight: About 8 lbs. Checkered walnut stock w/pistol grip, straight or Monte Carlo comb, recoil pad, beavertail forearm. Made 1973-74.

SKB CENTURY II . . . . NiB $773 Ex $623 Gd $432
Boxlock. Auto ejector. 12 ga. Bbls: 32- or 34-inch, vent rib, F choke. Weight: 8.25 lbs. Improved version of Century. Same general specifications except has higher comb on checkered stock stock, reverse-taper beavertail forearm w/redesigned locking iron. Made 1975-76.

SKB MODEL XL300 STANDARD AUTOMATIC
Gas-operated. Gauges: 12, 20 (3-inch). Five round capacity. Bbls.: Plain or vent rib; 30-inch F choke (12 ga. only), 28-inch F or M, 26-inch IC. Weight: 6 to 7.5 lbs. depending on ga. and bbl. Checkered pistol-grip stock, forearm. Made 1972-76.
W/plain barrel . . . . NiB $298 Ex $242 Gd $169
W/ventilated rib . . . . NiB $324 Ex $262 Gd $184

SKB MODEL XL900
DELUXE AUTOMATIC . . . . NiB $376 Ex $304 Gd $212
Same as Model XL300 except has game scene finished in silver on receiver, vent rib standard. Made 1972-76. See illustration previous page.

SKB MODEL XL
900 SKEET GRADE . . . . NiB $456 Ex $368 Gd $257
Gas-operated. Gauges: 12, 20 (3-inch). Five round tubular magazine. Same as Model XL900 Deluxe except has scrolled receiver finished in black chrome, 26-inch bbl. only, SK choke, skeet-style stock. Weight: 7 or 7.5 lbs. depending on ga. Made 1972-76.

SKB MODEL XL
900 SLUG GUN . . . . NiB $404 Ex $327 Gd $229
Same as Model XL900 Deluxe except has 24-inch plain bbl. w/slug boring, rifle sights. Weight: 6.5 or 7 lbs. depending on ga. Made 1972-76.

SKB MODEL
XL900 TRAP GRADE . . . . NiB $445 Ex $360 Gd $252
Same as Model XL900 Deluxe except 12 ga. only, has scrolled receiver finished in black chrome, 30-inch bbl. only, IM or F choke, trap style w/straight or Monte Carlo comb, recoil pad. Weight: About 7.75 lbs. Made 1972-76.

SHOTGUNS

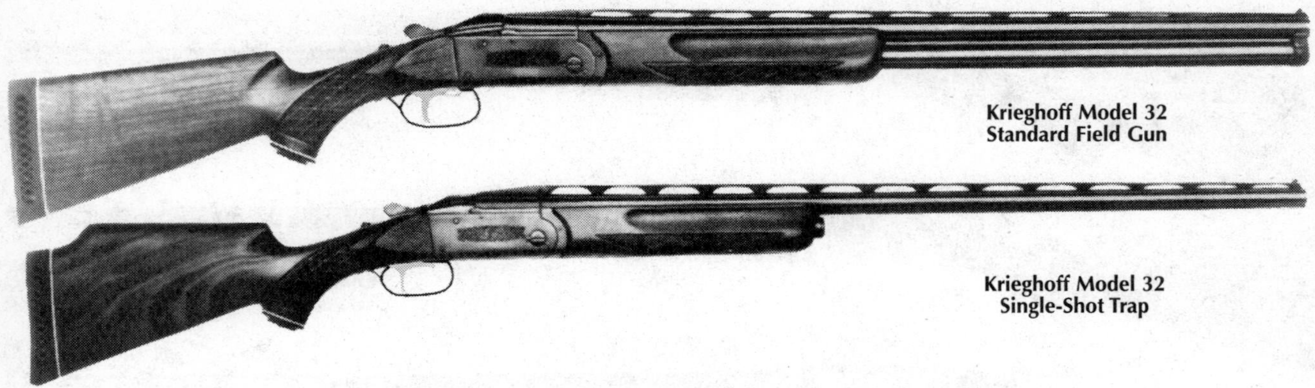

Krieghoff Model 32
Standard Field Gun

Krieghoff Model 32
Single-Shot Trap

IVER JOHNSON ARMS & CYCLE WORKS — Fitchburg, Massachusetts. Currently a division of the American Military Arms Corp., Jacksonville, Arkansas

CHAMPION GRADE SINGLE-SHOT HAMMER SHOTGUN

Auto ejector. Gauges: 12,16, 20, 28 and .410. Bbls.: 26- to 36-inch, F choke. Weight: 5.75 to 7.5 lbs. depending on ga. and bbl.length. Plain pistol-grip stock and forend. Extras include checkered stock and forend, pistol-grip cap and knob forend. Known as Model 36. Also made in a Semi-Octagon Breech, Top Matted and Jacketed Breech (extra heavy) models. Made in Champion Lightweight as Model 39 in gauges 24, 28, 32 and .410, .44 and .45 caliber, 12 and 14mm w/same extras. $200; add $100 in the smaller and obsolete gauges. Made 1909-73.

Standard model . . . . NiB $195 Ex $158 Gd $110
Semi-octagon breech. . . . . NiB $312 Ex $252 Gd $174
Top matted rib (disc. 1948) . . . . . . NiB $294 Ex $237 Gd $164

HERCULES GRADE HAMMERLESS DOUBLE

Boxlock. (Some made w/false sideplates.) Plain extractors and auto ejectors. Double or Miller single triggers (both selective or non-selective). Gauges: 12, 16, 20 and .410. Bbl. lengths: 26- to 32-inch, all chokes. Weight: 5.75 to 7.75 lbs. depending on ga. and bbl. length. Checkered stock and forend. Straight grip in .410 ga. w/both 2.5- and 3-inch chambers. Extras include Miller single trigger, Jostam Anti-Flinch recoil pad and Lyman ivory sights at extra cost. Disc. 1946.

W/double triggers, extractors . . . . NiB $747 Ex $606 Gd $425
W/double triggers, auto. ejectors . . . . . NiB $891 Ex $720 Gd $503
W/non-selective single trigger, add $100
W/selective single trigger, add. $135
.410 ga., add $185

MATTED RIB SINGLE-SHOT HAMMER SHOTGUN IN SMALLER GAUGES. . . . . NiB $378 Ex $306 Gd $214

Same general specifications as Champion Grade except has solid matted top rib, checkered stock and forend. Weight: 6 to 6.75 lbs. Disc. 1948.

SILVER SHADOW O/U SHOTGUN

Boxlock. Plain extractors. Double triggers or non-selective single trigger. 12 ga., 3-inch chambers. Bbls.: 26-inch IC/M; 28-inch IC/M, 28-inch M/F; 30-inch both F choke; vent rib. Weight: w/28-inch bbls., 7.5 lbs. Checkered pistol-grip stock/forearm. Made by F. Marocchi, Brescia, Italy 1973-78.

Model 412 w/double triggers . . . . NiB $508 Ex $410 Gd $285
Model 422 w/single trigger . . . . . NiB $632 Ex $509 Gd $353

SKEETER MODEL HAMMERLESS DOUBLE

Boxlock. Plain extractors or selective auto ejectors. Double triggers or Miller single trigger (selective or non-selective). Gauges: 12, 16, 20, 28 and .410. 26- or 28-inch bbls., skeet boring standard. Weight: About 7.5 lbs.; less in smaller gauges. Pistol- or straight-grip stock and beavertail forend, both checkered, of select fancy-figured black walnut. Extras include Miller single trigger, selective or non-selective, Jostam Anti-Flinch recoil pad and Lyman ivory rear sight at additional cost. Disc. 1942.

W/double triggers, plain extractors . . . . NiB $1441 Ex $1162 Gd $804
W/double triggers, automatic ejectors . . . . NiB $1753 Ex $1412 Gd $975
W/non-selective single trigger, add $150
W/selective single trigger, add $200
20 ga., add 25%
28 ga., add 75%
.410 ga., add 90%

SPECIAL TRAP SINGLE-SHOT HAMMER SHOTGUN . . . . NiB $417 Ex $336 Gd $234

Auto ejector. 12 ga. only. 32-inch bbl. w/vent rib, F choke. Checkered pistol-grip stock and forend. Weight: about 7.5 lbs. Disc. 1942.

SUPER TRAP HAMMERLESS DOUBLE

Boxlock. Plain extractors. Double trigger or Miller single trigger (selective or non-selective), 12 ga. only, F choke 32-inch bbl., vent rib. Weight: 8.5 lbs. Checkered pistol-grip stock and beavertail forend, recoil pad, Disc. 1942.

W/double triggers . . . . NiB $1174 Ex $810 Gd $446
W/non-selective single trigger, add $100
W/selective single trigger, add. $100

KBI INC. SHOTGUNS

See listings under Armscor, Baikal, Charles Daly, Fias, & Omega

KESSLER ARMS CORP. — Silver Creek, New York

LEVER-MATIC REPEATING SHOTGUN

. . . . . NiB $191 Ex $154 Gd $108

Lever action. Takedown. Gauges: 12, 16, 20; three-round magazine. Bbls.: 26-, 28-, 30-inch; F choke. Plain pistol-grip stock, recoil pad. Weight: 7 to 7.75 lbs. Disc. 1953.

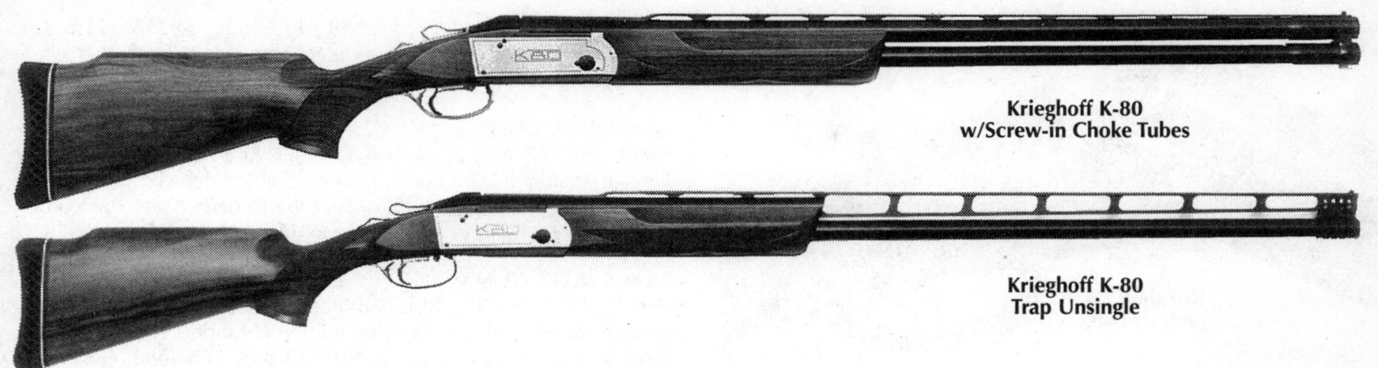

Krieghoff K-80
w/Screw-in Choke Tubes

Krieghoff K-80
Trap Unsingle

THREE SHOT BOLT-ACTION REPEATER . . NiB $106 Ex $86 Gd $62
Takedown. Gauges: 12, 16, 20. Two-round detachable box magazine. Bbls.: 28-inch in 12 and 16 ga.; 26-inch in 20 ga.; F choke. Weight: 6.25 to 7.25 lbs. depending on ga. and bbl. length. Plain one-piece pistol-grip stock recoil pad. Made 1951-53.

H. KRIEGHOFF JAGD UND SPORTWAFFEN-FABRIK — Ulm (Donau), West Germany

MODEL 32 FOUR-BARREL SKEET SET
Over/under w/four sets of matched bbls.: 12, 20, 28 and .410 ga., in fitted case. Available in six grades that differ in quality of engraving and wood. Disc. 1979.
Standard grade . . . . NiB $11,524 Ex $9218 Gd $6269
München grade . . . . NiB $12,811 Ex $10,249 Gd $6969
San Remo grade. . . . . NiB $15,772 Ex $12,617 Gd $8580
Monte Carlo grade . . . . . . NiB $20,536 Ex $16,428 Gd $11,171
Crown grade. . . . . NiB $25,428 Ex $20,342 Gd $13,833
Super Crown grade. . . . . . NiB $27,681 Ex $22,145 Gd $15,059
Exhibition grade . . . . NiB $38,561 Ex $30,849 Gd $20,977

MODEL 32 STANDARD GRADE O/U
Similar to prewar Remington Model 23. Boxlock. Auto ejector. Single trigger. Gauges: 12, 20, 28, .410. Bbls.: Vent rib, 26.5- to 32-inch, any chokes. Weight: 12 ga. Field gun w/28-inch bbls., about 7.5 lbs. Checkered pistol-grip stock and forearm of select walnut; available in field, skeet and trap styles. Made 1958-1981.
W/one set of bbls. . . . . NiB $3683 Ex $2961 Gd $2037
Low-rib two-bbl. trap combo . . NiB $4716 Ex $3788 Gd $2599
Vandalia (high-rib) two- bbl. trap combo . . NiB $4961 Ex $3984 Gd $2733

MODEL 32 STANDARD GRADE SINGLE-SHOT TRAP GUN . . . . . NiB $1818 Ex $1459 Gd $999
Same action as over/under. 12 ga. 32- or 34-inch bbl. w/high vent rib on bbl.; M, IM, or F choke. Checkered Monte Carlo buttstock w/thick cushioned recoil pad, beavertail forearm. Disc. 1979.

MODEL K-80
Refined and enhanced version of the Mdl. 32. Single selective mech. trig., adj. for position; release trigger optional. Fixed chokes or screw-in choke tubes. Interchangeable front bbl. Hangers to adjust point of impact. Quick-removable stock. Color casehardened or satin grey fin. rec.; alum. alloy rec. on lightweight models. Avail. in stand. plus 5 engraved grades. Made 1980 to date. Standard grade shown except where noted.

SKEET MODELS
Skeet International . . . . NiB $6114 Ex $4903 Gd $3353
Skeet Special . . . . NiB $5225 Ex $4319 Gd $2956

(*cont'd.*) MODEL K-80
Skeet standard model . . . . NiB $5146 Ex $4128 Gd $2827
Skeet w/choke tubes . . . . .NiB $6176 Ex $4952 Gd $3387
SKEET SETS
Standard grade 2-bbl. set. . . . . . NiB $9698 Ex $7758 Gd $5276
Standard grade 4-bbl. set. . . NiB $13,279 Ex $10,623 Gd $7224
Bavaria grade 4-bbl. set . . NiB $18,926 Ex $15,141 Gd $10,296
Danube grade 4-bbl. set. . . . NiB $24,643 Ex $19,714 Gd $13,405
Gold Target grade 4-bbl. set. . . . NiB $28,969 Ex $23,175 Gd $15,759
SPORTING MODELS
Pigeon . . . . NiB $6709 Ex $5379 Gd $3677
Sporting Clays . . . . NiB $6752 Ex $5413 Gd $3700
TRAP MODELS
Trap Combo. . . . . NiB $9106 Ex $7305 Gd $5000
Trap Single. . . . . NiB $6434 Ex $5158 Gd $3527
Trap Standard . . . . NiB $5976 Ex $4793 Gd $3279
Trap Unsingle . . . . NiB $6684 Ex $5359 Gd $3664
RT models (removable trigger) add $1385

KRIEGHOFF MODEL KS-5 SINGLE-BARREL TRAP
Boxlock w/no sliding top-latch. Adjustable or optional release trigger. Gauge: 12; 2.75-inch chamber. Bbl.: 32-, 34-inch w/fixed choke or screw-in tubes. Weight: 8.5 lbs. Adjustable or Monte Carlo European walnut stock. Blued or nickel receiver. Made from 1980 to date. Redesigned and streamlined in 1993.
Standard model w/fixed chokes . . . NiB $3332 Ex $2674 Gd $1834
Standard model w/tubes . . . . . . NiB $3904 Ex $3132 Gd $2146
Special model w/adj. rib & stock . . . . NiB $4162 Ex $3339 Gd $2286
Special model w/adj. rib & stock, choke tubes . . . . NiB $4755 Ex $3814 Gd $2611

TRUMPF DRILLING . . . . NiB $9342 Ex $7901 Gd $6057
Boxlock. Steel or Dural receiver. Split extractor or ejector for shotgun bbls. Double triggers. Gauges: 12, 16, 20; latter w/either 2.75- or 3-inch chambers. Calibers: .243, 6.5x57r5, 7x57r5, 7x65r5, .30-06; other calibers available. 25-inch bbls. w/solid rib, folding leaf rear sight, post or bead front sight; rifle bbl. soldered or free floating. Weight: 6.6 to 7.5 lbs. depending on type of receiver, ga. and caliber. Checkered pistol-grip stock w/cheekpiece and forearm of figured walnut, sling swivels. Made 1953 to date.

NEPTUN DRILLING . . . . NiB $12,296 Ex $9836 Gd $6689
Same general specifications as Trumpf model except has sidelocks w/hunting scene engraving. Currently manufactured.

NEPTUN-PRIMUS DRILLING . . . . NiB $14,099 Ex $11,278 Gd $7669
Deluxe version of Neptun model; has detachable sidelocks, higher grade engraving and fancier wood. Currently manufactured.

SHOTGUNS

Krieghoff Neptun Drilling

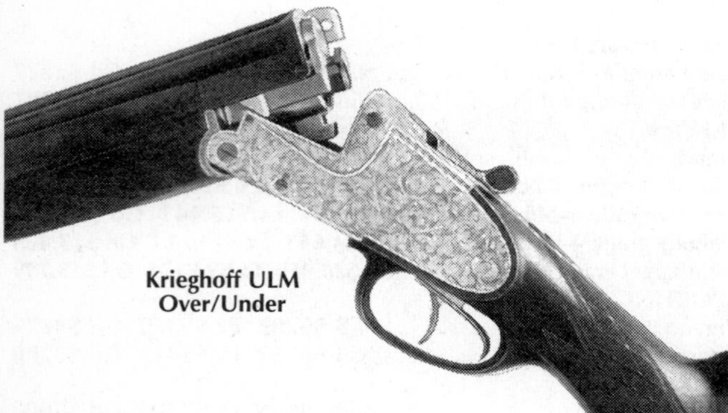
Krieghoff ULM Over/Under

TECK O/U RIFLE-SHOTGUN . . . . NiB $7014 Ex $5635 Gd $3872
Boxlock. Kersten dble. crossbolt system. Steel or Dural receiver. Split extractor or eject. for shotgun bbl. Single or double triggers. Gauges: 12, 16, 20; latter w/either 2.75- or 3-inch chamber. Cal: .22 Hornet, .222 Rem., .222 Rem. Mag., 7x57r5, 7x64, 7x65r5, .30-30, .300 Win. Mag., .30-06, .308, 9.3x74R. 25-inch bbls. With solid rib, folding leaf rear sight, post or bead front sight; over bbl. is shotgun, under bbl. rifle (later fixed or interchangeable; ext. rifle bbl., $175). Wt: 7.9-9.5 lbs. depending on type of rec. and caliber. Checkered pistol-grip stock w/cheekpiece and semi-beavertail forearm of fig. walnut, sling swivels. Made 1967 to date. Note: This comb. gun is similar in appearance to the same model shotgun.

TECK O/U SHOTGUN . . . . NiB $6569 Ex $5280 Gd $3630
Boxlock. Kersten double crossbolt system. Auto ejector. Single or double triggers. Gauges: 12, 16, 20; latter w/either 2.75- or 3-inch chambers. 28-inch vent-rib bbl., M/F choke. Weight: About 7 lbs. Checkered walnut pistol-grip stock and forearm. Made 1967-89.

ULM O/U RIFLE-SHOTGUN . . . . NiB $16,416 Ex $14,162 Gd $11,279
Same general specifications as Teck model except has sidelocks w/leaf Arabesque engraving. Made from 1963 to date. Note: This combination gun is similar in appearance to the same model shotgun.

ULM O/U SHOTGUN . . . . . NiB $12,225 Ex $10,192 Gd $7590
Same general specifications as Teck model except has sidelocks w/leaf Arabesque engraving. Made 1958 to date.

ULM-P LIVE PIGEON GUN
Sidelock. Gauge: 12. 28- and 30-inch bbls. Chokes: F/IM. Weight: 8 lbs. Oil-finished, fancy English walnut stock w/semi-beavertail forearm. Light scrollwork engraving. Tapered, vent rib. Made from 1983 to date.
Bavaria . . . . NiB $18,154 Ex $14,935 Gd $10,815
Standard . . . . NiB $14,099 Ex $11,690 Gd $8609

ULM-PRIMUS O/U. . . . . NiB $11,619 Ex $9296 Gd $6321
Deluxe version of Ulm model; detachable sidelocks, higher grade engraving and fancier wood. Made 1958 to date.

ULM-PRIMUS O/U RIFLE-SHOTGUN . . . . NiB $18,663 Ex $16,269 Gd $13,206
Deluxe version of Ulm model; has detachable sidelocks, higher grade engraving and fancier wood. Made 1963 to date. Note: This combination gun is similar in appearance to the same model shotgun.

ULM-S SKEET GUN
Sidelock. Gauge: 12. Bbl.: 28-inch. Chokes: Skeet/skeet. Other specifications similar to the Model ULM-P. Made 1983-86.
Bavaria . . . . NiB $11,839 Ex $9883 Gd $7380
Standard . . . . NiB $9779 Ex $8235 Gd $6259

ULM-P O/U LIVE TRAP GUN
Over/under sidelock. Gauge: 12. 30-inch bbl. Tapered vent rib. Chokes: IM/F; optional screw-in choke. Custom grade versions command a higher price. Disc. 1986.
Bavaria . . . . NiB $17,832 Ex $14,678 Gd $10,640
Standard . . . . NiB $14,099 Ex $11,690 Gd $8609

ULTRA O/U RIFLE-SHOTGUN
Deluxe Over/Under combination w/25-inch vent-rib bbls. Chambered 12 ga. only and various rifle calibers for lower bbl. Kickspanner design permits cocking w/thumb safety. Satin receiver. Weight: 6 lbs. Made from 1985 to date.
Ultra O/U combination. . . . . . . NiB $4966 Ex $4298 Gd $3443
Ultra B w/selective front trigger . . . NiB $5224 Ex $4504 Gd $3582

LANBER SHOTGUNS — Spain

MODEL 82 O/U SHOTGUN. . . . . . NiB $555 Ex $452 Gd $320
Boxlock. Gauge: 12 or 20; 3-inch chambers. 26- or 28-inch vent-rib bbls. w/ejectors and fixed chokes. Weight: 7 lbs., 2 oz. Double or single-selective trigger. Engraved silvered receiver. Checkered European walnut stock and forearm. Imported 1994.

MODEL 87 DELUXE . . . . NiB $844 Ex $684 Gd $478
Over/Under; boxlock. Single selective trigger. 12 or 20 gauge w/3-inch chambers. Barrels: 26- or 28-inch w/choke tubes. Silvered engraved receiver.Imported 1994 only.

MODEL 97 SPORTING CLAYS . . . . NiB $877 Ex $709 Gd $495
Over/Under; boxlock. Single selective trigger. 12 ga. w/2.75-inch chambers. Bbls: 28-inch w/choke tubes. European walnut stock, forend. Engraved receiver. Imported 1994 only.

MODEL 844 MST MAGNUM O/U . . . . NiB $472 Ex $385 Gd $275
Field grade. Gauge: 12. 3-inch Mag. chambers. 30-inch flat vent-rib bbls. Chokes: M/F. Weight: 7 lbs., 7 oz. Single selective trigger. Blued bbls. and engraved receiver. European walnut stock w/hand-checkered pistol grip and forend. Imported 1984-86.

MODEL 2004 LCH O/U . . . . NiB $652 Ex $529 Gd $373
Field grade. Gauge: 12. 2.75-inch chambers. 28-inch flat vent-rib bbls. 5 interchangeable choke tubes: Cyl, IC, M, IM, F. Weight: About 7 lbs. Single selective trigger. Engraved silver receiver w/fine-line scroll. Walnut stock w/checkered pistol-grip and forend. Rubber recoil pad. Imported 1984-86.

MODEL 2004 LCH O/U SKEET . . . . NiB $806 Ex $653 Gd $457
Same as Model 2004 LCH except 28-inch bbls. w/5 interchangeable choke tubes. Imported 1984-86.

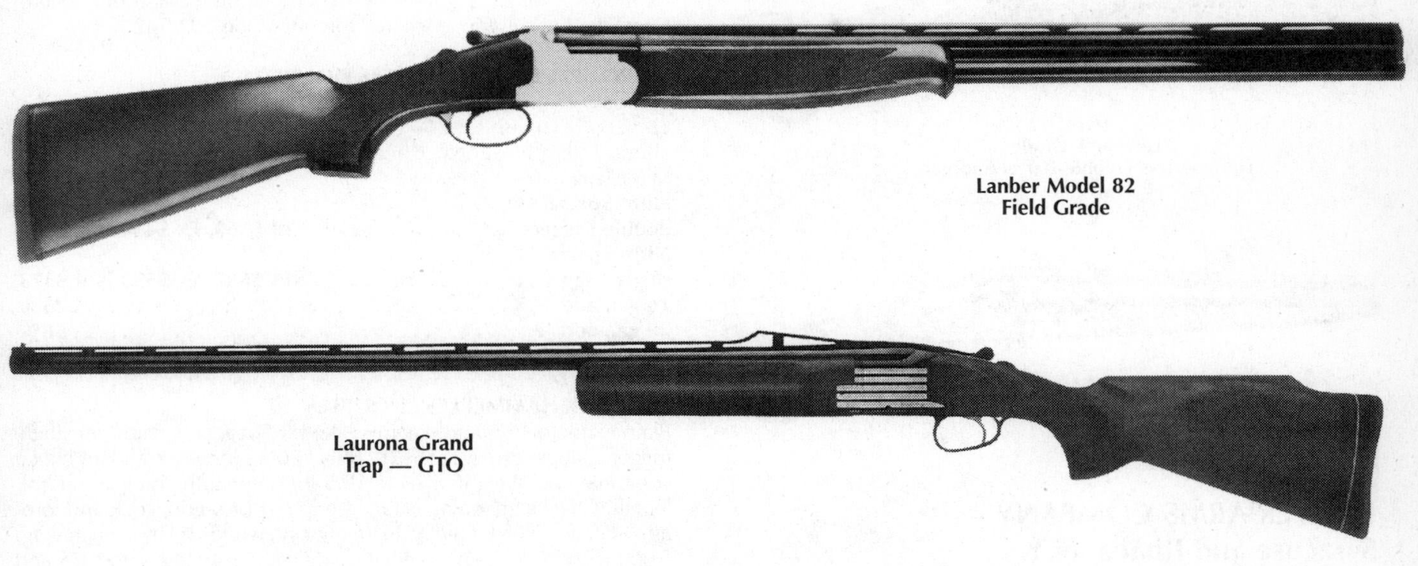

MODEL 2004
LCH O/U TRAP . . . . NiB $773 Ex $622 Gd $430
Gauge: 12. 30-inch vent-rib bbls. Three interchangeable choke tubes: M, IM, F. Manual safety. Other specifications same as Model 2004 LCH O/U. Imported 1984-86.

CHARLES LANCASTER — London, England

"TWELVE-TWENTY" DOUBLE-BARREL
SHOTGUN . . . . NiB $15,313 Ex $12,250 Gd $8330
Sidelock, self-opener. Gauge: 12. Bbls.: 24 to 30 inches standard. Weight: About 5.75 lbs. Elaborate metal engraving. Highest quality English or French walnut buttstock and forearm. Imported by Stoeger in the 1950s.

JOSEPH LANG & SONS — London, England

HIGHEST QUALITY
O/U SHOTGUN. . . . . NiB $27,000 Ex $21,600 Gd $14,688
Sidelock. Gauges: 12, 16, 20, 28 and .410. Bbls.: 25 to 30 inches standard. Highest grade English or French walnut buttstock and forearm. Selective single trigger. Imported by Stoeger in 1950s.

LAURONA SHOTGUNS — Eibar, Spain

GRAND TRAP COMBO
Same general specifications as Model 300 except supplied w/29-inch over/under bbls., screw-in choke tubes and 34-inch single barrel. Disc. 1992.
Model GTO (top single). . . . . . . NiB $2331 Ex $1872 Gd $1286
Model GTU (bottom single) . . . NiB $2467 Ex $1981 Gd $1360
Extra Field O/U bbls.
(12 or 20 ga.), ... NiB $885 Ex $716 Gd $499

SILHOUETTE 300 O/U
Boxlock. Single selective trigger. Selective automatic ejectors. Gauge: 12; 2.75-, 3- or 3.5-inch chambers. 28- or 29-inch vent-rib bbls. w/flush or knurled choke tubes. Weight: 7.75 to 8 lbs. Checkered pistol-grip European walnut stock and beavertail forend. Engraved receiver w/silvered finish and black chrome bbls. Made 1988-92.
Model 300 Sporting Clays . . . . . NiB $1347 Ex $1064 Gd $730
Model 300 Trap . . . . NiB $1347 Ex $1064 Gd $730
Model 300 Trap, single . . . . NiB $1347 Ex $1064 Gd $730
Model 300 Ultra-Magnum. . . . . NiB $1399 Ex $1116 Gd $730

SUPER MODEL O/U SHOTGUNS
Boxlock. Single selective or twin single triggers. Selective automatic ejectors. Gauges: 12 or 20; 2.75- or 3-inch chambers. 26-, 28- or 29-inch vent-rib bbls. w/fixed chokes or screw-in choke tubes. Weight: 7 to 7.25 lbs. Checkered pistol-grip European walnut stock. Engraved receiver w/silvered finish and black chrome bbls. Made from 1985 to date.
Model 82 Super Game (disc.) . . . . . NiB $706 Ex $572 Gd $400
Model 83 MG Super Game . . . . . . NiB $1111 Ex $906 Gd $643
Model 84 S Super Trap . . . . NiB $1430 Ex $1161 Gd $816
Model 85 MG Super Game . . . . . . NiB $1125 Ex $917 Gd $651
Model 85 MG 2-bbl. set . . . . . . NiB $1997 Ex $1586 Gd $1115
Model 85 MS Special Sporting (disc.). . . NiB $1395 Ex $1133 Gd $797
Model 85 MS Super Trap . . . . . . NiB $1366 Ex $1139 Gd $804
Model 85 MS Pigeon . . . . NiB $1437 Ex $1139 Gd $782
Model 85 S Super Skeet. . . . . . . NiB $1437 Ex $1166 Gd $819

LEBEAU-COURALLY SHOTGUNS — Belgium

BOXLOCK SIDE
BY-SIDE SHOTGUNS. . . . . NiB $17,438 Ex $13,950 Gd $9486
Gauges: 12, 16, 20 and 28. 26- to 30-inch bbls. Weight: 6.5 lbs. average. Checkered, hand-rubbed, oil-finished, straight-grip stock of French walnut. Classic forend. Made from 1986 to date.

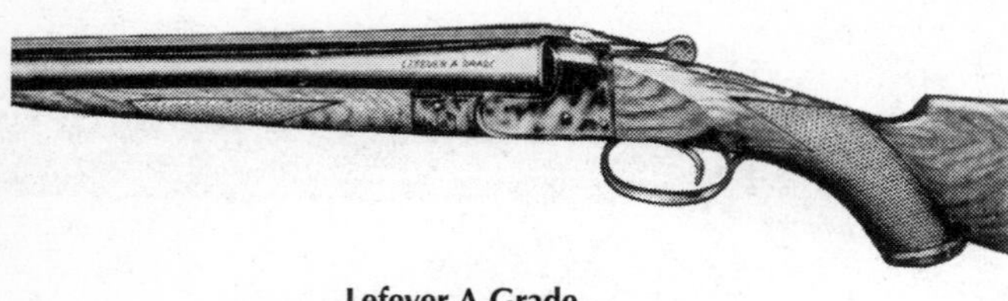

Lefever A Grade
Hammerless Double-Barrel Shotgun

LEFEVER ARMS COMPANY — Syracuse and Ithaca, N.Y.

Lefever sidelock hammerless double-barrel shotguns were made by Lefever Arms Company of Syracuse, New York from about 1885-1915 (serial numbers 1 to 70,000) when the firm was sold to Ithaca Gun Company of Ithaca, New York. Production of these models was continued at the Ithaca plant until 1919 (serial numbers 70,001 to 72,000). Grades listed are those that appear in the last catalog of the Lefever Gun Company, Syracuse. In 1921, Ithaca introduced the boxlock Lefever Nitro Special double, followed in 1934 by the Lefever Grade A; there also were two single-barrel Lefevers made from 1927-42. Manufacture of Lefever brand shotguns was disc. in 1948. Note: "New Lefever" boxlock shotguns made circa 1904-06 by D. M. Lefever Company, Bowling Green, Ohio, are included in a separate listing.

GRADE HAMMERLESS DOUBLE-BARREL SHOTGUN

Boxlock. Plain extractors or auto ejector. Single or double triggers. Gauges: 12, 16, 20, .410. Bbls.: 26-32 inches, standard chokes. Weight: About 7 lbs. in 12 ga. Checkered pistol-grip stock and forearm. Made 1934-42.

W/plain extractors, double triggers. NiB $1040 Ex $838 Gd $580
W/automatic ejector, add $250
W/single trigger, add $100
W/Beavertail Forearm, add $75
16 ga., add 25%
20 ga., add 45%
.410 ga., add 200%

GRADE SKEET MODEL

Same as A Grade except standard features include auto ejector, single trigger, beavertail forearm; 26-inch bbls., skeet boring. Disc. 1942.

A grade skeet model, 12 ga. . . . . NiB $1244 Ex $999 Gd $690
16 ga., add 45%
20 ga., add 90%
.410 ga., add 200%

HAMMERLESS SINGLE-SHOT TRAP GUN . . . . NiB $608 Ex $490 Gd $339

Boxlock. Ejector. 12 ga. only. 30- or 32-inch bbl.; vent rib. Weight: About 8 lbs. Checkered pistol-grip stock and forend, recoil pad. Made 1927-42.

LONG RANGE HAMMERLESS SINGLE-BARREL FIELD GUN . . . . . NiB $378 Ex $306 Gd $214

Boxlock. Plain extractor. Gauges: 12, 16, 20, .410. Bbl. lengths: 26-32 inches. Weight: 5.5 to 7 lbs. depending on ga. and bbl. length. Checkered pistol-grip stock and forend. Made 1927-42.

NITRO SPECIAL HAMMERLESS DOUBLE

Boxlock. Plain extractors. Single or double triggers. Gauges: 12, 16, 20, .410. Bbls.: 26- to 32-inch, standard chokes. Weight: about 7 lbs. in 12 ga. Checkered pistol-grip stock and forend. Made 1921-48.

Nitro Special W/ double triggers . . . . NiB $563 Ex $434 Gd $269
Nitro Special W/ single trigger . . . . NiB $667 Ex $538 Gd $373
16 ga., add 25%
20 ga., add 50%
.410 ga., add 200%

SIDELOCK HAMMERLESS DOUBLES

Plain extractors or auto ejectors. Double triggers or selective single trigger. Gauges: 10, 12, 16, 20. Bbls.: 26-32 inches; standard choke combinations. Weight: 5.75 to 10.5 lbs. depending on ga. and bbl. length. Checkered walnut straight-grip or pistol-grip stock and forearm. Grades differ chiefly in quality of workmanship, engraving, wood, checkering, etc.; general specifications are the same. DS and DSE Grade guns lack the cocking indicators found on all other models. Suffix "E" means model has auto ejector; also standard on A, AA, Optimus, and Thousand Dollar Grade guns.

H grade . . . . NiB $1930 Ex $1552 Gd $1069
HE grade . . . . NiB $2546 Ex $2046 Gd $1405
G grade . . . . NiB $2248 Ex $1807 Gd $1243
GE grade . . . . NiB $3004 Ex $2412 Gd $1655
F grade. . . . . NiB $2010 Ex $1616 Gd $1111
FE grade. . . . . NiB $3058 Ex $2455 Gd $1683
E grade. . . . . NiB $2911 Ex $2338 Gd $1604
EE grade. . . . . NiB $4464 Ex $3581 Gd $2451
D grade . . . . NiB $3592 Ex $2884 Gd $1977
DE grade . . . . NiB $5576 Ex $4470 Gd $3056
DS grade . . . . NiB $1565 Ex $1258 Gd $865
DSE grade . . . . NiB $1934 Ex $1553 Gd $1066
C grade . . . . NiB $4926 Ex $3954 Gd $2711
CE grade . . . . NiB $9184 Ex $7365 Gd $5037
B grade . . . . NiB $5914 Ex $4745 Gd $3249
BE grade . . . . NiB $10,559 Ex $8447 Gd $5744
A grade. . . . . NiB $18,339 Ex $16,054 Gd $14,829
AA grade. . . . . NiB $27,170 Ex $21,736 Gd $14,780
Optimus grade . . . . NiB $37,050 Ex $29,640 Gd $20,155
Thousand Dollar grade . . . NiB $55,250 Ex $44,200 Gd $30,056
W/single trigger, add 10%
10 ga., add 15%
16 ga., add 45%
20 ga., add 90%

D. M. LEFEVER COMPANY — Bowling Green, Ohio

In 1901, D. M. "Uncle Dan" Lefever, founder of the Lefever Arms Company, withdrew from that firm to organize D. M. Lefever, Sons & Company (later D. M. Lefever Company) to manufacture the "New Lefever" boxlock double- and single-barrel shotguns. These were produced at Bowling Green, Ohio, from about 1904-1906, when Dan Lefever died and the factory closed permanently. Grades listed are those that appear in the last catalog of D. M. Lefever Co.

HAMMERLESS DOUBLE-BARREL SHOTGUNS

"New Lefever." Boxlock. Auto ejector standard on all grades except O Excelsior, which was regularly supplied w/plain extractors (auto ejector offered as an extra). Double triggers or selective single trigger (latter standard on Uncle Dan Grade, extra on all others). Gauges: 12, 16, 20. Bbls.: Any length and choke combination. Weight: 5.5 to 8 lbs. depending on ga. and bbl. length. Checkered walnut straight-grip or pistol-grip stock and forearm. Grades differ chiefly in quality of workmanship, engraving, wood, checkering, etc. General specifications are the same.

O Excelsior grade
w/plain extractors . . . . NiB $3395 Ex $2731 Gd $1882
O Excelsior grade
w/automatic ejectors. . . . . NiB $3843 Ex $3090 Gd $2127
No. 9, F grade . . . . NiB $4753 Ex $3818 Gd $2622
No. 8, E grade . . . . NiB $5608 Ex $4502 Gd $3088
No. 7, D grade. . . . . NiB $5630 Ex $4840 Gd $3317
No. 6, C grade. . . . . NiB $6836 Ex $5485 Gd $3756
No. 5, B grade . . . . NiB $9049 Ex $7256 Gd $4962
No. 4, AA grade. . . . . NiB $13,000 Ex $10,400 Gd $7072
Uncle Dan grade . . . . NiB $19,500 Ex $15,600 Gd $10,608
W/single trigger, add 10%
16 ga., add 45%
20 ga., add 15%

D. M. LEFEVER SINGLE-BARREL
TRAP GUN. . . . . NiB $6564 Ex $5265 Gd $3603
Boxlock. Auto ejector. 12 ga. only. Bbls.: 26- to 32 inches, F choke. Weight: 6.5 to 8 lbs. depending on bbl. length. Checkered walnut pistol-grip stock and forearm.

MAGTECH SHOTGUNS — San Antonio, Texas Mfd. By CBC in Brazil

MODEL 586.2 SLIDE-ACTION SHOTGUN

Gauge: 12; 3-inch chamber. 19-, 26- or 28-inch bbl.; fixed chokes or integral tubes. 46.5 inches overall. Weight: 8.5 lbs. Double-action slide bars. Brazilian hardwood stock. Polished blued finish. Imported 1992 to date.

Model 586.2 F
(28-inch bbl., fixed choke) . . . . NiB $237 Ex $192 Gd $135
Model 586.2 P
(19-inch plain bbl., cyl. bore) . . . . . NiB $237 Ex $192 Gd $135
Model 586.2 S
(24-inch bbl., rifle sights, cyl. bore) . . . NiB $243 Ex $198 Gd $139
Model 586.2 VR
(vent rib w/tubes) . . . . NiB $237 Ex $192 Gd $135

MARLIN FIREARMS CO. — North Haven (formerly New Haven), Conn.

MODEL 16 VISIBLE HAMMER SLIDE-ACTION REPEATER

Takedown. 16 ga. Five round tubular magazine. Bbls.: 26- or 28-inch, standard chokes. Weight: About 6.25 lbs. Pistol-grip stock, grooved slide handle; checkering on higher grades. Difference among grades is in quality of wood, engraving on Grades C and D. Made 1904-10.

Grade A . . . . NiB $434 Ex $351 Gd $245
Grade B . . . . NiB $594 Ex $479 Gd $332
Grade C . . . . NiB $727 Ex $586 Gd $406
Grade D. . . . . NiB $1474 Ex $1187 Gd $820

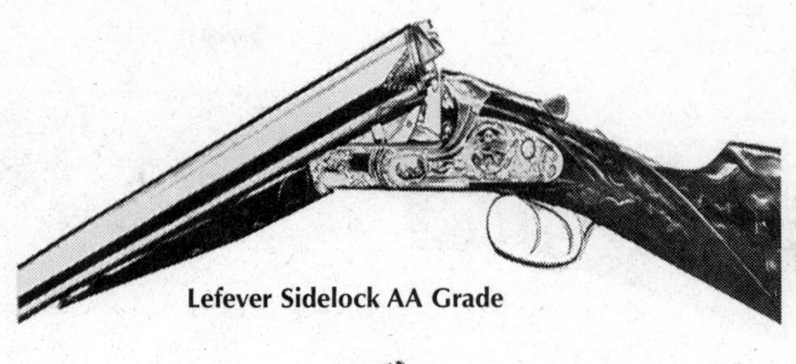
Lefever Sidelock AA Grade

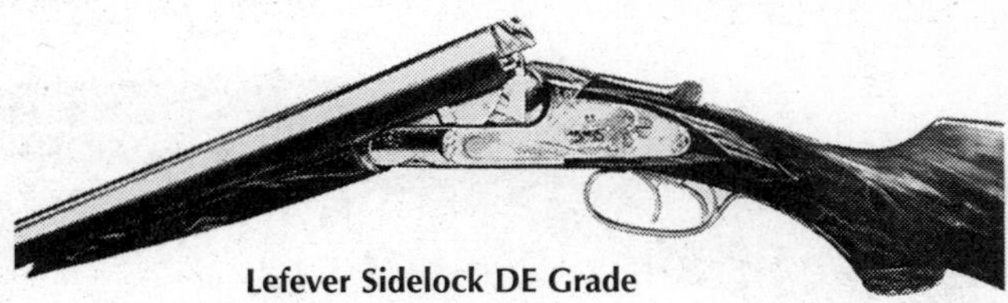
Lefever Sidelock DE Grade

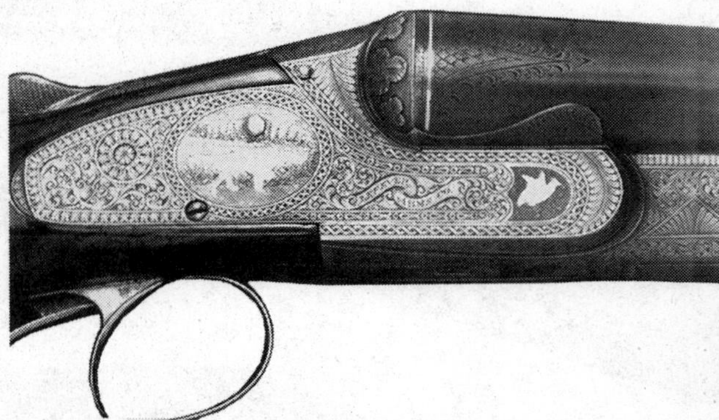

Lefever Sidelock Sideplate BE Grade

Lefever Sidelock Sideplate CE Grade

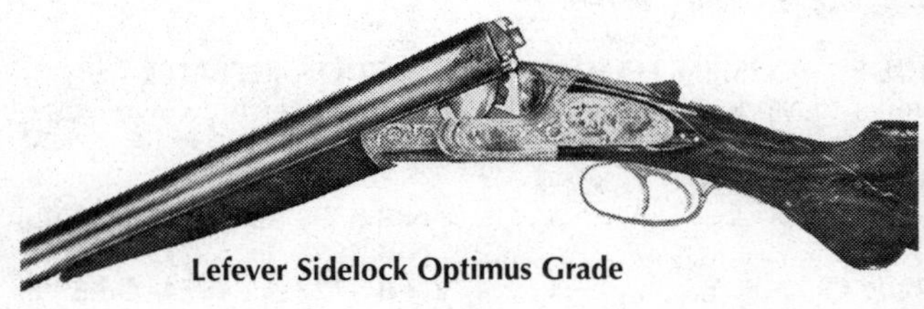
Lefever Sidelock Optimus Grade

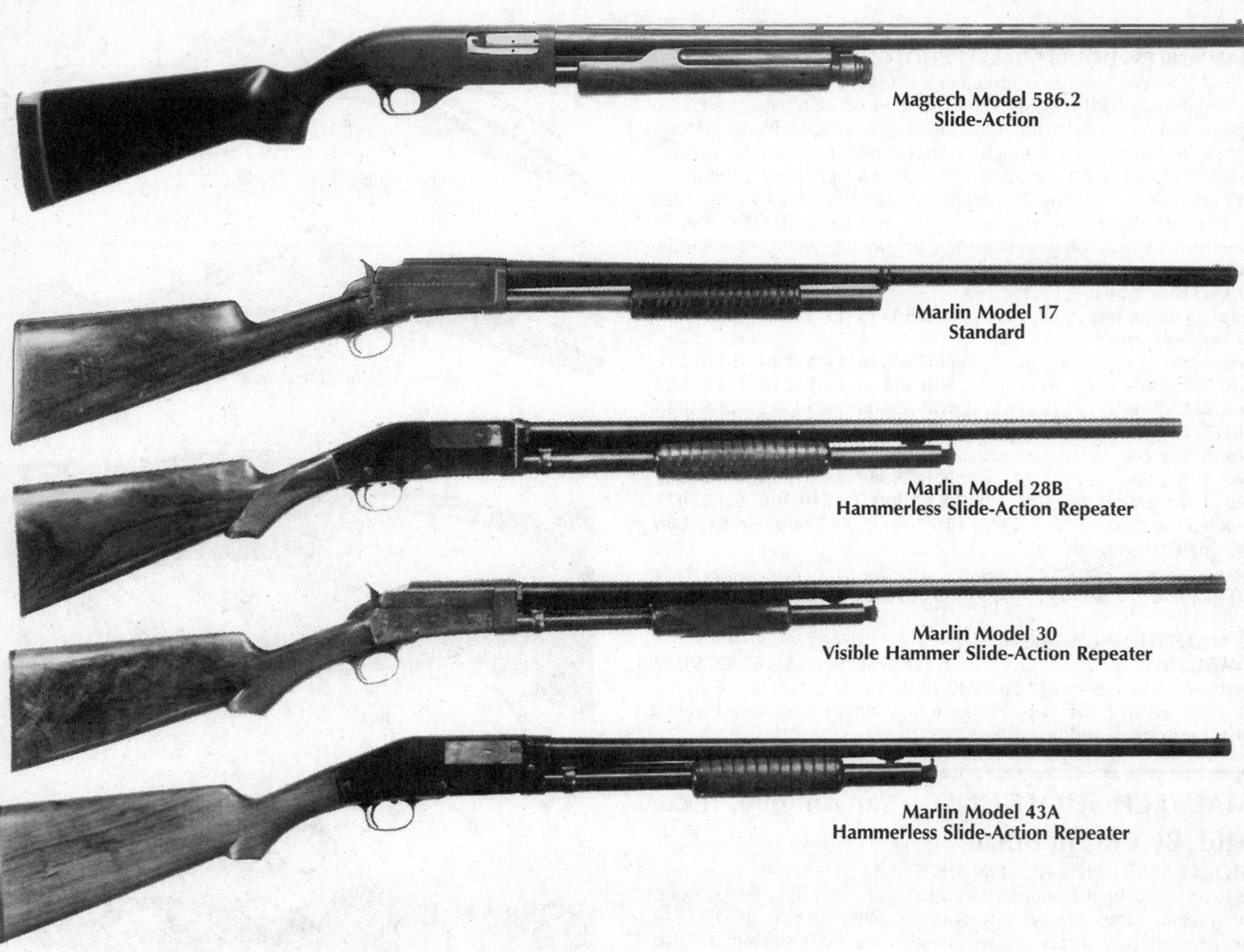

Magtech Model 586.2 Slide-Action

Marlin Model 17 Standard

Marlin Model 28B Hammerless Slide-Action Repeater

Marlin Model 30 Visible Hammer Slide-Action Repeater

Marlin Model 43A Hammerless Slide-Action Repeater

MODEL 17 BRUSH GUN . . . . NiB $395 Ex $314 Gd $222
Same as Model 17 Standard except has 26-inch bbl., cylinder bore. Weight: About 7 lbs. Made 1906-08.

MODEL 17 RIOT GUN . . . . NiB $410 Ex $333 Gd $235
Same as Model 17 Standard except has 20-inch bbl., cylinder bore. Weight: About 6.88 lbs. Made 1906-08.

MODEL 17 STANDARD VISIBLE HAMMER SLIDE-ACTION REPEATER . . . . NiB $395 Ex $314 Gd $222
Solid frame.12 ga. Five round tubular magazine. Bbls.: 30- or 32-inch, F choke. Weight: About 7.5 lbs. Straight-grip stock, grooved slide handle. Made 1906-08.

MODEL 19 VISIBLE HAMMER SLIDE-ACTION REPEATER
Similar to Model 1898 but improved, lighter weight, w/two extractors, matted sighting groove on receiver top. Weight: About 7 lbs. Made 1906-07.

Grade A . . . . NiB $391 Ex $319 Gd $226
Grade B . . . . NiB $657 Ex $531 Gd $371
Grade C . . . . NiB $722 Ex $574 Gd $399
Grade D . . . . NiB $1436 Ex $1157 Gd $800

MODEL 21 TRAP VISIBLE HAMMER SLIDE-ACTION REPEATER
Similar to Model 19 w/same general specifications except has straight-grip stock. Made 1907-09.

Grade A . . . . NiB $395 Ex $314 Gd $222
Grade B . . . . NiB $554 Ex $449 Gd $315
Grade C . . . . NiB $694 Ex $560 Gd $390
Grade D . . . . NiB $1379 Ex $1111 Gd $768

MODEL 24 VISIBLE HAMMER SLIDE-ACTION REPEATER
Similar to Model 19 but has improved takedown system and auto recoil safety lock, solid matted rib on frame. Weight: About 7.5 lbs. Made 1908-15.

Grade A . . . . NiB $362 Ex $296 Gd $211
Grade B . . . . NiB $581 Ex $471 Gd $329
Grade C . . . . NiB $727 Ex $587 Gd $408
Grade D. NiB $1491 Ex $1202 Gd $811

MODEL 26 BRUSH GUN . . . . NiB $323 Ex $262 Gd $184
Same as Model 26 Standard except has 26-inch bbl., cylinder bore. Weight: About 7 lbs. Made 1909-15.

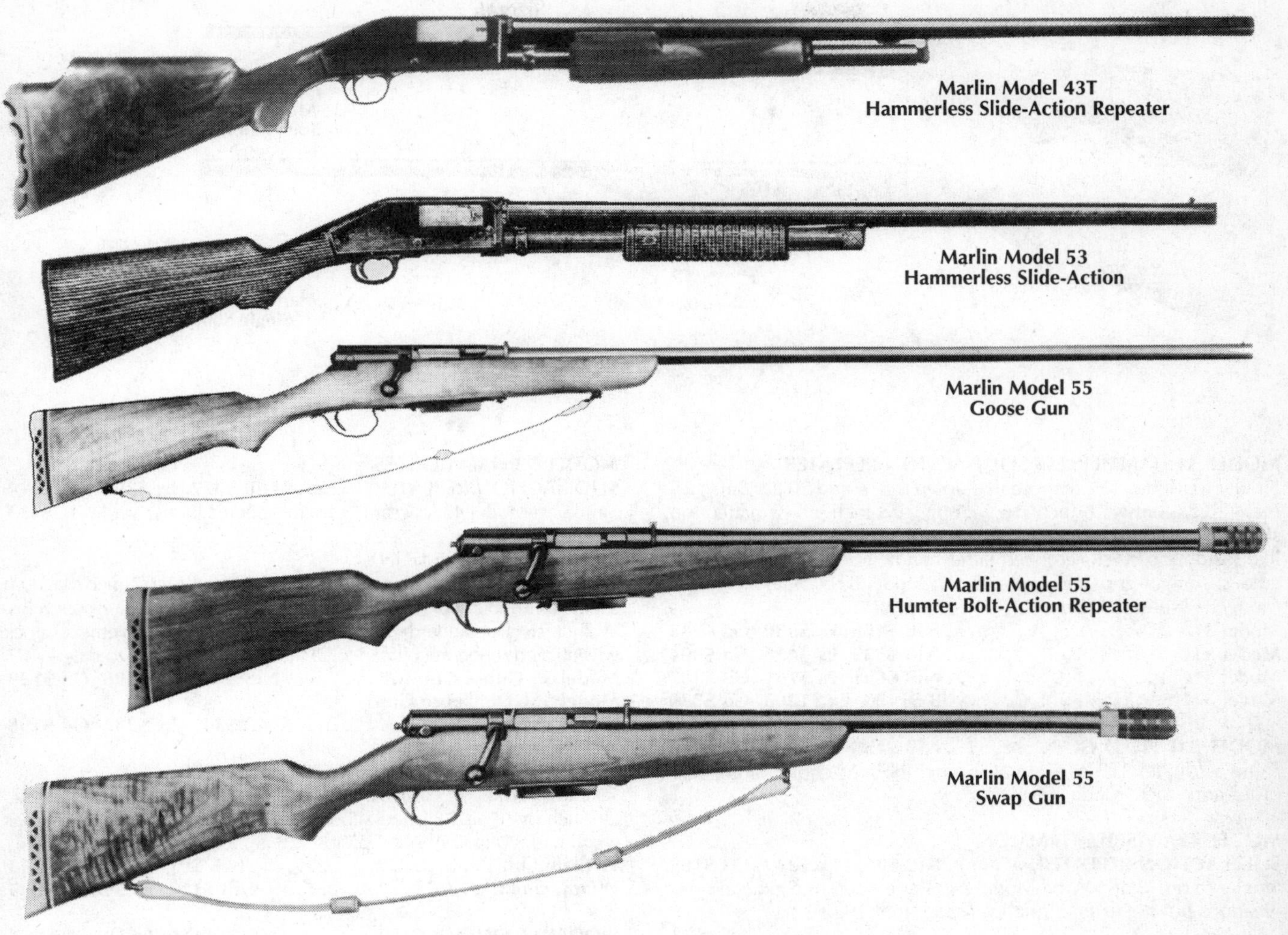

Marlin Model 43T
Hammerless Slide-Action Repeater

Marlin Model 53
Hammerless Slide-Action

Marlin Model 55
Goose Gun

Marlin Model 55
Humter Bolt-Action Repeater

Marlin Model 55
Swap Gun

MODEL 26 RIOT GUN . . . . NiB $291 Ex $237 Gd $168
Same as Model 26 Standard except has 20-inch bbl., cylinder bore. Weight: About 6.88 lbs. Made 1909-15.

MODEL 26 STANDARD VISIBLE HAMMER SLIDE-ACTION REPEATER. . . . . . . NiB $305 Ex $247 Gd $175
Similar to Model 24 Grade A except solid frame and straight-grip stock. 30- or 32-inch full choke bbl. Weight: About 7.13 lbs. Made from 1909-15.

MODEL 28 HAMMERLESS SLIDE-ACTION REPEATER
Takedown. 12 ga. Five round tubular magazine. Bbls.: 26-, 28-, 30-, 32-inch, standard chokes; matted-top bbl. except on Model 28D, which has solid matted rib. Weight: About 8 lbs. Pistol-grip stock, grooved slide handle; checkering on higher grades. Grades differ in quality of wood, engraving on Models 28C and 28D. Made 1913-22; all but Model 28A disc. in 1915. See illustration previous page.

Model 28A . . . . NiB $359 Ex $290 Gd $204
Model 28B . . . . NiB $507 Ex $410 Gd $285
Model 28C . . . . NiB $659 Ex $533 Gd $371
Model 28D . . . . NiB $1371 Ex $1106 Gd $766

MODEL 28T TRAP GUN . . . . NiB $630 Ex $509 Gd $355
Same as Model 28 except has 30-inch matted-rib bbl., F choke, straight-grip stock w/high-fluted comb of fancy walnut, checkered. Made in 1915.

MODEL 28TS TRAP GUN . . . . NiB $455 Ex $368 Gd $257
Same as Model 28T except has matted-top bbl., plainer stock. Made in 1915.

MODEL 30 FIELD GUN . . . . NiB $355 Ex $287 Gd $202
Same as Model 30 Grade B except has 25-inch bbl., M choke, straight-grip stock. Made 1913-14.

MODEL 30 VISIBLE HAMMER SLIDE-ACTION REPEATER
Similar to Model 16 but w/Model 24 improvements. Made 1910-14. See illustration previous page.

Grade A . . . . NiB $388 Ex $314 Gd $220
Grade B . . . . NiB $588 Ex $475 Gd $329
Grade C . . . . NiB $749 Ex $603 Gd $417
Grade D . . . . NiB $1602 Ex $1290 Gd $890

MODELS 30A, 30B, 30C, 30D
Same as Model 30; designations were changed in 1915. Also available in 20 ga. w/25- or 28-inch bbl., matted-top bbl. on all grades. Suffixes "A," "B," "C" and "D" correspond to former grades. Made in 1915.

Model 30A . . . . NiB $453 Ex $368 Gd $258
Model 30B . . . . NiB $560 Ex $474 Gd $316
Model 30C . . . . NiB $822 Ex $661 Gd $458
Model 30D . . . . NiB $1411 Ex $1136 Gd $786

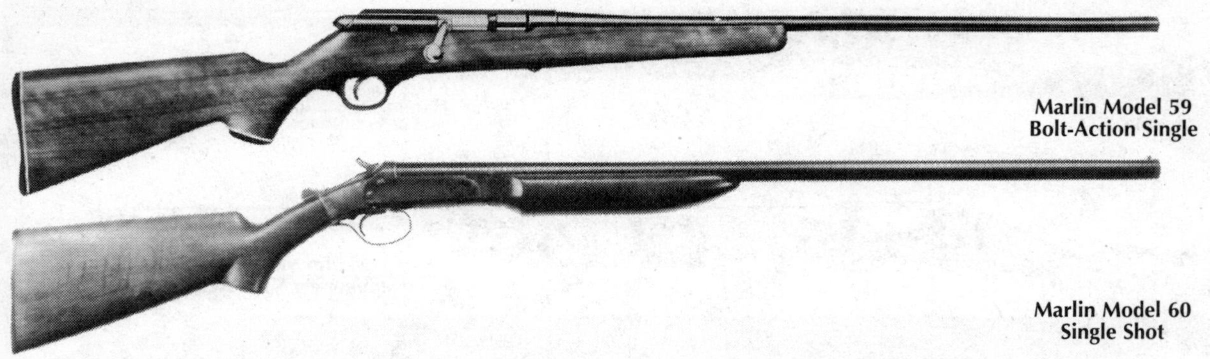

Marlin Model 59
Bolt-Action Single

Marlin Model 60
Single Shot

MODEL 31 HAMMERLESS SLIDE-ACTION REPEATER
Similar to Model 28 except scaled down for 16 and 20 ga. Bbls.: 25-inch (20 ga. only), 26-inch (16 ga. only), 28-inch, all w/matted top, standard chokes. Weight: 16 ga., about 6.75 lbs.; 20 ga., about 6 lbs. Pistol-grip stock, grooved slide handle; checkering on higher grades; straight-grip stock optional on Model 31D. Made 1915-17; Model 31A until 1922.
Model 31A . . . . NiB $406 Ex $330 Gd $232
Model 31B . . . . NiB $539 Ex $436 Gd $304
Model 31C . . . . NiB $691 Ex $761 Gd $387
Model 31D . . . . NiB $1493 Ex $1203 Gd $830

MODEL 31F FIELD GUN. . . . . NiB $433 Ex $382 Gd $280
Same as Model 31B except has 25-inch bbl., M choke, straight- or pistol-grip stock. Made 1915-17.

MODEL 42A VISIBLE HAMMER
SLIDE-ACTION REPEATER. . . . . NiB $265 Ex $239 Gd $163
Similar to pre-World War I Model 24 Grade A w/same general specifications but not as high quality. Made from 1922-34.

MODEL 43 HAMMERLESS SLIDE-ACTION REPEATER
Similar to pre-World War I Models 28A, 28T and 28TS, w/same general specifications but not as high quality. Made 1923-30.
Model 43A . . . . NiB $297 Ex $240 Gd $166
Model 43T . . . . NiB $598 Ex $484 Gd $339
Model 43TS . . . . NiB $632 Ex $511 Gd $357

MODEL 44 HAMMERLESS SLIDE-ACTION REPEATER
Similar to pre-World War I Model 31A w/same general specifications but not as high quality. 20 ga. only. Model 44A is a standard-grade field gun. Model 44S Special Grade has checkered stock and slide handle of fancy walnut. Made 1923-35.
Model 44A . . . . NiB $399 Ex $325 Gd $229
Model 44S . . . . NiB $480 Ex $389 Gd $274

MODEL 49 VISIBLE HAMMER SLIDE-
ACTION REPEATING SHOTGUN . . NiB $481 Ex $390 Gd $274
Economy version of Model 42A, offered as a bonus on the purchase of four shares of Marlin stock. About 3000 were made 1925-28.

MODEL 50DL BOLT
ACTION SHOTGUN . . . . NiB $291 Ex $227 Gd $168
Gauge: 12 w/3-inch chamber. Two round magazine. 28-inch bbl. w/modified choke. 48.75 inches overall. Weight: 7.5 lbs. Checkered black synthetic stocks w/ventilated rubber recoil pad. Made 1997 to date.

MODEL 53 HAMMERLESS
SLIDE-ACTION REPEATER. . . . . NiB $377 Ex $306 Gd $214
Similar to Model 43A w/same general specifications. Made 1929-30.

MODEL 55 GOOSE GUN
Same as Model 55 Hunter except chambered for 12-ga. 3-inch Magnum shell, has 36-inch bbl., F choke, swivels and sling. Weight: About 8 lbs. Walnut stock (standard model) or checkered black synthetic stock w/ventilated rubber recoil pad (GDL model). Made 1962 to date.
Model 55 Goose Gun . . . . NiB $240 Ex $196 Gd $139
Model 55GDL Goose Gun
(intro. 1997) . . . . NiB $347 Ex $282 Gd $198

MODEL 55 HUNTER BOLT-ACTION REPEATER
Takedown. Gauges: 12, 16, 20. Two round clip magazine. 28-inch bbl. (26-inch in 20 ga.), F or adj. choke. Plain pistol-grip stock; 12 ga. has recoil pad. Weight: About 7.25 lbs.; 20 ga., 6.5 lbs. Made 1954-65.
W/plain bbl. . . . . NiB $91 Ex $74 Gd $53
W/adj. choke . . . . NiB $113 Ex $92 Gd $65

MODEL 55 SWAMP GUN. . . . . NiB $116 Ex $95 Gd $67
Same as Model 55 Hunter except chambered for 12-ga. 3-inch Magnum shell, has shorter 20.5-inch bbl. w/adj. choke, sling swivels and slightly better-quality stock. Weight: About 6.5 lbs. Made 1963-65.

MODEL 55S SLUG GUN. . . . . NiB $158 Ex $128 Gd $91
Same as Model 55 Goose Gun except has 24-inch bbl., cylinder bore, rifle sights. Weight: About 7.5 lbs. Made 1974-79.

MODEL 59 AUTO-SAFE
BOLT-ACTION SINGLE . . . . NiB $119 Ex $98 Gd $70
Takedown. Auto thumb safety, .410 ga. 24-inch bbl., F choke. Weight: About 5 lbs. Plain pistol-grip stock. Made 1959-61.

MODEL 60 SINGLE-SHOT
SHOTGUN . . . . NiB $213 Ex $172 Gd $121
Visible hammer. Takedown. Boxlock. Automatic ejector. 12 ga. 30- or 32-inch bbl., F choke. Weight: About 6.5 lbs. Pistol-grip stock, beavertail forearm. Note: Only about 600 were produced in 1923.

MODEL 63 HAMMERLESS SLIDE-ACTION REPEATER
Similar to Models 43A and 43T w/same general specifications. Model 63TS Trap Special is same as Model 63T Trap Gun except stock style and dimensions to order. Made 1931-35.
Model 63A . . . . NiB $352 Ex $286 Gd $200
Model 63T or 63TS . . . . NiB $444 Ex $359 Gd $250

Marlin Model 90
Standard Over-and-Under

Marlin Model 120
Magnum Slide-Action Repeater

Marlin Model 410
Lever-Action Repeater

Marlin Model 512
Slugmaster

Marlin Model 55-10
Super Goose 10

Marlin Premier Mark I
Slide-Action Repeater

Marlin Premier Mark IV

Marlin-Glenfield
Model 50 Bolt-Action Repeater

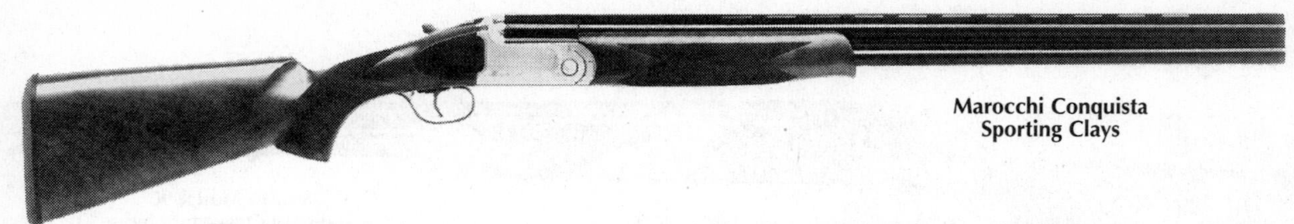

Marocchi Conquista
Sporting Clays

MODEL 90 STANDARD O/U SHOTGUN
Hammerless. Boxlock. Double triggers; non-selective single trigger was available as an extra on pre-war guns except .410. Gauges: 12, 16, 20, .410. Bbls.: Plain; 26-, 28- or 30-inch; chokes IC/M or M/F; bbl. design changed in 1949, eliminating full-length rib between bbls. Weight: 12 ga., about 7.5 lbs.; 16 and 20 ga., about 6.25 lbs. Checkered pistol-grip stock and forearm, recoil pad standard on prewar guns. Postwar production: Model 90-DT (double trigger), Model 90-ST (single trigger). Made 1937-58.
W/double triggers .... NiB $538 Ex $442 Gd $320
W/single trigger .... NiB $660 Ex $539 Gd $386
Combination model............. NiB $780 Ex $636 Gd $452
16 ga., deduct 10%
20 ga., add 15%
.410, add 30%

MODEL 120 MAGNUM
SLIDE-ACTION REPEATER........ NiB $328 Ex $268 Gd $191
Hammerless. Takedown. 12 ga. (3-inch). Four round tubular magazine. Bbls.: 26-inch vent rib, IC; 28-inch vent rib M choke; 30-inch vent rib, F choke; 38-inch plain, F choke; 40-inch plain, F choke; 26-inch slug bbl. w/rifle sights, IC. Weight: About 7.75 lbs. Checkered pistol-grip stock and forearm, recoil pad. Made 1971-85.

MODEL 120 SLUG GUN......... NiB $309 Ex $253 Gd $178
Same general specifications as Model 120 Magnum except w/20-inch bbl. and about .5 lb. lighter in weight. No vent rib. Adj. rear rifle sights; hooded front sight. Disc. 1990.

MODEL 410 LEVER-ACTION REPEATER
Action similar to that of Marlin Model 93 rifle. Visible hammer. Solid frame. .410 ga. (2.5-inch shell). Five round tubular magazine. 22- or 26-inch bbl., F choke. Weight: About 6 lbs. Plain pistol-grip stock and grooved beavertail forearm. Made 1929-32.
Model 410 w/22-inch bbl....... NiB $1493 Ex $1204 Gd $823
Model 410 w/26-inch bbl....... NiB $2097 Ex $1010 Gd $702
Deluxe model, add.................................. 30%

MODEL 512 SLUGMASTER SHOTGUN
Bolt-action repeater. Gauge: 12; 3-inch chamber, 2-round magazine. 21-inch rifled bbl. w/adj. open sight. Weight: 8 lbs. Walnut-finished birch stock (standard model) or checkered black synthetic stock w/ventilated rubber recoil pad (GDL model). Made 1994 to date.
Model 512 Slugmaster........... NiB $321 Ex $261 Gd $183
Model 512DL Slugmaster
(intro. 1998) .... NiB $347 Ex $282 Gd $198
Model 512P Slugmaster
w/ported bbl. (intro. 1999) .... NiB $355 Ex $287 Gd $202

MODEL 1898 VISIBLE HAMMER SLIDE-ACTION REPEATER
Takedown. 12 ga. Five shell tubular magazine. Bbls.: 26-, 28-, 30-, 32-inch; standard chokes. Weight: About 7.25 lbs. Pistol-grip stock, grooved slide handle; checkering on higher grades. Difference among grades is in quality of wood, engraving on Grades C and D. Made 1898-05. Note: This was the first Marlin shotgun.
Grade A (Field) .... NiB $377 Ex $300 Gd $224
Grade B .... NiB $606 Ex $525 Gd $326
Grade C .... NiB $932 Ex $761 Gd $555

(cont'd.) **MODEL 1898 VISIBLE HAMMER**
Grade D .... NiB $1870 Ex $1620 Gd $791

MODEL 55-10 SUPER GOOSE 10.. NiB $240 Ex $196 Gd $139
Similar to Model 55 Goose Gun except chambered for 10 ga. 3.5-inch Magnum shell, has 34-inch heavy bbl., F choke. Weight: About 10.5 lbs. Made 1976-85. See illustration on page 495.

PREMIER MARK I
SLIDE-ACTION REPEATER........ NiB $230 Ex $188 Gd $134
Hammerless. Takedown. 12 ga. Magazine holds 3 shells. Bbls.: 30-inch F choke, 28-inch M, 26-inch IC or SK choke. Weight: About 6 lbs. Plain pistol-grip stock and forearm. Made in France 1960-63.

PREMIER MARK II AND IV
Same action and mechanism as Premier Mark except engraved receiver (Mark IV is more elaborate), checkered stock and forearm, fancier wood, vent rib and similar refinements. Made 1960-63.
Premier Mark II .... NiB $307 Ex $249 Gd $176
Premier Mark IV (plain barrel) .... NiB $339 Ex $275 Gd $193
Premier Mark IV (vent rib barrel) .... NiB $396 Ex $321 Gd $225

GLENFIELD MODEL 50
BOLT-ACTION REPEATER .... NiB $88 Ex $71 Gd $50
Similar to Model 55 Hunter except chambered for 12-or 20-ga., 3-inch Magnum shell; has 28-inch bbl. in 12 ga., 26-inch in 20 ga., F choke. Made 1966-74.

GLENFIELD 778 SLIDE-ACTION
REPEATER .... NiB $246 Ex $199 Gd $139
Hammerless. 12 ga. 2.75-inch or 3-inch. Four round tubular magazine. Bbls.: 26-inch IC, 28-inch M, 30-inch F, 38-inch MXR, 20-inch slug bbl. Weight: 7.75 lbs. Checkered pistol-grip. Made from 1979-84.

MAROCCHI SHOTGUNS — Brescia, Italy Imported by Precision Sales International of Westfield, MA

CONQUISTA MODEL O/U SHOTGUN
Boxlock. Gauge: 12; 2.75-inch chambers. 28-, 30- or 32-inch vent rib bbl. Fixed choke or internal tubes. 44.38 to 48 inches overall. Weight: 7.5 to 8.25 lbs. Adj. single-selective trigger. Checkered American walnut stock w/recoil pad. Imported since 1994.
Lady Sport Grade I .... NiB $1977 Ex $1594 Gd $1103
Lady Sport Grade II.......... NiB $2365 Ex $1905 Gd $1318
Lady Sport Grade III .... NiB $4209 Ex $3380 Gd $2322
Skeet Model Grade I .... NiB $1701 Ex $1388 Gd $968
Skeet Model Grade II .... NiB $2129 Ex $1818 Gd $1193
Skeet Model Grade III........ NiB $3387 Ex $2724 Gd $1876
Sporting Clays Grade I .... NiB $1881 Ex $1519 Gd $1057
Sporting Clays Grade II....... NiB $2177 Ex $1553 Gd $1212
Sporting Clays Grade III ...... NiB $3320 Ex $2670 Gd $1839
Trap Model Grade I.......... NiB $1936 Ex $1561 Gd $1081
Trap Model Grade II .... NiB $2305 Ex $1859 Gd $1288
Trap Model Grade III......... NiB $3236 Ex $2851 Gd $1962
Left-handed model, add........................ 10%

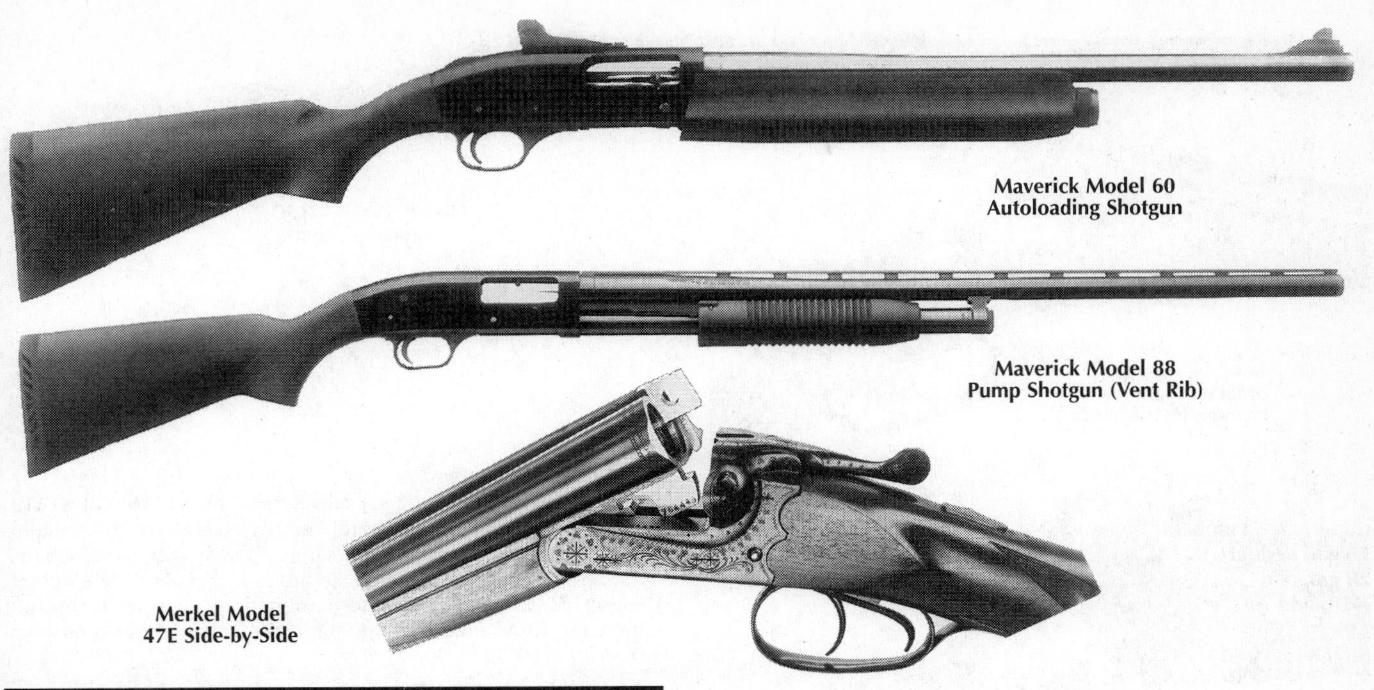

MAVERICK ARMS, INC. — Eagle Pass, Texas

MODEL 60 AUTOLOADING SHOTGUN
Gauge: 12, 2.75- or 3-inch chamber. Five round capacity. Bbls.: Magnum or non-Magnum; 24- or 28-inch w/fixed choke or screw-in tubes, plain or vent rib; blued. Weight: 7.25 lbs. Black synthetic buttstock and forend. Announced in 1993, but not produced.
Standard model . . . . NiB $381 Ex $310 Gd $219
Combo model
w/extra 18.5 inch bbl. . . . . NiB $423 Ex $343 Gd $241
Turkey/Deer model
(w/ghost ring sights) . . . . NiB $438 Ex $355 Gd $229

MODEL 88 BULLPUP . . . . NiB $312 Ex $254 Gd $181
Gauge: 12; 3-inch chamber. Bbl.: 18.5-inch w/fixed choke, blued. Weight: 9.5 lbs. Dual safeties: Grip style and crossbolt. Fixed sights in carrying handle. High-impact black synthetic stock; trigger-forward bullpup configuration w/twin pistol-grip design. Made 1991-94.

MODEL 88 DEER GUN . . . . NiB $204 Ex $165 Gd $115
Crossbolt safety and dual slide bars. Cylinder bore choke. Gauge: 12 only w/3-inch chamber. Bbl.: 24-inch. Weight: 7 lbs. Synthetic stock and forearm.

MODEL 88 PUMP SHOTGUN
Gauge: 12; 2.75- or 3-inch chamber. Bbl.: 28 inches/M or 30 inches/F w/fixed choke or screw-in integral tubes; plain or vent rib, blued. Weight: 7.25 lbs. Bead front sight. Black synthetic or wood buttstock and forend; forend grooved. Made from 1989 to date.
Synthetic stock
w/plain bbl. NiB $182 Ex $148 Gd $104
Synthetic stock
w/vent-rib bbl.. . . . . NiB $202 Ex $163 Gd $114
Synthetic Combo
w/18.5 inch bbl. . . . . NiB $227 Ex $183 Gd $128
Wood stock
w/vent-rib bbl./tubes. . . . . NiB $220 Ex $178 Gd $124
Wood Combo w/vent-rib bbl./tubes . . . . NiB $259 Ex $209 Gd $146

MODEL 88 SECURITY. . . . . NiB $191 Ex $154 Gd $108
Crossbolt safety and dual slide bars. Optional heat shield. Cylinder bore choke. Gauge: 12 only w/3-inch chamber. Bbl.: 18.5-inches. Weight: 6 lbs., 8 ozs. Synthetic stock and forearm. Made 1993 to date.

MODEL 91 PUMP SHOTGUN
Same as Model 88, except w/2.75-, 3- or 3.5-inch chamber, 28-inch bbl. W/ACCU-F choke, crossbolt safety and synthetic stock only. Made 1991-95.
Synthetic stock w/plain bbl. . . . . . NiB $240 Ex $194 Gd $134
Synthetic stock w/vent-rib bbl. . . . . NiB $253 Ex $204 Gd $142

MODEL 95 BOLT-ACTION . . . . NiB $169 Ex $137 Gd $97
Modified, fixed choke. Built-in two round magazine. Gauge: 12 only. Bbl.: 25-inch. Weight: 6.75 lbs. Bead sight. Synthetic stock and rubber recoil pad. Made 1995 to date.

GEBRÜDER MERKEL — Suhl, Germany
Mfd. by Suhler Jagd-und Sportwaffen GmbH, *Imported by GSI, Inc., Trussville, AL, (Previously by Armes de Chasse)*

MODEL 8 HAMMERLESS DOUBLE. . NiB $1250 Ex $1009 Gd $700
Anson & Deeley boxlock action w/Greener double-bbl. hook lock. Double triggers. Extractors. Automatic safety. Gauges: 12, 16, 20; 2.75- or 3-inch chambers. 26-or 28-inch bbls. w/fixed standard chokes. Checkered European walnut stock, pistol-grip or English-style w/or w/o cheekpiece. Scroll-engraved receiver w/tinted marble finish.

SIDE-BY-SIDE MODEL 47E . . . . NiB $2430 Ex $2370 Gd $1625
Hammerless boxlock similar to Model 8 except w/automatic ejectors and cocking indicators. Double hook bolting. Single selective or double triggers. 12, 16 or 20 ga. w/2.75-inch chambers. Standard bbl lengths, choke combos. Hand-checkered European walnut stock, forearm; pistol-grip and cheekpiece or straight English style; sling swivels.

Merkel Model 47LSC
Sporting Clay

Merkel Model 47S
Hammerless Sidelock

Merkel Model 247S
Hammerless Sidelock

Merkel Model 347S
Hammerless Sidelock

Merkel Model 122
Hammerless Double

MODEL 47LSC
SPORTING CLAYS S/S . . . . . NiB $2901 Ex $2336 Gd $1613
Anson & Deeley boxlock action w/single-selective adj. trigger, cocking indicators and manual safety. Gauge: 12; 3-inch chambers. 28-inch bbls.w/Briley choke tubes and H&H-style ejectors. Weight: 7.25 lbs. Color case-hardened receiver w/Arabesque engraving. Checkered select-grade walnut stock, beavertail forearm. Imported 1993-94.

MODELS 47SL, 147SL, 247SL, 347SL, 447SL
HAMMERLESS SIDELOCKS
Same general specifications as Model 147E except has sidelocks engraved w/Arabesques, borders, scrolls or game scenes in varying degrees of elaborateness.
Model 47SL . . . . NiB $5216 Ex $4198 Gd $2895
Model 147SL . . . . NiB $5719 Ex $4600 Gd $3168
Model 147SSL. . . . . NiB $6207 Ex $4991 Gd $3434
Model 247SL . . . . NiB $5675 Ex $4651 Gd $3203
Model 347SL . . . . NiB $6144 Ex $4940 Gd $3449
Model 447SL . . . . NiB $6633 Ex $5331 Gd $3665
28 ga. .410, add 20%

NOTE: Merkel over/under guns were often supplied with accessory barrels, interchangeable to convert the gun into an arm of another type; for example, a set might consist of one pair each of shotgun, rifle and combination gun barrels. Each pair of interchangeable barrels has a value of approximately one-third that of the gun with which they are supplied.

MODEL 100 O/U SHOTGUN
Hammerless. Boxlock. Greener crossbolt. Plain extractor. Double triggers. Gauges: 12, 16, 20. Made w/plain or ribbed bbls. in various lengths and chokes. Plain finish, no engraving. Checkered forend and stock w/pistol grip and cheekpiece or English-style. Made prior to WWII.
W/plain bbl. . . . . NiB $1975 Ex $1584 Gd $1085
W/ribbed bbl. . . . . NiB $2042 Ex $1638 Gd $1121

MODELS 101 AND 101E O/U
Same as Model 100 except ribbed bbl. standard, has separate extractors (ejectors on Model 101E), English engraving. Made prior to World War II.
Model 101 . . . . NiB $2097 Ex $1682 Gd $1152
Model 101E . . . . NiB $2255 Ex $1809 Gd $1237

MODEL 122
HAMMERLESS DOUBLE . . . . NiB $3845 Ex $3081 Gd $2103
Similar to the Model 147S except w/nonremovable sidelocks in gauges 12, 16 or 20. Imported since 1993.

MODEL 122E
HAMMERLESS SIDELOCK. . . . . NiB $4343 Ex $3494 Gd $2408
Similar to the Model 122 except w/removable sidelocks and cocking indicators. Importation disc. 1992.

MODEL 126E
HAMMERLESS SIDELOCK . . . . NiB $28,969 Ex $23,175 Gd $15,759
Holland & Holland system, hand-detachable locks. Auto ejectors. Double triggers. 12, 16 or 20 gauge w/standard bbl. lengths and chokes. Checkered forend and pistol-grip stock; available w/cheekpiece or English-style buttstock. Elaborate game scenes and engraving. Made prior to WW II.

MODEL 127E
HAMMERLESS SIDELOCK . . . . NiB $29,549 Ex $23,639 Gd $16,074
Similar to the Model 126E except w/elaborate scroll engraving on removable sidelocks w/cocking indicators. Made prior to WW II.

MODEL 128E
HAMMERLESS BOXLOCK DOUBLE. . . NiB $12,554 Ex $10,042 Gd $6829
Scalloped Anson & Deeley action w/hinged floorplate and removable sideplates. Auto-ejectors. Double triggers. Elaborate hunting scene or Arabesque engraving. 12, 16 or 20 gauge w/various bbl. lengths and chokes. Checkered forend and stock w/pistol grip and cheekpiece or English-style. Made prior to WW II.

MODEL 130
HAMMERLESS BOXLOCK DOUBLE. . . NiB $12,554 Ex $10,042 Gd $6829
Similar to Model 128E except w/fixed sideplates. Auto ejectors. Double triggers. Elaborate hunting scene or Arabesque engraving. Made prior to WW II.

MODESL 147 & 147E HAMMERLESS BOXLOCK DOUBLE-BARREL SHOTGUN
Anson & Deeley system w/extractors or auto ejectors. Single selective or double triggers. Gauges: 12, 16, 20 or 28 ga. (Three-inch chambers available in 12 and 20 ga.). Bbls.: 26-inch standard, other lengths available w/any standard choke combination. Weight: 6.5 lbs. Checkered straight-grip stock and forearm. Disc. 1998.
Model 147 w/extractors . . . . . . NiB $2679 Ex $2165 Gd $1508
Model 147E w/ejectors . . . . NiB $3136 Ex $2530 Gd $1756

MODELS 200, 200E, 201, 201E, 202 AND 202E O/U SHOTGUNS
Hammerless. Boxlock. Kersten double crossbolt. Scalloped frame. Sideplates on Models 202 and 202E. Arabesque or hunting engraving supplied on all except Models 200 and 200E. "E" models have ejectors, others have separate extractors, signal pins, double triggers. Gauges: 12, 16, 20, 24, 28, 32 (last three not available in postwar guns). Ribbed bbls. in various lengths and chokes. Weight: 5.75 to 7.5 lbs. depending on bbl. length and gauge. Checkered forend and stock w/pistol grip and cheekpiece or English-style. The 200, 201, and 202 differ in overall quality, engraving, wood, checkering, etc.; aside from the faux sideplates on Models 202 and 202E, general specifications are the same. Models 200, 201, 202, and 202E, all made before WW II, are disc. Models 201E &202E in production w/revised 2000 series nomenclature.
Model 200 . . . . NiB $2441 Ex $1982 Gd $1396
Model 200E . . . . NiB $3363 Ex $2720 Gd $1838
Model 200 ES Skeet. . . . . NiB $4908 Ex $3956 Gd $2738
Model 200ET Trap . . . . NiB $4721 Ex $3806 Gd $2636
Model 200 SC Sporting Clays . . . . NiB $5294 Ex $4265 Gd $2948
Model 201 (disc.). NiB $2919 Ex $2364 Gd $1656
Model 201E (Pre-WW II) . . . . NiB $3323 Ex $2689 Gd $1876
Model 201E (Post-WW II) . . . . NiB $4670 Ex $3765 Gd $2609
Model 201 ES Skeet. . . . . NiB $7354 Ex $5913 Gd $4069
Model 201 ET Trap. . . . . NiB $7296 Ex $5867 Gd $4037
Model 202 (disc.). NiB $3813 Ex $3080 Gd $2143
Model 202E (Pre-WW II) . . . . NiB $4464 Ex $3600 Gd $2496
Model 202 E (Post-WW II & 2002EL). . . . . NiB $6871 Ex $5627 Gd $3806

Merkel Model 147E
Hammerless Boxlock Double-Barrel Shotgun

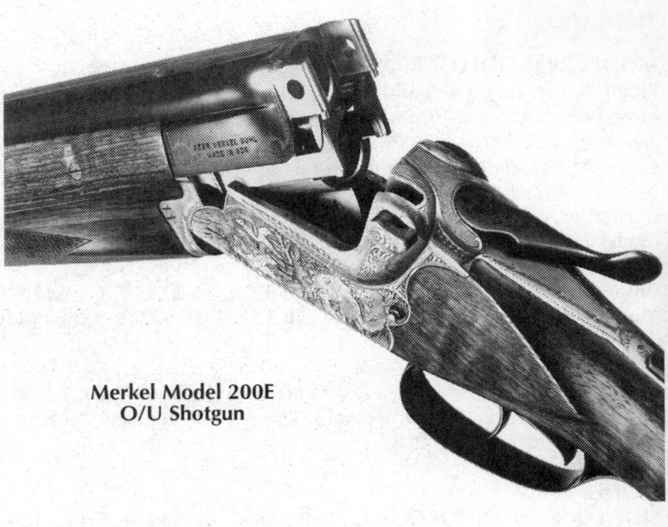
Merkel Model 200E
O/U Shotgun

SHOTGUNS

Merkel Model 203E
Sidelock O/U Shotgun

Merkel Model 303E O/U Shotgun

MODEL 203E SIDELOCK O/U SHOTGUNS
Hammerless action w/hand-detachable sidelocks. Kersten double cross bolt, auto ejectors and double triggers. Gauges: 12 or 20 (16, 24, 28 and 32 disc.). 26.75- or 28-inch vent rib bbls. Arabesque engraving standard or hunting engraving optional on coin-finished receiver. Checkered English or pistol-grip stock and forend. See illustration previous page.
Model 203E sidelock (disc. 1998) . . NiB $6311 Ex $5083 Gd $3512
Model 203ES skeet
(imported 1993-97) . . . . NiB $8924 Ex $7174 Gd $4850
Model 203ET trap (disc. 1997) . . . . NiB $8975 Ex $7215 Gd $4962

MODEL 204E
O/U SHOTGUN . . . . NiB $7579 Ex $6097 Gd $4202
Similar to Model 203E; has Merkel sidelocks, fine English engraving. Made prior to World War II.

MODEL 210E
SIDE-LOCK O/U SHOTGUN. . . NiB $6055 Ex $4959 Gd $3429
Kersten double cross-bolt, scroll-engraved, casehardened receiver. 12, 16 or 20 ga. Double-triggers; pistol-grip stock w/cheekpiece.

MODEL 211E
SIDE-LOCK O/U SHOTGUN. . . NiB $7311 Ex $5964 Gd $4112
Same specifications as Model 210E except w/engraved hunting scenes on silver-gray receiver.

MODELS 300, 300E, 301, 301E AND 302 O/U
Merkel-Anson system boxlock. Kersten double crossbolt, two underlugs, scalloped frame, sideplates on Model 302. Arabesque or hunting engraving. "E" models and Model 302 have auto ejectors, others have separate extractors. Signal pins. Double triggers. Gauges: 12, 16, 20, 24, 28, 32. Ribbed bbls. in various lengths and chokes. Checkered forend and stock w/pistol grip and cheekpiece or English-style. Grades 300, 301 and 302 differ in overall quality, engraving, wood, checkering, etc.; aside from the dummy sideplates on Model 302, general specifications are the same. Manufactured prior to World War II.
Model 300 . . . . NiB $2754 Ex $2218 Gd $1531
Model 300E . . . . NiB $3354 Ex $2696 Gd $1856
Model 301 . . . . NiB $7016 Ex $5627 Gd $3849
Model 301E . . . . NiB $8375 Ex $6713 Gd $4588
Model 302 . . . . NiB $14,803 Ex $11,842 Gd $8052

MODEL 303EL O/U
SHOTGUN . . . . NiB $17,349 Ex $13,879 Gd $9438
Similar to Model 203E. Has Kersten crossbolt, double underlugs, Holland & Holland-type hand-detachable sidelocks, auto-ejectors. This is a finer gun than Model 203E. Currently manufactured.

MODEL 304E O/U
SHOTGUN. . . . . NiB $22,306 Ex $17,752 Gd $12,134
Special version of the Model 303E-type, but higher quality throughout. This is the top grade Merkel over/under. Currently manufactured.

MODELS 400, 400E, 401, 401E O/U
Similar to Model 101 except have Kersten double crossbolt, Arabesque engraving on Models 400 and 400E, hunting engraving on Models 401 and 401E, finer general quality. "E" models have Merkel ejectors, others have separate extractors. Made prior to World War II.
Model 400 . . . . NiB $2295 Ex $1856 Gd $1294
Model 400E . . . . NiB $2896 Ex $2337 Gd $1621
Model 401 . . . . NiB $2437 Ex $1969 Gd $1371
Model 401E . . . . NiB $3958 Ex $3187 Gd $2199

O/U COMBINATION GUNS ("BOCKBÜCHSFLINTEN")
Shotgun bbl. over, rifle bbl. under. Gauges: 12, 16, 20; calibers: 5.6x35 Vierling, 7x57r5, 8x57JR, 8x60R Mag., 9.3x53r5, 9.3x72r5, 9.3x74R and others including domestic calibers from .22 Hornet to .375 H&H. Various bbl. lengths, chokes and weights. Other specifications and values correspond to those of Merkel over/under shotguns listed below. Currently manufactured. Model 210 & 211 series disc. 1992.
Models 410, 410E, 411E
(see shotgun models 400, 400E, 401, 401E)
Models 210, 210E, 211, 211E, 212, 212E
(see shotgun models 200, 200E, 201, 201E, 202, 202E)

MODEL 2000EL O/U SHOTGUNS
Kersten double cross-bolt. Gauges: 12 and 20. 26.75- or 28-inch bbls. Weight: 6.4 to 7.28 lbs. Scroll engraved silver-gray receiver. Automatic ejectors and single selective or double triggers. Checkered forend and stock w/pistol grip and cheekpiece or English-style stock w/luxury grade wood. Imported 1998 to date.
Model 2000EL Standard . . . . . NiB $5172 Ex $4167 Gd $2880
Model 2000EL Sporter . . . . NiB $5379 Ex $4331 Gd $2992

MODEL 2001EL O/U SHOTGUNS
Gauges: 12, 16, 20 and 28; Kersten double cross-bolt lock receiver. 26.75- or 28-inch IC/mod, mod/full bbls. Weight: 6.4 to 7.28 lbs. Three-piece forearm, automatic ejectors and single selective or double triggers. Imported 1993 to date.
Model 2001EL 12 ga. . . . . NiB $6120 Ex $4925 Gd $3396
Model 2001EL 16 ga. (disc. 1997)
. . . . . NiB $6120 Ex $4925 Gd $3396
Model 2001EL 20 ga. . . . . NiB $6120 Ex $4925 Gd $3396
Model 2001EL 28 ga.
(made 1995). . . . . NiB $6729 Ex $5411 Gd $3726

MODEL 2002EL. . . . . NiB $6866 Ex $5522 Gd $3801
Same specifications as Model 2000EL except hunting scenes w/Arabesque engraving.

ANSON DRILLINGS
Three-bbl. combination guns; usually made w/double shotgun bbls., over rifle bbl., although "Doppelbüchsdrillingen" were made w/two rifle bbls. over and shotgun bbl. under. Hammerless.

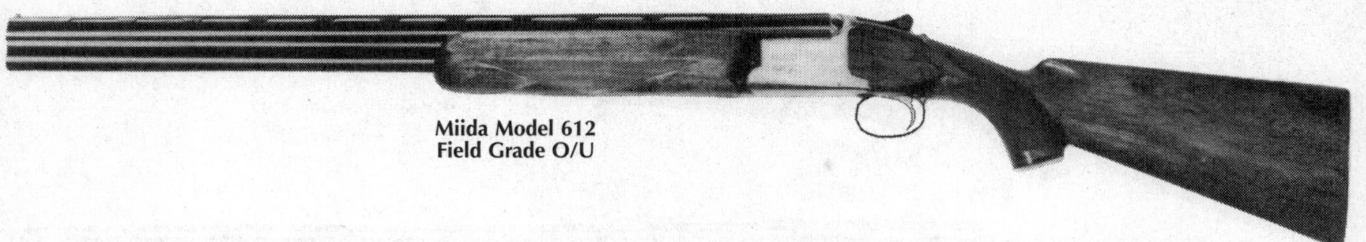

Miida Model 612
Field Grade O/U

(*cont'd.*) **ANSON DRILLINGS**
Boxlock. Anson & Deeley system. Side clips. Plain extractors. Double triggers. Gauges: 12, 16, 20; rifle calibers: 7x57r5, 8x57JR and 9.3x74R are most common, but other calibers from 5.6mm to 10.75mm available. Bbls.: standard drilling 25.6 inches; short drilling, 21.6 inches. Checkered pistol-grip stock and forend. The three models listed differ chiefly in overall quality, grade of wood, etc.; general specifications are the same. Made prior to WW II.
Model 142 Engraved . . . . NiB $5449 Ex $4381 Gd $3015
Model 142 Standard . . . . NiB $4140 Ex $3334 Gd $2302
Model 145 Field . . . . NiB $3474 Ex $2800 Gd $1939

MIIDA SHOTGUNS — Manufactured for Marubeni America Corp., New York, N.Y., by Olin-Kodensha Co., Tochigi, Japan

MODEL 612 FIELD GRADE O/U. . . NiB $885 Ex $720 Gd $509
Boxlock. Auto ejectors. Selective single trigger. 12 ga. Bbls.: Vent rib; 26-inch, IC/M; 28-inch, M/F choke. Weight: W/26-inch bbl., 6 lbs., 11 oz. Checkered pistol-grip stock and forearm. Made 1972-74.

MODEL 2100 SKEET GUN . . . . NiB $993 Ex $807 Gd $568
Similar to Model 612 except has more elaborate engraving on frame (50 percent coverage), skeet-style stock and forearm of select grade wood; 27-inch vent-rib bbls., SK choke. Weight: 7 lbs., 11 oz. Made 1972-74.

MODEL 2200T TRAP GUN,
MODEL 2200S SKEET GUN . . . . . NiB $1032 Ex $838 Gd $588
Similar to Model 612 except more elaborate engraving on frame (60 percent coverage), trap- or skeet-style stock and semi-beavertail forearm of fancy walnut, recoil pad on trap stock. Bbls.: Wide vent rib; 29.75-inch, IM/F choke on Trap Gun; 27-inch, SK choke on Skeet Gun. Weight: Trap, 7 lbs., 14 oz.; Skeet, 7 lbs., 11 oz. Made 1972-74.

MODEL 2300T TRAP GUN,
MODEL 2300S SKEET GUN . . . . . NiB $1111 Ex $903 Gd $635
Same as models 2200T and 2200S except more elaborate engraving on frame (70% coverage). Made 1972-74.

GRANDEE MODEL GRT/IRS
TRAP/SKEET GUN. . . . . NiB $2662 Ex $2150 Gd $1494
Boxlock w/sideplates. Frame, breech ends of bbls., trigger guard and locking lever fully engraved and gold inlaid. Auto ejectors. Selective single trigger. 12 ga. Bbls.: Wide vent rib; 29-inch, F choke on Trap Gun; 27-inch, SK choke on Skeet Gun. Weight: Trap, 7 lbs., 14 oz.; Skeet, 7 lbs., 11 oz. Trap- or skeet-style stock and semi-beavertail forearm of extra fancy wood, recoil pad on trap stock. Made 1972-74.

MITCHELL ARMS — Santa Ana, California

MODEL 9104/9105 PUMP SHOTGUNS
Slide action in Field/Riot configuration. Gauge: 12; 5-round tubular magazine. 20-inch bbl.; fixed choke or screw-in tubes. Weight: 6.5 lbs. Plain walnut stock. Made 1994 to date.

(*cont'd.*) **MODEL 9104/9105 PUMP SHOTGUNS**
Model 9104 (w/plain bbl.) . . . . NiB $258 Ex $211 Gd $149
Model 9105 (w/rifle sight). . . . . NiB $526 Ex $221 Gd $974
W/choke tubes, add $20

MODEL 9108/9109 PUMP SHOTGUN
Slide action in Military/Police/Riot configuration. Gauge: 12, 7-round tubular magazine. 20-inch bbl.; fixed choke or screw-in tubes. Weight: 6.5 lbs. Plain walnut stock and grooved slide handle w/brown, green or black finish. Blued metal. Made 1994 to date.
Model 9108 (w/plain bbl.) . . . . NiB $265 Ex $216 Gd $154
Model 9109 (w/rifle sights) . . . . NiB $286 Ex $231 Gd $164
W/choke tubes, add $20

MODEL 9111/9113 PUMP SHOTGUN
Slide action in Military/Police/Riot configuration. Gauge: 12; 6-round tubular magazine. 18.5-inch bbl.; fixed choke or screw-in tubes. Weight: 6.5 lbs. Synthetic or plain walnut stock and grooved slide handle w/brown, green or black finish. Blued metal. Made 1994 to date.
Model 9111 (w/plain bbl.) . . . . NiB $258 Ex $211 Gd $151
Model 9113 (w/rifle sights) . . . . NiB $283 Ex $231 Gd $164
W/choke tubes, add $20

MODEL 9114/9114FS
Slide action in Military/Police/Riot configuration. Gauge: 12; 7-round tubular magazine. 20-inch bbl.; fixed choke or screw-in tubes. Weight: 6.5-7 lbs. Synthetic pistol-grip or folding stock. Blued metal. Made 1994 to date.
Model 9114. . . . . NiB $309 Ex $251 Gd $178
Model 9114FS . . . . NiB $341 Ex $277 Gd $195

MODEL 9115/9115FS
PUMP SHOTGUN. . . . . NiB $341 Ex $277 Gd $195
Slide action in Military/Police/Riot configuration. Gauge: 12; 6-round tubular magazine. 18.5-inch bbl. w/heat-shield handguard. Weight: 7 lbs. Gray synthetic stock and slide handle. Parkerized metal. Made 1994 to date.

MONTGOMERY WARD

See shotgun listings under "W"

MORRONE SHOTGUN — Manufactured by Rhode Island Arms Company, Hope Valley, RI

STANDARD MODEL 46 O/U . . . . NiB $1010 Ex $816 Gd $567
Boxlock. Plain extractors. Non-selective single trigger. Gauges: 12, 20. Bbls.: Plain, vent rib; 26-inch IC/M; 28-inch M/F choke. Weight: About 7 lbs., 12 ga.; 6 lbs., 20 ga. Checkered straight- or pistol-grip stock and forearm. Made 1949-53. Note: Fewer than 500 of these guns were produced, about 50 in 20 ga.. A few had vent-rib bbls. Value shown is for 12 ga. w/plain bbls.. The rare 20 ga. and vent-rib types should bring considerably more.

Mossberg Model 83D

Mossberg Model 85D
Bolt-Action Repeating Shotgun

Mossberg Model 183K

Mossberg Model 185K

Mossberg Model 200K
Slide-Action Repeater

Mossberg Model 395K
Bolt-Action Repeater

O. F. MOSSBERG & SONS, INC. — North Haven, Connecticut, Formerly New Haven, Conn.

MODEL 83D OR 183D .... NiB $144 Ex $118 Gd $83
3-round. Takedown. .410 ga. only. Two shell fixed top-loading magazine. 23-inch bbl. w/two interchangeable choke tubes (M/F). Later production had 24-inch bbl. Plain one-piece pistol-grip stock. Weight: about 5.5 lbs. Originally designated Model 83D, changed in 1947 to Model 183D. Made 1940-71.

MODEL 85D OR 185D BOLT-ACTION REPEATING SHOTGUN .... NiB $124 Ex $102 Gd $71
Takedown. Three-round. 20 ga. only. Two-shell detachable box magazine. 25-inch bbl., three interchangeable choke tubes (F, M, IC). *(cont'd.)* **MODEL 85D OR 185D**
Later production had 26-inch bbl. w/F/IC choke tubes. Weight: About 6.25 lbs. Plain one-piece, pistol-grip stock. Originally designated Model 85D, changed in 1947 to Model 185D. Made 1940-71.

MODEL 183K .... NiB $138 Ex $112 Gd $80
Same as Model 183D except has 25-inch bbl. w/variable C-Lect-Choke instead of interchangeable choke tubes. Made 1953-86.

MODEL 185K .... NiB $145 Ex $118 Gd $83
Same as Model 185D except has variable C-Lect-Choke instead of interchangeable choke tubes. Made 1950-63.

MODEL 190D .... NiB $138 Ex $112 Gd $80
Same as Model 185D except in 16 ga. Weight: About 6 lbs. Made 1955-71.

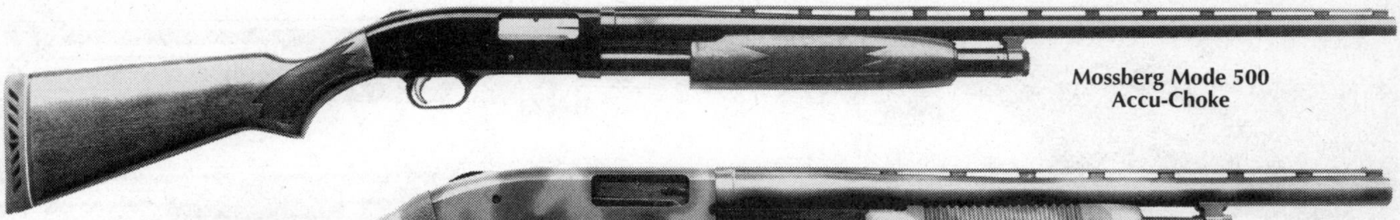

Mossberg Mode 500
Accu-Choke

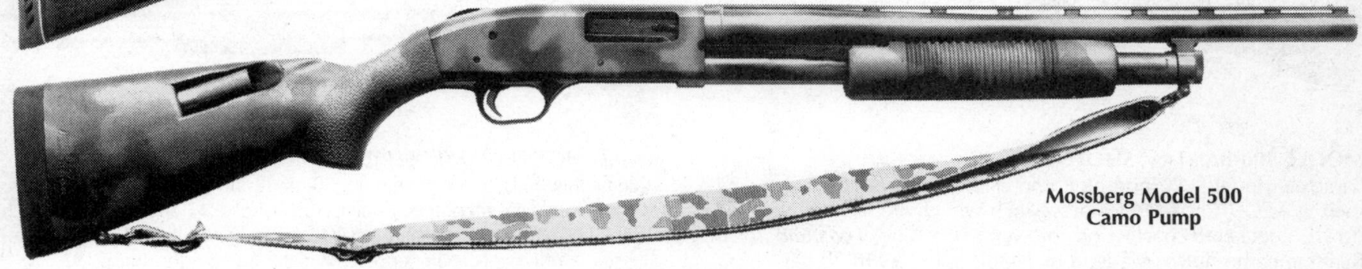

Mossberg Model 500
Camo Pump

Mossberg Model 500
Bullpup Shotgun

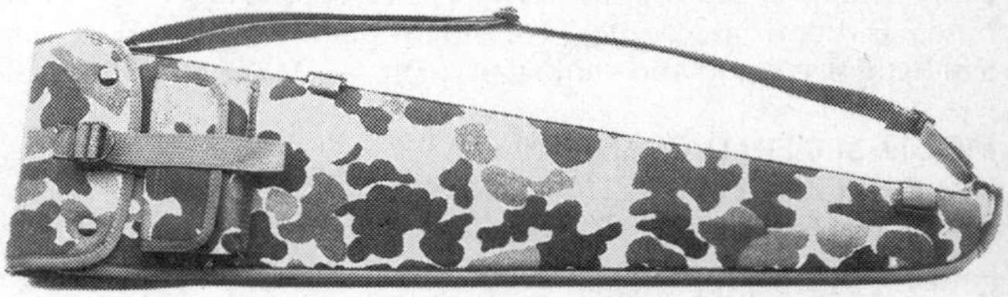

MODEL 190K . . . . NiB $145 Ex $118 Gd $83
Same as Model 185K except in 16 ga. Takedown. Three round capacity; 2-round magazine. Weight: About 6.75 lbs. Made 1956-63.

MODEL 195D . . . . NiB $145 Ex $117 Gd $83
Same as Model 185D except in 12 ga. Takedown. Three round capacity; 2-round magazine. Weight: About 6.75 lbs. Made 1955-71.

MODEL 195K . . . . NiB $145 Ex $117 Gd $83
Same as Model 185K except in 12 ga. Takedown. Three round capacity; 2-round magazine. Weight: About 7.5 lbs. Made 1956-63.

MODEL 200D . . . . NiB $150 Ex $122 Gd $86
Same as Model 200K except w/two interchangeable choke tubes instead of C-Lect choke. Made 1955-59.

MODEL 200K
SLIDE-ACTION REPEATER. . . . . NiB $165 Ex $134 Gd $93
12 ga. 3-round detachable box magazine. 28-inch bbl. C-Lect choke. Plain pistol-grip stock. Black nylon slide handle. Weight: About 7.5 lbs. Made 1955-59.

MODEL 395K BOLT-ACTION REPEATER . . . . . . NiB $139 Ex $113 Gd $80
Takedown. Three round (detachable-clip magazine holds two rounds).12 ga. (3-inch chamber). 28-inch bbl. w/C-Lect-Choke. Weight: About 7.5 lbs. Monte Carlo stock w/recoil pad. Made 1963-83.

MODEL 385K . . . . NiB $139 Ex $113 Gd $80
Same as Model 395K except 20 ga. (3-inch), 26-inch bbl. w/C-Lect-Choke. Weight: About 6.25 lbs.

Mossberg Model 500
Camper

MODEL 390K . . . . NiB $150 Ex $122 Gd $86
Same as Model 395K except 16 ga. (2.75-inch). Made 1963-74.

MODEL 395S SLUGSTER. . . . . NiB $178 Ex $144 Gd $101
Same as Model 395K except has 24-inch bbl., cylinder bore, rifle sights, swivels and web sling. Weight: About 7 lbs. Made 1968-81.

MODEL 500 ACCU-CHOKE SHOTGUN . . . . . NiB $284 Ex $229 Gd $159
Pump-action. Gauge: 12. 24- or 28-inch bbl. Weight: 7.25 lbs. Checkered walnut-finished wood stock w/ventilated recoil pad. Available w/synthetic field or Speed-Feed stocks. Drilled and tapped receivers, swivels and camo sling on camo models. Made from 1987 to date.

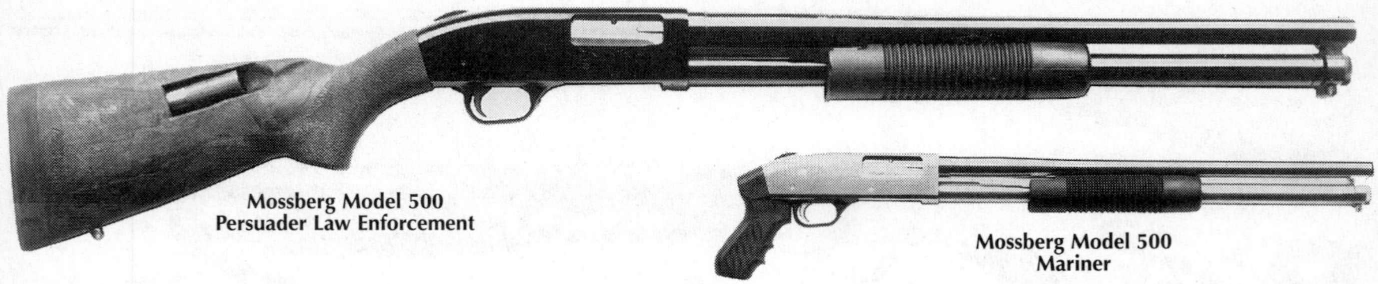

Mossberg Model 500
Persuader Law Enforcement

Mossberg Model 500
Mariner

MODEL 500 BANTAM SHOTGUN
Same as Model 500 Sporting Pump except 20 or .410 ga. only. 22-inch w/ACCU-Choke tubes or 24-inch w/F choke; vent rib. Scaled-down checkered hardwood or synthetic stock w/standard or Realtree camo finish. Made from 1990-96 and 1998-99.
Bantam Model (hardwood stock) . . . . NiB $246 Ex $198 Gd $138
Bantam Model (synthetic stock) . . . . NiB $232 Ex $188 Gd $130
Bantam Model (Realtree camo), add. $50

MODEL 500 BULLPUP SHOTGUN . . . . . . NiB $501 Ex $404 Gd $281
Pump. Gauge: 12. Six or 8-round capacity. Bbl.: 18.5 to 20 inches. 26.5 and 28.5 inches overall. Weight: About 9.5 lbs. Multiple independent safety systems. Dual pistol grips, rubber recoil pad. Fully enclosed rifle-type sights. Synthetic stock. Ventilated bbl. heat shield. Made 1987-90.

MODEL 500 CAMO PUMP
Same as Model 500 Sporting Pump except 12 ga. only. Receiver drilled and tapped. QD swivels and camo sling. Special camouflage finish.
Standard model . . . . NiB $253 Ex $200 Gd $141
Combo model (w/ext. Slugster bbl.) . . . NiB $321 Ex $252 Gd $176

MODEL 500 CAMPER . . . . NiB $261 Ex $213 Gd $149
Same general specifications as Model 500 Field Grade except .410 bore, 6-round magazine, 18.5-inch plain cylinder bore bbl. Synthetic pistol grip and camo carrying case. Made 1986-90.

MODEL 500 FIELD GRADE HAMMERLESS SLIDE-ACTION REPEATER
Pre-1977 type. Takedown. Gauges: 12, 16, 20, .410. Three inch chamber (2.75-inch in 16 ga.). Tubular magazine holds five 2.75-inch rounds or four three-inch. Bbls.: Plain- 30-inch regular or heavy Magnum, F choke (12 ga. only); 28-inch, M or F; 26-inch, IC or adj. C-Lect-Choke; 24-inch Slugster, cylinder bore, w/rifle sights. Weight: 5.75 to lbs. Plain pistol-grip stock w/recoil pad, grooved slide handle. After 1973, these guns have checkered stock and slide handles; Models 500AM and 500AS have receivers etched w/game scenes. The latter has swivels and sling. Made 1962-76.
Model 500A, 12 ga., ... NiB $264 Ex $215 Gd $151
Model 500AM, 12 ga., hvy. Mag. bbl. . . . . NiB $272 Ex $221 Gd $155
Model 500AK, 12 ga., C-Lect-Choke . . . . NiB $304 Ex $247 Gd $173
Model 500AS, 12 ga., Slugster . . . . NiB $302 Ex $253 Gd $177
Model 500B 16 ga., ... NiB $264 Ex $215 Gd $151
Model 500BK, 16 ga., C-Lect-Choke . . . . . NiB $318 Ex $257 Gd $180
Model 500BS, 16 ga., Slugster . . . . NiB $304 Ex $247 Gd $173
Model 500C 20 ga., ... NiB $266 Ex $216 Gd $152
Model 500CK, 20 ga., C-Lect-Choke . . . . . NiB $337 Ex $273 Gd $190
Model 500CS, 20 ga., Slugster . . . . NiB $304 Ex $247 Gd $173
Model 500E, .410 ga., ... NiB $330 Ex $267 Gd $187
Model 500EK, .410 ga., C-Lect-Choke . . . . NiB $369 Ex $298 Gd $208

MODEL 500 "L" SERIES
"L" in model designation. Same as pre-1977 Model 500 Field Grade except not available in 16 ga., has receiver etched w/different game scenes; Accu-Choke w/three interchangeable tubes (IC, M, F) standard, restyled stock and

(*cont'd.*) MODEL 500 "L" SERIES
slide handle. Bbls.: plain or vent rib; 30- or 32-inch, heavy, F choke (12 ga. Magnum and vent rib only); 28-inch, Accu-Choke (12 and 20 ga.); 26-inch F choke (.410 bore only); 18.5-inch (12 ga. only), 24-inch (12 and 20 ga.) Slugster w/rifle sights, cylinder bore. Weight: 6 to 8.5 lbs. Intro. 1977.
Model 500ALD, 12 ga., plain bbl. (disc. 1980) . . . . NiB $296 Ex $242 Gd $173
Model 500ALDR, 12 ga., vent rib . . . . NiB $337 Ex $273 Gd $190
Model 500ALMR, 12 ga., Heavy Duck Gun (disc. 1980) . . . . NiB $337 Ex $273 Gd $190
Model 500ALS, 12 ga., Slugster (disc. 1981) . . . NiB $738 Ex $221 Gd $155
Model 500CLD, 20 ga., plain bbl. (disc. 1980) . . . . NiB $266 Ex $216 Gd $152
Model 500CLDR, 20 ga., vent rib . . . . NiB $304 Ex $247 Gd $173
Model 500CLS, 20 ga., Slugster (disc. 1980) . . . . NiB $337 Ex $273 Gd $190
Model 500EL, .410 ga., plain bbl. (disc. 1980) . . . . NiB $292 Ex $236 Gd $165
Model 500ELR, .410 ga., vent rib . . . . NiB $337 Ex $273 Gd $190

MODEL 500 MARINER SHOTGUN . . . . . . NiB $427 Ex $324 Gd $169
Slide action. Gauge: 12. 18.5 or 20-inch bbl. Six round and 8-round respectively. Weight: 7.25 lbs. High-strength synthetic buttstock and forend. Available in extra round-carrying Speed Feed synthetic buttstock. All metal treated for protection against saltwater corrosion. Intro. 1987.

MODEL 500 MUZZLE LOADER COMBO . . NiB $341 Ex $284 Gd $197
Same as Model 500 Sporting Pump except w/extra 24-inch rifled .50-caliber muzzleloading bbl. w/ramrod. Made from 1992 to date.

MODEL 500 PERSUADER LAW ENFORCEMENT
Similar to pre-1977 Model 500 Field Grade except 12 ga. only, 6- or 8-round capacity, has 18.5- or 20-inch plain bbl., cylinder bore, either shotgun or rifle sights, plain pistol-grip stock and grooved slide handle, sling swivels. Special Model 500ATP8-SP has bayonet lug, Parkerized finish. Currently manufactured.
Model 500ATP6, 6-round, 18.5-inch bbl., shotgun sights . . . . NiB $264 Ex $215 Gd $151
Model 500ATP6CN, 6-round, nickle finish "Cruiser" pistol-grip. . . . . NiB $279 Ex $225 Gd $158
Model 500ATP6N, 6-round, nickel finish, 2.75- or 3-inch Mag. shells . . . . NiB $271 Ex $220 Gd $154
Model 500ATP6S, 6-round, 18.5-inch bbl., rifle sights . . . . NiB $264 Ex $215 Gd $151
Model 500ATP8, 8-round, 20-inch bbl., shotgun sights . . . . NiB $291 Ex $236 Gd $164
Model 500ATP8S, 8-round, 20-inch bbl., rifle sights . . . . NiB $305 Ex $247 Gd $173
Model 500ATP8-SP Spec. Enforcement . . . NiB $358 Ex $290 Gd $203
Model 500 Bullpup . . . . NiB $554 Ex $446 Gd $310
Model 500 Intimidator w/laser sight, blued . . . NiB $512 Ex $414 Gd $288
Model 500 Intimidator w/laser sight, parkerized . . . . NiB $527 Ex $425 Gd $295
Model 500 Security combo pack . . . . NiB $223 Ex $182 Gd $130
Model 500 Cruiser w/pistol grip . . . . NiB $223 Ex $182 Gd $130

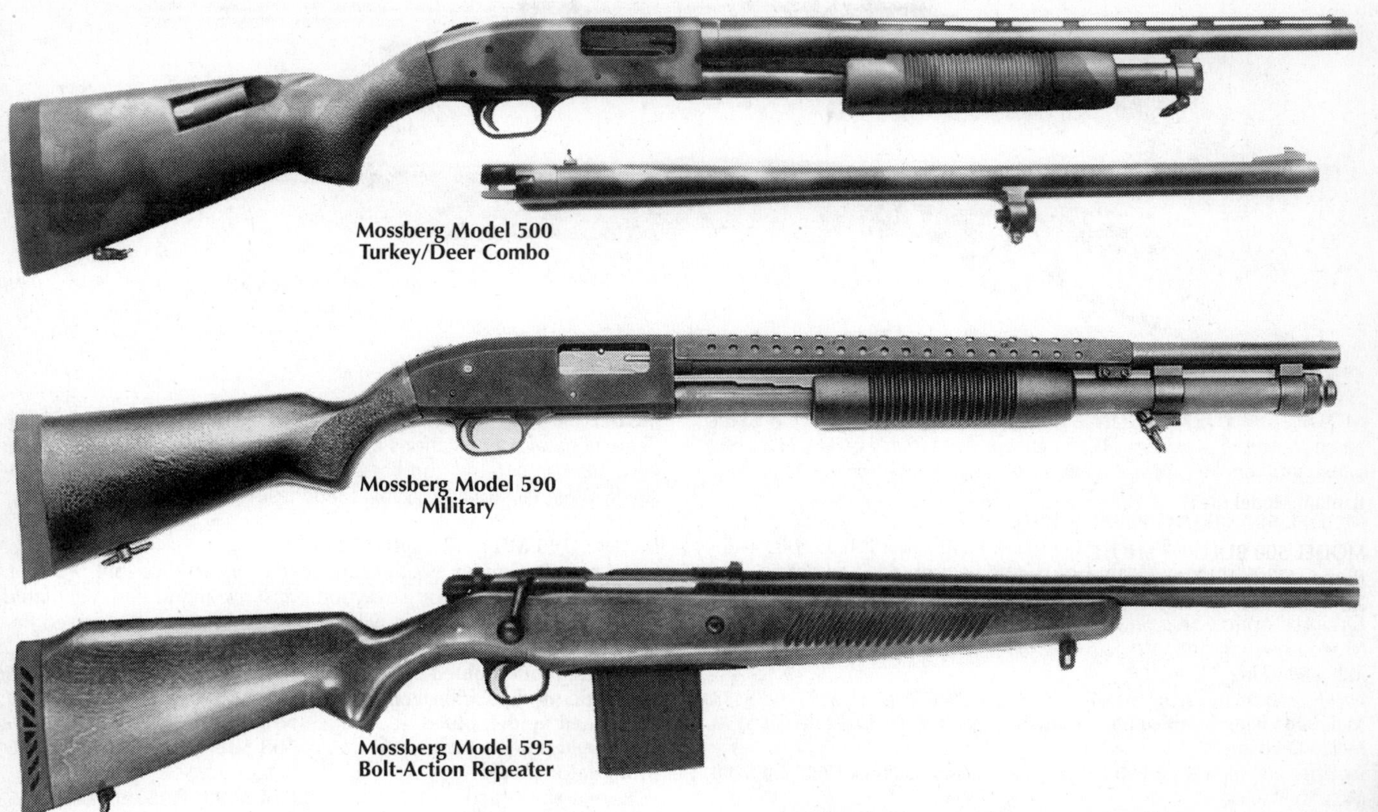

Mossberg Model 500 Turkey/Deer Combo

Mossberg Model 590 Military

Mossberg Model 595 Bolt-Action Repeater

MODEL 500 PIGEON GRADE
Same as Model 500 Super Grade except higher quality w/fancy wood, floating vent rib; field gun hunting dog etching, trap and skeet guns have scroll etching. Bbls.: 30-inch, F choke (12 ga. only); 28-inch, M choke; 26-inch, SK choke or C-Lect-Choke. Made 1971-75.

Model 500APR, 12 ga., field, trap or skeet . . . NiB $476 Ex $385 Gd $270
Model 500APKR, 12 ga.
field gun, C-Lect-Choke . . . . NiB $488 Ex $396 Gd $277
Model 500 APTR, 12 ga.,
Trap gun, Monte Carlo stock . . . . NiB $572 Ex $463 Gd $323
Model 500CPR, 20 ga., field or skeet gun . . . . NiB $495 Ex $401 Gd $280
Model 500EPR, .410 ga.
field or skeet gun . . . . NiB $508 Ex $411 Gd $288

MODEL 500 PUMP COMBO SHOTGUN . . . . NiB $340 Ex $277 Gd $197
Gauges: 12 and 20. 24- and 28-inch bbl. w/adj. rifle sights. Weight: 7 to 7.25 lbs. Available w/blued or camo finish. Drilled and tapped receiver w/sling swivels and camo web sling. Made from 1987 to date.

MODEL 500 PUMP SLUGSTER SHOTGUN
Gauges: 12 or 20 w/3-inch chamber. 24-inch smoothbore or rifled bbl. w/adj. rifle sights or intregral scope mount and optional muzzle break (1997 porting became standard). Weight: 7 to 7.25 lbs. Wood or synthetic stock w/standard or Woodland Camo finish. Blued, matte black or Marinecote metal finish. Drilled and tapped receiver w/camo sling and swivels. Made 1987 to date.

Slugster (w/cyl. bore, rifle sights) . . . . NiB $267 Ex $218 Gd $154
Slugster (w/rifled bore, ported) . . . . NiB $331 Ex $269 Gd $190
Slugster (w/rifled bore, unported) . . . . NiB $296 Ex $240 Gd $170
Slugster (w/rifled bore, ported,
integral scope mount) . . . . NiB $366 Ex $297 Gd $208
Slugster (w/Marinecote and
synthetic stock), add $60
Slugster (w/Truglo fiber optics), add $30

MODEL 500 REGAL SLIDE-ACTION REPEATER
Similar to regular Model 500 except higher quality workmanship throughout. Gauges: 12 and 20. Bbls.: 26- and 28-inch w/various chokes, or Accu-Choke. Weight: 6.75 to 7.5 lbs. Checkered walnut stock and forearm. Made 1985 to date.

Model 500 w/Accu-Choke . . . . NiB $269 Ex $220 Gd $156
Model 500 w/fixed choke . . . . NiB $250 Ex $203 Gd $145

MODEL 500 SPORTING PUMP
Gauges: 12, 20 or .410, 2.75- or 3-inch chamber. Bbls.: 22 to 28 inches w/fixed choke or screw-in tubes; plain or vent rib. Weight: 6.25 to 7.25 lbs. White bead front sight, brass mid-bead. Checkered hardwood buttstock and forend w/walnut finish.

Standard model . . . . NiB $271 Ex $221 Gd $157
Field combo (w/extra Slugster bbl.) . . . . NiB $335 Ex $272 Gd $192

MODEL 500 SUPER GRADE
Same as pre-1977 Model 500 Field Grade except not made in 16 ga., has vent rib bbl., checkered pistol grip and slide handle. Made 1965-76.

Model 500AR, 12 ga. . . . . NiB $284 Ex $230 Gd $163
Model 500AMR, 12 ga.,
heavy magnum bbl. . . . . NiB $317 Ex $258 Gd $182
Model 500AKR, 12 ga., C-Lect-Choke . . . . NiB $324 Ex $263 Gd $185
Model 500CR 20 ga. . . . . NiB $304 Ex $247 Gd $174
Model 500CKk, 20 ga., C-Lect-Choke . . . . NiB $392 Ex $338 Gd $271
Model 500ER, .410 ga.. NiB $276 Ex $225 Gd $159
Model 500EKR, .410 ga., C-Lect-Choke . . . . . . NiB $344 Ex $280 Gd $196

MODEL 500 TURKEY/DEER COMBO. . . . . NiB $364 Ex $295 Gd $206
Pump (slide action). Gauge: 12. 20- and 24-inch bbls. Weight: 7.25 lbs. Drilled and tapped receiver, camo sling and swivels. Adj. rifle sights and camo finish. Vent rib. Made from 1987 to date.

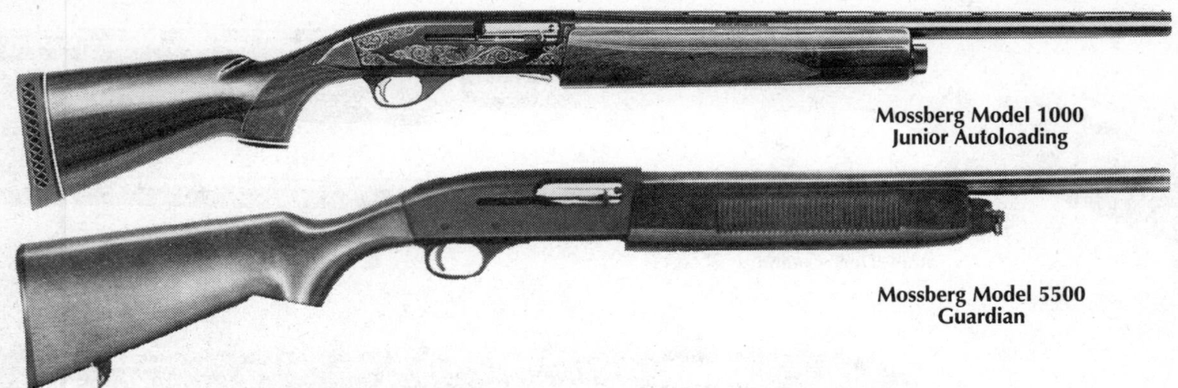

Mossberg Model 1000
Junior Autoloading

Mossberg Model 5500
Guardian

MODEL 500 TURKEY GUN....... NiB $332 Ex $269 Gd $188
Same as Model 500 Camo Pump except w/24-inch ACCU-Choke bbl. w/extra full choke tube and ghost ring sights. Made from 1992 to date.

MODEL 500 VIKING PUMP SHOTGUN
Gauges: 12 or 20 w/3-inch chamber. 24-, 26- or 28-inch bbls. available in smoothbore w/Accu-Choke and vent rib or rifled bore w/iron sights and optional muzzle brake (1997 porting became standard). Optional optics: Slug Shooting System (SSS). Weight: 6.9 to 7.2 lbs. Moss-green synthetic stock. Matte black metal finish. Made 1996-98.
Mdl. 500 Viking
(w/VR & choke tubes, unported)........... NiB $237 Ex $193 Gd $135
Mdl. 500 Viking (w/rifled bore, ported) ... NiB $291 Ex $226 Gd $158
Mdl. 500 Viking
(w/rifled bore, SSS & ported) .... NiB $369 Ex $298 Gd $208
Mdl. 500 Viking
(w/rifled bore, unported) .... NiB $266 Ex $216 Gd $155
Mdl. 500 Viking Turkey
(w/VR, tubes, ported) .... NiB $241 Ex $195 Gd $138

MODEL 500
WATERFOWL/DEER COMBO.......... NiB $356 Ex $288 Gd $200
Same general specifications as the Turkey/Deer combo except w/either 28- or 30-inch bbl. along w/the 24-inch bbl. Made from 1987 to date.

MODEL 500 ATR SUPER
GRADE TRAP .... NiB $449 Ex $363 Gd $253
Same as pre-1977 Model 500 Field Grade except 12 ga. only w/vent-rib bbl.; 30-inch F choke, checkered Monte Carlo stock w/recoil pad, beavertail slide handle. Made 1968-71.

MODEL 500DSPR DUCK STAMP
COMMEMORATIVE .... NiB $713 Ex $575 Gd $399
Limited edition of 1000 to commemorate the Migratory Bird Hunting Stamp program. Same as Model 500DSPR Pigeon Grade 12-Gauge Magnum Heavy Duck Gun w/heavy 30-inch vent-rib bbl., F choke; receiver has special wood duck etching. Gun accompanied by a special wall plaque. Made in 1975.

MODEL 590 BULLPUP .... NiB $471 Ex $380 Gd $265
Same general specifications as the Model 500 Bullpup except 20-inch bbl. and 9-round magazine. Made 1989-90.

MODEL 590 MARINER PUMP
Same general specifications as the Model 590 Military Security except has Marinecote metal finish and field configuration synthetic stock w/pistiol-grip conversion included. Made from 1989 to date.
Model 590 Mariner (w/18.5-inch bbl.)...... NiB $334 Ex $270 Gd $188
Model 590 Mariner (w/20-inch bbl.) .... NiB $349 Ex $282 Gd $196
Model 590 Mariner (w/grip conversion), add $20
Model 590 Mariner (w/ghost ring sight), add $50

MODEL 590 MILITARY SECURITY.......... NiB $409 Ex $331 Gd $231
Same general specifications as the Model 590 Military except there is no heat shield and gun has short pistol-grip style instead of buttstock. Weight: About 6.75 lbs. Made from 1987 to date.

MODEL 590 MILITARY SHOTGUN
Slide-action. Gauge: 12. 9-round capacity. 20-inch bbl. Weight: About 7 lbs. Synthetic or hardwood buttstock and forend. Ventilated bbl. heat shields. Equipped w/bayonet lug. Blued or Parkerized finish. Made from 1987 to date. See illustration Previous Page.
Synthetic model, blued .... NiB $361 Ex $293 Gd $205
Synthetic model Parkerized ...... NiB $387 Ex $314 Gd $220
Speedfeed model, blued .... NiB $380 Ex $308 Gd $216
Speedfeed model, Parkerized ..... NiB $380 Ex $308 Gd $216
Intimidator model
w/laser sight, blued .... NiB $490 Ex $396 Gd $275
Intimidator model
w/laser sight, Parkerized .... NiB $503 Ex $406 Gd $283
For ghost ring sight, add $75

MODEL 595/595K
BOLT-ACTION REPEATER .... NiB $190 Ex $153 Gd $107
12 ga. only. Four round detachable magazine. 18.5-inch bbl. Weight: About 7 lbs. Walnut finished stock w/recoil pad and sling swivels. Made 1985-86.

MODEL 695 BOLT-ACTION SLUGSTER
Gauge: 12 w/3-inch chamber. Two round detachable magazine. 22-inch fully rifled and ported bbl. w/blade front and folding leaf rear sights. Receiver drilled and tapped for Weaver style scope bases. Also available w/1.5x-4.5x scope or fiber optics installed. Weight: 7.5 lbs. Black synthetic stock w/swivel studs and recoil pad. Made 1996 to date.
Model 695 (w/ACCU-choke bbl.) .. NiB $220 Ex $178 Gd $123
Model 695
(w/open sights) .... NiB $284 Ex $228 Gd $158
Model 695
(w/1.5x-4.5x Bushnell scope) ..... NiB $304 Ex $326 Gd $226
Model 695 (w/Truglo fiber optics) .... NiB $319 Ex $258 Gd $180
Model 695 OFM Camo .... NiB $272 Ex $219 Gd $152

MODEL 695 BOLT-ACTION TURKEY GUN NiB $274 Ex $220 Gd $153
Similar to 695 Slugster Model except has smoothbore 22-inch bbl. w/extra-full turkey Accu-choke tube. Bead front and U-notch rear sights. Full OFM camo finish. Made 1996 to date.

MODEL 712 AUTOLOADING SHOTGUN
Gas-operated, takedown, hammerless shotgun w/5-round (4-round w/3-inch chamber) tubular magazine. 12 ga. Bbls.: 28-inch vent rib or 24-inch plain bbl. Slugster w/rifle sights. Fixed choke or ACCU-choke tube system. Weight: 7.5 lbs. Plain alloy receiver w/top-mounted ambidextrous safety. Checkered.

(cont'd.) **MODEL 712 AUTOLOADING SHOTGUN**

Mdl. 712 w/fixed chokes . . . . NiB $290 Ex $236 Gd $166
Mdl. 712 w/ACCU-Choke tube system . . . . . NiB $324 Ex $263 Gd $185
Mdl. 712 Regal w/ACCU-Choke tube system . NiB $358 Ex $290 Gd $203
Mdl. 712 Regal w/ACCU-Choke II tube sys. . . NiB $392 Ex $317 Gd $222

MODEL 835 FIELD PUMP SHOTGUN

Similar to the Model 9600 Regal except has walnut-stained hardwood stock and one ACCU-Choke tube only.

Standard model . . . . NiB $297 Ex $241 Gd $170
Turkey model . . . . NiB $309 Ex $252 Gd $178
Combo model (24- & 28-inch bbls.) NiB $335 Ex $272 Gd $192

MODEL 835 "NWTF" ULTI-MA SHOTGUN

National Wild Turkey Federation pump-action. Gauge: 12, 3.5-inch chamber. 24-inch vent-rib bbl. w/four ACCU-MAG chokes. Realtree camo finish. QD swivel and post. Made 1989-93.

Limited Edition model . . . . NiB $471 Ex $380 Gd $265
Special Edition model . . . . NiB $400 Ex $324 Gd $227

MODEL 835 REGAL ULTI-MAG PUMP

Gauge: 12, 3.5-inch chamber. Bbls.: 24- or 28-inch vent-rib w/ACCU-Choke screw-in tubes. Weight: 7.75 lbs. White bead front, brass mid-bead. Checkered hardwood or synthetic stock w/camo finish. Made 1991-96.

Special model . . . . NiB $309 Ex $252 Gd $178
Standard model . . . . NiB $380 Ex $308 Gd $216
Camo Synthetic model . . . . NiB $406 Ex $329 Gd $230
Combo model . . . . NiB $438 Ex $355 Gd $248

MODEL 835 VIKING PUMP SHOTGUN

Gauge: 12 w/3-inch chamber. 28-inch smoothbore bbl. w/Accu-Choke, vent rib and optional muzzle brake (in 1997 porting became standard). Weight: 7.7 lbs. Green synthetic stock. Matte black metal finish. Made 1996-98.

Model 835 Viking (w/VR and choke tubes, ported) . . . . NiB $296 Ex $241 Gd $169
Model 835 Viking (w/VR and choke tubes, unported) . . . . NiB $284 Ex $230 Gd $163

MODEL 1000 AUTOLOADING SHOTGUN

Gas-operated, takedown, hammerless shotgun w/tubular magazine. Gauges: 12, 20; 2.75- or 3-inch chamber. Bbls.: 22- to 30-inch vent rib w/fixed choke or ACCU-Choke tubes; or 22-inch plain bbl, Slugster w/rifle sights. Weight: 6.5 to 7.5 lbs. Scroll-engraved alloy receiver, crossbolt-type safety. Checkered walnut buttstock and forend. Imported from Japan 1986-87.

Junior model, 20 ga., 22-inch bbl. . NiB $446 Ex $362 Gd $255
Standard model w/fixed choke . . . . NiB $459 Ex $382 Gd $260
Standard model w/choke tubes . . . NiB $483 Ex $392 Gd $274

MODEL 1000 SUPER AUTOLOADING SHOTGUN

Similar to Model 1000, but in 12 ga. only w/3-inch chamber and new gas metering system. Bbls.: 26-, 28- or 30-inch vent rib w/ACCU-Choke tubes.

Standard model w/choke tubes . . . NiB $535 Ex $435 Gd $305
Waterfowler model (Parkerized) . . NiB $575 Ex $466 Gd $326

MODEL 1000S SUPER SKEET . . . . . NiB $634 Ex $512 Gd $358

Similar to Model 1000 in 12 or 20 ga., except w/all-steel receiver and vented jug-type choke for reduced muzzle jump. Bright-point front sight and brass mid-bead. 1 and 2 oz. forend cap weights.

MODEL 5500 AUTOLOADING SHOTGUN

Gas-operated. Takedown. 12 ga. only. Four round magazine (3-round w/3-inch shells). Bbls.: 18.5- to 30-inch; various chokes. Checkered walnut finished hardwood. Made 1985-86.

Model 5500 w/ACCU-Choke . . . . . NiB $309 Ex $252 Gd $178
Model 5500 modified junior . . . . . NiB $316 Ex $256 Gd $180

(cont'd.) **MODEL 5500 AUTOLOADING SHOTGUN**

Model 5500 Slugster . . . . NiB $326 Ex $265 Gd $187
Model 5500 12 ga. . . . . NiB $280 Ex $228 Gd $161
Model 5500 Guardian . . . . NiB $269 Ex $219 Gd $155

MODEL 5500 MKII AUTOLOADING SHOTGUN

Same as Model 5500 except equipped w/two Accu-Choke bbls.: 26-inch ported for non-Magnum 2.75-inch shells; 28-inch for magnum loads. Made 1988-93.

Standard model . . . . NiB $294 Ex $239 Gd $169
Camo model . . . . NiB $326 Ex $264 Gd $186
NWTF Mossy Oak model . . . . NiB $356 Ex $289 Gd $202
USST model (Made 1991-92) . . . . . NiB $307 Ex $250 Gd $177

MODEL 6000 AUTO SHOTGUN. . . NiB $307 Ex $250 Gd $177

Similar to the Model 9200 Regal except has 28-inch vent-rib bbl. w/mod. ACCU-Choke tube only. Made from 1993 to date.

MODEL 9200 CAMO SHOTGUN

Similar to the Model 9200 Regal except has synthetic stock and forend and is completely finished in camouflage pattern (incl. bbl.). Made from 1993 to date.

Standard model (OFM camo) . . . . . NiB $423 Ex $342 Gd $239
Turkey model (Mossy Oak camo) . . . . . NiB $466 Ex $376 Gd $262
Turkey model (Shadow Branch camo) . . . NiB $550 Ex $444 Gd $308
Comb. model (24 & 28-inch bbls. w/OFM camo) . . . . NiB $515 Ex $417 Gd $289

MODEL 9200 CROWN (REGAL) AUTOLOADER

Gauge: 12; 3-inch chamber. Bbls.: 18.5- to 28-inch w/ACCU-Choke tubes; plain or vent rib. Weight: 7.25 to 7.5 lbs. Checkered hardwood buttstock and forend w/walnut finish. Made from 1992 to date.

Model 9200 Bantam (w/1-inch shorter stock) . . . . NiB $409 Ex $331 Gd $231
Model 9200 w/ACCU-Choke . . . . NiB $423 Ex $342 Gd $239
Model 9200 w/rifled bbl. . . . . NiB $437 Ex $354 Gd $248
Model 9200 Combo (w/extra Slugster bbl.). . . . NiB $488 Ex $394 Gd $273
Model 9200 SP (w/matte blue finish, 18.5-inch bbl.) . . . . NiB $338 Ex $274 Gd $193

MODEL 9200 PERSUADER . . . . NiB $361 Ex $293 Gd $205

Similar to the Model 9200 Regal except has 18.5-inch plain bbl. w/fixed mod. choke. Parkerized finish. Black synthetic stock w/sling swivels. Made 1996 to date.

MODEL 9200 A1 JUNGLE GUN . . . NiB $648 Ex $545 Gd $262

Similar to the Model 9200 Persuader except has mil-spec heavy wall 18.5-inch plain bbl. w/cyl. bore designed for 00 Buck shot. 12 ga. w/2.75-inch chamber. Five round magazine. 38.5 inches overall. Weight: 7 lbs. Black synthetic stock. Parkerized finish. Made 1998 to date.

MODEL 9200 SPECIAL HUNTER . . NiB $423 Ex $342 Gd $239

Similar to the Model 9200 Regal except has 28-inch vent-rib bbl. w/ACCU-Choke tubes. Parkerized finish. Black synthetic stock. Made from 1998 to date.

MODEL 9200 TROPHY

Similar to the Model 9200 Regal except w/24-inch rifled bbl. or 24- or 28-inch vent-rib bbl. w/ACCU-Choke tubes. Checkered walnut stock w/sling swivels. Made from 1992-98.

Trophy (w/vent rib bbl.) $317
Trophy (w/rifled bbl. & cantilever scope mount) $338
Trophy (w/rifled bbl. & rifle sights) $306

MODEL 9200 USST AUTOLOADER $331

Similar to the Model 9200 Regal except has 26-inch vent-rib bbl. w/ACCU-Choke tubes. "United States Shooting Team" engraved on receiver. Made from 1993 to date.

SHOTGUNS

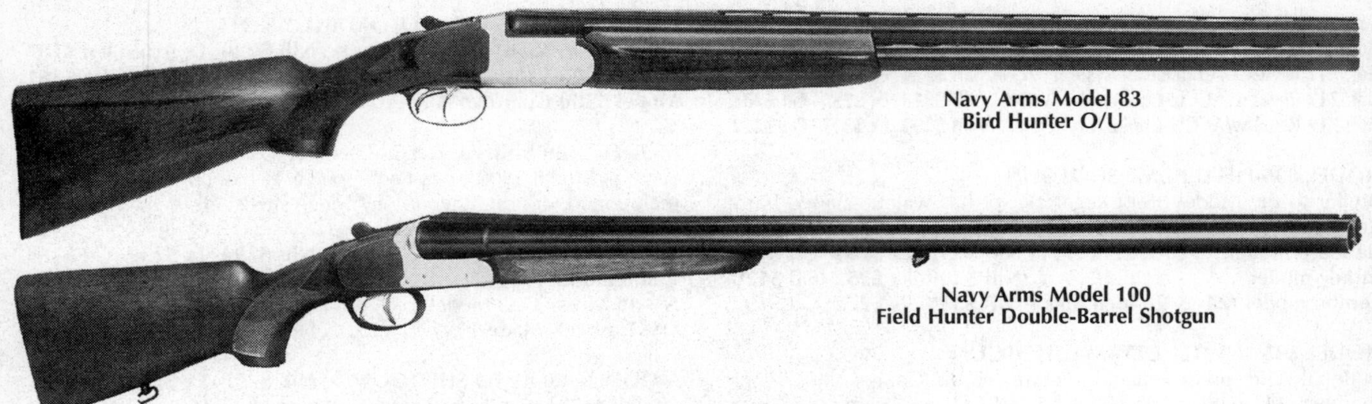

Navy Arms Model 100
Field Hunter Double-Barrel Shotgun

MODEL 9200
VIKING AUTOLOADER. . . . . NiB $387 Ex $312 Gd $217
Gauge: 12 w/3-inch chamber. 28-inch smoothbore bbl. W/Accu-Choke and vent rib. Weight: 7.7 lbs. Green synthetic stock. Matte black metal finish. Made 1996-98.

MODEL HS410
HOME SECURITY PUMP SHOTGUN
Gauge: .410; 3-inch chamber. Bbl.: 18.5-inch w/muzzle brake; blued. Weight: 6.25 lbs. Synthetic stock and pistol-grip slide. Optional laser sight. Made from 1990 to date. A similar version of this gun is marketed by Maverick Arms under the same model designation.
Standard model . . . . NiB $253 Ex $206 Gd $149
Laser model . . . . NiB $433 Ex $350 Gd $243

LINE LAUNCHER. . . . . NiB $897 Ex $723 Gd $501
Gauge: 12 w/blank cartridge. Projectile travels from 250 to 275 feet.

"NEW HAVEN BRAND" SHOTGUNS
Promotional models, similar to their standard guns but plainer in finish, are marketed by Mossberg under the "New Haven" brand name. Values generally are about 20 percent lower than for corresponding standard models.

NAVY ARMS SHOTGUNS — Ridgefield, New Jersey

MODEL 83/93 BIRD HUNTER O/U
Hammerless. Boxlock, engraved receiver. Gauges: 12 and 20; 3-inch chambers. Bbls.: 28-inch chrome lined w/double vent-rib construction. Checkered European walnut stock and forearm. Gold plated triggers. Imported 1984-90.
Model 83 w/extractors . . . . NiB $309 Ex $252 Gd $178
Model 93 w/ejectors . . . . NiB $361 Ex $293 Gd $205

MODEL 95/96 O/U SHOTGUN
Same as the Model 83/93 except w/five interchangeable choke tubes. Imported 1984-90.
Model 95 w/extractors . . . . NiB $400 Ex $324 Gd $227
Model 96 w/ejectors . . . . NiB $528 Ex $426 Gd $295

MODEL 100/150 FIELD HUNTER
DOUBLE-BARREL SHOTGUN
Boxlock. Gauges: 12 and 20. Bbls.: 28-inch chrome lined. Checkered European walnut stock and forearm. Imported 1984-90.
Model 100 . . . . NiB $377 Ex $306 Gd $214
Model 150 (auto ejectors) . . . . . . NiB $490 Ex $396 Gd $275

MODEL 100 O/U SHOTGUN . . . . . NiB $258 Ex $211 Gd $150
Hammerless, takedown shotgun w/engraved chrome receiver. Single trigger. 12, 20, 28, or .410 ga. w/3-inch chambers. Bbls.: 26-inch (F/F or SK/SK); vent rib. Weight: 6.25 lbs. Checkered European walnut buttstock and forend. Imported 1986-90.

NEW ENGLAND FIREARMS — Gardner, Massachusetts

In 1987, New England Firearms was established as an independent company producing selected H&R models under the NEF logo after Harrington & Richardson suspended operations on January 24, 1986. In 1991, H&R 1871, Inc. was formed from the residual of the parent H&R company and then took over the New England Firearms facility. H&R 1871 produced firearms under both their logo and the NEF brand name until 1999, when the Marlin Firearms Company acquired the assets of H&R 1871.

NEW ENGLAND FIREARMS NWTF TURKEY SPECIAL
Similar to Turkey and Goose models except 10 or 20 gauge w/22- or 24-inch plain bbl. w/screw-in full-choke tube. Mossy Oak camo finish on entire gun. Made from 1992-96.
Turkey Special 10 ga. . . . . NiB $209 Ex $180 Gd $164
Turkey Special 20 ga. . . . . NiB $128 Ex 108 Gd $77

NRA FOUNDATION YOUTH . . . . . NiB $191 Ex $156 Gd 112
Smaller scale version of Pardner Model chambered for 20, 28 or .410 w/22- inch plain bbl. High luster blue finish. NRA Foundation logo laser etched on stock. Made 1999 to date.

PARDNER SHOTGUN
Takedown. Side lever. Single bbl. Gauges: 12, 20 and .410 w/3-inch chamber; 16 and 28 w/2.75-inch chamber. 26-, 28- or 32-inch, plain bbl. w/fixed choke. Weight: 5-6 lbs. Bead front sight. Pistol grip-style hardwood stock w/walnut finish. Made from 1988 to date.
Standard model . . . . NiB $116 Ex $95 Gd $70
Youth model . . . . NiB $123 Ex $102 Gd $73
Youth Turkey model . . . . NiB $137 Ex $112 Gd $81
W/32-inch bbl., add $15

PARDNER SPECIAL PURPOSE 10 GA. SHOTGUN
Similar to the standard Pardner model except chambered 10 ga. only w/3.5-inch chamber. 24- or 28-inch, plain bbl. w/full choke tube or fixed choke. Weight: 9.5 lbs. Bead front sight. Pistol-grip-style hardwood stock w/camo or matte black finish. Made from 1989 to date.
Special Purpose model w/fixed choke . . NiB $143 Ex $117 Gd $85
W/camo finish, add $15
W/choke tube, add $20
W/24-inch bbl. turkey option, add $30

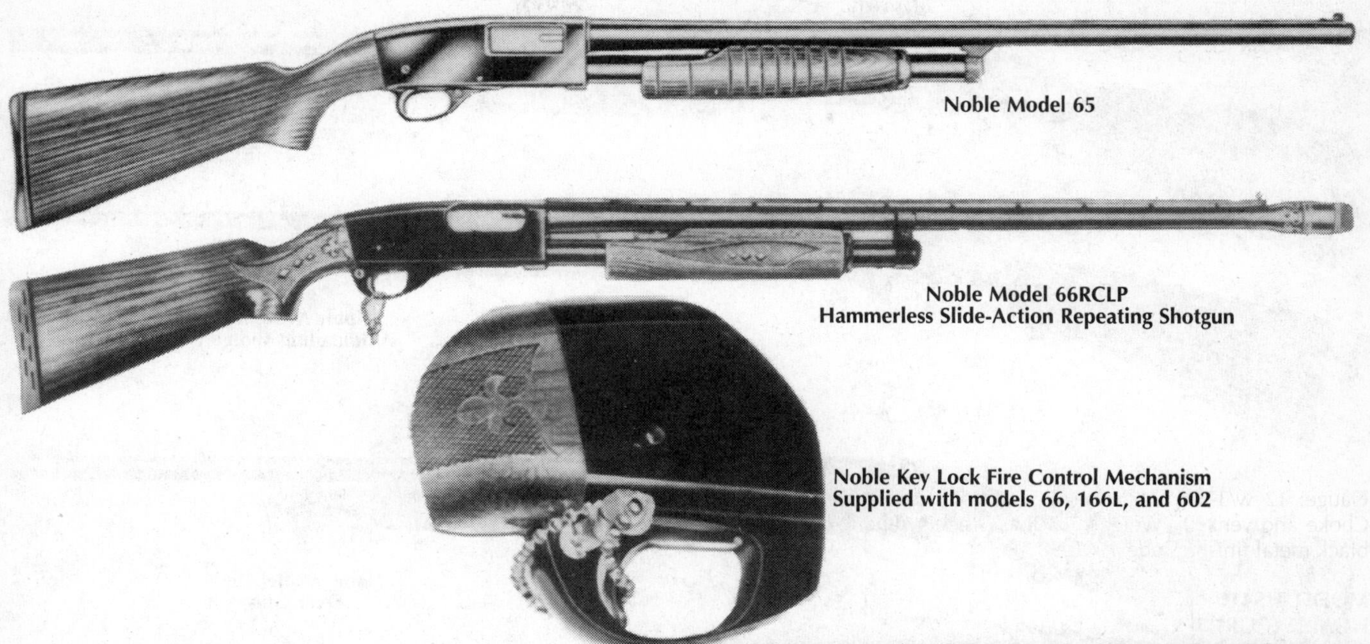

Noble Model 65

Noble Model 66RCLP
Hammerless Slide-Action Repeating Shotgun

Noble Key Lock Fire Control Mechanism
Supplied with models 66, 166L, and 602

PARDNER SPECIAL PURPOSE
WATERFOWL SINGLE-SHOT . . . . . . NiB $169 Ex $137 Gd $96
Similar to Special Purpose 10 Ga. model except w/32-inch bbl. Mossy Oak camo stock w/swivel and sling. Made 1988 to date.

PARDNER TURKEY GUN
Similar to Pardner model except chambered in 12 ga. w/3.0- or 3.5-inch chamber. 24-inch plain bbl. W/turkey full-choke tube or fixed choke. Weight: 9.5 lbs. American hardwood stock w/camo or matte black finish. Made from 1999 to date.
Standard Turkey model . . . . NiB $150 Ex $121 Gd $85
Camo Turkey model . . . . NiB $163 Ex $132 Gd $92

SURVIVOR SERIES
Takedown single bbl. shotgun w/side lever release, Automatic ejector and patented transfer-bar safety. Gauges: 12, 20, and .410/.45 ACP w/3-inch chamber. 22-inch bbl. w/modified choke and bead sight. Weight: 6 lbs. Polymer stock and forend w/hollow cavity for storage. Made 1992-93 and 1995 to date.
12 or 20 ga.
w/blued finish . . . . NiB $128 Ex $104 Gd $73
12 or 20 ga.
w/nickel finish . . . . NiB $160 Ex $130 Gd $91
.410/.45 ACP, add . . . . NiB $46 Ex $38 Gd $28

TRACKER SLUG GUN
Similar to Pardner model except in 10, 12 or 20 ga. w/24-inch w/cylinder choke or rifled slug bbl. (Tracker II). Weight: 6 lbs. American hardwood stock w/walnut or camo finish, Schnabel forend, sling swivel studs. Made from 1992 to date.
Tracker Slug
(10 ga.) . . . . NiB $131 Ex $106 Gd $75
Tracker Slug
(12 or 20 ga.) . . . . NiB $132 Ex $101 Gd $60
Tracker II (rifled bore) . . . . NiB $163 Ex $132 Gd $70

NIKKO FIREARMS LTD. — Tochigi, Japan

See listings under Golden Eagle Firearms, Inc.

NOBLE MANUFACTURING COMPANY — Haydenville, Massachusetts

Series 602 and 70 are similar in appearance to the corresponding Model 66 guns.

MODEL 40 HAMMERLESS SLIDE-ACTION
REPEATING SHOTGUN . . . . NiB $156 Ex $126 Gd $88
Solid frame. 12 ga. only. Five round tubular magazine. 28-inch bbl. w/ventilated Multi-Choke. Weight: About 7.5 lbs. Plain pistol-grip stock, grooved slide handle. Made 1950-55.

MODEL 50
SLIDE-ACTION . . . . NiB $156 Ex $126 Gd $88
Same as Model 40 except w/o Multi-Choke. M or F choke bbl. Made 1953-55.

MODEL 60 HAMMERLESS SLIDE-ACTION
REPEATING SHOTGUN . . . . NiB $219 Ex $177 Gd $123
Solid frame. 12 and 16 ga. Five round tubular magazine. 28-inch bbl. w/adj. choke. Plain pistol-grip stock w/recoil pad, grooved slide handle. Weight: About 7.5 lbs. Made 1955-66.

MODEL 65 . . . . NiB $182 Ex $147 Gd $103
Same as Model 60 except without adj. choke and recoil pad. M or F choke bbl. Made 1955-66.

MODEL 66CLP . . . . NiB $169 Ex $137 Gd $96
Same as Model 66RCLP except has plain bbl. Introduced in 1967. Disc.

MODEL 66RCLP HAMMERLESS SLIDE-ACTION
REPEATING SHOTGUN . . . . NiB $211 Ex $170 Gd $118
Solid frame. Key lock fire control mechanism. Gauges: 12, 16. 3-inch chamber in 12 ga. Five round tubular magazine. 28-inch bbl., vent rib, adj. choke. Weight: About 7.5 lbs. Checkered pistol-grip stock and slide handle, recoil pad. Made 1967-70.

MODEL 66RLP . . . . NiB $194 Ex $157 Gd $110
Same as Model 66RCLP except w/F or M choke. Made 1967-1970.

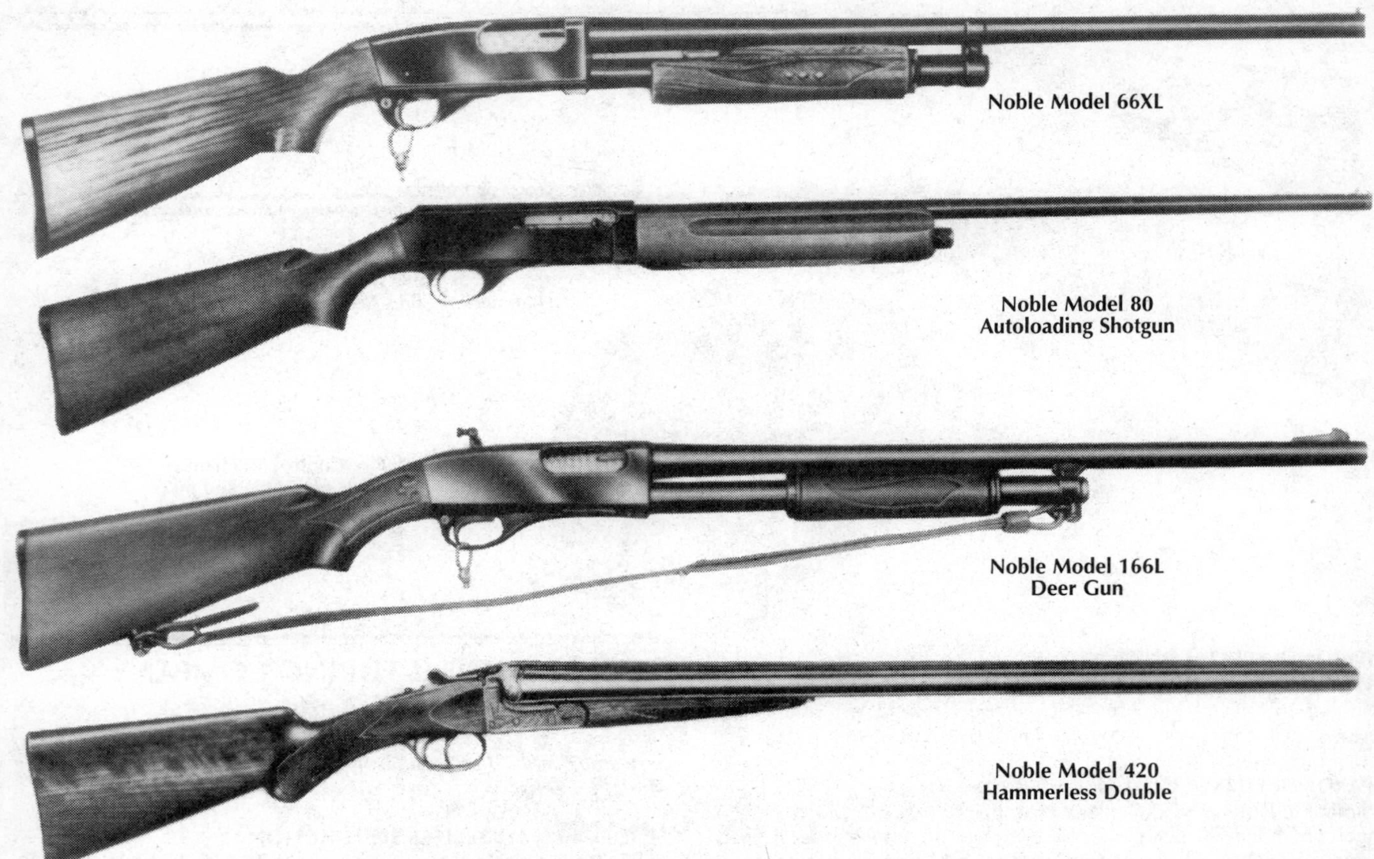

Noble Model 66XL

Noble Model 80
Autoloading Shotgun

Noble Model 166L
Deer Gun

Noble Model 420
Hammerless Double

MODEL 66XL .... NiB $169 Ex $137 Gd $96
Same as Model 66RCL except has plain bbl., F or M choke, slide handle only checkered, no recoil pad. Made 1967-70.

MODEL 70CLP HAMMERLESS SLIDE-ACTION REPEATING SHOTGUN .... NiB $194 Ex $157 Gd $110
Solid frame. .410 gauge. Magazine holds 5 rounds. 26-inch bbl. w/adj. choke. Weight: About 6 lbs. Checkered buttstock and forearm, recoil pad. Made 1958-70.

MODEL 70RCLP .... NiB $202 Ex $162 Gd $113
Same as Model 70CLP except has vent rib. Made 1967-70.

MODEL 70RLP................ NiB $188 Ex $152 Gd $106
Same as Model 70CLP except has vent rib and no adj. choke. Made 1967-70.

MODEL 70XL .... NiB $143 Ex $116 Gd $81
Same as Model 70CLP except without adj. choke and checkering on buttstock. Made 1958-70.

MODEL 80 AUTOLOADING SHOTGUN...... NiB $246 Ex $198 Gd $138
Recoil-operated. .410 ga. Magazine holds three 3-inch shells, four 2.5-inch shells. 26-inch bbl., full choke. Weight: About 6 lbs. Plain pistol-grip stock and fluted forearm. Made 1964-66.

MODEL 166L DEER GUN .... NiB $274 Ex $220 Gd $153
Solid frame. Key lock fire control mechanism. 12 ga. 2.75-inch chamber. Five round tubular magazine. 24-inch plain bbl., specially bored for rifled slug. Lyman peep rear sight, post ramp front sight.

(cont'd.) **MODEL 166L DEER GUN**
Receiver dovetailed for scope mounting. Weight: About 7.25 lbs. Checkered pistol-grip stock and slide handle, swivels and carrying strap. Made 1967-70.

MODEL 420 HAMMERLESS DOUBLE .... NiB $358 Ex $289 Gd $201
Boxlock. Plain extractors. Double triggers. Gauges: 12 ga. 3-inch mag.; 16 ga.; 20 ga. 3-inch mag.; .410 ga. Bbls.: 28-inch, except .410 in 26-inch, M/F choke. Weight: About 6.75 lbs. Engraved frame. Checkered walnut stock and forearm. Made 1958-70.

MODEL 450E HAMMERLESS DOUBLE .... NiB $399 Ex $322 Gd $224
Boxlock. Engraved frame. Selective auto ejectors. Double triggers. Gauges: 12, 16, 20. 3-inch chambers in 12 and 20 ga. 28-inch bbls., M/F choke. Weight: About 6 lbs., 14 oz., 12 ga. Checkered pistol-grip stock and beavertail forearm, recoil pad. Made 1967-70.

MODEL 602CLP .... NiB $214 Ex $174 Gd $122
Same as Model 602RCLP except has plain bbl. Made 1958-70.

MODEL 602RCLP HAMMERLESS SLIDE-ACTION REPEATING SHOTGUN .... NiB $226 Ex $184 Gd $129
Solid frame. Key lock fire control mechanism. 20 ga. 3-inch chamber. Five round tubular magazine. 28-inch bbl., vent rib, adj. choke. Weight: About 6.5 lbs. Checkered pistol-grip stock/slide handle, recoil pad. Made 1967-70.

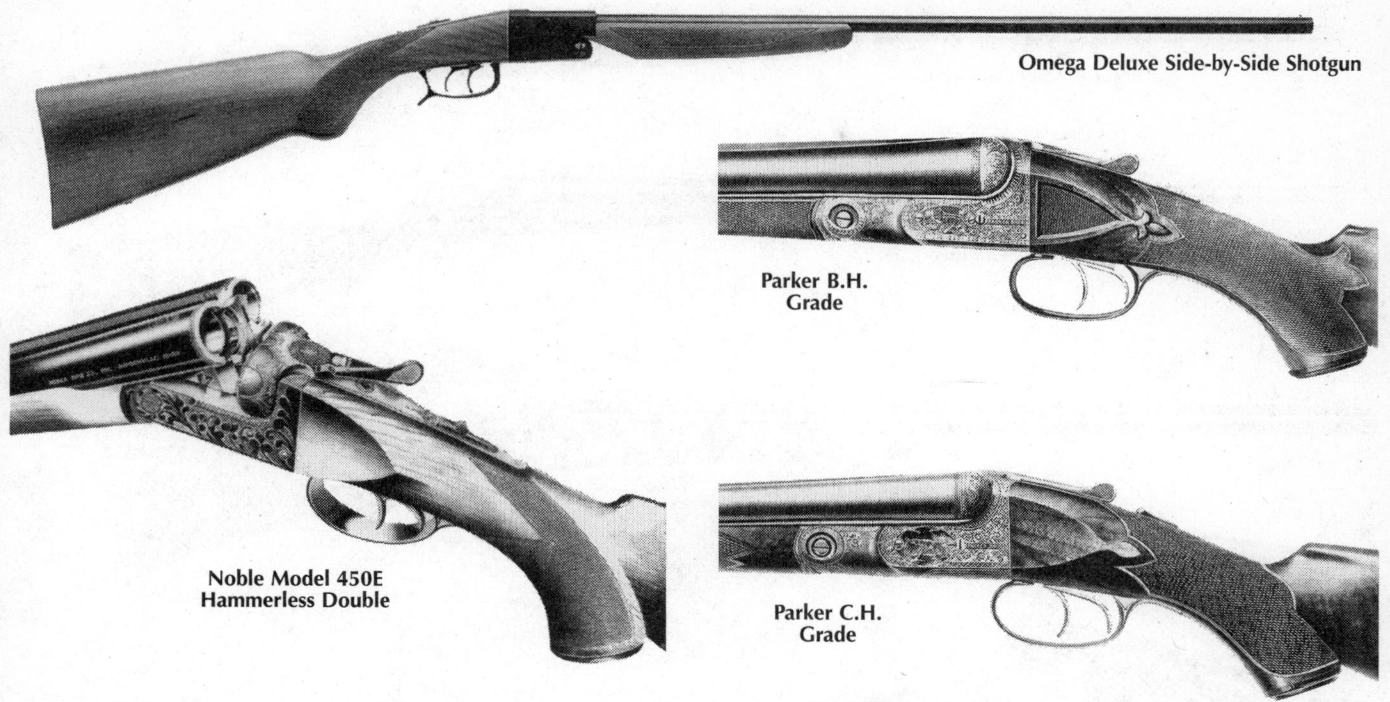
Omega Deluxe Side-by-Side Shotgun

Parker B.H. Grade

Noble Model 450E Hammerless Double

Parker C.H. Grade

MODEL 602RLP . . . . **NiB $204 Ex $164 Gd $115**
Same as Model 602RCLP except without adj. choke, bored F or M choke. Made 1967-70.

MODEL 602XL . . . . **NiB $171 Ex $139 Gd $98**
Same as Model 602RCL except has plain bbl., F or M choke, slide handle only checkered, no recoil pad. Made 1958-70.

MODEL 662 . . . . **NiB $210 Ex $170 Gd $118**
Same as Model 602CLP except has aluminum receiver and bbl. Weight: About 4.5 lbs. Made 1966-70.

OMEGA SHOTGUNS — Brescia, Italy, and Korea

FOLDING OVER/UNDER SHOTGUN, STANDARD
Hammerless Boxlock. Gauges: 12, 20, 28 w/2.75-inch chambers or .410 w/3-inch chambers. Bbls.: 26- or 28-inch vent-rib w/fixed chokes (IC/M, M/F or F/F (.410). Automatic safety. Single trigger. 40.5 inches overall (42.5 inches, 20 ga., 28-inch bbl.). Weight: 6 to 7.5 lbs. Checkered European walnut stock and forearm. Imported 1984-94.
Standard model (12 ga.) . . . . **NiB $463 Ex $365 Gd $231**
Standard model (20 ga.) . . . . **NiB $463 Ex $365 Gd $231**
Standard model (28 ga. & .410) . . . . **NiB $534 Ex $432 Gd $302**

O/U SHOTGUN, DELUXE . . . . **NiB $453 Ex $367 Gd $258**
Gauges: 20, 28 and .410. 26- or 28-inch vent-rib bbls. 40.5 inches overall (42.5 inches, 20 ga., 28-inch bbl.). Chokes: IC/M, M/F or F/F (.410). Weight: About 5.5-6 lbs. Single trigger. Automatic safety. European walnut stock w/checkered pistol grip and tulip forend. Imported from Italy 1984-90.

OMEGA DELUXE SIDE-BY-SIDE SHOTGUN . . . . **NiB $223 Ex $181 Gd $126**
Same general specifications as the Standard Side-by-Side except has checkered European walnut stock and low bbl. rib. Made in Italy from 1984-89.

STANDARD SIDE-BY-SIDE SHOTGUN, ...**NiB $222 Ex $180 Gd $125**
Gauge: .410. 26-inch bbl. 40.5 inches overall. Choked F/F. Weight: 5.5 lbs. Double trigger. Manual safety. Checkered beechwood stock and semi-pistol grip. Imported from Italy 1984-89.

DELUXE SINGLE-SHOT SHOTGUN . . . . **NiB $116 Ex $94 Gd $68**
Same general specifications as the Standard single bbl. except has checkered walnut stock, top lever break, fully-blued receiver, vent rib. Imported from Korea 1984-87.

STANDARD SINGLE-SHOT SHOTGUN
Gauges: 12, 16, 20, 28 and .410. Bbl. lengths: 26-, 28- or 30-inches. Weight: 5 lbs., 4 oz. to 5 lbs., 11 oz. Indonesian walnut stock. Matte-chromed receiver and top lever break. Imported from Korea 1984-87.
Standard fixed . . . . **NiB $93 Ex $77 Gd $55**
Standard folding . . . . **NiB $171 Ex $139 Gd $98**
Deluxe folding . . . . **NiB $210 Ex $170 Gd $118**

SHOTGUNS

PARKER BROTHERS — Meriden, Connecticut

This firm was taken over by Remington Arms Company in 1934 and its production facilities moved to Remington's Ilion, New York, plant.

HAMMERLESS DOUBLE-BARREL SHOTGUNS
Grades V.H. through A-1 Special. Boxlock. Auto ejectors. Double triggers or selective single trigger. Gauges: 10, 12, 16, 20, 28, .410. Bbls.: 26- to 32-inch, any standard boring. Weight: 6.88-8.5 lbs.,12 ga. Stock and forearm of select walnut, checkered; straight, half-or full-pistol grip. Grades differ only in quality of workmanship, grade of wood, engraving, checkering, etc. General specifications are the same for all. Disc. about 1940.
V.H. grade, 12 or 16 ga. . . . . **NiB $3362 Ex $2720 Gd $1898**
V.H. grade, 20 ga. . . . . **NiB $4850 Ex $3909 Gd $2706**
V.H. grade, 28 ga. . . . . **NiB $7811 Ex $6278 Gd $4317**
V.H. grade, .410 ga. . . . . **NiB $19,249 Ex $15,398 Gd $10,471**
G.H. grade, 12 ga. . . . . **NiB $4521 Ex $3647 Gd $2528**
G.H. grade, 16 ga. . . . . **NiB $4721 Ex $3806 Gd $2636**

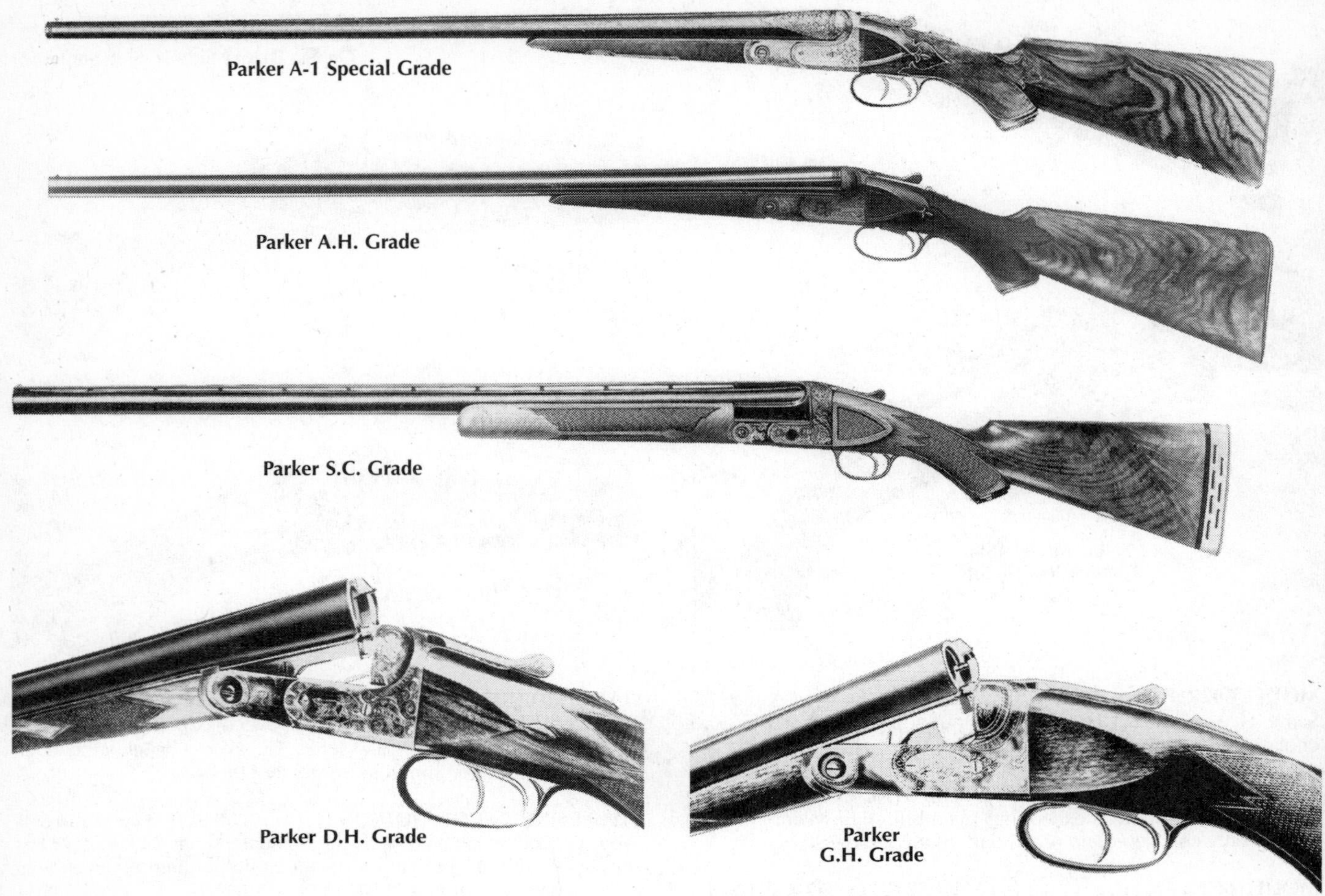

Parker A-1 Special Grade

Parker A.H. Grade

Parker S.C. Grade

Parker D.H. Grade

Parker G.H. Grade

(*cont'd.*) HAMMERLESS DOUBLE-BARREL SHOTGUNS

G.H. grade, 20 ga. NiB $6172 Ex $4938 Gd $3358
G.H. grade, 28 ga. NiB $9656 Ex $7725 Gd $5253
G.H. grade, .410 ga. . . . . NiB $24,463 Ex $19,714 Gd $1405
D.H. grade, 12 or 16 ga. . . . . NiB $7030 Ex $5624 Gd $3823
D.H. grade, 20 ga. NiB $9038 Ex $7230 Gd $4916
D.H. grade, 28 ga. . . . . NiB $13,588 Ex $10,871 Gd $7392
D.H. grade, .410 ga. . . . . NiB $45,577 Ex $36,462 Gd $24,794
C.H. grade, 12 or 16 ga. . . . . NiB $7802 Ex $6242 Gd $4240
C.H. grade, 20 ga. . . . . NiB $10,189 Ex $8151 Gd $5543
C.H. grade, 28 ga. NiB $1931 Ex $1545 Gd $1051
B.H. grade, 12 or 16 ga. . . . . NiB $11,665 Ex $9332 Gd $6345
B.H. grade, 20 ga. . . . . NiB $20,471 Ex $16,377 Gd $11,136
B.H. grade, 28 ga. . . . . NiB $38,239 Ex $30,591 Gd $20,802
A.H. grade, 12 or 16 ga. . . . . NiB $27,038 Ex $21,630 Gd $14,708
A.H. grade, 20 ga. . . . . NiB $33,604 Ex $26,883 Gd $18,280
A.H. grade, 28 ga. . . . . NiB $59,482 Ex $47,586 Gd $32,080
A.A.H. grade, 12 or 16 ga. . . . . NiB $61,723 Ex $49,378 Gd $33,577
A.A.H. grade, 12 or 16 ga. . . . . NiB $51,371 Ex $41,097 Gd $27,946
A.A.H. grade, 20 ga. . . . . NiB $74,932 Ex $59,946 Gd $40,763
A.A.H. grade, 28 ga. . . . . NiB $111,626 Ex $89,301 Gd $60,724
A-1 Special grade, 12 or 16 ga. . . . . . NiB $96,562 Ex $77,250 Gd $52,530
A-1 Special grade, 20 ga. . . . . NiB $142,140 Ex $113,712 Gd $77,324
A-1 Special grade, 28 ga. . . . . . . NiB $190,035 Ex $152,028 Gd $103,379
W/selective-single trigger, add 20%
W/ventilated rib, add 35%
For non-ejector guns, deduct 30%

SINGLE-SHOT TRAP GUNS

Hammerless. Boxlock. Ejector. 12 ga. only. Bbl. lengths: 30-, 32-, 34-inch, any boring, vent rib. Weight: 7.5-8.5 lbs. Stock and forearm of select walnut, checkered; straight, half-or full-pistol grip. The five grades differ only in quality of workmanship, grade of wood, checkering, engraving, etc. General specifications same for all. Disc. about 1940.

S.C. grade . . . . NiB $5031 Ex $4027 Gd $2742
S.B. grade . . . . NiB $6151 Ex $4923 Gd $3349
S.A. grade . . . . NiB $6885 Ex $5510 Gd $3750
S.A.A. grade . . . . NiB $8808 Ex $7049 Gd $4796
S.A.1 Special . . . . NiB $27,038 Ex $21,630 Gd $14,708

SKEET GUN

Same as other Parker doubles from Grade V.H.E. up except selective single trigger and beavertail forearm are standard on this model, as are 26-inch bbls., SK choke. Discontinued about 1940. Values are 35 percent higher.

TROJAN HAMMERLESS DOUBLE-BARREL SHOTGUN

Boxlock. Plain extractors. Double trigger or single trigger. Gauges: 12, 16, 20. Bbls.: 30-inch both F choke (12 ga. only), 26- or 28-inch M and F choke. Weight: 6.25-7.75 lbs. Checkered pistol-grip stock and forearm. Disc. 1939.

12 ga. . . . . NiB $2367 Ex $1899 Gd $1301
16 ga. . . . . NiB $3139 Ex $2516 Gd $1721
20 ga. . . . . NiB $4067 Ex $3259 Gd $2225

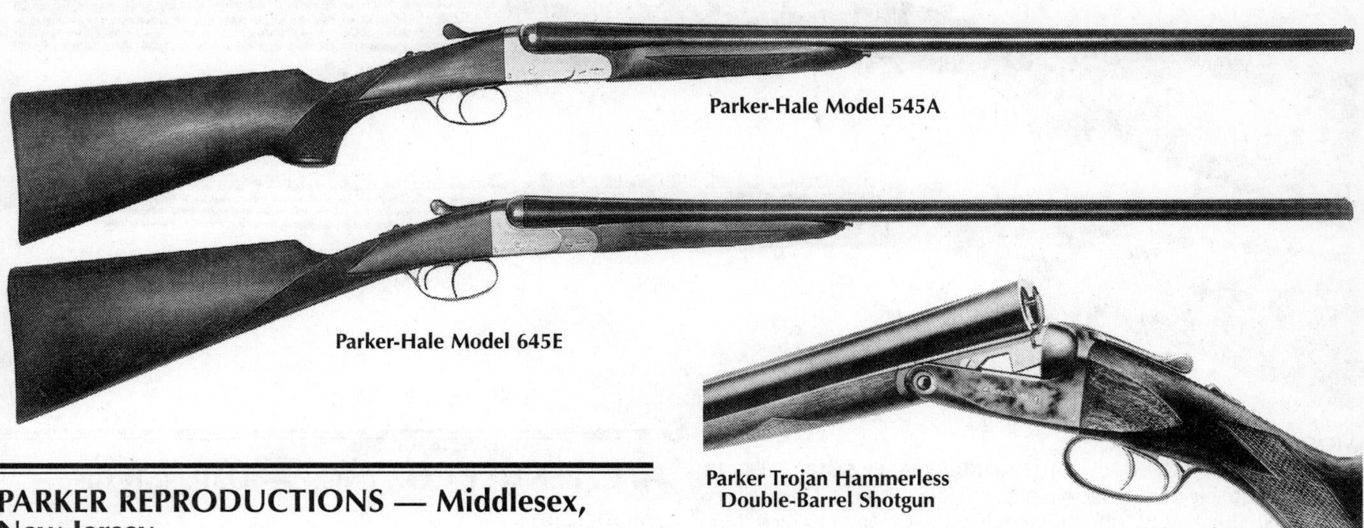

Parker-Hale Model 545A

Parker-Hale Model 645E

Parker Trojan Hammerless Double-Barrel Shotgun

PARKER REPRODUCTIONS — Middlesex, New Jersey

HAMMERLESS DOUBLE-BARREL SHOTGUNS

Reproduction of the original Parker boxlock. Single selective trigger or double triggers. Selective automatic ejectors. Automatic safety. Gauges: 12, 16, 20, 28 or .410 w/2.75- or 3-inch chambers. Bbls.: 26- or 28-inch w/fixed or internal screw choke tubes SK/SK, IC/M, M/F. Weight: 5.5-7 lbs. Checkered English-style or pistol-grip American walnut stock w/beavertail or splinter forend and checkered skeleton buttplate. Color casehardened receiver with game scenes and scroll engraving. Produced in Japan by Olin Kodensha 1984-88.

DHE grade, 12 ga.................... NiB $3512 Ex $2829 Gd $1956
DHE grade, 12 ga Sporting Clays........ NiB $4381 Ex $3525 Gd $2429
DHE grade, 20 ga.................... NiB $2926 Ex $2361 Gd $1638
DHE grade, 28 ga.................... NiB $3255 Ex $2623 Gd $1816
DHE grade 2-barrel set (16 & 20 ga.)..... NiB $5572 Ex $4477 Gd $3077
DHE grade 2-barrel set (28 & .410) ...... NiB $6216 Ex $4992 Gd $3427
DHE grade 3-barrel set .... NiB $7690 Ex $6172 Gd $4229
B grade Bank Note Lim. Ed., 12 ga. ...... NiB $5501 Ex $4421 Gd $3039
B grade Bank Note Lim. Ed., 20 ga. ...... NiB $6860 Ex $5507 Gd $3777
B grade Bank Note Lim. Ed., 28 ga...... NiB $10,551 Ex $8441 Gd $5740
B grade Bank Note Lim. Ed., .410 ga...... NiB $9979 Ex $8600 Gd $5782
A-1 Special grade, 12 ga. .... NiB $9779 Ex $7833 Gd $5320
A-1 Special grade, 16 ga.............. NiB $11,524 Ex $9218 Gd $6269
A-1 Special grade, 20 ga. .... NiB $9393 Ex $7514 Gd $5109
A-1 Special grade, 28 ga. .... NiB $14,099 Ex $11,278 Gd $7669
A-1 Special gr. 2-barrel set .... NiB $11,009 Ex $8806 Gd $5988
A-1 Special gr. 3-barrel set ..... NiB $26,394+ Ex $21,115+ Gd $14,358+
A-1 Special gr. custom engraved...... NiB $16,094 Ex $12,875 Gd $8955
A-1 Special gr. custom 2-barrel set ..... NiB $12,296 Ex $9836 Gd $6689
Extra barrel set, add $250

PARKER-HALE SHOTGUNS — Mfd. by Ignacio Ugartechea, Spain

MODEL 645A (AMERICAN) SIDE-BY-SIDE SHOTGUN

SIDE-BY-SIDE SHOTGUN .... NiB $1132 Ex $920 Gd $648

Gauges: 12, 16 and 20. Boxlock action. 26- and 28-inch bbls. Chokes: IC/M, M/F. Weight: 6 lbs. average. Single non-selective trigger. Automatic safety. Hand-checkered pistol grip walnut stock w/beavertail forend. Raised matted rib. English scroll-design engraved receiver. Discontinued 1990.

MODEL 645E (ENGLISH) SIDE-BY-SIDE SHOTGUN

Same general specifications as the Model 645A except double triggers, straight grip, splinter forend, checkered butt and concave rib. Disc. 1990.

(*cont'd.*) MODEL 645E (ENGLISH) SIDE-BY-SIDE SHOTGUN

MODEL 645E
12, 16, 20 ga. with 26- or 28-inch bbl...... NiB $1196 Ex $970 Gd $683
28, .410 ga. with 27-inch bbl............ NiB $1600 Ex $1293 Gd $901
MODEL 645E-XXV
12, 16, 20 ga. with 25-inch bbl. .... NiB $1132 Ex $944 Gd $648
28, .410 ga. with 25-inch bbl. .... NiB $1510 Ex $1222 Gd $854

PEDERSEN CUSTOM GUNS — North Haven, Connecticut, Div. of O. F. Mossberg & Sons, Inc.

MODEL 1000 O/U HUNTING SHOTGUN

Boxlock. Auto ejectors. Selective single trigger. Gauges: 12, 20. 2.75-inch chambers in 12 ga., 3-inch in 20 ga. Bbls.: Vent rib; 30-inch M/F (12 ga. only); 28-inch IC/M (12 ga. only), M/F; 26-inch IC/M. Checkered pistol-grip stock and forearm. Grade I is the higher quality gun with custom stock dimensions, fancier wood, more elaborate engraving, silver inlays. Made 1973-75.

Grade I .... NiB $2377 Ex $1914 Gd $1321
Grade II .... NiB $1924 Ex $1551 Gd $1075

MODEL 1000 MAGNUM

Same as Model 1000 Hunting Gun except chambered for 12-ga. Magnum 3-inch shells, 30-inch bbls., IM/F choke. Made 1973-75.

Grade I .... NiB $2571 Ex $2068 Gd $1426
Grade II .... NiB $2114 Ex $1703 Gd $1178

MODEL 1000 SKEET GUN

Same as Model 1000 Hunting Gun except has skeet-style stock; 26- and 28-inch bbls. (12 ga. only), SK choke. Made 1973-75.

Grade I .... NiB $2218 Ex $1786 Gd $424
Grade II .... NiB $1806 Ex $1457 Gd $1010

MODEL 1000 TRAP GUN

Same as Model 1000 Hunting Gun except 12 ga. only, has Monte Carlo trap-style stock, 30- or 32-inch bbls., M/F or IM/F choke. Made 1973-75.

Grade I .... NiB $1965 Ex $1584 Gd $1096
Grade II .... NiB $1600 Ex $1292 Gd $896

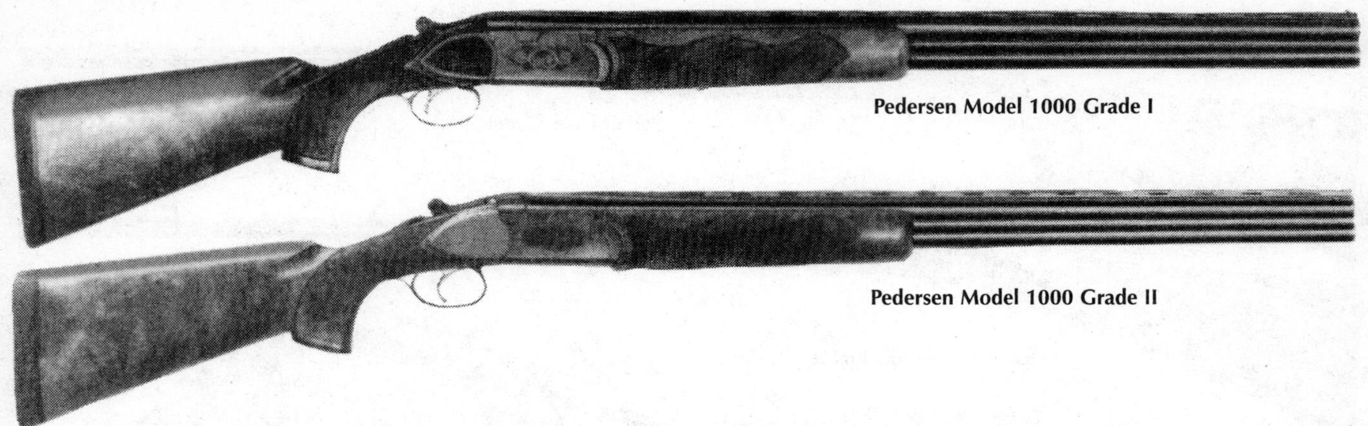
Pedersen Model 1000 Grade I

Pedersen Model 1000 Grade II

MODEL 1500 O/U
HUNTING SHOTGUN . . . . NiB $806 Ex $648 Gd $448
Boxlock. Auto ejectors. Selective single trigger. 12 ga. 2.75- or 3-inch chambers. Bbls.: vent rib; 26-inch IC/M; 28- and 30-inch M/F; Magnum has 30-inch, IM/F choke. Weight: 7-7.5 lbs., depending on bbl. length. Checkered pistol-grip stock and forearm. Made 1973-75.

MODEL 1500 SKEET GUN . . . . NiB $829 Ex $668 Gd $463
Same as Model 1500 Hunting Gun except has skeet-style stock, 27-inch bbls., SK choke. Made 1973-75.

MODEL 1500 TRAP GUN . . . . NiB $691 Ex $557 Gd $387
Same as Model 1500 Hunting Gun except has Monte Carlo trap-style stock, 30- or 32-inch bbls., M/F or IM/F chokes. Made 1973-75.

MODEL 2000 HAMMERLESS DOUBLE
Boxlock. Auto ejectors. Selective single trigger. Gauges: 12, 20. 2.75-inch chambers in 12 ga., 3-inch in 20 ga. Bbls.: Vent rib; 30-inch M/F (12 ga. only); 28-inch M/F, 26-inch IC/M choke. Checkered pistol-grip stock and forearm. Grade I is the higher quality gun w/custom dimensions, fancier wood, more elaborate engraving, silver inlays. Made 1973-74.
Grade I . . . . NiB $2588 Ex $2085 Gd $1443
Grade II . . . . NiB $2188 Ex $1926 Gd $1335

MODEL 2500
HAMMERLESS DOUBLE . . . . NiB $485 Ex $391 Gd $270
Boxlock. Auto ejectors. Selective single trigger. Gauges: 12, 20. 2.75-inch chambers in 12 ga., 3-inch in 20 ga. Bbls.: Vent rib; 28-inch M/F; 26-inch IC/M choke. Checkered pistol-grip stock and forearm. Made 1973-74.

MODEL 4000 HAMMERLESS SLIDE-ACTION
REPEATING SHOTGUN . . . . NiB $498 Ex $401 Gd $278
Custom version of Mossberg Model 500. Full-coverage floral engraving on receiver. Gauges: 12, 20, .410. Three-inch chamber. Bbls.: Vent rib; 26-inch IC or SK choke; 28-inch F or M; 30-inch F. Weight: 6-8 lbs. depending on ga. and bbl. Checkered stock and slide handle of select wood. Made in 1975.

MODEL 4000 TRAP GUN . . . . NiB $507 Ex $409 Gd $283
Same as standard Model 4000 except 12 ga. only, has 30-inch F choke bbl., Monte Carlo trap-style stock w/recoil pad. Made in 1975.

MODEL 4500 . . . . NiB $454 Ex $366 Gd $254
Same as Model 4000 except has simpler scroll engraving. Made in 1975.

MODEL 4500 TRAP GUN . . . . NiB $466 Ex $375 Gd $260
Same as Model 4000 Trap Gun except has simpler scroll engraving. Made in 1975.

J. C. PENNEY CO., INC. — Dallas, Texas

MODEL 4011
AUTOLOADING SHOTGUN. . . . . . NiB $235 Ex $190 Gd $133
Hammerless. Five round magazine. Bbls.: 26-inch IC; 28-inch M or F; 30-inch F choke. Weight: 7.25 lbs. Plain pistol-grip stock and slide handle.

MODEL 6610
SINGLE-SHOT SHOTGUN . . . . NiB $110 Ex $90 Gd $63
Hammerless. Takedown. Auto ejector. Gauges: 12, 16, 20 and .410. Bbl. length: 28-36 inches. Weight: About 6 lbs. Plain pistol-grip stock and forearm.

MODEL 6630
BOLT-ACTION SHOTGUN . . . . NiB $149 Ex $120 Gd $84
Takedown. Gauges: 12, 16, 20. Two round clip magazine. 26- and 28-inch bbl. lengths; with or without adj. choke. Plain pistol-grip stock. Weight: About 7.25 lbs.

MODEL 6670
SLIDE-ACTION SHOTGUN . . . . . . NiB $174 Ex $141 Gd $103
Hammerless. Gauges: 12, 16, 20, and .410. Three round tubular magazine. Bbls.: 26- to 30-inch; various chokes. Weight: 6.25-7.25 lbs. Walnut finished hardwood stock.

MODEL 6870 SLIDE-ACTION
SHOTGUN . . . . NiB $250 Ex $199 Gd $142
Hammerless. Gauges: 12, 16, 20, .410. Four round magazine. Bbls.: Vent rib; 26- to 30-inch, various chokes. Weight: Average 6.5 lbs. Plain pistol-grip stock.

PERAZZI SHOTGUNS — Manufactured by Manifattura Armi Perazzi, Brescia, Italy

See also listings under Ithaca-Perazzi.

DB81 O/U TRAP . . . . NiB $5019 Ex $4035 Gd $2774
Gauge: 12; 2.75-inch chambers. 29.5- or 31.5-inch bbls. w/wide vent rib; M/F chokes. Weight: 8 lbs., 6 oz. Detachable and interchangeable trigger with flat V-springs. Bead front sight. Interchangeable and custom-made checkered stock; beavertail forend. Imported 1988 to date.

DB81 SINGLE-SHOT TRAP . . . . NiB $5019 Ex $4035 Gd $2774
Same general specifications as the DB81 over/under except in single bbl. version w/32- or 34-inch wide vent-rib bbl., F choke. Imported 1988 to date.

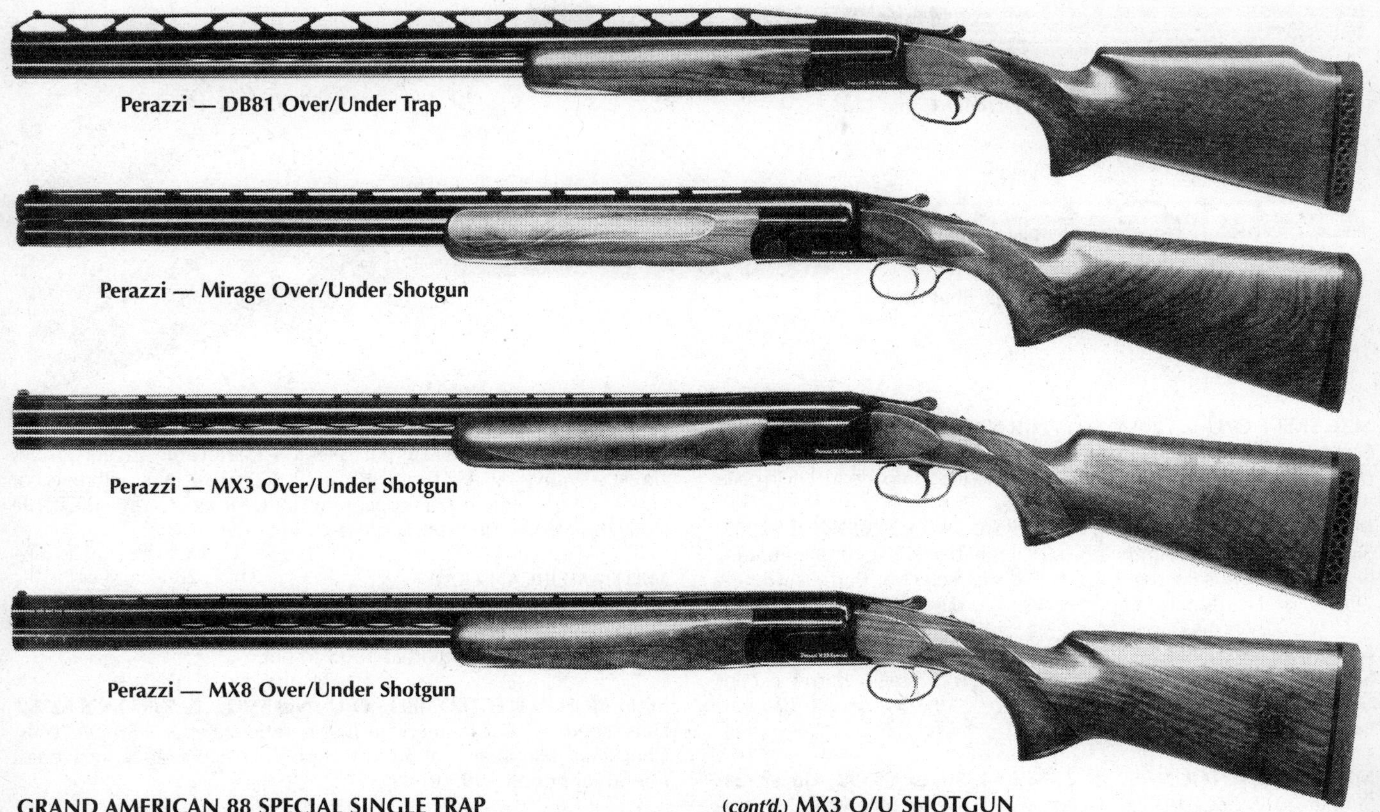
Perazzi — DB81 Over/Under Trap

Perazzi — Mirage Over/Under Shotgun

Perazzi — MX3 Over/Under Shotgun

Perazzi — MX8 Over/Under Shotgun

GRAND AMERICAN 88 SPECIAL SINGLE TRAP
Same general specifications as MX8 Special Single Trap except w/high ramped rib. Fixed choke or screw-in choke tubes.
Model 88 standard . . . . NiB $4441 Ex $3571 Gd $2459
Model 88 w/interchangeable choke tubes . . . . NiB $4724 Ex $3798 Gd $2613

MIRAGE O/U SHOTGUN
Gauge: 12; 2.75-inch chambers. Bbls.: 27.63-, 29.5- or 31.5-inch vent-rib w/fixed chokes or screw-in choke tubes. Single selective trigger. Weight: 7 to 7.75 lbs. Interchangeable and custom-made checkered buttstock and forend.
Competition Trap, Skeet, Pigeon, Sporting . . . . NiB $6218 Ex $4975 Gd $3383
Skeet 4-barrel sets . . . . NiB $13,197 Ex $10,557 Gd $7179
Competition Special (w/adj. 4-position trigger) add $350

MX1 O/U SHOTGUN
Similar to Model MX8 except w/ramp-style, tapered rib and modified stock configuration.
Competition Trap, Skeet, Pigeon & Sporting . . . . NiB $3304 Ex $2656 Gd $1824
MXlC (w/choke tubes) . . . . NiB $3484 Ex $2800 Gd $1922
MXlB (w/flat low rib) . . . . NiB $3175 Ex $2553 Gd $1754

MX2 O/U SHOTGUN
Similar to Model MX8 except w/broad high-ramped competition rib.
Competition-Trap, Skeet, Pigeon & Sporting . . . . NiB $3987 Ex $3201 Gd $2196
MX2C (w/choke tubes) . . . . NiB $4534 Ex $3639 Gd $2494

MX3 O/U SHOTGUN
Similar to Model MX8 except w/ramp-style, tapered rib and modified stock configuration.

(cont'd.) **MX3 O/U SHOTGUN**
Competition Trap, Skeet, Pigeon & Sporting . . . . . . NiB $46,289 Ex $37,032 Gd $25,181
Competition Special (w/adj. 4-position trigger) add $300
Game models . . . . NiB $4174 Ex $3351 Gd $2298
Combo O/U plus SB . . . . NiB $5146 Ex $4128 Gd $2827
SB Trap 32- or 34-inch . . . . NiB $3530 Ex $2836 Gd $1968
Skeet 4-bbl. sets . . . . NiB $11,009 Ex $8806 Gd $5988
Skeet Special 4-bbl. sets . . . . NiB $11,233 Ex $8987 Gd $6111

MX3 SPECIAL PIGEON SHOTGUN. . . NiB $4984 Ex $4000 Gd $2739
Gauge: 12; 2.75-inch chambers. 29.5- or 31.5-inch vent rib bbl.; IC/M and extra full chokes. Weight: 8 lbs., 6 oz. Detachable and interchangeable trigger group w/flat V-springs. Bead front sight. Interchangeable and custom-made checkered stock for live pigeon shoots; splinter forend. Imported 1991 to date.

MX4 O/U SHOTGUN
Similar to Model MX3 in appearance and shares the MX8 locking system. Detachable, adj. 4-position trigger standard. Interchangeable choke tubes optional.
Competition Trap, Skeet, Pigeon & Sporting . . . . NiB $4760 Ex $3819 Gd $2616
MX4C (w/choke tubes) . . . . NiB $5075 Ex $4072 Gd $2788

MX5 O/U GAME GUN
Similar to Model MX8 except in hunting configuration, chambered in 12 or 20 ga. Non-detachable single selective trigger.
MX5 Standard . . . . NiB $3250 Ex $2616 Gd $1794
MX5C (w/choke tubes) . . . . NiB $3589 Ex $2878 Gd $1962

MX6 AMER. TRAP SINGLE-BARREL . . NiB $2999 Ex $2407 Gd $1649
Single shot. Removable trigger group. 12 ga. Barrels: 32- or 34-inch with fixed or choke tubes. Raised vent rib. Checkered European walnut Monte Carlo stock, beavertail forend. Imported 1995 to date.

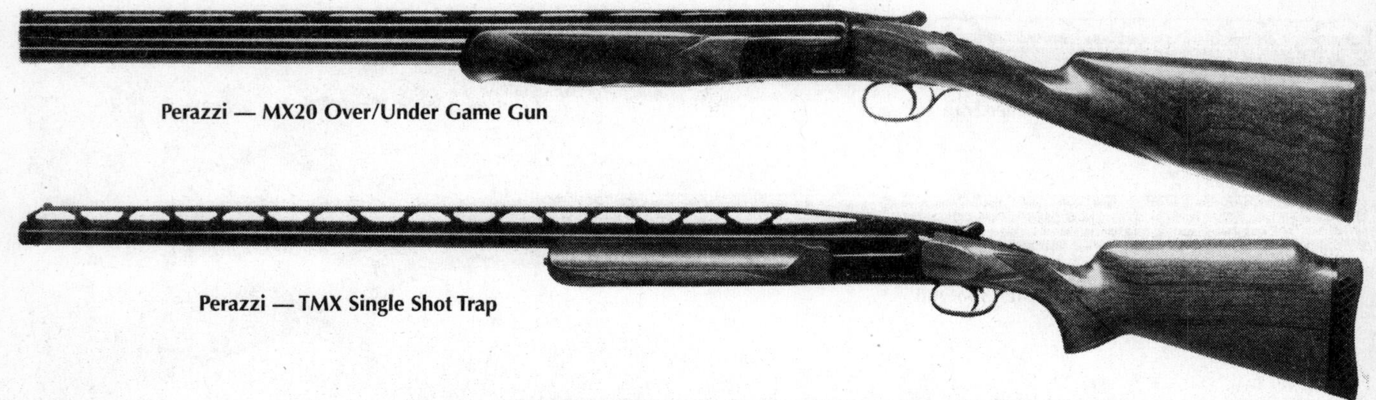
Perazzi — MX20 Over/Under Game Gun

Perazzi — TMX Single Shot Trap

MX6 SKEET O/U . . . . NiB $3393 Ex $2723 Gd $1866
Same general specs as MX6 American Trap single barrel except over/under; boxlock. Barrels: 26.75- or 27.50-inch. Imported 1995 to date.

MX6 SPORTING O/U . . . . NiB $3559 Ex $2857 Gd $1957
Same specs as MX6 American Trap single barrel except over/under; boxlock. Single selective trigger; external selector. Barrels: 28.38-, 29.50-, or 31.50-inch. Imported 1995 to date.

MX6 TRAP O/U. . . . . NiB $2981 Ex $2391 Gd $1635
Same general specs as MX6 American Trap single barrel except over/under; boxlock. Barrels: 29.50-, 30.75-, or 31.50-inch. Imported 1995 to date.

MX7 O/U SHOTGUN . . . . NiB $4230 Ex $3392 Gd $2321
Similar to Model MX12 except w/MX3-style receiver and top-mounted trigger selector. Bbls.: 28.73-, 2.5-, 31.5-inch w/vent rib; screw-in choke tubes. Imported 1992 to date.

MX8 O/U SHOTGUN
Gauge: 12, 2.75-inch chambers. Bbls.: 27.63-, 29.5- or 31.5-inch vent-rib w/fixed chokes or screw-in choke tubes. Weight: 7 to 8.5 lbs. Interchangeable and custom-made checkered stock; beavertail forend. Special models have detachable and interchangeable 4-position trigger group w/flat V-springs. Imported 1988 to date.
MX8 Standard . . . . NiB $3851 Ex $3090 Gd $2115
MX8 Special (adj. 4-pos. trigger) . . . . . . NiB $3954 Ex $3172 Gd $2172
MX8 Special single
(32-or 34-inch bbl.) . . . . NiB $3748 Ex $3007 Gd $2060
MX8 Special combo . . . . NiB $7682 Ex $6159 Gd $4211

MX8/20 O/U SHOTGUN. . . . . NiB $3907 Ex $3135 Gd $2146
Similar to the Model MX8 except w/smaller frame and custom stock. Available in sporting or game configurations with fixed chokes or screw-in tubes. Imported 1993 to date.

MX9 O/U SHOTGUN . . . . NiB $7016 Ex $5627 Gd $3849
Gauge: 12; 2.75-inch chambers. Bbls.: 29.5- or 30.5-inch w/choke tubes and vent side rib. Selective trigger. Checkered walnut stock w/adj. cheekpiece. Available in single bbl., combo, O/U trap, skeet, pigeon and sporting models. Imported 1993 to date.

MX10 O/U SHOTGUN . . . . NiB $6863 Ex $5504 Gd $3766
Similar to the Model MX9 except w/fixed chokes and different rib configuration. Imported 1993 to date.

MX10 PIGEON-ELECTROCIBLES O/U . . . . NiB $6685 Ex $5361 Gd $3668
Over/Under; boxlock. Removable trigger group; external selector. 12 gauge. Barrels: 27.50- or 29.50-inch. Checkered European walnut adjustable stock, beavertail forend. Imported 1995 to date.

MX11 AMERICAN TRAP COMBO . . NiB $5438 Ex $4365 Gd $2990
Over/Under; boxlock. External selector. Removable trigger group; single selective trigger. 12 ga. Bbls: 29-1/2- to 34-inch with fixed or choke tubes; vent rib. European walnut Monte Carlo adjustable stock, beavertail forend. Imported 1995 to date.

MX11 AMERICAN TRAP
SINGLE BARREL . . . . NiB $4823 Ex $3871 Gd $2653
Same general specs as MX11 American Trap combo except 32- or 34-inch single bbl. Imported 1995 to date.

MX11 PIGEON-ELECTROCIBLES O/U . NiB $5022 Ex $4030 Gd $2762
Same specs as MX11 American Trap combo except 27.50 O/U bbls. Checkered European walnut pistol grip adjustable stock, beavertail forend. Imported 1995 to date.

MX11 SKEET O/U . . . . NiB $5080 Ex $4077 Gd $2793
Same general specs as MX11 American Trap combo except 26.75 or 27.50-inch O/U bbls. Checkered European walnut pistol-grip adjustable stock, beavertail forend. Imported 1995 to date.

MX11 SPORTING O/U . . . . . . NiB $5537 Ex $4442 Gd $3042
Same general specs as MX11 American Trap combo except 28.38, 29.50-, or 31.50-inch O/U bbls. Checkered European walnut pistol-grip adjustable stock, beavertail forend. Imported 1995 to date.

MX11 TRAP O/U. . . . . NiB $5022 Ex $4030 Gd $2762
Same general specs as MX11 American Trap combo except 29.50,-30.75, or 31.50-inch O/U bbls. Checkered European walnut pistol-grip adjustable stock, beavertail forend. Imported 1995 to date.

MX12 O/U GAME GUN
Gauge: 12, 2.75-inch chambers. Bbls.: 26-, 27.63-, 28.38- or 29.5-inch, vent rib, fixed chokes or screw-in choke tubes. Non-detachable single selective trigger group w/coil springs. Weight: 7.25 lbs. Interchangeable and custom-made checkered stock; Schnabel forend.
MX12 Standard . . . . NiB $5022 Ex $4030 Gd $2762
MX12C (w/choke tubes) . . . . . . NiB $5537 Ex $4442 Gd $3042

MX14 AMERICAN TRAP
SINGLE-BARREL . . . . NiB $4230 Ex $3397 Gd $2331
Single shot. Removable trigger group; unsingle configuration. 12 ga. Bbl: 34-inch with fixed or choke tubes; vent rib. Checkered European walnut Monte Carlo adjustable stock, beavertail forend. Imported 1995 to date.

MX15 AMERICAN TRAP
SINGLE-BARREL . . . . NiB $4706 Ex $3778 Gd $2590
Full choke. Detachable trigger group. Gauge: 12 only with 2.75-inch chamber. Bbls: 32 and 34-inch. Weight: 8 lbs., 6 oz. .

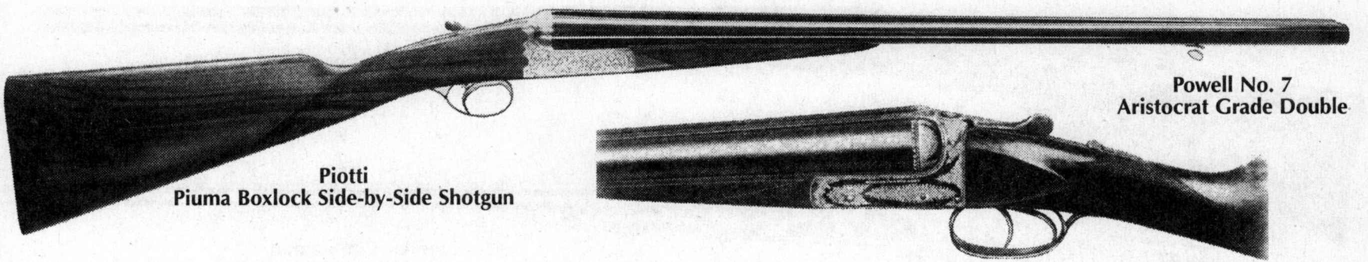

Powell No. 7
Aristocrat Grade Double

Piotti
Piuma Boxlock Side-by-Side Shotgun

MX20 O/U GAME GUN
Gauges: 20, 28 and .410; 2.75- or 3-inch chambers. 26-inch vent-rib bbls., M/F chokes or screw-in chokes. Auto selective ejectors. Selective single trigger. Weight: 6 lbs., 6 oz. Non-detachable coil-spring trigger. Bead front sight. Interchangeable and custom-made checkered stock w/Schnabel forend. Imported from 1988 to date.
Standard grade .... NiB $4966 Ex $3969 Gd $2718
Standard grade
w/gold outline.............. NiB $8561 Ex $6860 Gd $4684
MX20C w/choke tubes .... NiB $5313 Ex $4262 Gd $2917
SC3 grade .... NiB $9252 Ex $7418 Gd $5069
SCO grade............. NiB $12,660 Ex $10,127 Gd $6887

MX28 O/U GAME GUN ... NiB $14,098 Ex $11,278 Gd $7669
Similar to the Model MX12 except chambered in 28 ga. w/26-inch bbls. fitted to smaller frame. Imported 1993 to date.

MX410 O/U GAME GUN..... NiB $14,098 Ex $11,278 Gd $7669
Similar to the Model MX12 except in .410 bore w/3-inch chambers, 26-inch bbls. fitted to smaller frame. Imported 1993 to date.

TM1 SPECIAL
SINGLE-SHOT TRAP .... NiB $4286 Ex $3440 Gd $2358
Gauge: 12- 2.75-inch chambers. 32- or 34-inch bbl. w/wide vent rib; full choke. Weight: 8 lbs., 6 oz. Detachable and interchangeable trigger group with coil springs. Bead front sight. Interchangeable and custom-made stock w/checkered pistol grip and beavertail forend. Imported 1988 to date.

TMX SPECIAL
SINGLE-SHOT TRAP .... NiB $4451 Ex $3572 Gd $2448
Same general specifications as Model TM1 Special except w/ultra-high rib. Interchangeable choke tubes optional.

PIOTTI SHOTGUNS — Italy

BOSS O/U .... NiB $34,000 Ex $28,000 Gd $13,000
Over/Under; sidelock. Gauges: 12 or 20. Barrels: 26- to 32-inch. Standard chokes. Best quality walnut. Custom-made to customer's specifications. Imported 1993 to date.

KING NO. 1 SIDELOCK ... NiB $20,900 Ex $17,000 Gd $7000
Gauges: 10, 12, 16, 20, 28 and .410. 25- to 30-inch bbls. (12 ga.), 25- to 28-inch (other ga.). Weight: About 5 lbs. (.410) to 8 lbs. (12 ga.) Holland & Holland pattern sidelock. Double triggers standard. Coin finish or color casehardened. Level file-cut rib. Full-coverage scroll engraving, gold inlays. Hand-rubbed, oil-finished, straight-grip stock with checkered butt, splinter forend.

KING EXTRA SIDE-BY-SIDE
SHOTGUN............ NiB $21,125 Ex $17,000 Gd $10,000
Same general specifications as the Piotti King No. 1 except has choice of engraving, gold inlays, plus stock is of exhibition-grade wood.

LUNIK SIDE-LOCK
SHOTGUN
.... NiB $21,438 Ex $17,950 Gd $13,486
Same general specifications as the Monte Carlo model except has level, file-cut rib. Renaissance-style, large scroll engraving in relief, gold crown in top lever, gold name, and gold crest in forearm, finely figured wood.

MONTE CARLO
SIDE-LOCK SHOTGUN ..... NiB $10,938 Ex $8750 Gd $5950
Gauges: 10, 12, 16, 20, 28 or .410. Bbls.: 25- to 30-inch. Holland & Holland pattern sidelock. Weight: 5-8 lbs. Automatic ejectors. Double triggers. Hand-rubbed oil-finished straight-grip stock with checkered butt. Choice of Purdey-style scroll and rosette or Holland & Holland-style large scroll engraving.

PIUMA BOXLOCK
SIDE-BY-SIDE SHOTGUN.... NiB $10,494 Ex $8395 Gd $5709
Same general specifications as the Monte Carlo model except has Anson & Deeley boxlock action w/demi-bloc bbls., scalloped frame. Standard scroll and rosette engraving. Hand-rubbed, oil-finished straight-grip stock.

WILLIAM POWELL & SON LTD. — Birmingham, England

NO. 1 BEST GRADE
DOUBLE-BARREL
SHOTGUN............ NiB $50,112 Ex $39,000 Gd $18,000
Sidelock. Gauges: Made to order with 12, 16 and 20 the most common. Bbls.: Made to order in any length but 28 inches was recommended. Highest grade French walnut buttstock and forearm with fine checkering. Metal elaborately engraved. Imported by Stoeger about 1938-51.

NO. 2 BEST GRADE
DOUBLE-BARREL ...... NiB $27,500 Ex $22,000 Gd $14,960
Same general specifications as the Powell No. 1 except plain finish without engraving. Imported by Stoeger about 1938-51.

NO. 6 CROWN GRADE
DOUBLE-BARREL .... NiB $13,750 Ex $11,000 Gd $7480
Boxlock. Gauges: Made to order with 12, 16 and 20 the most common. Bbls.: Made to order, but 28 inches was recommended. Highest grade French walnut buttstock and forearm w/fine checkering. Metal elaborately engraved. Uses Anson & Deeley locks. Imported by Stoeger about 1938-51.

NO. 7 ARISTOCRAT GRADE
DOUBLE-BARREL
SHOTGUN .... NiB $6965 Ex $5590 Gd $830
Same general specifications as the Powell No. 6 except w/lower quality wood and metal engraving.

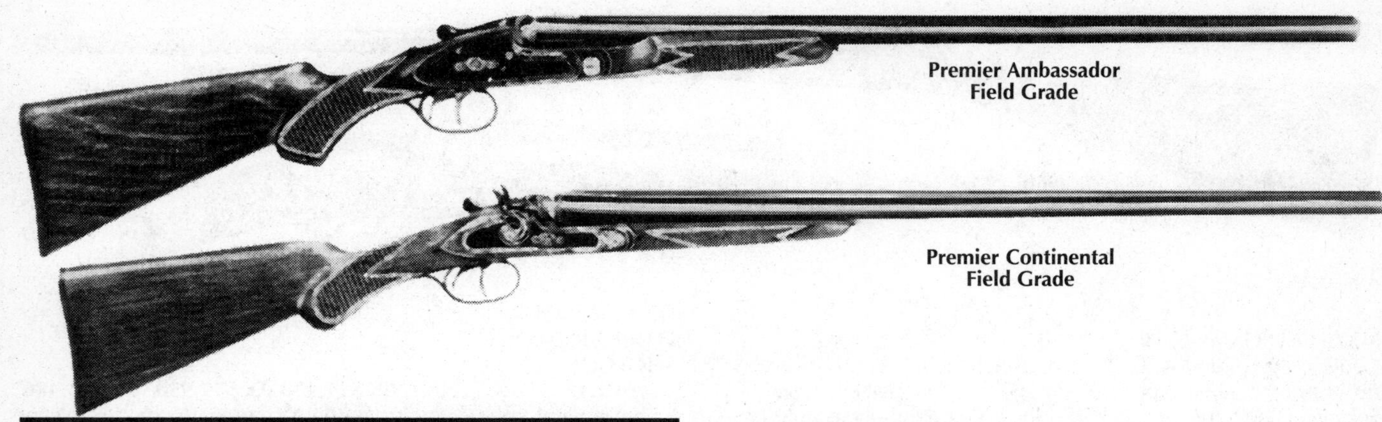

Premier Ambassador
Field Grade

Premier Continental
Field Grade

PRECISION SPORTS SHOTGUNS — Cortland, New York, Manufactured by Ignacio Ugartechea, Spain

600 SERIES AMERICAN HAMMERLESS DOUBLES
Boxlock. Single selective trigger. Selective automatic ejectors. Automatic safety. Gauges: 12, 16, 20, 28, .410; 2.75- or 3-inch chambers. Bbls.: 26-,27- or 28-inch w/raised matte rib; choked IC/M or M/F. Weight: 5.75-7 lbs. Checkered pistol-grip walnut buttstock with beavertail forend. Engraved silvered receiver with blued bbls. Imported from Spain 1986-94.

640A (12, 16, 20 ga. w/extractors) ...... NiB $901 Ex $727 Gd $504
640A (28, .410 ga. w/extractors) .... NiB $1052 Ex $849 Gd $589
640 Slug Gun (12 ga. w/extractors) ..... NiB $1031 Ex $832 Gd $579
645A (12, 16, 20 ga. w/ejectors) .... NiB $977 Ex $789 Gd $549
645A (28, .410 ga. w/ejectors) .... NiB $1187 Ex $957 Gd $662
645A (20/28 ga. two-bbl. set) .... NiB $1383 Ex $1113 Gd $769
650A (12 ga. w/extractors, choke tubes) ... NiB $915 Ex $738 Gd $511
655A (12 ga. w/ejectors, choke tubes) .. NiB $1010 Ex $814 Gd $563

600 SERIES ENGLISH HAMMERLESS DOUBLES
Boxlock. Same general specifications as American 600 series except w/double triggers and concave rib. Checkered English-style walnut stock w/splinter forend, straight grip and oil finish.

640E (12, 16, 20 ga. w/extractors) ...... NiB $780 Ex $629 Gd $437
640E (28, .410 ga. w/extractors) .... NiB $875 Ex $706 Gd $489
640 Slug Gun (12 ga. w/extractors) ..... NiB $1023 Ex $824 Gd $571
645E (12, 16, 20 ga. w/ejectors) .... NiB $1052 Ex $849 Gd $589
645E (28, .410 ga. w/ejectors) .... NiB $1004 Ex $810 Gd $563
645E (20/28 ga. two-bbl. set) .... NiB $1315 Ex $1068 Gd $733
650E (12 ga. w/extractors, choke tubes) .... NiB $909 Ex $732 Gd $508
655E (12 ga. w/ejectors, choke tubes) .... NiB $969 Ex $781 Gd $541

MODEL 640M MAGNUM 10 HAMMERLESS DOUBLE
Similar to Model 640E except in 10 ga. w/3.5-inch Mag. chambers. Bbls.: 26-, 30-, 32-inch choked F/F.

Model 640M Big Ten, Turkey ..... NiB $899 Ex $725 Gd $503
Model 640M Goose Gun......... NiB $925 Ex $746 Gd $517

MODEL 645E-XXV HAMMERLESS DOUBLE
Similar to Model 645E except w/25-inch bbl. and Churchill-style rib.

645E-XXV (12, 16, 20 ga. w/ejectors) ...... NiB $969 Ex $781 Gd $541
645E-XXV (28, .410 ga. w/ejectors) ...... NiB $1104 Ex $889 Gd $615

PREMIER SHOTGUNS

Premier shotguns have been produced by various gunmakers in Europe.

AMBASSADOR MODEL FIELD GRADE HAMMERLESS DOUBLE-BARREL SHOTGUN..... NiB $448 Ex $363 Gd $255
Sidelock. Plain extractors. Double triggers. Gauges: 12, 16, 20, .410. 3-inch chambers in 20 and .410 ga., 2.75- inch in 12 and 16 ga. Bbls.: 26-inch in .410 ga., 28 inch in other ga.; choked M/F. Weight: 6 lbs., 3 oz.-7 lbs., 3 oz. depending on gauge. Checkered pistol-grip stock and beavertail forearm. Intro. in 1957; disc.

BRUSH KING .... NiB $325 Ex $266 Gd $188
Same as standard Regent model except chambered for 12 (2.75-inch) and 20 ga. (3-inch) only; has 22-inch bbls., IC/M choke, straight-grip stock. Weight: 6 lbs., 3 oz. in 12 ga.; 5 lbs., 12 oz. in 20 ga. Introduced in 1959; disc.

CONTINENTAL MODEL FIELD GRADE HAMMER DOUBLE-BARREL SHOTGUN..... NiB $448 Ex $363 Gd $255
Sidelock. Exposed hammers. Plain extractors. Double triggers. Gauges: 12, 16, 20, .410. Three inch chambers in 20 and .410 ga., 2.75-inch in 12 and 16 ga. Bbls.: 26-inch in .410 ga.; 28-inch in other ga.; choked M/F. Weight: 6 lbs., 3 oz.-7 lbs., 3 oz. depending on gauge. Checkered pistol-grip stock and English-style forearm. Introduced in 1957; disc.

MONARCH SUPREME GRADE HAMMERLESS DOUBLE-BARREL SHOTGUN..... NiB $478 Ex $387 Gd $273
Boxlock. Auto ejectors. Double triggers. Gauges: 12, 20. 2.75-inch chambers in 12 ga., 3-inch in 20 ga. Bbls.: 28-inch M/F; 26-inch IC/M choke. Weight: 6 lbs., 6 oz., 7 lbs., 2 oz. depending on gauge and bbl. Checkered pistol-grip stock and beavertail forearm of fancy walnut. Introduced in 1959; disc.

PRESENTATION CUSTOM GRADE .... NiB $1221 Ex $990 Gd $695
Similar to Monarch model but made to order of higher quality with hunting scene engraving, gold and silver inlay, fancier wood. Introduced in 1959; disc.

REGENT 10 GA. MAGNUM EXPRESS .... NiB $377 Ex $306 Gd $214
Same as standard Regent model except chambered for 10-ga. Magnum 3.5-inch shells, has heavier construction, 32-inch bbls. choked F/F, stock with recoil pad. Weight: 11.25 lbs. Introduced in 1957; disc.

REGENT 12 GA. MAGNUM EXPRESS .... NiB $340 Ex $276 Gd $194
Same as standard Regent model except chambered for 12-ga. Magnum 3-inch shells, has 30-inch bbls. choked F and F, stock with recoil pad. Weight: 7.25 lbs. Introduced in 1957; disc.

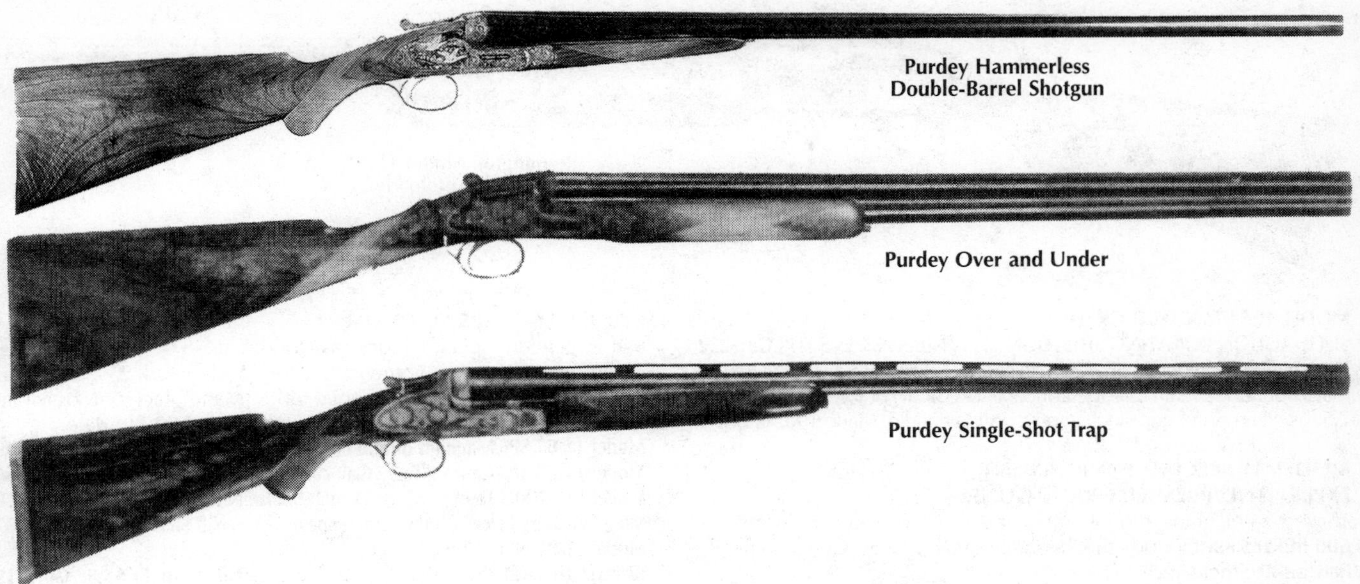
Purdey Hammerless Double-Barrel Shotgun

Purdey Over and Under

Purdey Single-Shot Trap

REGENT FIELD GRADE HAMMERLESS DOUBLE-BARREL SHOTGUN . . . . . NiB $302 Ex $245 Gd $171
Boxlock. Plain extractors. Double triggers. Gauges: 12,16, 20, 28, .410. Three inch chambers in 20 and .410 ga., 2.75-inch in other gauges. Bbls.: 26-inch IC/M, M/F (28 and .410 ga. only); 28-inch M/F; 30-inch M/F (12 ga. only). Weight: 6 lbs., 2 oz.-7 lbs., 4 oz. depending on gauge and bbl. Checkered pistol-grip stock and beavertail forearm. Introduced in 1955; disc.

JAMES PURDEY & SONS, LTD. — London, England

HAMMERLESS DOUBLE-BARREL SHOTGUN

Sidelock. Auto ejectors. Single or double triggers. Gauges: 12, 16, 20. Bbls.: 26-, 27-, 28-, 30-inch (latter in 12 ga. only);any boring, any shape or style of rib. Weight: 5.25-5.5 lbs. depending on model, gauge and bbl length. Checkered stock and forearm, straight grip standard, pistol-grip also available. Purdey guns of this type have been made from about 1880 to date. Models include: Game Gun, Featherweight Game Gun, Two-Inch Gun (chambered for 12 ga. 2-inch shells), Pigeon Gun (w/3rd fastening and side clips), values of all models are the same.
With double triggers. . . . . NiB $40,625 Ex $32,500 Gd $22,100
With single trigger . . . . . . NiB $43,438 Ex $34,750 Gd $23,630

OVER/UNDER SHOTGUN

Sidelock. Auto ejectors. Single or double triggers. Gauges: 12 16, 20. Bbls.: 26-, 27-, 28-, 30-inch (latter in 12 ga. only); any boring, any style rib. Weight: 6-7.5 pounds depending on gauge and bbl. length. Checkered stock and forend, straight or pistol grip. Prior to WW II, the Purdey Over/Under Gun was made with a Purdey action; since the war James Purdey & Sons have acquired the business of James Woodward & Sons and all Purdey over/under guns are now built on the Woodward principle. General specifications of both types are the same.
With Purdey act., double triggers . . . NiB $80,000 Ex $50,000 Gd $22,000
With Woodward action, double triggers . . . . NiB $55,750 Ex $45,000 Gd $31,240
W/single trigger, add . . . . NiB $1875 Ex $1500 Gd $1020

Purdey Hammerless Double-Barrel Shotgun

Purdey Hammerless Double-Barrel Shotgun w/Single Trigger

SINGLE-BARREL TRAP GUN . NiB $11,625 Ex $9300 Gd $6324
Sidelock. Mechanical features similar to those of the over/under model with Purdey action. 12 ga. only. Built to customer's specifications. Made prior to World War II.

REMINGTON ARMS CO. — Ilion, New York

Eliphalet Remington Jr. began making long arms with his father in 1816. In 1828 they moved their facility to Ilion, N.Y., where it remained a family-run business for decades. As the family began to diminish, other people bought controlling interests and today, still a successful gunmaking company, it is a subsidiary of the DuPont Corporation.

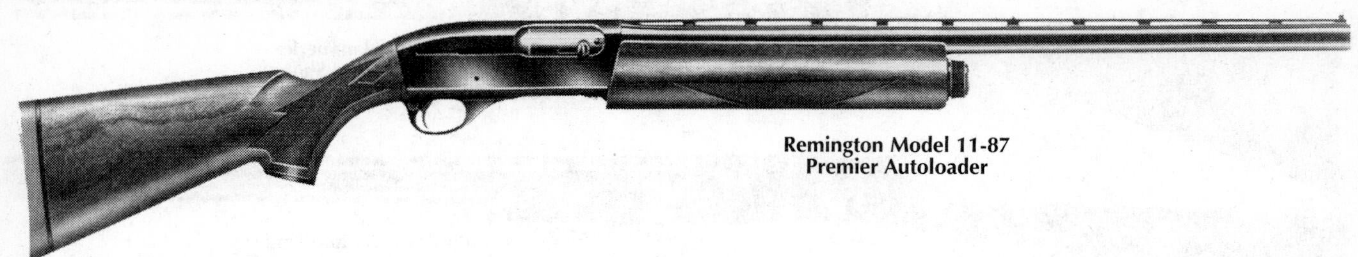

Remington Model 11-87
Premier Autoloader

MODEL 10A STANDARD GRADE
SLIDE-ACTION REPEATING SHOTGUN . . . . . NiB $392 Ex $317 Gd $222
Hammerless. Takedown. Six-round capacity. 12 ga. only. Five shell tubular magazine. Bbls.: Plain; 26- to 32-inch; choked F, M or Cyl. Weight: About 7.5 lbs. Plain pistol-grip stock, grooved slide handle. Made 1907-29.

MODEL 11 SPECIAL, TOURNAMENT, EXPERT AND PREMIER GRADE GUNS
These higher grade models differ from the Model 11A in general quality, grade of wood, checkering, engraving, etc. General specifications are the same.
Model 11B Special grade . . . . NiB $604 Ex $489 Gd $342
Model 11D Tournament grade . . . NiB $1174 Ex $964 Gd $669
Model 11E Expert grade . . . . . . NiB $1660 Ex $1337 Gd $924
Model 11F Premier grade . . . . . NiB $2647 Ex $2127 Gd $1460

MODEL 11A STANDARD GRADE AUTOLOADER
Hammerless Browning type. Five round capacity. Takedown. Gauges: 12, 16, 20. Tubular magazine holds four rounds. Bbls.: Plain, solid or vent rib, lengths from 26-32 inches, F, M, IC, Cyl., SK chokes. Weight: About 8 lbs., 12 ga.; 7.5 lbs., 16 ga.; 7.25 lbs., 20 ga. Checkered pistol grip and forend. Made 1905-49.
With plain barrel . . . . NiB $342 Ex $278 Gd $195
With solid-rib barrel . . . . NiB $438 Ex $355 Gd $248
With ventilated-rib barrel . . . . NiB $490 Ex $396 Gd $275

MODEL 11R RIOT GUN . . . . NiB $392 Ex $317 Gd $222
Same as Model 11A Standard grade except has 20-inch plain barrel, 12 ga. only. Remington Model 11-48. (See Remington Sportsman-48 Series.)

MODEL 11-87 PREMIER AUTOLOADER
Gas-operated. Hammerless. Gauge: 12; 3-inch chamber. Bbl.: 26-, 28- or 30-inch with REMChoke. Weight: 8.13- 8.38 lbs., depending on bbl. length. Checkered walnut stock and forend in satin finish. Made 1987 to date.
Premier Deer Gun . . . . NiB $575 Ex $466 Gd $327
Premier Deer Gun w/cantilever scope mount . . . . NiB $720 Ex $524 Gd $331
Premier Skeet . . . . NiB $589 Ex $477 Gd $334
Premier Sporting Clays . . . . NiB $700 Ex $566 Gd $395
Premier Sporting Clays SCNP (nickel plated) . . . . . . NiB $739 Ex $596 Gd $415
Premier Standard Autoloader . . . . NiB $589 Ex $477 Gd $334
Premier Trap . . . . NiB $688 Ex $556 Gd $387
Left-hand models, add $55

MODEL 11-87 SPECIAL PURPOSE MAGNUM
Same general specifications as Model 11-87 Premier except with non-reflective wood finish and Parkerized metal. 21-, 26- or 28-inch vent-rib bbl. with REMChoke tubes. Made 1987-93.
Model 11-87 SP Field Magnum . . . . NiB $686 Ex $555 Gd $386
Model 11-87 SP Deer Gun (w/21-inch bbl.) . . . NiB $624 Ex $506 Gd $353
Model 11-87 SP Deer Gun w/cantilever scope mount . . . . NiB $674 Ex $545 Gd $380

MODEL 11-87 SPS MAGNUM
Same general specifications as Model 11-87 Special Purpose Magnum except with synthetic buttstock and forend. 21-, 26- or 28-inch vent-rib bbl. with REMChoke tubes. Matte black or Mossy Oak camo finish (except NWTF turkey gun). Made 1990 to date.
Model 11-87 SPS Magnum (matte black) . . . . . NiB $617 Ex $500 Gd $349
Model 11-87 SPS Camo (Mossy Oak camo) . . NiB $646 Ex $522 Gd $365
Model 11-87 SPS Deer Gun (w/21 inch bbl.) . . NiB $560 Ex $454 Gd $318
Model 11-87 SPS Deer Gun w/cant. scope mt. . . . . NiB $632 Ex $511 Gd $357
Model 11-87 NWTF Turkey Gun (Brown Trebark) disc. 1993 . . . . NiB $730 Ex $590 Gd $411
Model 11-87 NWTF Turkey Gun (Greenleaf) disc. 1996 . . . . NiB $703 Ex $568 Gd $396
Model 11-87 NWTF Turkey Gun (Mossy Oak) disc. 1996 . . . . NiB $716 Ex $579 Gd $404
Model 11-87 NWTF Turkey Gun (Mossy Oak Breakup) introduced 1999 . . . . . . NiB $730 Ex $590 Gd $411
Model 11-87 NWTF 20 ga. Turkey Gun (Mossy Oak Breakup) Produced 1998 only . . . NiB $688 Ex $556 Gd $387
Model 11-87 SPST Turkey Gun (matte bl.) . . . NiB $632 Ex $511 Gd $356

MODEL 11-96 EURO LIGHTWEIGHT
AUTOLOADING SHOTGUN . . . . NiB $684 Ex $553 Gd $385
Lightweight version of Model 11-87 w/reprofiled receiver. 12 ga. only w/3-inch chamber. 26- or 28-inch bbl. w/6mm vent rib and REM Choke tubes. Semi-fancy Monte Carlo walnut buttstock and forearm. Weight: 6.8 lbs. w/26-inch bbl. Made 1996 to date.

MODEL 17A STANDARD GRADE SLIDE-ACTION REPEATING SHOTGUN
Hammerless. Takedown. Five round capacity. 20 ga. only. Four round tubular magazine. Bbls.: plain; 26- to 32-inch; choked F, M or Cyl. Weight: About 5.75 lbs. Plain pistol-grip stock, grooved slide handle. Made 1921-33. Note: The present Ithaca Model 37 is an adaptation of this Browning design.
Plain barrel . . . . NiB $399 Ex $318 Gd $217
Solid rib . . . . NiB $534 Ex $426 Gd $290

MODEL 29A STANDARD GRADE
SLIDE-ACTION REPEATING SHOTGUN . . . . . NiB $459 Ex $372 Gd $263
Hammerless. Takedown. Six round capacity. 12 ga. only. Five round tubular magazine. Bbls.: plain- 26- to 32-inch, choked F, M or Cyl. Weight: About 7.5 lbs. Checkered pistol-grip stock and slide handle. Made 1929-33.

MODEL 29T TARGET GRADE . . . . . NiB $522 Ex $424 Gd $298
Same general specifications as Model 29A except has trap-style stock with straight grip, extension slide handle, vent rib bbl. Disc. 1933.

MODEL 31 AND 31L SKEET GRADE
Same general specifications as Model 31A except has 26-inch bbl. with raised solid or vent rib, SK choke, checkered pistol-grip stock and beavertail forend. Weight: About 8 lbs., 12 ga. Made 1932-1939.
Model 31 Standard w/raised solid rib . . . . NiB $799 Ex $647 Gd $451
Model 31 Standard w/ventilated rib . . . . . NiB $954 Ex $770 Gd $536
Model 31L Lightweight w/raised solid rib . . . . . NiB $730 Ex $591 Gd $413
Model 31L Lightweight w/ventilated rib . . NiB $876 Ex $709 Gd $493

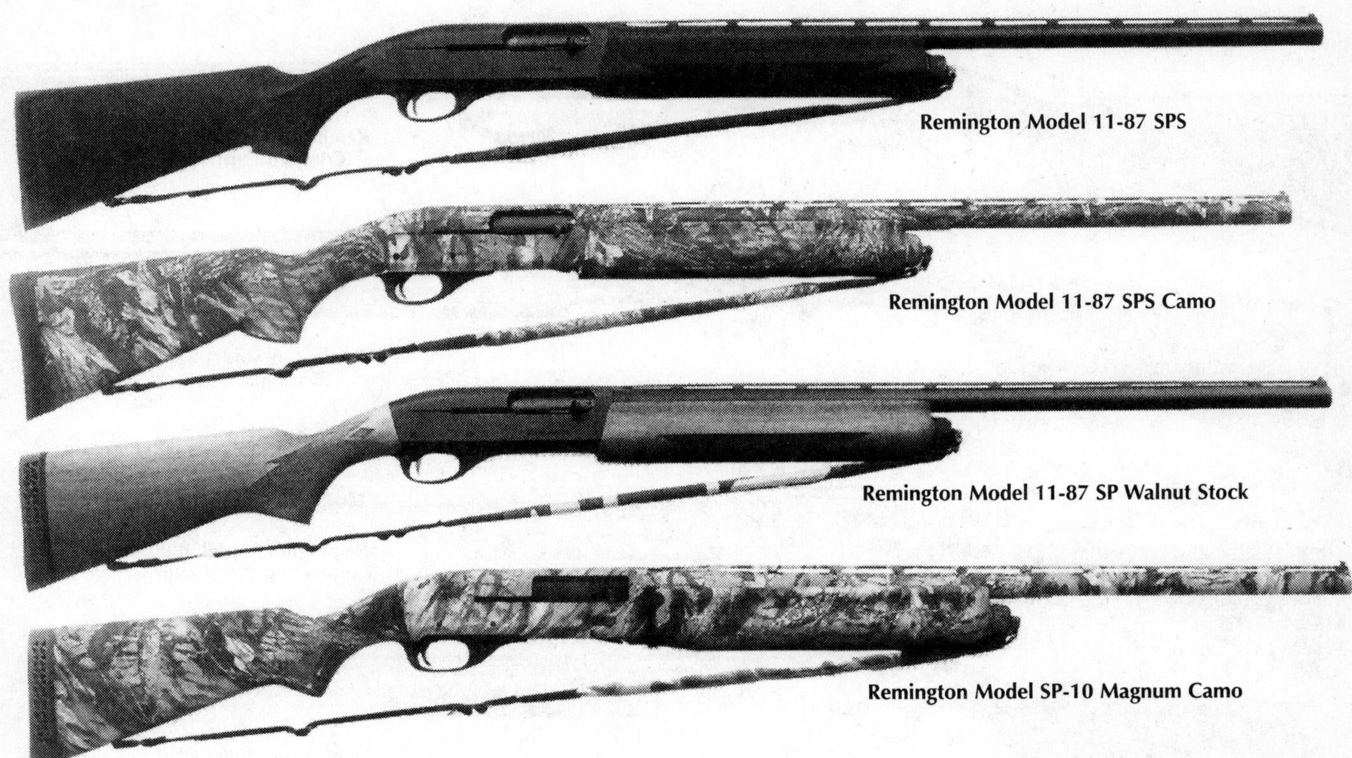

MODEL 31 SPECIAL, TOURNAMENT, EXPERT AND PREMIER GRADE GUNS
These higher grade models differ from the Model 31A in general quality, grade of wood, checkering, engraving, etc. General specifications are the same.
Model 31B Special grade . . . . NiB $703 Ex $568 Gd $396
Model 31D Tournament grade . . . NiB $1002 Ex $808 Gd $558
Model 31E Expert grade . . . . NiB $1399 Ex $1131 Gd $788
Model 31F Premier grade . . . . . NiB $2258 Ex $1821 Gd $1263

MODEL 31A SLIDE-ACTION REPEATER
Hammerless. Takedown. 3- or 5-round capacity. Gauges: 12, 16, 20. Tubular magazine. Bbls.: Plain, solid or vent rib; lengths from 26 -32 inches; F, M, IC, C or SK choke. Weight: About 7.5 lbs., 12 ga.; 6.75 lbs., 16 ga.; 6.5 lbs., 20 ga. Earlier models have checkered pistol-grip stock and slide handle; later models have plain stock and grooved slide handle. Made 1931-49.
Model 31A with plain barrel . . . . . NiB $422 Ex $342 Gd $240
Model 31A with solid rib barrel . . . NiB $508 Ex $411 Gd $288
Model 31A with vent rib barrel . . . NiB $544 Ex $440 Gd $307
Model 31H Hunters' Special w/sporting-style stock . . . . NiB $508 Ex $411 Gd $288
Model 31R Riot Gun w/20-inch plain bbl., 12 ga. . . . . NiB $363 Ex $295 Gd $208

MODEL 31S TRAP SPECIAL/31TC TRAP GRADE
Same general specifications as Model 31A except 12 ga. only, has 30- or 32-inch vent-rib bbl., F choke, checkered trap stock with full pistol grip and recoil pad, checkered extension beavertail forend. Weight: About 8 lbs. (Trap Special has solid-rib bbl., half pistol-grip stock with standard walnut forend).
Model 31S Trap Special . . . . NiB $549 Ex $445 Gd $312
Model 31TC Trap grade . . . . NiB $719 Ex $581 Gd $405

MODEL 32A STANDARD GRADE O/U
Hammerless. Takedown. Auto ejectors. Early model had double triggers, later built with selective single trigger only. 12 ga. only. Bbls.: Plain, raised matted solid or vent rib; 26-, 28-, 30-, 32-inch; F/M choke standard, option of any combination of F, M, IC, C, SK choke. Weight: About 7.75 lbs. Checkered pistol-grip stock and forend. Made 1932-42.
With double triggers . . . . NiB $2031 Ex $1631 Gd $1121
With selective single trigger . . . NiB $2289 Ex $1837 Gd $1261
With raised solid rib, add $200
With ventilated rib, add $300

MODEL 32 TOURNAMENT, EXPERT AND PREMIER GRADE GUNS
These higher-grade models differ from the Model 32A in general quality, grade of wood, checkering, engraving, etc. General specifications are the same. Made 1932-42.
Model 32D Tournament grade . . . . . . NiB $3926 Ex $3155 Gd $2168
Model 32E Expert grade . . . . . . NiB $4902 Ex $3935 Gd $2698
Model 32F Premier grade . . . . NiB $6626 Ex $5323 Gd $3642

MODEL 32 SKEET GRADE
Same general specifications as Model 32A except 26- or 28-inch bbl., SK choke, beavertail forend, selective single trigger only. Weight: About 7.5 lbs. Made 1932-42.

MODEL 32TC TARGET (TRAP) GRADE . . . . . . NiB $3198 Ex $2573 Gd $1773
Same general specifications as Model 32A except 30- or 32-inch vent-rib bbl., F choke, trap-style stock with checkered pistol-grip and beavertail forend. Weight: About 8 lbs. Made l932-42.

MODEL 89 (1889). . . . . NiB $1254 Ex $1008 Gd $695
Hammers. Circular action. Gauges: 10, 12, 16, 28- to 32-inch bls.; steel or Damascus twist. Weight 7-10 lbs. Made 1889-1908.

MODEL 90-T SINGLE-SHOT TRAP . . . . . NiB $2125 Ex $1714 Gd $1188
Gauge: 12; 2.75-inch chambers. 30-, 32- or 34-inch vent-rib bbl. with fixed chokes or screw-in REMChokes; ported or non-ported. Weight: 8.25 lbs. Checkered American walnut standard or Monte Carlo stock with low-luster finish. Engraved sideplates and drop-out trigger group optional. Made 1990-97.

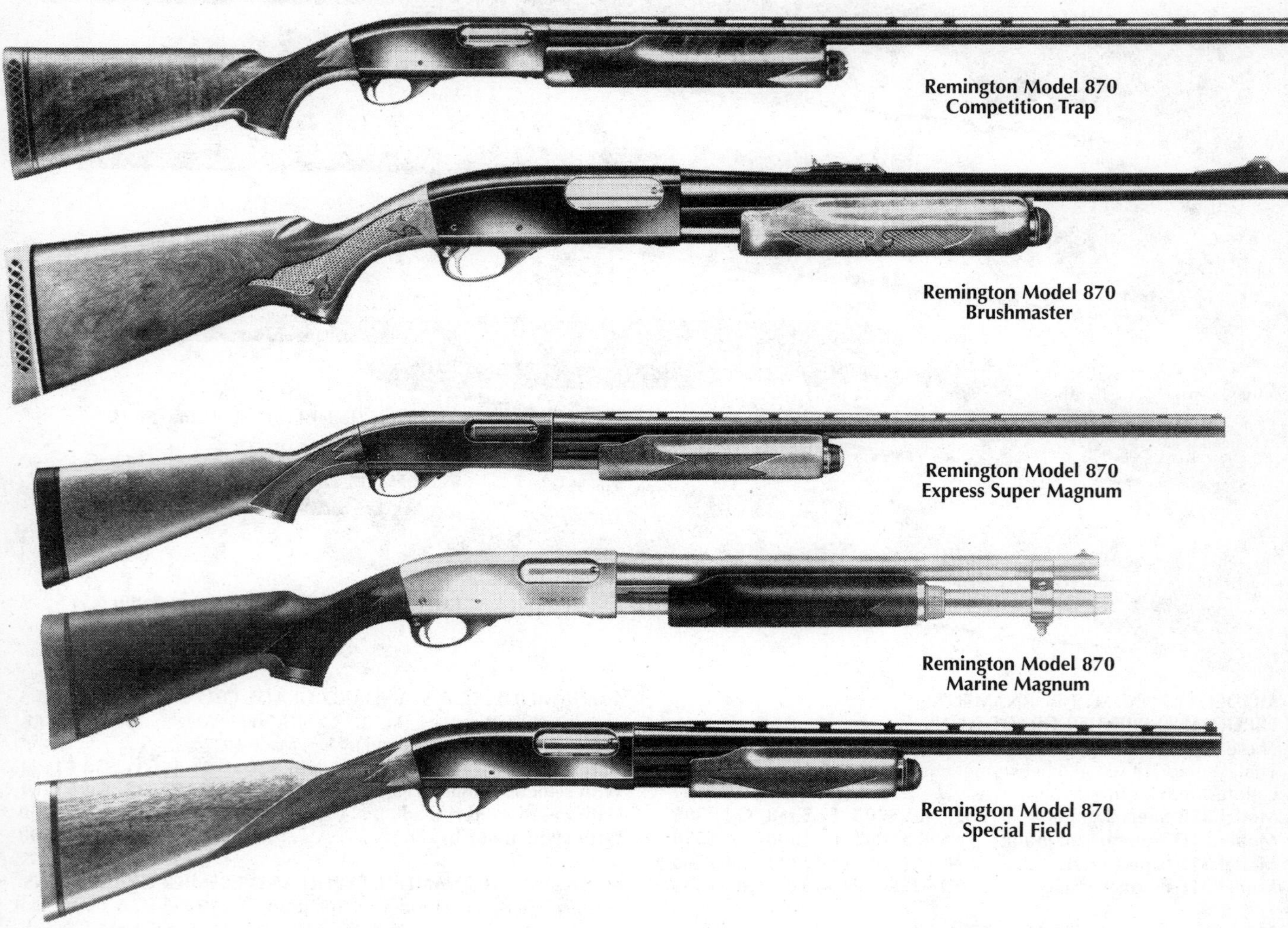

Remington Model 870 Competition Trap

Remington Model 870 Brushmaster

Remington Model 870 Express Super Magnum

Remington Model 870 Marine Magnum

Remington Model 870 Special Field

MODEL 396 O/U

Boxlock. 12 ga. only w/2.75-inch chamber. 28- and 30-inch blued bbls. w/Rem chokes. Weight: 7.50 lbs. Nitride-grayed, engraved receiver, trigger guard, tang, hinge pins and forend metal. Engraved sideplates. Checkered satin-finished American walnut stock w/target style forend. Made 1996 to date.

396 Sporting Clays . . . . NiB $1991 Ex $1605 Gd $1111
396 Skeet. . . . . NiB $2060 Ex $1660 Gd $1149

MODEL 870 "ALL AMERICAN" TRAP GUN . . . NiB $1086 Ex $881 Gd $618

Same as Model 870TB except custom grade with engraved receiver, trigger guard and bbl.; Monte Carlo or straight-comb stock and forend of fancy walnut; available only with 30-inch F choke bbl. Made 1972-77.

MODEL 870 COMPETITION TRAP . . . . NiB $613 Ex $496 Gd $348

Based on standard Model 870 receiver except is single-shot with gas-assisted recoil-reducing system, new choke design, a high step-up vent rib and redesigned stock, forend with cut checkering and satin finish. Weight: 8.5 lbs. Made 1981-87.

MODEL 870 STANDARD. . . . . NiB $406 Ex $330 Gd $233

Same as Model 870 Wingmaster Riot Gun except has rifle-type sights.

MODEL 870 BRUSHMASTER DELUXE

Same as Model 870 Standard except available in 20 ga. as well as 12, has cut-checkered, satin-finished American walnut stock and forend, recoil pad.

Right-hand model . . . . NiB $443 Ex $360 Gd $254
Left-hand model . . . . NiB $514 Ex $416 Gd $292

MODEL 870 EXPRESS

Same general specifications Model 870 Wingmaster except has low-luster walnut-finished hardwood stock with pressed checkering and black recoil pad. Gauges: 12, 20 or .410, 3-inch chambers. Bbls.: 26- or 28-inch vent-rib with REMChoke; 25-inch vent-rib with fixed choke (.410 only). Black oxide metal finish. Made 1987 to date.

Model 870 Express (12 or 20 ga., REMChoke) . . . . NiB $271 Ex $221 Gd $157
Model 870 Express (.410 w/fixed choke) . . . . NiB $304 Ex $247 Gd $175
Express Combo (w/extra 20-inch deer bbl.) . . . . NiB $361 Ex $293 Gd $205

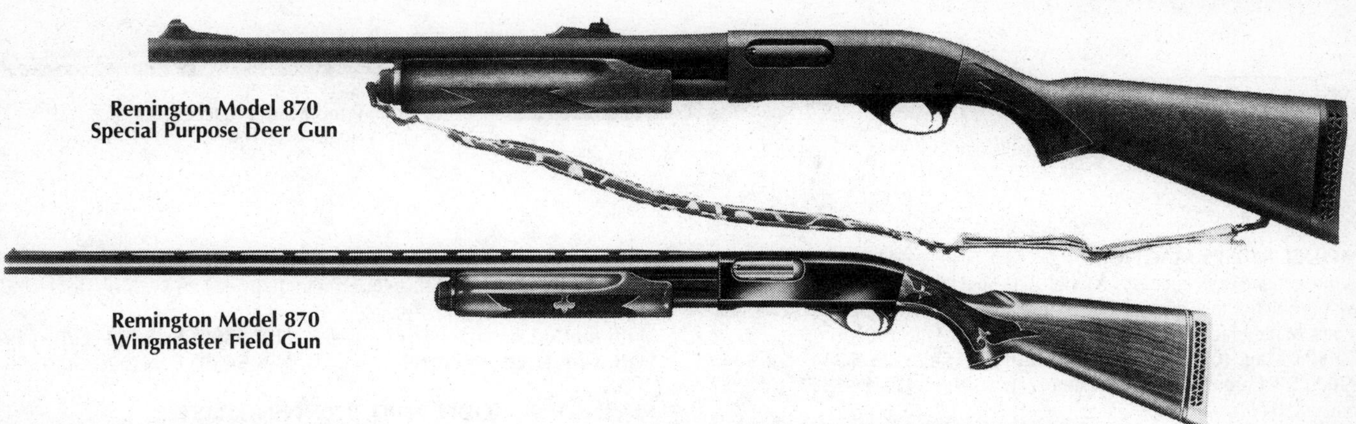

Remington Model 870
Special Purpose Deer Gun

Remington Model 870
Wingmaster Field Gun

MODEL 870 EXPRESS DEER GUN
Same general specifications as Model 870 Express except in 12 ga. only, 20-inch bbl. with fixed IC choke, adj. rifle sights and Monte Carlo stock. Made 1991 to date.
Express Deer Gun w/standard barrel . . . . NiB $296 Ex $241 Gd $169
Express Deer Gun w/rifled barrel . . . . NiB $331 Ex $268 Gd $188

MODEL 870 EXPRESS SUPER MAGNUM
Similar to Model 870 Express except chambered for 12 ga. mag. w/3.5-inch chamber. Bbls.: 23-, 26- or 28-inch vent rib w/REM Choke. Checkered low-luster walnut-finished hardwood, black synthetic or camo buttstock and fore-arm. Matte black oxide metal finish or full camo finish. Made 1998 to date.
Model 870 ESM (w/hardwood stock) . . . . NiB $282 Ex $229 Gd $162
Model 870 ESM (w/black synthetic stock) . . . . NiB $296 Ex $240 Gd $170
Model 870 ESM (w/camo synthetic stock) . . . . NiB $400 Ex $325 Gd $229
Model 870 ESM Synthetic Turkey (w/synthetic stock) . . . . NiB $301 Ex $245 Gd $175
Model 870 ESM como Turkey (w/full camo) . . . . NiB $379 Ex $308 Gd $218
Model 870 ESM combo (w/full camo, extra bbl.) . . . . NiB $442 Ex $359 Gd $253

MODEL 870 EXPRESS SYNTHETIC HOME DEFENSE . . . . . NiB $269 Ex $220 Gd $156
Slide action, hammerless, takedown. 12 ga. only. 18-inch bbl. w/cylinder choke and bead front sight. Positive checkered synthetic stock and forend with non-reflective black finish. Made 1995 to date.

MODEL 870EXPRESS TURKEY GUN. . . NiB $296 Ex $229 Gd $240
Same general specifications as Model 870 Express except has 21-inch vent-rib bbl. and Turkey Extra-Full REMChoke. Made 1991 to date.

MODEL 870 EXPRESS YOUTH GUN . . NiB $282 Ex $229 Gd $162
Same general specifications as Model 870 Express except has scaled-down stock with 12.5-inch pull and 21-inch vent rib bbl. with REMChoke. Made 1991 to date.

MODEL 870 LIGHTWEIGHT
Same as standard Model 870 but with scaled-down receiver and lightweight mahogany stock; 20 ga. only. 2.75-inch chamber. Bbls.: plain or vent rib; 26-inch, IC; 28-inch, M or F choke. REMChoke available from 1987. Weight 5.75 lbs. w/26-inch plain bbl. American walnut stock and forend with satin or Hi-gloss finish. Made 1972-94.
With plain barrel . . . . NiB $307 Ex $250 Gd $177
With ventilated rib barrel . . . . NiB $337 Ex $274 Gd $193
With REMChoke barrel . . . . NiB $380 Ex $308 Gd $216

MODEL 870 LIGHTWEIGHT MAGNUM
Same as Model 870 Lightweight but chambered for 20 ga. Magnum 3-inch shell; 28-inch bbl., plain or vent rib, F choke. Weight: 6 lbs. with plain bbl. Made 1972-94.
With plain barrel . . . . NiB $373 Ex $303 Gd $215
With ventilated rib barrel . . . . NiB $421 Ex $342 Gd $240

MODEL 870 MAGNUM DUCK GUN
Same as Model 870 Field Gun except has 3-inch chamber 12 and 20 gauge Magnum only. 28- or 30-inch bbl., plain or vent rib, M or F choke, recoil pad. Weight: About 7 or 6.75 lbs. Made 1964 to date.
With plain barrel . . . . NiB $442 Ex $359 Gd $253
With ventilated rib barrel . . . . NiB $484 Ex $393 Gd $275

MODEL 870 MARINE MAGNUM . . . . NiB $462 Ex $374 Gd $284
Same general specifications as Model 870 Wingmaster except with 7-round magazine, 18-inch plain bbl. with fixed IC choke, bead front sight and nickel finish. Made 1992 to date.

MODEL 870 SA SKEET GUN, SMALLBORE. . . . . NiB $443 Ex $360 Gd $253
Similar to Wingmaster Model 870SA except chambered for 28 and .410 ga. (2.5-inch chamber for latter); 25-inch vent rib bbl., SK choke. Weight: 6 lbs., 28 ga.; 6.5 lbs., .410. Made 1969-82.

MODEL 870 MISSISSIPPI MAGNUM DUCK GUN . . . . NiB $453 Ex $367 Gd $258
Same as Remington Model 870 Magnum duck gun except has 32-inch bbl. "Ducks Unlimited" engraved receiver, Made in 1983.

MODEL 870 SPECIAL FIELD SHOTGUN . . . . NiB $443 Ex $359 Gd $253
Pump action. Hammerless. Gauge: 12 or 20. 21-inch vent-rib bbl. with REMChoke. 41.5 inches overall. Weight: 6-7 lbs. Straight-grip checkered walnut stock and forend. Made 1987-95.

MODEL 870 SPECIAL PURPOSE DEER GUN
Similar to Special Purpose Magnum except with 20-inch IC choke, rifle sights. Matte black oxide and Parkerized finish. Oil-finished, checkered buttstock and forend with recoil pad. Made 1986 to date.
Model 870 SP Deer Gun . . . . NiB $379 Ex $308 Gd $218
Model 870 SP Deer Gun, cant. scope mt. . . . . NiB $443 Ex $360 Gd $253

MODEL 870 SPECIAL PURPOSE MAGNUM . . . . NiB $443 Ex $359 Gd $253
Similar to the 870 Magnum duck gun except with 26-, 28- or 30-inch vent rib REMChoke bbl.12 ga. only; 3-inch chamber. Oil-finished field-grade stock with recoil pad, QD swivels and Cordura sling. Made 1985 to date.

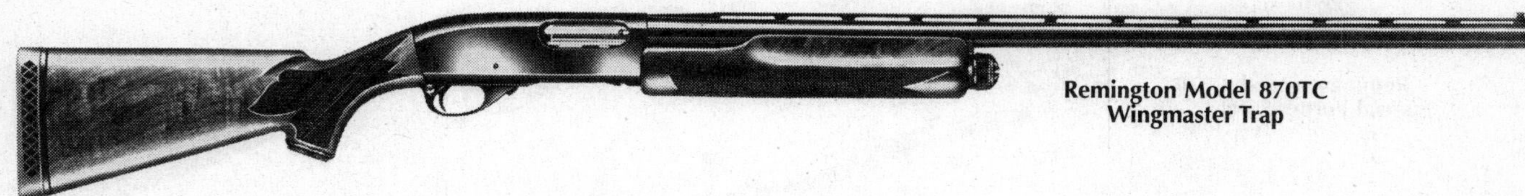

Remington Model 870TC Wingmaster Trap

MODEL 870SPS MAGNUM
Same general specifications Model 870 Special Purpose Magnum except with synthetic stock and forend. 26- or 28-inch vent-rib bbl. with REMChoke tubes. Matte black or Mossy Oak camo finish. Made 1991 to date.
70 SPS Mag. (black syn. stock) .... NiB $425 Ex $344 Gd $242
870 SPS-T Camo (Mossy Oak camo)...... NiB $439 Ex $357 Gd $250

MODEL 870 WINGMASTER FIELD GUN
Same general specifications as Model 870AP except checkered stock and forend. Later models have REMChoke systems in 12 ga. Made 1964 to date.
With plain barrel .... NiB $299 Ex $243 Gd $163
With ventilated rib barrel .... NiB $347 Ex $282 Gd $200

MODEL 870 WINGMASTER FIELD GUN, SMALL BORE
Same as standard Model 870 except w/scaled-down lightweight receivers. Gauges: 28 and .410. Plain or vent rib 25-inch bbl. choked IC, M or F. Weight: 5.5-6.25 lbs. depending on gauge and bbl. Made 1969-94.
With plain barrel .... NiB $548 Ex $444 Gd $311
With ventilated-rib barrel .... NiB $626 Ex $498 Gd $348

MODEL 870 WINGMASTER
MAGNUM DELUXE GRADE ...... NiB $552 Ex $448 Gd $314
Same as Model 870 Magnum standard grade except has checkered stock and extension beavertail forearm, bbl. with matted top surface. Disc. in 1963.

MODEL 870 WINGMASTER
MAGNUM STANDARD GRADE ... NiB $488 Ex $397 Gd $279
Same as Model 870AP except chambered for 12 ga. 3-inch Magnum, 30-inch F choke bbl., recoil pad. Weight: About 8.25 lbs. Made 1955-63.

MODEL 870 WINGMASTER REMCHOKE SERIES
Slide action, hammerless, takedown with blued all-steel receiver. Gauges: 12, 20; 3-inch chamber. Tubular magazine. Bbls.: 21-, 26-, 28-inch vent-rib with REM Choke. Weight: 7.5 lbs. (12 ga.). Satin-finished, checkered walnut buttstock and forend with recoil pad. Right- or left-hand models. Made 1986 to date.
Standard model, 12 ga. .... NiB $367 Ex $298 Gd $210
Standard model, 20 ga. .... NiB $390 Ex $316 Gd $223
Youth model, 21-inch barrel ...... NiB $384 Ex $312 Gd $220

MODEL 870ADL WINGMASTER DELUXE GRADE
Same general specifications as Wingmaster Model 870AP except has pistol-grip stock and extension beavertail forend, both finely checkered; matted top surface or vent-rib bbl. Made 1950-63.
With matted top-surface barrel.... NiB $373 Ex $303 Gd $215
With ventilated-rib barrel .... NiB $416 Ex $338 Gd $238

MODEL 870AP WINGMASTER STANDARD GRADE
Hammerless. Takedown. Gauges: 12, 16, 20. Tubular magazine holds four rounds. Bbls.: Plain, matted top surface or vent rib; 26-inch IC, 28-inch M or F choke, 30-inch F choke (12 ga. only). Weight: About 7 lbs., 12 ga.; 6.75 lbs., 16 ga.; 6.5 lbs., 20 ga. Plain pistol-grip stock, grooved forend. Made 1950-63.
With plain barrel .... NiB $277 Ex $226 Gd $160
With matted surface barrel .... NiB $291 Ex $236 Gd $167
With ventilated rib barrel .... NiB $317 Ex $257 Gd $181
Left-hand model .... NiB $329 Ex $267 Gd $188

MODEL 870BDL WINGMASTER DELUXE SPECIAL
Same as Model 870ADL except select American walnut stock and forend. Made 1950-63.
With matted surface barrel .... NiB $399 Ex $324 Gd $229
With ventilated-rib barrel .... NiB $439 Ex $357 Gd $250

REMINGTON MODEL 870D, 870F WINGMASTER TOURNAMENT AND PREMIER GRADE GUNS
These higher-grade models differ from the Model 870AP in general quality, grade of wood, checkering, engraving, etc. General operating specifications are essentially the same. Made 1950 to date.
Model 870D Tournament grade ...... NiB $2622 Ex $2113 Gd $1463
Model 870F Premier grade .... NiB $5674 Ex $4555 Gd $3123
Model 870F Premier gr. w/gold inlay..... NiB $8957 Ex $7181 Gd $4909

REMINGTON MODEL 870R
WINGMASTER RIOT GUN .... NiB $383 Ex $311 Gd $219
Same as Model 870AP except 20-inch bbl., IC choke, 12 ga. only.

REMINGTON MODEL 870SA WINGMASTER SKEET GUN
Same general specifications as Model 870AP except has 26-inch vent-rib bbl., SK choke, ivory bead front sight, metal bead rear sight, pistol-grip stock and extension beavertail forend. Weight: 6.75 to 7.5 lbs. depending on gauge. Made 1950-82.
Model 870SA Skeet grade (disc. 1982) ...... NiB $395 Ex $320 Gd $225
Model 870SC Skeet Target grade (disc. 1980) .... NiB $557 Ex $449 Gd $313

REMINGTON MODEL 870TB
WINGMASTER TRAP SPECIAL .... NiB $474 Ex $383 Gd $268
Same general specifications as Model 870AP Wingmaster except has 28- or 30-inch vent rib bbl., F choke, metal bead front sight, no rear sight. "Special" grade trap-style stock and forend, both checkered, recoil pad. Weight: About 8 lbs. Made 1950-81.

REMINGTON MODEL
870TC TRAP GRADE .... NiB $646 Ex $524 Gd $370
Same as Model 870 Wingmaster TC except has tournament-grade walnut in stock and forend w/satin finish. Over-bored 30-inch vent rib bbl. w/ 2.75-inch chamber and RemChoke tubes. Reissued in 1996. See separate listing for earlier model.

REMINGTON MODEL 870TC WINGMASTER TRAP GRADE
Same as Model 870TB except higher-grade walnut in stock and forend, has both front and rear sights. Made 1950-79. Model 870 TC reissued in 1996. See separate listing for later model.
Model 870 TC Trap (Standard)..... NiB $652 Ex $529 Gd $373
Model 870 TC Trap (Monte Carlo) .. NiB $678 Ex $550 Gd $387

REMINGTON MODEL
878A AUTOMASTER .... NiB $297 Ex $239 Gd $166
Gas-operated Autoloader. 12 ga., 3-round magazine. Bbls.: 26-inch IC, 28-inch M choke, 30-inch F choke. Weight: About 7 lbs. Plain pistol-grip stock and forearm. Made 1959-62.

NOTE: *New stock checkering patterns and receiver scroll markings were incorporated on all standard Model 1100 field, magnum, skeet and trap models in 1979.*

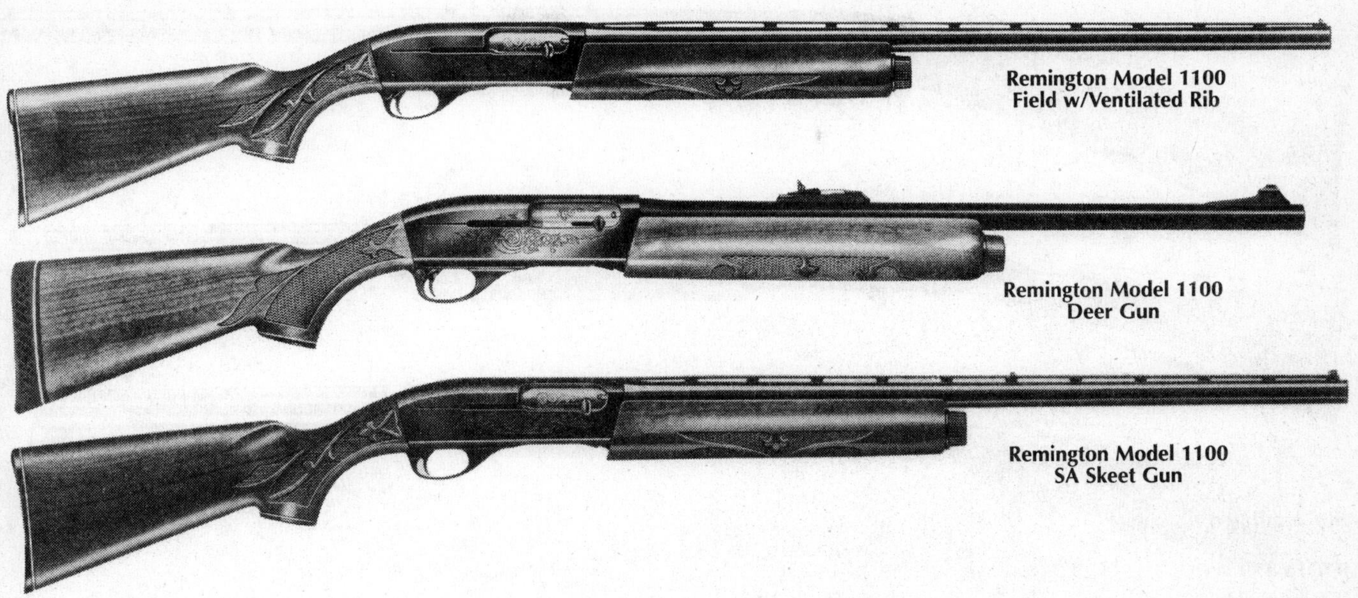

Remington Model 1100
Field w/Ventilated Rib

Remington Model 1100
Deer Gun

Remington Model 1100
SA Skeet Gun

MODEL 1100 AUTOMATIC FIELD GUN
Gas-operated. Hammerless. Takedown. Gauges: 12, 16, 20. Bbls.: plain or vent. rib; 30-inch F, 28-inch M or F, 26-inch IC; or REMChoke tubes. Weight: Average 7.25-7.5 lbs. depending on ga. and bbl. length. Checkered walnut pistol-grip stock and forearm in high-gloss finish. Made 1963 to date. 16 ga. discontinued.
With plain barrel .... NiB $371 Ex $303 Gd $215
With ventilated-rib barrel .... NiB $422 Ex $344 Gd $243
REMChoke model .... NiB $462 Ex $375 Gd $265
REMChoke, Left-hand action ..... NiB $499 Ex $406 Gd $285

MODEL 1100 DEER GUN .... NiB $469 Ex $381 Gd $269
Same as Model 1100 Field Gun except has 22-inch barrel, IC, with rifle-type sights; 12 and 20 ga. only; recoil pad. Weight: About 7.25 lbs. Made 1963-96.

MODEL 1100 DUCKS UNLIMITED
ATLANTIC COMMEMORATIVE... NiB $1030 Ex $834 Gd $583
Limited production for one year. Similar specifications to Model 1100 Field except with 32-inch F choke, vent rib bbl. 12-ga. Magnum only. Made in 1982.

MODEL 1100 DUCKS UNLIMITED "THE CHESAPEAKE" COMMEMORATIVE NiB $754 Ex $613 Gd $441
Limited edition 1 to 2400. Same general specifications as Model 1100 Field except sequentially numbered with markings "The Chesapeake." 12 ga. Magnum with 30-inch F choke, vent rib bbl. Made in 1981.

REMINGTON MODEL 1100 FIELD GRADE, SMALL BORE
Same as standard Model 1100 but scaled down. Gauges: 28, .410. 25-inch bbl., plain or vent rib; IC, M or F choke. Weight: 6.25-7 lbs. depending on gauge and bbl. Made 1969-94.
With plain barrel .... NiB $545 Ex $436 Gd $342
With ventilated rib .... NiB $689 Ex $560 Gd $394

MODEL 1100 LIGHTWEIGHT
Same as standard Model 1100 but scaled-down receiver and lightweight mahogany stock; 20 ga. only, 2.75-inch chamber. Bbls.: Plain or vent rib; 26-inch IC; 28-inch M and F choke. Weight: 6.25 lbs. Made 1971 to date.
With plain barrel .... NiB $511 Ex $416 Gd $294
With ventilated rib .... NiB $572 Ex $464 Gd $328

MODEL 1100 LIGHTWEIGHT MAGNUM
Same as Model 1100 Lightweight but chambered for 20 gauge Magnum 3-inch shell; 28-inch bbl., plain or vent rib, F choke. Weight: 6.5 lbs. Made 1971 to date.
With plain barrel .... NiB $537 Ex $435 Gd $305
With ventilated rib .... NiB $597 Ex $484 Gd $339
With choke tubes .... NiB $639 Ex $516 Gd $361

MODEL 1100 LT-20
DUCKS UNLIMITED
SPECIAL COMMEMORATIVE ..... NiB $668 Ex $540 Gd $377
Limited edition 1 to 2400. Same general specifications as Model 1100 Field except sequentially numbered with markings, "The Chesapeake." 20 ga. only. 26-inch IC, vent-rib bbl. Made in 1981.

MODEL 1100 LT-20 SERIES
Same as Model 1100 Field Gun except in 20 ga. with shorter 23-inch vent rib bbl., straight-grip stock. REMChoke series has 21-inch vent rib bbl., choke tubes. Weight: 6.25 lbs. Checkered grip and forearm. Made 1983 to date.
Model 1100
LT-20 Special .... NiB $550 Ex $446 Gd $313
Model 1100
LT-20 Deer Gun............... NiB $522 Ex $424 Gd $298
Model 1100
LT-20 Youth .... NiB $537 Ex $436 Gd $305

REMINGTON MODEL
1100 MAGNUM .... NiB $481 Ex $390 Gd $275
Limited production. Similar to the Model 1100 Field except with 26-inch F choke, vent rib bbl. and 3-inch chamber. Made in 1981.

MODEL 1100 MAGNUM DUCK GUN
Same as Model 1100 Field Gun except has 3-inch chamber,12 and 20 ga. Mag. only. 30-inch plain or vent rib bbl. in 12 ga., 28-inch in 20 ga.; M or F choke. Recoil pad. Weight: About 7.75 lbs. Made 1963-88.
With plain barrel .... NiB $429 Ex $348 Gd $247
With ventilated
rib barrel.................... NiB $482 Ex $392 Gd $276

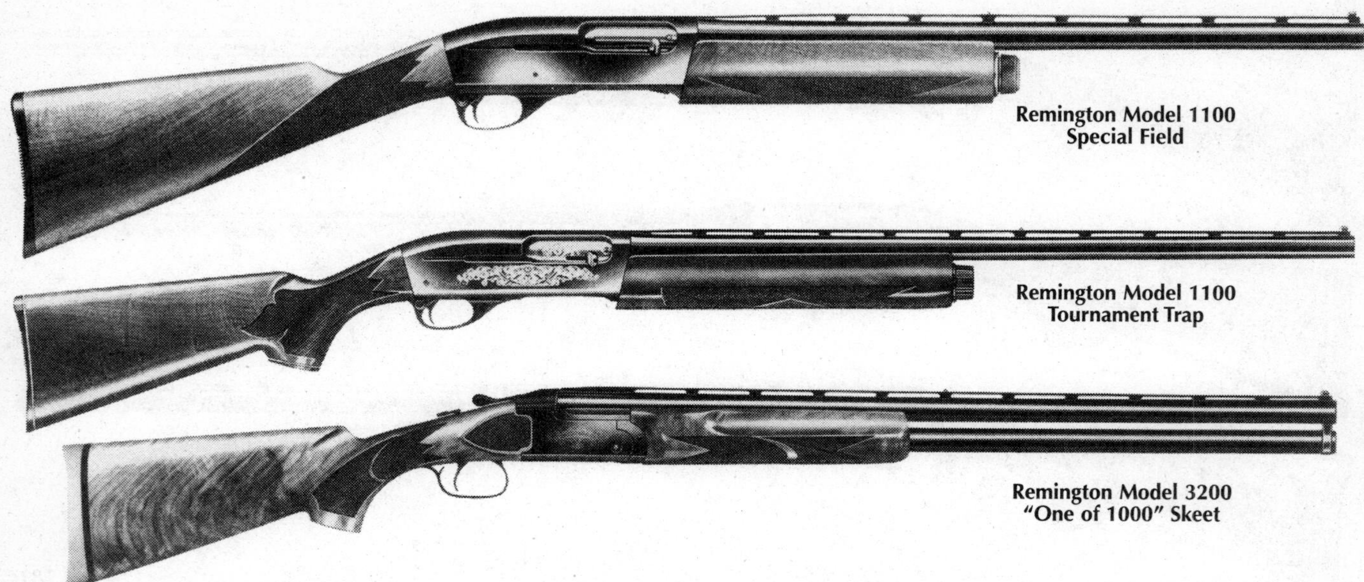

Remington Model 1100 Special Field

Remington Model 1100 Tournament Trap

Remington Model 3200 "One of 1000" Skeet

MODEL 1100 ONE OF 3000 FIELD .... NiB $1276 Ex $1133 Gd $722
Limited edition, numbered 1 to 3000. Similar to Model 1100 Field except with fancy wood and gold-trimmed etched hunting scenes on receiver. 12 gauge with 28-inch Mod., vent rib bbl. Made in 1980.

MODEL 1100 SA SKEET GUN
Same as Model 1100 Field Gun, 12 and 20 ga. except has 26-inch vent-rib bbl., SK choke or with Cutts Compensator. Weight: 7.25-7.5 lbs. Made 1963-94.

With skeet-choked barrel .... NiB $543 Ex $441 Gd $311
With Cutts Comp. .... NiB $562 Ex $457 Gd $321
Left-hand action .... NiB $581 Ex $472 Gd $332

MODEL 1100 SA LIGHTWEIGHT SKEET .... NiB $513 Ex $416 Gd $293
Same as Model 1100 Lightweight except has skeet-style stock and forearm, 26-inch vent-rib bbl., SK choke. Made 1971-97.

MODEL 1100 SA SKEET SMALL BORE .... NiB $582 Ex $473 Gd $333
Similar to standard Model 1100SA except chambered for 28 and .410 ga. (2.5-inch chamber for latter); 25-inch vent-rib bbl., SK choke. Weight: 6.75 lbs., 28 ga.; 7.25 lbs., .410. Made 1969 to date.

MODEL 1100 SB LIGHTWEIGHT SKEET .... NiB $569 Ex $461 Gd $325
Same as Model 1100SA Lightweight except has select wood. Introduced in 1977.

MODEL 1100 SB SKEET GUN .... NiB $542 Ex $440 Gd $310
Same specifications as Model 1100SA except has select wood. Made 1963-97.

MODEL 1100 SPECIAL FIELD SHOTGUN .... NiB $569 Ex $461 Gd $325
Gas-operated. Five round capacity. Hammerless. Gauges: 12 and 20. 21-inch vent-rib bbl. with REMChoke. Weight: 6.5-7.25 lbs. Straight-grip checkered walnut stock and forend. Made 1987 to date.

MODEL 1100 SP MAGNUM
Same as Model 1100 Field except 12 ga. only with 3-inch chambers. Bbls.: 26- or 30-inch F choke; or 26-inch with REM Choke tubes; vent rib. Non-reflective matte black, Parkerized bbl. and receiver. Satin-finished stock and forend. Made 1981 to date.

With fixed choke .... NiB $446 Ex $363 Gd $256
With REMChoke .... NiB $498 Ex $404 Gd $283

MODEL 1100 TOURNAMENT AND PREMIER
These higher grade guns differ from standard models in overall quality, grade of wood, checkering, engraving, gold inlays, etc. General specifications are the same. Made 1963 to date.

Model 1100D Tournament .... NiB $2748 Ex $1975 Gd $1409
Model 1100F Premier .... NiB $5941 Ex $4396 Gd $2910
Model 1100F Premier with gold inlay .... NiB $9031 Ex $5168 Gd $3495

MODEL 1100 TOURNAMENT SKEET .... NiB $682 Ex $613 Gd $389
Similar to Model 1100 Field except with 26-inch bbl. SK choke. Gauges: 12, LT-20, 28, and .410. Features select walnut stocks and new cut-checkering patterns. Made 1979-89.

MODEL 1100TA TRAP GUN ...... NiB $485 Ex $384 Gd $272
Similar to Model 1100TB Trap Gun except with regular-grade stocks. Available in both left- and right-hand versions. Made 1979-86.

MODEL 1100TB TRAP GUN
Same as Model 1100 Field Gun except has special trap stock, straight or Monte Carlo comb, recoil pad; 30-inch vent-rib bbl., F or M trap choke; 12 ga. only. Weight: 8.25 lbs. Made 1963-79.

With straight stock .... NiB $516 Ex $419 Gd $265
With Monte Carlo stock .... NiB $541 Ex $439 Gd $308

MODEL 1900 HAMMERLESS DOUBLE .... NiB $1143 Ex $924 Gd $643
Improved version of Model 1894. Boxlock. Auto ejector. Double triggers. Gauges: 10, 12, 16. Bbls.: 28 to 32 inches. Value shown is for standard grade with ordnance steel bbls. Made 1900-10.

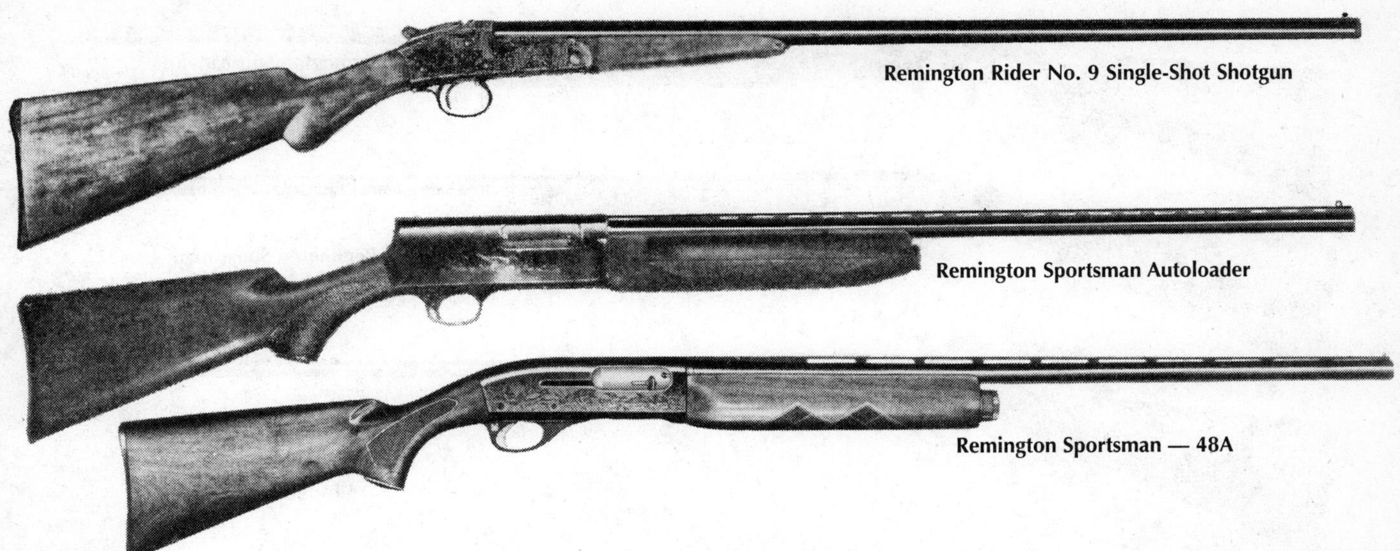
Remington Rider No. 9 Single-Shot Shotgun

Remington Sportsman Autoloader

Remington Sportsman — 48A

MODEL 3200
COMPETITION SKEET GUN . . . . NiB $1760 Ex $1424 Gd $994
Same as Model 3200 Skeet Gun except has gilded scrollwork on frame, engraved forend, latch plate and trigger guard, select fancy wood. Made 1973-84.

MODEL 3200
COMPETITION SKEET SET . . . . NiB $5450 Ex $4381 Gd $3011
Similar specifications to Model 3200 Field. 12-ga. O/U with additional, interchangeable bbls. in 20, 28, and .410 ga. Cased. Made 1980-84.

MODEL 3200
COMPETITION TRAP GUN. . . . NiB $2165 Ex $1752 Gd $1224
Same as Model 3200 Trap Gun except has gilded scrollwork on frame, engraved forend, latch plate and trigger guard, select fancy wood. Made 1973-84.

MODEL 3200
FIELD GRADE MAGNUM . . . . . NiB $1815 Ex $1466 Gd $1020
Same as Model 3200 Field except chambered for 12 ga. mag. 3-inch shells 30-inch bbls., M and F or both F choke. Made 1975-84.

MODEL 3200 FIELD GRADE O/U . . . NiB $1223 Ex $993 Gd $697
Boxlock. Auto ejectors. Selective single trigger. 12 ga. 2.75-inch chambers. Bbls.: Vent rib, 26- and 28-inch M/F; 30-inch IC/M. Weight: About 7.75 lbs. with 26-inch bbls. Checkered pistol-grip stock/forearm. Made 1973-78.

MODEL 3200
"ONE OF 1000" SKEET . . . . NiB $1985 Ex $1602 Gd $1111
Same as Model 3200 "One of 1000" Trap except has 26- or 28-inch bbls., SK choke, skeet-style stock and forearm. Made in 1974.

MODEL 3200
"ONE OF 1000" TRAP. . . . . NiB $2180 Ex $1763 Gd $1231
Limited edition numbered 1 to 1000. Same general specifications as Model 3200 Trap Gun but has frame, trigger guard and forend latch elaborately engraved (designation "One of 1,000" on frame side), stock and forearm of high grade walnut. Supplied in carrying case. Made in 1973.

MODEL 3200 SKEET GUN . . . . . NiB $1577 Ex $1273 Gd $885
Same as Model 3200 Field Grade except skeet-style stock and full beavertail forearm, 26- or 28-inch bbls., SK choke. Made 1973-80.

MODEL 3200
SPECIAL TRAP GUN . . . . NiB $1448 Ex $1174 Gd $824
Same as Model 3200 Trap Gun except has select fancy-grade wood and other minor refinements. Made 1973-84.

MODEL 3200 TRAP GUN . . . . . . NiB $1339 Ex $1086 Gd $764
Same as Model 3200 Field Grade except trap-style stock w/Monte Carlo or straight comb, select wood, beavertail forearm, 30- or 32-inch bbls. w/ventilated rib, IM/F or F/F chokes. Made 1973-77.

RIDER NO. 9
SINGLE-SHOT SHOTGUN . . . . NiB $453 Ex $370 Gd $263
Improved version of No. 3 Single Barrel Shotgun made in the late 1800s. Semi-hammerless. Gauges 10, 12, 16, 20, 24, 28. 30- to 32-inch plain bbl. Weight: About 6 lbs. Plain pistol-grip stock and forearm. Auto ejector. Made 1902-10.

SP-10
MAGNUM AUTOLOADER . . . . NiB 1076 Ex $871 Gd $605
Takedown. Gas-operated with stainless steel piston. 10 ga., 3.5-inch chamber. Bbls.: 26- or 30-inch vent-rib with REMChoke screw-in tubes. Weight: 11 to 11.25 lbs. Metal bead front. Checkered walnut stock with satin finish. Made 1989 to date.

SP-10
MAGNUM TURKEY COMBO . . . . NiB $1087 Ex $879 Gd $614
Same general specifications as Model SP-10 Magnum except has extra 22-inch REMChoke bbl. with M, F and Turkey extra-full tubes. Rifle sights. QD swivels and camo sling. Made 1991 to date.

PEERLESS O/U. . . . . NiB $1120 Ex $906 Gd $632
Boxlock action and removable, engraved sideplates. Gauge: 12 only with 3-inch chambers. Barrels: 26-, 28-, or 30-inch with vent rib and REMChoke system. Automatic safety and single selective trigger. Weight: 7.25 lbs. to 7.5 lbs. Blued receiver and bbls. Checkered American walnut stock. Made 1993-98.

SPORTSMAN A STANDARD GRADE
AUTOLOADER
Same general specifications as Model 11A except magazine holds two shells. Also available in "B" Special Grade, "D" Tournament Grade, "E" Expert Grade, "F" Premier Grade. Made 1931-48. Same values as for Model 11A.
48D . . . . NiB $1183 Ex $900 Gd $513

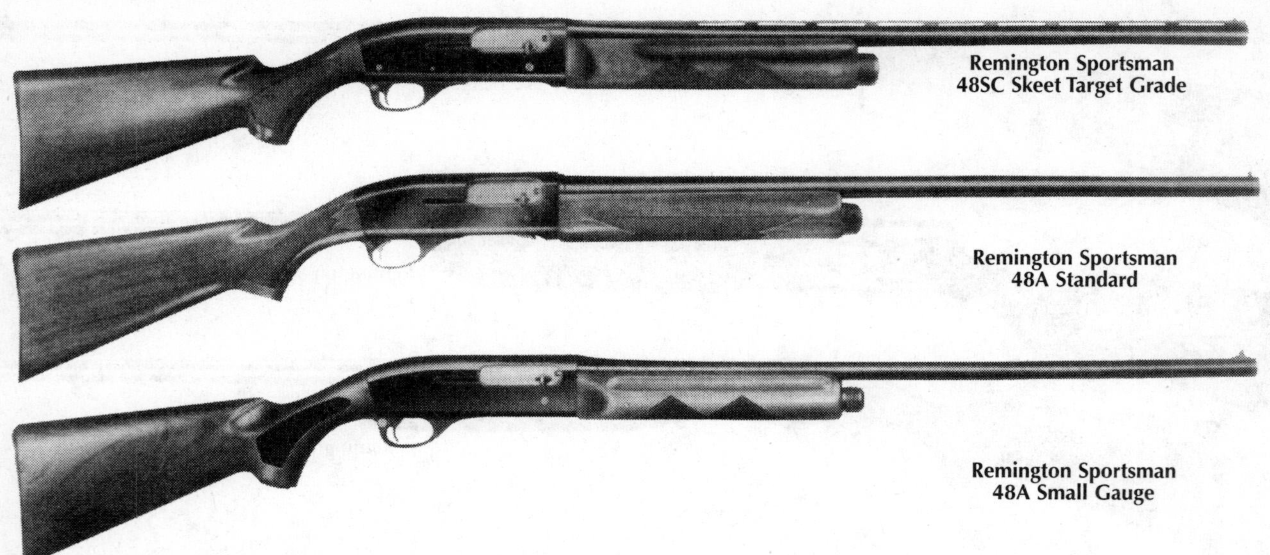

Remington Sportsman 48SC Skeet Target Grade

Remington Sportsman 48A Standard

Remington Sportsman 48A Small Gauge

SPORTSMAN SKEET GUN
Same general specifications as the Sportsman A except has 26-inch bbl. (plain, solid or vent rib), SK choke, beavertail forend. Disc. 1949.
With plain barrel .... NiB $433 Ex $250 Gd $251
With solid-rib barrel .... NiB $519 Ex $422 Gd $299
With ventilated rib barrel .... NiB $567 Ex $461 Gd $325

SPORTSMAN-48A STANDARD GRADE AUTOLOADER
Streamlined receiver. Hammerless. Takedown. Gauges: 12, 16, 20. Tubular magazine holds two rounds. Bbls.: Plain, matted top surface or vent rib; 26-inch IC, 28-inch M or F choke, 30-inch F choke (12 ga. only). Weight: About 7.5 lbs., 12 ga.; 6.25 lbs., 16 ga.; 6.5 lbs., 20 ga. Pistol-grip stock, grooved forend, both checkered. Made 1949-59.
With plain bbl. .... NiB $396 Ex $340 Gd $222
With matted top-surface bbl. ...... NiB $432 Ex $353 Gd $251
With ventilated rib bbl. .... NiB $457 Ex $373 Gd $266

SPORTSMAN-48 B, D, F SPECIAL, TOURNAMENT AND PREMIER GRADE GUNS
These higher grade models differ from the Sportsman-48A in general quality, grade of wood, checkering, engraving, etc. General specifications are the same. Made 1949-59.
Sportsman-48B Special grade ..... NiB $470 Ex $383 Gd $271
Sportsman-48D Tournament grade ... NiB $984 Ex $794 Gd $551
Sportsman-48F Premier grade .... NiB $2153 Ex $1738 Gd $1208

SPORTSMAN-48SA SKEET GUN
Same general specifications as Sportsman-48A except has 26-inch bbl. with matted top surface or vent rib, SK choke, ivory bead front sight, metal bead rear sight. Made 1949-60.
With matted top-surface barrel ... NiB $389 Ex $318 Gd $228
With ventilated rib barrel .... NiB $465 Ex $370 Gd $263
Sportsman-48SC Skeet
Target grade .... NiB $550 Ex $447 Gd $315
Sportsman-48SD Skeet
Tournament grade .... NiB $962 Ex $777 Gd $540
Sportsman-48SF Skeet
Premier grade .... NiB $2263 Ex $1826 Gd $1268

MODEL 11-48A RIOT GUN ...... NiB $268 Ex $273 Gd $193
Same as Model 11-48A except 20-inch plain barrel and 12 ga. only. Disc. in 1969.

MODEL 11-48A STANDARD GRADE 4-ROUND AUTOLOADER .410 & 28 GAUGE
Same general specifications as Sportsman-48A except gauge, 3-round magazine, 25-inch bbl. Weight: About 6.25 lbs. 28 ga. introduced 1952, .410 in 1954. Disc. in 1969. Values same as shown for Sportsman-48A.

MODEL 11-48A STANDARD GRADE AUTOLOADER
Same general specifications as Sportsman-48A except magazine holds four rounds, forend not grooved. Also available in Special Grade (11-48B), Tournament Grade (11-48D) and Premier Grade (11-48F). Made 1949-69. Values same as shown for Sportsman-48A.

MODEL 11-48SA
.410 AND 28 GA. SKEET .... NiB $423 Ex $342 Gd $240
Same general specifications as Model 11-48A 28 gauge except has 25-inch vent rib bbl., SK choke. 28 ga. introduced 1952, .410 in 1954.

SPORTSMAN-58 SKEET, TARGET, TOURNAMENT AND PREMIER GRADES
These higher grade models differ from the Sportsman-58SA in general quality, grade of wood, checkering, engraving, and other refinements. General operating and physical specifications are the same.
Sportsman-58C Skeet Target ...... NiB $620 Ex $503 Gd $345
Sportsman-58D Skeet Tournament..... NiB $890 Ex $720 Gd $502
Sportsman-58SF Skeet Premier .. NiB $1728 Ex $1394 Gd $967

SPORTSMAN-58 TOURNAMENT AND PREMIER
These higher grade models differ from the Sportsman-58ADL with vent-rib bbl. in general quality, grade of wood, checkering, engraving, etc. General specifications are the same.
Sportsman-58D Tournament ...... NiB $968 Ex $783 Gd $549
Sportsman-58F Premier........ NiB $1766 Ex $1425 Gd $988

SPORTSMAN-58ADL AUTOLOADER
Deluxe grade. Gas-operated. 12 ga. Three round magazine. Bbls.: plain or vent rib, 26-, 28- or 30-inch; IC, M or F choke, or Remington Special Skeet choke. Weight: About 7 lbs. Checkered pistol-grip stock and forearm. Made 1956-64.
With plain barrel .... NiB $363 Ex $294 Gd $206
With ventilated rib barrel .... NiB $417 Ex $338 Gd $236

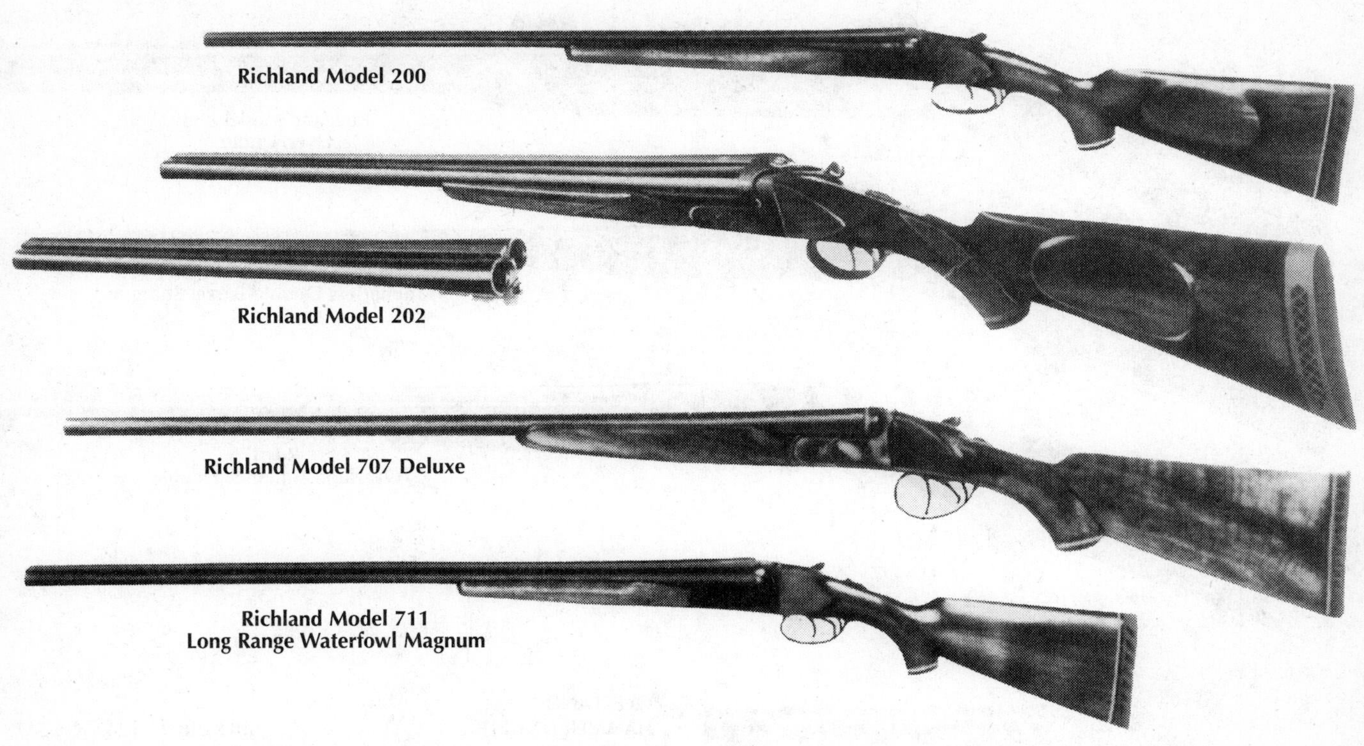
Richland Model 200

Richland Model 202

Richland Model 707 Deluxe

Richland Model 711
Long Range Waterfowl Magnum

SPORTSMAN-58BDL DELUXE SPECIAL GRADE
Same as Model 58ADL except select grade wood.
With plain barrel .... NiB $388 Ex $316 Gd $224
With ventilated rib barrel .... NiB $450 Ex $365 Gd $258

SPORTSMAN-58SA
SKEET GRADE .... NiB $438 Ex $356 Gd $250
Same general specifications as Model 58ADL with vent-rib bbl. except special skeet stock and forearm.

REVELATION SHOTGUNS

See Western Auto listings.

RICHLAND ARMS COMPANY — Blissfield, Michigan; Manufactured in Italy and Spain

MODEL 200
FIELD GRADE DOUBLE .... NiB $354 Ex $319 Gd $206
Hammerless, boxlock, Anson & Deeley-type. Plain extractors. Double triggers. Gauges: 12, 16, 20, 28, .410 (3-inch chambers in 20 and .410; others have 2.75-inch). Bbls.: 28-inch M/F choke, 26-inch IC/M; .410 with 26-inch M/F only; 22-inch IC/M in 20 ga. only. Weight: 6 lbs., 2 oz. to 7 lbs., 4 oz. Checkered walnut stock with cheekpiece, pistol grip, recoil pad; beavertail forend. Made in Spain 1963 to date.

MODEL 202
ALL PURPOSE FIELD GUN .... NiB $340 Ex $278 Gd $198
Hammerless, boxlock, Anson & Deeley-type. Same as Model 200 except has two sets of barrels same gauge. 12 ga.: 30-inch bbls. F/F, 3-inch chambers; 26-inch bbls. IC/M, 2.75-inch chambers. 20 gauge: 28-inch bbls. M/F; 22-inch bbls. IC/M, 3-inch chambers. Made 1963 to date.

MODEL 707
DELUXE FIELD GUN .... NiB $372 Ex $303 Gd $215
Hammerless, boxlock, triple bolting system. Plain extractors. Double triggers. Gauges: 12, 2.75-inch chambers; 20, 3-inch chambers. Bbls.: 12 ga., 28-inch M/F, 26-inch IC/M; 20 ga., 30-inch F/F, 28-inch M/F, 26-inch IC/M. Weight: 6 lbs., 4 oz. to 6 lbs., 15 oz. Checkered walnut stock and forend, recoil pad. Made 1963-72.

MODEL 711 LONG-RANGE WATERFOWL MAGNUM DOUBLE-BARREL SHOTGUN
Hammerless, boxlock, Anson & Deeley-type, Purdey triple lock. Plain extractors. Double triggers. Auto safety. Gauges: 10, 3.5-inch chambers; 12, 3-inch chambers. Bbls.: 10 ga., 32-inch; 12 ga., 30-inch; F/F. Weight: 10 ga., 11 pounds; 12 ga., 7.75 lbs. Checkered walnut stock and beavertail forend; recoil pad. Made in Spain 1963 to date.
10 ga. magnum .... NiB $449 Ex $331 Gd $225
12 ga. magnum .... NiB $386 Ex $280 Gd $191

MODEL 808
O/U SHOTGUN .... NiB $452 Ex $369 Gd $262
Boxlock. Plain extractors. Non-selective single trigger. 12 ga. only. Bbls. (Vickers steel): 30-inch F/F; 28-inch M/F; 26-inch IC/M. Weight: 6 lbs., 12 oz. to 7 lbs., 3 oz. Checkered walnut stock/forend. Made in Italy 1963-68.

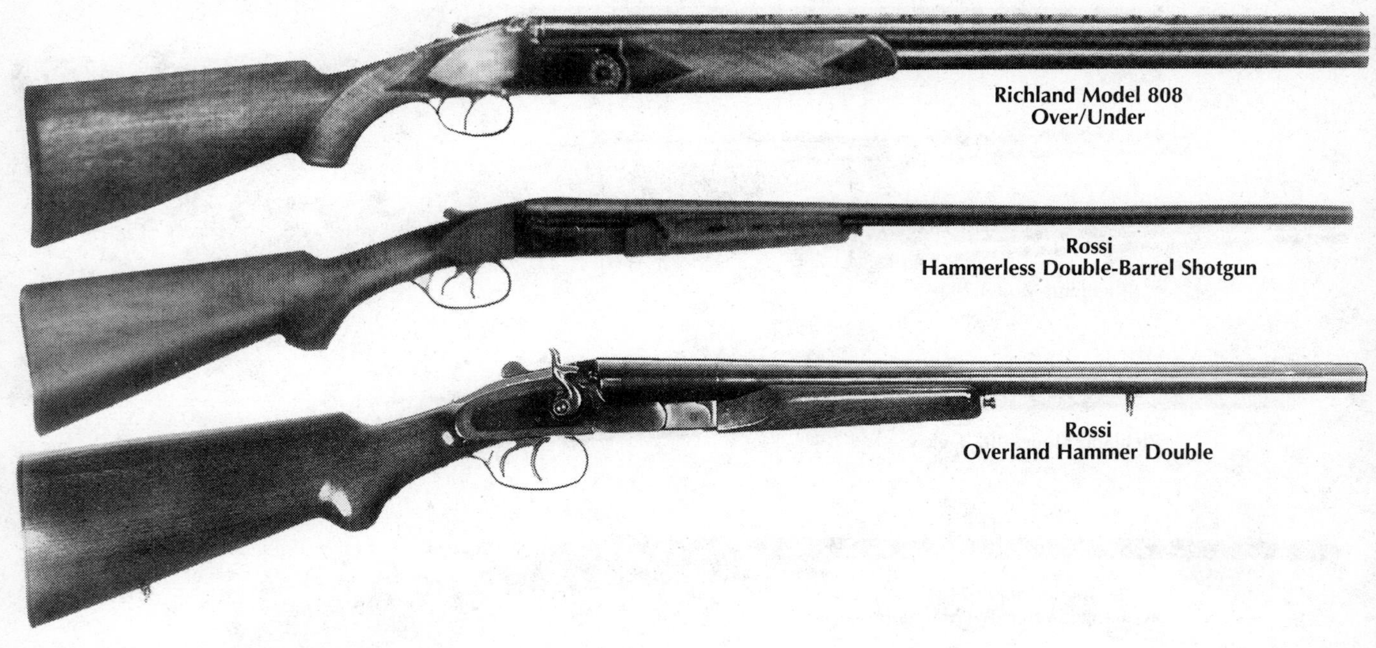

Richland Model 808 Over/Under

Rossi Hammerless Double-Barrel Shotgun

Rossi Overland Hammer Double

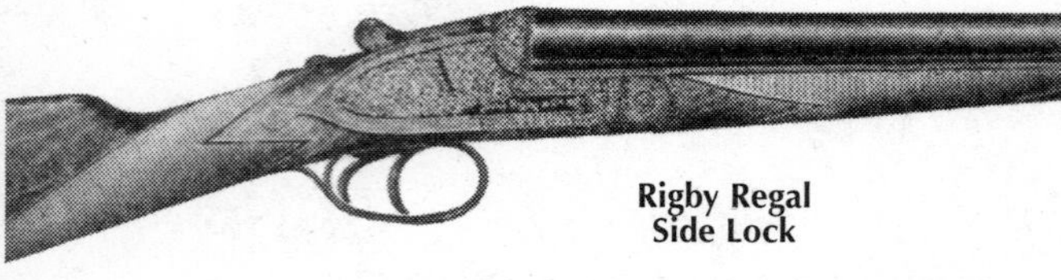

Rigby Regal Side Lock

JOHN RIGBY & COMPANY — London, England

HAMMERLESS BOX LOCK DOUBLE-BARREL SHOTGUNS
Auto ejectors. Double triggers. Made in all gauges, barrel lengths and chokes. Checkered stock and forend, straight grip standard. Made in two grades: Sackville and Chatsworth. These guns differ in general quality, engraving, etc.; specifications are the same.
Sackville grade .... NiB $6048 Ex $4860 Gd $3340
Chatsworth grade .... NiB $4566 Ex $3674 Gd $2534

HAMMERLESS SIDE LOCK DOUBLE-BARREL SHOTGUNS
Auto ejectors. Double triggers. Made in all gauges, barrel lengths and chokes. Checkered stock and forend, straight grip standard. Made in two grades: Regal (best quality) and Sandringham; these guns differ in general quality, engraving, etc., specifications are the same.
Regal grade .... NiB $12,500 Ex $10,000 Gd $6000
Sandringham grade .... NiB $9500 Ex $7500 Gd $3775

AMADEO ROSSI, S.A. — Sao Leopoldo, Brazil

HAMMERLESS DOUBLE-BARREL SHOTGUN..................... NiB $366 Ex $298 Gd $212
Boxlock. Plain extractors. Double triggers. 12 ga. Three-inch chambers. Bbls.: 26-inch IC/M; 28-inch M/F choke. Weight: 7 to 7.5 lbs. Pistol-grip stock and beavertail forearm, uncheckered. Made 1974 to date. Note: H&R Model 404 (1969-72) is same gun.

OVERLAND HAMMER DOUBLE .... NiB $296 Ex $242 Gd $173
Sidelock. Plain extractors. Double triggers. Gauges: 12, .410; 3-inch chambers. Bbls.: 20-inch, IC/M in 12 g.; 26-inch, F/F choke in .410. Weight: 7 lbs. (12 ga.); 6 lbs. (.410). Pistol-grip stock and beavertail forearm, uncheckered. Note: Because of its resemblance to the short-barreled doubles carried by guards riding shotgun on 19th-century stagecoaches, the 12 ga. version originally was called the "Coach Gun." Made 1968-89.

ROTTWEIL SHOTGUNS — West Germany

MODEL 72 O/U SHOTGUN......................... NiB $2031 Ex $1640 Gd $1141
Hammerless, takedown with engraved receiver. 12 ga.; 2.75-inch chambers. 26.75-inch bbls. with SK/SK chokes. Weight: 7.5 lbs. Interchangeable trigger groups and buttstocks. Checkered French walnut buttstock and forend. Imported from West Germany.

MODEL 650 FIELD O/U SHOTGUN .... NiB $828 Ex $676 Gd $480
Breech action. Gauge: 12. 28-inch bbls. Six screw-in choke tubes. Automatic ejectors. Engraved receiver. Checkered pistol grip stock. Made 1984-86.

AMERICAN SKEET........... NiB $1976 Ex $1596 Gd $1111
Boxlock action. Gauge: 12. 27-inch vent-rib bbls. 44.5 inches overall. SK chokes. Weight: 7.5 lbs. Designed for tube sets. Hand-checkered European walnut stock with modified forend. Made 1984-87.

INTERNATIONAL TRAP SHOTGUN.................... NiB $2031 Ex $1640 Gd $1141
Box lock action. Gauge: 12. 30-inch bbls. 48.5 inches overall. Weight: 8 lbs. Choked IM/F. Selective single trigger. Metal bead front sight. Checkered European walnut stock w/pistol grip. Engraved action. Made 1984-87.

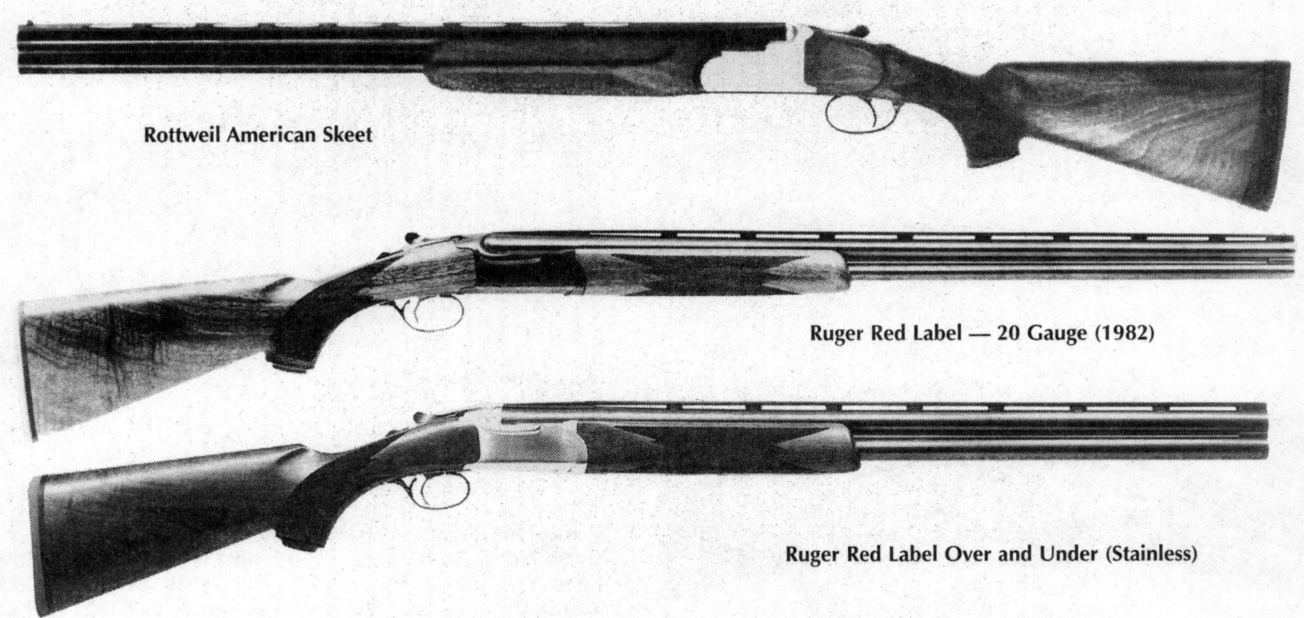

Rottweil American Skeet

Ruger Red Label — 20 Gauge (1982)

Ruger Red Label Over and Under (Stainless)

STURM, RUGER & COMPANY, INC. — Southport, Connecticut

PLAIN GRADE RED LABEL O/U

Boxlock. Auto ejectors. Selective single trigger. 12, 20 or 28 ga. w/2.75- or 3-inch chambers. 26-inch vent-rib bbl., IC/M or SK choke. Single selective trigger. Selective automatic ejectors. Automatic top safety. Standard gold bead front sight. Pistol-grip or English-style American walnut stock and forearm w/hand-cut checkering. The 20 ga. Model was introduced in 1977; 12 ga. version in 1982 and the stainless receiver became standard in 1985. Choke tubes were optional in 1988 and standard in 1990. Weight: 7.0 to 7.5 lbs.

Red Label w/fixed chokes . . . . NiB $877 Ex $709 Gd $495
Red Label w/screw-in tubes . . . . . NiB $1132 Ex $918 Gd $643
Red Label w/grade 1 engraving. . . . NiB $2258 Ex $1821 Gd $1263
Red Label w/grade 2 engraving . . . NiB $2598 Ex $2094 Gd $1447
Red Label w/grade 3 engraving . . . NiB $2954 Ex $2378 Gd $1641

RED LABEL O/U ALL-WEATHER STAINLESS

Gauges: 12 ga. Only. Bbls.: 26- 28- or 30-inch w/various chokes, fixed or screw-in tubes. Stainless receiver and barrel. Checkered black synthetic stock and forearm. Weight: 7.5 lbs. Made 1999 to date.

All-weather stainless model . . . . . NiB $1209 Ex $977 Gd $680
W/30-inch bbl., add $56

RED LABEL "WOODSIDE" O/U

Similar to the Red Label O/U Stainless except in 12 ga. only with wood sideplate extensions. Made 1995 to date.

Standard Woodside . . . . NiB $1567 Ex $1263 Gd $875
Engraved Woodside . . . . NiB $2213 Ex $1785 Gd $1236

RED LABEL SPORTING CLAYS O/U

Similar to the standard Red Label model except chambered 12 or 20 ga. only w/30-inch vent-rib bbls., no side ribs; back-bored w/screw-in choke tubes (not interchangeable w/other Red Label O/U models). Brass front and mid-rib beads. Made 1992 to date.

Standard Sporting Clays. . . . . NiB $1377 Ex $1112 Gd $772
Engraved Sporting Clays . . . . . . NiB $2423 Ex $1951 Gd $1349

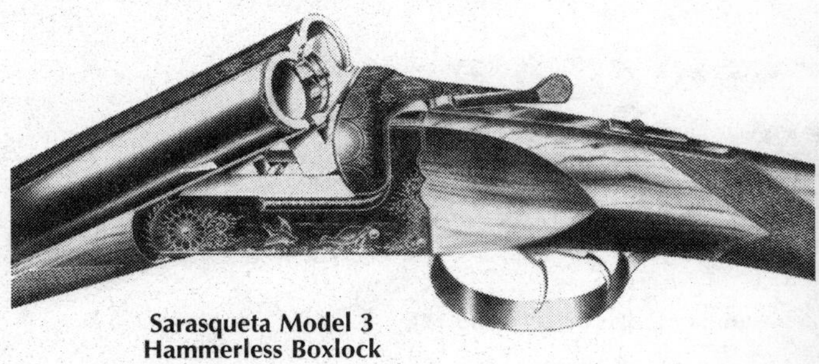

Sarasqueta Model 3
Hammerless Boxlock

RED LABEL SPECIAL EDITION - WILDLIFE FOREVER

Limited edition commemorating the 50th Wildlife Forever anniversary. Similar to the standard Red Label model except chambered 12 ga. only w/engraved receiver enhanced w/gold mallard and pheasant inlays. 300 produced in 1993.

Special edition. . . . . NiB $1769 Ex $1430 Gd $994
Special edition w/hard case . . . NiB $1919 Ex $1549 Gd $1075

VICTOR SARASQUETA, S. A. — Eibar, Spain

SARASQUETA MODEL 3 HAMMERLESS BOXLOCK DOUBLE-BARREL SHOTGUN

Plain extractors or auto ejectors. Double triggers. Gauges: 12, 16, 20. Made in various bbl. lengths, chokes and weights. Checkered stock and forend, straight grip standard. Imported 1985-87.

Model 3, plain extractors . . . . NiB $487 Ex $396 Gd $279
Model 3E, automatic ejectors . . . . . NiB $604 Ex $488 Gd $342

HAMMERLESS SIDELOCK DOUBLES

Automatic ejectors (except on Models 4 and 203 which have plain extractors). Double triggers. Gauges: 12, 16, 20. Barrel lengths, chokes and weights made to order. Checkered stock and forend, straight grip standard. Models differ chiefly in overall quality, engraving, grade of wood, checkering, etc.; general specifications are the same. Imported 1985-87.

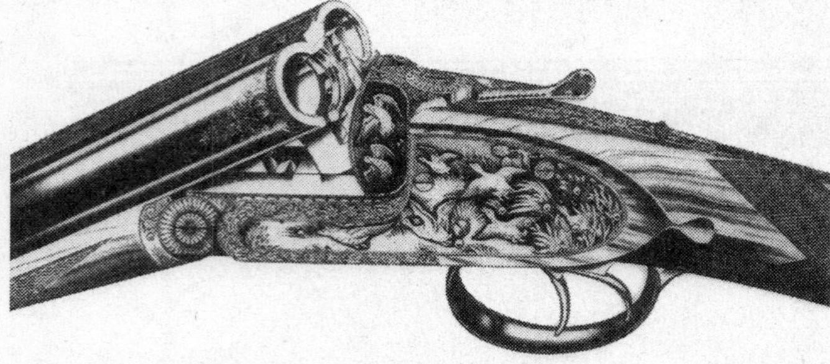

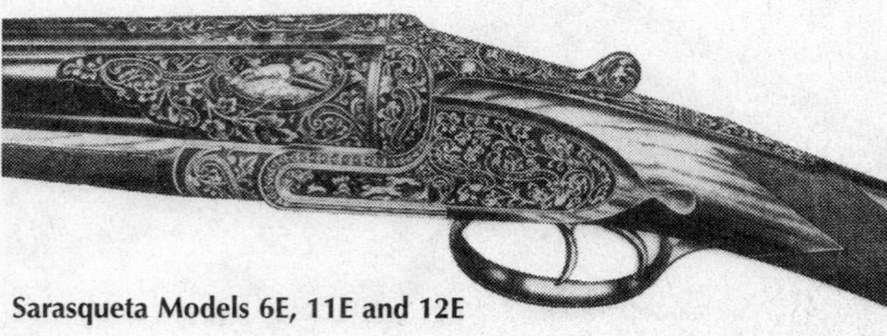

Sarasqueta Models 6E, 11E and 12E

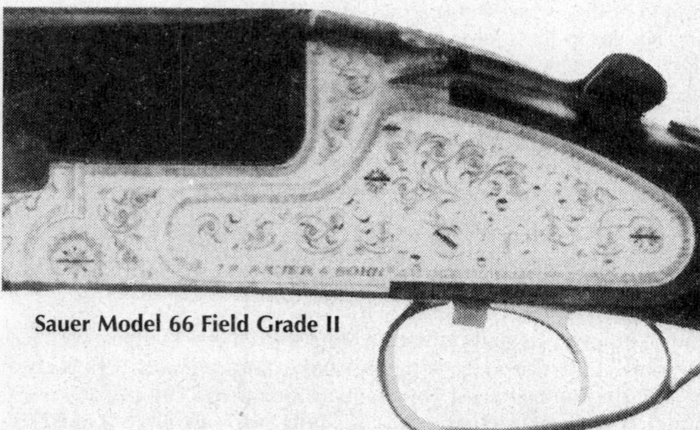

Sauer Model 66 Field Grade II

(cont'd.) HAMMERLESS SIDELOCK DOUBLES

Model	NiB	Ex	Gd
Model 4	NiB $638	Ex $510	Gd $346
Model 4E	NiB $689	Ex $551	Gd $375
Model 203	NiB $666	Ex $533	Gd $362
Model 203E	NiB $723	Ex $579	Gd $393
Model 6E	NiB $839	Ex $672	Gd $456
Model 7E	NiB $898	Ex $718	Gd $488

Sauer Model 66 Field Grade III

(cont'd.) HAMMERLESS SIDELOCK DOUBLES

Model	NiB	Ex	Gd
Model 10E	NiB $1703	Ex $1374	Gd $954
Model 11E	NiB $1759	Ex $1420	Gd $984
Model 12E	NiB $2012	Ex $1621	Gd $1124

J. P. SAUER & SOHN — Eckernförde, Germany, Formerly located in Suhl, Germany

MODEL 66 O/U FIELD GUN

Purdey-system action with Holland & Holland-type sidelocks. Selective single trigger. Selective auto ejectors. Automatic safety. Available in three grades of engraving. 12 ga. only. Krupp special steel bbls. w/vent rib 28-inch, M/F choke. Weight: About 7.25 lbs. Checkered walnut stock and forend; recoil pad. Made 1966-75.

Grade	NiB	Ex	Gd
Grade I	NiB $2495	Ex $2015	Gd $1401
Grade II	NiB $3279	Ex $2641	Gd $1826
Grade III	NiB $4337	Ex $3488	Gd $2402

MODEL 66 O/U SKEET GUN

Same as Model 66 Field Gun except 26-inch bbls. with wide vent rib, SK choked- skeet-style stock and ventilated beavertail forearm; non-automatic safety. Made 1966-75.

Grade	NiB	Ex	Gd
Grade I	NiB $2426	Ex $1960	Gd $1363
Grade II	NiB $3282	Ex $2644	Gd $1828
Grade III	NiB $4620	Ex $3714	Gd $2557

MODEL 66 O/U TRAP GUN

Same as Model 66 Skeet Gun except has 30-inch bbls. choked F/F or M/F; trap-style stock. Values same as for Skeet model. Made 1966-75.

MODEL 3000E DRILLING

Combination rifle and double barrel shotgun. Blitz action with Greener crossbolt, double underlugs, separate rifle cartridge extractor, front set trigger, firing pin indicators, Greener side safety, sear slide selector locks right shotgun bbl. for firing rifle bbl. Gauge/calibers12 ga. (2.75-inch chambers); .222, .243, .30-06, 7x65R. 25-inch Krupp-Special steel bbls.; M/F choke automatic folding leaf rear rifle sight. Weight: 6.5 to 7.25 lbs. depending on rifle caliber. Checkered walnut stock and forend; pistol grip, Monte Carlo comb and cheekpiece, sling swivels. Standard model with Arabesque engraving; Deluxe model with hunting scenes engraved on action. Currently manufactured. Note: Also see listing under Colt.

Model	NiB	Ex	Gd
Standard model	NiB $4489	Ex $3609	Gd $2485
Deluxe model	NiB $5419	Ex $4354	Gd $2991

ARTEMIS DOUBLE-BARREL SHOTGUN
Holland & Holland-type sidelock with Greener crossbolt double underlugs, double sear safeties, selective single trigger, selective auto ejectors. Grade I with fine-line engraving, Grade II with full English Arabesque engraving. 12 ga. (2.75-inch chambers). Krupp special steel bbls., 28-inch, M/F choke. Weight: About 6.5 lbs. Checkered walnut pistol-grip stock and beavertail forend; recoil pad. Made 1966-77.
Grade I .... NiB $5758 Ex $4626 Gd $3178
Grade II .... NiB $7110 Ex $5708 Gd $3913

BBF 54 O/U COMBINATION RIFLE/SHOTGUN
Blitz action with Kersten lock, front set trigger fires rifle bbl., slide-operated sear safety. Gauge/calibers: 16 ga.; .30-30, .30-06, 7x65R, 25-inch Krupp special steel bbls.; shotgun bbl. F choke, folding-leaf rear sight. Weight: About 6 lbs. Checkered walnut stock and forend; pistol grip, mod. Monte Carlo comb and cheekpiece, sling swivels. Standard model with Arabesque engraving; Deluxe model with hunting scenes engraved on action. Currently manufactured.
Standard model .... NiB $2763 Ex $2227 Gd $1540
Deluxe model .... NiB $3188 Ex $2566 Gd $1771

ROYAL DOUBLE-BARREL SHOTGUNS
Anson & Deeley action (boxlock) with Greener crossbolt, double underlugs, signal pins, selective single trigger, selective auto ejectors, auto safety. Scalloped frame with Arabesque engraving. Krupp special steel bbls. Gauges: 12, 2.75-inch chambers, 20, 3-inch chambers. Bbls.: 30-inch (12 ga. only) and 28-inch, M/F- 26-inch (20 ga. only), IC/M. Weight: 12 ga., about 6.5 lbs.; 20 ga., 6 lbs. Checkered walnut pistol-grip stock and beavertail forend; recoil pad. Made 1955-77.
Standard model .... NiB $1649 Ex $1332 Gd $926
20 ga. .... NiB $2160 Ex $1743 Gd $1211

SAVAGE ARMS — Westfield, Massachusetts Formerly located in Utica, New York

MODEL 24 22-.410
O/U COMBINATION .... NiB $178 Ex $145 Gd $102
Same as Stevens No. 22-.410 with walnut stock and forearm. Made 1950-65.

MODEL 24C
CAMPER'S COMPANION .... NiB $207 Ex $148 Gd $105
Same as Model 24FG except made in .22 Magnum/20 ga. only; has 20-inch bbls., shotgun tube Cyl. bore. Weight: 5.75 lbs. Trap in butt provides ammunition storage; comes with carrying case. Made 1972-89.

MODEL 24 .... NiB $248 Ex $201 Gd $141
Same as Models 24DL and 24MDL except frame has black or casehardened finish. Game scene decoration of frame eliminated in 1974; forearm uncheckered after 1976. Made 1970-88.

MODEL 24DL .... NiB $186 Ex $152 Gd $108
Same general specifications as Model 24S except top-lever opening; satin-chrome-finished frame decorated with game scenes, checkered Monte Carlo stock and forearm. Made 1965-69.

MODEL 24F-12T TURKEY GUN ... NiB $471 Ex $381 Gd $266
12- or 20-ga. shotgun bbl./.22 Hornet, .223 or .30-30 caliber rifle. 24-inch blued bbls., 3-inch chambers, extra removable F choke tube. Hammer block safety. Color casehardened frame. DuPont Rynite camo stock. Swivel studs. Made 1989 to date.

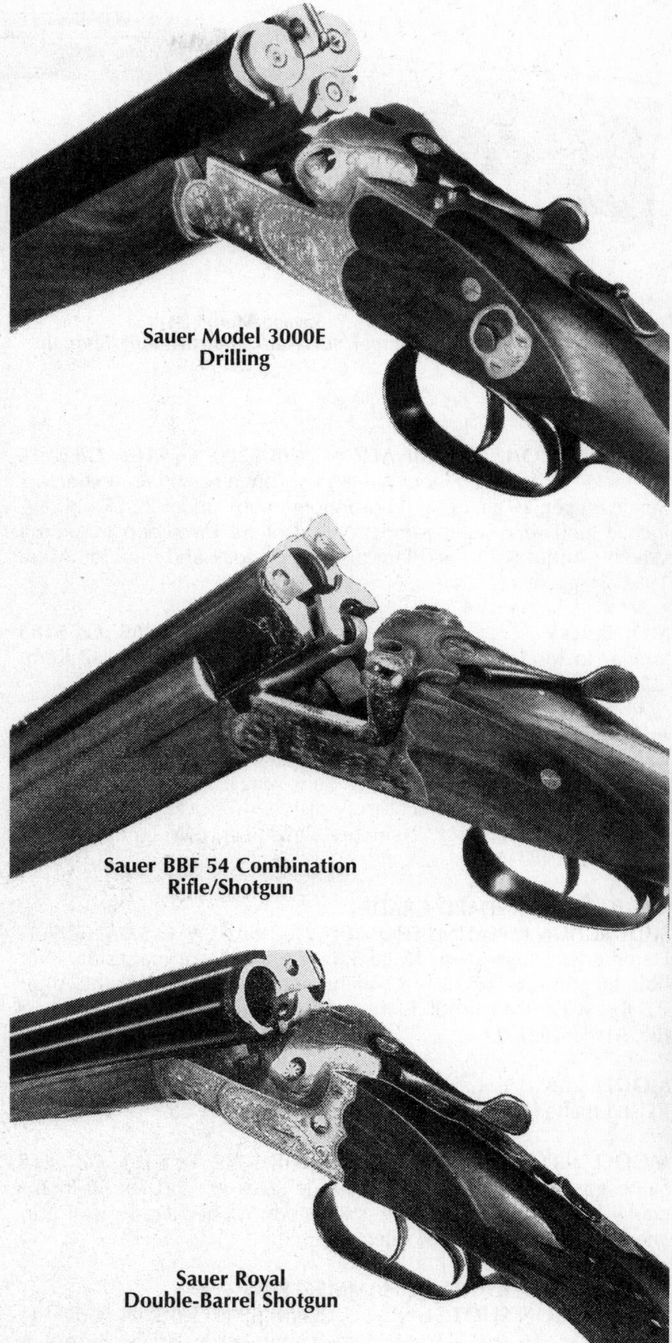
Sauer Model 3000E Drilling

Sauer BBF 54 Combination Rifle/Shotgun

Sauer Royal Double-Barrel Shotgun

MODEL 24FG FIELD GRADE ..... NiB $186 Ex $154 Gd $111
Same general specifications as Model 24S except top lever opening. Made 1972 to date.

MODEL 24MDL .... NiB $198 Ex $163 Gd $117
Same as Model 24DL except rifle bbl. chambered for 22 WMR. Made 1965-69.

MODEL 24MS .... NiB $186 Ex $154 Gd $111
Same as Model 24S except rifle bbl. chambered for 22 WMR. Made 1965-71.

Savage Model 24 .22-/.410 O/U Combination

Savage Model 24-VS Camper/Survival/Centerfire Rifle/Shotgun

MODEL 24S O/U COMBINATION . NiB $200 Ex $163 Gd $116
Boxlock. Visible hammer. Side lever opening. Plain extractors. Single trigger. 20 ga. or .410 bore shotgun bbl. under 22 LR bbl., 24-inch. Open rear sight, ramp front, dovetail for scope mounting. Weight: About 6.75 lbs. Plain pistol-grip stock and forearm. Made 1965-71.

MODEL 24V .... NiB $327 Ex $265 Gd $185
Similar to Model 24D except 20 ga. under .222 Rem., .22 Rem., .357 Mag., .22 Hornet or .30-30 rifle bbl. Made 1971-89.

MODEL 24-VS CAMPER/SURVIVAL/ CENTERFIRE RIFLE/SHOTGUN.... NiB $276 Ex $223 Gd $157
Similar to Model 24V except .357 Rem. Mag. over 20 ga. Nickel finish full-length stock and accessory pistol-grip stock. Overall length: 36 inches with full stock; 26 inches w/pistol grip. Weight: About 6.5 lbs. Made 1983-88.

MODEL 28A STANDARD GRADE SLIDE-ACTION REPEATING SHOTGUN .... NiB $339 Ex $275 Gd $193
Hammerless. Takedown. 12 ga. Five round tubular magazine. Plain bbl., lengths: 26-,28-, 30-, 32-inches, choked C/M/F. Weight: About 7.5 lbs. with 30-inch bbl. Plain pistol-grip stock, grooved slide handle. Made 1928-31.

MODEL 28B .... NiB $358 Ex $290 Gd $204
Raised matted rib; otherwise the same as Model 28A.

MODEL 28D TRAP GRADE...... NiB $383 Ex $311 Gd $218
Same general specifications as Model 28A except has 30-inch F choke bbl. w/matted rib, trap-style stock w/checkered pistol grip, checkered slide handle of select walnut.

MODEL 30 SOLID FRAME HAMMERLESS SLIDE-ACTION SHOTGUN....... NiB $249 Ex $204 Gd $144
Gauges: 12, 16, 20, .410. 2.75-inch chamber in 16 ga., 3- inch in other ga. Magazine holds four 2.75-inch shells or three 3-inch shells. Bbls.: Vent rib; 26-, 28-, 30-inch; IC, M, F choke. Weight: Average 6.25 to 6.75 lbs. depending on ga. Plain pistol-grip stock (checkered on later production), grooved slide handle. Made 1958-70.

MODEL 30 TAKEDOWN SLUG GUN .. NiB $232 Ex $189 Gd $135
Same as Model 30FG except 21-inch cyl. bore bbl. with rifle sights. Made 1971-79.

MODEL 30AC SOLID FRAME ..... NiB $256 Ex $209 Gd $148
Same as Model 30 Solid Frame except has 26-inch bbl. with adj. choke; 12 ga. only. Made 1959-70.

MODEL 30AC TAKEDOWN....... NiB $254 Ex $207 Gd $146
Same as Model 30FG except has 26-inch bbl. with adj. choke; 12 and 20 ga. only. Made 1971-72.

MODEL 30ACL SOLID FRAME .... NiB $269 Ex $219 Gd $156
Same as Model 30AC Solid Frame except left-hand model with ejection port and safety on left side; 12 ga. only. Made 1960-64.

MODEL 30D TAKEDOWN........ NiB $232 Ex $189 Gd $135
Deluxe Grade. Same as Model 30FG except has receiver engraved with game scene, vent rib bbl., recoil pad. Made 1971 to date.

MODEL 30FG TAKEDOWN HAMMERLESS SLIDE-ACTION SHOTGUN....... NiB $190 Ex $156 Gd $112
Field Grade. Gauges: 12, 20, .410. Three-inch chamber. Magazine holds four 2.75-inch shells or three 3-inch shells. Bbls.: plain; 26-inch F choke (.410 ga. only); 28-inch M/F choke; 30-inch F choke (12 ga. only). Weight: Average 7 to 7.75 lbs. depending on gauge. Checkered pistol-grip stock, fluted slide handle. Made 1970-79.

MODEL 30L SOLID FRAME ...... NiB $222 Ex $180 Gd $128
Same as Model 30 Solid Frame except left-handed model with ejection port and safety on left side; 12 ga. only. Made 1959-70.

MODEL 30T SOLID FRAME TRAP AND DUCK .... NiB $252 Ex $205 Gd $145
Same as Model 30 Solid Frame except only in 12 ga. w/30-inch F choke bbl.; has Monte Carlo stock with recoil pad, weight: About 8 lbs. Made 1963-70.

MODEL 30T TAKE DOWN TRAP GUN .... NiB $228 Ex $185 Gd $131
Same as Model 30D except only in 12 ga. w/30-inch F choke bbl. Monte Carlo stock with recoil pad. Made 1970-73.

MODEL 69-RXL SLIDE-ACTION SHOTGUN .... NiB $215 Ex $175 Gd $124
Similar to Model 67 (law enforcement configuration). Hammerless, side ejection top tang safe for left- or right-hand use. 12 ga. chambered for 2.75- and 3-inch magnum shells. 18.25-inch bbl. Tubular magazine holds 6 rounds (one less for 3-inch mag). Walnut finish hardwood stock with recoil pad and grooved operating handle. Weight: About 6.5 lbs. Made 1982-89.

MODEL 210F BOLT-ACTION SLUG GUN .... NiB $371 Ex $301 Gd $211
Built on Savage 110 action. Gauge: 12 w/3-inch chamber. Two round detachable magazine. 24-inch fully rifled bbl. Receiver drilled and tapped for scope mounts w/no sights. Weight: 7.5 lbs. Checkered black synthetic stock w/swivel studs and recoil pad. Made 1997 to date.

MODEL 210FT BOLT-ACTION SHOTGUN ... NiB $441 Ex $357 Gd $248
Similar to Model 210F except has smoothbore 24-inch bbl. w/choke tubes. Bead front and U-notch rear sights. Advantage Camo finish. Made 1997 to date.

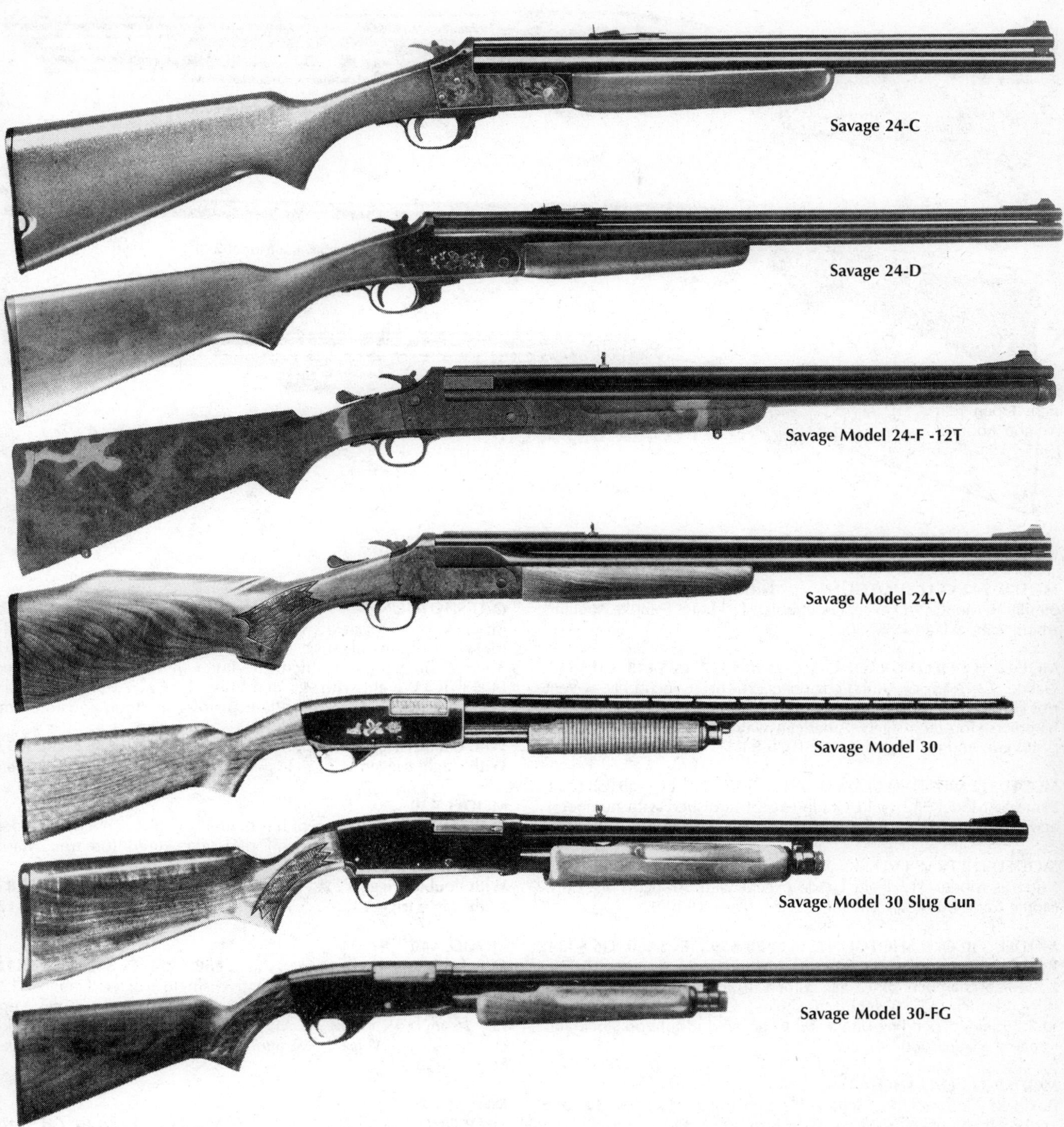
Savage 24-C

Savage 24-D

Savage Model 24-F -12T

Savage Model 24-V

Savage Model 30

Savage Model 30 Slug Gun

Savage Model 30-FG

MODEL 220 SINGLE-BARREL SHOTGUN. . NiB $138 Ex $113 Gd $81
Hammerless. Takedown. Auto ejector. Gauges: 12,16, 20 .410. Single shot. Bbl. lengths: 12 ga., 28- to 36-inch, 16 ga., 28- to 32-inch; 20 ga., 26- to 32-inch; .410 bore, 26-and 28-inch. F choke. Weight: about 6 lbs. Plain pistol-grip stock and wide forearm. Made 1938-65.

MODEL 220AC . . . . NiB $163 Ex $132 Gd $94
Same as Model 220 except has Savage adj. choke.

MODEL 220L. . . . . NiB $120 Ex $99 Gd $71
Same general specifications as Model 220 except has side lever opening instead of top lever. Made 1965-72.

MODEL 220P . . . . NiB $138 Ex $113 Gd $80
Same as Model 220 except has PolyChoke bbl., made in 12 ga. with 30-inch bbl., 16 and 20 ga. with 28-inch bbl., no .410 bore; recoil pad.

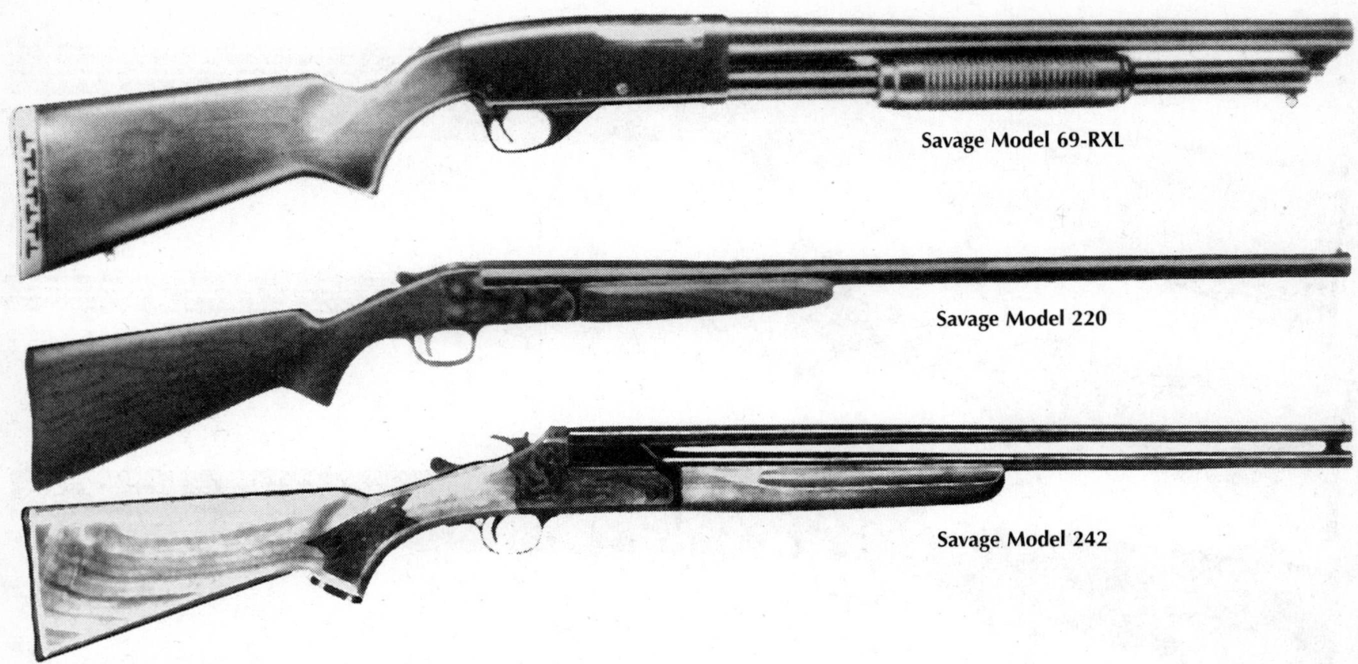
Savage Model 69-RXL

Savage Model 220

Savage Model 242

MODEL 242 O/U SHOTGUN. . . . . NiB $383 Ex $314 Gd $218
Similar to Model 24D except both bbls. .410 bore, F choke. Weight: About 7 lbs. Made 1977-80.

MODEL 312 FIELD GRADE O/U. . . NiB $557 Ex $448 Gd $312
Gauge: 12; 2.75- or 3-inch chambers. 26- or 28-inch bbls. w/vent rib; F/M/IC chokes. 43 or 45 inches overall. Weight: 7 lbs. Internal hammers. Top tang safety. American walnut stock with checkered pistol grip and recoil pad. Made 1990-93.

MODEL 312 SPORTING CLAYS O/U . . . . . NiB $593 Ex $480 Gd $334
Same as Model 312 Field Grade except furnished with number 1 and number 2 Skeet tubes and 28-inch bbls. only. Made 1990-93.

MODEL 312 TRAP O/U. . . . . NiB $633 Ex $512 Gd $355
Same as Model 312 Field Grade except with 30-inch bbls. only, Monte Carlo buttstock, weight: 7.5 lbs. Made 1990-93.

MODEL 330 O/U SHOTGUN. . . . . NiB $593 Ex $480 Gd $334
Boxlock. Plain extractors. Selective single trigger. Gauges: 12, 20. 2.75-inch chambers in 12 ga., 3-inch in 20 gauge. Bbls.: 26-inch IC/M; 28-inch M/F; 30-inch M/F choke (12 ga. only). Weight: 6.25 to 7.25 lbs., depending on gauge. Checkered pistol-grip stock and forearm. Made 1969-78.

MODEL 333 O/U SHOTGUN
Boxlock. Auto ejectors. Selective single trigger. Gauges: 12, 20. 2.75-inch chambers in 12 ga., 3-inch in 20 ga. Bbls.: vent rib; 26-inch SK choke, IC/M; 28-inch M/F; 30-inch M/F choke (12 ga. only). Weight: Average 6.25 to 7.25 lbs. Checkered pistol-grip stock and forearm. Made 1973-79.
Model 333 12 ga. . . . . NiB $673 Ex $543 Gd $377
Model 333 20 ga. . . . . NiB $812 Ex $654 Gd $452

MODEL 333T TRAP GUN . . . . NiB $599 Ex $484 Gd $337
Similar to Model 330 except only in 12 ga. with 30-inch vent-rib bbls., IM/F choke; Monte Carlo stock w/recoil pad. Weight: 7.75 lbs. Made 1972-79.

MODEL 420
O/U SHOTGUN
Boxlock. Hammerless. Takedown. Automatic safety. Double triggers or non-selective single trigger. Gauges: 12, 16, 20. Bbls.: Plain, 26- to 30-inch (the latter in 12 ga. only); choked M/F, C/IC. Weight with 28-inch bbls.: 12 ga., 7.75 lbs.; 16 ga., 7.5 lbs.; 20 ga., 6.75 lbs. Plain pistol-grip stock and forearm. Made 1938-42.
With double triggers . . . . NiB $447 Ex $362 Gd $253
With single trigger . . . . NiB $507 Ex $410 Gd $285

MODEL 430
Same as Model 420 except has matted top bbl., checkered stock of select walnut with recoil pad, checkered forearm. Made 1938-42.
With double triggers . . . . NiB $508 Ex $410 Gd $285
With single trigger . . . . NiB $557 Ex $448 Gd $312

MODEL 440
O/U SHOTGUN . . . . NiB $534 Ex $431 Gd $332
Boxlock. Plain extractors. Selective single trigger. Gauges: 12, 20. 2.75-inch chambers in 12 ga., 3-inch in 20 ga. Bbls.: Vent rib; 26-inch SK choke, IC/M; 28-inch M/F; 30-inch M/F choke (12 ga. only). Weight: Average 6 to 6.5 lbs. depending on ga. Made 1968-72.

MODEL 440T
TRAP GUN . . . . NiB $552 Ex $446 Gd $310
Similar to Model 440 except only in 12 ga. with 30-inch bbls., extra-wide vent rib, IM/F choke. Trap-style Monte Carlo stock and semibeavertail forearm of select walnut, recoil pad. Weight: 7.5 lbs. Made 1969-72.

MODEL 444 DELUXE
O/U SHOTGUN . . . . NiB $557 Ex $448 Gd $312
Similar to Model 440 except has auto ejectors, select walnut stock and semi-beavertail forearm. Made 1969-72.

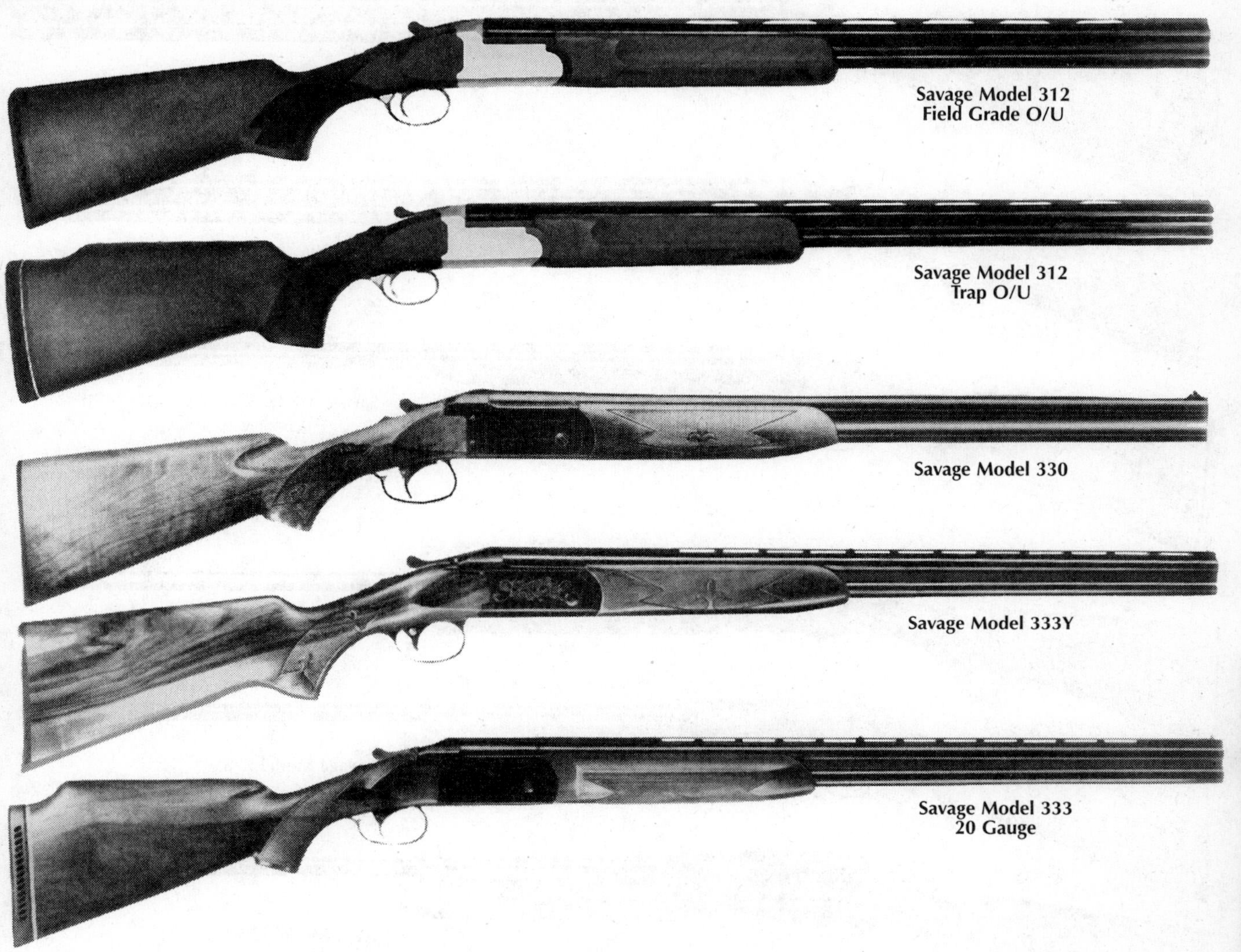

Savage Model 312
Field Grade O/U

Savage Model 312
Trap O/U

Savage Model 330

Savage Model 333Y

Savage Model 333
20 Gauge

MODEL 550
HAMMERLESS DOUBLE . . . . NiB $289 Ex $235 Gd $167
Boxlock. Auto ejectors. Non-selective single trigger. Gauges: 12, 20. 2.75-inch chamber in 12 ga., 3-inch in 20 ga. Bbls.: Vent rib; 26-inch IC/M; 28-inch M/F; 30-inch M/F choke (12 ga. only). Weight: 7 to 8 lbs. Checkered pistol-grip stock and semi-beavertail forearm. Made 1971-73. See illustration page 516.

MODEL 720 STANDARD GRADE
5 SHOT AUTOLOADING
SHOTGUN . . . . NiB $291 Ex $193 Gd $168
Browning type. Takedown. 12 and 16 ga. Four round tubular magazine. Bbl.: plain; 26- to 32-inch (the latter in 12 ga. only); choked IC, M, F. Weight: About 8.25 lbs., 12 ga. with 30-inch bbl.; 16 ga., about .5 lb. lighter. Checkered pistol-grip stock and forearm. Made 1930-49.

MODEL 726 UPLAND SPORTER GRADE
3-SHOT AUTOLOADING
SHOTGUN . . . . NiB $295 Ex $240 Gd $169
Same as Model 720 except has 2-round magazine capacity. Made 1931-49.

MODEL 740C
SKEET GUN. . . . . NiB $369 Ex $290 Gd $252
Same as Model 726 except has special skeet stock and full beavertail forearm, equipped with Cutts Compensator. Bbl. length overall with spreader tube is about 24.5 inches. Made 1936-49.

MODEL 745LIGHT-WEIGHT
AUTOLOADER . . . . NiB $291 Ex $237 Gd $168
Three- or five-round models. Same general specifications as Model 720 except has lightweight alloy receiver, 12 ga.only, 28-inch plain bbl. Weight: About 6.75 lbs. Made 1940-49.

MODEL 750
AUTOMATIC SHOTGUN . . . . NiB $300 Ex $244 Gd $173
Browning-type autoloader. Takedown. 12 ga. Four round tubular magazine. Bbls.: 28-inch F or M choke; 26-inch IC. Weight: About 7.25 lbs. Checkered walnut pistol-grip stock and grooved forearm. Made 1960-67.

MODEL 750-AC. . . . . NiB $335 Ex $272 Gd $191
Same as Model 750 except has 26-inch bbl. with adj. choke. Made 1964-67.

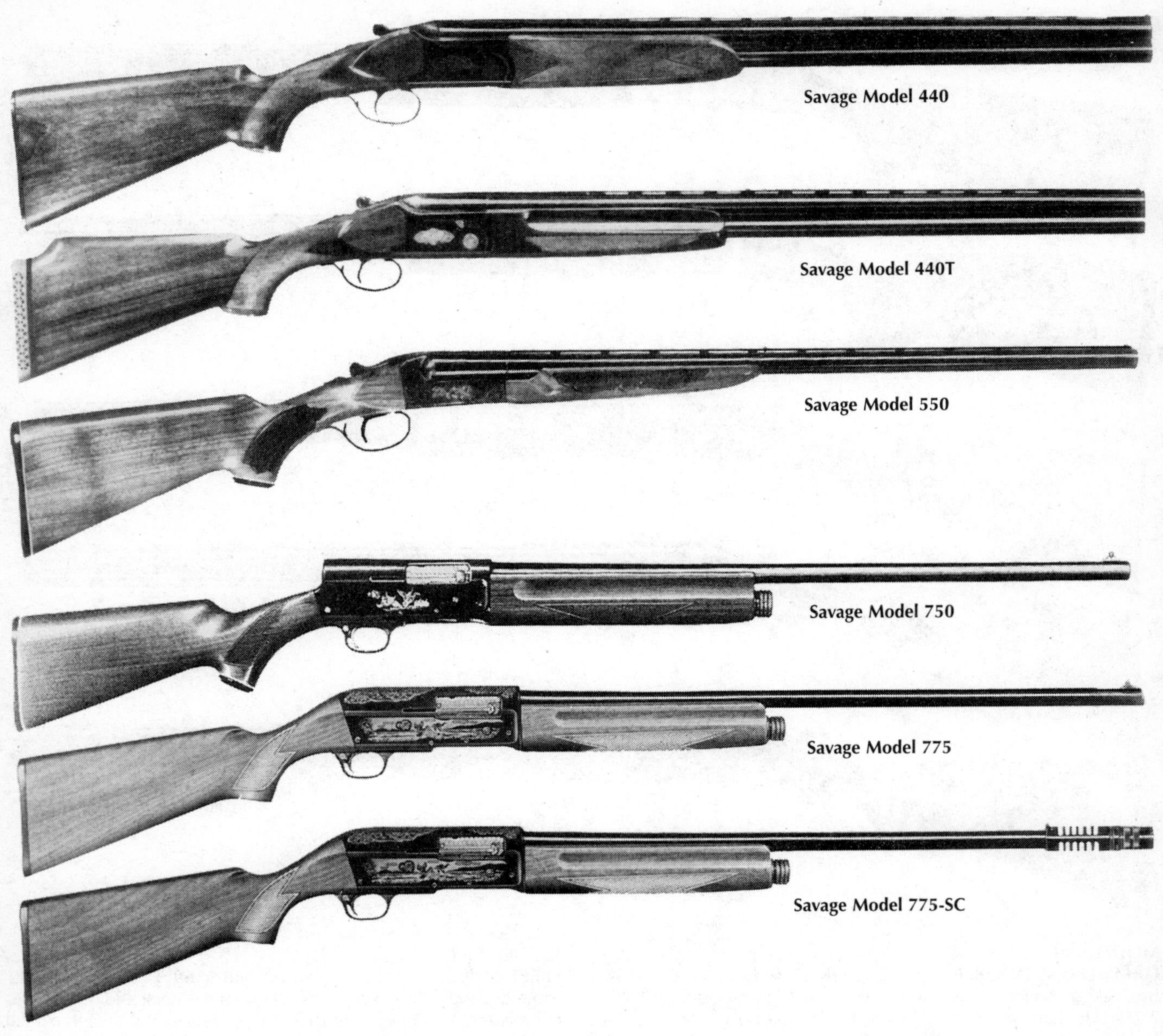

Savage Model 440

Savage Model 440T

Savage Model 550

Savage Model 750

Savage Model 775

Savage Model 775-SC

MODEL 750-SC . . . . NiB $307 Ex $249 Gd $176
Same as Model 750 except has 26-inch bbl. with Savage Super Choke. Made 1962-63.

MODEL 755 STANDARD GRADE AUTOLOADER . . . . NiB $291 Ex $237 Gd $168
Streamlined receiver. Takedown.12 and 16 ga. Four round tubular magazine (a three-round model with magazine capacity of two rounds was also produced until 1951). Bbl.: Plain, 30-inch F choke (12 ga. only), 28-inch F or M, 26-inch IC. Weight: About 8.25 lbs., 12 ga. Checkered pistol-grip stock and forearm. Made 1949-58.

MODEL 755-SC . . . . NiB $287 Ex $234 Gd $165
Same as Model 755 except has 26-inch bbl. w/recoil-reducing, adj. Savage Super Choke.

MODEL 775 LIGHTWEIGHT. . . . . . NiB $294 Ex $239 Gd $169
Same general specifications as Model 755 except has lightweight alloy receiver, weight: About 6.73 lbs. Made 1950-65.

MODEL 775-SC . . . . NiB $307 Ex $249 Gd $176
Same as Model 775 except has 26-inch bbl. with Savage Super Choke.

MODEL 2400 O/U COMBINATION . . . . NiB $651 Ex $606 Gd $549
Boxlock action similar to that of Model 330. Plain extractors. Selective single trigger. 12-ga. (2.75-inch chamber) shotgun bbl., F choke over .308 Win. or .222 Rem. rifle bbl.; 23.5-inch; solid matted rib with blade front sight and folding leaf rear, dovetail for scope mounting. Weight: About 7.5 lbs. Monte Carlo stock w/pistol grip and recoil pad, semibeavertail forearm, checkered. Made 1975-79 by Valmet.

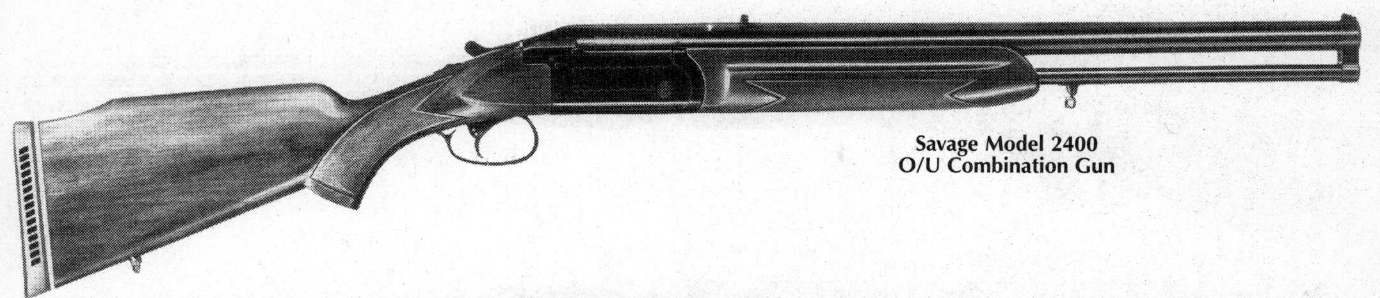

Savage Model 2400
O/U Combination Gun

SEARS, ROEBUCK & COMPANY — Chicago, Illinois. (J. C. Higgins and Ted Williams Models)

Although they do not correspond to specific models below, the names Ted Williams and J. C. Higgins have been used to designate various Sears shotguns at various times.

MODEL 18
BOLT-ACTION REPEATER .... NiB $118 Ex $97 Gd $69
Takedown. Three round top-loading magazine. Gauge: .410 only. Bbl.: 25-inch w/variable choke. Weight: About 5.75 lbs.

MODEL 20 SLIDE-ACTION REPEATER .. NiB $224 Ex $181 Gd $126
Hammerless. Five round magazine. Bbls.: 26- to 30-inch w/various chokes. Weight: 7.25 lbs. Plain pistol-grip stock and slide handle.

MODEL 21 SLIDE-ACTION REPEATER ..... NiB $246 Ex $199 Gd $139
Same general specifications as the Model 20 except vent rib and adj. choke.

MODEL 30 SLIDE-ACTION REPEATER... NiB $233 Ex $188 Gd $131
Hammerless. Gauges: 12, 16, 20 and .410. Four round magazine. Bbls.: 26- to 30-inch, various chokes. Weight: 6.5 lbs. Plain pistol-grip stock, grooved slide handle.

MODEL 97 SINGLE-SHOT SHOTGUN....... NiB $92 Ex $76 Gd $55
Takedown. Visible hammer. Automatic ejector. Gauges: 12, 16, 20 and .410. Bbls.: 26- to 36-inch, F choke. Weight: Average 6 lbs. Plain pistol-grip stock and forearm.

MODEL 97-AC SINGLE-SHOT SHOTGUN..... NiB $112 Ex $92 Gd $65
Same general specifications as Model 97 except fancier stock and forearm.

MODEL 101.7 DOUBLE-BARREL
SHOTGUN .... NiB $224 Ex $181 Gd $126
Boxlock. Double triggers. Gauges: 12, 16, 20, .410. Bbls.: 26- to 32-inch, choked M and F. Weight: From 6 to 7.5 lbs. Plain stock and forend.

MODEL 101.7C DOUBLE-BARREL
SHOTGUN .... NiB $239 Ex $183 Gd $102
Same general specifications as Model 101.7 except checkered stock and forearm.

MODEL 101.25 BOLT-ACTION SHOTGUN.... NiB $112 Ex $92 Gd $65
Takedown. .410 gauge. Five round tubular magazine. 24-inch bbl., F choke. Weight: About 6 lbs. Plain, one-piece pistol-grip stock.

MODEL 101.40 SINGLE-SHOT SHOTGUN .. NiB $97 Ex $79 Gd $57
Takedown. Visible hammer. Automatic ejector. Gauges: 12, 16, 20 and .410. Bbls.: 26- to 36-inch, F choke. Weight: Average 6 lbs. Plain pistol-grip stock and forearm.

MODEL 101.1120 BOLT-ACTION REPEATER ..... NiB $112 Ex $92 Gd $65
Takedown. .410 ga. 24-inch bbl., F choke. Weight: About 5 lbs. Plain one-piece pistol-grip stock.

MODEL 101.1380 BOLT-ACTION REPEATER .. NiB $125 Ex $102 Gd $72
Takedown. Gauges: 12, 16, 20. Two round detachable box magazine. 26-inch bbl., F choke. Weight: About 7 lbs. Plain one-piece pistol-grip stock.

MODEL 101.1610 DOUBLE-BARREL
SHOTGUN .... NiB $329 Ex $266 Gd $186
Boxlock. Double triggers. Plain extractors. Gauges: 12, 16, 20 and .410. Bbls.: 24- to 30-inch. Various chokes, but mostly M and F. Weight: About 7.5 lbs, 12 ga. Checkered pistol-grip stock and forearm.

MODEL 101.1701 DOUBLE-BARREL
SHOTGUN .... NiB $327 Ex $265 Gd $185
Same general specifications as Model 101.1610 except satin chrome frame and select walnut stock and forearm.

MODEL 101.5350-D
BOLT-ACTION REPEATER .... NiB $107 Ex $88 Gd $62
Takedown. Gauges: 12, 16, 20. Two round detachable box magazine. 26-inch bbl., F choke. Weight: About 7.25 lbs. Plain one piece pistol-grip stock.

MODEL 101.5410
BOLT-ACTION REPEATER .... NiB $112 Ex $90 Gd $64
Same general specifications as Model 101.5350-D.

SKB ARMS COMPANY — Tokyo, Japan *Imported by G.U. Inc., Omaha, Nebraska*

MODEL 385 SIDE-BY-SIDE ..... NiB $1738 Ex $1404 Gd $977
Boxlock action w/double locking lugs. Gauges: 12, 20 and 28 w/2.75- and 3-inch chambers. 26- or 28-inch bbls. w/Inter-Choke tube system. Single selective trigger. Selective automatic ejectors and automatic safety. Weight: 6 lbs., 10 oz. Silver nitride receiver w/engraved scroll and game scene. Solid rib w/flat matte finish and metal front bead sight. Checkered American walnut English or pistol-grip stock. Imported 1992 to date.

MODELS 300 AND 400 SIDE-BY-SIDE DOUBLES
Similar to Model 200E except higher grade. Models 300 and 400 differ in that the latter has more elaborate engraving and fancier wood.
Model 300 .... NiB $972 Ex $787 Gd $550
Model 400 .... NiB $1176 Ex $950 Gd $663

MODEL 400 SKEET .... NiB $112 Ex $900 Gd $628
Similar to Model 200E Skeet except higher grade with more elaborate engraving and full fancy wood.

MODEL 480 ENGLISH .... NiB $1432 Ex $1156 Gd $802
Similar to Model 280 English except higher grade with more elaborate engraving and full fancy wood.

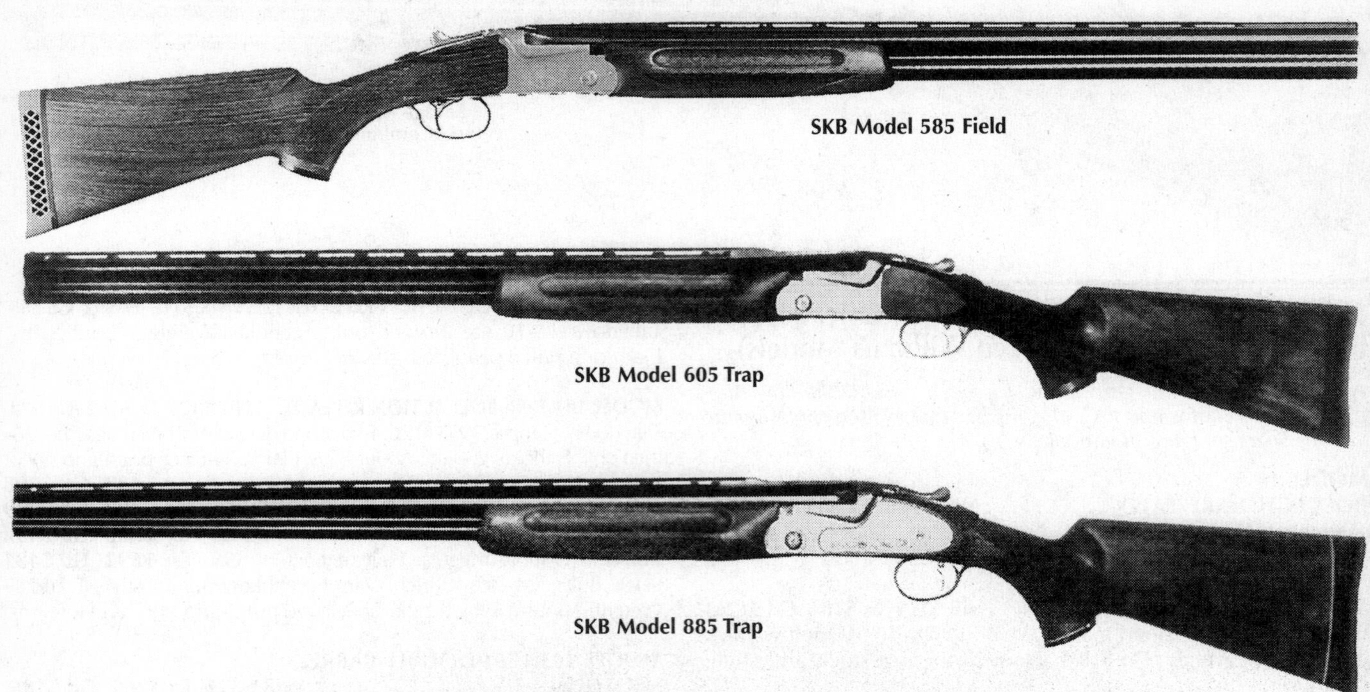
SKB Model 585 Field

SKB Model 605 Trap

SKB Model 885 Trap

MODEL 500 SERIES O/U SHOTGUN
Boxlock. Gauges: 12 and 20 w/2.75-or 3-inch chambers. Bbls.: 26-, 28- or 30-inch with vent rib; fixed chokes. Weight: 7.5 to 8.5 lbs. Single selective trigger. Selective automatic ejectors. Manual safety. Checkered walnut stock. Blue finish with scroll engraving. Imported 1967-80.
500 Field, 12 ga. . . . . NiB $566 Ex $458 Gd $319
500 Field, 20 ga. . . . . NiB $667 Ex $538 Gd $374
500 Magnum, 12 ga.
3-inch chambers . . . . NiB $634 Ex $501 Gd $356

MODEL 500 SMALL
GAUGE O/U SHOTGUN . . . . NiB $698 Ex $563 Gd $391
Similar to Model 500 except gauges 28 and .410; has 28-inch vent-rib bbls., M/F chokes. Weight: About 6.5 lbs.

MODEL 505 O/U SHOTGUN
Blued boxlock action. Gauge: 12, 20, 28 and .410. Bbls.: 26-, 28, 30-inch; IC/M, M/F or inner choke tubes. 45.19 inches overall. Weight: 6.6 to 7.4 lbs. Hand checkered walnut stock. Metal bead front sight, ejectors, single selective trigger and ejectors. Introduced 1988.
Standard Field, Skeet or Trap grade. . . . . . . NiB $923 Ex $743 Gd $513
Standard Two-bbl. Field set . . . . . NiB $1406 Ex $1132 Gd $782
Skeet grade, three-bbl. set . . . . NiB $1989 Ex $1598 Gd $1099
Sporting Clays . . . . NiB $984 Ex $792 Gd $547
Trap grade two-bbl. set . . . . NiB $1689 Ex $1358 Gd $936

MODEL 585 DELUXE O/U SHOTGUN
Boxlock. Gauges: 12, 20, 28 and .410; 2.75-or 3-inch chambers. Bbls.: 26-, 28-, 30-, 32- or 34-inch with vent rib; fixed chokes or Inter-choke tubes. Weight: 6.5 to 8.5 lbs. Single selective trigger. Selective automatic ejectors. Manual safety. Checkered walnut stock in standard or Monte Carlo style. Silver nitride finish with engraved game scenes. Made 1987 to date.
Field, Skeet, Trap grades . . . . NiB $1259 Ex $1014 Gd $701
Field grade, two-bbl. set . . . . . . NiB $2204 Ex $1773 Gd $1221
Skeet set (20, 28, .410 ga.) . . . . NiB $2667 Ex $2144 Gd $1473
Sporting Clays . . . . NiB $1524 Ex $1228 Gd $847
Trap Combo (two-bbl.) . . . . NiB $2204 Ex $1773 Gd $1221

MODEL 600 SERIES O/U SHOTGUN
Similar to 500 Series except w/silver nitride receiver. Checkered deluxe walnut stock in both Field and Target Grade configurations . Imported 1969-80.
600 Field, 12 ga. . . . . NiB $708 Ex $573 Gd $401
600 Field, 20 ga. . . . . NiB $900 Ex $704 Gd $550
600 Magnum, 12 ga.
3-inch chambers . . . . NiB $777 Ex $550 Gd $370
600 Skeet or Trap grade . . . . NiB $756 Ex $601 Gd $447
600 Trap Doubles Gun. . . . . NiB $708 Ex $573 Gd $401

MODEL 600 SMALL GA. . . . . NiB $911 Ex $807 Gd $503
Same as Model 500 Small Gauge except higher grade with more elaborate engraving and fancier wood.

MODEL 605 SERIES O/U SHOTGUN
Similar to the Model 505 except w/engraved silver nitride receiver and deluxe wood. Introduced 1988.
Field, Skeet, Trap grade . . . . NiB $956 Ex $771 Gd $535
Skeet three-bbl. set . . . . NiB $2058 Ex $1659 Gd $1147
Sporting Clays . . . . NiB $967 Ex $781 Gd $542

MODEL 680 ENGLISH O/U SHOTGUN
Similar to 600 Series except w/English style select walnut stock and fine scroll engraving. Imported 1973-77.
680 English, 12 ga. . . . . NiB $812 Ex $656 Gd $457
680 English, 20 ga. . . . . NiB $921 Ex $822 Gd $517

MODEL 685 DELUXE O/U
Similar to the 585 Deluxe except with semi-fancy American walnut stock. Gold trigger and jeweled barrel block. Silvered receiver with fine engraving.
Field, Skeet, Trap grade . . . . NiB $1327 Ex $1074 Gd $749
Field grade, two-bbl. set . . . . . . NiB $2036 Ex $1640 Gd $1134
Skeet set . . . . NiB $2787 Ex $2247 Gd $1557
Sporting Clays . . . . NiB $1379 Ex $1118 Gd $782
Trap Combo. two bbl. . . . . NiB $2021 Ex $1630 Gd $1131

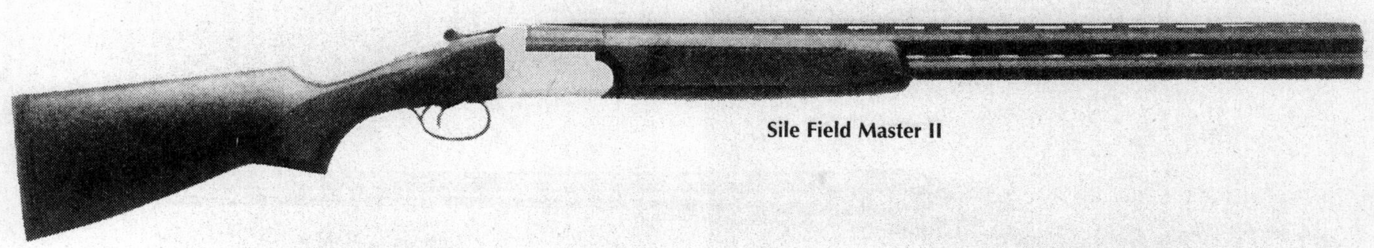
Sile Field Master II

MODEL 800 SKEET/TRAP O/U
Similar to Model 700 Skeet and Trap except higher grade with more elaborate engraving and fancier wood.
Model 800 Skeet .... NiB $372 Ex $1071 Gd $734
Model 800 Trap .... NiB $1231 Ex $993 Gd $688

MODEL 880 SKEET/TRAP
Similar to Model 800 Skeet except has sideplates.
Model 880 Skeet .... NiB $1484 Ex $1276 Gd $882
Model 880 Trap .... NiB $1622 Ex $1307 Gd $903

MODEL 885 DELUXE O/U
Similar to the 685 Deluxe except with engraved sideplates.
Field, Skeet, Trap grade .... NiB $1297 Ex $1047 Gd $727
Field grade, two-bbl. set ...... NiB $2021 Ex $1625 Gd $1119
Skeet Set .... NiB $3268 Ex $2634 Gd $1821
Sporting Clays .... NiB $1659 Ex $1337 Gd $924
Trap Combo................ NiB $2708 Ex $2185 Gd $1514

The following SKB shotguns were distributed by Ithaca Gun Co. from 1966-76. For specific data, see corresponding listings under Ithaca.

CENTURY SINGLE-BARREL TRAP GUN
The SKB catalog does not differentiate between Century and Century II; however, specifications of current Century are those of Ithaca-SKB Century II.
Century (505) .... NiB $985 Ex $800 Gd $563
Century II (605) .... NiB $1132 Ex $918 Gd $643

GAS-OPERATED AUTOMATIC SHOTGUNS
Model XL300 with plain barrel .... NiB $388 Ex $320 Gd $232
Model XL300 with vent rib .... NiB $427 Ex $351 Gd $260
Model XL900.................. NiB $383 Ex $316 Gd $229
Model XL900 Trap .... NiB $446 Ex $366 Gd $264
Model XL900 Skeet .... NiB $457 Ex $375 Gd $269
Model XL900 Slug .... NiB $407 Ex $335 Gd $246
Model 1300 Upland, Slug .... NiB $505 Ex $414 Gd $296
Model 1900 Field, Trap, Slug...... NiB $562 Ex $459 Gd $327

SKB OVER/UNDER SHOTGUNS
Model 500 Field .... NiB $594 Ex $485 Gd $343
Model 500 Magnum .... NiB $689 Ex $558 Gd $396
Model 600 Field .... NiB $798 Ex $649 Gd $459
Model 600 Magnum .... NiB $826 Ex $672 Gd $475
Model 600 Trap .... NiB $790 Ex $607 Gd $430
Model 600 Doubles .... NiB $770 Ex $627 Gd $444
Model 600 Skeet—12 or 20 ga. .... NiB $834 Ex $678 Gd $478
Model 600 Skeet—28 or .410........... NiB $900 Ex $731 Gd $514
Model 600 Skeet Combo........... NiB $2144 Ex $1733 Gd $1208
Model 600 English .... NiB $782 Ex $637 Gd $451
Model 700 Trap.................... NiB $963 Ex $782 Gd $549
Model 700 Doubles .... NiB $853 Ex $694 Gd $489
Model 700 Skeet.................... NiB $924 Ex $750 Gd $528
Model 700 Skeet Combo........... NiB $2345 Ex $1893 Gd $1314

SKB RECOIL-OPERATED AUTOMATIC SHOTGUNS
Model 300—with plain barrel .... NiB $343 Ex $282 Gd $205
Model 300—with vent rib .... NiB $381 Ex $313 Gd $225
Model 900 .... NiB $425 Ex $348 Gd $249
Model 900 Slug .... NiB $407 Ex $334 Gd $240

SKB SIDE-BY-SIDE DOUBLE-BARREL SHOTGUNS
Model 100..................... NiB $531 Ex $433 Gd $308
Model 150..................... NiB $590 Ex $480 Gd $339
Model 200E.................... NiB $864 Ex $700 Gd $492
Model 200E Skeet .... NiB $853 Ex $692 Gd $487
Model 280 English .... NiB $1179 Ex $954 Gd $669

SIG SAUER — (SIG) Schweizerische Industrie-Gesellschaft, Neuhausen, Switzerland

MODEL SA3 O/U SHOTGUN
Monobloc boxlock action. Single selective trigger. Automatic ejectors. Gauges: 12 or 20 w/3- inch chambers. 26-, 28- or 30-inch vent rib bbls. w/choke tubes. Weight: 6.8 to 7.1 lbs. Checkered select walnut stock and forearm. Satin nickel-finished receiver w/game scene and blued bbls. Imported 1997-98.
Field model .... NiB $1291 Ex $1036 Gd $724
Sporting Clays model .... NiB $1385 Ex $1120 Gd $781

MODEL SA5 O/U SHOTGUN
Similar to SA3 Model except w/detachable sideplates. Gauges: 12 or 20 w/3- inch chambers. 26.5-, 28- or 30-inch vent rib bbls. w/choke tubes. Imported 1997-99.
Field model .... NiB $2344 Ex $1893 Gd $1315
Sporting Clays model .... NiB $2530 Ex $2041 Gd $1416

SILE SHOTGUNS — Sile Distributors, New York, NY

FIELD MASTER II O/U SHOTGUN.......... NiB $600 Ex $483 Gd $335
Gauge: 12, 3-inch chambers. 28-inch bbl., IC, M, IM, F choke tubes. 45.25 inches overall. Weight: 7.25 lbs. Satin-finished walnut, checkered stock and forend. Introduced 1989.

L. C. SMITH SHOTGUNS — Made 1890-1945 by Hunter Arms Company, Fulton, N.Y.; 1946-51 and 1968-73 by Marlin Firearms Company, New Haven, Conn.

L. C. SMITH DOUBLE-BARREL SHOTGUNS
Values shown are for L. C. Smith doubles made by Hunter. Those of 1946-51 Marlin manufacture generally bring prices about 1/3 lower. Smaller gauge models, especially in the higher grades, command premium prices: Up to 50 percent more for 20 gauge, up to 400 percent for .410 gauge.

SHOTGUNS

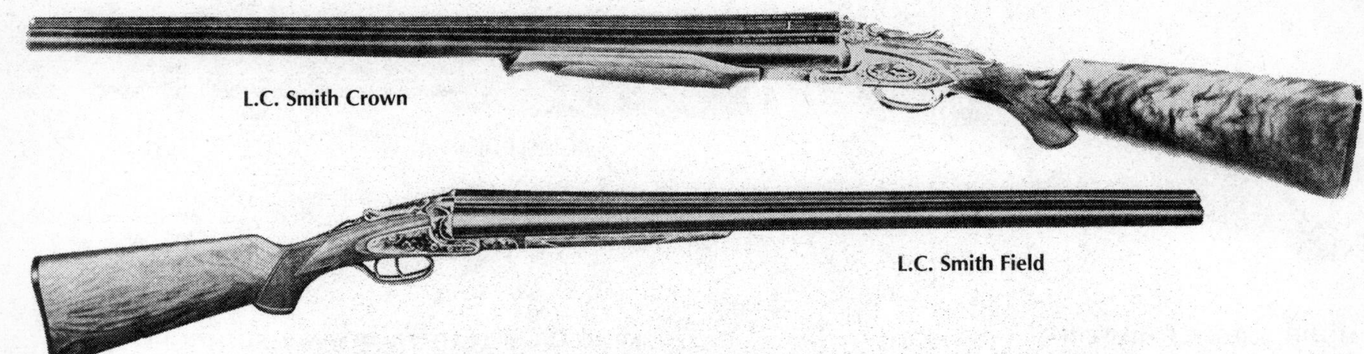
L.C. Smith Crown

L.C. Smith Field

(*cont'd.*) **L. C. SMITH DOUBLE-BARREL SHOTGUNS**

Crown grade, double triggers,
automatic ejectors . . . . NiB $6447 Ex $5177 Gd $3553
Crown grade, selective single trigger,
automatic ejectors . . . . NiB $7528 Ex $5069 Gd $4141
Deluxe grade, selective single trigger,
automatic ejectors . . . NiB $22,531+ Ex $18,025+ Gd $12,257+
Eagle grade, double triggers,
automatic ejectors . . . . NiB $5270 Ex $4235 Gd $2912
Eagle grade, selective
single trigger . . . . NiB $5616 Ex $4513 Gd $3100
Field grade, double trigger
plain extractors . . . . NiB $1269 Ex $1027 Gd $718
Field grade, double triggers
auto. ej. NiB $1675 Ex $1352 Gd $939
Field grade, non-selective single trigger,
plain extractors . . . . NiB $1580 Ex $1276 Gd $887
Field grade, selective single trigger,
automatic ejectors . . . . NiB $1675 Ex $1352 Gd $939
Ideal grade, double triggers,
plain extractors . . . . NiB $1750 Ex $1411 Gd $979
Ideal grade, double triggers,
auto. ej. NiB $2375 Ex $1917 Gd $1331
Ideal grade, selective single trigger,
automatic ejectors . . . . NiB $2736 Ex $2208 Gd $1534
Monogram grade, selective single trigger,
automatic ejectors . . . . NiB $12,971 Ex $10,376 Gd $7057
Olympic grade, selective single trigger,
automatic ejectors . . . . NiB $2519 Ex $2035 Gd $1415
Premier grade, selective single trigger
automatic ejectors . . . NiB $17,703+ Ex $14,162+ Gd $9630+
Skeet Special, non-selective single trigger,
automatic ejectors . . . . NiB $2431 Ex $1965 Gd $1368
Skeet Special, selective single trigger,
auto ejectors . . . . NiB $3142 Ex $2533 Gd $1754
.410 ga. . . . . NiB $13,519 Ex $10,815 Gd $7354
Specialty grade, double triggers,
auto ejectors . . . . NiB $4013 Ex $3230 Gd $2229
Specialty grade, selective single trigger,
automatic ejectors. . . . . NiB $4284 Ex $3446 Gd $2376
Trap grade, sel. single trigger,
auto ej. NiB $1798 Ex $1448 Gd $1001

L C. SMITH HAMMERLESS DOUBLE-BARREL SHOTGUNS

Sidelock. Auto ejectors standard on higher grades, extra on Field and Ideal Grades. Double triggers or Hunter single trigger (non-selective or selective). Gauges: 12, 16, 20, .410. Bbls.: 26- to 32-inch, any standard boring. Weight: 6.5 to 8.25 lbs., 12 ga. Checkered stock and forend; choice of straight, half or full pistol grip, beavertail or standard-type forend. Grades differ only in quality of workmanship, wood, checkering, engraving, etc. Same general specifications apply to all. Manufacture of these L. C. Smith guns was discontinued in 1951. Production of Field Grade 12 ga. was resumed 1968-73. Note: L. C. Smith Shotguns manufactured by the Hunter Arms Co. 1890-13 were designated by numerals to indicate grade with the exception of Pigeon and Monogram.

00 grade . . . . NiB $1557 Ex $1253 Gd $865
0 grade . . . . NiB $1891 Ex $1520 Gd $1046
1 grade . . . . NiB $2114 Ex $1703 Gd $1210
2 grade . . . . NiB $2323 Ex $1870 Gd $1291
3 grade . . . . NiB $3279 Ex $2635 Gd $1811
Pigeon . . . . NiB $4107 Ex $3299 Gd $2265
4 grade . . . . NiB $8567 Ex $6868 Gd $4699
5 grade . . . . NiB $9271 Ex $7432 Gd $5079
Monogram . . . . NiB $11,118 Ex $8894 Gd $5047
A1 . . . . NiB $6859 Ex $3885 Gd $2674
A2. . . . . NiB $11,491 Ex $9193 Gd $6251
A3 . . . . NiB $25,750+ Ex $20,600+ Gd $14,008+

L. C. SMITH HAMMERLESS DOUBLE
MODEL 1968 FIELD GRADE. . . . . NiB $787 Ex $642 Gd $456

Re-creation of the original L. C. Smith double. Sidelock. Plain extractors. Double triggers. 12 ga. 28-inch vent-rib bbls., M/F choke. Weight: About 6.75 lbs. Checkered pistol-grip stock and forearm. Made 1968-73.

L. C. SMITH HAMMERLESS DOUBLE
MODEL 1968 DELUXE . . . . NiB $1148 Ex $937 Gd $669

Same as 1968 Field Grade except has Simmons floating vent rib, beavertail forearm. Made 1971-73.

L. C. SMITH SINGLE-SHOT TRAP GUNS

Boxlock. Hammerless. Auto ejector.12 gauge only. Bbl. lengths: 32- or 34-inch. Vent rib. Weight: 8 to 8.25 lbs. Checkered pistol-grip stock and forend, recoil pad. Grades vary in quality of workmanship, wood, engraving, etc.; general specifications are the same. Disc. 1951. Note: Values shown are for L. C. Smith single-barrel trap guns made by Hunter. Those of Marlin manufacture generally bring prices about one-third lower.

Olympic grade. . . . . NiB $1885 Ex $1520 Gd $1052
Specialty grade . . . . NiB $2360 Ex $1901 Gd $1315
Crown grade . . . . NiB $4063 Ex $3265 Gd $2244
Monogram grade . . . . NiB $6016 Ex $4827 Gd $3307
Premier grade . . . . NiB $9286 Ex $7448 Gd $5098
Deluxe grade. . . . . NiB $14,194 Ex $11,356 Gd $7722

SMITH & WESSON SHOTGUNS — Springfield, Massachusetts, Mfd. by Howa Machinery, Ltd., Nagoya, Japan

In 1985, Smith and Wesson sold its shotgun operation to O. F. Mossberg & Sons, Inc.

L.C. Smith 1968 Field Grade

L.C. Smith 1968 Deluxe

L.C. Smith Single-Shot Trap Gun

Smith & Wesson Model 1000 Magnum

Smith & Wesson Model 3000 Slide Action

MODEL 916 SLIDE-ACTION REPEATER
Hammerless. Solid frame. Gauges: 12, 16, 20. Three inch chamber in 12 and 20 ga. Five round tubular magazine. Bbls.: plain or vent rib; 20-inch C (12 ga., plain only); 26-inch IC- 28-inch M or F; 30-inch F choke (12 ga. only). Weight: With 28-inch plain bbl., 7.25 lbs. Plain pistol-grip stock, fluted slide handle. Made 1972-81.
With plain bbl. .... NiB $193 Ex $159 Gd $115
With ventilated rib bbl. .... NiB $242 Ex $197 Gd $140

MODEL 916T
Same as Model 916 except takedown, 12 ga. only. Not available with 20-inch bbl. Made 1976-81.
With plain bbl. .... NiB $208 Ex $170 Gd $121
With ventilated rib bbl. .... NiB $242 Ex $197 Gd $140

MODEL 1000 AUTOLOADER ..... NiB $355 Ex $290 Gd $205
Gas-operated. Takedown. Gauges: 12, 20. 2.75-inch chamber in 12 ga., 3-inch in 20 ga. Four round magazine. Bbls.: Vent rib, 26-inch SK choke, IC; 28-inch M or F; 30-inch F choke (12 ga. only). Weight: With 28-inch bbl., 6.5 lbs. in 20 ga.,7.5 lbs. in 12 ga. Checkered pistol-grip stock and forearm. Made 1972 to date.

MODEL 1000 MAGNUM .... NiB $431 Ex $349 Gd $245
Same as standard Model 1000 except chambered for 12 ga. magnum, 3-inch shells; 30-inch bbl. only, M or F choke; stock with recoil pad. Weight: About 8 lbs. Introduced in 1977.

MODEL 1000P .... NiB $377 Ex $307 Gd $216
Same general specifications as Model C 3000 Slide Action, but an earlier version.

MODEL 3000
SLIDE ACTION .... NiB $382 Ex $411 Gd $219
Hammerless. 20-ga. Bbls.: 26-inch IC; 28-inch M or F. Chambered for 3-inch magnum and 2.75-inch loads. American walnut stock and forearm. Checkered pistol grip and forearm. Introduced 1982.

SPRINGFIELD ARMS — Built by Savage Arms Company, Utica, New York

SPRINGFIELD DOUBLE-BARREL
HAMMER SHOTGUN .... NiB $439 Ex $356 Gd $250
Gauges: 12 and 16. Bbls.: 28 to 32 inches. In 12 ga., 32-inch model, both bbls. have F choke. All other gauges and barrel lengths are left barrel, Full; right barrel, Mod. Weight: 7.25 to 8.25 lbs., depending on gauge and barrel length. Black walnut checkered buttstock and forend. Disc. 1934.

SQUIRES BINGHAM CO., INC. — Makati, Rizal, Philippines

MODEL 30
PUMP SHOTGUN .... NiB $214 Ex $173 Gd $121
Hammerless. 12 ga. Five round magazine. Bbl.: 20-inch Cyl.; 28-inch M; 30-inch F choke. Weight: About 7 lbs. Pulong Dalaga stock and slide handle. Currently manufactured.

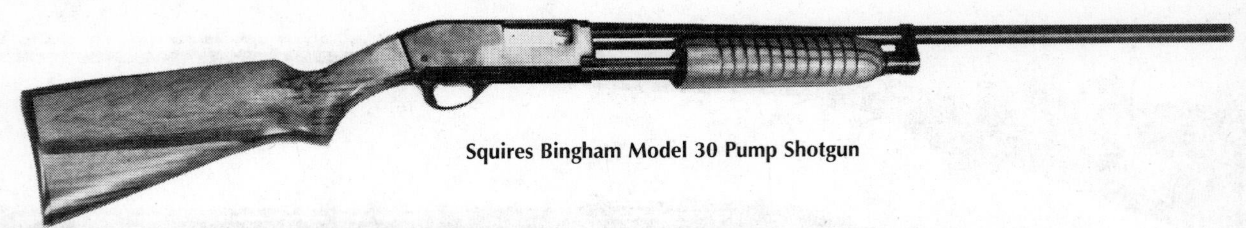
Squires Bingham Model 30 Pump Shotgun

J. STEVENS ARMS COMPANY — Chicopee Falls, Massachusetts, Division of Savage Arms Corporation

NO. 20 "FAVORITE" SHOTGUN . . NiB $355 Ex $287 Gd $202
Calibers: .22 and .32 shot. Smoothbore bbl. Blade front sight; no rear. Made 1893-1939.

NO. 39 NEW MODEL POCKET SHOTGUN . . . . NiB $675 Ex $545 Gd $381
Gauge: .410. Calibers: .38-40 shot, .44-40 shot. Bbls.: 10, 12, 15 or 18 inches, half-octagonal smoothbore. Shotgun sights. Made 1895-1906.

NO. 22-.410 O/U COMBINATION GUN
.22 caliber rifle barrel over .410 ga. shotgun barrel. Visible hammer. Takedown. Single trigger. 24-inch bbls., shotgun bbl. F choke. Weight: About 6 lbs. Open rear sight and ramp front sight of sporting rifle type. Plain pistol-grip stock and forearm; originally supplied with walnut stock and forearm. "Tenite" (plastic) was used in later production. Made 1938-50. Note: This gun is now manufactured as the Savage Model 24.
With wood stock and forearm . . . . NiB $243 Ex $199 Gd $141
With Tenite stock and forearm . . . . NiB $185 Ex $153 Gd $111

MODEL 51 BOLT-ACTION SHOTGUN . . . . NiB $120 Ex $99 Gd $71
Single shot. Takedown. .410 ga. 24-inch bbl., F choke. Weight: About 4.75 lbs. Plain one-piece pistol-grip stock. checkered on later models. Made 1962-71.

MODEL 58 BOLT-ACTION REPEATER . . . . NiB $146 Ex $119 Gd $84
Takedown. Gauges: 12, 16, 20. Two round detachable box magazine. 26-inch bbl., F choke. Weight: About 7.25 lbs. Plain one piece pistol-grip stock on early models w/takedown screw on bottom of forend. Made 1933-81. Note: Later production models have 3-inch chamber in 20 ga., checkered stock with recoil pad.

MODEL 58-.410 BOLT-ACTION REPEATER. . . . . NiB $138 Ex $113 Gd $81
Takedown. .410 ga. Three round detachable box magazine. 24-inch bbl., F choke. Weight: About 5.5 lbs. Plain one piece pistol-grip stock, checkered on later production. Made 1937-81.

MODEL 59 BOLT-ACTION REPEATER . . . . NiB $184 Ex $150 Gd $106
Takedown. .410 ga. Five round tubular magazine. 24-inch bbl., F choke. Weight: About 6 lbs. Plain, one piece pistol-grip stock, checkered on later production. Made 1934-73.

MODEL 67 PUMP SHOTGUN
Hammerless, side-ejection solid-steel receiver. Gauges: 12, 20 and .410, 2.75- or 3-inch shells. Bbls.: 21-, 26-, 28- 30-inch with fixed chokes or interchangeable choke tubes, plain or vent rib. Weight: 6.25 to 7.5 lbs. Optional rifle sights. Walnut-finished hardwood stock with corncob-style forend.

(cont'd.) **MODEL 67 PUMP SHOTGUN**
Standard model, plain bbl. . . . . NiB $243 Ex $198 Gd $141
Standard model, vent rib . . . . NiB $256 Ex $209 Gd $149
Standard model, w/choke tubes . . . NiB $269 Ex $219 Gd $156
Slug model w/rifle sights . . . . NiB $230 Ex $188 Gd $134
Lobo model, matte finish . . . . NiB $284 Ex $239 Gd $169
Youth model, 20 ga. . . . . NiB $256 Ex $209 Gd $149
Camo model. w/choke tubes . . . . . NiB $307 Ex $249 Gd $176

MODEL 67 WATERFOWL SHOTGUN . . . . NiB $281 Ex $228 Gd $162
Hammerless. Gauge: 12. Three round tubular magazine. Walnut finished hardwood stock. Weight: About 7.5 lbs. Made 1972-89.

MODEL 77 SLIDE-ACTION REPEATER . . . . NiB $221 Ex $180 Gd $129
Solid frame. Gauges: 12, 16, 20. Five round tubular magazine. Bbls.: 26-inch IC, 28-inch M or F choke. Weight: About 7.5 lbs. Plain pistol-grip stock with recoil pad, grooved slide handle. Made 1954-71.

MODEL 77-AC. . . . . NiB $256 Ex $209 Gd $139
Same as Model 77 except has Savage Super Choke.

MODEL 79-VR SUPER VALUE . . . . . NiB $243 Ex $198 Gd $141
Hammerless, side ejection. Bbl.: Chambered for 2.75-inch and 3-inch mag. shells. 12, 20, and .410 ga. vent rib. Walnut finished hardwood stock with checkering on grip. Weight: 6.75-7 lbs. Made 1979-90.

MODEL 94 SINGLE-SHOT SHOTGUN. . NiB $129 Ex $106 Gd $76
Takedown. Visible hammer. Auto ejector. Gauges: 12, 16, 20, 28, .410. Bbls.: 26-, 28-, 30-, 32-, 36-inch, F choke. Weight: About 6 lbs. depending on gauge and barrel. Plain pistol-grip stock and forearm. Made 1939-61.

MODEL 94C . . . . NiB $173 Ex $131 Gd $101
Same as Model 94 except has checkered stock, fluted forearm on late production. Made 1965-90.

MODEL 94Y YOUTH GUN . . . . NiB $171 Ex $139 Gd $99
Same as Model 94 except made in 20 and .410 ga. only; has 26-inch F choke bbl., 12.5-inch buttstock with recoil pad; checkered pistol grip and fluted forend on late production. Made 1959-90.

MODEL 95 SINGLE-SHOT SHOTGUN. . NiB $129 Ex $106 Gd $76
Solid frame. Visible hammer. Plain extractor. 12 ga. Three-inch chamber. Bbls.: 28-inch M- 30-inch F choke. Weight: About 7.25 lbs. Plain pistol-grip stock, grooved forearm. Made 1965-69.

MODEL 107 SINGLE-SHOT HAMMER SHOTGUN . . . . NiB $122 Ex $101 Gd $73
Takedown. Auto ejector. Gauges: 12, 16, 20, .410. Bbl. lengths: 28- and 30-inch (12 and 16 ga.), 28-inch (20 ga.), 26-inch (.410); F choke only. Weight: About 6 lbs., 12 bore ga. Plain pistol-grip stock and forearm. Made about 1937-53.

MODEL 124 CROSS-BOLTREPEATER . . NiB $183 Ex $150 Gd $106
Hammerless. Solid frame. 12 ga. only. Two round tubular magazine. 28-inch bbl.; IC, M or F choke. Weight: About 7 lbs. Tenite stock and forearm. Made 1947-52.

Stevens Model 51

Stevens Model 58

Stevens Model 58-410

Stevens Model 67 Pump Shotgun

Stevens Model 67 Waterfowl Shotgun

Stevens Model 77

Stevens Model 94C

Stevens Model 95

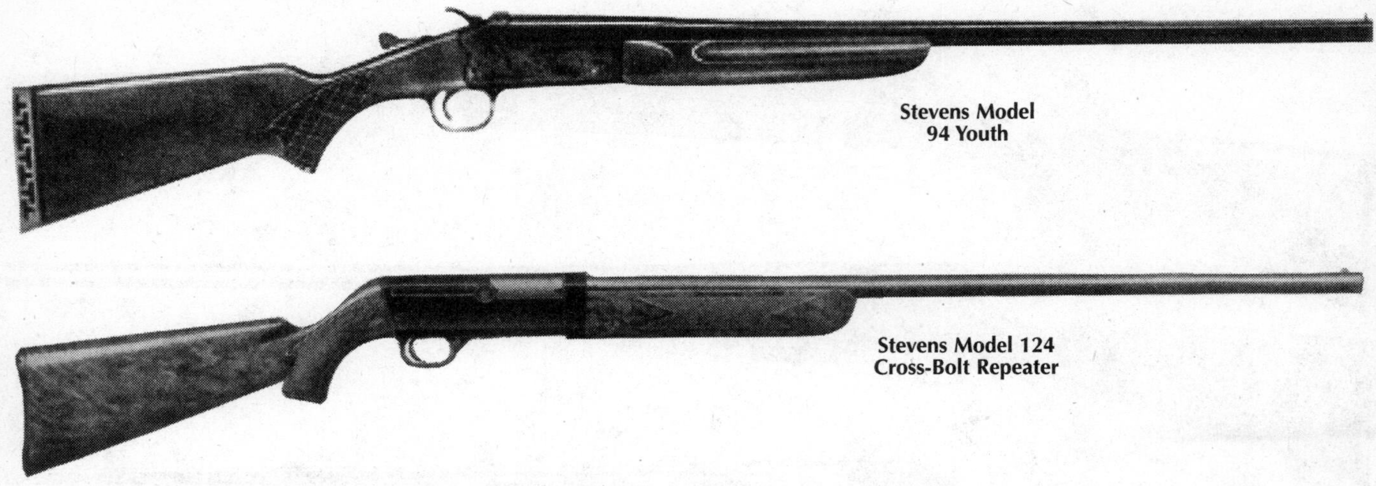

Stevens Model 94 Youth

Stevens Model 124 Cross-Bolt Repeater

MODEL 240 O/U SHOTGUN. . . . . NiB $335 Ex $272 Gd $191
Visible hammer. Takedown. Double triggers. .410 ga. 26-inch bbls., F choke. Weight: 6 lbs. Tenite (plastic) pistol-grip stock and forearm. Made 1940-49.

MODEL 258 BOLT-ACTION REPEATER . . . . NiB $123 Ex $109 Gd $78
Takedown. 20-gauge. Two round detachable box magazine. 26-inch barrel, Full choke. Weight: About 6.25 lbs. Plain, one piece pistol-grip stock. Made 1937-65.

MODEL 311 SPRINGFIELD HAMMERLESS DOUBLE
Same general specifications as Stevens Model 530 except earlier production has plain stock and forearm; checkered on current guns. Originally produced as a "Springfield" gun, this model became a part of the Stevens line in 1948 when the Springfield brand name was discontinued. Made 1931-89.
Pre-WW II . . . . NiB $405 Ex $327 Gd $229
Post-WW II . . . . NiB $359 Ex $290 Gd $204

MODEL 311-R HAMMERLESS DOUBLE . . . . NiB $296 Ex $240 Gd $170
Same general specifications as Stevens Model 311 except compact design for law enforcement use. Bbls.: 18.25-inch 12 gauge with solid rib, chambered for 2.75 and 3-inch Mag. shells. Double triggers and auto top tang safety. Walnut finished hardwood stock with recoil pad and semi-beavertail forend. Weight: About 6.75 lbs. Made 1982-89.

MODEL 530 HAMMERLESS DOUBLE . . . . NiB $358 Ex $290 Gd $204
Boxlock. Double triggers. Gauges: 12, 16, 20, .410. Bbl. lengths: 26- to 32-inch; choked M/F, C/M, F/F. Weight: 6 to 7.5 pounds depending on gauge and barrel length. Checkered pistol-grip stock and forearm; some early models with recoil pad. Made 1936-54.

MODEL 530M. . . . . NiB $265 Ex $216 Gd $153
Same as Model 530 except has Tenite (plastic) stock and forearm. Disc. about 1947.

MODEL 530ST DOUBLE GUN . . . . NiB $329 Ex $269 Gd $187
Same as Model 530 except has non-selective single trigger. Disc.

MODEL 620 HAMMERLESS SLIDE-ACTION REPEATING SHOTGUN . . . . NiB $335 Ex $272 Gd $191
Takedown. Gauges: 12, 16, 20. Five round tubular magazine. Bbl. lengths: 26-, 28-, 30-, 32-inch; choked F, M IC, C. Weight: About 7.75 lbs., 12 ga.; 7.25 lbs., 16 ga.- 6 lbs., 20 ga. Checkered pistol-grip stock and slide handle. Made 1927-53.

MODEL 620-C. . . . . NiB $335 Ex $272 Gd $191
Same specifications as Model 620 except equipped with Cutts Compensator and two choke tubes.

MODEL 620-P . . . . NiB $349 Ex $283 Gd $200
Same specifications as Model 620 equipped with Aero-Dyne PolyChoke and 27-inch bbl.

MODEL 620-PV. . . . . NiB $349 Ex $283 Gd $200
Same specifications as Model 620 except equipped with ventilated PolyChoke and 27-inch bbl.

MODEL 621 . . . . NiB $406 Ex $328 Gd $229
Same as Model 620 except has raised solid matted-rib barrel. Disc.

MODEL 820 HAMMERLESS SLIDE-ACTION REPEATING SHOTGUN . . . . NiB $269 Ex $219 Gd $156
Solid frame. 12 gauge only. Five round tubular magazine. 28-inch barrel; IC, M or F choke. Weight: About 7.5 lbs. Plain pistol-grip stock, grooved slide handle. Early models furnished w/Tenite butt-stock and forend. Made 1949-54.

MODEL 820-SC. . . . . NiB $294 Ex $239 Gd $169
Same as Model 820 except has Savage Super Choke.

MODEL 940 SINGLE-SHOT SHOTGUN . . . . NiB $123 Ex $103 Gd $75
Same general specifications as Model 94 except has side lever opening instead of top lever. Made 1961-70.

MODEL 940Y YOUTH GUN . . . . NiB $146 Ex $121 Gd $88
Same general specifications as Model 94Y except has side lever opening instead of top lever. Made 1961-70.

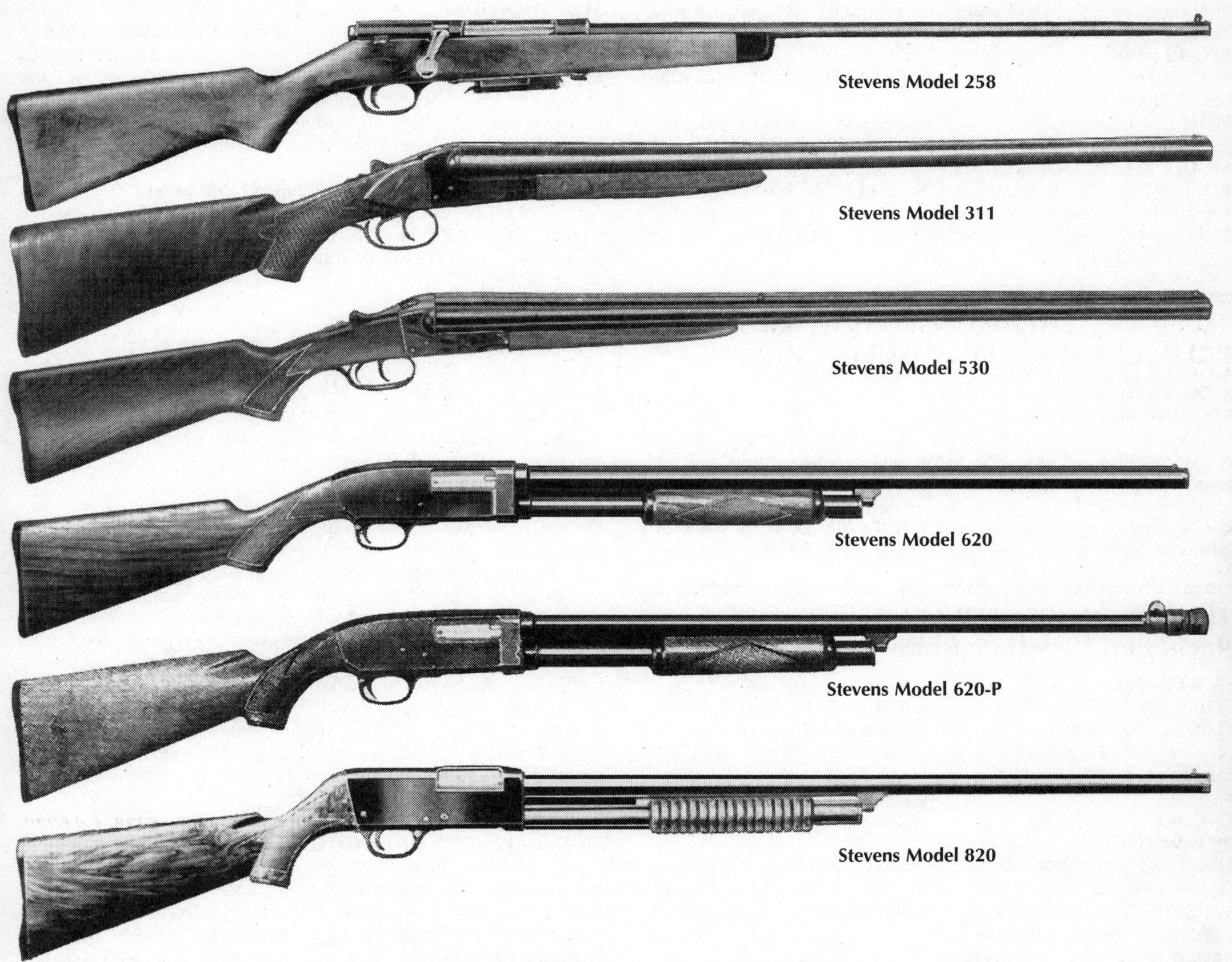
Stevens Model 258

Stevens Model 311

Stevens Model 530

Stevens Model 620

Stevens Model 620-P

Stevens Model 820

MODEL 9478 .... NiB $119 Ex $97 Gd $69
Takedown. Visible hammer. Automatic ejector. Gauges: 12, 20, .410. Bbls.: 26-, 28-, 30-, 36-inch; Full choke. Weight: Average 6 pounds depending on gauge and barrel. Plain pistol-grip stock and forearm. Made 1978-85.

MODEL 5151 SPRINGFIELD...... NiB $413 Ex $334 Gd $233
Same specifications as the Stevens Model 311 except with checkered grip and forend; equipped with recoil pad and two ivory sights.

STOEGER SHOTGUNS

See IGA and Tikka Shotguns

TAR-HUNT CUSTOM RIFLES, INC. — Bloomsburg, PA

MODEL RSG-12 MATCHLESS
BOLT-ACTION SLUG GUN.... NiB $1810 Ex $1460 Gd $1013
Similar to Professional model except has McMillan Fibergrain stock and deluxe blue finish. Made 1995 to date.

MODEL RSG-12 PEERLESS
BOLT-ACTION SLUG GUN.... NiB $1885 Ex $1520 Gd $1052
Similar to Professional model except has McMillan Fibergrain stock and deluxe NP-3 (Nickel/Teflon) metal finish. Made 1995 to date.

MODEL RSG-12 PROFESSIONAL BOLT-ACTION SLUG GUN

Bolt action 12 ga. w/2.75-inch chamber, 2-round detachable magazine, 21.5-inch fully rifled bbl. w/ or w/o muzzle brake. Receiver drilled and tapped for scope mounts w/no sights. Weight: 7.75 lbs. 41.5 inches overall. Checkered black McMillan fiberglass stock w/swivel studs and Pachmayr Deacelerator pad. Made 1991 to date.

RSG-12 model W/O muzzle brake (disc. 1993) .... NiB $1479 Ex $1197 Gd $836
RSG-12 model W/muzzle brake .... NiB $1620 Ex $1310 Gd $914

MODEL RSG-20 MOUNTAINEER BOLT ACTION SLUG GUN..... NiB $1337 Ex $1084 Gd $759

Similar to Professional model except 20 ga. w/2.75 inch chamber. Black McMillan synthetic stock w/blind magazine. Weight: 6.5 lbs. Made 1997 to date.

TECNI-MEC SHOTGUNS — Italy, Imported by RAHN Gun Work, Inc., Hastings, MI

MODEL SPL 640 FOLDING SHOTGUN

Gauges: 12, 16, 20, 24, 28, 32 and .410 bore. 26-inch bbl. Chokes: IC/IM. Weight: 6.5 lbs. Checkered walnut pistol-grip stock and forend. Engraved receiver. Available with single or double triggers. Imported 1988-94.

640 w/single trigger .... NiB $486 Ex $396 Gd $280
640 w/double trigger............ NiB $544 Ex $442 Gd $312

THOMPSON/CENTER ARMS — Rochester, New Hampshire

CONTENDER .410 GA. CARBINE .... NiB $390 Ex $318 Gd $226

Gauge: .410 smoothbore. 21-inch vent rib bbl. 34.75 inches overall. Weight: About 5.25 lbs. Bead front sight. Rynite stock and forend. Made 1991 to date.

ENCORE 20 GA. SHOTGUN

Gauge: 20 smoothbore w/rifled slug bbl. or 26-inch vent-rib bbl. w/three internal screw choke tubes, 38 to 40.5 inches overall. Weight: About 5.25 to 6 lbs. Bead or fiber optic sights. Walnut stock and forend. Made 2000 to date.

Encore 20 ga. W/vent rib.................... NiB $564 Ex $456 Gd $320
Encore 20 ga. w/rifled slug bbl................ NiB $522 Ex $424 Gd $298
W/extra bbl., add $262

MODEL '87 HUNTER SHOTGUN............ NiB $500 Ex $406 Gd $285

Single shot. Gauge: 10 or 12, 3.5-inch chamber, 25-inch field bbl. with F choke. Weight: 8 lbs. Bead front sight. American black walnut stock with recoil pad. Made 1987 to 1992.

MODEL '87 HUNTER SLUG .... NiB $513 Ex $416 Gd $293

Gauge: 10 (3.5-inch chamber) or 12 (3-inch chamber). Same general specifications as Model '87 Hunter Shotgun except with 22-inch slug (rifled) bbl. and rifle sights. Made 1987 to 1992.

TIKKA SHOTGUNS — Manufactured by: Armi Marocchi, Italy, (formerly by Valmet), Riihimaki, Finland

M 07 SHOTGUN/ RIFLE COMBINATION .... NiB $1094 Ex $889 Gd $627

Gauge/caliber: 12/.222 Rem. Shotgun bbl.: About 25 inches; rifled bbl.: About 22.75 inches. 40.66 inches overall. Weight: About 7 lbs. Dovetailed for telescopic sight mounts Single trigger with selector between the bbls. Vent rib. Monte Carlo-style walnut stock with checkered pistol grip and forend. Made 1965-87.

M 77 O/U SHOTGUN.......... NiB $1193 Ex $1150 Gd $745

Gauge: 12. 27-inch vent-rib bbls., approx. 44 inches overall, weight: About 7.25 lbs. Bbl. selector. Ejectors. Monte Carlo-style walnut stock with checkered pistol grip and forend; rollover cheekpiece. Made 1977-87.

M 77K SHOTGUN/ RIFLE COMBINATION .... NiB $1427 Ex $1156 Gd $810

Gauge: 12/70. Calibers: .222 Rem., 5.6x52r5, 6.5x55, 7x57r5, 7x65r5, .308 Win. Vent-rib bbls.: About 25 inches (shotgun); 23 inches (rifle), 42.3 inches overall. Weight: About 7.5 lbs. Double triggers. Monte Carlo-style walnut stock with checkered pistol grip and forend; rollover cheekpiece. Made 1977-86.

412S/512S SHOOTING SYSTEM

Boxlock action with both under lug and sliding top latch locking mechanism designed to accept interchangeable monobloc barrels, including O/U shotgun, combination and double rifle configurations. Blued or satin nickel receiver w/cocking indicators. Selective single trigger design w/barrel selector incorporated into the trigger (double triggers available). Blued barrels assemblies w/extractors or auto ejectors as required. Select American walnut stock with checkered pistol grip and forend. Previously produced in Finland (same as the former Valmet Model 412) but currently manufactured in Italy by joint venture arrangement with Armi Marocchi. From 1990-93, Stoeger Industries imported this model as the 412/S. In 1993 the nomenclature of this shooting system was changed to 512/S and is now imported under that designation. Note: For double rifle values, see Tikka Rifles.

MODEL 412S/512S O/U SHOTGUN

Gauge: 12 w/3-inch chambers. 24-, 26-, 28- or 30-inch chrome-lined bbls. w/blued finish and integral stainless steel choke tubes. Weight: 7.25 to 7.5 lbs. Blue or matte nickel receiver. Select American walnut stock with checkered pistol grip and forend. Imported 1990 to date.

Standard Field model .... NiB $831 Ex $671 Gd $465
Standard Trap model .... NiB $986 Ex $794 Gd $549
Premium Field model .... NiB $896 Ex $722 Gd $500
Premium Trap model .... NiB $1183 Ex $952 Gd $657
Sporting Clays model .... NiB $1002 Ex $808 Gd $558
Standard Trap model .... NiB $1183 Ex $952 Gd $657
W/Extra O/U shotgun bbl., add $575
W/Extra O/U combination bbl., add $695
W/Extra O/U rifle bbl., add $995

MODEL 412S/512S OVER/UNDER COMBINATION

Gauge: 12 w/3-inch chamber. Calibers: .222 Rem., .30-06 or .308 Win. Blue or matte nickel receiver, 24-inch chrome-lined bbls. w/extractors and blued finish. Weight: 7.25 to 7.5 lbs. Select American walnut stock with checkered pistol grip and forend. Imported 1990 to date.

Standard Combination model .... NiB $1056 Ex $862 Gd $615
Premium Combination model .... NiB $1114 Ex $909 Gd $647
Extra barrel options.................. NiB $1114 Ex $909 Gd $647

TRADITIONS PERFORMANCE FIREARMS — Importers of shotguns produced by Fausti Stefano of Brescia, Italy and ATA Firearms, Turkey.

CLASSIC SERIES, FIELD I O/U
Available in 12, 20, 28 (2 3/4-inch chamber) and .410 gauge, 26- or 28-inch vent rib bbls. W/fixed chokes and extractors. Weight: 6 3/4 to 7 1/4 lbs. Blued finish, silver receiver engraved with game birds. Single, selective trigger. Brass bead front sight. European walnut stock. Overall length 43 to 45 inches. Intro. 2000. .... **$637**

FIELD HUNTER MODEL
Same as Field I except 12 and 20 gauge, 3-inch chambers, screw-in chokes and extractors.................................. **$689**

FIELD II MODEL
Same as Field I except with screw-in chokes and automatic ejectors. **$813**

FIELD III GOLD MODEL
Same as Field I model except 12 gauge only, high-grade, oil-finish walnut, coin-finish receiver with engraved pheasants and woodcock, deep blue finish on barrels, automatic ejectors and non-slip recoil pad.. **$1029**

CLASSIC SERIES O/U SPORTING CLAY III
Available in 12 and 20 gauge, 3-inch chambers, high grade walnut stock, oil-satin finish, palm swell Schnabel forend. 28- and 30-inch bbls. with 3/8-inch top and middle vent rib, red target front bead sight. Automatic ejectors, extended choke tubes. Weight: 8 1/4 lbs. Intro. 2000... **$1225**

SPORTING CLAY II MODEL
Same as Sporting Clay III model but with European walnut stocks, cut checkering and extended choke tubes. Overall length: 47 inches. Weight: 7 3/4 lbs.................................... **$988**

UPLAND III MODEL
Same as Sporting Clay III model but round pistol grip and Schnabel forend, blued receiver with engraved upland scene, weight: 7 1/2 lbs **$1091**

UPLAND II MODEL
Same as Upland III model except with English walnut straight-grip stock and Schnabel forend, 24- and 26-inch vent rib bbls., floral engraving on blued receiver, automatic ejectors. **$864**

MAG 350 SERIES
TURKEY II O/U
Magnum 3 1/2-inch chambers in 12 gauge only, 24- and 26-inch bbls., screw-in flush fitting chokes: F and XF. Matte finish, engraved receiver, Mossy Oak or Realtree camo. Intro. 2000. .... **$916**

WATERFOWL II MODEL
Same as Turkey II model except with Advantage Wetlands camo stock and barrels, weight: 8 lbs., overall length 45 inches. Waterfowl model has 28-inch bbls. **$916**

MAG HUNTER II
Same as Turkey II model except blued engraved receiver and matte finish walnut stocks, 3 1/2-inch chambers, 28-inch bbls. with screw-in chokes... **$823**

ELITE SERIES DOUBLE-BARREL SHOTGUNS
ELITE FIELD III ST
Checkered English walnut straight stock, splinter forend, fixed chokes. Available in 28 and .410 gauge, 26-inch chrome-lined bbls., Cylinder and Modified chokes. Silver trigger guard and receiver with hand-finished engraving of upland game scenes with gold inlays. Automatic ejectors. Brass front sight bead. Weight: About 6 1/2 lbs. Intro. 2000.................................... **$2162**

ELITE HUNTER ST
Same as Elite Field model except 12 and 20 gauge, European walnut stock, beavertail forend, screw-in choke tubes, extractors, three-inch chambers. Blued finish. Vent-rib, tang safety.
Weight: 6 1/2 pounds **$1029**

ELITE FIELD I ST
Same as Elite Field III except single trigger, fixed chokes, extractors; European walnut stock. Available in 12, 20, 28 (2 3/4-inch chambers) and .410 gauge; fixed IC/M chokes. Weight: 5 3/4 to 6 1/2 lbs. **$947**

ELITE FIELD I DT
Same as Elite Field I except with double triggers, fixed chokes, extractors. Available in 12, 20, 28 (2 3/4-inch chambers) and .410. Bbls: 26 inches, fixed IC/M chokes. Weight: 5 1/2 to 6 1/4 lbs **$895**

ALS 2100 SEMI-AUTOMATIC SHOTGUNS
FIELD SERIES, WALNUT MODEL
Gas-operated, 12 and 20 gauge, 3-inch chambers, cut-checkered Turkish walnut stock and forend, blued 26- and 28-inch vent rib bbls., multi-choke system, chrome bore lining. Weight: About 6 lbs. Rifled barrel with cantilever mount available Intro. 2001.... **$494**

SYNTHETIC STOCK MODEL
Same as the ALS 2100 Walnut model except with synthetic stock, matted finish on receiver and bbl., weight: About 6 lbs **$473**

YOUTH MODEL
Same as ALS 2100 Walnut model except with a shorter walnut stock (length of pull: 13 1/2 inches). Available in 12 or 20 gauge with 24-inch vent rib barrel, weight: 5 1/2 to 6lbs................. **$494**

HUNTER COMBO MODEL
Same as ALS 2100 Walnut model except comes with two bbls. (28-inch vent rib and 24-inch slug), TruGlo adjustable sights and cantilever mount. Available with Turkish walnut or synthetic stock with matte barrel finish. Weight: 6 1/2 lbs.
(Walnut) **$649**
(Synthetic) **$596**

SLUG HUNTER MODEL
Same as ALS 2100 Walnut except with fully-rifled barrel, choice of walnut or synthetic stocks, matte or blue finish; rifle or TruGlo adjustable sights. Weight: About 6 1/4 lbs................. **$565**

TURKEY HUNTER/WATERFOWL MODEL
Same as ALS 2100 Walnut except with synthetic stock, 3-inch chambers, 26-inch vent rib bbl., screw-in chokes, Mossy Oak or Realtree camo stocks... **$535**

HOME SECURITY MODEL
Same as ALS 2100 Walnut but with 20-inch cylinder-bore bbl., synthetic stock, 3-inch chambers, six-round capacity with 2 3/4-inch shells. Weight: About 6 lbs.............................. **$411**

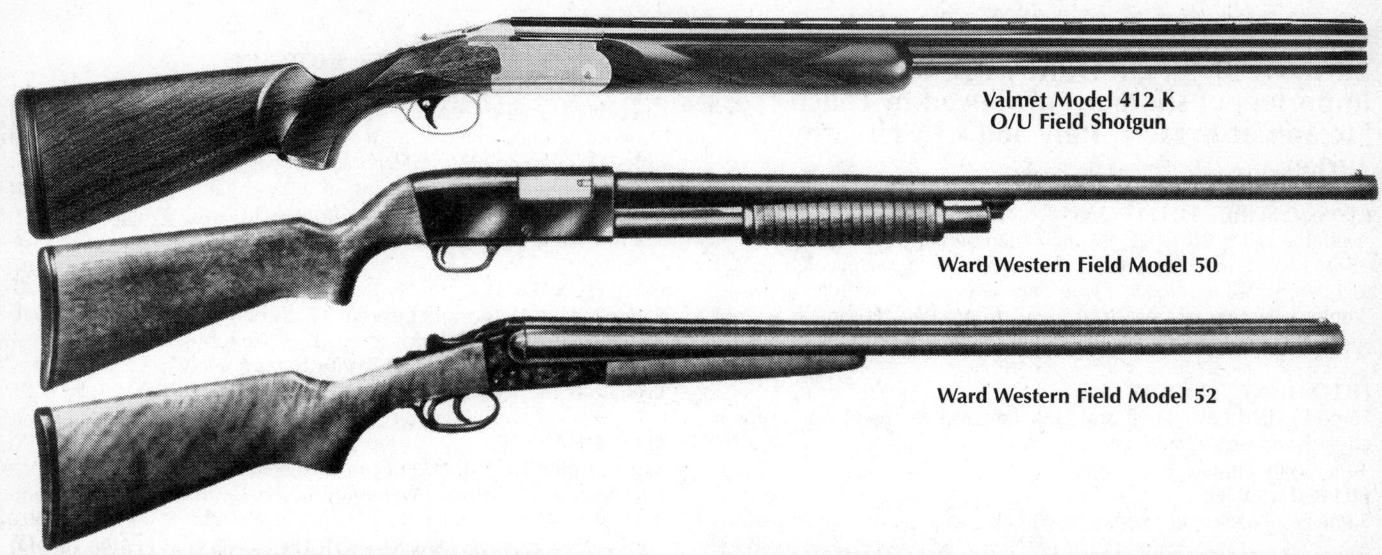

Valmet Model 412 K O/U Field Shotgun

Ward Western Field Model 50

Ward Western Field Model 52

TRISTAR SPORTING ARMS — North Kansas City, MO

MODEL 1887 LEVER-ACTION REPEATER . . . . NiB $610 Ex $494 Gd $345
Copy of John Browning's Winchester Model 1887 lever-action shotgun. 12 ga. only. 30-inch bbl. which may be cut down to any desired length of 18 inches or more. Version shown has 20-inch bbl. Imported 1997-98.

MODEL 300 O/U SHOTGUN . . . . . NiB $448 Ex $365 Gd $258
Similar to the Model 333 except 12 ga. only w/3-inch chambers, 26- or 28-inch vent rib bbls. w/extractors and fixed chokes. Etched receiver w/double triggers and standard walnut stock. Imported 1994-98.

MODEL 311 SIDE-BY-SIDE SHOTGUN
Boxlock action w/underlug and Greener cross bolt. 12 or 20 ga. w/3-inch chambers, 20, 28- or 30-inch bbls. w/choke tubes or fixed chokes (311R). Double triggers. Extractors. Black chrome finish. Checkered Turkish walnut buttstock and forend. Weight: 6.9 to 7.2 lbs. Imported 1994-97.
311 Model (w/extractors and choke tubes) . . . NiB $610 Ex $493 Gd $335
311R Model
(w/20-inch bbls. and fixed chokes) . . . . NiB $448 Ex $365 Gd $258

MODEL 330 O/U SHOTGUN
Similar to the Model 333 except 12 ga. only w/3-inch chambers. 26-, 28- or 30-inch vent rib bbls w/extractors or ejectors and fixed chokes or choke tubes. Etched receiver and standard walnut stock. Imported 1994 to date.
330 model (w/ extractor and fixed chokes) . . . NiB $539 Ex $437 Gd $307
330 D model (w/ejectors and choke tubes) . . . NiB $706 Ex $571 Gd $398

MODEL 333 O/U SHOTGUN
Boxlock action. 12 or 20 ga. w/3-inch chambers. 26-, 28- or 30-inch vent rib bbls. w/choke tubes. Single selective trigger. Selective automatic ejectors. Engraved receiver w/satin nickel finish. Checkered Turkish fancy walnut buttstock and forend. Weight: 7.5 to 7.75 lbs. Imported 1994 to date..
333 Field model . . . . NiB $807 Ex $651 Gd $452
333 Sporting Clays model (1994-97) . . . . . NiB $909 Ex $732 Gd $508
333 TRL Ladies Field model . . . . NiB $820 Ex $662 Gd $460
333 SCL Ladies Sporting Clays model
(1994-97) . . . . NiB $928 Ex $749 Gd $518

SHOTGUNS OF ULM — Ulm, West Germany

See listings under Krieghoff.

U.S. REPEATING ARMS CO. — New Haven, Connecticut

See Winchester Shotgun listings.

VALMET OY — Jyväskylä, Finland

NOTE: In 1987, Valmet and Sako merged and the Valmet production facilities were moved to Riihimaki, Finland. In 1989 a joint venture agreement was made with Armi Marocchi, and when production began in Italy, the Valmet name was changed to Tikka (Oy Tikkakoski Ab).

See also Savage Models 330, 333T, 333 and 2400, which were produced by Valmet.

VALMET LION O/U SHOTGUN . . . NiB $517 Ex $419 Gd $293
Boxlock. Selective single trigger. Plain extractors. 12 ga. only. Bbls.: 26-inch IC/M; 28-inch M/F, 30-inch M/F, F/F. Weight: About 7 lbs. Checkered pistol-grip stock and forearm. Imported 1947-68.

MODEL 412 K O/U FIELD SHOTGUN . . . . NiB $860 Ex $694 Gd $482
Hammerless. 12-ga., 3-inch chamber, 36-inch bbl., F/F chokes. American walnut Monte Carlo stock. Made 1982-87.

MODEL 412 K SHOTGUN RIFLE
COMBINATION . . . . NiB $1035 Ex $835 Gd $580
Similar to model 412 K except bottom bbl. chambered for .222 Rem., .223 Rem., .243 Win., .308 Win. or .30-06. 12-ga. shotgun bbl. with IM choke. Monte Carlo American walnut stock, recoil pad.

MODEL 412 KE O/U
FIELD SHOTGUN . . . . NiB $834 Ex $674 Gd $468
12-ga. chambered for 2.75-inch shells. 26-inch bbl., IC/M chokes; 28-inch bbl., M/F chokes; 12-ga. chambered for 3-inch shells, 30-inch bbl., M/F chokes. 20-ga. (3-inch shells); 26-inch bbl., IC/M chokes; 28-inch bbl., M/ F chokes. American walnut Monte Carlo stock.

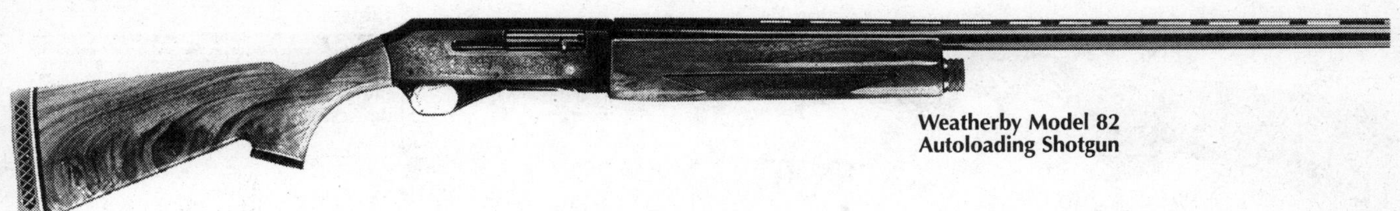
Weatherby Model 82
Autoloading Shotgun

MODEL 412 KE SKEET........... NiB $969 Ex $781 Gd $541
Similar to Model 412 K except skeet stock and chokes. 12 and 20 ga. Disc. 1989.

MODEL 412 KE TRAP .... NiB $1010 Ex $814 Gd $583
Similar to Model 412 K Field except trap stock, recoil pad. 30-inch bbls., IM/F chokes. Disc.1989.

MODEL 412 3-BARREL SET ....NIB $2644 EX $2130 GD $1473

MONTGOMERY WARD — Chicago, Illinois Western Field and Hercules Models

Although they do not correspond to specific models below, the names Western Field and Hercules have been used to designate various Montgomery Ward shotguns at various times.

MODEL 25 SLIDE-ACTION REPEATER ...... NiB $224 Ex $183 Gd $131
Solid frame. 12 ga. only. Two- or 5-round tubular magazine. 28-inch bbl., various chokes. Weight: About 7.5 lbs. Plain pistol-grip stock, grooved slide handle.

MODEL 40 O/U SHOTGUN...... NiB $742 Ex $602 Gd $421
Hammerless. Boxlock. Double triggers. Gauges: 12, l6, 20, .410. Bbls.: Plain; 26- to 30-inch, various chokes. Checkered pistol-grip stock and forearm.

MODEL 40N SLIDE-ACTION REPEATER........ NiB $230 Ex $188 Gd $134
Same general specifications as Model 25.

(WESTERN FIELD) MODEL 50 PUMPGUN ... NiB $237 Ex $193 Gd $138
Solid frame. Gauges: 12 and 16. Two- and 5-round magazine. 26-, 28- or 30-inch bbl., 48 inches overall w/28-inch bbl. Weight: 7.25 - 7.75 lbs. Metal bead front sight. Walnut stock and grooved forend.

(WESTERN FIELD) MODEL 52 DOUBLE-BARREL SHOTGUN..... NiB $267 Ex $218 Gd $155
Hammerless coil-spring action. Gauges: 12, 16, 20 and .410. 26-, 28-, or 30-inch bbls., 42 to 46 inches overall, depending upon bbl. length. Weight: 6 (.410 ga. w/26-inch bbl.) to 7.25 lbs. (12 ga. w/30-inch bbls.), depending upon gauge and bbl. length. Casehardened receiver; blued bbls. Plain buttstock and forend. Made circa 1954.

MODEL 172 BOLT-ACTION SHOTGUN .... NiB $118 Ex $97 Gd $69
Takedown. Two-round detachable clip magazine.12 ga. 28-inch bbl. with variable choke. Weight: About 7.5 lbs. Monte Carlo stock with recoil pad.

MODEL 550A SLIDE-ACTION REPEATER .... NiB $265 Ex $215 Gd $152
Takedown. Gauges: 12, 16, 20, .410. Five-round tubular magazine. Bbls.: Plain, 26- to 30-inch, various chokes. Weight: 6 (.410 ga. w/26-inch bbl.) to 8 lbs. (12 ga. w/30-inch bbls.). Plain pistol-grip stock and grooved slide handle.

MODEL SB300 DOUBLE-BARREL SHOTGUN............................ NiB $285 Ex $232 Gd $163
Same general specifications as Model SD52A.

MODEL SB312 DOUBLE-BARREL SHOTGUN... NiB $323 Ex $263 Gd $185
Boxlock. Double triggers. Plain extractors. Gauges: 12, 16, 20, .410. Bbls.: 24- to 30-inch. Various chokes. Weight: About 7.5 lbs. in 12 ga.; 6.5 lbs in .410 ga. Checkered pistol-grip stock and forearm.

MODEL SD52A DOUBLE-BARREL SHOTGUN.... NiB $243 Ex $198 Gd $141
Boxlock. Double triggers. Plain extractors. Gauges: 12, 16, 20, .410. Bbls.: 26- to 32-inch, various chokes. Plain forend and pistol-grip buttstock. Weight: 6 (.410 ga., 26-inch bbls.) to 7.5 lbs. (12 ga., 32-inch bbls.).

WEATHERBY, INC. — Atascadero, California (previously South Gate, California)

MODEL 82 AUTOLOADING SHOTGUN
Hammerless, gas-operated. 12 ga. only. Bbls.: 22- to 30-inch, various integral or fixed chokes. Weight: 7.5 lbs. Checkered walnut stock and forearm. Imported 1982-89.
Standard Autoloading Shotgun .... NiB $447 Ex $364 Gd $257
BuckMaster Auto Slug w/rifle sights (1986-90).................. NiB $454 Ex $369 Gd $261
W/fixed chokes, deduct.. $40

MODEL 92 SLIDE-ACTION SHOTGUN
Hammerless, short-stroke action. 12 ga.; 3-inch chamber. Tubular magazine. Bbls.: 22-, 26-, 28-, 30-inch with fixed choke or IMC choke tubes; plain or vent rib with rifle sights. Weight: 7.5 lbs. Engraved, matte black receiver and blued barrel. Checkered high-gloss buttstock and forend. Imported from Japan since 1982.
Standard Model 92 .... NiB $363 Ex $296 Gd $210
BuckMaster Pump Slug w/rifle sights (intro. 1986)........ NiB $387 Ex $316 Gd $224
W/fixed chokes, deduct.............................. $25

ATHENA O/U SHOTGUN
Engraved boxlock action with Greener crossbolt and sideplates. Gauges: 12, 20, 28 and .410; 2.75- or 3.5-inch chambers. Bbls.: 26-, 28-, 30- or 32-inch with fixed or IMC Multi-choke tubes. Weight: 6.75 to 7.38 lbs. Single selective trigger. Selective auto ejectors. Top tang safety. Checkered Claro walnut stock and forearm with high-luster finish. Imported 1982 to date.
Field Model w/IMC multi-choke (12 or 20 ga.)......................... NiB $2255 Ex $1824 Gd $1272
Field Model w/fixed chokes (28 or .410 ga.)... NiB $2200 Ex $1660 Gd $1189
Skeet Model w/fixed chokes (12 or 20 ga.).... NiB $1906 Ex $1544 Gd $1082
Skeet Model w/fixed chokes (28 or .410 ga.) .... NiB $2118 Ex $1714 Gd $1197
Master skeet tube set .... NiB $3579 Ex $2883 Gd $1992
Trap Model w/IC tubes .... NiB $1946 Ex $1577 Gd $1104
Grade V (1993 to date) .... NiB $2359 Ex $1907 Gd $1329

Weatherby Model 92 Slide-Action Shotgun

Weatherby Athena O/U Shotgun

Weatherby Centurion Automatic Shotgun

Weatherby Olympian Trap O/U Shotgun

Weatherby Orion O/U Shotgun

Weatherby Patrician Deluxe Grade

Weatherby Regency Trap Gun

CENTURION AUTOMATIC SHOTGUN
Gas-operated. Takedown. 12 ga. 2.75-inch chamber. Three round magazine. Bbls.: Vent ribs; 26-inch SK, IC or M 28-inch M or F; 30-inch Full choke. Weight: With 28-inch bbl., 7 lbs. 10.5 oz. Checkered pistol-grip stock and forearm, recoil pad. Made in Japan 1972-81.

Centurion Field grade . . . . NiB $372 Ex $313 Gd $215
Centurion Trap Gun (30-inch full choke bbl.) . . . . NiB $427 Ex $347 Gd $245
Centurion Deluxe (etched receiver, fancy wood) . . . . NiB $548 Ex $444 Gd $311

OLYMPIAN O/U SHOTGUN
Gauges: 12 and 20. 2.75- (12 ga.) and 3-inch (20 ga.) chambers. Bbls.: 26-, 28-, 30, and 32-inch. Weight: 6.75 - 8.75 lbs. American walnut stock and forend.

Field Model . . . . NiB $976 Ex $793 Gd $560
Skeet Model . . . . NiB $1000 Ex $813 Gd $574
Trap Model . . . . NiB $983 Ex $798 Gd $564

ORION O/U SHOTGUN
Boxlock with Greener crossbolt. Gauges: 12, 20, 28 and .410; 2.75- or 3-inch chambers. Bbls.: 26-, 28, 30-, 32- or 34-inch with fixed or IMC Multi-Choke tubes. Weight: 6.5 to 9 lbs. Single selective trigger. Selective auto ejectors. Top tang safety. Checkered, high-gloss pistol-grip Claro walnut stock and forearm. Finish: Grade I, plain blued receive; Grade II, engraved blued receiver; Grade III, silver gray receiver. Imported 1982 to date.
Orion I Field w/IC (12 or 20 ga.) .... NiB $1157 Ex $938 Gd $656
Orion II Field w/IC (12 or 20 ga.) .... NiB $1201 Ex $974 Gd $681
Orion II Classic w/IC (12, 20 or 28 ga.)..... NiB $1189 Ex $960 Gd $673
Orion II Sporting Clays w/IC (12 ga.)...... NiB $1373 Ex $1111 Gd $774
Orion III Field w/IC (12 or 20 ga.)......... NiB $1242 Ex $1006 Gd $703
Orion III Classic w/IC (12 or 20 ga.) ...... NiB $1483 Ex $1199 Gd $835
Orion III English Field w/IC (12 or 20 ga.).. NiB $1442 Ex $1166 Gd $812
Orion Upland w/IC (12 or 20 ga.) .... NiB $1334 Ex $1079 Gd $763
Skeet II w/fixed chokes .... NiB $1442 Ex $1166 Gd $812
Super Sporting Clays .... NiB $1751 Ex $1413 Gd $981

PATRICIAN SLIDE-ACTION SHOTGUN
Hammerless. Takedown. 12 ga. 2.75-inch chamber. Four round tubular magazine. Bbls.: Vent rib; 26-inch, SK, IC M; 28-inch, M F; 30-inch, F choke. Weight: With 28-inch bbl., 7 lbs., 7 oz. Checkered pistol-grip stock and slide handle, recoil pad. Made in Japan 1972-82.
Patrician Field grade .... NiB $305 Ex $247 Gd $175
Patrician Deluxe (etched receiver,
fancy grade wood) .... NiB $353 Ex $286 Gd $201
Patrician Trap Gun (30-inch F choke bbl.) .... NiB $323 Ex $262 Gd $184

REGENCY FIELD GRADE O/U SHOTGUN .. NiB $1312 Ex $1062 Gd $743
Boxlock with sideplates, elaborately engraved. Auto ejectors. Selective single trigger. Gauges: 12, 20. 2.75-inch chamber in 12 ga., 3-inch in 20 ga. Bbls.: Vent rib; 26-inch SK, IC/M, M/F (20 ga. only); 28-inch SK, IC/M, M/F; 30-inch M/F (12 ga only). Weight with 28-inch bbls.: 7 lbs., 6 oz., 12 ga.; 6 lbs., 14 oz., 20 ga. Checkered pistol-grip stock and forearm of fancy walnut. Made in Italy 1965-82.

REGENCY TRAP GUN.......... NiB $1344 Ex $1088 Gd $761
Similar to Regency Field Grade except has trap-style stock with straight or Monte Carlo comb. Bbls. have vent side ribs and high, wide vent top rib; 30- or 32-inch, M/F, IM/F or F/F chokes. Weight: With 32-inch bbls., 8 lbs. Made in Italy 1965-1982.

WESTERN ARMS CORP. — Ithaca, New York Division of Ithaca Gun Company

LONG RANGE HAMMERLESS DOUBLE
Boxlock. Plain extractors. Single or double triggers. Gauges: 12, 16, 20, .410. Bbls.: 26- to 32-inch, M/F choke standard. Weight: 7.5 lbs., 12 ga. Plain pistol-grip stock and forend. Made 1929-46.
With double triggers .... NiB $340 Ex $277 Gd $196
With single trigger .... NiB $427 Ex $346 Gd $243

WESTERN AUTO SHOTGUNS — Kansas City, Missouri

MODEL 300H SLIDE-ACTION REPEATER .... NiB $274 Ex $224 Gd $161
Gauges: 12,16, 20, .410. Four round tubular magazine. Bbls.: 26- to 30-inch, various chokes. Weight: About 7 lbs. Plain pistol-grip stock, grooved slide handle.

MODEL 310A SLIDE-ACTION REPEATER .... NiB $261 Ex $214 Gd $154
Takedown. 12 ga. Five round tubular magazine. Bbls.: 28- and 30-inch. Weight: About 7.5 lbs. Plain pistol-grip stock.

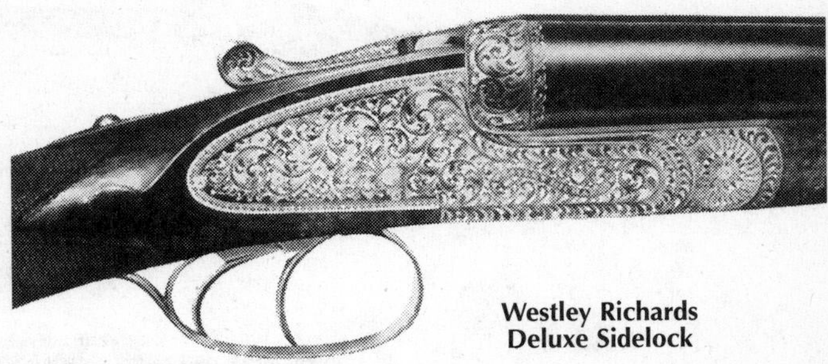
Westley Richards Deluxe Sidelock

MODEL 310B SLIDE-ACTION REPEATER..... NiB $243 Ex $198 Gd $141
Same general specifications as Model 310A except chambered for 16 ga.

MODEL 310C SLIDE-ACTION REPEATER .... NiB $269 Ex $219 Gd $156
Same general specifications as Model 310A except chambered for 20 ga.

MODEL 310E SLIDE-ACTION REPEATER..... NiB $307 Ex $249 Gd $176
Same general specifications as Model 310A except chambered for .410 bore.

MODEL 325BK BOLT-ACTION REPEATER..... NiB $133 Ex $111 Gd $81
Takedown. Two round detachable clip magazine. 20 ga. 26-inch bbl. with variable choke. Weight: 6.25 lbs.

WESTERN FIELD SHOTGUNS

See "W" for listings under Montgomery Ward.

WESTLEY RICHARDS & CO., LTD. — Birmingham, England

The Pigeon and Wildfowl gun, available in all of the Westley Richards models except the Ovundo, has the same general specifications as the corresponding standard field gun except has magnum action of extra strength and treble bolting, chambered for 12 gauge only (2.75- or 3-inch); 30-inch full choke barrels standard. Weight: About 8 lbs. The manufacturer warns that 12-gauge magnum shells should not be used in their standard weight double-barrel shotguns.

BEST QUALITY BOXLOCK HAMMERLESS DOUBLE-BARREL SHOTGUN
Boxlock. Hand-detachable locks and hinged cover plate. Selective ejectors. Double triggers or selective single trigger. Gauges: 12, 16, 20. Barrel lengths and boring to order. Weight: 5.5 to 6.25 lbs. depending on ga. and bbl. length. Checkered stock and forend, straight or half-pistol grip. Also supplied in Pigeon and Wildfowl models with same values. Made from 1899 to date.
With double triggers .... NiB $21,312 Ex $17,050 Gd $11,594
With selective single trigger........ NiB $24,062 Ex $19,250 Gd $13,090

BEST QUALITY SIDELOCK HAMMERLESS DOUBLE-BARREL SHOTGUN
Hand-detachable sidelocks. Selective ejectors. Double triggers or selective single trigger. Gauges: 12, 16, 20, 28, .410. Bbl. lengths and boring to order. Weight: 4.75 to 6.75 lbs., depending on ga. and bbl. length. Checkered stock and forend, straight or half-pistol grip. Also supplied in Pigeon and Wildfowl models with same values. Currently manufactured.
With double triggers............. NiB $25,031 Ex $20,225 Gd $14,073
With selective single trigger........ NiB $27,250 Ex $22,000 Gd $15,280

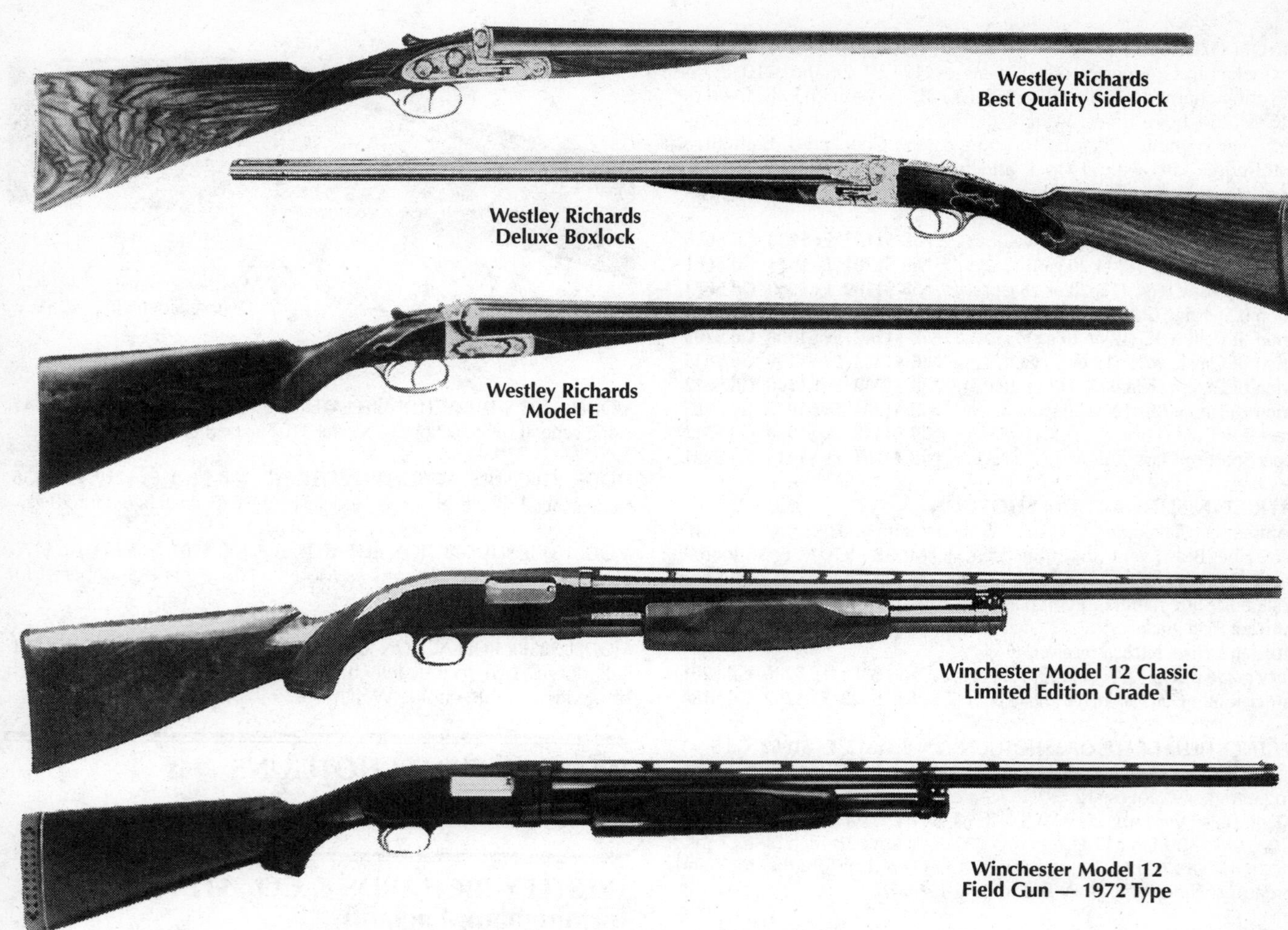

Westley Richards Best Quality Sidelock

Westley Richards Deluxe Boxlock

Westley Richards Model E

Winchester Model 12 Classic Limited Edition Grade I

Winchester Model 12 Field Gun — 1972 Type

MODEL DELUXE BOX LOCK HAMMERLESS DOUBLE-BARREL SHOTGUN

Same general specifications as standard Best Quality gun except higher quality throughout. Has Westley Richards top-projection and treble-bite lever-work, hand-detachable locks. Also supplied in Pigeon and Wildfowl models with same values. Currently manufactured.

With double triggers .... NiB $11,188 Ex $8950 Gd $6086
With selective single trigger .... NiB $30,000 Ex $28,000 Gd $12,000

MODEL DELUXE SIDELOCK

Same as Best Quality Sidelock except higher grade engraving and wood. Currently manufactured.

With double triggers .... NiB $25,000 Ex $20,000 Gd $13,600
With single trigger ...... NiB $30,000 Ex $24,000 Gd $16,320

MODEL E HAMMERLESS DOUBLE

Anson & Deeley-type boxlock action. Selective ejector or non-ejector. Double triggers. Gauges: 12, 16, 20. Barrel lengths and boring to order. Weight: 5.5 to 7.25 lbs. depending on type, ga. and bbl. length. Checkered stock and forend, straight or half-pistol grip. Also supplied in Pigeon and Wildfowl models with same values. Currently manufactured.

Ejector model .... NiB $4814 Ex $3865 Gd $2651
Non-ejector model .... NiB $4195 Ex $3370 Gd $2314

OVUNDO (O/U) .... NiB $18,744 Ex $14,995 Gd $10,197

Hammerless. Boxlock. Hand-detachable locks. Dummy sideplates. Selective ejectors. Selective single trigger. 12 ga. Barrel lengths and boring to order. Checkered stock/forend, straight or half-pistol grip. Mfd. before WW II.

TED WILLIAMS SHOTGUNS

See Sears shotguns.

WINCHESTER SHOTGUNS — New Haven, Connecticut

Formerly Winchester Repeating Arms Co., now mfd. by Winchester-Western Div., Olin Corp., and by U.S. Repeating Arms Company. In 1999, production rights were acquired by Browning Arms.

MODEL 12 CLASSIC LIMITED EDITION

Gauge: 20; 2.75-inch chamber. Bbl.: 26-inch vent rib; IC. Weight: 7 lbs. Checkered walnut buttstock and forend. Polished blue finish (Grade I) or engraved with gold inlays (Grade IV). Made 1993 to 1995.

Grade I (4000) .... NiB $925 Ex $746 Gd $517
Grade IV (1000) .... NiB $1440 Ex $1158 Gd $797

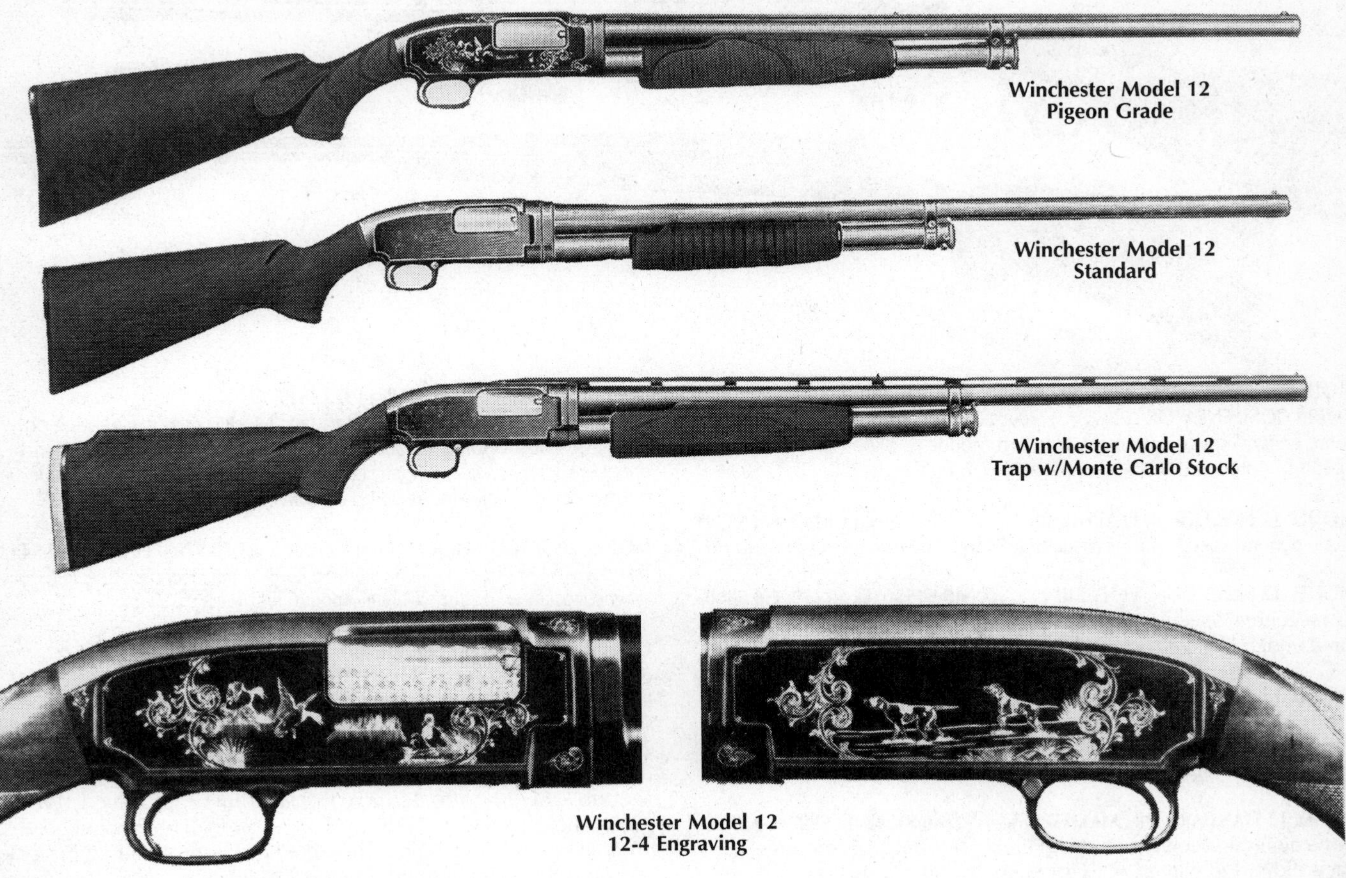

Winchester Model 12 Pigeon Grade

Winchester Model 12 Standard

Winchester Model 12 Trap w/Monte Carlo Stock

Winchester Model 12 12-4 Engraving

MODEL 12 FEATHERWEIGHT. . . . . NiB $551 Ex $447 Gd $313
Same as Model 12 Standard w/plain barrel except has alloy trigger guard. Modified takedown w/redesigned magazine tube, cap and slide handle. 12 ga. only. Bbls.: 26-inch IC; 28-inch M or F; 30-inch F choke. Serial numbers with "F" prefix. Weight: About 6.75 lbs. Made 1959-62.

MODEL 12 FIELD GUN, 1972 TYPE . . . . . . NiB $668 Ex $540 Gd $376
Same general specifications as Standard Model 12 but 12 ga. only, 26- 28- or 30-inch vent rib bbl., standard chokes. Engine-turned bolt and carrier. Hand-checkered stock/slide handle of semifancy walnut. Made 1972-75.

MODEL 12 HEAVY DUCK GUN
Same general specifications as Standard Grade except 12 ga. only chambered for 3-inch shells. 30- or 32-inch plain, solid or vent rib bbl. w/full choke only. Three round magazine. Checkered slide handle and pistol-grip walnut buttstock w/recoil pad. Weight: 8.5 to 8.75 lbs. Made 1935-63.

Heavy Duck Gun, plain bbl. . . . . NiB $880 Ex $710 Gd $492
Heavy Duck Gun, solid rib (disc. 1959). . . . . NiB $1341 Ex $1085 Gd $757
Heavy Duck Gun, vent rib (Special order only) . . . . NiB $1728 Ex $1394 Gd $967

MODEL 12 PIGEON GRADE
Deluxe versions of the regular Model 12 Standard or Field Gun, Duck Gun, Skeet Gun and Trap Gun made on special order. This grade has finer finish throughout, hand-smoothed action, engine-turned breech bolt and carrier, stock and extension slide handle of high grade walnut, fancy checkering, stock dimensions to individual specifications. Engraving and carving available at extra cost ranging from about $135 to over $1000. Disc. 1965.

Field Gun, plain bbl. . . . . NiB $1836 Ex $1481 Gd $1028
Field Gun, vent rib. NiB $2224 Ex $1792 Gd $1239
Skeet Gun, matted rib . . . . NiB $2041 Ex $1645 Gd $1139
Skeet Gun, vent rib . . . . NiB $2543 Ex $12048 Gd $1413
Skeet Gun, Cutts Compensator . . . . NiB $1516 Ex $1226 Gd $854
Trap Gun, matted rib. . . . . NiB $2181 Ex $1758 Gd $1217
Trap Gun, vent rib . . . . NiB $2402 Ex $1934 Gd $1336
16 ga. (Field), add 20%
16 ga. (Skeet), add 90%
20 ga. (Field), add 25%
20 ga. (Skeet), add 45%
28 ga. (Skeet), add 350%

MODEL 12 RIOT GUN . . . . NiB $844 Ex $684 Gd $478
Same general specifications as plain barrel Model 12 Standard except has 20-inch cylinder bore bbl.,12 gauge only. Made 1918-1963.

MODEL 12 SKEET GUN . . . . NiB $1147 Ex $927 Gd $647
Gauges: 12, 16, 20, 28. Five round tubular magazine. 26-inch matted rib bbl., SK choke. Weight: About 7.75 lbs., 12 ga.; 6.75 lbs., other gauges. Bradley red or ivory bead front sight. Winchester 94B middle sight. Checkered pistol-grip stock and extension slide handle. Disc. after WWII.

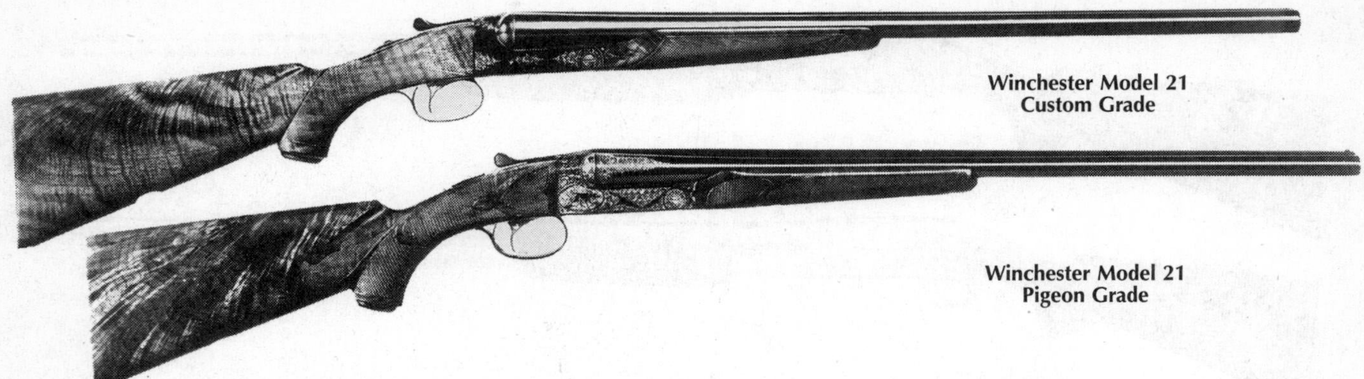

Winchester Model 21
Custom Grade

Winchester Model 21
Pigeon Grade

MODEL 12 SKEET GUN, CUTTS COMPENSATOR . . . . NiB $978 Ex $793 Gd $558
Same general specifications as standard Model 12 Skeet Gun except has plain bbl. fitted with Cutts Compensator, 26 inches overall. Disc. 1954.

MODEL 12 SKEET GUN, PLAIN-BARREL . . . . . NiB $910 Ex $740 Gd $522
Same general specifications as standard Model 12 Skeet except w/no rib.

MODEL 12 SKEET GUN, VENT RIB . . . . NiB $1556 Ex $1259 Gd $880
Same general specifications as standard Model 12 Skeet Gun except has 26-inch bbl. with vent rib, 12 and 20 ga. Disc. in 1965.

MODEL 12 SKEET GUN, 1972 TYPE. . . . . NiB $993 Ex $807 Gd $568
Same gen. specifications as Standard Model 12 but 12 ga. only. 26-inch vent rib bbl., SK choke. Engine-turned bolt and carrier. Hand-checkered skeet-style stock and slide handle of choice walnut, recoil pad. Made 1972-75.

MODEL 12 STANDARD GR., MATTED RIB. . . . . . NiB $1242 Ex $997 Gd $714
Same general specifications as plain bbl. Model 12 Standard except has solid raised matted rib. Disc. after World War II.

MODEL 12 STANDARD GR., VENT RIB. . . . NiB $1395 Ex $1130 Gd $792
Same general specifications as plain barrel Model 12 Standard except has vent rib. 26.75- or 30-inch bbl.,12 ga. only. Disc. after World War II.

MODEL 12 STANDARD SLIDE-ACTION REPEATER
Hammerless. Takedown. Gauges: 12, 16, 20, 28. Six round tubular magazine. Plain bbl. Lengths: 26- to 32-inches; choked F to Cyl. Weight: About 7.5 lbs., 12 ga. 30-inch, 6.5 lbs. in other ga. with 28-inch bbl. Plain pistol-grip stock, grooved slide handle. Made 1912-64.
12 ga., 28-inch bbl. (full choke) . . . . NiB $806 Ex $653 Gd $457
16 ga. . . . . NiB $816 Ex $581 Gd $408
20 ga. . . . . NiB $935 Ex $756 Gd $527
28 ga. . . . . NiB $3956 Ex $3185 Gd $2198

MODEL 12 SUPER PIGEON GRADE . NiB $3184 Ex $2567 Gd $1778
Custom version of Model 12 with same general specifications as standard models. 12 ga. only. 26-, 28- or 30-inch vent-rib bbl., any standard choke. Engraved receiver. Hand-smoothed and fitted action. Full fancy walnut stock and forearm made to individual order. Made 1965-72.

MODEL 12 TRAP GUN
Same general specifications as Standard Model 12 except has straighter stock, checkered pistol grip and extension slide handle, recoil pad, 30-inch matted-rib bbl., F choke, 12 ga. only. Disc. after World War II; vent rib model disc. 1965.
Matted rib bbl. . . . . NiB $1055 Ex $858 Gd $606
With straight stock, vent rib . . . . . NiB $1048 Ex $852 Gd $601
With Monte Carlo stock, vent rib . . . . NiB $1371 Ex $1115 Gd $787

MODEL 12 TRAP GUN, 1972 TYPE . . . . NiB $985 Ex $806 Gd $577

***(cont'd.)* MODEL 12 TRAP GUN, 1972 TYPE**
Same general specifications as Standard Model 12 but 12 gauge only. 30-inch vent-rib bbl., F choke. Engine-turned bolt and carrier. Hand-checkered trap-style stock (straight or Monte Carlo comb) and slide handle of select walnut, recoil pad. Intro. in 1972. Disc.

MODEL 20 SINGLE-SHOT HAMMER GUN . . . . NiB $763 Ex $619 Gd $433
Takedown. .410 bore. 2.5-inch chamber. 26-inch bbl., F choke. Checkered pistol-grip stock and forearm. Weight: About 6 lbs. Made 1919-24.

ORIGINAL MODEL 21 DOUBLE-BARREL SHOTGUNS (ORIGINAL PRODUCTION SERIES - 1930 TO 1959)
Hammerless. Boxlock. Automatic safety. Double triggers or selective single trigger, selective or non-selective ejection (all postwar Model 21 shotguns have selective single trigger and selective ejection). Gauges: 12, 16, 20, 28 and .410 bore. Bbls.: Raised matted rib or vent rib; 26-, 28-, 30-, 32-inch, the latter in 12 ga. only; F, IM, M, IC, SK chokes. Weight: 7.5 lbs., 12 ga. w/30-inch bbl.; about 6.5 lbs. 16 or 20 ga. w/28-inch bbl. Checkered pistol- or straight-grip stock, regular or beavertail forend. Made 1930-59.
Standard grade, 12 ga. . . . . NiB $5011 Ex $4034 Gd $2783
Standard grade, 16 ga. . . . . NiB $6276 Ex $5045 Gd $3470
Standard grade, 20 ga. . . . . NiB $6492 Ex $5218 Gd $3589
Tournament grade, 12 ga. (1933-34). . . . . NiB $5269 Ex $4240 Gd $2923
Tournament grade, 16 ga. (1933-34). . . . . NiB $6499 Ex $5213 Gd $3592
Tournament grade, 20 ga. (1933-34). . . . . NiB $7740 Ex $6222 Gd $4279
Trap grade, 12 ga. (1940-59) . . . . . NiB $5082 Ex $4090 Gd $2822
Trap grade, 16 ga. (1940-59) . . . . . NiB $5681 Ex $4569 Gd $3147
Trap grade, 20 ga. (1940-59) . . . . . NiB $7020 Ex $5641 Gd $3875
Skeet grade, 12 ga. (1936-59). . . . . NiB $5011 Ex $4034 Gd $2783
Skeet grade, 16 ga. (1936-59). . . . . NiB $5745 Ex $4621 Gd $3182
Skeet grade, 20 ga. (1936-59). . . . . NiB $6672 Ex $5363 Gd $3776
Duck Gun, 12 ga. 3-inch (1940-52) . . . NiB $5526 Ex $4446 Gd $3064
Magnum Gun, 12 ga. 3-inch (1953-59). . . . . NiB $5340 Ex $4296 Gd $2962
Magnum Gun, 20 ga. 3-inch (1953-59). . . . . NiB $6499 Ex $5223 Gd $3592
Cust. built/deluxe gr., 12 ga.(1933-59). . . . . NiB $7899 Ex $6355 Gd $4379
Cust. built/deluxe gr., 16 ga. (1933-59) . . . . NiB $9129 Ex $7338 Gd $5048
Cust. built/deluxe gr., 20 ga. (1933-59). . . . . NiB $10,030 Ex $8059 Gd $5538
Custom built/deluxe grade, 28 ga.(1933-59) . . . . Very Rare*
Custom built/deluxe grade, .410 1933-59) . . . . Very Rare*
*Fewer than 100 sm. bore models (28 ga. and .410) were built, which precludes accurate pricing, but projected values could exceed $30,000. Such rare specimens should be authenticated by factory letter and/or independent appraisals.

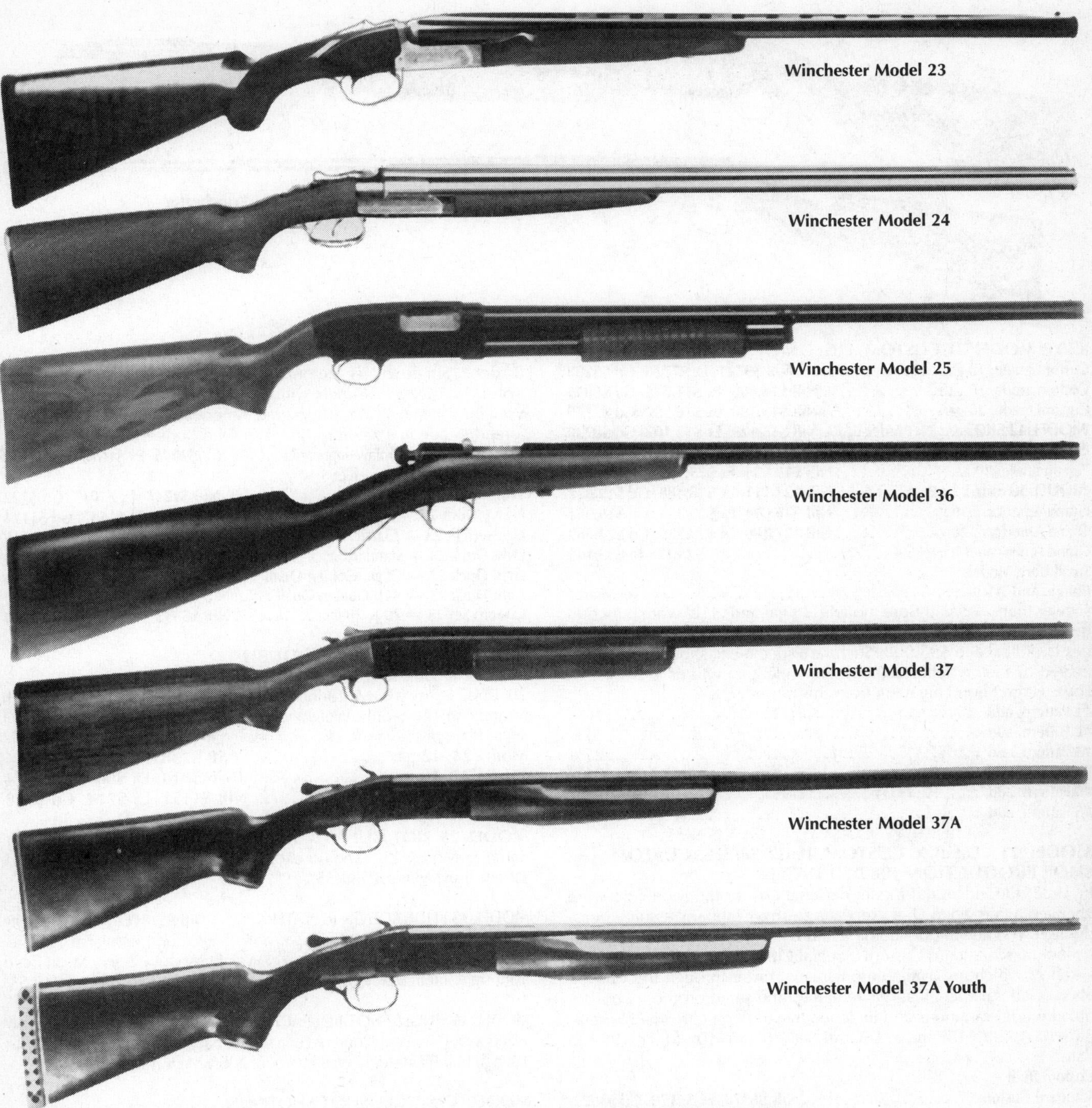
Winchester Model 23

Winchester Model 24

Winchester Model 25

Winchester Model 36

Winchester Model 37

Winchester Model 37A

Winchester Model 37A Youth

(cont'd) **ORIGINAL MODEL 21**

W/vent rib on 12 ga. models, add $690
W/vent rib on 16 ga. models, add $1600
W/vent rib on 20 ga. models, add $1100
W/double triggers ans extractors, deduct 30%
W/double trigger, selective ejection, deduct 20%

For Custom Engraving from this period:

No. 1 Pattern, add 25%
No. 2 Pattern, add 35%
No. 3 Pattern, add 50%
No. 4 Pattern, add 35%
No. 5 Pattern, add 65%

(cont'd) **ORIGINAL MODEL 21**

No. 6 Pattern, add 75%

MODEL 21 CUSTOM, PIGEON, GRAND AMERICAN (CUSTOM SHOP SERIES - PRODUCTION 1959 TO 1981)

Since 1959 the Model 21 has been offered through the Custom Shop in deluxe models. (Custom, Pigeon, Grand American) on special order. General specifications same as for Model 21 standard models except these custom guns have full fancy American walnut stock and forearm with fancy checkering, finely polished and hand-smoothed working parts, etc.; engraving inlays, carved stocks and other extras are available at additional cost. Made 1959-81.

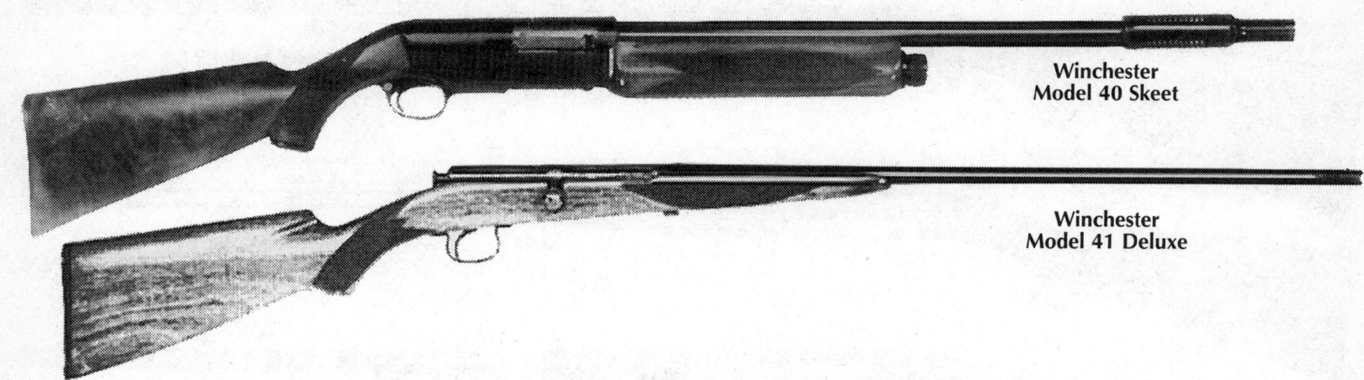
Winchester Model 40 Skeet

Winchester Model 41 Deluxe

(*cont'd*) **MODEL 21 CUSTOM, PIGEON,**

Custom grade, 12 ga.................. NiB $9721 Ex $7776 Gd $5288
Custom grade, 16 ga............... NiB $14,806 Ex $11,845 Gd $8055
Custom grade, 20 ga............... NiB $13,198 Ex $10,557 Gd $7179
Pigeon grade, 12 ga. .... NiB $15,129 Ex $12,102 Gd $8230
Pigeon grade, 16 ga. .... NiB $21,244 Ex $16,995 Gd $11,557
Pigeon grade, 20 ga. .... NiB $19,635 Ex $15,707 Gd $10,681
Grand American, 12 ga. .... NiB $23,111 Ex $18,488 Gd $12,572
Grand American, 16 ga. .... NiB $36,694 Ex $29,355 Gd $19,961
Grand American, 20 ga. .... NiB $27,360 Ex $29,355 Gd $14,883
Grand American 3-barrel Set .... $23,175 to $39,140
Small Bore Models
(28 ga. And .410) .... Very Rare*

*Fewer than 20 Small Bore models (28 ga. and .410) were built during this period, which precludes accurate pricing, but projected values could exceed $35,000. Such rare specimens should be authenticated by factory letter and/or independent appraisals.

For Custom Shop Engraving from this period:

#1 Pattern, add 10%
#2 Pattern, add 15%
#3 Pattern, add 25%
#4 Pattern, add 35%
#5 Pattern, add 45%
#6 Pattern, add 50%

MODEL 21 - U.S.R.A. CUSTOM-BUILT SERIES (CUSTOM SHOP PRODUCTION 1982 TO DATE)

In 1982, the individual model designations for the Model 21 were changed again when U. S. Repeating Arms Company assumed production. The new model nomenclature for the Custom/Built catagory, includes: Standard Custom, Special Custom and Grand American — all of which are available on special order through the Custom Shop. General specifications remained the same on these consolidated model variations and included the addition of a Small Bore 2-Barrel Set (28/.410) and a 3-Barrel Set (20/28/.410). Made 1982 to date.

Custom Built -
Standard Custom...................... NiB $6370 Ex $5120 Gd $3522
Custom Built -
Special Custom .... NiB $7529 Ex $6047 Gd $4152
Custom Built - Grand American ...... NiB $13,519 Ex $10,815 Gd $7354
Custom Built - Grand
American 2-barrel set............ NiB $44,999 Ex $35,998 Gd $24,479
Custom Built - Grand
American 3-barrel set............ NiB $67,594 Ex $54,075 Gd $36,771

The values shown above represent the basic model in each catagory. Since many customers took advantage of the custom built options, individual gun appointments vary and values will need to be adjusted accordingly. For this reason, individual appraisals should be obtained on all subject firearms.

MODEL 23 SIDE-BY-SIDE SHOTGUN

Boxlock. Single trigger. Automatic safety. Gauges: 12, 20, 28, .410. Bbls.: 25.5-, 26-, 28-inch with fixed chokes or Winchoke tubes. Weight: 5.88 to 7 lbs. Checkered American walnut buttstock and forend. Made in 1979 for Olin at its Olin-Kodensha facility, Japan.

Classic 23 — Gold inlay, engraved .... NiB $2046 Ex $1610 Gd $1125
Custom 23 — Plain receiver,
Winchoke system .... NiB $1248 Ex $1017 Gd $722
Heavy Duck 23 — Standard .... NiB $1982 Ex $1546 Gd $1124
Lightweight 23 — Classic .... NiB $1972 Ex $1597 Gd $1115
Light Duck 23 — Standard .... NiB $1872 Ex $1513 Gd $1061
Light Duck 23 — 12 ga. Golden Quail ... NiB $2211 Ex $1794 Gd $1259
Light Duck 23 — .410 Golden Quail ..... NiB $3756 Ex $3030 Gd $2100
Custom Set 23 — 20 & 28 ga............ NiB $5833 Ex $4692 Gd $3230

MODEL 24 HAMMERLESS DOUBLE

Boxlock. Double triggers. Plain extractors. Auto safety. Gauges: 12, 16, 20. Bbls.: 26-inch IC/M; 28-inch M/F (also IC/M in 12 ga. only); 30-inch M and F in 12 ga. only. Weight: About 7.5 lbs., 12 ga. Metal bead front sight. Plain pistol-grip stock, semi-beavertail forearm. Made 1939-57.

Model 24, 12 ga. .... NiB $738 Ex $605 Gd $434
Model 24, 16 ga. .... NiB $814 Ex $664 Gd $474
Model 24, 20 ga. .... NiB $1151 Ex $714 Gd $508

MODEL 25 RIOT GUN .... NiB $575 Ex $469 Gd $3333

Same as Model 25 Standard except has 20-inch cylinder bore bbl., 12 ga. only. Made 1949-55.

MODEL 25 SLIDE-ACTION REPEATER....... NiB $518 Ex $421 Gd $298

Hammerless. Solid frame. 12 ga. only. Four round tubular magazine. 28-in. Plain bbl.; IC, M or F choke. Weight: About 7.5 lbs. Metal bead front sight. Plain pistol-grip stock, grooved slide handle. Made 1949-55.

MODEL 36 SINGLE-SHOT BOLT ACTION.... NiB $625 Ex $508 Gd $360

Takedown. Uses 9mm Short or Long shot or ball cartridges interchangeably. 18-inch bbl. Plain stock. Weight: About 3 lbs. Made 1920-27.

MODEL 37 SINGLE-SHOT SHOTGUN

Semi-hammerless. Auto ejection. Takedown. Gauges: 12, 16, 20, 28, .410. Bbl. lengths: 28-, 30-, 32-inch in all gauges except .410; 26- or 28-inch in .410; all barrels plain with F choke. Weight: About 6.5 pounds, 12 ga. Made 1937-63.

12 ga. .... NiB $343 Ex $280 Gd $200
16 ga. .... NiB $281 Ex $231 Gd $167
20 ga. .... NiB $390 Ex $318 Gd $226
20 ga. (Youth w/red dot indicator) .... NiB $470 Ex $402 Gd $284
28 ga. (red letter only) .... NiB $1559 Ex $1260 Gd $877
410 ga. .... NiB $463 Ex $377 Gd $268
Other "Red Letter" models, add 20%
W/32-inch bbl., add 15%

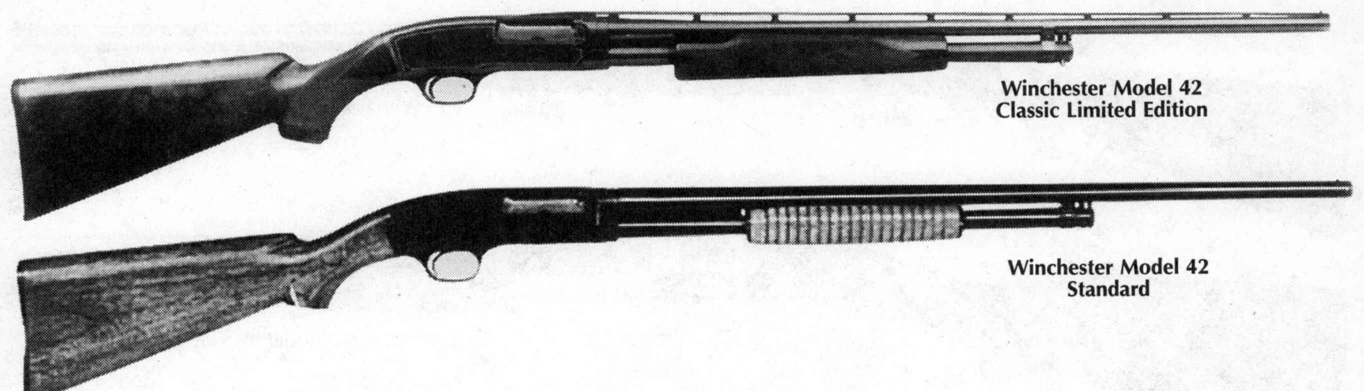
Winchester Model 42 Classic Limited Edition

Winchester Model 42 Standard

MODEL 37A SINGLE SHOT SHOTGUN
Similar to Model 370 except has engraved receiver and gold trigger, checkered pistol-grip stock, fluted forearm; 16 ga. available with 30-inch bbl. only. Made 1973-80.
Model 37A, 12, 16, or 20 ga. . . . . . NiB $177 Ex $145 Gd $104
Model 37A, 28 ga.. . . . . NiB $258 Ex $211 Gd $150
Model 37A, .410 ga. . . . . NiB $309 Ex $252 Gd $178
W/32-inch bbl., add $20

MODEL 37A YOUTH. . . . . NiB $190 Ex $155 Gd $111
Similar to Model 370 Youth except has engraved receiver and gold trigger, checkered pistol-grip stock, fluted forearm. Made 1973-80.

MODEL 40 STANDARD AUTOLOADER. . NiB $768 Ex $619 Gd $429
Streamlined receiver. Hammerless. Takedown. 12 ga. only. Four round tubular magazine. 28- or 30-inch bbl.; M or F choke. Weight: About 8 lbs. Bead sight on ramp. Plain pistol-grip stock, semi-beavertail forearm. Made 1940-41.

MODEL 40 SKEET GUN . . . . NiB $1046 Ex $852 Gd $605
Same general specifications as Model 40 Standard except has 24-inch plain bbl. w/Cutts Compensator and screw-in choke tube, checkered forearm and pistol grip, grip cap. Made 1940-1941.

MODEL 41 SINGLE-SHOT BOLT ACTION
Takedown. .410 bore. 2.5-inch chamber (chambered for 3-inch shells after 1932). 24-inch bbl., F choke. Plain straight stock standard. Also made in deluxe version. Made 1920-34.
Standard model . . . . NiB $692 Ex $563 Gd $399
Deluxe model. . . . . NiB $822 Ex $668 Gd $470

MODEL 42 CLASSIC LTD. EDITION. NiB $1685 Ex $1362 Gd $950
Gauge: .410 with 2.75-inch chamber. Bbl.: 26-inch vent rib; F choke. Weight: 7 lbs. Checkered walnut buttstock and forend. Engraved blue with gold inlays. Limited production of 850. Made 1993.

MODEL 42 DELUXE . . . . NiB $5877 Ex $4723 Gd $3247
Same general specifications as the Model 42 Trap Grade except available w/vent rib after 1955. Finer finish throughout w/hand-smoothed action, engine-turned breech bolt and carrier, stock and extension slide handle of high grade walnut, fancy checkering, stock dimensions to individual specifications. Engraving and carving were offered at extra cost. Made 1940-63. Note: Exercise caution on VR models not marked "DELUXE" on the bottom of the receiver. A factory letter will insure that the rib was installed during the initial manufacturing process. Unfortunately, factory authentication is not always possible due to missing or destroyed records. To further complicate this matter, not all VR ribs were installed by Winchester. From 1955-63, both Deluxe and Skeet Grade models were available with Simmons style ribs. After-market rib installations are common.

MODEL 42 PIGEON GRADE
This higher-grade designation is similar to the Deluxe grade and is available in all configurations. May be identified by engraved Pigeon located at the base of the magazine tube. Most production occurred in the late 1940's. *NOTE: To determine the value of any Model 42 Pigeon Grade, add 50 % to value listed under the specified Model 42 configuration.*

MODEL 42 SKEET GUN
Same general specifications as Model 42 Standard except has checkered straight or pistol-grip stock and extension slide handle, 26- or 28-inch plain, solid-rib or vent-rib bbl. May be choked F., Mod., Imp. Cyl. or Skeet. Note: Some Model 42 Skeet Guns are chambered for 2.5-inch shells only. Made 1933-63.
Model 42 Skeet
w/plain bbl. . . . . NiB $2580 Ex $2092 Gd $1467
Model 42 Skeet
w/solid rib. . . . . NiB $3352 Ex $2710 Gd $1887
Model 42 Skeet
w/vent rib . . . . NiB $4478 Ex $3615 Gd $2511
W/2.5-inch
chamber, add 35%

MODEL 42 TRAP GRADE
This higher grade designation was available in both field and skeet configurations and is fitted w/deluxe wood w/trap grade checkering pattern and marked "TRAP" on bottom of receiver. Made 1934-39. Superseded by the Deluxe model in 1940.
Model 42 Trap grade
w/plain bbl. . . . . NiB $8925 Ex $7380 Gd $3775
Model 42 Trap grade
w/solid rib. . . . . NiB $5815 Ex $4785 Gd $2210
Model 42 Trap grain
w/vent rib . . . . NiB $6845 Ex $5300 Gd $2467

MODEL 42 STANDARD GRADE
Hammerless. Takedown. .410 bore (3- or 2.5-inch shell). Tubular magazine holds five 3-inch or six 2.5-inch shells. 26- or 28-inch plain or solid-rib bbl.; cylinder bore, M or F choke. Weight: 5.8 to 6.5 lbs. Plain pistol-grip stock; grooved slide handle. Made 1933-63.
Model 42 Standard w/plain bbl. . NiB $1326 Ex $1080 Gd $742
Model 42 Standard w/solid rib . . . . NiB $2068 Ex $1914 Gd $1502

MODEL 50 FIELD GUN, VENT RIB . . . NiB $537 Ex $435 Gd $305
Same as Model 50 Standard except has vent rib.

MODEL 50 SKEET GUN . . . . NiB $609 Ex $493 Gd $343
Same as Model 50 Standard except has 26-inch vent-rib bbl. with SK choke, skeet-style stock of select walnut.

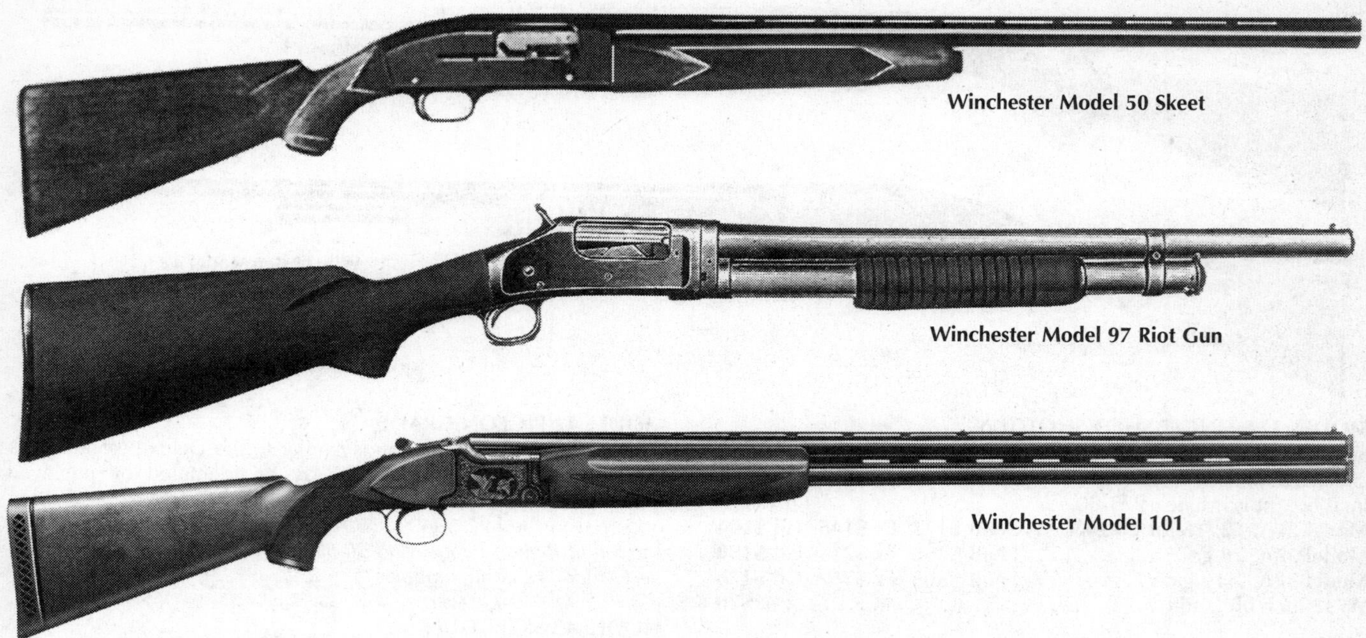

Winchester Model 50 Skeet

Winchester Model 97 Riot Gun

Winchester Model 101

MODEL 50 STANDARD GRADE . . . NiB $477 Ex $387 Gd $271
Non-recoiling bbl. and independent chamber. Gauges: 12 and 20. Two round tubular magazine. Bbl.: 12 ga. — 26-, 28-, 30-inch; 20 ga. — 26-, 28-inch; IC, SK, M, F choke. Checkered pistol-grip stock and forearm. Weight: About 7.75 lbs. Made 1954-61.

MODEL 50 TRAP GUN . . . . NiB $837 Ex $657 Gd $425
Same as Model 50 Standard except 12 ga. only, has 30-inch vent-rib bbl. with F choke, Monte Carlo stock of select walnut.

MODEL 59 AUTO-LOADING SHOTGUN . . . NiB $674 Ex $551 Gd $396
Gauge: 12. Magazine holds two rounds. Alloy receiver. Win-Lite steel and fiberglass bbl.: 26-inch IC, 28-inch M or F choke, 30-inch F choke; also furnished with 26-inch bbl. with Versalite choke (interchangeable F, M, IC tubes; one supplied with gun). Weight: About 6.5 lbs. Checkered pistol-grip stock and forearm. Made 1959-65.

MODEL 97 BUSH GUN
Takedown or solid frame. Same general specifications as standard Model 97 except w/26-inch cylinder bore bbl. Made 1897-1931.
Model 97 Bush Gun w/solid frame . NiB $812 Ex $562 Gd $437
Model 97 Bush Gun takedown . . . . NiB $1074 Ex $862 Gd $590

MODEL 97 RIOT GUN
Takedown or solid frame. Same general specifications as standard Model 97 except 12 ga. only, 20-inch cylinder bore bbl. Made 1898-1935.
Model 97 Riot Gun w/solid frame . . NiB $1259 Ex $1013 Gd $700
Model 97 Riot Gun takedown . . . . NiB $1097 Ex $885 Gd $613

MODEL 97 TRAP, TOURNAMENT AND PIGEON
These higher grade models offer higher overall quality than the standard grade. Made 1897-39.
Standard Trap grade . . . . NiB $1489 Ex $1199 Gd $828
Special Trap grade . . . . NiB $1604 Ex $1353 Gd $933
Tournament grade (Black Diamond) . . . . NiB $2624 Ex $2112 Gd $1457
Pigeon grade . . . . NiB $5032 Ex $4040 Gd $2771

MODEL 97 TRENCH GUN . . . . NiB $2083 Ex $1672 Gd $1147
Solid frame. Same as Model 97 Riot Gun except has handguard and

***(cont'd.)* MODEL 97 TRENCH GUN**
is equipped with a bayonet. World War I government issue, 1917-18.
Model 97 Trench Gun
w/solid frame . . . . NiB $3048 Ex $2445 Gd $1674
Model 97 Trench Gun takedown. . . . NiB $1304 Ex $1050 Gd $723

MODEL 97 SLIDE-ACTION REPEATER
Standard Grade. Takedown or solid frame. Gauges: 12 and 16. Five-round tubular magazine. Bbl.: Plain; 26 to 32 inches, the latter in 12 ga. only; choked F to Cyl. Weight: About 7.75 lbs. (12 ga. w/28-inch barrel). Plain pistol-grip stock, grooved slide handle. Made 1897-1957.
Model 97, 12 ga. w/solid frame . . . NiB $901 Ex $731 Gd $512
Model 97, 16 ga. w/solid frame . . NiB $1160 Ex $938 Gd $654
Model 97, 12 ga. takedown. . . . . . NiB $931 Ex $755 Gd $529
Model 97, 16 ga. takedown. . . . . NiB $1197 Ex $968 Gd $674

NOTE: All Winchester Model 101s are mfd. for Olin Corp. at its Olin-Kodensha facility in Tochigi, Japan. Production for Olin Corp. stopped in Nov. 1987. Importation of Model 101s was continued by Classic Doubles under that logo until 1990. See separate heading for additional data.

MODEL 101 DIAMOND
GRADE TARGET . . . . NiB $1781 Ex $1430 Gd $1003
Similar to Model 101 Standard except silvered frame and Winchoke interchangeable choke tubes. Made 1981-90.

MODEL 101 FIELD GUN O/U
Boxlock. Engraved receiver. Auto ejectors. Single selective trigger. Combination bbl. selector and safety. Gauges: 12 and 28, 2.75-inch chambers; 20 and .410, 3-inch chambers. Vent rib bbls.: 30- (12 ga. only) and 26.5-inch, IC/M. Weight: 6.25 to 7.75 lbs. depending on gauge and bbl. length. Hand-checkered French walnut and forearm. Made 1963-81. Gauges other than 12 introduced 1966.
12 and 20 ga. . . . . NiB $1011 Ex $817 Gd $570
28 and .410 ga. . . . . NiB $1236 Ex $997 Gd $693
12 and 20 ga. mag. . . . . NiB $1069 Ex $864 Gd $602

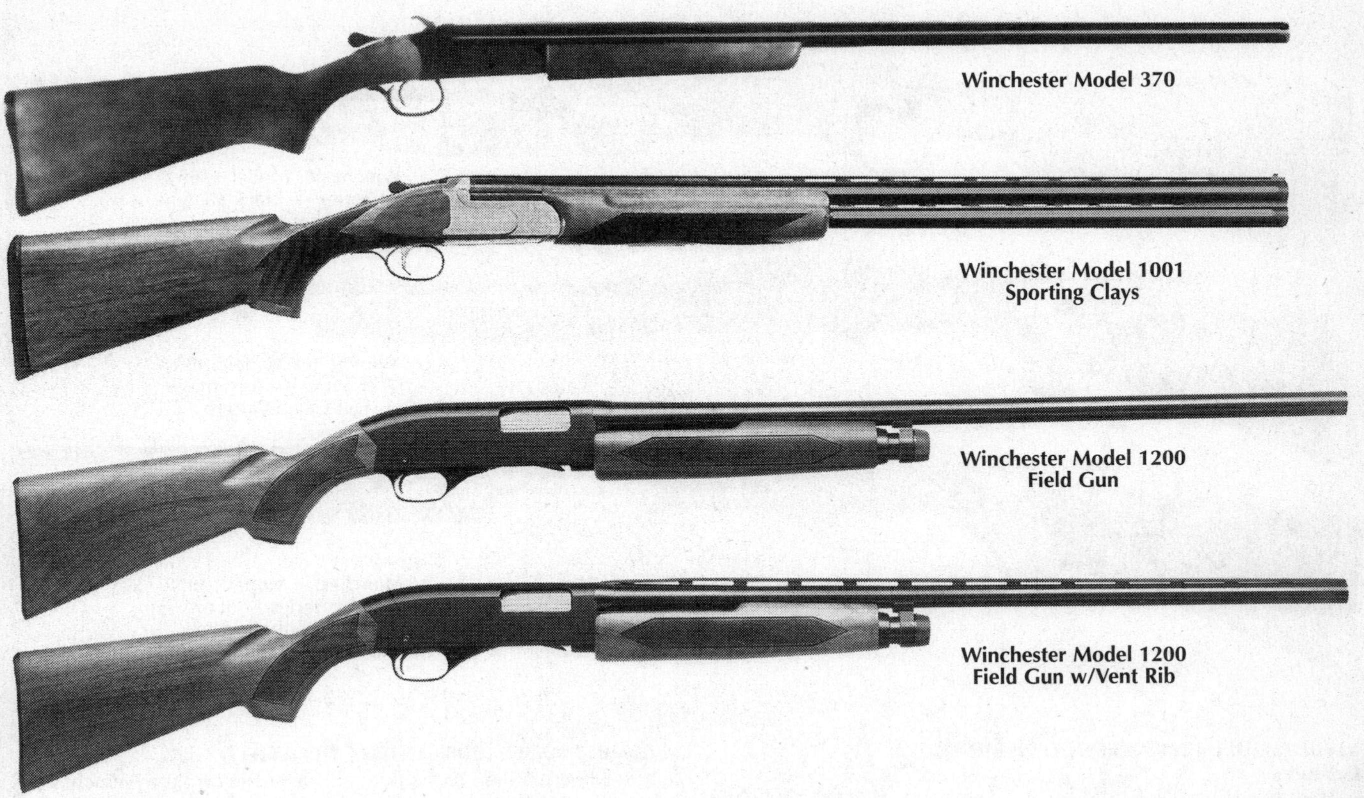
Winchester Model 370

Winchester Model 1001 Sporting Clays

Winchester Model 1200 Field Gun

Winchester Model 1200 Field Gun w/Vent Rib

MODEL 101 QUAIL SPECIAL O/U
Same specifications as small-frame Model 101 except in 28 and .410 ga. with 3-inch chambers. 25.5-inch bbls. with choke tubes (28 ga.) or M/F chokes (.410). Imported from Japan in 1984-87.
12 ga. . . . . NiB $2231 Ex $1799 Gd $1248
20 ga. . . . . NiB $2637 Ex $2124 Gd $1469
28 ga. . . . . NiB $3272 Ex $2636 Gd $1873
.410 ga. NiB $2306 Ex $1859 Gd $1288

MODEL 101 SHOTGUN/RIFLE COMBINATION GUN. . . . . . . NiB $2370 Ex $1912 Gd $1326
12-ga. Winchoke bbl. on top and rifle bbl. chambered for .30-06 on bottom (over/under). 25-inch bbls. Engraved receiver. Hand checkered walnut stock and forend. Weight: 8.5 lbs. Mfd. for Olin Corp. in Japan.

MODEL 370 SINGLE-SHOT SHOTGUN . . . . NiB $137 Ex $113 Gd $82
Visible hammer. Auto ejector. Takedown. Gauges: 12, 16, 20, 28, .410. 2.75-inch chambers in 16 and 28 ga., 3-inch in other ga. Bbls.: 12 ga., 30-, 32- or 36-inch,16 ga; 30- or 32-inch; 20 and 28 ga., 28-inch; .410 bore, 26-inch, all F choke. Weight: 5.5-6.25 lbs. Plain pistol-grip stock and forearm. Made 1968-73.

MODEL 370 YOUTH
Same as standard Model 370 except has 26-inch bbl. and 12.5-inch stock with recoil pad; 20 gauge with IM choke, .410 bore with F choke. Made 1968-73.
Model 370, 12, 16, or 20 ga. . . . . NiB $156 Ex $128 Gd $91
Model 37A, 28 ga. . . . . NiB $217 Ex $176 Gd $125
Model 37A, .410 ga. . . . . NiB $182 Ex $150 Gd $107

MODEL 1001 O/U SHOTGUN
Boxlock. 12 ga., 2.75- or 3-inch chambers. Bbls.: 28- or 30-inch vent rib; WinPlus choke tubes. Weight: 7-7.75 lbs. Checkered walnut buttstock and forend. Blued finish with scroll engraved receiver. Made 1993 to date.
Field model (28-inch bbl., 3-inch) . . . . NiB $1032 Ex $838 Gd $588
Sporting Clays . . . . NiB $1155 Ex $935 Gd $655
Sporting Clays Lite. . . . . NiB $1068 Ex $866 Gd $608

MODEL 1200 DEER GUN . . . . NiB $271 Ex $221 Gd $120
Same as standard Model 1200, except has special 22-inch bbl. with rifle-type sights, for rifled slug or buckshot; 12 ga. only. Weight: 6.5 lbs. Made 1965-74.

MODEL 1200 DEFENDER SERIES SLIDE-ACTION SECURITY SHOTGUNS
Hammerless. 12 ga. w/3-inch chamber. 18-inch bbl. w/cylinder bore and metal front bead or rifle sights. Four- or 7-round magazine. Weight: 5.5 to 6.75 lbs. 25.6 inches (PG Model) or 38.6 inches overall. Matte blue finish. Synthetic pistol grip or walnut finished hardwood buttstock w/grooved synthetic or hardwood slide handle. NOTE: Even though the 1200 series was introduced in 1964 and was supplanted by the Model 1300 in 1978, the Security series (including the Defender model) was marketed under 1200 series alpha-numeric product codes (G1200DM2R) until 1989. In 1990, the same Defender model was marketed under a 4-digit code (7715) and was then advertised in the 1300 series.

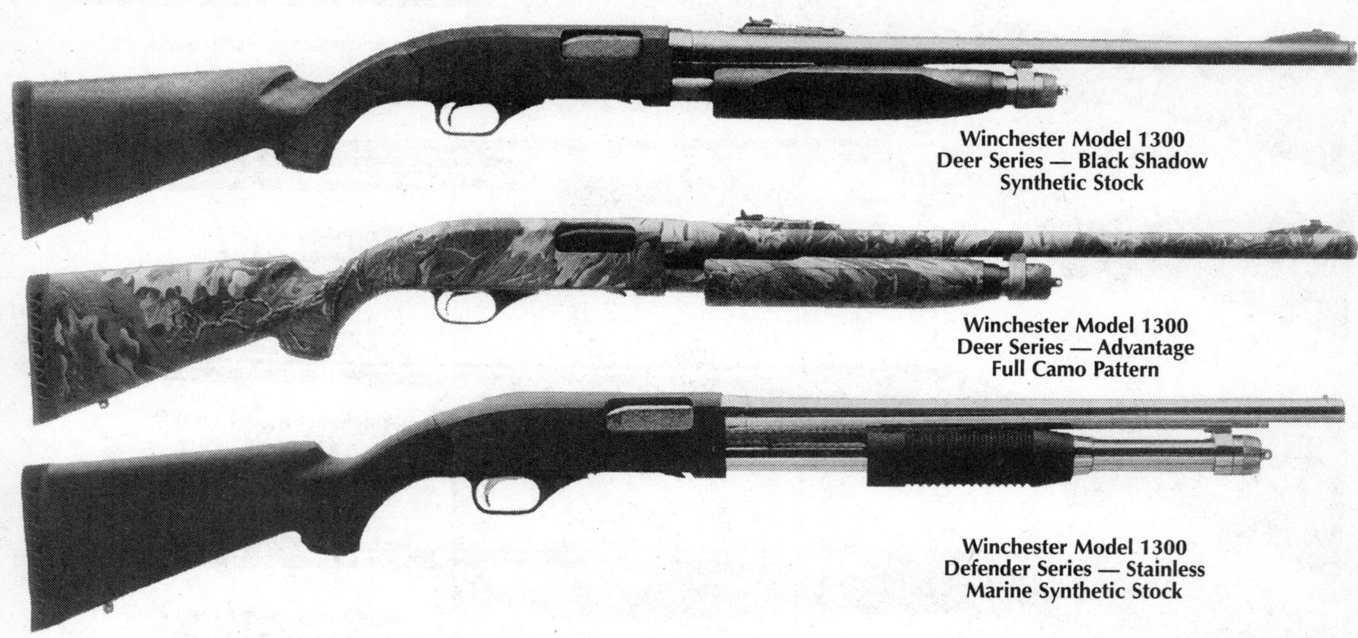

Winchester Model 1300 Deer Series — Black Shadow Synthetic Stock

Winchester Model 1300 Deer Series — Advantage Full Camo Pattern

Winchester Model 1300 Defender Series — Stainless Marine Synthetic Stock

(*cont'd*) MODEL 1200 DEFENDER SERIES

Defender w/hardwood stock,bead sight . . . . . NiB $230 Ex $188 Gd $134
Defender W/hardwood stock, rifle sights . . . . NiB $243 Ex $199 Gd $141
Defender model w/pistol-grip stock . . . NiB $250 Ex $204 Gd $144
Defender Combo model W/extra 28-inch plain bbl. . . . . . . NiB $281 Ex $229 Gd $162
Defender Combo model W/extra 28-inch vent rib bbl. . . . . NiB $301 Ex $244 Gd $173

MODEL 1200 FIELD GUN — MAGNUM

Same as standard Model 1200 except chambered for 3-inch 12 and 20 ga. magnum shells; plain or vent-rib bbl., 28- or 30-inch, F choke. Weight: 7.38 to 7.88 lbs. Made 1964-83.

With plain bbl. . . . . NiB $262 Ex $204 Gd $144
With vent rib bbl. . . . . NiB $277 Ex $226 Gd $160
Add for Winchester recoil reduction system $65

MODEL 1200 RANGER SLIDE-ACTION SHOTGUN. . . . . . . NiB $249 Ex $204 Gd $144

Hammerless. 12 and 20 ga.; 3-inch chambers. Walnut finished hardwood stock, ribbed forearm. 28-inch vent-rib bbl.; Winchoke system. Weight: 7.25 lbs. Made 1982 to 1990 by U. S. Repeating Arms.

MODEL 1200 RANGER YOUTH SLIDE-ACTION SHOTGUN. . . . . . . NiB $243 Ex $199 Gd $141

Same general specifications as standard Ranger Slide-Action except chambered for 20 ga. only, has Four round magazine, recoil pad on buttstock, weight: 6.5 lbs. Mfd. by U. S. Repeating Arms.

MODEL 1200 SLIDE-ACTION FIELD GUN

Front-locking rotary bolt. Takedown. 4-round magazine. Gauges: 12, 16, 20 (2.75-inch chamber). Bbl.: Plain or vent rib; 26-, 28-, 30-inch; IC, M, F choke or with Winchoke (interchangeable tubes IC-M-F). Weight: 6.5 to 7.25 lbs. Checkered pistol-grip stock and fore

(*cont'd.*) MODEL 1200 SLIDE-ACTION FIELD GUN

arm (slide handle), recoil pad; also avail. 1966-70 w/Winchester recoil reduction system (Cycolac stock). Made 1964-83.

With plain bbl. . . . . NiB $243 Ex $199 Gd $141
With vent rib bbl. . . . . NiB $255 Ex $208 Gd $148
Add for Winchester recoil reduction system $65
Add for Winchoke $25

MODEL 1200 STAINLESS MARINE SERIES SLIDE-ACTION SECURITY SHOTGUN

Similar to Model 1200 Defender except w/6-round magazine. 18-inch bbl. of ordnance stainless steel w/cylinder bore and rifle sights. Weight: 7 lbs. Bright chrome finish. Synthetic pistol grip or walnut finished hardwood buttstock w/grooved synthetic or hardwood slide handle.Made 1984-90.

Marine model w/hardwood stock . . NiB $275 Ex $214 Gd $107
Marine model w/pistol-grip stock . NiB $275 Ex $214 Gd $107

MODEL 1200 STAINLESS POLICE SERIES SLIDE-ACTION SECURITY SHOTGUN

Similar to Model 1200 Defender except w/6-round magazine. 18-inch bbl. of ordnance stainless steel w/cylinder bore and rifle sights. Weight: 7 lbs. Matte chrome finish. Synthetic pistol grip or walnut-finished hardwood buttstock w/grooved synthetic or hardwood slide handle.Made 1984-90.

Police model w/hardwood stock . . . NiB $291 Ex $237 Gd $168
Police model w/pistol grip stock . . . NiB $353 Ex $286 Gd $201

MODEL 1200 TRAP GUN

Same as standard Model 1200 except 12 gauge only. Has 2-round magazine, 30-inch vent-rib bbl., Full choke or 28-inch with Winchoke. Semi-fancy walnut stock, straight Made 1965-73. Also available 1966-70 with Winchester recoil reduction system.

With straight-trap stock. . . . . NiB $348 Ex $283 Gd $201
With Monte Carlo stock . . . . NiB $427 Ex $346 Gd $243
Add for Winchester recoil reduction system $75
Add for Winchoke $30

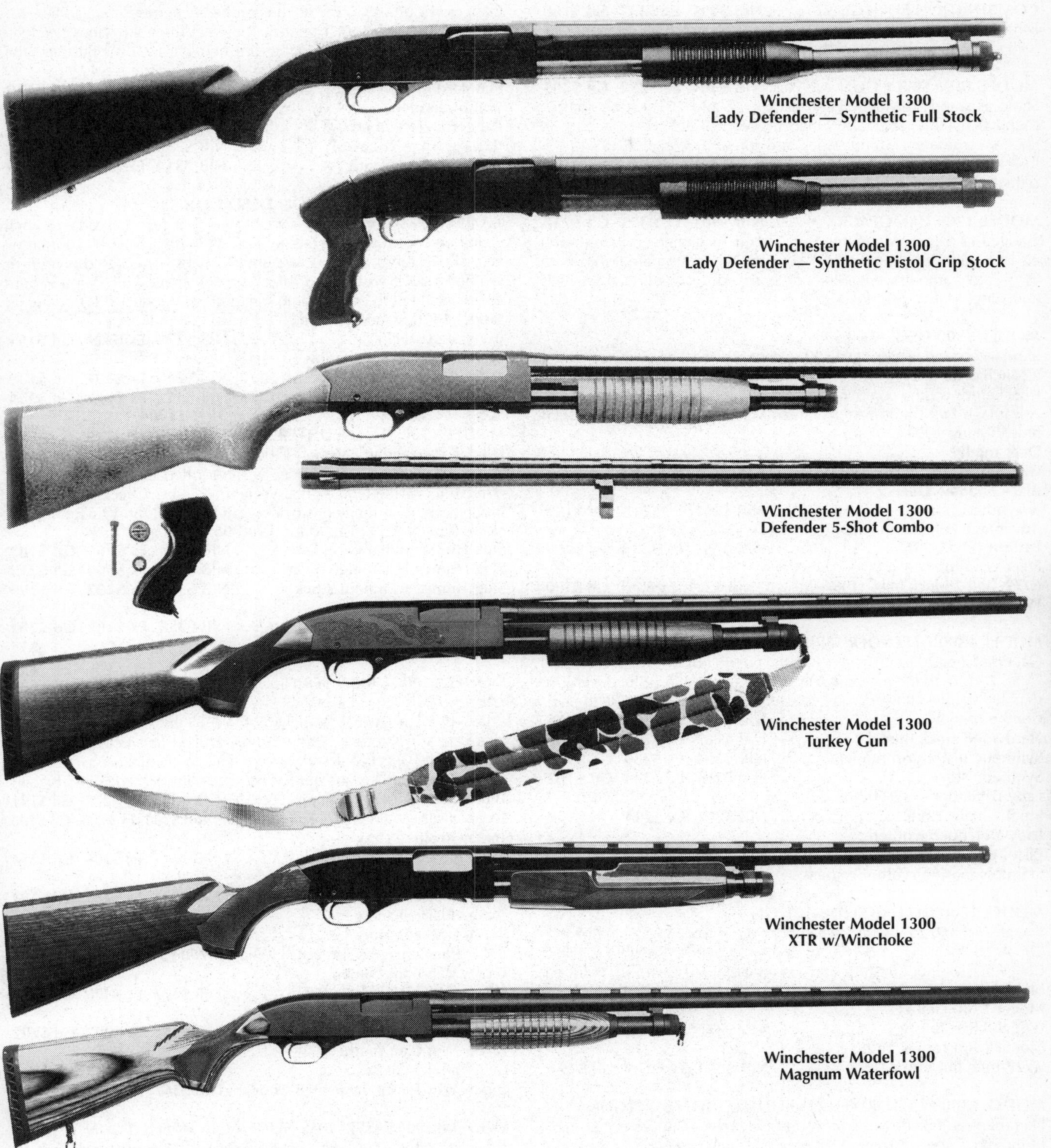

Winchester Model 1300
Lady Defender — Synthetic Full Stock

Winchester Model 1300
Lady Defender — Synthetic Pistol Grip Stock

Winchester Model 1300
Defender 5-Shot Combo

Winchester Model 1300
Turkey Gun

Winchester Model 1300
XTR w/Winchoke

Winchester Model 1300
Magnum Waterfowl

MODEL 1200 RANGER COMBINATION SHOTGUN...... NiB $291 Ex $237 Gd $168
Same as Ranger Deer combination except has one 28-inch vent-rib bbl. with M choke and one 18-inch Police Cyl. bore bbl. Made 1987-90.

MODEL 1200 SKEET GUN .... NiB $361 Ex $292 Gd $205
Same as standard Model 1200 except 12 and 20 ga. only; has 2-round magazine, specially tuned trigger, 26-inch vent-rib bbl. SK choke, semi-fancy walnut stock and forearm. Weight: 7.25 to 7.5 lbs. Made 1965-73. Also avail. 1966-70 with Winchester recoil reduction system (add $50 to value).

MODEL 1300 CAMOPACK .... NiB $401 Ex $325 Gd $227
Gauge: 12.3-inch Magnum. Four round magazine. Bbls.: 30-and 22-inch with Winchoke system. Weight: 7 lbs. Laminated stock with Win-Cam camouflage green, cut checkering, recoil pad, swivels and sling. Made 1987-88.

MODEL 1300 DEER SERIES
Similar to standard Model 1300 except 12 or 20 ga. only w/special 22-inch cyl. bore or rifled bbl. and rifle-type sights. Weight: 6.5 lbs. Checkered walnut or synthetic stock w/satin walnut, black or Advantage Full Camo Pattern finish. Matte blue or full-camo metal finish. Made 1994 to date.
Deer model w/walnut stock (intro. 1994)...... NiB $374 Ex $304 Gd $213
Black Shadow Deer w/synthetic stock (intro. 1994).... NiB $261 Ex $213 Gd $151
Advantage Full Camo Pattern (1995-98) .... NiB $361 Ex $292 Gd $205
Deer Combo w/22- and 28-inch bbls. (1994-98).... NiB $321 Ex $261 Gd $150
W/rifled bbl. (intro. 1996), add......................... $25

MODEL 1300 DEFENDER SERIES
Gauges: 12 or 20 ga. 18- 24- 28-inch vent rib bbl. w/3-inch chamber. Four-, 7- or 8- round magazine. Weight: 5.6 to 7.4 lbs. Blued, chrome or matte stainless finish. Wood or synthetic stock. Made 1985 to date.
Combo model .... NiB $453 Ex $366 Gd $256
Hardwood stock model.......... NiB $267 Ex $218 Gd $155
Synthetic pistol-grip model .... NiB $294 Ex $239 Gd $168
Synthetic stock .... NiB $281 Ex $228 Gd $162
Lady Defender synthetic Stock (made 1996) .... NiB $301 Ex $254 Gd $172
Lady Defender synthetic Pistol-grip (made 1996).......... NiB $269 Ex $219 Gd $156
Stainless marine synthetic stock ... NiB $434 Ex $352 Gd $245

MODEL 1300 DELUXE SLIDE-ACTION
Gauges: 12 and 20 w/3-inch chamber. Four round magazine. Bbl.:22, 26 or 28 inch vent rib bbl. w/Winchoke tubes. Weight: 6.5 lbs. Checkered walnut buttstock and forend w/high luster finish. Polished blue metal finish with roll-engraved receiver. Made 1984 to date.
Model 1300 Deluxe w/high gloss finish.............. NiB $377 Ex $306 Gd $214
Model 1300 Ladies/Youth w/22-inch bbl.(disc. 1992) .... NiB $334 Ex $271 Gd $191

MODEL 1300 FEATHERWEIGHT SLIDE-ACTION SHOTGUN
Hammerless. Takedown. Four round magazine. Gauges: 12 and 20 (3-inch chambers). Bbls.: 22, 26 or 28 inches w/plain or vent rib w/Winchoke tubes. Weight: 6.38 to 7 lbs. Checkered walnut buttstock, grooved slide handle. Made 1978-94.
Model 1300 FW (plain bbl.) ...... NiB $301 Ex $244 Gd $172
Model 1300 FW (vent rib) .... NiB $349 Ex $283 Gd $200
Model 1300 FW XTR .... NiB $363 Ex $294 Gd $207

MODEL 1300 RANGER SERIES
Gauges: 12 or 20 ga. w/3-inch chamber. Five round magazine. 22- (Rifled), 26- or 28-inch vent-rib bbl. w/Winchoke tubes. Weight: 7.25 lbs. Blued finish. Walnut-finished hardwood buttstock and forend. Made 1984 to date.
Standard model .... NiB $307 Ex $250 Gd $176
Combo model .... NiB $371 Ex $301 Gd $211
Ranger Deer combo (D&T w/rings & bases) .... NiB $390 Ex $316 Gd $221
Ranger Ladies/Youth .... NiB $314 Ex $255 Gd $179

MODEL 1300 SLIDE-ACTION FIELD GUN
Takedown w/front-locking rotary bolt. Gauges: 12, 20 w/3-inch chamber. Four round magazine. Bbl.: Vent rib; 26-, 28-, 30-inch w/ Win-choke tubes IC-M-F). Weight: 7.25 lbs. Checkered walnut or synthetic stock w/standard, black or Advantage Full Camo Pattern finish. Matte blue or full-camo metal finish. Made 1994 to date.
Model 1300 Standard Field (w/walnut stock) .... NiB $279 Ex $227 Gd $161
Model 1300 Black Shadow (w/black synthetic stock)......... NiB $240 Ex $197 Gd $139
Model 1300 Advantage Camo ..... NiB $341 Ex $277 Gd $194

MODEL 1300 SLUG HUNTER SERIES
Similar to standard Model 1300 except chambered 12 ga. only w/special 22-inch smoothbore w/sabot-rifled choke tube or fully rifled bbl. w/rifle-type sights. Weight: 6.5 lbs. Checkered walnut, hardwood or laminated stock w/satin walnut or WinTuff finish. Matte blue metal finish. Made 1988-94.
Slug Hunter w/hardwood stock ... NiB $321 Ex $261 Gd $183
Slug Hunter w/laminated stock.... NiB $374 Ex $303 Gd $213
Slug Hunter w/walnut stock ...... NiB $347 Ex $282 Gd $199
Whitetails Unlimited w/beavertail forend .... NiB $355 Ex $287 Gd $202
W/sabot-rifled choke tubes, add $15

MODEL 1300 TURKEY SERIES
Gauges: 12 or 20 ga. 22-inch bbl. w/3-inch chamber. Four round magazine. 43 inches overall. Weight: 6.4 to 6.75 lbs. Buttstock and magazine cap, sling studs w/Cordura sling. Drilled and tapped to accept scope base. Checkered walnut, synthetic or laminated wood stock w/low luster finish. Matte blue or full camo finish. Made 1985 to date.
Turkey Advantage Full Camo......... NiB $335 Ex $272 Gd $191
Turkey Realtree All-Purpose Full Camo.... NiB $365 Ex $295 Gd $208
Turkey Realtree Gray All-Purpose Full Camo .... NiB $377 Ex $306 Gd $214
Turkey Realtree All-Purpose Camo (matte metal) .... NiB $321 Ex $261 Gd $183
Turkey Black Shadow (black synthetic stock) .... NiB $227 Ex $185 Gd $132
Turkey Win-Cam (green laminated wood)... NiB $340 Ex $276 Gd $194
Turkey Win-Cam Combo (22- and 30-inch bbls.)............ NiB $377 Ex $306 Gd $214
Turkey Win-Cam NWTF (22- and 30-inch bbls.)............ NiB $355 Ex $287 Gd $202
Turkey Win-Cam Youth/ Ladies model (20 ga.) .... NiB $415 Ex $335 Gd $235
Turkey Win-Tuf (br. laminated wood) .. NiB $347 Ex $282 Gd $199

MODEL 1300 WATERFOWL SLIDE-ACTION SHOTGUN
Similar to 1300 Standard model except has 28- or 30-inch vent rib bbl. w/Winchoke tubes. Weight: 7 lbs. Matte blue metal finish. Checkered walnut finished hardwood or brown laminated Win-Tuffwood stock w/camo sling, swivels and recoil pad. Made 1984-92.
Model 1300 Waterfowl w/hardwood stock ... NiB $321 Ex $261 Gd $183
Model 1300 Waterfowl w/laminated stock.... NiB $347 Ex $282 Gd $199

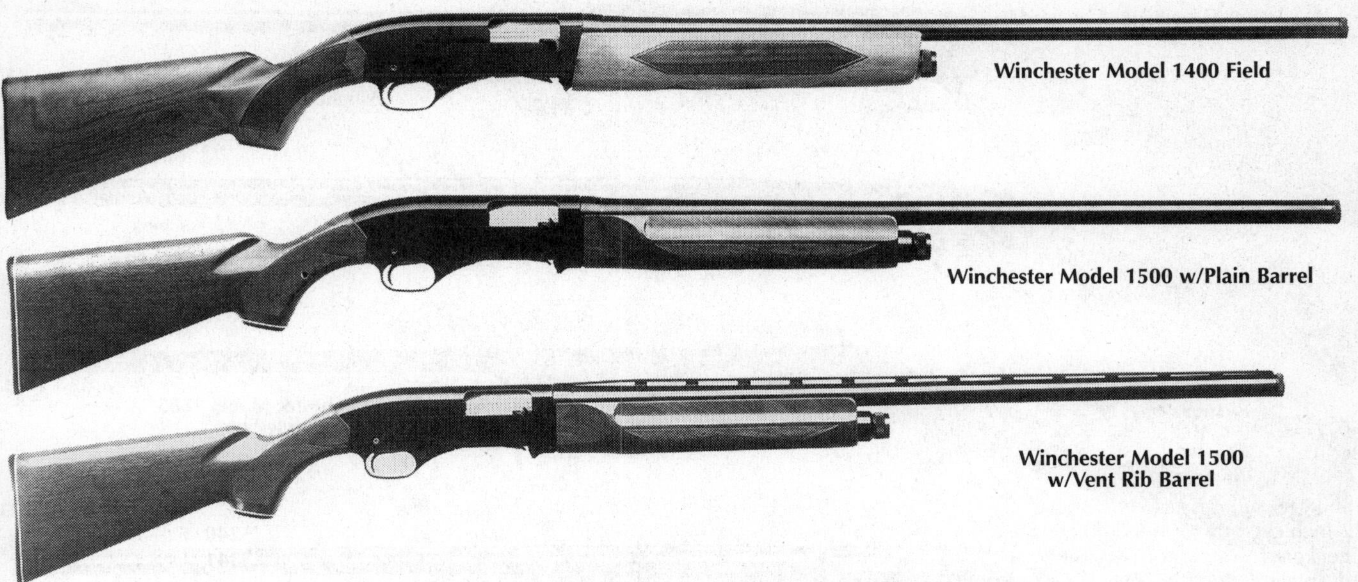

Winchester Model 1400 Field

Winchester Model 1500 w/Plain Barrel

Winchester Model 1500 w/Vent Rib Barrel

MODEL 1300 XTR SLIDE-ACTION . NiB $415 Ex $335 Gd $235
Hammerless. Takedown. Four shot magazine. Gauges: 12 and 20 (3-inch chambers). Bbl.: Plain or vent rib; 28-inch bbls.; Winchoke (interchangeable tubes IC-M-F). Weight: About 7 lbs.

MODEL 1400 AUTOMATIC FIELD GUN
Gas-operated. Front-locking rotary bolt. Takedown. Two round magazine. Gauges: 12, 16, 20 (2.75-inch chamber). Bbl.: Plain or vent rib; 26-, 28-, 30-inch; IC, M, F choke, or with Winchoke (interchangeable tubes IC-M-F). Weight: 6.5 to 7.25 lbs. Checkered pistol-grip stock and forearm, recoil pad, also available with Winchester recoil reduction system (Cycolac stock). Made 1964-68.
With plain bbl. . . . . NiB $323 Ex $262 Gd $184
With vent rib bbl. . . . . NiB $353 Ex $286 Gd $201
Add for Winchester recoil reduction system $100
Add for Winchoke $25

MODEL 1400 DEER GUN . . . . NiB $321 Ex $261 Gd $183
Same as standard Model 1400 except has special 22-inch bbl. with rifle-type sights, for rifle slug or buckshot; 12 ga. only. Weight: 6.25 lbs. Made 1965-68.

MODEL 1400 MARK II DEER GUN. NiB $371 Ex $301 Gd $211
Same general specifications as Model 1400 Deer Gun. Made 1968-73.

MODEL 1400 MARK II FIELD GUN
Same general specifications as Model 1400 Field Gun, except not chambered for 16 gauge; Winchester Recoil Reduction System not available after 1970- only 28-inch barrels w/Winchoke offered after 1973. Made 1968-78.
With plain bbl. . . . . NiB $341 Ex $277 Gd $194
With plain bbl. and Winchoke. . . . . NiB $368 Ex $298 Gd $212
With vent-rib bbl. . . . . NiB $388 Ex $314 Gd $220
With vent-rib bbl. and Winchoke . . NiB $415 Ex $335 Gd $235
Add for Winchester recoil reduction system $100

MODEL 1400 MARK II SKEET GUN . . . . NiB $434 Ex $335 Gd $245
Same general specifications as Model 1400 Skeet Gun. Made 1968-73.

MODEL 1400 MARK II TRAP GUN
Same general specifications as Model 1400 Trap Gun except also furnished with 28-inch bbl. and Winchoke. Winchester recoil reduction system not available after 1970. Made 1968-73.
With straight stock . . . . NiB $479 Ex $389 Gd $274
With Monte Carlo stock . . . . NiB $521 Ex $422 Gd $296
With Winchester recoil reduction system, add $100
With Winchoke, add $25

MODEL 1400 MARK II UTILITY SKEET NiB $366 Ex $299 Gd $213
Same general specifications as Model 1400 Mark II Skeet Gun except has stock and forearm of field grade walnut. Made 1970-73.

MODEL 1400 MARK II UTILITY TRAP . NiB $401 Ex $327 Gd $232
Same as Model 1400 Mark II Trap Gun except has Monte Carlo stock/forearm of field grade walnut. Made 1970-73.

MODEL 1400 RANGER SEMIAUTOMATIC SHOTGUN . . . . NiB $281 Ex $228 Gd $162
Gauges: 12, 20. Two round magazine. 28-inch vent rib bbl. with F choke. Overall length: 48.63 inches. Weight: 7 to 7.25 lbs. Walnut finish, hardwood stock and forearm with cut checkering. Made 1984 to 1990 by U. S. Repeating Arms.

MODEL 1400 RANGER SEMIAUTOMATIC DEER SHOTGUN. . . . . NiB $294 Ex $239 Gd $169
Same general specifications as Ranger Semiautomatic except 24.13-inch plain bbl. with rifle sights. Mfd. by U.S. Repeating Arms.

MODEL 1400 SKEET GUN . . . . NiB $406 Ex $328 Gd $229
Same as standard Model 1400 except 12 and 20 ga. only, 26-inch vent-rib bbl., SK choke, semi-fancy walnut stock and forearm. Weight: 7.25 to 7.5 lbs. Made 1965-68. Also available with Winchester recoil reduction system (add $50 to value).

MODEL 1400 TRAP GUN
Same as standard Model 1400 except 12 ga. only with 30-inch vent-rib bbl., F choke. Semi-fancy walnut stock, straight or Monte Carlo trap style. Also available with Winchester recoil reduction system. Weight: About 8.25 lbs. Made 1965-68.
With straight stock . . . . NiB $464 Ex $378 Gd $267
With Monte Carlo stock . . . . NiB $498 Ex $404 Gd $284
Add for Winchester recoil red. system. $100

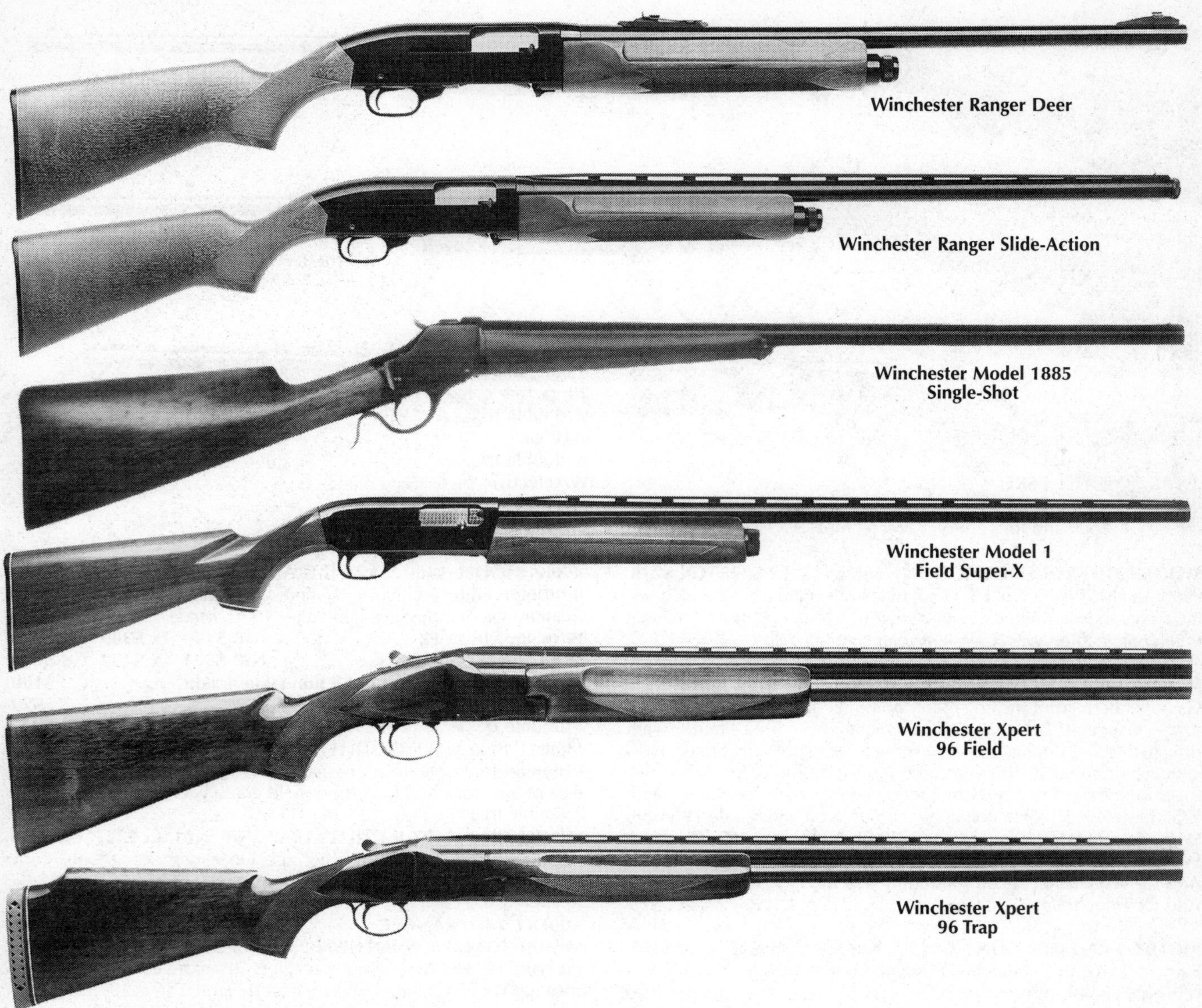
Winchester Ranger Deer

Winchester Ranger Slide-Action

Winchester Model 1885 Single-Shot

Winchester Model 1 Field Super-X

Winchester Xpert 96 Field

Winchester Xpert 96 Trap

MODEL 1500 XTR SEMIAUTOMATIC . . NiB $344 Ex $280 Gd $198
Gas-operated. Gauges: 12 and 20 (2.75-inch chambers). Bbl.: Plain or vent rib; 28-inch; WinChoke (interchangeable tubes IC-M-F). American walnut stock and forend; checkered grip and forend. Weight: 7.25 lbs. Made 1978-82.

MODEL 1885
SINGLE-SHOT SHOTGUN . . . . NiB $3919 Ex $3185 Gd $2198
Falling-block action, same as Model 1885 Rifle. Highwall receiver. Solid frame or takedown. 20 ga. 3-inch chamber. 26-inch bbl.; plain, matted or matted rib; Cyl. bore, M or F choke. Weight: About 5.5 lbs. Straight-grip stock and forearm. Made 1914-16.

MODEL 1887 LEVER-ACTION SHOTGUN
First of John Browning's patent shotgun designs produced by Winchester. 10 or 12 ga. on casehardened frame fitted w/20-inch blued, cylinder bore or full choke 30- or 32-inch bbl. Plain or checkered walnut stock and forend. Made 1887 to 1901.
Model 1887 10 or 12 ga. standard . . . . NiB $2499 Ex $2020 Gd $1406
Model 1887 10 or 12 ga. deluxe. . . NiB $5196 Ex $4192 Gd $2907
Model 1887 10 or 12 ga. riot gun . . . . NiB $2385 Ex $1928 Gd $1343

(cont'd.) **MODEL 1887 LEVER-ACTION SHOTGUN**
W/.70-150 Ratchet rifled bbl.
.70 cal. rifle/87 produced) . . . . NiB $3404 Ex $2735 Gd $1906
W/3 or 4 blade Del. Damascus bbl., add. 20%

MODEL 1901 LEVER-ACTION SHOTGUN
Same general specifications as Model 1887, of which this is a redesigned version. 10 ga. only. Made 1901-20.
Model 1901 Standard. . . . . NiB $2110 Ex $1711 Gd $1199
Model 1901 Deluxe . . . . NiB $2659 Ex $2149 Gd $1496

MODEL 1911 AUTO-
LOADING SHOTGUN. . . . . NiB $672 Ex $549 Gd $393
Hammerless. Takedown. 12 gauge only. Four round tubular magazine. Bbl.: plain, 26- to 32-inch, standard borings. Weight: About 8.5 lbs. Plain or checkered pistol-grip stock and forearm. Made 1911-25.

RANGER DEER COMBINATION . . . NiB $309 Ex $250 Gd $175
Gauge: 12, 3-inch Magnum. Three round magazine. Bbl.: 24-inch Cyl. bore deer bbl. and 28-inch vent rib bbl. with WinChoke system. Weight: 7.25 lbs. Made 1987-90.

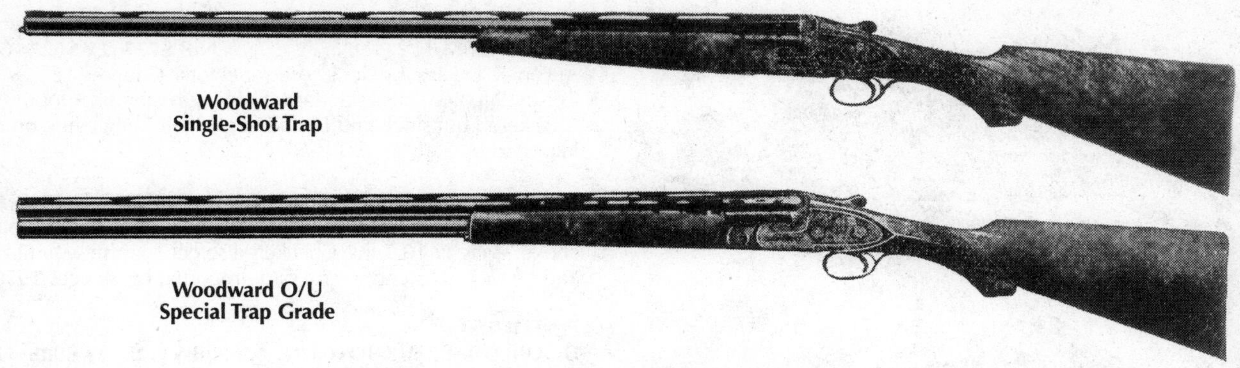

Woodward
Single-Shot Trap

Woodward O/U
Special Trap Grade

SUPER-X MODEL I AUTO FIELD GUN... NiB $4503 Ex $406 Gd $282
Gas-operated. Takedown.12 ga. 2.75-inch chamber Four round magazine. Bbl.: Vent rib 26-inch IC; 28-inch M or F; 30-inch F choke. Weight: About 7 lbs. Checkered pistol-grip stock. Made 1974-84.

SUPER-X MODEL I SKEET GUN ... NiB $765 Ex $610 Gd $424
Same as Super-X Field Gun except has 26-inch bbl., SK choke, skeet-style stock and forearm of select walnut. Made 1974-84.

SUPER-X MODEL I TRAP GUN
Same as Super-X Field Gun except has 30-inch bbl., IM or F choke, trap-style stock (straight or Monte Carlo comb) and forearm of select walnut, recoil pad. Made 1974-84.
With straight stock .... NiB $599 Ex $484 Gd $337
With Monte Carlo stock .... NiB $693 Ex $560 Gd $389

XPERT MODEL 96 O/U FIELD GUN ..... NiB $973 Ex $789 Gd $555
Boxlock action similar to Model 101. Plain receiver. Auto ejectors. Selective single trigger. Gauges: 12, 20. 3-inch chambers. Bbl.: Vent rib; 26-inch IC/M; 28-inch M/F, 30-inch F/F choke (12 ga. only). Weight: 6.25 to 8.25 lbs. depending on ga. and bbls. Checkered pistol-grip stock and forearm. Made 1976-81 for Olin Corp. at its Olin-Kodensha facility in Japan.

XPERT MODEL 96 SKEET GUN... NiB $1026 Ex $852 Gd $585
Same as Xpert Field Gun except has 2.75-inch chambers, 27-inch bbls., SK choke, skeet-style stock and forearm. Made 1976-1981.

XPERT MODEL 96 TRAP GUN
Same as Xpert Field Gun except 12 ga. only, 2.75-inch chambers, has 30-inch bbls., IM/F or F/F choke, trap-style stock (straight or Monte Carlo comb) with recoil pad. Made 1976-81.
With straight stock .... NiB $945 Ex $769 Gd $542
With Monte Carlo stock .... NiB $970 Ex $788 Gd $555

JAMES WOODWARD & SONS — London, England

James Woodward & Sons was acquired by James Purdey & Sons after World War II.

BEST QUALITY HAMMERLESS DOUBLE
Sidelock. Automatic ejectors. Double triggers or single trigger. Built to order in all standard gauges, bbl. lengths, boring and other specifications. Made as a field gun, pigeon and wildfowl gun, skeet gun or trap gun. Manufactured prior to World War II.
12 ga.
w/double triggers ...... NiB $26,906 Ex $21,525 Gd $14,637
20 ga.
w/double triggers ...... NiB $30,516 Ex $24,412 Gd $16,600

(cont'd.) **BEST QUALITY HAMMERLESS DOUBLE**
28 ga.
w/double triggers ...... NiB $37,731 Ex $30,187 Gd $20,527
.410 ga.
w/double triggers ...... NiB $42,656 Ex $34,125 Gd $23,205
W/selective single trigger, add 5%

BEST QUALITY O/U SHOTGUN
Sidelock. Automatic ejectors. Double triggers or single trigger. Built to order in all standard gauges, bbl. lengths, boring and other specifications, including Special Trap Grade with vent rib. Woodward introduced this type of gun in 1908. Made until World War II.
12 ga.
w/double triggers ...... NiB $29,531 Ex $23,425 Gd $16,065
20 ga.
w/double triggers ...... NiB $39,703 Ex $31,762 Gd $21,598
28 ga.
w/double triggers ...... NiB $52,172 Ex $41,737 Gd $28,381
.410 ga.
w/double triggers .... NiB $59,062 Ex $47,250+ Gd $32,130
W/single trigger, add 5%

BEST QUALITY SINGLE-SHOT TRAP........ NiB $12,406 Ex $9925 Gd $6749
Sidelock. Mechanical features of the O/U gun. Vent rib bbl. 12 ga. only. Built to customer's specifications and measurements, including type and amount of checkering, carving and engraving. Made prior to World War II.

ZEPHYR SHOTGUNS — Manufactured by Victor Sarasqueta Company, Eibar, Spain

MODEL 1 O/U SHOTGUN .... NiB $1281 Ex $1043 Gd $738
Same general specifications as Field Model O/U except with more elaborate engraving, finer wood and checkering. Imported by Stoeger 1930s-51.

MODEL 2 O/U SHOTGUN .... NiB $1651 Ex $1338 Gd $939
Sidelock. Auto ejectors. Gauges: 12, 16, 20, 28 and .410. Bbls.: 25 to 30 inches most common. Modest scroll engraving on receiver and sideplates. Checkered, straight-grain select walnut buttstock and forend. Imported by Stoeger 1930s-51.

MODEL 3 O/U SHOTGUN.... NiB $2245 Ex $1814 Gd $1263
Same general specifications as Zephyr Model 2 O/U except with more elaborate engraving, finer wood and checkering. Imported by Stoeger 1930s-51.

Zephyr Crown, Premier and Royal Grades

MODEL 400E FIELD GRADE DOUBLE-BARREL SHOTGUN
Anson & Deeley boxlock system. Gauges: 12 16, 20, 28 and .410. Bbls.: 25 to 30 inches. Weight: 4.5 lbs. (.410) to 6.25 lbs. (12 ga.). Checkered French walnut buttstock and forearm. Modest scroll engraving on bbls., receiver and trigger guard. Imported by Stoeger 1930s-50s.

12, 16 or 20 ga. . . . . NiB $1477 Ex $1195 Gd $834
28 or .410 ga. . . . . NiB $1654 Ex $1337 Gd $831
W/selective single trigger, add $200

MODEL 401 E SKEET GRADE DOUBLE-BARREL SHOTGUN
Same general specifications as Field Grade except with beavertail forearm. Bbls.: 25 to 28 inches. Imported by Stoeger 1930s-50s.

12, 16 or 20 ga. . . . . NiB $1750 Ex $1414 Gd $984
28 or .410 ga. . . . . NiB $1918 Ex $1518 Gd $1075
W/selective single trigger, add $350
W/nonselective single trigger, add $250

MODEL 402E DELUXE
DOUBLE-BARREL SHOTGUN. . NiB $2210 Ex $1782 Gd $1234
Same general specifications as Model 400E Field Grade except for custom refinements. The action was carefully hand-honed for smoother operation; finer, elaborate engraving throughout, plus higher quality wood in stock and forearm. Imported by Stoeger 1930s-50s.

CROWN GRADE. . . . . NiB $1599 Ex $1297 Gd $901
Boxlock. Gauges: 12, 16, 20, 28 and .410. Bbls.: 25 to 30 inches standard but any lengths could be ordered. Weight: 6 lbs., 4 oz. (.410) to 7 lbs., 4 oz. (12 ga.). Checkered Spanish walnut stock and beavertail forearm. Receiver engraved with scroll patterns. Imported by Stoeger 1938-51.

FIELD MODEL
O/U SHOTGUN . . . . NiB $777 Ex $627 Gd $437
Anson & Deeley boxlock. Auto ejectors. Gauges: 12, 16 and 20. Bbls.: 25 to 30 inches standard- full-length matt rib. Double triggers. Checkered buttstock and forend. Light scroll engraving on receiver. Imported by Stoeger 1930s-51.

HONKER SINGLE-SHOT SHOTGUN . . . . . NiB $540 Ex $438 Gd $307
Sidelock. Gauge: 10; 3.5-inch magnum. 36-inch vent rib barrel w/F choke. Weight: 10.5 lbs. Checkered select Spanish walnut buttstock and beavertail forend; recoil pad. Imported by Stoeger 1950s-72.

PINEHURST
DOUBLE-BARREL SHOTGUN. . . . NiB $1125 Ex $906 Gd $625
Boxlock. Gauges: 12, 16, 20, 28 and .410. Bbls.: 25 to 28 inches most common. Checkered, select walnut buttstock and forend. Selective single trigger and auto ejectors. Imported by Stoeger 1950s-72.

PREMIER GRADE
DOUBLE-BARREL SHOTGUN . . . . NiB $2440 Ex $1965 Gd $1357
Sidelock. Gauges: 12, 16, 20, 28 and .410. Bbls.: Any length, but 25 to 30 inches most popular. Weight: 4.5 lbs. (.410) to 7 lbs. (12 ga.). Checkered high-grade French walnut buttstock and forend. Imported by Stoeger 1930s-51.

ROYAL GRADE
DOUBLE-BARREL SHOTGUN . . . . NiB $3743 Ex $1010 Gd $2073
Same general specifications as the Premier Grade except with more elaborate engraving, finer checkering and wood. Imported by Stoeger 1930s-51.

STERLINGWORTH II
DOUBLE-BARREL SHOTGUN. . . . . NiB $986 Ex $801 Gd $566
Genuine sidelocks with color-casehardened sideplates. Gauges: 12, 16, 20 and .410. Bbls.: 25 to 30 inches. Weight: 6 lbs., 4 oz. (.410) to 7 lbs., 4 oz. (12 ga.). Select Spanish walnut buttstock and beavertail forearm. Light scroll engraving on receiver and sideplates. Automatic, sliding-tang safety. Imported by Stoeger 1950s-72.

THUNDERBIRD
DOUBLE-BARREL SHOTGUN . . . . NiB $987 Ex $802 Gd $567
Sidelock. Gauges: 12 and 10 Magnum. Bbls.: 32-inch, both F choke. Weight: 8 lbs., 8 oz. (12 ga.), 12 lbs. (10 ga.). Receiver elaborately engraved with waterfowl scenes. Checkered select Spanish walnut buttstock and beavertail forend. Plain extractors, double triggers. Imported by Stoeger 1950-72.

UPLAND KING
DOUBLE-BARREL SHOTGUN . . . NiB $1136 Ex $922 Gd $648
Sidelock. Gauges: 12, 16, 20, 28 and .410. Bbls.: 25 to 28 inches most popular. Checkered buttstock and forend of select walnut. Selective single trigger and auto ejectors. Imported by Stoeger 1950-72.

UPLANDER 4E
DOUBLE-BARREL SHOTGUN . . . . NiB $934 Ex $760 Gd $538
Same general specifications as the Zephyr Sterlingworth II except with selective auto ejectors and highly polished sideplates. Imported by Stoeger 1951-72.

WOODLANDER II
DOUBLE-BARREL SHOTGUN . . . . NiB $659 Ex $536 Gd $381
Boxlock. Gauges: 12, 20 and .410. Bbls.: 25 to 30 inches. Weight: 6 lbs., 4 oz. (.410) to 7 lbs., 4 oz. (12 ga.). Checkered Spanish walnut stock and beavertail forearm. Engraved receiver. Imported by Stoeger 1950-72.

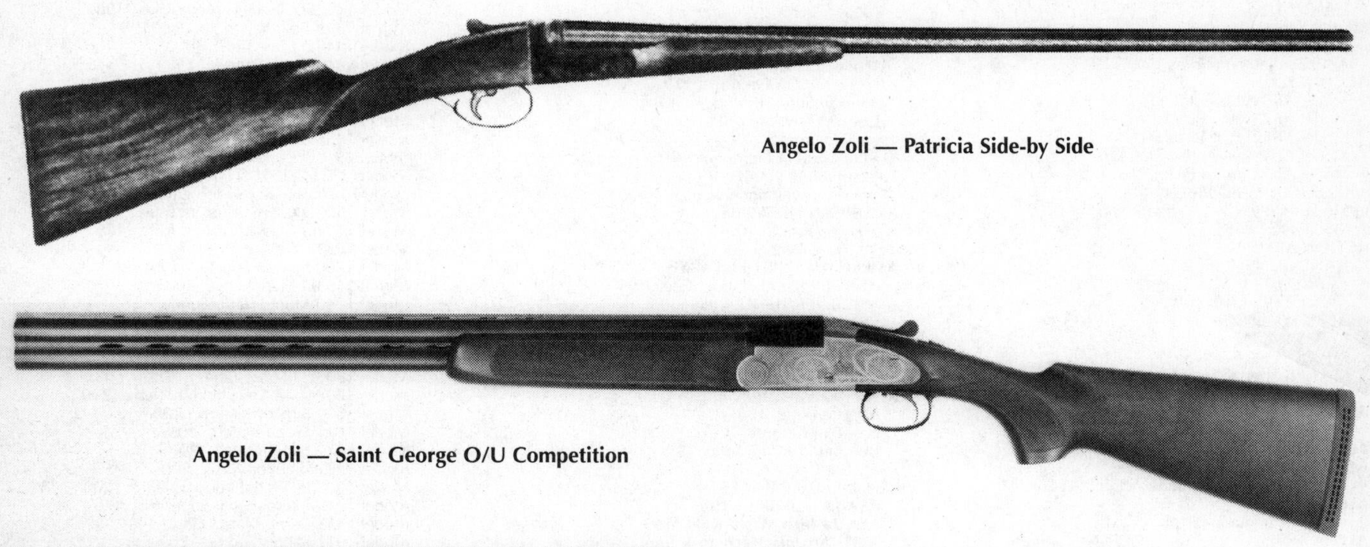

Angelo Zoli — Patricia Side-by Side

Angelo Zoli — Saint George O/U Competition

ANGELO ZOLI — Mississauga, Ontario, Canada

ALLEY CLEANER S/S SHOTGUN .... **NiB $698 Ex $570 Gd $406**
Gauges: 12 and 20. 20-inch bbl. 26.5 inches overall. Weight: 7 lbs. average. Chokes: F/M, F, IM, M, IC, SK. Chrome-lined barrels. Walnut stock and engraved action. Made 1986-87.

APACHE O/U FIELD SHOTGUN
Gauge: 12. Chokes: F/M, F, IM, M, IC and stock fixed or tubes. 20-inch bbl. Short vent rib. Weight: 7.5 lbs. Checkered walnut stock and forearm. Lever action. Pistol grip. Made 1986-88.
Apache w/fixed chokes .... **NiB $488 Ex $402 Gd $293**
Apache w/choke tubes .... **NiB $579 Ex $475 Gd $342**

DAINO I AND II FOLDING SINGLE SHOT
Gauges: 12, 20 and .410. 28- or 30-inch bbl. Weight: 6 lbs. average. Choke: Full. Chrome-lined barrel, vent rib. Pistol-grip walnut stock. Engraved action. Made 1986-88.
Daino I w/top lever .... **NiB $170 Ex $140 Gd $100**
Daino II w/bottom lever .... **NiB $183 Ex $150 Gd $108**

HK 2000 SEMIAUTOMATIC SHOTGUN .... **NiB $716 Ex $581 Gd $403**
Gauge: 12. Five round capacity. Bbls.: 24-, 26-, 28- and 30-inch; vent rib. Weight: 6.5 to 7.5 lbs. Checkered walnut stock and forearm. Glossy finish. Pistol grip. Engraved receiver. Made 1988.

PATRICIA SIDE-BY-SIDE SHOTGUNS ..... **NiB $1409 Ex $1141 Gd $798**
Gauge: .410 only. 28-inch bbl. Choke: F/M. Weight: 5.5 lbs. Automatic ejectors; Zoli single selective trigger, box lock. Hand-checkered walnut stock with English straight grip, splinter forearm. Made 1986-88.

SAINT GEORGE O/U COMPETITION .... **NiB $2034 Ex $1641 Gd $1138**
Gauge: 12. 30- and 32-inch vent rib barrels. Weight: 8 lbs. Single selective trigger. Oil-finished, pistol-grip walnut stock. Made 1986-88.

SILVER SNIPE O/U SHOTGUN .... **NiB $663 Ex $542 Gd $368**
Purdey-type box lock with crossbolt. Selective single trigger. Gauges: 12, 20; 3-inch chambers. Bbls.: 26-, 28- or 30-inch with a variety of choke combinations. Weight: 5.75 to 6.75 lbs. Checkered European walnut buttstock and forend. Made in Italy.

Z43 STANDARD O/U SHOTGUN .... **NiB $435 Ex $353 Gd $247**
Gauge: 12 or 20. 26-, 28- or 30-inch bbls. Chokes: F/M, M/IC Weight: 6.75 to 8 lbs. vent lateral ribs, standard extractors, single non-selective trigger. Glossy-finished walnut stock and forearm. Automatic safety. Made 1986-88.

ANTONIO ZOLI, U.S.A., INC. — Fort Wayne, Indiana, Manufactured in Italy

SILVER FALCON O/U .... **NiB $1236 Ex $1003 Gd $704**
Gauges: 12 and 20; 3-inch chambers. 26- or 28-inch blued barrels. Weight: 6.25 to 7.25 lbs. Antiqued silver finish on receiver. Pistol-grip stock of Turkish Circassian walnut with polyurethane-type finish. Imported 1989-1990.

UPLANDER SIDE/SIDE SHOTGUN .... **NiB $816 Ex $663 Gd $467**
Gauges: 12 and 20. Casehardened receiver. Checkered oil-finished, hand-rubbed stock of Turkish Circassian walnut; splinter forend. Imported 1989-90.

SHOTGUNS

Index

INDEX

INDEX

INDEX

INDEX